Peace and Conflict Studies

Fifth Edition

Sara Miller McCune founded SAGE Publishing in 1965 to support the dissemination of usable knowledge and educate a global community. SAGE publishes more than 1000 journals and over 800 new books each year, spanning a wide range of subject areas. Our growing selection of library products includes archives, data, case studies and video. SAGE remains majority owned by our founder and after her lifetime will become owned by a charitable trust that secures the company's continued independence.

Los Angeles | London | New Delhi | Singapore | Washington DC | Melbourne

Peace and Conflict Studies

Fifth Edition

David P. Barash
University of Washington

Charles P. Webel
University of New York in Prague

Los Angeles | London | New Delhi
Singapore | Washington DC | Melbourne

FOR INFORMATION:

SAGE Publications, Inc.
2455 Teller Road
Thousand Oaks, California 91320
E-mail: order@sagepub.com

SAGE Publications Ltd.
1 Oliver's Yard
55 City Road
London, EC1Y 1SP
United Kingdom

SAGE Publications India Pvt. Ltd.
B 1/I 1 Mohan Cooperative Industrial Area
Mathura Road, New Delhi 110 044
India

SAGE Publications Asia-Pacific Pte. Ltd.
18 Cross Street #10-10/11/12
China Square Central
Singapore 048423

Printed in the United States of America

ISBN: 978-1-5443-6905-1

This book is printed on acid-free paper.

Sponsoring Editor: Lara Parra
Product Associate: Kenzie Offley
Production Editor: Astha Jaiswal
Copy Editor: Diana Breti
Typesetter: Hurix Digital
Cover Designer: Gail Buschman
Marketing Manager: Victoria Velasquez

21 22 23 24 25   10 9 8 7 6 5 4 3 2 1

• Brief Contents •

• Detailed Contents •

Chapter 14 • International Cooperation 352

• Preface •

Welcome to the fifth edition of *Peace and Conflict Studies*. Not surprisingly, a lot has happened since we wrote the fourth edition, about five years ago. Although it isn't clear whether the pace of events is quicker now than in the past, it often feels that way.

In any event, it is striking to consider how rapidly the world changes compared to that of any academic discipline: That's why it's called "current events"! Since the fourth edition of this book, the United States of America and Russia have gone from a situation of cautious collaboration to increasingly overt distrust, bordering on another Cold War and including threats of renewed nuclear competition. Somewhat less volatile, but if anything more economically and politically consequential, China has assumed an increasingly prominent international role as the world's second-largest economy, soon to surpass the United States in total gross national product and with an ever more assertive footprint when it comes to world politics generally.

Much of the Arab world went from an exciting time of prodemocracy movements to deep disillusionment, disappointment, and violence. One "terrorist" organization (al-Qaeda) diminished in importance and was replaced by another (ISIS), which has been militarily defeated, at least in Iraq and Syria, but nonetheless remains a potentially potent force worldwide, especially in North Africa, Afghanistan, and other parts of Asia. The Trump administration (2017–2021) engaged in a hyper-nationalistic "go-it-alone" policy that disrupted many of the prior relationships among countries, notably the stability and reliability of Western collaboration, which had previously counted on US support and collaboration. Along the way, numerous assumptions about the stability of global relationships—especially those based on the assumption of US stability—were shattered; their future remains to be seen. Moreover, the global environmental situation has further deteriorated, notably with respect to two crises: climate and the novel coronavirus pandemic that emerged in 2020.

Although this book is directed to a global audience, it will doubtless continue to be especially relevant to students and teachers in the United States in particular and to the English-speaking world and Scandinavia, more generally. Given the many missteps of the recent Trump administration, not the least of which are the incitement of violent mob insurrections—most notably on the US Capitol on January 6, 2021—along with the importance of the United States when it comes to world events, it is critical how the Biden administration deals with the many crises it has inherited: especially those involving the economy, the pandemic, racial justice, social inequities, and climate change. Only the future will reveal whether the extraordinary malfeasance of the Trump administration and the unprecedented threat to American democracy posed by its leader and base were an aberration from the norms and processes of the US system—and whether they will be successfully surmounted.

All things considered, the rate of change sometimes seems so dizzying that it has been hard to keep up, and periodically we wish that we were specialists in such "stable" fields as ancient languages or Baroque harpsichord music.

Fortunately, not all changes have been for the worse. There are encouraging signs of global cooperation when it comes to environmental awareness, including global campaigns to mitigate climate change and the development and distribution of vaccines to fight Covid-19. Millions of people—especially in Asia—enjoy greater prosperity and health than ever before. Global communication and other indications of connectedness have expanded. By some measures, even as world attention has been riveted on specific acts of terrible violence and disunity, our world has actually grown more peaceful, statistically speaking.

At the same time, and fortunately (at least for those who write textbooks and teach about these events and their significance), some things remain unchanged, namely, the historical and philosophical background of world affairs as well as the implications of what has happened, and is happening, and—perhaps—what is likely to take place in the future.

Probably more than any other discipline, peace and conflict studies (the subject) as well as *Peace and Conflict Studies* (the book) are deeply enmeshed in and concerned about that world. You are therefore about to enter an academic discipline but also much more than that. Everyone is welcome; indeed, you are unavoidably engaged in issues of peace and conflict, contentment and dissatisfaction, life and death, whatever your current "course load"! The Russian revolutionary Leon Trotsky once commented that although you might not be interested in war, war is interested in you. So are peace, social justice and injustice, environmental phenomena, and much more.

In the fourth edition of this book, written immediately following the 2016 election of Donald Trump as president of the United States, we added a "Supplementary Preface," in which we analyzed some of the implications of the election and made some tentative predictions. The ensuing four years have, unfortunately, demonstrated that our expectations regarding the Trump administration were, if anything, too measured and "optimistic," although our fear that the United States would engage in one or more gratuitous wars was not realized. We now revisit and supplement what we wrote then, with some reflections regarding the possible "legacy" of Donald Trump and Trumpism.

In November 2020, Joe Biden was elected president of the United States, disappointing the more than 74 million voters who had supported the re-election of Donald J. Trump, while providing welcome relief to most of the American electorate and to much of the rest of the world as well. Biden carried the US Electoral College 306–232 and had the highest popular vote in US history, with more than 81 million and a margin of more than 7 million votes over Trump. The long-term consequences of Biden's victory are unforeseeable, as are the responses of the millions of voters who supported Trump, especially the most violent and seditious fringes. The refusal of Donald Trump, his enablers, and his supporters to accept the clear results of that election not only roiled the US political environment, but it has threatened to undermine the fundamental democratic institutions of the United States, with likely negative consequences for the future—within the United States and abroad because many countries have, until recently, regarded the United States as a model of democratic government. Other notable downsides of the Trump administration include the following:

1. A reversal of climate change policies; withdrawal of the United States from international treaties and accords, most notably the Paris Agreement, as a result of which coordinated efforts to reverse climate change have to some extent faltered worldwide; increased domestic focus on coal, oil,

and nuclear energy, with decreases in funding and support for alternative sources of energy; and the dilution or elimination of much environmental protection regulation with increasingly grave consequences for water, air, land, and the biosphere domestically and globally.

2. The loss of health insurance by about 20 million or more Americans who had obtained coverage from the Obama-sponsored Affordable Care Act, plus the danger of yet more uninsured people; the spread of infectious diseases and epidemics (Covid-19 in particular); and underfunding of the National Institutes of Health, Centers for Disease Control and Prevention, National Institute of Mental Health, along with scientific and scholarly research more generally; reduced public acknowledgment of the validity of science as a whole, along with increased distrust of mainstream news reporting: a kind of "truth-decay"; and pressure to reverse gains in reproductive rights, especially for women, including the possible eventual reversal of *Roe v. Wade,* the Supreme Court decision that legalized abortion.

3. The deportation of thousands of immigrants and refugees, leading to a significant worsening of the global refugee crisis and to a rise in the number of victims of civil and regional wars; an upsurge in racism, sexism, ultranationalism, jingoism, Islamophobia, violent right-wing extremism, and xenophobia in the United States and in other countries undergoing waves of "populist nationalism," followed by uprisings and violence across the United States; and protests against US policies around the world and a worsening of relations with many other nations, with the exception of Israel and some Persian Gulf States.

4. The "packing" of the Supreme Court and other judicial and federal agencies with far-right conservatives who may be seeking to enforce measures protective of corporate and religious fundamentalist interests and to reverse legal protections for women, minorities, the disabled, immigrants, the impoverished, LGBTQ individuals, and the disadvantaged.

5. The encouragement of far-right, nativist, nationalist, and neo-fascist political movements within the United States and in other countries, notably in Europe, although possibly elsewhere as well, as in Brazil and the Philippines.

6. The disparagement and debasement of longstanding democratic political ideals and practices, including the federal election; and degrading of the office of the US presidency itself, leading to dismay and alarm within the United States and around the world, along with a substantial reduction in the esteem that the United States had previously enjoyed.

To address these disturbing trends, we propose for our readers' consideration the following potential courses of action, individually and collectively, should the legacy of the Trump administration persist after Trump's departure from the White House:

1. Remain silent, accept the policies of the new Biden administration, and hope that Trump and his policies will prove to be a singularly disruptive anomaly in the history of the American presidency.

2. Have individual conversations and debates about the strengths and weaknesses of the new and previous administrations, supporting

what one favors and objecting to what one dislikes about its policies, proposals, and actions.

3. Join and support the ongoing but thus-far unsuccessful movement to abolish or reform the Electoral College, which was originally set up in large measure to protect Southern slave-owning and rural agricultural interests against Northern urban interests and elites, and replace it with either a national popular vote or the proposed National Popular Vote Interstate Compact, in which each participating state agrees to allocate its electors to the winner of the vote nationwide.

4. Become part of a mass domestic and international nonviolent political revolution to resist the legacy of the Trump administration and its policies and to catalyze the new administration to pursue policies supportive of social, racial, and gender equity and justice, both domestically and internally.

As we emphasize throughout this text, peace and conflict studies differs from other branches of scholarship, not merely in the overall richness of its intellectual material but in its commitment to help create a better world and in its overt hope that you, the reader, will undertake your own commitment actively to support this effort.

Toward that end, we have sought to combine our own sociopolitical orientation with informed scholarship, to analyze recent events while not getting mired in short-term issues of the moment, and, where appropriate, to engage in advocacy without sacrificing academic rigor. As is often the case with co-authored books, we are not in complete accord about everything in this book, notably the degree to which academic style and detailed referencing are always suitable for a project of this kind. But we are in agreement about virtually every substantive issue covered in this long book, which is remarkable considering the number and range of topics covered, not to mention the degree to which issues of peace, war, and conflict themselves tend to generate their own opportunities for conflict, even among scholars! We also concur that you, the readers, should reflect on and debate the issues of greatest interest to you, to humanity, and to our shared planet in general.

We encourage feedback in this regard—and, indeed, on anything related to either the style or substance of this book—from students as well as faculty, just as we welcome all of you to this important subject, something as challenging, frustrating, rewarding, and important as anything we can imagine.

David P. Barash
University of Washington, Seattle, WA

Charles P. Webel
University of New York in Prague, Czech Republic

Acknowledgments

SAGE gratefully acknowledges the contributions of the following reviewers:

Carol Shaw Austad, Central Connecticut State University

Walton Brown-Foster, Central Connecticut State University

Mark Davidheiser, Nova Southeastern University

David Drews, Juniata College

The Promise of Peace, the Problems of War

In the third decade of the 21st century, we are faced with many problems. The Earth is composed of finite resources whose limits may soon be reached. Moreover, global climate change has been ongoing, already resulting in unprecedented catastrophes. Human societies contain gross maldistributions of wealth and power, another problem that has grown worse in recent years, preventing most human beings from realizing their potential and driving millions of people to despair, violent political extremism, and premature death.

Many cultural systems perpetuate regrettable patterns of economic, social, and political injustice in which racism, sexism, homophobia, militarism, ageism, religious intolerance, and other forms of unfairness abound and in which representative government is relatively rare and torture and other forms of oppression are distressingly common. The natural balance upon which all life depends has been increasingly disrupted. Global pandemics are not infrequent. Threats may also include super-intelligent and potentially malicious computers, existential risks of asteroid collisions, super-volcano eruptions, and, especially, thermonuclear war, the risk of which may well be increasing for the first time since the end of the Cold War between the United States and the former Soviet Union. And this is only a partial list.[1]

Yet, despite all of these difficulties, the remarkable fact is that enormous sums of money and vast resources of material, time, and energy are expended, not in solving what we might call the "problems of peace" but rather in threatening and actually making war on one another. Although it seems unlikely that human beings will ever achieve anything approaching heaven on Earth, or what the philosopher Immanuel Kant called "Perpetual Peace," it seems reasonable to hope—and perhaps even to demand—that we will someday behave more responsibly and establish a global community based on the needs of the entire planet and the beings who inhabit it, a planetary society that is just and sustainable and not characterized by repeated major outbreaks of violence. Seriously, along with the many problems confronting us, there is also the hopeful reality that to some degree these problems have generated social and political involvement among people increasingly committed to solving them.

This book explores some of the aspirations, needs, prospects, and obstacles involved in achieving a genuinely peaceful world. After opening chapters on the meanings and measurement of peace, it proceeds to examine war—its causes and prevention. This is one of humanity's most serious challenges because behind the threat of war—especially nuclear and/or biochemical war—lies the prospect that human beings may end their civilization and perhaps all life on Earth.

Part I looks specifically at the promise of peace and the problems of war. Although war and peace are not polar opposites, there is a fundamental tension between them, two differing ways in which people interact. Part II considers war and its apparent causes, and Part III looks at possible routes toward preventing and abolishing war and other forms of collective violence. Part IV turns to deeper aspects of peace, examining our shared dilemmas and considering some solutions, including the creation of positive structures of peace—steps that go beyond just preventing war. Each chapter concludes with some questions for further thought and discussion, along with a few recommended readings; however, because peace and conflict are a moving target, and this book aims to emphasize material with a longer "shelf life," it will go light on transient issues-of-the-moment. This 5th edition of *Peace and Conflict Studies* is intended not just to inform you but also to challenge you, not only intellectually but also in other dimensions of your life, and ideally to inspire you to work toward a better world.

The Meanings of Peace

War is one of humanity's most pressing problems; peace is almost always preferable to war and, moreover, it can and must include not only the absence of war but the establishment of positive, life-enhancing values, political institutions, and social structures. We know that there is no simple solution to the problem of war. Many aspects of the war-peace dilemma are complex, interconnected, and, even when well understood, difficult to move from theory to practice. On the other hand, much can be gained by exploring the various dimensions of war and peace, including the possibility of achieving a more just and sustainable world—a way of living that can nurture life.

Throughout this book, we maintain that there is good reason for such hope, not simply as an article of faith, but based on the realistic premise that human beings are capable of understanding the global situation and

The Meanings of Peace

War is one of humanity's most pressing problems; peace is almost always preferable to war and, moreover, it can and must include not only the absence of war but the establishment of positive, life-enhancing values, political institutions, and social structures. We know that there is no simple solution to the problem of war. Most aspects of the war-peace dilemma are complex, interconnected, and, even when well understood, difficult to move from theory to practice. On the other hand, much can be gained by exploring the various dimensions of war and peace, including the possibility of achieving a more just and sustainable world—a way of living that can nurture life.

Throughout this book, we maintain that there is good reason for such hope, not simply as an article of faith but based on the realistic premise that human beings are capable of understanding the global situation and recognizing their own species-wide best interests. People can behave rationally, creatively, with compassion, and, over time and with collective good will, can diminish—and, ideally, eliminate—most if not all forms of violence.

Most people think they know what *peace* means, but in fact different people often have very different understandings of this seemingly simple word. And although most would agree that some form of peace—whatever it means—is desirable, there are often vigorous, even violent, disagreements over how to obtain it.

The Meanings of Peace

Peace is surprisingly difficult to define. Like happiness, harmony, justice, and freedom, it is something we often recognize by its absence. Johan Galtung, a founder of peace studies and peace research, has proposed an important distinction between "positive" and "negative" peace. "Positive" peace denotes the presence of many desirable states of mind and society, such as harmony, justice, equity, and so on. "Negative" peace has historically meant the "absence of war." By contrast, positive peace refers to a condition in which exploitation is minimized or eliminated and in which there is neither overt violence nor the more subtle phenomenon of underlying *structural violence*. Positive peace denotes the continuing presence of an equitable and just social order as well as ecological harmony.

Many philosophical, religious, and cultural traditions refer to peace in its positive sense. In Chinese, for example, the word *heping* denotes world peace, or peace among nations, while the words *an* and *mingsi* denote an "inner peace," a tranquil and harmonious state of mind and being akin to a meditative mental state. Other languages also frame peace in its "inner" and "outer" dimensions.

The English language has many terms that refer to peace. In *Webster's Third New International Dictionary,* for example, peace is initially defined as "freedom from civil clamor and confusion" and also as "a state of public quiet," as well as "a state of mutual concord between governments: absence of hostilities or war." In some cases and some cultures, the word *peace* even has an undesirable connotation. The Roman writer Tacitus spoke of making a desert and calling it "peace," an unwanted situation of sterility and emptiness. To be *pacified,* derived from *pax,* the Latin word for peace, often means to be subdued or lulled into a false and misleading quietude. Indeed, *appeasement*—buying off a would-be aggressor—has acquired a very bad name. In probably the most notorious example of appeasement, former British prime minister Neville Chamberlain appeased Hitler in September 1938, famously declaring as he signed the Munich Agreement, which essentially gave in to all of Hitler's demands: "I believe it is peace for our time." (Less than a year later, Hitler invaded Poland, effectively starting World War II on the European continent.) At the time, however, public opinion had generally supported "appeasement," seeing it as a reasonable and far-seeing effort to meet the legitimate needs of an aggrieved party and to do so short of war. Today, appeasement stands as a warning to genuinely peace-loving people that even efforts toward peace can backfire if unwisely pursued.

By contrast, even the most peace-loving among us recognize the merits of certain martial and aggressive attitudes, especially when referring to something other than direct military engagements: President Lyndon Johnson's "war on poverty," for example, or the medical "war on cancer," and "battle against AIDS."

Some Eastern Concepts of Peace

The foregoing is not simply a matter of playing with words. Fighting, striving, and engaging in various forms of conflict and combat (especially when they are successful) are widely associated with vigor, courage, and other positive virtues. Nonetheless, it is no exaggeration to claim that peace, along with happiness, may be the most longed-for human condition.

Chinese philosopher Lao Tzu (6th century BCE), founder of Taoism and author of the *Tao Te Ching,* emphasized that military force is not the recommended *Tao,* or "Way." He frequently referred to peaceful images of water or wind—both soft and yielding yet ultimately triumphant over such hard substances as rock or iron. The teachings of Confucius (approximately 551–479 BCE) are often thought by most Westerners to focus on respect for tradition, including elders and ancestors. But Confucius did not hold to these ideas because he valued obedience and order as virtues in themselves; rather, he maintained that the attainment of peace was the ultimate human goal and that it came from social harmony and equilibrium. His best-known collection of writings, the *Analects,* also emphasizes the doctrine of *jen* (empathy), founded on a kind of hierarchical Golden Rule: treat your subordinates as you would like to be treated by your superiors.

The writings of another renowned ancient Chinese philosopher and religious leader, Mo Tzu (468–391 BCE), took a more radical perspective. He argued against war and in favor of all-embracing love as a universal human virtue and the highest earthly goal, yet one that is within the grasp of each of us. Mo Tzu said, "Those who love others will also be loved in return. Do good to others and others will do good to you. Hate people and be hated by them. Hurt them and they will hurt you. What is hard about that?"[2] In what is now India, the Buddhist monarch Ashoka (3rd century BCE) was renowned for abandoning his successful military campaigns in the middle of his career and devoting himself to the religious conversion of his adversaries by nonviolent means.

The great ancient Indian text, the Hindu epic *Mahabharata* (written about 200 BCE), contains as perhaps its most important segment the *Bhagavad Gita.* This is a mythic account of a vicious civil war in which Arjuna, one of the principal warriors, is reluctant to fight because many of his friends and relatives are on the opposing side. Arjuna is ultimately persuaded to engage in combat by the god Krishna, who convinces Arjuna that he must fight, not out of hatred or hope for personal gain but out of selfless duty. Although the *Gita* can be and has been interpreted as supporting caste loyalty and the obligation to kill when bidden to do so by a superior party, it also inspired the great 20th-century Indian leader Mohandas Gandhi as an allegory for the de-emphasis of individual self in the pursuit of higher goals. The *Gita* was also cited by the "father of the atomic bomb," J. Robert Oppenheimer, when he described the first atomic explosion as a contemporary incarnation of Krishna: "I am become Death, the Destroyer of Worlds."

Some Judeo-Christian Concepts of Peace

Peace per se is not prominent in the Old Testament. The God (Yahweh) of Abraham, Moses, and David is frequently portrayed as bellicose, even bloodthirsty, and the ancient Israelites were often merciless warriors. Exceptions exist, however, such as the prophet Isaiah, who praised the reign of peace and described war as a punishment to be inflicted on those who have failed God.

Under the influence of Isaiah and later Hebrew prophets—and despite the ostensibly defensive violence of the Maccabees and Zealots (who opposed Roman rule in the lands now called Israel and Palestine and who have sometimes been called history's first recorded terrorists)—Jewish tradition has tended to strongly endorse peacefulness. On the other hand, it can also be argued that with the emergence of Israel as a militarily threatened—and threatening—state, this tradition has substantially changed. In fact, Jewish, Christian, and Islamic traditions all have bellicose components and elements in their history. A key question is whether such militarism—often persistent and widespread—is part of a pattern of faithfulness to, or a deviation from, their underlying religious worldview.

A deep irony underlies the concept of peace in these three great Western religious systems. "My peace I give unto you," declares Jesus, according to the New Testament, along with "the peace of God, which passeth all understanding" and the Sermon on the Mount, which famously urges followers to turn the other cheek. Christianity is, in fact, unique among Western religions in the degree to which it was founded upon a message of peace, love, and nonviolence, and yet it gave rise to one of the great warrior traditions. Although definitions of peace often vary and hypocrisy is not infrequent, most people share a positive presumption in favor of peace, in accord with the stated aspirations of most major religions.

Positive and Negative Peace

Let us recall the important distinction between positive and negative peace. Negative peace usually denotes the absence of war. It is a condition in which little, if any, active, organized military violence is taking place. When the noted 20th-century French intellectual Raymond Aron defined peace as a condition of "more or less lasting suspension of rivalry between political units," he was thinking of negative peace.[4] Aron's is the most common understanding of peace in the context of conventional political science and international relations, and it epitomizes the so-called realist view that peace is found whenever war or other direct forms of organized state violence are absent. From this perspective, the peace proclamations of Pharaonic Egypt, the *Philanthropa*, were actually statements of negative peace, expressions of benevolence from a stronger party toward those who were weaker. Similarly, the well-known *pax* of Roman times indicated little more than the absence of overt organized violence, typically a condition of nonresistance or even acquiescence enforced by local arrangements and the military might of the Roman legions. The negative peace of the *Pax Romana* was created and maintained, in large measure, through social and political repression of those who lived under Roman law.

An alternative view to this realist (or *Realpolitik*) perspective is one that emphasizes the importance of positive peace and that has been particularly advanced by Norwegian peace researcher Johan Galtung. Positive peace refers to a social condition in which exploitation is minimized or eliminated and in which there is neither overt violence nor the subtle phenomenon of underlying *structural violence*. It denotes the continuing presence of an equitable and just social order as well as ecological harmony.

Structural and Cultural Violence

Violence is usually understood to be physical and readily apparent. But it is important to recognize the existence of other forms of violence that are more indirect and insidious. This structural and cultural violence is typically built into the nature of social, cultural, and economic institutions. For example, both ancient Egypt and imperial Rome practiced slavery and were highly despotic, although they were technically in states of negative peace for long periods of time.

Structural violence usually has the effect of denying people important rights, such as economic well-being; social, political, and sexual equality; a sense of personal fulfillment and self-worth, and the like. When people starve to death or go hungry, violence is taking place. Similarly, when people suffer from preventable diseases or when they are denied a decent education, afford- able housing, freedom of expression and of peaceful assembly, or opportuni- ties to work, play, or raise a family, violence is occurring, even if no bullets are shot or no clubs wielded. A society commits violence against its members when it forcibly stunts their development and undermines their well-being, whether because of religion, ethnicity, gender, age, sexual preference, social class, or some other factor. Structural violence is a form of oppression that can also involve mistreatment of the natural environment. However defined, structural violence is widespread, hurtful, and often unacknowledged.

Under conditions of structural violence, many people who behave as good citizens and who think of themselves as peace loving may, as Galtung puts it, participate in "settings within which individuals may do enormous amounts of harm . . . without ever intending to do so, just performing their regular duties as a job defined in the structure."[3] Analyzing the role of "normal" people, such as Adolf Eichmann, who helped carry out the Holocaust during World War II, philosopher Hannah Arendt referred to the "banality of evil," emphasizing that routine, workaday behavior by otherwise normal, decent people can con- tribute to mass murder, social oppression, and structural violence.

In contrast with structural violence of starvation, underlying racism, eco- nomic impoverishment, and psychological alienation, direct violence gener- ally works faster and is more visible and dramatic. In cases of overt violence, even those people not specifically involved in the conflict may be inclined to take sides. News coverage of these events is often intense, and because the outcome is typically visible and undeniable (e.g., wars, terrorism, as well as acts of domestic repression such as the murder and violent removal of Chinese citizens from Tiananmen Square by Chinese Army troops in 1989), the public is more likely to pay attention to what they can see rather than to the underlying structural but less visible factors that may have led to the conflict.

The concept of *cultural violence* can be seen as a follow-up to the idea of structural violence. Cultural violence is any aspect (often symbolic) of a cul- ture that can be used to legitimize violence in its direct or structural forms. Symbolic violence built into a culture does not kill or maim like direct vio- lence or that built into a social structure. However, it is used to legitimize either or both, as in the Nazi theory of a *Herrenvolk* or superior ("master") race.

Structural and cultural violence are, however, contested concepts. Clearly, they occur wherever there is slavery or gross political, cultural, and/or eco- nomic oppression; it remains debatable, on the other hand, whether social inequality constitutes structural violence and whether culture-specific norms and practices can even constitute violence. And what about skewed access to education, jobs, or medical care? Does simple social hierarchy (as, for example, in a family or classroom) constitute structural violence, and do culturally relative forms of life amount to cultural violence?

Achieving Positive Peace

Many cultural and spiritual traditions have identified political and social goals that are closer to positive than negative peace. The ancient Greek concept of *eireinei* (the related English word is *irenic*) means harmony and justice as well as peace. Similarly, the Arabic *salaam* and the Hebrew *shalom* connote not only the absence of violence but also the presence of well-being, wholeness, and harmony within one's self, a community, and among all nations and peoples. The Sanskrit word *shanti* refers not only to peace but also to spiritual tranquility, an integration of outward and inward modes of being, just as the Chinese *ping* denotes harmony and the achievement of unity from diversity. In Russian, *mir* means peace, a village community, and the world.

Public awareness of negative peace, or the simple absence of war, usually comes about via a diplomatic emphasis on peacekeeping or peace restoring (if war has already broken out). Negative peace is a conservative, status-preserving goal, as it seeks to keep things the way they are (if a war is not actually taking place), whereas positive peace is more ambitious and bolder, implying the creation of something that, in most cases, does not currently exist.

Moreover, just as there is disagreement about how best to avoid a war—that is, how to achieve negative peace—even among decision makers who may be well intentioned, there is often disagreement about the best routes toward positive peace. Peace in its positive form is more difficult to articulate, and possibly more difficult to achieve, than its negative version. Although there is relatively little current debate about the desired end point in pursuing negative peace (most people agree that war is a bad thing), there is considerable controversy over *how* to prevent (or terminate) specific wars, as well as war generally.

People often disagree about the justification for any particular war. When it comes to positive peace, there is substantial disagreement about goals and the means to achieve them. Some theorists have argued, for example, that only negative peace should be pursued because once defined idealistically as a goal to be achieved, peace becomes something to strive for, even perhaps to the point of going to war! As Quincy Wright, one of the 20th century's preeminent researchers into the causes of war, put it:

> Wars have been fought for the sanctity of treaties, for the preservation of law, for the achievement of justice, for the promotion of religion, even to end war and to secure peace. When peace assumes a positive form, therefore, it ceases to be peace. Peace requires that no end should justify violence as a means to its attainment.[4]

Other notable figures have maintained that a free society may justify—or even require—occasional violence. Thomas Jefferson, for example, wrote in 1787 that "the tree of liberty must be refreshed from time to time with the blood of patriots and tyrants." This apparent paradox—violence as a precondition for attaining its alternative—is a recurring theme in the study of and quest for peace.

Supporters of positive peace nonetheless agree that a repressive society, even if it is not at war, should be considered at peace only in a very narrow sense. In addition, a nation at peace that tolerates outbreaks of domestic violence on a widespread level, despite an absence of violent conflicts with other nations, is not really at peace with itself.

Social Justice

Having recognized the importance of positive peace, we now turn to a related notion: social justice. Although almost everyone today agrees that a just society is desirable, there is often widespread disagreement as to what, exactly, a just society looks like, or how to achieve it. For example, whereas capitalists and individualists tend to privilege economic freedom from state intervention along with individual liberty—often at the cost of mass poverty, malnutrition, and homelessness—socialists and collectivists tend to value economic and social security, sometimes at the price of individual freedoms. Also, many Western individualists assert that nations with capitalist economies and democratic political systems seldom, if ever, go to war with one another, whereas many non-Western and dissident Western critics of capitalism claim that capitalism by its very expansionistic nature is inherently predatory and militaristic, impelling ostensibly democratic nations to invade and occupy undemocratic but economically and/or strategically important countries, usually in the non-Western world.

The Peace-War Continuum

"War is not sharply distinguished from peace," according to Quincy Wright. Moreover,

> Progress of war and peace between a pair of states may be represented by a curve: the curve descends toward war as tensions, military preparations, and limited hostilities culminate in total conflict; and it rises toward peace as tensions relax, arms budgets decline, disputes are settled, trade increases, and cooperative activities develop.[5]

Although a quick look at war and peace gives the impression that the two are clearly distinguished, a more detailed examination suggests that *war and peace are two ends of a continuum,* with only a vague and uncertain transition between the two. But the fact that two things may lack precise boundaries does not mean that they are indistinguishable. Thus, at dawn, night grades almost imperceptibly into day and vice versa at dusk. Yet when two things are very distinct, we say that "they are as different as night and day." The transition from war to peace may often be similarly imprecise (although the move from peace to war may be all too clear and dramatic, as was evident at the beginning of World War II, both in Europe and in the Pacific).

Consider, for example, that the US involvement in Vietnam and much of the rest of Southeast Asia began in the early 1950s with economic and military aid to French forces seeking to retain their colonial possessions. It progressed to include the deployment of relatively small numbers of "technical advisers" in the early 1960s to what was then called South Vietnam. Larger numbers of American "advisers" were then added, accompanied by combat troops in small numbers, followed by limited and eventually massive bombing of all Vietnam (and its neighbors Laos and Cambodia). Finally, even though more than 500,000 American troops were eventually committed to propping up a corrupt and autocratic South Vietnamese government engaged in both a civil war and in hostilities against what was then called North Vietnam, and even though more than 50,000 Americans died as did perhaps more than 2 million Vietnamese, Cambodians, and Laotians, the United States never formally declared war! Yet there was no doubt that a state of war existed.

There is an increasing tendency—especially since the Vietnam War and notably during America's "War on Terror(ism)"—for nations to fight wars without a formal declaration and, similarly, without solemn peace ceremonies or treaties signaling their end. The Korean War, for example, which began in 1950, was never officially declared and has never technically ended (although there has been a prolonged ceasefire, with rare outbreaks of violence, between North and South Korea over more than a half-century). One of the most destructive wars of the second half of the 20th century, the conflict between Iran and Iraq in the 1980s, was never declared, although it produced casualties that may have numbered in the millions (and Iraq probably used chemical weapons and may have been developing biological weapons). In fact, most of the world's armed conflicts involve revolutionary, counter-revolutionary, genocidal, and/or terrorist violence with no declarations of war whatsoever. Examples include East Timor, Kashmir, Sudan, Democratic Republic of the Congo, Rwanda, and much of the rest of central Africa; the former Yugoslavia and several independent nations spawned from the former Soviet Union; and El Salvador, Nicaragua, Guatemala, Afghanistan, Angola, Syria, Libya, Yemen, and Cambodia. By the same token, the US-led invasions of Afghanistan and Iraq were not preceded by formal declarations of war and seem unlikely to conclude with official announcements of peace.

The reluctance of most governments to declare war, as opposed to their willingness to fight or promote wars, may also result from the fact that although wars continue to be fought and to break out, most citizens and politicians are not proud of that fact. And despite theoretical arguments over the precise transitions between different stages of conflicts, most people know at a gut level what is meant by war. There is also little doubt that, given the choice, most would prefer peace.

Measuring Peace

Defining and Redefining Peace

The concept of peace remains nonetheless difficult to define. This may partly explain why there have been so few attempts to measure states of peace across nations. Although scholars have made numerous attempts to measure and operationalize "war," it is only recently that similar efforts have been made to measure peace.

The Global Peace Index

Unlike such economic indices as gross national product or unemployment rates, the peacefulness of a country does not readily lend itself to direct measurement. However, the Global Peace Index (GPI), produced by the Institute for Economics and Peace in Sydney, Australia and updated annually, has succeeded in generating a credible assessment.[6]

The GPI offers us the opportunity not only to rank countries with regard to their peacefulness, but—more importantly—to begin assessing what factors correlate with peaceful versus nonpeaceful societies. For example, the 2019 GPI examined 163 countries, comprising more than 99% of the world's population, and used 23 qualitative and quantitative indicators that reflect three broad themes: (1) level of internal safety and security, (2) involvement in domestic or international conflict, and (3) degree of militarization. Measurements used include number of external conflicts, internal conflicts, violent domestic demonstrations, incarceration and murder rates, relations with neighboring countries, and so forth.

According to the 2019 GPI, Europe is the most peaceful region, while the Middle East and North Africa are the least peaceful. The 10 most peaceful countries are, in order: Iceland, New Zealand, Portugal, Austria, Denmark, Canada, Singapore, Slovenia, Japan, and the Czech Republic. The United States ranks rather poorly—128th out of 163 countries—while the least peaceful country is Afghanistan, closely followed by Syria, South Sudan, Yemen, Iraq, Somalia, Central African Republic, Libya, Democratic Republic of the Congo, Russia, and Pakistan. Democracies consistently have the strongest level of positive peace but represent the minority of countries. Similarly, high-income countries generally rate very highly in the Positive Peace Index. The most militarized country is Israel, followed in turn by Russia, the US, North Korea, and France.

Importantly, peace is becoming more unevenly distributed. While Europe continues its long-term trend of pacification, the Middle East continues its recent tendency for belligerence, further increasing the distance between the most and least peaceful regions and countries. In Europe and in many other developed countries, homicide rates and other forms of interpersonal violence continue to drop and are at historic lows. By contrast, rates of interpersonal violence have climbed in Central America.

The economic impact of violence on the global economy in 2018 was substantial and is estimated at more than $15 trillion, equivalent to the combined economies of Brazil, Canada, France, Germany, Spain, and the United Kingdom.

The United States

In 2012, the United States was chosen for the first national peace index (Mexico and the UK were subsequently selected, and a second US Peace Index appeared more recently) principally due to the high quality of state-level data, dating back to the early 1980s, and the existence of a large literature of related studies, which estimate the various costs of violence as well as the costs associated with containing it.[7] The United States performs well on citizen perception of crime within the country and on the low likelihood of violent demonstrations. But as already noted, the United States fares comparatively poorly on the GPI, especially when compared to other highly developed Western-style democracies, mainly due to its involvement in numerous wars, its exceptionally high level of military expenditures, and its civil unrest.

The United States also has a higher rate of violence than most other developed economies, although trends in crime over the past 20 years have fluctuated substantially, for reasons that have been much debated. At the beginning of the 1980s, the US crime rate was comparable to that of other developed nations, after which violence steadily increased to a peak in the mid-1990s and has since been falling. However, this reduction has been accompanied by a steadily *increasing* incarceration rate leading to an unrivaled percentage of its population behind bars—especially people of color—which has significant economic, racial, and social consequences.

Here are some significant findings from the US Peace Index: Compared to most other countries, relatively more data are available for the United States, permitting a more fine-grained analysis:

1. During the last 25 years, there has been a substantial decrease in the rates of homicide and violent crime. (Because of a drumbeat of misinformation, however, due in large part to Trump and his supporters as well as some social media, the majority of Americans mistakenly believe otherwise.) These improvements have been largely offset by increases in the incarceration rate, which, as of year-end 2018,

stood at 0.7% of resident adults, the highest in the world. Although some political conservatives claim that this is due to the greater effectiveness of US criminal enforcement activities, most experts reject this interpretation and associate the high US incarceration rate with unusually punitive social traditions and the targeting by law enforcement agencies of people of color, especially males.

2. The five most peaceful states are Maine, New Hampshire, Vermont, Minnesota, and North Dakota. The Northeast is the most peaceful region in the United States, with all of its states ranking in the top half of the US Peace Index. This includes the heavily populated states of New York, Pennsylvania, and New Jersey. The least peaceful states are Louisiana, Tennessee, Nevada, Florida, and Alabama.

3. Peace is linked to opportunity, health, education, and the economy. Statistically significant correlations exist between a state's peacefulness (notably low crime rate) and 15 different social and economic factors, such that higher scores in peacefulness are associated with higher scores in health, education, and economic opportunity, but not with political affiliation.

4. The potential economic gains from improvements in peace are significant. Improvements in peace would result in the realization of substantial savings for both governments and society as a whole. If the United States reduced its violence to the same levels as Canada, for example, local governments would collectively save about $89 billion. For instance, lost productivity from assault and from incarceration constitutes the greatest share of the total cost of violence, so states with high levels of incarceration and assault tend to have a higher per capita cost. The release of "trapped productivity" via a reduction of violence would create a stimulus that could generate an additional 1.7 million new jobs. And the benefit of transferring state and federal expenditures from violence-containment industries (including the military, police, and prison-industrial complex) to more economically productive industries is significant. This can be exemplified by building more new schools than jails and by employing more new teachers than missile designers. Although such efforts would not necessarily generate additional economic activity in themselves, they would create the foundation for a more productive economy. The implementation of such additional economic activity is defined as the "dynamic peace dividend," which can result in a substantial lift in GDP, employment, and quality of life.

5. Growing incarceration is a drag on the economy and in recent years has not had a significant effect on violent crime. While homicide and violent crime rates have fallen, the economic benefits to flow from these decreases have been largely offset by the costs associated with the increase in the incarceration rate. In recent years, there has been no statistically meaningful relationship between increases in incarceration rates and decreases in violent crime.

6. There is a strong correlation between peacefulness within each state and people's satisfaction with their access to such basic services as clean water, medicine, a safe place to exercise, affordable fruits and vegetables; enough money for food, shelter, and health care; perceptions of safety within one's community, and access to necessary medical care.

Culture of Peace

In 1999, the United Nations (UN) General Assembly launched a program of action to build a "culture of peace" for the world's children, which envisaged working toward a positive peace of justice, tolerance, and plenty. The UN defined a culture of peace as involving values, attitudes, and behaviors that

- reject violence,

- endeavor to prevent conflicts by addressing root causes, and

- aim at solving problems through dialogue and negotiation.

The UN proposed that such a culture of peace would be furthered by actions promoting education for peace and sustainable development, which it suggested was based on human rights, gender equality, democratic participation, tolerant solidarity, open communication, and international security. However, these links between the concept of peace and its alleged causes were presumed rather than systematically measured. For example, although advocates of liberal peace theory have held that democratic states rarely attack each other, the ongoing wars in Iraq, Afghanistan, and elsewhere demonstrate how some democratic countries can be militant or belligerent— the justification for war often being that peace is ultimately secured through violence or the threat of violence.

A Final Note on the Meanings of Peace

Neither the study nor the pursuit of peace ignores the importance of conflict. Peace and conflict studies does not aim to abolish conflict any more than peace practitioners expect to eliminate rivalry or competition in a world of finite resources and imperfect human conduct. (Analogously, medicine and public health do not realistically seek to eliminate all bacteria or viruses from the world, although they are committed to human betterment by struggling against those that generate diseases.)

Where possible, peace and conflict studies seeks to develop new avenues for cooperation, as well as to reduce violence, especially organized, state-sanctioned violence and the terrorizing violence perpetrated both by and against non-state actors. It is this violence, by any definition the polar opposite of peace, that has so blemished human history and that—with the advent of nuclear weapons, biochemical weapons, and other mechanisms of global destruction—now threatens the future of life on this planet. And it is the horror of such violence, as well as the hope for peace (both negative and positive), that make peace and conflict studies especially frustrating, fascinating, and essential.

Questions for Further Reflection

1. Is peace an absolute, or are there degrees of peace, both outer and inner?

2. To what extent are peace and war mutually exclusive?

3. Under which circumstances, if any, is conflict inescapable and perhaps even desirable?

4. Under which circumstances, if any, is violence inescapable and perhaps even desirable?

5. Assess the strengths and weaknesses of empirical tools such as the GPI for measuring peace and its absence.

Suggestions for Further Reading

David P. Barash, ed. 2018. *Approaches to Peace: A Reader in Peace Studies*, 4th ed. New York and Oxford: Oxford University Press.

Elise Boulding. 2000. *Cultures of Peace: The Hidden Side of History.* Syracuse, NY: Syracuse University Press.

Richard Caplan. 2019. *Measuring Peace.* Oxford and New York: Oxford University Press.

David Cortright. 2009. *Peace: A History of Movements and Ideas.* Cambridge and New York: Cambridge University Press.

Michael Mandelbaum. 2019. *The Rise and Fall of Peace on Earth.* New York: Oxford University Press.

Oliver Richmond. 2016. *Peace Formation and Political Order in Conflict Affected Societies.* New York and Oxford: Oxford University Press.

Oliver Richmond, Sandra Pogodda, and Jasmin Ramovic, eds. 2016. *The Palgrave Handbook of Disciplinary and Regional Approaches to Peace.* New York: Palgrave Macmillan.

Charles Webel and Jorgen Johansen, eds. 2012. *Peace and Conflict Studies: A Reader.* London and New York: Routledge.

Houston Wood. 2017. *Current Debates in Peace and Conflict Studies.* New York: Oxford University Press.

Nigel J. Young, ed. 2010. *The Oxford International Encyclopedia of Peace.* Four vols. Oxford and New York: Oxford University Press.

Notes

1. For an overview and analysis of existential risks to humanity and the Earth, see Nick Bostrom, ed. 2008. *Global Catastrophic Risks.* Oxford: Oxford University Press; Toby Ord. 2020. *The Precipice Existential Risk and the Future of Humanity.* London: Bloomsbury.

2. Mo Tzu. 1967. *Basic Writings of Mo Tzu.* New York: Columbia University Press.

3. Johan Galtung. 1985. "Twenty-Five Years of Peace Research: Ten Challenges and Responses." *Journal of Peace Research* 22: 141–158.

4. Quincy Wright. 1964. *A Study of War.* Chicago: University of Chicago Press.

5. Ibid.

6. For the *Global Peace Index* and related documents, including *COVID and Peace*, see http://www.visionofhumanity.org/gpi-data/

7. The 2012 United States Peace Index (USPI) is available at https://www.visionofhumanity.org/maps/us-peace-index/#/

Taylor Hill via Getty Images

Peace Studies, Peace Education, and Peace Research

Peace studies is a child of its time, notably the Cold War and the nuclear era from 1945 to the present. It is a transdisciplinary inquiry that has grown considerably since its birth during the mid-20th century, although its precursors go back to ancient times. On the other hand, the practice of peace education began in the early 20th century, partly in reaction to World War

I. It took off after World War II, as did the earliest peace studies programs at certain colleges and universities.

Similarly, although the origins of peace research date back to religious and ethical traditions across many world cultures and traditions, and the forerunners of scientific approaches to investigating peace and war emerged out of frustration over the advent of World War I (which was often called "the war no one wanted"), peace and conflict research as a distinct scholarly discipline gained momentum after World War II. It continues to be vibrant today.

Peace Studies, War Studies, and Peace and Conflict Studies

Whereas there have been different approaches to studying peace, contemporary Western peace studies (or *irenology,* from the Greek "Irene," the goddess of peace) focuses on the analysis, prevention, de-escalation, and solution of conflicts by peaceful or nonviolent means, thereby seeking satisfactory outcomes for all parties involved, rather than winners and losers. This is in contrast to traditional international and so-called security studies, which focus on factors leading to victory or defeat in conflicts waged principally by violent means and to the increased or decreased "security" of one—but typically not all—of the parties involved.

Because peace studies investigates the reasons for and outcomes of large- and small-scale conflicts, as well as the preconditions for peace, the discipline is also known as *peace and conflict studies* (PCS). Its focus allows one to examine not only war but also the various forms of violence, including structural violence—notably social oppression, discrimination, exploitation, and marginalization—while also addressing the effects of political, cultural, and physical violence. The rigorous analysis of peace and conflict lends itself, as well, to the assessment and promotion of various peacemaking strategies, in response to growing popular alarm about the many perils facing today's world.

Peace Education

The first organized initiatives in peace education focused on the horrors of war and generated statistics about weapon systems. Today, peace education consists of a wide variety of courses and programs aimed at giving students the tools to reduce violence and oppression. These include nonmilitary strategies for avoiding bullying and increasing citizen empowerment.

According to Betty Reardon, a noted American peace educator,

> the general purpose of peace education . . . is the development of an authentic planetary consciousness that will enable us to function as global citizens and to transform the present human condition by changing the social structures and patterns of thought that have created it.[1]

Like her fellow progressive peace educators, Reardon takes "a transformational approach," aiming not only to inform students but also to shift current conventional values, thinking, behaviors, and institutions away from violence and toward nonviolent solutions to interpersonal, social, and political disputes.

Toward this end, The Peace Education Foundation writes and publishes materials for conflict-resolution curricula currently used in more than 20,000 schools worldwide. Peace education is also strongly supported by the UN. Koichiro Matsuura, past director-general of the United Nations Educational, Scientific and Cultural Organization (UNESCO), has written that peace education is of "fundamental importance to the mission of UNESCO and the United Nations." Peace education has been increasingly integrated with education for democracy; women's rights as well as those of children, indigenous peoples, and LGBT (lesbian, gay, bisexual, and transgender) individuals; and human rights more generally, along with nonviolent conflict resolution.

The Israeli peace educator Gavriel Salomon has described some major challenges facing peace educators around the world today, especially those working in zones of ongoing and seemingly intractable conflict such as Israel and Palestine. In addition to political opposition to their programs and severe socioeconomic inequalities in the regions where they operate, peace educators face such challenges as conflicting collective narratives, divergent historical memories, and contradictory beliefs.

To maximize the enduring social impact of peace education, effective programs of peace education should take ethnic and social differences into account and combine general dispositions to peace with specific context-sensitive applications of peace pedagogy and practice. Peace and conflict studies may be viewed, in part, as the dimension of peace education that is present in institutions of higher learning.

The Dimensions of Peace and Conflict Studies

As a scholarly enterprise, PCS is multi- or transdisciplinary, incorporating important theories and research findings from anthropology, sociology, political science, international relations, psychology, biology and zoology, ethics and philosophy, theology, history, and aspects of contemporary neuroscience. Ideally, PCS is also multilevel because it examines inner peace and conflict, as well as peaceful and conflictual relations between individuals, neighbors, ethnic groups, organizations, states, and civilizations (or outer peace and conflict).

Central to peace studies, peace education, and peace research is a concern not just with understanding the world but with changing it. This is a bone of contention for academics who espouse "value neutrality and scientific impartiality," especially by such more conventional disciplines as political science, international relations, and strategic or security studies.

PCS is both normative (or prescriptive) and analytic (or descriptive). As a normative discipline, peace and conflict studies often makes value judgments, such as the assertion—often, the unspoken assumption—that peace and nonviolence are *better* than war and violence. But it makes these judgments both on the basis of ethical postulates (i.e., humans *should* resolve conflicts as nonviolently as possible) and of analytic descriptions (i.e., most violent efforts to resolve conflicts *in fact* result in less social stability than nonviolent means of conflict resolution). Also assumed is that violence is in itself undesirable. Importantly, such value judgments are not unusual in the academic world: medical science values health over disease, literary studies often focus on "classics of literature" rather than on "junk novels," just as art, music, mathematics—indeed, all scholarly enterprises—make value judgments regarding the material they study and teach. Even physical science, which might seem the least overtly value-oriented of disciplines, has value judgments at its core: prizing honesty, accuracy, replicability of results, correspondence between scientific propositions with the natural world, and the possible falsifiability of truth claims.

Therefore, the normative components of PCS are little different from many other scholarly endeavors. What distinguishes PCS from most academic fields is principally its subject matter—peace, violence, conflict, and power—its inter- (or multi-) disciplinary methodology, and its aim of identifying, testing, and implementing many different strategies for dealing with conflict situations. In addition, of course, its subject matter and recommendations are often controversial and politically fraught, in contrast with the lack of debate over, say, whether cancer and schizophrenia are bad whereas physical and mental health are good.

Peace and conflict studies is both theoretical and applied, including history and concepts as well as "hands-on" experiences when possible. It also focuses not merely on conflict resolution (as crucial as that is in specific cases), but on conflict transformation and reconciliation, thereby aiming to heal old wounds and establish sustainable peace among antagonistic parties.

At the theoretical level, PCS aims to uncover the roots of conflict and cooperation by examining and proposing theoretical models to explain violent and nonviolent individual and collective behaviors, both historically and cross-culturally. By revealing the underlying structures that give rise to human conflict and that support conflict resolution, PCS aims to transform the underlying causes, develop preventive strategies, and teach conflict transformation skills.

Fieldwork is often an important part of peace studies, with students often taking extended internships in conflict zones or with local nongovernmental organizations (NGOs), where they can learn and apply dialogue, negotiation, and mediation skills. The fruits of peace studies may sometimes be difficult to see and take long to come to fruition, but given that human beings have been engaging in violent conflict for thousands of years, it is unrealistic to expect enduring solutions in months or even years. At the same time, the dangers and sheer horror of recent history combined with worries about the future lend a sense of urgency to the practical necessity for peaceful and—no less important—sustainable change.

Peace and conflict studies also aspires to be multicultural and cosmopolitan, in part citing the lives and works of Gandhi and Martin Luther King, Jr. as paragons. However, true multiculturalism and cosmopolitanism remain more an aspiration than a reality for the field because most peace studies programs and centers are located in the West (although their influence is increasing elsewhere, particularly in Asia).

Peace and conflict studies is both a pedagogical activity, in which teachers and learners come together to understand the roots of peace and conflict, and a research enterprise, in which researchers propose rigorous theories and methods for formulating and testing hypotheses about the sources of conflict and the institutionalization of lasting cultures of peace. In the process, researchers also interact with peace and antiwar activists and political movements engaged in "peace work" because the goal is not just to study but also to achieve peace.

Teaching PCS

Everyday citizens, teachers, and students have long been motivated by an interest in peace. American student interest in what is today considered peace studies first appeared in the form of campus clubs at US colleges in the years immediately following the Civil War. Similar movements appeared in Sweden at the end of the 19th century and elsewhere in Europe soon after. These were usually student-originated discussion groups, not formal courses included in college and university curricula.

Because of its destructiveness, World War I, or "The War to End All Wars," was a turning point in many Western attitudes to war. When the leaders of France, Britain, and the United States (led by Georges Clemenceau, David Lloyd George, and Woodrow Wilson, respectively) met to sign the Treaty of Paris in 1919 and to decide the postwar future of Europe, President Wilson proposed his famous Fourteen Points for peacemaking, which included breaking up European empires into nation-states and establishing a League of Nations. The failures of both these aspirations contributed, paradoxically, to heighten focus on how international peace could be established and maintained. As a result, PCS gradually emerged as an academic discipline.

Peace studies was initiated by scholars who were intentionally separating themselves from the older, more established discipline of international relations (or IR, whose first professorial chair was established in 1919 at Aberystwyth University in Wales). IR is still seen by many peace studies professionals, including the distinguished scholar-activist Elise Boulding, as principally devoted to maintaining a Eurocentric, pro-establishment orientation toward "negative" peace, for the world as well as for their discipline. Other peace studies educators have argued that the field of international relations itself was initially developed with a peace studies focus to avoid war and that the disciplines can and should be complementary, albeit in fact they are sometimes competitive. Peace studies started out on most American college campuses within departments emphasizing international relations, which, to many scholars and activists, had reneged on the study and promotion of war avoidance in favor of a self-identified "hard-headed realism."

Just after World War II, many university courses on peace and war were established. The first undergraduate academic program in peace studies in the United States was created in 1948 at Manchester College in Indiana. It was not until the late 1960s in the United States that student and professorial objections to the Vietnam War stimulated more universities to offer courses about peace, whether in an undergraduate major or postgraduate degree program, or as a course within such traditional majors as political science and sociology. In the US, notable peace studies programs were initiated in 1968 at Manhattan College, which is a Catholic school and hence representative of the support for peace studies by many religious institutions of higher education, as well as by the secular Colgate University in 1969. In England, the first school of peace studies was founded in 1973 at Bradford University. By the early 1970s, many North American universities were offering courses about the Vietnam War, with faculty responding to student demands for courses that were "relevant to their own lives."

Growth in peace studies programs accelerated during the 1980s, as students and the general public became increasingly concerned about the prospects of nuclear war. This spurred the creation of a host of new courses and programs aimed at promoting global survival.[2] Key components of peace studies during this period included courses on violence and war, the nuclear arms race and the threat of nuclear destruction, international conflict, alleged aggressive tendencies in human nature, disarmament, discrimination against minorities, group conflicts, nonviolent action, defense policy, group dynamics, environmental damage, cultural integration, the unequal distribution of wealth, women's roles, Central America, apartheid in South Africa, and structural violence.

With the dissolution of the Soviet Union and the formal end of the Cold War in 1991, the emphasis of peace studies courses at many North American colleges shifted somewhat from international politics to the domestic scene, emphasizing structural, domestic, and civil violence. In 1991, the United States Institute of Peace published *Approaches to Peace: An Intellectual Map,* which listed the following headings for the study of peace: traditional approaches (collective security and deterrence); international law approaches (international law, interstate organizations, third-party dispute settlement); new approaches (transnationalism, behavioral approaches, conflict resolution); and political systems approaches (internal systems and systemic theories/world systems). Many international organizations, agencies, and NGOs, from the United Nations, the Organization for Security and Cooperation in Europe (OSCE), the European Union (EU), and the World Bank to the International Crisis Group, International Alert, and others, began to draw on PCS research. By the mid-1990s, peace studies curricula in the United States had somewhat shifted from research and teaching about negative peace to positive peace.

Since the beginning of the new millennium, course offerings in peace studies have expanded to include topics such as north-south relations; development, debt, and global poverty; the environment, population growth, and resource scarcity; feminist perspectives on peace, militarism, and political violence; zones of local peace; ecology and climate change; nonviolent alternatives to terrorism; and in-depth treatments of conflict resolution and transformation.

Research in PCS

Such notable thinkers as Plato, Jesus, Immanuel Kant, Leo Tolstoy, and various Eastern religious leaders long recognized the centrality of peace for inner and outer harmony. But it was not until the 1950s and 1960s that peace studies began to emerge as an academic discipline with its own research tools, a specialized set of concepts, and such forums for discussion as conferences and journals. Peace research institutes were established in Europe in the 1960s, although many of these do not offer formal peace studies courses. Some of the oldest and most prominent peace research centers include PRIO in Oslo, founded in 1959; the Department of Peace and Conflict Research at Uppsala University in Sweden; and the Stockholm International Peace Research Institute (SIPRI). Scholarly journals such as *The Journal of Conflict Resolution* and *The Journal of Peace Research,* begun in the 1950s and 1960s, reflected the growing interest in and academic stature of the field.

In 1963, the Peace Research Society was founded in Sweden. The group of initial members included Walter Isard, Kenneth Boulding, and Anatol Rapoport. In 1973, this group became the Peace Science Society. Peace science was viewed by these academics as an interdisciplinary and international effort to develop a set of theories, techniques, and data to better understand and mitigate conflict. Peace science attempts to use quantitative techniques developed in economics and political science, especially game theory and econometrics, otherwise seldom used by researchers in peace studies. The Peace Science Society website makes available the *Correlates of War,* one of the best-known collections of data on international conflict. The society also publishes two scholarly journals: *The Journal of Conflict Resolution* and *Conflict Management and Peace Science.*

In 1964, the International Peace Research Association (IPRA) was formed at a conference organized by Quakers in Switzerland. The IPRA holds a biennial conference. In 2001, the Peace and Justice Studies Association (PJSA) was created after the merger of two precursor organizations. It publishes a news-letter (*The Peace Chronicle*); lists programs in peace, justice, and conflict stud-ies; and holds annual conferences on themes related to the organization's mission "to create a just and peaceful world" through research, scholarship, pedagogy, and activism.

PCS Today

The number of universities offering peace and conflict studies courses is hard to estimate because it is often difficult to identify whether a course takes a basically PCS perspective, given that suitable courses may be taught in differ-ent departments and have different names.

Of the several hundred North American colleges and universities with peace studies programs, about one-half are in church-related schools, about a third are in large public universities, approximately one-fifth are in non-church-related private colleges, and a smaller number are in community colleges. About half of the church-related schools that have peace studies programs are Roman Catholic. Other religious denominations with more than one college or university offering a peace studies program are the Men-nonites, Quakers, United Church of Christ, and Church of the Brethren. About 80% of these programs are at the undergraduate level and the rest at the graduate level. Despite the growth in courses related to PCS, only about 10% of North American colleges and universities have both under-graduate and graduate programs, both of which are noticeably absent at elite private universities (such as the US's "Ivy League"), where departments of political science and government hold sway along with programs in secu-rity and international studies. By contrast, many elite private colleges offer coursework readily associated with a PCS perspective. Most international PCS programs offer primarily graduate-level degrees, notably including the UN-mandated University for Peace in Costa Rica.

PCS programs and international security and diplomacy research agendas have also become common in institutions located in conflict, post-conflict, and developing countries and regions, for example, the National Peace Council (Sri Lanka), Centre for Human Rights (University of Sarajevo, Bosnia), Chulalongkorn University (Thailand), National University of Timor (Timor-Leste), University of Kabul (Afghanistan), Makerere University (Uganda), Tel Aviv University (Israel), the University of Sierra Leone, and so on.

Until 2017, PCS had mostly shifted its focus from interstate rivalry to intrastate conflict, as well as to problems caused by interpersonal violence. However, because of the Trump administration's hostility to China and Iran, and its appeasement policies toward Russia and North Korea, international conflict is again on the agenda of much contemporary PCS research and teaching. In addition, PCS is also now addressing such hot-button issues as wars, terrorism, trafficking, refugees, treaties, climate change, the pros and cons of nonviolent resistance, and multilateral efforts to curtail war and the arms trade and to promote an ecologically sustainable future.

Some Contributions of PCS

Scholars and others working in peace and conflict studies have made sig-nificant contributions to the policies of many NGOs, development agencies, international financial institutions, and the UN system, as well as to human knowledge more generally. Social scientists and other peace researchers, although still concerned with assessing historical trends in warfare and violence, have also increasingly analyzed the comparative efficacy or failure of violent and nonviolent strategies and tactics of revolutionary and other movements. This represents a shift in interest from conflict management approaches, or a strictly negative peace orientation to conflict resolution, to peacebuilding approaches aimed at positive peace. This shift started at the end of the Cold War and was encapsulated in the report of then–UN secretary-general Boutros Boutros-Ghali, *An Agenda for Peace.*

What has been called *liberal peacebuilding,* or democratic *state-building,* is based largely on the work that has been carried out in this area. The techniques of nonviolence protest and resistance, initially developed by peace researcher Gene Sharp, have been so widely (and sometimes success-fully) adopted that Sharp has been called a modern-day godfather of this approach, as it has been practiced in, for example, prodemocracy protests in Russia and Hong Kong. Other notable cases of bringing nonviolent theory to progressive political practice have been the "Arab Spring," the "Occupy Movement," "Extinction Rebellion," the "Umbrella Movement" and its suc-cessor in Hong Kong, and such recent other peace and democracy political movements as those in Belarus and Burma (Myanmar).

On a cautionary note, the once-inspiring "Arab Spring" of about a decade ago across North Africa and the Middle East appears to have led to signifi-cant democratic progress only in Tunisia, although there are some reasons for cautious optimism in Algeria, Morocco, the UAE, and Jordan as well—in sharp contrast with the restoration of military dictatorship in Egypt and the ongoing catastrophic wars in Syria, Yemen, and Libya.

Liberal peacebuilding or state-building has been successful at times in places as diverse as Cambodia, Colombia, the Balkans, Timor-Leste, Sierra Leone, Liberia, Nepal, Tunisia, and for a while, in Burma/Myanmar, although in all such cases, stability has been fragile and old conflicts (notably between military and civilian sectors) have re-emerged, especially in Burma. Some PCS scholars have advocated an emancipatory form of peacebuilding, based upon an international "responsibility to protect" (R2P), human security, local ownership, and popular participation in democracy-building processes. Ultimately, however, the success or failure of PCS will depend on the impact it has on peace movements, which will ideally include students and teachers of the subject.

Conflicts Within PCS

Not surprisingly, there are disagreements within PCS. Although many PCS observers and critics smile when they hear about conflicts among those studying conflicts, the reality is that just as doctors sometimes get diseases, PCS scholars and practitioners now and then have disputes. (Thus far, how-ever, they have all been resolved nonviolently.)

For example, peace studies is now often referred to as peace and conflict studies, reflecting an integration of both studying peace and understanding conflict. But some leaders in the field believe that by doing so, peace stud-ies risks becoming more like war studies as attention in peace research is devoted to war research and to conflict resolution rather than to building peace and transforming conflicts by peaceful means.

The inclusion of the analysis of (violent) conflict within peace studies has sparked a debate not only with mainstream international relations and its dominant *Realpolitik* orientation but also in the field of peace studies itself.

Most research on large-scale conflicts looks at wars, which have been studied by pioneers such as Lewis Richardson, who developed a series of mathematically sophisticated models, and Quincy Wright, a political scientist best known for his attention to international law as it relates to the causes, effects, and prevention of war.

Some PCS researchers and activists claim that if we could simply persuade people to be more tolerant and open-minded, conflicts would no longer be harmful, or may even disappear altogether. Others focus on how people behave, maintaining that the problem is humanity's use of violent and aggressive means of trying to resolve conflict. And some conflict transformers argue that what matters is that existing social and economic contradictions must be resolved or transcended, that "social justice" is a necessary precondition for the establishment of a durable peace. All three perspectives have some "fundamentalists," but a growing majority of PCS researchers and conflict specialists see the need to include them all.

An old controversy within PCS concerns the relation between inner and outer peace. Should one first strive to achieve peace within one's self or initially try to create greater peace in society at large? Which comes first, healing one's self to gain inner peace, or changing a violent world to gain outer peace? Despite different views, many peace researchers and activists view this as a false dilemma and see the need for both.

Some peace scholars and educators are absolute pacifists, proponents of "principled nonviolence" who oppose use of military force in *all* circumstances, but many are not, advocating what is called "strategic nonviolence." People in both camps see themselves as contributing to a body of knowledge and practice that historically has been neglected in favor of the study and practice of war. But peace studies is not antimilitary. Many peace scholars are in conversations with the military, and at least some in the military support peace studies.

As in other social and human sciences, there is considerable debate about methodology within PCS. To get the best understanding of a conflict or a peace movement, should the emphasis be on quantitative or qualitative investigations? At present, the majority of those close to the political science and international relations side tend to use more quantitative methodologies, while the social movement and nonviolent side usually conducts more qualitative analyses.

When initiatives are taken to have new PCS programs at universities, there have often been spirited discussions regarding whether the best way to create a PCS degree is to include PCS in existing fields (like international relations) and within academic disciplinary divisions (like social science) or to set up separate PCS centers. Around the world there is now an expansion of both types. Many academic fields have a theoretical component, PCS included. Good theories are essential for anyone who wants to understand the world. The complexity of conflicts makes it a challenge to have a complete understanding of such multifaceted political realities. As with most human sciences, PCS finds it difficult to do experiments and repeatable tests, so empirical observation and case studies are much needed and highly regarded.

Comparing PCS with meteorology and the early history of public health may help clarify some of the challenges faced by the field. The complexity of weather forecasting is probably similar to the complexity of many conflicts. Meteorologists today are pretty good at predicting a five-day weather forecast. By identifying, measuring, and analyzing the many variables that influence the weather, they are able to forecast the probability of how weather will develop in the near future. However, it is almost impossible to accurately predict the more distant future. Early warning systems for predicting the development of human conflicts face similar or even more difficult challenges. Human beings significantly alter the Earth's climate, especially by causing global warming, but have little influence on day-to-day weather. Natural forces create weather and human behavior creates conflicts. Although both are to some extent predictable, neither is rigidly so.

Understanding human behavior is necessary but not sufficient for students of PCS because it is an ethical and applied social science as well as an analytical one. Like public health professionals who were trying about a century ago simultaneously to forge a disciplinary identity separate from the medical establishment and to scientifically analyze and treat epidemics, contemporary peace scholars, researchers, and students attempt not merely to understand the world but to improve it. But before acting, one must have sufficient knowledge and skills. For a practicing surgeon or a public health worker combating a mass infection, this is obvious. Many soldiers are normally given at least a year of training prior to being sent to a conflict zone, and medical doctors and other public-health workers must also have rigorous training before going into the field. Similarly, peace and conflict workers should be equipped with a comparable toolbox of conflict resolution skills and nonviolent techniques before they intervene in a conflict.

All tools, theories, and kinds of knowledge can be misused. Medical science is a gift to humanity, but it was misused by some doctors in Nazi Germany. Governments and individuals employing tactics of torture often use legally, psychologically, and medically trained personnel to help them be more efficient. Many PCS scholars and activists accordingly feel a need to include a humanitarian ethic in their teaching, research, and politically engaged practices.

Criticisms of PCS and Some Responses

Critics of the field have sometimes claimed that PCS research is diffuse, imprecise, and insufficiently rigorous. Such views have been strongly opposed by scholars who have done interdisciplinary, theoretical, methodological, and empirical research into the causes of violence and dynamics of peace. Others assert that PCS is not objective, is derived from mainly leftist and/or inexpert sources, is not practical, supports certain forms of violence and terrorism rather than rejecting them, or has not led to useful policy developments.

PCS supporters respond that other social and human sciences are also normatively oriented and involve subjective choices; sociology, political science, psychology, and even economics, for example, are not neutral, value-free sciences. They typically value, for example, social stability (in the case of sociology), democracy and freedom (political science), sanity (psychology), and capitalism (economics), just as medicine values health. The sources on which PCS educators and researchers rely are often the same books, journals, and databases as other academic fields and reflect the full range of ideological and political orientations. PCS action proposals are almost entirely nonviolent and antiterrorist in orientation; whether or not these proposals are operationalized, they are neither more nor less practical than those formulated outside PCS.

Furthermore, the development of UN and major donor policies (including the EU, United States, United Kingdom, Japan, Canada, Norway, etc.) in conflict and post-conflict countries has been heavily influenced by PCS. Since roughly the year 2000, a range of key policy statements has been developed by these governments, as have such UN (or UN-related) documents as "Agenda for Peace," "Agenda for Development," "Agenda for Democratization," the "Millennium Development Goals," and the "Responsibility to Protect." PCS research has also been influential in the work of, among others, the United Nations, the United Nations Development Programme (UNDP), the UN Peacebuilding Commission, the UN High Commissioner for Refugees (UNHCR), the World Bank, the EU, and OSCE.

PCS has also significantly influenced such international NGOs as International Alert, International Crisis Group, Amnesty International, Human Rights Watch, and many local NGOs. And PCS scholars have generated major databases such as "The Correlates of War" project by the Peace Science Society at the University of Michigan, as well as the resources of PRIO in Oslo and SIPRI in Stockholm. Finally, peace and conflict studies debates have generally confirmed, not undermined, a broad global consensus on the importance of human security, human rights, equitable and sustainable economic development, democracy, and the rule of law.

The Future of PCS

The growth of peace studies programs in Canada, the United States, Australia, New Zealand, China, India and the developing world, Western and Central Europe, and elsewhere indicates a concern for the future of life on this planet. Faculty members are using their professional skills to educate students about the causes of war while pointing out concrete alternatives to violent behavior. PCS programs vary considerably as to their scope, content, and structure. More conventional programs that emphasize the study of treaty arrangements, alliance systems, deterrence theories, and the study of war between sovereign nation-states have been complemented by newer programs focusing on sub-national groups and movements that cut across the boundaries of nation-states.

As we move further into the 21st century, there is a danger that many peace studies courses and programs will disappear as faculty and administrators who were attracted to peace studies as a result of the war in Vietnam, the original Cold War between the Soviet Union and the West, and/or the nuclear threat, retire. Many graduate programs produce young scholars committed to peace paradigms who have difficulty finding work at universities that are downsizing and whose faculty and administrators are committed to traditional subject matter and disciplinary boundaries. More conventional academic departments (notably political science and international relations), feeling threatened by large peace studies enrollments and themselves having to cope with fewer institutional resources (which are increasingly devoted to STEM fields—Science, Technology, Engineering, and Mathematics—as well as to programs in Business, Economics, and Computer Science/Information Technology), and often supported by budget-conscious university administrators, sometimes seek to roll back if not terminate peace studies degree programs.

The undergraduate peace and conflict studies major at the University of California at Berkeley, for example, has been "retired," as was the program at the University of Oslo in Norway (until recently a global leader in the field). Other peace studies graduate and other graduate programs are being "merged" into social science and international or global studies divisions and are losing their disciplinary autonomy. And many younger scholars, originally attracted to the idealistic visions of peace education, may become frustrated and disappointed at the academy's inability to incorporate them. Whether the field of peace studies as a whole is in a period of global retrenchment remains to be seen.

Scholarly debate about the value of multidisciplinary programs also provides a challenge for PCS. Most scholars are accustomed to looking at the world through the lenses of the disciplines in which they were trained. Peace studies, rather than relying on a single disciplinary perspective, can provide a potentially unifying center for political scientists, educators, sociologists, theologians, psychologists, biological scientists, lawyers, anthropologists, economists, diplomats, historians, and philosophers. Nonetheless, although colleges and universities typically pay lip service to interdisciplinary studies, the reality is that such programs are difficult to establish and to maintain; in this regard, PCS, sadly, is no exception.

An unexpected development following the US election of Donald Trump in 2016, along with the (re-)emergence of right-wing authoritarianism in many other nations, was widespread revulsion at the growth of militarism resulting from heightened inward-looking nationalism and the (more expected) concomitant indifference of many authoritarian and illiberal elites to human rights, economic inequality, and environment destruction. This, in turn, has energized movements for peace, democracy, and climate change mitigation, as citizens turn to strategies of resistance and political transformation. Nonetheless, the mainstream politicians who emphasize responding to violence with greater violence and who, along with some mass and social media, substitute "fake news" and outright falsehoods for the truth, make it hard to build support for peace studies among citizens and decision makers who see the pursuit of peace by peaceful means as idealistic, unglamorous, impractical, and/or unprofitable.

The pursuit of peace is often labeled idealistic because it is assumed that human beings will always be violent due to "human nature" and that any talk about building a peaceful global community is naïve and dangerous. Peace work for nonviolent conflict transformation is also widely considered unglamorous because bloody and dramatic events make headlines; an old saying in journalism is "If it bleeds, it leads."

Peacemaking successes are usually not covered by mainstream mass media seeking to titillate an audience that has been raised on unrealistic macho images of violence promoted on television, in novels, movies, video games, and popular music. News reports obsessively cover the protagonists in violent conflicts but generally ignore the peacemakers who may be present and working to resolve conflicts nonviolently. Importantly, the business of war and preparations for war (a.k.a. the military-industrial complex) is a multitrillion-dollar global enterprise whose economic and political clout currently dwarfs that of the world's peacemakers. Accordingly, PCS needs to find ways to dramatize the work of peace heroes and heroines and to signal the successes of nonviolent movements. It is crucial that the struggle to build a peaceful world be a dynamic part of the public debate, so that the rest of the 21st century will not be as dominated by violence and war as it has been for its first two decades, as was much of the 20th century, especially the period from 1914 to mid-century.

A Final Note on Peace and Conflict Studies, Education, and Research

When Gandhi said that the theory and practice of nonviolence was at the same level as electricity in Edison's day, he was probably right. "Peace by peaceful means" is an important concept, especially because it modifies the more traditional justification of war-making as a way to achieve peace. With disciplined research, creative action, and compassion, PCS educators, activists, and students can better address global and local challenges.

We hope this textbook will be a useful tool for those taking that path. At the same time, we note with alarm and regret that violence continues to plague the world, such that the need for PCS and its approaches has never been greater.

Like peace itself, peace studies, peace research, and peace education are very much works in progress. We invite you to discuss and debate the values and methods that have been used thus far, and, where possible, to add to this necessary and dynamic endeavor.

Questions for Further Reflection

1. Based on what you have now read about peace and conflict studies, what would you consider to be the strengths and weaknesses of this field?

2. If you were to design a peace education program for your community/nation, what would you include?

3. Do you think global peace is achievable in your lifetime? Why or why not?

4. What are the most and least fruitful areas for peace and conflict research?

5. How do you envision the future of PCS?

Suggestions for Further Reading

Robin Cooper and Laura Finley, eds. 2014. *Peace and Conflict Studies Research: A Qualitative Perspective.* New York: Information Age.

Ronald Edsforth, ed. 2020. *A Cultural History of Peace.* Six volumes. London: Bloomsbury.

B. Jeannie Lum. 2016. *Peace Education: Past, Present and Future.* New York: Routledge.

Borislava Manojlovic. 2018. *Education for Sustainable Peace and Conflict Resilient Communities.* New York: Palgrave Macmillan.

Timothy A. McElwee, B. Welling Hall, Joseph Liechty, and Julie Garber, eds. 2009. *Peace, Justice, and Security Studies: A Curriculum Guide.* Boulder and London: Lynne Rienner.

Ian Harris and Mary Lee Morrison. 2012. *Peace Education,* 3rd ed. New York: McFarland.

Oliver Richmond. 2006. *Peace in International Relations.* London: Routledge.

Oliver Richmond. 2014. *Peace: A Very Short Introduction.* New York and Oxford: Oxford University Press.

Gavriel Saloman and B. Nevo, eds. 2002. *Peace Education: The Concepts, Principles, and Practices Around the World*. Mahwah, NJ: Lawrence Erlbaum Associates.

Rita Verma. 2017. *Critical Peace Education and Global Citizenship*. New York: Routledge.

Peter Wallensteen. 2011. *Peace Research: Theory and Practice*. New York: Routledge.

Charles Webel and Johan Galtung, eds. 2009. *The Handbook of Peace and Conflict Studies*. London and New York: Routledge.

Scholarly Journals

The International Journal of Peace Studies: http://www.gmu.edu/programs/icar/ijps/

Journal of Conflict Resolution: http://jcr.sagepub.com/

Journal of Peace Research (JPR): http://jpr.sagepub.com/

Peace and Change: http://www.wiley.com/bw/journal.asp?ref=0149-0508

Peace and Conflict: Journal of Peace Psychology: http://www.apa.org/pubs/journals/pac/

Peace Review: http://www.tandf.co.uk/journals/titles/10402659.asp

Notes

1. Betty Reardon. 1988. *Comprehensive Peace Education: Educating for Global Responsibility*. New York and London: Teachers College Press, Columbia University.

2. David Barash offered a course on nuclear war at the University of Washington

between 1982 and 1990; it typically enrolled a thousand students, the maximum possible. By 1990, enrollment had dropped substantially.

The Meaning of War

Most human activities—buying and selling, sowing and reaping, loving, learning, eating, sleeping, parenting, worshipping—take place with a minimum of overt conflict and without anything remotely like war. Warfare nonetheless has a special importance for human beings, particularly since the invention of nuclear weapons in 1945, which raised the very real possibility that war could extinguish human civilization and, possibly, life on Earth.

Peace researcher Quincy Wright began his *A Study of War* by noting that

to different people war may have very different meanings. To some it is a plague which ought to be eliminated; to some, a mistake which should be avoided; to others, a crime which ought to be punished; to still others, it is an anachronism which no longer serves any purpose. On the other hand, there are some who take a more receptive attitude toward war and regard it as an adventure which may be interesting, an instrument which may be useful, a procedure which may be legitimate and appropriate, or a condition of existence for which one must be prepared.[1]

If wars are to be understood and, ultimately, overcome, we must first agree what they are. In this text, we will mainly consider "hot" wars—that is, overt violent conflicts between governments or rival subnational groups hoping to overthrow existing regimes and/or to establish new governments: in short, international and civil wars. In recent times, an official declaration of war has been relatively rare; nonetheless, in many cases, "war" can still easily be recognized, not only between different nation-states but also as civil wars and so-called wars of liberation. We shall largely exclude feuds, disputes, or cases of banditry, as well as trade wars, propaganda wars, or "cold" wars, except insofar as these have a bearing on hot ones.

Defining War

The term *war* ultimately derives from the Old High English noun *werra*, meaning "confusion." Many people have tried to compile data on wars throughout history, both to help identify the issue and to test various empirical hypotheses about their causes (thereby diminishing at least one aspect of war's confusion). However, researchers have not always agreed on what qualifies as a war. There is little doubt, for example, that World Wars I and II qualify, but what about the War of the Bavarian Succession (1778–1779), in which war was declared, fully armed Prussian and Austrian troops marched while drums rolled, but not a shot was fired and no one died? By contrast, in the Korean War more than 2 million people (military and civilian) were killed, the US and China were major protagonists, and yet war was never declared. (In fact, neither was peace. This conflict is still officially unresolved, with an ongoing armed truce.) Instead, it was officially known as a United Nations "police action." Likewise for the Vietnam War, in which, once again, no official state of war was ever acknowledged.

Quincy Wright considered a war to have taken place either when it was formally declared or when a certain number of troops were involved; he suggested 50,000 as a baseline. Lewis Richardson, another pioneering peace researcher, sought to define war by the number of deaths incurred. J. D. Singer, M. Small, and the Uppsala Conflict Date Program have focused on a minimum of 1,000 combat-related fatalities incurred between conflict parties, at least one of which is the government of a nation-state, in a calendar year. Whatever the technicalities involved, most people likely agree that war can be described in much the same way as a jurist's observation about pornography: "I may not be able to define it, but I know it when I see it."

Similarly, there can be debate over exactly when a given war began. The United States entered World War II in December 1941, after the Japanese attack on Pearl Harbor. The Soviet Union had entered it six months earlier, after it was attacked by Germany in June 1941. Most historians (and virtually all Europeans), however, believe that World War II began with Hitler's invasion of Poland in September 1939, after which France and Great Britain declared war on Germany. On the other hand, some argue that World War II began with Italy's invasion of Ethiopia (1935) or even earlier, with Japan's initial incursion into northern China (1931). And others maintain that in fact World Wars I and II were really a continuation of the same basic struggle, separated by a brief period of relative peace, followed by remilitarization. The long Cold War (1945–1991) between the United States and the Soviet Union was never declared, but when the Soviet Union collapsed, the Cold War was widely considered to have been "won" by the United States. This induced considerable resentment among many Russians, especially regarding the expansion of NATO to include the Baltic States (Estonia, Latvia, and Lithuania, formerly Soviet republics), leading, in part, to the current "new Cold War" between Russia and much of the West.

Psychologically, the essence of war is the intensely hostile attitudes among two or more contending groups. Economically, war often involves the forced diversion of major resources from civilian to military pursuits. Sociologically, it typically results in a rigid structuring of society, with prominence given to military functions. Perhaps the most famous definition of war, however, speaks to its *political* significance.

Karl von Clausewitz (1780–1831), a Prussian army officer best known for his treatise *On War,* defined it as "an act of violence intended to compel our opponents to fulfill our will." He further emphasized that war was "the continuation of politics by other means." In other words, war should not simply reflect senseless fury. Rather, it should be orchestrated with a particular political goal in mind. Very often, that goal is the preservation of the power of those statesmen and other elites who organize and hope to benefit from a particular war. It is the victors among warring elites who, in its aftermath, will normally declare the war to have been "good" and/or "just." The losers and victims of wars generally have a different view.

The Frequency and Intensity of Wars

By some measures, wars have been relatively infrequent. Based on the number of nation-states existing since 1815, there have been between 16,000 and 20,000 nation-years, and during this time, war has occupied about 4% of the possible total. The 20th century was a very warlike one, with about 87 million war deaths (60/40 civilian to military fatalities). More than 85% of these occurred during the two World Wars, whereas between 1945 and 2010, direct wars between major states (the "Great Powers") have been virtually nonexistent, and wars between other states declined dramatically. Recently, however, according to the Uppsala Conflict Data Program (UCDP) and the Peace Research Institute of Oslo (PRIO), state-based, non-state, and one-sided violent conflicts have increased, and so has the number of casualties of these conflicts, with almost 2.75 million fatalities between 1989 and 2018, averaging approximately 90,000 deaths per year.

These numbers notwithstanding, modern warfare, even with its enormous devastation, has been directly responsible for fewer than about 2% of all deaths during the past century. Diseases, many of which are preventable or manageable, kill far more people than violent conflicts. Nonetheless, in addition to their tangible and direct lethal consequences, wars have also generated many indirect casualties, by disease, starvation, social disruption and the diversion of resources from domestic needs.

For example, between 1991, when the first Gulf War began in Iraq, and 2019, the number of civilian casualties has far exceeded the number of direct military and civilian deaths. Total deaths from Western interventions in Iraq and Afghanistan since the 1990s "War on Terror"—from direct killings and the longer-term impact of war-imposed deprivation and disruption —likely amount to around 4 million and could be as high as 6 to 8 million. The exact number may never be known because, as a matter of policy, US-led armed forces refuse to track the civilian death toll of military operations.

Between 1500 and 1942 there was an average of nearly one declared war per year. This does not include armed revolutions, of which there were approximately 350 between 1900 and 1965, an average of 5 or more per year. Between 1820 and 1946 there were at least 59 million deaths from human violence, of which fewer than 10 million were due to individual and small-group violence; the remainder resulted from wars. (However immense and uncertain is the human toll of war, its impact on the natural world—animals, plants, ecosystems—is also enormous but even less clearly known.)

Although wars between nations in the early 21st century have been less frequent than in the past, they are nonetheless ongoing in many places and imminent in others. Since 1955, the number of armed conflicts has ranged from about 20 (in the late 1950s) to nearly 60 (in the late 1980s). During the 1990s and until 2019, the overall number of wars declined somewhat but remained between 30 and 40 per year. Major armed conflicts in recent years have occurred in Afghanistan, Ukraine, Democratic Republic of Congo, Iraq, Yemen, Libya, Pakistan-India, Sri Lanka, and Syria. Prior to this, genocides in Rwanda and Sudan (its Darfur region) were especially egregious, along with Burmese atrocities against its Muslim Rohingya population.

Nonetheless, the attention-grabbing organized violence in the post–World War II years does not contradict the trend that overall levels of mass killings have been declining in and between the major industrial countries, mostly Western. A notable exception has been the ongoing conflict in eastern Ukraine. In contrast, large parts of the Middle East and Africa remain venues of armed conflict and mass violence.

Indirect Killing

In addition to the direct casualties, war kills indirectly, particularly by disease among armed forces personnel, as well as by starvation as a result of disrupted food production and distribution services. For example, more than 8 million soldiers and 1 million civilians died during World War I, while approximately 18 million people were killed by an influenza epidemic in 1918. Historically, more soldiers have died of diseases and of exposure than from enemy fire: More than eight times as many French soldiers died from cholera during the Crimean War (1853–1856) than from battle. Similarly, of Napoleon's forces who invaded Russia in 1812, many more succumbed to pneumonia than to Russian military resistance. During the Thirty Years' War (1618–1648), the armies of Gustavus Adolphus (Sweden) and Albrecht von Wallenstein (Bohemia, part of the modern-day Czech Republic) faced each other outside Nuremberg and lost 18,000 men to typhus and scurvy and then separated without a shot having been fired.

In modern times, deaths due to disease have become less prominent during war, as a result of improved medical technology. At the same time, advances in military technology have made wars themselves more deadly, especially for nearby civilians: Military deaths were roughly the same in World Wars I and II (about 17 million in each war), but civilian deaths in World War II (approximately 35 million) were about seven times greater than in World War I, whose carnage was more concentrated on the various battlefields. In the past, civilians suffered horribly during wars, notably during the Thirty Years' War, when an estimated one-third of the German population was killed, and during the sacking of fallen cities, such as Carthage at the end of its three Punic Wars with the Roman Republic (264 BCE to 146 BCE).

Through most of human history, war casualties were nonetheless concentrated among military forces. With advances in technology combined with such phenomena as city bombing, the intentional infliction of firestorms, and of course, the atomic bombings of Hiroshima and Nagasaki, the ratio of civilian to military deaths rose to unprecedented levels during the 20th century, a trend that appears to be continuing in the 21st. In the event of thermonuclear or biochemical war, the casualties could well include essentially all the civilian population on both sides—and possibly billions of bystanders in other countries as well.

The Waste of War

The sheer wastefulness of war has been appalling, even with conventional (non-nuclear) weapons. During the Battle of the Somme (1916) in World War I, for example, the British sought to pierce the German lines, gaining a mere 120 square miles at a cost of 420,000 men while the Germans lost 445,000. At the Battle of Ypres (1917), the British advanced 45 square miles, in the process losing 370,000 men. During World War I alone, Europe lost virtually an entire generation of young men. Here is F. Scott Fitzgerald's description of the Somme battlefield, from his novel *Tender is the Night*:

> See that little stream—we could walk to it in two minutes. It took the British a month to walk to it—a whole empire walking very slowly, dying in front and pushing forward behind. And another empire walked very slowly backward, a few inches a day, leaving the dead like a million bloody rugs.[2]

Numbers can be numbing. For example, of the 2,900,000 men and women who served in the US armed forces during the Vietnam War (average age 19), 300,000 were wounded and about 55,000 were killed. Yet these figures convey very little of the war's significance or of its horror, both for those who served and for the country at large—especially for the people of Vietnam. They also ignore the war's devastating socioeconomic consequences for Vietnam, Laos, and Cambodia, as well as for the United States, where it had profound social effects, including widespread alienation of millions of young people and massive antiwar demonstrations around the country. There were also political consequences, not all of them negative, including a hesitancy to engage US servicemen and servicewomen in foreign conflicts (the "Vietnam syndrome"). In Vietnam itself, the economy and natural environment were devastated, and several million Vietnamese were killed.

Decades after they have ended, the Iraq, Afghanistan, Yemen, and Syrian wars may similarly have devastating consequences not only for the millions of Iraqis, Afghans, Yemenis, and Syrians displaced, killed, or maimed by the conflict but also for coalition soldiers and civilians who return home only to be afflicted by epidemics of brain injuries, posttraumatic stress disorder (PTSD), and attendant suicides. Improved medical care has reduced the per capita battlefield death rate—at least for serving military from the "developed" countries—while also increasing the number of surviving soldiers who are seriously injured, often permanently.

It is deceptively easy to present a sanitized statistical summary of warfare's carnage and misery. In this book, we plead guilty to this form of euphemism and linguistic sanitation, offering only the excuse that the demands of space (and cost) do not permit reproducing photos that would reveal the atrocity of warfare far better than does a written text.

Historical Trends in War

The following list of (admittedly bloodless) facts and figures should give some idea of how war has evolved over the past half millennium. Consider, for example, these trends:

1. *An increase in the human, environmental, and economic costs of war; a decrease in the casualty rate among combatants; and an increase in the number of civilian casualties.* In the Middle Ages, for example, the defeated side, typically the one that broke and ran, would be cut down by the victors, often losing as many as 50% of its fighting men. By modern standards, however, the total numbers were small: thousands or, at most, tens of thousands involved in combat, in contrast with modern armies numbering in the hundreds of thousands. Up to the 16th century, about 25% of combatants died; by the 17th century, this proportion was about 20%, declining to 15% in the 18th century, 10% in the 19th century, and 6% in the 20th century (perhaps fewer in the first two decades of the 21st).

This is partly because with modern technology, a larger proportion of "combatants" are engaged in support and supply rather than actual fighting. In addition, the proportion of combat injuries leading to death has decreased because of better medical care for the wounded. And disease, once a major scourge during wartime, now causes fewer combat fatalities (although the indirect effects of combat may kill many civilians, as in Iraq since 1991 and in Syria and Yemen more recently).

On the other hand, the proportion of the civilian population in the armed services has increased, and because the number and duration of battles have increased as well, the percentage of the national population dying in war has also gone up. In France, for example, approximately 11 out of every 1,000 deaths during the 17th century were due to military service; in the 18th century, this number had increased to 27; by the 19th century, 30; and in the 20th century, 63. During the 20th century, large-scale attacks were initiated on civilian shipping, especially with the use of submarines. Attacks on noncombatants became particularly pronounced with the use of air bombardment—of Ethiopians by Italy; of Spanish Loyalists by German and Italian "volunteers" during the Spanish Civil War; of Chinese by Japan; of Poles, Dutch, and English by Germany; of Finns by the USSR; of Japanese and Germans by the United States and Britain during World War II; and of Iraq, Afghanistan, Serbia, Syria, and Libya by the United States and its allies, especially Saudi Arabia, which has bombed many civilian quarters in Yemen. The ratio of civilian to military casualties at Hamburg, Dresden, Tokyo, Hiroshima, and Nagasaki was on the order of thousands to one.

2. *An increase in the speed at which wars spread to additional belligerents, in the number of belligerents involved in a given war, and in the area covered.* In ancient times, battles typically took place in, and were named for, cities or mountain passes: the Battles of Thermopylae, Waterloo, Gettysburg. During the 15th and 16th centuries, each war had, on average, just slightly more than two major antagonists. By the 20th century, the number of states involved had jumped to five. In World War II, many battles expanded to

whole countries (the "Battle of Britain"), even continents or oceans (the "Battle of the Atlantic"); the tides of battle swept across all of Europe, as well as across much of northern Africa, East Asia, and the Pacific Ocean. Continuing this trend, a World War III involving the use of weapons of mass destruction would most likely be global in its impact.

3. *Since World War II, an increase in the frequency of so-called low-intensity conflicts (LICs), which indirectly involve the United States and the former Soviet Union in many Third World conflicts, revolutions, and counterrevolutions.* During the 20th century, both the United States and, to a lesser degree, the former Soviet Union tended to consider that their "national interests" included the outcome of struggles taking place virtually anywhere on the globe. Often, they interpreted strictly indigenous conflicts, especially those reflecting revolutionary nationalism, as evidence of meddling by the other side and regarded the nations involved, therefore, as pawns in the Cold War conflict. As war has become potentially more destructive and more likely to involve nuclear powers, military strategy has focused increasingly on fighting comparatively limited wars—for example, US support for the contras in Nicaragua and for the mujahideen (notably including Osama bin Laden and his supporters) in the 1980s against the Soviets in Afghanistan.

These activities were perceived as less threatening to the major powers, allowing them to carry on their rivalry on someone else's soil and mostly shedding someone else's blood. The US experience in the Vietnam War (and, quite possibly, the Russian experiences in Afghanistan and Chechnya) also sensitized government leaders to the difficulties of conducting wars that are expensive, in terms of money as well as lives, and that do not enjoy strong public support. As a result, one might expect increased interest in the 21st century by the great powers in orchestrating LICs that are comparatively low profile and hence less controversial and domestically disruptive.

At the same time, the phrase "low-intensity conflict" is a euphemism, dangerously misleading as to the death and misery it may produce. Similar euphemisms include the "police actions" in Korea (1950–1953) and Vietnam (1962–1974), "peacekeeping" in the Dominican Republic (1965), and the "rescue operation" in Grenada (1983). To many defense strategists in the United States, who by the late 1980s were especially committed to the concept, a LIC is really a war, typically in the Third World, in which the number of US combatants and casualties is kept low; for those directly affected, by contrast, the damage can be staggering. For example, consider the death toll of Nicaraguans during the US-sponsored contra war of the 1980s: more than 29,000. To gain a better perspective on this, imagine that Nicaragua's population (3.5 million) were that of the United States (about 285 million at the time). A comparable cost to the United States would have been more than 2 million lives. Proportionately, the Nicaraguan death toll in this "low-intensity war" exceeded all US losses in all the wars of its history, from the Revolutionary War to Iraq and Afghanistan.

Even "small" conventional wars can be devastating; for example, the Six-Day War between Israel and its Arab opponents in 1967 resulted in 21,000 battle-related deaths, far greater than the rate of killing per day that occurred during the Korean War. And between 1980 and 1988, the war between Iran and Iraq, generally considered a "minor" conflagration because the major powers were not directly involved, may have claimed more than a million lives. Between 1991 and 2000, wars and "ethnic cleansing" in Rwanda, Burundi, Iraq, East Timor, and some parts of the former Soviet Union and Yugoslavia claimed vast numbers of civilian casualties. Millions of Iraqis,

Afghans, Syrians, Yemenis, Burmese, and Uighurs have been displaced, wounded, or killed since 1991. The civil war in Sudan, between an Islamic government in the northern part of that country and Christian and animist secessionists in the south, claimed perhaps 2 million lives, both from direct fighting and from subsequent disease and mass starvation.

4. *A continuing increase in "asymmetrical" conflicts between nations or empires on the one hand and guerrillas, "freedom fighters," and/or "terrorists" on the other.* During the late 18th and early 19th centuries, the Napoleonic era of revolutionary wars initiated the phenomenon of guerrilla warfare. Resistance and "terrorist" fighters had existed since antiquity. Best known, historically, were the Zealots, dagger-wielding Jewish opponents of Roman rule in ancient Palestine. But the concept of guerrilla warfare as an uprising against existing authority originated with the Spanish resistance to Napoleon during the Peninsular War in 1800. During the 5 years of French occupation, Spanish guerrillas (aided by English forces in Portugal) accounted for as many French casualties as Napoleon's forces suffered during their ill-fated Russian campaign.

5. *A likely increase in religiously inspired armed conflicts.* The phenomenon of resistance to imperial dominion by dedicated fighters in small groups has taken on an increasingly religious cast. The Soviet occupation of Afghanistan during the 1980s and the American-led occupations of Afghanistan and Iraq (and emplacement of military bases throughout the Middle East and Islamic world more generally) have been met by fierce resistance on the part of "freedom fighters" and "God's warriors" who believe that "Christian-Jewish crusaders," and their "infidel" Muslim backers, have desecrated the Islamic "holy land." Jihadists claim that they are defending their faith from an American-led attack against Islam itself. On the other hand, some conservative Western commentators have called militant Islam "Islamo-Fascism" and called for a modern-day Crusade. While violent Islamists believe their "holy war" *(jihad)* to be a just struggle against "imperialists and infidels," many Westerners consider the global "War on Terror(ism)" to be a "just war." Self-styled warriors for god come in all denominations, and their escalated violence has had consequences for countless victims caught in the ostensibly "divinely inspired" crossfire.

6. Finally, although the future—by definition—cannot be predicted with certainty, many experts anticipate extension of certain recent trends, such as use of child soldiers, especially in impoverished regions (e.g., sub-Saharan Africa) that are better endowed with people than with financial resources; increased reliance on robotically controlled munitions, space-based weapons, cyberwarfare, and drones; and increased reliance on private, mercenary armed forces, especially by wealthier countries.

Modern Weaponry

We can identify four major eras of weaponry: (1) the earliest period (encompassing the entire preindustrial period), based primarily on muscle power; (2) an intermediate period (from approximately the Renaissance until the first half of the 20th century in the West and still the case in most of the rest of the world), powered by chemicals, especially gunpowder, as well as steam and internal combustion engines; (3) the second half of the 20th century, dominated by the threat of nuclear weapons and other weapons of potential mass destruction (especially biochemical), and (4) the early 21st century, which, while preserving the dubious legacy of the late 20th century, may also be increasingly characterized by military adaptations of such cutting-edge technologies as robotics, drones (unmanned controllable devices that kill at a distance), nanotechnology, space-based weaponry, and cyberwarfare. This progression from stone ax to hydrogen bomb and satellite gives particular urgency to peace and impels us to understand the instruments of war so as to appreciate the need for developing nonviolent alternatives to armed conflict.

Before 1939, it was assumed by many strategic thinkers that World War II would largely be a replay of the static trench warfare of World War I. Instead, the German Army used quick-moving armored forces closely coordinated with air strikes, in a new style of rapidly penetrating battle known as *Blitzkrieg,* or "lightning war," which benefited the offense. In contrast with trench warfare, there were relatively few casualties in the Nazi conquest of Poland, the Low Countries (Holland, Belgium, and Luxembourg), and France (Holocaust victims excluded, of course). The major loss of life in the European theater during World War II occurred during prolonged fighting on the eastern front, where the Soviet Union suffered more than 20 million casualties and Germany sustained nearly 90% of its wartime losses.

Toxic gas was used extensively by all sides during World War I. Japan employed chemical weapons against unprepared Chinese forces during the 1930s; Italy did the same in Ethiopia. Subsequently, advances in chemical and biological warfare (CBW) have raised new fears about the potentially devastating consequences of future wars, along with their possible use by terrorists (as in the 1995 attack on the Tokyo subway system by *Aum Shinrikyo,* a religious cult). Iraqi forces apparently used chemical weapons (mustard gases) in their war with Iran during the 1980s, as well as against Kurdish rebels inside Iraq itself, in both cases violating international law. The deployment of bioengineered weapons and increases in cyberattacks against key civilian and military infrastructures may well replace potentially fraught armed confrontations between major states

There have been many innovations in war-fighting technology within the past hundred years: breech-loading artillery, landmines, grenades, torpedoes, machine guns, tanks, chemical warfare, powered ships (first steam, later diesel), iron-hulled ships, submarines, and aircraft, including fighters and bombers. Advances in rocketry have permitted swift, stealthy, and relatively accurate attacks on distant targets. The Battle of Leyte Gulf, during World War II, for example, was the most intense naval engagement of all time: In 5 days, Japan lost 4 aircraft carriers, 3 battleships, 6 heavy cruisers, and 11 destroyers (and, of course, many thousands of sailors), all destroyed by torpedoes launched by submarines or by bombs dropped by airplanes; there were no direct encounters between the surface vessels of the two sides.

Other developments in conventional weaponry involved armor plating for tanks and ships, as well as highly accurate *precision-guided munitions—* relatively inexpensive, highly accurate rocket-propelled devices that can be fired by small groups of soldiers and that endanger costly targets, such as tanks, ships, and aircraft. Many military analysts believe that the future will see further development of highly lethal munitions and robots, used on an increasingly automated, even electronic, battlefield, possibly conducted in space as well. These trends have culminated in what is probably the most important technological development in war making: the invention and high-speed delivery of nuclear weapons (discussed in Chapter 5).

Cutting-Edge Military Technologies

In their never-ending search for "winning weapons," military planners have increasingly appropriated scientific and engineering innovations with dual-use applications; that is, innovations intended for civilian as well as military purposes. During the early 21st century, cutting-edge and futuristic military technologies include nanotechnological devices; drones, robots, and other *Terminator*-like weapons; chemical and biological warfare agents; cyberwarfare technologies; satellites and other space-based weapons systems; and new hypersonic missiles.

Nanotechnological Devices

Nanotechnology (also nanotech, or NT) is the engineering of functional systems on an atomic and molecular scale. Its military applications include building materials and parts for machines and weapons, materials to enhance soldiers' clothing, and, according to the US Defense Advanced Research Projects Agency (DARPA), sensor microchips implantable in soldiers to monitor their health and vital signs during combat. DARPA is also developing chips allowing for treatment of medical conditions from within the body. Because these chips are meant for military uses, they could be developed to harm the body from the inside, potentially as a means of torture or of controlling one's own soldiers. There is also the possibility that NT could be developed for surveillance purposes (via nanoscale microphones or cameras) to be used for such covert military operations as spying.

Despite the possible civilian benefits of molecular nanotechnology, such as the potential to improve medical procedures and treatments and to develop alternative energy sources, there are risks associated with its military applications. These risks include potential dangers to soldiers' health; the threat of technologically "improved nuclear" warfare; social and economic disruption; and the threat of criminal or terrorist use.

Nanoparticles used on weapons and machinery (i.e., drones, tanks, planes, etc.) to make surfaces harder, smoother, and stealthier for covert military operations could erode and enter the body through the respiratory system, possibly leading to lung infections or cancers that could spread to the rest of the body and cause a multitude of health problems. NT that is used to improve human performance can also pose human health risks, especially if injected into the bloodstream. Another example of NT that can be used to improve human performance is nanoscale receptor enhancers that are designed to increase alertness and reduce reaction times. With repeated use, however, these enhancers could cause addiction and, with chronic use, other currently unidentified problems.

NT is also risky because weapons can be developed to destroy specific targets with considerable ease and speed, once NT itself has sufficiently progressed for its incorporation into the design and deployment of inexpensively manufactured military products. NT-based weapons have the potential not only to be devastating on the battlefield but also to become the driving force of a new and unstable arms race because NT is easier to use, to transport, to manufacture, and to develop into weaponry than most current conventional and nuclear technologies. Consequently, restrictions are needed on the applications of NT to weapons, especially those of mass destruction.

As nations are increasingly encouraged to get involved in nanotechnology research due to its implications for military weaponry, superpowers could well lose their current ability to "police" the international arena, thus encouraging the breakup of existing relationships and alliances between nations and contributing to additional global instability.

Hypersonic Missiles, Drones, Robots, and *Terminator*-Like Weapons

Hypersonic missiles are designed to travel extremely fast—between 5 and 10 times the speed of sound—and thus are capable of striking their targets with near-nuclear impact, although they seem likely in the near term to be equipped with conventional explosives, or even with no detonation devices at all, relying instead on the kinetic effect of such high speeds. As of early 2020, hypersonic missiles were actively being developed by the US, Russia, and China. As with nanotechnology, there have been no negotiated restraints on these weapons, illustrating a persistent dilemma whereby the development of new military technology nearly always outpaces diplomatic efforts to set limits on them. Arms races today are often less between competing countries than between the forces promoting and profiting from new weapons and those seeking to reduce them—a struggle that the arms peddlers nearly always win.

Drones, otherwise known as unmanned aerial vehicles (UAV), are aircraft without a human pilot onboard. Its flight is either controlled autonomously by computers in the vehicle or under the remote control of a navigator on the ground—in the US case, often on the other side of the world—or in another vehicle. Although they are also used in a small but growing number of civil applications, such as firefighting or nonmilitary security work (e.g., the surveillance of pipelines), drones are increasingly noted for their military applications and are often preferred for missions that are too dull, dirty, or dangerous for manned aircraft.

Between September 11, 2001 and early 2012, the Pentagon increased the drone inventory from a handful to 7,500, comprising approximately one-third of all US military aircraft, including Predator and Reaper drones equipped with air-to-ground rockets. As advances in artificial intelligence (AI) continue, drones and other robotic systems designed for military use (e.g., ground-based robots assigned a wide variety of tasks, such as evacuating wounded soldiers and locating and detonating explosive mines) may eventually be tasked with making combat decisions without human input. If so, they would likely be immune to human operator issues associated with adrenaline, hunger, sleep deprivation, or anything else that has the potential to influence a person's judgment; they would also likely be insensitive to traditional concepts of morality. This could have the potential to remove human forces completely from the battlefield and therefore minimize casualties—something that is a top priority in combat situations. But this could also generate major problems.

This technology still has a long way to go; drones have already been responsible for major war crimes, such as attacking supposed Taliban, al-Qaeda, or ISIS operatives in Afghanistan, Pakistan, Somalia, and Yemen that turn out to be wedding parties and other purely civilian events, resulting in the deaths of hundreds of innocent people and generating immense anger in the host/victim countries. In such cases, official US policy is to pay reparations to surviving family members, consistent with local Islamic tradition in such regions. However, it is appropriate to ask whether the perceived benefit of remotely killing alleged terrorists exceeds the cost of civilian lives, in addition to the added cost of antagonizing people whose hearts and minds are supposedly being courted.

Another dilemma arises when considering accountability: Who is accountable for, say, the killing of civilians in a strike? The commander who can override its orders? The politician(s) who authorized its use? The manufacturer of the robot if its equipment is proven to be faulty?

Since late 2012, authorization of drone attacks has been handled by the Central Intelligence Agency, not the US military command. Using unmanned military technology removes certain psychological barriers to wars (e.g., the cost of human lives, distances), which could well make them easier to start. Across Pakistan, Yemen, and Somalia, the Obama administration launched more than 390 drone strikes in its first 5 years in office, many times more than were launched in the entire Bush presidency. The number of civilian deaths due to drone strikes during the Trump administration was not reported, although there appears to be a reduction in civilian casualties per attack, perhaps because of improvements in drone and missile technology, rising tensions between host/victim countries and the United States over such events, and greater scrutiny of covert drone campaigns both at home and abroad. At the same time, military drone technology has advanced and thus become affordable to the point that many smaller countries, as well as subnational fighting groups, can now afford to deploy them, not only for surveillance but for violent attacks.

Space Technologies

No longer just science fiction, space technologies are becoming more useful for military purposes, including tiny disposable satellites, material breakthroughs to maximize the efficiency of solar cells for satellites, and even small nuclear reactors for satellite systems and other spacecraft. An additional technology is the unmanned Boeing X-37, or OTV (Orbital Test Vehicle). The OTV is a reusable robotic spacecraft that is boosted into space by a launch vehicle, then re-enters Earth's atmosphere and lands as a space-plane. The X-37 is currently operated by the United States Space Force and was deployed by the Air Force Space Command until 2019 for orbital space-flight missions intended to demonstrate reusable space technologies. This clearly has potential military uses.

DARPA's "SeeMe" program includes the use of tiny satellites that could focus on battlefields, allowing soldiers to have much wider and constant surveillance coverage and therefore be instantly updated during combat situations. It could also be cost effective, much less expensive than the flying robots that comprise the US drone fleet. The US Air Force has plans to increase the amount of energy available for use by its satellite systems for military-based missions. Additional technologies that can be utilized to provide energy for even ground-based facilities include small modular nuclear reactors and space tethers, which—if developed—could harvest energy from the Earth's geomagnetic field. Although space tethers are in the distant future, small modular nuclear reactors are not. In fact, nuclear energy has already been utilized for several satellite systems and has been shown to provide a consistent source of power at a much higher level than current technologies. As the size of these nuclear reactors decreases, their utility onboard satellite systems and other spacecraft increases. However, such a technology can easily have catastrophic consequences if not properly maintained or if it ends up in the wrong hands. Russia, for example, was reported to have been experimenting with a missile powered by a miniature nuclear reactor when a prototype exploded. Attached to missiles, rockets, or even hand grenades, if small enough, this type of nuclear technology could prove extremely dangerous both physically and politically.

Biological and Chemical Weapons

Biological and chemical agents have long been used during warfare. Such weapons are sometimes known as "the poor man's nuclear weapon" because of the ease of developing them compared with nuclear weapons.

Biological agents include pathogens or other microscopic organisms such as bacteria (e.g., anthrax), viruses (e.g., smallpox), fungi, and toxins. Biological agents differ from chemical agents in that their release and their effects are not immediately noticeable, simply because infection of the human body requires time to become an illness.

Chemical weapons include (1) nerve agents (e.g., GB, or sarin), (2) blister agents (e.g., sulfur mustard), and (3) choking agents (e.g., phosgene). Nerve agents are particularly toxic: VX, or methylphosphonothioic acid, causes death after 15 minutes of absorption, and GB can cause death in 1 to 2 minutes if enough is absorbed. Blister agents do not immediately kill like nerve agents; they are primarily meant to limit fighting ability. Sulfur mustard is particularly toxic, due to its stability; it attacks not only the skin but also the eyes and the respiratory tract. Choking agents use chemicals that attack lung tissue. Phosgene is the most dangerous of these, as it causes massive pulmonary edema and can result in death within 24 to 48 hours of exposure.

Clearly, these weapons pose a significant ethical issue, although it is also worth considering why they should be considered less internationally acceptable than traditional explosive or penetrating weaponry based on gunpowder. Biological agents are generally easier to develop, requiring only that pathogens be aerosolized so that they can spread easily and rapidly. However, as with chemical weapons, their spread is susceptible to local weather conditions, making them potentially dangerous for the side employing them as well as the intended victims. The risk of chemical terrorism and/or bioterrorism is growing.

The Convention on the Prohibition of the Development, Production and Stockpiling of Bacteriological (Biological) and Toxin Weapons and on their Destruction (often known as the Biological and Toxin Weapons Convention, or BTWC) was the first multilateral disarmament treaty banning the production of an entire category of weapons. It resulted from prolonged efforts to establish a new instrument that supplemented the 1925 Geneva Protocol, which prohibited use but not development or possession of chemical and biological weapons. The BTWC became effective in 1975. It currently commits the states that are party to it (not Israel, Kazakhstan, or about 20 other nations) to prohibit the development, production, and stockpiling of biological and toxin weapons. However, the absence of any formal verification regime to monitor compliance has limited its effectiveness. The Chemical Weapons Convention (CWC) is a similar arms agreement outlawing chemical weapons, resulting in the destruction of about 90% of the world's declared stockpile of chemical weapons. However, credible reports of violations, even by signatories such as Syria, have been persistent.

Chemical agents, like NT and drones, pose their own ethical, legal, and political problems. For example, what might be done about countries that possess chemical weapons and are not under any legal imperatives to surrender them or to allow for their inspection and control? Although there is widespread public revulsion regarding chemical and biological weapons, they remain appealing to the armed forces of less economically and techno-logically advanced countries that lack nuclear or other advanced weapons, especially the Syrian regime, which has been widely reported to have used them against opposition forces and civilians.

Cyberwarfare

Cyberwarfare is computer hacking conducted by a country or a criminally minded subnational group or individual. Its goal could be to disrupt essential domestic functions of the intended target or to introduce computer worms or viruses into designated systems, causing their functioning to go awry. It is a form of information warfare sometimes seen as analogous to conventional war. In 2009, President Barack Obama declared America's digital infrastruc-ture to be a "strategic national asset," and in 2010, the Pentagon set up a new US Cyber Command (USCYBERCOM) to defend American military networks and attack other countries' systems. The European Union has set up the European Network and Information Security Agency (ENISA). The United Kingdom has established a cybersecurity and "operations centre." The USCYBERCOM is intended to protect only military assets, whereas civilian government and corporate infrastructures are primarily the responsibility of the Department of Homeland Security and private companies, respectively.

Numerous key sectors of national economies are potential targets, including cyberthreats to public and private facilities, banking and finance, transportation, manufacturing, medicine, education, electrical grids, and government, all of which are dependent on computers for daily operations. Many countries are currently preparing for cyberwar, including China, Israel, North Korea, Russia, Iran, and the United States. Iran has been the subject of more cyberattacks than has any other country, reflecting efforts by Israel and the United States to stall and, if possible, cripple purported Iranian nuclear programs.

Cyberwarfare is often depicted in movies as intense yet easy; with just one click of the mouse and a few keystrokes, the "good guys" (or the "bad guys") successfully hack into a multimillion dollar security system or insert a com-puter virus undetected. In reality, however, cyberattacks are complicated, time-consuming, and expensive. They can be multifunctional and used for a variety of purposes, including propaganda, espionage, and even imper-sonation, in addition to destroying physical infrastructures (e.g., factories, power plants, or nuclear enrichment centrifuges, in the case of Iran).

There is also the growing possibility of cyberterrorism. Many impor-tant infrastructures and services rely on the Internet to function, and so in theory can be controlled or manipulated from the Internet. Potentially, the most serious form of cyberwarfare is a targeted attack, designed to breach defenses and disable computerized functions of an individual, company, or organization. Defensive measures against such attacks include not only such standard techniques as security software, firewalls, and encryption but also procedures for what to do after an attack has been successful. Preven-tive measures include backing up information on a secure outside source, developing advanced analytic software, and setting up network intelligence systems to create awareness of possible attacks and develop means of defense against them. Identification of a highly sophisticated targeted attack involves (1) detection, or recognizing the attack; (2) situational awareness, or deter-mining its context; and (3) intelligence, or finding the solution to the prob-lem. Most successful targeted attacks are designed to take advantage of vulnerabilities in software or programs.

A conspicuous American and Israeli cyber-effort (later called "Stuxnet" by computer security experts) attacked Iran's Natanz nuclear plant in 2007. Additional attacks in the weeks following the initial assault temporarily disabled approximately 1,000 of the 5,000 uranium-enrichment centrifuges in that facility. Then, in 2016, a coordinated effort by the US cyber-command succeeded in disabling much of ISIS's Internet recruiting and propaganda activities. The implications of these successes are considerable, including the fact that the United States, whose economy relies greatly on computer networks, would appear to have the most to lose if and when cyberattack capabilities become widespread, including by "rogue" non-state actors with what the US regards as malign intentions. Programs in other countries can also be disrupted or sabotaged; however, it is not an easy matter, for there are significant disadvantages associated with using any cyberweapon. The US revealed in 2020 that some of its supposedly most secure computer networks, including those of the Defense Department, were breached over an extended period, apparently by Russia.

Cyberweapons are time-consuming in their development as well as in their transfer to the physical site of the target. The team that developed Stuxnet had to physically transfer it via thumb drives into the Natanz facility, an operation that was both risky and arduous. Because many Middle Eastern infrastructure systems aren't accessible via the Internet, other measures have to be taken in order to infect them; this is why using a cyberweapon to attack Syrian armed forces, for instance, might be futile. In addition, cyberweapons have shown the capability to jump from one computer system to another; Stuxnet, for example, "escaped" into the Internet. If a successor worm were capable of attacking targets other than nuclear centrifuges, catastrophic damage might ensue, with this form of pseudo-life running amuck and becoming a kind of Frankenstein's cyber-monster. Although potentially available as an alternative to actual warfare (Stuxnet was designed, at least in part, to disrupt Iran's nuclear program, thereby forestalling a possible Israeli military attack), cyber-attacks can easily morph into a *casus belli*: a cause of war. The US government's Nuclear Posture Review, issued in 2018, announced that nuclear weapons might be used in response to a variety of nonnuclear provocations, including cyber-attacks. At the same time, cyber-security has become a large and growing enterprise, increasingly seen as crucial to national security.

Like other new cutting-edge military technologies, for good and ill, future developments of cyberwarfare are unpredictable, risky, and ethically contentious. The growth of technology is exponential whereas that of human institutions and societies is much slower. Cyberweapons are currently being developed outside any regulatory framework. The Stuxnet computer worm was the starting point for what may become a unique kind of international competition. Unlike nuclear warfare, for example, in which countries enter into arms races while ostensibly hoping that those weapons will not be used, cyberwarfare is already upon us: Countries are not only developing various computer worms, viruses, and so on, and then storing them for possible use in the future, they are currently using these weapons, analogous to traditional espionage activities, absent an overt state of war.

Has Technology Made War Obsolete?

In the age of nuclear, biochemical, and cyber weapons, some people claim that the destructiveness of these devices has made war obsolete.

Interestingly, this suggestion is not unique to contemporary weapons of mass destruction: Throughout history, people have regularly claimed that the latest advances in weaponry, by their very lethality, will somehow prevent war. And then comes the next war. (This brings to mind Mark Twain's comment: "It is easy to stop smoking; I've done it many times.")

Following the invention of the bayonet, for example, an English editor wrote in 1715 that "perhaps Heaven hath in Judgment inflicted the Cruelty of this invention on purpose to fright Men into Amity and Peace, and into an Abhorrence of the Tumult and Inhumanity of War." Similarly, Alfred Nobel hoped that his new invention, dynamite, would make war impossible. In 1910, an Englishman, Norman Angell, wrote a best-selling book, *The Great Illusion,* in which he argued that because of the economic interconnectedness of nations, as well as the increased destructiveness of modern military forces, war had finally become impossible. The "great illusion" was that no one could rationally wage war in the 20th century; ironically, World War I began just 3 years after the publication of Angell's book. And in that conflict, the invention of the machine gun made neither people nor war obsolete. Rather, it led to the deaths of hundreds of thousands, often in just a single military engagement, such as the Battle of the Somme.

Since the dawn of the nuclear age in 1945, some observers of the global military scene have suggested once again that because war has become unacceptably destructive—to a would-be aggressor and even to a supposed "victor"—the likelihood of war has actually decreased. Although this line of reasoning may appear somewhat comforting, it is also seriously flawed. Let us grant that nuclear war, because of its potential for global annihilation, may appear to be its own deterrent. States possessing nuclear weapons (especially the major superpowers) may be especially cautious during a conflict with other nuclear weapons' states. But at the same time, theorists of mutual nuclear deterrence seem to have produced the expectation that because of the seriousness of nuclear war, each side can count on the other to refrain from anything resembling a nuclear provocation, which in turn makes the world "safe for conventional war."

In addition, there is the great danger that in a nuclear confrontation, each side will presume that the other will be deterred by the prospect of annihilation and, therefore, expect the other to back down, while remaining determined to stand firm itself. Moreover, nuclear weapons carry with them an inherent ambiguity: Because the consequences of using them are so extreme, the threat to do so lacks credibility. As a result, although technological "progress" in war-making has made war—especially nuclear war—horrifically destructive, it remains uncertain whether such developments have actually made war any less likely. In fact, it may well be that a nuclear conflict, detonation, or accident is more, not less, likely in this century than in the previous one because of the increased likelihood of "accidental" local (or *theater*) nuclear wars, as well as the possible proliferation of small nuclear devices (which might even be deliverable in suitcases) and of "rogue states" and "terrorists" seeking to acquire and deploy them.

Perhaps most disturbing of all, the fact remains that human beings, including decision makers, are influenced by many things beyond a cool, rational calculation of their perceived best interests. Wars have been initiated for many reasons, often including mistaken judgment or faulty information. And when war takes place, the combatants make use of whatever weapons they have. Never in the history of human warfare to date has an effective weapon been invented and then allowed to rust without at some time being used. (The problems related to nuclear deterrence will be explored more deeply in Chapter 5.)

Historically, the impact of "war is obsolete" reasoning has also been ironic: It has not so much discouraged governments from waging war as diminished whatever hesitation scientists, engineers, and industrialists might otherwise have had about lending their talents to the production of ever-more-destructive weapons. Even the liberal view of the perfectibility of human nature helped justify science's contribution to the manufacture of cannons, no less than steam engines or new techniques of manufacturing metal alloys. From the late 1980s to the present, many scientists similarly justify their participation in "Star Wars" research (a.k.a. Ballistic Missile Defense), which, as explored in Chapter 5, actually *increases* the danger of nuclear war.

Total War

One of the most important changes in modern warfare has been the combination of (1) increased destructiveness of the weapons and (2) decreased selectivity as to their targets. The weapons, in short, have become more deadly while at the same time increasingly directed at civilians, even as their actual targeting has become more accurate. Traditionally, noncombatants have been granted immunity during war—in theory, if not always in practice. In his book *A Sentimental Journey Through France and Italy,* English author Laurence Sterne recounted how, in the 18th century, he went to France, entirely omitting the fact that at the time England and France were fighting the Seven Years' War!

There was a time when states engaged in war without the lives of all their citizens poisoned, corrupted, or otherwise focused on the conflict. In 1808, for example, with the Napoleonic Wars raging, the French Institute conferred its gold medal on Sir Humphry Davy, an Englishman, who blithely crossed the English Channel to accept his award to the enthusiastic cheers of great scientists of France. However, this separation between civilian and military, between the lives of the people and the behavior of their states, has changed dramatically with the "hardening" of political boundaries as well as the advent of what has come to be called *total war.*

Historically, although military forces were raised primarily by the crown or the state taxing the population at large, armies in the field largely supported themselves by foraging, purchasing, or pillaging. With the advent of huge national defense forces that employed advanced technology they were unable to provide for themselves, policymakers decided to mobilize the "home front" in order to generate needed food, clothing, support facilities, and munitions for their armies. As entire populations were enlisted in the war effort, it became increasingly difficult to distinguish between combatants and noncombatants. After all, it was argued, how can the enemy be limited to the person who pulls a trigger, ignoring those who build the bombs, guns, ships, and other articles of war? Furthermore, why shouldn't war also be waged against those who support armies or even those who grow the food without which a belligerent country could not continue to make war?

During the Russian retreat from Napoleon's invading French army in 1812, partisans destroyed crops and other civilian articles that might be useful to the invader, and the Russians even permitted Moscow to be burned, in order to ensnare the French into remaining in the heart of Russia during a cruel winter. And toward the end of the War Between the States in the United States, also known as the Civil War, the Union's General Sherman marched destructively through Georgia, punishing the civilians in that part of the Confederacy more than the rebel military. Total war was, therefore, not unknown prior to the 20th century; civilians, moreover, have in many cases suffered greatly after their side was militarily defeated, especially if their city was sacked. New to 20th- and early-21st-century total war, however, was the organized use of military force directly and explicitly against an opponent's homeland in order to wage a war.

Total war became institutionalized during World War I, with the first use of the term *home front* and the deliberate targeting of civilians constituting that front. Italy initiated military bombing of noncombatants during its 1911 campaign in Libya, but Germany's use of zeppelins to bomb London was the first major attack on a home front. To appreciate some of the ambivalence that this tactic raised among the perpetrators, consider the following letter from Captain Peter Strasser, chief of Germany's naval airship division, to his mother:

> We who strike the enemy where his heart beats have been slandered as "baby- killers" and "murderers of women." . . . What we do is repugnant to us too, but necessary. Very necessary. Nowadays there is no such animal as a non-combatant; modern warfare is total warfare. A soldier cannot function at the front without the factory worker, the farmer and all the other providers behind him. You and I, mother, have discussed this subject, and I know you understand what I say. My men are brave and honorable. Their cause is holy, so how can they sin while doing their duty? If what we do is frightful, then may frightfulness be Germany's salvation.[3]

Loosening of Restraints

The tendency toward total war at that time was not limited to Germany. For example, the British naval blockade of Germany during World War I caused great suffering and widespread malnutrition, leading to an estimated 800,000 additional civilian deaths. As the historian John Nef put it, "One consequence of industrialization was to loosen the restraints upon war. With the growing material power to make war, what was needed was more politeness, more art, more wit in the conduct of international relations. What came was more grossness."[4]

What also came, as a result of national commitments to total war, was an inability on the part of the belligerents to call a halt to the carnage. For example, the disputes leading up to World War I were in their own way no more serious than those of the 18th century, which were resolved with much less bloodshed. What happened in part was that, according to the military historian Gwynne Dyer,

> the techniques of war had completely overpowered the ability of governments to limit their commitment to it. The axiom that force can only be overcome by greater force drove them to make war total, and the scale of the sacrifices they then had to demand of their citizens required that the purposes of the war must also be great. . . . When the people's willingness to go on making sacrifices has been sustained in every country by hate propaganda that depicts the war as a moral crusade against fathomless evil—then governments cannot just stop the fighting, sort out the petty and obscure Balkan quarrel that triggered it, swap around a few colonies and trade routes, and thank the

surviving soldiers and send them home. Total war requires the goal of total victory, and so the propaganda has become the truth: the future of the nation (or at least the survival of the regime) really does depend on victory, no matter what the war's origins were.[5]

Strategic Bombing

The invention of airplanes, and with it the possibility of long-range, strategic bombing, opened up yet another phase in the march of total war. Following the horrors of trench warfare in World War I, some military analysts initially welcomed the possibility of attacking an enemy's homeland as a means, they thought, of making future wars short and, on balance, less destructive than in the past. Foremost among these theorists was Italian Air Force General Guido Douhet (1869–1930), who argued that air power, applied directly to an enemy's industry and to the workforce that sustained its war effort, would destroy that side's "will to resist" and break its morale, resulting in a relatively quick and painless victory:

A complete breakdown of the social structure cannot but take place in a country being subjected to . . . merciless pounding from the air. The time will soon come when, to put an end to horror and suffering, the people themselves, driven by the instinct of self-preservation, will rise up and demand an end to the war.[6]

Exemplifying total war, during the 1930s and continuing through World War II, numerous civilian targets were attacked. German bombers initiated the process—as an intentional experiment—by destroying the town of Guernica during the Spanish Civil War (an event immortalized in Picasso's renowned painting illustrating Guernica's obliteration) During World War II, the Luftwaffe (Nazi Germany's air force) bombed Rotterdam (Holland) as well as Coventry and London (Britain), while British and American strategic bombers later retaliated and then exceeded the initial German bombings, conducting large-scale raids against many German urban areas, including the especially destructive fire-bombings of Hamburg and Dresden, killing tens of thousands of civilian noncombatants. In the Far East, US bombers attacked Japanese civilian targets, culminating in the firebombing of Tokyo and the use of atomic bombs against the cities of Hiroshima and Nagasaki, killing hundreds of thousands of civilians.

With the possible exceptions of these latter two cases, there is no evidence that the national will to resist was ever seriously shaken by total war; on the contrary, national will was typically hardened by such attacks, even as the civilian casualty toll mounted. It is estimated, for example, that German bombs killed 60,000 British civilians during World War II and that Allied bombs about 600,000 Germans and an equivalent number of Japanese.[7] Perhaps most troubling, today many decision makers take civilian casualties for granted, as "collateral damage," even as they ostensibly attempt to minimize them. Admittedly, however, we have not (yet?) reached Shakespeare's prediction in *Julius Caesar*:

Blood and destruction shall be so in use
And dreadful objects so familiar,
That mothers shall but smile when they behold
Their infants quartered with the hands of war.

Wars, Empires, Colonialism, and National Liberation

To some extent, the history of war *is* the history of civilization or, more accurately, a history of failures in our struggle to be civilized. The earliest peace treaties known are clay tablets dating from about 3000 BCE, which resulted from wars among the city-states of the Tigris and Euphrates valley. The rise and fall of empires and states have been marked—if not specifically caused—by a pattern of military successes followed eventually by defeats. Empires that rose by the sword generally died by the sword.

Some Ancient Empires

In the ancient Near East, the Sumerian empire was established around 2500 BCE and replaced by that of Sargon of Akkad, which in turn ended about 2000 BCE. Hammurabi then forged a Babylonian empire, which lasted about 200 years, until it was conquered by the Mitanni and the Assyrians around 1400 BCE. Egypt began uniting in approximately 3000 BCE, whereupon it spread via conquest and contacted the Mitanni, signing a nonaggression pact with them and with the Hittites around 1400 BCE. But the Assyrians eventually conquered Egypt as they did the Babylonians. In turn, the Assyrian capital of Nineveh was destroyed by the Egyptians and Medes in 612 BCE.

Next to rise to prominence were the Persians, who conquered Babylon in 538 BCE. The Persian Empire under Darius I in the 5th century BCE extended from what is now southern Russia to southern Egypt and from the Danube to the Indus Rivers. But the Greeks held off the Persians, and following its rather unexpected success, Athenian Greece entered into its Golden Age, 500–400 BCE. However, this period of prosperity and cultural creativity was shattered by the devastating Peloponnesian War between Sparta and Athens, and the Greeks never regained their civic and military glory.

Ultimately, the Greeks were defeated by the Macedonians under Philip. Philip's son, Alexander the Great, unified the Greek city-states and enabled them to conquer Egypt and virtually everything previously held by the Persians. Meanwhile, Rome developed as a major force, conquering Macedonia and Greece and defeating its arch-rival, Carthage, in the Punic Wars by the 3rd century BCE. The ensuing *Pax Romana* lasted about 500 years, but the western Roman Empire ceased to exist after CE 476 because of successful attacks by such "barbarians" as the Huns, Visigoths, and Vandals. The eastern (Byzantine) part of the Roman Empire, centered around Constantinople, later came under attack by Muslim Saracens and ultimately fell to the Turks in 1453. Before this, Islamic forces had conquered Egypt, northern Africa, Palestine, and Spain and were engaged in periodic wars with the Christian Crusaders. (Empires, created, maintained, and ended by wars, also existed in China, India, Africa, and Latin America).

Medieval to Modern Empires

Muslim armies were stopped in their advance into Europe at Tours, in modern-day France, by forces under the leadership of Charles Martel. Charlemagne, Martel's grandson, was subsequently crowned Holy Roman Emperor by the pope, in the forlorn hope of rekindling the power of ancient Rome.

Several centuries later, in the 12th century, Genghis Khan, leader of nomadic Mongol herdsmen from central Asia, established the largest land empire ever known, while massacring perhaps tens of millions of people. Although Genghis's army was never conclusively defeated, the Mongol empire eventually gave way as well, largely because the various subjugated peoples retained their cultural identity even as they assimilated certain Mongol traditions.

As the Mongol and Islamic empires receded, others grew dominant, each relying heavily on military power and each relatively short-lived. Thus, the Italian city-states, as well as Spain, Portugal, and the Netherlands, have all had their periods as major world powers, especially through their trading activities, secured by naval power. England and France contested the spoils of the New and Old Worlds for centuries, essentially to a draw. Napoleon, and, in more recent times, Hitler, attempted to conquer large parts of the known world, and although they succeeded briefly (at least in continental Europe), their imperial ambitions were defeated by countervailing military force.

From the 18th to the mid-20th centuries, Britain was the dominant world power, but the British Empire also declined, in large measure hastened by the bloodletting and economic costs of World Wars I and II. Neither the "thousand-year Reich" (Hitler's imperial design for Germany) nor the "greater east Asia co-prosperity sphere" (Japan's euphemism for its brief imperial sway over Asia) lasted for more than a decade or two. World War I brought about the end of most European monarchism and four empires. World War II left the United States and the Soviet Union as the two preeminent global powers; soon thereafter, the Cold War was initiated between them. The end of European colonialism in the 20th century was hastened by numerous wars of national liberation. In the 21st century, what some regard as American imperialism has been increasingly challenged by China's rise as a global superpower, a development that so far has been driven more by economic ascendency than by military might.

Wars and Social Change

Although wars have been crucial to many of the most important geopolitical changes, they have often also served to prevent significant social and economic changes. The *Pax Romana*, during the period of Roman hegemony, was due largely to the ability of Rome to act essentially as the Mediterranean world's police. The same was true, but to a lesser extent, during the so-called *Pax Britannica*, from the late 18th to the early 20th century. Following World War II, the United States attempted to forge a kind of *Pax Americana*; some would claim that it succeeded. But it may well be that the only kind of peace likely to be truly lasting and socially significant will have to be something as yet unknown in modern times, a *Pax Mundi*—that is, a global peace associated not with an individual nation but with the entire world and designed to protect and enhance human, not simply national, security.

Owing largely to their advantages in science, socioeconomic and educational development, and military technology, the major European powers—and, to a lesser extent, the United States and the former Soviet Union—were able to conquer, or at least to dominate militarily and politically, large areas of the globe. In the early stages of European colonial expansion, such indigenous peoples as Native Americans, Africans, and Chinese had numerical superiority, but they lacked modern firearms and often the necessary social and political organization to resist effectively. The Spanish conquistador Cortés, for example, conquered 8 million Aztecs with 400 men with muskets, 16 horses, and 3 cannons. Another Spanish conqueror, Pizarro, was similarly successful in Peru, as was the English-man Clive in India. The American Commodore Perry "opened" Japan with a handful of naval vessels. An Englishman, Hilaire Belloc, offered this sardonic commentary on the crucial role of technology in 19th-century British imperial conquest:

> Whatever happens we have got
>
> The Maxim gun, and they have not.

But just as Native Americans eventually obtained rifles (especially during the late 19th century), anti-*junta* rebels in El Salvador during the 1980s captured large amounts of military hardware, provided initially by the United States to the repressive, neocolonial Salvadoran government. Much of Saddam Hussein's Iraqi arsenal, as well as the arms controlled by the anti-Soviet mujahideen in Afghanistan, came by way of their eventual US enemies. And when the American-trained and equipped Iraqi Army collapsed under pressure from ISIS in 2014, the latter obtained large amounts of modern, US-supplied military hardware.

Revolutionary nationalism, especially in the form of guerrilla warfare, has been very successful, particularly since World War II, in evicting the weakened European powers from such regions as eastern Africa, Algeria, Vietnam, and Indonesia. By contrast, revolutionary forces have only rarely triumphed over locally based, nationalist governments, except when those governments were corrupt and generally out of touch with their citizenry, as happened in Russia in 1917, China in 1949, Cuba in 1959, and in Nicaragua and Iran in 1979.

Another, often unappreciated effect of war is that when unsuccessful, it can lead to the collapse of governments, and not only in the aftermath of defeat and occupation by the victors. Although wars often begin in a surge of enthusiasm, if they drag on longer than expected and especially if com-bined with unacceptable casualties, popular dissatisfaction can set in, with negative consequences for the government in power. When the Argentin-ian military junta took over the Falklands (which the Argentines call the Malvinas), the Argentine government's public support was fleeting; shortly after the United Kingdom retook those islands, that government fell—not to the British military but, in large part, as a result of angry protests by the people of Argentina, who blamed the generals (correctly) for the debacle.

In the middle of the inconclusive and costly Korean War, US president Harry Truman was succeeded by Dwight Eisenhower, a World War II general who had promised to "go to Korea" and end that war. A ceasefire was in fact achieved in the next year (1953), although a permanent peace treaty has yet to be achieved. Another US president, Lyndon Johnson, chose to forego a run for re-election in 1968, in large measure due to American discontent with the course of the Vietnam War. He was replaced by Richard Nixon, who had claimed to have "a secret plan to end the war," but didn't. The Vietnam War dragged on for another 5 years. And, ultimately, the US was defeated and forced to make an embarrassing exit from Vietnam.

A singularly disruptive political effect of an unpopular war occurred in 1917. The Russian Revolution of 1917 was, to a large extent, precipitated by the immense losses and misery experienced by Russian armies fighting Germany on the "eastern front" during World War I. The moderate Keren-sky government that initially replaced the czar and that was committed to continuing the war, initiated a massive offensive against the much better prepared and equipped German armies, which resulted in huge Russian casu-alties and in turn generated widespread rebellion by the Russian military.

This contributed significantly to the Kerensky government being promptly overthrown by the Bolsheviks—later to become the Communist Party of the Soviet Union—led by Vladimir Lenin and Leon Trotsky.

The Desirability of Peace Versus Justifications for Wars

Given the positive response that most people have to the word *peace*, it is fair to question why so few large-scale human societies have attained it, at least on an enduring basis. In fact, for many centuries, war has been considered acceptable, even honorable, by large numbers of people and many governments. How can one explain the conundrum that the same human beings who say they want peace will nonetheless kill other human beings, sometimes ruthlessly and indiscriminately, to obtain it and to protect their own "vital interests" and "national security"? What justifications are provided for violent conflicts, and what are the motivations that underlie decisions made by leaders who make war?

Biological Justifications for Wars

War has long been an ultimate arbiter of human disputes and a way of achieving glory, both for individuals and for entire peoples and nations. Ares, the Greek god of war (Roman equivalent: Mars), was a major deity, whereas Irene, the Greek goddess of peace, was a minor figure at best. According to Heraklitos, a pre-Socratic philosopher, war (or strife) "is the father of all things." And an influential 19th- and 20th-century intellectual movement, Social Darwinism, maintained that war was not only rewarding, virtuous, and manly but also biologically appropriate.

Social Darwinism misapplied the evolutionary concept of natural selection to human political and social activities, thus providing a faulty biological rationale for national conquests, imperialism, military dictatorships, and the subjugation of "weaker" by "stronger" peoples. But in fact, Social Darwinism is not scientifically valid because natural selection, and thus the process of organic evolution, favors living things that are most successful reproductively, not necessarily those that are the most aggressive. Moreover, there is no objective basis for assuming that just because something may be biologically underpinned it is therefore socially desirable, ethically defensible, or even characteristic of human beings. AIDS, typhoid fever, and Covid-19, for example, are all "natural" and "organic," yet virtually all people agree that none of them is desirable.

Social and Political Justifications for Wars

Some influential Western philosophers, including Hobbes, Hegel, and "philosophical" precursors of and contributors to Fascist, Nazi, and Maoist political ideologies, have at times expressed views that deem war not merely natural but beneficial to humanity because, in Hegel's words (partially intended as a critique of Immanuel Kant's pathbreaking essay *Perpetual Peace*), "war prevents a corruption of nations which a perpetual, let alone an eternal peace would produce."[8]

Although this view may be in widespread disrepute today, throughout most of the "civilized" world, wars have frequently shaken up existing (and often unjust) sociopolitical orders and have resulted in many changes, not all of them for the worse. Through revolutionary wars and wars of national liberation, many peoples have achieved independence from colonial powers, both by overthrowing despotic governments and by repulsing the efforts of other powers to force them back into subjugation. In some cases, however, revolutionary struggles have resulted in newer forms of autocracy, as in the Iranian revolution of 1979, in which the despotic pro-Western Shah was overthrown, only to be replaced by the despotic Islamic fundamentalist Ayatollah Khomeini. Ditto for the autocratic and arguably genocidal consequences of the Russian and Chinese Revolutions. Still, revolts against oppression should not automatically be condemned because they sometimes go astray after the insurrectionary groups have seized state power.

Thus, wars have at times served the enticing ends of generating, at least for a short time, national self-determination and political liberty. Indigenous peoples, no less than those in advanced technological societies, also tend to "rally 'round the flag" in times of perceived military danger, and this sense of patriotic fervor and national unity is usually achieved at the cost of projecting a stereotyped, and often dehumanized, image of "the enemy." Indeed, domestic political elites often employ the unifying effect of war and the threat of war to distract their citizenry from domestic problems and scandals in order to increase electoral support for themselves.

Social Justice and War

Social injustices, such as economic exploitation and political autocracy, are important not only as contributors to structural violence but also as factors in the outbreak of wars. Perhaps ironically, although the United States of America originally arose following a war of independence from Great Britain in the late 18th century, during the final decades of the 20th century and continuing into the first decades of the 21st, the United States became widely perceived as both an antirevolutionary force and a "status quo power," "the policeman of the world" often supporting repressive regimes, especially if they had anti-communist pretensions, and not uncommonly in opposition to nationalist aspirations. The Vietnam War is a "textbook" example of this phenomenon.

Not coincidentally, for most American citizens, as well as for privileged Europeans and other economic elites in less affluent societies, the military, cultural, and political hegemony of the United States at the beginning of this millennium was welcomed as the guarantor of their wealth, power, and status. For them, peace has meant the continuation of things as they are, with the additional hope that overt violence would be minimized or prevented altogether. Others yearn for dramatic social and economic change from the status quo. And for some of the most militant people, peace is, paradoxically, something to kill and die for—if it can bring about greater social justice and economic equity. As a Central American peasant is reported to have said, "I am for peace, but not peace with hunger."

The great 18th-century French philosopher Denis Diderot was convinced that a world of justice and plenty would mean a world free from tyranny and war. Hence, in his magisterial work, the *Encyclopédie,* Diderot hoped to establish peace by disseminating globally all of humanity's accumulated scientific and technical knowledge, from beekeeping and leather tanning to iron forging. Similar efforts continue today, although few advocates of economic and social development and equity claim that the problem of war can be solved simply by spreading knowledge or even by keeping everyone's belly full.

It is indeed disquieting that in a time of historically unprecedented affluence in many nations; the global dissemination of some Western political, economic, and cultural ideals; and increasing environmental and existential threats, the inhabitants of our planet continue to dissipate resources and lives fighting among themselves, or preparing to do so. Although there is nothing new in the human experience about recourse to war and political violence, what is new is the global risk involved in these potentially cataclysmic squabbles.

Political Ideologies and Militarism

The noted British historian Michael Howard introduced the term *bellicist* to refer to cultures "almost universal in the past, far from extinct in our own day, in which the settling of contentious issues by armed conflict is regarded as natural, inevitable and right." For example, Howard continues, bellicism during World War I "accounts not only for the demonstrations of passionate joy that greeted the outbreak of war but sustained the peoples of Europe uncomplainingly through years of hardship and suffering."[9]

Although this account may overstate toleration of horrific loss of life, it does point to the fact that many people are inclined (or manipulated) to identify perceived adversaries as bellicist, while claiming that they and their governments are peace loving, albeit not pacifist. The latter is a term of opprobrium often hurled by many political leaders against opponents they wish to caricature as weak.

Some Conservative Viewpoints

In contrast with their more liberal and progressive counterparts, some conservatives have tended on occasion to regard war quite favorably, considering it the "lesser of two evils" to defend liberty and one's native land against aggression and tyranny. Nonetheless, even most conservative ideologists have espoused a preference for peace and war prevention.

The mainstream Anglo-American conservative perspective traces its roots to a pessimistic view of human nature. One of the philosophical founders of this tradition, the 17th-century English philosopher Thomas Hobbes, who was reflecting on the horrors of the English civil war, warned that because of humanity's inherent aggressiveness and competitiveness, life in what Hobbes termed "the state of nature" consisted of *bellum omnium contra omnes* (the war of everyone against everyone). For Hobbes, this "natural state" of war required people who wished to avoid violent death to impose on themselves an absolute political authority (which he called the "Leviathan," after a biblical sea monster) and to be prepared to defend themselves by any means necessary against those would do them harm.

More than 2,000 years earlier, in Plato's *Republic,* Socrates is depicted as arguing that only philosopher-kings should rule, rather than the people as a whole. Plato also concluded from the Peloponnesian War (as a result of which Athens was defeated by Sparta) that city-states, in part following the Spartan example, must be hierarchically and stringently organized if they are to survive in a violent, unruly world in which war seems an unavoidable fact of life.

The mainstream Western conservative tradition also suggests that strong moral and governmental controls over individual conduct are necessary if social order and peace are to be secured. To many conservatives, wars usually occur because we are, at bottom, predatory and aggressive by nature and also because social order and political stability constantly threaten to break down. Since social organizations are regarded by most conservatives as basically unstable and often irrational, peace, security, and stability can be safeguarded only by strong laws and the efficacious use of force, thereby achieving a desirable combination of deterrence (to prevent breaches of the peace) and punishment (in case deterrence fails). Hence, many conservatives, although generally opposed to government intervention in most areas, support police and military forces.

For Hobbes, and for many in the mainstream Western conservative tradition, virtually nothing justifies the overthrow of a monarch or duly elected political authority. From this perspective, the "state of nature" is so dangerous and abhorrent that the people make a *social contract* with political authority, whereby they cede to the "Leviathan," the absolute state, their allegiance (and forgo their right to rebel) in return for protection against real and alleged enemies, foreign and domestic, who might engage in lethal violence against them. This is a social contract whose purpose is to minimize the risk of anarchy and maximize political order within a state. But Hobbes also noted that states interacted with other nations in what was essentially an anarchic situation. "The state of Commonwealths considered in themselves is natural, that is to say, hostile," he declared in *The Citizen,* and so "neither if they cease from fighting, is it therefore to be called peace; but rather a breathing time."[10]

According to mainstream Western conservative political ideology, if power is properly and securely held and wielded, there should be little reason for international wars or domestic insurrections, except perhaps in response to another state's real or alleged aggression or to adjust the "international state system"—that is, for what has come to be called "reasons of state." War may be acceptable, even laudable, if it also serves to prevent civic and moral breakdown. For example, the Roman historian Livy (59 BCE to 17 CE) reported approvingly in *The Early History of Rome* that the Roman Senate had "ordered an immediate raising of troops and a general mobilization on the largest possible scale" in the hope that the revolutionary proposals that some Roman tribunes were bringing forth might be forgotten in the bustle and excitement of three imminent military campaigns against Rome's perceived enemies. The Roman general Vegetius is first credited with having coined the phrase *si vis pacem, para bellum* ("if you wish peace, prepare for war"). And in more recent times, the doctrines of "balance of power," "peace through strength," "national security," and *"Realpolitik"* have continued this line of conservative political thought.

Probably the most articulate spokesperson for conservative political theory in the English-speaking world was the 18th-century orator and statesman Edmund Burke. Reacting to the violent extremes of the French Revolution, Burke articulated mainstream Anglo-American conservative political doctrine by stressing the primacy of "community" and "tradition," the importance of preserving existing institutional order, and skepticism about the perfectibility of human societies and individual persons. According to Burke, society is a partnership "not only between those who are living, but between those who are living, those who are dead, and those who are to be born."[11]

Not surprisingly, most conservatives have been especially concerned about the threat of disorder and subversion being imported from abroad. Writing about the French Revolution, Burke observed, "It is a war between the partisans of the ancient, civil, moral, and political order of Europe—the monarchy—against a set of fanatical and ambitious atheists which means to change them all." For most conservatives, the traditions inherited from past generations must be respected and defended, by military force if need be. Social cohesion and political stability are seen to come from reverence for and deference to, established authority—which is one reason why Confucius, despite counterindications in his moral philosophy, is also considered a conservative social thinker.

In the 19th and 20th centuries, with the overthrow of hereditary monarchy in most of Europe, mainstream Western conservatism shifted away from veneration of established political authorities and began to advocate "rugged individualism," "free enterprise," and "free markets," unimpeded by "state interference," while also revering patriotism and loyalty to duly elected governments. During the late 1990s into the 21st century thus far, a new trend gained momentum within conservative circles, especially in the United States. So-called neo-cons (for "new conservatives") advocated a pro-interventionist foreign policy aimed at toppling regimes deemed unfriendly to the United States and installing governments that are ostensibly sympathetic to both democracy and free enterprise.

This approach differs from the older, "paleo-conservatives," including the influential political strategists Henry Kissinger and Hans Morgenthau (especially prominent in Republican Party circles beginning in the 1950s) who, although generally more bellicist than their liberal counterparts, take a more pessimistic view of human nature and thus of the prospects of changing political and socioeconomic systems in other countries. Neo-cons were especially influential during the presidency of George W. Bush (2001–2009); however, their impact waned somewhat during the presidency of Barack Obama (2009–2017) as the failures of the Iraq War became increasingly apparent even to traditional war-supporting conservatives.

Some Liberal Viewpoints

Most Anglo-American political liberals have valued highly the autonomous individual, free from political and ecclesiastical authority. Major liberal theorists in this tradition include John Locke, Thomas Jefferson, Jeremy Bentham, John Stuart Mill, John Maynard Keynes, John Kenneth Galbraith, and John Rawls. According to the mainstream liberal tradition in the English-speaking world, political and legal equality are preferable to social hierarchy, giving greater scope for war in defense of equality and human rights. A major strand in Western liberal political thought addresses the issue of peace and war from an economic perspective. The early defense of capitalism by classical liberals may come as a surprise to many contemporary conservatives, who have associated liberalism with advocacy of the welfare state. But the two leading theorists and early defenders of capitalist economics, Adam Smith and David Ricardo, were considered the leading liberals of their day. The liberal theorist Norman Angell even claimed in 1910 that capitalists were necessarily opposed to war because "the capitalist has no country, and he knows . . . that arms and conquests and juggling with frontiers serve no ends of his and may very well defeat them, through the great destruction that such wars will generate."[24]

In *The Spirit of Laws*, the 18th-century French political philosopher Montesquieu proposed that international trade and commerce would naturally promote peace: "Two nations which trade with each other become reciprocally dependent; if it is to the advantage of one to buy, it is to the advantage of the other to sell; and all unions are founded on mutual needs." This foreshadows the widespread view, sometimes known as "liberal peace theory," that democracies do not go to war against each other in large measure because their economic interests would be severely undermined by international conflicts.

Montesquieu also argued that trade leads to an improvement in manners and basic civility: "It is almost a general rule that wherever there are tender manners, there is commerce, and wherever there is commerce, there are tender manners."[12] In a similar vein, John Stuart Mill claimed that "it is commerce which is rapidly rendering war obsolete, by strengthening and multiplying the personal interests which act in natural opposition to it."[13]

Mill's and Montesquieu's views soon became part of the liberal antiwar credo: By expanding commerce and spreading capitalism around the world, as well as by promoting democracy and harnessing public opinion, war could be made obsolete. In the late 19th century, the leaders of the so-called Manchester School of British economic theory, Richard Cobden and John Bright, opposed foreign interventionism by the British crown and maintained that maximum trade between peoples would make war not only unnecessary but impossible. As economic globalization gathered steam at the beginning of the 21st century, others have argued similarly that increased trade and economic interdependence would contribute not only to enhanced wealth for most nations but also to peace. The opponents of contemporary globalization disagree vehemently.

In a reversal of theoretical roles, however, 20th-century liberals, especially in the United States, placed greater emphasis on social responsibility and community than have the conservative champions of free enterprise and possessive individualism, except possibly in the area of civil liberties, where liberals defend individual rights and freedom and most conservatives prioritize traditional social units, such as the family, church, and state.

With regard to the establishment of peace and the cause of wars, Anglo-American liberals have decried what they deem the excessive power of nation-states and their often imperious leaders. At the same time, because of their generally positive view of human nature and rational thought, many liberals were caught off guard by the rise of Fascist, racist, and xenophobic movements in 20th-century central Europe, especially in Austria, Germany, and Italy. Many American liberals and progressives were also perplexed and horrified by the electoral successes of Donald Trump and other contemporary political leaders they considered illiberal and autocratic.

After World War II, Western conservatives generally saw the rise of communism in the Soviet Union and in "Red China" as the chief peril to "the free world," and were prepared to use any military, economic, and propaganda means necessary to defeat it. By contrast, most Western liberals were less rhetorically aggressive in promoting the Cold War while nonetheless continuing to allocate massive expenditures to military and espionage activities aimed at defeating left-wing governments, many of which were fundamentally nationalist in their political aspirations. Nonetheless, compared with conservatives, Anglo-American liberals, including the Biden administration, tend to be more favorably disposed to arms control agreements, placing more hope in the peacemaking and peacekeeping roles of international organizations such as the United Nations than do most conservatives, who tend to be skeptical of supranational institutions.

Liberals have, however, supported specific wars on occasion. The Spanish Civil War (1936–1939), for example, was initially seen by virtually all Western progressives as an unambiguously just war, the defense of a popularly elected socialist and secular government against an attack by reactionary forces aided by Fascist dictatorships in Germany and Italy. America's entry into World War II occurred under the administration of Franklin Delano Roosevelt, probably the most liberal American president of the 20th century.

Many liberals associated with the Kennedy and Johnson administrations initially supported America's war in Southeast Asia, primarily Vietnam.

Virtually all prominent liberal congressional figures in the United States also were in favor of American involvement in the Persian Gulf War, the war in Kosovo, the invasion of Afghanistan in late 2001, NATO's 2011 bombing of Libya, and the bombings and armed interventions in Syria by the Obama and Trump administrations. Nonetheless, the rationale for American involvement in wars since the 1990s has shifted somewhat from its previous anticommunist rhetoric to a defense of human rights in the face of potentially genocidal "ethnic cleansing" (a term that depicted the actions by ethnic Serbs in Bosnia against Bosnian Muslims and Croats) and in opposition to terrorists and, in the formulation of President George W. Bush, "the states that support or harbor them."

Liberals have typically been more ambivalent about war than most conservatives and they usually require a "better rationale" for military action. By the early 21st century, traditional liberal and conservative perspectives on war and peace had become even more fractionated. Some conservatives, for example, embraced an isolationist approach to international relations, while others, especially in the United States, favored selective military interventions in order to maintain and enhance the global military and economic preeminence of the United States as well as in ostensible defense of human rights abroad. But while some liberals favor military intervention for allegedly humanitarian purposes or to vanquish terrorism, others oppose any military incursion into another country.

The Iraq War (begun in 2003) created strange political bedfellows within the United States: just as some old-line conservatives, such as Kissinger and Morgenthau, opposed that war (while neo-cons orchestrated it), an important contingent of "liberal internationalists" or "Wilsonian liberals" (named for their parallel to President Woodrow Wilson's enthusiasm for World War I as a means of "making the world safe for democracy") supported the US overthrow of Saddam Hussein. The ongoing conflict in Syria has also provoked both liberal and conservative hawks to advocate US military intervention, opposing both the Assad regime and such militant Islamist groups as ISIS.

The Trump administration, although distinctly right wing in nearly all respects, exhibited an avowed reluctance to intervene militarily in other countries (especially for "democratic nation building"), while at the same time threatening war with Iran and opposing not only arms control agreements but nearly all kinds of international cooperation. This was exemplified by its withdrawal of the US from the Paris Agreement on climate change, from membership from the World Health Organization (WHO), and from the Joint Comprehensive Plan of Action (JCPOA), more commonly known as the Iran nuclear deal. In its first week in office, the Biden administration committed the US to rejoining both the Paris Agreement and the WHO. Its policy toward Iran, as of the writing of this book, has yet to be determined, although the US and Iran began negotiations aimed at having the US rejoin the JCPOA, in return for which Iran would agree to constrain its nuclear program.

Some Leftist Viewpoints

Political movements of the far right have rarely professed peace as an important goal. By contrast, most left-wing (progressive and/or radical) thinkers and parties have traditionally claimed a strong association with world peace, although with some exceptions. The most explicit and best-known example of a radical left-wing (communist) leader supporting war is Mao Zedong, who wrote,

> Political power grows out of the barrel of a gun. . . . All things grow out of the barrel of a gun. . . . Some people ridicule us as advocates of the "omnipotence of war." Yes, we are advocates of the omnipotence of revolutionary war; that is good, not bad. . . . We are advocates of the abolition of war, we do not want war; but war can only be abolished through war, and in order to get rid of the gun it is necessary to take up the gun.[14]

Ironically, whereas the purported goals of left-wing revolutionary wars differ from the those of right-wing military campaigns, people from all political perspectives have justified the use of organized state violence as a defensible (if sometimes regrettable) means of attaining allegedly "higher" political, social, and economic goals, such as freedom and national security.

Within left-wing political traditions, stemming from Karl Marx and continuing through Lenin, Mao, and Che Guevara to the present, there is further justification for the "selective" use of revolutionary violence (and even of terror) against established "reactionary" regimes or in defense of "revolutionary" ones: the emancipation of workers and other oppressed peoples from capitalist domination and exploitation and the ultimate construction of communism domestically and globally.

This radical political tradition is often in opposition to another viewpoint—namely, an antimilitarist, socialist-pacifist tradition, represented in the 20th-century European progressive movements by Rosa Luxemburg, Karl Liebknecht, and Bertrand Russell, and in the United States by Eugene V. Debs, Norman Thomas, Emma Goldman, Noam Chomsky, and A. J. Muste. For Muste in particular, religious considerations loomed large, such as the necessity of personal, faith-based "witness" against war. Muste is particularly well known for his insistence that "there is no way to peace; peace is the way" and that "wars will end when men refuse to fight."

Prior to World War I, European pacifists and socialists had hoped that workers' solidarity would prevent the outbreak of war. But the war that erupted between 1914 and 1918 was an enormous blow to the optimism of many socialist-pacifists, especially since overwhelming majorities in the European Socialist and Social Democratic parties elected to support their governments' war efforts (with such notable exceptions as Rosa Luxemburg and Karl Liebknecht), rather than to engage in antiwar activities. Eighty-five years later, in 1999, many members of the European Left—especially those with important political offices in England and Germany—enthusiastically supported NATO's bombing campaigns in Serbia and Kosovo, despite the protests of many more pacifistically inclined members of their own political parties (such as the Labour, Social Democratic, and Green parties). In response to attacks on the United States, Madrid, London, Paris, Brussels, Berlin, and elsewhere, many hitherto "pacifists" on the red/green left sanctioned the use of violence against terrorists. There are also often vehement, but usually nonviolent, disputes within both the Israeli and Palestinian peace and social justice movements regarding the means viewed necessary to secure a just and lasting peace between the antagonists as well as to create a viable Palestinian state.

In summary, radical leftists and other political progressives have long advocated opposition to war in general, although many have believed that the abolition of war, the prevention of genocide, and the struggle against terrorism—and in some cases, even social justice itself—can be accomplished only via war. With the fall of the Soviet Union and the end of the 20th-century Cold War, many progressives have become more involved in local, often environmentally related activities, sometimes creating local "zones of peace," rather than engaging in the mass antiwar and antinuclear movements with which they had been closely identified between 1950 and 1990—notwithstanding opposition to the invasion and occupation of Iraq. Whether this continues in the third decade of the 21st century remains to be seen.

Asymmetries

Troublesome issues often arise when there is a significant disparity in wealth and power between two contending parties, with the militarily stronger one satisfied with the status quo and the weaker dissatisfied. This is largely the case, for example, in Israel and Palestine: most Israelis want peace, as do most Palestinians. However, most Israelis are also content with the current situation, whereas most Palestinians are not. Peace, for most Israelis, therefore involves keeping things as they are, whereas for most Palestinians, peace requires change. As a result, insofar as nonviolent means fail to induce such change, many Palestinians—as well as their sympathizers—have become increasingly convinced that only violence will get the other side's attention, never mind actually achieving their desired results.

From a mainstream Israeli perspective, as a senior adviser to the government has pointed out, Israel "cannot make peace while there is violence and when there is no violence it sees little reason to make peace." The situation that emerges is like the paradox of when to repair a leaky roof: You don't want to do it while it is raining (i.e., while violence is occurring, since this can appear to be appeasement), and when it isn't raining, there seems little reason to do anything! This perpetuates a status quo that at least one major party in the conflict, the Palestinians, finds unacceptable and increases the risk of an escalation of violence by all involved.

Another frequent and painful asymmetry concerns the suffering imposed on a country (often a less-developed one) that finds itself a battlefield. For example, the US-led war in Afghanistan resulted in the loss of more than 2,200 American lives, while more than 100,000 Afghans were killed. This occurred after more than 40 years of near-continuous warfare initiated and prolonged by covert operations and overt invasions by the former USSR and then by US-led forces. A similar asymmetry occurred in Iraq and—even more dramatically—in Vietnam during what is known in the US as the Vietnam War and in Vietnam as the American War.

Is War Inevitable?

Many 19th-century liberals viewed war as a deplorable interruption in the linear progression of our species to a better, more peaceful world. Even today, most liberal views of the causes of wars emphasize the role of misperceptions and cognitive errors, rather than iniquity or malign intentions on the part of leaders. War is, in this view, a blunder, the consequence of human fallibility: If decision makers would only operate more carefully and thoughtfully, most wars could be prevented.

In contrast, there is another, sterner tradition associated with conservative viewpoints. The emphasis here is on innate human weakness, sin, and/

or the allegedly unalterable fact of "evil" human nature. According to one of the most important conservative politicians of the 20th century, Winston Churchill, "The story of the human race is war." From this perspective, wars do not in general occur because one side, presumably the more peace-loving one, misunderstands the other. Rather, wars are usually forced on otherwise rational and peace-loving national leaders because their "vital interests" have been assaulted or because they realistically perceive an impending threat to their national security and hence must defend themselves and others against those who would do them harm. According to this view, epitomized by the administration of George W. Bush but not, in practice, revoked by either the Obama or the Trump administrations, the defense of freedom requires a political willingness by national statesmen to go to war if need be.

Regardless of one's thinking about the ultimate, underlying causes of war, the belief that war is inevitable carries a great danger. Consider, for instance, the idea of a self-fulfilling prophecy, in which something that is not necessarily true may become true if enough people believe it. Thus, if one believes that another person or country is an enemy and acts on this assumption, this belief may create a new reality. Similarly, if war is deemed inevitable and countries therefore prepare to fight against each other—by drafting an army, procuring and deploying weapons systems that threaten their neighbors, and/or engaging in bellicose foreign policy— war may well result. Such a war may then be cited as "proof" that it was inevitable from the start. Moreover, it may be used to justify similar bellicose behavior in the future. In this way, the most war-prone, hawkish members of a country's leadership often act to support and legitimize the most war-prone, hawkish leaders on another side. This pattern was exemplified during much of the Cold War (1945–1991) between the US and Soviet Union, and it may also be in play as part of the more recent hostilities between the US and North Korea, Iran, and, most ominously, Russia and China.

A reason for cautious optimism, however, is that many social practices once common and widely viewed by many as inevitable—such as slavery and dueling—are virtually unknown today. If opponents of slavery and dueling had simply conceded the inevitability of these ancient social practices, they would not have struggled to end them—although slavery, often in the form of human trafficking, still persists in some parts of the world. Nonetheless, ending widespread slavery and dueling may have been easy compared with ending war because those social changes were feasible irrespective of what other nation-states were doing. A country that renounces war, by contrast, may find itself vulnerable to threats made by other, better-armed nations. In short, unlike the case of slavery in the United States, an end to war cannot be simply declared by a unilateral Lincoln-like "emancipation proclamation." Ending war seems to require a wider will to do so, although this does *not* mean that individual countries are powerless until everyone agrees.

Can Nations Change?

There are some other reasons for guarded optimism. For example, history provides many examples of countries changing dramatically from warlike to peaceful. During the early Middle Ages, the Swiss were among Europe's most bellicose people, fighting successfully against the French in northern Italy and for their own independence against the Holy Roman Empire. But Switzerland hasn't fought a war since 1515, when it adopted a policy of permanent neutrality. Switzerland's vaunted "neutrality" (most keenly compromised during World War II due to the support by many Swiss for Nazi Germany) has long been undergirded by a large, well-equipped, defensively oriented modern army and by a civilian network of underground shelters, and also by its perceived usefulness as a center for banking and international diplomacy.

Japan has also changed notably over the centuries. It gave birth to one of the world's great warrior traditions, the code of *Bushidō* and the very aggressive samurai. Within several decades after European firearms reached Japan via Portuguese traders in 1543, Japanese musketry was among the most advanced in the world. But a century later, guns were virtually absent from all of Japan. And when Commodore Matthew Perry "opened" Japan (for Western trade) in 1853, Japanese warfare was technologically medieval.

The process of Japan's transformation had been remarkable. The 16th-century shōgun (literally, a "barbarian-quelling generalissimo") Tokugawa, upon being victorious over his rivals, centralized all firearms manufacture and arranged for all gunpowder weapons gradually to be destroyed, without replacement. His decision was not based on a wholehearted devotion to peace; rather, it reflected the samurais' great distaste for muskets and cannons, which threatened to ruin the cult of the warrior/nobleman who could be shot by a mere commoner. Despite the reasons for this "conversion," the Japanese example is nonetheless instructive because it demonstrates that militarism can be curtailed and whole societies reorganized along more peaceful lines, once the authorities (and in democracies, the citizenry) consider such changes to be in their interest.

However, demilitarization can be reversed, as was the case in Japan during the latter half of the 19th century. After being humiliated by Perry, Japan modernized very rapidly and initiated successful wars against China (1894) and Russia (1904–1905). But Japan's increasingly aggressive and warlike ventures, including its attacks on China and much of the rest of Asia in the late 1930s and on the United States in 1941 at Pearl Harbor, culminated in its defeat in 1945. Since the end of World War II, Japan has kept its military force considerably smaller than that of comparably affluent nations (in part because it has been "protected by America's nuclear umbrella") and has, instead, devoted its energies to economic growth, although there is currently pressure within Japan to increase its military role and even to consider renouncing the American-imposed "pacifist" clause of its constitution and to consider acquiring nuclear weapons.

Germany has been similarly variable in its war/peace behavior. After the devastating Thirty Years' War (1618–1648), the principalities and kingdoms in the German-speaking world went on to become the philosophical, musical, and scientific centers of central Europe, although militarism continued to flourish in Prussia, the most influential of the German states. Beginning about 1860, with the wars of German unification under Bismarck, the newly constituted state of Germany became increasingly militarized, culminating in Germany's aggression during World Wars I and II and its defeat by the Allies in 1945. Since then, Germany, like Japan, has been partially demilitarized, although it participated in NATO's military strikes against Serbia in 1999 and has played a support role in Afghanistan, much to the consternation of Germany's considerable antiwar movement.

Peaceful traditions can be ruptured by war, just as peaceful societies can become militarized. For example, despite long-standing Jewish advocacy of peace and nonviolence, modern-day Israel's military spending comprises an international high of roughly 30% of its gross national product, and it has been involved in five wars (1948, 1956, 1967, 1974, and 2006), as well as many military incursions into Lebanon and Gaza, during its brief existence.

On the other hand, nations that had previously been rent by war and domestic violence can renounce those behaviors, as did Costa Rica in 1948, when the government abolished its military.

War can become a national habit and militarism a way of life. But so can peace. Long-standing traditions of war and conflict may, with sufficient popular support, give way to non-bellicose traditions. Great Britain and France, for example, which were bitter opponents for centuries and had fought many devastating wars against each other, have become close allies since the turn of the 20th century, as have such other longtime enemies as the United States and Great Britain. Kenneth Boulding, one of the founders of Peace Studies, pointed out that a zone of "stable peace" has spread to include most of Western Europe (though notably not in the Balkans and the Basque and Catalan regions of Spain), North America, and Oceania (Australia and New Zealand). Within these zones, war seems very unlikely to break out.

The case of Northern Ireland provides another, more recent example of a transition from war to peace. In 2005, the (Catholic) Irish Republican Army disarmed and pledged never to resume its unsuccessful, violent campaign to drive Britain out of Northern Ireland, while the (Protestant) Ulster Volunteer Force made a parallel commitment, with both sides agreeing to share political power. There had been violent conflict between Irish Catholics and Protestant English settlers in Ireland since the Norman conquest in 1066 and more actively since Henry VIII sought to impose Protestantism and English land ownership on an overwhelmingly Catholic Irish population. It is possible that the current agreement will break down at some point, especially following the UK's departure from the European Union ("Brexit"), which threatens the smoothly functioning border between Northern Ireland—part of the United Kingdom—and the Republic of Ireland, which remains in the EU. The fact that these belligerents agreed to peace—the Good Friday Agreement—after centuries of violence is nonetheless a hopeful step and a powerful statement of the capacity of people to change.

Are We Winning the War Against War?

The answer, perhaps surprisingly, is a qualified yes, according to psychologist Steven Pinker, because long-term historical trends indicate the following:[15]

1. Wars today are measurably fewer and smaller than 40 years ago.

2. The number of people killed directly by war violence decreased by 75% in that period.

3. Interstate wars have become very infrequent and relatively small.

4. Wars between "great powers" have not occurred for more than 55 years.

5. The number of civil wars is also shrinking, although less dramatically.

The reasons for these encouraging changes are complex, but they seem to include modest successes by international peacekeepers, NGOs, diplomats, and peace movements, as well as a continuing delegitimation of war itself as a way of solving disputes. Pinker has also provided evidence that counter-intuitively perhaps, violence—at least in its tangible physical manifestations—is generally declining, at least in most of the Western world. Thus:

1. Homicide rates in Europe have gone down thirtyfold since the Middle Ages.

2. Human sacrifice, slavery, punitive torture, and mutilation have been officially abolished around the world (although slavery, torture, and mutilation—especially female genital mutilation—still persist in certain regions).

3. Wars between developed countries have vanished, and even in the developing world civil wars cause substantially fewer casualties than they did decades ago.

4. Rape, battering, hate crimes, deadly riots, child abuse, cruelty to animals—every category of violence has declined.

Pinker also anticipates that forms of institutionalized violence that can be eliminated by the stroke of a pen—such as capital punishment, the criminalization of homosexuality, and the corporal punishment of children in schools—will also continue to decline.

Not all scholars and peacemakers are as optimistic because these trends are not irreversible, but it is increasingly clear that peace and war—along with violence/nonviolence generally—exist on a continuum whose balance constantly fluctuates. Neither should be taken for granted, and neither is humanity's "natural state." The human condition—whether to wage war or to build an enduring peace—is for us to decide.

The Nature and Functions of Conflict

We end this chapter with a brief discussion of various ways of conceptualizing conflict. The word *rivalry,* for example, originated with the Latin *rivus* (river or stream). Rivals were literally "those who use a stream in common." Competitors, by contrast, are those who seek to obtain something that is present in limited supply, such as water, food, mates, or status. But the word *enemy* derives from the Latin *in* (not) plus *amicus* (friendly), and it implies a state of active hostility. Rivals necessarily compete, if there is a scarcity of a sought-after resource, but they do not have to be enemies. The word *conflict,* on the other hand, derives from the Latin *confligere,* which means literally "to strike together." It is impossible for two physical objects, such as two billiard balls, to occupy the same space. They conflict, and if either is in motion, the conflict will be resolved by a new position for both of them.

Within the human realm, conflict occurs when different social groups are rivals or otherwise compete. Such conflicts can have many outcomes: one side changed, one side eliminated, both sides changed, neither side changed, or (rarely) both sides eliminated. They can be resolved in many ways: by violence, by the issues changing over time, by the deaths (natural or otherwise) of one or more of the conflicting parties, or by mutual agreement. Most people agree that the latter is best.

A Final Note on War

Today's armed conflicts, as previously noted, rarely involve a formal declaration of war, probably because, in general, diplomatic formalities are currently less prominent, and war is increasingly considered an illegitimate way to settle grievances. Although there is substantial evidence that countries can become less war-prone and, moreover, some trends in warfare and violence are at least mildly encouraging, wars—often under various euphemisms—are still taking place, causing immense destruction and misery. Moreover, the threat of war remains great, with its likely consequences more severe and potentially far-reaching than ever.

The history of war shows that human life certainly is not considered priceless and also that some lives—especially those of white privileged elites—are valued more than others. Moreover, a great danger lurks in a unique calamity—nuclear war—that could be catastrophic not only for all humans but also, perhaps, for all life on Earth. We return to this theme in Chapter 5.

Questions for Further Reflection

1. Are there any persuasive justifications for war? If so, which justifications and which wars? If not, why not?

2. Is it possible to end war? Why or why not?

3. Consider the statistical definitions mentioned in this chapter to define wars in particular and violent conflicts in general. What are their strengths and weaknesses?

4. Can and should there be ways of resolving bitter conflicts without going to war?

5. Do you think we, as a species, are becoming more or less belligerent and violent? Why or why not?

Suggestions for Further Reading

Raymond Aron. 1966. *Peace and War*. New York: Doubleday.

Ronan Farrow. 2018. *War on Peace: The End of Diplomacy and the Decline of American Influence*. New York: W. W. Norton.

Joshua Goldstein. 2011. *Winning the War on War: The Decline of Armed Conflict Worldwide*. New York: Dutton.

A. C. Grayling. 2006. *Among the Dead Cities: The History and Moral Legacy of the WWII Bombing of Civilians in Germany and Japan*. New York: Walker & Company.

Michael Howard. 1986. *The Causes of Wars*. Cambridge, MA: Harvard University Press.

John Keegan. 1994. *A History of Warfare*. New York: Vintage Books.

Judith Eve Lipton and David P. Barash. 2018. *Strength Through Peace: Demilitarization in Costa Rica, and What We Can Learn From a Small Tropical Country*. New York: Oxford University Press.

Jeff McMahan. 2009. *Killing in War*. New York: Oxford University Press.

Steven Pinker. 2011. *The Better Angels of Our Nature: Why Violence Has Declined*. New York: Viking.

Anatol Rapoport. 1997. *The Origins of Violence: Approaches to the Study of Conflict*. New Brunswick, NJ: Transaction.

Arnold J. Toynbee. 1950. *War and Civilization*. New York: Oxford University Press.

Quincy Wright. 1964. *A Study of War*. Chicago: University of Chicago Press.

Notes

1. Quincy Wright. 1964. *A Study of War*. Chicago: University of Chicago Press.

2. F. Scott Fitzgerald. 1934. *Tender Is the Night*. New York: Scribner.

3. From A. Normal. 1969. *The Great War*. New York: Macmillan.

4. John U. Nef. 1950. *War and Human Progress*. Cambridge, MA: Harvard University Press.

5. Gwynne Dyer. 1985. *War*. New York: Crown.

6. Guido Douhet. 1942. *The Command of the Air*. New York: Coward-McCann.

7. A. C. Grayling. 2006. Among the Dead Cities: The History and Moral Legacy of the WWII Bombing of Civilians in Germany and Japan. New York: Walker & Company.

8. G. W. F. Hegel. 1942. *Philosophy of Right*. T. M. Knox, trans. Oxford: Clarendon.

9. Michael Howard. 1986. *The Causes of Wars*. Cambridge, MA: Harvard University Press.

10. Thomas Hobbes. 1949. *The Citizen*. New York: Appleton-Century-Crofts.

11. Edmund Burke. 1961. *Reflections on the Revolution in France*. New York: Doubleday.

12. C. L. Montesquieu. 1977. *The Spirit of Laws*. David Carrithers, trans. Berkeley: University of California Press.

13. John Stuart Mill. 1958. *Considerations on Representative Government*. New York: Liberal Arts Press.

14. Mao Zedong. 1966. *Basic Tactics*. Stuart R. Schram, trans. New York: Praeger.

15. Steven Pinker. 2011. *The Better Angels of Our Nature*. New York: Viking.

4

Terrorism and Counterterrorism

A War Without End?

On September 11, 2001, the cities of New York and Washington, D.C. were attacked by Islamic terrorists. The toll of American life in a single day (about 3,300 civilians) was exceeded in US history only by battles during the Civil War. Especially unprecedented is that these attacks occurred on American soil, that US civilian airplanes were transformed into weapons of mass destruction, that the United States was not in a declared state of war at

David Surowiecki via Getty Images

Terrorism and Counterterrorism

A War Without End?

On September 11, 2001, the cities of New York and Washington, D.C. were attacked by Islamic terrorists. The loss of American life in a single day (about 3,000 civilians) was exceeded in US history only by battles during the Civil War. Especially unprecedented is that these attacks occurred on American soil, that US civilian airplanes were transformed into weapons of mass destruction, that the United States was not in a declared state of war at the time, and although the leadership of certain countries (notably Afghanistan) was sympathetic to the attacks, the actual perpetrators were nonstate actors, mostly citizens of Saudi Arabia.

The instigators of the 9/11 attacks—and of bombings in Madrid in 2004, London in 2005, in Paris and other metropolises in 2015, in Brussels, Berlin, and Nice in 2016, in New Zealand in 2019, and in other cities around the world since 9/11—have been decried as terrorists in most of the non-Islamic world and in many Islamic countries as well. On the other hand, they have been praised as martyrs by some Muslims. Although terrorism and terrorists predated the attacks on New York and Washington, D.C., since 9/11 they have emerged as headline political and military issues—although there is little global consensus on the meaning of terrorism, the identity of terrorists, and what to do about the problem.

What Is Terrorism? Who Are Terrorists?

Terrorism is a vexing term. Any actual or threatened attack against civilian noncombatants (and, arguably, against government and military agents as well) may be considered an act of terrorism, generally carried out by people who feel unable to confront their perceived enemies directly and who, accordingly, use violence, or the threat of violence, against noncombatants—and, as argued by some analysts and advocates, against police, soldiers, and civilian government officials as well—to achieve their political aims.

Terrorism is also a contemporary variant of what has been described as guerrilla or insurrectionary warfare, dating back at least to the anti-colonialist and anti-imperialist struggles for national liberation conducted in North America and Western Europe during the late 18th and early 19th centuries and continuing after World War II in Africa and South Asia against such European empires as the British, French, Dutch, and Portuguese.

Placing "terrorist" in quotation marks may be jarring for some readers, who consider the designation self-evident. We shall often do so, however, not to minimize the horror of such acts but to emphasize the value of qualifying righteous indignation by recognizing that often one person's "terrorist" is another's "freedom fighter." Thus, who is or is not a terrorist and what may or may not be acts of terrorism depend largely on the perspective of those using these terms. "Terrorism," in one form or another, is as old as violent human conflict.

Here are some contemporary and contending definitions: Terrorism is "premeditated, politically motivated violence perpetrated against noncombatant targets by sub-national groups or clandestine agents, usually intended to influence an audience."[1] This is perhaps the most commonly understood contemporary definition of terrorism in the West, and it was penned by the US Central Intelligence Agency (CIA).

A second, widely held definition is articulated by an influential American terrorism expert, Bruce Hoffman (formerly of the RAND Corporation, a think tank funded largely but not exclusively by the US government and military):

Terrorism is fundamentally a form of psychological warfare. Terrorism is designed, as it has always been, to have profound psychological repercussions on a target audience. Fear and intimidation are precisely the terrorists' timeless stock-in-trade. . . . It is used to create unbridled fear, dark insecurity, and reverberating panic. Terrorists seek to elicit an irrational, emotional response.[2]

Western analysts and officials generally view terrorism as politically motivated violence perpetrated by *subnational* groups *against citizens or noncombatants*. There is less consensus, though as to whether attacks by these groups, or by individuals, against military personnel or government officials also constitutes terrorism. In any event, terrorism is widely seen as a "weapon of the weak," as a means used by groups or individuals ("lone-wolf terrorists") lacking sophisticated weaponry to confront real and perceived enemies

There is another perspective, however, one that also identifies terrorism as conducted by existing governments, or by government agents, against those who present "targets of opportunity" and are usually unable to defend themselves. A growing number of scholars and terrorism analysts, including ourselves, identify non-state terrorism as "terrorism from below" and state and state-sponsored terrorism as "terrorism from above." This equation of what is widely seen as legitimate violence (from above) with illegitimate (from below) often seems discordant to people from the industrialized West, who are accustomed to considering terrorism as something that "they" rather than "we" do. Importantly, from this point of view, which may be the dominant perspective outside the Western world, both nation-states—which commit "terrorism from above" (TFA)—and subnational entities (individuals and groups alike)— which engage in "terrorism from below" (TFB)—may commit acts of terrorism.[3]

Work conducted by the political scientist Robert Pape and also by the National Consortium for the Study of Terrorism and Responses to Terrorism (START) at the University of Maryland challenges some other long-accepted notions: for example, that terrorists are pathological, driven by religious fanaticism, and/or spurred by poverty. They emphasize that many terrorists are well educated and, within their worldview, quite rational. In this light, it should come as little surprise that some of yesterday's "terrorists" have become heads of state and even Nobel Peace Prize winners.

The Politics of Terrorism and a Very Brief History

"Terrorism" is at bottom a political construct, a historically variable and ideologically useful way of branding those who may violently oppose a particular circumstance as beyond the moral pale, hence not suitable for diplomacy and negotiations. Moreover, yesterday's "terrorist" may become today's or tomorrow's chief of state—if successful in gaining state power.

Historical examples abound, from the "barbarian" Teutonic insurgents who overthrew the Roman Empire to the Jacobins during the early days of the French Revolution. Prior to the US Civil War, militant abolitionists such as John Brown were considered terrorists and are now widely seen as freedom fighters, albeit quite extreme in their methods, sometimes verging on the fanatical. During the 1940s, Menachem Begin—who subsequently became prime minister of Israel and a close ally of the United States—headed a militant Zionist group known as the *Irgun;* this organization conducted numerous acts of violence, primarily against British-occupied Palestine, including, in 1946, the notorious bombing of the King David Hotel, killing almost 100 people.

Yasser Arafat, longtime head of the Palestine Liberation Organization, was similarly denounced in the West and in Israel as a terrorist, whereas among Palestinians, he was widely regarded as a heroic leader. The government of Pakistan, which criticized the 9/11"terror attacks" on the United States as un-Islamic, has long sponsored violent agitators in Kashmir, who are considered terrorists by the government of India. The Irish Republican Army

(IRA) was widely regarded in Great Britain as a terrorist organization, yet many Irish Catholics consider this group laudably patriotic, and much of its funding came from donations raised in the United States. Nelson Mandela and other leaders of the antiapartheid resistance movement in South Africa used violence to promote their political ends. When asked if he and his African National Congress (ANC) were terrorists, Mandela replied, "Of course." Mandela later won the Nobel Peace Prize, as did Yasser Arafat and Menachem Begin. (On the other hand, so did Henry Kissinger, an architect of the Vietnam War and of the "Christmas bombing" campaign that killed many Vietnamese civilians just before the American withdrawal from Vietnam.) After accession to state power, the victors often rewrite the history books to label themselves as freedom fighters, patriots, and/or proponents of national liberation, while demoting and denigrating their vanquished adversaries as "terrorists," "autocrats," "imperialists," "dictators," and so on.

Terrorism therefore may acquire its political content *retrospectively*, based on its success or failure in achieving such political goas as independence and victory over an occupying power. Many politically powerful contemporary opponents of "terrorism" claim for themselves a kind of moral superiority, an ethical high ground that justifies virtually any means (often designated "counterterrorism" and/or "preemptive war")—including bombings that result in many civilian casualties—to win their particular struggle against what they label terrorism. This often results in an escalating series of attacks and counterattacks, potentially leading to wars without end (as in the Middle East and elsewhere).

A Brief History of Terrorism: From Above and From Below

The lexicography and history of terrorism are important. The term derives originally from the French Revolution, when *la Terreur* ("The Terror") was initially used approvingly in 1793–1794 by newly installed defenders of the revolutionary regime to deploy state-sanctioned violence against alleged "enemies of the state." In a speech in 1794, Maximilien Robespierre—one of the most influential leaders of revolutionary France—announced to the National Convention that "If the basis of popular government in peacetime is virtue, the basis of popular government during a revolution is both virtue and terror; virtue, without which terror is baneful; terror, without which virtue is powerless." (Robespierre himself eventually fell victim to The Terror.)

The noted political conservative Edmund Burke decried the terrorism of the French revolutionaries, who had executed their king, killed many aristocrats, and guillotined thousands of alleged traitors and counter-revolutionaries. In fact, the word *terrorist* first entered the English language in Edmund Burke's *Letters on a Regicide Peace*, published in 1795 and 1796. At the turn of the 19th century, therefore, *terrorism denoted political violence deployed by agents of a government against its real and alleged internal and external foes*—"enemy combatants"—and those who supported them.

Two centuries later, the term has been inverted so that TFA (terrorism from above) has largely been excluded from official and even popular understanding. Instead, most people in the West have learned to identify "terrorism" exclusively with TFB (terrorism from below). *This is a profoundly important shift, because it permits states and the media to legitimize the violence, intimidation, and coercion of state-sanctioned "counterterrorist" operations, ostensibly conducted in defense of freedom and national security.* It also delegitimizes and morally condemns domestic and foreign opponents of state authority. The ongoing "global war on terrorism" exemplifies this transformation and is, to a large extent, the logical extension of trends in warfare dating back to World War II, when "total war" included the massive bombing of civilian noncombatants.

Warfare as Terrorism From Above

Terror bombings of civilians during wartime have resulted in many more casualties (numbered in the millions) than all acts of terrorism from below combined. In fact, more than 99% of the victims of political violence between 1968 and 1988 were killed by state agents of terror.[4]

Furthermore, aerial bombings of civilians have rarely achieved their goals. Massive city bombing during World War II did not by themselves significantly induce the German and Japanese governments to surrender; rather, they tended to harden the resolve of the indigenous populations to fight harder (as did the German *Blitz* of England during 1940). Some historians have also made the case that even the nuclear bombings of Hiroshima and Nagasaki did not significantly accelerate the outcome of the War in the Pacific because the Japanese government had already signaled its willingness to capitulate before the bombings; the major stimulus for Japanese surrender, according to this view, was the USSR's declaration of war against Japan.

On the other hand, the firebombing of Rotterdam in 1940 (which may not have been intended by the *Luftwaffe*) was followed almost immediately by the surrender of the Dutch to the Germans. Similarly, Serbia withdrew from Kosovo soon after Belgrade and other Yugoslavian cities were bombed by NATO in 1999 (although some Serbs claim that their government began exiting Kosovo before then). NATO's bombing of Muammar Gadhafi's forces in Libya in 2011 eventually resulted in his being driven from power and killed, leading to Libya becoming a failed state. In any event, in these two cases the bombing was brief and civilian casualties were probably in the hundreds, not the hundreds of thousands, as in Germany and Japan during World War II. US bombing of North Korea during the Korean War and of North Vietnam two decades later did not lead to capitulation by either country. In these cases, terrorism from above, like its TFB counterpart, succeeded in terrorizing and dehumanizing huge numbers of people, treating them as means toward political ends.

What might be called this Age of Global Terrorism, dating from the early 20th century—when total war and strategic bombing became acceptable components of military and diplomatic strategy—has caused the progressive obliteration of important, previously held moral and military distinctions. Notably, there has been a collapse of the distinction between illegitimate (i.e., civilian noncombatants) and legitimate (i.e., military) targets, as well as of the distinction between terrorists and the states that support them.

Finally, this century-long process has eroded the boundary between "terrorism" and "war." Since at least the early days of World War II, for the civilian populations of the affected states, war has become indistinguishable from terrorism. Terrorism, as an extreme form of psychological warfare, whether from above or below, has become a tool employed by war planners and policy makers as well as by the enemies of governments, both locally and globally.

Homegrown American Terrorists From Below

The United States has its own tradition of homegrown insurrectionary groups and terrorist actions. From the standpoint of the British government, during the American War of Independence (1776–1783), such American "founding fathers" as Paul Revere, George Washington, John Adams, and Thomas Jefferson were deemed by their British adversaries as the equivalent of terrorists because of their opposition to colonial rule and espousal of revolutionary, insurrectionary, and belligerent strategies and tactics to gain independence from England. Immediately prior to the American Civil War, proslavery and antislavery groups had frequent battles, particularly in "Bleeding Kansas," their principal battleground, where more than 200 people were killed.

Following the Civil War, Confederate veterans, some organized in the Ku Klux Klan (KKK), terrorized the newly freed blacks of the American South as well as their white Republican allies. The Klan worked to curb education, economic advancement, voting rights, and the right of black citizens to bear arms. In the late 1860s, the Klan spread into nearly every southern state, launching a "reign of terror" against Republican leaders, black and white. The KKK continued to lynch blacks and to murder white liberals well into the 20th century, especially during the early days of the civil rights movement.

During the 1990s, the number of violent right-wing groups and hate crimes increased dramatically. White Protestant militia groups, such as The Order and similar Christian Patriot organizations, promoted fiercely anti-Semitic, anti-Islamic, anti-government, and xenophobic views. And such neo-Nazi groups as the *Volksfront* and *White Revolution* have hoped for an "Aryan Revolution," with many believing that a "racial holy war" is inevitable.

On April 19, 1995, white supremacist Timothy McVeigh—a US Army veteran and security guard—detonated a truck bomb in front of the Alfred P. Murrah Federal Building in Oklahoma City, killing 168 people and injuring more than 800 in the deadliest act of terrorism within the United States prior to the attacks of September 11, 2001. McVeigh hoped to inspire a revolt against what he considered a tyrannical federal government. He was convicted of 11 federal offenses and executed in 2001; two others were also convicted and sentenced to life imprisonment as co-conspirators.

Various homegrown "militia movements" have grown in mostly rural areas, some inspired by a shadowy organization called the Army of God (AOG), which has intimidated, assaulted, and even murdered workers and physicians at abortion clinics. There have also been such "lone wolf" homegrown jihadists as the Boston Marathon bombers in 2013 and the San Bernardino, California, killers of 14 people in late 2015. Perhaps the most notorious "lone-wolf" event of this kind occurred in late 2017 and was not perpetrated by jihadists, but rather by a single individual, who fired more than 1,000 rounds of ammunition at participants in a music festival in Las Vegas, Nevada, killing 60 people and wounding more than 400. His motives remain unclear. This incident—the deadliest mass shooting committed by an individual in modern United States history—along with other attacks ending in mass murder and perpetrated by US civilians, have not been classified as "domestic terrorism."

Following his inauguration as US president in 2017, Donald Trump repeatedly used incendiary rhetoric against various immigrant and minority groups, which may have provided inspiration for a large number of right-wing white supremacist and neo-Nazi groups. Thus, the Southern Poverty Law Center reported a dramatic increase in the number of white nationalist groups, from 100 chapters in 2017 to 148 in 2018. According to the Anti-Defamation League, the first two years of Trump's presidency saw a 182 percent increase in the distribution of white supremacist propaganda, and a 25 percent increase in the number of rallies and demonstrations by white supremacy groups during that same time. Similarly, the Center for Strategic and International Studies found that the number of terrorist attacks by far-right perpetrators quadrupled in the US between 2016 and 2017, while according to the FBI, there was a 17 percent increase from 2016, with massive increases in the frequency of hate crimes directed toward African Americans, Muslims (especially of Arab ancestry), Hispanics, and Jews.

Continuing this trend, the most dramatic and potentially violent event in modern American history was the assault on the US Capitol by Trump supporters on January 6, 2021, leading to many casualties, Trump's second impeachment, and constituting an alarming wake-up for the civilized world regarding the dangers posed by far right-wing insurgents.

Like their terrorist fellow travelers at other times and in other cultures, many of these American terrorists believe they are conducting a righteous, even God-ordained struggle against evil, no longer limited to federal and state authorities, and thus including civilians identified by their religion, skin color, and ethnic origin. During the Trump administration, internal security forces were induced to focus on left-wing agitators ("antifa," for anti-fascist) and to largely ignore the more organized and violent threats coming from the far right. By the end of the Trump administration in early 2021, most experts had concluded that home-grown violent right-wing terrorists—most of them White nationalist and often antisemitic as well as anti-Black and anti-Muslim—constituted a greater danger to US peace and security than did groups originating outside the country and certainly more than did home-grown and largely nonviolent demonstrators such as Black Lives Matter, who protested lethal police violence against African Americans.

Terrorism and the Middle East

Because the Middle East today is widely (although inaccurately) considered the font of all terrorism and the birthplace of most terrorists, it is useful to consider it as an illustration of the tension between state and anti-state violence. From biblical times until the zenith of the Roman Empire (roughly from just before the time of Christ to the early 5th century CE), the Middle East was a hodge-podge of nomadic ethnic groups and city-states within what we now call the nation-states of Egypt, Israel (and Palestine), Tunisia, Libya, Greece, Jordan, Syria, Lebanon, Saudi Arabia, Iraq, the Gulf States, and Turkey. By the 1st century BCE, almost all these territories lay within the Roman Empire. It is here that the blood-curdling dialectic between state terrorism (TFA) and nonstate terrorism (TFB) may have begun, and—after some long intervals of relative peace, mainly under Islam— was revived during and shortly after World War I.

Conventional histories of terrorism depict the Roman Empire as having deployed its considerable resources to quash popular revolts against its rule in the Roman province of Judea (contemporary Israel and Palestine). In so doing, according to the Christian theologian and philosopher St. Augustine, the Romans created a desert and called it peace: "Peace and war had a contest in cruelty, and peace won the prize."[5] The Romans were challenged by the rebelliousness of some Middle Eastern peoples, especially Jews, and strove to control them.

Terrorism from below was initiated in large part by the political revolts and religious uprisings by Rome's Jewish opponents, especially the dagger-wielding Zealots of the 1st century CE. At the same time, terrorism from above was practiced by the Roman occupiers in their efforts to create, expand, and defend their empire. About two centuries after the fall of the Roman Empire, Islam replaced Christianity and Rome as the dominant religious and political force in the Middle East, after which it began to establish its own empires at an extremely rapid pace.

Islam

Former president George W. Bush, supported by some American Muslim clerics, once announced that Islam was "a religion of peace" that had been "hijacked" by such violent groups as al-Qaeda. But this apparently reassuring statement was immediately disputed by others who claimed that Islam is more accurately seen as "a religion of war." Those who take the latter view cite the Muslim belief that the world is divided by a continuous struggle between the *dar al-Islam* (the unified house of Islam) and the *dar al-Harb* (the house of war); allegedly, the Muslim believer is therefore duty-bound to participate in jihad (holy war). In Arabic, the word *Islam* means "submission" to the will of God, or Allah, and is also related to *salaam,* "peace." This implies that peace is a prerequisite of Islam.

But belief in jihad is also central to Islam, as attested by many sacred texts. For example, as one *hadith* (saying of the Prophet Muhammad) proclaims: "There is no monasticism in Islam; the monasticism of this community is the holy war." It is also historically true that Islam began in battle. Exiled for his subversive beliefs, the Prophet Muhammad gained warrior allies in the Arabian hinterlands, defeated his numerically superior opponents, and returned as a conqueror to his natal city of Mecca.

Muhammad was a great war leader as well as a spiritual redeemer, promising his followers not only admission to heaven in the next world but also concrete spoils of victory in this one. Those early Muslims who did not participate in jihad were considered lacking in religious merit. Those who fell in battle were guaranteed immediate entrance into paradise. (A similar claim was widespread among militant Christians, especially during the Crusades.)

Nor did Islam become exclusively a religion of peace after Muhammad's death (632 CE). Instead, Muslim warriors battled against the powerful Persian and Byzantine empires. Their eventual victory validated their message for their millions of followers and also established the foundation for the great Islamic dynasties that were eventually to rule from Spain and Morocco to India.

Yet a portrait of Islam as a warlike religion is as simplistic as the alternative image of Islam as one of peace. Consider, as a parallel, how misleading it is to describe Christianity as simply a "religion of peace" or a "religion of war," given that Christ's redeeming message is widely seen as intimately bound up with peace while Christianity also became one of the world's great warrior religions! Although many Muslims divide the world into warring camps of believers and nonbelievers or heretics, in real life it is not so easy to decide who is who, since "only God knows" the true content of the human heart.

In this context, many Muslims interpret the injunction for jihad as a command to purify one's self (the "greater jihad"). With self-doubt, spiritual introspection, and resigned acceptance of the inevitable plurality of beliefs as major religious themes in Islam, war against the external heathen (the "lesser jihad") has usually been secondary to an internal war against negative personal inclinations, that is, an individual battle for self-control and submission to Allah's will.

Jihad and Terrorism: Are They Synonymous?

In many Western and even in some Muslim-jihadist circles, jihad and terrorism appear related, even synonymous. But according to the contemporary Muslim writer Yasmeen Ali,[6]

> Terrorism is no Jihad. Western media is more often than not, awash with the details of "jihadists" who commit atrocious acts in the name of religion. More and more, Islam is projected as a religion of violence, hatred and vengeance. However, Islam comes from the root word Salaam, which means peace. It also means submitting one's will to Allah. The word Salaam is also an attribute of God. In this context, it means "The Giver of Peace." Terrorism, is a different concept altogether.[7]

But does Islam condone terrorism? Are terrorism and jihad ever one and the same? Not according to Ali:[8]

> Military conflict is to be directed only against fighting troops and not against civilians. As a matter of fact, all religions of "The Book," promote peace and tolerance, not violence. Attacking innocent civilians, women, children, sick in hospitals, people going about their daily chores who are not at war with you is terrorism. If there is a threat to human life, property and honor, fighting for defending life, property and honor is deemed as Jihad.[9]

For some violent jihadists, however, the West and its Middle Eastern surrogates do present such a threat to their lives, property, honor, and sacred polity, thus providing a "justification" for terrifying acts of violence against both "heathens" and Muslim apostates.

Reestablishing the Sacred Polity

Similar to recent times, when many Muslims have felt assaulted by "heathens" inside and outside their community, more than a millennium ago many Muslims who had participated in Muhammad's *umma* (Muslim community) could not accept the disintegration of their unified and charismatic collective. They nostalgically and imaginatively remembered the promises of the Prophet and what they perceived as the divinely consecrated commune of all Muslims—memories (or longings) that continue today to activate religious resistance to secular government. Muslims have thus constantly sought more sanctified candidates to fill the post of ruler over an Islamic collective. This quest, in its most extreme manifestations, has animated the unique brand of religious-political terrorism practiced in the name of Islam since the death of the Prophet Muhammad.

In addition, contrary to common Western misconceptions, conversion to Islam by former nonbelievers usually has usually not been at the point of a sword; instead, it has most often been a voluntary response to Muslim egalitarianism, generosity, and the Prophet's expansive message of salvation. In this environment, Islamic pogroms against Jews, Christians, and other minorities were considerably less common in the premodern Middle East than in premodern Christian Europe. For much of the Islamic world, all the descendants of Abraham (including Jews and Christians) are honored as fellow "people of the book" and recognized as sharing a fundamental kinship.

Traditional Islam, for example, venerates both Moses and Jesus as inspired prophets—albeit not on the same level as Mohammed, who is believed to have received direct transmission from Allah through the angel Gabriel, recorded in the Muslim holy book, the *Koran*.

Divisions Within Islam

Many Muslims who had participated in Muhammad's original *umma* (religious community) during the 7th century CE refused to accept its subsequent disintegration. They nostalgically recalled the promises of the Prophet and what they perceived as the divinely consecrated commune of all Muslims—memories (or longings) that continue today to activate religious resistance to secular governments. Some have accordingly sought more sanctified candidates to fill the post of ruler over an Islamic collective. This quest, in its most extreme manifestations, has animated the unique brand of religious-political terrorism practiced in the name of Islam since the death of the Prophet Mohammed. Hence, Islamist jihadists denounce their moderate opponents as apostates for accepting the "un-Islamic" commands of the corrupt and despotic rulers of secular Islamic states—whose political leaders are widely perceived to be manipulated and paid off by the West in general and by the United States in particular.

The Shiites: Partisans of Ali
and Opponents of Sunni Traditionalists

The schism between the two major denominations of Islam—Shia and Sunni—began over disagreement over Mohammed's succession. Shiites reject as usurpers the first three caliphs who followed the Prophet Muhammed. For the Shiites, Muhammad's authority was reincarnated in his descendants, beginning with Ali, who served as the fourth caliph after the Prophet's death. These "partisans of Ali," or Shiites, argue that since Muhammad had no sons, Ali—his son-in-law, first cousin, and closest male relative—had inherited Muhammad's spiritual power and must be recognized the Prophet's only legitimate heir and hence as the sacred ruler of all Islam. For those following Ali or other lineal descendants of the Prophet, the first crisis of faith occurred when Ali was assassinated by a poisoned sword wielded by an Islamic "Kharijite" (former partisans of Ali who turned on him) fanatic.

In contrast, Sunni (from the Arabic word *sunna*, meaning "tradition") Islam rapidly became the largest branch of Islam, currently comprising up to 90% of all Muslims. Sunnis recognize an order of succession originally decided by a council and leading to the first four caliphs who succeeded the Prophet Muhammad. Unlike Shiite Islam, Sunnism has no centralized clerical institution; it comprises four schools of law (*sharia*), and its adherents range ideologically from the expressive and mystical Sufis to the puritanical Wahhabis (discussed later in this chapter).

Shiite resentment over Sunni rule and the perceived injustices of this world developed within a decade after Mohammed's death and continues to fan subversive acts of intra-Islamic conflict, not altogether different from historical disputes—often violent—between Protestant and Catholic Christians. Shiites are a majority of the indigenous Muslim population only in Azerbaijan, Bahrain, and, most notably, in Iraq and Iran. Shiite-Sunni animosity undergirds the current antagonisms between Saudi Arabia, which is largely Sunni, and Shiite Iran, as well as within Saudi Arabia and Bahrain.

(Nonetheless, Shiite solidarity was not strong enough to prevent a devastating war between Iraq and Iran during the 1980s.)

But despite numerous disputes between Shiite and Sunni Muslims and by Shiite and Sunni rebels against despised secular state authorities, rarely has insurrectionary violence directed against political elites kindled general rebellion among the disenfranchised masses, with the exceptions of the early days of the "Arab Spring" and Syrian civil war. Most Muslims in the past, like most today, have been satisfied (or perhaps been reluctantly acquiescent) to have a stable, if autocratic, regime in power.

The Iranian Revolution and Shiite Militancy

The great oppositional Islamic upheaval of modern times was the Iranian revolution of 1979, led by Ayatollah Khomeini. Throughout the Middle East as a whole, the Shiite clergy has had greater independence than Sunni clerics, and Shiites, unlike most Sunnis, believe that certain scholars, known as Ayatollahs, are sacred authorities. Because Iranian Ayatollahs (the "sign of Allah," or God) have had such great spiritual authority and wealth, they have been largely able to resist secularizing trends in government, even prior to the advent of the deposed former despot of Iran, Reza Shah. The shah was convincingly—and to a large extent accurately—portrayed by the Ayatollah Khomeini and his mainly student followers as a puppet of the Western powers, namely the United Kingdom and, especially, what many Iranians deem "the great Satan," the United States.

The old Shiite belief system was reawakened and transformed by Khomeini and his acolytes; his followers could now redeem the ancient stain of betrayal by actively purging this world of evil, starting in Iran and expanding to combat such alleged enemies of righteousness as the US. This message inspired acts of self-sacrifice, leading to the overthrow of the shah in 1979 and also to terrorist attacks against Americans and others. Americans were especially outraged by the holding of US embassy personnel for more than a year, just as Iranians have long been enraged that the shah had been placed on his throne in 1953 as a result of a coup orchestrated by US and British intelligence services, which overthrew Mohammed Mossadegh, the democratically elected Iranian president—a coup orchestrated because Mossadegh was perceived in Washington and London as unfriendly to Western oil interests.

Islamic Fundamentalists and Terrorists: The Wahhabi Movement, the Muslim Brotherhood, al-Qaeda, and the Islamic State

Although there are significant doctrinal differences between Shiite and Sunni clerics, dating back to the struggle over the succession to the Prophet Muhammad, the political cleft between the majority Sunnis and the minority Shiites has widened in recent decades and engulfed the Middle East in factional violence.

Wahhabism denotes a Sunni, fundamentalist, or "Salafist" (the "righteous ancestors") movement that seeks to emulate the original, 7th-century Islamic community, although it dates back mostly to the late 18th century, when it was founded by Muhammad al-Wahab, who preached the controversial message that all modifications to Islam after the late 10th century must be purged. Al-Wahab converted the Saudi tribe to this ascetic branch of Sunnism, and Wahhabis have remained extremely influential in Saudi Arabia, the birthplace of Osama bin Laden and many of his most militant followers. Despite its avowed friendship with the US, the current Saudi government, true to its Wahhabi history and popular influence, has launched a war against Yemen (during which it may have committed war crimes by attacking civilians), has continued to fund virulently anti-Western propaganda, and perhaps has even sponsored terrorism and targeted assassinations (notably the torture and murder in 2018 of Jamal Khashoggi, a Saudi dissident, journalist for *The Washington Post,* and former general manager and editor-in-chief of *Al-Arab News*).

Egypt has, however, been the home of perhaps the most significant Sunni Islamist movement of the 20th century, the Muslim Brotherhood. For more than a millennium, Cairo was the prime center of Sunni scholasticism; modern Sunni militancy arose there following the end of World War I. The Muslim Brotherhood, initially a religious and social reform movement whose followers are called "Islamists," has also inspired contemporary *jihadis* ("holy warriors"), as well as the *mujahideen* ("strugglers for jihad") since its 1928 founding in Egypt.

Long suppressed by more-or-less pro-Western Egyptian leaders, following the Arab Spring and the removal of Hosni Mubarak from power in 2011, the Muslim Brotherhood temporarily enjoyed political success, even having one of its own, Mohamed Morsi, democratically elected in 2012 as president of Egypt. However, the Egyptian Army overthrew Morsi in 2013, launching a bloody crackdown that left 1,400 dead and detained 16,000, and replaced him a year later with a military strongman, General Abdel Fattah el-Sisi, who is friendly to the West and who sought to suppress the Brotherhood once again and—at least temporarily—has succeeded.

Militant Islamists today—although comprising a small fraction of the world's one billion plus Muslims—hope to revive the original Islamic community. This entails relentless opposition to all existing "infidels," especially corrupt and ruthless local Muslim rulers and their "Christian-Zionist" supporters. In addition to religious ideology, a major unifying force among militant Islamists is antipathy toward Israel, which is widely considered to be politically illegitimate, in part because its founding involved expropriation of what had been Palestinian land.

For many current Sunni Islamists, the most important figure was the Egyptian political rebel and writer Sayyid Qutb. For 3 years he lived in the US, which he found empty, decadent, sexually depraved, materialistic, and godless. (This, incidentally, should be a cautionary note for those who assume that Islamic exposure to the West will automatically result in the acceptance of Western ideals and lifestyles.) Qutb then returned to Cairo and, in 1953, joined the Muslim Brotherhood. He was subsequently imprisoned, tortured, and hanged by the Egyptian government. While in prison, Qutb wrote in his influential book *Milestones* of the need for a purified Islam, which became a very influential ideology for militant Sunni Islamists. The organization known as "al-Qaeda" has heard, and acted on, Qutb's appeal.

Al-Qaeda

In Arabic, *al-Qaeda* refers to a base or foundation of a house (or of a political movement), as well as to a principle, rule, formula, or model. Its primary initial leaders, Osama bin Laden and Ayman al-Zawahiri, were reared in Sunni antiestablishment circles and gained their political experience in the 1980s as Arab volunteers for the predominantly Shiite mujahideen resistance to the Soviet occupation of Afghanistan. Ironically, funding for the

Afghan mujahideen groups was provided by the United States and channeled through the Pakistani government, as well as by the Saudi government and Persian Gulf–based mosque charities. About 20 years later, the US, Pakistan, Saudi, and Gulf governments—early backers of anti-Soviet Islamic jihadis and mujahideen—became targets of al-Qaeda.

For the three decades or so that Western intelligence and counterterrorist agencies have focused on it, al-Qaeda appears to have operated less like a formal organization and more like a network with an ideology that inspires a worldwide political movement. Most of bin Laden's Islamist radicalization efforts revolved around the alleged failures of the House of Saud, rulers of Saudi Arabia and custodians of the holy cities of Mecca and Medina. According to bin Laden in his 1996 "Declaration of War Against the Americans Occupying the Land of the Two Holy Places" (Saudi Arabia, home of Mecca and Medina), the Saudis committed an unpardonable sacrilege when, in the early 1990s, they accepted American military assistance to defend their kingdom against the Iraqi Army of Saddam Hussein, which had invaded and occupied Kuwait and seemed poised to do the same in Saudi Arabia. The subsequent stationing of US military forces in their "holy land" and more generally throughout the Islamic world shocked and angered millions of Muslims. (This event, interestingly, barely registered on the Western public at the time.)

Bin Laden's proclamations were designed not just to evoke Muslim fury about the US-led occupation of Islamic lands but also to arouse Arab resentment regarding a century of Western exploitation and a millennium of what he called "aggression, iniquity, and injustice imposed by the Zionist-Crusader alliance and their collaborators," with Bin Laden pointing to Muslim blood being "spilled in Palestine and Iraq . . . . in Tajikistan, Burma, Kashmir, Assam, the Philippines . . . Ogaden, Somalia, Eritrea, Chechnya and Bosnia-Herzegovina." For him, the US occupation of the holy sites in Saudi Arabia and the Israeli occupation of Palestinian territory (especially Al-Aqsa Mosque in Jerusalem) were against the will of Allah. Consequently, bin Laden called for jihad "to expel the occupying enemy out of the country of the two holy places, to re-establish the greatness of the *umma* and to liberate its occupied sanctuaries."[10]

To accomplish this mission, al-Qaeda views itself—like numerous TFB groups throughout history—as the vanguard of a local and global jihad against occupying forces in the Middle East. Also targeted are the states that sponsor them and the civilians—Christian, Jewish, and Muslim—who wittingly or unwittingly perpetuate occupation and other alleged anti-Islamic policies. On September 11, 2001, supporters of al-Qaeda–inspired jihad hijacked commercial airplanes and flew them into the World Trade Center in New York and the Pentagon: tangible symbols of American economic power and military might.

Since 9/11 and the US-led invasions and occupations of Iraq and Afghanistan— where al-Qaeda had operated training camps dating back to 1996—Al-Qaeda has metamorphosed from a relatively small group of Sunni-led Islamic terrorists to the ideological fringe of a broad Islamist movement. But unlike their forefathers, today's jihadis wage their war on a global as well as a local scale. Although the future of this struggle is unclear, it has become evident since 9/11 that suicide terrorism is a prime weapon in al-Qaeda's and the Islamic jihadis' arsenal—a weapon of the weak, but a troublesomely effective one nonetheless.

Al-Qaeda as an entity may or may not survive the US-instigated assassinations of Osama Bin-Laden (in 2011), his son, Hamza (in 2019), and other

Sunni (and Shiite) leaders that the US and Israel deem threats to their interests, notably including top Iranian military leaders and nuclear research scientists. These actions have likely accelerated Iran's nuclear programs and may have strengthened rather than weakened the fundamentalist Shiite Iranian regime. Despite these setbacks, the mission and appeal of fundamentalist Islam, whether Sunni or Shiite, are likely to endure, unless the social and political conditions that give rise to such groups as al-Qaeda and ISIS, and to such regimes as those in Iran and their emulators are transformed. Despite the dream of Western "neocons," regime change itself will almost certainly be impossible to orchestrate from abroad, and if done by military means, will almost certainly be short-lived.

ISIL/ISIS

The Islamic State of Iraq and the Levant (ISIL), or, alternatively, the Islamic State of Iraq and al-Sham (ISIS), is a jihadist militant group that follows an Islamic fundamentalist, Wahhabi doctrine of Sunni Islam. The group is also known as Daesh, an acronym derived from its Arabic name. Since 2004, a significant goal of this group has been the founding of a fundamentalist Sunni Islamic state, specifically a "caliphate" led by religious authorities under a supreme leader—the caliph. The group has referred to itself as the Islamic State, or IS, ever since it proclaimed a worldwide caliphate in June 2014. The group initially pledged allegiance to al-Qaeda in 1999 and participated in the Iraqi insurgency following the 2003 invasion of Iraq by Western (mostly US) forces. In 2011, following the outbreak of the Syrian Civil War, ISIS delegated a mission to Syria and established a major presence in some Sunni-majority provinces. They were, however, rejected by the leaders of al-Qaeda, and ISIS has challenged al-Qaeda for leadership of the global jihadist cause; its direct and indirect sponsorship of attacks against other Muslims and many Western targets has simultaneously provoked outrage and envy from its jihadist rivals.

ISIS gained the West's attention in early 2014 when it drove Iraqi government forces out of key cities in a western Iraq offensive, followed by the capture of Mosul (Iraq's second-largest city) and the massacres and much-publicized beheadings of alleged infidels and traitors, among others. The subsequent possibility of a collapse of the Iraqi government in Baghdad prompted a renewal of US military action in the country.

At its peak, ISIS controlled significant parts of Syria and Iraq, and its numbers swelled with the addition of overseas volunteers. For a few years it functioned in those countries as an effective, if very brutal, government, until almost all of its territory had been recaptured by US forces and local armies, mostly Kurds. ISIS follows an extremist, largely Wahhabi interpretation of Islam. It promotes religious violence and capital punishment, prohibiting any deviating religious practice (even by fellow Muslims) and regarding Muslims who dispute its interpretations as infidels or apostates. Importantly, during its brief existence as a geographic entity, ISIS killed, maltreated, and impoverished far more Muslims than Westerners (although for a number of reasons, some "radicalized" Western volunteers became foot soldiers and wives for ISIS warriors, leading to a continuing challenge of reintegrating these former ISIS adherents into the societies they abandoned). There has been no love lost between followers of ISIS and other Sunni groups labeled "terrorist," such as the militant Palestinian group Hamas, which controls Gaza.

In late 2019, following the targeted killing of ISIS's leader, Abu Bakr al-Baghdadi, it was claimed by US officials that the Islamic State had been defeated, which is true insofar as most of its physical territory in Iraq and Syria has been retaken, mostly by Kurds or by Syrian government forces backed by Russian and Iranian supporters. However, an unknown number of hardened and radicalized fighters have returned to their countries of origin, while ISIS affiliates also remain active in areas of Libya, Nigeria, Afghanistan, the Sahel of Africa, Indonesia, and elsewhere. In addition, insofar as ISIS and al-Qaeda sympathizers persist in other countries, including many Western ones, it is premature for the West to congratulate itself that this particular threat has been eliminated. As long as the reasons that have led to the rise and fall of ISIS and al-Qaeda have not been addressed, the lure of violent jihad—at least for some Muslims—will remain.

What to Do to Counter Islamic Terrorism Without Escalating the Conflict?

As of early 2021, although ISIS and al-Qaeda's military presence has been greatly diminished in the Middle East, their ideology continues to attract adherents worldwide. Furthermore, even as the less militant Muslim Brotherhood has had much of its leadership killed or imprisoned in Egypt and elsewhere, it still maintains the loyalty of millions of Sunni Muslims across the Middle East.

To counter and diminish the appeal of violent Islamist movements and to promote lasting peace in the Middle East and elsewhere, it seems important for peacemakers and anti-terrorism planners to

1. Learn from history that military force rarely "works" against terrorist groups from below and/or religious-political movements and, instead, try seriously to negotiate either directly or indirectly (via third parties). Steps in this direction have been made, albeit hesitantly, by the US and representatives of the Afghan Taliban (who, according to the 2019 Global Terrorism Index, caused more fatalities that year than any other group labeled terrorist by the West). Rely more on dialogue, intelligence gathering, police work, and cultural integration than on militaristic counterinsurgency strategies and tactics, which—even if they seem successful in the short run in killing violent Islamists—typically create more enemies.

2. Recognize that for millions of angry and disaffected Muslims (almost all Sunni, in the case of ISIS), the policies of the West in general and of the United States and Israel in particular have spawned violent jihadist opposition movements to both the local brutal and repressive regimes in Iraq and in Syria and to Western/Israeli interests and representatives, both military and civilian.

3. Recognize that other groups—Kurds, Shiites, as well as Christians, Jews, and various smaller sects, notably the powerful Alawites in Syria and Druze in Lebanon—also have legitimate grievances, needs, and aspirations. In short, be informed about and sensitive to the diversity and complexity of the populations inhabiting what can too easily be lumped together as the "Middle East" or Islam in general.

4. Remember that the current borders and nation-states of most of the region were created by colonial powers (especially the United Kingdom and

France) about a century ago and do not reflect the cultural and sectarian realities on the ground. These borders are not carved in stone and might need to be adjusted to reflect political, social, and religious realities.

Suicide Terrorism

Islamist terrorist groups have grabbed the headlines of the mass media since 9/11. But it is important to note that this is a relatively recent development and that until the formation of the state of Israel just after the end of World War II and the US-led occupation of Middle Eastern lands several decades later, terrorism from below in that part of the world was committed mainly by Arab subnational groups against other Arabs, principally against secular political authorities.

There is also a popular conception in the West that most suicidal terrorists are Muslim and that virtually all of them have predominantly religious motivation: seeking martyrdom. In fact, suicide terrorism was committed by Jewish Zealots against the Romans centuries before Islam even existed and, until recently, the most frequent suicide attacks have been perpetrated by Hindus—the Tamil Tigers in Sri Lanka. Other notably destructive terrorist groups include the Hindu-extremist RSS, the Lord's Resistance Army of Uganda, Boko Haram, al-Shabaab, and, until recently, Colombia's FARC. In the late 20th century, the United States supported antigovernment, right-wing terrorist groups such as UNITA in Angola and the *contras* in Nicaragua. In addition, during the 19th and 20th centuries, Christian, Sikh, Buddhist, and Shinto terrorists also carried out suicide attacks, only sometimes with explicitly religious motivations. Moreover, Islamist suicide terrorists display a range of secular and/or religious motivations for their actions, most often revenge against Israeli raids and "targeted assassinations" and/or to end the Israeli occupation of Palestinian territory.

Also contrary to popular belief that a single terrorist suffices to carry out a suicide terrorist attack, there are always several people involved in preparing a human bomb for explosion. In the 1990s, when religious terrorist organizations such as Hamas and the Islamic Jihad were the primary sources for suicide bombers, they were often recruited in a mosque, and the recruiter was someone connected to that mosque. When such secular terrorist organizations as the People's Front for Liberation of Palestine have employed suicide bombers, recruitment has taken place anywhere, from hospitals or restaurants to primary schools—the youngest suicide bomber arrested by Israeli security services was just 13 years old, and the youngest who blew up was 16.

Contemporary suicide bombings fit into an ancient tradition as a tactic employed by political groups too weak to confront their enemies directly, so instead they kill (or, from a jihadi point of view, "martyr") themselves and as many opposing soldiers or civilians as they can. Most often, this is done in hopes of pressuring a vastly more powerful force—the state—to change its policies once it becomes luridly evident that the price of continuing them will be the lives of many of its citizens. In explaining and preventing terrorism from below, it is important to understand that terrorist actions would have little popular resonance if it were not for one other aspect of terrorism—namely, the terror perpetrated by many states on their own people.

State and State-Sponsored Terrorism

In contrast to subnational terrorism from below, state-sponsored terrorism from above rarely makes any claim to sacred justification. It is quite baldly the assertion of ruthless force for the purpose of breaking resistance to the central authority. For many Muslims, such brutal violence confirms the widely perceived illegitimacy of the secular state which, from earliest times, has suffered in comparison with the history of sacred rule by the Prophet and his succeeding caliphs.

Lacking any sacred justification, popular compliance with the decrees of corrupt rulers—secular or religious—has typically been coerced by mass terror from above. In the Islamic world, popular resentment has historically been directed at the ruling elites of oil-rich Arab states, which are perceived to be backed by the United States and other "Christian-Zionist" nations. The Arab Spring movement that began in 2010 and briefly offered hope (largely unfulfilled) of instituting genuine democracy in traditionally autocratic countries was a quintessential expression of this long-held attitude.

Structural violence committed by the state—its neglect of basic human rights and its promotion of repressive and self-aggrandizing policies—is rarely confronted directly by those who are its everyday victims. The reason is terrorism from above, a phenomenon that has in no way been limited to the Middle East. Thus, although TFA is most readily conceived as occurring literally, when bombs are dropped on a foreign opponent, it has long been practiced by dictatorial regimes against their own population, using not only terrifying military methods (e.g., chemical warfare by Iraq's Saddam Hussein and Syria's Bashar al-Assad) but also subtler but nevertheless powerful methods of internal repression by intelligence surveillance, secret police, midnight raids, and control of propaganda (e.g., by Fascist regimes such as Francisco Franco in Spain as well as during the Stalinist period in the USSR). For most of their post-colonial history, Latin American regimes maintained substantial armed forces, ostensibly for national defense but in reality to intimidate and directly repress their own citizens; similarly, much of post-colonial Africa experienced more internal terrorism from above than warfare between countries.

In earlier times, the violence and terrorism of many rulers were restrained both by traditional standards of honor and by the relative weakness of the regimes themselves. As a consequence, in the Middle East, for example, most Sultans (the word simply means "power") were content to torture, maim, and kill mainly members of their own immediate entourage, leaving the populace relatively unscathed as long as taxes were paid and order was maintained. However, contemporary Middle Eastern rulers (irrespective of their religious or political leanings) have greater ambitions as well as greater means at their disposal for the infliction of violence and mass terror. As a result, state-sponsored terrorism in that region has substantially increased— evidenced, for example, by the mass violence orchestrated by Syria's ruling elites against popular resistance to the rule of President Bashar al-Assad and also by the current Egyptian military dictatorship against its real and imagined opponents.

Prior to Assad, Iraq under Saddam Hussein may have been the most frightening and well-publicized instance of state terror. A conservative estimate is that more than 100,000 citizens "disappeared" during the reign of Saddam Hussein. Compare this to the 30,000 who "disappeared" during the "dirty war" in Argentina. Other regimes, from Algeria to Sudan and from Libya to Taliban Afghanistan, have numerically lesser, but equally horrifying, human rights records. One cannot understand the appearance of religion-based terrorist movements in the modern Middle East without also taking into account the ways such states maintain their power through coercion of and violence against their own people, thus prompting violent revolts against state autocracies, with ensuing state repression, leading to a vicious cycle of tit for tat—even without Western heavy-handedness, which often stokes violent nationalist fervor in opposition.

As a result, terrorism from above and from below reinforce each other, the latter clad variously in the garb of liberty, equality, democracy, religious purity, certain specified rights, revenge of historical wrongs, and the like, and the former often proclaiming stability, national unity, independence, and so forth. *The crucial difference between recent history and the past is that terrorism from below has gone global*, ostensibly in the name of oppressed people rising up (for whatever reason), just as terrorism from above—especially in the 21st century—has increasingly been described as "counterterrorism." For example, this has been the official and public-relations-generated rationale for state-sponsored terror applied by the governments of China, Russia, Myanmar, and Syria against their own peoples, especially those labeled dissidents or "terrorists" by their respective governments.

Terrorism in the Name of God

It is easy to paint Islam as either essentially pacifist or bellicose—just as it is easy to draw passages from the Bible or from the Torah to make either case about Christians and Jews. The truth about all great religions is that the written record is ambiguous: Islamic scripture, like that of the Christians and Jews (or Hindus or Buddhists, for that matter), can be interpreted in various ways for various purposes.

It is the protean character of great religions that makes them so appealing—and so dangerous. Islam is no different in this respect. Its adherents can be pacifists, terrorists, or somewhere in between, including the great majority who are likely politically indifferent, merely wanting to get on with their daily lives. All faiths can equally call on holy writ to "justify" themselves and their murderous deeds. Neither terrorism nor pacifism reflects some essential aspect of Islam any more than the slavery and genocide that stain European and American history are a direct and inevitable consequence of Christianity. The problem lies in neither the Koran nor the Bible but in the violent behavior of some who believe not only that "God is on our side" but that their terrorizing acts are morally, divinely, and politically sanctioned, while the other side is irredeemably evil. Regrettably, a kind of terrorism industry plays an important role in framing these perceptions.

The Official Terrorism Industry

During and immediately after the Vietnam War, there arose a caste of political and military pundits who have "advised" Western governments about the real and alleged threats posed by subnational groups to Western—particularly American—economic and geopolitical interests around the world. Since the Reagan administration in the 1980s, they also have actively worked for the mass media. Most have military, CIA, and/or US State Department backgrounds. Since 9/11, these consultants and advisers have contributed to a revived and influential "terrorism industry" (which also includes mercenaries and the purveyors of military hardware and services).

The wars conducted by the United States in Central America, Africa, and South Asia from the 1980s to the present have routinely been cast as defensive and necessary to promote freedom and democracy in nations allegedly endangered by "terrorists and by the governments that harbor them." Much of this originated in 1979, when both the Sandinistas in Nicaragua and the Islamic clerics in Iran swept to power in relatively nonviolent revolutions against US-supported autocracies. To combat these "antidemocratic" "extremists," "fanatics," and "militants," governments allied with the West frequently deployed death squads and other paramilitary forces (as in El Salvador, Guatemala, and Honduras) to quell populist insurrections.

Until 2000, the United States Army School of the Americas (USARSA)—alternatively known as the "School of the Assassins"—was the principal training site for US and Latin American military and police personnel. Critics note that much of the training that occurred at USARSA, located at Fort Benning, Georgia, provided expertise in antidemocratic "counterterrorism," whereby right-wing military dictatorships, supported by the US government, practiced TFA against their citizens.

Millions of civilian noncombatants worldwide have been casualties of what have been called counterinsurgency operations, ranging from Indonesia and Vietnam in the 1960s and 1970s, to Central America and central Africa in the 1980s, and to Iraq and Afghanistan from 1991 to the present. These "casualties of war" have rarely been portrayed (at least in the West) as innocent victims of state and state-supported terrorism. And yet, counterinsurgency and counterterrorist operations, especially in Asia, Africa, and Latin America, have frequently inflamed rather than quelled popular resistance to local authorities and to Western intervention. Such "blowback" is, in part, due to the widespread perception in many impoverished countries that these activities serve principally to prop up corrupt and despotic regimes and to channel indigenous natural resources—such as oil, precious minerals, and such valuable crops as coca and vanilla—to affluent consumers in industrialized countries while benefiting the local elites rather than the native population. In addition, the civilian and noncombatant casualties caused by "precision bombing" and other counterterrorist measures further enrage those people who are to be "liberated" from "terrorists" and/or "rogue regimes." This often serves to radicalize disaffected youth and abets the efforts of violent insurgents who would recruit them as suicide bombers.

The mass media tend to follow the agenda framed by powerful political and economic elites, and only later, if at all, do they question the vision, strategy, tactics, and motives of decision makers and their lobbyists. The rationales provided by the US and British governments for their initiation of war in Iraq, as part of the global war on terrorism, are prime examples.

The Global War on Terrorism

After the attacks on the World Trade Center in New York City and the Pentagon just outside Washington, D.C., many Americans agreed with pronouncements that the United States was at war with terrorism. Yet, to many disempowered people, especially in poorer countries, Americans, principally US government, military, and police officials, are also terrorists (from above).

Following 9/11, then-President George W. Bush announced that the United States "would make no distinction between terrorists and the countries that harbor them." For large numbers of frustrated, impoverished, infuriated people—who view the United States as a terrorist country—attacks on American civilians were justified in precisely this way: making no distinction between a "terrorist state" and the citizens who aid and abet it.

Militarists within the United States and elsewhere have found the existence of "worldwide terrorism" to be especially convenient. This is particularly true since the end of the US-USSR Cold War in 1991 deprived them of a suitable enemy. The case can even be made that if al-Qaeda and the Islamic State/ISIS did not exist, the West would have been obliged to invent them. A more perfect foil to replace "the communist threat" could scarcely be imagined than a worldwide conspiracy of Islamic terrorists bent on our destruction. Whatever the real structure and function of violent Islamist groups and cells, the image of Islamic terrorism, like "The Red Menace" before it, creates an ideal vehicle for motivating a global war in defense of freedom. In addition, because terrorists are only rarely manifested in the government of a particular country, against which a declaration of war could be declared or which could be clearly defeated, such a "war" can never be definitively won. It therefore threatens (or, for its supporters, promises) to go on indefinitely. This not to downplay the reality of violent threats, especially against Westerners and Western interests. But as the saying goes, even paranoids can have real enemies—albeit sometimes their behavior helps create those enemies.

Countering Terrorism From Below

What seems particularly novel and terrorizing about the political state of affairs in the 21st century is the global scope of terrorist and counterterrorist operations and the suddenness and lethality of such actions. In addition, whereas people often demand swift and decisive responses from their government in the face of violent events of this sort, the perpetrators are typically elusive and often difficult to identify, much less to apprehend or punish.

Counterterrorism, the dominant Anglo-American mode of dealing with TFB, consists of the practices and strategies that governments, militaries, police departments, and corporations adopt to deal with real and perceived terrorist threats and/or acts. If the terrorist opponents are part of a broader insurgency, counterterrorism may also form part of a broader counterinsurgency doctrine, but political, economic, and other measures—often poorly funded and less utilized in contrast with military counterterrorist operations—may focus more on the insurgency than on the specific acts of terror.

According to the Department of Homeland Security, created after 9/11:

> Protecting the American people from terrorist threats is the founding purpose of the Department and our highest priority. The Department's efforts to battle terrorism include detecting explosives in public spaces and transportation networks, helping protect critical infrastructure and cybernetworks from attack, detecting agents of biological warfare, and building information-sharing partnerships with state and local law enforcement that can enable law enforcement to mitigate threats.[11]

Efforts to counter terrorism are part of an increasingly recognized 21st century pattern: so-called asymmetric warfare, in which large, wealthy, heavily armed, and technologically sophisticated countries find themselves militarily aligned against small, poor, lightly armed, low-tech opponents, who are often willing to die for their cause. Although the latter can typically be defeated in straightforward set-piece battles, the former—in part because of the comparative openness of their societies as well as the fact that they offer a target-rich environment—are likely to remain vulnerable.

In this regard, another major concern is the law of unintended consequences, whereby actions (especially violent ones) often bring about results that are unpredictable as well as undesirable. This can apply to those responding to terrorism no less than to the perpetrators. Thus, violent retribution by the leaders of a victimized country runs the risk not only of killing additional innocent civilians but also of generating yet more attacks, in a potentially endless cycle of violence. (This problem is exacerbated when terrorist perpetrators are difficult to identify and target, all the more so when they reside within civilian populations.)

In the case of those events unleashed by the attacks of 9/11, what some Muslims regard as a US-led "crusade"[12] against terrorism has been perceived as a war against Islam. This has, in turn, threatened to destabilize certain moderate Islamic regimes, resulting in governments that are yet more extremist and violence prone. Tunisia and Libya are contrasts in the mixed legacy of the Arab Spring: the former relatively stable (occasional terrorist attacks directed against Western tourists notwithstanding) and the latter a chaotic failed state in which groups including ISIS and al-Qaeda are still active. Given that the United States has a long history of supporting military dictatorships—for example, in Pakistan, now a nuclear weapons state—such concerns are especially cogent.

There is even a term for this sort of thing: *blowback,* which, according to the former CIA employee and Berkeley professor Chalmers Johnson, does not just mean

retaliation for things our government has done to, and in, foreign countries. It refers specifically to retaliation for illegal operations carried out abroad *that were kept totally secret from the American public.* These operations have included the clandestine overthrow of governments various administrations did not like, the training of foreign militaries in the techniques of state terrorism, the rigging of elections in foreign countries, interference with the economic viability of countries that seemed to threaten the interests of influential American corporations, as well as the torture or assassination of selected foreigners. The fact that these actions were, at least originally, secret meant that when retaliation does come—as it did so spectacularly on September 11, 2001—the American public is incapable of putting the events in context. Not surprisingly, then, Americans tend to support speedy acts of revenge intended to punish the actual, or alleged, perpetrators. These moments of lashing out, of course, only prepare the ground for yet another cycle of blowback.[13]

Historically, terrorists have sought not only to cause terror but often to induce their victims to strike back: the bloodier and more indiscriminating the retaliation by governments, the more perceived benefit derived by the terrorists themselves. This is because a lethally violent response tends not only to delegitimize the retaliators, it also plays into the hands of the original perpetrators by recruiting others, newly victimized, to their cause (i.e., blowback). When there is an asymmetry between perpetrators and responders, such that the perpetrators are indigenous—as with the Taliban in Afghanistan and Pakistan—and the responders are foreigners, usually United States' and NATO forces, the local population has tended to blame the responders while exonerating the original perpetrators.

Then there are the internal costs, both economic and human, of conducting a "war" against terrorism. Torture; "extraordinary rendition" (abduction of others in foreign countries without due process and their deportation to countries where they are likely to be tortured); the use of detention camps and jails in which human rights are typically denied, such as Guantánamo Bay (the US base in Cuba) and Abu Ghraib (a notorious prison in Iraq); violations of civil liberties; unlawful surveillance; and the targeted assassinations of real and suspected terrorists have all occurred in the name of protecting the homeland and apprehending terrorists.

There is also the expenditure of trillions of dollars and euros, funds that could have been devoted to such other "wars" as against cancer, poverty, Covid-19, global climate change, and so on. In two decades of the "global war on terrorism," the number of deaths on American soil due to terrorist attacks remains at the approximately 3,000 killed on September 11, 2001, averaging fewer than 200 deaths per year. From a utilitarian perspective—seeking the greatest good for the greatest number of persons—the high costs of the war on terrorism just from the Western perspective (notably, the death of more than 7,800 coalition troops, which averages about 350 per year) are hard to justify when compared to the following annual fatalities in the US alone, many of which are preventable: more than 1700 premature childhood deaths as a result of abuse and/or neglect, at least 42,000 victims of vehicle-related accidents and similar numbers due to medical errors and gun violence, and 440,000 deaths per annum due to tobacco use. And then there are the more intangible costs to US credibility and leadership, due in large measure to its seemingly endless wars in Afghanistan and elsewhere in the Middle East, justified in large measure by US government lies, misrepresentations, and false promises.

The Victims and Perpetrators of Global Terrorism and Counterterrorism

No one can say with certainty how many civilians have died since 9/11 in wars between Western nations and their alleged Islamist adversaries. During the first decade or so of the "Global War on Terror" (2001–2011), between 12,000 and 14,000 noncombatants are estimated to have perished in Afghanistan and at least 120,000 in Iraq. Thousands more have since perished. The disheartening fact that each year brings many thousands of civilian war deaths worldwide points to an urgent need to reconsider the efficacy of lethal military solutions. This applies particularly to what Pope Francis has called the "Third World War."

As tempting as it may be to view the absence of large-scale successful terrorist attacks in the United States after September 11, 2001, as evidence that the war on terror has succeeded in its primary mission to protect the US, there is no demonstrable causal relationship between these two variables. *There may have been no additional attacks even if the war had never been waged, and nonmilitary reasons, such as good police work and intelligence, may be responsible for the absence of additional attacks.*

According to the Global Terrorism Index, an annual report produced by the Australian Institute for Economics and Peace using data from the Global Terrorism Database and other sources, the most frequent perpetrators of nonstate terrorist attacks worldwide from 2014–2019 were the Taliban, ISIS (especially by its operatives in Afghanistan and Pakistan since the decline of "ISIS Central" in Syria), al-Shabaab, and Boko Haram, and the countries most victimized were Afghanistan, Iraq, Pakistan, Ukraine, Somalia, India, Yemen, Libya, Nigeria, and the Philippines.

Cumulative deaths attributed to subnational terrorism fell in 2019, after peaking in 2014. This decline in deaths corresponds with military successes against ISIS (in Syria and Iraq) and Boko Haram (in Nigeria), with the total number of deaths falling by 15 percent between 2017 and 2018 to just under 16,000. The largest decline was in Iraq, which recorded 3,217 fewer deaths from terrorism in 2018, a 75 percent decrease from the prior year. For the first time since 2003, Iraq is no longer the country most impacted by terrorism.

Although the total number of deaths from terrorism has fallen in recent years, the impact of terrorism remains widespread. In 2018, 71 countries experienced at least one death from terrorism, which is the second highest number of countries recording one or more deaths in the past 20 years. In addition, the global economic impact of terrorism was estimated at $33 billion in 2018.

Furthermore, these estimated costs of terrorism are conservative, as they do not account for the indirect impacts on business, investment, and the costs associated with security agencies in countering terrorism. Terrorism also has wide-ranging economic consequences that have the potential to spread quickly through the global economy with significant social ramifications. One of the more worrying recent trends is the surge in far-right political terrorism over the past 5 years. In North America, Western Europe, and Oceania, far-right attacks increased by 320 percent over the past 5 years.

Including 9/11, fewer than 3 percent of the deaths due to nonstate terrorists occurred in the West; most were victims of lone-wolf perpetrators. Despite a widespread perception in the United States that the West in general and the United States in particular are under constant and ruthless attack, such that Western civilization itself is imperiled, *the reality is that almost 99.9 percent of the victims of global terrorist attacks are not Americans. Globally, most victims of terrorist attacks are Muslims.*

When counting worldwide costs associated with terrorism and counterterrorism, one should also include the damage to mainstream Islamic culture and traditions, not to mention the affront to the collective self-esteem of Muslims. In sum, the conventional counterterrorist strategy, put into effect since September 2001,

- Has not defeated radical Islamism and has almost certainly recruited many new fighters,
- Has resulted in hundreds of thousands of casualties,
- Has led to a global clash between extreme elements of Western and Islamist civilizations and threatens to escalate to a war of the world in which nonstate terrorists and state counterterrorists may both employ weapons of mass destruction.

That said, it's important to put terrorism in perspective. Compared to other forms of violence, such as homicide, armed conflict, and military expenditures, *terrorism causes a small percentage of the total global cost of violence*, which has been credibly estimated at *$14.1 trillion in purchasing power parity for 2018.*

A peace-oriented perspective condemns terrorist attacks, seeing them as criminal activities calling for a law enforcement response rather than military mobilization; it also decries violent, and usually counterproductive, responses to them. Nonetheless, an alternative view also deserves attention. Consider a country that refuses to respond forcefully after large numbers of its citizens are attacked: some well-meaning, well-informed people honestly believe that such a policy might actually encourage more attacks, resulting in reduced overall security. Although vengeance is not highly regarded by most civilized persons, justice is. Accordingly, the best response to such terrible events is often maddeningly unclear and should not be made precipitously, in the heat of the moment. How does one "counter" terrorism without resorting to terror? Any policy for countering terrorism should profit by an understanding of when, where, how, and why officially designated subnational terrorist groups have ended.

How Do Terrorist Groups End?

The RAND Corporation is a global think tank largely but not exclusively funded by the US government, especially via military contracts. In 2008, RAND researchers presented to the US House Armed Services Committee the results of a comprehensive study, concluding that "By far the most effective strategy against terrorist groups has been the use of local police and intelligence services, which were responsible for the end of 73% of such groups since 1968." The RAND report recommended that

- "the US military should generally resist being drawn into combat operations in Muslim countries where its presence is likely to increase terrorist recruitment;" and

- "ending the notion of a 'war' on terrorism" and "moving away from military references would indicate that there was no battlefield solution to countering terrorism."[14]

The report concluded that groups labeled "terrorist" by governments are more likely to achieve their aims via political negotiations with the governments they oppose, leading to inclusion within the available political processes, than by force of arms. Furthermore, insurgent/terrorist groups are far more likely to end by "splintering" (i.e., through internal disagreements leading to disintegration) or by effective government intelligence gathering and police work than by violent state counterterrorism efforts. For both sides, military force unaccompanied by dialogue is usually a losing strategy.

And yet, perhaps paradoxically, the RAND authors also conclude that a political solution between the West and al-Qaeda and its offshoots and between the latter and existing Middle East governments is "not possible"— ostensibly due to the alleged inflexibility of religiously motivated terrorist groups. But if the incorporation of official terrorist groups in the political process, combined with the efforts of police and intelligence services to prevent terrorist attacks, results in a success rate (ending terrorist actions) far greater than other strategies, why shouldn't this strategy replace the global war on terrorism, with its associated counterproductive counterterrorist strategy and extraordinarily high costs?

Antiterrorism

A feasible alternative to counterterrorism is antiterrorism. It includes those measures taken to protect society while focusing on nonmilitary preventive actions. It is part of a "human security paradigm" that outlines a nonmilitary approach that aims to address the enduring underlying inequalities and injustices (both real and perceived) that fuel terrorist activity. Causal factors need to be delineated and measures implemented that allow equal access to resources and sustainability for all people, providing "freedom from fear" and "freedom from want," with details varying with the specific complaints and historical/societal details of each local situation. It would also include bringing violent terrorists to justice (legally sanctioned justice and not simple revenge), as well as negotiations with anti-state terrorist groups.

Antiterrorism is a multilateral strategy congruent with human security that advocates ethical, legally sanctioned methods for establishing effective communication and just relations between adversaries, resolving conflicts peacefully, and bringing terrorists to justice. Antiterrorism is a less violent, or even a nonviolent, alternative to counterterrorism (TFA). One possibility is to replace *counter*terrorist violence with *anti*terrorist prevention and interception measures. This may include negotiations with members or representatives of anti-state terrorist groups.

An additional course of nonviolent but potentially effective action would be to empower international organizations such as the United Nations and the International Court of Justice to bring to trial such perpetrators of crimes against humanity as those involved in the mass murder of civilians. Implied in such an approach is that "terrorism" should evoke a response involving international police activity and that "terrorists" should be brought to justice in the same way as other alleged lawbreakers.

At the same time, the West would need to recognize that colonialist, imperialist, and military occupations of non-Western lands constitute a principal political reason for terrorist attacks both against uniformed representatives of occupying powers as well as against their citizens locally and in their home countries. Therefore, the United States, France, Russia, and Great Britain should seriously consider dramatically altering their Middle East strategic policy, which would necessitate withdrawing non-Islamic combat forces from the countries in question and redeploying some of those forces offshore—until a comprehensive Middle East peace plan could be negotiated by all the affected parties, whereupon those forces would be brought home. In addition—and this, too, is easier said than done—there must be increased efforts by the West to motivate existing undemocratic governments, especially those enjoying substantial Western financial and/or military support (such as Egypt), to relinquish their autocratic hold on power and to maximize democratic processes so that their nations' citizens play a dominant role in determining their own affairs, even if this means reducing the influence of existing pro-Western financial and military elites.

Direct negotiations currently seem unlikely between many major adversaries: The United States, Great Britain, and their allies on the one hand, and a shifting congeries of radical Islamist cells ostensibly directed and/or inspired by al-Qaeda, ISIS, Hamas, and the Taliban on the other hand, with the governments of Russia, Pakistan, India, Saudi Arabia, Turkey, and China somewhat in between. But negotiations also seemed out of reach for much of the 20th century between Northern Ireland and Great Britain on the one hand and the Irish Republic and IRA on the other. Then came the Good Friday Accords, agreements signed in 1998 that officially disarmed the "terrorist" IRA and brought a fragile but continuing peace to Ireland after "the troubles" that had persisted for centuries. Just as there is now substantial mutual demonization between successive US administrations and militant, violent Islamists, a related dynamic characterized the IRA and pro-British "loyalists" in Northern Ireland. But eventually, due in part to the skillful intervention of third parties, including U.S. mediators, they came to coexist peacefully and even to share power.

Similarly, following years of torture and terrorism on both sides, the French negotiated their withdrawal from Algeria with the National Liberation Front. And few thought that apartheid in South Africa would end peacefully, but the ANC (another onetime "terrorist" organization) and the racist Afrikaner-led government in Pretoria negotiated a mostly nonviolent transition to majority black rule and, ultimately, to national reconciliation as well (although a kind of economic apartheid between the rich white minority and the mostly poor black majority persists).

The FARC, an intermittently violent insurrectionist group in Colombia, reached a milestone agreement with the national government that included disarmament of the rebels and their incorporation into civilian life; unfortunately, as of early 2021, this accommodation was showing signs of unravelling. The Palestinian Liberation Organization (*Fatah*), a longtime "terrorist group" in the eyes of many Israelis and Americans that currently speaks for the Arab population on the West Bank, has been negotiating, off and on, with the Israeli government for decades. It is likely that no "peace process" will succeed until all parties—including Hamas, a more radical organization that holds power in the Gaza Strip—are included and until all sides agree to accept less than their full demands. There are also sporadic efforts among the West, Russia, and China, on the one hand, and North Korea and Iran, respectively, on the other hand, to reach some accommodation on the latter nations' nuclear programs, with tentative deals, particularly with Iran, being reached and suspended. In short, although the work is not nearly complete, there are numerous examples of governments doing business and concluding peace with what they long deemed "terrorist groups," "state sponsors of terrorism," "rogue nations," and "liberation fronts," with these non-state actors laying down their arms in return for political and economic concessions.

It is, however, difficult to negotiate directly with an adversary that is geographically distant, decentralized, culturally unfamiliar, and that has alienated many with their rhetoric as well as frequently murderous violence. Nearly always, national governments—especially when fighting for their political power and, not uncommonly, their lives—have also done their share of alienating and murdering even greater numbers of people. But on more than one occasion, both al-Qaeda and the Afghan Taliban, for example, have publicly indicated willingness to suspend hostilities and to declare a kind of truce with their Western and Islamic adversaries. (ISIS may or may not be similarly willing.) With the exception of recurrent but inconsistent negotiation overtures between Washington and the Afghan Taliban, Western governments have officially refused to take up this invitation . . . which was also the case for years with the IRA, the ANC, and the FARC.

It is at best uncertain whether good-faith negotiations between the Western powers and militant Islamists, possibly through back channels conducted by third parties such as the Arab League, the Organization of the Islamic Conference, and/or the United Nations, might result in a reduction of both terrorist attacks and counterterrorist operations. But the alternative—an open-ended conflict with the potential to escalate to widespread war in the entire region and even possibly the use of nuclear and other weapons of mass destruction—is liable to be so destructive as to warrant that all nonviolent efforts should be made to end the current inflammatory situation. Any antiterrorism policy must, of course, be chosen with the greatest care and respect for human life and with a prospect of having a lasting positive result for all sides involved. To end terrorism means, among other things, to change the political, economic, and social realities that gave rise to it.

A Final Note on Terrorism

Terrorism is simultaneously one of the oldest and most recent incarnations of political violence. Whether employed from above or below, it has existed for millennia. Accordingly, it is wishful thinking to believe that terrorism can be ended overnight or even, perhaps, within the lifetimes of the writers and readers of this book.

It is not, however, wishful thinking to believe that we can begin now to struggle forcefully, but if possible nonviolently, against all forms of political violence, no matter the perpetrators. Although we may not see the end of terrorism in the foreseeable future, perhaps by confronting political mass murder with reason and understanding rather than with corresponding violence, we may see the beginning of the end of terrorism.

Questions for Further Reflection

1. Consider the contending definitions of terrorism. Which seem most appropriate, and why? Try to suggest your own definition.

2. Is TFA by states comparable to TFB by subnational agents, or is one worse than the other? Why?

3. To what degree do you consider the current wars and terrorism in the Middle East to be a continuity of, or a rupture with, Middle Eastern political history since the rise of Islam in the 7th century? To what extent is terrorism similar worldwide? Provide examples.

4. In what ways should the struggle against home-grown domestic terrorism be similar to that waged against terrorism that originates in other countries? In what ways should it be different?

5. Discuss the proposition that TFA is something for which Westerners are principally responsible.

Suggestions for Further Reading

B. J. Balleck. 2018. *Modern American Extremism and Domestic Terrorism*. Santa Barbara, CA: ABC-CLIO.

Martha Crenshaw and Gary LaFree. 2017. *Countering Terrorism*. Washington, DC: Brookings Institution Press.

Bruce Hoffmann. 2017. *Inside Terrorism,* 3rd ed. New York: Columbia University Press.

Richard Jackson and D. Pisoiu, eds. 2018. *Contemporary Debates on Terrorism*. London: Routledge.

Haig Khatchadourian. 2011. *The Morality of Terrorism*. New York: Peter Lang.

Gus Martin. 2020. *Understanding Terrorism,* 7th ed. Thousand Oaks, CA: SAGE.

Robert A. Pape. 2005. *Dying to Win: The Strategic Logic of Suicide Terrorism*. New York: Random House.

Mark Tomass. 2016. *The Religious Roots of the Syrian Conflict*. New York: Palgrave Macmillan.

Charles Webel. 2007. *Terror, Terrorism, and the Human Condition*. New York: Palgrave Macmillan.

Charles Webel and John Arnaldi, eds. 2011. The Ethics and Efficacy of the Global War on Terrorism: Fighting Terror With Terror. New York: Palgrave Macmillan.

Charles Webel and Mark Tomass, eds. 2017. *Assessing the War on Terror: Western and Middle-Eastern Perspectives*. London and New York: Routledge.

Lawrence Wright. 2007. *The Looming Tower: Al-Qaeda and the Road to 9/11*. New York: Vintage.

Notes

1. Derived from Title 22 of the US Code, Section 2656f(d). US Department of State, Office of the Coordinator for Counterterrorism, Country Reports on Terrorism, April 30, 2007. Also see http://www.nij.gov/topics/crime/terrorism/pages/welcome.aspx.

2. Bruce Hoffman. 2002. "Lessons of 9/11." Santa Monica, CA: RAND. http://www.rand org/pubs/testimonies/CT201/.

3. Two examples of the minority of Western scholars who accept the distinction between TFA and TFB are Haig Khatchadourian. 2011. *The Morality of Terrorism*. New York: Peter Lang; and Gus Martin. 2020. *Understanding Terrorism*, 7th ed. Thousand Oaks, CA: SAGE.

4. See Edward S. Herman and Gerry O. Sullivan. 1991. "'Terrorism' as Ideology and Culture Industry." In *Western State Terrorism*, ed. Alexander George. Oxford, UK: Polity Press, 41–42.

5. Quoted in Jean Bethke Elshtain. 2003. *Just War Against Terror*. New York: Basic Books, 50.

6. Yasmeen Ali. 2010, July 17. "Jihad and Terrorism: Are Both Synonymous?" Web

log post. http://pakpotpourri2.blogspot.cz/2010/07/jihad-and-terrorism-are-both-synonymous.html.

7. Ibid.

8. Ibid.

9. Ibid.

10. Quoted in Jason Burke. 2015. *The New Threat: The Past, Present, and Future of Islamic Militancy*. New York: New Press.

11. Department of Homeland Security website: https://www.dhs.gov

12. Muslims, especially in Arab countries, are especially sensitive to reminders of those bloody medieval wars in which European armies sought to wrest the Holy Lands from Muslim control.

13. Chalmers Johnson. 2004. *The Sorrows of Empire: Militarism, Secrecy, and the End of the Republic*. New York: Holt.

14. See Seth Jones and Martin C. Libicki. 2008. *How Terrorist Groups End: Lessons for Countering al Qa'ida*. Santa Monica, CA: RAND; and Audrey Kurth Cronin. 2009. *How Terrorism Ends: Understanding the Decline and Demise of Terrorist Campaigns*. Princeton, NJ: Princeton Unive rsity Press.

5

Bettmann via Getty Images

Nuclear Weapons

Albert Einstein once noted that as a child, he had been taught that modern times began with the fall of the Roman Empire. But everything changed with the atomic bombings of Hiroshima and Nagasaki: Now, Einstein observed, we must say that modern times began in 1945, when the first nuclear explosions were detonated.

There is indeed something special about nuclear weapons. They represent a dramatic discontinuity in human history, and they offer the possibility of an even more dramatic break: a canceling of the past, an end to the present, and a negating of the future. As destructive and dangerous as conventional warfare has been—and continues to be—it clearly takes a backseat to the sheer terror and horrific consequences of a global nuclear war.

One of the ironies of the 21st century is that with the end of the Cold War between the US and the former Soviet Union other concerns (including global warming, economic inequality, abuse of human rights, environmental deterioration, and terrorism) have eclipsed public anxiety about nuclear weapons as such. And yet, even as the risk of all-out global thermonuclear war—"World War III"—seems to have abated, the risk that nuclear weapons will be used intentionally or accidentally has not lessened; it may even have increased.

Moreover, as President Barack Obama has noted, "as the only nuclear power to have used a nuclear weapon, the United States has a particular moral responsibility to act." And according to Takashi Hiraoka, mayor of Hiroshima, in the "Hiroshima Peace Declaration," on the 50th anniversary of that city's nuclear destruction (August 6, 1995), "So long as such weapons exist, it is inevitable that the horror of Hiroshima and Nagasaki will be repeated—somewhere, sometime—in an unforgivable affront to humanity itself." And so, we turn to a consideration of these uniquely terrible weapons.

At least four factors must be understood if one is to grasp the nature of nuclear war and the urgency as well as the prospects of preventing it: (1) the weapons—bombs and warheads—and their effects; (2) delivery systems, the means by which nuclear weapons are to be directed to their targets; (3) strategic doctrine, concerned with the plans and strategies for the use of nuclear weapons; and (4) the problems of nuclear proliferation, nuclear terrorism, and new emerging threats.

The Nature of Nuclear Weapons

Nuclear weapons derive their explosive power from the conversion of matter into energy. This takes place according to Einstein's well-known equation, $E = mc^2$, in which E is the amount of energy released, m is the mass to be converted into energy, and c is the speed of light. Because the speed of light is itself a very large number (186,000 miles or 300,000 kilometers per second), which is squared in the equation, the resulting energy release is truly enormous. Nuclear fusion drives the sun and the stars; prior to 1945, the explosive power of nuclear energy had never been released by humans.

The power of nuclear weapons exceeds that of most conventional explosives by approximately a factor of 1 million. Herein rests the underlying significance of nuclear weapons and nuclear war: Something radically new and qualitatively different from previous human experience has been introduced into the world and into strategic thinking about conflicts. "The splitting of the atom has changed everything but our way of thinking," wrote Albert Einstein on the first anniversary of the atomic bombing of Hiroshima, "and thus we drift toward unparalleled catastrophe."

Atomic bombs result from nuclear fission, the splitting of large, unstable atoms, most commonly uranium-235 (a radioactive isotope of the element uranium) or plutonium-239 (another radioactive element, one that is essentially human made). When enough fissionable material is gathered together in one place and exposed to a barrage of neutrons, some of the unstable nuclei are split, releasing energy as well as additional neutrons. These neutrons, in turn, split the nuclei of other atoms, releasing yet more energy and neutrons, which continue to split additional nuclei in a chain reaction that accelerates geometrically and, thus, at extraordinary speed. The material has reached critical mass when each nucleus, after being split (or "fissioned"), releases enough neutrons to split approximately two nearby nuclei. As a result, an immense amount of energy can be released in a very short time. For example, in 0.00000058 second, 2^{57} nuclei (approximately 2 followed by 24 zeros) will have been split, releasing the energy equivalent to 100,000 tons of TNT.

Atomic, or fission, explosions are typically measured in kilotons (kt)—that is, the equivalent energy that would be released by the detonation of thousands of tons of TNT. Thus, a 12-kt atomic explosion—the size that destroyed the Japanese city of Hiroshima—releases the same amount of energy as would be released if 12,000 tons of TNT were to detonate.

The first nuclear weapons were based on fission. Most nuclear weapons today, however, are fusion, or thermonuclear, devices. They derive much of their energy from the squeezing together of very small atoms, notably deuterium and tritium, two isotopes of hydrogen. In the process, the element helium is produced, and through the conversion of mass into energy, a vast amount of energy is released. When plutonium, for example, is split, the total mass of the fission products that are formed—such as iron, cobalt, and manganese—is slightly less than that of the parent nucleus with which the process started. Similarly, the total mass of the helium nuclei produced by fusion is slightly less than the mass of the hydrogen isotopes with which a fusion reaction begins. This mass has not been "lost." Rather, it has been converted into a very large amount of energy: $E = mc^2$.

Fusion is more efficient than fission in that more energy per starting mass is released. But fusion is also more difficult to initiate than fission because great heat and pressure are required to literally squeeze the hydrogen nuclei together. Therefore, fusion explosions—or "hydrogen bombs," as they are commonly known—start with a relatively small "atomic" explosion, which serves as a trigger to initiate the much more powerful fusion reaction. This requirement of great heat and pressure is why fusion reactions are also known as *thermo*nuclear explosions. Fusion explosions are also typically boosted with an additional fission component, as the energy released by the fusion is captured by a lower-grade form of uranium, usually U-238, which is split by the high temperature and pressure of the fusion explosion. So the typical thermonuclear explosion is fission-fusion-fission, all occurring in a minuscule fraction of a second. The energy released in such detonations can extend into the range of megatons (Mt), equivalent to millions of tons of TNT.

Although nuclear explosives are often referred to as bombs, if deployed by nation-states, they are in fact more likely to be carried by a missile, in which case they are known as warheads. If deployed by some subnational actors, small nuclear devices and "dirty" bombs may be carried in a variety of ways, possibly including backpacks and suitcases. In addition, nuclear weapons are often designated as either tactical or strategic. The former usually refers to weapons intended for use on a battlefield; the latter are normally intended for use against an adversary's homeland and intended to win—or, according to deterrence theory, prevent—a war rather than to win a particular battle. As a result, tactical nuclear weapons are usually smaller than their strategic counterparts.

The Effects of Nuclear Weapons

Given that nuclear weapons have only twice been exploded in wartime (both in 1945, at Hiroshima and Nagasaki), it may seem strange that they should command so much attention. The reason is simple and related primarily to their effects: Nuclear explosions are extraordinarily powerful and devastating. Consider this account of the first atomic bomb test, at Alamogordo, New Mexico, in July 1945:

> No man-made phenomenon of such tremendous power had ever occurred before. The lighting effects beggared description. The whole country was lighted by a searing light with the intensity many times that of the midday sun. It was golden, purple, violet, gray and blue. It lighted every peak, crevasse and mountain range with a clarity and beauty that cannot be described but must be seen to be imagined. It was the beauty the great poets dream about but describe most poorly and inadequately. Thirty seconds after the explosion came . . . to be followed almost immediately by the strong, sustained, awesome roar which warned of doomsday and made us feel that we puny things were blasphemous to dare tamper with the forces heretofore reserved to the Almighty. Words are inadequate tools for the job of acquainting those not present with the physical, mental and psychological effects. It had to be witnessed to be realized.[1]

For insight into the effects of a nuclear explosion, however, it is more useful to consider eyewitness accounts of the actual use of atomic weapons, such as this one describing the impact on Nagasaki:

> For some 1,000 yards, or three-fifths of a mile, in all directions from the epi-center . . . it was as if a malevolent god had suddenly focused a gigantic blow-torch on a small section of our planet. Within that perimeter, nearly all unprotected living organisms . . . perished instantly. Flowers, trees, grass, plants, all shriveled and died. Wood burst into flames. Metal beams . . . began to bubble, and the soft gooey masses twisted into grotesque shapes. Stones were pulverized, and for a second every last bit of air was burned away. The people exposed within that doomed section neither knew nor felt anything, and their blackened, unrecognizable forms dropped silently where they stood.[2]

During the height of the Cold War, pronuclear strategists on both sides argued for "civil defense" as a way of minimizing damage in a nuclear war, although anti-nuclear opponents maintained that such efforts were neither "civil" nor "defense" because they would provide no real safety and, if anything, increased the risk that such weapons might be used insofar as they were perceived to be survivable. Former Soviet Communist Party chairman Nikita Khrushchev once observed that following a nuclear war, the survivors would envy the dead.

Both Nagasaki and Hiroshima were hit with atomic bombs carrying the explosive power of about 20 kt and 12 kt, respectively. These are very small compared with the bombs and warheads now available: Hydrogen bombs have been produced and deployed in the multimegaton range. Because 1 Mt is equivalent in energy to 1 million tons of TNT, it follows that a 9-Mt bomb is slightly less than 1,000 times more powerful than the one that destroyed Hiroshima. Most bombs and warheads in the strategic arsenal of the United States and Russia are about 100 to 500 kt, or approximately 8 to 40 times more powerful than the Hiroshima explosion. In 2010, the total US strategic arsenal was about 1,700 Mt; by comparison, the entire explosive force detonated by all sides during World War II was approximately 3 Mt.

Despite substantial cuts in the nuclear arsenals of the two nuclear super-powers (the United States and Russia) since the end of the Cold War, by 2020 there were still about 14,000 nuclear weapons in the world. Of these, some 3,750 are operationally deployed, of which roughly one-half of US and Russian warheads are on high alert, ready for use on short notice. The exact number of nuclear weapons in each country's possession is a closely held national secret, although it is generally agreed that the United States has about 6,200 and Russia, 6,500. The other "declared nuclear states"—the United Kingdom, France, China, India, Pakistan—possess roughly 100 to 300 nuclear warheads and/or bombs each, as does another undeclared nuclear state: Israel.

North Korea possesses a nuclear arsenal of uncertain number (variously estimated at about 30 to 60) and questionable reliability. Iran is widely sus-pected of having attempted to develop nuclear weapons, a capability that had been thwarted (at least for the next 15 years or so) by an international agreement reached in 2015; however, the US announced in 2019 that it was withdrawing from this agreement, technically freeing Iran to "go nuclear" at its own pace. And as of late 2020, Iran had responded to that withdrawal by increasing its nuclear stockpile eight-fold and concentrating fissionable uranium to just short of bomb grade. It is also widely believed that subna-tional and terrorist groups, as well as possibly a few nonnuclear states, have been seeking to develop, or acquire, nuclear devices, thus far unsuccessfully.

Immediate Effects of Nuclear War

Most estimates of nuclear war fatalities are lower than they should be because the relevant effects—blast, burns, and radiation—are generally considered separately. In reality, however, all would occur simultaneously. In addition to those immediately vaporized or incinerated, many people would be trapped in collapsing buildings (blast), which would then likely burn (heat), while the survivors would also have to contend with radiation. Infections are a serious complication of burns, and radiation reduces the body's ability to ward off infection. Many victims would likely be burned and irradiated and might also suffer from crushing or piercing injuries. In addition, most hospitals and medical personnel are located in major cities, which would almost certainly be targeted and destroyed, and pharmaceu-ticals would be almost entirely unavailable; ditto for emergency services of all sorts. Firefighting would also be virtually impossible because streets would be impassably blocked with the debris of collapsed buildings, water pressure would be nonexistent because of the rupture of pipes, and poten-tial firefighters would likely be dead or contending with their own personal tragedies.

Of the 90,000 to 150,000 fatalities resulting from the bombing at Hiro-shima, about 50% were due to burns and about 30% to lethal doses of radia-tion. Another 40,000 to 80,000 people eventually perished due to the atomic bombing of Nagasaki. Although technical knowledge of this sort is impor-tant, such sanitized data are grossly inadequate for conveying the horror of nuclear war. Numbers are numbing. Another kind of knowledge, more personal and visceral, may be more meaningful.

There are harrowing accounts of people with empty eye sockets whose eyeballs were literally melted, of infants attempting to nurse at the corpses of dead mothers, of burn victims with their skin hanging in loose strips, and of family members trying to rescue relatives who had been trapped under collapsed and burning buildings. One survivor gives this account:

The sight of the soldiers was more dreadful than the dead people . . . I came upon . . . many, burned from the hips up . . . where the skin had peeled, their flesh was wet and mushy . . . And they had no faces! Their eyes, noses, and mouths had been burned away, and it looked like their ears had melted off. It was hard to tell front from back.[3]

Even for those not physically injured, the psychological effects of such an immense and sudden disaster were overwhelming for most survivors. A Hiroshima physician describes some survivors leaving the rubble:

Those who were able walked silently toward the suburbs in the distant hills, their spirits broken, their initiative gone . . . . They were so broken and confused that they moved and behaved like automatons . . . a people who walked in the realm of dreams . . . . A spiritless people had forsaken a destroyed city.[4]

To repeat: the Hiroshima and Nagasaki bombs were very small by today's standards. Moreover, at that time there was an "outside world" from which aid eventually reached the survivors. In the event of full-fledged nuclear war today, the experience would be many times worse, with virtually no prospect of recovery.

Societal Effects of Nuclear War

In addition to the radioactive fallout that would follow nuclear explosions, a major mid-range effect of nuclear war would be its impact on social, economic, and political systems. Food storage would likely be destroyed or inaccessible; cities would be devastated, with rescue, firefighting, and medical services largely unavailable; transportation might well cease altogether. Electricity-generating plants would almost certainly be destroyed, along with oil refineries. Most sources of power—for communication, transportation, manufacturing, and agriculture—would be eliminated, perhaps permanently. A simple barter system would probably replace traditional money-based economies for any possible survivors. As economist John Kenneth Galbraith has emphasized, communism and capitalism (as well as socialism, Christianity, Islam, Judaism, Hinduism, Buddhism, etc.) would likely be indistinguishable in the ashes. Diseases such as cholera would spread rapidly, with sanitation and public hygiene virtually eliminated and billions of insects and trillions of bacteria multiplying in the rotting, unburied corpses.

Shortly before he was assassinated in 1979, Great Britain's Lord Mountbatten gave a speech in which he asked,

And when it is all over, what will the world be like? Our . . . great buildings, our homes will exist no more. The thousands of years it took to develop our civilization will have been in vain. Our works of art will be lost. Radio, television, newspapers will disappear. There will be no means of transport. There will be no hospitals. No help can be expected for the few mutilated survivors . . . there will be no neighboring towns left, no neighbors . . . there will be no hope.[5]

By contrast, many nuclear strategists calculated that nuclear war might be survivable, at least for some people and with appropriate precautions, such as (in the early 1960s) blast and/or fallout shelters and (in the 1980s) crisis relocation plans, which were intended to organize the evacuation of the citizenry from high-risk areas to other regions, thought to be untargeted. Such thinking was especially prominent among those nuclear strategists who fretted that "excessive" anxiety about the effects of nuclear war might erode US willingness to stand up to its possible adversaries. They worried also about the possibility that antinuclear fears would diminish the credibility of the stated US intention to resort to nuclear weapons under certain circumstances, such as an invasion of Western Europe, South Korea, or Japan; or in retaliation for a nuclear attack on the United States or its NATO allies. In addition, some conservative politicians were long concerned that nuclear fears might undermine a continuing commitment by the United States to ever-more weaponry and likely undercut the "better dead than red" mentality that had been prevalent among many Cold Warriors.

By the 1990s, however, such thinking became increasingly difficult to defend, largely as a result of the widespread publicity concerning the horrific prompt and intermediate effects of nuclear war, as well as revelations concerning their likely long-term effects. The peace movement, both in the United States and worldwide, can take substantial credit for awakening many government leaders to the unacceptable consequences of nuclear war, as epitomized in the belated observation by President Reagan (who took office with a seemingly cavalier attitude toward the effects of nuclear war) that a "nuclear war can never be won and must never be fought."

Long-Term Consequences of Nuclear War

Long-term effects of nuclear weapons would include dramatically increased levels of background radiation (due to radioactive fallout) as well as significant depletion of stratospheric ozone (O^3), which otherwise protects the Earth's inhabitants from dangerous cancer- and blindness-inducing levels of natural ultraviolet radiation from the sun. Undoubtedly, however, the most serious long-term consequence would be the phenomenon of nuclear winter. This refers to the cooling and darkening of the planetary environment that most atmospheric scientists believe would result from an all-out nuclear war. The basic scenario for a nuclear winter is as follows: A nuclear war would produce not only immense amounts of dust but—far more important—enormous fires, which in turn would generate huge quantities of smoke and soot. Rising into the upper atmosphere, this material would absorb incoming heat and light from the sun, thereby making the Earth very cold and very dark.

Some estimates show that nuclear winter could be triggered by the detonation of as "little" as 100 Mt, a tiny fraction of the world's arsenals. The effects would be worldwide and catastrophic: Temperatures could plummet as much as 50° F, which would result in extreme freezing over widespread areas and total disruption of agriculture and natural ecosystems, as well as perhaps making fresh water unavailable for people, plants, and/or animals for prolonged periods of time. Certainly, such an event would greatly complicate the problems of survival in what is sometimes, in a sanitized way, referred to as the "postattack environment."

The nuclear winter scenario generated controversy, as specialists questioned some of its assumptions, such as precisely how much smoke would be produced, how it would be distributed globally, and how intense and how persistent the climatic darkening and freezing would therefore be. There is also debate over the possible modulating effect of the oceans and the effect of increased cloud cover, as well as questions as to what proportion of the targeted cities would actually burn.

Thus far, however, most of the conclusions reached by scientists study-ing the issue have proven to be quite robust; a study reported by the Inter-national Physicians for the Prevention of Nuclear War (which received the Nobel Peace Prize in 1985) concluded that even a "limited" nuclear war between India and Pakistan—using roughly one-half of their current arsenals—would likely trigger worldwide famine, resulting in upwards of one billion deaths due to starvation alone, and would "probably cause the end of modern industrial civilization as we know it."[6] It is clear that any significant use of nuclear weapons is liable to be an act of global suicide.

Part of the objection to the robust science of nuclear winter has accord-ingly been political because this highly destructive long-term consequence of nuclear war makes the use of such weapons—whether as attack or retaliation—self-inhibiting. At present, and despite a growing consensus that nuclear war is an unacceptable option, some aspects of nuclear strategy nonetheless depend on the willingness of governments to employ nuclear weapons or, at least, they depend on the belief by an adversary that such willingness exists. Hence, one comes across such statements as the observation by Henry Kissinger (now a self-professed nuclear abolitionist) that nuclear diplomacy "requires strong nerves" and that, accordingly, the United States should "leave no doubt about our readiness and our ability to face a final showdown."[7]

During the early years of the Reagan administration, for example, offi-cial pronouncements sought to minimize the likely consequences of nuclear war. In 1982, then deputy undersecretary of defense T. K. Jones claimed that "everybody's going to make it if there are enough shovels to go around. . . . Dig a hole, cover it with a couple of doors and then throw three feet of dirt on top. It's the dirt that does it."[8] Other pronouncements of this sort, combined with a massive and unprecedented military buildup of both conventional and nuclear weapons, stimulated renewed interest in—and anxiety about—the effects of nuclear war. This, in turn, contributed to delegitimizing (at least somewhat) the concept of nuclear war fighting as a strategic doctrine.

Delivery Systems

The technology—and the peace/war implications—of delivering nuclear weapons to their targets is almost as important as that of the weapons them-selves. The strategic nuclear forces of both the United States and Russia are based on a "triad" of three distinct components: long-range bombers, land-based intercontinental missiles, and missile-carrying submarines. Each of the other nuclear powers— China, France, Great Britain, India, Pakistan, Israel, and North Korea—employs one or, at most, two "legs" of such a triad. (As of early 2020, North Korea has not demonstrated the capacity to miniatur-ize nuclear warheads, thereby rendering them capable of being carried on a missile; that country's ICBM, or intercontinental ballistic missile, capacity is very likely but not as yet proven.)

Bombers

Bombers were originally intended to attack targets by dropping gravity bombs. That role has, to some extent, been superseded by the use of bomb-ers as "launch platforms" for a variety of conventionally armed air-to-land cruise missiles. More recently, interest has also been revived in using bomb-ers as "penetrating aircraft"—so-called stealth bombers, designed to deflect radar when at altitude and which, like cruise missiles, are also intended to duck under radar detection. The wars conducted by the North Atlantic Treaty Organization (NATO) on Serbia, Kosovo, and Libya, and by the United States and its allies on Iraq and Afghanistan, made heavy use of both high-altitude conventional bombing as well as missile-launched conventional warheads, which resulted in very few (in some cases, zero) casualties for the fliers but significant casualties for civilians and soldiers who happened to be in the path, whether of "precision-guided" or errant munitions.

Intercontinental Ballistic Missiles

Ballistic missiles are rockets. They travel very rapidly, reaching speeds of greater than 10,000 miles per hour, and during intercontinental flight they leave the Earth's atmosphere, to reenter before striking their targets. Intercontinental ballistic missiles (ICBMs) are usually located underground, in steel-and concrete-reinforced silos, making them relatively invulnerable to all but a direct hit. The United States maintains up to 1,000 ICBMs (as with all such weapons for all countries, the exact numbers keep changing, when older models are phased out and new ones brought into service). Russia has also invested heavily in ICBMs, primarily because their bomber and submarine fleets are fewer and less advanced. As of 2020, China's strategic nuclear weapons are entirely based on ICBMs; this seems likely to change in the future, although China's nuclear doctrine involves substantially fewer launch vehicles and warhead numbers than does that of either the US or Russia.

ICBMs in the US and Russian arsenals have usually been *MIRV*ed, that is, equipped with Multiple, Independently targeted Reentry Vehicles. A single MIRVed missile can carry 10 or more warheads, each of which can be aimed at a different target. Fifty MIRVed missiles can thus destroy 500 distinct targets, each with a warhead of between 350 kt (nearly 30 times the power of the Hiroshima bomb); 2 Mt Russian missiles have historically tended to be bigger than their US counterparts, a fact that has caused great consternation to some in the United States and that was long used to buttress claims that the United States was "behind" in ICBMs, thereby helping generate support for additional missile programs. But in fact, the smaller size of US ICBMs was an indication of the superiority, not inferiority, of US missile technology.

According to the physics of nuclear explosions, the accuracy of a warhead is far more important than its explosive size: When it comes to the probability of destroying a given "hardened" target, a small increase in accuracy is equivalent to a very large increase in total explosive force. Making a warhead twice as accurate is equivalent, with regard to its probability of destroying an ICBM silo, to increasing its explosive force by a factor of eight. The US arsenal achieved very high degrees of accuracy (thanks in part to the same satellite technology employed in global positioning system devices); as a result, it has been possible to decrease the megatonnage and also to deploy ICBMs that are significantly smaller than the first, relatively bulky and less accurate missiles. It would take approximately 30 minutes for ICBMs fired by one nuclear superpower to devastate the other and much less time for such regional nuclear powers as India and Pakistan to obliterate one another.

Submarine-Launched Ballistic Missiles

Submarines can be "nuclear" in two senses: They are often propelled by nuclear power plants, and they also carry nuclear missiles known as Submarine-Launched Ballistic Missiles (SLBMs). These missiles are designed to be fired while the submarine remains submerged. The particular advantage of strategic submarines is that unlike bombers or ICBMs, once they are on deep-ocean patrol they cannot be targeted by an adversary. In terms of strategic doctrine, they have therefore been considered an ideal deterrent weapon because they offer the prospect of a secure "second strike" force—that is, one that could permit their country to absorb a "first strike" and still be able to deliver retaliation that would be devastating for a would-be nuclear aggressor. However, SLBMs have certain disadvantages, notably the fact that communication with deeply submerged submarines is often difficult.

Strategic submarines carry many SLBMs; US Trident submarines, for example, carry up to 24 missiles, with that number reduced to 20 following the US-Russia New Start Treaty of 2010. Like ICBMs, SLBMs tend to be MIRVed, with the United States having progressed further than Russia in this regard. When it comes to strategic submarines, the United States also enjoys a geographic advantage over Russia because of its extensive, ice-free ocean coastlines (which is one reason Russia was committed to the defense of the Assad regime in Syria, where it maintains a naval station). The US is also acknowledged to have a substantial lead over any competitors in submarine technology, including antisubmarine warfare.

Strategic Doctrine: Deterrence

Strategic doctrine refers to the plans that purportedly underlie the accumulation of nuclear weapons, the justifications for their existence, and the expectations as to their use. The major component of US strategic doctrine is alleged to be deterrence, the idea that nuclear war will be prevented by the threat that any attacker would suffer unacceptable retaliation. Realizing this, the would-be attacker should therefore be deterred.

Deterrence as such is not unique to nuclear weapons. What is unique to nuclear deterrence, however, is the consequence of failure and the fact that, heretofore, military forces that ostensibly provided deterrence also did double duty in providing defense, should deterrence fail. For centuries, for example, Rome relied primarily on "deterrence by punishment." Although serious efforts were made to defend Rome itself, the perimeter of its far-flung territory was so extensive that it was not possible to prevent various enemy incursions. Much of Rome's military was therefore configured to punish invasions by "barbarians." The intent was to respond so violently that such actions would be deterred, that is, never attempted again. By contrast, "deterrence by denial" seeks to deter attack by presenting a would-be invader with defenses that are so intimidating as to be likely to deny any success. The Great Wall of China is a notable manifestation of this strategy, as was France's Maginot Line (which was considerably less successful).

In the nuclear age, despite efforts at achieving strategic missile defense, the offense is all-powerful, despite hopes by some that a National Missile Defense (NMD) program might lessen the dominance of offense; if nuclear deterrence between nuclear superpowers should fail, there is currently no effective defense, leaving all nuclear countries reliant on deterrence by punishment. Moreover, most independent experts agree that any conceivable missile defense system—dubbed "Star Wars" by its critics—would readily be overwhelmed by a concerted ballistic missile attack, as well as easily confused by such countermeasures as decoys, including chaff (material such as metal foil, which appears as an indeterminate cloud, camouflaging possible incoming warheads).

Shortly after World War II, American strategic analyst Bernard Brodie recognized the qualitative change in deterrence ushered in by nuclear weapons:

> The first and most vital step in any American security program for the age of atomic bombs is to take measures to guarantee . . . in case of attack the possibility of retaliation in kind. [The issue is not] . . . who will *win* the next war in which atomic bombs have been used. Thus far the chief purpose of our military establishment has been to win wars. From now on its chief purpose must be to avert them. It can have almost no other useful purpose.[9]

Advocates of missile defense nonetheless maintain that even though it could not function effectively against a concerted attack by a well-armed opponent (e.g., Russia), it might be useful against a very limited first strike by a nuclear "mini-power" such as North Korea. At present, the United States has been the country most committed to developing strategic missile defense, which has emerged as a favorite of conservative "hawks" even though the technical problems are immense and not nearly solved; US tests have been less than 50% successful, even when the timing and flight path of test launches were known in advance. When he was Soviet premier, Nikita Khrushchev likened the problem of mounting a successful defense against ballistic missiles as "hitting a bullet with a bullet."

Strategic deterrence theory has been modified many times, varying with the state of US-Russian—previously, US-Soviet—relations and weaponry. However, the basic premise of deterrence remains that no country would use nuclear weapons against the other so long as the victim retains the ability to cause unacceptable damage to the attacker. In such thinking, the initial attack is referred to as a first strike, and a first-strike capability is generally taken to mean the ability to conduct an initial assault that will render the victim unable to retaliate.

According to conventional deterrence theory as it applies to nation-states, therefore, it behooves each country to maintain a second-strike capability, the capacity to absorb a first strike and still retaliate. If one side has a second-strike capability, the other, by definition, lacks a first-strike capacity. The result is considered strategic stability, a situation in which neither side can profit by striking first; thus, nuclear war should not occur. This, of course, is not peace at all but rather a kind of suspended animation in which overt warfare is merely postponed (in theory).

Skeletons in the Closet of Deterrence

Deterrence theory is not as cut and dried, or as reliable, as its proponents might wish. A number of factors—or "skeletons in the closet"—have consistently undermined the presumed goal of strategic nuclear stability based on mutual deterrence.

Skeleton 1: How much is enough? No simple rule of thumb or straightforward quantitative measure can assure national leaders that they have accumulated enough retaliatory force to deter an adversary. Indeed, if one side is willing to be annihilated in a counterattack, it cannot be deterred. And if one side is convinced of the other's implacable hostility, or of its presumed indifference to loss of life (as seems to be the case with some violent Islamist and other subnational groups), no amount of weaponry can ever be "enough." So long as money is made by accumulating weapons, and so long as prestige and careers are served by designing, producing, and deploying new "generations" of nuclear forces, there will be continuing insistence on yet more of them. Finally, insofar as nuclear weapons also in part serve symbolic, psychological needs, such as conveying prestige to otherwise insecure leaders and countries—thereby ostensibly demonstrating the scientific and technological accomplishments of a nation—then once again, there is no rational way to put a cap on the optimum size of one's arsenal.

Strategic planners in the United States declared in the 1960s that to be "prudent," each leg of the strategic triad should be able to destroy two-thirds of the then-USSR's population and industrial capacity. However, because of the many factors that drive nuclear arms races—and, to some extent, arms races in general—the arsenals of both the United States and Russia expanded to many times this amount. Given that a single nuclear bomb or warhead delivered on any major city would cause staggering loss of lives and property, it is difficult to understand the deterrent rationale for maintaining literally thousands of times that destructive capacity.

Skeleton 2: Credibility. A second major difficulty of deterrence theory is the problem inherent in basing security on the threat to do something that is grossly self-destructive and therefore lacking in credibility. Thus, granted that one side would be irrational to attack a nuclear-armed opponent that had a second-strike capability, the victim would be equally irrational to reply with nuclear weapons. Critics compare the problem of credible nuclear deterrence to the situation of a police officer, armed with a huge stick of dynamite, with which he or she is expected to deter a bank robber; the robber might well find its use to be literally incredible. Thus, not only would the threat of nuclear retaliation likely be useless because it lacks credibility, but it would almost certainly be counterproductive, adding to worldwide destruction (through fallout, ozone depletion, nuclear winter, etc.) while also raising the possibility of yet another attack from the aggressor's remaining nuclear forces. In addition, given the ethical issues raised by a willingness to commit mass murder on the largest scale in human history, there might be additional reasons to doubt a nuclear state's willingness to do so.

"One cannot fashion a credible deterrent out of an incredible action," wrote former defense secretary Robert McNamara. "Thus, security for the United States and its allies can only arise from the possession of a range of graduated deterrents, each of them fully credible in its own context."[10] Such thinking led, in turn, to the notion of "flexible response," according to which a country should possess a range of military options, including a diversity of nuclear responses, proceeding up what is called the "escalation ladder" from the limited or "tactical" (short-range "theater") nuclear weapons, which are claimed to have the potential of determining winners and losers short of global thermonuclear war. Belief in such flexible responses has been touted as providing alternatives to mutually assured destruction, or MAD.

There are, however, serious problems with doctrines of limited war fighting. First, to be credible, such threats must be based on weapons and tactics that are in fact usable: generally, missiles, bombs, and warheads that are smaller and highly accurate and that produce relatively less collateral damage (the killing of civilians and the destruction of property and other non-targets). So in order to be effective, which in the case of nuclear weapons means in order *not to be used,* these weapons must be made *more usable!* This is not merely a paradox but a very dangerous reality, one that may someday be catastrophic: The more usable, hence credible, they are, the more likely they are actually to be used. And numerous war game scenarios (simulations of actual conflict) have shown that in the event of nuclear war between nuclear powers, no matter how small and controlled the opening shots, the confrontation is very likely to escalate to an all-out strategic exchange, with disastrous consequences for all involved. Moreover, even without such escalation, a limited nuclear war, in Europe or between regional nuclear powers (such as between India and Pakistan, or Israel and its adversaries) would appear quite unlimited to the Europeans, South Asians, or people in the Middle East, for whose benefit the war was ostensibly being fought. As a result of all this, even limited nuclear war—hence, nuclear deterrence—may be not only unacceptably dangerous, but lacking in credibility after all.

Skeleton 3: Vulnerability. As already mentioned, deterrence requires that the nuclear weapons of each side remain invulnerable to attack or, at least, that the probability of them being destroyed in a first strike be very low. Over time, however, as nuclear missiles have become increasingly accurate, concerns have been raised about the growing vulnerability of these weapons (note: not vulnerability of the population, which is fundamental to deterrence). This alleged vulnerability of nuclear weapons has been enhanced by the development of so-called counterforce doctrines: policies and capabilities that focus on targeting an adversary's weapons rather than population centers. Although counterforce appears less unethical than its alternative, countervalue targeting (or the deliberate intent to destroy civilian populations in cities), it also raises concerns that the other side may be planning a first strike because, in theory at least, a successful counterforce attack would preclude retaliation.

This perception of vulnerability can lead to "strategic instability." On the one hand, the side possessing a first-strike capability may be tempted to make such an attack, especially under conditions of crisis, when war seems likely and perhaps inevitable. On the other hand, the vulnerable side might well calculate that because its opponent has the ability to strike a devastating first blow, it ought to preempt such an attack by striking first. This is also more likely during an international crisis. There is virtually no limit to this chain of reasoning: Side A, fearing that side B is about to preempt in this way, may be tempted to pre-preempt, leading side B, which anticipates such a pre-preemption, to consider pre-pre-preempting, and so forth. The result—so-called crisis instability—is profoundly dangerous and, as with the problem of credibility, threatens to undermine stability.

One of the most important contributions toward reducing crisis instability was the Anti-Ballistic Missile (ABM) Treaty, according to which signatories agreed to forgo the deployment of antimissile defenses. Although the evidence is overwhelming that such "Star Wars" antiballistic missile systems could not successfully defend major population centers, it is at least theoretically possible that they might succeed in protecting some of a country's nuclear arsenal after it had first launched a nuclear attack against its opponent's weapons. If a would-be attacker had confidence that its ballistic missile defenses could be somewhat successful against a "ragged retaliation," it might in theory be tempted to launch such an attack in the first place, thereby undermining deterrence. And this, in turn, could also frighten a nervous victim into pre-empting such an anticipated attack with one of its own! The George W. Bush administration withdrew the United States from the ABM Treaty in 2001 and announced plans to install a limited ABM system, ostensibly to defend against a possible attack from Iran. Both Russia and China objected vigorously, worried—or claiming to worry—that this presaged a possible first strike attack against them.

The Russian government claimed that such a system—even if technologically flawed and susceptible to countermeasures—would dangerously erode nuclear stability. The Bush administration nonetheless announced plans to deploy ABM components in Poland and the Czech Republic, which was vigorously opposed by many Czechs and Poles, along with the Russian government. Subsequently, the Obama administration backed away from this proposed land-based ABM system in favor of a more limited one, to be based primarily on warships in the open ocean. In 2019, the Trump administration began deploying a limited anti-missile system in South Korea, ostensibly as protection against North Korea and despite vigorous protests by South Koreans and also by China, which claims that it is actually directed against them.

Skeleton 4: Human psychology. Deterrence theory assumes optimal "rationality" in decision makers or, at least, that those with their fingers on the nuclear triggers will remain calm and cognitively unimpaired under extremely stressful conditions. It also assumes that leaders will always retain control over their nuclear forces and that, moreover, they will always retain control over their emotions as well, making decisions based solely on a cool calculation of the costs and benefits associated with each course of action. Deterrence theory thus maintains that each side will scare the other with the prospect of the most hideous, unimaginable consequences and that those political and military leaders thus terrified will then behave with the utmost in deliberate, precise instrumental rationality. Virtually everything known about human psychology suggests precisely the opposite.

Deterrence theory also ignores that even without intense fear, many people often behave in ways that are irrational, vengeful, and even spiteful and self-destructive (i.e., hurtful to themselves as well as others). Moreover, they may be the victims of insufficient or faulty information or of various other perceptual distortions that cause them to make incorrect judgments of others' intentions, the likely outcomes of various alternative courses of action, and so on. It requires no arcane strategic wisdom to know that people often act out of anger, despair, insanity, stubbornness, revenge, and/or dogmatic conviction. And finally, in certain situations—as when either side is convinced that war is inevitable or when the pressures to avoid losing face are especially intense—an irrational act, even a lethal one, may appear quite "rational," and therefore appropriate, even unavoidable.

Skeleton 5: Deterring terrorists. How can people who do not fear violent death and who do not have a fixed location be deterred? Deterrence theory is therefore of dubious relevance for dedicated terrorists, many of whom may be immersed within the very societies they are inclined to attack, or in remote and unknown locations (who therefore cannot be targeted for retaliation), and/or might not be "deterred" because they do not fear—and may even welcome— "martyrdom." How can people who believe their violence is sacred and will be rewarded, either by God or by their community, be deterred, or even found and retaliated against, especially if they are within urban, civilian communities? Moreover, a sudden nuclear detonation within a city would not likely be accompanied with a return address, especially because any potential evidence would probably be annihilated along with the victims.

Even more problematic is that the cycle of terrorist/counterterrorist violence may spiral out of control. Tit for tat, an eye for an eye, a city for a city, a nation for a nation: There is no lasting security in a world in which terror matches terror and neither the terrorists nor the counterterrorists are deterred by the prospect of greater violence. This extends from the local detonation of car bombs and precision-guided weaponry to the deployment, locally and globally, of weapons of mass destruction (WMDs).

Has Nuclear Deterrence Worked?

Many strategic analysts would say, "Of course nuclear deterrence has worked." Even while acknowledging that the Emperor Deterrence has no clothes, they claim that he is still emperor; that is, no effective alternative exists. They also argue that we can thank nuclear deterrence for the fact that there has been no nuclear or major conventional war between nuclear states, notably between the United States and the Soviet Union, even when tensions between the two superpowers were quite high. Some also maintain that the fall of the Soviet Union and the defeat of communism were brought about by the West's nuclear deterrent, which allegedly prevented the former Soviet Union from invading Western Europe.

Others, however, argue that the absence of a war between the United States and its NATO allies on the one hand, and the former Soviet Union and its Warsaw Pact allies on the other hand, was not due to nuclear deterrence but to other factors, such as the absence of any wars between America and Russia prior to the advent of the nuclear age and to internal domestic considerations within each country. The fact that there has not been a nuclear war could be due to many factors, although it is tempting—but not necessarily accurate—to attribute an event to the factor of one's choice. This brings to mind the story about the man who sprays perfume on his lawn every morning, explaining that he does so to keep the elephants away. When confronted with the fact that there aren't any elephants within 10,000 miles, he exclaims, "You see? It works!" There is also this logical conundrum: If there had been a nuclear war (and it would probably require just one), we likely wouldn't be around to complain about deterrence having failed.

It is widely agreed, moreover, that the closest we came to nuclear war was during the Cuban Missile Crisis (1962), a conflict that was caused, almost exclusively, by the presence of nuclear weapons. Given the logical inconsistencies and threats generated by deterrence itself, it can credibly be claimed that thus far, rather than having been prevented by the threat of nuclear retaliation, nuclear war has been avoided in spite of it.

Do Nuclear Weapons Convey National Power?

Nuclear weapons are immensely powerful and throughout history, powerful weapons have conveyed social, political, and recently, national power. It is doubtless no coincidence that the permanent members of the Security Council are all nuclear armed, or that the government of North Korea—a small, impoverished, and largely ostracized country—gained a major profile on the international stage once it obtained its own nuclear arsenal. And yet, the historical record is clear that possessing nuclear weapons has not enabled countries to get their way in the world, and it has not even provided immunity against military provocations by nonnuclear states.

For example, in 1951, China was still more than a decade from obtaining nuclear weapons and yet was not deterred from sending nearly 500,000 troops into Korea in a massive undeclared war with a mostly US-led military; the resulting stalemate prolonged the Korean War by years, tens of thousands of casualties, and as of 2020, is still unresolved. Similarly, the UK's nuclear weapons did not deter conventionally armed Argentina from invading the British-held Falkland Islands in 1982, just as during the first Gulf War (in 1991), Saddam Hussein's nonnuclear Iraq was not deterred from lobbing dozens of Scud missiles into nuclear-armed Israel—which did not retaliate, at least in part because incinerating Baghdad would not have benefitted Israel, something that the Iraqi government evidently understood.

Nor have nuclear weapons enabled nuclear-armed countries to get their way in other respects. The Soviet arsenal did not help it maintain control over its East European satellite states after 1990, nor did it assist Russia in its wars with rebels in Chechnya or Afghanistan. Similarly, the US nuclear arsenal did not help it succeed in the Vietnam War or its wars in Afghanistan or Iraq, just as nuclear-armed France was unable to hold onto Algeria. Other examples abound, leading to the conclusion that nuclear weapons—although unimaginably destructive—are not especially useful as geopolitical tools, except perhaps by reassuring nationalists that their country is particularly powerful . . . even though the evidence is at best equivocal.

How a Nuclear War Could Start

There are many possible scenarios (hypothetical sequences of interactions) according to which nuclear war could occur. What follows are some examples. Although these were originally developed with an eye to the Cold War between the United States and the Soviet Union, most could apply to other confrontations, notably between India and Pakistan, between Israel and a nuclear-armed Iran, and so forth. (And, regrettably, between the US and Russia, or between the US and China, if in fact new Cold Wars develop further between these nuclear, economic, and political rivals.)

Bolt Out of the Blue. Although most laypeople imagine a surprise, middle-of-the-night attack, experts agree that a so-called bolt out of the blue (BOOB) attack is the least likely scenario. Neither side would come out ahead, and unless other factors are operating, deterrence might prevent any such calculated madness. On the other hand, strategic analysts worry constantly that one side may be tempted to attack preemptively if it becomes convinced that its perceived adversary's weapons could be destroyed in a surprise first strike. More realistic scenarios for BOOB attacks generally depend on some combination of other interactions discussed next.

A Game of "Chicken." A popular but risky game played by teenagers, and captured memorably in the classic 1950s film *Rebel Without a Cause* (starring James Dean), was to play "chicken" in automobiles. Two drivers would drive toward a cliff at high speed. The first one to bail out lost; the one who persevered was the winner. In a game of chicken, therefore, the goal is to induce the opponent to turn aside and not to do so oneself until the last possible moment, if at all.

Philosopher and antinuclear campaigner Bertrand Russell made an even more dramatic analogy between strategic games of chicken and two drivers heading toward each other, straddling a white line, each seeking to induce the other to turn aside. The most dramatic example of nuclear chicken occurred during the Cuban Missile Crisis in 1962, when the Soviet Union had furtively installed medium-range nuclear missiles in Cuba, hoping to deter the United States from invading Cuba and to "balance" the American deployment of nuclear-tipped missiles in Turkey (bordering the former Soviet Union) and Great Britain.

The United States demanded that the missiles be withdrawn; the Soviets refused. After considering and rejecting various options—including a conventional attack on the missile sites, an invasion of Cuba, and a preemptive nuclear strike against the Soviet Union—President John F. Kennedy decided on a naval blockade (designated at the time a "quarantine"). The situation was exceedingly tense, and President Kennedy subsequently stated that he thought the chance of nuclear war had been between one in two and one in three. Premier Khrushchev ordered Soviet naval vessels to turn back, and an accommodation was reached in which the Soviet missile site was dismantled and the United States promised not to invade Cuba. (An unofficial part of the deal was that the United States would quietly decommission its medium-range missiles in Turkey, something it had already planned to do before the Cuban Missile Crisis.)

As then-Secretary of State Dean Rusk put it, "We were eyeball to eyeball, and the other guy blinked." In other words, the Soviets turned aside in that game of nuclear chicken. They may have been induced to do so, at least in part, by the fact that the Soviet Union was militarily inferior to the United States at the time, both in conventional forces in the Caribbean region and in nuclear arms as well. However, the United States and Russia now appear equally capable of destroying each other, as well as the rest of the world, and neither side is likely to accept the ignominy of being the one to swerve. In contests of nuclear chicken, when each side insists that the other one turn aside, the result is likely to be "fried chicken."

Escalated Conventional War. Military forces of the United States and Russia have not engaged in direct hostilities since the US—along with other major Western powers—tried unsuccessfully to undo the Bolshevik Revolution by invading eastern parts of the nascent Soviet Union. It is at least possible (some would say, likely) that such restraint has been due to the shared possession of nuclear weapons. Nonetheless, each side has been engaged in conventional fighting—the Soviets, for example, in Hungary (1956), Czechoslovakia (1968), and Afghanistan (1979–1988); the Russians in Chechnya (1996–2009), Georgia (2008), Ukraine (2014–present), as well as Syria (2015–present); and the United States in Korea (1950–1953), Vietnam (1962–1974), Beirut (1982), Grenada (1983), Panama (1989), the Persian Gulf (1990–1991), the former Yugoslavia (1999), Afghanistan (2001–present), and Iraq (2003–present), to mention just a few cases.

The United States has seriously considered the use of nuclear weapons many times, including during the Vietnam War, in 1968, when American generals considered the possible use of nuclear weapons to help lift the siege of a major US marine base at Khe Sanh. The administration of George W. Bush refused to rule out the first use of nuclear weapons, although President Obama also revised US policy on the use of nuclear weapons in a "nuclear posture review" required of all presidents, declaring for the first time that the United States would not use nuclear weapons against *non*nuclear states that were compliant with the nuclear Non-Proliferation Treaty. Subsequently, the Trump administration affirmed in the 2018 Nuclear Posture Review and elsewhere that US policy includes possible first use of nuclear weapons under a variety of conditions, including a cyberattack against the US homeland.

Thus far, existing international threats and confrontations have been resolved short of nuclear war, but there is no assurance that this can continue indefinitely. There is also an ongoing danger that during conventional warfare, nuclear weapons will be used in a last-ditch effort to win the war or simply to prevent one's homeland from being overrun. Israel is believed to have been on the verge of using nuclear weapons against Egypt after having suffered an initially successful surprise attack in 1973, during the Yom Kippur War. Many experts believe that the greatest current threat of nuclear use is posed by India and Pakistan, two nuclear-armed countries with shared borders, a long-simmering conflict over a disputed geographic region (Kashmir), and a long history of wars during the past few decades. It is all too possible that should a conventional war break out between these two countries, the losing side might resort to nuclear weapons. Ironically, it is even possible that the winning side would also be tempted, out of fear that the other might do so in desperation and, thus, in the hope of beating it to the punch!

Nearly 20 years after leaving the Defense Department, Robert McNamara also warned that "we face a future in which . . . in the tense atmosphere of a crisis, each side will feel pressure to delegate authority to fire nuclear war weapons to battlefield commanders. As the likelihood of attack increases, these commanders will face a desperate dilemma: use them or lose them."[11] There is a real prospect that in the Indian subcontinent, the future is now; thus, because of the substantial conventional superiority of India over its rival, Pakistan, the latter's military doctrine has been modified to give battlefield commanders authority to use tactical nuclear weapons if their forces are in danger of losing. Of course, this may be a strategic bluff, intended to deter India in the event of war; but it may also be a genuine threat.

Nuclear Accidents. An accidental nuclear detonation has never taken place, although both Russia and the United States have come terrifyingly close. In several cases, the conventional explosive that is part of a nuclear weapon has detonated, scattering large amounts of radioactive material. Furthermore, nuclear-armed bombers and submarines have crashed, exploded, and/or sunk. Given the chaos that would doubtless follow an accidental nuclear explosion, it is always possible that such an event would lead to retaliation for an "attack" that didn't occur. A full-fledged nuclear detonation would dwarf such accidents as those that occurred at the Three Mile Island (United States), Chernobyl (Ukraine, at the time part of the Soviet Union), and Fukushima (Japan) nuclear power plants.

Nor is the United States immune from other possible nuclear blunders: In 2007, a B-52 bomber flew from North Dakota to Louisiana carrying five armed nuclear warheads, apparently unbeknownst to the crew or any higher authorities. The plane and its super-lethal cargo remained unguarded on a runway for 11 hours before the situation was discovered. Moreover, if a nuclear explosion occurred during a time of international tension, the consequences may well be extremely grave for all parties. In addition, given boredom as well as reduced opportunities for career advancement among nuclear warriors (because ostensibly preventing war carries less charisma than actually fighting in one), it is not surprising that low morale and lax oversight appear to be endemic within the US nuclear establishment and seem likely within Russia and other nuclear states, especially those with less technological sophistication and command and control (like Pakistan) as well. Under such circumstances, nuclear accidents seem more likely than any sane person would desire.

Unauthorized Use, "Loose Nukes," and Nuclear Terrorism. Both the United States and Russia until the late 1990s kept relatively tight, centralized control over their nuclear weapons, in an effort to make certain that they will be employed only in response to orders from the highest level of political leadership. Numerous fail-safe devices are incorporated into US weapons design, and until the 1990s it was widely assumed that comparable controls existed on the Russians' part as well. However, there is no guarantee that something could not go wrong, and as a result, someone relatively low in military/political rank could wind up starting a nuclear war. Such worries seem especially acute when it comes to other nuclear armed states, among whom budgets and, thus, fail-safe mechanisms are presumed to be more limited.

After the collapse of the Soviet Union in 1991, the danger of "loose nukes" not subject to stringent command and control procedures emerged as a major worry, in response to which the United States invested hundreds of millions of dollars in its Fissile Material Disposition and Global Threat Reduction programs, designed to improve security around nuclear facilities in the former Soviet Union, as well as transporting high-level nuclear materials for disposal. It remains debatable, however, whether these measures have been adequate to the task.

Fissionable materials could be stolen and then fabricated into nuclear weapons, or small nuclear bombs or warheads could be sold to interested buyers. It has also been suggested that given the economic and social decline of post-Soviet Russia, formerly well-paid weapons designers may have been willing to sell their expertise to the highest bidder. (A paradoxical benefit of Russia's renewed nuclear weapons program initiated by President Putin may be that this particular danger may have diminished because of tightened control by Moscow over its nuclear forces). Governments or terrorist groups could conceivably steal ready-made bombs, warheads, or bomb-ready fissile material while they are in transit or in storage depots. Israel's nuclear weapons program benefited when that country commandeered a shipload of enriched uranium in the late 1960s. In addition, governments could purchase ready-made nuclear weapons: At one time, Libya, for example, attempted unsuccessfully to buy nuclear bombs from China.

Many Western terrorism experts believe it is only a matter of time before subnational terrorist groups succeed in acquiring and/or detonating nuclear devices, dirty bombs (that would spew radioactive materials, although without a nuclear explosion), and/or other WMDs. Enormous resources are being devoted by law enforcement, military, information technology, intelligence-gathering, counterterrorist, and customs agencies to prevent nuclear and WMD attacks by official and as-yet-unknown terrorist groups. But if these prevention and interdiction measures should fail—even once—there will be tremendous pressure on the attacked nation to retaliate quickly and with overwhelming force, as there was in the United States immediately after the attacks of 9/11. Use of nuclear weapons against alleged nuclear terrorists might well be favored by decision makers who are understandably angry, but this would likely not be the most prudent or rational course of action, especially because identifying perpetrators might well be impossible, as well as likely resulting in such potentially catastrophic unintended (but foreseeable) consequences as massive civilian casualties and possible escalation to global thermonuclear war.

Irrational Use. It can be argued that any use of nuclear weapons constitutes irrational use. Beyond this, however, the possibility exists that those persons exercising the highest political authority may themselves go insane or behave irrationally. Many famous leaders throughout history were emotionally disturbed and/or experienced psychotic episodes: probably including Caligula, Nero, Adolf Hitler, and Joseph Stalin. Woodrow Wilson and Dwight Eisenhower suffered major strokes while in office, which may have compromised their ability to perform their duties and to think clearly. During the final days before resigning his presidency in 1974, Richard Nixon is said to have acted irrationally, possibly due in large measure to the stress of the Watergate investigations and threatened impeachment. And credible questions were raised by mental health professionals about the mental stability of US President Donald Trump.

No precedent and no guidelines currently exist for countermanding the orders of a sitting president, no matter how dangerous or unwise such orders might be; moreover, the use of nuclear weapons could legally be ordered without a formal declaration of war by Congress and even without any prior consultation. In Russia, China, India, Pakistan, Israel, and North Korea, the possibility of unnerved political decision makers or "rogue officers" authorizing the use of nuclear and/or other WMDs is at least as high as in the United States, especially if a conventional war appears to be going badly.

False Alarms. One of the most chilling—because the most likely—scenarios for nuclear war involves failure in the command, control, communications, and intelligence (C3I) systems of a nuclear state. Before the nuclear age, decision makers in many countries worried about being the victims of a surprise attack, as happened twice in 1941: to the United States at Pearl Harbor, and to the Soviet Union when Germany suddenly invaded. In the era of nuclear weapons, a danger even greater than surprise attack is that one side—thinking it is under attack—may "retaliate" when in fact it had not actually been struck or, in the case of a nuclear and/or WMD attack by unidentified terrorists, may retaliate massively against a nation or people unconnected with the initial assault.

The leadership of nuclear states is essentially hostage to the correct functioning of their warning systems. And during times of international stress or crisis, this connection may be especially perilous. Thus, there have been many false alarms: According to the US Senate's Armed Services Committee, in the United States alone there were 151 "serious" nuclear false alarms and 3,703 lesser alerts during a (presumably representative) period between January 1979 and July 1980. In the past, radar signals bouncing off the newly risen moon have been taken for enemy missiles, migrating geese have been similarly misinterpreted, and a fire in a Siberian natural gas pipeline set off a satellite sensor, which identified it as the exhaust of a Soviet missile launch. Once, a practice war-games tape was erroneously read by military computers as an actual attack, and faulty microchips have several times generated inappropriate alerts. The former Soviet Union, and present-day Russia, have been exceptionally close-mouthed about their history of false alarms, but one case is well documented. In 1983, during an especially tense time in US-USSR relations, a mid-ranking Soviet officer received notice that a new satellite warning system detected a handful of ICBMs heading toward the USSR from the US. That officer, one Stanislav Petrov, decided it was likely an error by the recently installed system (which it was), and—contrary to explicit orders—did not pass the alert to Kremlin authorities. He was punished for this insubordination, but he has also been called "The Man Who Saved the World."

Because the extreme destructive power of nuclear weapons is combined with exceedingly high-speed missile velocities and short warning times—literally minutes—there would be great pressure on decision makers to know quickly whether an attack is really under way and, if so, to respond immediately. In addition, as nuclear delivery systems have become increasingly accurate, counterforce weapons have made it more and more feasible (at least in theory) for the attacking side to demolish an adversary's nuclear forces. As that feasibility increases, reports of such an attack become more believable, particularly in times of crisis. The result is to put great pressure on a prospective victim of a nuclear attack to "use 'em or lose 'em," with a resulting increased risk of severe miscalculation and premature launch.

The hot line between the White House and the Kremlin—installed in 1963 as a result of the Cuban Missile Crisis of 1962—and various crisis control centers are supposed to reduce the danger that similar false alarms will lead to nuclear war by miscalculation. But it remains unclear what sort of communication would reassure a side that believes it is being attacked and feels that it must respond promptly: "You are not really about to be obliterated. Please believe me and don't do anything"?

Launch on warning. Nuclear deterrence depends, essentially, on a would-be aggressor believing that if attacked, the victim will retaliate, causing unacceptable damage. But as we have seen, nuclear deterrence has a credibility problem: Having suffered immense destruction in an initial attack, the victim would have literally nothing to gain by retaliating and, moreover, a great deal to lose, both via the global effects of nuclear war and also if the attacker responds by firing yet more missiles. In addition, the great speed and increasing accuracy of strategic missiles have led some strategic analysts to conclude that, at least in theory, an opponent could target a large proportion of the adversary's land-based missiles. So it has been argued that to shore up the credibility of nuclear deterrence, it is necessary to employ a system known as launch on warning, in which the decision to launch is made upon warning of an attack, rather than waiting until the attacker's warheads have literally begun exploding on the victim's soil.

Moreover, to bolster the credibility that the victim will actually retaliate, launch on warning is also often taken to involve removing the decision to launch from human beings and instead transferring it to computers preprogrammed to do so when alerted to an impending attack. As noted, there have been numerous reports of near launches based on computer, satellite sensor, and/or human mistakes. And with increased reliance on computer systems (which, like people, are never perfect), the danger of nuclear retaliation to avenge a real or perceived attack on either side has not decreased since the formal end of the Cold War.

Launch on warning, the supremely "logical" consequence of nuclear deterrence theory itself, thus carries immense dangers. First, it drastically reduces the time span in which a decision must be made—perhaps the most fateful one in world history. Second, it places the fate of the Earth in the hands of potentially fallible sensor and warning systems, with, by definition, no possibility of human override.

It is widely thought that Russian, Chinese, Indian, Pakistani, and North Korean computer systems are less reliable than those used by the Pentagon, the United Kingdom, France, and Israel, which are themselves hardly

fail-safe. Moreover, if other countries with less robustly developed technological infrastructure develop their own nuclear arsenals, their command
and control systems will likely be even more vulnerable to accidents and
false alarms, especially when and if their governments are engaged in a tense
diplomatic, political, and/or military standoff.

In any event, should "deterrence fail"—a bloodless construct often used
by the nuclear priesthood—there will likely be no strategists or historians left
to debate the reasons for its failure.

Nuclear Proliferation

We have focused mainly on the two nuclear superpowers because the United
States and Russia still account for roughly 95 percent of the world's nuclear
weapons. In addition, the United States and Russia are responsible for the
qualitative as well as the quantitative dimensions of nuclear arms escalation.
We have accordingly examined what has been called vertical proliferation,
the accumulation of weapons and delivery systems by the nuclear superpowers. However, there is substantial reason to be concerned as well about
horizontal proliferation, the acquisition of nuclear weapons by other, previously nonnuclear countries, especially those with long-standing traditions
of hostility (notably between India and Pakistan and between Israel and its
Middle Eastern neighbors, especially Iran).

There are numerous potential routes to nuclear proliferation, including
the following:

1. Buying, stealing, or otherwise obtaining already-made nuclear weapons
   that are currently deployed or stockpiled by countries possessing them.

2. Somehow obtaining sufficient quantities of plutonium or highly
   enriched uranium to be able to construct one's own nuclear weapons.

3. Making illegal or clandestine use of the products of nuclear power plants
   or research reactors, especially plutonium. Plutonium is unavoidably
   created in all currently operating reactors, and although it is difficult
   to safely separate it from other, nonfissile byproducts, it is technically
   feasible; the United States did so when generating the fissile material
   for the Nagasaki bomb. There aren't two distinct kinds of radioactive
   plutonium—the "good" kind produced in power and research reactors
   and the "bad" kind used in nuclear weapons. Rather, there is only one
   kind of plutonium atom. North Korea's weaponization program was
   achieved using reactor-generated plutonium.

4. Using various chemical or mechanical processes to increase the
   concentration of uranium-235. Although present in only minute
   concentrations (less than 1 percent) in natural uranium ore, once
   concentrated to 3 percent to 5 percent, U-235 can power nuclear
   reactors. Increased to 90 percent or more, it can constitute an atomic
   bomb. Because all uranium atoms are chemically identical, it is difficult
   to separate the radioactive isotope U-235 from relatively inert U-238,
   which makes up the overwhelming bulk of raw uranium ore. However,
   this can be done using ultra-high-speed centrifuges, which take
   advantage of the slightly lesser weight of U-235. Iran's disputed pursuit
   of nuclear weapons followed this route.

Regardless of the means of proliferation, it is widely believed that following the end of the Cold War, horizontal proliferation may have equaled vertical proliferation as a source of worry.

But there is also another view. It has been argued—albeit by a small minority of analysts—that because nuclear weapons in the hands of the Great Powers ostensibly helped "keep the peace," these same weapons, widely proliferated, might conceivably be a stabilizing influence on world affairs. (After all, if the US and Russian publics are supposed to believe that nuclear weapons are good for them, why wouldn't nuclear weapons be equally good for, say, Iran, Nigeria, North Korea, Egypt, Brazil, South Africa, Saudi Arabia, Japan, South Korea, or Argentina?) This is the so-called porcupine theory, that a world composed of many nuclear-armed states would be a safe one because each state would carefully avoid antagonizing its neighbors, just as porcupines walk in relative safety through the forest. (And as the joke goes, how do they even make love? Carefully.) More often, however, the argument is reversed, with the assumption that horizontal proliferation is, in fact, profoundly dangerous. Nonetheless, insofar as some people argue in favor of certain countries (notably the United States) maintaining their nuclear weapons, how can they sincerely oppose nuclear weapons in the hands of any country that might want them?

From the perspective of a would-be proliferator, perhaps even more significant than how to "go nuclear" is the question of whether to do so. Thus, numerous countries that could readily go nuclear (including Sweden, Canada, Germany, Japan, Australia, the Netherlands, Switzerland, and possibly Saudi Arabia) have not done so, and others (Ukraine, Kazakhstan, South Africa) have voluntarily given up their nuclear weapons. On the other hand, Pakistan and India, with considerably less developed economic and technological bases than most of the countries just enumerated, have joined the nuclear "club," while other nations are possible future entrants.

Among the acknowledged nuclear powers, the proliferation path has been much like a chain of dominoes. The United States initiated a nuclear weapons program largely out of fear of being beaten to the punch by Germany during World War II and to intimidate the Soviet Union; the Soviet Union followed suit, in response to the US nuclear monopoly; China went nuclear largely because of the Soviet Union; India developed nuclear weapons primarily because of China; and Pakistan developed its nuclear arsenal in response to India. For its part, Israel furtively became a nuclear power ostensibly to deter its Arab neighbors and Iran. And North Korea's rationale for its nuclear stockpile is to deter the United States. If Iran or some other Islamic country were eventually to develop nuclear weapons and the systems to deliver them, the likely rationale would also be to deter a possible attack by Israel and/or the United States.

In any event, whether a country actually intends to become nuclear-armed, or whether its government plans to use the threat as a lever by which to negotiate certain benefits from the international community, such actions are criticized by some as blackmail but considered by others to be geopolitical realism. Either way, it is a dangerous "game" because possible proliferation by a country (e.g., Iran) that also expresses belligerent antagonism toward another country (e.g., Israel) runs the risk of evoking a preemptive attack, with unforeseeable consequences for the region and the world.

Saudi Arabia and Egypt (both primarily Sunni), in particular, have threatened to respond with their own nuclear programs if their rival, Iran (primarily Shiite), goes nuclear. Similarly, the presence of North Korea's nuclear arsenal has pressured South Korean militarists to do the same. Japan, also, feels threatened by a nuclear North Korea, although thus far, it has effectively resisted calls for nuclearization from its far right, in large part because the destruction of Hiroshima and Nagasaki in the last days of World War II has, so far, immunized that country against developing its own indigenous nuclear force. A disastrous near-meltdown, with substantial release of nuclear radioactivity, at Japan's Fukushima power plant following a massive tsunami in 2011 also reduced the likelihood that Japan will join the nuclear "club" . . . at least in the immediate future.

In some cases of proliferation, states went nuclear after they discovered that the superpowers could not be counted on to provide a "nuclear guarantee"— that is, to risk nuclear war on their behalf. Nuclear states cannot really be blamed for hesitating to run such a grave risk as nuclear war, even on behalf of an ally. Concern over whether the US would risk, say, the destruction of Chicago to "defend" London or Paris was influential in the decision by the UK and France to go nuclear. The problem is closely intertwined with that of state sovereignty: States insist on their absolute freedom of action, even in a world that is increasingly interdependent.

There is also another motivation behind would-be proliferators: pride and political status. Britain and France, for example, had little strategic motivation for developing their own nuclear arsenals, but both countries in the 1950s and 1960s were contending with the dismantling of their overseas empires and with the psychological stress of having to forgo their previous position as Great Powers. If it possesses nuclear weapons, a state is virtually guaranteed a place in world councils, and many leaders in less economically advanced nations believe that their country, their people, and their culture deserve the same recognition that more affluent societies have arrogated to themselves.

Recent international developments appear to have motivated the decision by North Korea, for example, to go nuclear. After Moammar Gaddafi gave up his incipient WMD program, the Libyan government—engaged in a brutal civil war—was essentially overthrown by NATO intervention, and Gaddafi was killed. This arguably served as a lesson for North Korea's dictator, Kim Jong-un, that nuclear weapons might be necessary to avoid a similar fate. It was also not lost on the political leadership of North Korea that the US invasions of Iraq and Afghanistan would probably not have occurred had those countries possessed their own nuclear arsenals. Combined with a willingness on the part of the United States to support regime change, it is not unlikely that the North Korean government concluded that acquiring nuclear weapons may be in its survival interest.

Many legitimate reasons for opposing nuclear proliferation exist, including the following:

1. As more people, small groups, and political-religious organizations have their "finger on the button," it becomes more likely that someone, somewhere, will for some reason press it. (Note that there is no one "button"; the word is simply a convenient metaphor.)

2. In many less economically developed countries, political power is held by dictators and autocrats who are not accountable to their citizenry, who have obtained power without democratic checks and balances, and who may be especially unstable.

3. Countries with a limited technological base may be hesitant to invest heavily in various fail-safe protective devices, thereby increasing the

danger of accidental detonations, unauthorized use, or war by false alarm. This is particularly true of subnational groups.

4. According to standard deterrence theory, states with a very small nuclear arsenal may actually be more at risk of preemptive attack than those having an ability to absorb such an attack and then retaliate. In this sense, it is paradoxically true that a comparatively large nuclear arsenal may actually lead to greater "crisis stability" than a small arsenal like North Korea's.

5. Many would-be proliferators are currently engaged in active or smoldering hostilities directly on their borders. This is especially the case along the India-Pakistan border, in the Israeli-Palestinian conflict, and in some of the southern Russian republics bordering recently independent states, such as Georgia.

The existing nuclear powers have a shared interest in restricting nuclear proliferation, and they have established an international framework toward that end, the Non-Proliferation Treaty, which, regrettably, has not been signed by India, Pakistan, or Israel, and from which North Korea has withdrawn. Signatories agree to forgo nuclear ambitions (if they are nuclear "have-not" states) and to permit inspection of their declared nuclear facilities, while in return, states possessing nuclear weapons agree to cooperate in sharing nuclear power technology with them. This itself is problematic because there is no clear dividing line between the technology necessary for nuclear power and that enabling the development of nuclear weapons. In addition, nuclear states are also bound by the Non-Proliferation Treaty to make good-faith efforts to reduce and eventually eliminate their nuclear arsenals, although the major nuclear powers have not done so. They are thus ill situated to criticize others for seeking to obtain nuclear weapons so long as they continue to add to and modernize their own vast arsenals: "Do as I say," they appear to be saying, "not as I do."

In addition to continuing international anxiety about possible nuclear proliferation, there is, ironically, a growing risk that efforts to prevent proliferation might actually precipitate conventional war—or that claims of would-be proliferation will serve as a trumped-up excuse for such a war. In 1981, Israeli warplanes destroyed an Iraqi nuclear reactor, evidently in an effort to prevent Iraq from developing nuclear weapons. A similar attack occurred again in 2007, with Israeli warplanes this time attacking a facility in Syria believed (although never proven) to be associated with nuclear weapons development. The US government claimed, falsely, that Iraqi possession of WMDs was the major justification for its invasion of Iraq in 2003 and has since threatened war with North Korea over its nuclear weapons programs. Short of military strikes, nonproliferation efforts likely to be encountered by other would-be proliferators in the future have included strenuous economic and political sanctions as well as such other illegal but widely acknowledged measures as cyberattacks (e.g., the "Stuxnet" computer worm, engineered by Israel and the United States, which temporarily disabled Iranian enrichment facilities) and even the assassination of military officials and leading nuclear scientists.

Less prominent than nuclear proliferation as such, but nearly as important, is proliferation of delivery systems (most commonly ballistic missiles) capable of conveying nuclear warheads to a potential target. First-generation nuclear weapons—of the sort initially developed by North Korea, for example—are too large and heavy to be placed atop a missile;

with increasing sophistication, however, the warheads are miniaturized and thus rendered more "deliverable." In this regard, much international attention focused on North Korea's test launch of a long-range missile in 2012 and of its more recent successes in missile design and delivery. Although ostensibly intended for placing a weather satellite in Earth's orbit, the reality is that any missile capable of doing this is also capable of delivering a nuclear warhead at intercontinental range. (MIRVing—the placement of multiple, independently targeted warheads on a single missile—was initially developed as a means of launching multiple satellites with a single rocket.)

There have also been clear signs of an emerging missile race in South Asia. Thus, India has launched a ballistic missile capable of reaching Shanghai and Beijing, thereby joining the small group of nations (all nuclear capable) that also possess long-range missiles. This, in turn, threatens to provoke an arms race between the two Asian giants, India and China, with Pakistan not far behind. Further underlining the growing militarization of this region is the fact that India has become the world's most active weapons importer, while pressure mounts in Japan and South Korea (both of whose industrial infrastructures are capable of expanding into missile design and production) to join their Asian neighbors/competitors.

The horror of nuclear war is so great that fear of nuclear weapons—with or without suitable delivery systems—falling into the "wrong" hands will continue to mount, along with the possible need for even well-intentioned governments to decide whether to risk preemptive war as a preventive measure. This raises the question of whether nuclear weapons can ever be in the right hands.

Other Proliferation Problems

In addition to the problem of nuclear proliferation, there are other, related issues, notably the proliferation of chemical or biological warfare capabilities, of conventional weapons with near-nuclear effects, and of ballistic missile and land and/or space-based antimissile and antisatellite technology. Chemical weapons have been called the "poor man's atomic bomb," and in fact, the manufacture of highly toxic chemical munitions is relatively easy and inexpensive. Iraq, under Saddam Hussein, used such weapons against Iran (obtained from the United States during the Reagan administration) and subsequently against its own Kurdish rebels. Libya, assisted by a German chemical firm, constructed a chemical warfare facility, which was subsequently dismantled. France, Russia, and the United States have maintained large chemical weapons stockpiles until very recently. Of these, the US arsenal has been the most sophisticated, consisting of binary chemicals—two subcomponents that are not lethal in themselves but become highly toxic when combined immediately prior to use.

The major holders of these weapons have indicated the intention of destroying their chemical arsenals but have not done so, while others—notably Syria—developed their own. When the Syrian government in 2013 used chemical weapons against rebels and civilians, worldwide outrage was such that it appeared for a time that the United States would attack the government of dictator Bashar al-Assad. An agreement was reached—thanks in large part to the intervention of Assad's ally, Russian president Vladimir Putin—to eliminate these weapons. Although many chemical weapons were subsequently removed from Syria, the Syrian government then used more primitive chemical weapons (notably chlorine gas) against its opponents.

In the final years of the Clinton administration and continuing through the two terms of George W. Bush's presidency, official US doctrine included the implied threat that the United States might employ nuclear weapons in response to nonnuclear (e.g., chemical and/or biological) attacks against its interests. Although this policy was rescinded under President Obama, it was reestablished during the Trump administration and matched by a declaration by President Putin that Russia might also use nuclear weapons to defend itself against a nonnuclear attack, a significant change in policy from its avowed "no first use" doctrine of the latter half of the 20th century.

Some New Worries

There have been worrisome new developments on the nuclear front. Even though the Cold War (between the United States and the former Soviet Union) ended when the latter dissolved in 1991, relations between the United States and Russia—the Soviet Union's primary successor state—have become increasingly fraught; because these two countries possess most of the world's nuclear weapons, this in itself is worrisome. Adding to this are some recent nuclear developments, suggesting that a new arms race has begun.

The Trump administration proposed the following weapons and delivery systems: 600 new ICBMs, 12 Columbia-class SLBM-carrying submarines outfitted with new missiles and warheads, and 100 enhanced stealth-equipped B-21 Raider long-range bombers. A single, current-generation Trident submarine is outfitted with 20 D-5 missiles, each MIRVed to carry eight warheads, each of about 450 kt (roughly 40 times the explosive power of the Hiroshima bomb). Hence, one such submarine carries the equivalent of 6,400 Hiroshima-level nuclear explosions (20 × 8 × 40), leading to the question: How much is needed for any reasonable definition of deterrence?

Because of a special, adjustable tail assembly, the proposed new generation of gravity bombs—known as the B61-12—would be the world's first guidable nuclear bomb; as noted earlier, enhanced accuracy greatly increases potential destructiveness against hardened targets, such as the ICBMs upon which Russia primarily relies. Also, this enhanced accuracy makes it feasible to employ lower-yield explosives, which might appear a good thing until we realize that lower yields make such weapons more "usable," something appealing to analysts planning to fight a future nuclear war but distinctly less attractive to those seeking to prevent one. In addition, the United States intends to develop and deploy a new generation of air-launched cruise missiles designed for dual use—that is, to be armed with either a conventional or nuclear explosive.

Cruise missiles are pilotless jet aircraft that travel slowly compared to ballistic missiles (about the speed of sound) but close to the ground and are therefore difficult to detect. They are also relatively inexpensive to produce, roughly $1 million each. Equipped with modern navigational and homing devices, they are also becoming extremely accurate. In addition, cruise missiles are quite short, perhaps 20 feet long. Thus, once they have been deployed in large numbers, verification that they have been eliminated at any time in the future, even if countries possessing them muster the political will to do so, becomes extremely difficult if not impossible.

Cruise missiles with conventional warheads were used by the United States in its two wars against Iraq, by NATO in Libya and Afghanistan, as well as by Russia in Syria beginning in 2015. The proposed new cruise missiles—1,000 of them, known as long-range standoff (LRSO) weapons—would be carried by strategic bombers, either by existing B-52s, B-1s, B-2s, or by the proposed B-21s. Of particular concern is that because these LRSO missiles could be armed with conventional or nuclear warheads (and at present there is no way to distinguish the two kinds from a distance), the danger exists that once a country discovers that such a missile is approaching its territory, it won't be able to tell whether it is under nuclear attack and might well assume the worst.

Nor is the United States the only source of alarming nuclear developments. Russian strategic plans are less publicized, but it appears that a form of submersible drone, capable of stealthily carrying a nuclear weapon into a port city, is under development, along with a cruise missile not only capable of carrying a nuclear warhead, but powered by a small nuclear reactor—a test version of which exploded in 2019. Russia unilaterally withdrew from a long-standing agreement with the United States that called for the safe, bilateral disposal of plutonium, and in 2019 the US, citing Russian violations of the Intermediate Nuclear Forces treaty, withdrew from that agreement—originally signed between Presidents Reagan and Gorbachev—which had resulted in the elimination of an entire class of nuclear-capable missiles.

Tensions between India and Pakistan (both nuclear states) remain high, exacerbated by terrorist attacks fomented by Pakistan on Indian soil and India's crackdown on its administered part of the disputed region of Kashmir, one of several Indian actions in 2019 widely perceived as directed at its Muslim citizenry. Considerably larger, both economically and demographically, India could almost certainly defeat Pakistan in a conventional war; this, in turn, gave impetus for Pakistan to develop nuclear weapons, as a presumed deterrent. Pakistan currently seems to have the world's fastest growing nuclear arsenal (the growth of North Korea's arsenal is a closely guarded secret). In response to a terrorist incursion from Pakistan in 2001, India mobilized its army, and although the crisis eventually subsided, it was evident that these Indian preparations were slow and relatively clumsy. In response, India developed a new, rapid mobilization strategy, dubbed Cold Start. And in response to this, Pakistan has been developing a new generation of smaller, more usable battlefield nuclear weapons.

Some Good News

Things aren't entirely bleak on the nuclear weapons front. In 2015, an agreement was reached between Iran and the so-called P5+1 (the permanent members of the UN Security Council plus Germany), whereby Iran agreed to significant restrictions on its nuclear program in return for a lifting of a severe UN-sanctioned economic embargo. As part of this agreement—technically known as the Joint Comprehensive Plan of Action (JCPOA)—Iran pledged to mothball 12,000 nuclear centrifuges; to ship more than 12 tons of low-enriched fuel (98 percent of that country's stockpile) out of the country; to fill the core of its giant plutonium reactor at Arak with concrete; to allow continuous, invasive inspections by the International Atomic Energy Administration (IAEA); and also to provide information to the IAEA regarding the military dimensions of its prior nuclear activities.

Most experts agree that although the JCPOA is not 100 percent foolproof, it would have prevented an Iranian nuclear weapon for at least the next 15 years. Although Iran had fully complied with its pledges and the plan was implemented, the Trump administration announced in 2019 that it had withdrawn from the JCPOA, claiming that it didn't go far enough in restraining Iranian nuclear ambitions and that the agreement's provision whereby Iran was to obtain roughly $100 billion of its own money that had been embargoed (and which critics claim might finance terrorist actions in the Middle East) is inimical to US interests. Iran responded to the unilateral US withdrawal by also going out of compliance, which, as of 2021, included pushing the fissionable uranium enrichment limits up to 20 percent. This limit had been set at 3.67 percent, substantially below weapons grade. Whereas Iran had been limited by the JCPOA to 447 pounds of uranium, as of 2021 it had stockpiled roughly 6,000 pounds. The JCPOA had permitted inspectors to investigate the entire Iranian nuclear fuel cycle, an option that was terminated when the US unilaterally withdrew.

Although both the Iranian government and the Biden administration have expressed desire to return to a version of the JCPOA, this has proven difficult because of the mutual distrust that had been generated as well as the need to synchronize and verify a return to the previous condition, with economic sanctions lifted by the US and Iran returning to compliance.

It is widely believed that the Union of South Africa had developed a small nuclear weapons capacity, which was eventually decommissioned by the majority black government. Following the breakup of the Soviet Union, three former republics—Belarus, Kazakhstan and Ukraine—voluntarily shipped to Russia the Soviet nuclear weapons that had been deployed on their soil. By the late 1990s, antinuclear peace movement activists had succeeded in making it unacceptable for politicians and strategic planners to speak lightly of precipitating a nuclear holocaust. Toward the latter years of the Reagan administration and during both Bush administrations, official pronouncements on this topic became much more circumspect, testimony to the impact of a populace that had become increasingly antinuclear because of these administrations' policies. President Obama then became the first US president to make nuclear abolitionism a centerpiece of foreign policy (at least rhetorically); in a much-touted speech in Prague in 2009, he laid out a possible road map toward a nuclear-free world.

In addition, in 2010 the Obama administration negotiated New START, a treaty that reduced the number of deployed strategic nuclear weapons to 1,550 on each side, set limits on the total number of strategic delivery systems, and provided for on-site verification. In return for Republican support in the Senate, the Obama administration agreed to support a range of new warheads and other nuclear escalations. The US nuclear "modernization" program, estimated to cost upwards of $1.4 trillion, was adopted and carried forward by the Trump administration. The New START treaty had been scheduled to expire in February 2021, and President Trump indicated that he would let it lapse, which would have left the US and Russia with no strategic nuclear restrictions; immediately following his election, however, President Biden announced that he would agree to renewing the treaty for another five years, until 2026.

From a long-range perspective, it is encouraging that compared to a high of roughly 60,000 nuclear weapons in the mid-1960s, as of 2020 the nations of the world were encumbered with "only" about 13,000. There may also be a growing antinuclear tide. In Scotland's 2015 elections and in the UK general election of 2019, for example, the Scottish National Party won overwhelmingly; its platform called for scrapping the United Kingdom's Trident nuclear submarine program, currently berthed in northern Scotland (however, the governing conservative party in the United Kingdom continued to support "modernizing" this program, including purchasing a new generation of submarines).

In addition, more than 150 countries have signed the UN Treaty on the Prohibition of Nuclear Weapons (TPNW), which makes it illegal to "develop, test, produce, manufacture, otherwise acquire, possess, or stockpile nuclear weapons or other nuclear explosive devices." It officially entered into force in January 2021, when it was ratified by the 50th UN member country. This ongoing multilateral effort to make nuclear weapons a violation of international law will obviously not be implemented immediately, but it goes a long way toward delegitimating nuclear weapons and the threat they embody. Although the nuclear states have thus far refused to sign (never mind ratify) this treaty, the inhabitants of nonnuclear countries, frustrated by the slow pace and regular backsliding of the nuclear states when it comes to denuclearization, have thus increasingly chosen to take their future in their own hands by formally delegitimizing nuclear weapons in the perhaps realistic hope that—as the saying goes—a journey of a thousand miles begins with a single step. Of additional possible relevance is Dornbusch's Law, which states that substantial change is often surprisingly slow in arriving but that once it begins, it can then be stunningly fast. (Examples include the legitimation of same-sex marriage in the US and, eventually perhaps, the delegitimation of nuclear weapons.)

What Might Be Done

Although it is beyond the scope of this book to detail all the possible ways of reducing the risk of nuclear war, a few scenarios can be outlined. Naturally, these vary in their desirability and feasibility.

1. Rely even more heavily on nuclear weapons, in the hope of increasing whatever benefits they are presumed to have provided thus far. This might include encouraging the spread of nuclear weapons to other, currently nonnuclear countries, consistent with the idea that a nuclear armed world would be one in which countries avoided antagonizing each other.

2. Continue with the status quo, hoping that catastrophe will somehow be averted—as, according to traditional deterrence theory, it has been in the past.

3. Engage in a vigorous effort at nuclear arms control via international treaties, including restrictions on bomb and warhead testing and development, on the production of plutonium and highly enriched uranium, as well as reductions in the allowable numbers of delivery vehicles.

4. Move away from the current focus on (negative) "peace" via traditional nuclear deterrence, especially as this doctrine was established during the Cold War vis-à-vis the Soviet Union. Shakespeare's play *The Winter's Tale* includes this famous stage direction, which generations of theater professionals have struggled to represent on stage: "Exit, pursued by a bear." Rethinking current nuclear strategy would require going beyond decades of assumptions about the need to devise nuclear weaponry and doctrine in response to the West and its allies, especially from the former Soviet empire, allegedly being pursued by the Russian "bear."

Russophobia is noticeably influencing (and possibly deforming) the thinking of many of today's strategic analysts and weapons procurers.

5. Engage in a vigorous policy of de-alerting, thereby granting decision makers more time before nuclear weapons can be employed. This could involve physically storing bombs and warheads separately from their delivery vehicles, imposing greater code restrictions on their arming and use, removing guidance systems from missiles, and pinning open the switches that fire missile motors. Such actions would not only diminish the likelihood of nuclear war by accident or false alarm, they would also enhance the confidence of all sides that others are unlikely to attempt a surprise attack or to "retaliate" without having been attacked.

6. Encourage the further spread of nuclear-free zones, regions within which— by treaty—(as in Latin America, much of Africa, and New Zealand) no nuclear weapons are permitted. This would require nations' willingness to subscribe to the latest in verification technology (a robust international monitoring system is already in place, capable of identifying very small nuclear tests as well as test missile launches), including submission to onsite inspection.

7. Engage in unilateral reductions in nuclear weaponry, including delivery systems. Given the excessive numbers of both—especially within the arsenals of the US and Russia—either side could afford to initiate substantial unilateral reductions without compromising its perceived national security. The likelihood is that such actions would stimulate other countries to do the same, and even if it does not, the initiator's security would not be compromised. By contrast, so long as the nuclear powers jealously guard and modernize their arsenals, other countries will likely keep theirs or plan to increase their stockpiles.

8. Establish verifiable international agreements that prohibit any cyberattacks, especially against another country's nuclear facilities, information and technology grids, and satellites.

9. Establish "no first use" as an irrevocable national commitment; also, eliminate the ability of any one person to order the use of nuclear weapons.

10. Encourage an international environment that helps delegitimize the development and deployment of nuclear weapons. Although this approach would not be sufficient in itself, and may appear to rely on wishful thinking, it is based on the power of comparable historical developments. Thus, it is inconceivable that France and the United Kingdom would now attack each other, even though they have a long history of violent competition. Various "soft power" connections (economic, social, cultural, diplomatic, and political ties) between the two countries have made war between them unimaginable. Similarly, the likelihood is quite low that biological weapons will deliberately be used by great powers against each other in the immediate future, largely because social and cultural norms—along with international treaty— have delegitimized their employment. By the same token, it is altogether possible that vigorous worldwide public efforts to label nuclear weapons "uncivilized," "unacceptable," and "illegal" could have the practical effect of literally making their deliberate use inconceivable by any civilized society, thereby making their development, deployment, and— most important—their use extremely unlikely.

A Final Note on Nuclear Weapons

There is an ancient Chinese proverb: "Unless we change direction, we shall end up where we are headed." The proliferation of nuclear weapons and of other WMDs—both vertically and horizontally—poses, along with global warming, the most serious threat to human beings and to the planet. It is our planet, our lives, and we have the right, even the duty, to aim high. Given the extraordinary dangers of nuclear war, mere prevention—from day to day, year to year—is not sufficient. Any satisfactory solution to the nuclear dilemma must be political and ethical, not just technological. But at the same time, peace in the nuclear age demands the elimination of the nuclear threat itself. In the long run, nothing less will do.

"We are not condemned to repeat the lessons of 40 years at the nuclear brink," said General Lee Butler, former commander of the US Strategic Air Command, in a speech at the State of the World Forum, in San Francisco, in 1996. "We can do better than condone a world in which nuclear weapons are enshrined as the ultimate arbiter of conflict. The price already paid is too dear, the risks run too great. The nuclear beast must be chained, its soul expunged, its lair laid waste. The task is daunting but we cannot shrink from it. The opportunity may not come again."

Questions for Further Reflection

1. What are the justifications for the development, possession, and deployment of nuclear weapons? How do you evaluate them?

2. What are the rationales for the reduction and elimination of nuclear arsenals? How do you assess them?

3. What encourages nuclear proliferation? Is it inevitable? Is it desirable?

4. Unlike global climate change, whose destructive consequences are now visible and thus easily identified, global nuclear war has not happened. What are the implications of this difference when it comes to the dangers they both pose as well as the issues associated with resisting them?

5. Were the atomic bombings of Hiroshima and Nagasaki justified? Is there any circumstance today that would justify the use of nuclear weapons?

Suggestions for Further Reading

David P. Barash. 2020. *Threats: Intimidation and Its Discontents*. New York: Oxford University Press.

Michael E. Brown, Owen R. Coté, Jr., Sean M. Lynn-Jones, and Steven E. Miller, eds. 2010. *Going Nuclear: Nuclear Proliferation and International Security in the 21st Century*. Cambridge, MA: MIT Press.

Daniel Ellsberg. 2018. *The Doomsday Machine: Confessions of a Nuclear War Planner*. New York: Bloomsbury.

Fred Kaplan. 2020. *The Bomb: Presidents, Generals and the Secret History of Nuclear War*. New York: Simon & Schuster.

William J. Perry and Tom Collins. 2020. *The Button: The New Nuclear Arms Race and Presidential Power from Truman to Trump*. Dallas, TX: Ben Bella Books.

Jonathan Schell. 2000. *The Fate of the Earth and the Abolition*. Stanford, CA: Stanford University Press.

Eric Schlosser. 2013. *Command and Control: Nuclear Weapons, the Damascus Incident, and the Illusion of Safety*. New York: Penguin.

Notes

1. Quoted in L. Groves. 1962. *Now It Can Be Told*. New York: Harper & Row.

2. Frank Chinnock. 1969. *Nagasaki: The Forgotten Bomb*. New York: World.

3. From John Hersey. 1946. *Hiroshima*. New York: Modern Library.

4. From M. Hachiya. 1955. *Hiroshima Diary*. Chapel Hill: University of North Carolina Press.

5. From a speech delivered by Lord Mountbatten in Strasbourg, France, 1979.

6. Ira Helfand. 2013. *Nuclear Famine: Two Billion People at Risk? Global Impacts of Limited Nuclear War on Agriculture, Food Supplies, and Human Nutrition*, 2nd ed.

http://www. ippnw.org/pdf/nuclear-famine-two-billion-at-risk-2013.pdf.

7. Henry Kissinger. 1957. *Nuclear Weapons and Foreign Policy*. New York: Norton.

8. Quoted in Robert Scheer. 1982. *With Enough Shovels*. New York: Random House.

9. Bernard Brodie. 1946. *The Absolute Weapon*. New York: Harcourt Brace Jovanovich.

10. Robert McNamara. 1968. *The Essence of Security*. New York: Harper & Row.

11. Robert McNamara. 1986. *Blundering Into Disaster: Surviving the First Century of the Nuclear Age*. New York: Pantheon.

The Causes
of Wars

In Part I, we presented an overview of peace and war. The absence of war is a necessary but not a sufficient condition for the realization of peace. It is insufficient because a life without war can nonetheless also be lacking in peace. But at the same time, the prevention of war is necessary if any meaningful peace is ever to be achieved. Enduring peace simply cannot coexist with war. And so our hopes for peace, and our work toward it, must take account of war; in particular, we must turn to the reasons for wars, if our suggestions, means, and goals are to enjoy any realistic prospect of success. Accordingly, we now turn to the causes of wars.

For too long, students of peace—in their eagerness to embrace a new and more peaceful world—have abandoned the understanding of war and other forms of violent human conflict to their "hardheaded," "realistic" colleagues in the more traditional academic disciplines of political science, security studies, and international relations. As a result of this division of responsibility, while centers for strategic studies and the like engage in the planning and legitimation of war and other acts of government-initiated violence, many people in peace and conflict studies and in peace movements spend much time trying to conceptualize peace while avoiding the very real problems of war and violence. In doing so, they run the risk of becoming increasingly marginalized, not only in academic circles but also with respect to their potential influence in the real world. This is not to propose that peace and conflict studies students and teachers should become handmaidens of the academic war establishment, whether cold or hot; rather, they should get to know their "enemy." And that enemy, more than anything else, is violence and war.

"War" does not exist; there are, rather, individual wars. Nonetheless, just as we can make useful generalizations about the human species, we can do the same about the "species" of violent human conflict known as war. In doing so, it is helpful to distinguish between the *actual* causes, often *underlying* reasons, of a particular war and the *ostensible* reasons (or pretexts) for each one. The former refer to the underlying factors that give rise to any given war; the latter refer to the propagandistic excuses frequently given by governments to justify them.

We are primarily concerned in Part II of this text with the causes of wars. Then in Part III, we assess various suggestions for preventing war. Both tasks are daunting. Indeed, trying to specify the reasons for war generally—that is, the motives that led decision makers to make war or even just the causes of any one war—is a bit like the story of the blind men and the elephant by the 19th-century American John Saxe:

> It was six men from Industan, to learning much inclined,
>
> Who went to see the elephant (though all of them were blind)
>
> That each by observation might satisfy his mind. . . .
>
> Each felt a different part, so the one touching the legs thought they were tree trunks, the one touching the tail thought it was a snake, and so on.
>
> And so, at the end, they disputed loud and long,
>
> Each in his opinion stiff and strong,
>
> Though each was partly in the right, and all of them were wrong.[1]

In reviewing the various proposed causes of wars, we shall proceed from the most reductionistic interpretations to the most inclusive. Thus, we begin by examining the personal level, moving through a consideration of wars among small groups of preindustrial and nontechnological peoples to the functioning of large, advanced social units and nation-states. Then we examine decision making by national leaders, assess the role of social and economic factors, and finally summarize what we have reviewed. Although we shall necessarily consider these explanations one at a time, let us try to avoid the blind men's blunder by recognizing at the outset that war, like an elephant, is a complex and integrated phenomenon, which to be understood must be taken in its entirety and with a hefty dose of humility.

Consider, for example, that someone has just died. We might ask, "What was the cause of death?" And perhaps we are told, "He or she died of disease." "What kind of disease?" "Heart disease." "What was the nature of the heart disease?" "Hardening of the arteries leading to a massive stroke—that is, a coronary thrombosis." And if we then inquire, "What was the cause of that?" we are likely to get any number of answers: poor dietary habits, a genetic predisposition to high cholesterol levels, a lack of regular medical care, too much stress, a history of heavy smoking, not enough exercise, and so forth. One of these might be the precipitating factor, but it is most likely that several of them, taken in combination, were ultimately responsible. The social, psychological, and historical reasons for wars can be at least as complex as the physical causes of one person's death.

We should also keep in mind the logical distinction between necessary and sufficient conditions. Thus, for war to occur, it may be necessary for human beings to exist in such forms of collective organization as tribes, nations, and societies, but it certainly is not sufficient—there are human societies that have apparently never known war. Similarly, it may be necessary for individuals to be motivated to participate in the preparations and conduct of war, but once again, this is not sufficient—people often get angry, but this does not necessarily mean that their country goes to war as a result. Moreover, wars often occur without very much personal anger being involved.

Virtually every scholar of peace and war, it appears, has a different framework for understanding the causes of organized human violence. The historian Quincy Wright, for example, identified four major factors—idealistic, psychological, political, and legalistic—arguing that individuals and masses have been moved to war (1) because of enthusiasm for ideals expressed in the impersonal symbols of a religion, a nation, an empire, a civilization, or humanity, the blessings of which it is thought may be secured or spread by coercion of the recalcitrant [idealistic]; or (2) because of the hope to escape from conditions which they find unsatisfactory, inconvenient, perplexing, unprofitable, intolerable, dangerous, or merely boring [psychological]. Conditions of this kind have produced unrest and have facilitated the acceptance of ideals and violent methods for achieving them. Governments and organized factions have initiated war (3) because in a particular situation war appeared to them a necessary or convenient means to carry out a foreign policy, to establish, maintain, or expand the power of a government, party, or class within the state; to maintain or expand the power of the state in relation to other states; or to reorganize the community of nations [political]; or (4) because incidents have occurred or circumstances have arisen which they thought violated law and impaired rights and for which war was the normal or expected remedy according to the jural standards of the time [legalistic].[2]

To this, we would add error, misunderstanding, and misperceptions. Although there is disagreement over the most useful way to categorize the causes of wars, there is consensus that every war—just like every human being—must have progenitors. Efforts at identifying warmongering culprits, as individuals rather than impersonal forces, have been especially frequent in the aftermath of every major war. One scholar described the chronology of such culprit hunting as follows:

In the eighteenth century many philosophers thought that the ambitions of absolute monarchs were the main cause of war: pull down the mighty, and wars would become rare. Another theory contended that many wars came from the Anglo-French rivalry for colonies and commerce: restrain that quest, and peace would be more easily preserved. The wars following the French Revolution fostered an idea that popular revolutions were becoming the main cause of international war. In the nineteenth century, monarchs who sought to unite their troubled country by a glorious foreign war were widely seen as culprits. At the end of that century the capitalists' chase for markets or investment outlets became a popular villain. The First World War convinced many writers that armaments races and arms salesmen had become the villains, and both world wars fostered the idea that militarist regimes were the main disturbers of the peace.[3]

Similarly, the Vietnam War—to take just one example—was said to have been caused by

the desire of American capitalists for markets and investment outlets, by the pressures for markets and investment outlets, by the pressures of American military suppliers, by the American hostility to communism, by the crusading ambitions of Moscow and Peking, the aggressive nationalism or communism of Hanoi, the corruption or aggression of Saigon, or the headlong clash of other aims.[4]

Clearly, a host of different causes can be identified for the Vietnam War— or any other—many of which might be operating simultaneously, some of which may involve individuals, while others involve more frustrating and faceless considerations. In their yearning for truth, however, many people are dissatisfied with complex, multifactorial explanations. For example, it is tempting to say that the country that initiates a war is the one that "started" it and, therefore, the one that "caused" it—that is, the culprit. But the real world is rarely this simple.

When the United States "started" the War of 1812 with Britain, it was at least partly in response to the impressment of American sailors by British naval forces. (It was also in part because of US imperialistic designs on British Canada.) And although nearly everyone considers that Nazi Germany initiated the European part of World War II, the fact remains that Britain and France first declared war on Germany, not the other way around . . . but only after Germany invaded Poland in 1939.

Wars, in short, often occur as a result of preexisting antagonisms that lead to provocations so that the underlying reasons for a war may lie further back in time. And of course, those provocations are themselves the result of yet earlier factors. The German invasion of Poland, for example, was itself "caused" or at least, facilitated, by Britain and France's earlier appeasement of Hitler, which convinced the German leader that aggression against Poland would go unpunished. Meanwhile, Hitler's aggressive and expansionist policies were also "caused," at least in part, not only by his own personal idiosyncrasies but also by German anger over the terms of the Treaty of Versailles, which ended World War I. And so it has gone.

The dominant Western conception of causality requires that for every effect there must be a preexisting cause. It also suggests that this cause should be clear-cut, direct, and linear. But even if we grant the ultimate legitimacy of cause and effect, there is no reason why causation—especially for something so complicated as war—should not be diffuse, indirect, curvilinear, and multifaceted. In short, war is, to borrow a psychoanalytic term, *overdetermined*: it has multiple reasons for its existence, both as a general phenomenon and in each specific case.

This is not to claim that efforts to answer the question "Why war?" are a waste of time, even though the results can sometimes be confusing, even misleading. Out of that search can come a deeper appreciation of the devastating conundrum that is war. Moreover, our judgment as to the reasons for war will have great influence on our preferred methods for preventing specific ones and our prospects for eliminating war altogether.

6

The Individual Level

Wars require the organized activity of large numbers of people. But even the facts of complex organization and massive numbers do not eliminate the personal involvement and responsibility of individuals. To some degree, individual people acquiesce to war, prepare for it, and often participate in it, either passively (by permitting it to occur) or actively (by providing material assistance or actually doing the fighting). If individuals didn't allow, encourage, or engage in them, wars wouldn't happen. As a popular bumper sticker has it, "What if they had a war and nobody came?" Hence, without denying the importance of other dimensions—which we shall explore in subsequent chapters—our search for the causes of war will commence by looking to the inclinations and behavior of individual people.

iStock.com/ipopba

The Individual Level

Wars require the organized activity of large numbers of people. But even the facts of complex organization and massive numbers do not eliminate the personal involvement and responsibility of individuals. To some degree, individual people acquiesce to war, prepare for it, and often participate in it, either passively (by permitting it to occur) or actively (by providing material assistance or actually doing the fighting). If individuals didn't allow, encourage, or engage in them, wars wouldn't happen. As a popular bumper sticker has it, "What if they had a war and nobody came?" Hence, without denying the importance of other dimensions—which we shall explore in subsequent chapters—our search for the causes of war will commence by looking to the inclinations and behavior of individual people.

The preamble to the constitution of the United Nations Educational, Scientific and Cultural Organization (UNESCO) states that "wars begin in the minds of men" (and, we must add, women, although possibly to a somewhat lesser extent). It takes no great stretch of imagination to charge the human psyche with prime responsibility for the initiation of war. Former senator J. William Fulbright emphasized the personal dimension of war making—and, thus, war preventing—when he wrote,

> The first, indispensable step toward the realization of a new concept of community in the world is the acquisition of a new dimension of self-understanding. We have got to understand . . . why it is, psychologically and biologically, that men and nations fight; why it is . . . that they always find *something* to fight about.[5]

When we concern ourselves with peace and war, we normally talk about the actions of large social units, often entire countries. But just as "a pot of water boils" means that individual molecules in the pot reach a certain temperature, when we say that a social unit "acts" in a particular way, what we really mean is that individuals within that unit act in such a manner.

First, we shall focus on the level of the individual person: instinct theory, sociobiology and evolutionary psychology, a brief overview of some relevant points made in Freudian and post-Freudian theory, and the idea of innate human depravity. These perspectives, while differing in significant ways, share an emphasis on the role of inborn, biological factors. Then, after considering some criticisms of these "human nature" approaches, we consider a variety of other factors believed to operate at the individual level, but which involve greater attention to social influences.

Aggression, Drives, and Instincts

Many thinkers have assumed that human beings are instinctively aggressive and violent, traits presumed to be human instincts. Thus, Hans Morgenthau's extremely influential textbook on international relations begins as follows: "The drives to live, to propagate, and to dominate are common to all men."[6]

Accordingly, human warfare might be traced to our biological heritage, attributable directly to genetic, hormonal, neurobiological, and/or evolutionary mechanisms, including a tendency to form dominance hierarchies, to defend territories, and to behave aggressively toward others. From this perspective, much emphasis is placed on the existence of comparable behavior patterns among certain animals and the presumption that the behavior of animals reflects underlying principles that hold for the human species as well.

The Lorenzian Approach

Perhaps the most influential exponent of this perspective was the Nobel Prize–winning Austrian animal behaviorist Konrad Lorenz. Lorenz helped conceptualize a view of instinctive behavior according to which animals are endowed with certain behaviors, called "fixed action patterns," whose physical performance is genetically fixed and unvarying from one individual to another. In his book *On Aggression,* Lorenz argued that certain "species preserving" aspects of aggression applied to human beings as well. They include the following:

1. Providing an opportunity for competition within a species, after which the most fit will emerge to produce the next generation

2. Achieving spacing and population control, to minimize the disadvantages of overpopulation

3. Establishing a means whereby the pair bond can be strengthened, as by shared aggression of a mated pair against competitors

Lorenz was not concerned with extolling human aggression but with understanding it. He noted that, in moderate amounts, aggression may well be functional and healthy, but, at the same time, he deplored its occurrence in excess, especially when combined with what he called "militant enthusiasm," the tendency of people to lose their normal inhibitions against violence when united with others similarly motivated.

Lorenz also emphasized that animals, such as wolves and hawks, that have lethal natural weapons also tend to possess innate inhibitions against employing such weapons against members of the same species. By contrast, animals such as rabbits, doves, and human beings—not naturally equipped with lethal weapons—lack such inhibitions. According to this line of thought, the human condition is especially perilous because although we have developed the ability, by technological means, to kill our fellow humans quickly, easily, and in great numbers, our biological evolution remains far behind our technological progress, and so we lack genetically based mechanisms to keep our newfound lethality in check.

The Lorenzian approach, which tends to "extrapolate war from human instinct," is in some ways a caricature of biological (ethological) views. According to what might be called the classical ethological approach, aggression is genetically controlled behavior, such that the actual behavior patterns are rigidly stereotyped, invariant, and independent of learning. From this perspective, aggression can also emerge spontaneously; that is, individuals have a need to discharge this drive by behaving aggressively.

Lorenz suggests that one way to deal with our instinctive penchant for aggression and militant enthusiasm is by rechanneling this biological energy in socially useful (or, at least, nondestructive) forms of competition, such as athletics, the exploration of space, or medical research. Nonetheless, Lorenz is led to a pessimistic assessment of the human future:

> An unprejudiced observer from another planet, looking down on man as he is today, in his hand the atom bomb, the product of his intelligence, in his heart the aggressive drive inherited from his anthropoid ancestors, which this same intelligence cannot control, would not prophesy long life for the species.[7]

Is War in Our Genes?

Although biology may well provide valuable insights into much animal and some human behavior, simplistic extrapolations from animal to human can be dangerously misleading. For example, it is no more valid to argue that human beings are naturally murderous because baboons sometimes kill other baboons than it is to conclude that human beings are naturally vegetarians because gorillas exclusively eat plants or that humans can fly because birds have wings.

There is a danger that by accepting war as part of "human nature," one thereby justifies war itself, in part by diminishing the human responsibility to behave more peacefully. If war is "in our genes," presumably we cannot act otherwise, so we should not be blamed for what we do; maybe, then, we shouldn't even bother trying to do anything about our warlike inclinations. At minimum—and perhaps, at its most pernicious—such biological fatalism supports a pessimistic perspective on the human condition, one that provides an excuse for the maintenance of large military forces and leads to profound and possibly lethal distrust of others. There is, indeed, evidence that people who are generally promilitary tend to be disproportionate believers in the doctrine that war is somehow etched in our DNA, whereupon it risks becoming a self-fulfilling prophecy.

To address (and scientifically refute) biological determinism, a group of prominent behavioral scientists from 12 nations met in 1986 in Seville, Spain, and agreed on the "Seville Statement." The document provides scientific information contradicting the myth that the human capacity for aggression makes war and violence inevitable and identifies sociocultural factors as the main causes of violence. Most importantly, it also highlights the role of education in preventing, diminishing, and eliminating violence. The document was also endorsed by a number of well-known significant scientific organizations, including the American Psychological Association, the American Anthropological Association, the American Sociological Association, and other scholarly organizations. Some excerpts from this statement are as follows:

- It is scientifically incorrect to say that we have inherited a tendency to make war from our animal ancestors. Warfare is a peculiarly human phenomenon and does not occur in other animals.

- It is scientifically incorrect to say that war or any other violent behavior is genetically programmed into our human nature.

- It is scientifically incorrect to say that in the course of human evolution there has been a selection for aggressive behavior more than for other kinds of behavior.

- It is scientifically incorrect to say that humans have a "violent brain." While we do have a neural apparatus to act violently, there is nothing in our neurophysiology that compels us to.

- It is scientifically incorrect to say that war is caused by "instinct" or any single motivation. The technology of modern war has exaggerated traits associated with violence both in the training of actual combatants and in the preparation of support for war in the general population.

- We conclude that biology does not condemn humanity to war, and that humanity can be freed from the bondage of biological pessimism. . . . The same species . . . [that] invented war is capable of inventing peace.

Approximately a quarter century after the original "Seville Statement," in September 2011, an international conference on violence was held in Rome. The conference was held to more effectively analyze the complex relationships among brain, aggression, and society. Participants concluded that the fundamental thesis enunciated in the original Seville Statement—that human violence is not inevitable because it is not biologically determined but is basically related to sociocultural factors—while still valid, needs to be further evaluated in the light of recent research findings.

Sociobiology and Evolutionary Psychology

A more sophisticated version of instinctivism is associated with sociobiology, whose best-known practitioner is Edward O. Wilson. The mainstream sociobiological approach, which in the 1990s was somewhat superseded by an even more recent discipline known as evolutionary psychology, differs from instinctivism in that it emphasizes evolution as a process rather than a historical event. (Evolutionary psychology is essentially sociobiology applied to human beings.) Both sociobiologists and evolutionary psychologists are particularly concerned with the adaptive significance of behavior, that is, how particular behavior patterns are maintained and promoted because they contribute to the reproductive success of individuals (not species) who possess these traits.

A sociobiological or evolutionary psychological view of human war examines such phenomena as ecological competition (for food, nesting sites, etc.), male-male competition (for dominance in the pecking order and for mates), and the role of kinship patterns in directing aggressive behavior in particular ways. Among many species, for example, males tend to be larger, showier, and more aggressive than females. In addition, biological differences between males and females mean, among other things, that one male can successfully fertilize many females. Sexual differences of this sort, in turn, convey a reproductive payoff (enhanced evolutionary fitness) to individuals, especially males, who succeed in defeating their rivals, whether in symbolic display or outright combat.

Consistent with this theory is the finding that men tend to be more aggressive than women and also that men are more likely to be involved in violence of all sorts, including war. Another important tenet of sociobiological theory is the role of genetic relatedness: Individuals who share genes probably will behave benevolently (altruistically) toward each other because such behavior tends to contribute to the success of genes predisposing toward such behavior; conversely, a low probability of genetic relatedness is likely to be associated with aggressiveness. Therefore, appeals to patriotism often involve what anthropologists call fictive kinship, calling on citizens to stand up for the motherland, fatherland, Uncle Sam, "brothers and sisters," and so forth.

Competition has been defined by Wilson as "the active demand by two or more individuals . . . for a common resource or requirement that is actually or potentially limiting."[8] Many studies have pointed to the role of primitive war in gaining access to mates, animal protein, and social prestige, such that warfare among preindustrial or nontechnological peoples, which in the past appeared to be irrational and nonadaptive, is now increasingly seen to possess an internal logic of its own—although not necessarily a logic that is consciously understood by the participants. Nor does this imply that war itself is innate, although a capacity for personal aggressiveness evidently is.

Both Nature and Nurture

It is misleading to ask whether a given behavior is either instinctive or learned because all behavior results from the interaction of genetic potential with experience; in other words, both nature and nurture are involved. "We are now sophisticated enough to know," writes Edward O. Wilson, "that the capacity to learn certain behaviors is itself a genetically controlled and there-fore evolved trait."[9]

Finally, another important evolutionary perspective considers war to have had a prominent role in the early evolution of the human species. Conceivably, proto-human warrior bands were a major selective force in our own early evolution, with successful groups killing off those that were less successful. Large brains could well have contributed to success in violent intergroup conflict by promoting relatively sophisticated communication, formation of social alliances, and effective use of weapons. Those experienc-ing such outcomes would presumably have left more descendants, who in turn were likely to possess these favored traits and capacities. According to this hypothesis, war helped select for our large brains.

Freudian and Post-Freudian Psychoanalytic Perspectives

Sigmund Freud was the founder of psychoanalysis, a branch of psychiatry and clinical psychology. He is particularly noteworthy for emphasizing the role of the unconscious in human behavior. Freud himself was a pacifist, and he deplored what he saw as a vicious, lethal streak among human beings.

To Freud, human history is in large part a history of violence, with people having exchanged "numerous, and indeed unending, minor wars, for wars on a grand scale that are rare but all the more destructive." In his later work, he attributed much of humanity's more "inhumane" behavior to the opera-tion of *Thanatos,* or the death instinct, which he saw as opposed to *Eros,* the life (or erotic) instinct, which, he claimed, "encourages the growth of emo-tional ties between men [and] must operate against war." In a famous letter to Albert Einstein, Freud noted, "We are led to conclude that this [death] instinct functions in every living being, striving to work its ruin and to reduce life to its primal state of inert matter."[10] When Thanatos is thwarted by Eros, in this view, its energy is displaced outward onto subjects other than oneself, resulting in aggression between individuals or among groups.

The Freudian formulation of a death instinct has virtually no sup-port among contemporary biologists and social scientists, in part because any genetically mediated tendency for self-destruction would be strongly selected against and would therefore disappear over evolutionary time. Moreover, social anthropologists have failed to find Thanatos in any human culture. Even some prominent psychoanalysts, notably Wilhelm Reich, as well as adherents of the more recent "critical psychology" movement have also rejected the notion of a death drive, arguing that social aggression and human destructiveness, especially in the past century or so, have been largely catalyzed by inequitable power relations and competition between classes and nation-states under modern capitalism.

A more plausible Freudian notion, expressed in Freud's late book *Civili-zation and Its Discontents,* is that if we are aggressive (not necessarily death-seeking) by nature, civilization demands that people repress such primitive and destructive tendencies if they are to live together successfully. This idea has enjoyed significantly more support than Freud's idea of the death drive. Parents must provide discipline for their children, society must restrict its citizens, and, ultimately, according to both Freud and Einstein, some form of supranational authority, like a fully-empowered United Nations, is neces-sary to enforce a system of world government over individual states, which would otherwise function anarchically.

Another Freudian concept relevant to understanding war is that of narcissistic injury. Narcissism involves infatuation with one's self and, in moderation, is considered a normal stage in personality development. But when the individual associates himself or herself with a larger group, especially the nation-state, slights or injuries to the group are easy to perceive as injuries to one's self. The resulting "narcissistic rage" may involve an unrelenting compulsion to undo the hurt; in the pursuit of this vengeful "justice," great violence may be employed. This phenomenon is also, of course, associated with prominent politicians and other leaders who, upon feeling threatened by a real or actual loss of power and status, may behave in a belligerent and paranoid manner, potentially leading to the instigation of collective violence, as seen in the Trump-inspired attack on the US capitol in early January, 2021.

Many of the most destructive wars in the 20th century were perpetrated by people seeking to retake territory that had been wrested from them by others: for example, the French yearning to recapture the provinces of Alsace and Lorraine from Germany—lost during the Franco-Prussian War—which was a major reason for World War I; and the Viet Cong and North Vietnamese, who sought during the Vietnam War to reunite their country. Other wars have been instigated by ethnic groups seeking to secede from a central governmental authority, only to precipitate intervention by armed forces from the nation-state from which they hoped to disconnect (as in Nigeria, Ethiopia, Indonesia, the former Yugoslavia, Sudan, Turkey, and Ukraine/Russia).

Like the Lorenzian—and to a lesser extent, evolutionary—approach, the orthodox Freudian perspective tends to be pessimistic about the prospects for ameliorating war, much less eliminating it. Thus, Freud maintained, for example, that we really shouldn't be surprised by atrocities during wartime because the notion that humankind is fundamentally civilized is itself illusory.

Some other psychoanalytically oriented observers of human behavior, including the "object-relations" theorists Melanie Klein and Donald Winnicott, concluded that much human misery, including to some degree even the penchant for war itself, derive in part from the consequences of being mistreated as children. Klein speculated that aggression is innate and is exacerbated by poor mother/infant bonding. Winnicott claimed that with "good enough mothering," an infant's proclivities toward aggression could be mollified and that a nurturing environment can lessen the risk of infants and children later engaging in destructive behaviors. Virtually all child psychologists concur that no acts of violence toward children—whether overt, such as beating or sexual abuse, or more subtle behaviors such as severe criticism and belittling—can be justified, even by the mistaken belief that human beings are inherently sinful and depraved. Although Winnicott himself analyzed the effects of World War II on British children and found that such effects vary and depend on children's ages, characters, and the impact of war news on them, it still remains to be determined if such clinical theories might be applicable to understanding the causes of war in general.

It remains to be determined whether and how these theories might be applicable to understanding the causes of war.

Innate Depravity?

Some important theorists have maintained that human beings are innately depraved, nasty, and evil, basing this claim on a loosely argued blend of biology, moral outrage, and, on occasion, theology. Looking over the bloodletting of the English Civil War (1642–1649), the philosopher

Thomas Hobbes concluded that there was "a general inclination of all mankind, a perpetual and restless desire for power after power that ceaseth only in death."[11] To some extent, Hobbes's pessimism can be traced to a biblical—especially a conservative Christian—tradition that sees human nature as inherently flawed.[12] According to this view, humans are suffused with original sin and deemed inherently incapable of becoming good. Consider these remarks by the 16th-century theologian John Calvin, perhaps the most influential advocate of this perspective: "Even infants themselves, as they bring their condemnation into the world with them, are rendered subject to punishment of their own sinfulness. . . . For though they have not yet produced the fruits of their iniquity, yet they have the seed of it in them."[13]

In Calvinist theology, because of our allegedly innate human sinfulness, we were cast out of the Garden of Eden, doomed to death. We therefore deserve—indeed, we require—to be treated sternly and punished vigorously. In any event, according to this pessimistic Christian view, a true state of personal peace can be achieved only by grace, just as a state of political peace requires the Second Coming of Christ. And until then, war is inevitable.

This attitude is not limited to conservative Christians, however. Another approach, rarely articulated, emphasizes that human beings have not only a capacity for violence but also a deep-seated love of bloodletting, hatred, and destruction. In the 17th century, John Milton wrote,

> even if our species were rendered somehow impervious to injury from all outside forces, yet the perverseness of our folly is so bent, that we should never cease hammering out of our own hearts, as it were out of a flint, the seeds and sparkles of new misery to ourselves, till all were in a blaze again.[14]

From this perspective, war is an evil unique to humanity. The influential 20th-century theologian Reinhold Niebuhr argued that it was the "sinful character of man" that necessitated "the balancing of power with power."[15] The philosophers Spinoza and Kant located human violence in the fact that our rational faculties are regularly overwhelmed by our irrational and untamed emotions.

This is only a very limited sampling of influential thinkers who have supported the widespread notion of our alleged depravity. Although it is impossible to verify, the idea of innate human sinfulness and iniquity remains popular, especially among the lay public. It has also been particularly influential among those who are sympathetic to the deployment of military force, if not to war itself. Thus, if human nature is inherently violent and warlike, we can have little confidence in ethics, law, or human rationality to deliver us from war because these are only frail, artificial institutions intended to paper over our fundamental flaws. Accordingly, from this perspective, because human nature presumably cannot be changed, the best way to safeguard personal or national security is by recourse to arms.

Rational War-Making?

Although war typically arouses great passions, it is not always true that it results from such passions. In some cases, wars appear to have been chosen by intelligent, instrumentally rational individuals, after carefully calculating the costs and benefits of alternative courses of action. According to military historian Michael Howard,

In general, men have fought during the past two hundred years neither because they are aggressive nor because they are acquisitive animals, but because they are reasoning ones: because they discern, or believe they can discern, dangers before they become immediate, the possibility of threats before they are made.[16]

Humans also fight when they can perceive—whether accurately or not—that they will gain substantially by doing so. One influential view, then, is that, rather than a result of instinctive "human nature," war (and not just the weapons employed) can be the consequence of our coolest, most cerebral faculties. Moreover, successful wars require elaborate and careful planning, plus, ironically, a high level of coordination and cooperation—at least among those on each side.

Individuals may fight with passion when placed in warlike situations, but throughout history, authorities have often had to force their supposedly vicious, hotheaded, and war-loving, but often in fact fearful and reluctant, citizens to fight at all. Traditionally, many soldiers have been goaded into battle with guns at their backs, hating and fearing their officers and military discipline more than the "enemy."

Criticisms of Human Nature Theories

The various human nature theories about the reasons for human violence all contain flaws. For example, human beings undoubtedly have the biological capacity to kill one another—demonstrated by the fact that they have often done so! The danger is that such a broad generalization may be useless in analyzing the past or predicting the future. Other, more specific problems in these theories exist as well. For example, consider the following:

1. Although war is a widespread human trait, it is not a universal one; certain cultures, such as the South African Bushmen (or San), the Semai (in Southeast Asia), and the Inuit (in northern North America), apparently never engaged in war, although interpersonal violence is not unknown. Yet the assumption that war derives irrevocably from human nature should apply to these peoples no less than to others. Although some societies are clearly more war-prone than others, there is also no evidence that such differences reflect inherent differences in human nature.

2. Even among war-prone cultures, there have been many years of peace. If human nature caused World War II or the Vietnam War, what about the peace that preceded and followed these wars? If human nature causes war, it must also cause peace—the neutrality of Sweden, the demilitarized U.S.-Canadian border, Gandhi's nonviolence, Costa Rica's abolition of its entire military, and so on.

3. Even within war-prone cultures, there have been war resisters, peace advocates, and such longtime nonviolent traditions as the Mennonites and the Quakers; are they less "human" or less "natural" than their more violent fellow citizens?

4. The fact that animals behave in certain ways does not necessarily mean that human beings do so; we have the capacity for complex, abstract, and symbolic thought, which gives us the opportunity to reason, to analyze, and to rise above our unpleasant or dangerous inclinations.

On the other hand, given that human beings are "rational animals" in Aristotle's terms, it is reasonable to assume that certain basic behavioral patterns found in other species apply to our own species too.

5. If war is a result of a fixed human nature, it seems predestined and unavoidable because, by definition, we cannot behave counter to our own nature (although we can struggle against and master most of our natural predispositions and inclinations). There is a special danger in the belief that war is inevitable because it is likely to discourage people from seeking to end war and to promote peace. Moreover, it can also serve to justify war by making it appear somehow good because it is natural. The noted astrophysicist Carl Sagan pointed out that extraordinary claims require extraordinary evidence. Similarly, claims with potentially dangerous social implications require especially persuasive evidence— and although there is no question that people are capable of great violence under certain predictable circumstances, there is no persuasive evidence that we harbor anything resembling a "war instinct."

The above criticisms oversimplify the more sophisticated human nature arguments. Most biologically inclined theorists recognize that genetic factors do not irrevocably commit a person, or a society, to a given course of action. Rather, they create predispositions for periodically aggressive or violent behavior. Similarly, nothing in sociobiological or evolutionary psychological theory suggests that such predispositions could not be overridden by religious beliefs, historical circumstances, ethical constraints, collective social action, and so on.

There is a great difference between a possible genetic influence on war-proneness and the doctrine of genetic determinism. The former denotes tendencies, or predispositions, that are likely to be subtle and capable of being overridden, whereas the latter refers to rigid, ironclad automatic responses. There may well be genetic and neurobiological influences that human beings, if they are to be more peaceful, must overcome or sublimate. But this is not to say that our genes, neurons, and/or hormones predetermine our behavior and condemn us to violence, much less to war.

Regarding ethics, advocates—and critics—of biologically based arguments should be wary of what the philosopher David Hume first identified and what was later labeled by the 20th-century British philosopher G. E. Moore as the naturalistic fallacy—the mistaken belief that "*is* implies *ought*." In other words, whatever descriptive claims that evolutionary theory, neuroscience, or a reductionist Freudian perspective might provide regarding natural tendencies (the "is") are distinct from prescriptive, ethical guidance as to what is right and good (the "ought"). Typhoid is natural; this does not mean that it is good. War may or may not be "natural" (although this book's authors think otherwise!). Whether war is "good," however, is a different matter. In any event, if typhoid, or war, is to be prevented or cured, we must understand its causation, whether or not we are pleased by what we find.

Social Learning Theories

Thinkers since Aristotle have debated the primary causes of human behavior, often dividing them into "nature" (biology) versus "nurture" (experience). Having just reviewed some of the main theories involving human nature, we now turn to the dominant competing paradigm: a variety of hypotheses involving the role of experience and the environment—in short, "nurture," which typically focus on social learning as well as cultural traditions and expectations.

Frustration-Aggression

Among explanations for war that do not depend on explicit assumptions about human nature, one of the most influential has been the frustration-aggression hypothesis, which was developed to explain individual aggressiveness. According to this theory, first proposed in 1939 by John Dollard and Neal Miller, aggressiveness is produced by frustration, which in turn is defined as "an interference with the occurrence of an instigated goal-response at its proper time in the behavior sequence."[17] Thus, if a hungry rat is presented with food, after which a glass wall is interposed between the animal and the object of its desire, the rat is likely to become aggressive.

A similar thing happens with people who have been seeking something unsuccessfully—food, political freedoms, access to a disputed territory, union with others who practice the same customs—or who have obtained partial success only to be prevented from achieving their ultimate goals. When circumstances prevent people from achieving their goals, individuals are likely to respond aggressively. This theory attempts to explain why people create scapegoats; when the source of the frustration cannot be challenged, the aggression gets displaced onto an innocent target.

In its initial formulation, frustration theory was presented rather dogmatically. "The occurrence of aggressive behavior always presupposes the existence of frustration, and contrariwise, the existence of frustration always leads to some form of aggression."[18] This rigidity led to problems comparable to those encountered with some human nature theories: The argument can become circular if all cases of aggression are defined as revealing preexisting frustration, and vice versa, if any behavior that follows frustration is defined as aggression. Additionally, aggression is not always the response to frustration. Furthermore, there is little empirical support for the initial formulation of frustration theory, even though researchers have studied it for more than 70 years.

Frustration theory has subsequently been modified to recognize that frustration creates a predisposition for aggression by producing an intervening emotional state: anger. In addition, an individual's learning experiences and society's expectations exert a powerful influence on the connection between frustration and aggression. Of course, other responses to frustration are also possible—namely submission, resignation, alienation, withdrawal, avoidance, or even acceptance—but this does not in itself argue against a possible frustration-aggression link.

Frustration can also result in resentment, which (like the above responses) may or may not subsequently produce aggressive behavior. Frustration may be especially high when there is a discrepancy between expectations and realities: Bad social conditions, such as poverty or political repression, are made to seem even worse by high expectations that conflict with unpleasant realities. Accordingly, the "revolution of rising expectations," particularly in the less-developed economies, has been associated with frustration and violence. In his influential book, *Why Men Fight*, political scientist Ted Gurr developed the concept of "relative deprivation"—people's sense of their socioeconomic standing relative to others—showing that higher relative deprivation correlated with a greater propensity for revolutionary violence.

Political and military authorities often respond to collective efforts to promote social change with increased repression, but the forceful repression of strongly-felt needs (such as the yearning for Palestinian self-determination and, before that, of Zionists for a Jewish state) can in itself be highly frustrating and thereby ultimately increase hostility and aggression. There is another possible twist to the connection between frustration and war: boredom. It has been suggested that war is especially appealing to those whose lives are lacking in excitement and interest. "The absence of delight in daily living," wrote the historian John Nef, "has helped to leave many lives empty and sterile and so, fair game for any excitement, including the most terrific of worldly excitements, that of war."[19]

Furthermore, once a society has elevated military values, has trained men and boys (and, increasingly, women and girls) to be warriors, and has institutionalized and mythologized the war experience, people may be especially prone to be frustrated and bored with peace. Of course, warfare itself actually involves prolonged periods of boredom and monotony. The endless repetition, drill, and "hurry up and wait" behavior that characterize military routine are poor antidotes for civilian ennui. Military boredom may lead, however, to frustration, which in turn may lead to greater willingness to go to war, if only to "see action" and thereby finally break the suspense.

Social Learning and Conditioning

Clearly, human beings are strongly influenced by their experiences as well as by their society's norms and expectations. Many psychologists and most sociologists and anthropologists maintain that human violence arises in response to experiences, rather than bubbling up out of our genetic constitution.

Social learning theory explains human behavior in terms of continuous reciprocal interaction among cognitive, behavioral, and environmental influences. According to the influential social psychologist Albert Bandura, people learn through observing others' behavior, attitudes, and outcomes of those behaviors: "Most human behavior is learned observationally through modeling: from observing others, one forms an idea of how new behaviors are performed, and on later occasions this coded information serves as a guide for action." Bandura, who was analyzing adolescent aggression, believed in "reciprocal determinism": the world and a person's behavior cause each other.

"The important fact," wrote psychologist John Paul Scott, "is that the chain of causation in every case eventually traces back to the outside. There is no physiological evidence of any spontaneous stimulation for fighting arising within the body."[20] In particular, individuals are likely to fight if they have fought successfully in the past, and that aggression often results from a breakdown in social structures. (It is also noteworthy, on the other hand, that some of the most aggressive societies have been highly structured: Nazi Germany as well as Fascist Italy and pre–World War II Japan, for example.)

One of the most important developments in 20th-century psychology that also emphasizes the role of experience is behaviorism, which is particularly associated with the work of B. F. Skinner. The basic idea is that behavior will be influenced by its consequences for the individual: Certain behaviors tend to be reinforcing—that is, they make it more likely that the individual will repeat the previous actions. (The classic model is a rat pressing a bar and then being reinforced by food.) Some social scientists influenced by behaviorism use the phrase *instrumental aggression* to refer to aggressive behavior that is oriented primarily toward attaining a goal, such as winning a war or recovering territory, rather than causing injury as such.

Conditioning theory applied to human aggressiveness suggests that people will behave aggressively when such behavior leads to reinforcing (i.e., positive) results and, conversely, that the likelihood of aggression will be reduced if it leads to negative results. By extrapolation, members of whole societies can presumably be influenced similarly, making war more probable if their behavior has been positively reinforced (rewarded) or negatively reinforced (punished).

For example, the international aggressiveness of Nazi Germany was positively reinforced during the 1930s by the appeasement policies of the West. In contrast, conditioning theory might maintain that overseas incursions into foreign countries by the United States were negatively reinforced by the US's divisive and ultimately unsuccessful involvement in Southeast Asia, resulting in a subsequent reluctance to commit American ground troops to foreign combat, the so-called "Vietnam syndrome." This behaviorist thesis is, however, at least disputable because it did not inhibit two subsequent U.S.-led invasions of Iraq as well as its invasion and occupation of Afghanistan; moreover, one of the expressed motivations for these military adventures was to "get rid of the Vietnam syndrome."

Socialization to Aggressiveness

Some cultures actively encourage aggressiveness from early childhood: for example, the Fulani people of northern Nigeria, among whom most males seek to embody the ideals of "aggressive dominance." As boys, young Fulani males are taught to beat their cattle to prevent them from wandering off and to fight back unhesitatingly whenever they have been attacked. If they refrain from retaliating, they are mocked as cowards. They show virtually no emotion when struck with sticks during increasingly violent fights, and by the time they are young men, the Fulani are proud of their battle scars. Not surprisingly, they are also prone to personal fighting as well as warfare.

Mark May, an influential social psychologist, summed up a dominant American view when he wrote that "men not only learn when it is best to fight or not to fight, whom to fight and whom to appease, how to fight and how not to; but they also learn whom, when, and how to hate." May went on to discuss the phenomenon of social learning for group aggressiveness:

> Learning to fight and to hate involves much more than learning to box, to duel, or to participate in other forms of group violence. Systematic education for aggressive warfare in ancient Sparta or in modern Germany included, besides physical education in games and contests, universal compulsory military training; the inculcation of certain attitudes, prejudices, beliefs; and devotion to leaders and ideals. The whole purpose and direction of such education is toward group aggression.[21]

Also important in this context is the phenomenon of "imitative learning," whereby individuals are prone to do something if they witness others doing the same thing. Thus, aggressiveness and hostility—or, alternatively, an inclination to settle disputes peacefully—can become part of the ethos of a society.

And finally, there is the very important social-psychological phenomenon of obedience to authority: Beginning with experiments conducted at Yale University in 1961—the ethics of which have been criticized—the social psychologist Stanley Milgram sought to understand the willingness of seemingly well-adjusted Germans to engage in heinous acts during the Second World War. Milgram's research apparently showed that "normal" Americans would be willing to administer what they thought were painful and even dangerous electric shocks, when they felt pressured to do so by authority figures. Later, another influential social psychologist, Herbert Kelman, and his associate, V. Lee Hamilton, in a similar but less ethically fraught manner, analyzed the situational and societal factors involved in the commission of what they call "crimes of obedience." These include the massacres committed by US forces at My Lai and elsewhere during the Vietnam War as well as the acts of politicians and others during the Watergate scandal in the US in the early 1970s. Like Milgram, Kelman and Hamilton concluded that the illegal and/or unethical acts committed by ordinary people are usually in response to orders or directions from authority figures.

Gender, War, and Peace

The recorded history of warfare is made up of wars waged and fought almost entirely by men. Only recently have women been admitted to most armed forces, and until 2013, women were excluded from combat in the U.S. military. In centuries past, women filled primarily supportive roles in society, beginning most obviously with motherhood. The question naturally arises whether women, regarded throughout history as "the weaker and gentler sex," might help to temper the bellicose tendencies of men, if only they were to occupy more high positions in government, from which the military takes orders. There have been female leaders who never waged or promoted any wars, but the same can be said of male leaders.

A few salient examples—including Britain's former prime minister Margaret Thatcher, former U.S. secretary of state Madeleine Albright, India's former prime minister Indira Gandhi, Israel's former prime minister Golda Meir, and former U.S. secretary of state Condoleezza Rice—appear on their face to challenge the idea that women might be intrinsically more pacific than men. In 1982, Thatcher sent British troops to respond to Argentina's attempted annexation of the Falkland Islands and earned the epithet "The Iron Lady," in part for her tough positions and willingness to wield the weapons of war.

Madeleine Albright was a staunch proponent of the 1999 NATO bombing of Kosovo. Earlier, while serving as the U.S. ambassador to the United Nations, Albright infamously asked then-head of the Joint Chiefs of Staff Colin Powell, "What's the point of having this superb military that you're always talking about if we can't use it?" And Condoleezza Rice was one of the most outspoken advocates of the 2003 invasion of Iraq, even in the face of vehement opposition by millions of people the world over; she joined her fellow male war architects in disdaining the Charter of the United Nations, according to which war must be waged only as a last resort and with the blessing of the UN Security Council.

How are we to understand such cases? One way is simply to take them as refutations of the thesis that women are inherently more pacific than men. In reality, however, it is important to understand how the corridors of power come to be filled in such militarily powerful lands as Britain and the United States. Such nations, with long histories filled with wars, have been shaped politically so as to preclude the ascent to power of nearly anyone who opposes, on principle, the use of deadly force as a means of resolving international conflict. Accordingly, the fact of militarily aggressive women in positions of power does not show anything more than that access to political authority requires a willingness to use military force—perhaps even more willingness, in a number of instances, than their male colleagues because of a felt need to prove their toughness.

On the other hand, during the early stages of the Covid-19 pandemic, many of the nations that were relatively "successful" in dealing with it were led by women, notably New Zealand, Germany, Finland, Iceland, and Slovakia. Their gender may or may not have "predisposed" them to be more compassionate, ready to listen to scientific and public health experts, and resistant to the counsel of those advocating "keeping the economy running" over restrictions on economic and other business-related activities. Time will tell whether this approach saved many thousands, or perhaps millions, of lives in the long run.

There are many reasons for this promilitary bias in the selection of most political and even business leaders. The rhetoric of defense is typically used in persuading voters to support candidates for political office, and those who spurn the use of military force are lambasted as weak, naive, and unfit for leadership. At the same time, powerful economic forces are poised to support promilitary candidates and, above all, those who can be counted on to pass legislation likely to be lucrative to the military industry and its many sub-contractors. Although the implements of war are very expensive and profitable to produce, those of peace, negotiation, and dialogue are not generally viewed as sufficiently profitable to powerful corporations and their associated interests. As a result, promilitary candidates are at a great advantage, enjoying political approval from the populace in general and the financial support of the military industry and its subcontractors as well.

This complex situation makes it extremely difficult to tease out the necessary variables to determine whether women are intrinsically more pacific than men. Not only are elected officials in the most powerful nations likely to be quite hawkish, but the people whom they appoint, such as secretaries of defense and national security advisors, share their views and values. To complicate matters, the few women who have achieved such positions may feel the need to flex their military muscle, so to speak, in order to refute the prevailing cultural dogma according to which women are weak. They may adopt and espouse exceptionally hawkish positions during times of conflict, as did Margaret Thatcher, Madeleine Albright, Condoleezza Rice, and others.

Most social institutions are by nature conservative, concerned first and foremost with their own preservation and perpetuation, and military institutions are no exception. The cases of female leaders such as Thatcher, Albright, and Rice reveal that access to the corridors of power nearly always presupposes a promilitary stance, given the structures already in place, which were usually erected by men. We do not know what contemporary social and political institutions might have looked like had they been created by women because they were not. But we do know that many cherished myths about the relation between gender and war/peace roles have gone down in flames due to lack of scientific support, such as the alleged causal link between testosterone levels and aggression on the one hand and between female hormones and peacefulness on the other hand, along with the allegation that most women oppose wars and hence choose not to participate in combat. Like most social phenomena, gender seems to matter when it comes to belligerent and peaceful behavior. But social and biological scientists are still investigating how much, or how little, it matters.

Self-Fulfilling Behaviors

An important sociological concept is the self-fulfilling prophecy. In the realm of aggressive behavior, hostility often begets hostility on the part of others, which in turn not only reinforces the initial hostility but also intensifies it. People may create their own interpersonal environments simply by behaving with a certain expectation: If someone is suspicious, secretive, and blameful, he or she is likely to elicit comparable behavior. This pattern has the makings of a vicious circle, in which hostility becomes self-reinforcing and thus self-fulfilling in a kind of positive feedback.

A similar pattern can apply to international relations as well: If country A, convinced of the hostility of country B, increases its armaments, B may well respond in kind. This reinforces the "enemy image" already present, leading to further militarily oriented actions, each of which may truly be intended as "defensive" but, taken as a whole, diminish the security of all participants. Such a process characterizes much of the history of arms races.

Redirected Aggression

Other patterns in behavioral development also occur, often without any intent to produce aggression. For example, in displaced or redirected aggression, a victim will attack an innocent third party who may have had nothing to do with the initial victimization. The Bible describes how the ancient Israelites designated an animal as a scapegoat, which would be abused and driven from the herd, ostensibly taking with it the sins and anger of those who remained behind.

Frequently, the victims of redirected aggression are smaller, weaker, or already the subjects of social abuse: a religious or ethnic minority, advocates of unpopular political doctrines, and so on. African Americans, communists, and dark-skinned immigrants to the United States; North African and Middle-Eastern migrants and refugees to the European Union; and religious and ethnic minorities (especially those with dark skin, such as the Roma, or Gypsies) in countries spawned by the collapse of the former Soviet Union and Yugoslavia have all borne the brunt of redirected aggression by people who are themselves deprived or disadvantaged.

Although local minorities provide convenient "targets of opportunity," foreign nationals are particularly targeted as objects of redirected group anger, and they have increasingly been the victims (and, less often, the perpetrators) of violent acts on the part of segments of the majority, particularly in the US and parts of Europe. The sources of ultra-nationalist "populism," xenophobia, and of the mass support by millions of urban and agricultural workers for autocratic and illiberal political leaders often lie in these groups' feelings of anxiety regarding their economic well-being, their resentment toward "new immigrants" and refugees from war-torn countries they (usually mistakenly) believe may take their jobs, and their desperate longing to believe the (usually false) promises made to them by political leaders. Instead of directing their rage toward those individuals and institutions who really exploit them—who are often the very demagogues who are playing on workers' anxieties as well as multinational corporations offshoring jobs and benefiting from a domestic labor surplus—the victims of mass manipulation may blame other victims of globalization and may then elect precisely the people most responsible for their plight.

Immediately prior to the US-led invasion of Iraq in 2003, the following ditty made its way around the Internet (to the tune of the children's song, "If You're Happy and You Know It, Clap Your Hands"):

If you cannot find Osama, bomb Iraq.

If the market's hurt your momma, bomb Iraq.

If they've repossessed your Audi, and the terrorists are Saudi,

And you're feeling kind of rowdy . . . bomb Iraq.

There are many possible reasons why the Bush administration chose to bomb Iraq and then either "liberate" or "invade" it (depending on one's perspective). What is clear, however, is that Saddam Hussein was not responsible for the terrorist attacks of 9/11. But for most Americans, the agony of that attack demanded that something be done—something violent—and that someone be held accountable and made to suffer, preferably someone already known to be nasty and who could readily be defeated. The initial object of American wrath was Afghanistan, whose appropriateness for US-led invasion and occupation will long be debated. But the Iraq invasion seemed a total nonsequitur as a response to 9/11. So why did it happen?

Here is Thomas Friedman, an influential American reporter and columnist, writing in *The New York Times*:

The "real reason" for this war, which was never stated, was that after 9/11 America needed to stick it to someone in the Arab-Muslim world. . . . Smashing Saudi Arabia or Syria would have been fine. But we attacked Saddam for one simple reason: because we could, and because he deserved it, and because he was right in the heart of that world.

According to former chief UN weapons inspector Hans Blix, in his book, *Disarming Iraq*, "It is clear that the U.S. determination to take on Iraq was not triggered by anything Iraq did, but by the wounds inflicted by Al-Qaeda." U.S. counterterrorism expert Richard Clarke noted that "Having been attacked by Al-Qaeda, for us to go bombing Iraq in response was like our invading Mexico after the Japanese attacked us at Pearl Harbor." As illogical as such actions may appear, they fit rather well into the phenomenon of redirected aggression.[22]

Authoritarian and Machiavellian Personalities

Following World War II and the Holocaust in which 6 million of Europe's Jews (as well as millions of pacifists, gays, Roma, war resisters, mentally disabled people, political dissidents, and civilian noncombatants) were murdered, researchers led by the German philosopher Theodor Adorno and the US social psychologist Nevitt Sanford sought to identify the personal traits and experiences that predispose people toward violent anti-Semitism and related antidemocratic ideologies and practices. The results were published as *The Authoritarian Personality* (1950). Their work utilized the F Scale (for Fascist), a personality test purported to provide a rough measure of an individual's tendency toward authoritarianism. It examines such alleged personality traits as conventionalism (conformity to the traditional societal norms and values of the middle class), submission to conventional norms and values, and aggression exhibited in punishing and condemning individuals who don't adhere to these expectations. Other alleged personality markers of Fascism include superstition and stereotype, power and "toughness," destructiveness, and cynicism.

The authoritarian personality is also supposedly positively correlated with a rigidly hierarchical family structure: the husband dominant over the wife, and parents (especially fathers) demanding unquestioned obedience and respect from their children. This moralistic and disciplinarian style of child rearing, according to Adorno and his colleagues, is often combined with a strongly nationalistic outlook, ready submission to powerful external authority, and fear of weakness and of moral "contamination" by "aliens and other outsiders." It is negatively associated with supporting peace, independent thought and action, and willingness on occasion to defy social conventions.

The F Scale has been heavily criticized by many psychologists and other social scientists because it may be a better indicator of conservatism, and an old-fashioned outlook, rather than a measure of authoritarianism. However, it does express sentiments tending toward the political right and sentiments characteristic of less-educated and less cognitively flexible people who are uncomfortable with nuance, ambiguity, and science. The F Scale may also reflect cultural norms rather than underlying authoritarian personality dimensions.

Similar to the authoritarian personality is "the Machiavellian personality," which describes people who are likely to support unjust and violent behavior if it is profitable for themselves. In opposition to the Machiavellian personality stands the altruistic personality—empathetic, moral, and highly peace-supportive (but also, perhaps, more likely to be taken advantage of).

The notion of an authoritarian personality has largely gone out of fashion among mainstream psychologists. Closely connected to it, however, is the psychoanalytic concept of "identification with the aggressor," first described by Anna Freud (Sigmund Freud's daughter). Here, the victim tends reflexively to adopt the attributes of a powerful punishing agent (teacher, parent, government) in order to alleviate anxiety; in the process, the victim is transformed into an aggressor, either directly or indirectly by supporting aggression by others. It may be significant that comparatively permissive societies seem to be less warlike than those with high levels of physical punishment of children and sexual repression.

Alienation and Totalism

Many psychologists today focus on the role of painful or traumatic experiences in the generation of a range of unpleasant feelings and behaviors. Their work was preceded by the studies done from the 1940s through the 1970s by psychoanalysts Erich Fromm and Erik Erikson.

Fromm distinguished between *defensive* and *malignant aggression,* with the latter involving a passionate drive to hurt others (sadism) or oneself (masochism). But unlike the human nature theorists, he attributed malignant aggression to *social conditions* rather than to innate human traits. In particular, Fromm blamed alienation, an enduring feeling of acute loneliness and disconnectedness from others, for the inclination of some people to avenge their pain by acts of extreme destruction. According to Fromm, those who are extremely alienated are also ripe candidates for inclusion in violent organizations, where they can find satisfaction in a group that is united by its hatred of others. This might include the Ku Klux Klan and other supremacists and neo-Nazis in the United States, skinheads in Great Britain, and numerous hate groups worldwide.

In a similar vein, Erikson pointed out that a society, especially when it is changing rapidly, may generate ambiguities and unresolved stresses that combine with the individual's developmental problems to produce total-ism, a susceptibility to all-or-nothing simplifications: us versus them, good versus evil, God versus the devil. War demands substantial sacrifices, not only economic and political but also a willingness to sacrifice one's life and to go against the standard societal prohibition against taking another's life. Accordingly, it is not surprising that totalistic thinking goes hand-in-hand with war.

Prejudice, Images of the Enemy, and Human Needs

During the 1950s, the psychologist Gordon Allport argued that individual prejudice is founded on ignorance of others; therefore, less ignorance would mean less prejudice. According to Allport's "contact hypothesis," an increase in social interaction between members of in- and out-groups could reduce intergroup prejudice. Intergroup contact would lead to reduced intergroup prejudice if the contact situation embodies four conditions: (1) equal status between the groups in the situation, (2) sharing common goals, (3) no competition between the groups, and (4) authority sanction for the contact. Subsequent research has shown that, in fact, increased intergroup contact does correlate with reduced intergroup prejudice. About a decade after Allport's work, the psychiatrist Jerome Frank and the political psychologist Ralph White emphasized the dangers of developing diabolical enemy images, especially when people feel threatened.

Many violent conflicts result from the suppression of human needs, in large part because, according to the noted peace researcher John Burton, such basic needs as the desire for security and such core values as freedom are not negotiable—unlike interests, which are often transactional and depend on circumstances. Johan Galtung, a founder of peace studies, also emphasizes the primacy of human needs, which, if frustrated, may engender intrastate and destructive identity conflicts. Galtung argues that sustainable peace requires the satisfaction of our needs for security, identity, well-being, and self-determination.

Attributions and Projection

Attributions refer to the causal explanations that people devise in order to rationalize both physical events and human behavior, especially acts perceived as successes or failures and that benefit or harm oneself and others. Attribution theory is especially relevant for understanding behavior that is based on cognitive errors and biases and that may lead to interpersonal and group conflict.

These attributions are governed by such biases as the "illusion of control," according to which there is a strong tendency for people to believe that the world is just, one in which people get what they deserve: "Good things happen to good people and bad things happen to bad people." Therefore, we tend to blame the victim for his or her misfortune and not the society, culture, economy, or environment. If our thinking is self-serving and other-blaming, it is easy to valorize one's group and demean or demonize others and to rationalize our good fortune and the misfortune of others.

Social psychologists have also identified the so-called "fundamental attribution error," whereby people tend to hold a double standard between self and other when it comes to explaining behavior, especially actions that are undesirable. In brief, when someone else does something hurtful, there is a powerful temptation to attribute it to internal weakness or malevolence on the part of the actor, but if and when a subject engages in comparably regrettable behavior, often this is not attributed to one's negative internal characteristics but to external pressures that allegedly left little or no alternative. Thus, when someone else does something "bad," it is because we often feel that *they* are in some sense bad; but when *we* ourselves do something bad, we tend to tell ourselves it was "because we had no choice." The result is to avoid blame for one's self while casting it on others.

Biased attributions may also be present at the level of larger-scale societal, class, religious, cultural, and even civilizational attributions. Often, from our perspective, *the other side* is aggressive, sneaky, violent, greedy, undisciplined, unethical, and so forth, whereas we are simply responding to their nastiness and perfidy. Many psychoanalysts describe this as an unconscious defensive mechanism of "projection," whereby in order to avoid unsettling feelings of guilt and anxiety for our having done something bad (for which we are in fact responsible), we displace, or project, the source of the vile deed onto others and proceed to blame them for what we have done.

In addition, many Westerners, especially affluent ones, tend to make dispositional attributions ("individuals make their own destinies"), based on shared cultural assumptions of Western individualism, whereas people in many non-Western and more collectivist cultures may attribute beneficial or harmful events and actions to fate, nature, the group, or the "will of God." This provides an ideological and motivational basis for large-scale misunderstandings, with all participants in the conflict believing they are good, their adversaries are evil, and "God is on our side."

Dehumanization, Altruism, and Reconciliation

The social-psychological process of categorizing individuals into in-groups and out-groups may lead to depersonalization: individuals are perceived as without distinctive features and as anonymous members of a "mass." They may also no longer be viewed as (fully) human, especially when language of dehumanization is at play. The discourse of dehumanization motivates and activates stereotypical and ethnocentric thinking and behavior; once viewed as subhuman, other individuals and groups are easily stripped of their dignity and their humanity denied. Discrimination, belligerence, and even genocide against nonpersons may therefore be legitimated.

In sharp contrast with the paradigm that human behavior is primarily individualistic and egoistic, altruism denotes activities that are costly to individuals themselves but may benefit others. According to the "empathy-altruism hypothesis," empathic concern (an emotional reaction brought about by the act of perspective-taking and characterized by such feelings as compassion, tenderness, soft-heartedness, and sympathy for another) leads to selfless motivation to help another person. Perhaps surprising to his "free market" admirers, Adam Smith, in his 1759 book, *The Theory of the Moral Sentiments*, was a major proponent of the cultivation of such aspects of human nature as pity and compassion.

In addition, the ethologist Frans de Waal argues against the allegedly antisocial character of aggression and instead proposes a "reconciliation hypothesis," according to which aggression is a well-integrated part of social life. The dynamics of social interactions among nonhuman primates, according to de Waal, are such that confrontation is not simply a barrier to sociality but rather is an unavoidable element upon which social relationships are often built and strengthened through reconciliation. Social animals, including human beings, seek contact with former opponents and engage in such post-conflict reunion practices as kissing, embracing, sexual intercourse, grooming, and so on. Reconciliation serves to decrease aggression and socially destabilizing anxiety. It occurs especially after a conflict between parties whose possible partnership may have a high eventual reproductive value.

De Waal's demonstration of reconciliation in both monkeys and apes supports the idea that forgiveness and peacemaking are widespread among nonhuman primates. The evolutionary advantages of reconciliation are obvious for animals that survive through mutual aid, that is, by cooperating even when the parties have interests that may partially conflict. These findings may have significant potential applications for understanding human conflict resolution, insofar as reconciliation may be a shared heritage of the primate order.

The Attractions of War

In *Notes From Underground,* Fyodor Dostoyevsky wrote, "In former days we saw justice in bloodshed and with our conscience at peace exterminated those we thought proper to kill. Now we do think bloodshed abominable and yet we engage in this abomination, and with more energy than ever."[23] This energy derives, at least in part, from the fact that some people find war a positive experience. Many combatants have extolled the sheer intensity of confronting the basic phenomena of life and death and, in the process, exploring the boundaries of one's capacities. For some soldiers, especially young men, there is something exhilarating about meeting death face to face, perhaps even heroically and for a noble cause, rather than being overtaken alone in one's bed. Pierre Teilhard de Chardin (who served in World War I) wrote,

> The front cannot but attract us, because it is . . . the extreme boundary between what you are already aware of, and what is still in the process of formation. Not only do you see there things that you experience nowhere else, but you also see emerge from within yourself an underlying stream of clarity, energy, and freedom that is to be found hardly anywhere else in ordinary life. . . . This exaltation is accompanied by a certain pain. Nonetheless it is indeed an exaltation. And that is why one likes the front in spite of everything, and misses it.[24]

For others, there may be a compelling sexual component, as revealed in this passage by the American novelist Norman Mailer:

> All the deep, dark urges of man, the sacrifices on the hilltops, the churning lusts of night and sleep, weren't all of them contained in the shattering, screaming burst of a shell? The phallus-like shell that rides through a shining vagina of steel. The curve of sexual excitement and discharge, which is, after all, the physical core of life.[25]

Most significant of all, perhaps, is the satisfaction of belonging, bonding, solidarity, and companionship, particularly a kind of male bonding, which most men do not experience during civilian life. Shakespeare's Henry V rhapsodizes about the pleasure the forthcoming battle holds for

> *We few, we happy few, we band of brothers;*
>
> *For he to-day that sheds his blood with me*
>
> *Shall be my brother.* (IV.iii.60–62)

Just prior to the commencement of World War I, the American philosopher and psychologist William James argued that the raw emotional appeal of war constituted one of the greatest difficulties in overcoming it. In a renowned essay titled "The Moral Equivalent of War," James presented a case for war's attractiveness:

> The war against war is going to be no holiday excursion or camping party. The military feelings are too deeply grounded to abdicate their place among our ideals until better substitutes are offered. . . . Showing war's irrationality and horror is of no effect upon him. The horrors make the fascination. War is the *strong* life; it is life in *extremis*. . . . Its "horrors" are a cheap price to pay for rescue from the only alternative supposed, of a world of clerks and teachers, of . . . consumer's leagues and associated charities, of industrialism unlimited. . . . Militarism is the great preserver of our ideals of hardihood, and human life with no use for hardihood would be contemptible. Without risks or prizes for the darer, history would be insipid indeed.[26]

James then suggested that these attractions could be overcome only by substituting other stressful and exciting tasks involving risk, daring, and hard work, which he called "the moral equivalent of war."

The preceding passages involve not so much enthusiasm for war as a grudging recognition that *even* war has not only its horrors but also its attractions. Other approaches have been more admiring of war itself. Thus, a famous *Bushidō* tract from ancient Japan advises that "when all things in life are false, there is only one thing true, death."[27] Although even the most war-prone ideologies generally claim that their long-term goals are to eliminate war, there is a notable modern exception: fascism.

Fascism glorifies war, and (judging by its success in the 20th century and its ominous recent comeback) it struck a favorable chord in many people. "War alone," wrote the Italian Fascist dictator Benito Mussolini,

> brings up to their highest tension all human energies and puts a stamp of nobility upon the people who have the courage to meet it. All other trials are substitutes, which never really put a man in front of himself in the alternative of life and death. A doctrine, therefore, which begins with a prejudice in favor of peace is foreign to Fascism.[28]

A final contributing reason for war, working at the individual level, is a kind of sanitized romanticizing of battle, found in many children's cartoons and toys, movies, music, art, and literature. For example, in "I Did Not Lose My Heart In Summer's Even," the English poet A. E. Housman wrote that he lost his heart to an enemy soldier who laughed and blew him a kiss as he was stabbed to death!

To be sure, there is also a rich catalog of antiwar songs, stories, movies, and poems, ranging from the delicate and plaintive (e.g., the songs "Where Have All the Flowers Gone?" and "The Drums of War") to the unrelentingly realistic and grotesque (e.g., the films *All Quiet on the Western Front, Johnny Got His Gun, Catch-22, Saving Private Ryan, Full Metal Jacket, Apocalypse Now,* and *The Hurt Locker*). Opponents of war, however, are obliged to recognize those aspects of war that have long exercised a positive appeal for many humans.

Inhibitions Against War

The history of warfare shows that people are capable of the most heinous acts of brutality. From American history alone, consider the massacres at Wounded Knee in South Dakota in the late 19th century and at My Lai in Vietnam about 100 years later: In both cases, hundreds of unarmed, non-combatant men, women, children, and even infants were slaughtered wantonly. Indeed, the preceding sections may leave the impression that war exerts a virtually irresistible attraction to human beings at the individual level, whether through our innate characteristics, our experiences, conducive psychological mechanisms, or via the lure of excitement, camaraderie, and ideology. But in fact, even beyond ethical and religious strictures, there are inhibitions that check the personal propensity for war.

One of these inhibiting factors is fear for one's own life. In Euripides's *The Suppliants,* the Theban herald points out that "if death had been before their own eyes when they were giving their votes, Hellas [Greece] would never have rushed to her doom in mad desire for battle." There are, in fact, very few authentic heroes during a war; most soldiers seek to do the minimum necessary to save themselves and their close colleagues.

As to alleged bloodlust and war fever, consider that during World War II, rarely did more than 25 percent of American soldiers fire their guns in battle; even during intense fire-fights, about 15 percent fired their weapons. And this applied to highly trained combat infantrymen. A study sponsored by the US Army concluded that "it is therefore reasonable to believe that the average and healthy individual—the man who can endure the mental and physical stresses of combat—still has such an inner and usually unrealized resistance toward killing a fellow man that he will not of his own volition take life if it is possible to turn away from that responsibility."[29] It can even be argued that in many wars before 1950, fear of killing, rather than fear of being killed, was the largest cause of battle failure.

By the Korean and Vietnam wars, however, the percentage of soldiers willing to fire their weapons appears to have gone up significantly, largely because of modified training and greater emphasis on establishing within-group solidarity among individual combat units. A major part of military training (especially in boot camp) seeks to countermand the basic moral teaching—not limited, incidentally, to Western tradition—"Thou shalt not kill." The goal of basic training, in the armed forces of most countries, has not so much been the teaching of new techniques and skills as the inculcation of new attitudes: unquestioning obedience to military superiors, bonding with one's peers, and a willingness to kill. Despite some resistance, most people can learn these things, usually in just a few weeks. This should not be surprising because a profound asymmetry of power exists between the recruits and the officers who train them: "Recruits usually have no more than twenty years' experience of the world, most of it as children, while the armies have had all of history to practice and perfect their techniques."[30]

Actual killing during combat was widely considered the role of enlisted men or, at most, junior officers. By 1914, for example, lieutenants and captains in the British Army led men into battle carrying only a swagger stick or, at most, a pistol. "Officers do not kill" was the common understanding at that time, and there is reason to believe that if they had the choice, most enlisted men would not have done so either. George Orwell, who fought as an anti-Fascist volunteer on the Loyalist side during the Spanish Civil War, recounted that he was unable to shoot an enemy soldier whom he observed

> half-dressed and . . . holding up his trousers with both hands. . . .
> I did not shoot partly because of that detail about his trousers. . . .
> A man who is holding up his trousers isn't a "Fascist," he is visibly a
> fellow-creature, similar to yourself, and you don't feel like shooting
> him.[31]

Some Issues in Nuclear Psychology

When it comes to nuclear war, feelings of attraction and revulsion are particularly intense. Some people evince a strange love for weapons of such all-encompassing power (hence the title of the famous satirical movie *Dr. Strangelove or: How I Learned to Stop Worrying and Love the Bomb*). Others are especially repelled by the grisly prospect of ending life on so massive a scale. And yet, because a full-fledged nuclear conflict has not occurred and because, in addition, the effects of nuclear explosions are so powerful as literally to stagger the human imagination, most people have difficulty focusing their minds and energies on such a topic, which is at once horrifying and yet strangely unreal.

When confronted with deeply unpleasant information, for example, people often respond with denial. This process is particularly well known with respect to personal death: Virtually every cognitively unimpaired adult recognizes that eventually he or she will die; however, most of us go about our lives as though our own death holds little reality. When confronted with profoundly unpleasant facts, people often practice denial. Something similar can be identified with respect to the nuclear danger: Most of us go about our daily lives as though the prospect of instantaneous nuclear holocaust does not hang over us, simply because such an overwhelming threat is too painful and emotionally disruptive to admit into our moment-by-moment consciousness.

This behavior, although presumably adaptive for the individual, also has unintended and potentially dangerous consequences. By refusing to confront unpleasant realities, people who might otherwise become mobilized in opposition to nuclear weapons are likely to place their attention and energy elsewhere. Moreover, they abandon the field to those who have insulated themselves from the negative consequences of their activities and who, by virtue of career advancement or ideology, have committed themselves to a more pronuclear and possibly even prowar orientation.

Denial is encouraged by the fact that nuclear weapons tend to lack psychological reality: They are kept in secret, restricted installations, and in the United States the Department of Defense consistently refuses either to "confirm or deny" their presence. This policy has ostensibly been adopted to keep information from would-be nuclear terrorists. Regardless, one important effect of official secrecy is to keep the American public uninformed and, to some extent, to facilitate denial. Hence, for most people, nuclear weapons cannot be seen, touched, smelled, or heard, so it requires a conscious effort to consider that they exist at all.

Closely related to denial is another personal, psychological phenomenon of the nuclear age, sometimes called *psychic numbing*. This phrase was originally applied by the distinguished psychiatrist Robert J. Lifton to the *hibakusha*, the victims of the atomic bombings of Hiroshima and Nagasaki. Psychic numbing refers to a loss of emotional sensitivity and awareness that appeared to result from the survivors' immersion in the mass death that characterized those events. It can be argued that, to some extent, we are all victims of Hiroshima and Nagasaki, in that all of us suffer from some degree of psychic numbing, even as the nuclear menace pervades our unconscious.

A Final Note on Individual-Level Explanations of Wars

It is notable that approximately 1 percent to 2 percent of human deaths during the 20th century were caused by other human beings. In other words, 98 percent to 99 percent of recent human deaths were *not* caused directly by intentional, individually inflicted violence. Moreover, of those deaths caused by other people, the majority are due to *collective* violence rather than to individual aggression. Individual humans often fight, and kill, when they can perceive—whether accurately or not—that they will gain substantially by doing so. A concerted effort to prevent war and to establish a just and lasting peace must therefore take into account the inclinations, needs, perceptions, and behavior of individual people, especially those with wealth and power, while not disregarding the role of "average" individuals.

However, analyzing and opposing war should not be confined to the level of individual psychology because, as we shall soon see, the behavior of organized groups may differ significantly from that predicted by many biological and psychological theories of personal motivation or individual experience.

Questions for Further Reflection

1. To what degree is aggression "in our genes"? Is it learned, innate, or something in between? What about war?

2. How do you evaluate the claim that human beings have an innate and universal "death drive?" What are arguments for and against this view?

3. Do the attractions of war outweigh our inhibitions against it? Why or why not?

4. To what extent is war a biological necessity or a human invention, a learned behavior that could be unlearned?

5. What are some of the strengths and weaknesses of individual-level explanations of wars? Which explanations do you find the most persuasive? The least?

Suggestions for Further Reading

David P. Barash and Judith Eve Lipton. 2011. *Payback: Why We Retaliate, Redirect Aggression, and Take Revenge.* New York: Oxford University Press.

Seyom Brown. 1987. *The Causes and Prevention of War.* New York: St. Martin's.

Albert Camus. 1972. *Neither Victims nor Executioners.* Chicago: World Without War.

D. J. Christie., R. V. Wagner., and D. D. Winter. 2001. *Peace, Conflict, and Violence: Peace Psychology for the 21st Century.* Upper Saddle River, NJ: Prentice Hall.

John Dippel. 2010. *War and Sex: A Brief History of Men's Urge for Battle.* Amherst, NY: Prometheus Books.

Sigmund Freud. 1963. *Character and Culture.* New York: Colliers Books.

Erich Fromm. 1973. *The Anatomy of Human Destructiveness.* New York: Holt, Rinehart & Winston.

Chris Hedges. 2004. *War Is a Force That Gives Us Meaning.* New York: Public Affairs.

David Livingstone Smith. 2007. *The Most Dangerous Animal: Human Nature and the Origins of War.* New York: St. Martin's Press.

Ervin Staub. 2003. *The Psychology of Good and Evil.* Cambridge, UK: Cambridge University Press.

Edward O. Wilson. 1979. *On Human Nature.* Cambridge, MA: Harvard University Press.

Notes

1. John Saxe. 1892. "The Blind Men and the Elephant." *The Poetical Works of John Godfrey Saxe.* Boston: Houghton.

2. Quincy Wright. 1966. "Analysis of the Causes of War." In *Toward a Theory of War Prevention*, eds. R. Falk and S. Mendlovitz. New York: World Law Fund.

3. Geoffrey Blainey. 1973. *The Causes of War.* New York: Free Press.

4. bid.

5. J. William Fulbright. Preface to Jerome D. Frank. 1967. *Sanity and Survival.* New York: Random House.

6. Hans Morgenthau. 1967. *Politics Among Nations.* New York: Knopf.

7. Konrad Lorenz. 1966. *On Aggression.* New York: Harcourt, Brace & World.

8. Edward O. Wilson. 1971. "Competitive and Aggressive Behavior." In *Man and Beast: Comparative Social Behavior,* eds. J. Eisenberg and W. Dillon. Washington, DC: Smithsonian Institution Press.

9. Edward O. Wilson. 1975. *Sociobiology: The New Synthesis.* Cambridge, MA: Harvard University Press.

10. Sigmund Freud. 1964. Reprinted in J. Strachey, ed. and trans., *The Standard Edition of the Complete Psychological Works of Sigmund Freud.* London: Hogarth.

11. Thomas Hobbes. 1930. *Selections.* F. J. E. Woodbridge, ed. New York: Scribner.

12. Although Hobbes himself appears to have been a semi-closeted atheist.

13. John Calvin. 1956. *On God and Man.* F. W. Strothmann, ed. New York: Frederick Ungar.

14. John Milton. 1953–1982. "The Doctrine and Discipline of Divorce." In *Complete Prose Works*. New Haven, CT: Yale University Press.

15. Reinhold Niebuhr. 1940. *Christianity and Power Politics*. New York: Scribner.

16. Michael Howard. 1984. *The Causes of War*. Cambridge, MA: Harvard University Press.

17. John Dollard et al. 1939. *Frustration and Aggression*. New Haven, CT: Yale University Press.

18. bid.

19. John Nef. 1950. *War and Human Progress*. Cambridge, MA: Harvard University Press.

20. John Paul Scott. 1975. *Aggression*. Chicago: University of Chicago Press.

21. Mark May. 1943. *A Social Psychology of War and Peace*. New Haven, CT: Yale University Press.

22. David P. Barash and Judith Eve Lipton. 2011. *Payback: Why We Retaliate, Seek Revenge and Redirect Aggression*. New York: Oxford University Press.

23. Fyodor Dostoyevsky. 1960. *Notes From Underground*. New York: E. P. Dutton.

24. Pierre Teilhard de Chardin. 1965. *The Making of a Mind: Letters From a Soldier-Priest, 1914–1919*. New York: Harper & Row.

25. Norman Mailer. 1968. *The Armies of the Night*. New York: New American Library.

26. William James. 1911. "The Moral Equivalent of War." In *Memories and Studies*. New York: Longmans, Green.

27. Z. Tamotsu. 1937. *Cultural Nippon*. Iwado, ed. and trans. Tokyo: Nippon Cultural Foundation.

28. Quoted in Seyom Brown. 1987. *The Causes and Prevention of War*. New York: St. Martin's.

29. S. L. A. Marshall. 1947. *Men Against Fire*. New York: William Morrow.

30. Gwynn Dyer. 1987. *War*. New York: Crown.

31. George Orwell. 1968. *Homage to Catalonia*. New York: Harcourt Brace Jovanovich.

7

The Group Level

War remains fundamentally a group activity, although individuals are necessarily involved. A single person may incite or catalyze an international or domestic conflict, as did the assassin who killed Archduke Franz Ferdinand in 1914, thereby initiating the events that led to World War I, or Adolf Hitler, who "caused" World War II in Europe. Similarly, individuals can go to war by enlisting or being conscripted. But an individual cannot make war because it is, by definition, a group endeavor. And strange things may happen when collective concerns become more important than individual difference is among the group members.

Let's take a brief look at the early history of warfare and quickly review its occurrence among premodern and nontechnological peoples. This is

AHMAD AL-RUBAYE via Getty Images

The Group Level

War remains fundamentally a group activity, although individuals are necessarily involved. A single person may incite or catalyze an international or domestic conflict, as did the assassin who killed Archduke Franz Ferdinand in 1914, thereby initiating the cascade that led to World War I, or Adolf Hitler, who "caused" World War II in Europe. Similarly, individuals can *go to* war by enlisting or being conscripted. But an individual cannot *make* war because it is, by definition, a group endeavor. And strange things may happen when collective concerns become more important than individual differences among the group members.

Let's take a brief look at the early history of warfare and quickly review its occurrence among premodern and nontechnological peoples. This is important because the "group-loving" as well as "group-opposing" aspects of humanity have extraordinary influence on our present as well as our future. Then we'll consider a key modern manifestation of human group orientation: nationalism.

War: Its Early History

War and Human Evolution

Very little is known about earliest human warfare. It seems likely, however, that social grouping among primitive human beings was highly adaptive—that is, it probably contributed to cultural and biological survival. By associating with other individuals living near them, our distant ancestors were able to share information and resources, to gain assistance in caring for their young, and to defend themselves against predators. Presumably, social grouping also enabled prehistoric human beings to bring down prey bigger and stronger than would have been possible for a solitary hunter.

Some anthropologists have suggested that the early stages of human social evolution were promoted by selection for effective hunting, which favored the ability to fashion and use tools, to walk upright (thereby freeing the hands), and to communicate effectively with one's fellow hunters. This "hunting hypothesis" has been disputed, however, by others who emphasize the importance of childcare, gathering, and digging roots. While the hunting hypothesis focuses on a dominant role for men, the foraging hypothesis places more emphasis on women.

The role of war in early human evolution has also been disputed. One view holds that war—even prehistoric or preindustrial war—is such a recent development that it exerted slight biological influence on the human species. The other view, perhaps equally extreme, claims that warfare was an essential component of human evolution, perhaps the major selective force operating in our early history. From this perspective, groups and their constituent individuals who were more successful in their conflicts with other groups were more likely to leave offspring who possessed traits leading to their success.

On the other hand, whereas individual aggression is at least somewhat encoded in our DNA—as is the potential for peaceful conflict resolution—war itself, as an organized human activity, is too recent to have been a driver of human evolution. In short, although aggressiveness (under certain circumstances) is "in our genes," war is not. The widespread geographical dispersion of early human groups probably made contact, and thus potential hostility, with other group members rare. Nonetheless, significant interactions likely still took place in regions of common interest: at waterholes, in areas of local food abundance, and so on.

Whatever the precise role group-level violence may have had in shaping human evolution, it seems unlikely that it has doomed the human species to unending war in the future. Moreover, war often entails such socially desirable elements as courage, initiative, coordination, self-restraint, and self-sacrifice. A winning group would presumably be one that cooperated well, at least internally. Making airborne weapons, for example, whether spears or intercontinental ballistic missiles, is not a frenzied act of passion but rather a labor of considered intelligence. (Launching these missiles, especially in retaliation, however, may in part involve more primitive mental processes.)

No clear evidence of warfare—as opposed to fighting and skirmishing between mobile bands—can be found during Paleolithic (early Stone Age) or Mesolithic times, from 10,000 to 8000 BCE. Hunting and gathering societies were slowly replaced by economies based on the domestication of plants and animals. War is first discernible during the early Neolithic period, which began around 8000 BCE. The remains of the ancient city of Jericho (dating from 7500 BCE) show clear signs of fortified towers and walls, suggesting that they were military defenses, probably necessitated by the accumulation of wealth via agriculture, artisanship, and trade, which in turn created targets for aggressive raiding or early war.

Why Study Premodern and Nontechnological Warfare?

Anthropologists studying modern non-high-tech peoples have found evidence of defensive fortification that may in some ways predate the maintenance of fixed and walled cities for the preservation of accumulated wealth. The actions of certain nontechnological societies, even if "primitive" by Western standards, are not the same as those that occurred in earlier stages of human history. Current traditional human societies were not our ancestors. Nonetheless, by examining nontechnological "war" among contemporary people (e.g., in the Amazon basin or the outback of Australia), we may learn something about our ancestors' behavior in pre-Neolithic days. And this, in turn, might yield some insight into underlying tendencies among human beings as a species.

A study of the diversity of human war-making might lead to some useful generalizations beyond the following claims articulated by the historian Arnold Toynbee: Extremes of climate (both very hot and very cold) are less conducive to the development of large-scale war-making than are temperate climates; prairie and seacoast dwellers tend to be more war-prone than mountain or forest inhabitants; pastoralists (nomads) are more war-prone than are settled agriculturalists. We can also go beyond the simplistic and misleading generalizations that human beings have always fought wars, that they have hardly ever fought wars, that they always fight wars for practical reasons, or that they never do so.

Functions of Nontechnological Wars

Most social scientists who have analyzed war agree that it is, in most cases, ethically a "bad thing." But there is general disagreement among an earlier generation of sociologists studying Western war and among anthropologists studying its traditional counterparts whether war is or has been adaptive or maladaptive. Ethics and morality aside—as is often the case during war—advocates of the maladaptive perspective emphasize the disruptive and retrogressive aspects of war: how it prevents growth, development, and material and social progress, as well as the negative effects of destruction, suffering, and death. Proponents of war-as-adaptive claim that preindustrial and nontechnological war can be functional— that is, it can serve an overall positive role for its participants by providing social solidarity within each competing unit, by yielding access to resources (notably food, territory, and/ or mates), or by enhancing the prestige of the victors.

Walter Bagehot, a noted 19th-century English economist, expressed a functional perspective when he wrote that "civilization begins because the beginning of civilization is a military advantage."[1] Herbert Spencer, a

19th-century proto-sociologist, also emphasized the prosocial aspects of war: "From the very beginning, the conquest of one people over another has been, in the main, the conquest of the social man over the antisocial man."[2] This is a challenging suggestion, especially for people who think of war as the extreme in antisocial behavior.

War is not a simple or unitary phenomenon among modern nation-states, nor is it readily explained—or even defined—among most traditional peoples. Premodern war may serve these social functions (note that war could, in theory, be advantageous for those who engage in it without it being "good" in an ethical or moral sense):

1. Provides outlets for aggressive young men and thus reduces within-society tensions.

2. Generates opportunities for social advancement via enhancement of prestige.

3. Gain access to food resources, notably animal protein.

4. Obtain women from neighboring groups.

5. Obtain land from neighboring groups.

6. Correct imbalance in the sex ratio—in certain societies, female infanticide creates an excess of males, which can be adjusted by mortality during war.

7. Achieve revenge, which often carries both symbolic and social payoffs.

8. Provide the opportunity for enlargement of tribal domain and (rarely) for certain individuals to establish large kingdoms or empires.

9. Deter incursions by neighboring groups, whether by intimidating other warrior groups enough that they don't attack, or by having defeated in combat previous aggressors.

At its simplest level, "primitive" war appears to be largely concerned with interpersonal competition and struggles to obtain individual prestige, rather than with large-scale conflicts between social groups or with the accumulation of land, women, or other resources. Thus, in premodern war, involvement and motivation tend to be at the individual level, as compared with its modern counterpart, which is mainly directed toward imperial or international conquest or the advancement of national or state interests. In modern large-scale technological warfare, personal involvement and motivation tend to be less intense because the benefits to be derived are more diffuse, often ideological rather than tangible. Anthropologists, however, are divided over the degree to which ecological forces are responsible for human war and, if so, which forces might predominate.

Characteristics of Premodern Wars

The renowned 20th-century anthropologist Bronislaw Malinowski identified six categories of armed aggressive behavior among nontechnological peoples:

1. "Fighting, private and angry," which also serves as the prototype of criminal behavior.

2. "Fighting, collective and organized," among groups within the same cultural unit.

3. "Armed raids, as a type of man-hunting sport, for purposes of headhunting, cannibalism, human sacrifices, and the collection of other trophies."

4. "Warfare as the political expression of early nationalism, that is, the tendency to make the tribe-nation and tribe-state coincide."

5. "Military expeditions of organized pillage, slave-raiding and collective robbery."

6. "Wars between two culturally differentiated groups as an instrument of national policy."[3]

Premodern war can be examined by considering its apparent functions. "Among almost all American Indians," according to H. H. Turner-High, "war existed to bring glory to the individual, and since war was relatively safe, everyone was happy even though few tactical, strategic and economic advantages for a whole people were obtained."[4] Even the causing of death or injury to one's opponents was not always a goal for premodern warriors, and mortality appears generally to have been low; premodern and nontechnological "wars" often end after a single death or a grave injury. The Dani people of New Guinea, for instance, traditionally did not use feathers on their war arrows, thereby reducing accuracy and keeping casualties down. And the Ibo of Nigeria used to count their dead after a war, after which the side losing fewer warriors would compensate the "losers" with money, to avoid any grudges.

Premodern war has typically been bounded by numerous rules specific to each tribe. For example, the Nuer of Sudan were forbidden from using spears against anyone living within a given proximity; beyond that distance such lethal weapons were allowed. Among the Dani, truces automatically occurred at nightfall, although a battle was considered unfinished until at least one person was killed on either side.

Premodern wars have usually been fought for limited goals and in a limited way. Warfare among traditional peoples today is generally of this sort—over revenge, women, animal protein, prestige, or, occasionally, access to physical space for hunting, farming, or living. It is virtually unknown for lethal group conflict to erupt due to contesting ideologies. In fact, neighboring groups, usually the opponents in nonindustrial wars, often share the same culture, language, and worldview. The goal of such conflicts only rarely includes complete destruction of the other side or anything approaching "unconditional surrender."

Among the most widespread customs associated with premodern warfare are those involving the extensive use of rituals to signal the initiation of warfare, as well as the change of one's status from civilian to warrior. Magic amulets were common, as were special ways of shaving or adorning the body, usually with paint and/or feathers. Such techniques ostensibly help ward off evil and bad luck, but their more practical function appears to be the promotion of group solidarity. This includes modern-day uniforms and such "totemic" symbols as insignias, regimental banners, national flags, and group-specific music. Ritual abstinence, notably from food or sex, apparently helped relieve the guilt of killing while also signifying that one was special, different, and thus permitted to do certain things that were forbidden during peacetime. Repetitive dancing and singing, often with the use of drugs, has been characteristic of warfare among some peoples in Asia, Africa, Polynesia, and certain Native American tribes; this apparently reduces fear and helps cement commitment among members of a war party. Rehearsals of battle serve to diminish anxiety and also provide practice for warriors going into combat.

Elaborate rituals are also often performed after a battle, especially if the warrior has killed somebody. Most societies regard anyone who kills—even in war—as somehow unclean and who must be ritually purified before being readmitted into civilian life: Fasting or abstinence is common, often with varying periods of isolation from the home group. In modern societies, returning soldiers are often accorded medals, parades, membership in special veterans' organizations, and their own cemeteries.

Alternatives to Traditional, Premodern Warfare

There are a variety of seemingly peaceful societies, defined variously as (1) not having wars fought on their soil, (2) not fighting wars with other groups, and/or (3) not experiencing any civil wars or internal collective violence. Whereas some human groups—notably the Yanomamo of Venezuela and Brazil—are considered archetypically war-prone, others (no less human) have no history of warfare. Examples of these peaceable societies include the Semai of Malaysia, the Siriono of Bolivia, the Mbuti pygmies of central Africa, the !Kung Bushmen of the African Kalahari Desert, and the Inuinnait of northern Canada.

Some traditional peoples are notable not so much for their lack of aggression as for their effective and nonviolent way of coping with it. For example, the Tunumiit of central Greenland slap each other's faces; in western and eastern Greenland, they engage in prolonged singing contests, with individuals competing to be more imaginative and to engage their audience more effectively. Many inhabitants of Alaska, Siberia, and Baffin Island have traditionally settled their disputes by wrestling. The Kwakiutl Indians of the northwest coast of North America used to compete via potlatch feasts, in which chiefs sought to outdo each other by demonstrating how much wealth they could sacrifice. And the African Bushmen (!Kung) and pygmies use laughter and ridicule to defuse conflicts.

In other stateless human societies, war is either absent or quite rare. Among those factors that help prevent the outbreak of organized civil violence, the following appear to be especially important, although not all are present at the same time: (1) socialization toward the peaceful settling of conflicts and disapproval of force or violence, (2) the presence of a group or tribal decision-making system that applies effective sanctions against violent transgressors, (3) the opportunity for dissidents to defect to other groups, and (4) the existence of economic interdependence within the group.

As to the maintenance of peace between groups, several factors can be identified, although the enormous diversity of human cultures makes any generalizations hazardous. The perception of shared ancestry between different groups tends to inhibit violence between them, although an emphasis on relatedness within a group (reflected in terms such as motherland, fatherland, brothers and sisters, etc.) tends to work in opposite directions: to foster greater internal group solidarity, combined with an increased willingness to close ranks against other groups perceived as unrelated, alien, and thus as enemies.

In addition, peaceful relations among groups are often enhanced by establishing kinship ties through marriage. According to the structuralist school of anthropology (whose most noted representative was the French anthropologist Claude Lévi-Strauss), a primary reason for the incest taboo is that by inducing people to marry outside the family, group members establish cooperative relationships with other groups, thereby minimizing the likelihood of violent conflict. Establishing politically useful alliances via marriage has a long history in the West as well, at least at the level of ruling houses among the European monarchies.

Encouragement as well as insight can also be gained by looking into what have been called "peace systems," arrangements among neighboring societies that are specifically designed to achieve peace among the members. A recent examination of three peace systems—the Upper Xingu River basin tribes of Brazil, the Iroquois Confederacy of upper New York State, and the European Union—highlighted six features considered important in the creation and maintenance of intersocietal peace: (1) a shared social identity among the participants; (2) interconnections among the subgroups, achieved by intermarriage, enhanced communication, and so forth; (3) interdependence, such that the well-being of the various subgroups is contingent upon peaceful coordination—as achieved, for example, via trade or other exchanges whereby all participants benefit; (4) "non-warring values," meaning the overt acknowledgment that peace is better than war, which includes valorizing peacemakers more than war makers; (5) symbolism and public ceremonies that reinforce peace as both an ideal and a practical goal; and (6) superordinate institutions that manage conflicts when they arise.[5] The existence of peace systems is consistent with what peace researcher Kenneth Boulding once proclaimed as his "First Law": If something exists, then it is possible!

Underlying Group Processes

Human beings are highly social creatures. One of the most powerful human tendencies is to form internal group bonds and develop ways to distinguish the members of different groups. This is typically achieved by shared language, customs, patterns of adornment, mythological and religious beliefs and practices, and so forth. Other groups who speak different languages (or even the same language but with a different accent), who worship different gods, whose physical appearance is different, or who follow a different political or economic system are readily identified as different (no surprise here!) and are often perceived as threatening. Such differences need not be substantial: Sigmund Freud wrote of the "narcissism of minor differences," whereby many people tend to focus on, and exaggerate, relatively inconsequential cultural traits that distinguish them from their neighbors.

Benefits and Costs

Group life has many important and empowering components, including the ability to pool resources, to cooperate, to achieve a division of labor, to learn and to teach, and simply to receive stimulation from the presence of one's fellows. Such benefits, however, likely also go beyond the ability to achieve more as part of a group than as an individual.

As philosopher and psychologist William James wrote, "All the qualities of a man acquire dignity when he knows that the service of the collectivity that owns him, need them. If proud of the collectivity, his own pride rises in proportion."[6] There is a powerful allure to being needed and appreciated and a strong tendency to associate oneself with a larger whole, thereby enhancing one's self-esteem and self-worth even as, paradoxically, the importance of each individual often declines as they are subsumed within a group.

Biologists debate whether evolution proceeds via comparative success among individuals and their genes or by the differential benefit accorded to groups. Either way, it is clear that as a general rule, larger groups have been able to defeat smaller ones, which itself may be responsible for the widespread preference for establishing group affiliations, regardless of whether they are composed primarily of genetic relatives.

But there are also disadvantages to group life. Of these, one of the most significant is the loss of inhibitions that can result from immersion in a crowd, as a result of which a mob psychology can take over, inducing individuals to engage in acts that would rarely, if ever, be done if individuals were acting alone. It can be debated whether war-making groups literally produce a new kind of entity, a social one having its own tendencies and characteristics, or whether groups sometimes merely give social sanction to potentially destructive individual tendencies—notably, aggressiveness, intolerance, and rage. Freud once commented that he could shame a single Nazi stormtrooper sent to search his apartment in Vienna, but when two were sent together, they became "good Nazis." And of course, once joining a group, individuals become vulnerable to the collectivity, whether or not such actions are in anyone's—or any group's—best interest.

Deindividuation

The process of deindividuation is an important part of group orientation and collective violence; it appears to have four major components:

1. *Validation by one's peers.* Members of homogeneous groups are more likely to respond to potential conflict situations with hostility than are groups whose membership is more heterogeneous. Individual aggressiveness, when validated by the expressed aggressiveness of others, is more likely to be released.

2. *Diminished individual profile.* Biologists have identified something known as the "selfish herd" phenomenon, whereby animals as diverse as fish or starlings appear to flock together because, by doing so, each individual increases the chances that its neighbor—rather than itself—will fall victim to an approaching predator. Similarly, a human crowd seems to provide not only a feeling (as well as the reality) of strength in numbers but also a shield of protective anonymity.

3. *Leadership.* Groups are usually associated with highly visible and persuasive leaders, who may provide the impetus for group hostility by actively fomenting as well as channeling violence that might not otherwise occur if individuals were left to their personal inclinations. The simple presence of leaders can also suggest to group members that the leaders, rather than the followers, are likely to be at risk for retaliation, which in turn diminishes the reluctance of the followers to participate.

4. *Contagious or imitative behavior.* A frustrated or angry person is more likely to behave aggressively if he or she perceives others doing so. This

may involve not only "getting the idea" of violence but also gaining a kind of social "permission" to behave in this way. Thus, violence (or, euphemistically speaking, "resistance to oppression") tends to spread when others witness or hear about precipitating events. Examples include the French Revolution of 1789, the Luddite uprising in early 19th-century Britain, the US African American ghetto uprisings of the late 1960s, and the mostly nonviolent protests following police shootings of African Americans from 2014 to the present. Other nonviolent cases worldwide include the active resistance of Chinese students and workers in 1989 (leading, alas, to the Tiananmen Square massacre) and of Buddhist monks and civilians in Myanmar in 2007, the Arab Spring from late 2010 to 2011, and the mass protests in 2019 in Hong Kong and France.

Dehumanization

Another prominent characteristic of group functioning is the tendency to dehumanize members of other groups—that is, to give the impression to compatriots and, at least on an unconscious level, to oneself, that the other group members are not really, or fully, human at all. It is especially easy to dehumanize those who are recognizably different because of language, appearance, cultural practices, religion, or political ideology.

Among some nontechnological peoples, the word for *human* is the same as the name for the tribe; members of other tribes are thus denied their humanity, as a result of which they can be killed with little or no remorse. Among modern technological societies, language patterns during times of hostility reflect this tendency, especially with the use of animal terms to describe the opponent: vermin, insects, rats, pigs, dogs, and others. Even nonanimal slang terms have a similar effect: wogs, slants, kikes, niggers, krauts, honkies, reds, and so on.

A terrorism expert at the RAND Corporation (a think tank heavily supported by the US Department of Defense) testified as follows to a US House of Representatives subcommittee in June 2007: "Unless we can impede radicalization and recruitment, then we are condemned to a strategy of stepping on cockroaches one at a time." Unless we can impede such dehumanizing language, future violent conflicts may continue to incorporate this rhetoric as a rationale for the extermination of "subhumans."

Brief Conclusion on Premodern and Nontechnological Warfare

We may never fully know either the earliest history of human warfare or whether violent conflicts between contemporary stateless societies casts much light on the evolution of human warfare. Nonetheless, the study of premodern war illuminates some facets of contemporary war that might otherwise be obscured by the complexity of modern society. Moreover, certain fundamental underlying principles of individual motivation, group psychology, and intergroup aggression today appear to be prefigured by premodern war. Still, peaceful and bellicose group interactions in the modern world are conducted in a different manner from those of premodern conflicts, namely the involvement of large groups most often functioning at the level of nations.

Nations, States, Ethnic Groups, and Nationalism

Nations and States

In a sense, nations are ethnic groups writ large. Just as tribal and ethnic groups are composed of individuals sharing a sense of shared social identity, nations are similarly united, but the populations are much larger and, typically, more complex internally.

Ethnic comes from the ancient Greek word *ethnos,* meaning a race, tribe, or group of people; the term *nation,* on the other hand, derives from the Latin *natio,* referring to birth (as in prenatal or native). Although the word *nation* is often used loosely in the United States to indicate a state—that is, a relatively large political and geographic entity usually with institutional structures—in fact it refers more precisely to a large group of people, typically united by a common language, origin, history, religion, and culture. No formal process exists for identifying nations; rather, a nation exists when a group considers itself a nation and is recognized as such. Within the United States, for example, indigenous groups often self-identify as the "Iroquois nation," "Cherokee nation," and so forth.

A state, by contrast, is a political unit, a region whose people are governed independent of other, comparable states. A nation-state exists if a nation and a state have the same geographic boundaries. For example, for a brief period after World War I, Lithuanians, Latvians, and Estonians each constituted separate nation-states, the Baltic states of Lithuania, Latvia, and Estonia. Then they were incorporated into a larger state, the Soviet Union, from which they eventually gained independence and became nation-states once more as the Soviet Union broke up.[7] Russia today, like the former Soviet Union, is a large state but not a single nation; rather, it is composed of many nationalities, including not only ethnic Russians but also Tatars, Chechens, and many other ethnic groups.

Nationalism

The phenomenon of nationalism is one of the most powerful sociopolitical forces of modern times. It refers to the yearnings of a people to constitute themselves as part of a nation, usually to form a nation-state and often to adjust geographic boundaries so as to increase the size of their domain, to incorporate others who share the same sense of national identity, and to establish themselves as distinct and self-governing. According to one definition, nationalism is "a people's sense of collective destiny through a common past and the vision of a common future."[8]

This hints at an important component of nationalism—namely, the emotional appeal of belonging, of shared deeds, and of extending the boundaries of one's individual identity to comprise a larger and seemingly more glorious whole. In the words of 19th-century French philosopher and historian J. Ernest Renan, "What constitutes a nation is not speaking the same tongue or belonging to the same ethnic group, but having accomplished great things in common in the past and the wish to accomplish them in the future." In perhaps the most famous definition of this phenomenon, Renan also suggested that nationalism is "a grand solidarity constituted by the sentiment of sacrifices which one has made and those that time is disposed to make again. It supposes a past, it renews itself especially in the present by a tangible deed: the approval, the desire, clearly expressed to continue the communal life. The existence of a nation is an everyday plebiscite."[9]

The 19th-century German philosopher G. W. F. Hegel noted a similarity between the ritual of reading a morning newspaper and morning prayer. A century and a half later, political scientist and historian Benedict Anderson developed this idea in his influential book *Imagined Communities* (1983): "Each communicant is well aware that the ceremony he performs is being replicated simultaneously by thousands (or millions) of others of whose existence he is confident, yet of whose identity he has not the slightest notion." Increasingly, however, the sense of national identity has moved beyond the standard textbook definition, which emphasizes cultural unity. To a great extent, large nation-states are not so much natural social constructs, whether "real" or imagined, as they are groupings of people, cobbled together for political and economic purposes. The result has been a strong tendency to confer unity by establishing national symbols shared by many persons, regardless of their other identities. National flags, heroes, myths, and anthems all have a remarkable hold over most people, and virtually all nation-states seek to inculcate recognition and respect for such symbols, typically requiring oaths, pledges, or other specific acts of allegiance.

During times of perceived stress, especially if the stress comes from an external threat, nationalist sentiments are likely to become particularly intense. Often the threat serves to enhance pronational emotions that may previously have been ebbing, as well as to distract public attention away from internal domestic challenges. The German invasion of the Soviet Union in 1941, for example, enabled Stalin to build on a "war nationalism" that overcame much disaffection with his purges and dictatorship. (At the same time, some nationalistic separatists, notably in the Baltic states and Ukraine, allied themselves with Nazi Germany during World War II, hoping to fulfill their own aspirations of separating from the Soviet Union.) The Japanese attack on China also evoked solidarity born of war nationalism, causing the government of Chiang Kai-shek and the revolutionary forces of Mao Zedong to make common cause, at least for a time, in the interest of Chinese national survival against the invaders.

Even long after national struggles have ceased, the existence of martyrs and of state holidays for remembrance also serve to whip up nationalist sentiment and keep it fresh. A notorious example of this was the former Serbian president and demagogue Slobodan Milošević whipping up Serbian nationalism just prior to the Bosnian War of 1992–1995 by invoking the memory of a famous Serb military defeat by Muslim Turks 500 years earlier. This led eventually to massacres of non-Serbs as well as to genocide against Bosnian Muslims,

Nationalism can, in theory, be limited to love for one's nation. In practice, however, it is often combined with antagonism toward other nations. "By nationalism," wrote George Orwell,

> I mean first of all the habit of assuming that human beings can be classified like insects and that whole blocks of millions or tens of millions of people can be confidently labeled "good" or "bad." But secondly—and this is much more important—I mean the habit of identifying oneself with a single nation or other unit, placing it beyond good or evil and recognizing no other duty than that of advancing its own interests.[10]

This occurs, in part, because the nation provides a way of submerging the comparatively small, vulnerable individual self into a much larger, more powerful Other. As the distinguished Protestant theologian H. Richard Niebuhr described the ardent nationalist,

The national life is for him the reality whence his own life derives its worth. He relies on the nation as a source of his own value. He trusts it; first, perhaps, in the sense of looking constantly to it as the enduring reality out of which he has issued, into whose ongoing cultural life his own actions and being will merge. His life has meaning because it is part of that context, like a word in a sentence. It has value because it fits into a valuable whole.[11]

Unfortunately, the tendency to identify one's group, tribe, or people as a "valuable whole" carries with it another tendency: to devalue other, similar groups or, worse yet, to see them as threatening to one's fundamental values, whereupon they often become targets for violence,

A Brief History of Nationalist Wars

Early Modern European Nationalism

The sense of nationhood, as opposed to ethnic group or tribal affiliation, is relatively recent. During the Middle Ages most individuals felt that they belonged to a rural community, a city, or to the domain of a local reigning monarch. Thus, the loyalty of someone whom we now identify as French might have included local affiliation to family and village and personal fealty to the duke of Lyon, the king of France, the Holy Roman Emperor, and the Pope, but not to "France" as such.

European nation-states began to develop during the late Middle Ages. After the Treaty of Westphalia (1648), which ended the Thirty Years' War, European peoples became increasingly aware of the existence of other collectivities who were similar to themselves, as well as others, generally farther away, who were quite different. Moreover, centralized authorities—abetted by gunpowder—were able to demolish the castles of local rulers and enforce a broader allegiance: to kings, whose domains also tended to include similar people. At the same time, loyalty to local rulers and religious leaders diminished. Spain, Portugal, France, and England were nation-states by the 16th century. During the early and mid-19th century, nationalism became explicitly articulated, particularly in central Europe. Nationalism had received an enormous boost, largely from the popular resistance of Spaniards and other nations that had been subjugated by Napoleonic France. French hegemony over much of continental Europe lasted for about a decade early in the 19th century, during which time nationalistic sentiments were magnified among people who resented being subordinated to a foreign emperor.

In the course of its revolution in the late 18th century, France developed the first truly national anthem, "La Marseillaise," and substituted adherence to the nation for fealty to a monarch. In addition, although Napoleon was initially welcomed by Europe's downtrodden as a populist liberator ("liberty, equality, fraternity")—in sharp contrast with the "ancient regime"—his empire building helped generate strong feelings of national identity among those whose lands had been invaded by French forces.

Nationalist sentiments were widespread by the early 19th century, largely coalescing around the doctrine of national self-determination, the belief that each national group had the right to form its own state. For example, Greece won its independence from Turkey in 1829, and Belgium was declared independent from the Netherlands in 1830. The Dutch republic had achieved its own national self-determination several centuries earlier, from the Spanish empire, after a protracted and bloody conflict; that Dutch revolt was the first modern successful war of national liberation.

Nationalism in the United States

For the American colonies under the sway of the British Empire, the Revolutionary War was largely a war of independence rather than of nationalism or of class-based social upheaval (the latter characterized the French Revolution). Nonetheless, US nationalism later expressed itself through the doctrine of manifest destiny, which claimed that it was "manifestly" (obviously) the destiny of the American people to expand across all of North America. Moreover, dreams of a major worldwide role for the United States led to other military adventures, including the little-remembered War of 1812. Senator Henry Clay of Kentucky, leader of an ultranationalist group known as the War Hawks, expressed both local pride and nationalist fervor when he proclaimed,

> It is said that no object is attainable by war with Great Britain. . . . I say that the conquest of Canada is in your power. I trust that I shall not be deemed presumptuous when I state that I verily believe that the militia of Kentucky are alone competent to place Montreal and all of Upper Canada at your feet.[12]

The resulting war was one of the least successful in US history—1,877 Americans killed, 9,700 taken prisoner, and a cost of $200 million (roughly $20 billion in today's dollars), including the burning of Washington, D.C., by the British. And no territory was gained. (Interestingly, this same war—which receives very little attention in US history books—is widely celebrated as a success in Canada because they avoided being engulfed by the "colossus to the south.") Nonetheless, US nationalist sentiment eventually contributed to such expansionist undertakings as the Mexican-American and Spanish-American Wars, the forced annexation of Hawaii, and genocidal appropriation of Native American lands, as well as to a growing series of armed interventions, notably in Latin America and the Far East.

European Nationalism in the 19th and 20th Centuries

By the late 19th century, Western European nationalism had become pronounced in Germany and Italy, each of which had been divided into numerous mini-states and principalities. After decades of struggles, Italian national unification was finally achieved in 1870, following a resistance to the Austrian empire (itself composed of many nations). Meanwhile, formal unification of such German mini-states as Saxony, Hanover, and Silesia was completed in 1871, with Prussia the undisputed leader of the new German nation-state. German unification was achieved by the Prussian leader Otto von Bismarck, who successfully engineered a series of wars, first against Denmark and then against Austria, culminating in the Franco-Prussian War, which was won by Prussia.

Whereas Western-European nationalism primarily involved the consolidation of previously disunited regions and states, nationalism in Eastern Europe took a somewhat different form, ultimately resulting in the carving out of nation-states from the large, heterogeneous Ottoman (Turkish), Austro-Hungarian, and Russian empires. The national yearnings and nationalistic demands by the diverse Balkan peoples and the tensions this provoked, especially within the Austro-Hungarian Empire from 1890–1914, played a major role in initiating World War I.

The Austrian leadership of the Habsburg Empire had been worried that it would not be able to hold together its unstable, heterogeneous assemblage of restive nations, consisting of Bosnians, Bulgarians, Hungarians, Serbs, Croats, Montenegrins, Slovenians, Czechs, Slovaks, and others. Following the assassination in 1914 of the Austrian archduke Franz Ferdinand by an extremist Serbian separatist, the Austrians feared that Serbian nationalism would ultimately result in the disintegration of their already rickety empire. And so it was decided to "punish" the Serbs. Russia stood by tiny Serbia, in a show of ethno-national solidarity of Slavic peoples (as it did 85 years later, during NATO's bombing of Serbia in 1999): Serbs, like Russians, are ethnically Slavic. In the run-up to World War I, Germany stood by Austria, which was its ally. France was already allied to Russia and was independently hungering to regain the provinces of Alsace and Lorraine, which had been lost to Germany 40 years before during the Franco-Prussian War and had been a continuing insult to French national pride. Furthermore, the war plans of Germany included an invasion of neutral Belgium, which in turn brought Great Britain into World War I. National passions, fears, demands, and misunderstandings thereby contributed mightily to the first global 20th-century war.

Following World War I (or, as it was called at the time, "the Great War"), numerous nations were *not* granted self-determination, although that had been an explicit goal of US president Woodrow Wilson. The state of Yugoslavia, for example, was created as a patchwork of seven "national republics"—consisting of Albanians, Bosnians, Croats, Macedonians, Montenegrins, Serbs, and Slovenians—all of whom considered themselves distinct nations. These groups were held together, at least in part, by a powerful leader, Josip Broz Tito, a renowned Croatian anti-Nazi partisan during World War II. Following Tito's death, nationalist unrest commenced in Yugoslavia in 1988–1989, culminating in the relatively nonviolent secession of Slovenia and Macedonia, the moderately violent withdrawal of Croatia, and extremely violent wars in Bosnia and Kosovo. (Kosovo is a predominantly Albanian national enclave inside Serbia that has been recognized as an independent nation by more than 100 states, but not by Serbia, which still claims it, or by Serbia's Slavic ally, Russia.)

Another example is the Ottoman Empire, which, after its dissolution at the end of World War I, gave rise to the current state of Turkey. It had been allied with the Central Powers (Germany and the Austro-Hungarian Empire) during the World War I. Most of the Arab peoples of the Middle East had been under Ottoman colonial control; in return for their assistance during World War I, the UK and France had promised them national independence. After the war, however, colonial control of what is now recognized as Lebanon, Syria, Jordan, Iraq, Egypt, and Israel was largely transferred to Britain and France. As a general principle, the national aspirations of defeated people are often trampled on by the victors. Although in this case the Arabs were on the side of the Allied victors, their national aspirations were squelched by their supposed allies, the British (poster-child for whom was T. E. Lawrence, better known as "Lawrence of Arabia"), so that they traded Ottoman oppressors for English ones. And much of today's international turmoil and resentment can be attributed to this betrayal.[13]

Nationalist sentiments can be extraordinarily resilient. For example, Poles retained their national identity for decades when "Poland" didn't exist; it had been gobbled up in the late 18th century by Germany, Russia, and Austria. Citizens of Venice considered themselves Italians even while part of Austria. French-speaking residents of Quebec have resisted anglicization of their culture by the rest of English-speaking Canada, periodically agitating for complete political independence. And most Basques and Catalans consider themselves first Basques and Catalans rather than Spaniards and seek independence from Spain, sometimes violently.

Kurds constitute the largest nation that is not associated with its own state; the Kurdish population is spread across Turkey, Iraq, Iran, and Syria. Despite continual yearnings—and frequent bloodshed—it seems unlikely that Kurdish nationalist aspirations will soon be gratified. This is largely because those states with substantial Kurdish populations resist any such separation, which would threaten their current boundaries. During the Syrian and Iraqi civil wars, Kurdish nationalist fighters—known as the *peshmurga* ("those who face death")—were effective military opponents of ISIS, the self-identified "Islamic State," but only when it came to reclaiming Kurdish regions of Iraq and Syria. There has, moreover, been substantial friction between Kurds and the Turkish government in particular, which calls many Kurdish nationalists "terrorists."

Intrastate nationalist movements have generally resisted the often militant efforts of states to deny their legitimacy. Nonetheless, there have been some examples of assimilation, in which isolated national groups lose their identity in favor of a larger group in which they are embedded. Despite awareness of their particular ethnic heritage and intermittent expressions of outrage at their historical mistreatment by the dominant Anglo culture, most American Indians, Hawaiians, Inuit, and First Nations, for example, still think of themselves as Americans or Canadians.

National Liberation and Revolutionary Nationalism

By the 19th century, the colonizing activities of the European powers had created a situation in which large parts of the Earth were under military domination by white colonizers who had little similarity with, or cultural affinity for, the much larger number of "natives" being subjugated. In Latin America, wars of national liberation during the 1800s—notably led by Simón Bolívar—were quickly successful, as the Spanish empire crumbled. A brief French ascendancy in Mexico was also ended, led by Benito Juarez. (The holiday Cinco de Mayo—"fifth of May"—is named for a victorious battle against French troops in 1862; interestingly, it is generally celebrated more vigorously in southwestern portions of the United States than in Mexico!)

Revolutionary nationalism during the 19th century was less successful, however, in Africa and Asia: The Zulus were eventually crushed by the British in South Africa, for example, and despite bloody uprisings (of which the so-called Sepoy Mutiny, 1857–1859, is best known) against its rule, Britain maintained control over India as well as Egypt and, indeed, over a large part of the inhabited planet. Although China was not directly occupied by imperialist powers, except for Hong Kong and Macao (both of which had been reclaimed by China by the end of the 20th century), during the 19th century the weak and decentralized Chinese government was regularly humiliated and forced to submit to economic exploitation, including the forced "opening" of the country to opium trading. The resulting Opium Wars (1839–1870)—won by Britain aided by French forces—caused yet more local resentment, adding to the growing urgency of Chinese nationalism, as did the Boxer Rebellion and, from 1850 to 1864, the failed Taiping Rebellion against the Manchu-led Qing dynasty. (This latter struggle, little known in the West, resulted in an estimated 20 million fatalities.)

In the aftermath of the two world wars of the first half of the 20th century, revolutionary nationalism, and counterrevolutionary and antimodern ethnocentrism, triumphed throughout much of the "postmodern" world. In some cases, this occurred through protracted conventional war (e.g., Algeria's and Vietnam's independence from France), in others by guerrilla operations (Kenya's independence from the UK), and in yet others by peaceful transitions (the Baltic countries of Estonia, Latvia, and Lithuania, as well as the "stans"—Kazakhstan, Tajikistan, Uzbekistan, and so forth—from the disintegrating USSR).

Since the geographical boundaries of erstwhile European possessions were often not identical with national boundaries, many newly independent former colonies have had to cope with substantial national and ethnic divisions, some of which have led to war. The borders of the current states of Iraq, Syria, Lebanon, and the Democratic Republic of Congo (or the DRC, formerly Zaire), for example, do not correspond to natural, ethnic, or tribal geographical entities due to British, French, or Belgian imperialism. Not surprisingly, these and other such arbitrary political units—often drawn on a map with no regard to realities on the ground—have been caught up in considerable postcolonial violence of their own.

Take, for example, Sudan. Previously one of the geographically largest countries in Africa, Sudan was a creation of joint British and Egyptian colonialism until it became independent in 1956. But even then, Sudan was a heterogeneous assemblage, consisting of light-skinned Muslims in the north, dark-skinned Muslims and animists in the west (Darfur), and dark-skinned Christians and animists in the south. After oppression and genocide promulgated by the dominant north against residents of Darfur, as well as a prolonged civil war initiated by forces in the south, an independent state of South Sudan was created and internationally recognized in 2011. However, even though in this case some nationalist aspirations have, to some extent, been met, the relationship between Sudan and South Sudan remains contentious, as well as within South Sudan itself, where a civil war was waged from 2013 to late 2018, at which time a fragile peace seemed to take hold.

Types of Nationalist Wars

National Independence

National independence need not always be preceded by war. Burma, Malaysia, the Slovak Republic (formerly part of and now separated from the Czech Republic), Ukraine, the Baltic states, and Slovenia, for example, achieved statehood and self-determination with relatively little bloodshed. Canada became independent from Britain (in 1867) with no violence whatsoever, as did Norway (1905) via a plebiscite to which the Swedish government acquiesced.

The eventual independence of India from Great Britain exemplifies the victory of a successful nonviolent, nationalist movement—to which the British did respond with violent episodes before eventually giving up. On the other hand, warfare is a frequent prelude to national independence, as witnessed by the birth of the United States. Indonesia fought for four years to gain independence from Holland, and East Timor successfully fought Indonesia for its autonomy. Algeria became separate from France only after eight years of fighting, which cost 250,000 Algerian and French lives. National independence for the former British colonies in East Africa (notably Kenya) occurred only after the bloody Mau nation Rebellion, which evoked even bloodier British responses. In South Africa, termination of the white-imposed domination (apartheid) of its black population came only after militant revolutionary actions led by the African National Congress, combined with international boycotts and other pressure. In this case, although South Africa was already an independent state, the end of apartheid effectively constituted a kind of national independence for its majority black population.

National Prestige

Many of the classic interstate wars of modern history have been engendered by issues of national prestige. Enthusiasm within the United States for the Mexican-American (1846–1848) and Spanish-American (1898) wars was largely generated by US desires to expand and to enter the arena of worldwide colonial acquisitions. In the former case, Mexican nationalism evoked resistance, whereas in the latter, the government of Spain appears to have fought back largely because it would have been embarrassing to give up its colonies in Cuba, Puerto Rico, and the Philippines without doing so.

Similarly, the aggressive appetites of Germany and Japan in the first half of the 20th century were whetted by a pervasive sense that these great nations had not achieved world status commensurate with their economic or technological accomplishments or their self-proclaimed racial superiority. Both Russia's takeover of Crimea and domination of parts of eastern Ukraine and (what some Westerners deem) Chinese expansionism in the western Pacific have been fueled, or at least justified domestically, by appeals to national prestige.

Following its independence from the UK, India took a leading position among developing nations in condemning worldwide militarism in general and the nuclear arms race in particular. But when Prime Minister Rajiv Gandhi announced in February 1988 that his country had successfully developed and tested a surface-to-surface liquid-fueled missile, entirely with Indian technology, he received a standing ovation in the Indian Parliament. A decade later, India publicly exploded nuclear devices, supposedly in response to the threat posed by Pakistan. Pakistan later claimed it tested and developed its nuclear arsenal in response to the alleged threat to its national identity posed by a nuclear-armed India.

Pride and prestige, sometimes on a personal level as well, can loom large. Thus, President Lyndon Johnson persevered in the Vietnam War in part because of his private determination not to be "the first US president to lose a war." For President Nixon, the worst outcome for the United States in that conflict was humiliation. "If, when the chips are down," he announced, "the world's most powerful nation, the United States of America, acts like a pitiful, helpless giant, the forces of totalitarianism and anarchy will threaten free nations and free institutions throughout the world. It is not our power but our will and character that is being tested."[14]

Frustration among America's ruling elites was particularly acute from late 1979 to early 1981, when revolutionary Iranians held captive the staff of the US embassy in Tehran. The resulting sense of national humiliation contributed to the defeat of Jimmy Carter and the election of Ronald Reagan to the US presidency in 1980, as well as to the military buildup that followed. Similarly, the US invasion of Grenada in 1983 served partly to assuage the emotional pain of a devastating car bomb attack on the temporary US Marine barracks in Beirut, Lebanon, just a few days before. Also during the Reagan administration, US bombers attacked Tripoli, Libya, in retaliation for acts of terrorism allegedly committed by Libyan nationals. Shortly afterward, the United States sank Iranian naval vessels in the Persian Gulf. These actions provided an outlet for frustration and an opportunity to redeem a sense of diminished national pride. At the same time, what redeems the pride of one nation usually diminishes that of another, leading in turn to a felt need for revenge, which creates yet more need to assuage the now-reinjured pride, and so on.

The maintenance of national prestige and the avoidance of humiliation loom large in the calculation of almost every major country. For example, immediately after NATO's air war over Serbia and Kosovo (which Russia opposed), Russian military units used a ruse to secure the airport in Priština (Kosovo's capital), thereby attempting to assert Russian national pride in the face of NATO's overwhelming military might and Russia's "defeat" in the Cold War. Comparable sentiments appear to have motivated the Russian takeover of Crimea in 2014.

Similarly, Arab pride was wounded by Israel's string of military victories in 1948, 1956, and 1967. The October War of 1973, although technically yet another Arab defeat, came close enough to victory to demolish the myth of Israeli invincibility and sufficiently restored Egyptian self-respect and prestige that President Anwar Sadat felt empowered to make his stunning trip to Jerusalem in 1977, to agree to the Camp David Accords in 1978, and to sign an Egyptian-Israeli peace treaty (the first one between Israel and an Arab state) in 1979. Many Arabs, even those who normally oppose militant Islamists, were pleased by Hezbollah's military performance during Israel's incursion into Lebanon in 2006. Iraqis, not surprisingly, are generally opposed to any large-scale redeployment of US troops in that country, at least in part because the invasion of 2003 injured local national pride, with intermittent protests against "foreign occupiers" continuing to the present.

Secessionism

Sentiments of national unity are often associated with yearnings of a group of people to secede from a larger collectivity of which they do not feel a part. In 1967, for example, about 50,000 Ibos, who had migrated to northern Nigeria, were slaughtered by the more numerous Hausas, who resented Ibo economic success. Another 1 million Ibos were driven out of the north, after which the Ibo "nation" sought to secede and form its own nation-state of Biafra. The result was a civil war in which hundreds of thousands died and many more suffered severe malnutrition and starvation. The war ended in 1970, unsuccessfully for the would-be secessionists.

Secessionism is a major factor in organized violence today; it was especially intense in the armed struggles by Kosovars and Chechens to secede from Yugoslavia and Russia, respectively, and for Hindu-affiliated Tamils seeking to separate from Buddhist-oriented Sinhalese in Sri Lanka. All of these wars ended with the secessionists defeated. Other disputes are ongoing as of 2020: For example, Russian-speaking inhabitants of eastern Ukraine (the Donbass), abetted by Russian military forces, seek to separate themselves from Ukrainian-speaking and largely Europe-oriented central and western Ukraine. Catalans seek even now to secede from Spain, just as Kurds yearn to secede from parts of Turkey, Iran, Iraq and Syria. There are also numerous secessionist movements that are generally below the Western radar.

For just two examples among many, during 2020 a secessionist movement within Tigray, a region of Ethiopia, resulted in hundreds of deaths and the threat of yet more violence. Similarly, the anglophone (English-speaking) minority in the African country of Cameroon has felt oppressed by the francophone (French-speaking) majority government; it is at least possible that this simmering conflict, involving a movement for anglophone secession, will someday erupt into civil war.

There have also been some recent secessionist successes: Eritrea seceded from Ethiopia and East Timor from Indonesia. Separatist movements, deploying degrees of violence and with varying prospects of success, but always cohering around nationalist associations and ambitions, are found on every continent except Antarctica. (And the US Civil War—better known in the South as the War Between the States—was, after all, an unsuccessful attempt at secession.)

International or Transnational Solidarity

A sense of nationhood and of national solidarity often extends across political boundaries (which have often been drawn without regard to "natural" national groupings), often resulting in strong feelings of empathy and connectedness with fellow nationals living in another state. When these people are considered abused, war can be evoked by a felt need to extend protection to fellow nationals living elsewhere. Thus, India felt justified in entering the 1971 Pakistani civil war between mostly Bengalis in what was then East Pakistan and Pashtuns in West Pakistan because India's Bengali population found it intolerable to stand idly by during Pakistan's slaughter of its own Bengali population. (Bengalis and Pashtuns are both predominantly Muslims, but each constitutes a different ethnic group—and thus, different nations—in terms of language, customs, and, to some extent, physical characteristics.)

Some Arab states send money in support of Palestinian nationalism, thereby expressing solidarity with fellow Arabs. The (mostly black) states of sub-Saharan Africa were especially opposed to South African apartheid because of the oppression by whites of its black population. Turkey has come to the aid of the Turkish population on Cyprus, just as Greece has been seen as the protector of the Greek population in the Greek-speaking component of that island. Many Irish Americans have historically supported Irish independence from the United Kingdom (including, to some degree, offering financial aid to violent constituents of the Irish Republican Army), just as many Jewish Americans tend to support Israel in its conflict with the Palestinians.

Of course, this is not the whole story, and extending cross-national solidarity can also be a pretext for aggression. For an example, Hitler annexed Czechoslovakia and invaded Poland, using alleged mistreatment of Czech and Polish "Germans" as an excuse. The US invasion of Grenada in 1983 was officially justified at the time by the claim that American medical students on that island were in danger of being taken hostage, just as the US invasion of Panama in 1989 was ostensibly undertaken to protect American lives in that country. In short, claims of cross-national solidarity have often been used to provide legal and political justifications that rationalize a conflict or military intervention whose roots may well lie elsewhere.

Closely related is "irredentism," a term derived from the Italian *irredento* (lost or unredeemed) and initially applied to regions of today's Italy, once controlled by the Austrian-Hungarian Empire but containing mostly ethnic

Italians. Irredentism refers to efforts at claiming or reclaiming territory that is justified by real or imagined connections to a particular territory and the people living there. When Argentina invaded the British-held Falkland Islands, it was acting on irredentist ambitions; the government in Buenos Aires considered itself the legitimate owner of what it called the Malvinas. Russian occupation of the Crimea was an irredentist act (the Crimea and, indeed, Ukraine as a whole had long been part of the Soviet/Russian Empire). There are many irredentist claims at work in the world, including the People Republic of China's wish to "reunite" with Taiwan, Northern Ireland as perceived by many in the Irish Republic, and so forth. All, in a sense, represent manifestations of nationalism, in some cases "genuine" and in others employed by the irredentist-leaning state as an excuse for its own expansion.

In many cases, states stop short of war but nonetheless provide "fraternal" aid to similar ethnic groups in other states. This is often done to promote their own interests, even if those interests are limited to satisfying otherwise restive, kindred national elements within their own borders. India, for example, was drawn into the fighting in Sri Lanka (formerly Ceylon) because both India and Sri Lanka have a large Tamil population, which is overwhelmingly Hindu. Russia is also an amalgamation of many ethnic groups (although much less so than the former Soviet Union, many of whose republics—which were to a large extent based on a degree of ethnic homogeneity—gained autonomy in 1991).

In addition, there are currently large ethnic Russian populations in many of the former states of the Soviet Union (in what Russia refers to as its "near abroad"). The danger therefore exists that a nationalist government in Russia might attempt to intervene in, say, Estonia, Latvia, or Kazakhstan, ostensibly on behalf of Russians in those countries, as already happened in the case of Ukraine when in 2015 Russia invaded and established a "fact on the ground," annexing Crimea, which, although part of Ukraine, also contains a large Russian-speaking and Russia-sympathetic population.

Russian nationalists were infuriated when the Baltic states joined NATO in 2004, contrary to US assurances after the break-up of the Soviet Union that NATO would not extend its membership any further east. Russia has had a long and painful history of being invaded from the West: in the Middle Ages by Lithuanian knights and Polish armies, in the 19th century by Napoleon's Grand Armée, and in the 20th by German forces during both World Wars. Moreover, Ukraine's European-leaning leadership in Kiev has been eager to join both NATO and the European Union. Russian political and military leadership has also been acutely concerned that Islamic fundamentalism might spread from the south to the heartland of Russia itself—a not unjustified worry given the numerous Islamist terrorist attacks in Russia during the past two decades. This, in turn, provided justification for Soviet/Russian wars in Afghanistan and Chechnya.

The future of nationalism is impossible to predict. On the one hand, transnationalism (communication and commerce across national borders, facilitated by the rise of cell phones and the Internet) was predicted to lead to enhanced nationalism, as members of various national diasporas (people who have migrated to other countries but nonetheless retain a sense of ethnic and national identity with their original homeland) connect with each other, thereby forming a potent social and political force. At the same time, however, others erroneously anticipated that globalization would generate a rapid decline in nation-states, with their parochial political and linguistic boundaries.

To date, neither prediction has clearly been confirmed, although growing numbers of nationalists object to what they see as globalization's dilution of their culture and traditions, whereas others eagerly anticipate that globalization will bring about prosperity and in the process strengthen nation-building and pronationalist sentiment. Just as the future of nationalism points in multiple directions, so do the effects of nationalist sentiment.

Nationalist Threats to States

One might ask why many governments so strenuously resist the various secessionist and reintegrationist national movements. Aren't the West Pakistanis better off not being artificially united with 100 million restless and resentful Bengalis? What would be the harm to Spaniards if the Basques (and Catalans) seceded and formed their own small nation-state(s)? Or to the US if Puerto Rico became an independent country?

Part of the answer may reflect a loss of national pride, the hope for the largest and greatest possible state, as well as fear of a slippery slope whereby other restive regions might be encourage to secede as well. In addition, the resisting peoples are often those who profit economically and socially from the presence of the would-be secessionists. British and American support for national self-determination for Kuwait (invaded by Iraq in 1990) and Brunei (long coveted by Indonesia) derives largely from interest in the oil resources of these small countries. Similarly, Belgium's support in 1960 for attempts by residents of Katanga to secede from the Congo was tied to the copper wealth of that province. Had Biafra been carved out of Nigeria, much of that state's industrial capacity and natural resources would have gone, along with the Ibo people. When Hitler seized the Sudetenland, he not only "liberated" 3 million Sudeten Germans but also—not coincidentally—seized about three-quarters of Czechoslovakia's industrial capacity, including an important armaments industry. South Sudan has oil, which north Sudan lacks, and Catalonia is the economic powerhouse of Spain.

When states are heterogeneous (i.e., composed of many ethnic groups and republics), political leaders often worry that demands for national self-determination may lead to additional popular demands and possibly to the breakup of the home country. This happened, for example, in the former Yugoslavia during the 1990s. Such fears drove the dying Habsburg Empire's policies at the onset of World War I, as well as many of the Russian government's international actions since the mid-1990s. Furthermore, further Balkanization (the breakup of a larger region into small constituent states, as happened in the Balkans) of Africa, India, or anywhere else may not necessarily further the cause of peace. Certainly, the Balkan Peninsula, known as the "tinderbox of Europe," has not been a good advertisement for the benefits of nationalist sentiment, as was abundantly clear during the last decade of the 20th century, when the former Yugoslavia violently splintered into separate states.

Although nationalism is generally seen as a force for unity within a political entity, this is only true if such an entity is mostly homogeneous. When diverse nations are contained within a single state, even if civil war and secessionism are avoided, the resulting social divisions may get in the way of unity rather than promoting it. Political leadership in such cases may be hamstrung, unable to provide coherent policies because of the danger of alienating one national faction or another. Examples include Egypt, divided between a Muslim majority and a minority Coptic Christian population, and

Lebanon, a small country that nevertheless includes numerous religious-ethnic factions, including Maronite Christian, Greek Orthodox, Palestinian refugee, Druze, and Chaldean Catholic minorities.

National heterogeneity has bedeviled peace in Iraq, divided into three primary groups: Sunni Arabs, Shiite Arabs (the majority), and Sunni Kurds. During 2020, tensions over Nagorno-Karabakh, a largely Armenian (Christian) enclave within Azerbaijan (mostly Muslim), resulted in short-lived but lethal warfare between Armenia and Azerbaijan. At the same time, multinational Switzerland is notably peaceful even though composed of German, French, Italian, and Romansh speakers, and nationalist sentiment in Scotland—although not quite strong enough to have generated a majority vote for separation from the United Kingdom in 2014 but resurging since Brexit in early 2020—has not evoked fears of violent secessionism (even though Scotland was incorporated into the United Kingdom following much bloodshed fomented by independence-minded Scots).

Racial and Cultural Intolerance

Whenever individuals associate, especially if they do so on the basis of shared characteristics that exclude others and make for a distinction between "Us" and "Them" and political leaders declare, "You're either with us or against us," there are the concomitant dangers of racism, ethnocentrism, xenophobia, and even genocide, not to mention wars against "foreigners."

Many of the world's hostilities involve different nationalities and ethnic groups in conflict. Of course, the mere fact of ethnic difference is not a sufficient cause of war; many pluralistic societies live peacefully, both *intra*nationally (e.g., the multiethnic population of Hawaii and of multilingual Switzerland) and *inter*nationally. In addition, distinct racial or cultural differences are not necessary for war, either. Paraguay and its racially and culturally similar neighbors fought some extraordinarily bloody wars in the 19th century, as did Austrians and Prussians, North and South Koreans, and North and South Vietnamese, not to mention the long and tragic history of civil wars within such relatively ethnically homogeneous nations as Spain and China.

Ethnic and Religious Antagonisms and "Ethnic Cleansing"

A high proportion of armed conflicts involve members of different ethnic/religious/cultural/linguistic groups, such as Iraq (Arab) versus Iran (Persian) and Jews versus Arabs in the Middle East, Irish Catholics versus UK-supportive Protestants in Northern Ireland, Tamils versus Sinhalese in Sri Lanka, Orthodox Christians (mostly Serbian) against Muslims (mostly Bosnian) in the former Yugoslavia, and Tutsis versus Hutus in Rwanda and Burundi. The horrific culmination of these conflicts has frequently been forced "ethnic cleansing"[15] conducted by militarily superior groups against ethnic minorities, as in large areas of the former Yugoslavia and central Africa. The result has been the slaughter of hundreds of thousands, perhaps millions, of people and often forced dislocation from their ancestral homelands.

In a sense, there is nothing new about this. Hatred based on ethnic and religious differences was at the root of many wars throughout history, including the Crusades of the Middle Ages (European Christians versus Arab Muslims) and the Thirty Years' War (mostly Catholics versus Protestants), which devastated central Europe in the 17th century. To a degree, no clear separation can be drawn between national antagonisms based on religion and those based on race and ethnicity. Many of the 20th-century intra-African wars (Ibo/Hausa, Hutu/Tutsi) have been more ethnic than religious. The India-Pakistan wars, on the other hand, have been primarily religious, although the differences between Hindus and Muslims are so fundamental to Indian and Pakistani society that they often include ethnic distinctions as well.

The Iran-Iraq and Arab-Israeli conflicts have involved both religious and ethnic differences, although economic and political factors are involved as well. The antagonism between Saudi Arabia (mostly Sunni) and Iran (over-whelmingly Shiite) is to some extent derived from religious differences, although ethnic and linguistic differences are also important (the Saudis are Arabs and speak Arabic, whereas the Iranians are Persian and speak Farsi), as are economic and geopolitical considerations. These include the straightfor-ward competitive "power politics" between two important, oil-rich states in the same geographical region.

Clearly, many other considerations apply to each of these conflicts: bor-der disputes, a history of antagonism based at least partly on generations of real or perceived oppression, economic rivalries, and the like. Usually, these various "causes" provide the immediate stimulus for each outbreak of violence. But national and often racial sentiments linger in the background as an underlying cause as well as an explanation for the persistence and intensity of many conflicts. In addition, once war erupts—even if for other immediate reasons—the belligerents often seize on any purported differ-ences between themselves and their opponents, typically magnifying these differences, elevating their own traits, and devaluing those of the other side. Usually it is sufficient just to point to the opponents as different (e.g., as Hondurans rather than Salvadorans. or as Koreans rather than Japanese) to evoke potent antagonisms. Dehumanizing language and racial/ethnic scape-goating are often introduced at this point as well.

A year after World War I began, Einstein lamented humanity's insistence on primitive hatred and its use of nationalism as the vehicle for that hatred:

> When posterity recounts the achievements of Europe, shall we let men say that three centuries of painstaking cultural effort carried us no fur-ther than from the fanaticism of religion to the insanity of national-ism? It would seem that men always seek some idiotic fiction in the name of which they can hate one another. Once it was religion; now it is the state.[16]

"State worship" and nationalism, of the sort that Einstein so decried, come together, especially in fascism and in other ultranationalist ideologies of statism.

Nationalism and the Public Mood

Public opinion counts, especially when it comes to issues of peace or war. Even dictators are concerned with their citizenry's mood, especially when it comes to rallying a nation for conflict. This is even truer in a democracy. "Opinion," wrote Alexander Hamilton, "whether well or ill-founded is the governing principle of human affairs."[17] And during one of his debates with Stephen Douglas, Abraham Lincoln noted that "he who molds public senti-ment goes deeper than he who enacts statutes or pronounces decisions."

Wars can be provoked for many reasons, including so-called reasons of state (*raisons d'état*), which, at the outset, evoke very little nationalist passion on the part of the participants; rather, they proceed in large part from the machinations of leadership. To prosecute wars, however, especially in the modern era, it has proven necessary for governments, through the mass media, to inflame the public, a role for which nationalist passions are well suited.

Manipulating Public Opinion by Arousing Public Passions

In modern times, war requires the mobilization of national sentiment, so if real affronts to national dignity, honor, or well-being are not available, pretexts are often arranged. Even Hitler, who sought to invade Poland in 1939, found it necessary to stage a phony "incident" to justify his actions and help arouse German national indignation: He staged an attack, allegedly by Polish forces (but actually by German prisoners wearing Polish uniforms), against a German radio station. The so-called Gulf of Tonkin incident, in which US destroyers were supposed to have been attacked by North Vietnamese forces in 1964, is now acknowledged to have been exaggerated and manipulated by the US government, so as to induce congressional authorization and public support for the unrestricted involvement of US combat units in Vietnam.

Effective orators and publicists have long been able to sway public mood, often generating enthusiasm for war and disregarding inconvenient facts. In his chronicle of the Peloponnesian War, the ancient Greek historian Thucydides recounted that the Athenian general Alcibiades stirred up irresistible public enthusiasm for glory, booty, and adventure. "With this enthusiasm of the majority," noted Thucydides, "the few that liked it not feared to appear unpatriotic by holding up their hands against it, and so they kept quiet." The result was an expedition against Syracuse (in modern-day Sicily) that ultimately proved as disastrous to Athens as it had been irresistible.

In the 2nd century BCE, when Carthage had long ceased to be a threat to Rome, the elderly and eloquent Roman orator Cato repeated to great effect after each of his speeches, *Carthago delenda est* ("Carthage must be destroyed"). And in the ensuing Punic War, it was. The US entry into the Spanish-American War was promoted by lurid and generally inaccurate accounts of alleged Spanish atrocities in Cuba, notably the so-called yellow journalism of the Hearst newspaper chain, which favored war. The US battleship *Maine* was blown up while in Havana harbor, allegedly by Spanish agents; this acutely inflamed American passions, and "Remember the *Maine*" became a slogan of that war. Many historians now maintain that the *Maine* was actually sunk by a prowar group to provide a pretext for the hostilities that followed; others argue that it sank due to a boiler accident.

One consequence of manipulating public opinion so as to arouse popular passion is that many of today's nationalist and ethnic wars remain unresolved, partly because relatively few recent wars have been successful in ending the underlying conflict that generated the war itself. Korea, for example, remains divided and heavily armed, nearly 70 years after cessation of the Korean War; India and Pakistan are in a state of ongoing antagonism, especially over control of Kashmir, terrorism, and the diminishing status of Muslims in India. The Middle East remains a tinderbox, and Cyprus, the Balkans, and much of central Asia and Africa are still divided among conflicting ethnic factions. Nationalist passions keep age-old rivalries simmering, interfering with the prospect of reconciling old disputes or healing ancient injuries.

In some cases, however, closure on a nationalist war has been achieved, generally when the most intensely pronationalist side wins: This happened in Vietnam, as in most anticolonial wars of national liberation. In other cases, a decisive move by a national leader—as with former Egyptian president Sadat's overtures to Israel—can overcome, or at least ameliorate, the prowar drift of nationalist passion.

Nationalism and Political Ideology

Even so potent a force as political ideology can appear pallid compared with the energies unleashed by nationalism, which is a primitive and pervasive ideology of its own. The Soviets and the Chinese Communists were both officially Marxist, but, for the most part, they remained Russians and Chinese first, as witnessed by their history of armed border clashes and persistent distrust in recent decades. Similarly, the Vietnamese and Chinese, despite a shared Marxist-Leninist ideology, fought a short but vicious war in 1979 and remain mutually distrustful today.

World War I: Ideology Loses to Nationalism

Perhaps the most dramatic case of the triumph of nationalism over ideology occurred in the early days of World War I. (More accurately, nationalist and imperialist ideology clashed with internationalist and socialist ideology, and the former won.)

In the years prior to World War I, many European Socialist and Social Democratic parties were powerful, seemingly united, and for the most part committed to opposing the institution of war, which was seen by most socialists as part of capitalist exploitation of the proletariat. Through various resolutions associated with the Second International, as well as within each major European country, major Socialist and Social Democratic parties (most influentially, those of Germany and France) asserted that if war ever appeared imminent, their memberships would smother it by general strikes and, if necessary, insurrections. Solidarity among the working class would, following this logic, make war impossible: "They" might declare a war, but no one would come.

Before war was declared, however, French socialists began worrying that German socialists would be unable to restrain German militarism, which would leave France powerless to withstand German aggression. German socialists, in turn, were afraid that antimilitary and antinationalist success on their part would leave Germany at the mercy of reactionary czarist Russia. In the end, an overwhelming majority within the socialist parties of each country announced support for the coming war because for *their* country, such a war would be defensive. The following declaration, by the Social Democratic Party of Germany in 1914, shows the tenor of thinking at the time:

> We are menaced by the terror of foreign invasion. The problem before
> us now is not the relative advisability of war or peace, but a consider-
> ation of just what steps must be taken for the protection of our country
> . . . . It devolves upon us, therefore, to avert this danger, to shelter the
> civilization and independence of our native land.[18]

Ideology and Nationalism Combined

In contrast, sometimes political ideology and nationalism go hand in hand, producing a combination that is especially potent. War-prone imperialist France during the 18th and 19th centuries, for example, was committed to its *mission civilisatrice,* the notion that France had a special mission to civilize the dark skinned, non-French world. Similarly, German national militarism in the 20th century was buttressed by Nazi yearnings for a "thousand-year *Reich*" peopled by a triumphant "Aryan race." The former Soviet Union's support for Third World national revolutions derived in part from its devotion to Marxist-Leninist ideology, just as the American ideology of free-market capitalism and the vision of the United States as the "new Jerusalem," a "shining city on the hill," uniquely pleasing to God and man, undergirded US territorial expansion during the 19th century and overcame its penchant for isolationism in substantial periods of the 20th and early 21st centuries.

In most cases, peace movements fare poorly during wartime, overwhelmed by militant national enthusiasm. There are exceptions, however. A kind of "war weariness" can set in, especially when the war is controversial or appears to be stalemated. The Vietnam War was such an example, controversial from the start and terminated in large part because the initial support of the American citizenry morphed increasingly into public outrage and mass war resistance. World War I turned out much bloodier than expected and, after several years, seemed nowhere near resolution. Although citizen support remained generally high (except in Russia), front-line mutinies became frequent. Fifty-four divisions (about half of the total) of the French Army mutinied in April 1917; 25,000 men were eventually court-martialed. Such behavior was contagious. The following month, 400,000 Italian troops deserted the field at Caporetto (although thousands stayed and were slaughtered, leading to one of the worst defeats in Italian military history), while around the same time, German and Russian troops were fraternizing openly.

President Obama inherited the wars in Afghanistan and Iraq from the administration of George W. Bush. As they dragged on, resulting in hundreds of thousands of casualties (mostly Afghan and Iraqi) and few demonstrable payoffs, both wars became increasingly unpopular with the American public, although neither war generated the kind of large-scale popular resistance that characterized, for example, public disaffection with the Vietnam War 40 years earlier. (Interestingly, estimated US and NATO combat casualties in Iraq and Afghanistan have so far been significantly lower than in the Vietnam War.)

The Tension Between Peace and Freedom

For all the legitimate criticism of war and of nationalism's frequent role in stimulating violent group-oriented passions, there has also been a positive side to nationalist sentiment in relation to war. Thus, some of humanity's most stirring visions and most memorable sacrifices have been made ostensibly on behalf of freedom—typically efforts of national groups to achieve self-determination.

Consider, for example, the blood-tingling sentiments of these lines from Robert Burns's poem (later set to music) "Scots Wha Hae," originally written in support of renewed Scottish national independence (Scotland was an independent state before being forcibly incorporated into the United Kingdom):

> *By oppression's woes and pain! By your sons in servile chains!*
>
> *We will drain our dearest veins, but they shall be free!*
>
> *Lay the proud usurpers low! Tyrants fall in every foe!*
>
> *Liberty's in every blow! Let us do or die.* [In Scottish dialect, "die" rhymes with "free."]

Many people think of nationalism and ethnocentrism as major reasons for wars, and they are at least partly correct. Certainly, nationalist sentiments, such as those expressed by Burns, are not likely to lead to the peaceful resolution of conflicts. It may be somewhat surprising, therefore, to learn that through much of the 19th and 20th centuries, nationalism was widely viewed as a potentially strong contributor to *peace*. Satisfying nationalist yearnings should, if nothing else, douse violent, frustrated passions, and, moreover, ethnically unified nations would seem less prone to civil war. However, the civil wars of Spain and China during the mid-20th century and, more recently, in Iraq, Afghanistan, Libya, Syria, and in much of central Africa give the lie to this somewhat wishful thinking.

On the other hand, by producing a crosscutting loyalty—one that transcends connections of economic class, local leadership, and even religion—feelings of national identity and ethnic solidarity may have sometimes contributed to peace and social stability. Thus, nationalism has helped end many instances of endemic subnational conflict. Following the establishment of nation-states in Western Europe, for example, the low-level feuding and banditry as well as the religious and class violence that had long characterized that region were virtually ended . . . to be followed, alas, by high-level war-making between these nation-states!

Although the future of Iraq, Syria, and Afghanistan remains unclear at the present time, the prospect of peace in those devastated countries depends, in part, on whether their citizens act upon a supranational identity as united "Iraqis," "Syrians," and "Afghans" rather than as ethnically based national groups—notably, as Sunni Arabs, Shiite Arabs, and Kurds (instead of "Iraqis"); as Kurds, Druze, Shiites, Alawites, Sunnis, and Christians (instead of "Syrians"); and as Pashtun, Tajik, Hazara, and Uzbek (instead of "Afghans"). On the other hand, it is possible that Syria and Iraq will come apart and become "failed states" like Libya, with the Western colonial borders of these artificial states being redrawn to reflect the ethnically divided realities on the ground, with Kurds, Shiites, and Sunnis controlling large swaths of these former nation-states.

The US Civil War took place in part because feelings of regional identity (especially in the South) were stronger than national identity. Perhaps stronger ties of allegiance by southerners to the nation of the United States of America might have kept the peace, at least in this instance. (What it would have done with slavery, however, remains unknowable.) The idea of nationalism as a route to peace is nonetheless ironic in that the first nation-state to have achieved what is generally regarded as a modern level of national self-consciousness—Napoleonic France—proceeded almost immediately to embark upon the most expansive, nationalistically motivated series of wars that Europe had experienced up to that time. Nonetheless, many one-time oppressed minorities—"captive nations" within autocratic empires—including Greeks under the yoke of the Ottoman Empire, Italians within the Austro-Hungarian, and so forth—have historically realized their national aspirations by successful, and mostly peaceful, struggles to form their own states.

By the turn of the 20th century, mainstream liberal European attitudes toward nationalism had become ambivalent. Rhetorical support for national self-determination clashed with reluctance to alienate powerful countries, no matter how oppressive. By the second decade of the 21st century, despite widespread sympathy in the United States for the national aspirations of various ethnic groups (e.g., Chechens and Tatars within Russia), the US government has avoided direct threats to the geographic and political integrity of Russia. Some analysts would say that smaller, less militarized, and less economically important countries are more subject to outside demands for national self-determination within their borders. Western foreign policy has consistently undercut the prospects of Kurdish nationalism, opting instead for the status quo, largely so as not to upset NATO ally Turkey. By the same token, the United States and Western countries tread carefully when it comes to questioning China's oppression of Buddhist Tibetans and of its indigenous Uighur people, who are Muslim and also ethnically different from the Han Chinese majority.

The Post–World War II International Scene

Europe was largely peaceful from World War II until the Balkan Wars in the former Yugoslavia and NATO's military intervention in 1999 during the breakup of that country. But Europe has also achieved a fair degree of national self-determination: Just about all French live in France and all Germans in Germany, nearly all Poles in Poland, and so forth. There are, however, Austrians in northern Italy (the Tyrol), Hungarians in Romania, and, until 1999, Albanians in Serbia (i.e., in Kosovo); there are also Gypsies (Roma) in much of eastern Europe and many "guest workers" from northern Africa, southern Europe, and Turkey in northern and western Europe, as well as millions of Arabs and other refugees and economic migrants from northern Africa and the Middle East, especially from Iraq, Afghanistan, and Syria.

The presence of minority groups in many European countries has led to a backlash against foreigners, who are (in most cases, incorrectly) perceived as taking jobs away from the ethnic majorities and of supporting or participating in well-publicized terrorist attacks on European cities. Right-wing politicians have in some European countries capitalized on widespread feelings of resentment and ethnic chauvinism. This has also led to substantial unease and occasional violence (especially in France, Germany, and Belgium, which have large minority populations). This manipulation of the racial attitudes and economic anxieties of ordinary citizens also contributed greatly to Brexit (Britain's exit from the European Union in January 2020).

There continue to be simmering separatist movements among Spanish Basques and Catalans, Catholics in Northern Ireland, and, occasionally, Swiss in the Jura region, as well as tension between Flemings (speaking a Dutch/German dialect) and French-speaking Walloons in Belgium, which is sometimes described as a "first-world failed state." Similar difficulties were most acute in the former Yugoslavia, which came apart violently in the 1990s. The resurgence of jingoism, ethnocentrism, and xenophobia in many parts of Europe shows few signs of abating and threatens to reverse the relatively halcyon conditions that prevailed in most of Europe during the second half of the 20th century, when the "Euro-project" of political as well as economic integration appeared successful.

Thus, the Euro (a shared European currency) has been under pressure, notably as a result of Greece's default on its national debt and Britain's exit from the European Union. In addition, the stability of the Schengen Zone, a region encompassing 26 countries within which most travel restrictions were eliminated, has been threatened by tensions over how to accommodate huge numbers of migrants and refugees, who are fleeing war and other abuses in their home countries. Local nationalists claim to fear loss of their "national identities," which has resulted in an upsurge in rightwing, nationalistic, and xenophobic political parties.

Other regions outside Europe did not experience the Cold War "peace" that prevailed in most of Europe between 1945 and 1990. Palestinians continue to strive for national self-determination, which may yet be attainable but only if Israel makes what it perceives to be concessions to the Palestinians as well as to the Arab nations surrounding it. India is a patchwork of numerous potential nations in which people speak more than a thousand languages. China, although relatively homogeneous, contains more than 50 million non-Chinese, of whom Tibetans and Uighurs are the most oppressed and resentful. Russia, like its predecessor, the former Soviet Union, remains a vast heterogeneous assemblage of territories and regions dominated by different ethnic groups. Finally, the boundaries of many postcolonial African states are contentious, in part because they were drawn (by Europeans) with virtually no regard to the nationalities of the indigenous peoples.

The Effects of Political Ideology

There is also the prickly question of fundamental values: Peace is a noble value, but is it preferable to anything else? Is it so worthy an end that it should be maintained at all costs? Similarly, what are the connections between peace and freedom or between peace and justice? What if justice—including national self-determination—seems unobtainable short of war?

Since 1945, many Western advocates of peace have tended to see nationalism as an evil if practiced by the Western powers, not only because it has led in the past to imperialism and major wars but also because it may contribute to the growing danger of nuclear war. At the same time, there is a tendency by many Western progressives to look favorably on wars of national liberation, if directed by the oppressed against their oppressors—for example, the Algerian struggles against France during the 1950s and 1960s, the Mau Mau movement for independence of Kenya from Britain during that same time, the Vietnamese conflict with the United States, and the struggles by Chechens and Kosovars to detach themselves from Russia and Serbia, respectively.

Before the collapse of the Soviet Union, right-wing anticommunists, while deploring revolutionary nationalist violence (which they have often labeled as "communist inspired" and therefore especially illegitimate), applauded various ultra-violent counterrevolutionary wars, including those conducted by the *contras* in Nicaragua, UNITA in Angola, and the anti-Soviet mujahideen in Afghanistan. Extreme right- and left-wing ideologues are often willing to value freedom (and "social justice") over peace, so long as freedom is defined as either (in the first case) freedom from Marxist governments or (in the second case) liberation from colonial or right-wing military dictators.

During the second half of the 20th century, there was a tendency among American conservatives to see antiestablishment revolutionary movements as aligned with worldwide, "monolithic communism." In contrast, leftists have been more likely to emphasize the nationalist, rather than the ideological, underpinnings of such activities. They point out, for example, that Josip Broz Tito, the anti-Nazi partisan leader and later president of Yugoslavia, was a nationalist first and a communist second (e.g., he withdrew Yugoslavia from the Soviet-dominated Warsaw Pact). Similarly, Ho Chi Minh, who led the North Vietnamese communists during the early days of the Vietnam War and had previously conducted independence struggles against Japan and France, was committed to Vietnamese nationalism more than to communism of either the Chinese or Soviet variety. The effort to achieve freedom via national struggle has produced many wars of liberation and of counter-liberation. At the same time, there has been widespread Western reluctance to acknowledge the role of nationalist sentiments in Iraq and Afghanistan in generating hostility toward US and NATO military forces.

The Question of "National Character"

There is no scientific evidence for any genetically influenced behavioral differences among people of differing nationalities. Nonetheless, there remains a persistent belief that a nation can in some cases be characterized by certain summed personality traits. There have accordingly been numerous errors of political judgment resulting from a misreading of the "national character" of a prospective opponent.

Hitler, for example—and Napoleon before him—believed that Britain was a "nation of shopkeepers" and therefore neither willing nor able to resist aggression. During the 18th century, Germans were deemed by the British and others to be either dreamy metaphysicians or incurable romantics, not cut out for heavy industry or any other practical undertakings; the Italians, in contrast, were about 200 years ago considered highly rational and scientifically inclined. Today, these two stereotypes have, to some extent, been reversed.

Often such perceptions are self-serving (or, rather, nation-serving) as well as incorrect. During World War II, for example, part of the Allied justification for bombing German cities was that unlike the allegedly dauntless British moral fiber, the German will to persevere would "crack" under bombardment, leading perhaps to revolt and thereby shortening the war. Official British government documents claim that "the evidence at our disposal goes to show that the morale of the average German civilian will weaken quicker than that of a population such as our own as a consequence of direct attack."[19] There is debate about whether strategic bombing actually shortened World War II by creating shortages of critical materials, notably ball bearings and petroleum, in its final months. However, it is now widely acknowledged that, if anything, bombing increased the will to resist. Certainly, the German "national character" did not crack.

During the 1960s and early 1970s, the United States underestimated the ability and willingness of the North Vietnamese to absorb bomb attacks and yet persevere in a war to which they, as a nation, were committed (whereas the United States, increasingly, was not). Despite what are perceived to be their eventual defeats, Serbs during the war over Kosovo and Chechens during the bombardments perpetrated by Russia held out longer than most Western political "experts" expected. This may in part be explained by a "rally 'round the flag" effect that strengthens ties of national and ethnic solidarity when people are under attack by a foreign power, even if the domestic regime is also perceived as corrupt and autocratic.

For example, German invasion of the USSR during World War II (known in Russia as the "Great Patriotic War") enhanced popular allegiance to the dictatorial Soviet leader Josef Stalin. Much of the resistance by Iraqi insurgents and by Afghan Taliban-followers to the US-led occupation—which was largely unanticipated by the Bush Administrations—was also due to a near-universal inclination toward national solidarity in the face of foreign occupation. This may be among the very few genuine components of national character, although it appears to be a human behavioral universal rather than limited to the character of any particular nation.

The persistence of the idea of national character is probably due to the fact that, although incorrect biologically, it has the appearance of psychological and sociological reality. Thus, a "national style," in speech, clothing, and even responses to stress or to potential enemies, can sometimes be exhibited. These styles can and do change over time, but they are nonetheless often inconsistent.

For example, some Mediterranean peoples (Italians, Greeks) seem to be relatively more voluble and excitable than peoples in more northern climates (Scandinavians, Germans, British, etc.). Latin Americans and Arabs tend to maintain less interpersonal distance than do Americans or Europeans, which sometimes leads to misunderstandings at international gatherings. Japanese and Chinese seem (by mainstream American standards) unusually concerned with politeness and social formality. And Russians and Americans often misinterpret each other. For example, when Soviet premier Khrushchev arrived in the US during a tense moment in the Cold War for a summit meeting with President Eisenhower, he unwittingly antagonized many Americans by clasping both hands above his head, in a gesture used to signal victory by US prizefighters; in the former Soviet Union, the same gesture communicated friendship and solidarity.

Whatever the role of national character and of shared experiences in molding collective traits and behaviors, the power of national self-image, or ethnic identity, is considerable. Nations and ethnic groups invariably see themselves as well-meaning and motivated only by the purest of goals; their adversaries, on the other hand, typically see them differently. For example, Americans generally perceived their efforts on behalf of post–World War II reconstruction (the Truman Doctrine and the Marshall Plan), which included assistance to defeated Germany and Japan along with economic aid to Greece and Turkey, as generous and laudable, a positive manifestation of their national character. To the Soviets, these actions appeared entirely self-serving, a form of economic imperialism, a device to relieve American post-war overproduction, and a political and military weapon directed against the Soviet Union.

More recently, many Americans saw the post–Cold War status of their nation (having emerged, at least for a time, as the sole superpower) as validating its political and economic ideology of "democratic capitalism" and of "American exceptionalism." At the same time, many other countries (especially Russia, much of the Islamic world, and, increasingly, China, much of Latin America, Africa, and even Western Europe) regard this posture as US arrogance and a dangerously inflated self-righteousness combined with a failure to acknowledge its diminished international standing.

A Final Note on Nationalism and Ethnocentrism

On the one hand, nationalism and ethnic solidarity can sometimes evoke compassion, love, and community pride. Love of one's land, people, culture, and ecosystems can contribute to dignity, caring, altruism, and some of the nobler emotions of which human beings are capable. At the same time, however, nationalism and ethnocentrism can become malevolent when they foster ethnic chauvinism, when they create violent divisions between people, and when they threaten to destroy the humanistic values they supposedly venerate. Nationalism and ethnocentrism pump people up, and they often generate conditions that bring them down as well.

In his essay "Christianity and Patriotism," Leo Tolstoy pitied "the good-natured foolish people, who, showing their healthy white teeth as they smile, gape like children, naively delighted at the dressed-up admirals and presidents, at the flags waving above them, and at the fireworks, and the playing bands." Tolstoy warned that this euphoria is typically short-lived, and the flags and cheerful bands are quickly replaced by "only the desolate wet plain, cold, hunger, misery—in front of them the slaughterous enemy, behind them the relentless government, blood, wounds, agonies, rotting corpses and a senseless, useless death."[20] One of the great challenges to students and practitioners of peace and conflict resolution is accordingly to channel the benevolent aspects of nationalism and ethnic solidarity while guarding against their horrors.

Questions for Further Reflection

1. What similarities and differences are there between premodern, nontechnological wars and contemporary warfare?

2. How does nationalism act as a force for peace? Or as a force for war? Or for something else?

3. Choose a current international or domestic conflict and describe the role played by either dehumanization, irredentism, or aspiration for political freedom.

4. What are some advantages and disadvantages of nationalism in late 20th- and early 21st-century political struggles?

5. To what extent and in what ways do national movements *influence* public opinion, in contrast with *responding* to it? Use specific examples such as the wars in Iraq and Afghanistan.

Suggestions for Further Reading

Benedict Anderson. 2006. *Imagined Communities: Reflections on the Origin and Spread of Nationalism.* New York: Verso.

John Coakley. 2012. *Nationalism, Ethnicity and the State: Making and Breaking Nations.* Thousand Oaks, CA: SAGE.

Douglas R. Fry. 2007. *Beyond War: The Human Potential for Peace.* New York: Oxford University Press.

Ernest Gellner. 2009. *Nations and Nationalism,* 2nd ed. Ithaca, NY: Cornell University Press.

Leah Greenfeld. 2019. *Nationalism: A Short History.* Washington DC: Brookings Institution Press.

Yoram Hazony. 2018. *The Virtue of Nationalism.* New York: Basic Books.

E. J. Hobsbawm. 2012. *Nations and Nationalism Since 1780.* Cambridge, UK: Cambridge University Press.

Yael Tamir. 2019. *Why Nationalism.* Princeton, NJ: Princeton University Press.

Notes

1. Walter Bagehot. 2010. *Physics and Politics*. Cambridge, UK: Cambridge University Press.

2. Herbert Spencer. 1993. *Political Writings*. Cambridge, UK: Cambridge University Press.

3. Bronislaw Malinowski. 1941. "An Anthropological Analysis of War." *American Journal of Sociology*, 46: 521–550.

4. H. H. Turner-High. 1949. *Primitive War*. Columbia: University of South Carolina Press.

5. D. Fry. 2012. "Life Without War." *Science*, 336: 879–894.

6. William James. 1911. "The Moral Equivalent of War." In *Memories and Studies*. New York: Longman, Green.

7. This process occurred over a period of roughly six months, during which there existed the UFFR: the Union of Fewer and Fewer Republics.

8. John Stoessinger. 1962. *The Might of Nations*. New York: Random House.

9. J. Ernest Renan. 1882. *Qu'est-ce qu'une nation?* Paris: Calmann-Levy.

10. George Orwell. 1953. *Such, Such Were the Joys*. New York: Harcourt, Brace.

11. H. Richard Niebuhr. 1970. *Radical Monotheism and Western Culture*. New York: Harper & Row.

12. Quoted in G. G. Van Deusen. 1937. *The Life of Henry Clay*. Boston: Little, Brown.

13. These events are highlighted in the concluding scenes of the movie *Lawrence of Arabia*, which chronicles the actions of the historical character T. E. Lawrence, a British officer who coordinated Arab resistance to the Turks, only to see his promises to the Arabs painfully broken after the war.

14. Richard M. Nixon. Radio and TV address to the nation, April 10, 1970.

15. A regrettable phrase first introduced by Eastern Orthodox Serbs committing genocide against Bosnian Muslims in the 1990s.

16. Albert Einstein. 1979. *Einstein: A Centenary Volume*. Cambridge, MA: Harvard University Press.

17. Hamilton Papers, Library of Congress; ALS, Hamilton Papers, Library of Congress. In *JCHW*, I, 56, letter dated 1778.

18. Quoted in Kenneth Waltz. 1959. *Man, the State, and War*. New York: Columbia University Press.

19. Quoted in C. Webster and N. Frankland. 1961. *The Strategic Air Offensive Against Germany*. London: HMSO.

20. Leo Tolstoy. 1987. *Writings on Civil Disobedience and Nonviolence*. Philadelphia: New Society.

8

The State Level

W e now come to the role of states in our examination of why wars occur. For many, or one, including most political scientists, states are the primary actors on the global stage. But although states are often sufficient for the genesis and resolution of worldwide conflicts, it is unclear if they are necessary, especially because in the 21st century, the boundaries between state and nonstate belligerents are becoming increasingly blurred.

Defining the State

Popular usage (especially in the United States) often refers to nation, when the correct word is state. The former correctly refers to a collection of people and the latter to an entity that is acknowledged to have legitimacy

8

Drew Angerer via Getty Images

The State Level

We now come to the role of states in our examination of why wars occur. For many people, including most political scientists, states are the prime movers on the global stage. But although states are often sufficient for the genesis and resolution of worldwide conflicts, it is unclear if they are necessary, especially because, in the 21st century, the boundaries between state and nonstate belligerents are becoming increasingly blurred.

Defining the State

Popular usage (especially in the United States) often refers to *nation,* when the correct word is *state*. The former correctly refers to a collection of people and the latter to an entity that is acknowledged to have legitimacy to function in the world political arena. (Thus, the United Nations should more properly have been called the United States . . . but that name was already taken!) More generally, a state can be defined as a sovereign political unit that may include many different communities and formal institutions and that operates via a centralized government, which has the authority and power to decree and enforce laws, collect taxes, and act as the legally recognized representative of its citizens in exchanges with other states, including the waging of war.

The relationship between nations and states is complex. Although there have long been efforts to make national and state borders coincide, thus creating nation-states, states also tend to suppress national movements within their borders. It has been estimated that there are about 200 states containing approximately 800 nationalist movements (more than 7,000 if ethnic identity alone is taken as the criterion for nationhood). At the same time, states promote their own forms of "nationalism," often calling it "patriotism," glorifying those who participate while denouncing those who don't. Thus, the leaders of states often seek to create a national or patriotic identity by unifying the diverse peoples living within state borders.

The concept of statehood has often been imbued with an idealistic and almost metaphysical significance; so, for that matter, has the concept of nationhood. "What is the State essentially?" asked Randolph S. Bourne.

> The more closely we examine it, the more mystical and personal it becomes. On the Nation we can put our hand as a definite social group, with attitudes and qualities exact enough to mean something. On the Government we can put our hand as a certain organization of ruling functions, the machinery of law-making and law-enforcing. The Administration is a recognizable group of political functionaries, temporarily in charge of the government. But the State stands as an idea behind them all, eternal, sanctified, and from it Government and Administration conceive themselves to have the breath of life.[1]

This abstract description notwithstanding, the modern state performs numerous specific functions and has immense power, including the power to wage war. When discussion of the state is not enveloped in emotional rhetoric ("wrapping one's self in the flag"), states often justify their existence by appeals to political realism and to principles of efficiency and solidarity. Yet scholars increasingly recognize that perhaps the most crucial characteristic of the state is its monopoly on the use of "legitimate" physical violence within its territory—that is, states reserve unto themselves the right to take human life, without being answerable to any higher secular authority.

The two political ideologies that particularly value the state—elevating it above the individual—are the authoritarian left and the far right. Thus, in some Communist Party–governed countries, individuals have been considered less important than the collectivity, typically represented by the state. Whereas Marxist theory calls for the eventual "withering away of the state," in practice, the governments of most Communist Party–ruled states are intrusive (as in China, Vietnam, North Korea, and Cuba).

Speaking from the perspective of the far right, Italian Fascist dictator Benito Mussolini wrote,

> The fascist conception of life stresses the importance of the State and accepts the individual only in so far as his interests coincide with those

of the State . . . the fascist conception of the State is all-embracing; outside of it no human or spiritual values can exist, much less have value.[2]

Mainstream liberals and conservatives have also placed considerable
emphasis on the role of the state, with many liberals looking toward the
promise of a benevolent "social welfare state" and conservatives lauding
the role of patriotism and the "national security state." Classical libertarians and extreme conservatives, on the other hand, wish to restrict the size
and functions of the state to the protection of private property and the prevention and punishment of crime. Peace activists and progressive scholars
frequently criticize what they regard as excessive emphasis on states. They
claim that an inordinately state-centered view of world politics makes the
continuation of states a foregone conclusion, thereby shutting out the possibility of other kinds of political organization. But however the state is imagined, whether we like it or not, and whatever our goals may be for states in
general and for our own in particular, states are the primary actors on the
world's political stage (just as multinational corporations have become the
major actors on the world's economic stage), so we should better understand
what they are about.

State Sovereignty

An important concept related to the theory and practice of states is sovereignty, defined by French political philosopher and jurist Jean Bodin
(in 1576) as "the state's supreme authority over citizens and subjects." In
other words, under the doctrine of sovereignty, states are the final arbiter of
earthly matters and disputes. There is no higher recourse. This is supposed to
be true during peacetime but is, if anything, exaggerated during war—at least
with respect to a state's control over its own citizens. Writing during the time
of monarchs believing in the "Divine Right of Kings," Bodin conceived of
sovereignty in the sense of one's "sovereign lord," emphasizing the relationship of a subject to his or her ruler.

The Dutch jurist Hugo Grotius, writing a century later, made major contributions to the development of international law by considering the relations
between sovereign rulers. He contended that in the light of state sovereignty,
no ruler could be subject to legal control by another state. This principle
still applies today, so in theory the United States is legally on a par with, for
example, Malta, an island state in the Mediterranean Sea, one-tenth the size
of Rhode Island and containing about one-third as many people.

The Price of State Sovereignty

A crucial consequence of state sovereignty is what many political scientists term *international anarchy*. In a world composed of separate states,
each of which is sovereign and thus legally equal, by definition there cannot be any higher authority in solving disputes. Conflicting claims among
cities can be adjudicated by the government of a province or whatever may
be designated the next higher administrative unit (confusingly known in
the United States as a "state," such as Illinois or California).

Conflicts among provinces can be adjudicated by a federal government
that, in some sense, sits above these provinces. But if different federal governments are truly sovereign, there is no guarantee of orderly process—much
less of harmony—when these entities quarrel. They may agree to submit

their dispute to mediation, arbitration, or other forms of negotiation, or they may seek to engage in diplomacy. But such efforts depend entirely on the voluntary goodwill of the leaders of the respective states; that is, they involve temporary, and readily revoked, surrender of sovereignty. The Charter of the United Nations, for example, clearly says that it does not seek to restrict the sovereignty of the states making up this international organization. By the same token, international weapons treaties, for example, usually include a provision by which any participating state can withdraw if it determines that its "supreme interests" require doing so.

When states have major disagreements, given that they are legally coequals, they are in theory "free" to engage in a violent test of strength: that is, war. To put it differently, one might say that sovereign states go to war when they agree that war is the most expedient way to resolve the issue between them. In short, the doctrine of state sovereignty results in the lack of an overriding central authority with the legitimacy and power to carry out its decrees. Note that this does not necessarily imply disorder, given that most diplomatic exchanges among states are highly structured. Rather, it follows from the absence of any overarching authority, superior to that of states themselves. Bodin, as well as the influential conservative political philosopher Thomas Hobbes, recognized that interstate violence, or war, is the price paid for the system of state sovereignty, which, they claimed, nonetheless maintains a degree of peace within and between states.

Other thinkers and policymakers have placed much of the blame for war on the state system, although this has not necessarily led to rejection (even in theory) of the system of nation-states. Frequently, their overall mood is one of resignation to the existing global state of affairs.

Violations of State Sovereignty

The doctrine of state sovereignty is powerful, although every treaty, whether on trade or arms control, cedes some freedom of action to reach a consensus about codified rules and norms that advance the interests of those "sovereign" countries that enter into them. Moreover, efforts at spying and subversion—which are frequent and sometimes continual between competing states—are common violations of sovereignty, along with coercion and, sometimes, outright invasion.

In 1979, for example, when the government of Tanzania, with the aid of Ugandan exiles, invaded Uganda and ousted the Ugandan despot Idi Amin, other governments generally applauded or remained silent, not so much out of disrespect for Ugandan sovereignty as because the Amin government was almost universally reviled. In 1956, the former Soviet Union trampled on Hungarian sovereignty, putting down efforts at liberalization; the same was done to Czechoslovakia in 1968, and Poland was implicitly threatened by the former USSR in 1981. These violations were tolerated by the international community largely because the Soviet Union was so powerful and also because of a tacit recognition that its de facto sovereignty included dominion over the "satellite states" of Eastern Europe.

Later, under Mikhail Gorbachev, the former Soviet Union peacefully allowed Poland, Hungary, Czechoslovakia, and other members of the Warsaw Pact to go their own way. Now, most of these Eastern European states are members of the North Atlantic Treaty Organization (NATO), to the consternation of many politicians in Russia. When a neo-Nazi political party became part of the governing coalition in Austria in 2000, many other governments expressed alarm, and the European Union (EU) nations sought to isolate Austria diplomatically. Others, including many people within Austria itself, expressed outrage at such actions and claimed these were efforts to interfere with that state's sovereignty. Austria, Germany, France, Hungary, Poland, and other nations within the EU have recently experienced alarming rises in the strength and militancy of far-right-wing movements, some of whose representatives have been elected to parliaments and formed powerful political parties in those countries. Yet virtually no nation would currently think of intervening forcefully in the internal affairs of a fellow EU member state.

The former Soviet Union may also be said to have violated the sovereignty of Afghanistan following its 1979 military move into that country; supporters of this action, however, claim that the Soviets were merely responding to requests for assistance at the time by the internationally recognized Afghan government. The US government sought repeatedly to arrange for the assassination of Cuba's Fidel Castro in the 1960s and attempted to kill Libya's leader, Moammar Gaddafi, by bombing his residence in 1986 (killing members of his household instead, including his 2-year-old daughter) and by supporting NATO's bombing of Libya in 2011, which led eventually to Gaddafi's death and Libya's failure as a unified state. The Central Intelligence Agency (CIA) engineered the forcible overthrow of democratically elected governments in Guatemala and Iran in the 1950s, and in 1973 it provided assistance to the right-wing forces that overthrew the democratically elected Socialist government of Salvador Allende in Chile. These are only some of the more widely acknowledged examples.

When Britain, France, and Israel invaded Egypt in 1956, capturing the Suez Canal, international pressure (especially by the United States) forced them to withdraw, with opponents of that invasion emphasizing the need to respect Egyptian sovereignty. Yet in 1984, the government of the United States secretly and illegally planted mines in Nicaraguan harbors, despite the fact that Nicaraguan sovereignty—at least in theory—is no less worthy of respect than that of Egypt (or of the United States). In 1988, the US government arranged for the extradition of an accused drug smuggler from Honduras, in clear violation of the Honduran constitution and Honduran sovereignty. Outraged Hondurans rioted in response. And in 1989, when the United States invaded Panama in clear violation of Panamanian sovereignty, worldwide condemnation of the action was widespread but ineffectual. There are questions, as well, regarding the legitimacy of military actions by the United States and its allies in Iraq (from the Persian Gulf War in 1990–1991 to the present), as well as in Serbia, Afghanistan, Iraq, Syria, Libya, and elsewhere.

As part of its "war on terror," the US government has made repeated use of missile attacks launched by unmanned drones on citizens of other sovereign states and within the territorial boundaries of these states, including in Yemen, Afghanistan, Syria, and, most frequently in Pakistan, whose government has publicly complained about such actions (while also covertly supporting Taliban rebels in Afghanistan). In 2011, a US Navy SEAL team killed Osama bin Laden, in a raid occurring within the sovereign state of Pakistan. Since 2014, Russia has provided military support for pro-Russian rebels in eastern Ukraine, while denying that it does so.

Russia has also annexed the Crimea, formerly part of Ukraine, in response to which Western states in particular have expressed outrage and imposed economic and political sanctions on Russia but have taken no further action. In short, although virtually all state governments pay lip service to the doctrine of state sovereignty, more powerful nations often invade and attack less powerful states as they see fit, violating state sovereignty in numerous ways. Very often, they get away with it.

At the same time, powerful states occasionally oppose international interventions into the domestic affairs of other states, claiming that such intrusions would violate state sovereignty. Ostensibly for this reason, China opposes UN intervention in Sudan, and Russia has vetoed UN intervention in Serbia. Both Russia and China oppose UN action against the Burmese military dictatorship. In these and other cases, however, the real motivation appears to be concern that such actions might constitute precedents that could diminish Russian sovereignty in Chechnya and Chinese dominion over Tibet and the ostensibly autonomous region of Xinjiang. And of course, all governments oppose foreign intervention in their own affairs!

Limitations of State Sovereignty

States have traditionally been hesitant to allow the armed forces of another state to be stationed within their territory or even to pass through it, out of concern for their sovereignty and also worry that a foreign armed force might turn against the "host" country. During World War II, for example, Spain's Falangist (basically fascist) government, led by the dictator Francisco Franco, was sympathetic to Nazi Germany but nonetheless did not permit German troops to cross its territory. However, sovereignty can be surprisingly flexible. The government of South Korea hosts thousands of US troops and many US nuclear weapons. South Korean military forces are essentially under US command, largely a consequence of the Korean War.

In a remarkable—if limited—surrender of sovereignty, in 1987, the government of Sri Lanka invited Indian troops to enter that country, so as to police an attempted truce with Tamil separatists; this led to Indian troops engaging in hostilities with Sri Lankans on Sri Lankan soil. From approximately 2004 until 2008, the United States claimed that the Iraqi government, installed by American military forces after overthrowing dictator Saddam Hussein, was sovereign, even as the new government in Baghdad "hosted" tens of thousands of foreign troops, and Iraq's sovereignty has been in doubt ever since.

The European Parliament continues to set some continent-wide economic and legal policy, in a sense over the heads of its constituent states; the same can be said for the EU generally. By eliminating tariffs among its members and by establishing rules for the conduct of trade among their participating states, the EU has established rules that partially circumscribe the economic sovereignty of each member state, presumably for the good of all—except the United Kingdom, of course.

In 1992, all trade barriers among EU member countries were lifted, and by the first decade of the 21st century, a common currency—the euro—had come into existence, replacing the currencies of many of the member states. Some suggest that this may be preliminary to the eventual establishment of a "United States of Europe."

On the other hand, voters in the United Kingdom surprised most experts by voting in 2016 to leave the EU (referred to as "Brexit"), a move completed at the end of December, 2020—to the chagrin of many Britons and most other EU member states. A slender majority of British voters were especially motivated by the (overstated) worry that the UK had surrendered its sovereignty to the EU.

Moreover, the European economic crisis in 2011—especially in some of those Eurozone countries with relatively weak economies, such as Greece,

Portugal, and Spain—may well have been exacerbated by the fact that countries suffering severe balance of payment deficits were unable to respond by devaluing their currency, thereby making their exports more affordable (which might have improved their financial situation). Such monetary adjustments require sovereign control of each state's money supply, something that was given up by the member states when the euro became the common currency of many, but not all, EU members.

Other economic alliances—including the Organization of Petroleum Exporting Countries (OPEC)—have often failed in getting their member states to subordinate their desires to those of the group as a whole, at least in part because these states have retained sovereign control over their own currencies as well as their foreign policies. When Saudi Arabia, the United Arab Emirates (UAE), or Venezuela, for example, refuses to restrict or to raise its crude oil production, thereby foiling OPEC efforts to keep the price of petroleum high by limiting supply, the members of OPEC often justify their actions by recourse to the principle of state sovereignty.

State sovereignty is largely enshrined in international law, which maintains that a procedure, if customary, has legal validity. In addition, there is an expectation of reciprocity, at least among states of roughly equal military and economic power: We'll respect your sovereignty and you'll respect ours. But underlying any legal niceties, the fundamental legitimacy of sovereignty appears to rest on force. Just as states have a monopoly on sanctioned violence within their borders, there are at present no suprastate structures legally or militarily capable of overriding a state's claim to sovereignty.

In *The City of God*, the fifth-century Christian philosopher-theologian St. Augustine tells the story of a pirate who had been captured by Alexander the Great. Alexander asked him what his justification was for "infesting" the sea, and the pirate answered, with uninhibited insolence, "The same as yours, in infesting the earth! But because I do it with a tiny craft, I'm called a pirate. Because you have a mighty navy, you're called an emperor."[3]

The State System

The Origins of States and the State System

Many theories have been proposed to explain the origin of the state. Aristotle maintained that it was "natural" and therefore needed no explanation. The 18th-century Swiss philosopher Jean-Jacques Rousseau viewed it as a historical curiosity. Some anthropologists have seen a relationship between the early production of agricultural surpluses and the presence of centralized organization to store, ship, and protect that surplus. Other scholars have emphasized the early association of pretechnological civilization with arid environments (as in Babylonia and Egypt) and the possible advantage of economies of scale in providing for irrigation canals. In some cases, however, including China and Mexico, states developed before irrigation. Orthodox Marxists maintain that states originated to police the dominance of one class over all others. Thomas Hobbes was less concerned with the origin of states than with their function, arguing in his masterwork, *The Leviathan*, that the state was crucial to maintaining social stability because it prevented people from acting on their violent, selfish, and antisocial inclinations.

Many social scientists and historians, however, ascribe special importance to interactions *among* states, leaning toward what may be called the "conquest" theory to explain the origins of the state. According to this view, larger, well-integrated sociopolitical groups succeeded in conquering smaller, less integrated rivals, eventually leading to the modern state system, which is widely thought to have originated in Europe with the Peace of Westphalia (1648). This agreement ended the carnage of the Thirty Years' War and defined the boundaries between states as reflecting the geographic limits of each sovereign's power; "sovereignty" thus emerged as the control exercised by each ruling sovereign.

Even before this, however, states had substantial force over their subjects. For example, in Sweden, during the Thirty Years' War, most of the taxes raised were appropriated for the war effort. From then on, European states began rationing food to the civilian population, as well as establishing armaments monopolies, appropriating private lands, and selling war bonds. In the pursuit of armed might, the state began to penetrate nearly every aspect of civilian life. Several centuries before the Thirty Years' War, distinctions had already been blurred between the sacred and the secular, that is, between religion and civil society. Similarly, in the conduct of modern war, boundaries were gradually erased between state and society. Just as medieval European knights were closely connected with the Catholic Church, 17th-century armies made virtually everyone into functionaries of the state.

War and the State System

Whatever their origins, states constitute a major fact of life in today's world, and the "state system" is crucial to issues of peace and war. Even though people are always organized in other ways as well—ethnically, vocationally, religiously, and so on—the state system has achieved a virtual monopoly not only over hard power (executions, wars, taxation) but also over political discourse, cultural exchanges, and diplomacy (soft power) and even the ability to imagine solutions to the problem of war. To a large extent, proposed courses of action within most peace-movement traditions are "state centered," and, within traditional government circles, policy options are focused almost entirely on the activities of states.

As states came to be accepted almost without question as sovereign over individuals within their boundaries, they were increasingly left free to act with other states to maintain and enhance their power and international standing. According to military historian Michael Howard, states usually don't fight "over any specific issue such as might otherwise have been resolved by peaceful means, but in order to acquire, to enhance, or to preserve their capacity to function as independent actors in the international system at all."[4]

The 20th-century French political theorist Raymond Aron argued that "the stakes of war are the existence, the creation or the elimination of states."[5] In short, the wars between states, which characterized so much of the state system, have typically been about states and the state system itself. On the other hand, since the end of World War II, the number of states in the world has tripled, largely because of decolonization, and yet the frequency of interstate wars has not increased correspondingly and has largely been replaced by intrastate, and often extraordinarily brutal "civil" wars, which have largely replaced interstate conflicts both numerically and in terms of civilian casualties. (We place this word "civil" in quotes because even by the lax ethical standards of wars, such events are notably *uncivil* and, if anything, more brutal than interstate wars.)

Historically, certain states have been disproportionately involved in wars. These tend overwhelmingly to be the "Great Powers," especially those of

Europe. According to Quincy Wright, of the 2,600 most important battles involving European states between 1480 and 1940, France participated in 47 percent, Austria-Hungary in 34 percent, Great Britain and Russia in 22 percent, Turkey in 15 percent, and Spain in 12 percent. Of 25 interstate wars since 1914, the Great Powers were involved in 19.[6] Today, the United States spends about 60 percent of the total worldwide military budget (more than the next seven countries combined, most of which are US allies), and the major powers of our time (the United States, Russia, Great Britain, France, Germany, China, and Japan) spend nearly 90 percent. A War Participation Index, based on the total number of wars in which a state has participated, divided by the years of the state's political existence, ranks the United States first, Israel second, Turkey and the Ottoman Empire third, and Great Britain fourth. Several centuries ago, Spain, Portugal, Turkey, Holland, and Sweden were involved in a high proportion of wars; with their decline as world powers, they have been substantially more peaceable as well.

Accordingly, perhaps the problem of war is not so much a function of the system of states but rather of *certain states and, particularly, of their relative power and status*. Furthermore, perhaps there is not, in fact, a "system" of states but rather simply a number of separate entities, each pursuing its own interest (*Realpolitik*). Yet states often seem to act not only to preserve themselves but also to maintain the international fabric of which they are part.

This leads to two different ways of thinking about the causes of wars: (1) a kind of *systemic* analysis, in which the most significant factor is the preexisting organization—of states, of ideologies, or of individual or group inclinations, versus (2) a *situational* analysis, which considers each crisis to be attributable largely to its own circumstances, a function of specific events, actors, and unique situations.

Importantly, the system of states is not irretrievably wedded to war. After all, there have been numerous peaceful boundaries between states, such as those between the United States and Canada since 1812, between the United States and Mexico since 1848, and between Norway and Sweden since their peaceful separation in 1905. In addition, a war between France and Germany, or Britain and France, is virtually inconceivable today, although the animosity between these pairs of states goes back hundreds of years.

From a "structural" or "defensive neorealist" perspective, cogently expressed by political scientist Kenneth Waltz,[7] states maneuver to maintain their position of relative power. In this view, states don't strive to maximize their power but rather to maintain it, often by engaging in various balance-of-power strategies.

An alternative view, known as "offensive neorealism," is particularly associated with another political scientist, John Mearsheimer.[8] It posits that the goals of states are more directly offensive, endeavoring to achieve unquestioned dominance (hegemony), if not worldwide then within their geographic sphere of influence. According to Mearsheimer,

> Great powers recognize that the best way to ensure their security is to achieve hegemony now, thus eliminating any possibility of a challenge by another great power. Only a misguided state would pass up an opportunity to be the hegemon in the system because it thought it already had sufficient power to survive.

Both these "neo" approaches focus on the role of international anarchy in driving potentially violent competition between states. They should be distinguished from classical realism, which emphasized the importance of flawed human nature. In any event, all of these viewpoints—whether realistic or not—are also pessimistic, in that they assume that war (although not desirable) is, for one reason or another, pretty much inevitable.

From a "structuralist-realist" perspective, the political scientist Steven van Evera claims that states fight[9]

- when they believe they'll win,
- when they think the strategic advantage will lie with the state the attacks first,
- when they fear their relative power may be declining,
- when they believe they can add to their resources, and
- if they think that conquest will be easy.

Van Evera argues that together these factors and perceptions explain much about the causes of modern wars, and in their absence, war rarely occurs. He also claims that while the actual structure of international power affects the risk of war, it is less important than the aforementioned factors, and that in modern times the structure of power has been relatively benign.

These "hardheaded" perspectives can be challenged, however, because enemies can and have become friends—antagonistic states can set aside their grievances and construct a relationship precluding the prospect of armed conflict. For example, political scientist Charles Kupchan argues that "enemies become friends"—warring states set aside their grievances and construct a relationship precluding the prospect of armed conflict—if the strategic necessity for stable peace unfolds in four phases:

1. a state faced with insufficient resources to deal with existing threats resorts to unilateral accommodation to befriend an adversary;
2. reciprocal restraint then regularizes cooperation and dampens rivalry between the states;
3. societal integration builds institutional and personal linkages between the former adversaries; and
4. changes in political discourse replace former bellicose narratives with new ones of amity and the consolidation of shared identities.[10]

Nations need not be democratic or have any particular form of government to make friends, but they do need leaders willing to take the initiative. The United States and Great Britain during the late 19th and early 20th centuries are examples of former foes making friends (as are the North and South of the United States following the Civil War). So are Iraq and Iran, which fought a bloody war between 1980 and 1988, with the United States supporting Iraq under Saddam Hussein. To some extent, similar reconciliation occurred between the United States and Vietnam, whose leadership continues to applaud former US President Bill Clinton for establishing diplomatic relations between the two erstwhile enemies in 1995.

Alliances Between States

States form alliances. They do so to increase their security, assuming that in unity there is strength. Surprisingly, perhaps, powerful states (including the United States, Russia, Britain, Japan, and France) are more likely to enter into alliances than are less-powerful ones. Large states consider themselves to have large responsibilities and commitments, with their obligations often exceeding their resources; hence, they seek to ally with others. Alliances are also often formed among states that share common cultural or ideological features. These usually involve mutual pledges of assistance, often including the willingness to go to war in support of another alliance member.

Alliances as a Cause of War

It has been claimed that alliances can help deter war by confronting a would-be aggressor with stronger opposition. But it can also be argued that overall, alliances have served principally as a cause of war. Even the signing of an alliance can be provocative, leading to efforts to test, undermine, or break rival alliances. The evidence is equivocal, although alliances clearly have a strong influence on who goes to war and on which side.

The events leading to World War I provide the most dramatic example of what George Washington had criticized more than a century earlier as "entangling alliances" among states dragging them to war. By the outbreak of war in 1914, the United Kingdom and France were allied (primarily against Germany) in an *entente cordiale*, in response to which Germany and Austria-Hungary formed a competing pact, the so-called Triple Alliance (which included Italy, although in fact Italy ultimately ended up fighting against Austria). When the Austrian Archduke Ferdinand was assassinated by a Serbian nationalist at Sarajevo—now part of Bosnia—Austria-Hungary sought to assert its power as an effective and unified state (although in fact it was a rickety multinational empire), while Russia felt compelled to back up tiny Serbia, with which it shared linguistic, ethnic, and religious ties.

The German Kaiser promised full support for Austria-Hungary, Russia did the same for Serbia, and France pledged to fight along with Russia (because of its alliance commitment as well as a long-held grudge over the loss of Alsace and Lorraine to Germany during the Franco-Prussian War several decades earlier). When Germany followed its long-prepared war plan and in 1914 invaded neutral Belgium to attack France, the United Kingdom felt compelled to enter the war as well. Many other factors were involved in precipitating World War I, which has been called "The War Nobody Wanted." The web of opposed alliances—some officially signed and equivalent to treaties, others based on strong feelings of connectedness—was therefore crucial in bringing most of Europe into war.

And the Absence of Alliances as a Cause of War

Ironically, just as World War I was caused in part by the state system of alliances, World War II was brought about in part by the absence of such alliances. Through much of the 1930s, as leader of the Soviet Union, Stalin had sought to involve the Western powers in an alliance against Nazi Germany, but the United Kingdom and France, apparently disliking the USSR even more than Hitler's Germany, resisted. Then, in 1938, French premier Édouard Daladier and British prime minister Neville Chamberlain agreed in Munich to allow Hitler to occupy the Sudetenland of Czechoslovakia. When Hitler also annexed Bohemia and Slovakia in the spring of 1939, the United Kingdom and France were ready to reinstate the World War I Triple Entente against Germany.

By this time, however, Stalin had given up on the West and had engineered his own pact with Hitler, calling for Germany and the Soviet Union to carve up Poland between them. When Germany invaded Poland in September 1939, France and the United Kingdom—having warned Hitler that they could not stand idly by—declared war on Germany. However, the ultimately successful alliance of the United Kingdom, France, the United States, and the Soviet Union did not come about until mid-1941, after Germany attacked its purported ally, the Soviet Union. Japan, allied to Germany, later that year attacked the United States at Pearl Harbor, after which Germany declared war on the United States. Just as the rigidities of the pre-1914 alliances in Europe helped precipitate World War I, the failure of the anti-Nazi and anti-fascist states to organize a united opposition appears to have encouraged German and Japanese expansionism.

In more recent times, supporters of NATO (and presumably supporters of the former Warsaw Pact as well) claim that these alliances kept the East-West peace between 1945 and the fall of the Soviet Union in 1991. An alternative view is that these alliances in fact heightened tensions that might otherwise have subsided. In any event, the end of the Cold War led to anxiety among many NATO officials that their alliance may become outdated, notwithstanding the leading role played by NATO in the militarily victorious campaign against Serbia in 1999 and in Libya in 2011, as well as NATO's less successful activities in Afghanistan since 2002. (In this last case, NATO was very much a junior partner to the United States.)

In summary, alliances among states can be double-edged swords: bringing about or preventing war, increasing or reducing tensions, or tying states together in ways that may not be anticipated by the leaders and can only be understood, with difficulty, later, by historians, if ever.

Alliances and the State System

Winston Churchill, for all his opposition to Hitler, detested Stalin and the Soviet Union at least as much—until Hitler's attack on the Soviet Union set the stage for Britain to ally itself with the Soviets against Nazi Germany. Again and again, alliances have been based primarily on matters of state convenience and power (*Realpolitik* considerations). Hence, they have shifted readily, depending on current perceptions of mutual advantage. As Great Britain's Lord Palmerston put it, "Great states have no permanent friends, only permanent interests."

States' interests often conflict, sometimes generating complex, interconnected, and antagonistic networks. In the Syrian civil war, for example, the competing regional powers—Saudi Arabia and Iran—backed different sides, with the Saudis opposed to Syrian president/dictator Bashar al-Assad and the Iranians supporting his regime. (Assad is an Alawite, a religious sect closer to Shiism, the predominant Iranian version of Islam, than to Sunni Islam, as practiced by the Saudis.) Toward this end, Iran encouraged engagement on behalf of the Syrian regime by Hezbollah, a Shiite militant group based in Lebanon and long supported by the Iranian government. The Turkish government opposes the Assad regime but has been even more antagonistic to the Syrian Kurds, who fight the self-proclaimed Islamic State, but only in Kurdish regions. (The Kurds have long demanded their own nation-state, with the current states from which it would emerge—Turkey, Syria, Iraq, and Iran— not surprisingly opposing them.)

Russia has long-standing ties to the Syrian government, including a naval base. In 2015, Russia entered the fray claiming to be fighting the self-proclaimed

Islamic State and all "terrorists" in Syria but, according to Western sources, it was more focused on attacking moderate anti-Assad forces that were, in turn, supported by the United States. The interests of traditional states (Saudi Arabia, Iran, Syria, Turkey, Russia, and the US) were entwined with those of such nonstate actors such as the Islamic State, Kurds, the al-Qaeda–linked al-Nusra Front, other anti-Assad forces, as well as non-Syrian–based groups.

Polarity and Connectedness

Conventional political scientists have attempted to characterize the state system, both past and present, in terms of the patterns of major state actors and their alliances. Two primary dimensions are generally considered: polarity and connectedness. Thus, a bipolar system consists of primarily two states (such as the United States and the former Soviet Union), with their associated allies as junior partners. By contrast, a multipolar system might consist of many states, some allied but others not.

Connectedness refers to the closeness with which the various states are linked and thus the probability that a disturbance in one state will cause some change in another. If this probability is high, the states are said to be tightly connected; if this probability is low, their connection is loose. Thus, the state system at any given time could conceivably be tight and bipolar, tight and multipolar, loose and bipolar, or loose and multipolar. Between 1945 and 1991 (during the Cold War), the world was essentially bipolar, or perhaps tripolar: the United States and its allies, the Soviet Union and its allies, and a "third world" consisting of non-aligned states of which India was the nominal leader

Much effort has been expended trying not only to assess the nature of the world state system but to predict its future as well. Theories also abound as to which patterns are most war-prone and which are most peace-stable. For example, perhaps bipolar systems are more stable because each side can more accurately monitor the behavior of the other. Or perhaps multipolar systems are more stable for the same reason that biologically diverse ecosystems are more stable than monocultures: there are more players available to take up the slack and to prevent catastrophic breakdown. Many other interpretations are possible; there is presently no consensus on the war/peace significance of differing patterns of interstate alliances.

These issues are especially the concern of political scientists and specialists in international relations, fields that are often closely allied with, and not infrequently apologists for, the state system. Many peace and conflict scholars and practitioners, in contrast, often argue that the state system is part of the problem and thus not likely to be part of the solution. Nonetheless and despite the many legitimate criticisms leveled at states, such "failed states" as Somalia and Libya, not to mention those undergoing civil war, including Syria, Yemen, and other parts of Africa, offer precious little security or well-being to their inhabitants. Although states can definitely be a problem for those concerned about peace, the chaotic breakdown of states has not offered an appealing alternative.

Realpolitik and *Raisons d'État*

When a state behaves in a particular way, supposedly doing so for its own good, it is acting for what the French label *raisons d'état,* the state's own reasons. The phrase also implies the "right" of a state to act in its own best interests. Insofar as states are totally sovereign, *raisons d'état* are sufficient justifications unto themselves, legally if not ethically. The phrase was initiated by Cardinal Richelieu, who, in the 17th century, guided French foreign policy leading to a period of French ascendancy in Europe. Although a devout Catholic clergyman, Richelieu placed the well-being and power of the French state above other considerations and justified military and political actions—including making alliances with Protestant powers—accordingly.

Closely related is the concept of *Realpolitik* (political realism), a German phrase referring to the conduct of international affairs under the assumption that a state's policy should be oriented toward and based on considerations of power and national security rather than on presumably utopian ethical ideals. *Realpolitik* is not necessarily any more "real" than other models of international relations, but its advocates fancy it to be.

In the early modern period, Niccolò Machiavelli was a major precursor of *Realpolitik*. During the 18th and 19th centuries, notable practitioners of *Realpolitik* included Prussian Emperor Frederick the Great, Austrian Chancellor Klemens von Metternich, British Prime Minister Lord Palmerston, and the first German Chancellor, Otto von Bismarck, who unified Germany, which had been a large number of separate states and princedoms. In the second half of the 20th century, former US secretary of state Henry Kissinger (a historian and student of Metternich) was a well-known practitioner of *Realpolitik*, as was the influential American political scientist Hans Morgenthau, both of whom maintained that policy decisions should be based primarily on considerations of power and national self-interest.

Realpolitik and Power

Hans Morgenthau, an influential American political scientist, was especially concerned with outlining the *Realpolitik*-basis for state conduct in world affairs. He maintained that the primary national interest was the quest for national security and that this was to be achieved fundamentally (although not exclusively) through national power. The goal of international politics, in Morgenthau's view, was therefore the maximization of national power, reducible to one of three basic goals: "to keep power, to increase power, or to demonstrate power." Power is to the national leader what wealth is to the economist, what morality is to the ethicist, what evolutionary fitness is to the biologist: the fundamental concept upon which their respective analyses are based. States are assumed to be concerned—almost exclusively—with enhancing their power and not hesitant about going to war to do so.

Power, however, is not strictly limited to military strength. In 1941, the United States was far more powerful than Japan may have realized, not primarily because of its military (which was relatively small at that time) but because of its population, industrial potential, geographic location, and, ultimately, its determination to prevail. Japan, similarly, is very powerful today, despite a relatively modest military force, because of the size of its economy and its ability to compete in international markets. (This, in turn, may be partly because Japan has invested largely in domestic industries, especially electronics and robotics, rather than weaponry, feeling protected, until recently, by the US "nuclear umbrella"; as anxiety about North Korea grows, however, this distribution of Japan's resources might be changing.) There is also moral power, enjoyed by such neutral states as Sweden, Switzerland, and, until recently, India because of its history of Gandhian nonviolence. (Following the wars between India and Pakistan, and then the intolerantly anti-Muslim policies of the highly nationalistic leader, Narendra Modhi, however, this moral authority diminished greatly.)

The power of a state can be defined as the ability of that state to influence the behavior of other states without physical coercion. This "soft power," in the words of political scientist Joseph Nye, can derive from unity, ideology, effective leadership, geographic position, cultural influence, the health and educational level of its citizens, and access to resources no less than raw military force and the willingness to use it, or "hard power."

Realpolitik and War

In the rough and tumble of *Realpolitik,* military power—however achieved, and whether direct or implied—is the "name of the game." Carl von Clausewitz, a prominent early 19th- century Prussian general and military theorist who stressed the centrality of *Realpolitik,* made the renowned observation that war is "the continuation of politics by other means." He emphasized the subordination of military to political goals and wrote that although war is often brutal, it should not be senseless, but rather "an act of violence to compel the enemy to fulfill our will." According to von Clausewitz, "Violence is therefore the means; imposing our will on the enemy, the end."[11]

Accordingly, part of the *Realpolitik* ideal in statecraft is that war is not a consequence of error or irrational factors but is rather a result of a cool-headed decision that more can be gained by going to war than by remaining at peace. By extension, wars begin when two parties disagree as to their relative strength and end when they are in agreement—that is, when the victor is revealed to be stronger than the vanquished. (Of course, given that most wars have a loser, it can be argued that 50 percent of the time, states are wrong, or that their initial decision process was faulty.)

But it would be misleading to assume that practitioners of *Realpolitik* are necessarily warmongers. Rather, they advocate a constant and, as they see it, hard-headed sense of the nature of international relations, limiting war only to those cases in which it will contribute to the "national interest." Hans Morgenthau, for example, strongly opposed the Vietnam War—but only because it damaged the security and economic interests of the United States, not because it was "wrong" in any other respect. If Western—especially US—policies toward the Islamic world were to be based on *Realpolitik*, this might help diminish any current Crusader-like inclinations to remake other countries in "our mold," which is to say, democratic, capitalist, and secular.

Realpolitik and Morality

When the *Realpolitik* of interstate behavior comes into conflict with more altruistic ethical principles, the latter almost always take a backseat. On the other hand, although states often use *Realpolitik* considerations in determining whether to go to war, they typically justify such a decision, publicly, in terms of morality or idealism. Consider the following argument from 19th-century British prime minister William Gladstone: "However deplorable wars may be, they are among the necessities of our condition; and there are times when justice, when faith, when the failure of mankind, require a man not to shrink from the responsibility of undertaking them." He argued, for example, that Britain had a moral obligation to aid the Bulgarians, at the time oppressed by the Turks, whose rule, according to Gladstone, involved "the basest and blackest outrage upon record within the present century, if not within the memory of man."[12] Yet, just 20 years earlier, Britain had gone to war in support of the Turkish-ruled Ottoman Empire against Russia (the Crimean War, 1853–1856). The issue at that time, far from the abuses and outrages of Turkish policy, was in fact *Realpolitik,* in this case competition between the United Kingdom and Russia for influence in the Black Sea region.

Realpolitik seems to transcend traditional liberal, leftist, and conservative political ideologies. Thus, the British liberal statesman James Bright resigned from the cabinet in 1882 to protest Britain's bombardment of Alexandria and occupation of Egypt: "Be the Government Liberal or Tory much the same thing happens: war, with all its horrors and miseries and crimes and cost."[13] Gladstone's attitude nonetheless represented something of an ethical advance over previous formulations of *Realpolitik* in that he emphasized the relation of war to the common interests of humankind rather than to simple considerations of state power.

Ethical considerations loom large in more recent history as well. Yet, when ideals of nonviolence, fairness, and noninterference conflict with *Realpolitik,* the latter has generally triumphed. Immediately after World War II, for example, US government officials harbored a number of former Nazis later deemed war criminals—especially those with expertise as rocket scientists or knowledge about left-wing movements in Europe and the strengths and weaknesses of the Soviet Union—in large part because it was believed these people could help the United States compete with and defeat the USSR. The United States has repeatedly refrained from criticizing the ruthless tactics of China in forcing its rule upon Tibet, and in brutally suppressing the prodemocracy movement in Tiananmen Square in 1989, because trade with China is deemed economically important to America and because, for a while, China served as a convenient ally in America's competition with the former Soviet Union.

Similarly, the United States was willing to wink at Pakistan's violation of nuclear nonproliferation obligations because of that nation's role as a conduit for American military aid to the anti-Soviet mujahideen guerrillas in Afghanistan during the 1980s. Pakistan has also been regarded by the United States as counterbalance to India, seen in the past by the United States as tilting toward the former Soviet Union. More recently, the United States has adopted a more positive stance toward India, perhaps in response to India's increasing technological and economic influence and its possible role of balancing China's growing economic and military power.

The United States experiences a difficult and complex relationship with Pakistan. It has funneled billions of dollars in military aid to the Pakistani government, which it claims to value as an anti-terrorism partner, even though the Islamabad government has long played a "double game" of fighting Islamic extremists within Pakistan itself while covertly supporting the Taliban inside Afghanistan. In doing so, the Pakistani government, especially its intelligence service, the ISI, may simply be acting according to *Realpolitik* calculations, which suggest that eventually the United States will depart Afghanistan, whereupon the Pakistani government may have to deal with an indigenous neighboring Islamist-fundamentalist government in Kabul.

In the recent past, the United States collaborated with right-wing dictators and despots, often ignoring their abominable human rights records, because their anti-communist stance was judged useful in competition with the former Soviet bloc. President Franklin Roosevelt, for example, is said to have observed in 1939 about the brutal Nicaraguan dictator Anastasio Somoza (who, after decades in power, was eventually overthrown by the

Sandinistas in 1979) that "he may be a SOB [son of a bitch] but he's *our* SOB!" US government policy toward developing countries also resulted, in large part, from a *Realpolitik* desire to oppose and undermine left-wing governments—in Nicaragua during the 1980s, in Venezuela during the presidencies of Hugo Chávez and Nicolás Maduro, and in Cuba since 1961—and also to oppose left-wing insurgencies against right-wing regimes friendly to the United States (including El Salvador, Honduras, Guatemala, Indonesia, and South Africa). During the Cold War, the Soviet Union was no less observant of *Realpolitik,* showing little hesitation about quashing prodemocracy movements in East Germany (1953), Hungary (1956), and Czechoslovakia (1968)—although it later allowed these and its other Eastern European client states to leave the Soviet orbit between 1989 and 1991, when the Soviet Union itself collapsed.

Status Quo Versus Revisionist States

Considerations of *Realpolitik* also influence whether states are satisfied with current circumstances or advocate for change. The former are "status quo states," such as the United States; they generally seek to keep things as they are. Their wars are fought against those who try to change things, notably aggressors such as Nazi Germany or, more recently, revolutionary nationalist and militant Islamist movements.

On the other hand, "revisionist states" are those whose leaders may believe that their international status is not commensurate with their economic and military power, and thus their geopolitical aspirations. Examples include Japan in 1905 (leading to the Russo-Japanese War) and again in the 1930s and early 1940s, when Japan initiated its wars against China and the states of the western Pacific; Germany in the 1870s and again in the 1930s; and possibly China in our own time. Despite its newly achieved Great Power status and growing economic clout as one of the world's two largest economies, China has thus far been notably reticent when it comes to projecting military power beyond its borders—with the exception of Tibet and the construction of a naval base in a disputed part of the South China Sea. In 2015, China also announced construction of another naval base in Djibouti—that country's first overseas military establishment. The United States and France already have facilities in Djibouti (as well as elsewhere), and China claims that its base is intended to assist Chinese antipiracy efforts in the ocean abutting the Horn of Africa. China also continues work on its "belt and road" initiative, announced in 2013 and scheduled for completion in 2049, which is intended to facilitate trade and possibly economic dominance by Chinese investments in nearly 70 countries.

It is arguable whether the Soviet Union in the late 20th century was a status quo or revisionist state. For decades, that country supported revisionist, anticolonial revolutionary movements, so long as they were directed against Western interests, while at the same time the USSR maintained the status quo with regard to its "satellite" states in Eastern Europe. Under Mikhail Gorbachev, the Soviet Union became increasingly revisionist at home and abroad, which culminated in ceding control over Bulgaria, Czechoslovakia, East Germany, Hungary, Poland, and Romania.

In contrast, the United States was for long periods of time, during the late 19th and early 20th centuries, a status quo power, both at home and abroad. More recently, from 2001 to 2008, the so-called Bush Doctrine, under which the United States pledged to promote democratization in other countries, suggests possible revisionist inclinations. It remains to be seen, however, whether this claim is simply rhetorical, retrospectively used to justify the Iraq War, or whether it will be acted upon by succeeding administrations with respect to such long-standing but undemocratic allies as Saudi Arabia or such other increasingly authoritarian states as Russia, Turkey, Hungary, Poland, India, China, Burma (a.k.a. Myanmar), and Brazil.

Israel has tended to act very much a status quo state in that most of its Jewish inhabitants are prosperous and relatively content. Despite Palestinian acts of "terrorism," there has been an unspoken assumption—especially by the right-wing spectrum of Israeli society—that occasionally "mowing the grass" (a euphemism for conducting regular military operations against militant Palestinians, with civilians often injured or killed as "collateral damage") is preferable to seeking a peaceful accommodation. The latter would likely require giving up territory seized by Israel during the 1967 war and making other concessions as well.

In contrast, the Palestinians are generally oppressed by the Israeli occupation and hence are very dissatisfied with the status quo. Former US President Jimmy Carter has called their situation tantamount to apartheid. Nearly 140 of the 193 member states of the United Nations, and two nonmember states, have recognized the state of Palestine. Many of the countries that do not do so nevertheless recognize the Palestinian Authority as the "representative of the Palestinian people." But because this recognition is not universal and Israel still occupies large parts of Palestinian territory, with Israel also fighting periodic wars in Hamas-controlled Gaza, Palestinians regularly seek to revise their current political status, occasionally through violence—which in this case is a weapon of the weak and desperate, especially given the vastly superior Israeli war machine.

Internal Cohesion

Considerations of *Realpolitik* and *raisons d'état* may lead politicians to engage in foreign wars so as to enhance their support and deflect public attention from domestic problems. Intense psychological and sociological pressures induce most citizens to "rally 'round the flag," ignoring or postponing complaints with the current government so as to present a united front to the enemy.

In the late 16th century, in his classic work *On Sovereignty*, Jean Bodin, a major early conceptualizer of state sovereignty, wrote,

> The best way of preserving a state, and guaranteeing it against sedition, rebellion, and civil war, is to keep the subjects in amity with another, and to this end, to find an enemy against whom they can make common cause.

Similarly, on the eve of the US Civil War, Secretary of State William Seward urged President Lincoln—unsuccessfully—to declare war on France and Spain so as to unite Americans and preserve the union.

In Shakespeare's *Henry IV, Part 2*, a dying King Henry advises his son how to respond when his subjects are unhappy with past abuses from their government: "Be it thy course, to busy giddy minds with foreign quarrels; that action, once borne out, May waste the memory of the former days." And in George Orwell's *1984*, the world was divided into three megastates, which constantly made war against each other, not to win but rather to preserve their internal stability:

> The war, therefore, if we judge it by the standards of previous wars, is merely an imposture. . . . The war is waged by each ruling group against its own subjects, and the object of the war is not to make or prevent conquests of territory, but to keep the structure of society intact.[14]

Wars can also serve states by providing an outlet for pent-up energy, resources, and surplus manpower. On the other hand, if wars have consistently been initiated so as to achieve internal cohesion, a correlation should exist between internal and external conflicts. Yet careful studies have not demonstrated any statistical relationship between these variables; that is, states are not more likely to go to war when they are seriously threatened with heightened dissension or internal violence. Moreover, wars initiated in the hope of achieving national unity and submerging domestic discontent don't always work out that way. If the war is prolonged and costly, citizen dissatisfaction can grow, despite the pressure for conformity that wars typically engender. Major reasons for resentment include the burden of added taxes to pay for the war, the mounting toll of casualties, unhappiness with the direction of the war, and, especially, anger if the war is lost. A significant cause of the Soviet withdrawal from Afghanistan in 1989, and its collapse two years later, was the economic and psychological toll paid by the USSR for its failed venture.

It is relatively rare that ethical considerations loom large in generating popular dissatisfaction with a regime's warlike behavior, although in the United States, the Vietnam War was an exception. Practical concerns are generally paramount. Thus, enormous Russian casualties during World War I were important in precipitating the Bolshevik Revolution of 1917, and popular resentment at the conduct and outcome of the Falklands War with the UK led to the downfall of General Galtieri's Argentine government in 1982.

On the other hand, Margaret Thatcher, prime minister of the UK during the 1980s, had been quite unpopular at home prior to the Falklands War; her political stock rose greatly following its success. The government of the Ayatollah Khomeini in Iran was, if anything, strengthened by its bloody war with Iraq in the 1980s, as was Saddam Hussein's regime in the 1990s, despite costly military defeats at the hands of the United States and its allies. Saddam was overthrown by the United States in 2003 and executed in 2006. A major part of the ostensible rationale for that US invasion was the (false) allegation that weapons of mass destruction were in Saddam's hands. When no such weapons were found, and as it became widely acknowledged that the Iraqi regime was not implicated in the 9/11 attacks on the United States, the "moral" justification shifted to removing a tyrant from power and ostensibly to "spread democracy" throughout the Middle East.

Finally, because warfare requires a degree of national unity and effective central coordination, states that are internally disunited may be especially cautious and therefore reluctant to engage in a war they could well end up losing.

Arms Races

Short of war itself, an arms race is the most prominent and bellicose form of competition between states. Arms races have been defined as "intense competitions between opposed powers or groups of powers, each trying to achieve an advantage in military power by increasing the quantity or improving the quality of its armaments or armed forces."[15]

Between 1945 and 1991, the nuclear arms race between the United States and the Soviet Union consumed considerable resources and attention, while generating extraordinary risk. Although the phrase "*the* arms race" generally connotes a nuclear competition, arms races existed long before the invention of nuclear weapons. Moreover, they have long been a major arena for interstate competition, from the city-states of Greece and competing feudal overlords during the Middle Ages to modern times. As William James put it, "The intensely sharp competitive preparation for war by the [states] is the real war: permanent, unceasing, and the battles are only a sort of public verification of the mastery gained during the 'peace' interval."[16] Writing about one of the first documented major wars in human history, the Peloponnesian War between Athens and Sparta, the historian Thucydides famously noted, "What made the war inevitable was the growth of Athenian power and the fear which this caused Sparta."

Numerous arms races have characterized sub-state actors during the early 21st century, notably including warring sides in the Syrian, Iraqi, Yemeni, and Afghan civil wars, and even North Korea—which is essentially "racing" with itself, having no prospect of militarily or economically equaling the US, or even South Korea or Japan. At the same time, the North Korean regime evidently hopes to preserve itself by further developing weapons of mass destruction and the means to deliver them to its perceived enemies.

Until relatively recently, there were few overt arms races between major powers, with the possible exception of renewed nuclear competition between Russia and the West, as well as a mostly nonnuclear competition between China and other Pacific states, including the United States. There are, on the other hand, substantial rivalries, including a military dimension involving Middle Eastern proxy wars between such regional powers as Saudi Arabia and Iran. Even these competitions, dangerous as they are, lack the terrifying momentum of the Cold War nuclear arms race between the United States and the former Soviet Union.

Mutual insecurity has often fueled arms races, with each side worried that the other was about to pull ahead or was already dangerously in the lead. Often, this involved incorrect estimates, which exaggerated the other side's forces. In 1914, for example, German intelligence estimated that the French Army had 121,000 more soldiers than the German Army; at the same time, the French calculated that the German Army exceeded the French by 134,000! From 1906 to 1914, when Great Britain and Germany were engaged in a vigorous naval arms race, each of the two states worried that the other was about to launch a preemptive attack. Such anxiety almost certainly played a part in the initiation of World War I. Edward Grey, British foreign secretary during the decade leading up to World War I, put it this way:

> Great armaments lead inevitably to war. The increase of armaments . . . produces a consciousness of the strength of other nations and a sense of fear. Fear begets suspicion and distrust and evil imaginings, till each Government feels it would be criminal and a betrayal of its country not to take every precaution, while every Government regards the precautions of every other Government as evidence of hostile intent.[17]

In Chapter 6, we considered the "fundamental attribution error," which is a cognitive mistake committed by individuals; this error also tends to characterize arms races between states. The failure of the Western powers—notably the United Kingdom and France—to engage Germany in an arms race may have helped bring about World War II, a case in which the allies, ironically, made a kind of reverse attribution error: not attributing sufficient malice to Hitler's motivations, which appears to have emboldened him in his aggressive designs. When Germany first began violating the provisions of the Versailles Treaty (which ended World War I and called for the demilitarization of Germany), the United Kingdom and France were considerably stronger than Germany, yet they did not respond.

When Germany rebuilt its military and reoccupied the Rhineland (which it had ceded to occupying powers as a result of the Treaty of Versailles) in 1936, in clear violation of its treaty obligations, Britain, France, and the United States failed to act or to engage in significant rearmament. The German General Staff is now known to have been initially quite apprehensive about Hitler's first aggressive moves. Had the Western allies responded more forcefully, it is entirely possible that Germany would have backed down, and Hitler's military momentum might have been ended before it gathered steam. In any event, historical counterfactuals, involving what "might have been" had one or more parties acted differently, are impossible to prove or disprove.

Peaceful Resolution of Arms Races

In some cases, arms races have been resolved peacefully:

1. Great Britain versus France, navy, 1841–1865

2. Germany versus France, army, 1870s–1890s

3. Great Britain versus France and Russia, navy, 1884–1905

4. Chile versus Argentina, navy, 1890–1902

5. United States versus Great Britain, navy (cruisers), 1920–1930

6. United States versus the former Soviet Union, nuclear weapons, and other weapons of mass destruction, 1945–1991, and to a lesser extent, the U.S. versus Russia, since 1991; and the US versus China, again, to some extent, since, roughly 2005.

In case 1, one side gave up. In case 2, the competition simply petered out, at least temporarily. Case 3 was resolved by an alliance among the racers, and case 4 ended with resolution of an existing boundary dispute. Case 5 (and 4 as well) ended with an arms limitation treaty. The outcomes of case 6 are uncertain.

Factors Driving Arms Races

Many things drive arms races, including the financial profits to be made by military-industrial complexes, the desires for advancement on the part of individuals whose careers depend on success in administering or commanding major new weapons programs, political leaders who pander to bellicose domestic sentiment, and interservice rivalry within a state. Another potential reason for these activities is concern about the genuine security needs of the state. Faced with an uncompromisingly hostile opponent, leaders have often believed that military might is their only real protection. This leads to what has aptly been called the security dilemma: When states perceive that they must increase their military power so as to achieve security, their rivals often feel obliged to do the same. As a result, both sides enter into a dangerous competitive spiral, whereby each side seeks to reduce its insecurity by acquiring more weapons and developing a more powerful military, which leads to even more insecurity, and which leads in turn to even greater military acquisitions, and so on.

British historian Herbert Butterfield suggested that perhaps "no state can ever achieve the security it desires without so tipping the balance that it becomes a menace to its neighbors."[18] In the process, it becomes a menace to itself. But this has not prevented states from trying to prevail over their real and perceived antagonists.

Arms Races and War

Do arms races lead to war? One influential point of view claims that they do. Another maintains just the opposite: By being militarily strong, a state prevents war. Arguing in favor of greater military expenditures, President Ronald Reagan, for example, claimed that the United States never got into a war because it was too strong. (This ignores the Mexican-American and Spanish-American wars, and perhaps the Vietnam and Iraq/Afghanistan wars as well.) Proponents of military strength and arms races point to the "lessons of Munich," when World War II may have been made more likely by the failure of the West to respond in kind to Germany's growing military strength. Opponents of arms races counter with the case of World War I, when arms races helped precipitate the European powers into an unwanted and unnecessary war.

It is virtually impossible to evaluate these claims, although most attempts to examine the historical record have shown that arms races seem more likely to lead to war than to prevent it. For example, one political scientist examined 99 serious international disputes between 1815 and 1965. Whereas 28 of these had been preceded by an arms race, 71 had not. Of the former, 23 (82 percent) resulted in a war, whereas of the 71 disputes not preceded by an arms race, only 3 (4 percent) resulted in war.[19] Although this does not prove that arms races cause war, it does suggest that when a serious dispute occurs in conjunction with an ongoing arms race, war is far more likely than when the disputing nations have not also been competing militarily.

Nonetheless, many military and political leaders as well as normal citizens remain convinced that security often demands hard power, and this pursuit often generates an arms race. This theme is described in the famous Latin motto formulated by the Roman general Vegetius: *Si vis pacem, para bellum* ("If you want peace, prepare for war"). "A wiser rule," according to sociologist William Graham Sumner, "would be to make up your mind soberly what you want, peace or war, and then to get ready for what you want; for what we prepare for is what we shall get."[20]

A Final Note on War and States

When it comes to war and preparing for violent conflict, states seem more often to be the problem than the solution, notwithstanding the fact that if there is to be a solution to the problem of war, states will have to be a part of that as well. Increasingly, states appear to exist for their own sake, not for the benefit of their citizens. They enter into wars for their own *raisons d'état* and terminate them for the same reasons. Nuclear weapons in particular exist in large part because of the purported *Realpolitik* benefits they confer on states that possess them; it is unlikely, however, that they enhance either national or human security. Indeed, citizens of such nonnuclear states as New Zealand, Canada, Switzerland, Costa Rica, Finland, and Sweden are in many ways more secure and prosperous than citizens of the nuclear powers.

The novelist E. L. Doctorow wrote,

> The time may be approaching when we will have to choose between two coincident reality systems: the historical human reality of feeling, of thought, of multitudinous expression, of life and love and natural death; or the supra-human statist reality of rigid, ahistorical, censorious and contending political myth structures, which may in our name and from the most barbaric impulses disenfranchise 99 percent of the world's population from even tragic participation in their fate.[21]

With the world in ecological, political, public health, and social crises, states have largely compounded these problems by focusing on wars and preparations for wars, which, among other things, diverts trillions of dollars from addressing these global crises. If one is to oppose war, is it also necessary, then, to oppose the state? Can positive peace be achieved within the current system of states? And if not, what about the various positive roles of the state, such as maintaining domestic order, social welfare systems, and common purpose among its citizens? Many of the most important factors affecting people's lives occur on a planetary scale—made painfully clear by global climate change and the Covid-19 pandemic—and generally exceed the ability of individual states to manage.

In the 21st century, some states may increasingly turn their attention toward the global problems facing all human beings, such as poverty, global warming, ecological destruction, energy shortages, displaced persons, worldwide epidemics, and the urgent need for demilitarization, especially weapons of mass destruction. But except for such nongovernmental organizations and international institutions as the United Nations, it seems likely that *Realpolitik* and a narrowly defined sense of state interest will continue to be the modus operandi for most states, particularly for such current and emerging great powers as the United States, China, and Russia. As a result, students of peace and conflict studies can anticipate efforts by many organizations to go beyond existing state boundaries and to seek alternative or additional ways of addressing these planetary concerns.

Questions for Further Reflection

1. What are the advantages and disadvantages of state sovereignty? Do the advantages outweigh the disadvantages?

2. If states are "the problem," the principal cause of war in the modern period, what is the solution?

3. To what degree is *Realpolitik* "realistic" in the contemporary world? What might be some alternatives to it?

4. To what degree do current arms races resemble or differ from those of the 20th century?

5. Are there any viable alternatives to the international state system? If so, can you describe some?

Suggestions for Further Reading

Anne Clunan and Harold Trinkunas, eds. 2010. *Ungoverned Spaces: Alternatives to State Authority in an Era of Softened Sovereignty.* Stanford, CA: Stanford University Press.

E. Dougherty and R. L. Pfalzgraff. 2000. *Contending Theories of International Relations,* 5th ed. New York: Longman.

Charles A. Kupchan. 2010. *How Enemies Become Friends.* Princeton, NJ: Princeton University Press.

Pierre Mament. 2013. *A World Beyond Politics? A Defense of the Nation-State.* Princeton, NJ: Princeton University Press.

Benjamin Miller. 2007. *States, Nations and the Great Powers: The Sources of Regional Wars and Peace.* New York: Cambridge University Press.

Hans Morgenthau. 1967. *Politics Among Nations.* New York: Alfred Knopf.

Joseph S. Nye, Jr. 2003. *Understanding International Conflicts,* 4th ed. New York: Pearson.

Steven van Evera. 1999. *Causes of War: Power and the Roots of Conflict.* Ithaca, NY: Cornell University Press.

Kenneth N. Waltz. 2001. *Man, the State, and War: A Theoretical Analysis.* New York: Columbia University Press.

Edward Weisband and Courtney I. P. Thomas. 2015. *Political Culture and the Making of Modern Nation-States.* London: Routledge.

Notes

1. Randolph S. Bourne. 1964. *War and the Intellectuals, Collected Essays 1915–1919.* New York: Harper & Row.

2. Benito Mussolini. 1963. "The Doctrine of Fascism." In *Social and Political Philosophy,* eds. J. Somerville and R. Santoni. New York: Anchor.

3. St. Augustine. 2006. *The City of God.* John Mark Mattox, ed. London: Continuum, 25.

4. Michael Howard. 1992. "The Causes of War." In *A Peace Reader,* eds. Joseph Fahey and Richard Armstrong. New York: Paulist Press, 25.

5. Quoted in Howard.

6. Quincy Wright. 1964. *A Study of War.* Chicago: University of Chicago Press.

7. Kenneth N. Waltz. 1979. *Theory of International Politics.* New York: McGraw Hill.

8. John J. Mearsheimer. 2001. *The Tragedy of Great Power Politics.* New York, NY: W.W. Norton.

9. Steven van Evera. 1999. *Causes of War: Power and the Roots of Conflict.* Ithaca, NY: Cornell University Press.

10. Charles A. Kupchan. 2010. *How Enemies Become Friends.* Princeton, NJ: Princeton University Press.

11. Carl von Clausewitz. 1989 (1832). *On War.* Princeton, NJ: Princeton University Press.

12. Quoted in J. Morley. 1903. *The Life of William Everett Gladstone.* New York: Macmillan.

13. Ibid.

14. George Orwell. 1949. *1984.* San Diego: Harcourt Brace Jovanovich, chap. 9.

15. Hedley Bull. 1961. *The Control of the Arms Race.* New York: Praeger.

16. William James. 1967. *The Writings of William James.* New York: Random House.

17. Quoted in John G. Stoessinger. 1985. *Why Nations Go to War.* New York: St. Martin's Press.

18. Herbert Butterfield. 1960. *International Conflict in the Twentieth Century.* London, UK: Greenwood.

19. William D. Wallace. 1979. "Arms Races and Escalation." *Journal of Conflict Resolution* 23: 3–16.

20. William Graham Sumner. 1919. *War, and Other Essays.* A. G. Keller, ed. New Haven, CT: Yale University Press, 40.

21. E. L. Doctorow. 1983. "It's a Cold War Out There, Class of '83." *The Nation,* July 2.

The Decision-Making Level

arge groups of people are usually led by smaller groups, and in many cases, the ultimate decisions of war and peace are made by very few people, sometimes just one person. It is therefore appropriate to consider decision making at the level of governmental and other influential leaders

The Role of Leaders

There has long been debate over the role of crucial individuals in the making of history. So-called "great man" theories maintain that the personality of certain select major figures has had a determining effect on world events. By

9

Pool via Getty Images

The Decision-Making Level

Large groups of people are usually led by smaller groups, and, in many cases, the ultimate decisions of war and peace are made by very few people, sometimes just one person. It is therefore appropriate to consider decision making at the level of governmental and other influential leaders.

The Role of Leaders

There has long been debate over the role of crucial individuals in the making of history. So-called "great man" theories maintain that the personality of certain select, major figures has had a determining effect on world events. By contrast, theories of "impersonal forces" claim that most significant events would have happened no matter who was in charge because they are the culmination of large ebbs and flows of societies and historical trends, rather than resulting from the actions of a small, influential minority.

In various writings, but most notably in his novel *War and Peace,* Leo Tolstoy argued for the impersonal forces theory. He portrayed Napoleon as a bit ridiculous, imagining himself making important decisions such as whether or not to go to war or how to conduct major battles, whereas self-proclaimed leaders are actually "history's slaves." In discussing the outbreak of war between France and Russia in 1812, Tolstoy raises the following questions:

> What produced this extraordinary occurrence? What were its causes? The historians tell us with naive assurance that its causes were the wrongs inflicted on the Duke of Oldenburg, the non-observance of the Continental System, the ambition of Napoleon, the firmness of [Czar] Alexander, the mistakes of the diplomats, and so forth and so on. . . . [But] there was no one cause for that occurrence; it had to occur because it had to! Millions of men, renouncing their human feelings and reason, had to go from West to East to slay their fellows. . . . The actions of Napoleon and Alexander were as little voluntary as the action of any soldier who was drawn into the campaign by lot or by conscription. . . . To elicit the laws of history we must leave aside kings, ministers and generals, and select for study the homogeneous, infinitesimal elements which influence the masses.[1]

Tolstoy's view that the common people are as responsible as their leaders derived from his conviction that individuals have the opportunity—indeed, the responsibility— to take things into their own hands and refuse to fight. Whether this is historically valid, however, is another question.

With regard to its causes, probably no war has been analyzed in greater detail than World War I because the interweaving factors that culminated in that war were unusually complex, and because so many relevant government documents are available to historians. No single villain (and, certainly, no hero) emerges from all this scholarship, and some respected observers have even proposed that somehow war was "in the air," a view that does not ignore other concerns or causal factors but that emphasizes the irrational and impersonal:

> No single cause will explain the First World War. But the formal causes—the commercial and colonial rivalries, the cocked war establishments of Europe designed to mobilize, deploy, and conquer by the execution of a single and irreversible general-staff plan, the strident minorities and grandiose nationalisms, the disintegration of the Austro-Hungarian empire, the colonial rivalries, the rot of Turkey, the instability of the balance of power—all these pale before the fact that Europe in 1914 wanted war and got it.[2]

Although this debate may be irresolvable, it is still necessary to attend to the specific issue of leaders and their decision making, if only because leaders do exist and make decisions, and, moreover, there is good reason to think that these decisions are important—although perhaps not as important as most military and political leaders themselves would like to think.

Strong Leaders

In the past, when rulers embodied the political and military power of their group, they clearly played a major role in deciding whether or not to go to war. In *The Education of a Christian Prince,* Erasmus (1456–1536) urged,

Although a prince ought nowhere to be precipitate in his plans, there is no place for him to be more deliberate and circumspect than in the matter of going to war. Some evils come from one source and others from another, but from war comes the shipwreck of all that is good and from it the sea of all calamities pours out.[3]

The role of individual leaders may well have been unduly glamorized, and decision makers often receive credit—and blame—that they do not entirely deserve. Yet certain individuals, by the force of their personalities and the decisions they made, have had enduring effects on history. Sometimes, they represent the culmination of currents within their societies, and they may also catalyze other events. Nonetheless, people such as Alexander the Great, Genghis Khan, Charlemagne, Joan of Arc, Napoleon, Bismarck, Hitler, Stalin, de Gaulle, Mao Zedong, Saddam Hussein, and George W. Bush have acted as lightning rods for popular discontent and, often, as precipitators of war. Less often have leaders of this ilk achieved renown as peacemakers.

On the other hand, when it becomes necessary for a state to accept defeat, a highly regarded leader may be the only person capable of getting the populace to swallow that bitter pill. Marshal Pétain played this role in France in 1940, as did Carl Mannerheim in Finland in 1944 and Charles de Gaulle in France in 1961 when he acquiesced to independence for Algeria. Similarly, the warming of Sino-American relations during the Nixon administration was facilitated by the fact that Richard Nixon's reputation as a hardline anti-communist insulated him against most accusations of "appeasement."

Many leaders may be moved by the desire to go down in history as peacemakers. Thus, the dramatic warming of relations between the United States and the former Soviet Union during the late 1980s and early 1990s must be attributed, at least partly, to a partial shift in perceptions and goals by President Reagan. Even more important was the commitment by the Soviet leader, Mikhail Gorbachev, to *glasnost* ("political opening") and *perestroika* ("economic restructuring"), which in turn helped lessen US-Soviet tensions and facilitated advances in arms control, such as a partial reduction of conventional forces in Europe and a decrease in the number of deployed nuclear warheads. This almost certainly would not have taken place had any of Gorbachev's more Stalinist rivals assumed power in the Kremlin.

On the other hand, Reagan's personal commitment to "Star Wars" (the Strategic Defense Initiative, or SDI) prevented even more dramatic cuts in US and Soviet nuclear weapons. By the same token, US withdrawal from the 1972 Anti-Ballistic Missile Treaty during the George W. Bush administration, ostensibly to build a Ballistic Missile Defense system—along with plans for substantial nuclear "modernization" initiated by the Obama administration—threaten to have a similar effect in the early 21st century. Even then, President Obama often expressed the desire to reduce both the number and the importance of nuclear weapons worldwide. President Donald Trump, by contrast, embraced nuclear weapons and orchestrated escalation in their importance and possible use, while also terminating a number of important agreements that had limited nuclear weapons prior to his presidency. Moreover, it is increasingly clear that his decisions were based at least as much on whim, impulse, and perceived opportunities for self-aggrandizement as on conceptions of public benefit.

The inspirational role of certain leaders was perhaps most clearly emphasized by events during the early days of World War II, when Great Britain stood virtually alone against Nazi Germany, which had conquered nearly all of continental Europe. Winston Churchill personified British defiance and determination at that time. He also helped generate it with such stirring rhetorical pronouncements as: "We shall fight on the beaches, we shall fight on the landing grounds, we shall fight in the fields and in the streets, we shall fight in the hills; we will never surrender."

Nor does strong leadership only promote war: When President Sadat of Egypt went to Israel and negotiated a historic peace treaty with Israel's Begin, through the mediating efforts of President Jimmy Carter, it was a triumph of vision and hard work by a few individuals. (Sadat was later assassinated by violent Islamists.) Making peace typically requires as much, if not more, courage and determination than does making war.

In many cases, of course, wars are imposed on their people by the decisions of their leadership. The various "wars of succession" during the 18th century, for example, did not arise from the upwelling of public anger or concern; rather, they were decreed by leaders for *raisons d'état* and obediently carried out by most of the populace. At other times, charismatic leaders from Alexander the Great to Hitler have succeeded in generating wartime enthusiasm—although admittedly their messages could flourish only on fertile soil. In his war message to the American people in 1917, President Wilson expressed the oft-spoken distinction between people and their leadership, one that—true or not—has proven especially convenient during war:

> We have no quarrel with the German people. . . . It was not upon their impulse that their government acted. . . . It was a war determined as wars used to be determined upon in the old, unhappy days when people were nowhere consulted by their rulers and wars were provoked and waged in the interest of dynasties or of little groups of ambitious men who were accustomed to use their fellow men as pawns or tools.[4]

Weak Leaders and the Role of "Villains"

It is not necessarily true that only strong leaders initiate wars. The weak political personalities of Germany's Kaiser Wilhelm and Russia's Czar Nicholas rendered them unable to hold their general staffs in check; stronger leadership on their part might have prevented World War I, just as stronger leadership in the UK and France during the 1930s might have averted World War II. In the former case, strength would have been needed to restrain those within their countries who felt bound to follow predesigned mobilization plans and who worried excessively about being preempted by the other side. In the latter case, strength would have been needed to restrain those outside the UK and France—notably Hitler and Mussolini.

The Cuban Missile Crisis—the closest humanity has come to general nuclear war—was brought about in part because a young John F. Kennedy felt browbeaten by Soviet premier Khrushchev at their 1961 summit meeting in Vienna and was further humiliated by the debacle of the failed American-supported invasion of Cuba at the Bay of Pigs. The following year, Kennedy was determined that he would not be pushed around again by the Soviet leader; fortunately for the world, Khrushchev was willing to back down.

The Vietnam War may well have been prolonged because Lyndon Johnson was personally determined not to be defeated by the North Vietnamese and the followers of Ho Chi Minh. The war between Iran and Iraq during the 1980s depended in large part on personal animosity between the two leaders, Saddam Hussein of Iraq and the Ayatollah Khomeini of Iran. The Persian Gulf War was animated in part by the hostility between Saddam Hussein and President George H. W. Bush, and the Iraq War was fed in turn by enmity between Hussein—widely believed to have tried to kill the first President Bush—and President George W. Bush. It has also been suggested that George W. Bush hoped to outdo his father, who, during the Persian Gulf War had ordered coalition forces to refrain from overthrowing Hussein.

Sometimes, wars result from the overwhelming personal ambition of leaders, a problem that is not restricted to modern tyrants or would-be conquerors. Consider this boast from Xerxes, King of Persia in 480 BCE (and recounted by Herodotus):

> Once let us subdue this people [the Greeks] . . . and we shall extend the Persian territory beyond our borders; for I will pass through Europe from one end to the other, and make of all lands which it contains one country. . . . By this course then we shall bring all mankind under our yoke.[5]

Sometimes, it is a matter of face-saving, in which case leaders are especially likely to precipitate a crisis—or respond aggressively to one—if they are wary of opposition at home. Thus, President Truman, stung by criticism that he had "lost" China to communists, may have felt especially driven to intervene when North Korea subsequently invaded South Korea. John F. Kennedy seriously worried in 1962 that he might be impeached if he did not respond forcefully to the discovery of Soviet missile sites under construction in Cuba. Also that year, Indian prime minister Nehru stirred up anti-Chinese feeling in India, and when the Chinese resisted Indian territorial encroachments, he had to choose between fighting and losing face, even though the Chinese had overwhelming logistic advantages and 10 times as many troops. The resulting brief war between India and China (little remembered these days in the West), ended with a painful defeat for India.

We know surprisingly little about what produces personalities that are likely to achieve national leadership or what distinguishes a peacemaker from a warmonger. Alexander the Great grew up as one of many children in a royal, polygynous household. Contact with his father (Philip of Macedon) was rare, and young Alexander apparently had a very intense relationship with his mother, who was ambitious, energetic, demanding, punitive, and rather violent. Perhaps it is not surprising that Alexander's quest for approval included conquering much of the known world before he was 33.

On the other hand, Prussia's Frederick—also known as the Great—had a submissive, ineffectual mother but a demanding, callous, and rather brutal father who forced him to witness the beheading of his boyhood friend, with whom he may have had a homosexual relationship. In his book *The Anatomy of Human Destructiveness,* psychoanalyst Erich Fromm argued that the early experiences of Hitler and Stalin produced a kind of malignant sadism (Stalin) and necrophilia (Hitler).

Genghis Khan, Attila the Hun, Timur, Hitler: These leaders often appear as villains, and rightly so, insofar as they figured prominently in precipitating wars that resulted in the deaths of millions. But what of Cecil Rhodes, an architect of British imperialism; Alfred Krupp, German weapons manufacturer extraordinaire; and J. Robert Oppenheimer and the other American physicists who created the first atomic bombs, President Truman who ordered their use, the bomber crews who dropped them; Edward Teller, "father" of the hydrogen bomb, or the patriotic citizens who paid their taxes in support of the war effort as well as the nuclear arms race that followed? The point is that it may be relatively easy to assign villainy to a select number of prominent individuals, but by most measures there is more than enough blame to go around.

Political revolutions are often precipitated by the popular perception that leadership is particularly corrupt, incompetent, or villainous. Although the new leadership may enjoy wider popular support (at least for a time), it may become as bad as, or worse than, what it replaces: Robespierre, for example, became more dreaded than the French King Louis XVI, who was rather mild and fumbling by contrast. Stalin was far worse than Czar Nicholas II. Ayatollah Khomeini, who replaced Mohammad Reza Pahlavi, Shah of Iran in 1979, was a very different leader in nearly every respect; it isn't at all clear, however, whether he was more or less dictatorial or war prone.

Moreover, heroes in one nation are often perceived as evildoers in another, and vice versa, as was the case during the Persian Gulf War, with Saddam Hussein and President George H. W. Bush being demonized in each other's country. Similar behavior occurred between Venezuelan president Hugo Chávez and US president George W. Bush. And although Osama bin Laden at the time of his death was substantially less popular in the Islamic world than had been the case shortly after 9/11, he was widely admired among many Muslims even as he was reviled in the West.

It is often difficult to assign villainy in matters of politics, and especially in war and peace, because supporting reasons often exist for even the most violent and inhumane acts. Nonetheless, in certain cases, responsibility and blame seem sufficiently clear that widely accepted moral judgments have been made. After Pol Pot and the Khmer Rouge took power in 1975, at least one million people out of Cambodia's total population of seven million were killed, including virtually anyone perceived by the Khmer Rouge leadership to have Western connections, training, language, uncalloused hands (suggesting intellectuality), or even eyeglasses. Idi Amin, formerly a Ugandan army sergeant, took over the government in 1971, initiating a reign of terror believed to have claimed more than 300,000 lives before Tanzanian troops, supported by Ugandan exiles, invaded that country in 1979 and drove Amin from power.

Even perceived villainy—or, at least, its extent—is open to dispute. The traditional, mainstream Anglo-American interpretation of the causes of World War II, for example, lays particular stress upon Hitler's aggressive designs plus, in a supporting role, British and French appeasement. But at least one highly regarded revisionist historian, A. J. P. Taylor, has refused to heap all the blame on Hitler, viewing World War II instead as a continued pattern of German expansionism and militarism traceable back at least as far as Bismarck in the second half of the 19th century. Also to blame in Taylor's view were the highly punitive Versailles Treaty that terminated World War II and faulty calculations by Hitler and also by the Western leaders.

Regardless of the specific historical details, there may be some validity to placing substantial blame for many and perhaps most wars on a limited number of individuals. This view, however, must reconcile itself with the likelihood that even with a different cast of major characters, the outcome might have been fundamentally the same. Much of this blame should also go to what has been called the "military mind," which, according to the influential American political scientist Samuel Huntington,

> emphasizes the permanence of irrationality, weakness and evil in human affairs. It stresses the supremacy of society over the individual and the importance of order, hierarchy and division of function. It accepts the nation state as the highest form of political organization and recognizes the continuing likelihood of war among nation states. . . . It exalts obedience as the highest virtue of military men. . . . It is, in brief, realistic and conservative.[6]

(Professor Huntington himself was widely recognized to be conservative, whether or not he was also realistic.)

Crisis Decision Making

Stimulated in particular by the close call of the Cuban Missile Crisis, psychologically minded students of international relations have directed considerable attention to the process whereby decisions are made—often focusing on issues of perception and misperception, communication and miscommunication, understanding and misunderstanding—and the effects of crisis conditions and of small group processes on decision making.

Small Groups

Major governmental decisions, especially regarding war or warlike actions, are often made by small ad hoc groups—that is, groups convened for that specific purpose. During the crisis at the beginning of the Korean War, for example, 14 people participated in the emergency deliberations of the US government; during the Cuban Missile Crisis, the committee convened by President Kennedy had 16 members. The Politburo, the core unit of decision making in the former Soviet Union, normally consisted of 14 full members. In this context, it has been suggested that the United Nations Educational, Scientific and Cultural Organization (UNESCO) charter should be rewritten to read, "Since wars begin in the minds of men [rarely, women] *in the core decisional groups of the nation-states,* it is in the minds of those men that the defenses of peace must be constructed."[7] (The actual version leaves out the phrase in italics.)

It is often hoped, even assumed, that a group will temper the enthusiasm and impetuosity of a leader. However, studies initiated by social psychologist Irving Janis suggested that the opposite is more likely: Group members tend to egg each other on, reinforcing tendencies present in the most dominant individual(s). Social psychologists have also found that risk taking tends to be more pronounced in groups than in individuals because no one person must (or can) take responsibility for the outcome. Janis coined the word *groupthink* to identify this tendency for groups to be no more rational than individuals, and often less so. Janis also emphasized that groupthink "is likely to result in irrational and dehumanizing actions directed against out-groups."[8]

Following General Douglas MacArthur's success in repelling the North Koreans early in the Korean War, the United States made the fateful decision to unify all of Korea by force of arms. This soon resulted in Chinese forces crossing the Yalu River into Korean territory and three years of stalemated war, with hundreds of thousands—perhaps more than one million—additional casualties. The earlier US decision was taken by a small group of officials, strongly influenced by MacArthur's overconfidence; we know almost nothing about the Chinese decision process. Discussion within the US group shared and reinforced an illusion of invulnerability based in part on racial stereotyping of the avowed enemy—North Korea—as well as the potential enemy, China. Experts with dissenting views were excluded from the decision-making process. Something similar appears to have occurred within the governments of both the United States and the UK during the run-up to the 2003 invasion of Iraq, which may provide a case study in how *not* to decide whether to initiate a war.

Excluding Bad News

During the Korean War, General MacArthur's commitment to conquering (he claimed, "liberating") North Korea made him insensitive to reports that would counsel caution to someone more open-minded. As a result, subordinates—eager to ingratiate themselves with their commander or, at least, to avoid antagonizing him—slanted intelligence reports to reinforce what they believed to be MacArthur's perception of the situation. Feeling threatened, China entered the war, which prolonged it at the cost of many thousands of casualties.

This is a widespread and dangerous phenomenon in crisis decision making: the fact that it may be based on incorrect information because the information sources have been hesitant to send bad news, namely anything that contradicts the preconceptions of those in power. There are two useful lessons here: (1) When the bearer of bad tidings is likely to fare poorly, he or she may well doctor the message, and (2) people—including state leaders—often exhibit selective attention, so if they are already committed to a course of action, they tend to disregard what they do not want to hear, focusing only on information that confirms their preexisting beliefs, a phenomenon known as confirmation bias.

Thus, Stalin actually ordered the execution of a Czech agent who warned in April 1941 (correctly, it turned out) that Nazi Germany was preparing an attack on the Soviet Union. At the time, Stalin maintained that the spy must be a British provocateur, so convinced was he of British animosity toward the Soviet Union and of the reliability of his alliance with Hitler. Prior to the US-led invasion of Iraq in 2003, White House officials not only cherry-picked intelligence information that supported their predetermined insistence on going to war, but Vice President Cheney also intimidated Central Intelligence Agency (CIA) and State Department officials who disagreed, thereby squelching alternative views and biasing reports in favor of war. At the same time, Defense Department officials were assuring Congress and the public that American troops would be welcomed enthusiastically and, moreover, that money derived from Iraqi petroleum sales would pay for the invasion. Neither were the case.

Decision-Making Pressures

Political crises may be defined as unanticipated threats to the values and institutions that leaders hold most important and that accordingly impel them to act promptly. Decisions made during perceived crises are likely to be especially crucial for war and peace; unfortunately, it is precisely under such conditions—when stress is unusually high—that decision making is most likely to be flawed.

Crisis decision making is likely to have the following characteristics:

1. *Time pressure.* There is frequently a need (or a perceived need) for leaders to make decisions quickly.

2. *Heavy responsibility.* Most leaders are aware—or, at least, claim to be aware—of the potential costs in human suffering if their decision results in war.

3. *Faulty and incomplete data.* Intelligence about the potential opponent (motivations, alternative options, strengths and weaknesses) is usually limited and inadequate. Under such conditions, decision makers tend to rely on simplistic and often inaccurate stereotypes of the opponent

4. *Information overload.* Many contemporary decision makers are inundated with large amounts of information, and although much of it may in fact be erroneous, it is often unclear what to ignore or believe.

5. *Limited options.* Decision makers frequently see themselves as having only a limited range of potential courses of action, in part because the stress of the situation itself tends to limit creative problem solving; at the same time, the opponent is often perceived as enjoying a wide latitude of possible choices.

6. *Short-term over long-term.* Decision makers' attention tends to be focused on the immediate, short-term effects of a course of action, with relatively little patience for assessing the possible long-term implications of their decision. Their chief desire is then to act in such a way as to relieve the current, pressing crisis.

7. *Surprise.* Although the situation may not be entirely unexpected, an element of surprise is often involved, so most crises appear to the decision makers as needing to be resolved on the spot, without benefit of pre-analyzed scenarios.

8. *Personal stresses.* Decisions of great import must often be made under conditions of sleep deprivation and sometimes under great anxiety, bordering on panic.

These factors combine to make it especially difficult for leaders—either singly or in small groups—to render intelligent and rational judgments. Writing of the Berlin Crisis of 1961, the Cuban Missile Crisis of 1962, and the US-Soviet tensions raised during the Arab-Israeli Six-Day War (1967), former US secretary of defense Robert McNamara noted that "on each of the occasions lack of information, misinformation, and misjudgments led to confrontation. And in each of them, as the crisis evolved, tensions heightened, emotions rose, and the danger of irrational decisions increased."[9]

Crisis Management

In view of the importance of such situations, an area of investigation has emerged known as crisis management. The goals of crisis management are (1) to prevent a crisis from escalating to war but also (2) to keep the leaders in control of the situation, and (3) to gain maximum advantage, whenever possible, from such crises when they occur. Crises that involve the danger of war, especially nuclear war, cause decision makers to want to appear strong, fear seeming weak, and be eager to gain advantages over the other that they would not like to see the other have over them. Crisis behavior thus tends to become an exercise in "competitive risk taking." Contrary to the widespread belief that "tough" leadership makes would-be aggressors back down, it seems equally plausible that the likelihood of war increases when leaders are willing to accept a high level of risk.

In crises, leaders on each side are inclined to engage in one-upmanship, hoping to induce the other to back down, in a situation dangerously reminiscent of the game of chicken, whether nuclear weapons are involved or not. For example, a senior aide to President Kennedy recounted that during the Cuban Missile Crisis in 1962, former secretary of state Dean Acheson recommended bombing the Soviet missile sites, which had just been discovered in Cuba. When asked by President Kennedy what, in his judgment, the Soviets would do in response, Acheson replied, "I think they'll knock out our missile bases in Turkey." "What do we do then?" "Under our NATO Treaty, we'd be obligated to knock out a base inside the Soviet Union." "What will they do then?" "Why, then we hope everyone will cool down and want to talk."[10]

Psychological Effects of Repetitive Crises

Even when an individual crisis is resolved peacefully (as with the Cuban Missile Crisis), repetitions can produce an expectancy of war. For example, preceding the outbreak of World War I, Germany had been embroiled in numerous situations of near war—with Russia over Austria's annexation of Bosnia and Herzegovina, with Britain and France over colonial control of Morocco—in addition to a naval arms race with Britain and an army arms race with France. Such situations can result in a feeling of fatalism as yet another crisis emerges or an existing one is painfully prolonged and things appear to be leading slowly but irrevocably toward war. In such cases, rationality and flexible decision making are often replaced by a sense on the part of leaders that they must accept the ensuing and apparently inevitable violence to come.

On the other hand, as a result of their having looked into the abyss of possible nuclear devastation, the US and Soviet decision makers who took part in the Cuban Missile Crisis seem to have been sobered, leading to a warming of relations the following year, which included signing the Atmospheric Test Ban Treaty and eventually a period of détente, if not friendship.

Crisis in the Nuclear Age

Prior to World War I, mobilization of the Great Powers was extraordinarily fast given the immense number of men and amount of material involved, but it still required several days. In the nuclear age, mobilization requires mere minutes, and entire wars could be fought within hours. The quick-reaction regime of ballistic missiles has resulted in a chronic crisis mentality in leaders, advisers, and military chiefs. Thomas Schelling, one of the founders of deterrence theory, offers the following metaphor:

> If I go downstairs to investigate a noise at night, with a gun in my hand, and find myself face to face with a burglar who has a gun in his hand, there is danger of an outcome that neither of us desires. Even if he prefers just to leave quietly, and I wish him to, there is danger that he may *think* I want to shoot, and shoot first. Worse, there is danger that he may think that I think *he* wants to shoot. And so on.[11]

In the idealized case, crisis decision making is based on instrumental or strategic rationality in which decision making is seen as a variant of mathematical economics, a process of maximizing the difference between benefits and costs; this approach is especially popular among devotees of nuclear deterrence theory. Strategist Herman Kahn, for example, developed an elaborate classification of 44 different rungs of nuclear escalation, beginning with precise, low-intensity options such as "slow-motion counter-property," moving through "augmented disarming attacks," and culminating in "spasm or insensate war"—sometimes labelled "wargasm."

The assumption that decision makers will remain rational during a full-fledged crisis, carefully picking and choosing among the various options while the bombs are going off all around, is one of the less credible aspects of modern strategic thinking. In 1974, Secretary of Defense James Schlesinger testified to Congress about his judgment as to the feasibility of rationally conducting a "limited" nuclear war:

> In spite of [the claims] that everything must go all out, when the existential circumstances arise, political leaders on both sides will be under powerful pressure to continue to be sensible. . . . Those are the circumstances in which I believe that leaders will be rational and prudent. I hope I am not being too optimistic.[12]

Evidence from history and psychology suggests that he almost certainly was.

Mental Illness in Leaders

Another source of uncalled-for optimism concerns the mental health of leaders. Here, the evidence is even more clear. There have been many examples of political leaders whose mental health has been questionable, and others who have been unquestionably crazy, such as the Roman emperor Caligula, who became infamous for sexual excess and for having people killed for his personal amusement, among other things; Charles VI of medieval France, who became convinced that he was made of glass and was terrified that at any moment he might break; Mad King Ludwig II of Bavaria, who likely suffered from Pick's disease (related to early Alzheimer's) along with frontotemporal dementia and schizotypal personality disorder; and King George III of England, who evidently suffered from logorrhea, an uncontrollable need to speak and write, to a degree that often became incomprehensible, as well as apparent bipolar disorder. And that is only a very limited sample. We can safely conclude that occupying a position of great political responsibility is no guarantee against mental illness

"Only part of us is sane," wrote Rebecca West. "Only part of us loves pleasure and the longer day of happiness, wants to live to our nineties and die in peace."[13] It requires no arcane wisdom to realize that chronic mental illness is not the only source of "crazy" behavior: People often act out of misperceptions, anger, despair, insanity, stubbornness, revenge, pride, and/or dogmatic conviction—particularly when under threat. Moreover, in certain situations—as when either side is convinced that war is inevitable or under pressure to avoid losing face—an irrational act, including a lethal one, may appear appropriate, even unavoidable. When he ordered the attack on Pearl Harbor, the Japanese Defense Minister observed that "Sometimes it is necessary to close one's eyes and jump off the Kiyomizu Temple" (a renowned suicide spot). During World War I, Kaiser Wilhelm wrote in the margin of a government document that "Even if we are destroyed, England at least will lose India." While in his bunker, during the final days of World War II, Adolf Hitler ordered what he hoped would be the total destruction of Germany because he felt that its people had "failed" him.[14]

Both Woodrow Wilson and Dwight Eisenhower suffered serious strokes while president of the United States. Boris Yeltsin, president of the Russian Federation from 1991 to 1999, was a known alcoholic who became incoherent and disoriented when on a binge. Nothing is known about what contingency plans, if any, were established within the Kremlin to handle potential war crises had they arisen during the Yeltsin period. Richard Nixon also drank heavily, especially during his stressful stint as US president during the Watergate crisis, which ultimately led to his resignation. During that time, Defense Secretary James Schlesinger took the extraordinary step of insisting that he be notified of any orders from the president that concerned nuclear weapons before they were passed down the command chain. Presumably, Schlesinger—and by some accounts, Henry Kissinger, who was then serving as National Security Adviser—would have inserted themselves, unconstitutionally, to prevent war, especially nuclear war, if Nixon had ordered it. As civilians, neither Yeltsin nor Nixon, when incapacitated by alcohol, would have been permitted to drive a car; yet they had full governmental authority to start a nuclear war by themselves.

During his time in office, Donald Trump was the first US president considered, by virtue of his own personal traits, to be a national security threat. Thus, he was renowned for repetitively lying, possibly to a pathological extent, and concerns were constantly raised about his mental stability, impulsiveness, narcissism, sociopathy, and many other ailments that in the opinion of many mental health professionals would have disqualified him for numerous military and government posts . . . but not the presidency.

It can plausibly be argued that no one, regardless of how psychologically sound, should be entrusted with the power to initiate nuclear war. Donald Trump's presidency nonetheless gave added momentum to proposals to restrict the unilateral authority of a US president in this regard.

The Effects of Crises on Rational Decision Making

What must be decided during a crisis? According to a renowned political scientist, the tasks include the following:

(a) Identify major alternative courses of action; (b) estimate the probable costs and gains of alternative policy choices; (c) distinguish between the possible and the probable; (d) assess the situation from the perspective of other parties; (e) discriminate between relevant and irrelevant information; (f) tolerate ambiguity; (g) resist premature action; and (h) make adjustments to meet real changes in the situation (and, as a corollary, to distinguish real from apparent changes).[15]

There have been numerous cases of crisis decisions made hastily, emotionally, and erroneously. The psychological data are also clear that mild stress tends to facilitate human decision making but that intense stress is likely to be especially disruptive, resulting in actions that are increasingly self-defeating. During severe crises, therefore, good policy decisions become both more important and less likely. Information overload, for example, becomes a substantial problem.

Laboratory studies have also shown that as perceived threat increases, messages sent and received reveal assessments of the situation that are increasingly stereotyped and simplistic. Moreover, during real-life international crises, time pressures are often intensified by the use of deadlines and ultimatums. "Nothing clarifies the mind," according to Samuel Johnson (several centuries before the nuclear age), "like the prospect of being hanged in the morning." This may be true, but it is equally predictable that nothing fogs the mind like the prospect of immediately having to make a potentially catastrophic decision in a stressful environment during a crisis.

Experimental research has also shown that severe stress is particularly likely to impede precisely those decision processes needed during international crises: Verbal and logical performance deteriorates; problem solving becomes more rigid; tolerance for complexity and ambiguity diminishes (this is especially crucial because in the real world of international affairs, issues are rarely simple matters of "either/or"); errors are more frequent; the focus of attention is reduced, both spatially and temporally; and decision makers become less able to discriminate the trivial from the crucial. In short, decision makers find themselves less able to see the problem clearly and to respond creatively.

Nonetheless, it remains uncertain whether simulation studies accurately reflect the real world. Speaking from his own experience in the Kennedy administration, Theodore Sorensen noted that "I saw first-hand, during the long days and nights of the Cuban crisis, how brutally physical and mental fatigue can numb the good sense as well as the senses of normally articulate men."[16]

Some Issues Regarding Perception and Cognition

It can be argued that most wars begin in error because each side often feels at the outset that it will win—or else it wouldn't go to war in the first place. Insofar as this is true, the process of war itself is a movement from error, through agony, to a more accurate appraisal of the situation because wars usually end when both sides agree which is the stronger. To be sure, some wars take place because one side is attacked or perceives the other as hostile and threatening, and it may fight back not because it expects to win but because it sees no viable alternative: for example, Poland after Germany invaded in 1939; Finland after the Soviet Union attacked in the same year; and Iraq during the Persian Gulf War. But in many other cases, human error—notably perceptual distortions—appears to have a role in causing war. Thus, Horatio, in Shakespeare's *Hamlet*, relates a tale,

> *Of carnal, bloody and unnatural acts,*
>
> *Of accidental judgments, casual slaughters,*
>
> *Of deaths put on by cunning and forced cause,*
>
> *And, in this upshot, purposes mistook*
>
> *Fall'n on th' inventors' heads.* (V.ii.382–386)

Insofar as blunders and misperceptions have an important role in the real world as well, it is advisable to be attuned to these sources of error. "We can never walk surely," wrote the British statesman Edmund Burke, "but by being sensible of our blindnesses."

There are cases, fortunately, in which such awareness has prevailed, to the benefit of all concerned. For example, in 1961, President Kennedy gave the go-ahead to the Bay of Pigs invasion of Cuba by anti-Castro dissidents. It turned out to be a military and political disaster, which left JFK with a deep distrust of overconfident and insufficiently thought-through military advice. As a result, during the Cuban Missile Crisis a year later, he resisted the urging of his Joint Chiefs of Staff that the US attack nuclear missile sites on that same island. It appears that neither the US nor the USSR "walked surely," as Edmund Burke had recommended, but being "sensible" of earlier blindness appears to have prevented the American president from blundering into disaster.

Even in the absence of a crisis, leaders and decision makers are often prevented from getting a clear, unbiased view of the situation. The outcome is a range of potential errors, resulting from misperceptions, misunderstandings, and/or miscalculations. Some of these, such as the tendency to disregard information that does not conform to one's preconceptions, have already been touched on. There are two major contending theories of perceptual distortion: cognitive theory, which is concerned with errors in the processing of information, and motivational theory, according to which the emotional needs of the decision makers are paramount. And, of course, in some cases of perceptual distortion, both cognitive and emotional factors are present. Here, we focus on the nature of misperceptions rather than their causes.

Inaccurate Perception of Others

History is replete with examples of inaccurate perceptions of others. Thus, Hitler disdained the British as "shopkeepers" and the Russians as "barbarians." Arabs who attacked the fledgling state of Israel with five armies in 1948 were highly (and wrongly) confident of victory over a Jewish nation that had been seen, in modern history, as nonmilitarist. Conversely, after their victory in the Six Day War (1967), the Israeli armed forces came to suffer from a misconception that Arabs were hopelessly incompetent in military matters; as a result, they nearly lost the 1973 October War and achieved, at best, a draw during a 2006 incursion into Lebanon.

Five different US presidents apparently misread the determination of the North Vietnamese and their leader, Ho Chi Minh. All seemed convinced that the North Vietnamese drive for unification would crumble if only more American military pressure were applied. Iraq, under Saddam Hussein, first apparently underestimated the resilience of the Ayatollah Khomeini and the Iranians and later misperceived the determination of President George H. W. Bush to undo Iraq's invasion of Kuwait as well as President George W. Bush's desire to topple Hussein's regime. (On the other hand, Bush misperceived the resilience of the Taliban in Afghanistan and woefully underestimated the subsequent insurgency in Iraq.) The dolorous list is very long; many decision makers have persistently underestimated their opponents. Of course, it may also be that we only become aware of such errors when the results are glaring. When, by contrast, decision makers correctly assess a would-be opponent or overestimate its strength, the resulting inaction doesn't make headlines.

Decision makers commonly misjudge the strength of allies as well. US political leadership underestimated the precarious status of the Shah of Iran in 1979, until it was too late. According to one expert on the role of misperceptions in international affairs, American officials were so slow in recognizing the Iranian revolution because it went counter to many preexisting and reinforcing beliefs:

> Not only were the Shah and his regime perceived as strong, but also the specific image was supported by the general belief—based on good historical evidence—that leaders who control large and effective internal security forces were not overthrown by popular protest. These preconceptions were reinforced by several others that were more peculiarly American: the menace to pro-Western governments comes from the left; modernization enjoys the support of the strongest political elements of society, and those who oppose it cannot be serious contenders for power; and religious motives and religious movements are peripheral to politics.[17]

As a result, American decision makers not only misinterpreted events in Iran but also made inappropriate decisions based on those misperceptions. This difficulty was enhanced by the anguish associated with making difficult decisions: The harder it is to make a decision and to set a policy, the greater the resistance to reversing that decision once it has been made.

Many preconceptions are self-serving. Hawks, for example, tend to see an opponent as unrelentingly hostile and aggressive, so even conciliatory moves are interpreted as clever maneuvers to make them let down their guard—thus further proving the correctness of the original impression. Doves tend to emphasize the role of perceptions, thereby sometimes excusing an unacceptably aggressive act as a consequence of misunderstanding or misperception. These "motivated errors" include, for example, the tendency among British leaders during the 1930s to underestimate German hostility. Some pro-military conservatives fear that a similar process may be occurring with regard to Western perceptions of Iran and North Korea, with antiwar sentiment ostensibly blinding many people in the West. At the same time, there is the risk that motivated misperceptions on the part of pro-militarists might precipitate unnecessary and avoidable war.

Misreading History

Decision makers' perceptions are often modified to minimize psychological distress and to support a congenial, often simplistic, view of current events. There is also an understandable yearning by many leaders to avoid repeating past errors and instead to repeat past successes. Following the Franco-Prussian War (1870–1871), for example, two assumptions were widespread among many European politicians and generals: (1) The next war would be intense and brief because (2) a long war would ruin a state's economy. The result was a desire to strike first and decisively; this contributed, in turn, to plans for prompt and total mobilization, with disastrous consequences: namely, World War I.

Past successes can also overshadow present realities. For example, NATO's history of inaction during the Bosnian War in the early 1990s emboldened Serbian president Milošević to assume he would have a comparably free hand in subduing rebels in Kosovo, but history did not repeat itself. Che Guevara's success during the Cuban revolution led him to believe that history would repeat itself in Bolivia; it also did not.

Professional "security managers" generally give special attention to cases that suit their own, often aggressive goals. For example, Argentine forces took over the Falkland Islands in 1982, with the Argentine military looking as a historical analogy to the Indian takeover of Goa, a small colonial enclave on the Indian mainland that had been forcibly retaken by India and whose loss was quickly accepted (without bloodshed) by the colonial Portuguese government. To the British, however, the relevant metaphor was Hitler and the origins of World War II, and they responded not as Portugal did in 1961 but rather as they wished they had done in 1938.

States such as the United States, which have relatively limited historical experience in world affairs, may be unusually susceptible to drawing inferences from the small number of international events that have been significant for them. And the more recent the event, the more likely it is to be salient in memory, even if it may not be especially relevant.

The Double Standard of Hostility

In 1970, during the Vietnam War, the United States bombed and invaded Cambodia, claiming that because Cambodia was providing haven and supply routes to the Viet Cong and the North Vietnamese, it could legally be attacked, even though it was a sovereign, nonbelligerent state. In 1988, however, after Nicaraguan forces pursued *contra* rebels to their staging and supply areas inside neighboring Honduras, the Reagan administration decried what it called an "unjustified invasion" and dispatched 3,000 US troops to Honduras.

In the late 1950s, the United States placed medium-range missiles, capable of reaching the Soviet Union, in Turkey and the UK; this was considered (by the United States) to be a defensive and justified action, for the sake of deterrence. But when, shortly afterward, the Soviet Union began placing medium-range missiles capable of reaching the United States in Cuba, this was deemed by the US government a dastardly, offensive, and unjustified act, and the Kennedy administration went to the brink of nuclear war to get them removed.

The principle sounds absurd but is widely followed: When *we* (Russia, the United States, whoever) do something, it is acceptable—often, laudable—but if *they* do the same thing, it is not. What is involved here, in part, is a profound absence of empathy, a failure to recognize that there is more than one way to look at a problem, and a refusal to consider that the motivations and actions of one side may be perceived quite differently by the other. Historian Herbert Butterfield attributed much of this widespread misperception to "Hobbesian fear":[18]

> You yourself may vividly feel the terrible fear that you have of the
> other party, but you cannot enter into the other man's counter-fear, or
> even understand why he should be particularly nervous. For you know
> that you yourself mean him no harm, and that you want nothing from
> him save guarantees for your own safety; and it is never possible for
> you to realize or remember properly that since he cannot see the inside
> of your mind, he can never have the same assurance of your intentions
> that you have.[19]

During a 1989 speech at an East-West conference on reducing conventional forces in Europe, then–secretary of state James Baker asserted, "Those in the West should be free of the fear that the massive forces under Soviet command might invade them. Those in the East should be free of the fear that armed Soviet intervention . . . would be used again to deny them choice."[20] Another, possibly more sensitive statesman might also have added something like "Those in the East should be free of the fear that the forces of the West will invade them, as they have so often in the past," and perhaps even "Those in the West should be free of the fear that their own military forces might precipitate a war, which, although ostensibly fought on their behalf, would destroy them."

Among psychologists, three related theories have sought to explain this tendency to perceive the other as hostile, while holding oneself blameless, and to minimize or misconstrue the concerns of others:

1. *Ego defense.* A theory of ego defense emphasizes that individuals would find it troublesome to admit that their activities threaten others; hence, they protect their self-images by maintaining their own innocence and benevolent intentions. When others then respond aggressively, this is regarded as demonstrating their hostility because it couldn't possibly have been evoked by us, "the good guys."

2. *Attribution.* Attribution theory suggests that individuals are intensely aware of the various external constraints on their behavior, including economic factors, the need to placate others within their own regime, and so on. Any threat or actual harm to others is therefore unintended. By contrast, it is much more difficult to understand the complex forces acting to produce the behavior of outsiders, which is often attributed to unreasoning hostile intent.

3. *Projection.* Projection is the phenomenon in which people take certain unacceptable tendencies of their own, displace them onto another person, and then identify those traits in the other instead of in themselves. Finding it painful to recognize nastiness, aggressiveness, and the like in themselves, many people project such characteristics onto an opponent.

Not surprisingly, wars fought because of the perception that an opponent is hostile, allied with an enemy, or bent on conquest tend to make that opponent hostile, allied with an enemy, and/or bent on conquest. Such wars vindicate the assumptions on which they were based. For example, the Vietnam War was presented by successive presidential administrations to the American public as a result of North Vietnam's invasion of South Vietnam—which came to pass *after* US bombing of North Vietnam triggered massive movement of North Vietnamese units into South Vietnam. Prior to that, the military struggle in South Vietnam was almost entirely carried out by indigenous South Vietnamese guerillas known as the Viet Cong.

Likewise, Soviet repression of reform efforts in Hungary and Czechoslovakia, in 1956 and 1968, out of the Kremlin's fear they were anti-Soviet, only increased anti-Soviet sentiment throughout Eastern Europe. The double standard of hostility prescribes not only that one's own actions are blameless but also that one's opponents are relentlessly hostile.

Similarly, to many Israelis, Israel seems small, isolated, and vulnerable. To many Arabs, and especially Palestinians, Israel is a dagger wielded by Western imperialists, stabbing right into the midsection of the Arab world. The Sandinistas in Nicaragua saw the Reagan administration as an imminent threat to their survival; at the same time, Nicaragua was rhetorically branded by President Reagan as an imminent threat to the security of the United States, located merely "two days' drive" from Harlingen, Texas.

Miscommunication

Some communication errors occur simply because people speak different languages and come from different cultures. For example, consider the "*mokusatsu* affair." In the early summer of 1945, the Allies, meeting in Potsdam, issued a surrender ultimatum to Japan. The official Japanese response was to *mokusatsu* the ultimatum, which was translated into English as "ignore." The Truman administration saw this as an outright rejection, whereas in fact it should more accurately have been rendered as "withhold comment, pending deliberation." It is at least possible that with better communication between Japanese and American decision makers, American atomic bombs might not have been dropped on Hiroshima and Nagasaki shortly thereafter.

In many other cases, and for diverse reasons, communication may result in what the French call *un dialogue des sourds,* "a dialogue of the deaf." Senders typically assume that if they spend much time and attention designing a message calibrated to convey a particular meaning, the receiver will necessarily understand it. Often, however, "messages" are not read as intended, whereupon warnings are not heeded, and the sender may even blame the receiver (unjustifiably) for intransigence or hostility.

In 1950, Secretary of State Acheson testified to Congress that Korea was outside the United States' Pacific defense perimeter; the North Koreans, not understanding that these words were intended more for domestic consumption than as an international signal, felt emboldened to attack the South Koreans. Later, when US forces were pushing far north of the 38th parallel (dividing North and South Korea), China sent numerous signals indicating that it would intervene if US troops continued military operations near the Chinese border. The United States, however, apparently did not pick up on these warnings. Furthermore, in seeking to reassure the Chinese that it did not wish to expand the Korean conflict, the United States referred frequently to long-standing friendship between the American and Chinese people. At the time, Chinese authorities had a very different perception of Sino-American relations, viewing the United States with deep distrust, as merely one of many imperialist exploiters of China during the 19th century and, more recently, as the inheritor of Japan's goal of an Asian empire.

Similarly, Saddam Hussein may have felt emboldened to invade Kuwait in 1990 because he misinterpreted the statements of a high-ranking American diplomat then stationed in Baghdad, who indicated that her government "does not take a stand" on Iraqi territorial claims to Kuwait; Saddam apparently thought this meant that the United States would not respond to Iraq's invasion, whereas it meant that the United States wasn't taking sides in the existing dispute, not that it would sit idly by if either side attempted to resolve the matter militarily.

Overconfidence

Many people have a habit of hearing what they want to hear and believing that something is true simply because they wish it were so. Military leaders tend to be "can-do" people; it is their job to take an assertive, problem-solving approach to their mission. Often there is no lack of intelligence, either data or IQ, but rather a reluctance to draw unpleasant conclusions. For example, prior to the 1962 Sino-Indian War—a stinging defeat for India—Indian leaders evidently assumed that the Chinese leadership was timid and that their military forces were superior to the Chinese, simply ignoring evidence to the contrary.

The same kind of unwarranted self-confidence led the United States into the quicksand of Vietnam, with most American decision makers confident that there was "light at the end of the tunnel" (subsequently identified by critics as an incoming train). In 1965, President Johnson was told by his Joint Chiefs of Staff that "the communists" would be defeated in Vietnam within 2 years, if only sufficient additional military pressure was applied. In 1971, the Pakistani leadership—ignoring all evidence that India enjoyed clear superiority—nonetheless attacked its archrival, seeking, unsuccessfully, to destroy the Indian Air Force on the ground, as Israel had succeeded against Egypt at the onset of the Six-Day War in 1967.

When the risks are high, one might expect that an uncompromising, self-critical honesty—if only for self-interested reasons—would prevail. But the opposite occurs at least as frequently: Self-delusion is rampant in the events before a war and in its early stages. For example, Lord Asquith, British prime minister in the early days of World War I, claimed that the War Office "kept three sets of figures: one to mislead the public, another to mislead the Cabinet, and a third to mislead itself." On the eve of their attack on Pearl Harbor, Japanese leaders realized that Japan could only hope to prevail over the United States in a brief and limited war, so they convinced themselves that this is what would probably happen, especially if the United States were sufficiently shocked and crippled militarily at the outset. And US vice president Dick Cheney claimed—and may even have believed—that the Iraqi people would welcome American invaders/liberators with "flowers and chocolates."

Overconfidence has often cost states and leaders dearly. In the autumn of 1914, the Kaiser promised Germany that its sons would be back "before the leaves had fallen from the trees." Hitler did not even have his quartermasters issue winter uniforms to his troops attacking the Soviet Union, so confident was he that the campaign would be over before winter; as it happened, many German soldiers died of exposure in Russia. In fact, most wars have been initiated on a note of excessive optimism, which, in many cases, may itself have been among the reasons for the war. Only rarely have soldiers marched off to war in a mood of grim determination and resignation—those emotions usually come after hostilities have dragged on.

It can also be argued, of course, that what is unintentional about most wars has not been the decision to fight but the outcome. Wars have typically turned out to be longer or costlier than expected at their outset. Above all, they typically result in the defeat of half the participants, virtually all of whom had initially expected to win.

Wishful Thinking

Wishful thinking is hardly a recent phenomenon. The defeat of its Armada, in 1588, marked the end of Spain as a global power. Before sailing, one Spanish commander "reasoned" as follows:

> It is well known that we fight in God's cause. So when we meet the English, God will surely arrange matters so that we can grapple and board them, either by sending some strange freak of weather, or more likely, just by depriving the English of their wits. . . . Unless God helps us by making a miracle, the English, who have faster guns and handier ships than ours, and many more long-range guns, and who know their advantage as well as we do, will . . . blow us to pieces with their

culverins, without our being able to do them any serious hurt. . . . So, we are sailing against England in the confident hope of a miracle.[21]

Military adventures are often launched on something more than the "confident hope of a miracle." Nearly three-quarters of all wars in the past 150 years have been won by the initiator, suggesting some tendency for accurate planning. However, there have also been notable exceptions, including the American Civil War, World War I, World War II, the Korean War, the 1973 October War, the Falklands War, the Iran-Iraq War, and the Persian Gulf War (when Iraq invaded Kuwait), all of which were initiated by the side that ultimately was defeated. Others become unanticipated quagmires, despite the initial appearance of success. The United States and the former Soviet Union became embroiled in their disastrous Vietnam and Afghanistan wars, each confident of relatively easy victory against a small, impoverished, Third World state.

Whereas the United States was quickly successful in its invasions of Afghanistan (2002) and Iraq (2003), the long-term consequences have not been nearly so positive. Not surprisingly, brief interventions by powerful states into much weaker states—such as the United States invasion of Grenada (1983) and of Panama (1989)—are more likely to be successful, at least in the short term. The long-term consequences of such events, however, are more difficult to predict, especially insofar as they may precipitate ongoing resentment and antagonism, whose effects can play out in subtle ways.

Negative, but Sometimes Accurate, Perceptions

The biases of certain leaders have clearly, on occasion, contributed to dangerous and costly misperceptions. But one should beware of assuming that international conflict arises solely from psychological errors and misperceptions. In some cases, negative assessments are, regrettably, all too accurate. Conflict may occur not because the adversaries misunderstand each other but rather because they understand each other all too well. In short, we must at least admit the possibility that sometimes states and their leaders are nefarious and war seeking. To seek peace and harmony or to strive for mutual understanding and confidence-building may not necessarily imply that one is naive or duped by the other side. But similarly, to be distrustful or to recognize danger or enmity is not necessarily to misperceive an adversary.

A Final Note on Decision Making

The making of war, and of peace, is the responsibility of human beings, typically of men (and, increasingly, women) who find themselves in positions of political and military leadership. To some degree, therefore, we are all at the mercy of those leaders whose decisions may be crucial for our survival. We thus have an interest in maximizing the quality of their decision making and of the information available to them. Nonetheless, even with perfect perception of all current issues, leaders are necessarily plunging into darkness.

Some influential members of Spain's aristocratic military tradition believed, in 1898, that a war with the United States was necessary in order to lose Cuba gracefully; they hadn't counted, however, on losing Puerto Rico and the Philippines, as well, to America. "The future," wrote the eminent historian A. J. P. Taylor, "is a land of which there are no maps, and historians err when they describe even the most purposeful statesman as though he were marching down a broad highway with his objective already in sight."[22] It is of the greatest importance, then, especially in the nuclear age, that leaders be as free as possible from emotional and perceptual blinders in making the crucial decisions of war and peace.

Questions for Further Reflection

1. In today's international context, which leaders do you perceive as "strong" or "weak," and why? Are there really "good" and "bad" guys?

2. Give some recent examples of "groupthink" at the decision-making level of nations embarking on recent military adventures. How did their peer groups influence these decisions for better or worse?

3. What were some of the pressures that may have affected the decision by the administration of President George W. Bush to invade Afghanistan and Iraq?

What about the subsequent military decisions of Presidents Obama and Trump?

4. How have (mis)perceptions and (faulty) cognitions influenced some of your personal "strategic" decisions? Would more accurate perceptions and cognitions have made a significant difference?

5. Taking a specific example of crisis management in the nuclear age, what factors led to the crisis and to its more or less successful management? Could the crisis have been managed better?

Suggestions for Further Reading

W. T. Coombs. 1999. *Ongoing Crisis Communication: Planning, Managing, and Responding.* Thousand Oaks, CA: SAGE.

Erika Hayes James and Lynn Wooten. 2010. *Leading Under Pressure.* New York: Routledge.

Irving Janis. 1982. *Groupthink: Psychological Studies of Policy Decisions and Fiascoes.* Boston: Houghton Mifflin.

R. Jervis. 2017. *Perception and Misperception in International Politics.* Princeton, NJ: Princeton University Press.

Robert F. Kennedy. 1999. *13 Days: A Memoir of the Cuban Missile Crisis.* New York: Norton.

Rose McDermott. 2007. *Presidential Leadership, Illness, and Decision-Making.* New York: Cambridge University Press.

Williamson Murray. 2011. *Military Adaptation in War: With Fear of Change.* Cambridge, UK: Cambridge University Press.

Thomas C. Schelling. 2007. *The Strategy of Conflict.* Cambridge, MA: Harvard University Press.

Notes

1. Leo Tolstoy. 1942. *War and Peace.* New York: Simon & Schuster.

2. E. Stilman & W. Pfaff. 1964. *The Politics of Hysteria.* New York: Harper & Row.

3. Desiderius Erasmus. 1936. *The Education of a Christian Prince.* New York: Columbia University Press.

4. Woodrow Wilson. 1965. *A Day of Dedication.* New York: Macmillan.

5. Herodotus. 1910. *History of Herodotus.* New York: E. P. Dutton.

6. Samuel P. Huntington. 1964. *The Soldier and the State.* New York: Vintage.

7. R. Falk and S. Kim. 1980. *The War System.* Boulder, CO: Westview.

8. Irving L. Janis. 1972. *Victims of Groupthink.* Boston: Houghton Mifflin.

9. Robert McNamara. 1986. *Blundering Into Disaster.* New York: Pantheon.

10. Quoted in Theodore Sorensen. 1965. *Kennedy.* New York: Harper & Row.

11. Thomas C. Schelling. 1960. *The Strategy of Conflict.* Cambridge, MA: Harvard University Press.

12. In John G. Stoessinger. 1985. *Why Nations Go to War.* New York: St. Martin's.

13. Rebecca West. 1940. *Black Lamb and Grey Falcon: A Journey Through Yugoslavia.* New York: Viking.

14. David P. Barash and Charles P. Webel. 2018. *Peace and Conflict Studies,* 4th ed. Thousand Oaks, CA: SAGE.

15. Ole Holsti. 1971. "Crisis, Stress and Decision-Making." *International Social Science Journal* 23(1).

16. Theodore Sorensen. 1964. *Decision-Making in the White House.* New York: Columbia University Press.

17. Robert Jervis. 1985. "Perceiving and Coping With Threat." In *Psychology and Deterrence,* eds. R. Jervis, N. Lebow, and J. G. Stein. Baltimore: Johns Hopkins University Press.

18. From the writings of 17th-century English philosopher Thomas Hobbes, who maintained that people are incorrigibly aggressive and power-seeking.

19. Herbert Butterfield. 1951. *History and Human Relations.* New York: Macmillan.

20. Quoted in the *New York Times,* March 7, 1989.

21. Quoted in B. Brodie and F. Brodie. 1962. *From Crossbow to H-Bomb.* New York: Dell.

22. A. J. P. Taylor. 1955. *Bismarck, the Man and the Statesman.* New York: Knopf.

The Ideological, Social, and Economic Levels

Wars are caused not only by individuals, groups, states, and leaders but also—at a less tangible level—by underlying ideological, social, cultural, and economic factors. We first consider some ideological and social reasons for wars before turning our attention to cases in which economic issues figure prominently. Then we briefly examine some of the social and economic effects of war and preparations for war. This is followed by a look at the contemporary notion of "the clash of civilizations" and a brief summary of the major causes of wars.

244

Conflicting Ideologies

An ideology is an integrated but often unarticulated network of ideas upon which social and political actions are often explained, justified, and implemented. Ideologies are usually characterized by a certain number of rigidly held and often implicit central propositions, a degree of comprehensiveness and systematization, and often a feeling of urgency on the part of the ideologues about the need for pursuing their favored approach. Ideologies are belief systems that pull together information, underlying assumptions, and global viewpoints that are generally not amenable to rational refutation. That is, differing ideologies weave together patterns of beliefs and basic premises that make up a self-contained thought system. Once accepted, such a belief system normally leads to only one admissible set of conclusions.

Ideologies can be organized around religious traditions or around such secular belief systems and institutions as capitalism, Marxism-Leninism, democracy, aristocracy, conservatism, liberalism, ethnocentrism, and nationalism. They can be powerful engines of human behavior, and when ideologies conflict, they can contribute to war.

Ideologies are not necessarily bad in themselves, nor is the word *ideology* necessarily pejorative, although the term *ideologue*, dating back to late 18th- and early 19th-century France and denoting a person who strongly adheres to a particular ideology, today generally conveys negative connotations of rigidity and closed-mindedness.

Because they are deeply and reflexively held, ideological differences can contribute to wars of extraordinary brutality, with little or no quarter asked or given. The 18th-century wars of monarchical succession, for example, were fought among states that all accepted the same political ideologies; hence, they were relatively brief and limited. By contrast, wars of religion, including the Crusades and the Thirty Years' War, and the little known (in the West) Taiping Civil War from 1850 to 1864, which caused something like 30 million deaths, involved passionately held conflicting ideologies and were exceptionally bloody.

Marxism, Capitalism, and Fascism

Among contemporary Western ideologies, Marxism has particularly addressed itself to the reasons for war and peace. According to orthodox Marxism (or Marxism-Leninism), modern capitalism results in two major antagonistic classes, the proletariat (workers) and the bourgeoisie, or capitalist ruling class, which owns the means of production and controls the government. War is the external manifestation of this class struggle: War will therefore be abolished when communism has triumphed worldwide over capitalism, following a possibly violent transition known as "the dictatorship of the proletariat," after which the state will "wither away." However, this has never happened, despite the seizures of state power by revolutionary leftists in Russia, China, Cuba, and Vietnam.

By contrast, mainstream Western capitalist ideology, of which current neo-liberalism is a major component, implies that individual success and social well-being are greatest in a situation of maximum economic "freedom" for markets from governmental regulations, along with freedom of thought, speech, and property ownership for individuals. In this view, wars are caused by many factors but most notably by perceived threats to human freedom, such as those allegedly posed by "communist-inspired" revolutionary social and political movements, as well as by "antidemocratic militants," often considered terrorists by many Western leaders.

Although Fascist ideology has not been as clearly articulated as its Marxist-Leninist and capitalist counterparts, it can be viewed as a far right-wing, nationalistic/militarist extension (or distortion?) of capitalism, a worldview that places great reliance on social rigidity and respect for hierarchy. It glorifies patriotism, the state, charismatic leadership, and militarism, harking back to a "golden" and romanticized past. Big business and conventional church-centered religion enjoy a prominent place in Fascist states, as long as the former cooperates with the regimes, especially in the production of war material, and so long as the latter espouses doctrines that emphasize obedience to secular authorities (including the promise of heavenly reward for patriotic loyalty to the state), while demonizing any opponents of Fascist rule. Racist and ethnocentric/nationalistic appeals have also been important to most Fascists, largely to buttress claims about the appropriateness of dominating other "inferior" peoples and achieving the nation's legitimate "place in the sun."

Ideologies and Wars

Ideologies can lead to perceptions, institutions, and activities that contribute to war making. For example, American supporters of the Vietnam War saw it as an example of the worldwide struggle against communism, whereas opponents saw it largely is as a manifestation of nationalistic yearnings for a unified Vietnam and of imperial overreach by the US. Similarly, those American decision makers during the administration of President Ronald Reagan who viewed the Sandinista government in Nicaragua as a manifestation of "international communism" were likely to consider it a threat to the peace and stability of the Western Hemisphere, whereas others who saw it as an example of revolutionary nationalism and whose ideology favored progressive or socialist values were more likely to recommend accommodation and friendly coexistence.

For their part, Communist Party ideologues within the former Soviet Union were quick to brand reform efforts in such former Eastern European bloc nations as Poland, Hungary, and Czechoslovakia as part of a global capitalist and counterrevolutionary offensive against socialism; Soviet citizens who supported these efforts were often marginalized or silenced.

World War II had clear ideological underpinnings: The Axis powers saw it as a crusade to make their nation-states great again, to support racial purity, and oppose communism, while the West saw it as the equally sacred defense of democracy against Nazi Germany (whose National Socialist ideology was an extreme form of fascism), as well as against Fascist Italy and Japan.

Although similar sentiments were expressed by political leaders before World War I, that conflict was not really an ideological war—until it began. World War I then evolved into a kind of ideological conflict, especially on the part of the United States, not only "to make the world safe for democracy" but also as "the war to end all wars," in the words of President Woodrow Wilson.

Before 1914, however, few people in the United States, Great Britain, or France had advocated war against Germany or Austria-Hungary, despite the fact that they were autocratic and certainly undemocratic. For the Germans, Austrians, and Turks, on the other hand, World War I soon became an ideological conflict in defense of their emperors and motherlands. Moreover, Russia under the czar, on whose side the US fought during World War I (and later in alliance with the Soviet Union during World War II) was an outright, violent dictatorship.

The following is part of an address in 1917 by President Wilson, in which he requested a congressional declaration of war:

> A steadfast concern for peace can never be maintained except by a partnership of democratic nations. We are glad . . . to fight thus for the ultimate peace of the world and for the liberation of its peoples, the German peoples included; for the rights of nations great and small and the privilege of men everywhere to choose their own way of life and of obedience. . . . America is privileged to spend her blood and her might for the principles that gave her birth and happiness and the peace which she has treasured . . . the world must be made safe for democracy.[1]

In the contemporary world, ideologies may make crosscutting demands. For example, although the state of Iran is Shiite-Islamic, its populace is ethnically Persian and not Arab, whereas Iraq is largely Arab and also has a Shiite majority. During the Iran-Iraq War (1980–1988), therefore, many Shiite Arabs were forced to choose between their religious ideology and their secular ideology (Arab nationalism). In most cases, they opted for the latter and supported Iraq over Iran.

Many wars, on the other hand, have been fought for non-ideological reasons: communist Vietnam against communist China in 1979, or right-wing capitalist Great Britain under Margaret Thatcher against right-wing capitalist Argentina under General Galtieri in 1982. And largely because of *Realpolitik* considerations, states that one might expect to be ideological enemies have become allies instead: officially communist and atheist China and authoritarian Islamic Pakistan, for example.

Although ideologies are undoubtedly important, the distinctions between them are not always clear. Twenty-first-century Chinese "communism," for example, is increasingly capitalist; Russian secular "democracy" under Vladimir Putin is distinctly authoritarian, with strong ties to the Russian Orthodox Church; "right-of-center" governments in Europe often follow social policies that are to the "left" of the mainstream of the Democratic Party in the United States; and Venezuelan "socialism" under President Hugo Chávez was avowedly Catholic as well as "anti-capitalist," even while its economy was largely based on oil sales to capitalist nations. Venezuela's economic collapse under Chavez's successor, Nicolás Maduro, who was elected president of that country in 2013 after the death of Chavez, has been due not only to colossal mismanagement but also in part to its overreliance on oil exports as well as the foreign currency controls established by President Chávez in an unsuccessful effort to manage the flourishing black market in US dollars.

Capitalism and War

It has been widely thought (except by Marxists) that capitalism would discourage war. This is because capitalism has historically tended to favor trade over the forcible seizure of land and political stability over instability.

Capitalist-industrial states have been no less warlike than others, although previously the pressure for war has come from classes in addition to the bourgeoisie. In the 19th century, for example, American agitation for the War of 1812 and the Civil War came primarily from the agrarian South and West rather than the mercantile East or North. In Britain, liberal merchants and industrialists were less supportive of imperialism than was the landed aristocracy. Japanese militarism was similarly spearheaded by the army and the peasantry rather than the capitalist classes, and in the lead-up to World War I, German militarism came primarily from the aristocratic Prussian *Junkers* (wealthy landed nobles in the eastern part of the empire) rather than from the business community. But since World War II, the behavior of leading capitalist states, in their search for energy, new markets, land, and cheap labor, may undermine the notion that inherently expansionist capitalist enterprises would contribute more to peace and global security than to war and insecurity (as in the Middle East and elsewhere).

Population Pressure and Other Social Stresses

Some scholars have argued that internal social stresses make war more likely, even though there is at present little evidence to support this contention. The Vietnam War was clearly associated with an increase in domestic conflict within the United States, but this increase was a result of that war rather than a reason for it. No strong and enduring correlations have yet been established between war proneness and population density, homicides, suicides, alcoholism, or urbanization. The role of population pressure, however, has repeatedly drawn attention.

The simplest claim is that expanding population drives a state to conquest, much as Hitler claimed that his conquests in Poland and the western Soviet Union were a result of the German need for *Lebensraum* (living space). Japan was, by many standards, overpopulated in the 1930s, when it was very aggressive. Today, however, it is still crowded, and yet its aggressiveness has largely been limited to competing with its rivals for exports for its products, especially automobiles and electronic goods.

Nor is this a recent phenomenon. Between the 3rd and 8th centuries CE, for example, the population of Europe fell, yet this was a time of Roman imperial wars followed by smaller "barbarian" wars and the end of the *Pax Romana*. Later, the European population was reduced drastically, by perhaps 30 percent to 60 percent, due to the Black Plague (14th century), and yet this period was also notable for the Hundred Years' War and an uneasy transition from the religious wars of the Crusades to feudal wars among opposing princes. Moreover, rapid population growth in the ancient and more recent past was associated not with increased war but rather with the *Pax Romana* and *Pax Britannica*.

At the same time, the leaders of smaller states have often worried that they were at risk of being attacked by larger, more populous ones: Belgium's fear of France, France's fear of Germany, Germany's fear of Russia, Vietnam's fear of China, Cambodia's fear of Vietnam; many nations' (including North Korea and Venezuela) fear of the United States, and the United States' concern about the military potential of China, are notable cases. Yet when they are not provoked, larger states seem if anything to be more inclined to overconfidence and complacency. Nevertheless, high unemployment, homelessness, mass poverty, starvation, and general social dissatisfaction, whether in industrial regions or in rural societies in which population growth has exceeded available land, may lead to a dangerous kind of national restlessness.

War Fatigue or Boredom?

The peace that typically follows a war may simply occur because there is nothing left to fight about, at least for a time. In other cases—when there was something to fight about—wars have followed one another, with little if any breathing space. For example, after fighting Japanese invaders during the early 1940s, the Viet Minh continued battling the French forces who reoccupied Vietnam (prior to World War II, Vietnam had been imperially dominated by France and before then fought intermittently for centuries against China). Then, they fought the Americans. As soon as their devastating war with the Japanese was finished in 1945, the Chinese communists resumed, with scarcely a pause, their comparably devastating civil war against Chiang Kai-shek's right-wing and American-backed government. If wars necessarily lead to national exhaustion and therefore to peace (or at least to a cease-fire), one might expect that periods of peace would lead to a lower threshold for war, as the immunizing effects of painful memories wear off. But states such as Switzerland and Sweden, which have enjoyed centuries of peace, do not seem any more war prone than others, such as Afghanistan, Ethiopia, Israel, Iraq, Sudan, Syria, Libya, and Yemen, which are, understandably, tired of war.

Following the Vietnam War, by contrast, the United States went through a period when it was hesitant to engage in other military adventures; American conservatives in particular criticized this as the "Vietnam syndrome." It did not, however, appear to be a weariness with war in general as much as a determination to avoid "bad" (i.e. unwinnable) wars. And the Vietnam syndrome was short-lived, as evidenced by America's military involvements against Iraq, Serbia, and other perceived foes during the 1990s, as well as the current "war against terrorism" around the globe. The former Soviet Union, following its unsuccessful military episode in Afghanistan, underwent a parallel "Afghanistan syndrome," which was also shed as Russia has battled "terrorists" in Chechnya from the mid-1990s to the present as well as wars against Georgia and in Eastern Ukraine, annexing the Crimea (despite the opposition of Ukraine and most of the international community), and conducting military operations in Syria as backers of Bashar al-Assad against his opposition.

Poverty as a Cause of War

According to orthodox Marxist thinking, wars are caused by class struggles, including conflicts within societies as well as between the upper classes of different societies for control over other countries, labor, and natural resources.

In *The Communist Manifesto*, Marx predicted that "in proportion as the antagonism between classes within the nation vanishes, the hostility of one nation to another will come to an end." But one doesn't have to be a Marxist to see that poverty can breed dissatisfaction, which in turn can lead to war. In 1962, for example, President John F. Kennedy, referring specifically to Latin America, warned, "Those who possess wealth and power in poor nations must accept their own responsibilities. . . . Those who make peaceful revolution impossible will make violent revolution inevitable."

Socioeconomic deprivation was a major factor in generating popular support for Fidel Castro's successful revolt against Cuban dictator Fulgencio Batista in 1959 and for the overthrow of Nicaraguan dictator Anastasio Somoza in 1979. Right-wing violence has also been spawned by economic conditions, as witnessed by the Central Intelligence Agency (CIA)-sponsored overthrow on September 11, 1973, of Salvador Allende, the democratically elected, socialist president of Chile. Whereas, for most Americans, "September 11" immediately conjures thoughts of the terrorist attacks of September 11, 2001, for millions of Chileans—and others in Latin

America—it connotes the anniversary of the coup that installed neo-Fascist General Augusto Pinochet. In contrast, September 11, 1906 is the date ascribed to Gandhi's formulation of his nonviolent doctrine of *satyagraha*. Efforts to destabilize a given regime by creating economic and social chaos testify to the widespread assumption that governmental stability can be diminished when domestic economic conditions are difficult.

Some of history's most notable revolutions (France in 1789, Russia in 1917, Italy's fascist one in 1922, Iran's Islamist revolution in 1979, Haiti and the Philippines in 1986, the "Velvet Revolution" in Czechoslovakia and elsewhere in Eastern Europe in 1989, as well in Tunisia and Egypt during the "Arab Spring" of 2011) have not, at least in their initial phases, involved lengthy civil wars but rather an array of strikes, demonstrations, and other mass actions, in which the government lost the ability to control its own armed forces as a result of the disaffection of the people. More recently, military governments have feared their own people more than an external enemy; accordingly, police expenditures in less economically advanced countries have increased much more rapidly than have expenditures for externally directed military forces. The large "defense" budgets of many Latin American, South Asian, and African countries, in particular, are aimed almost entirely against their own populace rather than against some threatening, external enemy.

Poverty and Domestic Unrest

Poverty does not, however, inevitably breed war or even revolution. The decade preceding the American Revolutionary War (1765–1775), for example, was a time not of poverty and deprivation but rather of prosperity and expansion: Business was booming, and the number of ships in New York's harbor had nearly doubled in a decade.

Even the French Revolution—long considered a classic case of hunger leading to violence—in fact took place at a time when economic conditions, although bad, were improving. According to Alexis de Tocqueville, "It is a singular fact that this steadily increasing prosperity, far from tranquilizing the population, everywhere promoted a spirit of unrest." Tocqueville also noted that "those parts of France in which the improvement in the standard of living was most pronounced were the chief centers of the revolutionary movement."[2] National misery and economic deprivation, in short, does not necessarily lead to war. Germany was not belligerent during a period of runaway inflation and economic collapse in 1923 but rather in 1914, at a time of unparalleled prosperity. Hitler may indeed have been aided in his rise to power by the Great Depression of the early 1930s, but by the time of German expansionism (the late 1930s), prosperity was already returning.

"The revolution of rising expectations," rather than declining conditions, may lead to social violence. Some theorists have proposed that the crucial point at which a society becomes unusually violent depends less on so-called objective conditions than on a gap between prevailing conditions and a public expectation—that is, when the "want-to-get ratio" is high. Propaganda and agitation can, of course, intensify the effect of this gap.

Frantz Fanon, advocate of anticolonial revolutionary violence in post–World War II Africa, maintained that "violence is a cleansing force. It frees the native from his inferiority complex and from his despair and inaction; it makes him fearless and restores his self-respect."[3] "Why does the guerrilla fighter fight?" asked Che Guevara, comrade-in-arms of Cuba's Fidel Castro.

We must come to the inevitable conclusion that the guerrilla fighter is a social reformer, that he takes up arms responding to the angry protest of the people against their oppressors, and that he fights in order to change the social system that keeps all his unarmed brothers in ignominy and misery.[4]

Wars and Social Change

Civil wars may occur when a disparity exists between the forces of socioeconomic change and the ability of existing political structures to accommodate these changes. Thus, the wars heralding the breakup of the Habsburg and Ottoman empires just after World War I occurred when nationalist sentiments could not be satisfied within those existing imperial systems. This is, however, a relatively new phenomenon: Prior to the late 18th century, wars had resulted largely from elite decision makers' ambitions for empire and conquest, from dynastic disputes and squabbles over state power and influence, as well as from messianic impulse, or for perceived self-defense. There had always been sporadic uprisings, such as that of the ill-fated Wat Tyler in 14th-century England or, before that, the Spartacus-led slave revolt against ancient Rome from 73–71 BCE.

But with the US War of Independence, and especially with the wars of the French Revolution, organized violence between large armed groups came to be seen as a potential instrument for social change. Prior to the Napoleonic Wars, which were to convulse Europe in the early 19th century, the newspaper *Patriote Français* exulted over the coming "expiatory war which is to renew the face of the world and plant the standard of liberty upon the palaces of kings, upon the seraglios [harems] of sultans, upon the chateaux of petty feudal tyrants and upon the temples of popes and muftis [Islamic legal authorities]."

Although economic and social deprivations appear to have been important in unleashing rebellions, such as the civil wars in China and Cuba, they seem less likely to have produced war between states. In many cases in ancient and medieval times, economic gain was a major motivating factor, especially the prospect of plunder obtained by looting the defeated side. For example, the successes of the Macedonians under Alexander the Great, the Huns under Attila, and the Mongols under Genghis Khan (who, during the early 13th century, may have been responsible for as many as 40 million deaths), and the remarkable advances of the armies of Islam during the 7th and 8th centuries CE, all were due at least in part to the lure of obtaining the "spoils" of successful conquest. However, these armies were not so much driven by desperation about their personal well-being as by the hope of obtaining yet more booty.

Poverty may drive war in unexpected ways. In 1966, President Johnson sought to justify the presence of US troops overseas (including, notably, those in Vietnam). "There are 3 billion people in the world," he said while reviewing US troops in Korea, "and we have only 200 million of them. We are outnumbered 15 to 1. If might did make right they would sweep over the United States and take what we have. We have what they want." Thus, when it comes to violence between states, poverty may be less influential in motivating the poor than in activating the wealthy to defend what they already have by taking measures ranging from "police actions" abroad to suppressing "civil disturbances" at home.

Economic conditions, however, can serve as an indirect cause of international war, as other state leaders become nervous at the success of recently established revolutionary regimes. The French Revolution was stimulated in part by the physical hunger of a significant part of the French people. In turn, the new republican government was seen as a threat to the established monarchies of Europe, and efforts were therefore made to invade France and suppress that revolution. The resulting French Revolutionary Wars led to the ascension to power of Napoleon Bonaparte and to the subsequent Napoleonic Wars that engulfed much of Europe.

Poverty as a Restraint on War

Overall, the correlations between poverty and war are unclear. Poor people are more likely to seek food and land locally than via overseas conquests. In the contemporary world, impoverished peasants may occasionally pose a threat to their own governments but not to their wealthy, well-armed neighbors. Few believe that the poor *campesinos* (peasant farmers) of Mexico, for example, are going to invade the United States (at least not militarily), although former President Donald Trump initiated building a wall along the southern border of the US to keep Latinos out and referred to refugees and asylum seekers as "invaders." A small number of poor and disenfranchised Mexicans have been responsible for an ongoing low-level insurgency against their government. If anything, however, poverty has been more likely to restrain the military adventuring of states than to encourage it. Wars are expensive; it is costly to equip infantries, navies, and air forces and to supply them in the field.

Truly desperate conditions, more often than not, reduce rather than enhance an army's motivation for fighting. For example, the terrible food, medicine, and supply situation (as well as despair over the high casualties and lack of battlefield success) led Russian forces to seek to end their war against Germany and Austria-Hungary in early 1917. These disaffected soldiers and sailors, together with many workers and peasants, comprised the bulk of the insurrection forces that, under the leadership of Lenin and Trotsky, generated the Bolshevik Revolution later that year as well as the defense of the new revolutionary government against what the Bolsheviks deemed counterrevolutionaries during Russia's civil war from 1918–1921.

When England introduced the world's first nationwide income tax in the early 19th century, it was to pay the costs of the Napoleonic Wars. Only rarely has poverty pushed a country to war; more often, leaders have hesitated to make war unless their economies were strong enough to withstand the strain. By contrast, a degree of prosperity can make leadership pushy and dangerously self-confident. (It can also make them relatively peace loving—although still militarized—like modern-day Switzerland and Sweden.)

Imperialism

Imperialism refers to the policy of extending political control over other, foreign peoples and their economic exploitation by the ruling class of the imperial states. It has an ancient history, beginning with the first efforts to conquer and dominate the populace of other lands. The Roman historian Tacitus commented, "Worldwide conquest and the destruction of all rival communities or potentates opened the way to the secure enjoyment of wealth and an overriding appetite for it."

Until the early 20th century, imperialism was widely accepted and even lauded—at least by the leadership of most imperialist states! At the same time, imperialism may have contributed directly to war and suffering—that is, by generating not only the direct violence of war but also the indirect, structural violence of colonial oppression.

By the end of the 20th century, it seemed to many mainstream Western analysts that the world had passed into a post-imperialist era. Therefore, suggestions that imperialism causes war may appear outdated. However, imperialism still occupies an important place in Marxist and post-colonialist thinking on war and even among some American conservatives and neo-liberals who argue the United States should be celebrating and securing rather than bemoaning and diminishing its "democratic empire." Hence, imperialism can be very resilient, cropping up in many different forms.

Lenin argued that imperialism necessarily led to war, especially when wedded to capitalism, which, in the Leninist view, inevitably generates over-production and, in turn, competition for new markets. Even today, "anti-imperialists," both in the less economically developed counties (especially in Latin America) and in advanced industrial nations (particularly in France, Italy, Spain, Portugal, and Greece), decry what they perceive to be the economic and cultural imperialism of Western multinational corporations and American mass media, as well as the continuing Israeli occupations of Arab land on the West Bank. At the same time, a strand within conservative thought, especially in the United States, has begun to favor a return to isolationism, arguing that the US and other countries should concentrate on their own strictly nationalist agendas.

A Brief History of Modern Imperialism

During its heyday from the 15th century through the end of World War I, overt imperialism had many backers, notably among such conservatives as Benjamin Disraeli, Lord Curzon, Rudyard Kipling, Cecil Rhodes, and, perhaps surprising to some, Winston Churchill in England; Jules Ferry in France; and Theodore Roosevelt, William McKinley, and other "manifest doctrine" supporters in the United States. Imperialism was lauded as helping "modernize and Christianize" the ostensibly savage and benighted peoples of the Earth, whose improvement and care were "the white man's burden." French apologists for imperialism similarly argued for their *mission civilisatrice* (civilizing mission).

Advocates of imperialism have also been generally unapologetic about the value of international conquests in providing raw materials for domestic industrial products and overseas markets for manufactured goods, as well as the prestige that befits a Great Power. "The issue is not a mean one," wrote Benjamin Disraeli, conservative prime minister of Great Britain during the 1870s. "It is whether you will be content to be a comfortable England, molded upon Continental principles, and meeting in due course an inevitable fate, or whether you will be a great country, an imperial country."[5]

But imperialism has had numerous critics as well, especially from the political left. In 1902, in his influential book *Imperialism,* the English economist John Hobson argued forcefully that imperialism was a social and economic wrong, indicating a defect in capitalism. In this view, imperialism results when nations enter the machine economy, with its advanced industrial methods, whereupon manufacturers, merchants, and financiers find it increasingly difficult to dispose profitably of their products. This, in turn, generates pressure for access to undeveloped overseas markets as well as to sources of raw materials. This overlooks the fact that ancient Rome was an imperium, as were ancient India, China, and many other empires through-out Africa and Asia during pre-capitalist eras.

Hobson's line of reasoning nonetheless seemed especially timely and influ-ential, coming as it did after such events as the Boxer Rebellion (1899–1901) and mid-19th-century Opium Wars in China, which in large part signified Chinese protests against Western economic domination of China and the insistence of the European imperialist powers (especially Great Britain) on opening China to the lucrative opium trade. The major intra-European con-flict of the 18th century, the Seven Years' War (from 1756–1763 and known in North America as the French and Indian War), was in some ways the first world war, brought about by worldwide colonial competition between England and France, a rivalry that was extended to India, the Caribbean, the west coast of Africa (over the highly profitable slave trade), Canada, the upper Ohio Valley, and eastern colonial America.

In addition, the Crimean (1853–1856) and Boer (or South African, 1899–1902) wars, as well as the Moroccan crises of 1905 and 1911, lent further weight to Hobson's depiction of imperialism as a cause of war. "As soon as one of our industries fails to find a market for its products," according to Anatole France in his novel *Penguin Island,* "a war is necessary to open new outlets. . . . In Third Zealand we have killed two-thirds of the inhabitants in order to compel the remainder to buy our umbrellas and braces."

Modern Manifestations of Imperialism

Imperialism can lead to war between the imperial government and the local population: Examples include wars of occupation and conquest, such as the Maori wars in New Zealand, the Zulu wars in southeast Africa, and the Indian wars in the United States. These were followed in turn by wars of national liberation—for example, the Huk rebellion against the United States in the Philippines, the Mau Mau rebellion in Kenya, the Algerian War of Independence from France, and so on.

Even though states do not directly compete for colonies these days, they are still likely to engage in various conflicts by intervening on behalf of their own nationals or by competing with local forces or the nationals of another country in some economically impoverished arena over economic, political, or ideological influence. Of the frequent US interventions in Latin America, many occurred on behalf of private US investments, notably those of the United Fruit Company. For example, in 1954 the Central Intelligence Agency organized the overthrow of the democratically elected Arbenz government in Guatemala. Arbenz, a leftist nationalist, had sought to nationalize the United Fruit holdings in his country, distributing them to landless peasants and insisting that the company accept, as fair compensation, the value it had declared for tax purposes to the US-supported Guatemalan government that preceded him.

By contrast, conflicts between the United States and Sandinista-led Nica-ragua in the 1980s and with Hugo Chávez's–led Venezuela, especially during the presidency of George W. Bush, seemed motivated largely by fear of a kind of ideological/social/economic domino effect: If such a small, poor state as Nicaragua, or an oil-rich but increasingly impoverished nation like Venezu-ela, were, like Cuba, to escape from the US orbit and—worse yet, from a right-wing US perspective—to prosper as a consequence, perhaps this would encourage others to do likewise. This is also consistent with the insistence by the Reagan administration on destroying the Nicaraguan economy, since by this strategy, even if the Sandinistas were not overthrown, their revolution could be discredited if Nicaraguan society could be sufficiently damaged. If nothing else, the suffering of the Nicaraguan people would serve as an object lesson for what will befall any other client state that might seek to go against the United States; to some extent, this is precisely what happened.

A similar interpretation might apply to the hostility by the government of the United States toward Castro-led Cuba, although in this case the political power of Cuban Americans, particularly in southern Florida, has also been key. Toward the end of its time in power, the Obama administration established better ties between the two former adversaries, a warming of relations that was largely reversed by the Trump Administration. It is unclear what the future holds for Cuban-American relations, although virtually all US allies have long maintained diplomatic relations with Cuba.

Neo-Imperialism and Dependency Theory

By the 1960s and 1970s, European imperial powers had dissolved their empires, and virtually all former colonies had gained political independence, even while their economic dependence on the West continued unabated. Contemporary neo-imperialism is now seen to operate more subtly, not through outright colonial control and only rarely via war. Rather, the great powers typically manipulate the economic, political, and sociocultural structures of less-developed economies, maintaining them in a condition of dependency, by a process that Lord Lugard, British governor of Nigeria, called "indirect rule": control via indigenous ruling classes. For example, long after the formal independence of their erstwhile colonies, many previous empires still maintain strong indirect influence (verging on rule) over their former possessions, notably including the United States in Central America, France in western Africa, Britain in parts of eastern Africa and of the Caribbean, Russia in its "near-abroad" (including Belarus and Kazakhstan), and China in parts of southeast Asia.

Previous colonial masters no longer rule by naked military power. Rather, they exercise control over local economies—and, often, sources of communication and information as well, such as the mass media and Internet access—typically relying on homegrown political allies recruited from the dominant socioeconomic classes. The emphasis in these cases is not so much on war as on the structural violence found when one state dominates another and when the indigenous elites within a state exploit the rest of the population.

Particularly influential in the development of what has become known as dependency theory are the Brazilian economist Andre Gunder Frank, the American global systems theorist Immanuel Wallerstein, and the Norwegian peace researcher Johan Galtung. Wallerstein and Galtung have developed models in which both the neo-imperial state and the neo-colony are divided into center (elites) and periphery (peasants and workers). According to this analysis, the neo-imperial system involves a connection whereby the center in the neo-imperial state is closely allied with the center in the neo-colony, with antagonism between center and periphery in the neo-colony and a perceived disharmony of interests between peripheries in the neo-colony and the neo-imperium. Instead of physical occupation, the imperial state provides limited economic aid, relatively abundant military aid, and intellectual underpinning and legitimacy to a colonial center that actively oppresses its own people for the benefit of the two centers, both imperial and colonial.

But it is difficult to argue, for example, that participation of the United States in the Vietnam War was primarily motivated by economic factors. Thus, Vietnam's teak, tungsten, and modest offshore oil deposits paled by contrast with the cost of that war for the United States: about $150 billion and the loss of more than 50,000 US lives. In addition, the stock market fell whenever it appeared that the Vietnam War would be prolonged, further suggesting that it was not good for American business. On the other hand, the invasion and occupation of Iraq and Afghanistan by the United States and its "coalition of the willing," as well as the continuing presence of American military bases throughout the Middle East and central Asia, are clearly related to the advanced industrial world's dependency on the oil resources and minerals in that region.

The lure of oil in generating the Iraq War has also been disputed, however. Thus, whereas Iraq's oil reserves (variously estimated as third, fourth, or fifth largest in the world) were used to buttress the Bush administration's internal arguments that the war's expense would be paid for by Iraqi oil, the war itself was likely caused by factors other than a mere yearning for "petro-dollars" as such. Ideological factors, such as an expectation that removal of Saddam Hussein's government would lead to pro-West political alignment in the Middle East, evidently contributed to George W. Bush's decision to overthrow the Iraqi regime and occupy that country. Bush was also motivated by a personal desire to avenge what he believed to have been a (now largely discredited) plot by alleged Iraqi operatives to kill his father, former President George H. W. Bush, in 1993. In any event, the region was lethally disrupted—and remains so today—with the primary regional beneficiary being Iran.

The Military-Industrial Complex

The link between economics and war is often a real one, particularly as this connection operates in contemporary capitalist societies through money making, the global reach of multinational corporations and the Internet, and the "military-industrial complex." Although this phrase has become especially popular among its left-wing critics, it was first introduced by the relatively conservative American president Dwight Eisenhower in his 1961 Farewell Address:

> We have been compelled to create a permanent armaments industry of vast proportions. . . . This conjunction of an immense military establishment and a large arms industry is new in the American experience. The total influence—economic, political, even spiritual—is felt in every city, every statehouse, every office of the federal government. . . . In the councils of government, we must guard against the acquisition of unwarranted influence, whether sought or unsought, by the military-industrial complex. The potential for the disastrous rise of misplaced power exists and will persist.[6]

This alliance of military, economic, and political interests, sometimes called "The Iron Triangle," has been joined by scientists and technologists, research universities, mainstream labor unions, the mass media, government, and, arguably, social media as well. And it is more firmly entrenched than ever.

Forerunners of the Military-Industrial Complex

The American military-industrial-science-labor-academic-government complex since World War II is not totally new in human experience. Those with a financial and social interest in making war have long had a dispropor-tionate influence on the policies of governments.

In the days of warrior-kings, they *were* the government. During ancient times, soldiers were rewarded with a proportion of the spoils of a sacked city. Mercenary armies, by definition, fought for pay and/or a share of the booty. Much of the martial enthusiasm that marked the Muslim conquests of much of Europe and the Mediterranean world during the Middle Ages, for exam-ple, has been attributed to the fact that Islamic warriors were fighting not only for their faith but also for personal enrichment. In the late 16th cen-tury, Spanish soldiers—fighting the Dutch effort at independence—sacked Antwerp (then the richest city in northern Europe) when Philip II of Spain went bankrupt and could not make good on their back pay.

"The orientation toward war," wrote the economist Joseph Schumpeter, "is mainly fostered by the domestic interests of ruling classes, but also by the influence of all those who stand to gain individually from a war policy, whether economically or socially."[7] From early in the industrial age, the great armaments manufacturers— Krupp in Germany, Vickers and Armstrong in England, Remington and Colt in the United States, and Dassault in France—all profited when their countries went to war. They even profited when other countries did the same, by selling arms to the belligerents—often to both sides.

During the 1930s, a US Senate committee chaired by Senator Gerald Nye investigated the charge that US arms manufacturers were responsible for American entry into World War I. Although the Nye Committee was unable to prove these allegations, the "merchants of death" theory gained credibility.

On the other hand, popular pressure in opposition to military spending has also influenced government decisions: Britain and France, for example, found it very difficult to maintain large military forces during the early 1930s because of popular antimilitary sentiment. And during the 1990s, the United States and Russia succeeded in restricting at least certain aspects of their nuclear competition, a kind of "peace dividend," due to the end of their long Cold War (1945–1991). Since 2001, however, both American and Russian defense expenditures and bellicosity have increased, as have Chinese and Indian, and tensions between the West and resurgent Russia and China have also increased, partially due to differing attitudes toward ballistic missile defense, nuclear proliferation, the perceived anti-Russian thrust of the North Atlantic Treaty Organization (NATO), and the perceived antidemocratic, militaristic, and anti–human rights conduct of Russian pres-ident Vladimir Putin and current Chinese, Indian, Brazilian, and Turkish political elites.

The Contemporary Military-Industrial Complex

Military expenditures and those who profit by them remain significant forces in the world today: Arms sales are the number one export for France and Israel and have been growing rapidly in Brazil. With the exception of Japan, arms comprise a major proportion of the exports of every industrial-ized state, with the United States, Russia, and France leading all others in absolute terms, and with the United States by far the largest arms peddler to the world.

Huge amounts of money are made on armaments, both through domestic weapons programs and in sales to other nations. Within the United States, during the latter part of the 20th century, about 10 percent of all business derived from military-related production—more yet for large corporations such as Lockheed, General Dynamics, Boeing, and Northrop, which in some cases derive up to 50 percent of their profits from military-related production. In certain regions of the United States, such as southern California and parts of the Southeast, military spending accounts for upward of one-third of all jobs.

In addition, influential politicians have often succeeded in bringing extraordinary amounts of military business, sometimes as "earmarks"—funds specifically designated by Congress to be spent in a particular way in a particular locality—to their local districts. Not only has this continued, but a growing trend for the privatization of war-related matters has resulted in an enormous growth of mercenary forces. This has also benefited many large private corporations that have emerged as "military contractors" that handle—and make enormous profits from—security arrangements, food, sanitation, and other logistics both domestically and abroad (notably in Iraq and Afghanistan, where local leaders hold them responsible for many civilian deaths).

There has long been a Soviet, and now a Russian and a Chinese, counterpart to the Western military-industrial complex. Nikita Khrushchev called them the "metal eaters," the alliance of industrial bureaucrats and military leaders in the former Soviet Union. In a society that long valued heavy industry and national defense over civilian goods, military production received highest priority in the former Soviet Union until Mikhail Gorbachev came to power in 1985 and initiated *glasnost* (openness) and *perestroika* (restructuring). Gorbachev's political liberalization policies have largely been reversed since then, however.

Instead, a somewhat different "military-industrial" complex, largely financed by Russia's immense oil, natural gas, and mineral resources, emerged with the accession to power of Boris Yeltsin in 1991 and during the presidency of Vladimir Putin since the beginning of this century. The recent process of capital accumulation in Russia was primarily based on the acquisition—at bargain prices—of former state enterprises by onetime government cronies and newly enriched "oligarchs." Loyalty to the Kremlin resulted in extremely lucrative contracts for these "New Russian" businesspeople. Perceived disloyalty, on the other hand, can result in Siberian imprisonment, voluntary or involuntary exile, or poisoning and untimely death, especially for journalists and politicians deemed "disloyal" to the Kremlin.

The reemergence of Russia as an economic and military power also induced a revived Russian nationalism, which sometimes expresses itself as xenophobia. Accompanying this has been a revival of Russian aspirations to Great Power status, which include a strong army with modernized nuclear weapons and delivery systems. Russian incursions, either overtly as in Georgia and the Crimean peninsula or more covertly in parts of eastern Ukraine, revived NATO defensive measures to protect Eastern European NATO members against possible Russian aggression and further chilled relations between Russia and its neighbors. Such developments show signs of a nascent new Cold War between Russia and the West.

There is also growing concern in many Western strategic quarters that China's booming economy has resulted in increased competition with American, European, and Japanese corporations for global markets, profits, and political dominance. Whether this also results in cold, or even hot, military conflicts between or among the West, Russia, and/or China remains to be seen. The wars between European empires during the 17th, 18th, and early

19th centuries were largely caused by competition for natural resources, political domination, profits on investments, and overseas markets. The global economic and energy conflicts of the 21st century between old (the United States and Europe) and emerging (Russia, China, India, and Brazil) great powers sooner or later may also accelerate arms races and lead to armed conflicts.

Because wars themselves typically impoverish countries, whereas preparing for them results in substantial—albeit concentrated—wealth, a key issue is not so much war profiteering as war-preparation profiteering. In limited cases, wars can help stimulate an economy; the Great Depression of the 1930s ended with the onset of World War II. However, peace researcher Lewis Richardson concluded that fewer than one-third of wars from 1820 to 1949 were generated by economic causes, and these were largely limited to small wars rather than large ones.

Economic considerations clearly influence military spending levels as well as specific procurement decisions, such as the purchase of one weapons system over another. The profit motive may contribute indirectly to war by supporting arms races and by creating important constituencies with an interest in the maintenance of international tension, which in turn makes it difficult to achieve disarmament or even arms control. Although it appears that the military-industrial complex does not always directly cause war, it is clear that wars have dramatic economic effects.

The Economic Effects of Wars

The location of the war is crucial: A war on one's own territory can be devastating; on someone else's, it is much less painful and can even help an economy. The Napoleonic Wars, for instance, put a special premium on iron, which in turn accelerated Britain's initiation of the Industrial Revolution.

There is, however, another view, namely that war has done little to stimulate industrial progress, whereas industrial progress has done much to stimulate war and to make it more horrendous when it occurs. Wars rely heavily on such peacetime scientific and economic achievements as advances in metallurgy, transportation, chemistry, medicine, communication, information technology, robotics, mathematics, and even food processing and preparation.

War is often a parasite on civilian economies, taking much and contributing little. During the 1980s, declines in American economic productivity and trade deficits were due largely to the Reagan administration's investment of substantial national resources—both human and material—in the military economy. By contrast, during the "economic boom" (for the affluent) in America during the 1990s, defense spending and investment were held relatively constant. This continued during the early 21st century for the Western financial and corporate elites, although not for most members of the working and middle classes or for impoverished people globally. During President Trump's administration, however, there were significant increases in defense and defense-related spending, which, along with a tax cut skewed to benefit corporations and the mega-rich, resulted in a boom for a tiny, mostly white, fraction of the American people.

As to the alleged spin-offs from military technology, if governments and corporations had really wanted no-stick frying pans or computer miniaturization, they would have been able to create these things much more rapidly, and cheaply, by investing directly in such technology. Moreover, military research and development are typically insensitive to cost while very demanding as to performance. As a result, advanced weaponry tends to be very expensive but not useful in the civilian marketplace. Consumers, for example, don't need toasters that will operate at 80 degrees below zero or mega-computers that can perform "Star Wars" calculations in nanoseconds; rather, they need reliable, inexpensive items that benefit their lives.

In the majority of less economically developed nations, wars have contributed little of benefit to the local economy, whereas the physical, economic, and social effects of wars have been immensely destructive. Wars lay waste to nations not only by the direct detonation of weapons but also by the disruption of economies, especially in those regions least able to afford it, such as Central Africa, Central America, and parts of the Middle East and South Asia.

Likewise, during its occupation by Western forces, Iraq increased expenditures for its nascent army and police but also experienced a precipitous deterioration in its infrastructure, as the provision of water and electricity fell dramatically below pre-invasion levels, domestic morbidity and mortality rates greatly exceeded those during the reign of Saddam Hussein, and millions of Iraqis emigrated or internally migrated to perceived safe havens. Since the beginnings of their civil wars, Syria, Yemen, Sudan/South Sudan, and Libya have undergone similar plights.

In Iraq, at least until the rise of ISIS in 2014, these conditions may have been somewhat ameliorated by the apparent cessation of active war-making by US-led occupation forces. In late 2011, the US defense secretary officially declared the Iraq War over, and the last US combat troops left Iraqi territory a few days later. Many US personnel then headed to Afghanistan, with special operations forces and American military "advisors" returning to Iraq in mid-2016 to spearhead the fight against ISIS through late 2019. Hundreds of contractors and US Special Forces remain in Iraq and Afghanistan, which are still torn by factional and sectarian violence.

Emergency and relief efforts—difficult enough to mount successfully in peacetime—can be lethally disrupted by war. In 1984 and 2000, Ethiopia suffered from severe famines in which hundreds of thousands starved and millions were malnourished. In 1988, Ethiopia received $534 million from abroad for famine and development aid; at the same time, the government was spending $447 million on military forces to fight secessionist wars against Eritrea and Tigre, as well as in the Ogaden region. Also, relief convoys conducted by the Red Cross were unable to make deliveries of needed food to people in the rebellious areas of Eritrea and Tigre. The Ethiopian government claimed that such convoys would not be safe, while critics accused it of withholding food as a weapon against the rebels and of spending three-fourths of the national budget on arms and internal security when poverty and hunger remain Ethiopia's most pressing needs.

A former army intelligence officer, Abiy Ahmed Alii, became prime minister of Ethiopia in 2018. He then launched a wide program of political and economic reforms and worked to broker peace deals in Eritrea, South Sudan, and a transition agreement in the Republic of the Sudan. Abiy was awarded the 2019 Nobel Peace Prize for his work in ending a 20-year post-war territorial stalemate between Ethiopia and Eritrea. However, since Abiy got the Prize, political and ethnic unrest and discrimination have increased in Ethiopia—leading to many episodes of violence, as well as to armed conflict between government forces under Abiy's command and the Tigray People's

Liberation Front (TPLF). This began in late 2020 between the Tigray Regional Government led by the TPLF and the central government of Ethiopia. The future of Ethiopia, like much of Africa, is far from clear.

Furthermore, the situation in the Darfur region of Sudan is also unstable, despite tepid emergency and relief efforts by the West, the United Nations, and some African states. Sudan itself separated into two states, the most recent of which, South Sudan, has undergone its own civil war. A comprehensive peace agreement was signed in August 2020 in Juba, South Sudan, between the Sudanese authorities and rebel factions to end armed hostilities.

In these conflicts as well as those in Syria and Yemen, desperately needed relief supplies for civilians have been held up by government agencies using the stall of delivery of life-saving supplies as a weapon against civilians seen to be opposed to the controlling forces.

The Effects of Military Spending

Some claim that military spending is economically beneficial, providing jobs, permitting federal governments to target areas needing financial investment, and generating demand that can stimulate a lagging economy. On the other hand, many analysts agree that, in the long run, military spending is economically damaging. (Of course, since the primary justification for military spending is not economic but rather the supposed enhancement of national security, economic arguments are generally seen as secondary.)

Economic criticisms of military spending focus on five areas:

1. *Employment.* Although military spending creates jobs, it almost invariably results in fewer jobs than would be generated by the same funds spent for civilian purposes. This is especially true for high-tech military procurement, notably for aerospace, robotics, and nuclear weapons. Such expenditures are capital-intensive—that is, they cost a lot of money but hire relatively few people—compared with such labor-intensive expenditures as education, health care, and rebuilding the civilian infrastructure.

2. *Inflation.* Military spending is perhaps the most inflationary way for a government to spend money. By using up major resources without producing consumable goods, military spending reduces supply while also increasing demand for raw materials, thereby contributing doubly to inflation. Moreover, costs tend to rise yet further when the supply of money and credit increases without corresponding increases in productivity. The result is the classic inflationary process: too much money chasing too few goods.

3. *Deficits.* Governments typically raise armies by paying for them. The immense federal deficits of the Reagan, George W. Bush, and Trump administrations, for example, occurred largely because the US government chose to lower taxes for the wealthiest Americans and corporations while dramatically increasing military expenditures.

4. *Productivity.* Industrial productivity is strongly influenced by the availability of scientists and engineers to provide innovative technologies and the ability of federal governments to invest in civilian research and development as well as the renovation of aging industrial plants. Military priorities tend to dominate government funded scientific

research and development activities, thereby robbing the civilian economy.

5. *Unmet social needs.* Resources spent on the military are not available to be spent in other ways. A "substitution effect" tends to operate, whereby expenditures for submarines, missiles, and machine guns, for example, are subtracted from money available for hospitals, daycare centers, schools, and so forth. One-half of 1 percent of one year's world military spending would purchase enough farm equipment, according to the Brandt Commission on North/South Issues, to permit the world's low-income countries to reach food sufficiency within a decade.

Military spending is a serious problem in the United States, Israel, Russia, and throughout much of the Middle East and in many less-developed countries. During most of the 1990s, Russia acknowledged the need to reduce military spending so as to address its inadequate domestic productivity. More recently, however, Russian politicians, led by President Vladimir Putin, have expressed their desire for Russia to resume Great Power status, which is usually acquired through military posturing, and Russia's incursions into Ukraine, Georgia, Moldova, and Syria exemplify this militaristic turn.

The problem is even more acute in many developing countries. In the 1990s, for example, military spending in Africa increased by 7.0 percent per year, while economic growth was only 0.3 percent. Taken as a proportion of gross national product (GNP), military expenditures by the world's richer states have actually declined since 1960, whereas those of the poorer states have increased; countries that cannot meet the basic social needs of their people have been spending a larger share of their meager incomes on weapons and soldiers than the richer states spend of their much more abundant income.

"Every gun that is made," said President Eisenhower,

> every warship launched, every rocket fired signifies, in the final sense, a theft from those who hunger and are not fed, those who are cold and are not clothed. The world in arms is not spending money alone. It is spending the sweat of its laborers, the genius of its scientists, the hopes of its children.[8]

Cultural Conflicts and the "Clash of Civilizations"

Cultures have always differed, and civilizations have clashed, on and off, since premodern times. "Western" (or "occidental") and "Eastern" (or "oriental") city-states and empires have coexisted peacefully and have also had violent interactions for millennia. Anthropologist Margaret Mead defined culture as "the systematic body of learned behavior which is transmitted from parents to children."[9] It may also be understood as a kind of "second nature," in which we are immersed from cradle to grave and that is usually taken for granted.

Cultures differ in many ways, especially in language, religion, and social customs; nonetheless, they usually manage to get along with one another. However, when one culture lacks important natural resources, such as grain or oil, it may invade another to get what it needs. And agglomerations of cultures that are urban based, sometimes called "civilizations," may also clash violently, especially when their differences involve significant ideological distinctions, such as religion, or such badges of identity as different languages. In many conventional texts, the history of human civilization reads like a story of civilizational conflicts.

For example, after centuries of relatively peaceful coexistence between the Greek city-states and their "barbaric" neighbors to the east and south, the Persian emperor Xerxes attempted to invade continental Europe but was defeated by the Greeks at the beginning of the 5th century BCE. (Interestingly, the word *barbaric* derives from the Greek cultural prejudice that anyone not speaking Greek was babbling incoherent nonsense that sounded to them like "bar-bar-bar.")

In 1993, the American political scientist Samuel P. Huntington wrote an article titled "The Clash of Civilizations." This was published in the mainstream journal *Foreign Affairs* and is one of the most cited and controversial pieces in the history of international relations. The following year, he expanded his argument in a book of the same name. The "Huntington thesis" regarding the rise, clash, and fall of civilizations is worth considering in some detail, both because of its intrinsic interest and because of its implications for the analysis of war and the prospects of peace in the multipolar world of the 21st century.

According to Huntington, in the 1920s, there was a bipolar (political) world: "the West and the Rest," the latter consisting of nations/cultures "actually or nominally independent of the West." During the 1960s—the peak of the Cold War—there was a tripolar world: the "Free World," led by the United States plus its allies; the "Communist Bloc," mainly the Soviet Union, China and their allies; and "Third World" unaligned nations, comprising much of Africa and South Asia, notably India. Since 1990, according to Huntington, there has arisen a multipolar "World of Civilizations," composed of nine centers: Western; Latin American; African; Islamic; Sinic (mainly Chinese); Hindu; Orthodox (mainly Slavic); Buddhist; and Japanese. In this new post–Cold War world, Huntington claims that "local politics is the politics of ethnicity; global politics is the politics of civilizations. The rivalry of the superpowers is replaced by the clash of civilizations."

"In the post–Cold War world," according to Huntington,

> for the first time in history, global politics has become multipolar *and* multicivilizational. . . . In the late 1980s the communist world collapsed, and the Cold War international system became history. In the post–Cold War world, the most important distinctions among peoples are not ideological, political or economic. They are cultural. The central and most dangerous dimension of the emerging global politics would be conflict between groups from differing civilizations . . . clashes between civilizations are the greatest threat to world peace.[10]

Huntington also claims that Islam has long had "bloody borders" and that conflict between Islam and the West was renewed after the fall of the Soviet Union. Moreover, the Soviet Union and, subsequently, Russia have had their own internal and "near abroad" conflicts with restive Muslim minorities within their borders, and with mujahideen and alleged terrorists outside, most notably in the Caucasus, Afghanistan, Syria, and Iran.

According to Huntington, the centuries-long rivalry between Christendom and Islam has been over power and culture, with Europe and the US on the frontlines of this conflict, as evidenced by terrorist bombings perpetrated by violent Islamists in many Western cities. For some Muslims, the struggle between Islam and the West is rooted in Western colonialism. For others, the clash is between the Judeo-Christian Western ethic and the Islamic revival movement, which now stretches from the Atlantic Ocean in the west to China in the east. Importantly, this "clash" is not always underpinned by religious differences; ethnic and ideological factors also contribute.

Perhaps unexpectedly, following the end of the Soviet Union in 1991, Western universalism in general and American triumphalism in particular have not led to a period of unparalleled Western military, cultural, and political dominance. Thus, many if not most non-Western cultures have not rushed to adopt such mainstream Western values as free markets and democracy.

Huntington observes that "all civilizations go through . . . processes of emergence, rise, and decline," and he claims that the greatest danger in our time is "major inter-civilizational war between core states," notably between the United States and China. Although a global conflict between the West and Islam would likely be immensely destructive, an "occidental/oriental" or Western/Sinic inter-civilizational war would likely be downright cataclysmic. It might be initiated, for example, by a local war between China and Taiwan, if the latter were to claim total political independence, or if China were to press territorial claims against Asian states such as the Philippines or Thailand, which are close US allies.

To avoid major inter-civilizational wars, Huntington posits three rules. The first is "the abstention rule," which he defines as the requirement that "core states" (the United States, Russia, China, etc.) abstain from intervention in the conflicts of other civilizations. The second prerequisite for the avoidance of war in our multipolar, multicivilizational post–Cold War world is "the mediation rule," which requires core states to negotiate with each other to halt or contain wars between states or groups within their civilization. And the final "rule for peace" (more precisely, for negative peace) in the world today is what Huntington calls "the commonalities rule," according to which "peoples in all civilizations should search for and attempt to expand the values, institutions, and practices they have in common with peoples of other civilizations."

While much of this analysis seems realistic, or even prophetic in light of the events since he penned these words, it is also necessary to consider the implications of Huntington's prescriptions. For instance, if one civilization were to follow strictly the "nonintervention" rule, it would entail, for example, that the West was wrong to intervene in Islamic "internal affairs" (as in Iraq, Syria, and Iran). But it would also imply that it would similarly be wrong to intervene in the intra-civilizational genocide in Rwanda or to stop the ethnic cleansing in the former Yugoslavia in the 1990s or in Myanmar more recently, which might amount to a politically and ethically painful toleration of some of the worst atrocities in human history.

Not surprisingly, many advocates and practitioners of peace studies are unenthusiastic about the Huntington thesis. Although some components, such as nonintervention and the elaboration of supra-civilizational commonalities, seem largely desirable, others are extremely troublesome, not least the explicit claim that all civilizations are equal—but that some (notably, the Western one) are more equal than others. More insidiously, the "clash of civilizations" threatens to become a self-fulfilling prophecy, by which the diagnosis of a problem, if taken seriously, risks creating its own reality: If countries act as though in the grip of civilizational conflicts, they are likely to exacerbate and/or generate precisely such conflicts.

The "clash of civilizations" thesis can thus be criticized as a recipe for the preservation and continuation of American/Western hegemony, one that risks generating yet more conflict even as it seeks to identify the sources of such conflict. Accordingly, it sounds like a post–Cold War version of "containment," with Islamic and Sinic civilizations substituted for the former Soviet Union. "The real 'clash of civilizations,'" according to the philosopher Martha Nussbaum,

> is not between "Islam" and "the West," but instead within virtually all modern nations—between people who are prepared to live on terms of equal respect with others who are different, and those who seek the protection of homogeneity and the domination of a single "pure" religious and ethnic tradition. At a deeper level, as Gandhi claimed, it is a clash within the individual self, between the urge to dominate and defile the other and a willingness to live respectfully on terms of compassion and equality, with all the vulnerability that such a life entails.[11]

A Final Note on the Complex Causes of War

Wars—and the preparations for wars—take place within contexts that usually transcend individuals and their group affiliations. These contexts include such diffuse but extremely important factors as ideologies, economic forces, sociocultural conditions, leadership, and perceptions of power. Accordingly, there are no simple cause-and-effect relationships in this realm. Rather, war, like other forms of violent human conflicts and human behavior more generally, is an overdetermined phenomenon: Multiple factors, some short term and relatively easy to discern (such as an assassination) and others that are long term and harder to pinpoint (such as cultural antagonisms), lead people and countries to go to war.

A possibly useful mnemonic device for remembering some of the multiple factors leading to wars is the acronym EGGGIEs: ego, greed, groups, governments, ideologies, and extenuating circumstances (of which the two most significant historical variables have been leadership and technology). From this perspective, wars are fought because powerful and influential individuals (political decision makers), usually in search of personal aggrandizement or revenge ("ego") and often motivated to increase their or their nations' wealth and/or power ("greed"), attempt to persuade, manipulate, and/or command their compatriots ("groups") and national resources ("governments") to pursue their personal and national agendas ("ideologies") by force of arms—despite the opposition of other individuals in different groups and/or nations, who would oppose them by violent means if necessary. Leadership, both good and bad, and technology (including the never-ending search for a "winning weapon") can sometimes make the difference between winning and losing any particular war, while also impacting its initiation.

Although wars are extremely complex phenomena, often eliciting the entire range of human motivations and conduct, they are, like all human artifacts, modifiable and preventable. In the remainder of this book, we consider ways to reduce the incidence and virulence of wars (building negative peace) and also to lay the groundwork for a world that enjoys positive peace.

Questions for Further Reflection

1. What are some principal ideological motivations for and inhibitions against the initiation of wars?

2. To what degree does imperialism still exist and operate as a war-making system?

3. Discuss the economic consequences—positive as well as negative—of a militarized economy.

4. What are the strengths and weaknesses of the "clash of civilizations" thesis? Is a reconciliation among conflicting cultures possible?

5. In assessing the reasons for wars, do you consider any particular level of analysis and explanation (the economic, political, ideological, etc.) as most helpful in understanding contemporary international conflicts? Why or why not?

Suggestions for Further Reading

Cynthia J. Arnson and I. William Zartman (eds.) 2005. *Rethinking the Economics of War: The Intersection of Need, Creed, and Greed*. Baltimore: Johns Hopkins University Press.

Richard K. Betts, ed. 2012. *Conflict After the Cold War: Arguments on Causes of War and Peace*. London: Routledge.

Seyom Brown. 1987. *The Causes and Prevention of War*. New York: Macmillan Education.

Ian Buruma and Avishai Margalit. 2004. *Occidentalism: The West in the Eyes of Its Enemies*. New York: Penguin Books.

Greg Cashman. 2013. *What Causes War?* 2nd ed. Lanham, MD: Rowman and Littlefield.

Jerome Frank. 1968. *Sanity and Survival: Psychological Aspects of War and Peace*. New York: Vintage.

Samuel P. Huntington. 1997. *The Clash of Civilizations and the Remaking of World Order*. New York: Touchstone.

Bernard Lewis. 1994. *Islam and the West*. New York: Oxford University Press.

Martha C. Nussbaum. 2007. *The Clash Within: Democracy: Religious Violence and India's Future*. Cambridge, MA: Harvard University Press.

Manfred B. Steger. 2009. *The Rise of the Global Imaginary: Political Ideologies from the French Revolution to the Global War on Terror*. Oxford, UK: Oxford University Press.

Notes

1. Woodrow Wilson. 1965. *A Day of Dedication*. New York: Macmillan.

2. Alexis de Tocqueville. 1955. *The Old Regime and the French Revolution*. New York: Doubleday.

3. Frantz Fanon. 1963. *The Wretched of the Earth*. New York: Grove.

4. Che Guevara. 1968. *Guerrilla Warfare*. New York: Monthly Review Press.

5. Quoted in Michael Howard. 1978. *War and the Liberal Conscience*. New Brunswick, NJ: Rutgers University Press.

6. Dwight D. Eisenhower. 1961. *Peace With Justice: Selected Addresses*. New York: Columbia University Press.

7. Joseph Schumpeter. 1955. *Imperialism and Social Classes*. New York: Meridian.

8. Eisenhower, 1961.

9. Margaret Mead. 1934/2005. "Preface." In Ruth Benedict, *Patterns of Culture*. New York: Houghton Mifflin, xiii.

10. Samuel P. Huntington. 1995. *The Clash of Civilizations*. New York: Simon & Schuster, 311.

11. Martha C. Nussbaum. 2007. *The Clash Within: Democracy, Religious Violence and India's Future*. Cambridge, MA: Harvard University Press.

Building "Negative Peace"

Throughout history, many people have recognized the absurdity and horror of war, even as they have engaged in it. There has been no shortage of proposed solutions to the problems posed by war. The simplest "solution," perhaps, may be derived from the failed yet ongoing "war on drugs": Just say no. But this turns out to be no solution at all, if only because it has been tried many times, yet war, like drug use, persists. Although seemingly straightforward moral judgments and outright condemnation are appealing to many people, most nations have been no more able to go "cold turkey" on war than individuals have on drugs. Mark Twain once noted that it was easy to stop smoking—he had done it many times! Similarly, it may seem easy to prevent war; many different solutions have been proposed, and some have even been implemented (to varying degrees).

Perhaps these solutions have not been not sufficiently innovative, forward thinking, or creative. Others may not be feasible. Perhaps the problem is that no single solution has been pushed hard and far enough. Or maybe war is still with us because these various solutions have not been attempted in the right combination. Perhaps they actually are working, only slowly, so that peace—like President Herbert Hoover's claim about prosperity during the Great Depression—is just around the corner. On the other hand, maybe something more radical is needed to end war as we know it, such as dramatic changes in global governance. In any event, let us hope that by considering humanity's efforts to prevent war, we can at least save peacemakers of the future from repeating the errors of the past. And, maybe, we can inspire greater efforts, and achieve greater success, in the decades to come.

"War is waged," wrote St. Augustine, "so that peace may prevail. . . . But it is a greater glory to slay war with a word than people with a sword, and to gain peace by means of peace and not by means of war."[1]

In the following chapters, we shall examine efforts to gain peace by peaceful means. It is no easy quest. As General Omar Bradley put it,

> The problem of peaceful accommodation in the world is infinitely more difficult than the conquest of space, infinitely more complex than a trip to the moon. . . . If I am sometimes discouraged, it is not by the magnitude of the problem, but by our colossal indifference to it. I am unable to understand why. . . we do not make greater more diligent and more imaginative use of reason and human intelligence in seeking. . . accord and compromise.[2]

What, then, do human reason and intelligence have to offer by way of preventing war and creating a durable and equitable peace? Maybe the question itself is inappropriate, and peace requires a fundamental change in the human mind-set rather than specific plans and protocols. "There is no way to peace," wrote the noted pacifist A. J. Muste, "peace is the way." But if we are to follow it, the route must at least be discerned, even if dimly. Like the reasons for war, the causes of peace are also multifaceted. Just as no one body part defines an elephant, if there is no one way to peace but instead many, some of them might lead down blind alleys, some to dangerous cliffs, and others to yet more paths, each with additional branching points and an unending series of twists and turns. In Part III, we shall walk a short way down some of the most prominent of these paths.

Figure 11.1   Courtesy of Donna Lyda/Getty Images

Peace Movements

Because virtually any war is a remainder of the human record, the work of peacemaking is not only essential but unfinished. By many measures, wars in recent times have become more destructive in somewhat less frequent, at least at the international level. Thus making the work of the peacemaker all the more urgent. There have been, nonetheless, numerous efforts at building peace, raising many possibilities and opportunities, some long-standing and others quite recent. There have also been fits of success, although paradoxically, whereas the toll of war can be tallied, it is impossible to assess how many wars—or how much destruction during wars—have been prevented by the efforts of people seeking peace—that is, the various peace movements.

Jeremy O'Donnell via Getty Images

Peace Movements

Because virtually any war is a tarnishing of the human record, the work of peacemaking is not only essential but unfinished. By many measures, wars in recent times have become more destructive (if somewhat less frequent, at least at the international level), thus making the work of the peacemaker all the more urgent. There have been, nonetheless, numerous efforts at building peace, raising many possibilities and opportunities, some long-standing and others quite recent. There have also been hints of success; although paradoxically, whereas the toll of war can be tallied, it is impossible to assess how many wars—or how much destruction during wars—have been prevented by the efforts of people seeking peace—that is, the various "peace movements."

Popular Attitudes Toward Peace

One difficulty faced by would-be peacemakers is that although most people claim to be in favor of peace, a considerable number seem to be more interested in war. At present, many people find peace boring and war exciting. We can readily identify a war novel, a war movie, a war song, a war painting, or a war toy; by contrast, how many of us can identify clearly a *peace* novel, movie, and so on? When war and other catastrophes are highlighted on the daily newscasts and by social media, people prick up their ears; when peace and related nonviolent stories are featured, most readers are more likely to yawn. The journalistic credo for attracting a wide audience goes "If it bleeds, it leads."

On the other hand, a distinct peace culture exists in the form of antiwar poetry (notably the works of Wilfred Owen and Siegfried Sassoon after World War I), novels (such as *All Quiet on the Western Front* and *Catch-22*), films (including *King of Hearts, Platoon, Dr. Strangelove, Fail-Safe, Gandhi, The War Game*), and folk and pop music, including Pete Seeger, John Lennon, and, more recently, Steve Earle and The Dixie Chicks. Opposition to war, interestingly, seems easier to express than is commitment to peace. Thus, not surprisingly, most peace movements have been fundamentally antiwar movements.

Attention, Success, and Failure

Human beings tend to use a variety of different terms to identify things in which they are particularly interested. The Inuit peoples of the far north, for example, are said to have 11 different words for what in English is known simply as "snow," and the Bedouins have 100 distinct words for "camel," depending on an animal's age, sex, health, and temperament. Similarly, we assign titles to our different wars (e.g., the War of the Roses, the Seven Years' War, the Balkan War, the Iraq War(s), the Syrian Civil War). By contrast, peace is a generic term used only in the singular, even though the peace that obtained, say, in Europe between World Wars I and II differed markedly from that of the 1950s as well as from the period just after the defeat of Napoleon. Perhaps when our interest in peace equals our interest in war, we shall begin to identify "peaces" as something more meaningful than simply the intervals between those things that "really matter" to many people and especially to the mass media: wars.

Peace entails more than the absence of war. However, a defining characteristic of most peace movements has long been their antiwar stance. Efforts to achieve ecological balance, economic fairness, social and racial justice, and human rights are crucially important, and they certainly belong within the purview of peace and conflict studies, but they are only just beginning to be integrated into what has generally been meant by a peace movement.

Significantly, there are virtually no "war movements"—at least, none that would identify themselves as such! A notable exception is fascism, which has often glorified war as necessary for the fullest expression of individual strength, racial "purity," and national identity. For the most part, however, a wide variety of doctrines and organizations espouse various (often contradictory) ways of achieving peace. Advocates of "peace through strength," for example, claim that, in the interest of peace, states must maintain large military forces, along with a willingness to employ them if necessary.

In this book, we shall consider peace movements as they are more traditionally identified—that is, as sources of popular opposition to war and to militarism and for the creation of structures and cultures of peace. Many 21st-century students of peace agree that war has reached its nadir: It has become less useful and less desirable than ever before. Virtually every modern war has been wasteful, destructive, and cruel. Moreover, in many cases, the state initiating a given war has not achieved its aims.

For example, during the 20th century, many international aggressors were either defeated or stymied in their goals: the Central Powers in World War I, the Axis in World War II, North Korea in the Korean War, Pakistan in the India-Pakistan Wars, Iraq in its war with Iran and its venture into Kuwait and the resulting Gulf War, and Serbia in Bosnia and Kosovo. Similarly, it appears that Israel's brief wars with Hezbollah in Lebanon (2006) and with Hamas in the Gaza Strip (2008–2009, 2012, 2014), and the US invasion and occupation of Iraq (2003–present), have left the initiating country worse off than before. As of this writing, the US-sponsored overthrow of the Taliban government in Afghanistan almost two decades ago appears to be less than successful; only time, and the outcome of fitful negotiations between the conflicting parties, will tell whether it, too, will eventually be judged a tragic failure.

At the same time, there have been some politically "successful" wars, notably those of imperial conquest, especially in the 19th century, as well as the wars of national liberation in Indonesia, Algeria, and Kenya, and, arguably, NATO's war against Serbia (although many Serbs make take a different view). The Vietnam War, or what the peoples of Southeast Asia call The American War, can also be seen as a successful war of unification for the Vietnamese, with distinctly anticolonial overtones as well, since it represented the culmination of struggles by the Vietnamese and their neighbors against France, Japan, and finally, the United States (although Vietnam's millennial-long conflict with China persists).

Historical and Current Perceptions of War

Although many contemporary readers may be surprised, until recently war has not generally been recognized as a serious human problem, nor has it been widely or deeply deplored. Indeed, war has not even been considered particularly unseemly. Rather, it was long accepted as an instrument of statesmanship, to be used under appropriate circumstances. Several factors seem to be involved in recent perceptions that war is a problem and that peace is not only a desirable goal but one that is—or must be—attainable:

1. *The potential for global destruction.* The development of increasingly destructive weapons, including various forms of conventional explosives, chemical and biological substances, and most ominously nuclear weapons, has given all people a stake in the permanent abandonment of armed hostilities.

2. *The social, economic, and environmental toll.* These costs of war and war preparations have induced antiwar efforts even when the fate of the Earth is not at stake.

3. *The evolution of the Earth into a "global village."* The increased means and speed of communications (especially via the Internet and social media) and, at least until the global pandemic, easily available intercontinental transportation have accelerated the connections among human

beings: economically, socially, and emotionally. More than ever before, people are directly affected by the experiences of others, as became painfully evident due to Covid-19. There is no real peace, or health, on Earth so long as war and pandemics are raging anywhere.

4. *The increase in political involvement.* With the growth in literacy and the post-World-War II spread of more democratic forms of government, even with recent and unpredictable antidemocratic backlashes, many people are more prone to accept personal responsibility for the actions of their country. To an extent not seen in the past, war is no longer considered a visitation of some god or an acceptable consequence of a monarch's whim. Likewise, peace is increasingly seen as everyone's business and also attainable, if enough people want it and are willing to work for it.

Before 1914, states were relatively unashamed to acknowledge their expansionist goals in starting a war. But since 1945 in particular, aggression without a self-justifying, "national security" rationale has become somewhat less frequent, with national leaders feeling obliged to proclaim their defensive and peace-loving intentions; even if their behavior has not become dramatically different, this change in emphasis is noteworthy.

Prior to 1947, for example, the United States had a War Department; its name was subsequently changed to the Defense Department. Indeed, the military branch of government of virtually every state in the world employs the word *defense,* rather than *war.* And since 1984, the United States Institute of Peace has been analyzing and attempting to resolve conflicts outside the United States, often in tandem with the State Department. Perhaps this switch to "Defense" and "Peace" is merely cosmetic. But even so, it might reflect a significant change of attitude: Defense is acceptable to policy makers and to most of the public; offensive war is not.

Movements: Theory and Practice

In English, the noun "movement" refers to a change of place or position or posture; it also refers to a tendency or trend. And it importantly denotes a series of organized activities working to promote or attain an end, especially such political and social movements as the civil rights movement, the women's and LGBTQ movements, the environmental and anti-globalization movements, and the peace movement.

Regarding "peace," the distinction between "theory" and "practice" is somewhat arbitrary because peace denotes both the idea or ideal of peace and the action or movement needed to bring it about. This unity of peace theory and practice is exemplified by the life and work of Mohandas Gandhi, for whom peace, or his preferred term, *nonviolence,* at both the individual and collective level, was simultaneously political, religious, psychological, legal, and ethical. For Gandhi and his successors, peace and social justice movements aim to change the political status quo and, in so doing, also to transform the lives and beliefs of the participants.

A political or social movement may be organized around a single issue or set of issues or around a set of shared concerns of a particular group. In contrast with a political party, a political movement is usually not organized to elect members of the movement to government office; instead, a political movement aims to convince citizens and/or government officials to take action on the issues and concerns that are its focus. Such movements may be local, regional, national, or international in scope, and they may be progressive, conservative, reactionary, or revolutionary.

History and Taxonomy of Peace Movements

One of the problems confronted by antiwar activists is that peace plans are usually far less specific and detailed—and typically less immediately workable—than are military plans for war. Peace campaigns, even the best organized and most generously funded, have rarely come close to rivaling the organization and funding behind virtually any pro-war campaign. Nonetheless, peace movements have a long and noble history. And many successes, often unreported, along with some notable failures.

In considering this history, an important distinction must be made between the proposals of specific individuals and the history of peace movements in general. Mass-mobilized peace movements as we understand them today are relatively recent developments, dating from the early 19th century. But they draw on a vast reservoir of popular discontent with war and have been nourished, in large part, by a belief in universalism, an idealist ethic that sees a common interest in peace and in shared humanity as overriding the political and ethnic dissension among peoples.

Early History

Perhaps the first organization specifically devoted to achieving lasting peace was the Amphictyonic League, organized among a number of city-states in ancient Greece; its members agreed not to attack one another or to cut off one another's water supply. The Olympic Games also served a peace-making function in ancient Greece. Every four years, any ongoing hostilities were halted by a one-month truce, during which Greeks were prohibited from bearing arms or making war and instead supported the athletic competition at Olympus. This tradition continued for about 12 centuries.

The early Christian church apparently was entirely pacifist. During the first few centuries BCE, Christians were persecuted by the Roman Empire for refusing to serve in the Roman legions. Renunciation of arms was inspired by the teachings of Jesus, especially as presented in the Sermon on the Mount. In addition, early Christian writing rejected service in the Roman legions as idolatry.

Pacifism also seemed especially appropriate to many Roman-era Christians because it involved renunciation of the secular world, in anticipation of the second coming of Christ. Subsequently, with the accession to power of the Emperor Constantine (a convert to Christianity) in the 4th century and the end of persecution by Roman authorities, mainstream Christianity also underwent its own conversion to a state-supportive view of the legitimacy of war and of military service. Earlier pacifist views came to be considered heresy by self-identified Christian realists, who believed that Christians must come to terms with the world of power and politics, as in the biblical injunction to "render unto Caesar that which is Caesar's." Christian realists, including St. Augustine—along with St. Thomas Aquinas, founders of the extremely influential Just War Theory—grant legitimacy to the secular world of military force.

Traditions of absolute pacifism nonetheless reemerged during the Middle Ages, most of which carried a strong anti-state flavor as well: The pacifist Waldensians of the 12th century and Anabaptists of the 16th century (both of them minority Christian "heretic" sects that briefly flourished in Europe) were aggressively persecuted by both church and state. Such more recent vigorous, if small-scale, pacifist groups as the Quakers, the Mennonites, and the Brethren—sometimes known as the "prophetic minorities"—nevertheless have maintained religiously oriented peace traditions. Much of their activity has been centered on individual statements of religious and ethical conscience, an individual refusal to participate in war often referred to as "personal witness."

Secular Peace Movements

By contrast, secular peace movements, as we know them today, are less than two centuries old. Numerous organizations sprang up during the 19th century. The New York and Massachusetts Peace Societies, for example, were both founded in 1815, and other organizations were established on both sides of the Atlantic, including the American Peace Society and the Universal Peace Union in 1866. Many international peace conferences were held during the mid-19th century, including gatherings in London (1843), Brussels (1848), Paris (1849), and Frankfurt (1850).

These efforts, however, were largely political fringe events. Other than legitimizing the concept of peace and spreading hope among those attending, they had virtually no concrete political successes. Later, The Hague Peace Conferences during the late 19th century had greater influence on government leaders, generating widespread expectations among many citizens as well. Although measurable successes were rare, by placing the concept of international peacemaking on the world agenda and keeping it there, international peace meetings helped set the stage for such peace-oriented multinational organizations as the League of Nations after World War I and the United Nations after World War II. They also gave voice to a growing international mood in which war was deemed uncivilized, and recourse to war became increasingly unpopular.

Probably the first organized efforts by any peace group to prevent a war took place in the United States, prior to the Mexican-American War (1845). Although they failed in preventing this expansionist war, peace groups did succeed in getting the antagonists to negotiate their differences, and a pro-peace viewpoint was forcefully expressed. During that war, the American writer Henry David Thoreau was jailed for refusing to pay a poll tax, which, in his judgment, supported that conflict. His essay "Civil Disobedience" has been enormously influential. In it, Thoreau argued that citizens of a democracy have a higher obligation than conformity to the policies of their government and that the conscientious citizen is obliged to do what is right and to refuse personal participation in wrongdoing—even if the wrongdoing is sanctioned by the legal authority of government and even if defiance leads to government retribution. When Thoreau was imprisoned for refusal to pay his taxes, he was visited by his close friend, the writer Ralph Waldo Emerson. The story goes that Emerson asked "Henry, what are you doing in *here*?" whereupon Thoreau responded "Ralph, what are you doing out *there*?"

The idea of civil disobedience has been greatly enlarged by modern practitioners of nonviolence. Each country is unique in its history of peace movements (or their absence). Within the past 100 years, the dominant periods of peace movement activism within the United States, and the primary theme of each, can be identified as follows:

- 1890–1914: Alarm about such modern armaments as accurate, breech-loading artillery, machine guns, and heavily armed naval vessels

- 1916–1921: Opposition to World War I and to Western intervention in the Soviet civil war

- 1920s: A variety of movements based on revulsion to World War I

- 1930–1939: Concern about a second world war and anxiety about the risks of aerial bombardment

- 1957–1963: Opposition to nuclear weapons, notably atmospheric nuclear testing with its resulting radioactive fallout

- 1965–1975: Opposition to the Vietnam War

- 1980–1985: Opposition to nuclear weapons, military bellicosity, and the growing danger of nuclear war; support for a nuclear freeze

- 1986–1990: Opposition to military involvement in Central America, concern regarding underground testing, deployment of "new generation" weapons, and the militarization of space

- 1991–1999: Concerns focused on military use of depleted uranium, child soldiers, and proliferation of small arms; greater emphasis on humanitarian intervention in such intrastate wars as Bosnia and Kosovo

- 2003–present: Opposition to the Iraq and Afghanistan wars (especially Iraq), increasing worry about possible future wars involving Iran, China, and North Korea, but ambivalence about direct American intervention in the civil wars in Syria, Libya, South Sudan, and Yemen. Local and global concerns about climate change and the proliferation of nuclear and other weapons of mass destruction.

The worldwide antiwar movement was probably at its peak after World War I, largely because despite mutual distrust among the great powers of the time and the long history of military and economic competitiveness that preceded that war, the European antagonists had no pre-war grudges that justified the immense slaughter that ensued. No nation was clearly identified as "good" or "evil," and, indeed, World War I appears to have been largely a consequence of blunders by all major belligerents. Hence, it has widely been labeled "the war nobody wanted," which in turn gave momentum to the prevalent Anglo-American understanding of pacifism. People who considered themselves peace-loving but who supported President Wilson's "war to end all wars" began calling themselves internationalists, and they placed their long-term hopes on agreements between states.

Strict or absolute pacifists were (and still are) associated with a firm personal refusal to fight in *any* war, a stance that typically is based on individual religious and/or moral convictions. In contrast, according to the noted peace scholar David Cortright, "pragmatic pacifism can be understood as a continuum of perspectives, beginning on the one hand with the rejection of military violence and extending across a range of options that allow for some limited use of force under specific conditions."[3]

In the United States, the antiwar movement of 1917 was eventually dismantled by wholesale arrests, brutal police raids (most notorious were the Palmer Raids in 1919, named for the attorney general at the time), and vigilante mobs. Many leaders were given long prison terms or expelled from the country.

Peace Movements in Historical Context

Historically, wars have been followed by periods in which peace is espoused with particular vigor. This is apparently due to potential adversaries' physical, economic, and social exhaustion, as well as to the inability of devastated societies to mobilize the resources—emotional and material—necessary to prosecute a lengthy war. The Greek historian Herodotus, called the "father of history" for his masterful treatment of the Greco-Persian Wars (500–479 BCE), pointed out that "in peace, children bury their parents; war violates the order of nature and causes parents to bury their children."[4] Insofar as such experiences are what psychologists describe as *aversive stimuli,* people are especially peace prone in the immediate aftermath of war.

For example, after the Peloponnesian War between Athens and Sparta, Greece experienced an upwelling of pacifist sentiment, as also occurred following the chaotic civil and imperial wars toward the end of the Roman Republic. Later, the Crusades from the late 11th through the late 13th centuries, as well as the various wars among dynastic rivals, including the Hundred Years' War between England and France in the 14th and 15th centuries, partially induced the pacifism of such humanists as the 16th-century writer Erasmus, as well as numerous suggestions for international law, especially by the 17th-century Dutch jurist Hugo Grotius.

The Thirty Years' War ended in 1648 with the establishment of the modern European state system, which was in large part motivated by widespread revulsion at how devastating that war had been. But the new system of states did not prevent war, at least not for long. The Napoleonic Wars, 150 years later, led not only to the so-called Holy Alliance and the "balance-of-power peace" of mid-19th-century Europe but also to an increased interest in international prohibitions on war and in the various peace conferences of that century.

Such late-19th-century nationalistic wars as the Franco-Prussian War (1871) led to renewed popular concern with the structure of international law. And, of course, the horrors of World War I were directly responsible for creation of the League of Nations and various disarmament efforts during the 1920s and 1930s, just as World War II led to the establishment of the United Nations as well as renewed interest in world government. The threat of global thermonuclear war, which intensified during the US-Soviet Cold War (1945–1991), was responsible for unprecedented concern about limiting and, if possible, abolishing nuclear weapons. With the end of the Cold War, such "nuclear abolitionism" became a much less prominent goal for both the public and mainstream US politicians than it was during the Gorbachev/Reagan era (1981–1991) and before, which had been characterized by a vigorous nuclear arms race and conspicuous saber rattling.

More recently, however, scientists, scholars, political activists, and significant segments of the public—especially younger voters—are once again becoming aware of the existential threats posed by weapons of mass destruction, especially nuclear weapons, as well as by climate change. For example, *The Bulletin of the Atomic Scientists* recently moved its "Doomsday Clock" to 100 seconds closer to midnight—closer to apocalypse than ever. In so doing, these scientists and global security analysts are explicitly warning leaders and citizens around the world that the international security situation is now more dangerous than it has ever been, even at the height of the Cold War.[5]

Unlike World War I, popular support for World War II was much broader. To some extent, in fact, and despite its immense carnage, World War II, sometimes referred to in the US as "The Good War," legitimized war in the minds of many and led to a lull in peace movement activity. In part, this war was widely viewed as having occurred because the Western democracies had been unwilling to confront Germany and Japan strongly and early enough (the so-called "lessons of Munich," when the UK's Prime Minister Neville Chamberlain acquiesced to Hitler's demand to annex a key part, the mostly German-speaking *Sudetenland*, of the then nation-state of Czechoslovakia).

In addition, because the aggressive militarism of Germany and Japan had represented a grave threat to the West as well as to such Asian allies as China, pacifism became widely discredited as a way of coping with international aggression. Moreover, during the decades following World War II, anticolonial liberation movements gave further credence to the legitimacy of organized violence, so long as it was for a "good cause," while the growth of Stalinism in the Soviet Union and Maoism in China served to justify militarism on the part of the United States and its NATO allies.

The resurgence of the peace movement during the 1950s and 1960s was due largely to growing popular anxiety about nuclear weapons, as well as opposition to specific wars, as in Korea and—to a much greater extent— Vietnam. The peace movement also was influenced by mass political and social actions in the so-called Third World, notably the nonviolence of Gandhi, as well as by increased antinuclear mobilization in the aftermath of the atomic bombings of Hiroshima and Nagasaki.

Following the Vietnam War, promilitary commentators worried that the United States had developed a "Vietnam syndrome," whereby Americans would be especially reluctant to wage war. Thus, President George H. W. Bush announced with pride following the first Iraq War—which violently removed Iraqi forces from Kuwait in 1990—that the United States had overcome this war reluctance. This, plus a dishonest but partially successful public relations effort to link the invasion of Iraq to the terrorist attacks against the US in September, 2001, might help explain the support of Congress and most of the US public for the second Iraq War, which began in 2003, at the prodding of President George W. Bush. British prime minister Tony Blair, Australian prime minister John Howard, and other national leaders also helped constitute a "coalition of the willing," which joined the US-led invasions and occupations of Afghanistan and Iraq. Given the consequences of these endeavors, it will be interesting to see if they lead to a return of the Vietnam syndrome and, if so, whether the US's onetime disinclination to invade weaker nations will be considered beneficial rather than worrisome.

A Typology of Peace Movements

Peace movements can usefully be divided into three categories:

1. Movements to eliminate war in general

2. Movements to stop particular aspects of war (e.g., conscription) or particular weapons (e.g., landmines and nuclear weapons)

3. Movements to stop particular wars (e.g., those in Vietnam or Iraq)

Of course, it is easier to stop specific wars than to stop war in general; hence, efforts to banish war altogether are also most likely to be associated with efforts to reshape public opinion and to establish firm structures of positive peace. These struggles are also more likely to be of indefinite duration, in contrast with opposition to particular wars or to specific means of waging war, which typically end along with the war in question or with the banning (or deployment) of the contested weapons.

Movements to eliminate war generally have given rise to such secular groups as the Peace Pledge Union in England, the Women's International League for Peace and Freedom, and Code Pink, as well as to such religious organizations and traditions as the Fellowship of Reconciliation, Pax Christi, the Quakers, and other religiously motivated advocates of nonviolence. Movements to stop particular aspects of war have included opposition to poison gas and landmines, to specific weapons delivery systems (Euromissiles, the MX missile, depleted uranium, Trident submarines), to nuclear weapons themselves (SANE, the Freeze campaign, the British Campaign for Nuclear Disarmament, the International Campaign for the Abolition of Nuclear Weapons), and against conscription (War Resisters League), as well as campaigns in support of converting military industries to civilian production, and opposition to specific wars.

The list in Table 11.1 contains a more detailed typology of peace movements (modified from Nigel Young. 1984. "Why Peace Movements Fail." *Social Alternatives* 4: 9–16) that identifies some of the major traditions, with an example of each.

Interconnections Between Peace and Other Social Movements

There have been many interconnections between peace movements and other popular social movements. For example, feminist antimilitarism, which emerged in the early years of the 20th century, was strongly infused with energy and leadership from the women's suffrage movement. Opposition

TABLE 11.1 ● Typology of Peace Movements	
Tradition	**Example(s)**
Religious pacifism	Conscientious objection: Society of Friends (Quakers), Pax Christi (Catholic), Fellowship of Reconciliation
Liberal internationalism	Associations, national peace councils, world disarmament campaigns
Anti-conscription	War Resisters League, Amnesty International
Socialist internationalism	No exact contemporary equivalents, but active until World War I, including the International Workers of the World ("Wobblies")
Feminist antimilitarism	Women for Peace, Women's International League for Peace and Freedom, Code Pink
Ecological pacifism	Greenpeace, Green Party (especially in Germany), Extinction Rebellion (especially in Great Britain and Germany)
Communist internationalism	World Peace Council
Nuclear pacifism	Europe: CND (Campaign for Nuclear Disarmament), END (European Nuclear Disarmament); United States: SANE/ Freeze, Physicians for Social Responsibility, International Physicians for the Prevention of Nuclear War, Global Zero, the International Campaign to Abolish Nuclear Weapons, and many others

to nuclear power—in the late 1960s, throughout much of the 1970s, and after the nuclear accidents in Chernobyl (1986); Three Mile Island, near Harrisburg, Pennsylvania (1979); and at Fukushima Daichi nuclear power plant in Japan (2011)—contributed to broader antinuclear sentiment in the 1980s and later.

Many people active in feminist, socialist, gay and lesbian rights, non-violent religious and environmental, and other social justice movements participate in peace movement activities as well. Such environmental organizations as Greenpeace and Friends of the Earth have found themselves increasingly involved in antinuclear protests. These groups express their antiwar and antinuclear concerns because of the threat of environmental destruction arising not only from nuclear war but also from the ongoing radioactive contamination emanating from nuclear weapons facilities, even while "nuclear peace" (less euphemistically, nuclear terror) prevails. Extinction Rebellion (XR) and its twin, Extinction Rebellion Peace (XRP), have mobilized mass demonstrations, occupations, and shut-downs of important facilities in London and other major cities in order to confront the inability of mainstream politicians, political parties, and multinational corporations to deal with the insidious consequences of global warming.

Other groups, which focus primarily on economic justice, have been drawn to the peace movement agenda as a result of their recognition of the social and economic costs of military expenditures. The era of avowedly conservative US government policies that included net tax cuts plus massive military expenditures—ushered in with the election of Ronald Reagan and followed by both Bush administrations, then amplified by Trump Administration policies—resulted in massive federal budget deficits and thus belt-tightening with respect to social expenditures. American activist groups, accordingly, became more aware of the opportunity costs of military spending—that is, the degree to which military expenditure diminishes a country's opportunity to invest money in ways that are socially more productive. During much of the 1990s, those who believed that the end of the Cold War would result in the end of peace movements were proven to be incorrect. At the same time, those who believed that these developments would result in greater domestic investment—the much hoped-for "peace dividend"—were also disappointed. Peace movements in reality have consistently exhibited a pattern of brief hiatus followed by regeneration around revised issues.

The United States

Despite the interconnections between peace and other social justice movements, contemporary peace-related movements in the United States have often been accused of being mainly a concern of middle-class white people. The reenergized antinuclear movement of the 1980s made efforts to reach out to progressive social justice groups organized by the poor and by people of color, to broaden their appeal and deepen their commitment to social justice, as did the Occupy Movements of 2011–2012. Nevertheless, antinuclear protesters as well as feminists, environmental, and anti-Wall Street activists were largely drawn from the relatively well-educated and well-to-do sectors of American society.

By contrast, opposition to US intervention in Central America and to apartheid in South Africa, as well as support for civil and gay rights, may well have been drawn from a wider socioeconomic cross section of American society. During the Reagan presidency, such organizations as Committee in Solidarity with the People of El Salvador (CISPES) and others opposing US sponsorship of the anti-Sandinista contra war in Nicaragua regularly underwent Federal Bureau of Investigation (FBI) harassment but nonetheless persevered and grew. Contemporary American and European opposition movements—especially those opposing the Iraq and Afghanistan Wars—also appear to have undergone similar scrutiny by federal governments, especially with various restrictions on civil liberties (notably a dramatic increase in electronic surveillance in the United States) in association with measures passed by the US Congress in support of the "war on terror."

Peace movements (and left-of-center movements generally) have tended to focus on one issue at a time, as earlier concerns are abandoned and the latest issue—cynics would say, the most recent fad—attracts most of the energy and outrage. Thus, in the late 1950s, it was opposition to widespread attacks on civil liberties during McCarthyism; in the early 1960s, protests against atmospheric testing and fallout shelters and in favor of arms control; in the mid-1960s, the civil rights movement; in the late 1960s and early 1970s, opposition to the Vietnam War; in the mid-1970s, defense of the environment; in the late 1970s, affirmation of feminism and human rights generally; in the early to mid-1980s, opposition to nuclear weapons and nuclear war fighting; in the late 1980s and early 1990s, protests against South African apartheid and US interventionism in Central America, along with support for gay rights; in the late 1990s, support of humanitarian intervention, economic conversion, and strategic nonviolence through various social movements, along with opposition to economically oppressive and environmentally destructive components of "globalization"; and during the first part of this century, opposition to the Iraq War and the economic hegemony of "the 1%" along with resistance to many aspects of the Trump Administration, from science denialism (especially climate-change science) to its inability to control the spread of racial, religious, and ethnic hate, as well as their associated far-right-wing white supremacy and neo-Nazi movements.

These shifting priorities of peace and social justice movements have been appropriate, reflecting changing global threats to peace. The Reagan administration, for example, with its verbal bellicosity and cavalier attitude toward nuclear war, generated the most vigorous antinuclear peace movement in US history, just as the Iraq War, with its accompanying doctrine of preemptive war, whereby the United States announced itself prepared to invade other countries at will, generated considerable political opposition around the world. So did the Trump Administration's withdrawal from international agreements, including the one constraining Iran's nuclear-weapons ambitions, the Paris Accords to reduce global climate change, and several important arms-control treaties with Russia.

Often, peace movements have been motivated by a surge of popular anxiety regarding a perceived threat that quickly subsides, even though the underlying problem remains as serious as ever. For example, the antinuclear movement of 1958–1963 declined rapidly after the Partial Test Ban Treaty was signed, although nuclear testing and the nuclear arms race simply went underground, increasing the number of such tests and the intensity of the arms race itself, rather than diminishing either. In other cases, peace movements that were narrowly focused on opposition to something specific tended to disband when that issue was resolved. A good example is resistance to the war in Vietnam, which ended when US ground forces withdrew. European opposition to the deployment of nuclear missiles by NATO sparked a virtual firestorm of antinuclear protests during the early 1980s.

However, during the Trump Administration there was no vigorous mass response by US peace movements protesting the many policies with which peace activists vehemently disagreed. That was not, however, the case in Western Europe and elsewhere, where movements such as Extinction Rebellion mobilized mass nonviolent resistance actions in support of climate-change mitigation and nuclear disarmament.

By exposing the absurdities of various nuclear war-fighting, war-surviving, and war-winning doctrines, the antinuclear movement of the 1980s temporarily succeeded in delegitimizing nuclear weapons to such a degree that even the previously bellicose Reagan administration eventually found itself proclaiming that "a nuclear war can never be won and must never be fought" and rescinding (at least for public consumption) its earlier pronuclear stance. In this way, the path of the US antinuclear movement has been similar to that of the environmental movement of the early 1970s, many of whose goals and ways of thinking have progressed from being widely perceived by the US public as radical to mainstream. The formal withdrawal of most American combat forces from Iraq and Afghanistan may have a similar consequence for peace movement activism, having both stimulated political opinion and having become absorbed into it.

Europe

Many important peace movement traditions have also developed in Europe, and a number are still active and influential. One is the Greens (*Die Grünen*), which originated in what was then West Germany. In the reunified Germany during the 1990s, the Greens gained political prominence, at one time forming part of a coalition government with the moderate Social Democrats. The Green movement also gave rise to other similar parties throughout Europe. The movement's underlying philosophy is a synthesis of ecology, feminism, political decentralization, community and workplace democracy, antiauthoritarianism, and antimilitarism. More recently, Green political parties have experienced a stunning rise to power-sharing in a number of European parliaments and as coalition partners in many cities and regions of Germany.

Like their American counterparts, European peace movements have long been dominated by direct opposition to war, a trend that has continued to the present. Anti-conscription advocates, especially the Berlin Appeal, became popular in both East and West Germany. Nearly 20 percent of those eligible for military service applied for conscientious objector status in West Germany, while the evangelical Lutheran churches of the German Democratic Republic (the former East Germany) also helped consolidate antimilitary sentiment. These church groups were particularly influential in organizing opposition to the former East German government, resulting in the dramatic events of late 1989 and 1990, when it (and other East European governments dominated by the Soviet Union) was toppled and the hated Berlin Wall dismantled.

The Campaign for Nuclear Disarmament (CND), founded in the United Kingdom in 1958, was stimulated initially by British opposition to nuclear testing. During the 1980s, largely in response to the intensification of the Cold War during the early Thatcher and Reagan years, the CND expanded dramatically as a broad-based, populist movement. In 1981, massive street demonstrations involving hundreds of thousands of people convulsed Bonn, Brussels, Athens, London, Rome, Madrid, and Amsterdam, largely in opposition to US-led NATO nuclear weapons policies. These demonstrations were part of a peace movement revitalization that united antinuclear protesters with antinuclear power activists. They included the women's and ecological movements, gay and lesbian rights supporters, and socialists and internationalists of a variety of orientations, including supporters of the United Nations, a sprinkling of pro-Kremlin peace fronts, and advocates of world government.

Although numerous peace movements exist in less-developed countries, they are almost always concerned with domestic issues. These typically focus on opposition to a government's oppression of its own indigenous people (e.g., Guatemala), political dictatorship (e.g., many African and Middle Eastern regimes), ethnic cleansing/genocide and military rule (Myanmar/ Burma), or governmental socioeconomic policies and corrupt leadership (e.g., Zimbabwe and elsewhere in Central and North Africa). It is mostly in the wealthier northern countries that peace movements respond to government actions in *other* parts of the world.

In early 2003, major European cities had huge demonstrations opposing the forthcoming US-led invasion of Iraq. For partisans of peace movement activism, these events offered both hope and disappointment: hope, because they were unprecedented in modern history, the first example of massive public opposition to a war before it began—but disappointment because they failed to prevent it.

Some Internal Debates Within Peace Movements

Peace movements are not homogeneous. They have fluctuated substantially in tactics, as well as in goals. They have periodically been galvanized by opposition to especially atrocious wars (Vietnam) or weapons (including poison gas, nuclear weapons, depleted uranium-tipped shells, and land mines), only to recede somewhat when the war is terminated (Vietnam, the Cold War) or when provocative actions have been removed (aboveground nuclear testing, Euromissiles, etc.). One observer of the European peace movement during the 1980s suggested that peace movements were like whales, which periodically break the surface and then disappear under the waves. "When the whale disappears in a dive, those on the right believe the movement no longer exists. Supporters of the movement, on the other hand, see the leaping whale and claim it can fly."[6] The truth may be somewhere in between.

In addition to their inconstancy, peace movements are notorious for their ideological heterogeneity and occasional combativeness. Ironically, peace activists fight a lot, at least with each other! (To be sure, not physically violent conflicts, but often with substantial conceptual and verbal aggressiveness—even including, we blush to admit, some peace textbook authors.) In part, this may be because movements advocating social change tend to attract adherents who are antiestablishment, strong-willed, and inclined to rebel against authority. In any event, here are some of the major controversies that have caused substantial splitting within peace movements but have also contributed to the vibrancy that comes from vigorous internal debate.

State-Centeredness

States (and multinational corporations, whose interests are often closely aligned with those of the major states) are the primary actors in the international war-peace arena. Therefore, some claim that it is essential to reform the way states behave toward one another—for example, by encouraging trade, democracy, disarmament conferences, and agreements on the rules of war; the abolition of certain weapons; and the establishment of such international agencies as the League of Nations and the United Nations. On the other hand, critics of the state-centered approach claim that focusing on the behavior of states merely perpetuates their behavior by exacerbating rather than alleviating nationalist biases. They think that states are the problem, not the solution, and that, accordingly, lasting solutions must be less state-centered.

Following the breakup of the Warsaw Pact in the 1990s, NATO's move to fill the Eastern European strategic vacuum and employ its military muscle in the former Yugoslavia, Libya, Iraq, and Afghanistan prompted new divisions in the peace movement. Some praise the international cooperation implicit in NATO's new interventionist role as a welcome challenge to state sovereignty and superpower policing of the world, as well as a defense of human rights. Others see the same actions as an attempted extension of Western hegemony and of inordinate American influence.

The Use of Military Force

Within the European peace movement, the same internal divisions resurfaced over NATO's bombing raids over Serbia and Libya and its use of "boots on the ground" in Afghanistan. Some defended military action as a means of assisting humanitarian causes, such as the violent—and possibly temporary—removal of the Taliban from power in Afghanistan. Opponents of any use of military force (absolute pacifists) disagree with relative pacifists, who believe in the possibility of a "good," "just," or permissible war or military action. Many but not all relative pacifists approved of Western interventions in Afghanistan, Kosovo, and Libya, the first Gulf War, the Spanish Civil War, and World War II, while also typically opposing such specific wars as those in Vietnam, Central America, and Iraq.

Even with so-called good wars, about which there is considerable debate, the question must be posed: Is the "evil" to be overcome (e.g., former Serbian President Slobodan Milošević's ethnic cleansing of non-Serbs in the former Yugoslavia, Saddam Hussein's alleged possession of weapons of mass destruction in Iraq, German Nazism and Japanese imperialism in World War II, the fascist takeover of Spain, slavery in the Civil War) greater than the "evil" of a war waged to overcome the malignancy? An analogy with cancer may be apt because some treatments for this disease can be as devastating as the illness itself.

A similar debate pertains to the use of smaller military forces. Was the "liberation" of Grenada worth the loss of life that resulted from the 1983 invasion of that island by the United States? Did the removal of Panama's former dictator Manuel Noriega warrant another American invasion in 1989, or did the end of the Gaddafi regime require the NATO bombing of 2011? Did American marines move too quickly into Somalia in 1993 and then conduct a too-hasty retreat when American lives were threatened by local tribal warlords? Some self-styled realists argue that under certain conditions, the use of force is appropriate; others—who see themselves as equally realistic—maintain that violence is ultimately self-defeating and also filled with unintended negative consequences for those who retaliate violently against an attack (so-called blowback).

Centralization Versus Grassroots Organization

One antiwar tradition favors the development of strong peace movement leadership and central authority. Another prefers local, grassroots organizing and "leaderless" or at least decentralized organization (e.g., within the US, the "Occupy Movements" of 2011–2012, the ongoing Extinction Rebellion movement, and the Indivisible and Sunrise Movements formed in response to the presidency of Donald Trump).

It is unclear whether peace movements have had greater success when they were composed primarily of large numbers of people mobilized as "objects" or of relatively fewer but more strongly motivated individuals, who saw themselves as "subjects" of their own intense actions and protests. Thus, the peace movement mobilization of 1 million people in New York City in June 1982 had an undeniable impact on the Reagan administration, but so did the handful of Buddhist monks who, a decade or so earlier, immolated themselves to protest the Vietnam War. Buddhist monks have also been a base of much nonviolent resistance, although some rabidly nationalist Buddhist monks have incited and even participated in violence against the Muslim Rohingya people in Myanmar (aka Burma).

US-based opposition to the Iraq and Afghanistan wars has been largely at the grassroots level, with peace proponents deeply impatient with the political leadership of both the Democratic and Republican parties. Despite a proliferation of antiwar organizations, their activities in the United States have not coalesced around any single issue. In much of Europe, Latin America, and the Muslim world, there is massive popular as well as selective elite political opposition to continuing Israeli occupations of Arab lands.

Single-Issue Versus Broader Social Agendas

Many peace groups have opposed specific aspects of war (such weapons as the MX missile and Trident submarines in the United States; neutron bombs and cruise missiles in Europe; conscription; war taxes; or specific wars, including Vietnam, Nicaragua, and Iraq), whereas some peace groups have emphasized the importance of broadening their agenda to embrace economic aspects of social justice (e.g., employment at decent wages, economic equity, medical care, affordable housing, and child care), environmental concerns (notably, opposition to anthropogenic climate change, along with support of clean air and water, preservation of open space, wildlife conservation, renewable energy sources, protection of tropical forests), support for gay rights, and opposition to racism and sexism.

In some cases, peace movements have become closely associated with a single political party (e.g., previously the Labour Party in the UK and more recently the Greens in Germany and the former Communist Party in Italy). In the United States, the Democratic Party has traditionally shied away from being too closely associated with peace movements, fearing that it would be tainted with an image of being "weak on national security," although its policies have been traditionally more pro-environment than those of many Republicans, who have increasingly denied even the overwhelming scientific consensus regarding climate change.

Supporters of the single-issue approach emphasize that by concentrating on a small number of manageable concerns, they are more likely to have a demonstrable effect, analogous to how a nail can penetrate a wall whereas broad pressure is far less effective. Supporters of a broader agenda counter with the argument that specific issues come and go and that the peace movement can actually be weakened whenever a single issue is resolved, no matter what the outcome (leaving the nail in a wall that still stands), and arguing that broad, programmatic, consensus-building blueprints for social change can bring pressure across a wider societal front, albeit often with less visible impact in any one area. Regardless of their perspective, peace advocates are increasingly aware of the importance of pointing out the linkages between various "single issue" considerations. For example, the Nuclear Freeze campaign in the United States during the 1980s received relatively little support from African Americans, at least in part because the US underclass was more concerned with economic and social justice.

Practicality Versus Idealism

How high should peace movements aim? Is there a risk that by setting their sights too high, peace movements will make "the best an enemy of the good"? On the other hand, don't peace movements have an obligation to be above politics-as-usual, which bills itself as the "art of the possible"?

At times of unprecedented danger and opportunity, perhaps peace movements should, as some peace advocates and leftist political organizers from the 1960s put it, "be realistic—demand the impossible." Thus, there can be a disadvantage in being too timorous: "Realism" on the part of the US Nuclear Freeze campaign, for example, appeared to be a step backward to many in the European peace movement, many of whom had long demanded substantial reductions in nuclear weapons, while others called for nuclear abolition. But—and it seems there is always a "but"—by choosing a more centrist goal, such movements are more likely to garner widespread support, making their goals more achievable.

Another dilemma of idealism versus practicality may be observed in Germany, where the Green Party since 2000 has enjoyed such electoral success that the elected Green Party members became insiders rather than protesters outside parliamentary politics. Earlier, the party had generated two factions within the Green movement: the "Fundis" ("fundamentalists"), who held out for such idealistic goals as the total abolition of nuclear weapons (a sentiment apparently shared, at least rhetorically, by former American president Barack Obama at the very beginning of his presidency) and refused to form coalitions with more conservative parties, and the "Realos" ("realists"), who were willing to make certain practical concessions in the interest of achieving immediate, although incomplete, political goals. In general, Green parties do well in societies with post-materialist conflicts caused by high levels of wealth and income inequality or the presence of a tangible environmental disputes—as evidenced by their recent electoral successes in numerous European countries, both at the national and at the local level.

One view of peace movements is that they serve as grit in the cogwheels of the world's war machines, preventing them from running smoothly and perhaps eventually causing them to break down altogether. Another analogy—and a more positive one—compares peace movements to bread yeast, helping dough to rise. Perhaps states are by their nature unqualified to promote creative transformations and are dependent on changes that emerge only from protest groups. In any case, peace movement activists remain divided as to whether they ought to compromise their principles in the interest of real but ambiguous progress.

Moreover, for politicians to act in support of a peace agenda, it is helpful—and perhaps necessary—for citizen activism to encourage them. When he met with A. Philip Randolph, who had spoken movingly about the need for federal action on civil rights, President Franklin Delano Roosevelt responded, "I agree with everything that you've said, including my capacity to be able to right many of these wrongs and to use my power and the bully pulpit. . . . But I would ask one thing of you, Mr. Randolph, and that is go out and make me do it."

Civil Disobedience

Supporters of civil disobedience maintain that when a government is engaging in ethically impermissible behavior—often in violation of international law—it is acceptable and even essential to oppose these practices, even if such opposition involves breaking domestic laws. Opponents of civil disobedience worry about the ethics and consequences of law breaking, and also about the possibility that such acts may alienate the majority of the citizenry and ultimately prove counterproductive.

This is part of a broader debate about tactics, especially between those who advocate grassroots (from the bottom up) activism "in the streets," by as many people as possible, and those who favor an approach that focuses more on working within the existing political system to influence decision-makers (lobbying, from the top down). In turn, the debate about tactics is part of an even larger issue: whether to oppose war through the electoral process, by writing, speaking, organizing and attending meetings, and passing resolutions, or actively to resist it, by strikes, tax resistance, and nonviolent civil disobedience, or even by violent confrontation with the warfare state.

Some Criticisms of Peace Movements

Although public opinion is often mobilized by peace movement activities, sometimes the political mainstream has also been alienated by them. In some cases, wars have been made more unpopular by peace movements but in others they may actually have been prolonged. Peace movement efforts nearly always have unseen, latent consequences as well as visible, immediate ones. This makes it difficult to declare a specific peace campaign—or the movement as a whole—a success or failure.

In the famous (some say, infamous) Oxford Peace Pledge Union during the 1930s, many students in England declared that they would not "fight for king and country," which, according to some commentators, emboldened Hitler by implying that his aggression might not be resisted. Similarly, other vigorous European peace movements of the 1930s may not only have made Nazi and Fascist aggression more likely but also diminished the degree of Allied preparedness when war finally came.

In addition, it has been suggested that peace movements, by excessive wishful thinking, may sometimes blind their fellow citizens to the provocative and dangerous behavior of others. By single-mindedly opposing military actions, or even nonengaged deployment, peace movements could undercut the hard-fought fragile stability in some conflict zones. For example, in 2019, President Trump suddenly withdrew and later redeployed a comparatively small contingent of US troops from northern Syria, thereby green-lighting attacks by Turkish armed forces against Syrian Kurds, who had fought effectively and at great cost to themselves against the Islamic State in Syria. This US action, justified by the Trump administration as an effort to terminate "unending wars," could be seen as a kind of peace movement success—because most peace activists have also been advocating the withdrawal of US-led coalition forces from Afghanistan, Iraq, and Syria—even though the decision to do so was clearly not in response to peace movement pressure and, given its murderous consequences for such US allies as the Kurds, might even cynically be caricatured as giving peace a bad name. Eventually, in light of withering criticism from his own military advisers, Trump partially reversed his decision and "redeployed" US forces to another part of Syria, ostensibly to "defend the oil" (which, it should be noted, is not American property).

In any event, this ostensibly pro-peace initiative by Trump constituted a bloody betrayal of the Kurds, who had been counting on a US "trip-wire" to prevent Turkey from carrying out what amounts to genocide against the Kurds. Some Kurdish groups have long been considered terrorists by the Turkish government, which feels threatened by Kurdish nationalist ambitions. Moral of the story: peace advocates—like pretty much all people—are well advised to be careful what they wish for: "Nothing is more promotive of war," writes peace researcher Quincy Wright, "than diversion of the attention of the prospective victims from the aggressor's preparations."[7]

However, as previously noted, there are many reasons for wars, few if any of which can plausibly be attributed to peace movements. Consequently, the occasional counterproductive effects of peace movements seem inconsequential. Few things are more disruptive of the pursuit of peace, it can be concluded, than blaming well-intentioned peace movements for the war-prone behavior of states and their leadership.

Peace movements often have a difficult time. During war, they are typically denounced and often banned or even attacked as unpatriotic, cowardly, or traitorous for giving "aid and comfort to the enemy." And during times of peace, they often are hard-pressed to make a dent in public complacency.

A critical view of peace movement activism sometimes claims that peace movement participants are "acting out" such personal needs as youthful ("Oedipal") rebellion; that is, youthful rebels are opposing authority at a predictable, age-appropriate stage in their own personal development and are exercising the opportunity of behaving outrageously while still relatively free of social or family responsibilities. This line of argument can be overused, especially by right-wing critics eager to discredit the often laudable goals of peace and antiwar activists. But it would also be a mistake to ignore the diverse personal motivations of those involved, who in fact represent a wide cross section of ages; many are peace movement veterans, some of whom may have "dropped out" for a while to develop careers or start families, only to return when the issues appear especially acute, when time allows (the children are grown, retirement is at hand), or when their conscience beckons. Many others are youthful activists, deeply anxious and justifiably concerned about the state of the planet and their own futures.

Another question arises: How vociferous should peace activists be in criticizing their own governments? Most devotees of peace studies point out that world peace, demilitarization, and an end to violence are not zero-sum games in which if one side wins, the other must lose. Rather, virtually everyone of good will stands to come out ahead if a peace agenda is actually realized (with the possible exception of some members of the military-industrial-governmental-academic complex, whose "good will" is often limited to their immediate financial and career payoff).

To this end, people are usually most able to influence the polities of which they are members: For US citizens, this is the government of the United States, just as for Russians it is the Russian government, and so on. In most cases, governments are all too happy to have their citizens—whether members of a peace movement or not—criticize and demonstrate against rival foreign powers. But in doing so, they are unlikely to have much impact on the conduct of their own governments. (During a peace conference during the Cold War, one of your authors was arguing with a Soviet journalist about the relative freedom of speech in the two countries. When he noted that he was free to stand on the steps of the US Capital and criticize President Reagan, whereupon nothing bad would happen to him, his counterpart responded that he, too, could stand on the steps of the Kremlin and criticize President Reagan . . . and nothing bad would happen to him, either!)

Peace movement activists generally operate on the assumption that people—especially, perhaps, those fortunate enough to be living in a genuine democracy, which is supposed to respond to their will—have a special responsibility to evaluate critically and, if necessary, to seek to reform the behavior of their own government. In this respect, they have much to do.

Maintaining the Momentum of Peace Movements

It is easy for peace activists to fall victim to personal fatigue, despair, and cynicism. But, in fact, peace workers worldwide have accomplished a great deal. In the 20th century, for example, conscientious objection became widely recognized in most Western countries as a basic legal right, although exercising that right was sometimes perilous. Interestingly, within many peace movements, even anti-conscription was not universally accepted as an appropriate goal. A segment of socialist antiwar activists at one time actually applauded conscription, hoping it would create a "people's army," whereas others feared that it would simply contribute to an "army against the people." The Vietnam War (for the Vietnamese, "The American War") was terminated in large part because of widespread popular discontent with the war in the US, fueled by immense pressure from the domestic peace movement, as well as, of course, by the fierce resistance of millions of Vietnamese to what they perceived as American imperialism.

Similarly, in the 1980s and 1990s, nuclear weapons underwent a rapid process of temporary delegitimation, much to the dismay of militarists and cold warriors. At the same time, many professed liberal internationalists supported NATO military engagement in Serbia and Afghanistan. Even the Iraq War was justified initially by the Bush administration's claim (later recognized to be bogus) that the Iraqi government was on the verge of obtaining weapons of mass destruction, and then the US administration claimed its invasion of Iraq to be in service of humanitarian intervention, ending the dictatorship of Saddam Hussein, liberating Iraqi women (who, in fact, had more political and economic freedom in that country than in most other Arab states in the Middle East), and initiating a process of democratizing the Middle East as a whole. The same debate arose over armed assistance to anti-Gaddafi and anti-Assad forces in Libya and Syria, respectively. Not surprisingly, peace advocates in good conscience have found themselves on different sides of these conflicts. Interestingly, many American "paleoconservatives" (as contrasted with so-called neoconservatives) joined traditional peace movement progressives in opposing the Iraq War along with Western armed interventions in Libya and Syria.

It remains to be seen whether contemporary peace movements can sustain their momentum if immediate, readily perceived threats no longer exist and also when governments modulate their rhetoric but not their policies, or co-opt various peace movement agendas by showy but relatively trivial concessions. More specifically, it is uncertain whether antiwar sentiment in the United States will outlast current crises in Africa, the Korean Peninsula, and the Middle East. Also in doubt: whether the antinuclear movement will resume its previous fervor or be co-opted or "pacified" by political rhetoric that equates nuclear weaponry with patriotism and security, or that makes superficially appealing but ultimately meaningless concessions.

Contemporary peace movements may well profit by developing alternative foreign policy concepts, alternative defense strategies, a pragmatic view of social goals, broader motivations beyond single-issue rallying points, a workable model of a disarmed (or, at least, substantially demilitarized) economy, and staying power. In addition, successful peace movements would likely benefit by realistically acknowledging, albeit not necessarily applauding, state and corporate power while also, when possible, breaking out of a strictly state-centered model of politics.

The overriding goal of many peace movement activists is not so much the elimination of states as their transformation from warfare states to peace-promoting agencies of social and environmental justice. Specifically, demilitarization could serve not only as a goal but also as a method of such change. And demilitarization, as such, is independent of the elimination of specific weapons or the pacification of particular "hot spots" around the world.

An important component of the peace movements of the 1980s and 1990s called for the denuclearization of military policy as well as the demilitarization of defense policy. It called into question the fundamental rationality of basing national security primarily on military strength. In addition, it called not only for widespread popular political and economic participation but also for the empowerment of ordinary citizens. Twenty-first-century peace movements appear to have a full agenda, especially given the threats posed not only by subnational terrorists from below, increasingly with extreme right-wing agendas and/or motivations, but also by the often violent responses of certain countries (e.g., United States, Russia, Turkey, China, India, Myanmar, Saudi Arabia, Pakistan, and Israel) to these real and perceived threats.

Peace movements are sometimes depicted in mainstream media and by their more *Realpolitik*-oriented critics as quixotic, hopelessly romantic quests, disproportionately peopled by refugees from the 1960s and 1980s. Yet evidence abounds that the movements of the past often influenced national policies, nearly always for the better. Both supporters and opponents of the war in Vietnam, for example, agree that the United States terminated its involvement in that conflict in large part because of an ebbing of political will to continue prosecuting the war. In addition, the Reagan administration, during its latter years, grew increasingly less pronuclear, in part due to peace movement pressure that was widespread, vocal, and highly visible. National policy in New Zealand has also been strongly influenced by that country's peace movement sentiment and its current Prime Minister, Jacinda Ardern, from the New Zealand Green Party. The result was a ban on all nuclear facilities in 1984, including visits by nuclear-armed or nuclear-powered naval vessels to New Zealand, much to the consternation of the US government, and, more recently, national support for global climate-change mitigation, responsible Covid-19 management, and—following a mass murder at a mosque—rigorous gun control. The United States' withdrawal of many of its occupation forces from Iraq and Afghanistan is, in part, due to domestic political pressure and the "war fatigue" felt keenly by some elected officials in Washington, D.C.

History also offers many examples of successful movements that initially appeared to be facing impossible odds: support for women's suffrage; opposition to monarchy; and resistance to slavery, which was an ancient and firmly rooted practice, at one time virtually worldwide and considered by many to be an immutable and irrevocable part of human society. As recently as the last few decades of the 20th century, few people would have imagined that

- decades-old Fascist dictatorships in Spain and Portugal would give way to modern parliamentary democracies;

- bloody tyrannies in the Philippines and Haiti could have been overthrown peacefully (although both countries, especially the Philippines, have significantly regressed to their autocratic legacies);

- the Soviet Union would renounce its Stalinist heritage and institute massive restructuring (*perestroika*) and political/ideological openness (*glasnost*) and, moreover, disappear as a political entity;

- the "captive nations" of Eastern Europe would throw off their shackles and emerge nonviolently as fledgling democracies eager to embrace free-market economic policies;

- the apartheid regime of South Africa would end, with remarkably little bloodshed, given its violent past and consistently oppressive governments; or that

- dictatorial regimes in Tunisia, Egypt, Ukraine, and Yemen would have been overthrown, initially at least, with very little violence (even though these gains, except for Tunisia, have been short-lived and, in the case of Ukraine, precipitated a violent backlash by Russia).

And this is just a partial list.

Maybe sometime in the future, people will look back wonderingly at the 21st century, noting with amazement that in such a war-prone world, persistent, widespread peace movements could mount so successful a campaign against war itself.

A Final Note on Peace Movements

What if they had a war and no one came? This old question seems never to go away—at least in part because it has never been tested. People always show up for wars. But what if "they" had a war and no one objected? What if no one protested the plans for future wars?

The alternative to vigorous peace movement activism is to continue "business as usual" in a world of war, injustice, glaring socioeconomic inequities, global climate change, and deprivation. Many people have long recognized that the traditional conduct of international power politics and warfare is unacceptable, a perception that has become even more widespread with the advent of weapons of mass destruction. Yet progress toward a different and more peaceful world has been painfully slow. With the end of the Cold War—and especially with the prospect of an unending "war on terrorism"—it seems that we have been, as Matthew Arnold put it,

Wandering between two worlds, one dead,

The other powerless to be born.[8]

There is no simple agreement among activists as to what peace movements should strive for: an end to specific wars or to particular weapons or governmental policies and/or various aspects of the complex tapestry of positive peace that we discuss in Part IV of this book. Regardless of the goals favored by each individual, the special promise of peace movements is that they might serve as midwives for a newer and better world, providing it with the impetus to be born at last.

Questions for Further Reflection

1. Make some specific suggestions for how contemporary peace movements might organize themselves in order to achieve general goals. Do the same for peace movements whose goals are more narrowly focused.

2. Suggest at least one classification of peace movements other than that presented in this book.

3. Investigate at least two current peace movements currently active. You may focus on Afghanistan, Central America, Israel, Russia, Syria, Yemen, Burma/ Myanmar, or any other non-Western country currently plagued by violence. How do they compare with the peace movements in the United States or Europe?

4. Describe your own position regarding the various controversies within modern peace movements, supporting that position with examples from history and/ or unfolding events.

5. Make the argument that, on balance, peace movements do more harm than good. Then take the opposite position.

Suggestions for Further Reading

Stefan Berger and Holger Nehring, eds. 2017. *The History of Social Movements in Global Perspective*. New York: Palgrave Macmillan.

April Carter. 1992. *Peace Movements in International Protest and World Politics Since 1945*. London: Longman.

Cynthia Cockburn. 2012. *Antimilitarism: Political and Gender Dynamics of Peace Movements*. New York: Palgrave Macmillan.

Robert Cooney and Helen Michalowski. 1987. *The Power of the People*. Philadelphia: New Society.

David Cortright. 2008. *Peace: A History of Movements and Ideas*. New York: Cambridge University Press.

Ted Gottfried. 2004. *The Fight for Peace: A History of Anti-War Movements in America*. New York: 21st Century.

Simon Hall. 2006. *Peace and Freedom: The Civil Rights and Antiwar Movements in the 1960s*. Philadelphia: University of Pennsylvania Press.

Scott Ritter. 2007. *Waging Peace: The Art of War for the Antiwar Movement*. New York: Nation Books.

Pam Solo. 1988. *From Protest to Policy*. Hagerstown, MD: Ballinger.

Notes

1. St. Augustine. 1950. *The City of God*. New York: Modern Library.

2. Quoted in Alan Geyer. 1982. *The Idea of Disarmament*. Elgin, IL: Brethren Press.

3. David Cortright. 2008. *Peace: A History of Movements and Ideas*. Cambridge and New York: Cambridge University Press.

4. Herodotus. 1910. *History*. G. Rawlinson, trans. New York: E. P. Dutton.

5. For the 2021 Doomsday Clock Announcement, and the rationale behind it, see https://thebulletin.org/doomsday-clock/current-time/.

6. Philip P. Everts. 1989. "Where the Peace Movement Goes When It Disappears." *Bulletin of the Atomic Scientists* 45: 26–30.

7. Quincy Wright. 1964. *A Study of War*. Chicago: University of Chicago Press.

8. Matthew Arnold. 1855. "Stanzas From the Grande Chartreuse." *Fraser's Magazine*, April.

Bettmann via Getty Images

Diplomacy, Negotiations, and Conflict Resolution

One way of achieving peace is for the contending sides in a dispute to reach a mutually acceptable agreement. When such agreements or understandings are obtained among states, through the efforts of trained government representatives, often employing stylized communication, we say that diplomacy has taken place. The people who practice this art are diplomats, although there is also a more cynical view of diplomats, who have been defined as "otherwise honest men [and, increasingly, women] sent abroad to lie for their country."

Peace researcher and political scientist Anatol Rapaport has usefully distinguished among fights, games, and debates. In a fight, the intent is to defeat the opponent, sometimes even to destroy him or her. Rules may exist, as in a prizefight, but they may also be ignored—as in a street fight or a vicious war—and the means are nonetheless violent. In a game, by contrast, each side tries to outwit the opponents, playing strictly within certain rules. And in a debate, the goal is to persuade the opponent of the justice or merits of one's position. The process of conflict resolution and management, ideally, is closest to a debate, just as wars are like fights, although conflict resolution bears some aspects of a game as well. However, even diplomacy and negotiations involve elaborate rules and, not uncommonly, the threat of fighting as well.

Although ways of fighting have changed through history, basic techniques of negotiation have changed little. Usually, negotiators have two things that they can offer: threats and promises. These can be backed up by varying degrees of good or ill will and a continuum of reassurance, ranging from blind trust to ironclad verification. Negotiations, however, can only succeed if there is a set of outcomes that each party prefers to no agreement. Dispute participants (especially if they are governments) occasionally engage in negotiations just to appear virtuous. But there is good reason to think that in most cases a negotiated settlement is preferred to either a failure to agree or the use of violence to determine an outcome. The challenge is to find a peaceful settlement acceptable to all conflicting parties.

Techniques for successful negotiations—often involving trained third parties—can contribute greatly to the peaceful resolution of conflicts. Ideally, one should also consider the techniques of conflict resolution and transformation more generally, not only in the international sphere but also with respect to domestic antagonisms and interpersonal as well as intrapsychic conflicts.

Conflict: A Brief Overview

Conflict may occur within a person, between two or more individuals or groups, or within or between large social organizations, most notably nation-states. As noted in Chapter 6, Sigmund Freud believed people are torn between innate drives for love and self-preservation on the one hand, and aggression and destruction on the other hand. Most contemporary social scientists tend to eschew such explanations, instead claiming that human conflicts are largely due to a real or perceived incompatibility, or contradiction between conflicting parties' attitudes, behaviors, interests, needs, positions, and/or values.

Modes of Conflict Analysis

There are two dominant and sometimes "conflicting" models of addressing conflicts: the realist and peace-oriented perspectives.

From a realist or ostensibly security-oriented perspective, actions taken to address conflicts include such measures as wars, espionage, and sanctions, often in tandem with diplomacy. The goal is to defend one's perceived interests and to defeat or neutralize the opponent, preferably by managing a conflict so that it does not spiral out of control and by resolving it through a mixture of violent and nonviolent means, such as mediation, arbitration, cease-fires, and treaties. The Cuban Missile Crisis is a classic example of international conflict *management*. But because the underlying reasons for such conflicts are typically not resolved or even addressed, hostilities may resume at a later time.

If conflicts are not dealt with early in a dispute, they may escalate so that the parties will deploy whatever means they choose, including threats, legal reprisals, and direct or indirect violence, to defeat the other and win the conflict. This happens frequently between such parties as couples in the process of a nasty divorce, as well as between nations (India and Pakistan, for example), existing states and nascent nation-states (Israel and Palestine), and states and nonstate adversaries (the United States and al-Qaeda, or between most established nation-states and the self-proclaimed Islamic State).

A peace-oriented perspective, in contrast, stresses the prevention rather than the management of conflicts and nonviolent conflict transformation as the preferred means of resolution. Because violence rarely works to control violence, nonviolent strategies and tactics must be utilized if conflicting parties are to transform their attitudes and behavior from enmity to tolerance. Gandhi's campaign for Indian independence, Martin Luther King's struggle for civil rights in the United States, and the Velvet Revolution in the former Czechoslovakia in 1989 are examples of nonviolent conflict resolution.

Conflict appears to be inherent in human relations and is therefore unlikely to be eliminated. Hence, the mission of nonviolent conflict transformers and peace workers is not to end conflict, but as peace and conflict researcher Kenneth Boulding said, to "make the world safe for conflict." This means to reduce the likelihood that social/political disputes erupt into violence and war.

Conflict Outcomes and Solutions

Conflicts have different outcomes. One side may win and the other lose (but not be eliminated), as in divorce settlements involving contested assets or child custody, or in many international disputes. Both sides may withdraw temporarily from the dispute, but because one or both parties may not believe its interests or needs were satisfactorily addressed, they might resume the conflict later. Many international conflicts fit this profile, and historians argue that World War II resulted, in part, from the failure to successfully address long-simmering resentments by Germany against the victors of World War I. Israel's ongoing conflicts with its Arab neighbors and many insurrections and terrorist actions against governments, especially vis-à-vis occupying powers, also conform to this model.

A conflict may infrequently result in the real or perceived total elimination of the other side, as with the destruction of the Nazi regime in 1945. In contrast, the Sri Lankan government, after defeating the rebel Tamil Tigers in 2011, claimed to have eliminated them. But because the Tamil people have not been eliminated, it remains to be seen whether the Sinhalese-Tamil (Buddhist-Hindu) conflict in Sri Lanka will persist, possibly breaking out in another, less lethal form. This situation provides a model for appreciating the difference between mere conflict management of violent outcomes and true conflict resolution and transformation.

Negotiating Solutions to Conflict via Peacemaking

People often negotiate solutions to conflict in their daily lives, typically at the interpersonal level. Everyday examples include disagreements among siblings over who gets to sit in a given chair, within families over what television program to watch, or between coworkers over whether or not to have an office party: such disputes are typically resolved, nearly always short of violence. This highlights the many routes available for dealing with conflict. It is something we do every day.

And yet, one of the most pervasive myths of cultures of militarism is that war and preparation for war are natural, unavoidable phenomena, whereas peace and conflict resolution strategies are hopelessly unrealistic. We are surrounded with subliminal messages to the effect that peacemaking is an impossible dream, whereas war making—or at best deterrence or a kind of armed standoff—is the only realistic option. Hence, it is important to demonstrate that peacemaking happens all around us, most of the time. Often, peacemaking receives society's attention only when it takes place at the highest government level, where it is in fact quite rare.

Summitry

In ancient times, leaders were often renowned warriors and, not uncommonly, would meet person-to-person to settle their disputes by individual combat. At other times, at least according to folklore, champions would be selected, one from each side, to fight it out: The classic example is David versus Goliath. Today, national leaders are more likely to be political figures, and their meetings are intended to help establish or cement relationships or to engage in personal resolution of disputes between their countries (while also playing to their domestic constituencies).

When the leaders of two major political entities meet, this is often referred to as a summit meeting. There have been many; for example, President Richard Nixon's meeting with Chinese leader Mao Zedong in 1972 was especially dramatic, as was Egyptian President Sadat's journey to Jerusalem and his meeting with Israeli Prime Minister Begin, which led to the Camp David Accords of 1978–1979. (Sadat was later assassinated by a Muslim nationalist army officer who believed that the Egyptian leader had sold out his country and his religion.) In both cases, the states involved had previously been bitter enemies—so antagonistic, in fact, that they were not even communicating with each other. Hence, the mere fact that political leaders were meeting and talking amicably sent a powerful signal about the possibilities of peaceful coexistence.

During the Cold War, the term *summit* was largely reserved for meetings between leaders of the United States and the Soviet Union. Here, too, it was widely thought that if only the leaders could meet and talk over their disagreements as reasonable, intelligent, and concerned human beings, peace between longtime adversaries might be possible.

Unfortunately, there is no reason to expect this always to be the case. On some occasions, summit meetings were merely cosmetic, perhaps improving the international atmosphere but offering few if any specific changes, thereby often disappointing those who had hoped for more. At other times, minor progress was achieved, largely by leaders signing agreements that the diplomats had laboriously worked out in advance, as in a 1972 summit between Richard Nixon and Leonid Brezhnev at which the Strategic Arms Limitation Talks (SALT I) agreement was signed, and the 1987 meeting in Washington, D.C., between Mikhail Gorbachev and Ronald Reagan, at which the Intermediate Range Nuclear Forces (INF) agreement was signed. More recently, American President Barack Obama and Russian President Dmitri Medvedev signed the New Strategic Arms Reduction Treaty (New START) in April 2010 in Prague. On the other hand, tensions between the United States and Russia have subsequently risen, to such a degree that the future of this treaty is in doubt upon its expiration in 2021.

Shortly after he took office, President Trump escalated a war of words with North Korean dictator Kim Jong-Il, threatening to destroy the latter, his government, and his country if the latter threatened the United States. A year or so later, Trump and Kim had a few face-to-face meetings after which President Trump, claiming success, announced that North Korea's nuclear weapons were no longer a threat—even though the Pyongyang government continued to modernize and expand its arsenal.

It is unclear whether the Trump-Kim meetings made things better, worse, or did not change the standoff between their countries. In any event, it created a smokescreen behind which Trump trumpeted what he contended as a great—and even a potentially Nobel Peace Prize–winning—accomplishment, although North Korean nuclearization proceeded unhindered. On the other hand, it reduced the sense of imminent threat on both sides, a threat that had been accelerated by North Korea's nuclear escalation as well as inflammatory rhetoric by both leaders. North Korean rhetoric was no less bellicose than Trump's, threatening to destroy the US in a "sea of fire," partly in response to Trump's verbal provocations, although such usage from the government in Pyongyang has been standard for many years.

Summit meetings have made things worse on occasion, resulting either in feelings of ill will or in dangerous misjudgments by one or both parties. For example, a 1961 meeting between John F. Kennedy and Nikita Khrushchev in Vienna appears to have been a personal embarrassment for Kennedy (who was younger and less experienced than his Soviet counterpart), and it led to Khrushchev's inaccurate estimation that the US president could be pushed around, which in turn set the stage for the Cuban Missile Crisis. It also evidently contributed to Kennedy's determination that he would be especially tough in the future.

With the end of the Cold War, meetings between world leaders have rarely carried the same emotional freighting as in the past and have generally received less public attention, the Trump/Putin and Trump/Kim meetings notwithstanding. Also contributing to their lowered visibility is the fact that such occasions have become more frequent, at least on a multilateral basis, with regular convocations of the world's major industrial states (the so-called Group of Eight, which included Russia until its suspension from the group in 2014, due to Russia's moves into Ukraine) as well as frequent trade and other ministerial meetings.

Summit meetings notwithstanding, it isn't clear that closer relations and greater communication among world leaders will make war less likely. Kaiser Wilhelm of Germany and Czar Nicholas of Russia, for example, were first cousins, and on the eve of World War I, they sent each other a flurry of telegrams signed "Willy" and "Nicky"! Summit meetings and personal relationships, in short, can be helpful, but they can also cause problems, depending on the issue and the personal dynamic between the leaders, or they can provide only an illusion of warmth and mutual understanding.

Probably the most dramatic example of successful summitry in modern times occurred at the Camp David meetings in 1978, which resulted in a historic agreement signed in 1979. Hosted by then–US president Jimmy Carter, who served as facilitator, Israel's prime minister Menachem Begin and Egypt's president Anwar Sadat spent 13 days at the rustic presidential retreat in Maryland. The meetings took place without the formalities, protocols, and rigid negotiations characteristic of traditional summit meetings or bargaining sessions. Rather, there was no formal agenda, no intrusive press, and—perhaps as a result—some highly personal and emotional interchanges. Although the Camp David meetings did not solve all Middle East problems, or even all areas of the Egyptian-Israeli dispute, they did turn out to be highly productive and led to the first mutual recognition between Israel and one of its Arab neighbors, as well as to a treaty.

The result has been a historic peace—although a "cold" one—between Israel and Egypt, followed in the late 1990s by a similar treaty between Israel and Jordan.

A Brief History of Diplomacy

Until recently, diplomats were usually drawn from the same social and economic class (upper), and in most cases they spoke the same language: French. Although there is a long history of monarchs sending ambassadors to the courts of other rulers, the current system of diplomatic protocol was established by Cardinal Richelieu, the chief minister—some would say, chief manipulator—of the early-17th-century French king, Louis XIII. Although there has always been a peculiar stiffness to official diplomatic discourse and protocol, such formalities have evolved over many years so as to enhance precision of communication and, whenever possible, to reduce the chances that personalities will interfere with formal and goal-oriented communication between governments.

Historically, ambassadors were the personal representatives of one sovereign to the court of another, and this polite fiction is still maintained, even in the case of democracies: Upon their arrival, ambassadors typically present their credentials to the head of state of the host country. In modern times, electronic communication has partially supplanted face-to-face negotiations when it comes to the establishment of important international agreements, but the role of person-to-person contact, even at the highest levels, remains important.

Ironically, states communicate with each other least frequently and least clearly during the run-up to war and during active hostilities—precisely when such communication is likely to be most needed. At such times, and occasionally when interactions become severely strained during peacetime, diplomatic relations are broken off, and each state recalls its ambassador. Otherwise, officials are available to correct possible misunderstandings, to clarify positions, and, when all else fails, simply to buy time, occasionally in the hope that tense situations will eventually blow over.

A point of contention is whether the prospect of negotiations itself should be used as a diplomatic lever. Most governments are adamant about not negotiating with "terrorists," a position that initially might appear reasonable insofar as doing so appears to be rewarding violent behavior by non-state actors. On the other hand, by foreclosing the option of negotiations, this stance runs the risk of blocking a potential avenue of nonviolent conflict resolution.

During the administration of George W. Bush, the United States leadership refused to "sit down at the table" with the governments of North Korea or Iran, although it did participate in multiparty talks. However, this posture proved unproductive and was to some extent replaced under the Obama administration by a willingness to discuss policy differences (especially regarding nuclear proliferation) with Iran, resulting in the 2015 nuclear framework between the Islamic Republic of Iran and a group of world powers: the P5+1 (the permanent members of the United Nations Security Council—the United States, the United Kingdom, Russia, France, and China, plus Germany) and the European Union. This agreement was subsequently abandoned by the Trump administration and as of early 2020 was teetering on the brink of abolition due to mutual recriminations between Iran and the United States in particular. It is widely expected that the Biden administration will re-enter the agreement, and as of 2021, negotiations between the two countries have resumed with this in mind. However, progress has been slow because of mutual distrust on the part of both governments, testimony to the fact that when it comes to international agreements—as with so many other things—it is much easier to destroy than to build.

To some extent, summit meetings—especially if conducted one-to-one—are seen as conveying political legitimacy on the participants. For most people devoted to peace, diplomacy and negotiation are not synonymous with capitulation, nor are they favors extended to the other side. Rather, they are important components of good-faith efforts to resolve conflicts short of violence. As a general proposition, Winston Churchill's quip that "Jaw, jaw, jaw is better than war, war, war" still holds.

Some Diplomatic Successes in Averting War

In 1987, Greece and Turkey exchanged threats over Turkish plans to prospect for oil near several eastern Aegean islands that were under Greek control but very close to the Turkish mainland. These two states have a long history of antagonism and warfare: Greece was once part of the Ottoman Empire, and the two states have engaged in threats as well as actual fighting over the fate of the Greek and Turkish communities on the island of Cyprus. Tensions have gradually declined, however, even though the Greek part of Cyprus is now part of the European Union and the long-term status of the Turkish enclave is still uncertain. This is in part because both sides fear antagonizing their NATO ally, the United States, which might cut off its military aid to the two countries.

In many cases, multilateral diplomacy has negotiated an end to fighting—for example, termination of the wars in Bosnia, Kosovo, Northern Ireland (mediated by the US) and between China and India (mediated by the USSR). It may be overly optimistic, however, to consider these cases as straightforward diplomatic successes because they may also be examples of diplomatic failures that later resulted in war (as in South Sudan), followed eventually by diplomacy-assisted termination once one or both sides tired of the war's costs. Nonetheless, these limitations notwithstanding, diplomacy can be useful, as a means whereby warring sides eventually achieve peace.

Some Diplomatic Failures

Sometimes, diplomats make things worse. Perceived slights between rulers and diplomats have occasionally endangered the peace. Late in the 17th century, France and Spain nearly came to blows when a coach carrying the Spanish ambassador to England cut in front of the French ambassador on a London street. In 1819, the Dey (ruler) of Algiers, angered about the failure of the French government to make good on a debt, struck the French consul three times with a fly swatter. This insult precipitated a naval blockade by the French and ultimately served as an excuse for what became the longtime occupation of Algeria.

Even at its best, diplomacy involves a certain deviousness and social artifice that many people find laughable, if not downright unpleasant. During the protracted negotiations leading to the Treaty of Paris after Napoleon's defeat, the famed Austrian diplomat Metternich was told that the Russian ambassador had died. Story has it that he responded, "Ah, is that true? I wonder what he meant by that."

Efforts at diplomatic clarification sometimes backfire: For example, in late July 1914, Sir Edward Grey, the British foreign secretary, warned Kaiser Wilhelm that if a general war occurred, Britain would enter on the side of France and Russia. Rather than deter Germany (as Grey had intended), this was seen as a threat to the Kaiser, which made him more belligerent, convinced of a plot against him by the Triple Entente. Similarly, public threats against a country—as with President Donald Trump's repeated verbal attacks against the Iranian government—generally serve to strengthen the hand of hawks on the receiving side.

Sometimes, statements by diplomats intended for domestic consumption have had grave international repercussions. In 1950, for example, Secretary of State Dean Acheson gave a speech in which he outlined the United States' "defense perimeter" in the Pacific; this appeared to exclude Korea, which gave the North Korean government the false impression that the United States would not forcibly resist an invasion of South Korea. Shortly before invading Kuwait, Iraqi leader Saddam Hussein met with the then–US ambassador to Iraq, who responded to a query by stating that the United States "takes no position" on Iraqi territorial claims to Kuwait. This was interpreted by the Iraqis, incorrectly, to mean that the United States would not become involved in the event of an Iraqi invasion. Of course, the United States did intervene and forcibly ejected Iraq from Kuwait.

Sometimes, ironically, war can be made more intense by the fact that diplomats are striving to bring the fighting to a close, as each side seeks to make or consolidate gains on the battlefield that might influence the ultimate peace settlement. Middle East diplomats noticed that the proposals put forward by Count Bernadotte, the first UN negotiator sent to settle the 1948 Israeli-Arab War, closely reflected the immediate battlefield situation; as a result, both sides paid less attention to him and put more effort into achieving military gains so as to influence the negotiations in their favor. During the end stages of the Bosnian War in the early 1990s, all sides tended to initiate offensives, hoping to improve their bargaining position in the eventual postwar settlement.

Starting in early 2016, just before the declaration of a cessation of hostilities, the Syrian government, buttressed by Russian air power, went on the offensive against its adversaries, labeled "terrorists" by both the Syrian and Russian administrations (although the major opposition groups deemed terrorist by the West, ISIS and the al-Qaeda–backed al-Nusra Front, were not parties to this agreement). For this reason, it is generally recommended that the first step in negotiating peace is an immediate ceasefire.

On occasion, diplomacy has even been consciously employed by political leaders who were eager to initiate war. The most famous example of this was the Ems Telegram, which was craftily edited by Prussian chancellor Otto von Bismarck to make it appear to the French that Prussia's Kaiser Wilhelm was snubbing the French ambassador. In Bismarck's own words, he "waved a red flag in front of the Gallic bull." The bull charged, as Bismarck had calculated, and ran into a Prussian steel wall in the ensuing Franco-Prussian War. In this case, Bismarck could have simply declared war on France, but he wanted to goad the French into appearing to be the aggressor.

Before the second half of the 19th century, European diplomacy often served to make peace in ways that avoided excessive humiliation of the loser, so as not to foment grievances that would lead promptly to more war. Some territory would be transferred; fortresses would be surrendered and frontiers adjusted; indemnities might be required and reparations exacted. But more recently, especially with intranational largely replacing interstate wars, concessions have often been cause for lasting resentment, which have in turn sowed the seeds for subsequent wars. Thus, France's loss of Alsace and Lorraine to what became Germany during the Franco-Prussian War in the late 19th century—and its national fervor for reclaiming these lost regions—did much to bring about World War I. The German anger and humiliation associated with the Treaty of Versailles (which ended that war) led in part to World War II. By contrast, the diplomatic settlements at the end of World War II, although imperfect, have had greater staying power.

Critics often note, however, that diplomacy is often not so much a means of avoiding war as it is an adjunct to national hostilities. "Diplomacy is a disguised war, in which States seek to gain by barter and intrigue, by the cleverness of wits, the objectives which they would have to gain more clumsily by means of war," wrote Randolph Bourne.

> Diplomacy is used while the States are recuperating from conflicts in which they have exhausted themselves. It is the wheedling and the bargaining of the worn-out bullies as they rise from the ground and slowly restore their strength to begin fighting again.[1]

Accordingly, let us now turn to the relationships between diplomacy and military force.

Diplomacy and Military Force

For many national leaders, diplomacy is only as effective as the military power available to each side, the threats that underwrite courteous diplomatic interchanges. "Diplomacy without armaments," according to Frederick the Great, "is like music without instruments."

There have been many examples of diplomatic intimidation, some successful, some not. Shortly after taking office in 1992, President Clinton sent diplomatic representatives to the Haitian colonels who had kept democratically elected Jean-Bertrand Aristide from assuming power. At the same time, a military invasion force was readied; only when reports reached Port-au-Prince that US aircraft were en route did the junta agree to step down, peacefully.

Also during the administration of Bill Clinton, after years in which NATO dithered and thousands of Bosnians died, the Serbs of Yugoslavia and Bosnia agreed to a settlement of the Bosnian War only after NATO actually initiated bombing of Serb positions. This is not a precedent that gladdens the hearts of peace advocates, but its reality must be acknowledged. Serbs claim, however, that they had already planned their exit from Bosnia and that the bombing did less to hurt Serb forces than to kill civilians, including Chinese diplomats, whose embassy in Belgrade was severely damaged by NATO bombs. On the other hand, the lack of US and Western intervention in Rwanda during its genocidal civil war in 1994, leading to the murder of perhaps 800,000

Rwandans, is often cited as a major failure of military resolve, especially by former president Clinton himself.

Otto von Bismarck, the 19th-century chancellor of Prussia and architect of German unification, was not a pacifist. Yet, while he freely employed military force, he also understood its limitations. During the Austro-Prussian War, for example, in 1866 the Austrians were badly defeated at the Battle of Königgrätz, far more soundly than most had expected. At this point, political pressure within Prussia called for a wider victory over Austria, including the dismemberment of the Habsburg Empire itself. But Bismarck insisted on limiting Prussian demands to the provinces of Schleswig and Holstein, thereby preventing war with France and possibly Russia and Britain. As the arch-diplomat Metternich once put it, "Diplomacy is the art of avoiding the appearance of victory."

In contrast to Bismarck's sensitivity to the dangers of pushing one's victories too far, during the Korean War American General Douglas MacArthur and President Harry Truman underestimated the costs of pressing the North Koreans and Chinese. After a surprise landing of US forces at Inchon resulted in dramatic gains in the autumn of 1950, UN (mostly US) troops advanced deeply into North Korea. This led to large-scale Chinese involvement and massive bloodshed on both sides, ending three years later in a stalemate, which might have been achieved with far fewer casualties had the Western leaders shown greater farsightedness and restraint. The lesson of Königgrätz—that military restraint can often lead to greater diplomatic and long-term success—had apparently not been learned.

Another kind of bargaining has occasionally been useful in diminishing levels of violence. Often termed *tacit bargaining,* this entails that conflicting parties reach agreements without explicitly spelling out the terms of the understanding. Because threats are strongly implied in such tacit bargains, they have most commonly taken place with the implications of war or other violence should bargaining fail. For example, during the Korean War, a tacit bargain existed on both sides: The Chinese would refrain from attacking US aircraft carriers, supply lines, and bases in Japan, while similarly there would be no bombing of North Korean supply lines in China.

In the Middle East today, there is another tacit bargain: Israel will not flaunt its stockpile of nuclear weapons, and Arab states will not repeatedly and publicly call attention to them. To some extent, this understanding serves the interests of both sides: The Israelis would rather not officially acknowledge their nuclear capability, and some Arab states would rather not have to respond publicly to its existence. This example is not especially satisfying to students of peace because it involves at best a kind of stand-off. Skilled diplomats and negotiators generally hope for better.

Diplomacy and *Realpolitik*

In *Poetry and Truth,* the great German writer Goethe acknowledged, "If I had to choose between justice and disorder, on the one hand, and injustice and order, on the other, I would always choose the latter." Many others—notably Metternich in the 19th century and one of the 20th century's best-known students of Metternich, Henry Kissinger—followed suit and made social and political stability a goal in itself, often tolerating repression and social injustice in the pursuit of a state's self-interest, so-called *Realpolitik.*

Hans Morgenthau, one of the 20th century's most influential advocates of *Realpolitik* in international relations, proposed numerous rules for diplomacy, which, he hoped, would help states resolve conflicts short of war while also pursuing their own self-interest in international affairs. These rules included the following:

- Do not be a crusader. Avoid "nationalistic universalism," the insistence that the goals of one's own nation are appropriate as universal goals for all nations. As the 19th-century French Foreign Minister Talleyrand put it, *pas trop de zèle* ("not too much zeal"). Such excessive zeal was shown in the enthusiasm of US National Security Council aides to assist the *contra* rebels in Nicaragua, even at the cost of illegal activities and, ultimately, at great harm to US influence and prestige. Ditto for neo-conservative enthusiasm in 2003 about overthrowing Saddam Hussein and "remaking the Middle East."

- Employ a narrow definition of vital national interests—namely, survival and the maintenance of socioeconomic well-being. Morgenthau emphasized that in the nuclear age, states cannot afford war—or the risk of war—for anything short of their supreme security interests.

- Be willing to compromise on all national interests that are not truly vital. Of course, there is disagreement about what is "vital."

- Try to see the other side's point of view, recognizing that all participants have vital national interests, and no one should be pushed into compromising them.

- Distinguish between what is real and what is illusory; do not allow considerations of honor, credibility, or prestige to override issues of real national security.

- Never paint yourself into a corner; always retain avenues of retreat (or advance).

- Do not allow an ally, especially a vulnerable one, to make decisions for you. As a corollary, do not allow yourself to be drawn into someone else's fight.

- Always keep military factors subordinate to political ones.

- "Neither surrender to popular passions nor disregard them."[2]

Following Napoleon's defeat in 1815, Western Europe entered into a period of relative stability, based in large part on the system established by the victors at the Congress of Vienna. Some of this "success" was because all the major players accepted the post-Napoleonic European state system as legitimate, and the dignitaries at the Congress felt equally rewarded and equally slighted by the outcome.

In contrast to Morgenthau's conception of value-free diplomacy is the notion that issues of right and wrong lie at the heart of international disputes. National leaders generally find it easier to look dispassionately at conflicts in which they are not themselves embroiled; once physically and emotionally involved, the process of moralizing often becomes intense, leaving only victory as a tolerable outcome. US president Woodrow Wilson urged the participants of World War I to seek a "peace without victory" and "a peace between equals" . . . until the United States entered that war. Then, even the American Peace Society declared, "This is not a war of territory, of trade routes or of commercial concerns, but of eternal principles. There can be no end of war until after the collapse of the existing German government."

Historically, many of the crucial aspects of diplomacy have been carried out largely in secret. Secrecy was subsequently blamed, by many, for the errors and miscalculations that led to World War I, and President Woodrow Wilson accordingly called for "open covenants openly arrived at." Diplomacy can be undermined by a failure of coordination within a government, as when, early in the Trump Administration, then-Secretary of State Rex Tillerson began negotiations with the North Korean government only to be contradicted by tweets from President Trump.

On the other hand, although secret diplomacy sounds unpalatable, especially to a democratic society, when conducted in public, diplomatic negotiating isn't usually conducive to compromise. Each side fears appearing soft or being duped and is inclined to play to domestic public opinion, making arguments and advancing proposals that may be politically popular, even if it knows that other solutions may be fairer and more desirable. So, there is much to be said for diplomacy that is carried out not so much "in secret" as under a mutual understanding that not every offer and counteroffer will be leaked. Some of the noteworthy diplomatic successes of recent years followed secret negotiations, such as the Oslo Accords, which brought a measure of peace (or, at least, hope) to the Middle East; the Dayton Accords, which ended the Bosnian War; and the termination of fighting in Kosovo.

Track II Diplomacy

Since the late 1970s, there has been growing interest in so-called Track II diplomacy, also sometimes called unofficial or "encounter group" diplomacy. Track II diplomacy is unofficial in that it need not involve formal negotiations between representatives of different states; rather, it revolves around relatively informal interactions among people from opposing groups. It contributes largely to laying the social and political groundwork needed in order for government leaders to act. It also can be seen as representing a way of solving problems independent of the nation-states themselves.

In Track II diplomacy, people are brought together, typically in the presence of an experienced third party or facilitator, for the purpose of achieving mutual understanding, exploring their commonalities as well as differences and establishing interpersonal relationships despite the political disagreements between their "home" groups.

This has been attempted, sometimes with considerable success, with groups of Catholics and Protestants from Northern Ireland, Greek and Turkish Cypriots, Israelis and Palestinians, and Tutsis and Hutus in East Africa. Usually, the individuals in question are relatively influential in their communities: doctors, lawyers, professors, journalists, midrange politicians, and military officials. Success is never guaranteed, and there is often substantial distrust and, frequently, minor incidents, especially at the outset. Over time, however, many of these "encounter groups" have produced positive results and have increasingly involved students participating in international exchange programs.

Third-Party Involvement

As an illustration of the potential usefulness of third-party involvements in disputes, consider a married couple who disagree over how to divide household chores. Left to themselves, the partners may be unable to reach agreement, in part because each individual considers only his or her viewpoint.

Moreover, each partner may hesitate to give in, even partially, for fear that any concession might be seen as an admission that he or she has a weaker case. Similar deadlocks arise in other situations of conflict, such as disputes between labor and management. In such cases, disputes between contending parties—whether individuals, organizations, or states—are sometimes more readily resolved if a third party is brought in. For domestic disputes, marital counselors may be helpful; for labor disputes, trained mediators or arbitrators, often provided by the government, might work well. A similar process can apply to international disputes.

An outside expert may be called in to help clarify the issues, resolve misunderstandings, and suggest areas of compromise and common ground. A third party— optimally unbiased and trusted by both sides—can sometimes help reach agreements for which everyone may be grateful but which (for a variety of reasons) neither party could suggest or even accept if it were proposed by the other side.

Imagine, for example, that two adjacent states are disputing the location of a shared border in a strip of land 100-kilometers wide. If state A proposes placing the border right down the middle, giving 50 kilometers to each side, state B might use this "opening" to bargain further, "splitting the difference" between them and proposing a border so that B gets 75 kilometers and A, 25 kilometers. In such a case, the side that first proposes a compromise finds itself at a disadvantage. One obvious solution, therefore, is for a third state, C, to propose independently that A and B agree to 50 kilometers each. (Unfortunately, international disputes are rarely this simple, given historical backgrounds, social factors, political passions, military alliances, and economic considerations, as well as such geographic factors as marshes, rivers, mountains, and so forth.) Importantly, disputes very often occur on at least two levels: the specific issue under dispute and also the underlying questions of who wins, who is more powerful, and what this portends for subsequent interactions.

Go-Betweens

There are several ways in which third parties can be helpful to disputants. First, they can serve as go-betweens, providing what is known as their "good offices," which may simply involve making a meeting place available on neutral ground. The Scandinavian states, as well as Austria and Switzerland, have often provided this service; when in doubt about a "neutral ground," international diplomats often meet in Geneva. Go-betweens can also be crucial when participants on one side (e.g., the Arab states, excepting Egypt and Jordan) do not officially recognize the existence or legitimacy of neighboring states deemed hostile to their interests (e.g., Israel). In the early 1990s, the Norwegian foreign minister was influential in facilitating the Oslo Accords between Israel and the Palestinians, and in 1999, the president of Finland served as go-between when NATO forces and Yugoslavian president Slobodan Milošević ended the war in Kosovo.

Of course, when the third party is a high-ranking representative of a major power, he or she presumably does not merely act as a messenger but also can engage in various forms of arm twisting—for example, threatening to cut off economic or military aid unless some proposed compromises are accepted. This further suggests why some forms of diplomacy are best conducted in secret: It may be politically unacceptable, for example, for a state to appear to buckle under to such pressure, although it may be better for everyone concerned if it does so. At the same time, powerful countries are able to "sweeten the deal," as with the United States providing billions of dollars in aid to both Israel and Egypt in the aftermath of the Camp David agreements. The possibility of financial and/or military assistance also underlines the prospects of further Arab-Israeli peace deals.

Third parties, if they have the respect of the conflicting sides, can also serve a valuable role as "fact finders," ascertaining, for example, whether a disputed border was crossed, how many political prisoners are held in specified jails, how large are the military forces involved, or what the economic situation is in a particular region. International organizations, notably the United Nations, have been especially helpful in this respect, establishing various "commissions of inquiry" to evaluate conflicting claims. In certain cases, basic facts are in dispute, but in others the disagreement is not over numbers or other data but rather over values—over what is perceived to be right rather than what is true.

Mediation and Arbitration

In addition to providing a place to meet, facilitating communication, and occasionally twisting a few arms, third parties can fulfill two diplomatic functions: mediation and arbitration. Mediators make suggestions that might be agreeable to both sides. Like marriage counselors, mediators try to resolve disputes, but adherence to their suggestions is voluntary. By contrast, in arbitration both sides agree in advance to accept the judgment of the arbitrator. Mediation therefore involves less of a threat to national sovereignty; it is accordingly more often acceptable than arbitration to contending states. A third procedure, adjudication, involves making decisions with reference to international law.

There is nothing new in the practices of mediation and arbitration, which were utilized frequently and often successfully in Europe from about the 13th to the 15th centuries. The success of third-party involvement at that time may have been due to several factors: Family ties among political leaders were frequent (not uncommonly, heads of state were cousins or even closer). The economic costs of war were widely recognized as extremely high, and local treasuries often teetered on the edge of bankruptcy. Finally, a powerful third party was available to aid in the settling of disputes—namely, the Catholic Church and its emissaries.

Adversarial governments often face a dilemma: Even when a compromise is feasible, both sides want to project an image of power and success. Accordingly, the mediator or arbitrator can suggest something that both sides privately want but neither is willing to propose.

For example, during the Geneva Conference in 1955—which formally ended the French occupation of Indochina—Britain, China, and the Soviet Union mediated between France and its primary Indochinese adversary, the Viet Minh. In this case, as with many others, mediation did not resolve the dispute; it only postponed it. But even apparent failures may sometimes be helpful: Sometimes there can be a real advantage in postponing war, if, over time, passions cool and peaceful solutions eventually become possible. And sometimes, of course, mediation is successful. American President Theodore Roosevelt, for example, won a Nobel Peace Prize for his successful mediation between Russia and Japan, which ended the Russo-Japanese War (1905). Pakistan and India had been engaged in military hostilities over control of the territories of Jammu and Kashmir when peace negotiations, mediated by Soviet Premier Alexei Kosygin, resulted in a ceasefire that called for a return to the *status quo ante* (the previous situation). Although the dispute between India and Pakistan was not settled by this arrangement, at least the killing between two highly militarized and hostile powers was ended—for the time being.

When both sides agree to abide by the judgment of a third party, the dispute has been submitted to arbitration. One of the most important cases is the so-called *Alabama* claim, known for a Confederate warship that had been purchased (illegally) in Britain, a neutral country, during the US Civil War. The US government subsequently demanded reparations for the damage done to US shipping by the *Alabama* and other similar ships, and in 1872 both sides consented to arbitration. An independent panel eventually awarded the United States more than $15 million in damages, which Britain paid, thereby lowering tensions between the two countries and paving the way for close ties between the former enemies. In fact, the now-close relationship between Britain and the United States can be counted as beginning with this successful arbitration.

Biased Mediation: The 2020 US-brokered Middle East "Peace Plan"

Third party diplomatic involvement presumes that the mediator is in fact an "honest broker," trusted by the contending sides and likely to come up with recommendations that are fair to everyone involved. It sometimes happens, however, that the mediator is biased; moreover, the proposed arrangements may be intended for political gain rather than to resolve an international dispute. One example is the Middle East "peace plan" unveiled by US President Donald Trump in 2020, allegedly intended to settle the long-standing Israeli-Palestinian dispute. It had been developed without any input from the Palestinians and strongly favored Israeli priorities; under it, the Palestinians would have had to make the only meaningful concessions.

This plan proposed, among other things, that Israel would be granted legal title to its settlements in Palestine (often called the West Bank) that it had taken in its 1967 Six Day War against its neighboring Arab states, the legitimacy of which the international community has consistently denied because this land had been illegally obtained by military force. The Palestinians were to be granted the semblance of an independent state, but one that is unlike any other because it would be forcibly demilitarized and would consist of a patchwork archipelago surrounded by Israeli territory. Israel, meanwhile, would be given full sovereignty over Jerusalem, which has been hotly contested by both peoples. Palestinians would receive, in return, a pledge of $50 billion in investments, ostensibly to come from other Arab countries, while they would be required to disarm Hamas—which controls Gaza. The former was in no way guaranteed, and the latter would almost certainly generate a civil war among Palestinians. Not surprisingly, the Palestinians rejected this offer outright.

Almost certainly, this supposed mediation was not intended to be accepted because it would have been political suicide (and possibly literal suicide as well) for any Palestinian government to accept so one-sided an arrangement. This plan was beneficial to the right-wing Israeli Likud Party government, led by Benjamin Netanyahu, a close ally of US President Donald Trump. As such, it also appears to have politically benefited Trump himself, by presenting him as an aspiring peacemaker while also endearing him to conservative supporters of Israel within the United States.

The take-home message of this sad story is that although diplomacy is nearly always preferable to overt conflict, even diplomatic initiatives should always be taken with a grain of salt and never at face value.

Negotiating Techniques for Resolving Conflict

Its occasional downsides and disappointments notwithstanding, arbitration and mediation offer much to aspiring peacemakers, and numerous techniques are available to genuinely honest brokers and to the contending sides themselves.

Last Best Offer

One promising example is the so-called last best offer. Imagine two sides disagreeing over the amount of money to be paid for ownership of a disputed island. Rather than making offers and counteroffers, each side is told to give the third party its last best offer, from which an arbitrator, for example, will choose the one that seems the fairest. The arbitrator cannot decide to split the difference because this might encourage each side to be intransigent. In the last-best-offer technique, by contrast, each side is nudged to be as conciliatory as possible, in hopes that its offer will be the one accepted.

Resolution Versus Dominance

In 1964, conservative American policy analyst Fred Charles Iklé wrote an influential book titled *How Nations Negotiate*. It focused on how one nation (the United States) can prevail over the other side, concluding that a good negotiator must, above all, "maintain the will to win."[3]

This view would probably still be endorsed by many diplomats and negotiators today. However, if negotiations are to help resolve rather than incite conflict, another perspective is needed, one that views negotiations as a means whereby contending parties seek to resolve their differences and not merely to prevail. It suggests that to be fruitful, negotiations must be seen as non-zero-sum solutions, interactions in which my gain is not necessarily balanced by your loss, or vice versa. Good-faith negotiations should aim to achieve "win-win" solutions in which all sides are better off than they were before.

Compromise

The most obvious and, in some cases, the most common negotiating technique is to compromise—that is, to reach an agreement that is in some sense intermediate between the demands of both sides. There are, however, several disadvantages to this method. For one, a compromise may leave both sides dissatisfied. In some cases, this may be desirable so that a "fair" decision may be defined—only somewhat tongue in cheek—as one that leaves everyone equally unhappy. This happens because although the immediate conflict has been "managed," the underlying reasons for the conflict have not been addressed or resolved, thus increasing prospects for the conflict's resumption at a later time.

In some cases, one side's claim may be just and the other's unjust; in such a case, a compromise simply rewards the unjust side while penalizing the just one. Compromise assumes that opponents are equally worthy, so that "splitting the difference" between them will produce a fair settlement.

But what if state A arbitrarily insists on imposing a 50 percent tariff upon all imports from state B but refuses to allow B to tax its imports? Clearly, a "compromise" that allows a 25 percent unilateral tariff would not be fair and is unlikely to be acceptable to state B.

In other cases, however, one side can "win" without the other "losing." For example, Franco-German relations were bedeviled through the first half of the 20th century by a dispute over ownership of the Saar region, a rich industrial sector of the Rhineland. Following World War I, occupation and mining rights to the Saar were ceded to France; French control was reasserted after World War II. But the region's population is overwhelmingly German-speaking, and the governments in Paris and Bonn eventually cooperated to resolve this issue: After a plebiscite in 1955, France permitted the Saar to rejoin what was then West Germany. This negotiated agreement, in which France ostensibly "lost," served everyone well because it proved to be a cornerstone for subsequent Franco-German cooperation and friendship.

Positional Versus Integrative Bargaining

Compromises are often the outcome of what has been called "positional bargaining," in which each side stakes out a position and then holds to it. Positional bargaining does not encourage flexibility and reasonable behavior; rather, intransigence is often rewarded, and willingness to compromise (or even to suggest compromise) is frequently penalized. Thus, in positional bargaining, the participants are rewarded for staking out a "hard" position and sticking to it, and they are penalized, in turn, for being "soft." As a result, "good" bargainers are those who remain relatively intransigent—that is, who make it difficult or unlikely that an agreement will be reached, except on their terms.

Fortunately, there is another way, known as "integrative" or "principled negotiating." It tries, among other things, to separate the actual dispute from the underlying interests of each side. The goal is to focus on the latter and avoid getting bogged down in the former.

As negotiators Roger Fisher and William Ury recount,[4] consider the story of two sisters who quarreled over an orange; they decided, finally, to compromise, each getting one half. One sister then proceeded to squeeze her half for juice while the other used the peel from her portion to flavor a cake. By compromising—an old and honorable solution—they overlooked the integrative solution of giving one all the peel and the other all the juice.

Or imagine once again that two nation-states disagree over a boundary. The real dispute may not be over territory as such but rather over one state's desire for access to certain transportation routes, while the other state is concerned that granting this access would diminish its military security. In such a case, integrative bargaining would seek to identify the underlying issues and solve them directly, perhaps reaching an understanding in which the needs of both sides are integrated into one solution: for example, access to the desired transportation routes for an agreed annual fee, along with a bilateral treaty specifying strict limitations on the nature of the vehicles or number of personnel permitted to travel along them. (An agreement of this general sort once permitted Palestinians living in the West Bank and the Gaza Strip to go back and forth, with Israel in between; given Israeli/Palestinian hostilities, this travel permission is regularly revoked by the Israelis.)

Numerous tactics may be employed by negotiators seeking to bridge differences between contending sides. They include focusing on the *shared interests* of both sides, rather than on the demands as such. This tactic often serves to diminish the role of personalities by separating the people from the problem. It thus "fractionates" the conflict, by separating a dispute into resolvable and intractable components and then working on the former, in the hope of building confidence between the antagonists, before tackling the latter. Such tactics may also contribute to a process of confidence building, which increases the probability that more difficult issues will be solved in the future. Researchers have shown that confidence-building measures (CBMs) are better than ICBMs at keeping the peace because by having made some degree of progress, disputants will likely try harder to reach additional agreements and be less inclined to resort to violence.

Certain disputes—such as the story of the oranges—have a high "integrative potential" in that they lend themselves to agreements that leave all parties satisfied. Others are more difficult, as when, for example, buyers and sellers disagree over the price of a house. Even here, however, there is room for integrative agreements: for example, by negotiating modifications in the interest rate, the date of occupancy, the amount of principal to be paid off by certain dates, and so on. In such cases, it may be possible to integrate the interests of both sides, by reaching agreement on other dimensions aside from those initially in dispute (in this case, the purchase price).

Methods of Integrative Bargaining

Let us now examine five different methods by which integrative agreements might be reached, taking as an example a hypothetical dispute between a husband and wife over where to spend their 2-week vacation: The wife wants to go to the seashore, the husband to the mountains. One solution is for the couple to compromise and spend one week at each desired destination; both partners would like, however, to find a more satisfactory settlement.

1. Expanding the Pie

Sometimes, solutions can be achieved by increasing a resource in short supply. Perhaps the couple could arrange to take 4 weeks of vacation, thereby spending 2 weeks at each location. This is not as utopian as it may seem because expanding the pie need not necessarily involve getting something for nothing. Thus, if they value their vacation enough, it might be possible for the couple to work overtime during the rest of the year to pay for it. For such solutions to work, however, each party must not find the other's preferred outcome to be aversive; that is, it could work if neither has an intrinsic objection to the other's preference but simply a stronger desire for his or her own choice. In this example, the husband must be able to tolerate going to the seashore and the wife to the mountains. Solutions of this sort are largely based on efforts to help each side get what it wants and to do so by increasing a limited resource (time, money, land, people, security, hard currency, etc.).

2. Nonspecific Compensation

In this case, one party "gives in" but is repaid in some other way. The husband, for example, may agree to go to the seashore but only if he is relieved of housecleaning chores for the next 4 months. By extension, a country may permit a neighbor to flood its markets with exported goods if the exporting country agrees to provide a certain number of jobs for citizens of the importing country. Solutions of this sort require information about what is particularly valued by both parties and what one party may be able (and willing) to provide to another in return for getting its way. An important factor is whether some form of compensation exists that may be of low cost to the donor and high value to the recipient: Perhaps the wife doesn't particularly mind doing the husband's share of the housecleaning, at least for a few months, and perhaps the exporting country actually needs the labor skills of the importer.

3. Logrolling

If both parties differ on the main issues under dispute, and if they differ in their priorities regarding these issues, the possibility exists for creative "logrolling," which is, in a sense, a variant of nonspecific compensation. For example, perhaps the husband-wife disagreement over vacations also involves differences of opinion about the preferred accommodations. Let us say that the wife favors simple, rustic beach cottages, whereas the husband is looking forward to an elegant mountain resort. Perhaps, then, the husband will be quite happy going to the seashore, so long as the wife agrees that they stay in a fancy seaside resort. For successful solutions based on logrolling, it helps to identify potential concessions and to ask, "Are some of my low-priority issues of high priority to the other?"

4. Cost Cutting

Solutions based on cost cutting are those in which one party essentially "wins," but the costs to the other party are reduced or eliminated. Thus, cost-cutting solutions are more one-sided than those discussed above but are nonetheless feasible and potentially stable if the side that "gives in" does not suffer any disadvantage from the agreement. In the case of the husband-wife vacation dispute, perhaps the husband had resisted going to the seashore because he feared being lonely and isolated while his wife was windsurfing; in this case, a cost-cutting solution—and one that could be entirely satisfactory to the husband—might be for the couple to agree to go to the seashore but to do so along with some of their friends, who could provide company for the husband.

5. Bridging

Bridging occurs when the two parties agree to a solution in which neither side wins or loses but rather both agree to a different option from whatever each originally favored. This solution must address the primary interests that underlie the specific issues in dispute. Thus, if the husband wanted to go to the mountains to hike and the wife wanted to go to the seashore for the sun, perhaps it would be possible to find a beach resort near hiking trails (or a vacation site where the mountain weather is dry and sunny). Successful bridging requires that the parties refocus their negotiations from an insistence on their *positions* to an examination of their underlying *interests*. Why are they pushing for their particular position? Is there some alternative outcome that would meet their real needs? Is it really the mountains or the seashore they want, or do these simply provide a means of achieving some other goal, such as sunshine, exercise, comfort, adventure, or simplicity?

Additional Negotiating Techniques

Apparently trivial details can become influential in the negotiating process. In some cases, for example, attention to the physical arrangement of participants may be important: Thus, it can be helpful to seat the rivals on the same side of a table—opposite the negotiator, whose job is to articulate the disagreement— thereby literally facing the problem together, rather than contentiously facing each other. This can encourage both sides to cooperate rather than compete, to concentrate on solving the problem rather than defeating each other. In other cases, a wise conflict resolver might ignore uncooperative statements, rather than allowing them to derail an agreement.

Efficacious Ignoring and Creative Ambiguity

During the Cuban Missile Crisis, for example, the US government received two communications from Nikita Khrushchev, Soviet premier at the time, one conciliatory and the other contentious. At Robert Kennedy's suggestion, the United States simply ignored the latter and responded to the former, thereby avoiding escalation leading to a possible nuclear conflict. (Kennedy was the brother of President John F. Kennedy, and was at that time US Attorney General.)

Clarity is generally a virtue; negotiated agreements can unravel or become a source of irritation when they are interpreted differently by the different parties. For example, British and American diplomats believed that, at the Yalta Conference toward the end of World War II, the Soviet Union had agreed to allow pluralistic democracy in postwar Poland. Soviet diplomats (and some US participants), on the other hand, argued differently. It is also possible, however, that if the expectations and intentions of each side had been spelled out in detail, an even greater falling out would have occurred. Part of the negotiator's art may therefore include recourse to equivocal and imprecise language. On the other hand, imprecise diplomatic language can impede action.

An important current example is United Nations Resolution 242, passed by the UN Security Council after the Six Day War in 1967, in which Israel captured the Gaza Strip (from Egypt), the Golan Heights (from Syria), and the West Bank (from Jordan). Resolution 242 calls for a classic "land for peace" swap between Israel and its Arab neighbors, including "withdrawal of Israeli armed forces from territories occupied in the recent conflict." Note that the wording specifies "withdrawal . . . from territories" rather than "withdrawal . . . from *the* territories." As a result, diplomats have argued for more than 50 years about whether Israel is obliged to remove its forces from all of the occupied territories or just some. (In any event, the outcome in this case has been consistent with the latter.)

Empathy

To avoid misunderstandings, a negotiator might also request that each side must state, as clearly as it can, the arguments of the opposing side. This can help build empathy, a deeper awareness and appreciation of the other's perspective and of the constraints felt by the other. Disputants are often intensely aware of the limitations on their own behavior while imagining that the opponent has great latitude; failure to reach agreement is then likely attributed—by each side—to the other's intransigence, an example of the attribution error discussed in Chapter 6.

Appropriate empathy can lead to a helpful exercise, the "yesable proposition." In this case, each party to a dispute is asked to consider formulating a proposition that the *other* side is likely to accept. This is a subtle but important shift: In most cases, each side makes demands—indeed, the nature of the negotiating process encourages them to do so—that are likely to be outrageous and unacceptable. In the search for "yesable propositions," both sides are more likely to uncover shared interests.

Intermediaries

In the course of seeking an agreement, it can be helpful for the contending parties to make proposals through an intermediary—often a low-ranking one—so that the proposals can be disowned if the other party rejects them out of hand. This avoids the embarrassment that could result from acrimony and ridicule; by having the capability of denying that any such opening was ever made, either side may be more willing to make an initial attempt. For example, during the Cuban Missile Crisis, Premier Khrushchev chose a low-ranking Soviet embassy official to convey his proposal: removal of Soviet missiles from Cuba in return for a US pledge not to invade that island (and, off the record, for the United States also to remove its Jupiter ballistic missiles from Turkey, which the United States had planned to do anyway). In addition, this message was sent to a news broadcaster rather than directly to US officials.

Avoiding Obstacles

Additional suggestions include avoid ultimatums, do not impugn the motives of the other side, try to keep from playing to the crowds, be flexible but not spineless, avoid ad hominem (personal) attacks, avoid nonnegotiable ploys, and do not be so desperate for agreement that you sacrifice future peace for short-term palliatives.

What counts, in the long run, is reaching agreements without either side giving in or resorting to violence. Sometimes it may be possible, even desirable, to paper over disagreements so as to buy time for new events to unfold or for old disputes to grow stale. Nobel Prize–winning Canadian diplomat Lester Pearson noted that he sometimes used language "not so much to record agreement as to conceal a disagreement" that, it was hoped, would disappear in time.[5]

Of course, there is no guarantee that all disputes can be resolved by negotiations. A positive outcome, for example, requires a degree of good will and a genuine desire to reach an agreement. It also requires willingness to "bargain in good faith." There have been cases in which good faith was not shown. For example, in 1939 the Soviet government was openly negotiating with Britain and France for a mutual defense pact against Nazi Germany while at the same time secretly organizing the now-infamous nonaggression (Molotov-Ribbentrop) pact that briefly allied Stalin with Hitler and paved the way for Germany's invasion of Poland. Similarly, Japanese diplomats were negotiating with their US counterparts on December 7, 1941, when Japanese forces attacked Pearl Harbor. And when, in 1955, Soviet negotiators accepted US disarmament proposals, complete with international verification procedures, the US delegation promptly withdrew them, having never thought they would be accepted!

Fortunately, there is good reason to believe that such cases are exceptions. The desire for nonviolent resolution of conflicts appears to be widespread—although it is always possible that governments make such claims, wishing to appear to be "on the side of the angels," while actually planning (even, sometimes, hoping) for a failure of negotiations in order to justify recourse to arms. Nonetheless, other factors—domestic opinion, international law, international organizations, the shared costs of violence—frequently combine to make nonviolent conflict resolution an attractive alternative to the use of force, so long as the participants (including the mediator or arbitrator, if there is one) are both skillful and persistent.

A Final Note on Conflict Resolution

Ultimately, belief in the feasibility of nonviolent conflict resolution—whether by diplomacy or negotiation, strictly between two parties, or with the assistance of a mediator or arbitrator—is just that, an exercise of faith in the underlying goodwill of most people and in their fundamental rationality. Such trust may or may not be warranted. Certainly, the human species has long displayed a penchant for irrational acts, personal as well as collective. But skeptics might consider that the alternative—war—is usually irrational and substantially less ethical.

Moreover, if it seems unrealistic to rely on the rationality of one's opponents, bear in mind that the fundamental strategy of great powers for avoiding direct conflict during the nuclear age—deterrence—relies precisely on just this kind of instrumental rationality and mutual dependence. It is much better, therefore, to employ tactics for the pursuit of conflict resolution than to resort to conflict prolongation or, worse yet, violence as the final arbiter of disputes.

Questions for Further Reflection

1. Identify some factors common to diplomatic successes in averting war; do the same for failures.

2. Analyze an interpersonal conflict you have experienced or observed. Who were the key actors; what were their interests and positions; which methods were used to "manage," "resolve," or "transcend" the conflict; and what were the outcomes for the parties involved? What, if anything, might have been done differently to produce a more "satisfactory" outcome?

3. Distinguish between positional and principled bargaining, giving some examples of each.

4. Choosing examples other than those in this chapter, illustrate at least two of the following negotiating techniques: expanding the pie, nonspecific compensation, logrolling, cost cutting, and bridging.

5. Apply Morgenthau's rules for diplomacy to a contemporary international conflict, such as the US-led war in Iraq, international attempts at stopping genocide in Darfur (Sudan), ending the civil wars in Syria or Yemen, or the efforts to prevent Iran from acquiring nuclear weapons.

Suggestions for Further Reading

G. R. Berridge. 2005. *Diplomacy: Theory and Practice*, 3rd ed. London: Palgrave Macmillan.

Bruce W. Darton and Louis Kriesberg, eds. 2009. *Conflict Transformation and Peacebuilding*. New York: Routledge.

Roger Fisher and William Ury. 1981. *Getting to YES*. Boston: Houghton Mifflin.

Louis Kriesberg. 1998. *Constructive Conflicts*. Oxford: Rowman & Littlefield.

John Paul Lederach. 2003. *The Little Book of Conflict Transformation*. Intercourse, PA: Good Books.

Roy J. Lewicki, David M. Saunders, and Bruce Barry. 2005. *Negotiation*. New York: McGraw Hill.

D. G. Pruitt. 1981. *Negotiation Behavior*. New York: Academic Press.

Oliver Ramsbotham, Tom Woodhouse, and Hugh Miall. 2005. *Contemporary Conflict Resolution*. Cambridge, UK: Polity.

Robert Trager. 2017. *Diplomacy: Communication and the Origins of International Order*. New York: Cambridge University Press.

Peter Wallensteen. 2015. *Understanding Conflict Resolution*, 4th ed. London: SAGE.

Notes

1. Randolph S. Bourne. 1964. *War and the Intellectuals, Collected Essays 1915–1919*. New York: Harper & Row.

2. Hans Morgenthau. 1978. *Politics Among Nations*. New York: Knopf.

3. Fred Charles Iklé. 1964. *How Nations Negotiate*. New York: Harper & Row.

4. R. Fisher and W. Ury. 1981. *Getting to YES*. Boston: Houghton Mifflin.

5. Lester B. Pearson. 1949. *Diplomacy in the Nuclear Age*. Cambridge, MA: Harvard University Press.

13

Disarmament and Arms Control

Virtually no one—not even the most ardent advocates of disarmament—claim that doing away with weapons, in general or with certain ones in particular, will solve the problem of violence. So long as the underlying causes of personal, group, and state conflict remain, and as long as human beings possess the capacity, and the inclination, to resort to violence under certain circumstances, war will continue to haunt us. Nonetheless, advocates of peace often favor eliminating weapons, or at least establishing strict control over them. In this chapter, we examine some aspect of disarmament and its cousin, arms control.

Jens Schlueter via Getty Images

Disarmament and Arms Control

Virtually no one—not even the most ardent advocates of disarmament—claim that doing away with weapons in general, or with certain ones in particular, will solve the problem of violence. So long as the underlying causes of personal, group, and state conflict remain, and as long as human beings possess the capacity and inclination to resort to violence under certain circumstances, war will continue to haunt us. Nonetheless, advocates of peace often favor eliminating weapons or, at least exercising strict control over them. In this chapter, we examine some aspects of disarmament and its cousin, arms control.

Different Visions of Disarmament

Arms Control and Gun Control

There have been many different visions of disarmament. Perhaps the simplest is General and Complete Disarmament, or GCD (General = all countries; Complete = all weapons). Not surprisingly, there are problems with this proposal, one of which is how to define a weapon. Dynamite, for example, can make an effective weapon, but it is also used for seemingly commercial purposes, such as mining or demolition. And what about firearms? Many citizens of the United States, for example, fervently maintain that "the right of the people to keep and bear arms shall not be infringed," as stated in the Second Amendment to the Constitution (aka the Bill of Rights). Others point to the article's precise wording, which begins, "A well-regulated militia being necessary to the security of a free State . . ." implying that this constitutional guarantee applies only to governmental entities, not to individuals.

In many ways, the heated debate over gun control in the United States mirrors issues of arms control and disarmament more generally: Opponents point to a perceived right (to keep guns) and to the supposedly comparable necessity of state sovereignty (to maintain national weaponry). They also maintain that "if guns are outlawed, only outlaws will have guns," just as opponents of arms control and disarmament point to the anarchy prevailing in international affairs and to the danger that a disarmed country will be at the mercy of aggressive armed states. At the same time, advocates of gun control emphasize that the easy availability of firearms contributes significantly to the high rate of violence, just as advocates of arms control and disarmament note the widespread "security dilemma," whereby the multilateral pursuit of military power tends to make everyone less secure. (From 2009 to 2016, 225,000 Americans died from gun violence, which is roughly the number of Syrians who died from the ongoing civil war in that country during the same period.)

Opponents of gun control argue that "an armed society is a polite society," whereas advocates point to the rate at which members of armed societies kill one another. Even as gun control opponents are fond of suggesting that "guns don't kill people; people do," arms control opponents emphasize that the problem is not military hardware but the aggressive designs of certain malevolent leaders, while to proponents of gun control as well as advocates of arms control and disarmament, it is absurd to think that more weapons—whether personal firearms or national military forces—make for safer individuals or a safer world.

In heavily armed societies, control and elimination of personal weapons might make disarmed individuals vulnerable to those who cheat by retaining their weapons; a similar concern is expressed with regard to the disarmament of states. In both cases, the possession of weaponry is like riding a tiger: Not only dangerous, it requires great care in extricating oneself from the perilous encounter. And many studies indicate that the folks most likely to be injured by firearms are their owners and/or their relatives. Most contemporary proposals for gun control in the United States call for elimination of those firearms that are especially lethal (e.g., semi-automatic weapons and large capacity magazines) or likely to fall into the wrong hands (e.g., "Saturday night specials"). A parallel can once again be drawn with proposals for arms control, which usually stop short of total disarmament.

Maintenance of National Security Capabilities

A less ambitious goal than general and complete disarmament was proposed at the end of World War I by President Woodrow Wilson in his Fourteen Points, which he recommended as international goals. Wilson called for national disarmament "to the lowest point consistent with domestic safety." This suggests that states would be allowed to retain police forces but nothing capable of threatening other states. A large police force sufficient for maintaining law and order inside China, however, might be quite threatening to Korea or Vietnam, just as a mobile Russian police force could threaten Ukraine, Estonia, and its other eastern and southern neighbors.

At the Versailles conference in 1918, Wilson's proposal was watered down to "the reduction of national armaments to the lowest point consistent with *national* safety," [italics added], terminology that leaves much open to interpretation. A state like Poland, for example, located on the wide plains of Europe and bordered by such historically threatening neighbors as Germany and Russia, would require a larger military force than does Switzerland, which has many natural mountain barriers. And the United States, with a friendly neighbor, Canada, to the north, a porous but protected border with Mexico to the south, and oceans to its east and west, would appear to need relatively little in the way of military force—unless (as has been the case for many decades) it considers that its national "safety" requires a military presence via bases, advisers, and/or the capacity for intervention in countries overseas.

Disarmament is not uniquely applied to sovereign governments. Among the most contentious issues arising between governments and insurgent movements are those involving potential disarmament of the latter.

Governments often refuse to negotiate with armed opponents; conversely, it is easy to see why revolutionary and other insurgent groups—especially those deemed "terrorist organizations"—typically resist being disarmed! This can readily lead to a kind of "chicken and egg problem," in which each side refuses to budge until the other does so.

For decades, for example, the Israeli government refused to negotiate with the Palestine Liberation Organization, considering it a group of armed "terrorists," just as "decommissioning" (disarming) of the Irish Republican Army was long a precondition set by the British government in Northern Ireland before any peace plan could be implemented. There have been some hopeful developments, however; in Colombia, scene of one of the longest-lasting insurrections, the government and the rebel group known as the FARC, agreed in 2015 to peace and disarmament, sponsored by the United Nations. Since then, violence between the government and rebel forces has resumed, and the outcome of this conflict is far from clear. More recently, the US and the Afghan Taliban have negotiated a fragile agreement to reduce the violence in that war-beleaguered country. The result of this negotiated ceasefire is also uncertain.

Selective Disarmament

One possibility for reducing the number and lethality of armaments is to disarm selectively, focusing on offensive weapons because they are especially destabilizing. This was the goal of the Geneva Disarmament Conference of 1932; it failed because of nations' collective inability to reach agreement on exactly which weapons are defensive and which are offensive (states typically define their own armaments as the former and those of their opponents as the latter). When the United States initially ended its occupation of South Korea in 1949, it removed airplanes and tanks, seeking in this way to ensure that South Korea would not be emboldened to attack the North. One result was that North Korea, instead, attacked South Korea, which found it difficult to mount an effective defense after being deprived of these "offensive" weapons. In response, the United States, under UN authorization, sent thousands of troops to the Korean peninsula, where they remain to this day, more than six decades after the ensuing Korean War.

The most popular version of selective or qualitative disarmament is the enthusiasm that countries have for disarmament of the *other*, allegedly more aggressive, countries but not for themselves. This was notable during the US–Soviet arms race, when many observers concluded that the two superpowers colluded in creating a "duopoly," whereby the two superpowers excluded others from being major players on the world stage.

There is a fable that describes a disarmament conference held among the animals. The eagle, eyeing the bull, recommends that all horns be cut off. The bull, looking at the tiger, suggests that sharp teeth and claws should be pulled. The tiger, sizing up the elephant, urges that tusks be filed down. The elephant, looking at the eagle, insists that all would be well if only wings and beaks were clipped. Then the bear speaks up in tones of sweetness and reason: "Come now, my friends, let us abandon these halfway measures and agree to abolish all weapons, and simply resolve any disagreements with a great, friendly hug."

Weapons of Mass Destruction

The possibility nonetheless exists for mutually agreed restrictions on demonstrably offensive weapons, such as bombers, motorized artillery, and the like. Perhaps the greatest prospect—as well as the greatest need—for selective disarmament concerns nuclear, biological, and chemical weapons ("weapons of mass destruction," or WMDs) because of the unique threats they pose. In addition, nuclear weapons— especially when combined with fast and highly accurate delivery systems—are especially unstable because they arouse fear of a preemptive strike. This makes enforceable and monitored selective disarmament agreements, particularly regarding WMDs, uniquely important.

Military Budgets

Reductions and restrictions in military budgets have often been considered by national leaders and their advisers. Not surprisingly, there have been problems. For example, if all states are restricted to the same total expenditure, then Luxembourg, a tiny country with few enemies, would have the same military budget as Russia, which has long borders and much greater need for defense. But if larger states are permitted larger military budgets based on their size (such as an internationally agreed percentage of area, population, or gross national product), then by virtue of their larger military, they could pose a threat to smaller states.

In addition, difficulties arise in determining the actual military expenditures of many states that do not publish reliable figures. Even the budget for the US Department of Defense (DOD) is misleading: It does not include the costs of nuclear bombs and warheads, for example, which are included in the Department of Energy budget. US military expenditures (including nuclear weapons and international military assistance, but not counting the Veterans Administration). For the fiscal year 2020, the DOD's budget totaled more than $700 billion. Including all military-related spending, the US defense expenditures for 2020–2021 amount to more than $900 billion, roughly equal to the military budgets of the next seven highest-spending countries in the world, many of which are members of NATO or other US allies

Weapons-Free Zones

The idea here is to agree on the elimination of weapons within a designated geographic area. For example, under the Treaty of Tlatelolco (named for a suburb of Mexico City), most of the states of the Western Hemisphere agreed not to develop or deploy nuclear weapons (the United States, of course, is not a party to this treaty, but, perhaps surprisingly, neither is Canada). The African Nuclear Weapon Free Zone Treaty, also known as the Treaty of Pelindaba (named after South Africa's main nuclear research center) has been ratified by 28 African nations and came into force in 2009. Similar proposals have been made for the Middle East, Australasia, the Balkans, and Scandinavia. Many local communities and districts in individual nations, including the United States, have also declared themselves Nuclear-Free Zones—although it is unclear what (if any) are the practical consequences.

Verifiable agreement to forgo all weapons within a designated zone, or even just those of a certain type, can help diminish concerns that a local rival is seeking to gain superiority. Consequently, such agreements could diminish pressure to push ahead with armaments that—when matched by the adversary—would ultimately diminish the security of all concerned. Thus, they offer the prospect of emerging from the Prisoner's Dilemma (discussed in Chapter 15).

For a little-known historical example that offers useful insight, consider the Rush-Bagot Treaty of 1817. This agreement laid the basis for the demilitarization of the US-Canada border, thus setting the stage for good relations between these two North American neighbors. It wasn't merely cosmetic, calling, among other things, for a 3,000-mile unfortified border and for the dismantling of a number of naval vessels, which had been built on the Great Lakes and were too large to be sailed. Significantly, this agreement was reached only 2 years after the United States and Great Britain—then governing Canada—had fought each other in the War of 1812, which included several naval battles on the Great Lakes.

Looking at US–Canadian relations today, we blithely take peace between these "good neighbors" for granted; but at the time of the Rush-Bagot Treaty, things were very different. Even the treaty itself did not immediately lead to peace; rather, distrust and several near-wars characterized the ensuing several decades. However, in this case, a disarmament agreement hastened a genuine peace. If threatening naval vessels had been allowed to continue patrolling the Great Lakes, and if military fortifications had been constructed along the US–Canadian border, relations between the two countries might have gone quite differently.

Another type of disarmament agreement, similar to the establishment of a weapons-free zone, occurs when all parties agree to preserve the political neutrality (nonalignment) of a particular country. Following World War II, for example, the victorious allies occupied Austria. By the Austrian State

Treaty of 1955, all sides agreed to end that military occupation, signing an accord whereby the state of Austria was essentially demilitarized and pledged to neutrality.

A Brief History of Disarmament

Self-Serving Plans

Governments have on occasion tried to reduce armaments, and sometimes they have even succeeded. But the history of such efforts is largely one of failure. After the Napoleonic Wars, for example, Czar Alexander led an (unsuccessful) effort to save governmental funds via multilateral disarmament. Later, Czar Nicholas II convened the first Hague Peace Conference in 1899, once again attempting to stave off an arms race that threatened to lead to bankruptcy.

But self-serving motivations—especially the desire to appear peace-loving—have also been important. After taking office in 1981, for example, President Reagan showed himself to be not only uninterested in disarmament but antagonistic to it, especially during his first term in office. Later, the US government begrudgingly entered into nuclear negotiations with the Soviet Union, almost certainly as a response to mounting political pressure, both within the United States and in Europe, and also as a result of the efforts of Soviet leader Mikhail Gorbachev and his advisers.

Other practical concerns have motivated disarmament efforts as well. For example, when Czar Nicholas II suggested a freeze on all military budgets in 1899, Russia already had the largest army in Europe; a freeze would have perpetuated that asymmetry. Winston Churchill proposed a naval-building "holiday" to the Germans during 1912 to 1914, when the UK was ahead, especially in battleships. Immediately following World War II, the United States proposed the Baruch Plan, which would have required that all states abandon the possibility of producing their own nuclear weapons, *after which* the United States would place its nuclear facilities under international supervision. This would have left the US the only state with the knowledge and ability to produce nuclear weapons in the future. The Soviets countered with a plan of their own, whereby the United States would dispose of its nuclear facilities *first*, after which other states would join in. It was argued in the West that the Soviet Union, as a vast and secretive society, would have had a greater opportunity to cheat if it sought to do so. The United States objected, and an arms race with the Soviet Union ensued. In short, disarmament negotiations and conferences have often served as a forum for advancing the interests of each state and for prosecuting interstate rivalry, rather than as a means of diminishing those rivalries.

During nuclear arms negotiations in the 1980s, the Soviet Union tried to restrict cruise missiles, forward-basing of nuclear forces, and most new technological developments in the arms race: all areas in which the United States was ahead. The US, in turn, urged reductions in large throw-weight intercontinental ballistic missiles (ICBMs, in which the Soviets were ahead), while zealously protecting its advantage in strategic bombers and submarine-based missiles.

Germany disarmed briefly after World Wars I and II; ditto for Japan after World War II. But in these cases, the victors of those wars simply imposed disarmament on the losers; there is no evidence that the people of Germany and Japan suddenly came to appreciate the merits of disarmament, although vigorous domestic peace movements had developed in both countries. Subsequently, the United States encouraged its new ally, West Germany, to rearm during the 1950s and eventually to join the North Atlantic Treaty Organization, much to the dismay of the Soviet Union. US government officials have long urged Japanese leaders to devote a larger share of Japan's national budget to its military. Following World War II, Japanese military spending had always been less than 1 percent of its GNP, and, according to its postwar constitution, Japan pledged never to maintain offensive forces. In 2015, however, the Japanese government approved a new policy under which its military could be deployed overseas if an ally (notably South Korea) were attacked and there is a continuing discussion in Japanese decision-making circles about increasing Japan's offensive military capabilities, and even the possibility of Japan—which has plutonium, rockets, and foes, especially nuclear-armed North Korea —developing its own nuclear stockpile.

Failed Attempts

At a disarmament conference held in 1931, considerable excitement ensued when several Afghans were found to be in attendance; the conference organizers were delighted that the idea of disarmament had spread so far and was being so widely pursued. But when asked why they were attending, the Afghans replied, "If these nations really are going to disarm themselves, perhaps we can pick up some weapons cheaply."

Disarmament policies have often served simply to show the general public that efforts are being made in a peaceful direction and that any failures are due to the stubbornness of other countries. Attempts at renouncing war by treaty have also been notable failures. By the early 1920s, the Treaty of Versailles appeared to be unraveling, with Germany refusing to pay its obligated World War I reparations and France responding by sending troops to occupy Germany's Ruhr Valley. The German foreign minister then organized a peace conference involving the major European powers, hoping to head off the establishment of a new anti-German alliance. At a meeting in Locarno, Italy, numerous agreements were reached, including demilitarization of the Rhineland and a mutual defense treaty linking France to both Poland and Czechoslovakia. Enthusiasm ran high for the outlawing of war altogether, and, shortly thereafter, French foreign minister Aristide Briand proposed to US secretary of state Frank Kellogg that, on the 10th anniversary of the US entry into World War I, France and the United States sign an agreement outlawing war between the two states.

The US government responded with unexpected enthusiasm, urging that the proposed instrument be expanded to a worldwide renunciation of "war as an instrument of national policy," in addition to a further agreement that "the settlement or solution of all international disputes or conflicts . . . shall never be sought except by peaceful means." Unfortunately, the Kellogg-Briand Pact of 1928 was unenforceable, and—along with the "Spirit of Locarno"—may have unwittingly done more harm than good because it gave a false sense of security to states that were already peace loving and a smokescreen behind which aggressive states were able to pursue their ambitions. The Kellogg-Briand Pact became a prototype of meaningless and often misleading "statements of principle." On the other hand, such agreements may be important in affirming a widespread yearning for dramatic reductions in armaments.

Violations of the Kellogg-Briand Pact were also part of the charges against former Nazi officials in the Nuremberg Trials, after World War II.

Modest Successes

When Albert Einstein was asked his opinion of the Geneva disarmament conference of 1926, he responded,

> What would you think about a meeting of a town council which is concerned because an increasing number of people are knifed to death each night in drunken brawls, and which proceeds to discuss just how long and how sharp shall be the knife that the inhabitants of the city may be permitted to carry?[1]

There have, however, been some modest examples of successful disarmament. The Washington Naval Conference resulted in a 1922 treaty that caused the United States, Britain, and Japan to scrap 40 percent of their capital ships (battleships and aircraft carriers). Certain minor restrictions on weapons systems have been imposed, including the elimination of expanding ("dum-dum") bullets, prohibitions against the use of poison gas, and a ban on landmines (unfortunately ignored or evaded by many countries, including the United States). Poison gas was used, however, by the Iraqi government against rebel Kurds during the late 1980s and also by the Damascus government, and possibly by other combatants as well, during Syria's civil war.

Arms Control

In the aftermath of World War II—widely seen in the United States not only as a "good war" but also as one that was hastened by the West's reluctance to arm adequately in the 1930s—public enthusiasm for disarmament waned significantly. The two emerging superpowers, the United States and the Soviet Union, each proposed plans for disarmament, but these were mostly a mixture of propaganda ploys and efforts to achieve unilateral advantage over the other. By the late 1950s, governments began to turn their attention from disarmament to a more modest and attainable goal, especially regarding nuclear weapons—namely, "arms control."

There were many reasons for this shift. Following Stalin's death in 1953, and spearheaded by Soviet premier Nikita Khrushchev and US president Dwight Eisenhower, the Cold War thawed somewhat. Improvements in technology permitted verification with greater confidence, especially by satellite surveillance. The ongoing arms race had heightened citizen anxiety and pushed the West in particular to recognize the growing dangers posed by radioactive fallout from above-ground nuclear testing. And, finally, with its acquisition of ICBMs and a growing nuclear arsenal, the Soviet Union essentially achieved strategic parity with the United States, thereby permitting both superpowers to negotiate in earnest, from a position of more or less equivalent strength. (It has been said that there are two rules for negotiators: Don't negotiate when you are behind, and don't negotiate when you are ahead. Hence, the best opportunity for progress often comes when two sides are functionally equal.)

To many dovish critics, arms control is a smokescreen, a thinly veiled excuse for continuing to accumulate weapons, all the while quieting the public with claims that "progress" is being made. Moreover, arms controllers are usually concerned with managing and stabilizing any existing arms race; disarmers, by contrast, do not seek to stabilize an arms race but rather to *destabilize* and end what physicist Herbert York called a "race to oblivion" altogether.

To its hawkish critics, arms control is only minimally more acceptable than unilateral disarmament, which is utterly anathema; it is considered a snare and a delusion whereby a country allows itself to be outmaneuvered at the bargaining table by its adversary. Their presumption is that the other side is untrustworthy and will cheat; moreover, that the other side will settle only for victory—or at least remaining continually ahead. To some extent, a free-for-all arms race, unfettered by international agreements, also reflects the economic free market, beloved by political conservatives and market fundamentalists.

These, then, are some of the hidden, unpeaceful goals of arms control: gaining a unilateral advantage either by ending competition when you are ahead or by steering competition into an area of one's advantage; establishing a monopoly that effectively subjugates other states; and creating the false impression of progress, thereby quieting domestic dissatisfaction. The official, legitimate goals of arms control are as follows:

1. *Reduce the likelihood that war will break out, by removing some of the more threatening situations or weapons.* For example, World War I might have been averted if some agreement had been reached that dampened competition for early mobilization on both sides. De-alerting of nuclear missiles can diminish fears of a surprise attack, thereby also reducing the danger of war being provoked by error or false alarm.

2. *Prevent competition that could be not only financially ruinous but also strategically destabilizing.* The Anti-Ballistic Missile (ABM) Treaty of 1972, in which the United States and the Soviet Union agreed to limit ABM's to 100 each at two different bases, and to refrain from developing and deploying updated missiles, headed off a militarily futile and economically wasteful escalating spiral between each side's offensive and defensive weapons. This treaty was, however, unilaterally abrogated by the George W. Bush administration in 2001, producing significant tension with Russia, which subsequently withdrew from the restrictions of a conventional forces treaty in Europe.

3. *Create an environment of increasing trust and confidence.* By reaching agreements—even over trivial issues—rival parties might progressively gain greater confidence in each other, as they become increasingly familiar with their counterparts, comfortable with their motivations, and thus more willing to engage in serious agreements in the future. Of course, such confidence-building measures (CBMs) also presuppose that the participants are well-meaning and that the agreements in question will be adhered to.

4. *To increase the probability that, in the event that war breaks out, it will be less destructive than it otherwise would have been without an arms control agreement between the belligerents.* The major powers appear to have destroyed biological warfare agents, following an international agreement in 1972, along with chemical weapons stocks, as called for in an international agreement in the late 1990s. One hypothetical danger is that in making war less destructive, it might also be rendered more tolerable and, therefore, a more acceptable instrument of national policy. After all, deterrence generally rests on the proposition that by making the costs of war *intolerable*, it will be prevented.

Some Current Agreements

Many arms control treaties have been signed since 1945, most of them related to nuclear weapons. Although the list of such treaties is long, the results are not impressive because the parties to these agreements have generally been willing to restrict only those arms-related activities that they were not interested in pursuing. For decades, arguably, the real arms race underlying the US/USSR's Cold War was between arms-builders and arms-controllers. And the arms promoters prevailed—as evidenced by the tens of thousands of weapons and delivery systems that were and are still being constructed. But the arms-controllers have had some successes.

Test Ban Treaties

Nuclear weapons have been banned from the Antarctic continent, from planetary orbit, and from the seabed. In 1963, the Partial Test Ban Treaty, or PTBT, capped many years of public protest against rising levels of worldwide fallout from atmospheric nuclear tests. Signatories agreed to refrain from atmospheric, outer space, and undersea nuclear testing, although testing was not stopped altogether. Instead, testing of new nuclear weapons was moved to underground sites or to controlled simulations in laboratories. In addition, the governments of China, France, India, and Pakistan refused to sign the PTBT and persisted in testing above ground (China) and beneath the ocean (France). Non-signatories India, Pakistan, and North Korea have detonated low-level nuclear explosions.

The United States hasn't tested nuclear weapons since 1992 and has no immediate plans to do so, arguing that it has already conducted more than 1,000 nuclear tests (more than any other state), and has therefore accumulated sufficient information plus the capacity for computer-based simulations to render actual explosions unnecessary. The real goal of most anti-testing advocates was—and continues to be—a Comprehensive Test Ban Treaty (CTBT), which would constrain all nuclear testing, underground as well as above ground.

In addition to its environmental benefits as a straightforward antipollution measure, a worldwide halt to nuclear testing would help to prevent proliferation. In particular, it would make it much more difficult—and perhaps impossible—for China, India, and Pakistan to deploy multiple warheads because doing so would require extensive testing to validate the reliability of new, more compact warhead designs. Finally, a global CTBT would offer a counterintuitive benefit. Although most weapons experts agree that testing is not required for confidence in the nuclear stockpile, the political reality is that without regular testing, some uncertainty is inevitable, and this uncertainty itself contributes to a kind of stability by making a first strike less likely: no country would want to be in the position of having launched an initial attack, only to have some of its warheads bump against another side's missile silos without detonating, leaving the would-be victim armed, presumably more than a bit annoyed (!) and likely inclined to massive retaliation.

A CTBT was signed in 1996 and ratified by the Russian Duma (legislature) in 2000. As of 2020, 184 states have signed—including the US—and 168 (not including the US) have ratified it. Of the 44 "Annex States," which are deemed nuclear capable and whose ratification are specifically required by the CTBT for its entry into force, India, Pakistan, and North Korea still have not signed, and only 36 have ratified the treaty.

Ratification of the CTBT by the United States might bring other countries along. China, for example, signed and has announced that it will ratify the CTBT if the United States does. Importantly, the Obama administration canceled plans to develop and deploy a new "reliable replacement warhead," electing to rely on a highly sophisticated "stockpile-stewardship program," and thus keeping the door open for an eventual worldwide CTBT. However, Trump Administration hawks made it clear that they would like the US to resume testing, while some conservatives have thus far prevented congressional ratification by the United States, claiming that (1) such a ban could not be satisfactorily verified and (2) even if it could, continued testing is necessary to ensure the reliability of the existing nuclear arsenal. Non-ratification of the CTBT has done much to deprive the US of any claim to leadership in promoting nuclear disarmament, or even arms control more generally. This also raises the possibility that other countries, notably Pakistan and India, will continue to expand their own nuclear arsenals and leaves the door open for Israel to do the same.

Verification

US President Ronald Reagan famously pronounced, with respect to nuclear arms negotiations with the Soviet Union: "trust, but verify" (a translation of a Russian proverb that, ironically, had been a favorite expression of Lenin). In this regard, the capacity of the United States to monitor nuclear testing unilaterally, as well as the capabilities of the International Monitoring System (IMS), now substantially exceed what had been predicted in 1999, such that any state attempting to cheat by testing a nuclear weapon would almost certainly be detected. Only one state, North Korea, has conducted nuclear tests since 1998. Each time, the IMS—although less robust than it is at present—successfully detected these rather feeble ("fizzle yield") tests. More recently, the successful North Korean tests have also been unambiguously detected.

More than a decade ago, a report by the US National Academy of Sciences, in consultation with senior scientific and military officials, concluded that the "U.S. is now better able to maintain a safe and effective nuclear stockpile and to monitor clandestine nuclear explosion testing than at any time in the past," and that a strong case can thus be made that there is little to be concerned about regarding the maintenance of the US nuclear stockpile and verification of a CTBT. The issue is currently one of political will rather than technological capability or strategic vulnerability.

Communications Agreements

The "Hot Line" agreement (1963) established an emergency communications link between Washington (the Pentagon) and the Kremlin. This was subsequently updated and modernized, with the addition of satellite links and so-called crisis control centers in each capital. In the Nuclear Accidents Agreement (1971), the two superpowers agreed to notify each other in the event of accidental or unauthorized nuclear detonations, and a High Seas Agreement (1972) sought to establish rules of conduct to minimize the chances of oceanic collisions and misunderstandings during naval maneuvers. In 1975, nearly all European states agreed to the Final Act of the Conference on Security and Co-operation in Europe (CSCE, better known as the Helsinki Accords), which ratified the post–World War II map of Europe and also arranged for advance notification of large military exercises.

Biological and Chemical Weapons

The Biological Weapons Convention (1972) committed the signatory states to refrain from developing, producing, or stockpiling biological weapons (primarily viruses and bacteria). The Environmental Modification Convention (1977) prohibited the alteration of the environment, including climate, of an adversary, and the "Convention on the Prohibition of the Development, Production, Stockpiling and Use of Chemical Weapons and on Their Destruction" entered into force in 1997.

Strategic Nuclear Weapons

The following two sections contain somewhat detailed descriptions of agreements and their numerical specifications; critics call this "bean counting," and we suggest to students less interested in it that they familiarize themselves with the general outlines but feel free to refrain from memorizing the precise arithmetic.

The first set of Strategic Arms Limitation Talks, or SALT I, resulted in an Interim Agreement (1972) that established numerical limits for American- and Soviet-guided missile submarines, submarine-launched ballistic missiles (SLBMs), and ICBMs. SALT II (1979) established various additional restrictions on strategic weaponry but fell victim to domestic US politics, having been strongly opposed by influential right-wing groups. Under the Reagan administration, the United States unilaterally breached certain terms of SALT II and then belatedly began negotiations on a replacement, known as START (Strategic Arms Reduction Treaty). Critics maintained that these talks were initiated with no serious expectation of success, but only to quiet the US peace movement. A START I treaty was, however, signed in 1991, ratified by the US Senate as well as by the Russian Duma, and came into effect in 1994. Among other things, it achieved a complex mix of reductions in missile launchers and in numbers of warheads to about 6,500 on each side.

In 2000, the Russian Duma ratified the START II agreement, by which the two sides agreed to a maximum of 3,500 strategic warheads each by 2007. Russia— seemingly eager to reduce the cost of maintaining its expensive arsenal—has urged that START III, the next step, ought to decrease the number of strategic warheads to 1,500, although during the Bush administration the United States resisted such reductions while also agitating for a new generation of warheads, including earth penetrators or "bunker busters." The Obama administration vowed not to develop these weapons, whereas the Trump Administration included these devices in its plans.

New START

Under this treaty, approved by the US Senate in late 2010, the United States and Russia agreed to significantly limit the numbers of deployed strategic weapons seven years from when the treaty enters into force. Under the terms of New START, each country can determine the structure of its own strategic forces but within aggregate limits specified by the treaty: 1,550 total strategic warheads, whether deployed ICBMs or SLBMs, with each deployed heavy bomber equipped to carry nuclear weapons counting as one warhead toward this limit. This opened the door for the development and deployment of a new generation of air-launched cruise missiles.

New Start permits each side one-quarter the strategic armament level allowed by the 1991 START treaty and only about one-third of the deployed strategic warhead limit allowed by the 2002 Moscow treaty. Under New START, thousands more warheads can, however, be kept in storage as a backup force; in addition, its restrictions do not apply to hundreds of short-range nuclear weapons in the US and Russian arsenals.

New START mandates a combined limit of 800 deployed and nonde-ployed ICBM launchers, SLBM launchers, and heavy bombers equipped for nuclear arms. The treaty also establishes a verification regime that mandates 18 onsite inspections per year, replacing a long-standing mutual inspection regime that lapsed in 2009. In addition, it mandates data exchanges and advance notification of any tests related to strategic offensive arms while also granting both countries unrestricted unilateral use of Earth-orbiting satel-lites and prohibiting interference with each other's satellites. Data exchanges are also organized with respect to the number, locations, and technical char-acteristics of all weapons systems and facilities subject to the treaty.

Unique among arms control treaties, New START also provides each ICBM, SLBM, and heavy bomber with an identifying number that allows its pres-ence or absence to be confirmed during every inspection. Both the United States and Russia have agreed to a mutual annual exchange of telemetric information to monitor missile performance during ICBM and SLBM test flights. The treaty also establishes a Bilateral Consultative Commission that will meet at least twice per year to iron out any difficulties in compliance. Part of the expressed motivation for supporting New START was the Obama administration's recognition that it cannot expect other countries to reduce or limit their weaponry unless the United States demonstrates its willingness to do the same. (A similar argument applies to restrictions in greenhouse gas emissions; see Chapter 20.)

However, in order to generate sufficient political support for ratifica-tion, treaties that limit nuclear weapons must often include compromises demanded by "hawks" within each country. In this case, a "Resolution of Advice and Consent" was certified by President Obama in early 2011 in which the administration undertook to *"modernize or replace* the triad of strategic nuclear delivery systems: a heavy bomber and air-launched cruise missile, an Intercontinental Ballistic Missile (ICBM), and a nuclear powered ballistic missile submarine (SSBN) as well as a new Submarine-Launched Ballistic Missile (SLBM)." President Trump denounced this treaty as some-how favoring Moscow. It is due to expire in January, 2021, one day after the forthcoming presidential inauguration. Given that renegotiation, and even simple renewal of such complex treaties takes considerable time, the fate of New START is uncertain at best.

Euromissiles and the INF Treaty

Euromissiles provide a notable example of successful albeit limited nuclear disarmament, yet it has subsequently been abrogated. The emplacement of US limited-range missiles in Germany, Italy, and the United Kingdom was a very contentious issue between 1979 and 1989, beginning with the Soviet deployment of medium-range, SS-20 ballistic missiles in Eastern Europe, which NATO insisted upon matching with Pershing II ballistic missiles and ground-launched cruise missiles. The ensuing situation was potentially dan-gerous because the Euromissiles on both sides not only were highly accurate but also had very short flight times, which threatened to precipitate a "hair-trigger" pattern of mutual apprehension and possible accidental or deliber-ate attacks. Opposition to these Euromissiles was very intense in Europe, leading to many huge protests, both in the UK and on the continent.

The Euromissile crisis was resolved when, just before the dissolution of the Soviet Union, both the West and the USSR accepted the "zero option," whereby the Intermediate Range Nuclear Forces (INF) Treaty—signed by US President Reagan and Soviet General Secretary Gorbachev in 1987—eliminated this entire class of nuclear delivery systems, specifically banning US and Russian missiles with ranges of 500–5,500 kilometers (310–3420 miles). For three decades, it was a successful nuclear weapons treaty, resulting in the destruction of hundreds of nuclear-capable missiles, launch systems, and transporter vehicles.

The INF Treaty has, however, subsequently encountered insurmountable challenges from both Russia and the United States, such that it is now defunct. The US formally withdrew from this treaty in 2019, and Russia followed suit a day later. President Trump had objected that it did not include China and also claimed that Russia had been violating it. Russia was accused of having tested both ballistic and cruise missiles that exceeded the 500 km limit, while Russian officials claimed that their ranges were just below this threshold and that the US was simply using this claim as a pretext to abrogate the treaty. (As with most such treaties, hawkish politicians and military people chafe at any restrictions on their freedom of action and escalation.) China was indeed not a signatory, in part because if it were, roughly 90 percent of its missiles would have to be eliminated.

Moreover, the INF Treaty did not place any restrictions on air- or sea-launched cruise missiles, an area in which the US has long had a substantial advantage. By abrogating this treaty rather than expanding it to include China as well as tightening verification and restrictions on permitted missile ranges, the US and Russia have eliminated one of the most important guardrails limiting nuclear weapons competition, resulting in the escalation of tensions between the two nuclear superpowers. Hence, it has thus far been a victory for pro-nuclearists on all sides.

Policy Modifications

Certain policy decisions, although not strictly treaty-based because they are made unilaterally, constitute important modifications of nuclear policy. In particular, every five years the US government develops a "Nuclear Posture Review."

During President Obama's first term, this strategic doctrine was revised, with the declaration that "the fundamental role" of nuclear weapons is to "deter nuclear attacks on the U.S., allies or partners," which constitutes a narrower policy statement than had existed in the past. This modified policy also eliminates much of the deliberate ambiguity that in the past had surrounded the possible use of nuclear weapons in that for the first time, the United States explicitly committed itself to *not using* such weapons "against nonnuclear states that are in compliance with the Nuclear Nonproliferation Treaty," even if they attacked the United States with such other weapons of mass destruction as biological or chemical weaponry.

The US government also renounced the development of any new nuclear weapons—part of an avowed policy first articulated by President Obama in Prague, Czech Republic, in the spring of 2009, which explicitly embraced the goal of eventually making nuclear weapons obsolete worldwide. For various reasons, however, neither the United States nor the other current nuclear powers have taken the dramatic steps needed to secure a nuclear-free world, in no small part because the Trump Administration reversed these stated goals and embraced an escalated nuclear weapons regime.

In the recent past, there were some revealing changes in the nuclear weapons component of the US military budget: an increase in funds allocated for "fissile material disposition" (safely isolating and when possible disposing of plutonium and highly enriched uranium within the United States) as well as in projects concerning global and cooperative "Threat Reduction Programs," focused primarily on securing fissionable material worldwide, sponsoring reactor conversions, and a variety of anti-smuggling initiatives aimed at combating prospects of such material falling into the hands of terrorists or "rogue governments." These changes, many of them reversed or halted by the Trump Administration, await revitalization by the incoming Biden Administration.

A growing consensus holds that nuclear weapons do not provide the security benefits that had once been attributed to them, with many strategists, including such former avowed nuclearists as Henry Kissinger and George P. Schultz (secretaries of state in the Nixon and Reagan Administrations, respectively), believing that the opposite is true: that world security would be enhanced by verifiably reducing US and Russian nuclear arsenals, which are largely relics of the Cold War. Even the Pentagon's 2012 strategy document *Sustaining U.S. Global Leadership: Priorities for 21st Century Defense* stated that "It is possible that our deterrence goals can be achieved with a smaller nuclear force, which would reduce the number of nuclear weapons in our inventory as well as their role in US national security strategy." It seems increasingly clear that the major threats facing the world today—including but not limited to proliferation, terrorism, cyberattacks, environmental degradation, energy shortages, global pandemics, and so forth—cannot be addressed by nuclear arms.

Once again, however, this perspective was not shared by the Trump Administration, whose 2018 Nuclear Posture Review called for, among other things: developing new low-yield (and thus more "usable") tactical nuclear bombs and warheads, explicitly rejecting "no first use," lowering the threshold for nuclear war by proclaiming that nuclear weapons can and should be used in response to even non-nuclear assaults against the US (such as cyberattacks), and developing a new generation of nuclear-capable cruise and hypersonic missiles.

The Nuclear Non-Proliferation Treaty

There is a widespread consensus that nuclear proliferation constitutes a real danger. International efforts to prevent horizontal proliferation are known generally as the "nonproliferation regime," the centerpiece of which is the Non-Proliferation Treaty (NPT). It took effect in 1970 and divides the world into "have" and "have not" countries with respect to nuclear weapons. Its most significant nonproliferation items are that

1. nuclear weapons states agree not to transfer nuclear weapons to non-weapons states or to help non-weapons states make their own weapons; and

2. non-weapons states agree neither to receive nor to manufacture their own. They also agree to accept inspection safeguards on their nuclear facilities to be monitored by the International Atomic Energy Agency (IAEA), under the auspices of the United Nations.

Not surprisingly, some of the non-weapons states objected to the NPT, believing they were forgoing weapons without receiving any tangible benefit in return. As a result, they insisted on these additional provisions:

1. weapons states agree to share "peaceful nuclear technology" with the non-weapons states; and

2. the weapons states agree to begin serious bargaining to end their arms race and to undertake genuine efforts at nuclear disarmament.

The NPT is reviewed every five years. At these review conferences, the non-weapons states have consistently expressed anger at what they initially saw as the superpowers' failure to live up to their agreement to work seriously to end their arms race, and, with the end of the Cold War, to make active efforts toward nuclear disarmament. Critics, led by Swedish disarmament expert (and Nobel Peace Prize winner) Alva Myrdal, criticized the United States and the then- Soviet Union as constituting a "duopoly" while insisting that the rest of the world do as they say, not as they do. Exhortations by the United States and the USSR that other countries refrain from going nuclear have rung hollow while those two nuclear superpowers clung to their own arsenals.

Despite an understandable tendency for public attention to focus on cases of real or suspected proliferation, the NPT is generally considered to have been successful in halting and preventing much horizontal nuclear proliferation. Whereas during the 1960s and 1970s, authorities worried that dozens of nations would shortly acquire nuclear weapons, the nuclear club has actually grown less rapidly in recent decades than most experts had feared. As of 2020, three states that developed nuclear weapons—India, Pakistan, and Israel—never signed the NPT, and North Korea renounced it in 2003. (Most international treaties contain a clause permitting adopters to withdraw in cases of "supreme national necessity," or the equivalent.)

In addition, critics of the NPT point out that a would-be proliferator can ratify the NPT, receive substantial assistance (including reactors, fuel, and the necessary technological expertise) and then, when it is on the threshold of building bombs or warheads, withdraw from the treaty and develop its nuclear arsenal. Hence, despite its many unsung successes, the NPT clearly is not foolproof and 100 percent proliferation resistant.

As noted, the NPT is an explicit bargain by which the nuclear nations have committed themselves to provide civilian nuclear technology to the non-weapons signers. According to its supporters, this is the only possible way to restrict proliferation because states desiring nuclear technology will somehow acquire it. Under the NPT, this will at least be supervised and therefore less likely to result in new nuclear arsenals. According to critics, however, there is no such thing as nonmilitary nuclear technology: Every reactor is a potential bomb factory. Moreover, the inclusion of reprocessing technology—which results in the production of plutonium—as "nonmilitary" further blurs the line between civilian and military.

Even aside from the problem of non-signers, who are not bound to the NPT in any way, the nonproliferation regime has a number of weaknesses:

1. The nuclear safeguards overseen by the IAEA are of questionable reliability because they include no means of enforcing compliance or of preventing diversion of plutonium for military use. Rather,

IAEA inspectors are empowered to report any possible violations they detect. A negative inspection report will in principle constitute "timely warning," after which it is up to the international community to respond as it sees fit, presumably with sanctions.

2. IAEA inspectors may examine only nuclear facilities that have been "declared" by the host country. They may not search for undeclared or secret facilities. Hypothetically, a state could be maintaining both safeguarded and unsafeguarded facilities at the same time.

3. Compliance is verified by allegedly tamperproof remote-control cameras, fuel components with special seals, and accounting checks, procedures that may nonetheless offer loopholes for would-be violators. It has been estimated that the "annual detection threshold" for plutonium may be as high as 18 pounds: That is, it may be possible to divert as much as 18 pounds (about one bomb) per country per year without being detected.

4. Although a nation's nuclear facilities are to be open for inspection at all times, IAEA inspectors must announce their visits weeks in advance, giving the host operators ample opportunity to prepare for such events. Moreover, host countries can veto inspectors from nations they consider unfriendly.

These weaknesses derive from a reluctance on the part of host nations to give up the perquisites of state sovereignty. They do not necessarily indicate an intent to circumvent the terms of the NPT. However, it rankles many non-weapons states that the requirements of inspection are asymmetric and discriminatory: The nuclear weapon states are not obligated to have their facilities inspected. Supporters of the safeguards and inspection system, while acknowledging its weaknesses, point out that it is better than no system at all.

Nuclear supplier states (including such technologically sophisticated countries as Canada, Holland, Australia, Germany, and Japan, which possess well-developed civilian nuclear capabilities but no nuclear weapons) tend to favor stricter safeguards than recipient nations deem appropriate. The IAEA was also charged with the job of promoting peaceful uses of nuclear energy, a role many critics feel poses a conflict of interest with its job as watchdog against proliferation.

In 1978, the US Congress passed the Non-Proliferation Act, which forbids US vendors from dealing with other countries, whether or not they are signatories to the NPT, if their nuclear facilities have not been placed under "full-scope" IAEA inspections and safeguards. (Under full-scope conditions, all of a nation's nuclear facilities are included, whether they were produced indigenously or acquired via outside assistance.) Exceptions have, however, been made in the cases of Pakistan and India, justified by the US both for supposed trade benefits and as a way of enhancing strategic cooperation in other realms.

The various nonproliferation strategies (excluding preemptive military attack) include the following:

1. Assume that nuclear proliferation, especially by one's allies, is in many states' national security interest and should be encouraged, but not prohibited. This is analogous to the position of the National Rifle Association in the United States that proliferation of weapons leads to greater security. The "Porcupine Theory" claims that nuclear armed

countries interact in a manner comparable to the NRA's assertion that "an armed society is a polite society," deriving its particular label from the joke "How do porcupines make love?" Answer: "Very carefully"!

2. Nuclear proliferation should be neither encouraged nor discouraged; rather, states should be free to avail themselves of any commercial opportunities to profit from nuclear exports. After all, states wanting nuclear technology are likely to buy it from somewhere, so the economic beneficiaries may as well be "us."

3. Nuclear proliferation should be stringently minimized, which would be enhanced if the nuclear states develop a record as reliable suppliers. As a result, nations will be able to meet their energy needs without relying heavily on Middle Eastern oil or developing their own reprocessing or enrichment operations.

4. All prospective nuclear supplier states should insist on rigorous IAEA safeguards, with stringent enforcement consequences for noncompliance.

5. Nuclear states do everything within their power to see that nuclear technology does not spread to other nations. This can and should include economic and social sanctions, and if necessary, various undercover methods such as industrial espionage, targeted assassinations, cyberattacks, and so forth.

The ABM Treaty and Star Wars

The Anti-Ballistic Missile (ABM) Treaty, signed in 1972 as part of SALT I, was a watershed in strategic policy in that both the US and the Soviet Union assumed the doctrine of mutually assured destruction (MAD): an agreement that nuclear deterrence between the two superpowers would be based on the mutual vulnerability of each state. It was unilaterally abrogated by the United States in 2001, so as to permit development, testing, and deployment of a form of Ballistic Missile Defense (BMD), or "Star Wars"—initially designated by the Reagan administration in the 1980's as the Strategic Defense Initiative.

First proposed as a "defensive" shield against Soviet nuclear missiles, a BMD system has been touted as offering possible protection against a terrorist attack or one conducted by such fledgling nuclear states as Iran and North Korea. Critics question whether BMD could work, given that offensive countermeasures have the advantage, especially because only a small number of warheads would have to penetrate such a system. Successful BMD has been likened to "hitting a bullet with a bullet," and, moreover, the target's radar systems can readily be confused by "chaff" and other decoys. In addition, BMD runs the risk of making other nuclear powers nervous because it could conceivably be paired with a first strike, as follows: Suppose that a surprise attack eliminated a substantial number of another country's missiles. A BMD system, although incapable of defending against a massive incoming first strike, could in theory nonetheless be effective against the "ragged retaliation" that would take place if the target sought to strike back with its reduced remaining forces.

A result of such a system—even one of limited effectiveness—could be to encourage its possessor to strike first, confident that the target could not retaliate. Hence, although described as defensive, BMD could also appear offensive, and therefore provocative, to a potential opponent, such as China, for instance, which fields a limited number of ICBMs and might well feel a need to increase its arsenal in response or to "use it or lose it," so as to be assured that it possesses a viable deterrent.

The Russian government has long been very critical of US plans to deploy a BMD system (previously planned by the Bush administration in Poland and Czechoslovakia), ostensibly to "shield" European and US forces stationed there from an accidental or limited attack by terrorists or a "rogue" state, such as Iran. Such a system's effectiveness and capabilities would be so questionable that it seems unlikely to threaten an arsenal as large as Russia's. Nonetheless, deployment encourages nationalists and militarists to resist any further decrease in Russian nuclear forces, and generates calls for increasing their numbers.

The US has deployed limited land-based BMD components in Alaska and California, as well as ship-based Aegis systems. Despite the billions of dollars being spent on development and production, however, their effectiveness is, at best, questionable. The US has also deployed its "THAD" (Terminal High Altitude Area Defense) system on Guam, Japan and South Korea, despite rumblings from the Chinese and North Korean governments. Current US plans call for airborne and possibly space-based Ballistic Missile Defense (probably a component of US Space Command), as well as for the development of early boost-phase interception, which would involve attacking missiles during their vulnerable take-off period; the latter would require not only intrusive surveillance but, because responses would have to be almost instantaneous, the prospect looms of an innocent or accidental rocket launch being misinterpreted as an attack, which could then precipitate war.

Future Prospects

Most arms-control measures were initiated during the Cold War between the United States and the former Soviet Union (1945–1991). More recently, there are worrisome indications of new Cold Wars because of rising US-Russia and US-China tensions. A great opportunity to reduce and even eliminate (as President Obama called for) weapons of mass destruction may have been missed in the interim. While the "genie cannot be put back in the bottle"— that is, the knowledge of how to make nuclear weapons cannot be undone— the weapons themselves can be dismantled and fissile materials recycled or otherwise disposed; the challenges are mostly political, not technical.

Numerous proposals have been made for large reductions in the stockpiles of the major nuclear states, as well as for physically separating warhead and missile components so that no country can quickly use whatever weaponry it may retain. With long-range (satellite) and onsite verification, the technical issues can be addressed, even if political willpower is lacking.

Ironically, at a time when it is most attainable, nuclear disarmament—or even meaningful reductions—seems unlikely in the near future. On the positive side, the total number of deployed warheads in the combined Russian and American nuclear arsenals has plummeted from a peak of around 65,000 in 1985 to about 6,000 deployed weapons in 2020 (with another 10,000 in storage, many of which could be quickly utilized). The collapse of the Soviet Union caused widespread concern about the control of nuclear weapons and materials in Russia and in other parts of the former Soviet Union (the problem of "loose nukes"), although the Soviet successor states of Ukraine, Kazakhstan, and Belarus all relinquished their nuclear arsenals following independence from the USSR. Most ominously, political and military developments in the United States and Russia threaten to reverse progress made in nuclear arms control, never mind disarmament.

Both the US and Russia have contributed to this situation. Thus, the United States orchestrated the expansion of the NATO alliance, including former Soviet satellites (such as Poland, Hungary, the Czech Republic, and the Baltic states), which moved NATO's borders closer to Russia and look offensive many wary Russians. US-orchestrated NATO expansion also abandoned a pledge by President George H. W. Bush to the Russian leadership that in the aftermath of the USSR's disintegration, NATO's borders would not be extended. Further unhelpful decisions by the US included terminating the ABM Treaty while insisting on deploying missile defenses, insistence on preserving the capability to rapidly expand the US strategic nuclear arsenal, aggressively sponsoring research on new nuclear weapons designs, and the US Senate's refusal to ratify the CTBT.

Under both the Clinton and George H. W. Bush administrations, the US government was lacking in creativity or even, perhaps, interest in pursuing nuclear disarmament, a hesitation that has long bedeviled all post–World War II US governments: fears of being considered "soft on defense." The George W. Bush Administration strongly opposed nuclear de-escalation, and although the Obama Administration appeared initially intent on reducing the nuclear threat, very little was accomplished, in part because of Republican opposition but also as a result of significant resistance among some Democrats and many "defense intellectuals." What followed was the Trump Administration, generally hostile to both international agreements and arms limitations most especially.

Meanwhile, Russian hardliners, xenophobes, and ultra-nationalists have also often gotten their way, in part by using US policies as justifications for resisting not only nuclear disarmament but also arms control. Some components of Russian nuclear escalation under President Vladimir Putin may have been due to Russian political elite's desire to reclaim the prior role that the USSR had experienced (within the USSR) as a global superpower, In the process, Russian military aggressiveness—in the Republic of Georgia and notably by seizing the Crimea and backing separatists in eastern Ukraine—has enhanced Western wariness of arms control agreements with Moscow and provided aid and comfort to their own pronuclear hardliners.

Nonetheless, opportunities still exist to take advantage of the (possibly closing) window of opportunity opened by the collapse of Soviet communism. These include a "consolidate-monitor-dismantle" initiative that would apply to the thousands of tactical nuclear warheads not covered by the strategic arms control reduction process and place them under secure control, in preparation for eventual dismantlement. US and Russian forces could also take thousands of strategic nuclear warheads off alert, which would reduce the risks of accidental nuclear war. Retraining, conversion, and alternative employment opportunities can be made available for nuclear weapons designers, to ensure that their expertise is not diverted to nuclear "wannabe" states. These measures would entail a change of attitude from the fantasy that national security can be enhanced by "winning" a new arms race to recognizing that security must be a collective endeavor, requiring coordinated and enforceable agreements.

Another related proposal is for the adoption of a Fissile Material Cut-Off Treaty, which would prohibit the production of weapons-capable highly enriched uranium, U-235, and plutonium, Pu-239. This might also allow

lower-level enrichment of U-235 and separation of the Pu-239 for purposes
of nuclear power generation—but under very strict controls. In 2004, under
the George W. Bush administration, the United States cast the only "No"
vote in the United Nations General Assembly against a resolution calling for
negotiations that might lead to such a treaty. However, in 2009, US President
Barack Obama reversed this position and proposed negotiating "a new treaty
that verifiably ends the production of fissile materials intended for use in
state nuclear weapons." Pakistan has opposed such a treaty. Despite prior rhetorical support for eventual nuclear disarmament, the US administration—
no matter who is president, but especially during the presidency of Donald
Trump—also remained by and large resistant to any serious efforts to do
away with nuclear weapons.

Some Conventional Arms-Control Efforts

Issues of disarmament and arms control are not limited to the nuclear arena.
Indeed, efforts (mostly unsuccessful) have also involved conventional weaponry. Here are some failures and successes.

Exporting Weapons

According to a report to Congress from the Congressional Research
Service, in 2019 the United States sold more than $10 billion in arms to
other countries, and signed deals during that year for $56 billion more.
The US thus continued its worldwide dominance in arms sales, with a total
exceeding that of the next four "leaders" combined (Russia, France, Germany
and Spain). China, South Korea and Brazil also export large amounts of
weapons, especially to developing countries and others undergoing violent
internal conflicts.

A proposed modification of the current "arms export regime" (which is
at present unregulated and thus not really a "regime" at all) would involve
adopting a code of conduct governing weapons transfers, requiring that
arms be made available only to governments that are democratic, respect
human rights, are not engaged in aggressive military policies, and that make
their military plans and activities "transparent"—that is, available for public
scrutiny. If such a code of conduct were enacted, this might reduce the likelihood of possible tragedies, such as the use of US-supplied weapons by the
Indonesian government during its army's slaughter of East Timorese, as well
as the use of cluster bombs provided to Israel as US military assistance and
dropped on civilian areas during the brief 2006 war between Israel and Hezbollah in Lebanon (Cluster munitions contain submunitions, or bomblets,
that disperse widely. Many bomblets can fail to explode, posing a threat to
civilians. A 2008 treaty bans the weapons, but major arms suppliers, including the United States and Russia, have not signed it.) Weapons provided to
the government of Saudi Arabia have been used in that country's attacks on
Houthis in Yemen, fueling one of the world's worst humanitarian crises.

In 1999, President Clinton, apparently for the first time in American history, apologized for the US's role in training and arming Guatemalan troops
who committed acts of genocide against the indigenous population during
the Reagan administration. It is unresolved whether, or to what extent, US
or UN forces should become involved in cases of within-country genocide
or "ethnic cleansing," the UN's 2005 "Responsibility to Protect" declaration (to prevent genocide, war crimes, ethnic cleansing, and crimes against

humanity) notwithstanding. Nonetheless, every country can act unilaterally to limit its own culpability by refusing to provide weapons and training to regimes likely to engage in major human rights abuses.

Prohibition of Landmines

There are more than 100 million antipersonnel landmines lurking underground in more than 40 countries, notably Cambodia, Angola, Mozambique, Bosnia, and Kosovo. Tens of thousands of persons—nearly all of them civilians, especially farmers working their fields or children at play—are maimed or killed by these devices every year.

In 1997, the International Campaign to Ban Landmines and its coordinator, Jody Williams, were awarded the Nobel Peace Prize for their efforts to eliminate these devices. Representatives from more than 100 countries gathered in Ottawa, Canada, to sign a comprehensive landmine treaty that prohibited the "use, stockpile, production, and transfer of anti-personnel landmines." This treaty entered into force in 1999, by which point it had been signed by 135 countries and ratified by 71. Although the United States has promised increased funding for humanitarian de-mining, it has refused to sign the Ottawa Treaty, claiming that military necessity requires it to retain the option of using landmines on the border separating North and South Korea.

Pitfalls of Arms Control Agreements

It might appear that the manufacture, deployment, and use of weapons systems can be ended via treaties and appropriate negotiated agreements. But even aside from the problem of underlying international hostilities, there are numerous pitfalls lurking along the road of efficacious arms control agreements.

Numerical Obsessions

Arms reduction treaties usually involve things that can be counted, which in turn gives greater importance to quantitative than qualitative factors. For example, the actual count of warheads or missiles can be misleading and distracting, especially because asymmetries in force structures make it possible for partisans from each side to point selectively to certain measures, thereby making it seem that their side is unacceptably behind. By focusing on the need for nuclear parity, moreover, excessive "bean counting" tends to discourage interest in sufficiency, in which states would assess what they need for their legitimate defense needs, rather than seeking to match or exceed potential opponents in every category.

Slowness

Arms control negotiations are almost always slow. It took 3 years for the United States and the Soviet Union to agree on SALT I, 7 years for them to agree on SALT II, and another 7 for the INF Treaty. Moreover, for reasons of pride and ideology, new presidents may disregard what their predecessors have accomplished, insisting on starting afresh. It is also more difficult to reach the political consensus needed to ban or even restrict a weapon than to meet the engineering requirements of designing and constructing it; as a result, by the time negotiators wind up banning a weapon, it may be nearly obsolete, while new weapons are being planned and produced. (On the other hand, when political will is present, agreements can be made quickly; the Partial Test Ban Treaty, for example, was negotiated in a matter of weeks.)

"Leveling Up"

It is relatively easy to decide to build more weapons; such decisions are *unilateral*. It is much harder, by contrast, to decide on a *bilateral* or *multilateral* halt, or even a ceiling on weapons and their delivery systems, because such decisions must be made in concert with others. There is also a reluctance to destroy expensive weapons that have already been deployed. So, rather than accept a limit below the current level, negotiators are inclined to accept—as a limit for all—the numbers possessed by the side that currently has the most. Often, treaty limits are even set above those of either side, whereupon they become production goals.

The "Balloon Principle"

When a weapon is restricted or banned, states tend to put effort into another weapons system, one that is unconstrained and then expands, like a balloon that is squeezed in one place and pops out somewhere else (or what might be called "weapons whack-a-mole"). For example, after the PTBT was ratified, the rate of underground nuclear testing *increased*. After SALT I, which did not restrict the number of warheads per missile, there was a significant increase in the strategic arsenals of each side, as both sides proceeded with MIRVing.

Bargaining Chips

According to many strategic decision makers, bargaining should proceed from a "position of strength"—that is, when one's side already has lots of weapons. At a time, for example, when even its advocates agreed that the MX ICBM missile was not justifiable on its merits, it was promoted as a way of buttressing then-ongoing strategic arms negotiations. Moreover, weapons that were ostensibly developed as bargaining chips tend to be retained if negotiations fail. And governments sometimes even begin negotiations specifically to build support for the procurement of weapons, ostensibly as bargaining chips. Governments also often find themselves having to bargain with their own military-industrial leadership. For example, the increase in underground testing that followed the PTBT took place because President Kennedy had to agree to it in order to garner support from the Joint Chiefs of Staff for the PTBT. And the Obama administration's consent to a "new generation" of nuclear delivery systems were the price paid for Republican support for the 2010 New START treaty.

Linkage

Arms control skeptics often claim that agreements should be held hostage—"linked"—to other aspects of the adversary's behavior. This suggests that such treaties are favors extended to the other side, whereas in fact if they are of any value, it is as positive-sum developments that are mutually beneficial.

Moreover, as President John Kennedy pointed out,

A sea wall is not needed when the seas are calm. Sound disarmament agreements, deeply rooted in mankind's mutual interest in survival,

must serve as a bulwark against the tidal waves of war and its destructiveness. Let no one, then, say that we cannot arrive at such agreements in troubled times, for it is then that their need is greatest.[2]

Legitimating Arms Competition

Only rarely (e.g., the INF Treaty, the ABM Treaty) have treaties actually
stopped weapons competition. More often, they are consistent with continuing trends and may have occasionally even ratified arms races themselves, providing government leaders with a touchstone by which they can
assure their citizenry that escalations in weaponry are consistent with treaty
obligations. The presence of arms control agreements thus sometimes allows
leaders to claim that they are seeking an end to a given arms competition
and escalation, while pursuing both.

False Confidence

In the 21st century, nuclear weapons have become so reviled in many
places that their legitimacy has once again been questioned. In the past,
however, popular revulsion at such weapons was bolstered by signs that
governments were not sincere about trying to restrain or abolish them. By
providing occasional arms control "successes," all the while ensuring that
weapons regimes remain fundamentally undiminished, governments may
succeed in quieting public opposition while maintaining a dangerous status
quo. Nuclearists in turn tend to worry that arms control agreements produce
a false sense of confidence that a country has benefited itself or at least not
fallen behind a potential opponent, while actually doing so.

The Paradox of Small Arsenals

By the peculiar logic of deterrence, there can be a kind of safety inherent
in relatively large nuclear arsenals because when a country has many potential nuclear weapons available for retaliation, an adversary would likely be
reluctant to initiate a first strike, knowing that some of the target's weapons
would probably survive and be available for retaliation. At the same time,
countries with a large nuclear arsenal would presumably be aware of the
reluctance by would-be attackers and would therefore be less nervous and
less likely to misinterpret false alarms or crisis conditions as indicating an
imminent attack on their own nation. A comparatively small nuclear arsenal, by contrast, is more vulnerable to a preemptive attack, both because
such an attack might theoretically succeed in eliminating any capacity to
retaliate (thereby undermining deterrence), and also because a country possessing a small arsenal might be especially worried that such a preemptive
attack might occur, as a result of which it could be tempted to preempt the
opponent's preemption, under the "use it or lose it" logic of deterrence.

Benefits and Methods of Achieving Arms Control Agreements

We live in a real world, not an ideal one. Just as a *Realpolitik* argument is
regularly used to justify the presence of armed forces, it also may provide
a rationale to reduce them. There are enormous risks in permitting an
uncontrolled arms build-up; hence, it seems essential that non-zero-sum
game solutions to humanity's shared dilemma be identified and acted upon.

In this regard, arms control and continued efforts at disarmament have a crucial role to play. Good agreements can inhibit wasteful competition (e.g., the ABM Treaty), reduce worldwide pollution (the PTBT) and the numbers of bombs, warheads and delivery systems (SALT I, START, New START), diminish the chances of accidental war (the Hot Line), and eliminate an entire class of dangerous weapons altogether (the INF Treaty).

Verification

Successful arms control (and disarmament) must rely on more than trust. Specifically, compliance must be verifiable. During the Cold War, the Soviet Union, largely a closed and secretive society, was consistently averse to onsite verification, which it long considered intrusive and a license for spying. So, just as the Soviets appears to have insincerely pressed for widespread (and unverifiable) disarmament schemes, the United States also insisted on iron-clad verification procedures it knew would be vetoed by the Soviets.

These issues are no longer likely to block agreements, and, in fact, Russia has in many ways been more open to US arms inspectors than have some US military contractors, who periodically object to what they fear might be industrial espionage. At the same time, verification has on occasion been hotly contested, notably in the aftermath of the Gulf War, because of Iraq's resentment of UN arms inspections and its periodic refusal to permit onsite monitoring of its weapons facilities. On several occasions, this issue was cited by the United States as a reason to bomb Iraq and also to delay the lifting of UN economic sanctions.

Verification is important. Most nations are understandably reluctant to consent to substantial cuts in their own arsenals unless they can be confident that other countries are abiding by the same agreements. Nonetheless, most reductions in arms—even if made unilaterally—will not diminish a state's security. So long as hundreds of nuclear warheads remain in a country's arsenals, it would not matter from a deterrence perspective if the other side squirrels away a few hundred more than are called for in any build-down agreement. Even in this case, however, verification may well be helpful, and perhaps necessary, if the reductions are to be acceptable to the hardliners on each side.

Techniques and Prospects

There is a distinction between "absolute," or legalistic, verification, by which *any* violation will be detected with absolute certainty, and "functional," or realistic, verification, according to which some relatively minor violations of an arms control agreement may not be detected, but strategically significant violations will be. With the advent of spy satellites and other detection techniques, functional verification can be enhanced; insistence on absolute verification, by contrast, is tantamount to insistence on no agreement at all.

A variety of verification procedures are available. Most treaties provide for the use of "national technical means," which denote a number of long-range reconnaissance procedures that do not directly intrude on the side being monitored. Of these, satellite observation is the most important, while infrared imaging can penetrate cloud cover and detect changes in work patterns inside factories.

Governments have additional sources for obtaining verification-related information. Radar, for example, provides for accurate detection, tracking, and monitoring of missile tests, thereby providing a means for assessing a country's compliance with treaty restrictions. Seismic instrumentation has become so sensitive that nuclear explosions as small as one kiloton can reportedly be distinguished from such natural events as earthquakes; this appears to hold even for so-called decoupled explosions, detonated in sites designed to absorb the blast effects. An array of tamper-proof black boxes, installed within national territory, can provide a very high level of reassurance that no party to the agreement is conducting nuclear tests. National technical means of verification also include electronic signal interception, whereby one country eavesdrops on the communications of another.

As a general rule, verification of military *capabilities* has been quite reliable, a notable exception having been faulty US and British intelligence reports that mistakenly alleged that the Iraqi government, under Saddam Hussein, had stockpiled weapons of mass destruction. It remains debatable, however, whether this represented a genuine breakdown in intelligence or a political ploy by the Bush and Blair administrations, which apparently had decided to invade Iraq for other reasons and then cherry-picked intelligence that supported the pretext for a fait accompli. Most often, intelligence failures have been in a "softer" area, notably political and military *intentions* (as opposed to *capabilities*). The West was caught off guard, for example, by the rapidity of the Soviet Union's disintegration, by the rampage of Hutus against Tutsis in Rwanda, by Serbian ferocity toward Kosovar Albanians, by the sudden Arab Spring uprisings against several dictatorial regimes, and by the extent of Chinese repressive measures against Uighurs.

Economic Conversion

The economy of the United States is heavily militarized, as was that of the Soviet Union; indeed, the severe economic pressure of keeping up an arms race appears to have contributed substantially to the Soviet Union's disintegration. The economies of such other states as Israel, Iraq, Saudi Arabia, North Korea, and South Korea are even more heavily oriented toward military expenditures and production, as measured by the proportion of GNP devoted to military purposes. Converting such economies from military to civilian functions poses special challenges as well as opportunities, and has long been a goal of peace activists.

It had been expected in many Western progressive political circles that the end of the Cold War would generate a substantial "peace dividend," as military spending might have been redirected toward the civilian economy. This has not happened in the United States, largely because of the "war on terror." Current military spending in the US is nearly double its earlier Cold War levels, leading to the suspicion that international terrorism has been used as an excuse to ramp up military investment in the absence of the Cold War. In any event, it seems clear that economic conversion—from a military to a civilian economy— deserves a place in the US national agenda, both to generate political pressure for the process itself and to ensure that, if and when it happens, it is carried out intelligently.

Challenges

Large military expenditures tend to create their own constituencies because millions of jobs depend on them. This in turn makes disarmament—and even arms control—politically difficult. When big corporations and their many employees make large amounts of money, the result is powerful pressure to continue business as usual, even if the military/strategic justification for such "business" has evaporated. Moreover, whole regions of the United States now rely on military spending, and many American politicians attribute their election and reelection to success in bringing some of the Pentagon "bacon" home to their constituents.

Disarmament—even if it is partial—can thus appear to threaten the livelihoods of many people. Economic factors therefore make disarmament politically unattractive to a large swath of government leaders in many countries besides the United States. In addition, large-scale demilitarization of an economy would require a major overhaul of existing economic arrangements, in some cases generating real hardships, at least until funds and priorities are rearranged. Thus, the closing of only a relatively small number of military bases in the United States during the 1990s generated heated political opposition.

Opportunities

On the other hand, military spending is, on balance, more hurtful than helpful to a national economy. In the long run—and aside from its presumed benefit in diminishing the likelihood of war—restructuring from a military to a civilian economy offers the promise of (1) reducing inflationary pressures, (2) increasing employment, (3) lowering the deficit, (4) improving productivity, and (5) freeing up resources—human as well as financial—for needed social programs, including rebuilding a nation's fragile infrastructure. Although skeptics may bemoan the potential problems, it is at least as plausible to consider economic conversion from military to civilian research and spending as an opportunity to yield a "disarmament dividend," which is yet another reason for moving toward a demilitarization of national and global security.

Economic conversion has been partially achieved in the past. Following World War II, the US military budget plummeted from nearly $76 billion in 1945 to less than $19 billion in 1947. As part of this postwar demobilization, the armed forces declined from 11 million troops in 1945 to 2 million just 2 years later, yet unemployment never exceeded 4 percent during this period. Skeptics point out, however, that successful post–World War II conversion in the United States was based in part on conditions that would probably not be repeated in the event of comparable conversion today. For example, many women who had been recruited into the workforce in the early 1940s returned home to raise families, thus making room in the workforce for demobilized servicemen. In addition, pent-up consumer demand had accumulated during the war years, when new automobiles, for example, were not produced because factories had been retooled to make jeeps, tanks, and other military hardware.

On the other hand, the US economy is far larger today than it was in 1945, and the number of people to be "demobilized" is far smaller. If substantial government expenditures are ever redirected from the military to the civilian sector, these funds will not simply evaporate; rather, they will be available for use in other areas (except for some portion left unspent, to diminish the federal deficit).

On balance, federal civilian-related expenditures produce *more* jobs, per dollar spent, than does military spending because the latter is "capital intensive," using large amounts of money to employ relatively few people. Moreover, national and global needs are immense and include funding for education, health, renewable energy, pollution abatement, housing, environmental protection, disaster emergency preparation and relief (as in New Orleans following Hurricane Katrina, in the New York City region following Hurricane Sandy, and in the entire country in response to the Covid-19 pandemic), and public transportation; rebuilding roads, bridges, and other structures; retooling the industrial base for the production of affordable consumer goods; reconstructing blighted cities; reforestation and other types of land reclamation; providing drug treatment and rehabilitation; establishing more humane penal institutions; and so on. Many billions of dollars and millions of workers would be better deployed if resources were redirected from militaristic to civilian purposes.

A problem, however, is that the additional jobs that would be made available as a result of conversion from a military to a civilian economy are in a sense "theoretical," in that the particular beneficiaries are not currently identified. By contrast, jobs lost to conversion are associated with those currently employed; therefore, such losses are often resisted more vigorously than the new ones are welcomed. It would nonetheless seem to indicate a stunted imagination to consider economic conversion a calamity to be avoided rather than an opportunity to be embraced.

Conversion Planning

Most people employed in today's military-industrial complex could be retrained for productive work in the domestic economy within about six months. Mid- and upper-level managers and engineers would require somewhat more extensive retraining because they are often specialized in making narrowly focused, cost-insensitive products, rigidly defined within certain bureaucratic guidelines. In short, they are accustomed to pleasing the Pentagon, not the public.

But there is no reason to think this cannot be changed. The United States already maintains an Office of Economic Adjustment, tasked with helping local communities mitigate the effects of changes in Defense Department activities, including plant and base closings. Such work could be expanded to a national scale. Some industries and labor unions have (often begrudgingly) begun making contingency plans for converting their activities to domestic and civilian purposes, although peace groups have thus far done the bulk of the work. Careful conversion planning could yield several payoffs: (1) In the event of a transition from a military to a genuinely nonmilitary economy, dislocation could be greatly reduced; and (2) the existence of realistic, mutually beneficial plans would make the disarmament process itself more feasible politically (which might help explain the reluctance of government, industry, and some communities to engage in such planning).

Economic conversion is important not only as a positive consequence of disarmament but also as a necessary prerequisite for movement in that direction. It is discouraging, therefore, that despite the immense opportunities afforded by the end of the Cold War, the US government generally remains resistant to the concept of economic conversion and averse even to planning for it.

GRIT

In his book, *An Alternative to War or Surrender* (1962), psychologist Charles Osgood proposed a practical strategy whereby states might achieve substantial progress in reducing tensions and the level of armaments. He called it

GRIT, for "Graduated and Reciprocated Initiatives in Tension Reduction." The idea is simple: just as individuals, or states, increase tension by a series of unilateral escalations, it is also possible to proceed down the tension ladder by a series of unilateral initiatives in the opposite direction. Arguments between two people, for example, often escalate through a series of mutual insults and affronts, with increasing distrust and animosity. However, individuals can also "make up," and this generally requires a reaching out to each other; that is, reconciliation may begin with some sort of unilateral initiative.

Comparable initiatives can be applied to international affairs, quite possibly with comparable results. These initiatives are not intended as appeasement. Rather, Osgood pointed out that when individuals or states make conciliatory gestures, substantial pressure builds for matching behavior from the other side.

It is quite possible — even likely — that the initial phases of GRIT will encounter skepticism. Over time, however, assuming that the initiatives are maintained and (better yet) intensified, powerful psychological and social forces encourage the other side to reciprocate—which, in turn, contributes to a process of mutual tension reduction that can be as real as the process of tension escalation that preceded it. Osgood recommended that a national policy of GRIT follow certain basic rules:

1. Each step should be small so the initiator does not at any time risk its military security.

2. Each initiative should be taken in the interest of reducing tension; initiatives should not be accompanied by threats or efforts at coercion, which tend to harden the opposition.

3. Each initiative should be publicly announced and carried out with maximum publicity.

4. Each action should be real and meaningful, not something that would be done in any case, like retiring an obsolete weapons system or withdrawing from territory already known to be indefensible or not wanted.

5. The GRIT initiatives should be continued, and if necessary repeated several times, in the hope of generating a similar response. If it fails, a GRIT strategy could always be abandoned, with little loss and no diminution to national security.

The United States and the Soviet Union apparently used a GRIT-like strategy of progressive mutual disengagement to defuse a tense situation during the Berlin crisis (1961), when US and Soviet tanks were almost literally muzzle to muzzle. President Kennedy apparently was aware of GRIT in the summer of 1963, when he initiated a series of outreaches to the Soviet Union, beginning with the announcement that the United States would stop atmospheric testing and not resume unless the Soviets did so first. Premier Khrushchev responded positively and announced a decrease in production of strategic bombers. Numerous tit-for-tat benefits followed, including the Hot Line agreement, a large wheat sale, the PTBT, and a lessening of East-West tensions. (The Soviets liked the interaction so much that they coined their own phrase to describe it, "the policy of mutual example," even claiming that they had invented it!)

There are many possibilities for GRIT-ty initiatives in today's world. If there is a possible benefit to being over-armed, perhaps it is that it provides an opportunity for all parties to initiate substantial reductions—in both armaments and tension—without diminishing security. GRIT might also be usefully applied to the many conflicts between adjacent rivals, such as India and Pakistan, Israel and its Arab neighbors, North and South Korea, Greece and Turkey, and so forth. In such cases, limitations on nations' will to adopt GRIT-ty initiatives include both the national security concerns and creativity of government leaders as well as anxiety by the general public about entering unknown waters. This makes peace-related education and outreach all the more important.

A Final Note on Disarmament and Arms Control

Disarmament is a long-standing, traditional value, to which—like peace, Mom, and apple pie—many people pay lip service. Yet efforts at disarmament often bog down when it comes to the specifics of implementation. This is not entirely surprising, nor should it be cause for despair. After all, human beings have used weapons and war in efforts to resolve their differences for thousands of years; it is not reasonable to expect that such ingrained habits will be overturned in quickly.

Whereas the goal of multilateral disarmament may at the present seem unattainable, short-term disappointment should not blind us to the benefits to be obtained from various arms-reduction accomplishments along the way. Most of all, it is vital to recognize that disarmament is a *process,* not an *event,* more a verb than a noun, a way of progressing rather than a finished masterpiece to be unveiled to the admiring world with a grand *"voilà!"* Like perfect peace or grace, disarmament may never be altogether achieved, but that doesn't mean that it is not a valid goal or even a route toward a pacified planet.

Questions for Further Reflection

1. What, in your opinion, have been some of the most important disarmament and/or arms control agreements since World War II? Why?

2. Distinguish between arms control and disarmament. What are some similarities and differences?

3. Identify one or more current areas of tension or violence in the world, and show how arms control agreements have either diminished or exacerbated the problem. Alternatively, describe how an agreement—not currently in force—might be helpful.

4. Look into current prospects for either enhanced verification of arms agreements or for economic conversion.

5. How does GRIT differ from traditional ways of reaching negotiated agreements? Can you propose some specific ways in which governments might apply this technique?

Suggestions for Further Reading

Helen Caldicott and Craig Eisendrath. 2007. *War in Heaven: Stopping the Arms Race in Outer Space Before It's Too Late*. New York: The New Press.

Thomas Graham. 2002. *Disarmament Sketches: Three Decades of Arms Control and International Law*. Seattle: University of Washington Press.

Oliver Meier and Christopher Diese, eds. 2012. *Arms Control in the 21st Century: Between Coercion and Cooperation*. London: Routledge.

Scott Ritter. 2010. *Dangerous Ground: America's Failed Arms Control Policy, From FDR to Obama*. New York: Nation Books.

SIPRI Yearbook. (Revised annually). *Armaments, Disarmament, and International Security*. New York: Oxford University Press.

Bard Steen. 2019. *Nuclear Disarmament*. New York: Routledge.

Lawrence Wittner. 2009. *Confronting the Bomb: A Short History of the World Nuclear Disarmament Movement*. Stanford, CA: Stanford University Press.

Notes

1. Albert Einstein. 1960. *Einstein on Peace*. New York: Meridian.

2. Quoted in A. Geyer. 1982. *The Idea of Disarmament*. Glencoe, IL: Brethren.

14

International Cooperation

Most people have experienced something like this: Trouble develops between two individuals, whereupon others step in and help resolve things short of violence. They may, in turn one or both of the rivals, or perhaps merely their presence help "cool" the situation. Maybe the contending parties will simply be urged to within us from the confrontation, or perhaps a genuine accommodation will be reached. In any event, conflict situations between combatants can then be resolved by separating or conciliating, and, in either case, the involvement of others is often crucial.

Peace researcher Kenneth Boulding identified two contrasting options: "associative" and "dissociative." Associative solutions are efforts to tear down walls, to join together. Dissociative ones involve relying on political

International Cooperation

Most people have experienced something like this: Trouble develops between two individuals, whereupon others step in and help resolve things short of violence. They may restrain one or both of the rivals, or perhaps merely their presence helps "cool" the situation. Maybe the contending parties will simply be urged to withdraw from the confrontation, or perhaps a genuine accommodation will be reached. In any event, conflict situations between countries can often be resolved by separating or connecting, and, in either case, the involvement of others is often crucial.

Peace researcher Kenneth Boulding identified two contrasting options: "associative" and "disassociative." Associative solutions are efforts to tear down walls, to join together. Disassociative ones involve relying on political separation and military strength, based on the idea that "good fences make good neighbors." As we have seen, prominent among the reasons for war—as well as a major obstacle to disarmament and even arms control—is the existence of bellicose, sovereign states, which are by definition disassociative relative to each other.

In the next few chapters, we shall examine possible mechanisms of war prevention that go beyond the current state-centered world system and look toward larger patterns of international integration. In this chapter, we consider associative possibilities based on ways of ameliorating—and perhaps one day even eliminating—the often bellicose role of states. It is an ancient dream: to establish world peace via international brother and sisterhood, based on some sort of administrative system that unites people rather than dividing them.

The United Nations

From the League of Nations to the United Nations

The most dramatic and conspicuously unsuccessful effort in the 20th century to create a multinational global organization was the League of Nations. Created in 1919, in the aftermath of World War I, the League was intended as a global guarantor of collective security. But the League of Nations proved unable to successfully address aggression by Japan in Manchuria (commencing in 1931) and by Italy in Ethiopia (then called Abyssinia), from 1936 to 1941. The League's demise was due to many factors, including the fact that the United States never joined and that the major powers were more interested in pursuing their perceived national interests than in banding together to prevent distant wars.

As World War II drew to a close, the victorious allies—traumatized by the second major war of the 20th century, and disillusioned at the failure of the state system to prevent it—decided once more to establish an international body that would work toward global security and especially the abolition of war. They also hoped that this new organization, known as the United Nations (UN), would avoid some of the pitfalls that had doomed the League of Nations. The formal idea of an international organization for preserving world peace was approved by Roosevelt, Churchill, and Stalin during a conference in Teheran in 1943. Specific plans for such an organization were drawn up at the Dumbarton Oaks Conference, in Washington, D.C., in late 1944.

It was agreed that all governments would be welcome, with membership in a large General Assembly, but that primary enforcement power would lie in a Security Council, with the United States, the Soviet Union, the United Kingdom, France, and China being permanent members, with each permanent Security Council member having a veto. In spring 1945, delegates from 50 countries met in San Francisco at the United Nations Conference on International Organization, which established a charter for the United Nations. The preamble to that charter reads as follows:

> We the peoples of the United Nations, determined to save succeeding generations from the scourge of war, which twice in our lifetime has brought untold sorrow to mankind, and to reaffirm faith in fundamental human rights, in the dignity and worth of the human person,

in the equal rights of men and women and of nations large and small, and to establish conditions under which justice and respect for the obligations arising from treaties and other sources of international law can be maintained, and to promote social progress and better standards of life in larger freedom, and for these ends to practice tolerance and live together in peace with one another as good neighbors, and to unite our strength to maintain international peace and security, and to ensure, by the acceptance of principles and the institution of methods, that armed force shall not be used, save in the common interest, and to employ international machinery for the promotion of the economic and social advancement of all peoples, have resolved to combine our efforts to accomplish these aims.

The UN's Basic Structure

There are several major differences between the United Nations and its predecessor, the League of Nations. For one, whereas the United States remained aloof from the League of Nations, it became a charter member and, in many ways, for better and worse, the most important single actor in the UN. For another, the UN, unlike the League, was constituted to have many other important functions beyond those dealing strictly with the avoidance or termination of wars. A branch of the UN, the Economic and Social Council, was established, with many specialized agencies concerned with various economic, educational, health, scientific, and social issues—such as the Food and Agriculture Organization (FAO), the World Health Organization (WHO), the World Bank and International Monetary Fund (IMF), the United Nations Children's Fund (UNICEF), and United Nations Educational, Scientific and Cultural Organization (UNESCO), as well as a number of professionally focused organizations with global reach, such as the International Civil Aviation Organization, the International Telecommunication Union, the World Meteorological Organization, and so on. The major organs of the UN and their prime missions are as follows:

- The Security Council: issues of war and peace

- The General Assembly: the main parliamentary organ

- The Economic and Social Council: quality of life worldwide

- The International Court of Justice (also known as the World Court) located at The Hague, Netherlands: adjudication of international legal disputes

- The Secretariat: the executive organ of the UN, led by one individual, the Secretary-General

The UN and the State System

To understand the United Nations and assess its actual and potential contributions to peace, it is important to realize what it is *not*. Thus, it is not a world government or even an effort at establishing one. It does not offer an alternative to state sovereignty; in fact, the United Nations was established with a number of guidelines to ensure that, if anything, state sovereignty supersedes it. Accordingly, although the UN often proclaims high-minded goals and resolutions, its decisions and actions are not above the more parochial interests of the states that comprise it. It is not a substitute or cure-all for the current state system; rather, the United Nations is in large part a *reflection* of that system: a mirror, not a panacea. It is not a solution to problems of personal aggressiveness, poor decision making, nationalism, oppression, and ethnic strife, and it did very little to ameliorate or end the Cold War.

It is limited to the actions of states and can solve only problems those states want to solve, in ways that are approved by the existing member states. Whatever one's disappointments in how the United Nations has functioned, the UN has not, for the most part, failed its member states. Rather, if there has been failure, it is the states—especially the permanent members of the Security Council—that have failed the UN.

Shortly after the United Nations was founded, it became apparent that the United States and the Soviet Union were not going to cooperate very often. In fact, the Cold War soon began. In the early years after the UN's founding, the United States had a number of allies in the General Assembly and was thus able to use the UN to prosecute its side of the Cold War. The Soviet Union, in turn, was isolated and used its veto in the Security Council on numerous occasions. However, UN membership expanded rapidly, due largely to an influx of newly independent former colonies of Britain and France. In 1946, there were only 55 members of the UN; by 1960, there were 99, and by 1982, 157. Now there are 193, including two non-member "observer states," Palestine and the Holy See (the Vatican).

By the late 1950s, the United States could no longer count on an automatic two-thirds majority in the General Assembly for support, as most of the new states considered themselves nonaligned, and in 1966, the United States cast its first veto in the Security Council. For decades, during which the United States refused to recognize the Communist government of mainland China, that country had been excluded from the UN. By 1971, however, a watershed was reached when—over US objections—China was seated in place of Taiwan (whose presence as a Security Council member had been something of a farce since 1949, when the government of "nationalist" China was defeated by Maoist insurgents and forced to take refuge—with US support—on the island of Formosa). UN security operations had earlier ceased to be a means whereby the United States prosecuted the Cold War, and the United Nations instead entered more clearly into a phase of limited peacekeeping and peacemaking.

Attitudes Toward the UN

Many conservatives in the United States have long been uncomfortable with the United Nations, seeing it as—at minimum—an infringement on national sovereignty. "Get the US out of the UN," read bumper stickers and the occasional roadside sign, "and get the UN out of the US" (Perhaps ironically, many less-powerful nations today have adopted these slogans in large part due to their anger at what they perceive to be undue influence of the United States over the United Nations.)

As economically developing countries have become a numerical majority in the United Nations, right-wing opposition within the United States to US membership intensified. Annoyance with the organization has been fueled by the fact that every state has one vote in the General Assembly, no matter how small it may be or how despotically governed. Moreover, the UN General Assembly has voted for numerous resolutions that many Americans have found repugnant, such as one in 1975 stating that Zionism (widely, if

perhaps erroneously, believed to be associated with violence and discrimination against Palestinians) is a "form of racism." Moreover, the United
Nations tends to address concerns that conservatives in the United States
generally oppose: disarmament, economic and social equality, environmental protection, and women's rights.

Conservatism and nationalism tend to be tightly linked, and many conservatives oppose any organization, such as the UN, that they see as threatening the absolute national sovereignty of their country. As a result, for a
long time the United States lagged behind other member states in paying its
dues, while regularly threatening to provide even less support unless various
demands—for organizational rearrangement as well as greater compliance to
United States wishes more generally—were met.

From a Peace Studies perspective, the major failing of the UN has been
its inability to achieve global disarmament, to prevent wars, and to end
quickly those armed conflicts it could not prevent. On the other hand, the
UN offers a vision of superordinate goals, including the coming together
of sovereign states because of a commitment— albeit sometimes a modest
one—to address planetary concerns. The UN may also help legitimize the
idea of world government. Meanwhile, the UN does good work in bettering
the world's social, economic, educational, medical, scientific, environmental, and cultural conditions. This is desirable in itself, and also helps create
conditions more conducive to positive peace. In addition, the UN has had
some, admittedly limited, success in acting directly to make peace and to
keep it.

Peacemaking Efforts

In the immediate aftermath of World War II, it was hoped that the
"grand alliance" that defeated Germany and Japan would hold together
and that the major powers, acting in concert, would fashion a truly functional system of collective security. The Security Council was empowered
to identify an aggressor and then to request various member states to provide military force as necessary to enforce the peace. To keep disagreements from escalating and possibly even causing war between them, the
permanent members of the Security Council were each given veto power
over any such decision: This meant, in effect, that the United Nations
would be paralyzed if any one of its permanent Security Council members
opposed a given action.

The Security Council veto has periodically acted as intended: As a circuit
breaker, preventing the multinational system from overloading and possibly
blowing itself apart when it faced situations that were quite contentious.
But, vetoes by members of the Security Council have also prevented UN
involvement in many cases where it might have been helpful, such as Syria.

As a result, the United Nations is virtually powerless to resolve disputes
which any of the permanent members believes the UN should not handle.
On the other hand, the UN has been able to function much longer than
its predecessor, the League of Nations, and—especially in issues involving
the less powerful member states—more effectively as well. The UN has been
involved in a wide array of armed disputes, and its roles have varied from
brokering peace to active *peacemaking* (which has sometimes come close to
war fighting) and peacekeeping. UN-sponsored commissions have arranged
ceasefires between Indonesian independence fighters and their Dutch colonial occupiers, as well as between India and Pakistan during two of their
wars over Kashmir. The United Nations supervised successful elections in a

number of war-torn countries, including East Timor, El Salvador, Cambodia, and the Democratic Republic of Congo.

The UN has also been involved as an armed intermediary, supervising ceasefires in Cyprus, Angola, Namibia, and Mozambique, among other trouble spots. Although the United Nations did not formally have armed peacekeepers during the conflicts in Bosnia, Kosovo, during the Gulf War, and during the Libyan civil war (military operations in these cases were carried out by the North Atlantic Treaty Organization, often with leadership by the United States), it was called in afterward, to help monitor ceasefires and attempt a degree of subsequent "nation-building." Nor has the UN acted to defend the rights of Tibetans (because of Chinese veto power), or of Chechens, Georgians, or Ukrainians (due to Russian veto power).

The United Nations played a key role, however, in ending the civil war in Sudan and in assisting the millions of displaced refugees from the Darfur region of that country. It may also be called upon to assist efforts to rebuild Iraq in the aftermath of that country's devastating wars, and quite possibly, to oversee negotiations between the West-supported government in Afghanistan and the Taliban, after NATO and US forces are no longer directly involved.

More controversially, the Korean War was officially prosecuted by the United Nations (although, in fact, the United States provided the vast majority of UN forces) against North Korea and its ally, China. The United Nations also held sway in the Congo during the 1960s. Perhaps the most prolonged UN involvement, however, has been in the Middle East, which provides a case study of both success and failure.

The Arab-Israeli Wars

Over Arab opposition, the General Assembly in 1947 approved a British plan dividing Palestine between a Jewish and an Arab state, with Jerusalem to be an international city governed under UN auspices. When Israel was declared an independent state, in 1948, it was invaded by armies from Egypt, Syria, Lebanon, Iraq, and Transjordan (now Jordan). The General Assembly and Security Council tried vainly to stop the fighting. That same year, a Swedish diplomat, Folke Bernadotte, was sent to the Middle East as a potential mediator, but was assassinated by Jewish extremists from a paramilitary Zionist organization. Eventually, US diplomat and UN mediator Ralph Bunche established an armistice in 1949, for which he received a Nobel Peace Prize. However, the issue was resolved not so much by UN diplomacy as by force of arms—that is, by Israel's defeat of Arab armies in the field. Indeed, the underlying issues, more than seven decades later, are still unresolved.

By the end of the initial round of fighting, Israel had expanded its borders beyond those approved by the UN, and hundreds of thousands of stateless Palestinian refugees fled to neighboring Arab states, including the West Bank and Gaza, where they remain today, largely unassimilated and demanding a homeland. In 1956, Egypt blockaded Israeli shipping in the Gulf of Aqaba and nationalized the Suez Canal, whereupon Britain and France, in coordination with Israel, invaded Egypt and captured the Sinai Peninsula as well as the Suez Canal. Britain and France vetoed action by the Security Council; the General Assembly then called for a ceasefire, which was achieved several months later. In this case, UN pressure was relatively unimportant because the UK and France were pushed to withdraw by the vigorous opposition of their close ally, the United States. But the General Assembly arranged for UN troops to guard the border between Egypt and Israel, which agreed to pull back to the 1949 ceasefire line.

This UN presence, the United Nations Emergency Force, represented an important and innovative step, first proposed by Canadian premier Lester Pearson (for which he won a Nobel Peace Prize) and administered by Secretary-General Dag Hammarskjöld: a new system that came to be known as "peacekeeping." The idea was not to favor either side but to enforce the peace by interposing a lightly armed UN presence between the belligerents. By what Hammarskjöld called "preventive diplomacy," UN peacekeepers help patrol and maintain otherwise shaky ceasefires. Minimally, this prevents further bloodshed; maximally, it gains time and helps create conditions under which creative diplomacy might help resolve the conflict.

In Hammarskjöld's conception—which has been retained ever since—the United Nations seeks to isolate local conflicts from big power involvement, in part by recruiting peacekeepers largely from smaller states. As of 2020, there were roughly 100,000 UN peacekeepers provided by more than 120 different countries, deployed in 20 different peacekeeping missions, the great majority in Africa. The six countries providing the most peacekeepers are, in order, Ethiopia, India, Pakistan, Bangladesh, Rwanda, and Nepal. And the six countries that provide the most funding for these activities are, in order, the US, China, Japan, Germany, France, and the UK.

Limitations on the UN's Use of Force

The UN's ability to serve as an active peacemaker and peacekeeper has been severely limited. For one thing, member states have never been able to agree on maintaining an independent UN force with sufficient military strength and political independence to deter possible adversaries.

In the case of many large-scale conflicts, the United Nations was uninvolved or ineffective, reduced to making futile pleas for peace or even—worse yet—failing to make any statement at all. Moreover, the UN has been hamstrung regarding conflicts involving the permanent members of the Security Council. The United Nations played no part, for example, in ending the struggle between Algeria and France—during which about 10 percent of the population of Algeria perished before they won their independence—because France, as a permanent Security Council member, wielded a veto. In response to the Iranian hostage crisis from 1979 to 1980, the Security Council toothlessly requested that Iran release the US hostages, but the Soviet Union vetoed a recommendation for economic sanctions. The United Nations also did essentially nothing to end the Vietnam War, the Soviet involvement in the civil war in Afghanistan, US military subversion of Nicaragua, Soviet incursions into Hungary and Czechoslovakia, Chinese oppression in Tibet and of the Uighurs, and Russian military actions in Chechnya and Ukraine.

The UN was also unable to intervene and prevent ethnic warfare in Bosnia and Kosovo, because Russia—ethnically and historically linked to Serbia—threatened to veto any such actions. (Eventually, NATO intervened militarily, with the United Nations subsequently enlisted to assist peacekeeping after the heavy fighting was over.) The UN eventually helped end famines in Somalia; but only after US forces suffered a small but humiliating military defeat. Shamefully, the United Nations (like the United States) did nothing to prevent genocide by the Khmer Rouge in Cambodia during the 1970s or by Rwandan Hutus against Tutsis in 1994. The US-led invasion of Iraq in 2003 was undertaken after it was clear that the UN would not support such an action, so the United States did not attempt to get a UN resolution to authorize the invasion.

At the time, such unilateralism on the part of the George W. Bush administration appeared to weaken the UN or, at least, to underscore its inability to prevent war; later, once the devastating effects of the Iraq War became clear, UN opposition to such adventurism may well have enhanced its prestige. The merits of concerted, multilateral intervention (assuming, of course, that any such intervention is warranted) may also have become more apparent as a result of the Iraq debacle. At the same time, the UN's inability to intervene significantly in the Syrian bloodletting because of threatened vetoes by Russia and China has not generated confidence in its willingness or ability to prevent future violent conflicts in which the major powers have differing interests.

Ups and Downs of Peacekeeping

The fact that the United Nations hasn't prevented or stopped many wars does not mean that it has not been effective in certain cases. Although the UN has not been a cure-all for the disease of war generally, it has achieved some notable successes: it has negotiated more than 200 different peaceful settlements, helping bring about an end to the Iran-Iraq War, as well as civil wars in El Salvador and Namibia, and it administered the withdrawal of Soviet troops from Afghanistan. It also supervised elections in Angola and East Timor.

Peacekeeping troops—lightly armed, blue-helmeted "soldiers without enemies"— currently serve as valuable buffers between contending forces in many past and potential hotspots worldwide (including Bosnia and Cyprus). They have also been important in monitoring compliance with ceasefires, supervision of disengagement lines, the maintenance of a "no man's land" between belligerents, and so forth. When neutral forces are interposed between armed adversaries, suspicious activities are less likely to be misinterpreted as a provocation, and intentional provocations themselves are less likely.

UN operations in the Golan Heights, for example, have been quite fruitful. This elevated region along the Israeli-Syrian border has great strategic value because it constitutes a high spot from which one can look down on Damascus and Jerusalem. Under UN supervision, the Golan Heights was effectively demilitarized, setting the stage for negotiations that might eventually lead to it being returned by Israel to Syria, presumably as part of a more comprehensive regional peace agreement.

However, in many cases the United Nations has only been "effective" after the guns have roared, and/or depleted treasuries, popular impatience, and exhaustion have forced governments to seek some kind of settlement as a result. A peacekeeping regime helps produce an atmosphere of calm, in which a peaceful solution can be negotiated. But even successful peacekeeping can have drawbacks. Although it may save lives at the time, UN-sponsored peacekeeping may also help perpetuate a crisis, by reducing the urgency of the conflicting parties to reach a political solution. By taking the edge off a conflict, UN peacekeeping may on occasion prolong the unresolved situation, making it more tolerable and even part of the way of life in the affected region.

Another disadvantage to peacekeeping is that, occasionally, UN forces have been inserted when there is no peace to keep. In addition, these forces may be inadequately trained and equipped, or provided with guidelines for military engagement that render them ineffective. For example, outgunned

UN forces were unable to prevent the slaughter of thousands of Bosnian Muslim men and boys in 1995 in Srebrenica during Bosnia's struggle for independence from the former Yugoslavia, and several hundred UN peacekeepers were taken hostage by Sierra Leone rebels in 2000. And, in at least a few cases, UN peacekeeping forces have even been accused of engaging in rape and other atrocities.

Even at its best, international peacekeeping is not merely an altruistic endeavor. Thus, peacekeeping directly serves the security, political, and commercial interests of most countries. But although the United Nations is often a first line of crisis response overseas, the United States (and, to a much lesser extent, a few other states) has fallen behind in paying dues and peacekeeping assessments. These overdue bills limit the UN's ability to respond rapidly to crises and to implement needed reforms. Ironically, given its reliance on the United Nations as a potential means of preserving peace and preventing genocide, the United States has often balked at paying its UN bill, which represents *less than one quarter of 1 percent* of planned US annual military budgets. Nonetheless, the US share of United Nations dues greatly exceeds that of any other country, and constitutes more than 20 percent of the overall UN budget.

If the United States—and, indeed, any country—is to avoid the costs and dangers of a unilateral role as world policeman, greater— not less—reliance upon and support of the United Nations is in order. According to the 2019 Global Peace Index, violence imposes a worldwide financial cost of about $14 trillion, or about 13 percent of the world's gross economic product. By contrast, investments in peacekeeping and peace building total roughly $15 billion: approximately 0.1 percent of the annual global cost of violence. The US alone has by some estimates spent about $4.1 trillion, just to conduct its wars in Afghanistan, Iraq, and Syria.

A Troublesome Example: Darfur

Since 2003, thousands of activists and celebrities urged support of the UN mission in Darfur, hoping that peacekeepers would end (or at least reduce) the violence, most of it initiated by the Sudanese government in Khartoum, which displaced nearly three million people, half of Darfur's population. The UN peacekeeping force in Darfur considerably mitigated the human suffering there, by providing and distributing humanitarian aid and by restraining violence on the part of nomadic government-sponsored militias.

These accomplishments, however, required that the UN team make substantial concessions to the Sudanese government and its military. As of 2019, mortality rates in Darfur had diminished to prewar levels, but rather than solving the Darfur problem, UN involvement may have frozen it, converting refugee camps into "instant city-slums" that threaten to become permanent, while the Sudanese government has acted as though the United Nations has relieved it of responsibility to clean up the mess it has largely created. Hence, rather than facilitating the return of displaced Darfurians to their former lives, or actively participating in pushing the Sudanese government to make needed social and economic adjustments, UN peacekeepers, while pursuing a humanitarian agenda, found themselves supporting the parlous status quo. The UN peacekeeping force in Darfur was underfunded, underequipped, and suffered casualties inflicted by organized groups of bandits. However unsatisfactory, this outcome was probably preferable to the fullscale genocide and human catastrophe that preceded UN involvement. In any event, this mission was terminated at the end of 2020.

The approved budget for UN Peacekeeping operations for 2020–2021 was about $6.85 billion, which is less than four hundredths of one percent of the $1.85 *trillion* that the total world military spending during that same year). Western countries in particular have largely been willing to shoulder this cost, seeing this as preferable to ignoring a preventable disaster or sending in their own troops; it is not certain however, how much longer this will continue.

Other Functions of the United Nations

Third-Party Mediation

UN mediators have occasionally served as trustworthy third parties, helping belligerents reach acceptable and face-saving agreements. Former Secretary-General Javier Pérez de Cuéllar and other UN diplomats were instrumental in helping reach the agreement that led to the withdrawal of Soviet troops from Afghanistan (1988–1989). UN secretaries-general and their deputies have also served as intermediaries in many conflicts, helping achieve ceasefires. In general, the world benefits considerably from the mediating work of the United Nations.

Dean Rusk—US secretary of state during the Cuban Missile Crisis—revealed that President Kennedy had prepared a memo to be proposed by then–Secretary-General U Thant in the event that the United States and the Soviet Union appeared headed toward war. This memo suggested a "compromise" that the US government had already decided would be acceptable, but only if it came from a disinterested third party, not the Soviet Union. This proposed deal—that the United States would remove its land-based missiles from Britain and Turkey in return for the Soviets dismantling their Cuban missile sites—proved unnecessary, because Premier Khrushchev eventually cut a deal with President Kennedy. It does, however, show the value of a respected and disinterested third party: even if the United Nations has only prevented one major war (never mind a nuclear war), this is sufficient to justify its existence.

A Forum for Debate

On occasion, the United Nations is derided as a mere debating society. But debating societies can be very useful, providing opportunity for government representatives to meet and exchange views, often without the glare of publicity. (In the words of one observer, the United Nations "has become indispensable before it has become effective.") There have also been cases in which outraged domestic public opinion has pressed a government to respond to some international crisis, while at the same time peace has been best served by a government's inactivity. "Blowing off steam" is less harmful than blowing up people. In such cases, the United Nations provides an opportunity for states to confront their adversaries rhetorically rather than through bloodshed.

For example, US authorities concurred that it would be unwise to intervene militarily when the Soviet Union put down a nationalist revolt in Hungary in 1956 by invading that Warsaw Pact country; instead, US delegates roundly condemned the Soviets at the United Nations, thereby giving the American public the impression that something was being done on behalf of the Hungarian resistance, while avoiding military confrontation with the USSR. Misleading? Yes. Useful? Also yes. The Soviets likewise protested but abstained from interventions when the United States unilaterally dispatched troops to Lebanon in 1958, to the Dominican Republic in 1965, and to Iraq in 2003. Similarly, Arab delegates castigate Israel regularly, attacking it verbally while Arab armies generally refrain from doing so militarily.

Preventing Major Power Conflicts

The United Nations has largely moved away from its original function of providing collective security (whereby an attack on one member state is to be considered an attack on all). Peacekeeping, on the other hand, has emerged as an intermittently successful UN innovation, not only in itself but also as a means of decreasing the likelihood that the major powers might intervene in conflicts between other nations and thereby further inflame the situation.

At the creation of the UN, its founders hoped that concerted military action by the major powers would keep the peace; now, the United Nations operates under an opposite assumption—namely, that peace will be usually enhanced by excluding the major powers from crises and instead recruiting peacekeepers from smaller, neutral states. Former Secretary-General Dag Hammarskjöld admitted in 1961 that the United Nations could not overcome superpower rivalry, as during US/USSR disputes over Berlin or when there are disagreements regarding nuclear weapons. But it could work, he maintained, to localize disputes in which the superpowers did not have an overriding interest. In Hammarskjöld's words, the job of the United Nations was "not to bring mankind to Heaven, but rather, to save it from Hell."

Constraints on the Use of Force

In theory, the UN has the authority, through its Charter, to raise military forces and inject them into a conflict without the permission of the conflicting parties. Article 42 of the UN Charter authorizes the Security Council to call for military operations against aggressors, and Article 43 calls on member states to provide such forces as requested. Moreover, Article 39 of the UN Charter says that the Security Council shall

> determine the existence of any threat to the peace, breach of the peace, or act of aggression and shall make recommendations, or decide what measure shall be taken . . . to maintain international peace and security . . . . Such action may include demonstrations, blockade, and other operations by air, sea, or land forces of Members of the United Nations.

The buildup of forces by adversarial nations, an oppressive domestic social system, or even the ascension to power of a militaristic government could plausibly be defined as a "threat to the peace." In theory, therefore, the United Nations has substantial discretionary powers for the use of force. In practice, however, it has been very cautious. Not only has it generally kept out of Big Power affairs, but it has also studiously avoided involvement in most civil wars as well. If the United Nations were to take its original mandate literally and attempt to squash any threat to peace, in the process it might well be squelching any hopes for national liberation on the part of Kurds, Basques, Kosovars, Catalans, and other groups. For better and worse, the United Nations operates under numerous constraints.

In summary, the weaknesses of the United Nations are more a reflection of the weakness of the world system as a whole: the fact that the world has been divided into contending and sovereign states, each of which nearly always evaluates a policy through the lens of national interest rather than international benefit.

Sensitivity to State Sovereignty

The UN attempts to be sensitive to issues of national sovereignty, trying not to force choices between allegiance to the state on the one hand and allegiance to the world body on the other. For example, since the Korean War and the UN's controversial Congo intervention in the early 1960s, prospective host countries have had the option of forbidding any UN peacekeeping presence; the United Nations can send observers into a country only if it is specifically invited to do so, or under a direct mandate from the Security Council. And the United Nations usually withdraws its forces when the host country so requests (as happened in Egypt in 1967). "The umbrella was removed," complained Israeli diplomat Abba Eban, "at the precise moment when it began to rain." As a result, the UN has been less forceful than it might otherwise be, but it has also been able to exist in a changing world of self-interested states. Such flexibility and adaptability have generally served the organization well and has kept it available for those cases in which it has been able to make its mark.

At the same time, rival superpowers have usually decided to handle their own controversies by themselves (e.g., during the Berlin and Cuban Missile crises and also during the various strategic arms negotiations among the great powers, in which the United Nations has had essentially no part). Similarly, the major powers continue to vigorously rebuff what they see as UN interference in their own foreign policy goals. For example, the United States did not consult with the United Nations before sending troops to the Dominican Republic in 1965 and to Grenada in 1983. The US-led invasion of Iraq in 2003 occurred in the face of explicit UN objections, although this breach of international peace was framed by the George W. Bush administration, in part, as an effort to enforce earlier UN resolutions directed against the regime of Saddam Hussein.

Increasingly, the United Nations has become a forum for addressing the tension between the industrialized, mainly wealthy North on the one hand and the largely impoverished South on the other hand, as well as for confronting worldwide, transnational environmental challenges. To some extent, the various economic and social agencies of the UN also have addressed the long-standing North/South economic imbalance.

Functionalism

When considering the possible role of the United Nations in promoting peace, one may be most likely to think about disarmament conferences and such measures as international peacekeeping and mediation. But according to advocates of another approach—"functionalism"—the long-term prospects of peace are enhanced more by other, clearly humanitarian activities that cut across state and national borders.

Doing Good

Functionalism, in sociology and social anthropology, examines how various parts of culture and society contribute to their smooth functioning as a whole. In international relations theories, functionalism usually refers to an approach to the work of international organizations that advocates international cooperation on scientific, humanitarian, social, and economic issues, as demonstrated by such agencies as the WHO, the FAO, and the Universal Postal Union, which are often given short shrift in popular discussions of the United Nations. The aims of these organizations do not include the establishment or maintenance of peace as such; rather, they include such goals as eradicating malaria, providing protein to undernourished children, and seeing to the fair exchange of international mail. Here is a sample of some of the humanitarian efforts and successes of the United Nations:

1. A 13-year effort by the WHO eradicated smallpox worldwide in 1980. The WHO also helped wipe out polio from the Western Hemisphere. In 1974, only 5 percent of children in developing countries had been immunized against these "preventable plagues": polio, tetanus, measles, whooping cough, diphtheria, and tuberculosis. By 1995, as a result of the efforts of UNICEF and the WHO, the immunization rate was close to 80 percent, saving the lives of more than 3 million children each year.

2. The UN has provided famine relief to millions of people. The International Fund for Agricultural Development, for example, provides economic credit for poor and marginalized groups, benefiting more than 230 million people in nearly 100 developing countries, while building the potential for long-term hunger relief.

3. Through sponsorship of several international treaties, the United Nations has been a leader in efforts to protect the ozone layer and curb global warming, notably through its Intergovernmental Panel on Climate Change.

4. UN forestry action plans help limit deforestation and promote sustainable forestry practices for 90 countries.

5. The United Nations has also been active in providing safe drinking water for 1.3 billion people in rural areas and maintains ongoing efforts to help prevent overfishing and to clean up pollution.

6. UN programs have helped raise the literacy rate of women in developing countries from 36 percent in 1970 to 77 percent in 2018.

7. The UN Mission for Emergency Ebola Response, established in September 2014, deployed financial, logistical and human resources to Guinea, Liberia, and Sierra Leone, under oversight by the World Health Organization (WHO), to support the push to zero cases of the Ebola virus in those countries; it was disbanded a year later, having largely achieved its goal, albeit with important contributions by individual states (notably the United States and Cuba), as well as such nongovernmental organizations as Doctors Without Borders. Similarly, the WHO took the lead in coordinating international responses to the coronavirus pandemic, especially beginning in 2020.

Deemphasizing the Role of States

For its proponents, functionalism is also a way of deemphasizing the role of states (although this is rarely admitted in public). Functionalism pins its hopes on a three-pronged strategy:

1. By reducing human misery through eradicating diseases, developing new strains of food crops, disseminating technological know-how, promoting literacy, and so forth, it is hoped that war will be made less likely.

2. By showing that institutions other than the state can attend to human needs—sometimes much better than states do—it is hoped that absolute state sovereignty will gradually be weakened (although this goal is not explicitly endorsed by the United Nations itself).

3. By providing opportunities for interactions across political borders, it is hoped that mutual understanding, tolerance, and respect will be enhanced.

It is difficult to evaluate the success, or the future prospects, of functionalism. Although many people think that misery leads to war, no clear evidence supports this claim, at least with regard to interstate war. Prosperity, in fact, often seems to have made violence more likely, not less, because strong and wealthy states, flushed with self-confidence, may be more inclined to engage in military adventures, whereas weaker ones—having fewer resources at their disposal—tend to be cautious. On the other hand, making a better life for people might well decrease the chances of rebellions and civil wars, which constitute the overwhelming majority of recent armed conflicts. And the humanitarian goals of functionalism are worthwhile in themselves, regardless of whether they result in fewer wars.

When it comes to undermining the authority of states, functionalism may be on strong footing. Thus, some social scientists (whose ideas often stem from the political philosophies of Hobbes, Locke, and Rousseau) emphasize the so-called social contract, whereby the loyalty of citizens to the state is supposed to result from a kind of exchange: the state provides certain benefits (most notably, security from violent attacks) to the populace, and, in return, the people support the state by, for example, paying taxes and going to war when told to do so. But if inoculations are provided by doctors from the WHO, new tractors are supplied by technicians from the FAO, and literacy programs are conducted by teachers from UNESCO, it is possible that in subtle ways the state's claim to the loyalty of its citizens is diminished. Many functionalists also hope that by experiencing the benefits of cooperation across traditional national and state boundaries, citizens could be weaned away from narrow, nationalistic concerns and gradually be imbued with an ethos that is cooperative and transnational.

Proponents of functionalism should take into consideration that states have historically asserted that patriotic loyalty supersedes other affiliations, often obtaining the cooperation and service of their subjects while providing little in return. States jealously guard their sovereignty and resist activities that might subvert the loyalty of their citizens. One difficulty impeding the worldwide campaign against AIDS, for example, has been the refusal of some states to admit that they have an HIV-related problem, for fear that it will result in a loss of international prestige and tourist dollars.

Nonetheless, by accepting the authority of various functional international agencies, states are agreeing to certain limitations on their sovereignty. For example, the use of airspace and sea lanes is now increasingly governed by decisions made by such low-profile UN entities as the International Civil Aviation Organization and the International Maritime Organization, respectively. In these dimensions of international behavior, a state no longer follows its own rules and procedures without regard to other nations. Also, in international telecommunications, the best frequencies are not simply preempted by the most powerful broadcasters; rather, it is universally recognized that to be legitimate, broadcasting frequencies must be allocated by the International Telecommunication Union.

In addition, communication and other related interactions provided by UN agencies are clearly beneficial. In his correspondence with Albert Einstein, Sigmund Freud declared, "Anything that creates emotional ties between human beings must inevitably counteract war . . . . Everything that leads to important shared action creates such common feelings." However, most wars have occurred between neighbors, who often know each other quite well. Close contact can breed greater antagonisms.

The possibility nonetheless exists that positive experiences among different and sometimes conflicting individuals and governments will lead to a snowballing, positive feedback effect, which in turn can lead to improved relations at the official level. There have been many gains from sister-city relationships and international pen pals, which serve to break down the political, geographical, and ideological barriers between states. Turkey and Greece, for example, have a long history of hostility. In 1999, both countries were devastated by earthquakes in rapid succession, and in each case aid was provided by the other state to the victims. The resulting "earthquake diplomacy" appears to have thawed relations between these old rivals, although Turkey and Greece still disagree about the status of the Turkish part of Cyprus. (Since 2016, the Greek government has been preoccupied by its financial and refugee crises, and Turkey by its own growing authoritarianism, an unsuccessful coup attempt, conflicts with Kurds and with ISIS, as well as with on-again, off-again relations with Russia plus its conflicted courtship of the European Union.)

For most states, a dramatic shared threat—such as an alien invasion, an asteroid on a collision course with Earth, or a global pandemic, such as Covid-19—might be needed to get feuding countries to put their antagonism and mistrust aside. Meanwhile, some governments have proposed multinational efforts to send a manned mission to Mars, to eradicate illiteracy and such diseases as malaria and tuberculosis, and so forth. Accordingly, transnational cooperative ventures of this sort offer the prospect of benefiting humanity in many ways.

The Newfound Folly of Fragmentation

There has also been a discernible trend, especially manifested by Brexit (the UK's withdrawal from the European Union) and in the growth of avowedly nationalist political parties and leaders in Hungary, India, Turkey, Russia, Brazil, Poland, and elsewhere, away from international cooperation and toward unilateralism and isolationism. Especially problematic was the retreat from international cooperation on the part of the United States, orchestrated by the Trump Administration. The US had been the leader in designing and implementing most of the post–World War II organized global intergovernmental systems, from such military alliances as NATO to financial and environmental collaborations.

These worldwide "rules-based systems," although not perfect, constituted a series of frameworks for dealing with problems on a global level. Recent movements by nationalist-populist and usually right-wing forces toward fragmentation, by contrast, have involved denouncing most of these arrangements, and, in the case of the United States, going so far as to withdraw from others, including nuclear agreements with Iran, the INF Treaty with Russia, the Paris Climate Accords, and even from such philanthropic activities as those carried out by UNESCO. The result of Trump's "America First" efforts were increasingly, America Alone, and the US and the world were almost certainly made worse off as a result.

By rejecting numerous rules and norms, increased fragmentation is a return to unilateralism and isolationism not seen since before World War II. It appears based on the belief that international interactions are inevitably zero-sum exchanges, in which a gain for one necessitates loss for another, so that each country—especially the strong and influential ones—are advised to accomplish what they can at the expense of others. It is an approach that denies several realities: that many problems are global and can only be solved globally; that win-win solutions are not only possible, but frequent; and that, conversely, a loss for one country often involves a loss for another. It seems to be not only a result of certain influential, short-sighted leaders, but also a response, in part, to right-wing populist pressures by people who have felt excluded from economic and social benefits, leading them to support policies that are not only nationalistic but also nihilistic.

In any event, insistence on "going it alone" and privileging myopic nationalism over global betterment has hobbled international cooperation in the short run. Whether policies of global coordination can be effectively reconstituted, and if so, how much time, effort, and painful adjustments will be required is yet to be seen.

Regional Organizations

Such competing military alliances as NATO and the former Warsaw Pact were directed *outward* against potential aggressors and were not designed as "collective security" organizations, which are intended to protect all members against an aggressor from *within* a given region. By many accounts, NATO has been among the most "successful" cooperative military alliances in history, originally founded to oppose the Soviet Union and having emerged "victorious" when the USSR fell apart. Even during the Cold War, however, there were substantial strains within NATO, over plans to deploy intermediate range nuclear weapons, as well as regarding details of the command structure and the threats that might justify a response by the organization as a whole.

Major disputes, continuing to the present day, concern the "rules of engagement" (as in Afghanistan, where the United States opposed the insistence of such NATO member states as Germany that their troops refrain from direct combat) as well as relative military budgets of member states. In 2019, for example, the United States devoted 3.1 percent of its gross domestic product to its military, whereas the other NATO states averaged less than 1.0 percent, leading to the complaint by some influential Americans— notably President Donald Trump—that these other states were "not doing their share," and that as a result, the US might not come to the aid of a NATO country if it were attacked. Critics of this threat point out NATO is not supposed to be a source of mutual protection via deterrence, not a "protection racket."

Other regional organizations include the Organization of African Unity (OAU), the Organization of American States (OAS), the Association of Southeast Asian Nations (ASEAN), the Arab League, and the Organization of Islamic Cooperation. In some cases, these organizations have helped maintain the peace, providing for third-party pressure to be brought against member states that might otherwise go to war. In other cases, they have helped terminate wars. For example, when the "Soccer War" broke out between El Salvador and Honduras in 1969, the OAS was able to arrange a ceasefire and provided independent observers to supervise its details. The OAU helped facilitate the settlement of border disputes between Morocco and Algeria and among Kenya, Somalia, and Ethiopia, and it played a major role in coordinating African opposition to South African apartheid. A military force from West African states, notably Nigeria, helped stabilize the chaotic post–civil war situation in Liberia.

The UN Charter explicitly endorses regional peacekeeping organizations. After an African Union Mission in Sudan was unable to end the genocide and keep the peace in that war-torn nation, a United Nations contingent replaced it in 2008. Prospects of success, however, have remained uncertain because Sudan and the newly independent South Sudan have fought over oil fields in the south, access to which requires pipelines running through the north. In other cases, the United Nations has taken a backseat to regional organizations, as evidenced by the role of NATO military forces in enforcing peace in Bosnia, Kosovo, and, less successfully, in Afghanistan after the US-led "coalition" overthrew the Taliban in 2001.

In the former Yugoslavia, the United Nations was initially unable to act because of Russian and Chinese opposition to UN intervention. Both countries were concerned that a precedent of UN intervention within a country's territorial borders might have serious implications for their treatment of some of their own rebellious provinces, notably Chechnya and Tibet. So, military action in Kosovo was carried out by NATO, in an extension of its traditional role, because the former Yugoslavia was outside the territory of any NATO member. NATO activities in Afghanistan occurred after the United States found that its military resources were stretched thin in Iraq. Similarly, NATO air power backed the rebels who overthrew Libya's strongman Muammar Gadhafi, might have prevented genocide but at the cost of making Libya a war-ridden "failed state."

On balance, regionalism has not been especially successful, for the same reason that the United Nations has been limited in its peacemaking: state sovereignty restricts its effectiveness. In addition, regional organizations have in the past become vehicles for superpower domination. OAS members, for example, were largely coerced by the United States into supporting sanctions against Cuba and into approving the 1983 US invasion of Grenada. On the other hand, OAS pressure succeeded in getting Nicaragua (under right-wing dictator Somoza) to back down from its brief invasion in 1955 of demilitarized Costa Rica.

Intergovernmental Organizations

States also cooperate by forming so-called intergovernmental organizations (IGOs), such as the Organization of Petroleum Exporting Countries (OPEC). If, as Mao said, power grows out of the barrel of a gun, it can also grow out of a barrel of oil: the oil revenues of the Middle East OPEC members in 1970 totaled $4 billion; just 4 years later, following price increases by the oil cartel, the figure was $60 billion. Today, it is approaching $1 trillion.

International cartels can be effective in raising prices of their goods for sale; although this helps states exporting these commodities, it hurts others, which have to pay more for these products. Moreover, increases in international prices do not always help the poor, even in exporting countries. For example, unroasted coffee rose from $0.60 per pound in the mid-1970s to more than $3 per pound in the late 1970s. As a result, the price to growers rose from $10.09 per pound to $10.40 per pound, which did not even keep up with inflation. And the pay raise for laborers was proportionately even less.

The OPEC oil embargo of 1973 was particularly painful for oil-poor developing countries, whose economic growth was strangled by their having to pay increased prices for petroleum. There is, accordingly, no clear evidence that monopoly cartels composed of producers, exporters, importers, etc. will further world peace, except perhaps indirectly by weakening the traditional, state-centered world system. Corporate monopolies seem as likely to foster war by generating intolerance, resentment, and further inequities of wealth. On the other hand, it is frequently difficult for OPEC member states to agree on a consistent policy: oil-rich states such as Saudi Arabia may prefer reducing output so as to maintain higher per-barrel prices, but are vulnerable to other states, like Russia, that wish to maximize production in order to obtain higher total revenue.

OPEC members' demands are often contradictory, as when Saudi Arabia, in 2015, maintained high output despite low per-barrel prices, seeking to keep prices low so as to punish its main competitors, Iran and Russia, which derive much of their income from oil exports, and also, perhaps, to discourage the "fracking" industry in the United States (which is an expensive way to access petroleum, and therefore vulnerable to low crude oil prices but has also led to the US becoming a net exporter of all oil products by 2019).

Another notable IGO—because of its subsequent transformation—was the European Coal and Steel Community (ECSC), established in 1950 to integrate the industrial economies of West Germany, France, Italy, and the Benelux countries (Belgium, the Netherlands, and Luxembourg). By 1958, the ECSC had become a larger, more integrated entity, the European Economic Community, also known as the Common Market. As of 2020, its successor, the European Union, comprises 27 states (nearly all of Western Europe, excepting Switzerland, Norway, and the United Kingdom) with a total population and gross national product exceeding that of the United States. Most trading and transportation barriers throughout Western and Central Europe have been eliminated, and 19 states are members of the European Monetary Union, employing a common currency, the euro.

The process of transnational integration exemplified by the EU could ultimately lead to eventual political union, a kind of United States of Europe; this, at least, had been the hope of at least some international-minded national leaders when the EU was first established. At minimum, it was hoped that this union would end the frequent wars that had long bedeviled Europe, in World War II.

Transnational integration of the sort experienced by Europe may also have disadvantages, such as a lack of flexibility on the part of member states to deal with specific needs and crises. For example, during the second decade of this century, the severe economic downturn that dramatically affected Greece and Spain starting in 2008 was precipitated, at least in part, by the fact that these countries were spending more than they were taking in. In the "old days," when Spain had its own currency, the *peseta*, and Greece had its *drachma*, it would have been possible for these countries to respond by devaluing their currency, which would have made their goods more affordable worldwide, and accordingly, improved their financial balance sheets by encouraging exports.

However, because the euro is a single currency for much of Europe, individual countries with struggling economies no longer have this option. Greece was forced to rely upon loans from wealthier EU countries—notably Germany—which precipitated resentment in Germany when these loans were not paid back, and anguish in Greece occasioned by the economic belt-tightening insisted upon by the lender countries. On top of this, economic and social pressures exerted by an influx of refugees and other migrants (especially from war-torn Muslim states), have threatened to disrupt trans-European unity and have also helped catalyze anti-immigrant sentiments and extreme right wing mobilization in much of otherwise "liberal" Europe. Another important contributor has been anger at the rules being dictated by what many ethno-nationalists call the "bureaucrats in Brussels" (seat of the EU). These were among the driving forces behind the vote for Brexit, whereby a narrow majority of British citizens voted in 2016 to exit the EU.

NGOs and MNCs

Importantly, networking and mobilization across international borders do not require the direct action of governments. There are many different kinds of nongovernmental organizations (NGOs), including many of the world's religions (e.g., the Roman Catholic Church, the Society of Friends, etc.) and other groups whose affiliations cut across political boundaries, such as Rotary International, the International Physicians for the Prevention of Nuclear War (winner of the 1986 Nobel Peace Prize), CARE, the International Olympic Committee, Amnesty International, Extinction Rebellion, and a wide array of scientific, educational, business, and other professional organizations.

Some of these groups seek as part of their agenda to break down the traditional barriers between states; most commonly, however, NGOs simply go about their affairs, which are usually best served by cutting across national and state borders. Thus, they are often subtly—benevolently—subversive of state authority. Whereas international organizations embody the principle of national sovereignty, transnational organizations try to ignore it. Among the most iconic such organizations (reflected in its name as well as its actions) is another Nobel Peace Prize winner, *Médecins Sans Frontières* (Doctors Without Borders).

A particularly important transnational phenomenon has been the emergence of powerful multinational corporations (MNCs). Such companies as Apple, Microsoft, General Electric, Royal Dutch Shell, BP, Google, Ciba/Geigy, Toyota, Lukoil, Amazon, Sony, Volkswagen, and others have commercial operations spread across many countries, as well as such transnational social media platforms as Facebook, Twitter, and so forth.

Controversy surrounds the role of these "multinationals." On the one hand, given their size—a number of MNC's have annual earnings larger than the GNP of many midsize countries—they could be powerful actors on behalf of transnational integration. And because profitable operations generally require a smooth international environment, multinationals theoretically could act to reduce the probability of war. Furthermore, by entangling different countries in a web of economic interdependence as well as rapid communication across state boundaries, multinational corporations may make war less likely, exemplifying a kind of benign functionalism—although one that is oriented more toward profits than altruism.

On the other hand, however, war has in the past often been precipitated by economic entanglements. During the 1930s, for example, rapidly growing Japan was dependent on the United States for oil and iron ore, and this dependence led to competition, resentment, and fear that the United States intended to contain further Japanese expansion. Japan's fears were not unfounded because once the US imposed an embargo, Japan lost access to three-fourths of its overseas trade and 88 percent of its imported oil. This act of "economic warfare" contributed significantly to the Japanese decision to attack Pearl Harbor in 1941.

Multinationals' pursuit of profits rather than peace can also sometimes involve the fomenting of revolution or coup (e.g., the role of Kennecott Copper and ITT in stimulating a coup against socialist Salvador Allende in Chile, in 1973), or counterrevolution (e.g., the influence of United Fruit in inducing the United States, through the Central Intelligence Agency, to overthrow the democratically elected Arbenz government in Guatemala in 1954).

In 1935, US Marine Corps commandant general Smedley Butler (winner of three Congressional Medals of Honor) offered this first-person testimony to the role of multinational corporations in generating military intervention:

> I spent 33 years in the Marines, most of my time being a high-class muscle man for big business, for Wall Street and the bankers. In short, I was a racketeer for capitalism. I helped purify Nicaragua for the international banking house of Brown Brothers in 1910–1912. I helped make Mexico and especially Tampico safe for American oil interests in 1914. I brought light to the Dominican Republic for American sugar interests in 1916. I helped make Haiti and Cuba a decent place for the National City [Bank] boys to collect revenue in. I helped in the rape of half a dozen Central American republics for the benefit of Wall Street. In China in 1927 I helped to see to it that Standard Oil went its way unmolested. I had a swell racket. I was rewarded with honors, medals, promotions. I might have given Al Capone a few hints. The best he could do was to operate a racket in three city districts. The Marines operated on three continents.[1]

Charles Wilson, US defense secretary during the Eisenhower administration, famously announced that "what's good for General Motors is good for the country." In many cases, government officials have apparently acted on this assumption, deploying military forces worldwide in support of various MNCs, especially in the developing world. There is nothing new about this: The British East India Company, for example, was arguably the primary guiding force behind English colonial expansion during the 18th and 19th centuries, just as the Hudson's Bay Company and the large railroads (such as Union Pacific) helped finance the often violent colonialist expansion of Canada and the United States throughout North America, at the expense of their indigenous peoples.

MNCs provide jobs in developing countries, and have therefore been lauded as helping to raise millions out of poverty. At the same time, however, these jobs are generally very low-paying, coming at the expense of employment in the multinationals' home countries; hence, multinationals are often criticized for "shipping jobs overseas," not out of humanitarian motives, but simply to save on labor costs and thereby to maximize their profits. In the process, multinationals also contribute to the long-term environmental degradation of host (i.e., often exploited) countries, while also keeping these countries economically and politically dependent on the MNC's. The resulting *dependencia* relationship (from the Spanish word for dependency) can be seen as a kind of neocolonialism that brings economic and social enslavement and neither prosperity nor peace.

The World Trade Organization (WTO), founded in the mid-1990s to replace the international economic framework known as GATT—the General Agreement on Tariffs and Trade—exemplifies the complexities of multinational financial integration, sometimes known as economic "global-ization." Worldwide communication and transportation have created what is increasingly a single, global economy. The WTO is dedicated to establish-ing "free trade," by eliminating tariffs and opposing—by economic sanc-tions if need be—national policies it perceives as constituting restraints on unfettered international trade. As a result of globalization, MNCs have been increasingly free to move factories to countries offering the lowest wage scales and minimal protection for human rights and the environment.

On the positive side, such corporate activities can provide jobs in devel-oping countries to impoverished people who might not otherwise be employed. Another benefit (albeit often short term) of globalization is the production of goods that can be purchased in countries other than one's own at lower prices than would otherwise be possible. On the other hand, union rights, worker safety laws and environmental protections are fre-quently minimal or nonexistent in countries where foreign corporations are active, and the WTO has been criticized as being a tool of the MNCs, simply fostering a "race to the bottom" when it comes to wages, human rights, and environmental stewardship. A major challenge for the WTO and for MNCs is to expand their activities to include more sustainable development for all people, not just for a privileged few.

World Government?

Most of the problems afflicting our planet and our species transcend the boundaries of the nation-state. A notable exception, war, in the modern era is a *product* of the nation-state, which leads to the question: What about the ultimate embodiment of "international cooperation"—world government? Many informed people have long sought alternatives to the nation-state sys-tem and in an age of diminishing resources, shrinking distances, and ever-more-devastating weaponry, and advocates of world government have long proposed thoughtful alternatives to international anarchy. They deserve a serious hearing.

Ever since the biblical Tower of Babel, human settlements have been plagued by their own political disunity. A potential solution has been to erase the existing political boundaries and to replace them with governmen-tal structures at the largest, most inclusive level. This suggestion has been raised most urgently with regard to war and its prevention because when it comes to war, nation-states have rarely been part of the solution; in the eyes of many, they are much of the problem. War-making has fractured the human community along ideological, social, and geopolitical lines. The pre-vention of war, accordingly, may well require that this community be recon-structed on a global scale.

Pre- and Post-Westphalian Worlds

In medieval times, most Europeans owed their allegiance to a feudal lord, who in turn may have been subject to the secular authority of the Holy Roman Emperor and the religious power of the Pope. Then came the so-called Wars of Religion, culminating with the Thirty Years' War and the signing, in 1648, of the Treaty of Westphalia, which inaugurated the European state system, eventually extended into the modern network of nation-states. For citizens in pre-Westphalian, medieval times, in much of Europe, day-to-day events were usually bounded by local surround-ings, nearby towns, and the closest castle with its protector (or oppressor) nobility. The Westphalian world expanded individual allegiance to include lands and people more distant than one's immediate surroundings. Technological advances, especially in transportation and communication, eventually made it unavoidable for individuals to travel to other places and to encounter people beyond their closest neighbors.

We might well currently now live in a post-Westphalian world, one in which the state or nation-state system is becoming as obsolete as its feudal antecedents. Our mounting problems—including global climate change, pollution, poverty, resource depletion, pandemics, runaway artificial intelligence, and the destructive effects of war—transcend the old traditional political boundaries, making it imperative that we think as planetary citizens. The world, in short, has become functionally integrated, even while it remains politically fragmented and economically segmented.

An Idea Whose Time Has Come?

A prime appeal of world government is that in a global super-community, political and legal authorities ought to be able to force quarreling subordinates to refrain from violence, to respect larger common interests, and to solve their disputes peacefully. When two individuals disagree about something, they are expected to resolve the issue in a law-abiding manner; they are generally not permitted to start shooting each other. Settling interpersonal disputes by a duel, common in previous centuries, is analogous to nation-states "settling" today's disputes by war. The former has been universally outlawed; the latter has not—or rather, to put it idealistically, not yet. Similarly, individual households are not "sovereign." They do not have the right to dump toxic chemicals into "their" stream, thereby poisoning their neighbors' water supplies. Why should states be permitted to do this?

International organizations, such as the United Nations, offer frameworks for transcending political boundaries, but as previously mentioned, they operate within the present system of sovereign states, which are free to disagree, overrule, or simply ignore these organizations if they choose because there is no larger authority that has the power to restrain states themselves. In modern times, the parts (states) claim to be greater than the whole: humanity and the planet Earth. With a just and globally recognized world government, this would likely change. States would be prohibited from violently imposing themselves on their neighbors whether economically, ecologically, or militarily, just as domestic governments now are empowered to prevent individuals from overstepping their legal bounds and as federal governments are tasked with keeping the peace among their smaller constituent parts.

A Brief History of Plans for World Government

By the 17th and 18th centuries, there were many proposals designed to establish worldwide restraints on war making. William Penn, in 1693, wrote *An Essay Towards the Present and Future Peace of Europe,* which proposed the establishment of a general parliament with sufficient military force to compel observance of its decrees. In 1713, the Abbé de Saint-Pierre, in his *Project for Perpetual Peace,* called for a "Senate of Europe" consisting of one representative from each European state, a plan that received much attention—and criticism. Voltaire, for example, noted that the states in question would overwhelmingly be monarchies. He maintained that for peace to be preserved, democracy was necessary; at that time—the 18th century, democracy, however—like world government today—was unachievable.

Notable among such proposals, in addition to Jeremy Bentham's *Plan for an Universal and Perpetual Peace* (1789), was one advanced by the philosopher Jean-Jacques Rousseau (1712–1778). In his *Discourse on the Origin of Inequality*, Rousseau claimed that ownership of private property (which Rousseau called "theft") was the underlying cause of war and that to achieve world peace, it would therefore be necessary to abolish private property worldwide. In *The Spirit of Laws* (1748), the French political philosopher Montesquieu claimed that war was not caused by human nature but by flaws inherent in the system of political states: "As soon as man enters a state of society . . . each particular society begins to feel its strength, whence arises a state of war between different nations."[2]

Like Montesquieu, Rousseau subsequently argued that war could be prevented by severing the bonds by which the state held people together: "It is only after he is a citizen," noted Rousseau in *The Social Contract*, "that he becomes a soldier." Rousseau also maintained that "conquering princes make war at least as much on their subjects as on their enemies" and that "all the business of kings . . . is concerned with two objects alone; to extend their rule abroad or make it more absolute at home."

Probably the most ambitious Enlightenment design for a potentially viable form of world government was put forth by the German philosopher Immanuel Kant. In *Perpetual Peace* (1795), Kant made the first major detailed effort to focus specifically on the dangers of arms races and armaments, rather than just proposing yet another kind of world parliament. He also argued strongly for "republican" governments—that is for representative democracies as being most likely to keep the peace, and that people ought to act upon a rational understanding of what is in their shared best interest.

Kant's views should be contrasted with those of Thomas Hobbes, who, in the mid-17th century, had argued that individual desires are fundamentally directed toward maximizing their own power, and are therefore bound to diverge, often violently. Accordingly, agreement among different and contending agents requires enforcement by fear of and obedience to an overarching power. Whereas Hobbes's emphasis on conflicting interests served to justify the existence of a powerful political state with an absolute sovereign (the "Leviathan"), Kant was concerned with preventing the excesses of state power, especially when states interact militarily with one another.

Kant proposed a worldwide organization that would be bound by international law and composed of a federation of free states. His theoretical proposals represented a tendency toward what may be called "optimistic internationalism" among peace theorists and devotees of world government. Rather than focusing on the problem posed by the state's very existence, Kant identified the cause of the problem in what he called the "lawlessness" of how states interact with one another. For Kant, some form of external coercion is therefore necessary to establish peace between states. Legal constitutions should safeguard and defend human rights, and, arguably, when these rights are violated and legal protections fail, what we would today call "humanitarian interventions"—nonviolent in nature—into the conduct of state are ethically and politically justified. Shortly after Kant's essay on peace appeared, the Napoleonic Wars convulsed Europe. For some, this showed the impossibility of peace; for others, it emphasized its necessity.

Twentieth-Century Proposals for World Government

The 19th century, was not notable important proposals concerning world government, at least in part because the post-Napoleonic Concert of

Europe did a reasonably good job at keeping the fragile peace within Western Europe. After World War I, however, and the subsequent failure of the
League of Nations, there was a flurry of renewed interest in world union, led
by such groups as the United World Federalists. Tensions arose between supporters of the United Nations and world federalists, who believed that international organizations of this sort tend to enhance state authority rather
than transcend it. Some argue that so long as international organizations
are structured around the preservation of state sovereignty, they are not so
much steppingstones to world government as threats and impediments to
its implementation.

The Clark-Sohn Plan

The most elaborate and detailed scheme since the end of World War II for
world government was developed in *World Peace Through World Law* (1958),
by the legal scholars Grenville Clark and Louis Sohn. It called for transforming the United Nations into a world peacekeeping unit, whereby states would
retain their sovereignty *except* in matters of disarmament (which would be
mandatory) and war (which would be prohibited). Clark and Sohn proposed
to increase the power of the General Assembly and to change its voting
procedures, so that decision making is largely proportional to population.
Under the Clark-Sohn Plan, the four most populous countries (China, India,
the Soviet Union, and the United States) would have 30 votes each, the next
eight largest would have 15 votes each, and so on.

An Executive Council would be authorized to intervene militarily worldwide, so as to prevent war. Unlike the present UN Security Council, however,
there would be no veto, although a clear majority (12 of 17 members) would
have to approve any armed action, and this vote would have to include a
majority of the largest states. An Inspection Commission would ensure that
disarmament is total; after a 2-year census of each country's military forces, it
would supervise a series of 10 percent annual reductions, across the board. A
World Peace Force, under UN auspices, would consist of 200,000 to 600,000
professional volunteers, initially using supplies and weapons obtained as the
member states disarmed themselves. Nuclear weapons would not be supplied to this force, but they could be obtained if needed—from a Nuclear
Energy Authority—to deter the real or threatened use of nuclear weapons by
any state that illegally retained a small cache.

The Clark-Sohn Plan, although very detailed and specific, does not offer
any suggestions as to the means of achieving its major goals, of getting from
"here" to "there." It does illustrate, however, that there is no shortage of well-
developed proposals for possible future world governments. Whatever the
strengths or weaknesses of any particular plan, world government has not
been stymied by a shortage of good ideas but rather by a lack of political will.

Pros and Cons of World Government

The Maintenance of Peace

The argument for peacefulness under world government is derived
largely from analogy with circumstances within most functioning countries.
Because domestic governments enforce peace (e.g., between New York and
Pennsylvania in the United States) a world government would presumably
do the same, treating nation-states much as municipal governments now
treat their citizens or as federal governments now treat their subordinate

provinces or constituent republics. But analogies do not always hold. More-over, federal governments do not always create or maintain peace: civil wars are common and often highly destructive. Europe during the 19th century, for example, was composed of feisty sovereign states, while the United States was a single, ostensibly united country. Yet, the war casualties suffered by the "United" States during its civil war (about 600,000) were almost precisely equal in number to the casualties suffered by Europe during the entire period between 1815 and 1913.

Perhaps if they were not held forcibly within a larger state, independent republics would be freer to work out their ethnic conflicts in peace. Alterna-tively, maybe they would go to war: ethnic antagonisms within the former Yugoslavia, for example, were kept from erupting into violence because of the inhibiting and unifying influence of the central government in Belgrade, under a widely respected leader, Josip Tito (a Croat). With that central force removed, the constituent republics—notably Serbia, Croatia, Bosnia, and, later, Kosovo—were vulnerable to violent appeals to previously submerged nationalistic passions.

The Danger of Oppression

To some, the prospect of a world government is truly frightening. These include many persons in the United States associated with various self-styled "militia" and "patriot" movements, who believe that an oppressive world government, most likely under the auspices of the United Nations, would be ready to swoop down in fleets of black helicopters and deprive them of their civil liberties (notably, their guns). Notwithstanding such fantasies, the claim that, as a cure, world government might be worse than the disease (state anarchy), needs to be taken seriously.

If large political units tend to be unresponsive to the needs of their citizens and are sometimes oppressive, imagine the danger inherent in government by a worldwide "super state" with the power to enforce its decrees on everyone. (The Clark-Sohn Plan envisioned that the armed forces of several countries, combined, would exceed those of the world force, thereby hedging against centralized despotism.)

Why, critics ask, should we expect better government from a world authority than we now get from national governments? And indeed, many states today do not have functioning representative democracies. So what, if anything, guarantees that a world government would not be a worldwide tyranny? Many people wish to have their proverbial cake and eat it too: Peace *and* freedom, international order *and* national sovereignty. But per-haps these goals are conflicting. If so, and if we have to choose, which is preferable? Or maybe we can hope for a compromise that offers restrictions on the state's ability to make war, without impinging on other aspects of domestic life.

Easier said than done, however. For one thing, powerful states are usu-ally not just uninterested in but vigorously opposed to world government because it would require that they give up some of the influence and power they exercise today. It might also make them subject to certain basic princi-ples of equality and fairness, from which they are at present largely exempt. In some cases—notably that of the United States—state sovereignty com-bined with military/economic/scientific/political might have been means of achieving and maintaining what many people believe to be inequitable access to the world's riches. What if, having surrendered its military auton-omy, the United States were faced with a demand from the economically less- developed states that it cease consuming an unfair share of the world's resources and polluting the planet out of proportion to its population, or that it redistribute its wealth? Would world government mean a responsibility to share? If so, many in the wealthy West might prefer autonomy and gluttony, even at the risk of occasional war.

Critics of world government also point to what they see as an inconsistency. World government is supposed to be necessary because the anarchic Hobbesian world of independent nation-states is simply too violent and irresponsible to continue unchecked. But what supports the assertion that fierce competitors and vicious inclinations will be rendered peaceful by a kind of world government modeled after the ideals of John Locke and other Euro-American liberals: a limited, tolerant, and democratic authority that is based largely on mutual consent? Such a "Lockean" government might indeed be more palatable than its Hobbesian alternative; but if the problem is so grave, the proposed solution might simply be inadequate. In short, a Hobbesian world may require a Hobbesian government, and the problem is that a Hobbesian government is likely to be brutal and authoritarian. Such a sovereign might be even more unpleasant—and more difficult to reform—if its resources and authority were global rather than national.

On the other hand, there is no reason why a future world government could not allow current national governments to continue exercising autonomy and sovereignty in their internal affairs. But rather than worrying about what the various states would have to surrender, perhaps one should focus on what they would be gaining. World government could then be viewed not so much as requiring us to give up something that we now have (state sovereignty and the ability to threaten and wage offensive wars) but rather as an opportunity to gain something now lacking: extending the peaceful rule of law to international affairs and, with it, a massive increase in human and global security.

As to the claim that world government would deprive states of one of the most important perquisites of state sovereignty—deciding whether or not to go to war—it is sobering to realize that the cherished independence of nation-states is in part illusory. The Soviet Union, for example, had essentially no choice about responding when it was attacked by Germany in June 1941. Similarly, the United States was propelled into World War II not so much by a declaration of war by the US House of Representatives as by decisions made by the Imperial War Council in Tokyo. And would it have been disadvantageous to world peace, not to mention to the United States, if the US had *not* been "free" to invade Iraq in 2003?

Advocates of world government emphasize that any viable world authority would have clearly delimited enforcement powers. As with the US federal government, rights not specifically granted to a world authority would be reserved for its constituent states. Similarly, in our private lives, we cherish certain personal rights while also accepting restrictions on them: One person's freedom to swing his or her arm ends, for example, where someone else's nose begins. Under a minimalist world government, nation-states would have to accept just two restrictions circumscribing their freedom: They would be obliged (1) not to maintain armed forces beyond police capacities needed to deal with domestic criminals and (2) not to behave aggressively against other states.

Similarly, world government would not necessarily mean the homogenization of national identities. Within the United States, Florida is still distinct from Alaska, and Maine from Arizona, just as national cultures within Russia range from urban Muscovites to tundra-dwelling indigenous peoples of Siberia, and from industrialism in European parts of Russia to seminomadic Islamic pastoralism in some of its Asian republics As Israeli prime minister Golda Meir once pointed out: "Internationalism doesn't mean the end of individual nations. Orchestras don't mean the end of violins."

The Dream of World Government: A Waste of Time?

There is one other potential problem with world government: By focusing on it, devotees may lose touch with the world and its current serious problems. Lost in dreams of utopia, hungering for what may turn out to be nothing more than "globaloney," proponents of world government risk being marginalized and considered irrelevant to "serious" discourse on issues of war and peace if they do not deal with the world as it is. And time itself is critical because world government will certainly not happen tomorrow, while wars are happening today. Even Freud, who supported the idea of world government, also warned (in his famous correspondence with Albert Einstein) about unrealistic dreams that "conjure up an ugly picture of mills which grind so slowly that, before the flour is ready, men are dead of hunger."

But no partisan of peace or devotee of world government recommends putting all of one's eggs in the one distant basket of global political union. It is not necessary to choose between nuclear arms reduction and world government, between peace in the Middle East and global disarmament, or between ecological harmony and transnational thinking and acting. In addition, even while addressing immediate, practical, pressing issues, isn't there also a need to focus on ultimate goals, even if they seem—at the moment—to exceed our grasp? As General Omar Bradley once pointed out, "It is time we steered by the stars and not by the lights of each passing ship."

Accordingly, we might ask the self-styled realists—the practical, hardheaded men (and, occasional female militarists notwithstanding, they are still largely *men*) if it is truly realistic to believe that the state system, with its divisions and contradictions and its history of never-ending warfare and state-centered militant nationalism, can be relied on to keep the peace and create a sustainable world into the future. Clearly, world government is unlikely to be perfect, but in view of the current state system's imperfections, it seems unlikely to be worse, or more dangerous, than our current plight. The dangers of a world with some form of centralized, war-suppressing government seem to pale in contrast to the dangers of a world without it.

The Prospects for World Government

A Penchant for Separating?

Despite the attractiveness of world government, many people—once organized into relatively large units—show more eagerness for separating than for joining together. There have been very few examples of the successful merging of states. The union of North and South Vietnam might be one such case, although it was only achieved via a prolonged and destructive war—and despite substantial resistance from many South Vietnamese themselves. Moreover, Vietnam had previously been a single country, so the outcome was not so much the merging of different states as the reunification of a state that had been artificially separated. The same can be said of the reunification of Germany in 1989 after its post–World War II separation into West and East.

From 1958–1961, Egypt and Syria attempted a peaceful merger, establishing the United Arab Republic, but that union was short lived. The former Yugoslavia now consists of independent states: Slovenia, Croatia, Bosnia, Serbia, Montenegro, Macedonia, and the partially recognized Republic of Kosovo. The former Czechoslovakia broke up into Slovakia and the Czech Republic formally renamed in 2016 as Czechia), and of course, what had been the Soviet Union now consists of numerous independent states, ranging from the Baltic republics of Latvia, Lithuania, and Estonia to the "stans" (Kazakhstan, Turkmenistan, and so forth) of central Asia.

When consolidation has occurred, a smaller unit was usually swallowed up by a larger one, often against the smaller's will: Tibet was incorporated into China, Goa into India, and, after World War I, the Baltic states into the Soviet Union. A major reason, indeed, for the breakup of the latter was the fact that it was an artificial entity, composed of numerous republics, many of which maintained their own distinctive national ethnic identities, which had resisted decades of domination and efforts to subordinate local ties to a larger Soviet whole. Furthermore, some of the tension in the world today is generated by regions desiring not to submerge their identities into a larger whole but rather to *separate* themselves from control by a larger entity: Catholics in Northern Ireland, Basques in Spain, Tamils in Sri Lanka, Kurds in Iraq, Turkey, Iran, and Syria, and so on.

Despite its flaws, dangers, and difficulties, world government may well be the least-bad solution for humanity's bellicosity and reluctance to act globally. However, just because something is desirable —even necessary—does not mean that it will come to pass. Thus, it is not sufficient simply to declare that world government ought to emerge because it is a prerequisite for survival. Maybe, with or without a world government, we will not survive. But given the current and likely future tensions among nuclear-armed states, it is hard to imagine a world government making things worse.

Commitment to States

The pressures against world government are strong. Most people retain a deep loyalty to their nation-states and also a powerful distrust of large, centralized systems. In addition, like so many proposals for dramatic reform (e.g., global disarmament), the "devil is in the details." How do we get from here to there?

In 1712, the French Abbé de Saint-Pierre proposed a pan–European Union, complete with a Senate of Peace, which would have authority over military forces sufficient to compel any recalcitrant ruler to submit to the will of the larger unit. Interestingly, the French foreign minister at the time, André Hercule de Fleury did not question the desirability of such a system, but he pointed out to Saint-Pierre: "You have forgotten an essential article, that of dispatching missionaries to touch the hearts of princes and to persuade them to enter into your views."

If state leaders agreed to a world government, it might be roughly equivalent to slaveholders banding together to outlaw slavery. But slavery has in fact been formally outlawed worldwide—although it remains in some parts of the world—sometimes (as in the United States) only after much bloodshed. Also consider how some nation-states (e.g., Sweden, Holland, Portugal, Spain) have made a seemingly healthy transition from imperial world power to secondary status in international politics. This might serve not only to prepare the United States for the possibility of its continuing decline as a global superpower in a world of continuing nation-states but also perhaps to suggest how the state system itself might be afforded lesser prominence and perhaps eventually eased out of existence.

At present, no powerful country seems inclined to relinquish its sovereignty and embrace world government; in most respects, states remain fiercely independent. Although the European Union seemed at one time to offer a blueprint for submerging national identity in a larger whole, economic stresses plus Brexit and possible Grexit, Italexit, Frexit, and the like have made that prospect less imminent. Whereas Marxist theory calls for the eventual "withering away" of the state, the former Soviet Union and its allies have long been unreceptive to world government—unless it were under Soviet control! When the state is considered to embody the needs and aspirations of its citizens, there is little reason to surrender the state's power. Even "peace groups" were described as unnecessary in most Soviet bloc states because the state itself was purported to be everybody's collective "peace group." (*It* was not the problem; *other* states were the problem!)

Traditionally, conservatives have engaged in relatively more militaristic flag-waving patriotism, while accusing the left of being part of, or duped by, various "international conspiracies," in the past alleged to be "communist inspired." However, the heyday of socialist internationalism was in the late 19th and early 20th centuries; in recent decades, many leftists have shown as much adherence to their own nation-state as have partisans of the political right. And in much of the developing world, militant nationalism is even more pronounced than in the industrialized North.

Examples of a Wider Transnational Identity

Although we do not yet know whether most people are capable of acting as part of a united species, the ultimate prospects for humanity as a whole may not be all that bleak. The United States of America, for example, is a very diverse country, made up of Caucasians, African Americans, Native Americans, Asian Americans, Hispanics, Catholics, Protestants, Jews, Buddhists, Muslims, and so on—and yet, the country as a whole enjoys a reasonable degree of solidarity, despite long-standing prejudices, ethnocentrism, and racial enmities. Although it may be claimed that US citizens are united by shared fear of "the other"—Chinese or North Korean "communists," Islamic "terrorists," international Mafia-style gangsters—the United States also has achieved a degree of unity via a shared cultural and social identity, a shared history, and shared ideals.

The human species is obviously capable of establishing even wider affiliations than those between the US states of Maine and Hawaii if feelings of connection are encouraged from birth and reinforced by teaching, symbols, slogans, and a range of appeals to emotion as well as reason. Most citizens of modern nation-states are subjected to vast amounts of pro-national and pro-state propaganda. More desirable would be education for a psychology of world citizenship.

People calling themselves "Germans" and "French" were historically at each other's throats, via their respective governments, those nation-states we identify as Germany and France. Yet, quite near these formerly warring states, several million very "French" people have lived peacefully for centuries with about three times as many equally "German" people. The difference is that in the former case, a sovereign state of Germany has confronted an equally sovereign France, whereas in the latter, "French" and "German" have submerged war-making authority under the sovereignty of a third shared entity, known as Switzerland (which also contains a third large subpopulation that is linguistically Italian). English and Irish, Italians and Austrians, Vietnamese and Chinese, and Arabs and Jews have waged brutal wars. But if they emigrate to the United States, they become citizens of the United States of America; they adopt a common identity, and, for the most part, live together peaceably. Clearly, transnational identifications are possible.

The Uniting of the United States of America: A Rehearsal for a Global Federal System?

Consider again the United States as it is now constituted: When California, for example, has a dispute with Arizona regarding water rights, the two state administrations do not call up their militias and fight it out. The "law of force" is subordinated to the "force of law," and both sides submit arguments, if need be, to the US Supreme Court. Then, they abide by the ruling. The states do not walk about like gunslingers from the American Wild West, revolvers on their hips, ready to settle disputes by the fastest draw.

Following the Revolutionary War, the United States under the Articles of Confederation was a loose amalgamation of mostly autonomous states, with no central authority to regulate their conduct and mediate their disputes. Maryland and Delaware fought an undeclared "oyster war" over fishing rights in the Potomac River; nine states had navies of their own; state militias were separate and distinct armies; seven of those states even printed their own currency; New York placed a tariff on wood from Connecticut and on butter from New Jersey; Boston boycotted grain from Rhode Island; various states imposed taxes on shipping from other states; and so on. Things were a mess within the not very united states, similar to how they are in the international arena today.

With the writing of the US Constitution, however, a strong federal system was created, out of whole cloth. Advocates of world government point to this transition from pluralism to unity that gave birth to the United States of America as "the great rehearsal" for world federalism, a transition that the global system might also make if and when the need and practicality are both recognized. Just as some people today fear a potential world "superstate," the delegates to the Constitutional Convention also were concerned about the possibility of establishing a despotic dictatorship. Yet, the framers of the Constitution recognized that the semi-independent 13 states were threatened with war and chaos, so they successfully designed a workable federal union, one that preserved the rights of states in regulating their internal affairs while establishing a strong federal system capable of providing unity and ensuring the peace. They did this by establishing a careful system of checks and balances.

At present, some of the member nation-states of the European Union have moved haltingly and erratically but with some success toward a limited and fragile form of economic and legal union. (Militarily, however, they have remained distinct, as are most issues connected with foreign policy). Many European states recognize the euro as a common currency; furthermore, despite a history of major wars and a present reality of numerous distinct and cherished linguistic and cultural traditions, passports and visas were largely unnecessary to cross member states' borders until the global refugee crisis of 2015–2016. Until the Covid-19 crisis of 2020, passage through international borders in nearly all of continental Europe—previously heavily controlled and guarded—was for the most part very fast and no more consequential than going from Texas to Oklahoma, despite a history of major wars and a present reality of numerous distinct and cherished linguistic and cultural traditions.

The reality of what the United States accomplished—in the face of grave doubts—suggests the magnitude of what can be achieved. The problem in 1787 was for new Americans to learn to think nationally about the United States, rather than locally. It wasn't until after the Civil War that this was achieved: prior to 1865, Americans were likely to discuss the "US" as a plural noun. Only by the late 19th century, was it consistently employed in the singular. Now, a major challenge is for people to learn to think internationally about the planet, rather than nationally.

Must world government then wait until humanity has achieved a different level of development? It is true that the "founding fathers" are currently revered in the United States, but they were human beings, just like us. It is also true that the US Constitution was not perfect (although it was certainly better than what preceded it in the former 13 colonies). Moreover, no one in the late 18th century claimed that a strong federal government could not be enacted until all the inhabitants of North America had first become saints.

Trans-Governmental Movements

Several trans-governmental movements have sought to go beyond the current state system by establishing links that intentionally defy present political boundaries. Thus, a number of international tribunals have worked toward delegitimizing select war-like actions of states (and, increasingly, of their bellicose leaders as well), trying to apply principles of international law, even though such proceedings have generally lacked enforcement capability. For example, the Russell Tribunal in the 1960s (named after the distinguished British philosopher and peace activist Bertrand Russell) excoriated the US war in Vietnam; in 1982, at a meeting held in Nuremberg, Germany, another tribunal of international legal experts heard testimony and condemned the existing nuclear weapons regime. The MacBride Commission in Britain investigated Israel's 1982 invasion of Lebanon and pronounced it a violation of international law. Such tribunals and peace movements generally are unpopular with the governments of the affected nation-states because they seek to restrict war-making capacity and also because they represent a budding transnational sensitivity, which might one day undermine state authority more generally. Of course, they also lack the "legitimacy" of recognized state-sponsored institutions.

If such activities truly threaten the current system of state sovereignty, it is an example of the important principle that "if people define situations as real, they are real in their consequences." If we define ourselves as bound irreparably to the current state system, we are so bound, by a kind of self-fulfilling prophecy. But the more we consider alternatives to the state system, the more we may find ourselves liberated from our customary allegiances.

One of the things that keeps people dependent on the state system is the difficulty in envisioning alternatives to it. "It is easier to imagine the end of the world," goes the saying, "than to imagine the end of capitalism." The same may be said about the difficulty of imagining the end of the global state system. Few people, as recently as 1989, would have predicted a

21st-century world in which South Africa has become a democratic, multiracial (albeit economically riven) state or in which the Soviet Union has dissolved. Two futures are easy to imagine: this world ending with the "bang" of nuclear war or with the "whimper" of continued degradation (ecological, economic, social, climatic, viral, etc.) plus ongoing conventional wars. Both are plausible but undesirable extrapolations of the status quo. World government—in whatever specific form—offers a potential third way.

Recently, there has been a proliferation of planetary gatherings, reflecting and dramatizing the fact that as advances in communication and transportation make the world smaller, the costs and responsibilities of technology—no less than its benefits—require attention on a global scale. Such conferences (sometimes webcast globally) include those on world population, women's rights, food, pollution, the status of indigenous people, the fights against racism and against AIDS, linkages between disarmament and development, the crisis of global climate change, ozone depletion, destruction of the world's rainforests, the need to protect biodiversity, to outlaw nuclear weapons, and to achieve global peace. With or without world government, worldwide problems will likely not be solved if governments remain stiffly chained to their traditional administrative boundaries.

Not surprisingly, the new social movements tend to be either local, community based, or region centered (and thus below the level of the state), or transnational and global (above the level of the state). Moreover, states themselves have already begun to surrender some aspects of sovereignty, as in the case of certain international organizations, as well as the general acknowledgment of—if not universal obedience to—international law. Perhaps this is the proverbial foot in the door. Or perhaps it simply reflects a defensive strategy by the states themselves: Make a few trivial concessions to "the common good" while at the same time remaining as unwilling as ever to permit any significant challenges to their authority.

However, many nation-states—even the strongest—are not entirely autonomous: The US government, for example, is not politically "free" to declare war on Canada. A kind of de facto (in fact) restriction of state sovereignty has thus already come into effect, even though it is not yet de jure (in law). War is also currently unimaginable between such historical rivals as Britain and France, Turkey and Russia, France and Germany, Japan and China, or between Mexico and the United States.

Interest in world government tends to increase after major world wars—notably, immediately following World Wars I and II. Then, just as predictably, when memories of the horrors of the last war fade, so do impassioned cries for trans-national solidarity. So, unfortunately, perhaps another major war, or a close brush with nuclear obliteration, might be necessary for people to rise up and demand a dramatic reworking—if not a surrender—of state sovereignty. Meanwhile, "futurism" need not be limited to technological panaceas and derring-do, to a "brave new world" of genetic engineering, cyborgs, and Star Wars. It can also include moving beyond national security to global security.

Furthermore, the role of vision and visionaries should not be dismissed. Before we can establish a better world, we must first imagine it. This is not to deny the importance of dealing with the world as it is. To "accept" current realities is not necessarily to accept them as God-given, engraved in stone, or immune to challenge and change. The world system of states, no matter how firmly entrenched, is a human creation—and, historically speaking, a relatively recent one at that. It is neither so perfect nor so powerful as to be a permanent part of the human condition. "The dogmas of the quiet past," wrote Abraham Lincoln, "are inadequate to the stormy present. We must think anew and act anew." Only if we think, plan, dream, and act for a future world that is better than today's or yesterday's can we have any hope of attaining such a future.

A Final Note on International Cooperation

Although their record has not been perfect, many activities of international organizations should be commended. Some of these organizations—especially the United Nations and its many branches—promote human and planetary betterment in numerous ways, including but not limited to the keeping of "negative peace." International organizations also represent a partial step in the progression from individualism, via nationalism, to globalism, a transition that may well be essential if humanity is ever to give peace on Earth a realistic chance. As such, international organizations can be seen as possible halfway houses toward the establishment and solidification of international norms, and perhaps even world government. And world government, although easily derided as impossible and unrealistic, may turn out to be the only viable antidote to humanity's self-inflicted maladies.

Questions for Further Reflection

1. What can be learned from the failure of the League of Nations? Is the United Nations similarly at risk?

2. In what way does the United Nations differ from world government? How is it similar?

3. Sketch the positive and negative effects of multinational corporations on the maintenance or disruption of peace.

4. Assess the realistic prospects for world government, paying particular attention to people's fears and hopes.

5. Describe how current and recent international events have affected the feasibility and/or the desirability of world government, as well as other forms of transnational cooperation.

Suggestions for Further Reading

Shamima Ahmed and David Potter. 2006. *NGOs in International Politics*. Bloomfield, CT: Kumarian Press.

Richard Falk. 1975. *A Study of Future Worlds*. New York: Free Press.

Linda Fasulo. 2015. *An Insider's Guide to the UN*, 2nd ed. New Haven, CT: Yale University Press.

Jean-Marie Guehenno. 2015. *The Fog of Peace: A Memoir of International Peacekeeping in the 21st Century*. Washington, DC: Brookings Institution Press.

Kelly-Kate S. Pease. 1999. *International Organizations: Perspectives on Governance in the Twenty-First Century*. Upper River Saddle, NJ: Prentice Hall.

Sebastian von Einsiedel, David M. Malone, and
Bruno Stagno Ugarte, eds. 2015. *The UN
Security Council in the 21st Century*. New
York: Lynne Rienner.

Thomas G. Weiss and Sam Daws, eds. 2018. *The
Oxford Handbook on the United Nations*. New
York: Oxford University Press.

Thomas G. Weiss and Rorden Wilkinson, eds.
2019. *International Organization and Global
Governance*, 2nd ed. New York: Routledge.

James Yunker. 2011. *The Idea of World
Government: From Ancient Times to the 21st
Century*. New York: Routledge.

Notes

1. Smedley D. Butler. 1935. In time of
peace. *Common Sense* 4 (11): 8–12.

2. Charles L. de Montesquieu. 1949. *The
Spirit of Laws*. New York: Hafner.

ED JONES/AFP via Getty Images

Peace Through Strength?

When asked about the most important way of maintaining peace, most people today—including governmental leaders—likely point to military strength. The slogan of the US Strategic Air Command proclaims, "Peace Is Our Profession." (Below this sign at SAC headquarters, someone once scrawled, "Mass Murder Is Our Specialty!") Not surprisingly, advocates of peace studies and peace activists generally look askance at the reliance on military force to maintain peace, viewing armed force as something to be transcended.

Like it or not, and agree with it or not, "Peace Through Strength" has probably been the most politically potent and influential concept of war prevention (and initiation) in recent times. It is also one of the most perilous.

Whether or not it "worked" in maintaining peace in the past, and whether it will work in the 21st century, "Peace Through Strength" succeeds in one sense at least: It legitimizes the expenditure of a significant percentage of national wealth, and virtually all major governments adhere to its precepts—in reality, if not in rhetoric. Accordingly, a major challenge for peace studies and the peace movement is to break away from the existing war system—which includes reliance on peace through strength—and to establish a viable ecology of peace, whose strength does not derive from violence or the threat of violence.

The motto "Peace Through Strength" is a modern version of the Latin *si vis pacem, para bellum* ("if you want peace, prepare for war"), which has been taken as axiomatic by entire generations of conventional politicians and military leaders. This perspective may be more than a rationalization for the maintenance of large and threatening armed forces, which exist for other reasons that are rarely acknowledged (such as economic gain, career benefits, distracting the populace, the satisfaction of personal psychological needs to feel powerful, to have clearly defined enemies, etc.). There have been, and still are, many people who sincerely believe that the only way to achieve peace is by the ability and willingness to employ military force. Significantly—and perhaps inconsistently—some advocates of peace through strength believe that this maxim applies only to their own country, and not to others—certainly, not to their potential adversaries!

Balance of Power

The idea of balancing power is an ancient one, reflected for example in the saying "any enemy of my enemy is my friend." At the geopolitical level, a "balance of power" occurs when contending states are roughly equal in their military strength. It is closely associated with the assumption of "peace through strength" and has often been used as an argument in its favor. The claim, in short, is that weakness invites aggression and so the power of one side must be balanced by that of others. Hence, what international relations theorists have called "bipolar" and "multipolar" worlds are allegedly more stable and less prone to war than are "unipolar" ones.

Peace through strength relies fundamentally on deterrence, the expectation that a would-be aggressor would refrain from attacking opponents who are more powerful than it or who are capable of inflicting unacceptable damage if attacked. Hence, adherence to balance of power implies a continuing arms race or, possibly, mutual agreements to keep the system relatively stable by keeping the mutual threat symmetrical. To some extent, the Cold War involved maintaining a balance of power (more accurately, a balance of terror) between the nuclear forces of the United States and those of the USSR. Before that, and especially during the 18th and 19th centuries, balance of power referred less to arms races than to a constantly shifting system of alliances, whereby states interacted to keep any one from being too powerful.

Until the end of World War II, Great Britain saw itself as the "balancer" in Europe, consistently aligning with weaker powers so as to prevent the emergence of stronger ones that might threaten its supremacy. Wars have often been fought in order to "maintain the balance," although in some cases countries have refrained from war so as not to upset a presumed balance. For example, at the conclusion of the first Gulf War in 1991, the United States avoided seizing Baghdad and overthrowing Saddam Hussein's government, in part out of concern that a stable, even if dictatorial, Iraq served as a useful counterbalance to the power of Syria, as well as Iran.

Hegemons and "Polarity"

Following World War II, the United States and the Soviet Union emerged as the two dominant states, initiating a "bipolar" balance of nuclear power, with each seeking to buttress its position by establishing competing alliances and courting the favor of neutral countries. With the end of the Cold War, that situation changed dramatically, and the United States emerged as the undisputed single great power, or unipolar "hegemon," especially in military terms. There are now increasing indications that other countries—especially Russia, China, Turkey, and Brazil—have come to fear and/or resent such an imbalance and also that international fear and resentment of an unbalanced "unipolar world" are precipitating new alliances seeking to reestablish a new balance.

The emergence of India, Brazil, and Japan (along with the "Asian tigers" of South Korea, Thailand, Malaysia, Singapore, and Taiwan), as well as of a partially united Europe, has created a kind of "multipolar" balance, especially in the economic sphere. Despite economic strains due especially to variations in the price of oil, along with Western sanctions following its seizure of Ukraine's Crimea, Russia, meanwhile, has become more assertive militarily. Moreover, with its rapid economic growth has come a greater inclination on the part of China to invest in its military as well as to flex its muscles—at least in the western Pacific, possibly presaging an eventual return to a bipolar world, with China replacing the former USSR as the primary rival of the United States.

Some analysts claim that multipolar systems are more stable and less warlike than bipolar ones because they involve (1) more cross-cutting loyalties, (2) less attention directed to any one state by another, and (3) the fact that increased armaments by one state (an incipient arms race) has less impact on the security of any other state. Other experts, however, point out that stable balances may be more difficult to achieve among the many different actors of a multipolar system, and also that the greater diversity of interests and demands provides more opportunities for conflict.

Problems With Balance of Power

Advocates of balance of power often assume and sometimes assert that such a balance deters war. It remains uncertain, however, whether wars are more or less likely during periods of alleged balance. Thus, the Peloponnesian War presumably would not have occurred if Athens and Sparta had not been so close in strength as to constitute a threat to each other. This may also have been the case for the Punic Wars between Rome and Carthage. During the *Pax Romana*, Rome was supreme in the Mediterranean world; there was no balance of power, yet there was comparative negative peace, at least for Rome. Similarly, there has never been a war between the Soviet Union and Bulgaria, or recently between the United States and either Canada or Mexico, in part because of the *imbalance* of power in these cases, with the United States being far economically and militarily superior to its northern and southern neighbors and the Soviet Union/Russia having vastly superior hard power to Bulgaria.

Promoting War

Wars often occur when rival states disagree about their relative strength, and they end when both sides agree: the stronger side is acknowledged as having won, and the weaker as having lost. Regarding postwar distributions of power, it is often the case that inconclusive wars were more likely to result in another war shortly thereafter, whereas decisive victories led more frequently to periods of negative peace. For example, many Germans felt that they had not been clearly defeated in World War I, attributing their loss to treason and insufficient governmental willpower (a "stab in the back"). World War II followed two decades later. By contrast, World War II was an indisputable defeat for the Axis Powers and has led to a more firmly established regime of peace, at least among the great powers that fought World War II.

Slight Imbalances and Their Effects

Wars tend to break out when there is a slight power imbalance, especially if one side has grown rapidly but has not yet matched the military strength of its major adversaries. In this situation, the status quo power (the one seeking to maintain things as they are) can feel threatened that the balance is about to tip against it, sometimes calculating that war now is preferable to waiting for the upstart power to become stronger.

States actively committed to a balance of power, in short, have an incentive to attack their major rivals if they perceive an adverse shift in that balance. Whether that attack is justified as preventive (to forestall gradual change and eventual war) or preemptive (jumping the gun to short-circuit an attack that is considered imminent), states sometimes leap through a "window of opportunity" and begin a war, lest it become a "window of vulnerability" through which they are attacked. Thucydides, writing about the Peloponnesian War, suggested that "the growth of the power of Athens, and the alarm which this inspired in Lacedaemon [Sparta], made war inevitable."

Something similar happened to Germany in 1914. In July of that year, General Helmuth von Moltke, the German chief of staff, wrote, "Basically, Russia is not at the moment ready for war. Nor does France or England want war now. In a few years, on all reasonable assumptions, Russia will be ready. By then it will overwhelm us with the number of its troops."[1]

Balance-of-power theories contain an important and often unstated assumption: Given the opportunity, a stronger state will attack a weaker one. This, presumably, is why severe imbalances must be prevented. Whereas there have been cases of aggression by very strong against very weak states (e.g., the Soviet Union attacking Finland in 1939, China attacking Vietnam in 1979, the United States attacking Iraq in 2003), the international system also abounds in unbalanced power relationships, many of them involving neighboring countries, which have not resulted in war. Brazil, for example, does not seem poised to invade Uruguay; nor is India about to attack Bhutan—but India may attack, or be attacked by, China or Pakistan, which are also nuclear powers. The fact that power imbalances do not necessarily produce war has not, however, diminished the cogency of this doctrine for those who believe strongly in it.

Upsetting a balance—or threatening to do so—may lead to war, even when the intent may have been to prevent it, as during the Cuban Missile Crisis of 1962. Thus, although power-seeking nations seek *imbalance* in their

own favor, such actions may backfire, generating a crisis and possibly leading to war.

Military Alliances

In his Farewell Address, George Washington reflected a widespread American distrust of foreign powers when he urged the United States to avoid
"entangling alliances." Of course, alliances—historically important to
balance-of-power systems—do not always lead to war. NATO, for example,
balanced by the Warsaw Pact, ostensibly promoted peace and stability in
Europe for 45 years after World War II. (Lord Ismay, the first NATO secretary
general, famously noted that NATO's purpose was "to keep the Russians out,
the Americans in, and the Germans down.")

Immediately prior to World War I, Kaiser Wilhelm sought to restrain his
Austrian imperial ally from attacking Serbia; had he succeeded, textbooks
might now be extolling the benefits of balanced alliances in preventing war!
At present, many historians point to the role of interlocking alliances in generating that war. Clearly, military alliances have often led to war, with the
major participants sometimes drawn in by the actions of their proxies and
because of their concern that inaction would mean a loss of national honor
(today referred to as "credibility").

Hegemonic US?

The United States has long seen itself, and, until relatively recently, was
widely considered the "leader of the Free World," especially after World War
II and during the Cold War. For centuries, the United Kingdom celebrated its
imperialistic success—noting proudly, for example, that "the sun never sets on
the British Empire." In contrast, the United States has usually been reluctant
to overtly embrace the role of imperial power or world hegemon. Despite
recently closing many installations in Iraq and Afghanistan, the United
States still maintains nearly 800 military bases in more than 70 countries and
territories abroad, from giant "Little Americas" (installations that are equal to
small cities) to small radar facilities and so-called lily pads with a few hundred
personnel and used for reconnaissance and increasingly, for deployment of
drones. These include facilities in Okinawa, Guam, Great Britain, Djibouti,
Germany, Bahrain, Saudi Arabia, Brazil, Cameroon, Italy, South Korea,
Afghanistan, and, until 2009, in Uzbekistan. Direct occupation of foreign
countries, however, has not been part of official US foreign policy. On the
other hand, there are no foreign military bases located in the United States.

Just as the conclusion of World War II marked the end of the British
Empire, and between 1989 and 1991 the Soviet Empire disintegrated, the
Great Recession and Global Economic Meltdown of 2008 and the coronavi-
rus-induced economic troubles of 2020 may be indicators of a gradual decline
in the American Empire. This may be due to a complex mix of internal financial strains and a reduction in international economic competitiveness, combined with the immense cost of wars in Iraq, Afghanistan, and elsewhere, as
well as of coping with global pandemics. Some would argue that for all its
faults, the United States has contributed positively to worldwide peace and
stability, such that its decline signals real peril. Others welcome a shift in
American international influence, pointing out that although the United
States didn't maintain an empire in the classic sense of British imperial control, it used economic pressure plus the adherence of local despots and the

threat of military intervention to maintain a system in which the United States and its closest allies enjoyed asymmetric benefits while much of the rest of the world did not share in the spoils.

Increasingly, especially following the inauguration of Donald Trump as US president in 2017, the role of the United States diminished internationally compared to its high point during the 1990s and early 2000s. This followed the collapse of the Soviet Union in 1991, leaving the United States as the world's sole superpower, sometimes calling itself, in the words of former US secretary of state Madeleine Albright, the "indispensable nation." It is possible—perhaps likely—that even without having been militarily stymied in Iraq and Afghanistan, the United States would never again be as dominant in the world as it recently was. On the other hand, after the humiliating retreat of the United States from Vietnam in 1975, it was widely, but mistakenly, assumed that the United States would not again commit itself to employing land forces abroad—and especially not in Asia. Such assumptions often require revision.

The Rise of the BRICS

The US military interventions in Iraq and Afghanistan, taken together, cost roughly 400,000 Iraqi and Afghan lives along with thousands of American lives, while also involving the expenditure, by some estimates, of four trillion US dollars. Many analysts argue that these blunders, combined with the diplomatic failures and botched response to the Covid-19 pandemic under President Trump, began an international decline in the situation of the United States that is likely to continue through the 21st century. Others maintain that this process began with the Great Recession in 2008 that was largely centered in the US, which reduced worldwide confidence in US economic wisdom and power. Others trace a history beginning with the US defeat in the Vietnam War. It is also possible, of course, that US international predominance will eventually resume.

In any event, it is undeniable that other countries, notably Brazil, Russia, India, South Africa, and especially China (the "BRICS") were collectively the most rapidly growing major emerging economies during the second decade of the 21st century, having become regional economic superpowers and, at least in the case of China, on track to surpass the United States in total economic output.

There has been a tectonic shift of growth and economic vitality from the developed world to some states in the developing world, notably the BRICS. India, for example, is more dynamic and has a gross domestic product (GDP) greater in absolute, though not in per capita terms, than its former colonial overlord, the United Kingdom. Similarly, the contemporary importance of Brazil far outstrips that of its European colonizer, tiny Portugal. This diffusion of power from the "West to the rest" has been accelerated by failed Western military adventures, as well as by Western nations' deindustrialization and outsourcing of manufacturing. This is combined with fiscal imbalances in trade, with most large Western states importing more goods than they export, as a result of which money flows out rather than in.

Consequently, Brazil and India (along with Germany, Japan, Nigeria, South Africa, etc.) have been lobbying for seats on the United Nations Security Council, a recognition of the presumed changing global geopolitical, economic, and military balance of power. China has already replaced Japan as the world's second largest economy, which in turn has generated worldwide interest in "state capitalism" as an appealing model for countries focused on the desirability of economic growth, albeit often at the cost of deemphasizing human rights and environmental values.

Although each of the BRICS has its own problems, notably widespread corruption as well as state-specific concerns, such as Russia's worries about its rapidly depopulating eastern regions, India's disorganization, Hindu nationalism, and pervasive poverty, and so forth, it is estimated that Brazil, India, Russia, and China alone accounted for nearly 45 percent of all the new investment money raised globally in 2019. China has been resurgent, not only economically but also politically and militarily. Historically, China perceived itself as the "Middle Kingdom" (because it occupied a special place in the middle of the world). For over a decade, the European Union and the United States have been economically and politically in relative stagnation. Until 2020, on the other hand, China enjoyed a spectacular rise in its GDP, along with favorable balance-of-payments (a great excess of goods exported over goods purchased).

The Case of China

The resulting Chinese accumulation of wealth, a significant proportion of which has been invested in US treasury notes and bonds, financed much of the US national debt. In addition, this inflow of money has been used by China to invest heavily in energy and resource extraction ventures, especially in Latin America, Africa, and Southeast Asia, as well as in some parts of Europe. In addition, China's "belt and road" initiative is intended to produce a 21st century version of the centuries old silk road that enabled trade between China and regions to its west, extending as far as Europe. At the same time, because of its immense population—around 1.4 billion people—China remains relatively impoverished on a per capita basis, although this is scarce comfort for those who worry that China will overtake the United States as the world's largest economy. On the other hand, the growth of the Chinese economy has varied substantially, and is declining significantly from its previous annual rate, which reached a high of 10 percent, to a more modest—but still impressive—annual growth rate of about 6 percent.

A significant source of friction between the United States and China has been China's reluctance to raise the value of its currency, the renminbi, or at least, not allowing it to fluctuate on the open market. If China permitted a significance increase in the exchange rate of the renminbi (also sometimes called the "yuan"), Chinese products would in turn be more expensive, which would mean less United States—and other countries—purchase of them, which would reduce the purchasers' trade imbalances and foreign debt. (There is some indication as of early 20220, however, that the renminbi may gradually be rising in value.)

Thus far, Chinese foreign policy has been notably cautious, focused on obtaining raw materials from developing countries and disinclined to engage directly (and not at all militarily) in their internal affairs. At the same time, however, China has expanded its military, producing new generations of fighter aircraft and a growing "blue ocean navy," which is increasingly capable of "projecting power" worldwide—although not nearly on the scale of the United States. Classical balance-of-power considerations would suggest that the other emerging Asian states (including Thailand, Burma/Myanmar, Malaysia, Indonesia, Singapore, the Philippines, and South Korea) might gradually restructure their international relationships so as to counter growing Chinese economic, military, and political influence. This acknowledges the new geostrategic reality that China in particular is a power to be reckoned with, as well as the fact that globalization, for better and worse, is no longer synonymous with Americanization.

China has an additional advantage compared to the United States and some of the other BRICS states: It isn't viewed with particular apprehension (except, possibly, by its neighbors Japan, Taiwan, and South Korea) because it lacks a modern history of being a colonial exploiter. Currently, Chinese efforts at "exploitation" appear limited to achieving access to raw materials and energy, the development of which is sought by many nations in sub-Saharan Africa and South America. China's chief goal—foreign and domestic—has long been consistent with its Confucian heritage: Stability at all costs and at least the appearance of harmony rather than conflict—something that has been recently called into question in Hong Kong, which has been subjected to increasingly harsh Chinese repression, contradicting its ostensible "One country, two systems" policy.

Declining US Influence?

A respected Indian-American analyst of international relations, noting the transition of world influence toward the BRICS, observed that American self-regard has been so exaggerated that on the one hand, the US has seen itself as the leading light of the world and yet also increasingly isolated. At the same time, Chinese influence—with its model of a vibrant economy combined with political authoritarianism—has made substantial inroads.[2] The historian Arnold Toynbee emphasized that all successful imperial powers eventually decline, despite their "mirage of immortality." To some extent, this was reflected in the US withdrawal from many of its commitments during the Trump administration, although this was presented to the public as an intentional decision rather than the retreat of a diminishing power.

In an increasingly interdependent world, once-local concerns have gone global, including pandemics, terrorism, human-induced climate change, energy and food insecurity, as well as resource depletion. Accordingly, globalization isn't only a fact of economic life but of political, economic, social, cultural, public health, and old-fashioned survival as well. Although some people (not all of them Americans) worry about a future world in which the United States is no longer the sole superpower, the rise of the BRICS generally, and of China in particular, is of increasing concern to some observers, both American and non-American. It is increasingly likely that the United States—which during the Obama administration announced a "strategic pivot" toward Asia—will come to function as "balancer" vis-à-vis China, as Great Britain did toward Europe in much of the 19th century.

Let us, accordingly, imagine a world of rising BRICS in which the United States is no longer the undisputed global heavyweight: Will this make the planet more or less safe and peaceful? How will the United States respond to its perceived/real loss of hegemony? If it behaves like such declining empires as Rome and the "Third Reich," there is much to fear. But if it skillfully adjusts to a new post-imperial, multipolar world, as the UK did during its waning days of empire, perhaps collective security will be enhanced and not undermined.

Collective Security

Advantages

Closely related to balance of power, but nonetheless distinct, is the concept of collective security. In collective security systems, states promise to refrain from using force against other members of the "collective," except that they agree to band together against any member who attacks another state within the group. Collective security differs from balance of power in that it relies on the participation of each state as an individual nonaligned entity, as opposed to a balance of unstable, constantly shifting alliances.

NATO and the former Warsaw Pact were not examples of collective security because they were established as mutual defense pacts against a potential aggressor from *outside* each alliance, whereas collective security pacts are specifically directed at defense against any aggression from *within* the pact. Early in NATO's history, some statesmen hoped it could exemplify collective security and would include the Soviet Union. However, the system of post–World War II alliances degenerated from collective security to "selective security," a series of bilateral and regional arrangements that—in the case of NATO and the Warsaw Pact—set themselves up as competing, alliances.

Disadvantages

There are problems with collective security. For example, it is debatable whether NATO and the Warsaw Pact prevented war or simply fostered nearly two generations of hostility. In addition, collective security agreements are only as good as the will of the participants to abide by them. Given the extreme destructiveness of war, states may be understandably reluctant to meet their treaty obligation if it entails going to war to defend an ally. This is true unless their populace strongly supports the military action that is called for. And finally, given the social and economic interdependence of modern states, even responses short of war—for example, boycotts and trade embargoes—may cause real hardship, thereby making political leaders hesitant to take such steps.

Also, collective security arrangements, when they involve states with large and powerful friends, can give rise to destructive and interminable wars. If North Korea and South Korea had been left to themselves, for example, the Korean War might have ended quickly. But instead the United States and China became involved, and the conflict was therefore prolonged and intensified. A similar process occurred in the struggle between North and South Vietnam, and between the *contra* rebels and the government of Nicaragua.

The Middle East was kept simmering, if not boiling, in part by assistance from the United States and the Soviet Union, primarily to the Israelis and the Arabs, respectively. By contrast, wars between India and China (1962) and between Britain and Argentina (1982) have been comparatively brief and decisive, in part because they were fought without significant military involvement by allies on either side of the conflict.

National Security via Military Force

Given the uncertainties of maintaining peace through balance of power or collective security, many government leaders opt for going it alone—not necessarily avoiding alliances but, rather, placing their primary emphasis on being sufficiently strong to deter war by the military power of the state, standing by itself.

Richard Perle, a hawkish assistant secretary of defense during the Reagan administration, also known among peace activists as "The Prince of Darkness," once said, "Those who believe that the way to maintain peace is by being weak are over and over again shown by history to be wrong." Here, the political right wing is in agreement with some more violence-prone elements of Maoism in particular.

Mao Zedong wrote that "we do not desire war, but war can only be abolished through war—in order to get rid of the gun, we must first grasp it in hand." In fact, the lessons of history are more equivocal. Diplomatic historian George Kennan suggested that "modern history offers no example of the cultivation by rival powers of armed force on a huge scale that did not in the end lead to an outbreak of hostilities," adding that "there is no reason to believe that we are greater, or wiser, than our ancestors." Moreover, there is every reason to believe that in the nuclear age, the consequences of worldwide hostilities could be far more catastrophic than they have ever been in the past.

Accordingly, strong states are far more likely than weak ones to be involved in wars, especially if the weak ones maintain a position of neutrality, and even more so if their "weakness" is really a refusal to provoke or threaten others. Thus, Switzerland and Sweden have been war-free for centuries, and although they appear weaker than their larger, more belligerent neighbors, they have long been rather strong militarily. In other cases, small, weak countries have indeed been conquered or absorbed by their more powerful neighbors: Latvia, Lithuania, and Estonia were annexed by the Soviet Union just prior to World War II; Hawaii was incorporated within the United States; Tibet was similarly overrun by China; and the Portuguese enclave of Goa was swallowed up by India.

Military Strength and Failure

There is a kind of logic to the notion that one is better off being strong than weak. Yet, overwhelming military strength has often resulted in failure. The United States, for example, was victorious in virtually every direct major military engagement of the Vietnam War. It dropped eight million tons of bombs (making more than 20 million craters) and nearly 400,000 tons of napalm, killing approximately 2.2 million Vietnamese, Cambodians, and Laotians; maiming and wounding about 3.2 million more; and leaving more than 14 million homeless—but was defeated. (At one point during that conflict, US Senator George Aiken suggested that because the United States had won every major battle, it should simple declare victory and withdraw!)

Israel is more than a military match for all its Arab neighbors combined and is vastly more powerful than the lightly armed Palestinians inhabiting the West Bank and Gaza, yet Israeli internal security and even control of the occupied Palestinian territories are not ensured. Many Israelis now argue that their overwhelming military defeat of Egypt, Syria, and Jordan during the Six Day War in 1967—as a result of which Israeli territory expanded to include Gaza, the West Bank, all of Jerusalem, and the Golan Heights—reduced Israel's security in the long run because it enhanced anti-Israeli sentiment while placing Israel in the difficult position of being overlord to millions of oppressed and resentful Palestinians.

Similarly, the Soviet Union was enormously more powerful, militarily, than the Afghan rebels who eventually compelled it to retreat. As with the United States in Vietnam, the Soviets were almost always victorious on the battlefield but were eventually forced to withdraw from Afghanistan by the lightly armed Afghan resistance (aided by the US).

A similar situation appears to be playing itself out for the United States in Afghanistan and Iraq. After stunning military successes that overthrew the Taliban government in 2002, and despite short-lived success of the Obama administration's military "surge" in 2009, only a residual contingent of US armed forces and a much smaller NATO contingent remained in Afghanistan after 2014, ostensibly not to engage in direct combat against the Taliban. However, as of mid-2020, significant numbers of US forces were deployed to "train and assist" the Afghan National Army in their combat missions. Despite billions of dollars in aid and ongoing Western training of its armed forces and police, it is unclear if the pro-Western Afghan government will survive.

Although the US military quickly and easily defeated the Iraqi army in 2003, subsequent instability, violence, and civil war kept US military forces in that country until 2011, when its direct combat role appeared to have concluded. However, a small contingent of US forces was reintroduced in Iraq in 2014, and additional US special operations troops were subsequently added to assist the Iraqi army (and military contractors) in battling ISIS and shoring up the unpopular Iraqi government.

Despite massive Western intervention, Iraq remains tumultuous because of its Sunni and Shi'ite factions, and in large part because in addition to the rise of ISIS and decline in that country beginning in 2014, US-backed Shi'ite central governments in Baghdad failed to integrate the Sunni minority into running that ethnically and religiously divided land. The duration of the US involvement in Afghan and Iraq wars, from October 2001 on, exceeds that of any previous US war and implies that overwhelming military strength, even when it leads to "victory" in nearly every battle, may often diminish a country's security.

Pyrrhus was a king in ancient Greece. During the 3rd century BCE, his forces defeated the Romans in the Battle of Asculum, although Pyrrhus lost nearly all of his men. Upon being congratulated for his victory, Pyrrhus replied, "One more such victory and we are utterly undone"—hence, the phrase, *Pyrrhic victory*. After Napoleon invaded Russia in 1812, his triumphant forces occupied Moscow but were soon thereafter obliged to withdraw, and in the subsequent retreat to France, the Grand Armée of 650,000 was reduced to a mere 25,000. The paradox is that military force, even military victory, does not necessarily lead ultimately to success or even enhanced security.

Part of the irony is that by committing a state's existence to military success, leaders paradoxically place its security in the hands of their opponents, and the ultimate outcome of a war—even a seemingly "successful" one—is not only impossible to predict but can often be counterproductive. As of 2020, it appears that a primary beneficiary of the American-led invasion of Iraq has been Iran, a country that, by some accounts, is considered a greater threat to such regional rivals as Israel and Saudi Arabia than Saddam Hussein's Iraq ever was.

Security Through Superiority?

Many government leaders argue that their prime responsibility is the maintenance of *national security,* a phrase that is readily invoked but only rarely scrutinized. It is easy to equate strength with safety and weakness with danger. Fearing to be seen as weak, accommodating, or easily pushed around, government leaders are prone to using threats of military force in efforts to coerce an opponent or to deter potential adversaries.

Sometimes this works; at other times, the bluff is called. After the Iraqi invasion of Kuwait in 1991, President George H. W. Bush demanded Iraq's withdrawal, and the United States eventually achieved this goal through the use of massive military force. At other times, preemptive saber-rattling may discourage unwanted actions; China, for example, threatened that it might respond militarily to any unilateral assertion of political independence on the part of Taiwan, which the Chinese maintain is an integral part of "one China." The United States has similarly threatened to respond with military force if China seeks to force a reunion with Taiwan; so far, Taiwan has not formally declared itself independent from China and China has not sought aggressively to annex Taiwan.

During times of international tension, adversaries are likely to be acutely suspicious that the other side is aggressive, dangerous, and likely to probe for weakness, being deterred only by strength. In the early days of the Korean War, and again during the Cuban Missile Crisis, US White House aides argued that the Soviets were following the Leninist maxim, "If you strike steel, pull back; if you strike mush, keep going." And as long as each side is determined to meet the other with steel rather than mush, each can justify its policy by pointing to the other's policy, as well as its steel.

The strategic dynamic of forever seeking superiority crumbles when one considers the role this logic plays in generating what has been called the security dilemma, which is that in pursuing their own perceived security, individual nation-states often diminish the security of their adversaries. As a result of this, those rivals seek to reestablish their security by building up their own forces whereupon invariably, everyone involved ends up being less secure and worse off. Thinking of this sort has nonetheless long dominated the national security managers of many states.

Through much of the 19th century, for example, Britain proclaimed the "two-power standard," by which the Royal Navy sought to be at least equal, and preferably superior, to the combined navies of the next two most powerful states. This was considered necessary to guarantee British national security. The British sought absolute security, despite the fact that, as former secretary of state and national security adviser Henry Kissinger put it, "the desire of one power for absolute security means absolute insecurity for all the others."

Hence, it is not surprising that the British and German naval establishments competed so vigorously during the first decade and a half of the 20th century that the tension generated by this competition contributed to the outbreak of World War I. The Anglo-German arms race also exemplified another difficulty in trying to achieve peace through strength: that new manifestations of "strength" can undermine a state's preexisting security. It is a classic case, worth exploring a bit further. Thus, the Royal Navy was far ahead of its German counterpart when, in 1906, the British Admiralty introduced a new class of extra-large, heavily armed and armored warships, known as "Dreadnoughts," after the name of the first such vessel. At a stroke, this unilateral act—which was the logical culmination of seeking to maintain peace through strength—made much of the Royal Navy obsolete and induced Britain to engage in a more intense competition with Germany, from a position of reduced advantage once the Germans began constructing their own Dreadnoughts, which quickly led to the construction of "super-Dreadnoughts."

The nuclear arms race also illustrated Kissinger's contention. The United States, the consistent leader and innovator in this "race to oblivion," has routinely introduced new delivery systems and warheads, only to find the Soviet Union (and subsequently Russia) following suit, after which both sides were less secure than they were before each escalation.

Military Interpretations of National Security and the Security Dilemma

As noted, national security is usually seen by conventional strategists and political decision makers as deriving from military strength. The "security" thereby gained is therefore mostly illusory and a "zero-sum game," in that the more one side gets, the less there is for the other. A peace studies perspective emphasizes, however, that it is an error to think of security as an exclusive, competitive gain, in which security for one party can only be purchased at the cost of insecurity for others. In fact, security can be a positive-sum game, in which all sides win. In a world of growing interdependence, as well as the shared danger posed by weapons of mass destruction, genuine and enduring national security can only be achieved multilaterally.

Moreover, government leaders may create "enemies" in order to enhance their own position of power and authority. This is an ancient pattern. For example, during the latter stages of the Roman Republic, the populace was wantonly exploited and pillaged by its own leadership in the name of security. Enemies were created to justify ruinously high taxes, the appropriation of private holdings, and the abridgement of personal liberties. Economist and historian Joseph Schumpeter unsparingly argued against "that policy which pretends to aspire to peace but unerringly generates war, the policy of continual preparation for war." He described these excesses on the part of Rome's rulers, which should serve as a warning to the excessively enemy-prone today:

> There was no corner of the known world where some interest was not alleged to be in danger or under actual attack. If the interests were not Roman, they were those of Rome's allies; and if Rome had no allies, then allies would be invented. When it was utterly impossible to contrive such an interest—why, then it was the national honor that had been insulted. . . . The whole world was pervaded by a host of enemies, and it was manifestly Rome's duty to guard against their indubitably aggressive designs.[3]

Following the end of the Cold War and the dissolution of the Soviet Union, American purveyors of new "enemies" were challenged to fill the gap, demonizing respectively, Cuba, Libya, Iraq, North Korea, Iran, international terrorism, fundamentalist Islamic extremism, Russia, China, and, when all else fails, a generalized worldwide "unpredictability." At the same time, notwithstanding the pronounced tendency for political leaders to exaggerate threats—especially for domestic political gain—such threats can also be genuine. The terrorist attacks of 9/11 in the United States and later in Madrid, London, Ankara, Bali, Paris, Istanbul, Brussels, Berlin, and elsewhere have demonstrated this all too clearly. Or as the saying has it, "Even paranoids have enemies."

Other National Security Considerations

Although it often has a legitimate military dimension, national security cannot be measured by military parameters alone. Security is also a function of economic strength, political cohesiveness, social equity and integration, cultural outreach, racial harmony, and environmental sustainability. National security is diminished if one's own populace is inadequately housed, fed, educated, and also if medical care is insufficient.

Historian Paul Kennedy has propounded the thesis that great powers tend to rise and fall in a predictable cycle, as their world ambitions make excessive demands on their domestic productivity: "A nation projects military power according to its economic resources, but eventually the high cost of maintaining political supremacy weakens the economic base. Great powers in decline respond by spending more on defense and weaken themselves further by directing essential revenues away from productive investment."[4]

Examples of this cycle include the rise and fall of Hapsburg and Spanish Empires, the British Empire, and the Soviet Union whose economy was unable to sustain a continuing 14 percent expenditure on the military sector. It also suggests that the United States might be undergoing a similar decline, especially as it increases its absolute level of military spending far beyond Cold War levels, such that it now exceeds the military spending of all of its potential rivals combined. According to the Stockholm International Peace Research Institute's report on military spending in 2018, global military expenditures exceeded $1.8 trillion, with the United States spending three times more than China and seven times more than Russia.

In contrast with the United States, whose military expenditures comprise about 3.5 percent of its gross national product (GNP), military spending in Japan has been only about 1 percent of its GNP, which freed money to help finance its remarkable post–World War II economic boom. Postwar Germany is a similar case. Significantly, about 10 percent of Japanese government investment in research and development goes into military production, whereas the analogous figure for the United States is 70 percent. The Japanese were pioneers in developing, marketing, and exporting VCRs, automobiles, cameras, robots, and so forth, and despite economic stagnation beginning in the 1990s, Japan has had a considerable financial surplus and the world's third largest economy. In contrast, by becoming the world's leading producer of high-tech military gadgetry, the United States has specialized in commodities that are not typically purchased by US taxpayers, contributing to a large trade deficit and national debt.

"The problem in defense," said President Eisenhower in 1953, "is how far you can go without destroying from within what you are trying to defend from without."

There is yet another problem with excessive reliance on peace through strength, in addition to running the risk of undermining one's security at home: the danger that by focusing on military considerations abroad, a country's long-term stability is sacrificed for short-term gains. Thus, as of 2018, the United States was spending 13 times more money supporting the military forces of Afghanistan and Pakistan than on all of its diplomatic and aid missions in those countries combined. International security is to some extent a prerequisite for domestic security, but "collateral damage" to civilians (via drone strikes, for instance) often generates alienation and hatred toward the perpetrators, while local populations resent the fact that their other needs—jobs, clean water, education, health care—are to a large extent ignored.

The pursuit of national security can also be destructive of domestic liberty, leading to a permanent "surveillance state," whereby personal freedoms are sacrificed. Although most people willingly submit to body searches before an airplane flight, there also arises an essential tension between democratic freedoms and personal safety, reflected in Benjamin Franklin's observation that "Those who would give up essential liberty to purchase a little temporary safety deserve neither." Or, to put it more gently: they risk obtaining neither.

Bargaining Chips Revisited

"We arm to parley," said Winston Churchill and, as we have seen, political leaders have long maintained that one of the benefits of armaments is that they provide leverage in disarmament or arms control negotiations with the other side. Generally, whenever two sides agree to divest themselves of weaponry (something that happens very rarely), or to refrain mutually from acquiring specified military forces—either by qualitative or quantitative restrictions—both sides are expected to forgo something comparable. If one side is militarily weak and the other strong, what incentive is there for the latter to build down? One answer is for both sides to make themselves comparably strong at the outset of any serious disarmament discussions.

Thus, joint efforts at nuclear arms control gathered momentum only in the late 1960s, when the Soviet Union achieved rough nuclear parity with the United States. Weapons originally justified as bargaining chips are only rarely cashed in. Rather, armaments tend to develop a powerful constituency— civilian contractors who build them, military commanders who deploy and command them, politicians in whose district they are constructed and/or sited, etc.—so they have often become part of the arsenal, whether needed or not.

Such considerations do not apply only to nuclear weapons, whose constituency may be declining. Rather, they are pertinent for such "big ticket" military procurement projects as destroyers ($2 billion apiece), ballistic missile submarines ($7 billion and more apiece), aircraft carriers (more than $10 billion each), for a US Navy that is currently larger than that of the next 13 countries combined—11 of whom are US allies. Another example: The United States is projected to spend an estimated $323 billion for development and procurement of nearly 2,500 F-35 air combat fighters, making it the most expensive defense program ever. The total lifecycle cost for the entire American fleet is estimated by the Congressional Budget Office to be $1.51 trillion or $618 million per plane. And yet, there is no other country that even comes close to possessing comparable weapons.

Military historian and retired US Army colonel Andrew Bacevich describes the situation as follows:

> The Pentagon presently spends more in constant dollars than it did at any time during the Cold War—this despite the absence of anything remotely approximating what national security experts like to call a "peer competitor." . . . What are Americans getting for their money? Sadly, not much. Despite extraordinary expenditures (not to mention exertions and sacrifices by U.S. forces), the return on investment is, to be generous, unimpressive. The chief lesson to emerge from the battlefields of the post-9/11 era is this: The Pentagon possesses next to no ability to translate "military supremacy" into meaningful victory.[5]

On the other hand, most American political conservatives recoil at any possible diminution in US military expenditures, pointing to the alleged impact of the Reagan-era military buildup in "defeating" the Soviet Union. They suggest that continued overwhelming US strength will provide immediate security and should also discourage other would-be rivals from increasing their military power to the point of eventually challenging the status of the United States as the world's superpower. Nonetheless, military buildups most commonly undercut doves on the opposing side and usually lead to a corresponding buildup in return. If, for example, the military had been in charge of negotiating the Montreal Protocols, which established standards for ozone protection, we might all be stockpiling chlorofluorocarbons as bargaining chips, all the while competing to be not only number one in the production of atmospheric pollutants but also to generate more than the rest of the world put together.

Appeasement, Provocation, and Deterrence

Just as political doves point to the dangers of over-arming and provocation—referring especially to the "lessons" of World War I—hawks point to the dangers of under-arming and appeasement, citing the "lessons of Munich" and World War II. Similarly, supporters of deterrence claim that being strong (including the possession of nuclear weapons) has deterred war; others take a different view.

World Wars I and II

The security dilemma is not unique to modern times or the nuclear age. In the decade before World War I, for example, German and British naval leaders each worried that the other might be planning a preemptive attack on the other's fleet. In addition, leaders in Germany and Russia were acutely aware that it would take a week or more to mobilize their armies using existing railroad lines, and each feared that if the other mobilized first, that side would have a potentially lethal advantage. The result was pressure on both to do so before the other. More generally, a would-be defender, seeking to achieve peace via strength, must walk a narrow line between, on the one hand, provoking the war it wants to prevent (the experience of all sides in World War I) and, on the other hand, failing to prevent war by being perceived as too weak or lacking in resolve (the "Munich syndrome," which helped precipitate World War II).

Does Deterrence Work?

Supporters of "peace through strength" like to point to the fact that no US–Soviet war took place in the nuclear age, even during periods of intense rivalry and antagonism. But this claim cannot be assessed. Perhaps peace prevailed between the two superpowers simply because they had no quarrel that justified fighting a terribly destructive war, even a conventional one. It is not at all clear, for example, that the Soviet leadership ever wished to invade Western Europe, and was restrained only by the other side's military strength. Such post facto arguments—especially negative ones, purporting to show why something has *not* happened—are in fact impossible to prove. (If a dog barks in the night, we might be able to say with confidence that it did so "because" someone walked by. If it does not bark, however, we may never know "why.")

In short, it may be inaccurate—even premature—to congratulate our leaders, or their weapons, for keeping the peace. The story is told about the man who sprayed perfume on his lawn every morning. When his perplexed neighbor asked about this strange behavior, the man replied, "I do it to keep the elephants away." The neighbor protested, "But there aren't any elephants within 10,000 miles of here," whereupon the man triumphantly announced, "You see, it works!"

In addition, the 45 years from World War II to the end of the Cold War was not really all that long. More than 20 years separated World Wars I and II; before that, there were more than 40 years of peace between the end of the Franco-Prussian War and World War I; and 55 years had elapsed since the previous major war, which ended with Napoleon's defeat at Waterloo in 1815. The point is that periods of peace have not been all that rare, even in war-prone Europe. And furthermore, when peace ended and the next war began, it was fought with the weapons available at that time—which, for the next major war, might well include nuclear and/or biological and chemical weapons.

There is also a logical fallacy at work: if nuclear weapons had failed to keep the peace and we had a nuclear war, there might well be no one around to argue about their effectiveness as peacekeepers. Moreover, although it is possible that the post-1945 US–Soviet peace was achieved "through strength," it is also possible that it has occurred *in spite of* the provocations of deterrence rather than because of them. Thus, the presence of nuclear weapons on hair-trigger alert capable of reaching each other's homeland has certainly made both sides nervous and edgy. The Cuban Missile Crisis—when by all reliable accounts the world came closer to nuclear war than at any other time—was dubious testimony to the effectiveness of deterrence because it was itself brought about by the provocative nature of the weapons themselves. Thus, it can be argued that we haven't been spared nuclear war because of deterrence but *in spite of it.*

There have also been many cases in which the possession of strong military forces—including nuclear weapons—has *not* deterred war. The Chinese, Cuban, Iranian, and Nicaraguan revolutions all took place despite the fact that the nuclear-armed United States was allied with the governments previously in power. Similarly, the United States lost the Vietnam War, just as the Soviet Union lost in Afghanistan, despite the fact that both countries were not only nuclear armed but also had more and better conventional weapons than their adversaries. Nuclear weapons also did not aid Russia in its unsuccessful war against Chechen rebels in 1994 to 1996 and again when its conventional weapons devastated Chechnya from 1999 to 2000; nor have they helped the United States achieve its goals in occupied Iraq or to insulate the United States from terrorist threats, which, in the future, are more likely to be made with nuclear weapons or other weapons of mass destruction than deterred by them. It was a nuclear-armed United States that "lost" China in 1949 and a nuclear-armed Soviet Union that "lost" China, in the early 1960s. (It is odd such a huge nation can have been so frequently misplaced!)

One of the most unstable world regions has long been south-central Asia. Unlike the United States and the Soviet Union during the Cold War, India and Pakistan share a common border and have fought four wars; by contrast, the United States and the Soviet Union were global and ideological competitors without a history of direct bloodshed or conflict over specific real estate (although the United States did have soldiers from 1918 to 1920 in Siberia in an "allied expeditionary force" as part of the unsuccessful Western effort to reverse the Bolshevik Revolution). Since 1998, India and Pakistan have been nuclear armed. Although it is possible that the possession of nuclear weaponry will induce both countries to be more cautious than they might otherwise be, there is little comfort to be derived from the fact that nuclear deterrence is potentially operating in this case, given the numerous terrorist attacks in both countries and the use of conventional weapons by both sides, especially in the disputed region of Kashmir.

Conventional Deterrence

Deterrence needn't only be nuclear. The Great Wall of China was intended—and to a large extent succeeded—to deter armed invaders by making it unlikely that an attack would succeed. A similar reliance on "deterrence by denial" was attempted by the French government when it built its Maginot Line: Fixed defensive fortifications along the Franco-German border. German armies simply went around it, through Belgium. For centuries, the Roman Empire practiced the alternative form of deterrence "by punishment" (similar to how deterrence is supposed to operate in the nuclear age), in that its legions were unable to deny initial success on the part of "barbarian" invaders; incursions, however, were met by punishing responses. In response to Russia's annexation of Crimea, the United States announced in 2016 that it would quadruple its conventional military expenditures in NATO's eastern states, hoping to deter—presumably by a combination of denial and punishment—any similar Russian provocations in Poland or the Baltic states (Estonia, Latvia, and Lithuania).

Arms races in general can be criticized as a kind of action-reaction sequence, in which an action by one side leads to a reaction by the other, which generates, in turn, yet another action. Closely related are "worst-case analyses," in which the military establishment on every side—seeking to be prudent—assumes the worst of their potential adversaries' capabilities and intentions. The result is a process of "threat inflation," in which every side takes an alarmist view of the threat their adversaries may pose, and overreacts as a result, thereby further intensifying the real or imaginary threats perceived by all sides.

The Use and Abuse of Threats

Deterrence—whether nuclear or conventional—is based on threat: That an attack will be met with retaliation so severe that the would-be attacker would be prevented (deterred) from attacking in the first place. Early in the 20th century, Sir John Fisher, First Sea Lord, Admiral of the Fleet, and widely regarded as the most important British naval figure after Horatio Nelson, emphasized the brutality of deterrence, that it is likely to be effective in proportion as the threatener has a fearsome reputation: "If you rub it in both at home and abroad that you are ready for instant war . . . and intend to be first in and hit your enemy in the belly and kick him when he is down and boil your prisoners in oil (if you take any), and torture his women and children, then people will keep clear of you."

The most extreme example of attempted peace through strength and threats has involved nuclear weapons. Arguments in their favor rely, as we have seen, on the concept of deterrence, as well as on the presumption that, in the absence of immense destructive power, possessors would be susceptible to attack, blackmail, and/or domination. Supposedly, states are made safe by their super-weapons and the threat they convey. In *Realpolitik* terms, it may not be the best of all imaginable worlds, but supporters claim that it is the best of all realistically possible worlds in that, as Admiral Fisher urged, "people will keep clear of you." As Shakespeare said in his play *Henry IV, Part I*, "Out of this nettle, danger, we pluck this flower, safety." And as Winston Churchill proposed, referring specifically to nuclear deterrence, "Safety will be the steady child of terror, and survival, the twin brother of annihilation."

Fear, Stubbornness, and Opportunity

When a nation seeks to maintain peace through strength, it relies on the effectiveness of threats. In *The Strategy of Conflict,* economist and strategic analyst Thomas Schelling distinguished between "compellent" and "deterrent" threats: the former are more aggressive, forcing the opponent to *do* something: withdraw from contested territory, surrender something of value, and so forth. The latter are intended to *prevent* the opponent from acting in a way that the threatener finds undesirable: deterring aggression, dissuading the opponent from subverting another state, and so on. Schelling also pointed out that force can be used for its punishment or shock effect, aside from its military usefulness: examples include General William Sherman's march through Georgia during the American Civil War; General Philip Sheridan's brutal tactics against the Comanche Indians about a decade later; German use of V1 and V2 weapons against Britain toward the end of World War II; and the atomic bombings of Hiroshima and Nagasaki in August 1945. States also tend to employ force when they see a need to shore up their credibility.

Deterrence theory and the assumptions underlying "peace through strength" can have a pernicious effect. Nuclear deterrence in particular depends on a mutually threatening posture, as every side seeks to impress the other with its toughness and willingness to use force. Thus, conflicts that may in themselves be of no intrinsic importance for those involved, and that may even occur far from the borders of either country, become imbued with a peculiar significance: by indicating the credibility, reliability, toughness, and hence buttressing the security of one side. It then becomes vital to intervene in virtually any struggle, just to prove that "we" will not be pushovers and to ensure that our "national will" is not about to be tested or doubted in the future. For example, concern about avoiding the image of the United States as a "pitiful, helpless giant" served as a major motivator for US perseverance in the Vietnam War and may motivate a long-term US military presence in the Middle East as well.

It is possible that deterrence made the superpowers cautious in their provocations of the other side. However, deterrence also encourages a kind of "competitive risk-taking," in which the bolder, tougher, more violence-prone player appears likely to win. When two sides collide, each determined to be the tougher, peace through strength can succumb to war through stubbornness, as with World War I.

Moreover, when political leaders are assessing whether or not to go to war, they may not follow the expectations of deterrence theory, which assumes that states regularly assess their potential prospects vis-à-vis one another and are likely to leap through any potential "windows of vulnerability." Thus, advocates of peace through strength warn that military weakness relative to another state invites attack, whereas strength deters it. But wars have often been precipitated by *fear* (of the other side being stronger or—more often—that it will shortly become stronger) rather than by overconfidence. Thus, at the eve of World War I, Germany and Austria feared being encircled and outmaneuvered by the Triple Entente (France, Russia, and Great Britain), just as the Israeli attack on Egypt and Syria in 1967 partially resulted from Israeli concerns that its Arab neighbors were getting too strong.

States are often more likely to be influenced by their own internal political needs than by their actual military strength vis-à-vis an opponent. Thus, Argentina was militarily inferior to Britain when it attacked the Falkland Islands in 1982, just as India was militarily inferior to China when it provoked the brief and (for India) disastrous Sino-Indian War over the disputed Himalayan region of Ladakh in 1962. (In both these cases, the unsuccessful attacker was not deterred by the fact that the "victim" possessed nuclear weapons.)

Similarly, the deteriorating political fortunes of India's ruling Hindu fundamentalist party were revived after India's nuclear testing in 1998 and its successful repulsion of Pakistan in Kashmir in 1999, just as the election of Russia's Vladimir Putin in 2000 was facilitated by his vigorous promotion of the Second Chechen War during its battle phase from 1999 to 2000.

Although it eventually proved to be a great political liability for President George W. Bush and his administration, in the early stages of the Iraq War, when the government of Saddam Hussein was quickly overthrown, the Bush administration's political popularity and prestige (as well as its electoral prospects) were enhanced. Moreover, the expectation of a positive domestic political outcome loomed large in the Bush administration's decision to invade Afghanistan and Iraq in the first place. And during those wars' initial phases, when it appeared that the Taliban had been defeated in Afghanistan, and Bush declared, "Mission accomplished" following the overthrow of Saddam Hussein, his administration's popularity and his party's electoral prospects reached a new high. When quick and relatively bloodless US victories in those countries were not forthcoming, however, American public opinion shifted against the Bush administration's policies in Iraq, particularly.

Finally, reliance on threat as an arbiter of victory may also lead to a false estimate of the other's threshold, which can be dangerous in the extreme if both sides engage in a game of chicken, each determined that the other must be the one to swerve.

The Prisoner's Dilemma

Advocates of peace through strength often maintain that states have no choice: they must maintain and even increase their armaments—as well as a credible threat to use them if called upon to do so—because if they relied less on military force, they would be at the mercy of another state that continued to arm heavily. Hence, every state may find itself forced into a warlike posture that none want but that all are unable to escape.

This scenario has long been recognized and modeled mathematically as the so-called Prisoner's Dilemma. Analyses based on the Prisoner's Dilemma have a prominent place in mathematical game theory, strategic analysis, political science, social psychology, behavioral economics, and even in evolutionary biology—fields that sometimes attempt to model competitive interactions. Understanding the "rationality" of the choices made by decision makers is therefore important, not only for the light it might shed on threats, competition, and problems of cooperation, but also for what it reveals about the mindset of people whose opinions are influential in shaping military and political doctrine and decisions.

The Prisoner's Dilemma is also a model for the evolution of cooperation versus competition. In its very simplified thought-experimental world, individuals (or states) have two options: "cooperate" (or disarm) and "defect" (or arm). If both cooperate, both receive payoff (R), the reward for cooperation; if both defect, both receive payoff (P), the punishment for mutual defection. But if one defects and the other cooperates, the defector receives T, the temptation to defect, and the one who cooperates (disarms, etc.) at the same time receives S, the sucker's payoff.

Basically, a Prisoner's Dilemma occurs when the payoffs are in the following relationship: $T > R > P > S$. In this case, the "players" are tempted to get T and fearful of getting stuck with S, so they wind up getting P (a punishing arms race) when the best mutual payoff would have been R, the reward for cooperation or mutual restraint. To understand this, imagine that you are inside the head of either player: "I don't know what the other will do, but I do know that if they defect (build up their weaponry), I had better do the same, or else I'll end up at a disadvantage compared to my heavily armed opponent. Alternatively, if the other side disarms, I could disarm too, but I have a more favorable option, namely to build up my own weapons, which would put me at a strong advantage. So either way, regardless of what the other side does, my best policy is to defect, either to keep from being at a disadvantage or to gain an advantage."

The dilemma here is that by following such a logical framework, both sides end up defecting—building up their weaponry—and therefore getting payoff P, the punishment of mutual defection (a punishing arms race), whereas if they had figured out a way to restrain themselves, they would each have gotten a higher payoff: R, the reward of mutual cooperation.

The Prisoner's Dilemma is a useful way of modeling the dilemma of thinking that one must be "nasty" for fear that anyone who is "nice" is at the mercy of others who persevere in being nasty, and similarly, because of the temptation to take advantage of the other side if that option arises. On the other hand, the Prisoner's Dilemma model may well be unduly pessimistic in that it assumes only two choices, whereas in reality individuals or states have a variety of options. They can try a mix of tactics: disarm in one dimension, build up in another, delay a modernization program, and so on.

This simplified model also requires that there is only one possible payoff and that "games" are one-time affairs. In reality, states interact many times in succession, and they can vary their behavior depending on what happened the previous time. And if both sides have an interest in generating a sequence of cooperative interactions, as political scientist Robert Axelrod has demonstrated in his book, *The Evolution of Cooperation,* cooperative outcomes can yield the highest payoff.

In short, the Prisoner's Dilemma can be useful in clarifying decision-making thinking, and, indeed, variants of it are used extensively by analysts in the promilitary strategic community. But such an approach carries many hidden assumptions and that individuals—and states—must avoid becoming prisoners of their own narrow-minded dilemmas.

Sanctions

Violence and the threat of violence are, by definition, coercive. Another way, ostensibly nonviolent, to influence the behavior of states is to rely on sanctions. These typically involve economic and cultural restrictions and boycotts, as well as refusal to trade with the targeted country, and punishments aimed specifically at political leaders: The latter include restrictions on their international travel, appropriation of foreign bank accounts, and occasionally indictment by international legal tribunals. International sanctions of this sort often seem appealing because they do not include overt violence.

To some extent, therefore, sanctions have become a preferred means of international "arm-twisting," as with efforts to induce North Korea and Iran to rethink their nuclear programs by isolating these countries diplomatically, economically, and, when possible, socially and even ideologically. However, while North Korea persists in developing its nuclear weapons program—despite a somewhat porous UN sanctions regime—Iran agreed in 2015 to dismantle its nuclear program, in large measure to have economic sanctions removed—until the Trump Administration unilaterally withdrew from this agreement and imposed even stricter sanctions on Iran, which appear to have led to a revival of Iran's nuclear program.

With the possible recent exception of the Iran case, it is uncertain whether such a "sanctions regime" has ever succeeded, although it appears that the apartheid government of South Africa was financially injured by persistent international boycotts, as has been the government of Iran. Moreover, the South African white population in particular—which has long valued athletic prowess—felt isolated from international sports competition. The former government of Libya, under Moammar Gaddafi, succumbed to a "carrot-and-stick" approach—combining economic pressures with the lure of financial incentives—when it agreed in 2003 to suspend its nuclear program and open its borders to inspectors.

On the other hand, sanctions typically exert their most painful effects on the poorest inhabitants of the target country, thereby compounding existing structural violence while having little impact on its wealthy, powerful rulers. According to a United Nations estimate, during the dozen years of punishing international sanctions against the regime of Saddam Hussein (from 1991 until 2003), as many as 500,000 Iraqi children died as a result of poverty and malnutrition. Accordingly, it must be concluded that international sanctions aren't nearly as nonviolent as their admirers like to claim, while their efficacy also remains in dispute.

Nonprovocative Defense

Having considered the major traditional doctrines related to peace through strength and found them wanting, we turn now to another concept, one that is somewhat congenial to military-minded seekers of peace. It is variously known as "alternative defense," "transarmament," and "nonprovocative defense." This approach seeks to make war less likely through a substantial restructuring of strategic planning and the disposition of armed forces.

Although most countries describe their military as "defensive," they almost always have a large offensive component, which leads to the security dilemma. By contrast, if they adopted nonprovocative defense, states would field only weapons that really are defensive, and would thus reconfigure their forces so as not to threaten other states. The goal would be to prioritize defense over offense, by which states would feel secure in their ability to repel an aggressor but insecure in their ability to successfully mount an attack.

How It Might Work

If nonprovocative defense were established on a national basis, tanks would be prohibited, but antitank defenses permitted; bombers prohibited, but antiaircraft batteries and short-range fighter-interceptors permitted; heavily armored mechanized forces prohibited, but lightly armed, mobile infantry units permitted; supplies would be prepositioned, and defensive networks constructed throughout the countryside. Such a posture would not be suitable for attack but could contribute to a formidable defense. US military thinking has not been receptive to nonprovocative defense, although some European strategic planners—especially in Switzerland and the Scandinavian countries—have shown substantial interest.

One difficulty with implementing nonprovocative defense is distinguishing unambiguously between defensive and offensive forces. Fighter aircraft, for example, can be used to supplement offensive operations, as well as to defend against invaders. Armored personnel carriers can be either aggressive or defensive, as can destroyers or submarines. Even fixed defensive fortifications can serve the offense: The Siegfried Line, built by Germany along its border with France, made it less likely that France would assist its Polish ally while the Nazis made war in Eastern Europe.

More recently, a possible Ballistic Missile Defense system (derided as "Star Wars") has long been touted as defensive by its American advocates. The prospect alarms other nations, especially Russia, which sees it as possibly *offensive* because it might encourage its possessor to initiate an attack with confidence (whether or not well-founded) that it will subsequently be immune to retaliation. In other cases, the distinction is more clear-cut: Minefields and immobile tank traps are unambiguously defensive, while nuclear weapons are offensive, even if they ostensibly provide deterrence.

Nonprovocative defense would require a substantial change in doctrine, compelling war planners to abandon existing designs for "forward-based defense," "deep strikes," and the like, tactics that call for "defending" a country by carrying the fight deep into opposing territory. Instead, countries would concentrate on "defense in depth," emphasizing small mobile units trained to mount disruptive partisan operations, if necessary far within their own borders.

Some powerful states—notably the United States—specialize in "projecting power" far from their shores. These forces—aircraft carriers, long-range fighter-bombers, mobile artillery, amphibious assault units—are not used for defending one's own borders; rather, their purpose is to massively intervene, or threaten to intervene, in other countries, often far from home. Nonprovocative defense would require states to forgo such activities.

A world in which interstate war is significantly less likely would be a potential advance on most current Western strategic planning. And the prospects for nonprovocative defense, although cloudy, are not altogether bleak. There is the practical appeal for budget-conscious strategic planners of the idea of confining each state's "defense forces" to real defense, thereby reducing the probability of war when either side misconstrues the intentions of the other, while also reducing tensions, and saving money to boot.

Importantly, nonprovocative defense would not offer any less defense than current military postures; in fact, by being less threatening to would-be opponents, it should reduce the likelihood of armed hostilities between disputing nations, thereby providing *more* defense for all sides. In addition, unlike most arms control or disarmament proposals, the transition to nonprovocative defense does not require complex bilateral or multilateral negotiated agreements. Any state that so wishes can make the shift unilaterally.

Several have already done so. A number of countries, notably the European states that practice "armed neutrality," are examples of successful nonprovocative defense. For example, Switzerland requires that all men between 20 and 50 years of age participate in the Swiss Army, which emphasizes antiaircraft systems, tank traps, and other unambiguously defensive capabilities, as well as a high degree of mobility, keyed to the natural defenses of the mountainous Swiss homeland. Supplies have been cached throughout the country; thousands of strategic demolition points have been identified and prewired, so as to slow any invader; and the Swiss Air Force features short-range fighter-interceptors, deliberately excluding long-range heavy bombers. In addition, a network of well-stocked, fortified underground civilian-defense bunkers has been built beneath the Alps to shelter Swiss citizens in case of attack or some other national catastrophe. The net result is a robust military capability, but one that is distinctly nonprovocative and also oriented toward deterrence by dissuasion rather than by threat.

Sweden, Finland, and Norway are other contemporary examples of affluent modern states that have achieved a kind of peace through strength, in part by emphasizing defensive and nonprovocative strategies. Norway, Finland, and Sweden have enhanced their own national security by promoting disarmament—especially nuclear disarmament—as a major issue on the world agenda. Thus, Swedish, Finnish, and Norwegian politicians have long been prominent in disarmament efforts, and their governments fund what are probably the preeminent peace institutes: the Stockholm International Peace Research Institute, The Tampere Peace Research Institute, and the International Peace Research Institute in Oslo, which is also home of the Nobel Peace Prize.

A Final Note on Peace Through Strength

In today's world, the pursuit of security should transcend the paradigm that prioritizes military strength as the only—or even the primary—source of "national security." Specifically, global human security should be recognized as encompassing economic, political, social, and environmental considerations, with national security no longer achievable by any country acting alone (if it ever was). That is, real security must be mutual or, better yet, collective or global. With the Cold War fading into memory, the inability of most states—notably, the United States, the richest and most powerful country on Earth—to articulate a nonmilitary, nonconfrontational vision of peace and global security is one of the great failures and missed opportunities of all time.

In an age of unparalleled technological and scientific achievement, most influential political decision makers still rely more on weapons than on peacemaking to prevent war, persistently claiming that increased military strength will result in increased peace.

Questions for Further Reflection

1. What are the relationships among balance of power, peace through strength, and the motto *si vis pacem, para bellum*?

2. What are some advantages and disadvantages of the Prisoner's Dilemma model in conceptualizing cooperation and competition?

3. Describe some merits and demerits of defining national security in strictly military terms.

4. It can be argued that for all its liabilities, "peace through strength" remains the most widespread conception of how to achieve negative peace. Why?

5. Discuss "nonprovocative defense" in the context of "the use and abuse of threats" as well as deterrence theory.

Suggestions for Further Reading

Max Blumenthal. 2019. *The Management of Savagery: How America's National Security State Fueled the Rise of Al Qaeda, ISIS, and Donald Trump*. New York: Verso.

Stuart Kaufman, Richard Little, and William C. Wohlforth. 2007. *Balance of Power in World History*. New York: Palgrave Macmillan.

Paul M. Kennedy. 1987. *The Rise and Fall of the Great Powers: Economic Change and Military Conflict 1500–2000*. New York: Harper & Row.

Henry Kissinger. 2013. *World Order*. New York: Penguin.

Rebecca Moore. 2007. *NATO's New Mission: Projecting Stability in a Post-Cold War World*. New York: Praeger.

Richard Rhodes. 2007. *Arsenals of Folly: The Making of the Nuclear Arms Race*. New York: Knopf.

Thomas Schelling. 1966. *Arms and Influence*. New Haven, CT: Yale University Press.

Notes

1. General von Moltke, quoted in Richard Ned Lebow. 1981. *Between Peace and War*. Baltimore: Johns Hopkins University Press.

2. Parag Khanna. 2008. "Waving Goodbye to Hegemony." *The New York Times Magazine*. http://www.nytimes.com/2008/01/27/magazine/27world-t.html

3. Joseph Schumpeter. 1988. "The Sociology of Imperialism." In *Two Essays by Joseph Schumpeter*. New York: Meridian.

4. Paul M. Kennedy. 1987. *The Rise and Fall of the Great Powers*. New York: Harper & Row.

5. Andrew Bacevich. 2011. "Cow Most Sacred: Why Military Spending Remains Untouchable." Retrieved from http://www.huffingtonpost.com/andrew-bacevich-cow-most-sacred-why-milit_b_814888.html

16

Paul Kemp/AP/Getty Images

International Law

Governments are supposed to operate by laws, the rules of conduct that specify what is permissible and, more often, what is not. Even in our own system of separate states, a legal framework underlies the relationships among states. This framework is known as international law.

The Sources of International Law

Most of us are familiar with domestic law, with its prohibitions against such violent crimes as murder, robbery, and assault, as well as the very laws regulate the nonviolent contacts of daily living, from the flow of traffic to the

439

Fred Ramage via Getty Images

International Law

Governments are supposed to operate by laws, the rules of conduct that specify what is permissible and, more commonly, what is not. Even in our current system of separate states, a legal framework undergirds the relationships among states. This framework is known as international law.

The Sources of International Law

Most of us are familiar with domestic law, with its prohibitions against such violent crimes as murder, robbery, and assault, as well as the way laws regulate the nonviolent conduct of daily living, from the flow of traffic to the work of businesses and the standards of licit conduct in private and public life. Less familiar, by contrast, is international law, the acknowledged principles that guide the interactions among states and set limits on what is and what is not permissible.

People live within societies and countries, not between them; accordingly, more has been done to encourage *intra*national law than *inter*national law. Yet, international law does exist; in fact, the current body of international law is quite large.

Just as daily life for most individuals in prosperous societies today is peaceful, most interactions among states on the world scene are also peaceful, in accord with expectations, and thus, in a sense, "legal." Unlike domestic law, which in the United States is codified in constitutions, amendments, and the specific laws passed by federal, state, and municipal law-making bodies, the body of international law is relatively diffuse and generated in many different ways. There are four major sources of international law: (1) classical writings that have become widely accepted, (2) custom, (3) treaties, and (4) the rulings of international courts.

Classical Writings

In the 16th century, the Spanish legal scholar Francisco de Vitoria developed the thesis that war must be morally justifiable and could not simply be fought over differences of religion or for the glory of a ruler. He also maintained that soldiers were not obliged to fight in unjust wars, even if so commanded by their king. But the best known and most influential example of classical international law was the work of the Dutch legal scholar Hugo Grotius. In his treatise *On the Law of War and Peace* (1625), Grotius claimed that there was a fundamental "natural law," which transcended that of nations and that emanated from the fact that people were ultimately members of the same human community. Grotius argued strongly for the sovereignty of individual states, within their own realms. From this, he concluded that states must avoid interference in the internal affairs of other states. Grotius pointed to the agreements that states had made with each other and that proved to be durable: peace treaties, decisions as to the allocation of fishing and navigation rights, commonly accepted boundaries, and so on.

The Grotian tradition thus derives the legitimacy of international law from the legitimacy of states themselves. But it goes further in seeking to generate principles whereby the behavior of one state toward another can be regulated, arguing that "natural right" must govern the interactions among states and this supersedes the authority of the states themselves. As Grotius saw it (and subsequent international law has affirmed), international "society" exists, which requires certain norms of conduct among states, including rules governing what is acceptable during war. For Grotius, war was not a breakdown in the law of nations but rather a special condition to which law still applies.

One of the earliest and most effective examples of international law in action was the European battle against international piracy, from the 16th to 18th centuries. It was widely agreed at the time—even by England and France, for example, which were then bitter enemies and which often outfitted or tacitly supported pirate raids against each other—that all states had jurisdiction over acts of piracy on the high seas; such unanimity permitted concerted and successful action against a growing threat to international trade and exploration. Importantly, however, pirates were apprehended by the military forces of individual, sovereign states and tried by domestic courts rather than by some international legal body. (In addition, even as states were enforcing such policies, they were also in the habit of sponsoring "privateers," who preyed on the merchant vessels of competing states.)

The term *international law* first appeared in 1783, with the publication of Jeremy Bentham's *Principles of International Law.* Whatever its shortcomings, international law has taken shape in just a few hundred years and has become increasingly important in the aftermath of World War II.

Beginning around 2009, piracy once again emerged as a significant threat to international trade and tourism, especially to shipping in the waters off the Horn of Africa, near Somalia in particular, where the absence of an effective government combined with extreme poverty has induced many Somalis to take up a modern form of piracy, in which cargo ships are taken over by small armed groups, who then demand ransom for the ship and crew. Although responses to this situation have generated a degree of cooperation from navies as diverse as those from the European Union, the United States, Iran, Russia, and China, it also poses a dilemma for international law because there are no clear venues or existing systems of international law under which apprehended modern-day pirates can be tried and, if convicted, punished.

Custom

Custom is one of the most important and least-appreciated sources of international law. For example, according to the "rules of diplomatic protocol," diplomats from one country are considered immune from arrest or detention in another country. This custom was established because it appeared to be in the interest of all countries: If the representatives of adversarial states could legally be harassed, communication between these states would quickly cease, to the disadvantage of all.

Diplomats are occasionally expelled from a host country, usually for "activities incompatible with their diplomatic status" (diplomat-speak for spying), in which case some of the other side's diplomats are typically expelled in retaliation. But normally—that is, customarily, and thus by customary international law—diplomats are allowed substantial leeway, including guarantees that they will be able to communicate freely with their home government. (The strength of this presumption is shown by the outrage generated when the custom of diplomatic immunity is violated, as when US diplomats were held hostage in Iran in 1979–1981, and when, during its attack on Serbia in 1999, NATO bombed the Chinese embassy in Belgrade, killing Chinese diplomats.)

Another example of international law derived from custom is the emerging concept of "common heritage of mankind" (CHOM). This notion has figured in the Law of the Sea and Antarctic treaties, as well as the Montreal Protocols directed at reducing the production of chemicals (especially chlorofluorocarbons) involved in damaging the Earth's ozone layer. According to CHOM, the fact that certain entities—for example, the ocean bed, Antarctica, the ozone layer—transcend state sovereignty means that individuals or states may not simply exploit or despoil them as they wish. Rather, as part of the CHOM, these resources (and, presumably, others as well) are entitled to protection under international law.

At present, CHOM is of uncertain status as an established principle of international law. It also exemplifies the important concept that international law, no less than domestic law, must be flexible and responsive to change and growth in accord accepted legal standards. Insofar as it has been successful, CHOM has thus far applied only to areas that are not within the accepted jurisdiction of existing states; the approach has not yet been widely effective, for example, in preserving tropical rainforests, whose ownership is zealously insisted upon by each state in question.

Despite its widely recognized importance, custom can be slippery as a touchstone for international legality. For example, when Russia annexed Crimea in 2014—which outraged many in the West, who consider it a clear violation of Ukraine's sovereignty and thus of international law—this same action was justified in the eyes of many Russians because Crimea had a long history of being considered, *by custom*, part of Russia.

Treaties

International treaties are analogous to contracts among individuals. Treaties have covered not only the termination of wars but also agreements about boundaries, fishing and navigation rights, and mutually agreed restrictions as to permissible actions during war.

Treaties are not always honored, but in the vast majority of cases, they have been. Backing away from treaty obligations results in substantial loss of face, and once branded a treaty breaker, a state may subsequently have difficulty establishing useful, reliable relationships with other states. Through treaties as well as customary practice, international law provides "rules of the road" by which international interaction, beneficial to each side, can be conducted. As a result, states have an interest in abiding by them. According to the US Constitution, international treaties are to be considered part of the "supreme law of the land," although in practice they are often accorded considerably less respect.

To become legally binding, most treaties have to pass two hurdles (depending on the domestic laws of the signatory states) and sometimes three. The first step, after the successful completion of negotiations, is signing, which affixes the approval of a state's head of government. Then, in the majority of cases, comes ratification by a national legislature (in the United States, treaty ratification requires a two-thirds affirmative vote by the Senate). In addition, many treaties specify that they are not in force until ratified by a specified number of states—and, sometimes, by particular states. Although there may be a substantial lag between signing and ratification, as well as between ratification and activation, countries traditionally abide by the terms of an international treaty once it has been signed. The reason for this is that a country typically does not agree to a treaty unless it is in its interest.

Short of treaties, but often taken seriously nonetheless, are a range of international agreements reached among heads of state. The multilateral agreement reached in 2015, whereby Iran agreed to refrain from acquiring nuclear weapons in return for the dropping of international sanctions, is an example of this, as is the Global Climate Change Agreement reached in Paris (also in 2015), whereby countries committed to individual restrictions in their greenhouse gas emissions. In both cases, the United States argued successfully for something short of formal treaties because two-thirds US Senate approval (constitutionally mandated for international treaties) was considered impossible due to the Republican majority in that house of Congress. In both cases, because these were agreements rather than formal treaties, the Trump Administration was readily able to withdraw. The incoming Biden Administration was, by the same token, free to rejoin — and did so.

Courts

Finally, international law—like domestic law—requires courts to hear disputed cases and render decisions. For example, the European Court of Human Rights, in Strasbourg (France), hears human rights cases involving citizens of any of its 47 signatory states. The International Court of Justice, located in The Hague (the Netherlands) is administered by the United Nations. Also known as the World Court, this institution consists of a rotating membership of world jurists; it issues decisions about international law that are generally considered authoritative, although often unenforceable.

An International War Crimes Tribunal was convened during the 1990s and has held trials against individuals accused of participating in genocide in Bosnia and Rwanda. This tribunal has tried some prominent government leaders once they were out of power—notably Serbian president Slobodan Milošević for war crimes in Bosnia and Kosovo. (Milošević died of natural causes before a verdict could be rendered.)

The International Criminal Court (ICC) came into existence in 2002, established by an international treaty known as the Rome Statute. As of early 2020, there were 104 ICC members, with 12 full members and 92 associate members, including all of Latin America, nearly all of Europe, and about one-half of African states. Its purpose is to prosecute individuals indicted for genocide, crimes against humanity, war crimes, and international aggression. The primary responsibility for such prosecutions is nonetheless left to sovereign states, and the ICC is empowered to act only when these states refuse to do so. Nonetheless, many prominent states—including India, China, Russia, Israel, and the United States—have not joined this court and have refused to sign on to the activities of the ICC. (The United States has objected to the possibility of its nationals being brought before the court but has been willing to support the indictment, trial, and imprisonment of citizens of other countries.)

Specific Actions (and Inactions)

In 2019, former president Laurent Gbagbo of the Ivory Coast was acquitted of crimes against humanity by the ICC. In early 2020, Sudan's rulers agreed to hand over ex-president Omar al-Bashir to the ICC to face genocide and war crimes charges. Nearly two decades after the wars in Bosnia and Kosovo, during which there were numerous serious human rights violations as well as genocide, especially by Serb forces against Bosnian and Kosovar Muslims, several major perpetrators were captured and brought to trial, including former Serbian president Slobodan Milošević, who died in 2006 before his trial was completed. But Ratko Mladić, the former Bosnian Serb military commander, was convicted and imprisoned, as was Vojislav Šešelj, founder and president of the nationalist Serbian Radical Party and from 1998 to 2000 Deputy Prime Minister of Serbia; they were found guilty of orchestrating murder, rape, and looting by murderous gangs of Serbian irregulars. The most significant conviction by the ICC so far has been that of Charles Taylor, who, while dictatorial president of Liberia (1997–2003), sponsored a brutal civil war in neighboring Sierra Leone, in which "blood diamonds" mined in Sierra Leone provided much of the financing for such atrocities as the amputations of the arms and legs of civilians.

In 2016, the International Court of Justice ruled that China had illegally encroached on Philippine territorial waters in the South China Sea by constructing artificial islands over which it claims sovereignty. China, however, has vowed to ignore this judgment, which makes it something of an international renegade, albeit a seemingly successful one. And Philippine President Duterte refused to enforce this historic ruling, arguing that his country does not want to go to war with China.

Within-State Violations

The wars of the late 20th and early 21st centuries have thus far taken place mainly within states rather than between them, a situation that seems likely to persist. Such wars—including those in Iraq, Bosnia, East Timor, Kosovo, Darfur, the Democratic Republic of Congo, Libya, Yemen, and Syria—although usually involving relatively light weapons, have included extreme brutality toward civilians. Increasingly, international courts have been called upon to apply the rule of law to the perpetrators, especially those in command (whether military or civilian) who violate basic international codes of conduct.

According to former Obama administration State Department official Anne-Marie Slaughter,

> When a government charged with making and enforcing laws systematically violates those laws by a deliberate decision to torture, murder, "disappear," or detain citizens without legal justification, domestic law gives way to international human rights law, and increasingly to international criminal law. When those citizens fight back in an organized fashion, or otherwise organize themselves against the state in a sustained military confrontation, then international human rights law gives way to the patchwork of international rules developed to apply to conflicts within states.

> The boundaries between all these categories are very blurred; witness the ongoing dispute over the past decade as to whether to try terrorists as criminals in a domestic court or as unlawful combatants under the laws of war. It will probably take many years to sort out when "the state" should be treated as one unit under international law, as a government accountable to its people under domestic constitutional and statutory law, or as a group of individuals responsible for their actions under domestic and international criminal law.[1]

Until recently, it was rare for major political or military leaders to be held criminally liable for their actions. More commonly, defeated heads of state, for example, were either executed by the victors, or they escaped or were driven into exile in other countries. As the various international criminal tribunals multiply, however, the legal decisions of these courts may have increasing influence on the development of international law. The great majority of ICC prosecutions have involved African leaders; consequently, the court has been criticized for focusing too much on Africa. Accordingly, the African Union (AU), an intergovernmental organization with 53 member states that was established in 2002, has created The African Court on Human and Peoples' Rights, which rules on African Union states' compliance with the African Charter on Human and Peoples' Rights.

A Verdict on International Courts

Thus far, the record of international courts is mixed. On the one hand, states are gradually becoming more accustomed to forgoing enough sovereignty to settle disputes in court instead of in combat. But on the other hand, adherence to the dictates of the various international courts is largely "consensual," whereas adherence to domestic law is obligatory. Moreover, even as individuals are increasingly held accountable for international crimes—including war crimes, genocide, and the like—there is currently no widely accepted legal framework for indicting, trying, and punishing transnational corporations. Imagine a community in which accused lawbreakers could be brought to trial only if they agreed that the laws applied to them, and further imagine that they could decide whether or not to abide by any ruling of the courts!

Enforcement of International Law

The major problem with international law, therefore, aside from its diffuseness, is enforcement. Because enforcement provisions are generally lacking, it has been claimed that international "law" is not, strictly speaking, law at all but rather a set of acknowledged customs or norms of behavior.

The importance of norms alone should not be underestimated; in fact, most human behavior occurs with regard to widely shared norms, not formal law. Nonetheless, domestic law is the last resort (short of violence, which domestic law typically prohibits), and law is effective at least in part because, if worse comes to worst and a lawbreaker is apprehended and found guilty of violating the law, he or she can be held accountable and ordered to pay fines, serve prison terms, etc.

In the case of domestic law, individuals acknowledge, whether overtly or not, that they are subordinate to the state and its machinery of enforcement: the police, court bailiffs, the national guard, and so on. When it comes to relations among states, by contrast, "individual" states insist on their sovereignty; they emphatically do not recognize that there is an authority that supersedes theirs. The major problem with international law, therefore, is that individual states demand a kind of latitude that they would rarely if ever allow their own citizens.

Consider the role of sanctions (punishments for noncompliance) in law more generally. There are three primary incentives for obeying any law, domestic or international: self-interest, duty, and coercion. For example, many individuals stop at red lights not because they fear getting a traffic ticket but rather because they know that, otherwise, they are more likely to have an accident. Rules may therefore be followed out of purely utilitarian concerns—in this case, citizens' interest in personal safety. Laws provide a way of regulating human conduct, ideally for the benefit of all. You can proceed with reasonable safety through an intersection when the light is green because you know that opposing traffic has a red light, and you have some confidence that other drivers will respect this law, just as you do.

In addition, individuals may follow the law because they feel duty-bound to contribute to an orderly society that functions with respect for authority. As members of society who benefit from orderly behavior, individuals assume a responsibility to behave accordingly. That is, many persons are influenced by "normative" considerations, or a kind of Kantian categorical imperative to do what is right because this is their duty as rational and responsible members of society. Finally, some people are induced to be law-abiding by fear that "violators may be prosecuted" and forced to succumb to the state's authority if they are apprehended and found guilty.

Although the role of such coercive factors is considerable, coercion by the state apparatus is not the only reason most people are law-abiding. Similarly, the absence of such coercion or mechanisms for enforcement does not invalidate international law or render it toothless. The fact that some people break the law and get away with it is not an argument for doing away with laws. Rather, it argues for greater vigilance and, when possible, enforceability.

Nation-states have numerous incentives, both positive and negative, for abiding by their legal obligations to other states. If a state abandons its legal responsibilities, adversaries may retaliate, friends and allies may disapprove, and world opinion is likely to be strongly negative, leading to ostracism and possible economic, political, and cultural sanctions. Moreover, governments themselves have a strong stake in their own legitimacy, and, even in authoritarian states, adherence to law is fundamental to such legitimacy.

Furthermore, enforcement per se may be less important in inducing compliance with any law, domestic or international, than the moral aura that surrounds law. Thus, in a law-abiding society, police forces do not make law respectable; rather, it is underlying respect for the law, or fear of punishment for breaking the law, that enables police forces to function effectively. According to this view, what is primarily needed for effective international law is not so much a mechanism for enforcement as a deeply felt sense that each law carries its own social and moral imperative. Examples include the 1951 Geneva Treaty on the Rights of Refugees and Migrants and the Convention on International Trade in Endangered Species.

The Conflict Between International Law and State Sovereignty

It simply isn't true that all is anarchy in the international arena any more than everyone is law-abiding in the domestic sphere. States generally obey the law—out of a combined sense of duty and self-interest—even though coercive sanctions, as understood in domestic law, are often absent. States engage in nonviolent commerce—exchange of tourists, diplomats, ideas, trade—according to certain regulations, and usually with good will. Moreover, states usually do not enter into treaties unless they intend to abide by them, and they only acquiesce to customary norms of behavior when they anticipate that, over the long run, they will benefit by doing so. But at the same time, they cling to various aspects of sovereignty. Most treaties include a provision permitting signatories to withdraw within a set period of time, typically three or six months, if their "supreme national interests" are jeopardized. And who makes this decision? The state itself.

States can be defined (following Max Weber and Lenin) as those political entities that claim a monopoly of "legitimate" violence within their borders. When they engage in what they claim is lawful violence outside their borders, states usually maintain that

1. they are acting in self-defense (e.g., the Soviet Union in World War II, Israel during the Six Days' War, and the United States after 9/11 when it invaded Afghanistan),

2. they are fulfilling treaty obligations (e.g., France and Britain in World War II),

3. they are intervening on the side of legitimate authority (e.g., the United States in Vietnam, the Soviet Union in Afghanistan, and Russia in Syria),

4. the situation is anarchic and lacks a legitimate authority (e.g., the United Nations in the Congo and Somalia, the United States in Syria),

5. the conflict is within the realm of international legal obligations (e.g., the United Nations in Korea), and/or

6. the conflict presents an overriding moral imperative, such as the prevention of genocide and the "responsibility to protect" civilian noncombatants (e.g., NATO in Kosovo, Libya, and the Democratic Republic of Congo, the United States briefly in Somalia).

In short, state sovereignty continues to reign—at least when it comes to the interveners. A semblance of international law is usually invoked as well, although states have been very hesitant, however, to circumscribe their day-to-day authority. Whereas The Hague Peace Conferences (1899 and 1907), for example, produced a few tentative restrictions on the waging of war, they were unable to establish any significant binding rules for peace.

States are also selective, even when it comes to accepting the jurisdiction of international courts, a process known as *adjudication*. Adjudication is very similar to arbitration in that the decision of the third party is binding. The only difference is that in adjudication, the decision is based on international law and rendered by a world court, rather than made by an independent and agreed-upon arbitrator.

When, in 1946, the United States formally agreed to refer all of its international disputes to the International Court of Justice, the Senate attached an amendment, known as the Connally Reservation, stipulating that the court's authority does not include anything within the domestic jurisdiction of the United States as determined by the United States. With this loophole, the United States is free to "determine" that any dispute is essentially within its domestic jurisdiction, thereby avoiding international adjudication whenever it wishes.

This stance by nation-states is not unusual. France, for example, refused to acknowledge the jurisdiction of the International Court of Justice when France tested nuclear weapons on its island territories in the Pacific, despite complaints of international illegality from New Zealand, Australia, and other Pacific states. And when the International Court of Justice ruled in 1986 against the United States and in favor of Nicaragua in a case involving US mining of Nicaraguan harbors during the "contra war" of 1983 and 1984, the United States simply shrugged aside this verdict, claiming that in this instance it did not recognize the court's authority.

Law, Power, and Social Change

Law is an important part of human life; some would even say that it is crucial to civilization. Despite widespread concerns about its enforcement—and anxiety when, as in the case of international law, enforcement powers are lacking—law is, in principle, the antithesis of rule by brute force. *Might* does not make normative *right*; law should reflect what is right and just, (although it often falls far short of this imperative). As a result, most people are presumed to be law-abiding, and, in fact, rule by law is almost inevitably seen as preferable to rule by force.

However, law can also be an instrument of oppression. Laws are made by those in power, and as such, they can serve to perpetuate that power and to prevent social and political change. Laws, international as well as domestic, therefore work best in a static, relatively unchanging environment. Developing and revolutionary states often point out that international laws were established by Western powers in support of their domination. One of the earliest and clearest examples is the Treaty of Tordesillas (1494), following Columbus's "discovery" of the New World, whereby the pope "legally" divided that world into Spanish and Portuguese domains, without any regard for the indigenous peoples already living there.

Similarly, Western international law relies heavily on the basic principle that *pacta sunt servanda* (treaties should be honored). But consider cases in which a puppet ruler, imposed by a foreign colonial power, signs a treaty granting economic privileges to that power. If an indigenous, representative government eventually replaces the colonial authorities, should the new government be obliged to fulfill those obligations? For example, the establishment of a US naval base at Guantánamo, Cuba, dates to a treaty between the two countries in 1903 following the Spanish-American War (when Cuba became a de facto ward of the United States) and another treaty in 1934 between the United States and the US-backed Batista dictatorship, which was later overthrown by the Cuban Revolution in 1959.

The power of previous treaties (plus, in the case of Guantánamo, the power of the United States) has generally been such that even those negotiated by an earlier and discredited regime are usually continued in force. When the Soviet Union dissolved, its major successor state, Russia, not only acceded to the previous Soviet Union's seat in the United Nations but also undertook to meet the Soviet Union's treaty obligations.

When Circumstances Change

Not surprisingly, however, economically developing and, to a lesser extent, revolutionary nationalist states are often inclined to repudiate *pacta sunt servanda* and to rely instead on an opposing doctrine, also recognized under law: *rebus sic stantibus* (circumstances have changed). This principle states that international laws must be living documents, subject to modification and, if necessary, annulment, whenever conditions become substantially different from those current when an agreement or treaty was reached. By the same token, agreements made under duress—like contracts signed with a gun to one's head—are not generally considered valid.

International law must be flexible, if only because of the march of technology. For several centuries, for example, since a Dutch ruling in 1737, *territorial waters* had been considered to extend three miles from shore, a distance based on the effective range of shore-based cannons at the time. New guidelines, however, established by the Law of the Sea Treaty after decades of wrangling, call for 200-mile limits. This treaty, known as the United Nations Convention on the Law of the Sea, also created mechanisms of dispute resolution, waste disposal, and navigation procedures. Under the Reagan administration during the 1980s, the United States refused to sign it, maintaining that the treaty's call for an intergovernmental body to supervise mining on the deep-sea bed constituted "international socialism."

This highlights, once again, the susceptibility of international law to asserted claims of state sovereignty, as well as the growing pressure of North-South cleavages. (The US administration eventually signed the Law of the Sea Treaty, but because Congress has yet to ratify it, the United States is not a party.)

Hidden Strengths of International Law

Governmental Respect for Law

Most governments do not routinely flout the law, not even their own domestic statutes, over which they have virtually complete control. In most democratic countries, governments accede to legal decisions, even those that go against them. Citizens of the United States, for example, often take for granted that in many cases, they can, if they wish, bring legal action against their own government. And if the courts—which are themselves organs of the government—rule against that government, citizens can receive compensation or other redress for their grievances, even though governments, not the courts, have the strong-arm potential of enforcing their will. This emphasizes the primacy of law over force. Although once again there are exceptions (including the US government's indefinite detainment of "enemy combatants" at Guantánamo Bay, Cuba, and the Central Intelligence Agency's renditions of purported terrorists) when the executive branch of a government acts "extra-legally" and only later, if at all, seeks court and/or congressional ratification of its actions.

During the Korean War, following a labor strike that supposedly threatened US war production at a critical time, President Truman sought to nationalize the US steel industry. The Supreme Court, however, overruled this action, and the government obeyed the law, albeit reluctantly. Because democratic governments have a long-range interest in settling disputes amicably, which usually supersedes its short-term interest in winning a given dispute, they tend to accept legal rulings, even those they dislike. On the other hand, such acceptance is generally less likely in international affairs, unless the opponents are so mutually balanced that the costs of losing a case are less than the costs of further wrangling and possible war.

Tacit Acceptance and Expectation

International law often appears weaker than it really is. This is because violations, when they occur, can be sensational and dramatic, whereas compliance is taken for granted and hence goes largely unnoticed.

When a domestic law is broken by individuals, only rarely are citizens moved to question the legitimacy of the law itself (mass civil disobedience during the US Civil Rights movement is a notable exception), and almost never do they doubt the law's existence. But a different standard is often applied to international law. When states violate international law, they may or may not be condemned by public opinion, but almost invariably, *the law itself* is called into question, and the purported weakness of international law is once again lamented. Just as we are not told about the vast majority of people who obey domestic law every day, we do not see headlines proclaiming, "Paraguay today complied with its treaty obligations regarding its border with Bolivia, and therefore no invasion took place."

Virtually the entire civilized world was shocked, by contrast, when, in the early days of World War I, German chancellor Theobald von Bethmann-Hollweg justified his country's invasion of Belgium by describing the international treaty guaranteeing Belgian neutrality as a "mere scrap of paper." On the one hand, this announcement—and, even more so, the invasion itself—demonstrated the truth of the chancellor's assertion: Belgian neutrality was in fact only an international agreement (the Treaty of London, signed in 1839), lacking any specific enforcement mechanism and certainly incapable, by itself, of keeping out the invading German Army. But on the other hand, the level of international outrage over Germany's invasion of Belgium showed that international law, even when it lacks a direct means of enforcement, is nonetheless real in its effects on public perception. Moreover, a major reason for the UK entering the war against Germany was the German violation of Belgium's neutrality. International treaty law was ultimately enforced in this case. Had Germany respected its treaty obligations under international law, the United Kingdom might well have stayed neutral, and Germany might have won World War I.

The Laws of War

War can be seen as the antithesis of law, whose goal is the ordering of relations without recourse to violence. Cicero first wrote that *inter arma silent legis* ("in war the law is silent"). This might be interpreted to mean that the justifiability of any given war is outside the purview of international law because states are sovereign authorities unto themselves and are thus free to make war or not, as they choose. Under this view, because there is no higher authority than a state, no one can claim that a state is making war *unlawfully*.

Nonetheless, a body of law is widely thought to apply to states under conditions of war. Legal scholar and war historian Quincy Wright has even defined war as "the legal condition which equally permits two or more hostile groups to carry on a conflict by armed force."[2] Therefore, at least according to some scholars and policymakers, war is a highly formalized occurrence when violence may legally be deployed by two opposing groups. Enough agreement exists within the community of nations that belligerent and neutral states alike recognize the existence of certain accepted standards for going to war: "Although war manifests the weakness of the community of nations," Wright claimed, "it also manifests the existence of that community."[3]

On occasion, members of the international community coalesce in opposition to acts that are deemed outrageous. For example, many states and nongovernmental organizations, to some extent reflecting the will of the world community as a whole, have been deeply offended by the use of children—some as young as eight years—in military engagements. In Geneva in 2000, the UN Convention on the Rights of the Child was revised, raising the minimum age for participation in armed conflicts from 15 to 18 and defining recruitment of soldiers under the age of 15 as a war crime. The United States eventually signed this convention, after having long objected to such a provision, insisting on its right to recruit 17-year-old volunteers and even to send them into combat. At the same time, rebel groups, especially in sub-Saharan Africa, rather than national armies, are prone to employ underage child soldiers, and such groups generally show little inclination to abide by the international laws of war.

The Nuremberg Principles

States that are party to international treaties may find themselves subject, even against their will, to the legal restraints of these treaties. Some captured officials from the losing countries in World War II, especially Nazi Germany, for example, were tried—and convicted—for having waged aggressive war in defiance of their obligations under the Kellogg-Briand Pact of 1928 (which has also served as the partial legal basis for the notion of "crimes against peace"). These trials, conducted in the German city of Nuremberg, were unique for having developed the legal doctrine that individuals are personally liable to criminal prosecution for crimes against international law and that "following orders" does not provide legal immunity. Such crimes include illegal resort to war as well as violations of accepted restraints on conduct during war—notably, the treatment of prisoners, the waging of genocide, and the intentional targeting of noncombatant civilians.

Telford Taylor, the chief Allied prosecutor at Nuremberg, wrote that

> war consists largely of acts that would be criminal if performed in time of peace—killing, wounding, kidnapping, destroying or carrying off other people's property. Such conduct is not regarded as criminal if it takes place in the course of war, because the state of war lays a blanket of immunity over the warriors. . . . But the area of immunity is not unlimited and its boundaries are marked by the laws of war.[4]

Some critics objected to these proceedings, claiming that the Nuremberg Trials were simply examples of "victors' justice" and not real international law. Nevertheless, the so-called Nuremberg Principles have served as a benchmark in efforts to introduce humane and reasoned limits to acceptable wartime behavior. Thus, the international military tribunal that convened in Nuremberg specified a series of international crimes. Article 6 of the Nuremberg Charter identified the following:

1. Crimes against the peace—planning; preparation; initiation or waging of a war of aggression or a war in violation of international treaties, agreements, or assurances; or participation in a common plan or conspiracy for the accomplishment of any of the foregoing

2. Crimes against humanity—murder, extermination, enslavement, deportation, and other inhumane acts committed against any civilian population, before or during the war, or persecutions on political, racial, or religious grounds . . . whether or not in violation of the domestic law of the country where perpetrated

3. War crimes—violations of the laws or customs of war. Such violations shall include, but not be limited to, murder; ill treatment or deportation to slave labor or for any other purpose of civilian population of or in occupied territory; murder or ill treatment of prisoners of war or persons on the seas; killing of hostages; plunder of public or private property; wanton destruction of cities, towns, or villages; and devastation not justified by military necessity

Article 7 specifies that "the official position of defendants, whether as Heads of State or responsible officials of Government departments, shall not be considered as freeing them from their responsibility or mitigating their punishment." And according to Article 8, "The fact that the defendant acted pursuant to orders of his Government or of a superior shall not free him from responsibility."

Whereas the German defendants at Nuremberg were tried for crimes they committed that were subsequently ruled to have been against international law, a series of lesser-known trials was conducted in Tokyo of Japanese officials accused in large part of crimes of *omission*—that is, illegal failure to prevent war crimes—as contrasted with the crimes of *commission* with which the Nuremberg Tribunal was concerned.

For example, Kōki Hirota, Japanese foreign minister from 1932 to 1937, failed to insist on an end to Japanese atrocities against civilian Chinese during the "rape of Nanking." Following the war, he was executed as an international war criminal. Several decades later, when US Army lieutenant William Calley was tried and found guilty for his role in the slaughter of hundreds of old people, women, and children—known as the My Lai Massacre—during the Vietnam War. This appears to have been the first time a state had accused one of its own soldiers of war crimes. (Calley was found guilty of directly murdering 22 unarmed civilians and was sentenced to life in prison; President Nixon commuted his sentence to three years of house arrest.) Calley's higher-ranking commanding officers were not tried, despite the fact that parallels can be drawn between the actions of senior US military and political leaders and those high-ranking Japanese officials who were tried and convicted after World War II. So again, whereas international laws exist and have been enforced, such enforcement has been highly selective.

Military Necessity?

Some of the treaties that were violated by the Nuremberg defendants, originating from the Geneva and Hague conventions, specified limitations on naval and aerial bombardment. But they also made allowances for "military necessity," which can be stretched to permit nearly any act in wartime, however brutal. Similarly, even the unenforceable Kellogg-Briand Pact, which officially outlawed war, was interpreted by many as permitting "wars of self-defense," as does the current UN Charter: Article 51 of that Charter grants states the "inherent right of individual or collective self-defense."

Self-defense would clearly have justified Poland's attempt to resist the German invasion in 1939, but it is not clear that France's declaration of war against Germany for its aggression against France's ally Poland would also have been considered legitimate self-defense. (France was bound by treaty to help defend Poland.) And what about the Israeli invasion of Egypt in 1967, in which Israel clearly struck first but argued that Egyptian behavior constituted a real provocation as well as an imminent threat that justified a "preemptive" attack? Similarly, the "Brezhnev Doctrine," by which the Soviet Union justified its invasion of Czechoslovakia in 1968, was described at the time as simply "self-defense by socialist people against Western-inspired counter-revolutionaries."

The "Carter Doctrine," articulated by President Jimmy Carter in 1980, stated that the United States would consider any attempt by an outside force (i.e., the Soviet Union) to gain control of the Persian Gulf region an assault on US vital interests that would be repelled by military force if necessary. And the "Reagan Doctrine," under which the United States assisted right-wing counter-revolutionaries seeking to overthrow leftist governments in Angola and Afghanistan, was also described by its supporters as aid to people seeking to defend themselves.

Governments have an old habit of declaring a "doctrine," as though that establishes a new component of international law. US president James Monroe, for example, announced the "Monroe Doctrine" in 1823, which declared that any efforts by European powers to colonize or otherwise "interfere" in the affairs of Western Hemisphere countries would be considered an act of aggression and would be met by US military force. Such doctrines might qualify as serving the cause of peace, insofar as they clarify what actions would likely lead to war, but as unilateral declarations, they do not establish new international law.

The administration of President George W. Bush showed very little respect for or patience with international law, announcing that the US invasion of Iraq in 2003 was an example of "preventive war," legitimated by the supposed possession by Saddam Hussein's government of weapons of mass destruction (which turned out to be fictitious). Moreover, when it comes to governments using force against their own citizens—such as Serbia in Kosovo; Sudan's persecution of its own citizens in Darfur; Russia's no-holds-barred bombing of the Chechen capital, Grozny; Chinese crackdown on Tibetan nationalists, on prodemocracy demonstrators in Tiananmen Square in 1989, and on its Muslim Uighur citizens beginning in 2018—obligations and restraints of international law are murkier yet, and such prima facie violations of human rights can rarely if ever be prosecuted by the international community.

In short, when states believe that their security interests require them, violations of international law occur, a situation likely to continue. Many scholars argue, incidentally, that the very possession of nuclear weapons runs counter to international law, because it involves preparations for genocide. Most of the nonviolent protests against US nuclear weapons has been based on a so-called "Nuremberg defense," according to which the protesters maintain that in opposing these weapons of mass destruction, they are acting in concert with the requirements established by the Nuremburg Principles. Thus far, judges have refused to permit testimony based on this concept, insisting instead that the issue is simply whether or not criminal law has been broken.

A Final Note on International Law

International law has many imperfections. It has nonetheless exerted useful restraints on unacceptable state conduct in some cases, while being woefully inadequate in others. The major powers tend to give international law less credence than do the militarily weaker states, in part because the former have recourse to their military strength, whereas the latter may be more invested in the rule of law, which offers them the possibility—or illusion—of a "level playing field" in conflicts with stronger opponents.

Some legal and political authorities recommend only a modest role for international law in the future, avoiding "the Charybdis of subservience to state ambitions and the Scylla of excessive pretensions of restraint," and recognizing that "it is in the interest of international law itself to put states' consciences neither to sleep nor to torture."[5] Another view is that international law is a good beginning, something on which to build a world with universally recognized legal guidelines or, at least, one in which the sanctity of state sovereignty is sometimes curtailed in the greater interest of human security and survival. In any event, as the world grows, in effect, smaller every day, the importance of international law grows larger.

Questions for Further Reflection

1. It has been said that to the extent that law is law, it is not international, and to the extent that it is international, it is not law. Analyze this contention.

2. How does the question of enforcement in international law differ from that of domestic law? How is it similar?

3. Are there any weaknesses in international law other than the problem of enforcement? If so, describe them.

4. In what sense can international law be seen as progressive? In what sense can it be seen as conservative?

5. What relevance, if any, do the Nuremberg Principles have to important international conflicts today? Your answer could be framed in general principles or specific examples.

Suggestions for Further Reading

Thomas Buergenthal and Sean Murphy. 2018. *Public International Law in a Nutshell*. St. Paul, MN: West Academic.

Simon Chesterman. 2002. *Just War or Just Peace? Humanitarian Intervention and International Law*. Oxford, UK: Oxford University Press.

Malcolm Evans, ed. 2014. *International Law*. Oxford, UK: Oxford University Press.

Jack L. Goldsmith and Eric A. Posner. 2006. *The Limits of International Law*. New York: Oxford University Press.

Christopher C. Joyner. 2005. *International Law in the 21st Century: Rules for Global Governance*. Lanham, MD: Rowman & Littlefield.

Christian Reus-Smit. 2004. *The Politics of International Law*. New York: Cambridge University Press.

Malcolm Shaw. 2017. *International Law*. Cambridge, UK: Cambridge University Press.

Notes

1. Anne-Marie Slaughter. 2011. "War and Law in the 21st Century: Adapting to the Changing Face of Conflict." *Europe's World*. http://europesworld .org/2011/10/01/war-and-law-in-the-21st-century-adapting-to-the-changing-face -of-conflict/#.V7TtrTVw6So.

2. Quincy Wright. 1982. *A Study of War*. Chicago: University of Chicago.

3. Ibid.

4. Telford Taylor. 1970. *Nuremberg and Vietnam*. Chicago: Quadrangle.

5. Stanley Hoffmann. 1971. "International Law and the Control of Force." In *The Relevance of International Law*, eds. K. Deutsch and S. Hoffmann. New York: Anchor.

Gilles BASSIGNAC/Gamma-Rapho via Getty Images

Ethical and Religious Perspectives

Killing another human being, except by accident, in self-defense, or because of insanity, is condemned in most contemporary societies—unless done during war or by the state against criminals within and enemies outside, in which case it is not only permitted but also frequently applauded. In war, skilled killers, and those who send them into combat, are often accorded high honors.

A Two-Sided View of Killing

Not surprisingly, war has received substantial attention from ethicists and theologians. The relationship between ethical doctrines and war has nonetheless long been ambiguous and their messages ambivalent; advocates of peace have often derived inspiration and strength from such principles, while at the same time, the war prone have also turned to religious and moral authorities (sometimes the same ones) to support their arguments.

Concerted opposition to war often derives considerable impetus from ethical and religious sources; nonetheless, some versions (or perversions) of ethics and religion have also fueled much warfare in the past and may continue to do so in the future. Many of the world's organized moral and theological institutions and preachers have been more likely to support militarism than to oppose it. Sometimes, religious authorities have been among the primary cheerleaders for war-making. At other times, their stance has been passive acquiescence.

In czarist Russia, for example, Russian Orthodox priests traditionally said a funeral mass for peasants when they were inducted into the army. Commonly, religious and ethical values were limited to self-protective and self-serving doctrines, such as immunity for the clergy and mixtures of reassurance and solace for the soldiery and endangered civilians. The following inscription (loosely translated) has been commonly seen on houses in small villages in Bavaria, Germany: "Saint Florian, protect our town, pass by my house, burn others down"! And religious fundamentalists from many denominations, most notably Islamic jihadists, Hindu ultranationalists, and Christian "freedom fighters," wage war against civilians and the "heathen," convinced that God is on their side.

On the other hand, religious and ethical concerns are often central to the establishment of peace. Moral decisions cannot always be avoided: There was, after all, virtually nothing technically wrong with Auschwitz, Dachau, or the bombings of Dresden and Hiroshima. (The latter, especially, was a major scientific and technical achievement.) Criticism, or condemnation, must come—if at all—in moral and/or spiritual terms.

In the modern world, religion has frequently been a force for social and political transformation. Examples include the respective roles of Shiite Islam in post-Shah Iran, Catholicism in Poland, Episcopal bishop Desmond Tutu and others who fought apartheid in South Africa, and Protestant Christianity in fueling the civil rights movement in the American South during the 1960s. Numerous American churches opposed the war in Vietnam, and during the 1980s church-led movements were instrumental in calling for the abolition of nuclear weapons and the end of East-West hostilities. The Berlin Wall fell in part because of nonviolent mass protests by Christians in the former East Germany.

Warfare is frequently overlain with numerous rules and elaborate structures of ostensibly permissible and impermissible conduct. But fundamentally, it is an inversion of one of the most basic strictures of social life: Thou shalt not kill. Hence, war carries the inherent ethical dilemma of whether killing in combat trumps religious and moral injunctions against taking human life. This, incidentally, may also be why war is so often the midwife of social change. Having broken out of the prescriptions of what is permissible and what is not, war occasionally opens up possibilities for rearranging the social order. Any meaningful turnabout in fundamental attitudes regarding the acceptability of war will often involve ethical and religious dilemmas; conversely, such switches are rarely possible if not anchored in ethical and/or religious precepts. This, plus the justifications provided by ethics and religion to peace workers and war boosters alike, make it all the more important that close attention be paid to these issues.

Ethics

Ethics, also known as moral philosophy, is concerned with the foundational principles of morality, which deals with the nature of right and wrong and of distinguishing good from bad actions from within the framework of often divergent cultural and social norms and customs. Applied ethics seeks an understanding of the moral dimensions of specific, real-life controversies and their potential solutions. It assesses how ethically justifiable outcomes can be achieved in specific situations. The discipline has many specialized subfields, such as business ethics, bioethics, medical ethics, environmental ethics, ethical codes for such professions as psychology, government or military ethics, as well as the ethics of war and peace.

Deontology

Deontology, or the theory of ethical duties and obligations, argues that the morality of an act is determined by an actor's good will—the *intent* to fulfill a moral duty or obey an applicable moral rule. Immanuel Kant's ethical theory and liberal political philosophy are closely identified with deontology.

From a Kantian deontological perspective, a rule is ethical when (1) it is *categorical*—there are no exceptions to its application; (2) it exhibits *universality*—when the rule is applied to one person or group, the resulting good must equal the good obtained when the same rule is applied to any other persons or groups; and (3) it does not use persons as a means to an ends—it respects all persons as ends in themselves.

According to Kant, war involves an inevitable moral descent from our privileged status as rational actors to our irrational and brutish animal nature, primarily because it deprives the enemy of the respect that is fundamentally due to all persons by virtue of their humanity. Kant emphasized that we should treat people as rational agents intrinsically deserving respect (i.e., as *ends*), whereas war often compels the combatants to see each other as mere *means*—as objects, numbers, or targets. Frequently, commanders even treat their own soldiers as cannon fodder. Because this underlying depersonalization runs counter to deep-seated humanistic moral precepts, there is a widespread need, especially on the part of aggressors, to justify their actions in moral terms. But overall, deontology tends to deem virtually all violence, especially warfare, as unethical.

Utilitarianism and Consequentialism

As compelling as deontological ethics may be, it is utilitarianism, or consequentialism, that is the dominant moral philosophy of our time, especially in the English-speaking world. From a consequentialist perspective, the morality or rightness of an act or belief depends on the *consequences* of that act or of something related to that act. The progenitors of this point of view are the English utilitarian philosophers Jeremy Bentham (1789), John

Stuart Mill (1861), and Henry Sidgwick (1907). For utilitarians, the morality of an act is determined by its utility (efficacy) in producing the greatest good for the most people; thus, good ends justify the means, so that the effect of an act has greater moral significance than the actor's intentions. Utilitarianism also places particular value on the balance of benefits and costs (also called the "utility") associated with any act.

For example, many thoughtful people maintain that violence—even war—can be justifiable if it occurs in pursuit of some lofty goal, such as human freedom or social justice. According to Herodotus, "the father of history," more than 2,500 years ago, when the invading Persians called for their opponents to surrender, the greatly outnumbered Greeks responded as follows: "A slave's life thou understandest, but, never having tasted liberty, thou canst not tell whether it be sweet or no. Ah! Hadst thou known what freedom is, thou wouldst have bidden us fight for it."

From a utilitarian or consequentialist perspective, the morality of an act is dependent upon how the outcome criteria are defined; for example, a drone attack may be judged a success by the nation that launched it because it met its criterion for killing alleged enemy combatants, while the villagers where the attack took place will likely judge it unethical if civilians were killed.

The same would be true for judging the ethics of using nuclear weapons and other weapons of mass destruction—the outcome might be judged a success by the attackers, but the survivors and other members of the global community probably won't agree. Additionally, judgment of results (especially by the perpetrators) often depends upon the length of time between the act and the evaluation of its consequences. In its immediate aftermath, a drone attack may be judged a success if it killed the targeted group of alleged terrorists, but over a period of several years it may be judged a failure if many of the family, friends, and community of those killed subsequently supported or joined terrorist groups or failed to cooperate with the armed forces or other representatives of the nation that launched the drone.

Critics of utilitarianism often claim that once the door is opened to official sanctioning of violence, consequentialist ethics can rapidly become apologies for mass murder. The deliberate killing of civilians, for example, can be deemed permissible by utilitarians if enough perceived benefits can be gained by it. The alternative, deontological ethics, often includes such stances as absolute pacifism. In this view, no killing is permissible, no matter what immediate "good" is achieved or what evil is averted thereby.

Realpolitik, Just War, and Pacifism

Specific applications of ethics to war usually encompass three applied ethical traditions: political realism/*Realpolitik*, just war, and pacifism. All three traditions presume that an individual has a natural right to life; however, they differ in the extent to which, if at all, war is acceptable as a possibly ethical means of protecting lives designated as innocent, and of preserving what is deemed to be national security.

Proponents of political realism, or *Realpolitik*, argue that the political behavior of nations and their adversaries is generally based not on civilian private morality, but on pragmatic considerations of national self-interest and power—and, they argue, when it is not so based, it should be. An alternate version is that the moral duty or political obligation of a ruler/government to protect the greatest number of innocent persons from harm, especially the citizens of the nation or the members of the group they represent, justifies using virtually any means necessary, including total war. In realism, it makes no sense to fight under rules that might give an advantage to the enemy and thereby prolong the war, when unrestricted military action might end the war more quickly and efficiently. Universality is generally not a consideration because the principal obligation is to the nation's defense of its own real and perceived interests, but often at the expense of the lives of its own and other nations' citizens.

The ethical criteria of the Just War tradition, discussed later in this chapter, presume that it is in the interest of all countries to restrict war within certain limits that will minimize harm to persons, especially civilians and other noncombatants. It seems, unfortunately, that Just War criteria have failed to reduce the frequency or destructiveness of war, in part due to the ease with which nations and their leaders can interpret these precepts in favor of their own interests. At the same time, it cannot be concluded that a given set of restraints upon war may have failed altogether because we don't know how things would have turned out if they hadn't been in place.

Pacifism, on the other hand, maintains the ethical premise that because the preservation of human life is the highest good, for "absolute" pacifists war is never defensible as an exception to society's fundamental prohibition against killing. "Relative" pacifists may justify occasional exceptions to this prohibition depending on the circumstances. Virtually all pacifists agree that the designation of groups of persons as innocent or guilty is irrelevant because all persons have a natural right to life that is not dependent upon fallible determinations made by human authorities. The extent to which individuals may use violence, reflexively or deliberately, in self-defense or for the protection of their kin, is an issue about which pacifists of either stripe have not as yet reached a consensus.

War, Ethics, and Religion

Mainstream Western ethical and religious thought typically condones war in particular cases; occasionally, as in Fascist doctrine, war is even enthusiastically embraced. But when considering war in general, ethical judgments tend to be critical of state-sanctioned violence. When ethical and religious thinkers approve specific wars (and mainstream figures tend to, in fact, approve), such support is largely restricted to specific wars, in which people are confronted with particular conflicts and identifiable threats called enemies.

One might argue that the specifics are what count: Just as there is no "war" in the abstract, but rather particular wars, it is of little help if ethicists and religious leaders condemn war in general but lend their approval to each individual war. But this misses a potentially important characteristic of most ethical thought: a predisposition *against* violence and killing. This fundamental and often unspoken precept may contribute importantly to the eventual delegitimation of war.

Presumptions Against War

Like the presumption of innocence in legal proceedings, virtually all ethical and religious traditions presume that the way of peace is better than the way of war. For war to be justified, therefore, the burden of proof must lie on those who initiate and defend it.

In addition, many reasonable citizens recognize that might does not make right . . . at least not usually. When trial by combat became legal in Burgundy in 501 CE, the clergy at the time objected, whereupon King Gundovald replied, "Is it not true that the event of national wars and private combats is directed by the judgment of God, and that his providence awards the victory to the juster cause?" Times have changed, and dramatically so: No modern state currently condones the settling of *private* disputes by violent combat between the contending individuals. When state or national disputes are settled by war, it is analogous to settling personal disputes by individual combat, with the outcome presumably a function of strength and cunning, rather than merit, and therefore difficult to justify.

One of the most dramatic and famous exceptions to the Western moral injunction against the politics of "might makes right" occurred in the ancient Athenian campaign against the residents of the island of Melos. The Melians had favored Sparta during the Peloponnesian War (in the 5th century BCE, between Athens and Sparta) but sought to maintain neutrality because they were geographically close to Athens, which was far stronger than tiny Melos. After a lengthy siege, the Athenians delivered an ultimatum to the inhabitants of Melos: Surrender and be enslaved or be exterminated. The Melians protested the unfairness of this choice, arguing that they had not given Athens any cause for such violence. According to Thucydides, the great historian of this war, the Athenian spokesman answered in a speech renowned for its brutal honesty: "Right only comes into question when there is a balance of power, while it is might that determines what the strong extort and the weak concede." Ultimately, all Melian males were killed by the Athenians, and the women and children were taken as slaves.

The Athenian disregard for modern conventional civil morality may seem shocking, and the fact that it is so upsetting is part of the reason why blame for the causation of war is nearly always heaped on the other side. It is almost unheard of for a belligerent to announce, "We have decided to make war on our neighbor, not because of any misdeeds on their part, or for any righteous cause, but because we desire to plunder their resources—including their women—settle on their territory, enhance our prestige, enrich our arms manufacturers, provide amusement and occupation for our dissatisfied young men, and/or deflect domestic criticism." Even when the aggressive design is transparent, the other side is typically blamed; such convenient fictions provide a shred of moral legitimacy to which the aggressor state's populace may cling and behind which its leadership may hide.

Blaming the Other Side

Wars are often preceded by efforts of antagonists to emphasize the alleged perfidy of the other side or, if necessary, to create "incidents" that make the war more acceptable. The sinking of the US battleship *Maine* in Havana harbor in 1898 generated great national anger and contributed directly to the United States declaring war on Spain. Today, most historians agree that this *casus belli* (immediate cause of a war) was actually an accident or a deliberate provocation, initiated by persons hoping to goad the United States into war. Similarly, Hitler repeatedly claimed that ethnic Germans within Czechoslovakia and Poland were being criminally maltreated, and prior to the invasion of 1939, German forces even staged a phony attack, ostensibly by Polish troops against a German radio station near the border. Such maneuvers are sometimes labeled false flag operations, as when ships in one nation's navy deliberately fly the flags of another country in order to deceive others and to make it appear that its own covert military or political operations had been undertaken by another party.

The Gulf of Tonkin Incident (1964) consisted of alleged hostile actions by North Vietnam against the US that were almost entirely manufactured by President Lyndon Johnson as a successful ploy to paint North Vietnam as an aggressor and to get Congress to approve direct US military intervention. The second Russian war in Chechnya (1999–2000) was justified domestically as a response to the bombing of several apartment houses in Moscow—alleged terrorist acts that were never proven to have been undertaken by Chechens and that some critics even suggest were initiated by the Russian government as an excuse for mobilizing public opinion in favor of crushing a troublesome, independence-minded republic.

The US-led invasion of Iraq in 2003 was preceded by claims that the government of Saddam Hussein was somehow involved in the terrorist attacks of 9/11 (it was not) and that the Iraqis were accumulating "weapons of mass destruction" for use against the United States (they were not). It is clear that the Bush administration wanted to invade Iraq for other reasons—the specifics of which will be debated for a long time—and that purported links to terrorism and weapons of mass destruction were pretexts for initiating war, and thus ways of mobilizing initial popular support, rather than actual reasons for the subsequent invasion and occupation.

Moral Claims

Government leaders are only rarely as direct as the Athenians who destroyed Melos. In addition to concocting justifications, often phony ones, statesmen almost invariably describe their wars as moral, often as crusades. Thus, for many in the United States, the Vietnam War was a crusade to defend the allegedly legitimate (capitalist and US-supported) government in Saigon against the allegedly illegitimate (communist) regime in Hanoi. The murderous *contras* in Nicaragua were likened by President Reagan to the American founding fathers. For Hitler, the belligerent expansion of the German Third Reich was required in part to "save the world from Jews and communists." The USSR's military interventionism in Afghanistan (1979–1989) was officially justified as a response to a request by the pro-Soviet government in Kabul and to protect the human rights of Afghans (especially the women, oppressed by Muslim fundamentalism). The Soviet Union also invaded Hungary in 1956 to "liberate" that country from an "anti-Soviet counterrevolution" (which was actually a failed indigenous attempt at liberalization and democratization). For India, the long-sought goal of dismembering Pakistan was clothed in the high moral purpose of aiding the supposedly persecuted Bengalis in East Pakistan, leading to a war between India and Pakistan in 1971. And for the Han-dominated government of China, its occupation of Tibet is explained as necessary to banish Tibetan feudalism.

Similarly, the oppression and forced detention of Uighurs in far-eastern China by the governing Communist Party since 2017—an action considered genocide by many Western critics—has been justified by the Chinese government on the grounds that members of this Muslim ethnic group have violated the ban on traveling to or contacting people from any of the 26 countries China considers sensitive, such as Turkey and Afghanistan; that they are attending services at mosques; that they have had more than three children per family; and that Uighurs are sending texts containing Quranic verses. The real reasons for this effort by the Chinse authorities in Beijing to "reeducate" their restive minorities through ethnic cleansing are unclear.

The US's violent eviction of Iraq from Kuwait during the Gulf War (1990–1991) was advertised as a high-minded pursuit of international justice, whereas it was probably done to safeguard Kuwaiti, and neighboring Saudi, oil for Western consumption, as well as for American domestic political needs. NATO's bombing of Serbia during the war in Kosovo (1999) may have been driven by that military alliance's desire to prove its relevance in a post–Cold War world, although it was publicly justified as a highly ethical, necessary action to prevent genocide by Serbia against native Kosovars. At the same time, the prevention of genocide, in itself, is a legitimate goal—which points to the complexity of ethical evaluations in such cases, especially when states feel predisposed to justify their own not infrequent violent behavior.

It is easy to criticize the ease with which moral indignation is aroused in support of organized killing, although ethical outrage serves many purposes, sometimes cynical in motivation, sometimes not. After all, politics is a difficult and messy occupation, and nowhere is it more difficult or messier than when it comes to decisions about war.

In the view of some distinguished theologians, including Reinhold Niebuhr, the necessity for hard choices and decisive, often violent, action in a world of moral ambiguity transforms politics into nothing less than tragedy: "Politics will, to the end of history, be an area where conscience and power meet, where the ethical and coercive factors of human life will interpenetrate and work out their tentative and uneasy compromises."[1]

An alternative view, however, is that especially when it comes to issues of war and peace, death and life, there is no room for compromises or moral equivocation. Accordingly, from this perspective, it is not enough to choose the lesser of two evils. One must choose to do what is right, which in this case is nearly always to refrain from war and other forms of violent conflict.

Religious Attitudes Toward War

Religious intolerance has provided motivation for many wars; in addition, religions have often contributed to war-making directly, by their own internal demands and expectations, thereby disrupting the peace rather than promoting it.

Judaism

Like most religions, Jewish doctrines and traditions are inconsistent with respect to war. Whereas many modern European Jews have traditionally been strongly peace oriented, the ancient Israelites were fearsome warriors, and indeed, the Old Testament is replete with bloody accounts of so-called commanded wars, in which God urged his people to destroy others: "When the Lord your God has given them over to you, and you defeat them, then you must utterly destroy them; you shall make no covenant with them, and show no mercy to them" (Deuteronomy 7:2).

However, after the subjugation of their ancient homeland by the Roman and Ottoman Empires, for centuries many Jews emphasized pacifism, only to be overcome by a renewed warlike ethos in association with the founding of the state of Israel and in the aftermath of the Holocaust during World War II, when approximately 6 million European Jews were slaughtered and the motto of Zionists (supporters of establishing and defending the Jewish state of Israel) became "Never again." Today, the Israeli army—formally known as the Israeli Defense Forces—is widely considered one of the most effective fighting forces in the world, although this vaunted reputation has been somewhat called into question by Israel's unsuccessful foray in 2006 into Lebanon as part of its conflict with Hezbollah and by the inconclusive outcome of its numerous past and ongoing battles with Hamas in and near the Gaza Strip.

Islam and Jihad

Many religious traditions have also intermittently displayed a positive attitude toward war. Perhaps the one that is best known—and most misunderstood—is *jihad,* which, for centuries, has been central to Islam but which has also been "globalized," particularly by Western mass media and politicians seeking to respond to such major terrorist attacks as 9/11. *Jihad* is the Arabic term for what can be variously translated as "struggle" or "fight," depending on the context. In the West, the word is generally understood to mean "holy war" and usually has exclusively military connotations; this, however, is inaccurate.

The *Quran* does call for "jihad" as a military struggle on behalf of Islam. But the *Quran* also refers to jihad as an *internal,* individual, spiritual struggle toward self- improvement, moral cleansing, and intellectual effort. It is said that the Prophet Muhammad considered the armed-struggle version of holy war "the lesser jihad," and regarded the spiritual dimension of holy war—the war within oneself—as "the greater jihad." Nonetheless, the lesser jihad against those outside oneself has been interpreted within some Islamic communities and sects (especially by violent jihadis) and by much of the non-Islamic world as calling, on occasion, for martyring oneself and slaying "apostates and infidels," in defense of Islam against its enemies.

Does Islam condone terrorism? Are terrorism and jihad the same? For most Muslims and Islamic scholars, the answer is No. Military conflict is to be directed only against armed soldiers and not against civilians. For the great majority of Muslims, those they call the "People of the Book"— that is, followers of monotheistic Abrahamic religions that are older than Islam, especially Christians and Jews—are their spiritual sisters and brothers. Attacking innocent civilians, women, children, the sick in hospitals, and people going about their daily chores who are not at war with one's people is considered terrorism, not jihad, as it is for most Jews and Christians. However, if there is a threat to human life, property, honor, and, above all, to Islam itself, then *jihad* to defend life, property, honor, and Islam is deemed appropriate (roughly, the equivalent of a Just War for Christians).

Even as Christianity is divided into numerous denominations (notably Protestant, Catholic, and Eastern Orthodox), Islam is similarly diverse, with the major distinction being between Sunni and Shiite (Sufis are a small Muslim minority). And just as Christianity has been riven by violence between Catholics and Protestants (as in the Wars of Religion within Europe during the late Middle Ages), armed struggle between Sunnis and Shiites has a long history, most recently reflected in what are essentially civil wars in Iraq and Afghanistan following the destabilization of those countries by the US-led invasions and occupations, as well as in continuing conflicts in Syria, Yemen, Libya, and elsewhere in the Muslim world.

Hinduism, Jainism, and Buddhism

Hinduism, as well as another ancient Indian spiritual tradition, Jainism, from which the important precept of *ahiṃsā,* or nonviolence, is derived, has contributed to the theory and practice of Gandhian nonviolence. But Hinduism also has a rigorous military tradition, one that still appeals to millions of contemporary Hindu nationalists and militarists. The great Hindu texts emphasize the duty of devout Hindus to fight even for a cause with which they may disagree: In the *Bhagavad Gita,* the main hero, Arjuna, is enjoined to kill even his friends and relatives, if his duty so demands. Moreover, battle is seen as a kind of divine, selfless action (*karma yoga*), and Arjuna, the man and warrior, is advised by Krishna, the warrior-god, to cease all personal striving on behalf of a greater goal.

In 2014, Narendra Modi became Prime Minister of India. He is a member of the Bharatiya Janata Party (BJP) and of the RSS, a fundamentalist, Hindu nationalist volunteer organization that has been especially intolerant of Muslims. (Importantly, although a majority Hindu country, India also contains the world's third-largest Muslim population, more than 200 million.) Since Modi's ascent to power, there has been a resurgence of militant, sometimes violent Hindu nationalism, with the evident support of the government. These activities included a Hindu religious conversion program and even attempts to celebrate Nathuram Godse, the far-right Hindu assassin of Gandhi. This Indian ethno-nationalist movement is also vociferously anti-Pakistani, leading to frequent skirmishes and even the possibility of an all-out war between these nuclear powers.

Peace has long been a central doctrine for Buddhism, but it has traditionally been more inward- than outward-looking. Resistance to particular wars, as a self-conscious Buddhist goal, has historically been rare; moreover, some Zen Buddhist practitioners in Japan strongly supported Japanese militarism during World War II. Notable exceptions were the Unified Buddhist Church of Vietnam and elsewhere in Indochina (the former name of France's colonial territories of Vietnam, Cambodia, and Laos prior to their independence). During the 1960s, some Buddhists committed self-immolation (suicide by burning themselves) to protest the US-backed regime in South Vietnam in particular and the Vietnam War more generally; more recently, Buddhists have protested the military junta in Burma (Myanmar).

Importantly, some Buddhists in Burma, especially in the military but also in the civilian Buddhist majority, have violently persecuted the Rohingya, a Muslim minority. They are actively supported, and some would argue incited, by Buddhist monks and members of the government, whose leader, the Nobel Prize–winner Aung San Suu Kyi (widely criticized for not sufficiently opposing this ethnic cleansing and possible genocide), was imprisoned in early 2021 after a military coup. Nonetheless, an intentional Buddhist peace tradition has persisted for the great majority of Buddhists, especially under the influence of the socially engaged Vietnamese teacher and writer, Thich Nhat Hanh.

Christianity

Christianity, too, has a complex relationship with war. Although many of its founding principles emphasize pacifism, turning the other cheek, and loving one's neighbor, Christianity (along with Islam, Hinduism, and Shinto, the predominant religious tradition of Japan) constitutes one of the great warrior religions of history. The fundamental Christian ambivalence toward war is reflected, for example, in attitudes toward the cross. On the one hand, it is supposed to be the ultimate symbol of God's peace and love, divine grace with which to replace violence and sin. But on the other hand, the cross has long been seen as a sword with which to smite the forces of evil. Thus, Saint Paul warned that "if thou dost what is evil, fear, for not without reason does it [government] carry the sword. For it is God's minister, an avenger to execute wrath on him who does evil" (Romans 13:4).

Christendom was the eventual heir to the disintegrating Roman Empire, and, as such, many of its early wars were unsuccessful, although fought with increasing fervor. The "holy war" tradition in Christianity is a direct descendant of the commanded wars of the Old Testament and was especially influential during the Middle Ages, most dramatically during the Crusades. For example, Saint Bernard of Clairvaux, in the 12th century, delivered the following sermon in support of Christian efforts to drive Muslims from Palestine:

> A new sort of army has appeared . . . . It fights a double war; first, the war of the flesh and blood against enemies; second, the war of the spirit against Satan and vice . . . . The soldier of Christ kills with safety; he dies with more safety still. He serves Christ when he kills. He serves himself when he is killed.[2]

In 1215, the Catholic Church forbade participation of priests or bishops in trials by combat. God, it was claimed, was not concerned with such demeaning matters; nonetheless, the tendency to see wars as divine judgment and retribution continued, in part, as a carryover from the time when various Old Testament prophets warned that the sinning city of Babylon would be punished by God, via war.

From the 16th to the 18th centuries, many Christians adhered to a similar perspective; war was widely seen as "God's beadle," chastising the ungodly, the sinners, those who were insufficiently devout and righteous. Not only did war represent God's vengeance on the wicked, it also served as a hair shirt, a kind of penance for the war maker, a chastisement for people who had been backsliding, who needed its miseries to remind them of their wickedness and smallness and of God's almighty power. At other times, religious zealotry served to legitimize the Christian conquest of nonbelievers.

Although "conversion by the sword" was a stimulus for the expansion of Islam from 700 to 1450 CE, it was also prominent among Christian war makers. Even as recently as 1914, the Bishop of London urged his countrymen to "kill Germans— kill them, not for the sake of killing, but to save the world, to kill the good as well as the bad, to kill the young men as well as the old . . . . As I have said a thousand times, I look upon it as a war for purity, I look upon everyone who dies in it as a martyr."[3] And bellicose German priests and ministers were simultaneously reassuring their countrymen that "*Gott (ist) mit uns*" (God is with us).

War is bad enough; when religious zealousness adds the conviction of absolute certainty of one's righteousness, it becomes even worse. "Men never do evil so completely and cheerfully," noted Blaise Pascal in his 17th-century *Pensées*, "as when they do it from religious conviction."

Religious Support for the Status Quo

Religious leaders and traditions have not only been accused of serving as cheerleaders for war but have also been condemned for hindering human freedom by serving as a bulwark in favor of the status quo. Christian doctrine in particular has been criticized for legitimating the oppression of women, blacks, sexual minorities, and the impoverished. The faithful have frequently been called upon to support law and order (often favored code words for government-sponsored repression), as a way of keeping human sinfulness under control. In short, religion has often served to keep people submissive and accepting of their oppression. Not surprisingly, therefore, revolutionary socialist doctrine has generally been antagonistic to organized religion, consistent with Karl Marx's famous statement that "religion is the opiate of the masses."

During World War II, Joseph Goebbels—the minister of propaganda in Nazi Germany—suggested to German religious leaders, "You are at liberty to seek your salvation as you understand it, provided you do nothing to change the social order." Similarly, the Russian Orthodox Church was permitted to operate more or less freely in the former Soviet Union, so long as it did not challenge the political dominance of the Communist Party. After the fall of communism, the Russian Orthodox Church became closely associated with the authoritarian government of Vladimir Putin.

Social Gospels

Christian doctrine is not inevitably wedded to entrenched power, supportive of government-sponsored war-making, or consistently opposed to social betterment. "Liberation theology," which originated in Latin America, proclaims a vigorously *social* gospel, emphasizing the social sensitivities of Christ and the need for the modern-day Catholic Church to align itself on the side of the poor, the despised, and the disenfranchised.

The General Conference of the Bishops of Latin America in Puebla, Mexico, in 1979 issued the following statement:

> From the heart of Latin America, a cry rises to the heavens ever louder and more imperative. It is the cry of a people who suffer and who demand justice, freedom, and respect for the fundamental rights of man . . . . We identify, as the most devastating and humiliating scourge, the situation of inhuman poverty in which millions of Latin Americans live.[4]

Among recent popes, John XXIII and Francis have, in contrast with their more status-quo-supportive predecessors, regularly made statements on behalf of the impoverished and critical of capitalist exploitation of people and the environment, sometimes seeming to echo Latin American liberation theology and, arguably, close to the social Gospel of Jesus. Despite the growth of conservative evangelicalism and "prosperity gospel" churches (overwhelmingly charismatic or Pentecostal Protestant) in the United States, most mainline Christian theologians maintain that Jesus's teachings were far removed from those of right-wing Republicans.

Christian "Realism"

To some extent, each Christian denomination has its own tradition with respect to war; often the same church has differing, even conflicting approaches. Thus, there are pacifist Baptists and highly militarist Baptists, nonviolent Lutherans and Lutheran paratroopers, and so on. The most influential Christian tradition with respect to war has been a somewhat middle-of-the-road approach between a highly militaristic, "crusading" mentality and one of fervent anti-war pacifism. Known as Just War doctrine, this perspective is sometimes called Christian realism and has for many centuries sought to provide ethical underpinnings for the initiation and conduct of war, although usually stressing that this must be a last resort while advocating traditional "balance of power" politics.

The Late Roman Empire

The early Christian Church appears to have been essentially pacifist; indeed, pacifism seems to have distinguished nascent Christianity from both the warlike Roman Empire and the violence-prone Old Testament Jewish tradition (including the "terrorist" Zealots). Many early Christian martyrs died for refusing to serve in the Roman legions. By the 4th century CE, the secular fortunes of Christianity improved, and shortly after the conversion of the Roman emperor Constantine, Christianity became the official religion of the Roman state. Almost overnight, Christians went from a persecuted minority and prophetic movement to being prime defenders of the Roman Empire. Its transformation was such that soon *only* Christians were permitted to serve in the Roman army! (It was in the context of taking up secular—especially war-related—burdens at that time that the Catholic Church became the *Roman* Catholic Church.) When the Roman Empire was threatened by such "barbarians" as the Goths, Vandals, and Huns, Christianity quickly developed a self-consciously practical and accepting view of organized violence, a middle ground between the bloodthirsty wars of the Old Testament and the uncompromising pacifism of the early Christian Gospels. The result was a series of careful rules by which a Christian could engage in a "just war."

The Augustinian View

The main contributor to early Christian Just War theory was St. Augustine, Bishop of Hippo in the 4th century CE, whose primary political concern was to justify Christian participation in the defense of Rome (Augustine also wished to absolve Christians from responsibility for Rome's defeat and occupation by "barbarians"). In *The City of God,* Augustine wrote that "it is the wrong-doing of the opposing party which compels the wise man to wage just wars" and that "war with the hope of peace everlasting" to follow was preferable to "captivity without any thought of deliverance."

To Augustine, and the influential tradition of "Christian realism" that followed him, peace was "tranquility in order." Augustine thus prefigured the tension between the devotees of order (often represented in modern times by the political right wing) and of justice (typically represented today by the political left). In the Augustinian view, the restoration or maintenance of what today can be called negative peace often requires violence against alleged evildoers, and the soldier who goes to war in defense of the Church—and the divinely sanctioned political order that it presumably incarnates—does not violate the commandment against killing.

War, in Augustine's view, must be based ultimately on "Christian charity"—that is, the defense of a neighbor who has been unjustly attacked. Nonetheless, a Christian was expected to go to war, if at all, with a heavy heart, and only after carefully examining their conscience, because the presumption was at all times supposed to be in favor of peace.

Whereas the City of God is founded on an act of loving grace, the City of Man, in Augustine's view, is founded on war and perdition: Because evil exists, the Christian is obliged to struggle against it. Much debate has arisen, however, over whether this is really a necessity, a permission, or an excuse. In certain hotly contested cases, wars themselves seem to be the greatest immorality. Opposition to the Vietnam War in the United States, for example, was fueled by a passionate sense that this war was unjust in its origins and also unjustly fought, which raises the difficult but unavoidable question of personal responsibility, especially when one's nation is perceived to be prosecuting an immoral war, even by Christian Just War criteria.

Just War Doctrine

There are two major components in Just War doctrine, especially as elaborated during the 13th century by another influential Catholic theologian, St. Thomas Aquinas. The first part refers to the justice of going to war, known by its Latin phrase, *jus ad bellum*. It spells out the requirements that must be met in order for a Christian to identify whether it is appropriate to enter into any given politically violent conflict. The second major component of Just War doctrine is *jus in bello,* or justice within a war. Whereas *jus ad bellum* concerns whether or not a war *ought* to be fought (the criteria for *initiating* a war versus maintaining the peace), *jus in bello* deals with *the manner* in which such a war must be fought (the rules for conducting in such a war). Thus, a just war, one that meets *ad bellum* criteria, may be fought unjustly (if it fails to accord with *in bello* restraints), and similarly, an unjust war can nevertheless be waged justly.

Jus ad Bellum

The generally acknowledged criteria for *jus ad bellum* are as follows (it may be a worthwhile exercise to examine specific wars with these principles in mind):

1. *Last resort:* War must not be entered into with undue haste or unseemly enthusiasm but only if all other means of conflict resolution have been explored and found inadequate.

2. *Legitimate authority*: The decision to go to war cannot be made by disgruntled individuals or self-appointed groups; it must come from a duly constituted state authority.

3. *Right intention and just cause*: War is unacceptable if motivated by aggression, revenge, or the hope of gain; it must be consistent with Christian charity and/or self-defense. (Interestingly, Augustine himself specifically excluded self-defense, arguing that it was acceptable only to wage war in defense of others.)

4. *Chance of success*: Futile resistance cannot be justified; only when there is reasonable chance of a beneficent outcome may the Christian consider that a war is justifiable.

5. *Goal of peace:* Looking ahead to the war's conclusion, it must be possible to envision a peace that is preferable to the situation that would prevail if the war were not fought.

Conditions 3 through 5 are sometimes summarized as the principle of proportionality, which states that for a war to be just, its overall moral benefits must exceed its costs. Thus, proportionality recognizes that war is inherently evil and can therefore be legitimated only if it leads to a greater overall good. In practice, once a state's leadership decides on war, many of its religious figures pronounce it to be just, whereupon the average citizen or soldier goes along (often literally). But at the same time, the requirements for *jus ad bellum* arguments provide—at least in theory—a yardstick whereby observant Christians can personally evaluate the legitimacy of a state's call to arms.

Jus in Bello

Once a war is under way, it can, in Just War doctrine, be fought justly or unjustly. The generally acknowledged *in bello* restraints can be summarized in two principles: double effect and discrimination. The principle of double effect is a specific application of the *ad bellum* doctrine of proportionality. Just as wars can be seen to have good and bad overall effects, the principle of double effect states that specific *in bello* actions—those taken during a war—typically have two effects: a good effect in bringing the war to a successful conclusion and a bad one in causing pain, death, and harm to combatants and often noncombatants as well. According to the principle of double effect, therefore, such actions as bombings and invasions can be countenanced only if the good effect outweighs the bad. Military means and the cost of war must be proportional to an ethical end and its presumed benefits.

The second component of *in bello* restraints, the principle of discrimination, is synonymous with noncombatant immunity. It states that civilians must not be the *direct, intentional* object of military attack. This principle recognizes that civilians will *in fact* often be killed during hostilities, but the direct targeting of noncombatants is prohibited. In practice, however, the principle of discrimination further acknowledges that noncombatants will often be targeted indirectly, and such activities, so long as they are inadvertent, are generally condoned. For example, when strategic bombardment seeks either to destroy war-production facilities or to diminish the other side's morale, as, arguably, in the allied fire-bombings of German and Japanese cities during World War II, the practical effect has been the incineration of hundreds of thousands of noncombatants.

Various attempts have been made to establish *in bello* restraints on the conduct of war. The medieval Truce of God defined certain days as unacceptable for fighting, and the Peace of God prohibited direct attack against certain persons: travelers, merchants, clergy, and farmers. The code of chivalry established rules concerning who may fight with whom and regarding the treatment of prisoners (if members of the nobility). The Second Lateran Council, in 1215, even banned the use of certain weapons, notably the crossbow. Significantly, however, these prohibitions applied only to use against Christians; the crossbow could still be employed against Muslims, during the Crusades for example. But even this prohibition eventually faltered, and in fact, there have been very few examples of weapons that have been effectively banned because their use was judged unethical.

Chemical and biological weapons appear to be an exception. Although used widely during World War I, they were also widely condemned and rarely employed during World War II. On the other hand, this restraint may have been more a function of deterrence than of ethical considerations because each side knew that the other was capable of retaliating with comparable weapons. Moreover, chemical weapons were used during the 1980s, notably by the Iraqis against the Iranians and also by Saddam Hussein's forces against Kurdish rebels in northern Iraq, and, more recently, by belligerents in Syria's civil war. Biological weapons are almost universally condemned and their use has been banned under international treaties, although stockpiles are still maintained by some nations in certain cases, ostensibly to facilitate the design of countermeasures.

Violations of Noncombatant Immunity

Perhaps the most notable feature of *in bello* restraint, however, and its most tragic failures, involve violations of noncombatant immunity, a trend that has been increasing since 1914. For example, although military casualties were roughly comparable during World Wars I and II, civilian casualties were substantially higher in the latter. This seems due to two factors: (1) the greater involvement of entire populations in a nationwide war effort, thereby blurring the distinction between military and civilian, and (2) the invention of increasingly more destructive and less discriminating weapons, many of which can be deployed from a great distance. Nuclear weapons represent a culmination of this trend.

Strategic bombing of cities became increasingly frequent during World War II. There had been great public outcry at the German and Italian air forces' bombing of the Basque city of Guernica during the Spanish Civil War, the Japanese bombing of such Chinese cities as Nanking, and the German bombing of Rotterdam and Warsaw. By the time of the London blitz and the subsequent Allied bombings of civilian populations in Germany and Japan, however, attacking cities ("countervalue" targeting) was virtually taken for granted. Night bombing was safer than daytime raids for the attacking side but was substantially less accurate than bombing by day; hence, it was virtually impossible to conduct precision attacks on specific military (or "counterforce") targets or even on war industries, so whole cities became targets. Hundreds of thousands of civilians died during American and British fire-bombings of Dresden, Hamburg, Tokyo, Osaka, and other German and Japanese cities. Munitions were specifically designed to increase the probability of creating firestorms, and bombing patterns were employed to create immense firestorms, trapping and killing as many civilians as possible.

The prominent American writer Lewis Mumford denounced the Allied saturation bombing of German civilian targets in World War II as "unconditional moral surrender to Hitler," and David Lilienthal, later the first chairman of the Atomic Energy Commission, warned, "The fences are gone. And it was we, the civilized, who have pushed standardless conduct to its ultimate." Others argued that strategic bombing in general and the atomic bombings of Hiroshima and Nagasaki in particular were ethically justified under the doctrine of double effect, claiming that the good effect (hastening the end of the war and saving the lives of great numbers of allied soldiers) overrode the bad (killing hundreds of thousands of civilians). In any event, ethical standards were not abandoned altogether. For instance, a plaque in Westminster Abbey commemorates the Royal Air Force pilots of Fighter Command who died defending Britain against German bombers, whereas there is no comparable recognition of the (equally courageous) fliers of Bomber Command who died while attacking German cities.

Such an ethical principle as noncombatant immunity has been influential in the propaganda associated with war, with each side accusing the other of causing civilian casualties. President Truman even described the first atomic target, Hiroshima, as "an important military base," which it was not. (By August, 1945, US bombers had been striking targets throughout Japan at will; all targets of military significance had already been attacked, most of them many times.) Rather, Hiroshima was chosen specifically because its military irrelevance had spared it from prior attacks, and, as an intact city, it could provide a clear demonstration of atomic destruction.

The principle of noncombatant immunity is sometimes accused of being a dangerous and misleading nicety that makes war seem civilized and, therefore, acceptable. Why is it considered an atrocity to throw a human being into a fire but a legitimate military activity to throw fire on a human being? The fire-bombing of Dresden, moreover, took place during the last days of World War II, when its outcome was already known and when the city itself was swollen with thousands of refugees during a children's carnival.

Given that actions which, during times of peace, are widely deemed unethical are at the same time inherent in the conduct of war itself, perhaps it is hypocritical to introduce restraints once organized violence has commenced. Yet, the horrors of unrestricted warfare are so great that it seems natural to be grateful for whatever *in bello* restraints may exist, however imperfect or frequently violated in practice. During the US-led bombing of Kosovo and, later, of Afghanistan, Iraq, and Syria, efforts apparently were made to minimize civilian casualties, the exact number of whom may never be known but is probably in the hundreds of thousands. Efforts to win "hearts and minds" (a phrase from the Vietnam War) of the people to be "liberated" are hobbled in direct proportion to the amount of death and destruction rained upon noncombatants.

Religious Pacifism

Neither holy wars nor just war doctrine constitute Christianity's unique contribution to the ethics of war: Holy wars trace their ancestry to the warlike traditions of the Old Testament, and Just War doctrine is in part a reworking of Greco-Roman ethics, notably Stoicism. It is in the doctrine of organized pacifism—at least in the sense of gospel-based refusal to participate in military service—that Christianity stands out in the Western religious tradition.

The Second Commandment calls us to love our neighbor as ourselves, but the New Testament, especially the Gospel according to John, goes further by having Jesus enjoin his disciples and followers to love their enemy and to actively return good for evil. Among modern Christian churches, the historic "peace churches," including the Society of Friends (Quakers), the Mennonites, and the Church of the Brethren, are notable for their literal adherence to pacifist doctrines as enunciated, for example, in Christ's Sermon on the Mount:

> You have heard that they were told, "An eye for an eye and a tooth for a tooth." But I tell you not to resist injury, but if anyone strikes you on your right cheek, turn the other to him too . . . . You have heard that they were told, "You must love your neighbor and hate your enemy." But I tell you, love your enemies and pray for your persecutors. (Matthew 5:38–46)

Many Christian religious traditions have had a clear conception of peace, although relatively few have specifically elevated it to central position in their dogma or practice. A notable exception is the Society of Friends (also known as the Quakers), established by George Fox in the mid-17th century. Quakers have long maintained a tradition of peacemaking, opposition to military conscription, and resistance to taxes for military purposes.

Pacifist traditions have also persisted as minority views within most mainstream Christian churches, including Catholicism, via such organizations as Pax Christi. The Fellowship of Reconciliation is an ecumenical effort to unite and coordinate religious pacifists of all faiths. In addition to opposing military policies, pacifists refuse personal participation in wars, most directly by resisting conscription. They often practice tax resistance as well, which frequently takes the form of refusing to pay the proportion of national taxes that goes toward the military. Some governments, including that of the United States, have reluctantly accepted the legitimacy of conscientious objectors, so long as some form of alternative service is available; on the other hand, war resisters have traditionally been persecuted and sometimes killed, and even today they may be imprisoned for their views.

Many pacifists agree with G. K. Chesterton's sardonic observation that "the Christian ideal has not been tried and found wanting. It has been found difficult and left untried." Mennonite theologian John Howard Yoder, who tried to live up to this idea, stated,

> Christians whose loyalty to the Prince of Peace puts them out of step with today's nationalistic world . . . are not unrealistic dreamers who think that by their objections all wars will end. The unrealistic dreamers are rather the soldiers who think that they can put an end to wars by preparing for just one more . . . . Christians love their enemies not because they think the enemies are wonderful people, nor because they believe that love is sure to conquer those enemies . . . . The Christian loves his or her enemies because God does, and God commands His followers to do so; that is the only reason, and that is enough.[5]

Religious pacifists, such as Yoder, emphasize that people are created in God's image and that Christ died for all humanity. Hence, they maintain that good Christians have no choice: They must follow Christ's injunctions and example, refusing to do violence against others, especially if this might entail refusing to take another's life and regardless of what the secular authorities might demand. The noted Dutch-born American pacifist A. J. Muste made numerous impassioned calls for noncompliance with the military draft, which he termed an act of "holy disobedience."[6]

Nuclear Ethics

Although considerable debate surrounds religious and ethical approaches to war, when it comes to nuclear war, the issues may appear more clear-cut. Despite the end of the US-USSR Cold War, there continue to be thousands of nuclear weapons maintained in different countries, and their use—by terrorists from below or from above, "rogue states," newly proliferated nuclear powers, or even the declared nuclear weapons states—cannot be precluded so long as they exist. This raises profound questions about the ethics of developing, maintaining, proliferating, and using such immensely destructive weapons.

Most religious and ethical authorities agree that a nuclear war could never meet Just War criteria. Noncombatant immunity could not be maintained, although some hawkish ethicists argue that civilians might legitimately be killed in such a war so long as they are not targeted directly. In 1966, the Second Vatican Council concluded that "any act of war aimed indiscriminately at the destruction of entire cities or of extensive areas along with their populations is a crime against God and man itself. It merits unequivocal and unhesitating condemnation." In their pastoral letter in 1983, the American Catholic bishops added that "this condemnation, in our judgment, applies even to the retaliatory use of weapons striking enemy cities after our own have already been struck." And in 2020, the Bishops stated,

The Church will heighten engagement on policy issues around nuclear disarmament as this issue remains a critical concern for the promotion of a sustainable peace. At the same time, in response to rising militarism and increased military spending, the Church will seek to prioritize the common good and advocate for dialogue, rather than reliance on military means, to resolve conflicts . . . . The United States has a responsibility to work to reverse the spread of nuclear, chemical, and biological weapons, and to reduce its own reliance on weapons of mass destruction by pursuing progressive nuclear disarmament.[7]

It is difficult to imagine what kind of "good effect" could balance the "bad effect" of killing millions of people, possibly billions, and maybe even threatening the continuation of life on Earth. Moreover, nuclear war is likely to fail all of the *ad bellum* criteria listed previously, except possibly the requirement of legitimate authority. Accordingly, the US Catholic bishops concluded that "our No to nuclear war must, in the end, be definitive and decisive." In late 2019, while visiting Hiroshima, Pope Francis declared,

the use of nuclear weapons is immoral, that is why it must be added to the *Catechism of the Catholic Church*. Not only their use, but also possessing them: because an accident or the madness of some government leader, one person's madness can destroy humanity. The words of Einstein come to mind: "The Fourth World War will be fought with sticks and stones" . . . . lasting peace cannot be achieved without disarmament.[8]

Ethics and Nuclear Deterrence

Although there is general (but by no means universal) agreement among civilians that nuclear war would be unethical, much debate surrounds the question of whether nuclear deterrence is equally unacceptable. The question is, can a country legitimately threaten something that would be unethical if carried out? Protestant ethicist Paul Ramsey used this metaphor to describe the dilemma:

Suppose that one Labor Day weekend no one was killed or maimed on the highways, and that the reason for the remarkable restraint placed on the recklessness of automobile drivers was that suddenly every one of them discovered that he was driving with a baby tied to his front bumper! That would be no way to regulate traffic even if it succeeds in regulating it perfectly, since such a system makes innocent human lives the direct object of attack and uses them as a mere means for restraining the drivers of automobiles.[9]

Ramsey's point is that ethical error lies first in the *intention* to do wrong and only later in the act itself. This is why intended wrong (such as attempted homicide) is considered more serious than accidental wrong (such as manslaughter), or doing the right thing for the wrong reason is nonetheless considered an ethical transgression. To rework Ramsey's metaphor, imagine that society decreed that, in the event of murder, punishment would befall not only the murderer but also all his friends and relatives. This would clearly be an unethical system, even if it worked to deter murder.

Nonetheless, Ramsey ended up defending the legitimacy of nuclear deterrence, so long as it is limited to counterforce (targeting of the other side's nuclear weapons). He admits that an adversary might be restrained by fears of collateral effects—the practical awareness that nuclear retaliation, even if ostensibly aimed at military targets only, would cause enormous destruction to the country and civilian populace at large. But so long as this "collateral damage" is a *byproduct* of the intended, discriminate targeting, defenders of nuclear deterrence deem it acceptable.

Other thinkers justify nuclear deterrence with the argument that sometimes it is necessary to commit an evil (threatening nuclear war) in order to prevent an allegedly greater one, such as defeat or subservience to an unacceptable foreign regime. On the other hand, the paradox remains that only by making credible threats can nuclear deterrence possibly work, and only by meaning these threats—that is, deploying weapons that are intended to be used—can the threat be credible. So the effectiveness of deterrence varies directly with the likelihood that, if one's bluff is called, nuclear war will follow; yet, should this happen, the outcome would be profoundly unacceptable.

In a speech at Hiroshima, Pope John Paul II said that "in current conditions, deterrence based on balance, certainly not as an end in itself but as a step on the way toward a progressive disarmament, may still be judged morally acceptable." As time goes on, however, ethicists may well ask whether deterrence has truly been used as a step toward disarmament or as an end in itself, and also as a means of justifying yet more weaponry (e.g., nuclear "modernization" typically justified as a means of enhancing deterrence). Moreover, deterrence has also been used to justify, after the fact, those weapons already used and in development by the US at the end of World War II.

The Council of Bishops of the United Methodist Church went further than their Catholic counterparts and refused to condone nuclear deterrence:

> The moral case for nuclear deterrence, even as an interim ethic, has been undermined by unrelenting arms escalation. Deterrence no longer serves, if it ever did, as a strategy that facilitates disarmament . . . . Deterrence must no longer receive the churches' blessing, even as a temporary warrant for the maintenance of nuclear weapons.[10]

Supporters of deterrence have argued that nuclear weapons are ethical and acceptable (at least in the hands of the US, France, and the UK) in part because they allegedly preserve the essential values of Western, Christian civilization. By attributing the collapse of Soviet communism to the West's perseverance in maintaining and adding to its nuclear arsenals, nuclear supporters justify the continued maintenance of such arsenals as a deterrent to other states and ideologies, as well as a hedge in case Soviet-style communism should reappear in Russia, China, North Korea, or elsewhere. Moreover, some pro-nuclear thinkers do not discount the possibility that "limited" nuclear wars could be fought and even won.

On the other hand, opponents of deterrence and of nuclear weapons maintain that they are themselves profoundly unethical and that willingness to engage in nuclear war is simply unacceptable. In the words of diplomat/historian George Kennan (an architect of the doctrine of "containment"):

> The readiness to use nuclear weapons against other human beings—against people whom we do not know, whom we have never seen, and whose guilt or innocence it is not for us to establish—and in doing so to place in jeopardy the natural structure upon which all civilization rests, as though the safety and the perceived interests of our own

generation were more important than everything that has ever taken place or could take place in civilization; this is nothing less than a presumption, a blasphemy, an indignity—an indignity of monstrous dimensions—offered to God![11]

A Final Note on Ethics and Religion

It remains unlikely that ethical and religious precepts and/or courageous leaders alone will someday abolish war. Absolute prohibitions—against killing, for example— have rarely been followed with absolute fidelity. And given that human beings have often used their creed of alleged moral or religious certainty to justify political repression, intolerance, and cruelty, there is good reason to be distrustful of any form of ethical absolutism. On the other hand, it may be that at this stage of human history, revulsion against organized violence is as much a necessity as a hope. Such remarkable changes as the collapse of the Soviet Union and the end of the Cold War, as well as of apartheid in South Africa, offer possibilities for redirecting human endeavors toward life instead of the mechanisms of oppression and death.

Having now completed our analysis of negative peace—that is, of the prospects and proposals for preventing war—let us bear in mind that, in the long run, such prevention will be a shallow victory if it does not include the establishment of positive peace as well. Hence, in Part IV, we turn from preventing war to building peace.

Questions for Further Reflection

1. Compare and contrast arguments that religion in general has been supportive of war with claims that it has largely been a force for peace.

2. Agree or disagree with the proposition that ethical support for war is necessarily an oxymoron—that is, a self-defeating or logically inconsistent proposition.

3. Pick a current war, or a smaller-scale violent conflict, and assess its morality according to just war criteria.

4. Make a case for why the prospect of nuclear war requires a rethinking of ethics and/or religious teaching as it has traditionally been applied to war. Alternatively, make a case for why it does not—that is, why the moral implications of nuclear weapons are quantitatively, not qualitatively, different than for nonnuclear weapons.

5. Pick a specific religious or ethical tradition and assess its strengths and weaknesses regarding its doctrines concerning war and peace.

Suggestions for Further Reading

Arnaud Blin. 2019. *War and Religion: Europe and the Mediterranean From the First Through the Twenty-first Centuries*. Berkeley: University of California Press.

Daniel R. Brunstetter and Cian O'Driscoll, eds. 2017. *Just War Thinkers*. New York: Routledge.

Joseph Fahey. 2005. *War and the Christian Conscience: Where Do You Stand?* Maryknoll, NY: Orbis Books.

T. Walter Herbert. 2014. *Faith-Based War.* New York: Routledge.

James Turner Johnson. 1984. *Can Modern War Be Just?* New Haven, CT: Yale University Press.

J. George Lucas. 2019. *Ethics and Military Strategy in the 21st Century.* New York: Routledge.

Paul Ramsey. 1978. *The Just War.* New York: Scribner.

Gregory M. Reichberg, Henrik Syse, and Endre Begby. 2006. *The Ethics of War: Classic and Contemporary Readings.* New York: Wiley-Blackwell.

Janusz Salamon, ed. 2015. *Solidarity Beyond Borders: Ethics in a Globalising World.* London: Bloomsbury.

Michael Walzer. 2006. *Just and Unjust Wars: A Moral Argument With Historical Illustrations.* New York: Basic Books.

Notes

1. Reinhold Niebuhr. 1932. *Moral Men and Immoral Society.* New York: Scribner.

2. Saint Bernard of Clairvaux. 1980. *Sermons.* Geneva, Switzerland: Slatkine Reprints.

3. Quoted in Roland Bainton. 1960. *Christian Attitudes Toward War and Peace.* Nashville, TN: Abingdon.

4. Quoted in Penny Lernoux. 1982. *Cry of the People.* New York: Penguin.

5. John Howard Yoder. 1982. "Living the Disarmed Life: Christ's Strategy for Peace." In *Waging Peace*, ed. J. Wallis. New York: Harper & Row.

6. One of Muste's best-known statements is "There is no way to peace; peace is the way." In Western religious traditions, disobedience is widely considered to be the primary human sin (e.g., Satan's disobedience of God and Adam and Eve's alleged transgressions in the Garden of Eden). And yet throughout human history, arguably far more harm has been done by obedience to authority than by disobedience.

7. For the full statement by the Bishops, see http://www.usccb.org/issues-and-action/human-life-and-dignity/war-and-peace/nuclear-weapons/backgrounder-on-nuclear-disarmament-and-challenging-increases-in-military-spending.cfm

8. This declaration occurred during a press conference Pope Francis gave after visiting Hiroshima and Nagasaki, during which he also commented on nuclear energy and the environment: https://www.vaticannews.va/en/pope/news/2019-11/pope-francis-press-conference-japan-airplane.html

9. Paul Ramsey. 1968. *The Just War.* New York: Scribner.

10. Council of Bishops of the United Methodist Church. 1986. *In Defense of Creation: The Nuclear Crisis and a Just Peace.* Nashville, TN: Graded Press.

11. George F. Kennan. 1982. "A Christian's View of the Arms Race." *Theology Today* 39:2.

Building "Positive Peace"

Preventing war is a necessary condition for establishing real peace, but negative peace is not sufficient. A world without war is certainly desirable, but it would not really produce a world at peace. Accordingly, it is not enough to be against war. Genuine, sustainable peace must be part of a broader, deeper effort to rethink the relationship of human beings to each other and to our planet. As difficult as it will be to obtain negative peace, it may be even more of a challenge to achieve positive peace because a world without violence would be a significant challenge to our basic way of living, not just our ways of killing and dying.

The study of peace and conflict is unusual not only in its transdisciplinary approach to the understanding and prevention of war, but also in its efforts to envision and help establish peace that is both desirable and attainable. But if war seems difficult to define—as evidenced by disagreement about the role of formal declarations, number of casualties, nature of the combatants, level of violence, and so on—getting to a consensual acceptance of the meaning of global peace can be even more elusive. Nonetheless, it is possible to sketch the outlines of a just and sustainable peace, recognizing that in a world that relies on violence and on the structures of violence, efforts toward such a peace may be not only visionary but also what conventional society may deem "radical."

Ideologically motivated political and military competitions are often inimical to humanity's fundamental needs, as well as being outdated and dangerous. Ardent militarists seem more and more to be ideological dinosaurs, formidable but dated, moving clumsily and even stupidly across a rapidly changing landscape. Military competition should slow and eventually cease, but that is insufficient. For positive peace advocates, conflicts that have plagued the post–World War II world must eventually give way to coordinated efforts to address planetary issues (many of which reveal tensions along a North-South axis) concerning human rights, poverty, the environment, and the promotion of nonviolence in politics and in personal life.

Much importance has been attributed to so-called Just War doctrine. The conditions for a "just peace" are no less important. For many in the West (at least, those who are relatively affluent and well educated), hope for a peaceful world is often equated with continuing the status quo, with some improvements around the margins, such as guaranteed health care, affordable college tuition, and improved financial security, whereas for many in the developing countries, struggles for human rights, national autonomy, and economic well-being are vitally important. For a growing number of people around the globe, just peace also entails achieving a viable relationship with the natural environment.

Although the absence of war is relatively easy to define—but still susceptible to dispute—reasonable people are even more likely to disagree about what constitutes positive peace. It brings up what we might call the "car-canine problem": Imagine a dog that has spent years barking and running after cars. Then one day it catches one. What does it do with it? Analogously, what would devotees of peace *do* with the world if they had the chance?

18

Human Rights

Like Mark Twain's celebrated remark about the weather, one can say that many people talk about human rights but relatively few do anything about it. Many of us lack some of the most basic human rights. Nearly one-half of the world's people are denied democratic freedoms and political participation; about one-third face severe restrictions on their right to own property; about one-half of Asians and sub-Saharan Africans do not have access to safe water; jails worldwide are filled with political prisoners; many of them held without trial and victimized by torture; child labor is widespread; women and sexual minorities are often deprived of the economic, social, and political rights that straight men take for granted; many workers are not only nonunionized but prohibited even from forming unions;

Human Rights

Like Mark Twain's celebrated remark about the weather, one can say that many people talk about human rights but relatively few do anything about it. Many of us lack some of the most basic human rights: Nearly one-half of the world's people are denied democratic freedoms and political participation; about one-third face severe restrictions on their right to own property; about one-half of Asians and sub-Saharan Africans do not have access to safe water; jails worldwide are filled with political prisoners, many of them held without trial and victimized by torture; child labor is widespread; women and sexual minorities are often deprived of the economic, social, and political rights that straight men take for granted; many workers are not only nonunionized but prohibited even from forming unions;

the right of conscientious objection to military service is not recognized in most countries; censorship is widespread; and billions of people are illiterate, chronically sick, without adequate shelter, and hungry. Slavery, which in the 21st century seems a hideous anachronism, not only persists but, by some accounts, has been increasing. Clearly, human rights advocates have much work to do.

A Brief History of Human Rights

It is tempting to claim that human rights are as old as the human species, but the truth is quite different. Even if human rights are God-given, inalienable, and fundamental, the conception of human rights as such—and respect for them—is relatively new. Rights and privileges have traditionally been considered a social benefit, to be bestowed or revoked by the larger unit (band, tribe, monarch, village, city, state) at will. In nearly all societies, for nearly all of human history, collective values have been derived from the social order, not the individual. Hence, a single human being could not claim entitlement to very much, if anything, simply because they existed.

Some representatives of traditional cultures support the concept of individual human rights as wide-ranging and universally derived. Confucius, for example, argued that "within the four seas all men are brothers," and Buddhists believe in "compassion for every sentient being." Nonetheless, human rights as currently understood are largely a Western tradition, deriving especially from the works of the English philosophers John Locke and John Stuart Mill. Locke maintained that a fundamental human right was the right to property, primarily to the security of one's own body; civil and political rights flowed, in his view, from this. There is some truth to the criticism that Westerners advocating human rights may occasionally be guilty of moral arrogance, seeking to export their own rather culture-bound ideas, especially their emphasis on civil/political freedom.

In addition, there is a strain in the Western intellectual tradition commanding respect for—and, occasionally, virtual worship of—the state. According to such influential 19th-century German political theorists as Hegel and Herder, rights are enlarged and even created for individuals only through the actions of the state. And for orthodox Marxists, value derives only from the social order: According to doctrinaire Marxist analysis, there is no meaning to individual rights, prior to them being granted by society. Although such nominally communist states as the former Soviet Union and contemporary China, Cuba, and Vietnam have been supposedly designed to maximize the benefits of every person, the "rights" of each individual may come to naught if they run counter to the presumed greater good of society as a whole. Individuals can expect to receive benefits from a community only insofar as they participate in it and further its goals. Even today, with Soviet-style communism largely a memory and ever-increasing agreement on the meaning and desirability of human rights, there continues to be substantial disagreement as to which rights should have priority.

Human Rights in Modern Times

There was little worldwide concern with human rights per se until after World War II. Despite the Enlightenment in late 18th-century Europe, modern capitalism's emphasis on individual property rights and Western democracy's emphasis on individual political rights, state sovereignty has usually taken precedence over *human* rights. When the modern state system was established in the mid-17th century, major European governments agreed— ostensibly in the interest of world peace—not to concern themselves very much with how other governments treated their own citizens. Within its own boundaries, each state was supreme and could do pretty much as it wished.

Gradually, however, human rights law developed, initially out of concern with protecting persons during armed conflicts. The Geneva Convention of 1864, for example, sought to establish standards for treatment of wounded soldiers and of prisoners. (It is ironic that war—one of the most inhumane of human situations—should have led to the first organized recognition of shared humanitarian values.)

The International Committee of the Red Cross is a nongovernmental organization long concerned with international human rights; it was organized by a group of Swiss citizens who had attended the 1864 Geneva Convention. The Red Cross remains active today, as does its Islamic equivalent, the Red Crescent, seeking especially to ensure fair treatment of people during armed conflict. It has also participated in several modifications and revisions of the Geneva Convention, most recently in 1977.

Following World War I, there was widespread recognition that one cause of that conflict was the denial of national rights to ethnic minorities within such large political entities as the Austro-Hungarian Empire. Hence, human rights received explicit attention from the League of Nations, which stressed that minorities must be respected by larger federal governments. Labor rights—to organize, to obtain decent working conditions and wages, and to impose restrictions on child labor—were the focus of the International Labour Organization, which later became part of the United Nations and won a Nobel Peace Prize. Opposition to slavery catalyzed numerous early human rights organizations, such as the Anti-Slavery League.

Many people do not realize that in some countries slavery was only formally abolished during the 1950s. Slavery is still practiced today, notably in Mauritania, where a tradition exists of farm laborers being indentured to other, local farm families, and also in Haiti, where under the *reste avec* ("stay with") system, young girls ostensibly receive food, lodging, and education in return for providing babysitting and other domestic services for wealthy urban households, but in actuality these girls become enmeshed in years-long enslavement. Pakistan is another notorious haven for de facto slavery, in which debtors find themselves forced to labor in brick factories, with essentially no hope of paying off their debts or gaining their freedom. It is estimated that nearly a million Uzbeks are similarly forced to labor in cotton fields.

The Global Slavery Index lists an extensive and shameful catalog of such human rights abuses. An estimated 40.3 million men, women, and children were victims of modern slavery on any given day in 2016. Of these, 24.9 million people were in forced labor and 15.4 million people were living in a forced marriage. Women and girls are vastly overrepresented, making up 71 percent of victims. Modern slavery is most prevalent in Africa, followed by the Asian and the Pacific regions, especially involving the unpaid use of domestics in Persian Gulf states and of trafficked women forced into prostitution in much of the world. The practices of slavery and human trafficking are also still prevalent in America, with an estimated 17,500 foreign nationals and 400,000 Americans being trafficked into and within the United States every year, with 80 percent of those being women and children. Much of this involves labor trafficking, by which seasonal workers, often from Mexico and Central America, who pick fruit or work on ranches in southern states are not compensated for their work.

Organized worldwide concern for human rights did not really coalesce until after World War II, perhaps in part as a reaction to the devastating denials of rights that occurred during that conflict. In the aftermath of the Nazi Holocaust, the conscience of some Western leaders was finally activated—partly out of regret for those who had suffered and partly out of self-interest. The German theologian Martin Niemöller put it memorably: "First they came for the Jews and I did not speak out—because I was not a Jew. Then they came for the communists and I did not speak out—because I was not a communist. Then they came for the trade unionists and I did not speak out—because I was not a trade unionist. Then they came for me—and there was no one left to speak out for me."[1] (In fact, Pastor Niemöller himself became a victim of the Nazis.)

Liberalism

In traditional liberal political thought, human rights exist not only because of their contribution to human dignity but also because human beings naturally possess such rights. "The object of any obligation in the realm of human affairs," according to philosopher Simone Weil, "is always the human being as such. There exists an obligation toward every human being for the sole reason that he or she is a human being, without any other condition requiring to be fulfilled."[2] Or, in Thomas Jefferson's phrase, people have certain "inalienable rights," which may not be denied. (In what must be counted a master-stroke of hypocrisy, Jefferson himself was a slave-holder.)

States with long traditions of social equity, including New Zealand and the Scandinavian nations, are also politically constructed along liberal lines but with a dose of socioeconomic egalitarianism. Thus, although the classical liberalism of the United States stresses equal civil and political rights with "freedom" of socioeconomic competition, institutions embedding legal egalitarianism and social welfare (present to some degree in Denmark, Iceland, Norway, Finland, and Sweden and, to a lesser extent, in Canada, New Zealand, Germany, and the Netherlands) place greater emphasis on citizens' rights to free or affordable health care and education.

Conservatism

Traditional Anglo-American conservatism has little to say today with respect to human rights because conservatism is in part a philosophy of *unequal* rights and privileges. But the unspoken tenets of conservatism are nonetheless influential in practice. Classical Western conservatism can be said to have originated with Plato, who argued in *The Republic* that all people are not equal and that the best form of government is therefore not democracy but rule by philosopher-kings. More than two millennia later, this belief in unequal rights underpins many right-wing governments, from the "classical conservatism" of the military juntas that ruled Brazil and Greece to the various US-sponsored Central American governments through most of the late 20th century (Guatemala, Honduras, El Salvador, Panama), to the neofascist dictatorships in Chile, Paraguay, Indonesia, and the Philippines, in which rights were reserved only for the most powerful.

Collectivism

Finally, the third branch of human rights philosophy might be called collectivist. It can be subdivided into several streams, Marxist, Sinic (East Asian, mainly Chinese), and national or ethnic identity. For Karl Marx, individuals are not fully independent actors; rather, they are largely dependent on economic forces, and as members of opposing classes, the working class and the capitalist class being the two most prominent in the modern world, are caught up in a relentless class struggle. In the Marxist view, the liberal emphasis on individual rights is therefore a misplaced bourgeois luxury, an ideological form without social substance. Instead, rights are conferred by society and belong mainly to the proletariat or working class. Such an approach leads to an embrace of socioeconomic rights and economic equity, with a downplaying of civil/political rights. Thus, in Marxist-oriented societies, freedom of speech and opinion are usually subordinated to the collective goals of group advancement and welfare. The state—prior to its "withering away" under communism—is ideally the embodiment of the working class.

Another variation of collectivism, based on its distinctive Confucian heritage, characterizes modern China. Here, special value is placed on "harmony," with individual rights subordinated to the smooth functioning of society. This orientation is quite suspect in the capitalist/democratic West, where it is perceived as permitting—even encouraging—government repression. Conversely, the Western focus on individualism and personal rights is usually interpreted by believers in collectivist values as justifying an unacceptable level of both societal chaos and inequality.

There is also a version of collectivist human rights that has a leftist flavor but is not, strictly speaking, Marxist. It derives in part from national liberation movements, and it places special emphasis on the rights to national self-determination and economic development, from which all other rights are then derived. Believers in the human right of national self-determination downplay the individual, although they remain committed to equal rights. Emphasis instead is on the rights of various identity groups. This approach lay behind the Universal Declaration of the Rights of Peoples, which grew out of an influential 1976 meeting of highly regarded, nongovernmental spokespeople from the developing world. Its concern with "people's rights" clearly distinguishes this approach from the Western focus on "individual rights."

Choosing the Appropriate Philosophy

Not surprisingly, there is debate over which human rights model is most appropriate for any given country. The two major contending Western systems of the past—capitalism based on classical free market liberalism and Soviet-style Marxism based on a collectivist philosophy—historically have produced deep structures of oppression. Thus, although Marx himself explicitly claimed that the state will eventually disappear, state structures dominated by self-identified Marxist or Communist political parties showed no tendency to do so. In fact, they became oppressive in their own right, until, as in the case of the Soviet Union, they simply crumbled—which is very different from Marx's original conception, under which the ideal workers' state would wither away by mutual consent only after its goals had been achieved. Even more than liberal capitalist states, Marxist-identified governments have tended to be super-states, abusing power via ossified bureaucratic structures that are generally insensitive to personal civil and political liberties.

By contrast, the supposedly "minimal states" envisioned by some Western political philosophers and established primarily in parts of Europe, Australia, and North America have focused on trying to balance the various political powers of government with popular sovereignty and corporate influence. Social and economic rights are here generally treated as secondary because capitalist/democratic societies rely on putative market mechanisms and an ethos of individual competition. Only begrudgingly have many capitalist/democratic states recognized a social responsibility toward their populace, although even ostensibly middle-of-the-road and relatively conservative states in much of Europe (e.g., Germany and France) have adopted such social welfare support systems as government-sponsored child care, universal health care at low or no cost to patients, and mandated parental leave. For such nations, health and a minimum standard of living are considered human rights. To many Americans, in contrast, this may appear quite "left-wing."

On balance, capitalist democracies pay scant attention to socioeconomic rights, while state socialist governments take inadequate account of civil/political ones. Economic development is generally more rapid under capitalism, especially the "state capitalism" of China today, and indeed, the economic stagnation of most state-socialist countries contributed mightily to their dramatic political decline relative to China's extraordinary economic development in the 21st century.

At the same time, relatively little benefit from economic development actually reaches the poorest citizens of most capitalist states, resulting in glaring economic inequality. The rapid transition to a primitive kind of capitalism on the part of post-Soviet Russia and some of its former satellite states has been accompanied, in most cases, by great wealth for a small minority of successful entrepreneurs and financiers, as well as for more than a few outright crooks and beneficiaries of rampant cronyism, after state assets were sold off at extremely low prices. Simultaneously, living conditions for the majority may have actually worsened.

In some cases, political freedoms expanded dramatically across the board, along with economic opportunities, although many people formerly living under Soviet-style communism and now experiencing Western-style "freedom" have experienced deterioration in their socioeconomic rights. China, once again, has been an exception, in that its unique embrace of state-sponsored capitalism along with political despotism has been associated with stunning economic advances, especially in the 21st century; hundreds of millions of people have been lifted from extreme poverty to middle class status.

Individual Liberty

Individual liberty is not unidimensional. It involves many things—including freedom from torture, unjust imprisonment, and execution; the intellectual freedom to speak, write, and worship; and political freedoms, including the right to peaceful assembly, freedom of association, and the right to vote by secret ballot. Similarly, socioeconomic rights include the right to work, decent housing, education, medical care, adequate food and clean water. To some extent, the United States and most other economically advanced capitalist states associate human rights with individual liberty, whereas state-socialist and many impoverished, Third World, "underdeveloped," or "developing" states, along with the Universal Declaration of Human Rights

(UDHR; adopted by the UN General Assembly in 1948), have given equal or greater weight to socioeconomic rights.

Those who are wealthy and privileged characteristically favor maximum individual freedom (especially freedom of economic competition, at which, not coincidentally, they have already succeeded, whether by virtue of luck, skill, graft, corruption, or inheritance) and a minimal role for government, which, at least in the United States, often leads in turn to opposition to the "welfare state." Those lacking in wealth and power, by contrast, are typically more in need of and favorable to protections ensured by society. Hence, there is a tendency among some Western governments to describe socioeconomic rights as not really human rights at all but either as aspirational social goals or as beneficial "externalities" for "free market" economies.

A global consensus has been developing that incorporates not only the traditional Anglo-American concern with political liberty but also an additional defense of socioeconomic rights, as well as other values that are difficult to pigeonhole. In some cases, alternative visions of human rights are different indeed: the "right to life" (of a fetus) versus a woman's "right to choose" (whether to have an abortion, or to use birth control). Many other putative rights are not quite as controversial—states' rights, consumer rights—but to claim that something is a human right is to claim something vital and universal, fundamental and weighty, including the right to security from mass destruction and to a healthy natural environment.

One influential conception of liberty was developed by the philosopher, Isaiah Berlin, who identified two kinds of freedoms (basically similar to rights): freedom *from* and freedom *to*. The former assures a degree of individual liberty, via the right to be spared various governmental abuses and infringements of personal activities. The latter, by contrast, emphasizes rights associated with freedom to achieve one's goals, and is thus more often associated with active governmental facilitation.

There are other rights that resemble the famous French motto "liberty, equality, fraternity": (1) political and intellectual rights, (2) economic and social rights, and (3) the right to peace and to a safe and fulfilling environment. Of these, the second and third ("equality," especially socioeconomic, and "fraternity," including civil rights broadly understood) are the most frequently contested—and, for some, most unsettling—of all.

Socioeconomic Rights

Many people, especially in developing countries, attribute great importance to socioeconomic rights. In the words of Léopold Senghor, former president of Senegal, "Human rights begin with breakfast." Without such an awareness, relatively well-off Westerners might sneer at the ostensibly poor human "rights" records of less developed countries, while remaining oblivious to their own shortcomings in the eyes of others, and thus miss what for many outside the West is the intimate connection between political and socioeconomic rights. In fact, there is also a long-standing recognition in Western political thought—albeit one that has been less influential than the traditional focus on political rights—that at least gestures toward socioeconomic rights Thus, in 1748 the prominent French thinker Montesquieu (who influenced the framers of the US Constitution) wrote that a republic owes its citizens "a certain subsistence, a proper nourishment, convenient clothing, and a kind of life not incompatible with health."

The structural violence under which people die from malnutrition and poverty, are poorly educated, and lack medical care, and the direct violence in which a society imprisons and tortures its political opponents, are also abuses of human rights. Also, if one acknowledges the existence of socioeconomic rights, then, for example, the state-socialist government of Cuba—which to many in the West is a failure because of its lack of representative government, widespread censorship, and imprisonment of political dissidents— might simultaneously be praised for its advances in other domains, such as public health and universal literacy. This is not to claim that success in some dimensions of human rights cancels outrages in another; rather, it helps permit a more balanced perception of systems that might otherwise seem unidimensionally evil and whose high level of local domestic acceptance is otherwise difficult for Americans to understand.

Indigenous People and Other "Peripheral Groups"

There are about 300 million indigenous people worldwide, constituting majorities in Guatemala and Bolivia, for example, and significant minorities in Brazil, Australia, Russia, Mexico, and the United States, among other countries. Regardless of their numbers, indigenous peoples are generally in dire straits, sometimes—as in Guatemala, Myanmar, and Brazil—having been the victims of state-sponsored genocide. For example, a UN investigation concluded in 1999 that three former Guatemalan presidents had been involved in genocide, state terrorism, and torture as part of a brutal counterinsurgency campaign conducted by the Guatemalan military during the 1970s and 1980s, which resulted in the deaths of more than 200,000 people, most of them Mayan Indians.

In other cases, indigenous people are severely maltreated and/or they enjoy dramatically fewer opportunities and privileges than their nonnative counterparts:

- Australian aborigines are, on a per capita basis, the most imprisoned people on Earth, with an incarceration rate 16 times that of Australia's Caucasian population.

- Even aside from being the targets of government-inspired atrocities, the life expectancy of Mayan Indians in Guatemala is 11 years shorter than that of the nonindigenous population.

- The average per capita income of Native Americans is half that of the rest of the US population; life spans are much shorter, incarceration and unemployment rates are much higher, along with high rates of drug abuse and, especially, alcoholism.

- Large dams have devastated the homelands of indigenous peoples in Canada, China, Brazil, Norway, the Philippines, and India, depriving them of an arguably crucial human right: to live in their ancestral homelands.

- The Rohingya, a Muslim minority, have lived in Myanmar for many centuries, and yet they have been subjected to ethnic cleansing, forcible expulsion, and genocide and denied citizenship.

- The Uighurs, another Muslim minority—especially in China—are being oppressed and subjected to "re-education camps" designed to eliminate their ethnic and religious identity.

Other groups can also be identified as having particular human rights claims and vulnerabilities: mentally ill persons, children, homeless persons, racial and sexual minorities, disabled persons, convicts, unskilled workers, migrant laborers, refugees, political dissidents, and the elderly. In the future, such human rights as civil liberties, economic opportunity, protection from violence, and the right to a safe and clean environment will be globally safeguarded. In practice, these rights must often be defended, most vigilantly for those groups that have been the most victimized.

Women's Rights

Women comprise roughly 52 percent of the world's population, yet for centuries they have suffered from patriarchal social structures that devalue their personhood and deny many of their basic human rights. This includes a diverse array of abuses, including foot binding in pre-communist China; the forced seclusion and isolation of women in some contemporary Hindu and Muslim societies; sexual mutilation, as currently done to millions of young women in numerous African societies; polygyny; restricted or nonexistent choice as to marriage; substantial discrimination regarding educational opportunities, especially in some conservative Islamic countries; and, even in such ostensibly liberated societies as the United States and the United Kingdom, restricted economic and professional opportunities and underrepresentation in political and business elites. Whatever the sources of well-being in the world, women as a group consistently enjoy fewer of them, including such intangibles as a fulfilling and freely chosen life as well as such physical assets as property.

Even though there are virtually no significant differences in men's and women's attitudes toward war, it is noteworthy that individuals who support gender equality are less likely to support war as a solution to international problems. Moreover, when civil wars break out, societies characterized by relative gender equality are more likely to experience successful UN peace-keeping than are societies in which males and females have more rigidly defined roles.

In the West

In the West, agitation for women's rights dates from the 18th-century Enlightenment. These rights were set out clearly, for example, in Mary Wollstonecraft's *A Vindication of the Rights of Woman,* published in England in 1792. This influential book emphasized the importance of providing education for women equal to that available to men. (Even in the 21st century, illiteracy rates remain consistently higher for women than for men, especially in developing countries.) During the late 19th and early 20th centuries, crusaders for women's rights were especially concerned about getting women the rights to vote and to hold political office.

By the mid-20th century, something of a shift occurred, with growing awareness in Western liberal circles of the degree to which women were also oppressed in the domestic sphere. Especially influential were these milestone books: *The Second Sex,* by Simone de Beauvoir, which raised consciousness by pointing out the extent to which men were traditionally considered the "subjects" of modern life whereas women were merely "others" and secondary objects; *The Feminine Mystique,* by Betty Friedan, which identified the deadening domesticity to which women were often relegated; and *The Female Eunuch,* by Germaine Greer, which castigated the sexual passivity to which many women were traditionally forced. Added to this were innovations in birth control technology (especially the development of contraceptive pills) as well as the US civil rights movement, which raised public awareness about the need to reevaluate and reconfigure the role of women in the home, the workplace, and the public sphere.

Although women's suffrage is virtually universal in the Western world, women's participation in the political process and in the business and professional world is often constricted by the traditional idea that "a woman's place is in the home" (which is not that far removed from the Nazi motto for women: *Kinder, Küche, Kirche* ("children, kitchen, church"). Advocates for women's rights point out that women are typically paid 80 percent of what men receive, leading to a demand for "equal pay for equal work." The number of women in executive-level positions in the US corporate world remains very low. The effort to expand women's social and political options involves a continuing effort to challenge social stereotypes of women as dependent, weak, passive, and hyperemotional, compared with most men. Although some countries (including the United Kingdom, New Zealand, Norway, Israel, India, Sri Lanka, Pakistan, Brazil, Chile, Finland, Argentina, the Philippines, and Germany) have had female prime ministers, the US Congress still has not passed a constitutional amendment guaranteeing equal rights for women. Women's reproductive rights remain precarious, evidenced by ongoing efforts on the part of social conservatives in the US and elsewhere to restrict access to birth control and to abortions. Efforts to roll back affirmative action programs that benefit women as well as minorities are also ongoing.

In addition, a continuing debate within the Western women's rights movement revolves around the degree of change to be sought: whether society (ranging from private domestic relationships to the sinews of public life) should be radically restructured or whether change should be incremental within the basic social structures that currently exist. Such a debate is not necessarily a weakness of the women's rights movement; rather, it reflects the vigor and heterogeneity of its devotees, paralleling ongoing discussions within other social justice movements. At the same time, some feminists are concerned that many members of the 21st-century generation of young women (and men) take for granted the advances of recent decades and are therefore less ardent in their pursuit of gender equality than are their elders.

In Developing Countries

In most economically developing countries, the goals of the women's movement tend to be more basic: increased literacy, health care, and an end to polygyny and bride price (whereby men literally purchase a wife). In some countries, women cannot own property and may not obtain a divorce without their husband's consent.

In many traditional societies, especially in Africa, millions of women are subjected to genital mutilation, which is often justified as a legitimate cultural practice but causes immense suffering, as well as diminished sexual pleasure and increased mortality. Many Muslim countries insist on very restrictive dress codes for women, legally sanctioned violent—often lethal—responses to sexual infidelity, and, frequently, the denial of educational, social, and economic opportunities. Until recently, women were prohibited from driving a car in Saudi Arabia, a country in which women were not granted suffrage until 2015, and even then, only in local and relatively inconsequential elections. The fundamentalist Taliban government of Afghanistan denied even basic education to women and prohibited them from working outside their houses. Indeed, in some conservative Islamic cultures, women are not permitted to go outside at all unless accompanied by a male relative, although this may be changing in Saudi Arabia.

Feminism and Peace

Women's rights have become increasingly tied to an integrated peace agenda. This reflects, among other things, the fact that whereas men are the primary wagers of war, women have long been among those who suffer. Feminists also point out a connection between patriarchy (male dominance) and war making, as reflected in an alleged greater male propensity for violence, in hierarchical structuring of systems of power, and in the use of threats and physical force over consensus building.

Feminist scholar and peace educator Betty Reardon has emphasized that "traditional gender roles have assigned the main functions and maintenance of quotidian [i.e., daily and domestic] security to women while excluding them from participation in the exercise of power over national and global security." She writes, moreover, that "this arrangement has made women more vulnerable to the violent consequences of militarized security," an arrangement that is especially unfair given that "the substance of daily life, the domestic and social chores upon which everyday human life depends, the functions that make all other human activities possible are women's work. Public decisions of life and death are not." In Reardon's view—and that of a growing number of feminist peace workers—this must change: "The feminist challenge is becoming a challenge to the war system itself."[3]

Ever since the classical Greek dramatist Aristophanes wrote *Lysistrata* (a satire in which women attempt to bring the Peloponnesian War to a halt by refusing sexual relations with their husbands until they stopped killing each other), women have taken part in efforts to end war and violence, although many have also participated in such activities or even instigated and, in rare cases, led them. Many women have also engaged in direct action in support of an avowedly feminist peace agenda.

The group Women in Black, for example, composed of Israeli and Palestinian women, has been urging an end to Israeli military occupation of the West Bank and Gaza and an end to terrorism from both sides. The Argentinean Mothers of the Plaza de Mayo, beginning in the 1970s, protested the "disappearances" (the kidnapping, torture, and murder) of their children, raising consciousness about crimes against humanity committed by the brutal Argentinian military junta and shaming political leaders into action. Similar courageous and effective moves were taken by the Chilean Association of the Relatives of the Detained and Disappeared. The Soldiers' Mothers' Movement in Russia actively disrupted the drafting and brutalization of Russian conscripts—especially in the Soviet Union's war in Afghanistan and Russia's war in Chechnya—in the process becoming a notable political force. In the United States, Code Pink has been a persistent thorn in the side of militarism and war. These and other groups have carried their message via direct actions and nonviolent public protest rather than by mere lamentation. Nonetheless, the practical impact of such activities remains uncertain, especially in authoritarian countries such as Russia.

The 2011 Nobel Peace Prize was given to three women—Tawakkol Karman of Yemen, Leymah Gbowee of Liberia, and Ellen Johnson Sirleaf of Liberia—for their devoted nonviolent efforts on behalf of human rights generally and women's rights in particular. In her Nobel Peace Prize acceptance speech, Ms. Johnson Sirleaf pointed to the "sisters and daughters" who had been "brutally defiled" and their lives devastated throughout history, and that crimes against women continue to be under-reported while laws ostensibly designed to be protective are persistently under-enforced. Yet she concluded by emphasizing that optimism is nonetheless warranted, as awareness of the universal legitimacy of human rights has been penetrating even into the world's remaining "dark corners."

Some Human Rights Controversies

It seems unavoidable that various rights will conflict. In a famous legal opinion, US Supreme Court Justice Oliver Wendell Holmes concluded that the right to free speech did not extend to yelling "Fire!" in a crowded theater. The "right" to a drug-free society may conflict with the "right" to privacy, just as the "right" of people in developing countries to healthy babies has conflicted with the "right" of the Nestlé Company, for example, to market infant formula in poor countries (which discourages the healthier practice of breast feeding).

In fundamentalist Islamic states, including Saudi Arabia, despite some tepid steps toward liberalization, women's rights are often subordinated to the "rights" of people (especially men) to practice the religion of their choice in the way they interpret it. A woman's right to control her own body, including an abortion if she desires, runs contrary to the perception of many that the fetus has a "right" to life. The right of religious freedom can conflict with a child's "right" to necessary medical care, as when fundamentalist Christian parents (including Jehovah's Witnesses and Christian Scientists) refuse lifesaving treatment for their child. The public's right to safe air travel appears to have trumped individual "rights" not to be searched without a warrant. The list goes on.

Many human rights are essentially claims against the authority of governments. As such, they are freedoms *from:* guarantees that governments will refrain from behaving badly toward their own people. As already noted, this can be distinguished from freedoms *to:* the asserted obligations of society to help its members achieve a better life. This is a distinction that somewhat parallels the one between negative and positive peace, between those rights asserted *against* governments (no war, no intrusions into personal freedom, etc.) and those expected *of* them: to establish positive peace, provide for basic human needs, and so on.

In most cases, the first category—negative rights—seems easier for governments to achieve. Certain states may lack the financial resources to make substantial improvements in socioeconomic conditions, but they all can stop torturing, murdering, and actively oppressing their people. A pervasive problem in this regard—and one about which oppressive governments are often aware although usually unwilling to acknowledge publicly—is the fear that absent such oppression, citizens may demand a change in those governments. Of course, this ignores the likelihood that revolutionary demands are often multiplied when governments, seeking to enhance control, resort to oppressive measures.

During the 1990s, Western countries did not intervene in the genocide perpetrated by Rwandan Hutus upon Tutsis; President Clinton subsequently apologized for this inaction. By contrast, NATO and the United States intervened with air power to prevent Libyan strongman Gaddafi from massacring his own people (who were in revolt, stimulated by the prodemocratic Arab Spring movement. The outcome, however, has been a fractured Libya, a failed state ruled by competing warlords, and continuing violations of human rights. Fearful of a similar scenario in Syria, the United States and NATO refrained from military action against President Assad, when his government used chemical weapons against rebels and cluster bombs against civilians.

Although human rights constitute a diverse and sometimes confusing array of causes, including movements for peace, women's rights, environmental protection, and penal reform to national independence, they share a common humanistic focus, placing individuals at the center of public policy. And yet, doing so poses numerous dilemmas, not least whether concern for human rights ought to mobilize states to use force against significant human rights abuses in other countries.

Refugees

There have always been refugees, as well as migrants, and although common sense and fundamental morality argues that both groups of people warrant human rights protection, it is important to distinguish between the two, if only because many countries make such a legal distinction. Migrants choose to change their location, whether within or between countries, in order to improve their socioeconomic condition. Refugees seek asylum, often in a new country, and are unable or unwilling to return to their natal lands because of a well-founded fear of persecution based on race, religion, nationality, political opinion, or membership in a particular social group. Refugees are usually given higher priority by the international community and in most cases are not returned to their home countries, whereas migrants are considered to have less pressing human rights claims.

Article 14(1) of the UDHR affords refugees the right to seek and enjoy asylum in other countries. The controlling international convention on refugee law, however, is the 1951 Convention Relating to the Status of Refugees and its follow-on 1967 Optional Protocol. These treaties established broad definitions of refugees and clarified the international legal principle of nonreturn, whereby host countries are prohibited from forcibly returning refugees to their persecutors. However, this principle does not clearly state how a refugee's status is to be evaluated. It also gives countries the right to refuse admittance to refugees who can be demonstrated to be threats to the hosts. Refugees raise many issues regarding human rights, including the high probability that their very existence testifies to a denial of human rights in their home country, the question of refugees' entitlements in host countries, and whether and under what conditions refugees can be forcibly repatriated without violating their human rights.

Beginning in 2014, there was a tremendous increase in the number of forcibly displaced people worldwide, approaching 71 million by mid-2019, with an average of 37,000 forced to flee their homes *every day* as a result of persecution or war; this is the highest level since World War II. The recent wave of refugees has been driven by many factors, notably the wars in Syria, Afghanistan, Iraq, Sudan, and Yemen, along with mass violence in Chad, Mali, Somalia, Eritrea, and Libya. The resulting human tragedy means that roughly one in every 120 people on Earth is currently fleeing one conflict or another. The international humanitarian relief system has been overwhelmed by the sheer numbers of refugees, who have greatly strained the resources of the "frontline" refugee-receiving states: Jordan, Lebanon, and Turkey. At the same time, international attention was riveted by the deaths of thousands of refugees attempting to cross the Mediterranean, often in rickety and overloaded boats. According to the president of Doctors Without Borders at the time, "A mass grave is being created in the Mediterranean, and European policies are responsible."

Thousands of refugees crossed into southern Europe from Libya to Italy, from Turkey to Greece, and from northwest Africa to Spain. Rescues at sea became humanitarian necessities, while European governments faced the dilemma that whereas doing nothing to assist the refugees is monstrously unethical, facilitating safe passage might only encourage greater numbers. In addition, political decision makers became acutely aware of the growing political unpopularity of accepting large numbers of people whose ethnic origin is foreign to most white, Christian Europeans.

Although the numbers of refugees declined somewhat in 2020 from a high of more than 1.2 million in 2015 alone, many Europeans continue to fear that such an influx of ethnically and religiously unfamiliar people threaten the traditional make-up of recipient states. This, in turn, injected new energy into various right-wing, nationalistic, and xenophobic political movements, and many European countries, especially in Hungary, Austria, Italy, France, and Germany, and even some Scandinavian countries (traditionally among the most welcoming) have rethought their openness to refugees. Immigration is the sincerest form of flattery, but many Western governments increasingly found themselves more threatened than flattered by refugees seeking entry into their countries.

In early 2016, for example, the Danish government passed legislation whereby refugees' cash assets exceeding roughly US$1,500 would be confiscated upon entry, ostensibly to help defray the costs of providing social services to these people but likely intended primarily to deter refugees from seeking asylum in Denmark. Australia—large, relatively underpopulated, and consisting almost entirely of immigrants (because most of the aboriginal population was killed off)—was once welcoming to refugees, particularly white Europeans but until recently also to Asians. However, because Australian legal doctrine calls for the detention of any refugee who arrives without a valid visa, potential immigrants (virtually all coming from Southeast Asia) are then shipped to squalid displacement camps on the tiny barren island of Nauru. To most human rights advocates, this draconian policy is inexcusable. Supporters claim, however, that instead of being callous, the Australian system is actually humane because it deters most asylum seekers from attempting a life-threatening ocean crossing.

Although the ongoing refugee crisis has evoked images of displaced persons flooding into Europe, there are, unfortunately, many other refugees, in equally desperate situations. To take just one example, the Rohingya are indigenous Islamic inhabitants of Myanmar (formerly Burma) who have been victimized in this largely Buddhist country. They have been deprived of citizenship, higher education, and free movement within Myanmar. Many are subjected to near slavery. As a result, more than two million Rohingya have become refugees, fleeing especially to Bangladesh, Thailand, and Pakistan, where they live in squalid conditions, while many others have resorted to dangerous boat travel, often paying traffickers who then abandon them on the open ocean.

Although many countries, especially those in northern Europe with low birth rates, seem likely to benefit socially and economically from an influx of young and energetic refugees, many of whom are well educated and highly motivated, the refugee crisis threatens to become a situation in which claims for human rights conflict with more parochial, protectionist, and political motivations.

LGBT Rights

When it comes to LGBT (lesbian, gay, bisexual, and transgender) rights, the situation is bifurcated: unprecedented improvement in some countries, backsliding in others. On the one hand, there is increased visibility and acceptance of LGBT people, especially in the Western Hemisphere and Europe, highlighted by widespread legalization of same-sex marriage. Thus, as of 2020, homosexual marriage is permitted in all European countries (except for the Turkish-controlled part of Cyprus), as well as in a growing number of Latin American states—30 different countries overall, and the US Supreme Court has ruled that laws prohibiting gay marriage are unconstitutional. This increased tolerance—unanticipated even by many ardent gay rights activists as recently as the turn of the 21st century—was reflected and perhaps encouraged by the following comment by Pope Francis: "If someone is gay and he searches for the Lord and has goodwill, who am I to judge?" (The Catholic Church, as well as most fundamentalist religious traditions, has long considered homosexuality a serious sin.)

On the downside, Russia has moved in the opposite direction, aligning itself against what President Putin considers Western "moral degeneracy." In Russia, gay rights activists, as well as out-of-the-closet homosexuals, are being persecuted by antigay laws and thugs, leading to calls for an international boycott of Russian goods and vacation sites.

It has been ludicrously claimed by some Iranian public figures that homosexuality doesn't exist in Iran (where it is punishable by death). Homosexuality, let alone gay marriage, remains illegal in 38 African countries, where gay persons are regularly beaten and even murdered, in some cases by enraged mobs while police stand by. In sub-Saharan Africa and in large parts of the Islamic world, it takes great courage to be openly gay. Homosexuality is criminalized in 71 countries (more than half of them former British colonies—homosexuality was illegal in the UK until it was decriminalized in 1967). The Human Dignity Trust challenges antigay laws worldwide; although it and other activist organizations have done a great deal to promote LGBT rights, they have much work yet to do.

The Legal Status of Human Rights

UN-Related Agreements

Although the UN Charter serves as a kind of international constitution, it lacks a binding Bill of Rights, specifying which human rights are to be protected. The aforementioned UN-sponsored UDHR was passed unanimously by the General Assembly in 1948, enumerating these rights. The United States was a major contributor to that document, with much of its impetus coming from Eleanor Roosevelt, at the time the widow of the recently deceased US president Franklin D. Roosevelt.

The UDHR consists of 30 articles, of which the first 21 are primarily civil/political, including prohibiting torture and arbitrary arrest, and guaranteeing freedom of assembly, religion, speech, and emigration—as well as the right to vote by secret ballot. The remaining articles are concerned with socioeconomic and cultural rights, including the right to work, to an "adequate" standard of living, to education, to some form of social security, and even to vacations with pay. The UDHR is not technically binding in the sense of an international treaty; it is a recommendation only, with no provisions for enforcement. Nonetheless, it is widely respected and has been a foundation for increasing global concern with human rights. It has even been incorporated into many national constitutions.

To some degree, the UDHR has become part of customary international law and, accordingly, many judicial scholars argue that it has the literal force of law, although it is often violated. Numerous worldwide legal instruments have built on the UN Charter and the UDHR, including an array of covenants, conventions, treaties, and declarations of diverse legal meanings but all helping further define the concept and ultimately the implementation of human rights. Of these, the most important are probably the Convention on the Prevention and Punishment of the Crime of Genocide (1948) and the International Convention on the Elimination of All Forms of Racial Discrimination (1965).

In addition, two UN human rights covenants were signed in 1966 and entered into force in 1977, when they were ratified by a sufficient number of national governments (but not by the United States). These are the International Covenant on Civil and Political Rights and the International Covenant on Economic, Social and Cultural Rights. There are also two 1977 Geneva Protocols on Armed Conflict, both controversial and not universally in force, in addition to various instruments concerned with specified rights, such as those of refugees and children, as well as denunciations of apartheid and numerous more informal declarations.

Scholars and political decision makers dispute precisely which obligations member states undertook when, in the UN Charter, they agreed to "promote universal respect for and observance" of human rights. Although early everyone agrees that human rights must include the right to be free from torture and arbitrary killing, what about the rights to live in a democracy, to free medical care, to a tolerable environment, to Internet access? Nonetheless, an underlying consensus has emerged that governments may not participate in a "consistent pattern of gross violations of human rights."

Whereas isolated incidents are unlikely to generate worldwide outrage, "gross violations," if they recur, merit condemnation and, ultimately, such actions as censure, economic boycott, and possible military intervention. Abuses of this sort could include widespread torture, mass arrests and imprisonment without trial, genocide, vicious policies of racial segregation and debasement, and forced relocation of entire populations. Small states engage in such activities at some risk, not only to their reputations but of possible armed intervention; large and powerful states, by contrast, are still literally able to "get away with murder."

Human Rights and the Nation-State

Encouragingly, some halting progress has been made as national courts have begun ruling to enforce international norms with respect to human rights. For example, in a celebrated legal case, Filártiga v. Peña-Irala, a US court ruled in 1980 that politically inspired torture and murder were so clearly prohibited by international agreements on human rights that the United States had jurisdiction to prosecute a Paraguayan national for crimes occurring in Paraguay. In 1998, the British government arrested former Chilean dictator Augusto Pinochet and nearly put him on trial for thousands of cases of torture and the "disappearance" of political prisoners during his dictatorship.

(Pinochet narrowly avoided legal action because he was judged too old and feeble to stand trial; he was deported to Chile, where he died before the legal process had run its full course.)

Nonetheless, the Pinochet case constitutes an important precedent, one that might well be expanded to allow prosecution of the many ex–heads of state—often living in comfortable exile—who ordered or condoned murder and torture while in office. The ultimate significance of such prosecutions might go beyond the satisfaction of justice, by putting current rights violators on notice that they might have to answer for crimes committed on "their watch."

Although the Pinochet case was controversial, there is nothing new about governments criticizing human rights abuses in *other* states, although it would be virtually unprecedented for them to place national leaders under arrest for human rights violations committed while they were heads of state.

Governments have long found it useful to complain loudly about the actions of foreign governments—especially those to which they are not allied—while turning a blind eye to their own misbehavior. The real tension between states and human rights concerns the degree to which a state is willing to forgo part of its sovereignty and permit its own human rights practices to be the subject of international scrutiny, judgment, and influence—if not control and, on occasion, punishment. Another issue is the disparity between enforcement of human rights violations when the countries are relatively small (e.g., Chile) versus when they are large and powerful (e.g., Russia, China, and the United States). For example, a US Senate report released in 2014 described details of the Central Intelligence Agency's use of torture during the "war on terror," which included waterboarding (repeated episodes of near drowning), as well as sexual and psychological abuse. Some former government officials defended such practices, whereas others decried them as "violating our most basic principles"; to date, no one has been held criminally liable as a result of these probable violations of human rights.

Resistance to Western Intervention

Although Western citizens often assume that people from other cultures would applaud their actions on behalf of worldwide human rights, sometimes the response is less than enthusiastic. Partly, this is because of the perceived moral arrogance with which the primarily Western concept of human rights is exported to other societies. Partly, it is because people from developing countries remain acutely aware of the legacy of Western imperialism as well as that, in the past, the West's sincere promotion of human rights has often been used as a moral pretext in connection with colonial conquest; for example, bringing an end to "barbarous" practices, such as the Indian custom of *suttee* (burning a widow on her deceased husband's funeral pyre), and female infanticide.

Various practices of female circumcision, widely practiced in northern Africa and elsewhere in the Muslim world, are increasingly seen—especially in the West—as unacceptable cases of genital mutilation. This leads to important and unresolved questions regarding the "rights" of national governments and regions to engage in their own religious/cultural traditions, versus increasingly widespread perception (generally in Westernized countries) that certain actions are cruel, "barbaric," inhumane and indeed, medically dangerous. The resulting tension is currently unresolved. At the same time, many developing countries are intensely committed to the pursuit of their people's socioeconomic rights, and they believe that progress in this respect may require that governments exert some restrictions on civil and political rights.

Following World War II, more than 80 former Western colonies won their political independence, liberating more than one billion people in the world's most massive transfer of political power from the "haves" to the formerly "have-nots." But national independence does not necessarily guarantee the rights of individuals. In some cases, quite the opposite takes place, especially when the newly established government is shaky; threats to the security of the nation serve as an excuse for denying individual rights, and many newly independent countries are politically insecure, for a variety of reasons. There is, accordingly, a strong tendency for such states to be run by authoritarian, often military, governments and for such governments to be quite repressive of human rights.

The Primacy of State Sovereignty

The greatest underlying conflict between human rights and the nation-state is one that is characteristic of virtually all governments. It derives from the nature of state sovereignty because a call for human rights is often a claim on behalf of individuals against the state. Whether demanding that states refrain from mistreating their people (negative rights) or that they commit themselves more aggressively to their citizens' betterment (positive rights), claimants for human rights often push governments in directions they would not otherwise choose.

International standards of human rights may represent claims against state power and sovereignty by restricting what a state can do (and, sometimes, telling it what to do), even within its own borders. This could include disapproval by the international human rights community of a country's internal policies, notwithstanding that such policies may be fully "legal" according to its own domestic laws.

For example, South African apartheid laws were not internationally acknowledged as legitimate, despite the fact that they were duly passed by that country's parliament. NATO's brief but violent air war in Kosovo was largely a response to the widespread perception that the Serbian government was abusing the human rights of Kosovars, leading to international intervention despite the fact that Kosovo was legally part of Yugoslavia. (This intervention derived in part from an earlier failure with respect to human rights intervention, namely, that other countries did nothing to prevent genocidal slaughter in Rwanda five years earlier.) NATO's air support of Libyan rebels in 2011 was similarly justified by strongman Gaddafi's brutal treatment of his own people. Subsequent violence and chaotic instability in Libya has, however, taken the glow off this intervention.

On the other hand, international concern about human rights may enhance states' sovereignty, or at least, their internal stability. States that by and large adhere to international standards of human rights—the Western democracies, generally—normally have a higher level of legitimacy and security than those that routinely trample on them. The US, Western European, Australian, and Japanese governments are extremely unlikely to be overthrown by coup or revolution—unlike other regimes that abused human rights, including those formerly led by Duvalier in Haiti, Somoza in Nicaragua, Ceauşescu in Romania, and Gaddafi in Libya. It is nonetheless unclear whether abuse of human rights leads to political instability and possible revolutionary violence, or if such instability inclines shaky govern-ments to abuse such rights in an effort to retain power.

At the same time, when governments trample on accepted norms of human rights—for example, by torturing suspected terrorists or incarcerating so-called enemy combatants indefinitely and without providing basic *habeas corpus* rights (the right to be confronted with evidence of a crime)—they often diminish their international standing. But some states, including Russia under Vladimir Putin, Turkey under Recep Tayyip Erdoğan, the Philippines under Rodrigo Duterte, Brazil under Jair Bolsonaro, India under Narendra Modi. and China under Xi Jin-ping, so value stability and the image of a "strong leader" that they not only tolerate but reward political elites that violate human rights as long as they also provide a sense of national pride along with protection from internal chaos.

The Role of Politics

Governments are often asked to report on the status of human rights within their own borders. Unsurprisingly, "investigations" by the state tend overwhelmingly to exonerate loyalists who abuse their own citizens' human rights. Allowing states to report on their own human rights situation is like having the fox report on the status of the chickens. The assessment by outside experts, including dissidents, is generally much more critical and believable than judgments made by official representatives about their own government's behavior.

The United Nations has also played politics with human rights. The UN Commission on Human Rights, for example, has generally been willing to criticize such "pariah" states as Israel and (during its apartheid regime) South Africa, but not the major powers. On the other hand, such organizations as the Red Cross, the International Labour Organization, United Nations Educational, Scientific and Cultural Organization (UNESCO), United Nations Children's Fund (UNICEF), the Food and Agriculture Organization (FAO), the World Health Organization (WHO), and the High Commissioner for Refugees have done much to improve human rights by offending states. Private nongovernmental organizations, notably Amnesty International (which won a Nobel Peace Prize in 1977), have sometimes been effective in improving conditions for specific political prisoners and, on many occasions, even winning their release. But such groups have tended to focus on individual cases, avoiding the more troublesome general issue of state sovereignty versus human rights.

The Problem of Enforcement

Faced with the sovereign power of states, the international human rights regime may seem to be weak and unreliable, given the general paucity of enforcement mechanisms. But legal systems always have difficulty control-ling powerful actors: for example, labor unions in France and large corpora-tions based in the United States. Ultimately, the international human rights regime relies on voluntary compliance. And some states, especially in Cen-tral America, have voluntarily improved their compliance with acknowl-edged human rights norms, largely to achieve international legitimacy as well as to avoid diplomatic ostracism.

Frustration with the rights-denying policies of states occasionally spills over into individual and group efforts to transcend or undermine state authority. Individuals of high moral and international standing have on occasion gathered together to fill what they see as a vacuum in the protection of human rights. So-called people's tribunals have periodically convened to draw attention to human rights abuses. Especially notable was the Russell Tribunal, which during the 1960s criticized US policy during the Vietnam War. The League for the Rights of Peoples, established in Rome in 1976, has held numerous sessions, condemning political repression under Ferdinand Marcos in the Philippines and offering retrospectives on the Turkish genocide against Armenians from 1915 to 1916, and on the Brazilian government's treatment of its indigenous Amazonian population. It has also criticized Indonesia's strong-arm tactics in East Timor, US interventions in Central America, and the Soviet Union's actions in Afghanistan, and has declared the illegitimacy of nuclear weapons. Such actions are of uncertain effectiveness, but they attract public attention and undercut the presumption that only state-centered approaches are relevant in dealing with human rights violations.

Human Rights and the United States

Many Americans think of their government as supporting human rights. After all, the Declaration of Independence states: "We hold these truths to be self-evident, that all men are created equal, that they are endowed by their Creator with certain inalienable Rights, that among these are Life, Liberty and the pursuit of Happiness—That to secure these rights, Governments are instituted among Men, deriving their just powers from the consent of the governed."

For most Americans, the right to "Life" presupposes the right to self-defense and protection against unwarranted attack and unjust government (as well as, for abortion opponents, the "right to life of unborn babies," i.e., human fetuses); the right to "Liberty" includes freedom of speech, of public association, of religion, and to establish a government of one's own choosing; the right to "pursuit of Happiness" includes the right to own property and to enjoy the fruits of one's labor. The US Constitution was later amended to include a much-cherished Bill of Rights, which specifically guarantees freedom of religion, speech, the press, and peaceable assembly; the right to petition the government for redress of grievances; the right to keep and bear arms (including, arguably, the right of state militias and much more controversially of all law-abiding citizens to own any weapons of their choice); freedom from unwarranted search and seizure and from self-incrimination; the right to a fair and speedy trial; and protection against excessive bail.

On the other hand, the behavior of the early government of the United States was not a paragon of human rights: Slavery was practiced in the South and in parts of the North, and women were denied the vote. Even today, and despite the election and reelection of a mixed-race president—Barack Obama—racial discrimination is widespread, including excessive police violence against African American men in particular. This gave rise to widespread reconsideration and occasional condemnation of the tactics of police enforcement, as well as to the Black Lives Matter movement. In 2020, the anger boiled over following the shocking murder of George Floyd, an African American, who was killed when a white police officer knelt on his neck for nearly nine minutes while Mr. Floyd died agonizingly. His death, seen by millions, ignited outrage that had been building over the repetitive killing of many unarmed African Americans by police.

The result was a proliferation of vigorous protests around the United States—and to some extent, around the world—leading to what may well be a much-delayed and much-needed recognition of the extent of inherent racial discrimination, not only in policing but in most aspects of the Western world's socioeconomic systems. A striking aspect of these protests and the soul searching that ensued was the extent to which White citizens sympathized and even participated. The long-term consequences of these developments, if any, remain to be seen.

Many other nations see the United States as an opponent of human rights. In the past, this was a response to a number of American government policies, including military interventions in Vietnam, Central America, and elsewhere; long-standing support for an array of oppressive right-wing dictatorships; US corporations' economic exploitation of many developing countries; as well as for American administrations' coddling of apartheid in South Africa; tacit support for Israeli oppression of Palestinians in the occupied territories, and its vigorous initiation and escalation of the nuclear arms race.

In addition, the United States is widely perceived to pursue a single-minded sponsorship of free enterprise capitalism as the sole acceptable solution to the world's ills, as well as publicly encouraging civil and political liberties while sometimes looking the other way when allies abuse these liberties (including the widely publicized cases of Saudi Arabia and Turkey), and opposing most efforts at promulgating universal socioeconomic rights. The US government's use of torture in its "war on terror" during the George W. Bush administration alienated many people throughout the world and threatened to make a mockery of any US embrace of human rights, even in its Western version, which traditionally focused mainly on civil liberties.

This tendency increased during the presidency of Donald Trump, who cozied up to authoritarian rulers in many places—notably Russia, China, North Korea, Hungary, Poland, Brazil, Turkey, Egypt, the Philippines, and Saudi Arabia—while explicitly denying that human rights abuses were of concern to the United States, except for those entailing property rights and freedom of worship. Under Trump's watch, the US withdrew from the UN Human Rights Council. This and other actions induced Human Rights Watch, in its annual report, to warn that US policies threatened to "reverse the accomplishments of the modern human-rights movement."

During the Trump administration, human rights abuses occurred most dramatically when families seeking refugee status in the US along the border with Mexico were often kept in inhumane conditions and—most notoriously—hundreds of young children were forcibly separated from their parents. In addition, a ban targeting immigrants from Muslim-majority countries, along with support for voter suppression efforts in many states, further tarnished the US as a self-proclaimed bastion of human rights. These policies were reversed by the Biden Administration. Nonetheless, substantial harm was done, not only to the victims but also to the reputation of the United States.

Messianic Zeal

One of the more pernicious doctrines under which human rights are violated is the notion that one's ideas are so good, pure, correct, and universally applicable that virtually anything is justified in pursuit of them. Totalitarian states, notably Nazi Germany and the Stalinist Soviet Union, justified violent repression of their own population in the name of a "greater good," either the glory of the fatherland (Fascist regimes) or the dictatorship of the proletariat (some Communist Party–led governments). The United States has not been immune from a dose of messianic ideology, beginning early in its history, when the fledgling country viewed itself as a "shining city on a hill" and a self-proclaimed "light unto the nations."

US National Security Council directive no. 68, issued in 1950 at the dawn of the Cold War, noted that "the integrity of our system will not be jeopardized by any measures, covert or overt, violent or nonviolent, which serve the purposes of frustrating the Kremlin's design." This directive has never been rescinded. In effect, it gives the US government license to intervene, both domestically and overseas, in ways destructive of human rights so long as such activities are aimed at "frustrating" the goals of its opponents, which, in the past, included the Soviet Union and, more recently, "international terrorism" and various "rogue nations." These actions included a range of interventions abroad, as well as the toppling of democratically elected governments, attempted assassination of Fidel Castro, likely collaboration in the murders of the Congolese prime minister Patrice Lumumba and Chilean president Salvador Allende, as well as bombing a presumed chemical warfare factory in Sudan—subsequently shown to be a pharmaceutical plant.

The United States' expressed concern for human rights has not been immune from a crusader-like ideology. Thus, its entry into World Wars I and II was facilitated in each case by the argument that these wars were in defense of liberty and democracy. Nonetheless, US foreign policy, like that of other countries, has not always been directly motivated concern about human rights abroad. More important has usually been the pursuit of national power and profits. When democratically elected leftist governments were believed by US political decision makers not to exhibit sufficient anticommunist zeal, and/or when such governments threatened to restrict the profits of US companies abroad, the United States often intervened to replace them with other regimes more friendly to US corporate interests, as happened in Iran (1953), Guatemala (1954), and Chile (1973). The human rights records of these new governments were far worse than those of their predecessors.

At other times, the export of human rights seems more like hypocrisy, as in George W. Bush's announcement, during his second inaugural address in 2005, that "it is the policy of the United States to seek and support the growth of democratic movements and institutions in every nation and culture, with the ultimate goal of ending tyranny in our world." These words might have had greater credibility if they had not occurred in the context of an increasingly failed war in Iraq, which was then being retroactively justified as part of a purported effort to export human rights, in the form of democracy, to the Middle East. It seems likely that such policies, because they are ultimately destructive of human rights, also feed anti-Western anger and may well contribute to terrorism more than they oppose it.

Traditional National Self-Interest

Despite its avowed commitment to human rights, US foreign policy has long been influenced by traditional self-serving Great Power concerns. Shortly before the outbreak of World War II, for example, the US government refused to permit the immigration of tens of thousands of German Jews attempting to flee murderous persecution by the Nazis. Motivated in part by anti-Semitism, as well as by concern to avoid the economic and social stresses immigration might produce, US decision makers chose to adhere strictly to narrowly written, blatantly racist laws governing immigration and naturalization rather than to a concern for the human rights of the victims of Nazism.

The Truman administration provided some initial support for human rights, through the UN Charter and the UDHR, but as the Cold War heated up, things changed, and during the second half of the 20th century, US human rights policy was subsumed within a foreign policy based largely on anticommunism and containment of the Soviet Union. This in turn produced alliances with many repressive governments, which were said by the US government to constitute part of the "free world," regardless of the degree of their own human rights violations, so long as they professed anticommunism.

Despite a partial respite during the presidency of Jimmy Carter, when human rights briefly became a genuine touchstone of foreign policy, the US government generally downgraded human rights, a tendency epitomized by the Reagan administration, which largely ignored socioeconomic rights and human rights violation by right-wing, anticommunist military dictatorships. A false distinction was made between "authoritarian" governments (rights-denying regimes that were, for the most part, anticommunist and thus allegedly deserving of US support) that were deemed capable of eventually moderating their oppression, and "totalitarian" governments, communist regimes that were ostensibly irredeemable.

During the presidency of Donald Trump, human rights were further downgraded as a US concern. The selectivity of current US human rights policy is exemplified by the contrast between decades of antagonism toward Cuba and political accommodation with China, although both violate civil/political rights, with China's offenses being perhaps more egregious than Cuba's. Considerations of *Realpolitik* appear to be paramount: Unlike Cuba, China is a major economic power and trading partner, whereas anti-Castro Cuban exiles represent a potent force within US politics, especially in the key state of Florida. The Obama administration, however, began to normalize relations with Cuba, starting in 2015, and diplomatic relations between the United States and Cuba were at that time largely restored—although downgraded again during the Trump administration—even while the American economic blockade on Cuba is retained.

The United States is not unique in its hypocrisy concerning human rights. China, for example, has trampled on the religious and political rights of Tibetans and Uighurs, and looked the other way with respect to the Sudanese genocide in Darfur (China imports oil from Sudan). The presumed Kurdish right to self-determination has been ignored by NATO countries worried about not alienating Turkey. In fact, when a country's "national interest" conflicts with its avowed concern for human rights, the latter nearly always loses.

Human Rights and Peace

Human rights and peace are inextricably connected. the denial of human rights is itself a denial of positive peace. A world in which there is no armed conflict but in which fundamental human rights are thwarted could not be considered peaceful in any meaningful sense. Speaking at the United Nations, Pope John Paul II explicitly linked human rights and war: "The Universal Declaration of Human Rights has struck a real blow against the many deep roots of war because the spirit of war in its basic primordial meaning springs up . . . wherever the inalienable rights of men are violated."

Not all rights-denying dictatorships are aggressive: Fascist Spain stayed neutral during World War II, and neither neo-fascist Paraguay nor neo-Stalinist Albania was an international aggressor. Similarly, for all its size and power, as well as political despotism, China has remained largely unthreatening to its neighbors (although, of course, Tibetans who wish to regain their autonomy from China, and the Vietnamese who have a millennial-long conflict with China, feel differently). This may be changing, however, as China is increasingly assertive concerning territorial claims against Vietnam and the Philippines in the South China Sea. On the other hand, there is also a connection between the way a state treats its own population and its behavior toward other states.

To some extent, the foreign policies of states reflect their domestic tendencies. While it existed, the Soviet Union largely denied political freedoms to its own people. Likewise, the relative disinterest of the United States in promoting economic justice at home has long paralleled its opposition to any substantive efforts at democratizing the international economic system.

The denial of human rights can also provoke breaches of international peace, if other states become involved. Humanitarian intervention may be legal; there is precedent in some classical writings of international law. Emer de Vattel's *The Law of Nations* (1760), for example, claimed that "nations have obligations to produce welfare and happiness in other states. In the event of civil war, for example, states must aid the party which seems to have justice on its side or protect an unfortunate people from an unjust tyrant." Great Britain, France, and Russia intervened in 1827 when Turkey used inhumane means to put down Greek aspirations for independence, and many nations supported US military actions against Spain during the Cuban War of Independence from 1895 to 1898 was intended, according to the congressional resolution at the time, to put an end to "the abhorrent conditions which have existed for more than three years in the island of Cuba, have shocked the moral sense of the people of the United States, and have been a disgrace to Christian civilization."[4]

On the other hand, claims of humanitarian intervention have often been used as excuses for aggression, of which the Spanish-American War may well be an example. Violations of Nicaraguan human rights, for another case, were cited by the United States as justification for its efforts to overthrow the Sandinista government, although no comparable justifications were ever used by the United States to overthrow murderous rightist regimes, including the earlier Somoza dictatorship, which had been far more abusive.

Finally, one of the widely recognized human rights—specified in the first article of both 1966 human rights covenants—is national self-determination, abuses of which have often led to war, especially civil war. The pursuit of human rights may, at least in the short term, lead to violence than to peace; history shows that human rights are often won by struggle and confrontation. Furthermore, there are claims for national self-determination that are not obviously legitimate. For example, should there be independent states of Kurdistan, Baluchistan, Chechnya, and/or Kosovo? And what about the national aspirations of Basques, Welsh, Scots, Québécois, native Hawaiians, Okinawans, and Puerto Ricans? The UN Security Council has determined that in certain cases, such as anticolonial struggles, a continuing denial of human rights constitutes a threat to international peace. (This was applied, for example, to apartheid South Africa but not to China's oppression of Tibet.)

In summary, the connection between human rights and peace is complex and multifaceted. It may be that the most useful connection is the claim that such a connection exists, which in turn can serve as an argument in favor of human rights, regardless of whether this actually promotes peace.

Competing Conceptions of Human Rights

Both defining and defending human rights will probably continue to be controversial, with competing conceptions, while the very notion of human rights often is contrary to the inclinations of most states to engage in *Realpolitik*. What should a state do, for example, when confronted with this choice: It desires a particular strategic relationship with another state, but that other state engages in abuses of human rights. Which should be sacrificed, national strategy or a commitment to human rights?

Theologian Reinhold Niebuhr argued that "group relations can never be as ethical as those that characterize individual relations."[5] Similar thinking inspired some Marxist-Leninist leaders to rationalize the power politics by which their states generally function, as well as their failure to "wither away," as Marx had originally predicted. During the 16th-century Italian Renaissance, Niccolò Machiavelli, in *The Prince*, wrote that "a man who wishes to make a profession of goodness in everything must necessarily come to grief among so many who are not good." This may have been largely a rationalization, justifying a ruler's conventional amorality, but it also expressed a genuine political dilemma for decision makers in modern times as well.

Perhaps, on the other hand, the "natural law" school is correct, and support of human rights is simply the right thing to do—period—regardless of its practical consequences. Consider this observation from German philosopher Karl Jaspers, who addressed the question of "metaphysical guilt" following the Holocaust: "There exists a solidarity among men as human beings that makes each co-responsible for every wrong and every injustice in the world, especially for crimes committed in his presence or with his knowledge. If I fail to do whatever I can to prevent them, I too am guilty."[6]

There is yet another possibility, a middle ground between the amorality of *Realpolitik* and the inflexibility of rigid ethical norms. Some argue that power (or, at least, security) can readily be reconciled with human rights. After all, the United States has discovered that brutal, oppressive regimes—Somoza's in Nicaragua, the Shah's in Iran, Marcos's in the Philippines—do not always make reliable allies, or at least, long-lasting ones. And Mikhail Gorbachev's reformist policies of *glasnost* ("openness") and *perestroika* ("restructuring") in the Soviet Union between 1985 and 1991 reflected in part the fact that, in the long run, national security may be enhanced, not diminished, by allowing human rights to flourish, even at the cost of traditional measures of state power. (At the same time, Gorbachev's embrace of political liberalization did not contribute to his own political security, since he lost power in 1991, when the Soviet Union collapsed.)

Former US secretary of state Cyrus Vance once offered the following observation: "We pursue our human rights objectives, not only because they are right, but because we have a stake in the stability that comes when people can express their hopes and find their futures freely." In short, when it comes to human rights, ideals and ethical security interests should coincide.

The Responsibility to Protect

A new and important concept has recently been articulated in the arena of human rights, known as the "responsibility to protect" (R2P). Former UN Secretary-General Kofi Annan raised the following question in the aftermath of the international community's failure to intervene during the 1994 mass murder of an estimated 800,000 people in Rwanda: "Under what circumstances, if at all, is the international community entitled—or even obliged—to intervene in a state's sovereignty, especially when that state is perpetrating genocide?" In response, the Canadian government established the International Commission on Intervention and State Sovereignty in 2000, to which was added the phrase "responsibility to protect" (which was thought better than "right" or "obligation" to intervene).

The basic idea of R2P is that under certain circumstances, other states—ideally in conjunction with the United Nations or some other international grouping—have a duty to protect civilians if their own sovereign state fails to do so or is complicit in oppression. It is a radical doctrine because it asserts that a sovereign state that engages in mass atrocities has sacrificed, by this behavior, some or all of its right to sovereignty.

R2P became a formal UN initiative in 2005, structured around the concept that sovereignty is not supreme; rather than being simply an unlimited right of governments, sovereignty carries with it a responsibility toward those being governed. R2P is especially concerned with preventing—or if that fails, halting—four crimes: ethnic cleansing, crimes against humanity, war crimes, and genocide. It is thus rather conservative and limited, in that it does not include a governmental responsibility to protect people from disease, illiteracy, and social injustice or to protect the environment. Instead, it focuses on the four most direct and egregious insults to a populace, which are identified as mass-atrocity crimes. R2P is currently an emerging global norm, although a controversial one, and not an established part of international law. In various forms it has been included in several international treaties. R2P is generally acknowledged to consist of three pillars:

1. Each state has a responsibility to protect its population from mass-atrocity crimes.

2. If the state is unable or unwilling to carry out pillar no. 1 on its own, the international community has a responsibility to assist that state in doing so.

3. In the initial stages of such an intervention, such coercive but nonviolent measures as economic sanctions are appropriate; if such efforts fail, however, military intervention is justified.

Not surprisingly, R2P has been disputed, mostly because of its challenge to traditional state sovereignty. In the UN report *Implementing the Responsibility to Protect,* Secretary-General Ban Ki-moon responded to this concern by pointing out that if a state is allowing mass atrocities to occur, it is committing what are widely recognized under international law (and affirmed in the Nuremberg Principles) as crimes of omission; similarly, if the state is directly committing these acts, it is guilty of crimes of commission. Either way, it has abrogated its responsibilities as a sovereign political entity, making corrective action from outside the state appropriate and legal.

It remains to be seen whether R2P will be abused. It is conceivable, for example, that in the future a state will insist upon intervening militarily in the domestic affairs of another state, claiming a responsibility to protect some of its inhabitants, analogous to Adolf Hitler's bogus claim in 1938 that Germany was annexing the Sudetenland because ethnically German inhabitants there were being abused by the Czech government. More likely, if R2P fails in the future, it will be because of failure at the other end of the spectrum, with the international community proving reluctant to enforce its responsibility against powerful states when they abuse their own people. For example, there has been no consensus as to an international obligation to restrain China from abusing the people of Tibet or Chinese Muslim Uighurs, or for Russia to treat its restive Chechen population more fairly, or for the Trump Administration to refrain from keeping refugees from obtaining asylum in the US, and to cease its policy of detaining asylum-seeking families— separating even very young children from their parents—and keeping them in degrading conditions.

R2P is also of dubious applicability when governments maintain (sometimes with good reason) that they are confronting a violent internal rebellion, which, they believe, the state has a responsibility to suppress, not to protect. Furthermore, in an age marked by terrorism, governments under internal threat are especially prone to describe their opponents, whether violent or nonviolent, as "terrorists" (as the Assad regime and the Russian government have branded all opposition forces in Syria) and therefore not entitled to protection. On the other hand, R2P was raised as a justification for NATO's support of the anti-Gaddafi rebels in Libya, at a time when that regime seemed poised to murder thousands of innocent noncombatant civilians in the port city of Benghazi, and R2P has long been contemplated with regard to the brutal Assad regime's repression of antigovernment activities in Syria.

The fact that R2P could be abused is not a refutation of the claim that the prime responsibility of governments should not be toward their own continuation and power, but rather, that they do in fact have a responsibility to protect their citizens. And if they do not—worse yet, if they actively persecute them—then perhaps other governments have a responsibility to become actively involved to prevent such abuses.

Human Rights Violations Under Authoritarian Regimes

Recent developments in human rights are not encouraging, in large part because of declines in the status of democracies worldwide (see Chapter 22). Even though human rights are not guaranteed even in countries with well-established democratic traditions, they are far more likely to be ignored or abused outright by autocratic or totalitarian governments. Thus, for the criticism levelled earlier in this chapter, it is incontrovertible that the United States is substantially more protective of human rights than are many other regimes. For example, Russia, Hungary, Egypt, Brazil, the Philippines, and Turkey, all of which are nominal democracies but have in practice become authoritarian with only a democratic veneer, have very poor records when it comes to inhibiting freedom of speech, of the press, and of assembly. And other countries, such as China, North Korea, and Saudi Arabia, which make no serious pretense of democracy, are even worse.

Some Examples

The Russian government under Vladimir Putin (who may remain as president for life) has prevented the rise of authentic opposition political parties and has also been credibly accused of orchestrating the murder of dissident journalists as well as some of the regime's political opponents, while the increasingly authoritarian Egyptian and Turkish governments have imprisoned the largest number of journalists. Dictatorial regimes in China and North Korea, which don't even claim democratic credentials, along with Iran (which does), have so severely restricted freedom of expression and of dissent that the number of people imprisoned for political disagreement in those countries cannot even be established.

The Philippines, a well-established democracy since the ouster of dictator Ferdinand Marcos in 1986, elected the thuggish Rodrigo Duterte as president in 2016; his brutal "war on drugs" has resulted in the death of more than 12,000 Filipinos, mostly urban poor and a large proportion due to "extrajudicial killings" by police, who have been encouraged to shoot suspected drug users and dealers without arrests or trials. The same is being done in Brazil under the presidency of Jair Bolsonaro.

Although Saudi Arabia has nominally improved the human rights of women, granting female suffrage, this only applies to relatively unimportant municipal elections. The same rigidly monarchical Saudi government, under the control of its crown prince, Mohammed bin Salman, is widely known to have ordered the 2019 murder and dismemberment of the dissident journalist Jamal Khashoggi. In such cases, an especially pernicious effect—but something doubtless intended—is that once the expectation of repression has become firmly established, would-be political dissidents often self-censor, thereby saving repressive governments the need to do so directly and also minimizing the opportunity for international outrage.

Human rights abuses have been particularly severe when directed against minority Muslim populations. India, which currently has the world's third-largest number (c. 200 million) of Muslims and may one day surpass Indonesia as the nation with the world's largest Muslim population, has been led by Narendra Modi, an extreme nationalist and uncompromising advocate of *Hindutva* (an ideology that strongly prioritizes the Hindu religion and Hindu cultural practices). In addition to violently repressing the Muslim majority in the Indian-administered part of Kashmir, the Modi government has modified its immigration laws regarding refugees from India's neighboring countries by privileging Hindus, Christians, and Buddhists—while denying comparable rights to Muslim immigrants—despite the fact that India's constitution explicitly identifies itself as secular.

Two decades ago, Modi was chief minister of Gujarat province when a murderous pogrom was launched against Muslims there that resulted in more than 2,000 civilian deaths. Although it was not formally conducted by the government, it also was not stopped by security forces. When asked if he regretted this outcome, Modi replied that he would regret the death of a dog under the wheels of his car: not a sentiment likely to reassure a vulnerable and persecuted population, or human rights activists!

In Myanmar (still called Burma by most Burmese) the military-controlled government has exploited episodic attacks by insurgents from its minority Rohingya Muslim community to engage in large-scale imprisonment, mass murder, gang rape, arson, ethnic cleansing, and possible genocide. These actions have resulted in nearly one million terrified Rohingya seeking refuge in neighboring countries, notably Bangladesh (which lacks adequate resources to care for them). Especially demoralizing for human rights advocates is that in 2019, Aung San Suu Kyi, a Nobel Peace Prize recipient who has been long known as a prodemocracy dissident, vigorously defended these actions at the International Court of Justice. Her supporters claim that she is seeking to balance her civilian authority against the still-powerful military.

China's treatment of its Muslim Uighur minority (a Turkic ethnic group of about 11 million persons) is another example of state-sanctioned human rights violations. Most of China's provinces are designated "autonomous regions," which means that they are nominally under local control, although they are actually governed by Han Chinese, who have installed puppet regional leaders. China's Uighurs largely inhabit Xinjiang province, where they have long been exploited ad discriminated against by ethnic Han Chinese. When a small-scale violent opposition movement by Uighurs was formed, the Beijing government used this as an opportunity to crack down, establishing prison-like "re-education camps," closing mosques, and installing an intrusive surveillance system. These human rights violations have evoked only mild criticism from other states, and although the government in Beijing may have temporarily tamped down Uighur resistance, the likelihood is that they will have generated immense resentment from those affected and—like most severe violations of basic liberty—will ultimately generate yet more unrest.

Promoting Human Rights

It is difficult to imagine exactly what a foreign policy, for any country, would be if it were organized primarily around the promotion of global human rights. However, the following specific actions, which have already been taken in different places at different times in support of human rights, suggest the benefits to be gained from a continuation and expansion of such policies, both by individual countries and also, whenever possible, the international community as a whole.

1. *Subtle diplomacy.* Quiet, persistent pressure applied to offending governments has the advantage that the government in question need not worry about losing face if and when human rights abuses are corrected. There may, however, be a disadvantage to subtle diplomacy beyond the possibility of its simply being ignored—namely, that a government may claim to be employing subtle diplomacy while actually doing nothing.

2. *Public statements.* This involves drawing world attention to specific abuses and to governments that violate human rights. It may include publicly dissociating one's own government from the unacceptable behavior of another. Human rights compliance can be promoted by the publication of reports of human rights violations. These documents gain widespread credence if the investigations have been conducted by respected, impartial commissions. Most governments seek to avoid the embarrassment that comes with being branded a violator of internationally acknowledged human rights.

3. *Symbolic acts.* Sending support to dissidents, either verbally, by contact with opposition figures, or by otherwise indicating disapproval of abuses, is a way of emphasizing to both the offending government and its people that human rights violations are noticed and decried.

4. *Cultural penalties.* If isolated as human rights offenders at international cultural events, including athletic exhibitions and other exchanges, the governments held responsible may become pariahs. National pride and the desire to be accepted add weight to such actions.

5. *Economic penalties.* Applying trade embargoes, calling for disinvestment in the offending country, and refusing to give development loans and other forms of foreign aid can hurt the economies of offending countries, thereby increasing pressure on the wealthiest and most influential citizens to modify abusive policies and/or oust the government. Both cultural and economic penalties were applied to the apartheid regime of South Africa. Even greater economic sanctions have been applied to North Korea. However, in this case economic penalties have been largely ineffective in changing the North Korean regime's behavior, in part because this "hermit kingdom" is already very isolated and also because its porous border with China, is unavailing in stopping trade between those neighboring countries.

6. *Immigration.* Human rights activists, dissidents, and those deprived of their human rights can be permitted to emigrate to receptive countries. In the past, the United States applied this "right" selectively, facilitating immigration by people fleeing leftist-governed countries (notably Cuba and Venezuela), whose human rights policies the United States has severely criticized, while restricting entry for refugees from rightist-led countries allied to the United States and whose human rights policies American administrations have been inclined to ignore or whitewash.

7. *Legal approaches.* International law can be applied more vigorously by identifying, indicting, and, when possible, arresting and trying overseas violators of human rights, just as some criminals involved in the international drug trade have occasionally been indicted and, when possible, extradited for trial. Such actions could serve as a substantial deterrent to future outrages.

8. *Multilateral approaches.* Countries can commit themselves to the various human rights organizations now active worldwide, especially the UN Commission on Human Rights. There are many other possibilities, such as the regular publication of a UN-sponsored catalog of human rights abuses, subject to international scrutiny. Regimes with disproportionately large military spending tend generally to be the worst human rights abusers, in part, perhaps, because the leaders of such states are usually acutely aware of their own instability and, accordingly, they invest in military power as a hedge against domestic unrest or civil war. At the same time, excessive military spending drains funds that might otherwise be available to help secure socioeconomic rights. Thus, the ratio of military to domestic national spending could be publicized for each state, and governments could be expected to explain and justify their priorities.

9. *Destabilization and regime change.* The United States has actively sought to destabilize the governments of certain countries (including the Sandinista-dominated government of Nicaragua, Castro-led Cuba, and the Chavez and Maduro regimes in Venezuela) because of their alleged human rights abuses. If it is to be seriously considered or used, the option of regime change, although of questionable legality and morality, ought to be applied even-handedly to all regimes that flagrantly violate human rights, regardless of ideology. The human rights abuses of Nazi Germany and imperial Japan may have served as justifications for the US decision to make war against them, although these abuses actually became more serious *after* war was declared. The Tanzanian invasion

of Uganda in 1979, which ultimately toppled the government of Idi Amin, won widespread support because Amin's human rights record was especially egregious.

A Final Note on Human Rights

In the short run, a country's respect for its citizens' human rights can be destabilizing once the citizenry detects possibilities that run counter to the policy of an existing government (as in the former Soviet Union and, more recently, in Hong Kong). But, in the long run, political stability—either within a state or between states—can best be maintained by the institutionalization of all human rights, socioeconomic as well as political. Thus, human rights not only are compatible with genuine personal and national security, but are necessary for it.

In the face of human cruelty, frailty, misunderstanding, power blocs, and *Realpolitik,* securing human rights is extremely difficult, conjuring up the Greek myth of Sisyphus, who was condemned to spend eternity pushing a boulder up a hill, only to have it roll back again. Yet, as the existential philosopher Albert Camus pointed out in a famous essay, "The Myth of Sisyphus," there may be no greater testimony to human dignity than the struggle to achieve such apparently "hopeless" goals. But unlike the fruitless labor of Sisyphus, sometimes human rights have been established, defended, and even expanded.

Questions for Further Reflection

1. To what extent can human rights be seen as an umbrella concept consisting of most of the social/political agendas of peace activists?

2. Compare a natural law approach to human rights (in which these rights are seen as belonging to all human beings) with the legal positivist approach, which restricts rights to those specified by common law.

3. What should states do when support for human rights appears to conflict with national security? Be specific with regard to one or more current cases.

4. The United States has consistently been inclined to define human rights in political rather than socioeconomic terms. Why? Agree or disagree with this policy.

5. In 2002, British prime minister Tony Blair stated in a speech at a Labour Party conference, "Our values are not Western values. They are human values, and anywhere, anytime people are given the chance, they embrace them." Agree or disagree.

Suggestions for Further Reading

Philip Alston, Ryan Goodman, and Henry J. Steiner. 2007. *International Human Rights in Context: Law, Politics, Morals.* New York: Oxford University Press.

Jack Donnelly. 2017. *International Human Rights.* New York and London: Routledge.

David P. Forsythe. 2012. *Human Rights in International Relations,* 3rd ed. New York: Cambridge University Press.

Michael Goodheart. 2016. *Human Rights: Politics and Practice.* New York: Oxford University Press.

Hurst Hannum. 2019. *Rescuing Human Rights: A Radically Moderate Approach.* Cambridge, UK: Cambridge University Press.

Lynn Hunt. 2008. *Inventing Human Rights: A History.* New York: Norton.

Paul Gordon Lauren. 2011. *The Evolution of International Human Rights: Visions Seen,* 3rd ed. Philadelphia: University of Pennsylvania Press.

Samuel Moyn. 2019. *Not Enough: Human Rights in an Unequal World.* Cambridge, MA: Belknap Press.

Notes

1. Quoted in J. Bentley. 1984. *Martin Niemöller.* New York: Free Press.

2. Simone Weil. 1952. *The Need for Roots.* New York: Putnam.

3. Betty Reardon. 1985. *Sexism and the War System.* Syracuse, NY: Syracuse University Press.

4. Testimony to the Senate Committee on Foreign Relations, 1980.

5. Reinhold Niebuhr. 1960. *Moral Man and Immoral Society.* New York: Scribner.

6. Karl Jaspers. 1961. *The Question of German Guilt,* trans. by E. B. Ashton. New York: Capricorn.

19

Environmental Well-Being

The word *ecology* comes from the Greek *oikos*, meaning "house." It refers to the interrelation of living things with other living things (e.g., plants, animals, and microorganisms) and with their physical environment (e.g., climate, rocks, water, and the Earth's atmosphere). Despite widespread dreams of space travel and the discovery of thousands of exoplanets outside our solar system, some of them possibly life-bearing, good planets are hard to find. For the foreseeable future, human beings have only one home, Earth, which also houses millions of other species, many becoming extinct and virtually all of them intimately connected to each other and, ultimately, to us.

An interesting milestone was reached in 2020: The total mass of all human-made objects (dominated by concrete and various aggregates) exceeded that of all living things. Moreover, the total "anthropogenic mass" has been doubling about every two decades, with the weight of buildings and other infrastructure already exceeding that of all the trees and shrubs on Earth, and the dry weight of plastics having become greater than that of all animals. Geologists have increasingly agreed that a new era, the Anthropocene, should be recognized, acknowledging the emergence of human beings as a uniquely powerful influence on the planetary environment. Regrettably, this influence is not altogether benign.

Enhanced Environmental Awareness

Environmental awareness has emerged fitfully over the centuries. Within the United States, it did not begin to achieve widespread public attention until the last third of the 20th century, in large part as a result of a number of worries that seemed to surface more or less simultaneously: increased public dismay about air and water pollution, the effects of persistent pesticides, worldwide reduction in biodiversity, anxiety about climate change, overpopulation, diminishing energy supplies, and others.

For a time, many social activists saw environmental concerns as a distraction from socioeconomic needs and even, in some cases, as a plot by Western economic elites to ensure the continued underdevelopment of impoverished countries. Now, the dependence of human beings on their planetary environment is clear to most observers; not only human happiness but human survival depends on the maintenance and proper functioning of natural systems. In addition, many people working closely with social movements in developing countries are convinced that environmental/ecological/resource issues are at the heart of their struggles. The web of life has been fraying; positive peace requires that it be rewoven or, at least, that the destruction must be slowed, eventually halted, and where possible, allowed to regenerate on its own.

From 1980 to the Present

By the 1980s, substantial progress in raising ecological awareness had been made in the United States, both in legislation and in public attitudes—but much of the environment itself continued to deteriorate, at least in part because of political policies that prized short-term economic growth over the natural environment. As part of their strong commitment to free enterprise, most political conservatives have remained opposed to government intervention on behalf of environmental protection, preferring to leave markets as free from regulations as possible, regardless of the environmental impact. Others, especially economic libertarians, argue that they are committed to sound environmental stewardship but that this goal will most effectively be achieved by relying on unfettered free-market mechanisms.

Environmental concern has become widespread in other countries as well. The Green Parties of Europe periodically make strong showings in national elections, especially in German-speaking and Scandinavian countries and in elections to the European Parliament. The environment has recently been very much on the front pages of the world's media: heat waves and droughts, alternating with occasional severe flooding, validate the overwhelming scientific consensus that climate change is real and is largely human-induced. (Global climate change is so pressing and well documented that it receives its own treatment in Chapter 20.) Far more people die each year because of environmental catastrophes than as a result of terrorist attacks.

Fires have ravaged the American West, including Yellowstone National Park, large swaths of California, as well as huge tracts in Mexico, the Brazilian Amazon, Greece, Australia, Portugal, Spain, and Indonesia. In Iran, the nation's largest lake, Lake Urmia, has shrunk by more than 80 percent as a result of climate change, irrigation for agriculture, and the damming of rivers that constituted a major contributor to Iran's cultural heritage as well as the livelihood—now destroyed—of thousands of Iranians.

The Earth's protective ozone layer has been thinning, dangerously and perhaps irreversibly. Nuclear accidents at Three Mile Island in the United States (1979), Chernobyl in the Soviet Union (1986), and Fukushima in Japan (2011), combined with the revelation that US nuclear weapons plants had secretly and recklessly fouled thousands of acres with radioactive waste, have tarnished the image of nuclear power as a "pollution-free" energy panacea. Waste disposal has become a worldwide problem, along with toxic contamination and floods exacerbated by forest destruction. Famines scourge Africa, soils are increasingly degraded, and the human population has surged to more than seven billion. The world's rainforests have diminished rapidly, and biodiversity has been drastically reduced, with many charismatic species (including giant pandas, tigers, rhinos, gorillas, and elephants), as well as a host of lesser known ones, pushed to the edge of extinction.

According to biologists and paleontologists, the Earth has experienced five major extinctions, in which a large proportion of its species have been decimated. Such events as asteroid impacts were especially involved. Our planet is currently experiencing a sixth major extinction, due to human intervention. Accordingly, the term *Anthropocene* has come into vogue, referring to a geological/biological epoch for which *Homo sapiens* is largely responsible.

The Environment and National Security

A world at peace must be one in which all living things are "at home." This does not require a state of perfect, unchanging harmony; indeed, the world has never known an extended period of stasis. Life itself involves change: consumption, synthesis, metabolism, locomotion, reproduction, competition, disintegration, and evolution. But life also depends on fundamental, underlying stability, at least in the long run—that is, over hundreds, thousands, or even millions of years. In recent times, some of the crucial relationships among the world's species and between those species and their environments have become increasingly tenuous, and this in turn has begun to threaten the quality of life for humans and nonhumans. It also threatens to undermine the integrity of our fundamental life-support systems: the air we breathe, the water we drink, the food we eat, and the diverse fabric of life that provides emotional and intellectual sustenance.

One of the most important shifts in human thinking has been the growing realization that national security must be defined in broader terms than just militarily. As our planet becomes increasingly interconnected politically, economically, culturally, technologically, and socially—and also increasingly endangered—the health, well-being, and security of every individual becomes gradually inseparable from the health, well-being, and security of the Earth. In his famous "strategy of peace" speech, delivered at American University in 1963, President Kennedy noted,

> We are devoting massive sums of money to weapons, that could be better devoted to combating ignorance, poverty and disease . . . . We

all inhabit this same small planet. We all breathe the same air. We all cherish our children's future. And we are all mortal.

Our connectedness—to each other and to other forms of life—is emerging as something beyond rhetoric or metaphor. Observing the growing numbers of species pushed to extinction, many people feel a sense of foreboding for the future. In the looming threats to clean air, clean water, and the integrity of the Earth's atmosphere, and in an era of diminishing resources, many people are recognizing threats to their own well-being that are as real as any military threat emanating from an armed opponent.

Prominent ecological thinkers maintain that human beings have an obligation to be something other than a predatory and destructive species. Rather, we must exercise wise stewardship over the planet's wild things and wild places, not just for our own benefit but as an ethical imperative. Environmentalists also see the connection between despoiled, depleted, and polluted lands and human misery. We cannot fully make "peace" until we make peace with our planetary environment.

Moreover, in responding—albeit belatedly—to environmental threats, we will not be running the risk of anything like the "security dilemma," in which military preparedness threatens to bring about the danger it is intended to surmount. Environmental sensitivity and protection seem likely to be largely win-win propositions, although there are also economic, social, and political conflicts to be faced and costs (at least in the short term) to be borne. Nonetheless, environmentalism, once considered an indulgence of the rich, is increasingly recognized as fundamental to a decent life for everybody.

In the absence of dramatic environmental disasters, public attention rarely focuses on the continuing plight of a silently deteriorating planet, except during such widely publicized natural catastrophes as earthquakes, floods, hurricanes, tsunamis, droughts, and fires, many of which are increasingly recognized as being human-influenced, by climate change in particular. Some of the most serious and adverse environmental effects (including climate change, resource depletion, and pollution) may not become fully apparent until later in this century, but if we wait until then before acting, we may well have foreclosed the opportunity to intervene effectively. As with the prevention of war, the prevention of ecological disaster requires that we intervene before catastrophe actually takes place, after which effective responses would be much more difficult and perhaps impossible.

The Tragedy of the Commons

A model first described in a much-noted scientific article by ecologist Garrett Hardin[1] helps us understand one of the key social factors underlying environmental problems. It considers the situation that long existed in pre-industrial Great Britain, in which some grassland was privately owned and another part, the "commons," was shared property of the community at large. Various citizens owned livestock, which they could graze on their own private lands or on the public commons. Overgrazing was harmful to the productivity of the grassland, so shepherds generally avoided overgrazing their own property. But they treated the commons differently: The shepherds recognized that a healthy commons benefited everyone, but each also reasoned that if they refrained from grazing their animals on the commons, others would probably take advantage of this restraint and fatten their flocks on the public lands. As a result, tendencies to be prudent and ecologically minded were suppressed because individuals concluded that if the commons were going to be degraded anyhow, they may as well be in on the profit. The result was deterioration of the commons, until it was no longer fit to support sheep or shepherds.

The tragedy of the commons, then, is that individuals—each seeking to gain personal benefit—find themselves engaging in behavior that hurts everyone. It is somewhat similar to the Prisoner's Dilemma, with all participants choosing to "defect" or be "nasty" (and exploit the shared environment) rather than to "cooperate" and conserve the resource. This model can be generalized to situations in which short-term perceptions of self-interest conflict with the long-term public good. For example, there may be immediate, selfish benefit for a factory owner to use the atmosphere as a public sewer; after all, even though their effluents pollute the air, the cost is borne more or less equally by everyone who breathes, whereas the owner personally is saved the expense of having to install pollution control devices.

It is the same with overuse of resources. If it is inconvenient to recycle and easier for individuals simply to throw their garbage "away" or to use more than their share of scarce commodities, they may derive some personal gain or enhanced convenience by doing so, while the cost—in overcrowded dumpsites or worldwide resource shortages—is diffuse and generally borne by all. Besides, if they don't abuse the environment, someone else will (which is just what the flock owners told themselves about the commons).

The tragedy of the commons has global dimensions: Scandinavian forests and lakes were polluted by acid rain because of the effluents of English smokestacks while Britain benefited. Japan, Norway, and Iceland periodically defy international outcry while hunting the world's great whales to the verge of extinction. Brazil benefits economically from the Amazon rainforest, even though logging, burning, and poaching are rapidly destroying the trees that have been described as "the lungs of the planet."

Some Major Environmental Problems

The best-known and quite likely the most serious environmental problem facing the planet is the global climate crisis, an issue so pressing that it will receive a separate chapter. The rest of this chapter focuses on other environmental issues, all of which must ultimately be mastered in order for positive planetary peace to be achieved.

Pollution

Modern industrial societies produce large amounts of byproducts, many of them toxic, such as pesticides, herbicides, nitrates, phosphates, heavy metals, petroleum products, and numerous other toxic substances, including contamination from military uses and abuses of the air, water, and soil. For many years, the atmosphere, fresh waters, and the oceans have been considered publicly owned (which is to say, unowned—another commons) and thus suitable for cheaply dumping all manner of unwanted substances. Automobiles spew out vast quantities of additional air pollutants, as do power generators and the widespread, large-scale burning of forests and grasslands, especially in the tropical, developing world. The American Lung Association estimates that air pollution alone is responsible for $45 billion in annual damage, counting medical expenses as well as damage to crops and buildings. And this is just in the United States, where air quality standards are among the highest in the world.

Even though industrialization generates much air and water pollution, wealthier countries still tend to have cleaner air and water, on average, than poorer ones. Because pollution control devices can be costly, they are often unaffordable for those poor countries. Environmental protection has thus become a luxury that most developing countries cannot afford, but in the long run, they cannot afford *not* to protect their environments. At present, many multinational corporations preferentially establish factories in countries where poverty and politically pliant leadership have resulted in low standards of environmental protection. The air in Mexico City, Manila, Beijing, Delhi, São Paulo, Lagos, and Mumbai, for example, is among the worst on Earth. Major rivers in such regions are often little more than open sewers.

This problem, however, is not intractable. Industrial pollution can be greatly diminished, not only by end-of-the-pipe treatment of effluents but also by reducing the waste stream itself. Nations do not have to wallow in their own toxic excrement, polluting the air and water and poisoning those people who usually cannot afford to live in safer, cleaner environments. A modest tax on carbon and other emissions can go far toward stimulating conservation and pollution reductions, although the decision makers of many domestic industries—and many developing countries—object vigorously, complaining that such a tax would inhibit their ability to compete internationally. Therefore, innovations of this sort would probably be most acceptable if adopted by many states simultaneously.

Attempts to respond in this manner have been bedeviled by demands from developing countries that they be given special dispensation when it comes to curtailing toxic emissions because their comparative poverty necessitates that they be permitted to develop their economies with minimal restraints. Moreover, because the wealthy, developed countries attained their status in part by despoiling the environment with minimal or no restraints, any insistence by them that the poorer countries act with ecological responsibility smacks of demanding that these countries act as the others say, not as they already did! Meanwhile, developed countries tend to insist that all states, rich and poor alike, should be treated equally.

Wealthy countries (notably the United States) argue that poorer countries should not be granted special privileges, especially when, as in the case of India and China, they have become huge mega-industrial states. In 2011, China exceeded the United States as the world's number one emitter of greenhouse gases, especially carbon dioxide, although per capita, the US remains far "ahead." China, however, argues that because it is still comparatively "underdeveloped" on a per capita basis, it shouldn't be held to the same standards as the countries of western Europe and the United States.

Pollution is not only hurtful but also wasteful. In a resource-limited world, mercury belongs in thermometers, not in fish; sulfur belongs in matches and pharmaceutical drugs, not as sulfuric acid in dead lakes, and so on. Environmental protection can thus be good economics as well as good ethics, with beneficial consequences in terms of diminished cost for health care and enhanced opportunities for fisheries, forestry, hunting, and ecotourism, among others. Thus, a thorough cleanup of air and water has practical benefits as well as ethical advantages. To make such changes, however, requires up-front capital investments.

There are signs of cooperation in cleaning up the planet, along with growing public awareness of the problem. International protocols have been signed restricting emissions of nitrogen, sulfur, and chlorofluorocarbons (which eat away the ozone layer) and reducing the production of greenhouse gases, notably carbon dioxide. Progress in this respect, however, has been slow, such that despite a worldwide scientific consensus as well as increasing political recognition of the problem, much-ballyhooed international meetings have generally accomplished little except for setting laudable goals and guidelines. A Law of the Atmosphere, comparable to the Law of the Sea, would be immensely helpful but does not seem likely in the near future—especially so long as many of the world's economies continue to struggle in the aftermath of the Covid-19 pandemic, in many cases having not even recovered from the 2008 Great Recession.

Nuclear energy constitutes one of the most pernicious environmental problems, even for economically developed nations (including France and Japan), which have come to rely on it for a significant percentage of their energy needs. Despite claims of the nuclear power industry, military contractors, and the government, nuclear power is not "clean." In the United States alone, more than 100 commercial reactors plus a handful of weapons reactors (as well as several hundred naval power plants) produce an average of 30 metric tons of nuclear waste per reactor per year. To this environmental risk must be added nuclear power's potential for weapons proliferation. Many experts believed that Iran, for example, was developing a nuclear weapons capability under the guise of civilian nuclear power. In addition, there are as-yet unresolved problems related to the permanent disposal of nuclear waste, which must be safely isolated for tens of thousands of years—longer than human civilization has existed.

In the aftermath of a huge tsunami in 2011, and the resulting destruction and partial meltdown of Japan's Fukushima nuclear power plant, Japan temporarily closed all of its nuclear reactors, and Germany pledged to end entirely its reliance on nuclear energy by 2022. This is especially notable for countries with advanced technological capacity that had been considered world leaders in the generation of "safe" electricity from nuclear power and—especially in the case of Japan—are lacking in indigenous energy resources and, accordingly, have been expected to be in the forefront of civilian nuclear power reactors. This emphasizes the uncertainty about nuclear energy's future, even as some observers and more than a few nuclear engineers, university departments, and corporations with a large investment in that technology tout its desirability as a nonpolluting alternative to fossil fuels.

Energy

As population increases globally, especially in less-developed countries, and industrialization along with it, the demand for energy rises exponentially. Although technological innovation (including the generation of energy from coal, oil, hydropower, nuclear power) has to some extent enabled economic development to continue despite the extraordinary increase in demand, the Earth's energy resources are limited. Moreover, all standard sources of energy employed thus far carry significant environmental downsides.

Wood

Wood burning, for example, is utilized throughout much of the world as a means of cooking and heating; however, it produces huge quantities of pollutants, including carbon dioxide, while also contributing to the planet's tragic deforestation, which is especially acute in the tropics, as well as to pulmonary diseases for people who cannot afford to cook outside dwellings in which wood is burned.

Coal

Nor is coal any better, even the supposed "low sulfur" variety. In addition to the overt destructiveness of coal mining, the burning of coal generates considerable amounts of carbon dioxide emissions, and although so-called clean coal is trumpeted as being on the horizon, it is a myth; the necessary technology simply does not exist. Moreover, cost-effective carbon dioxide sequestration technology has yet to be developed, let alone implemented. Natural gas is somewhat cleaner than coal, although as a heat-trapping gas, methane—released in huge quantities in extraction wells—is roughly 30 times more potent than is carbon dioxide. The burning of oil, too, releases large quantities of greenhouse gases, while oil wells, pipelines, and super-tankers regularly pollute the oceans.

Oil

In 2010, a devastating oil spill in the Gulf of Mexico from the BP Corporation's Deepwater Horizon offshore well was a dramatic example of just how costly energy extraction can be. The explosion killed 11 workers and spilled upward of 5 million barrels of oil into the Gulf of Mexico. This disaster exposed major structural flaws in US federal oversight of offshore drilling, including a cozy relationship between the oil industry and its ostensible regulators in the Interior Department.

BP eventually paid $14 billion in cleanup costs, $6.3 billion in damages to individuals and businesses, and pledged another $7.8 billion in additional payments, once subsequent claims are evaluated. (BP also changed its logo, apparently seeking to minimize the bad publicity associated with its earlier image.) This corporation is also likely to owe several billion dollars for damages to natural resources under the Oil Pollution Act, and approximately $14 billion in penalties under the Clean Water Act, after a court found BP guilty of "gross negligence."

The devastation from this spill was augmented by the fact that prior to the event, Gulf Coast wetlands and barrier islands were already seriously compromised by rampant industrialization and mismanagement of the Mississippi River as well as by Hurricane Katrina. In addition, Arctic conditions are such that a spill in the far North would be even more difficult to control and to remediate, although pressure for Arctic oil exploration and drilling continues, especially in the Arctic National Wildlife Refuge, strongly encouraged by the Trump administration, which aggressively rolled back many anti-pollution laws and regulations, especially any initiated by the Obama administration. As testimony to the costs and uncertainties associated with Arctic undersea oil exploration and drilling, Royal Dutch Shell eventually abandoned its Arctic drilling efforts, after having invested $7 billion in a high-stakes bet that didn't pay off.

Significant amounts of oil have been extracted from the tar sands of north-central Canada. Extracting this resource is very energy intensive and produces immense quantities of greenhouse gases. The Obama administration had vetoed applications for the controversial Keystone XL pipeline intended to carry tar sands oil to US gulf ports, a decision greeted with enthusiasm by environmental activists, but which was then reversed by the Trump administration, under which former oil, coal, and gas lobbyists were appointed to such agencies as the Department of the Interior and the Environmental Protection Agency. The Biden administration then cancelled this pipeline project once again and reversed many of the anti-environment measures of its predecessor.

Natural Gas

Although natural gas has been touted as a relatively "clean" energy source, it, too, produces carbon dioxide when burned. Hydraulic fracturing, or "fracking" (which extracts natural gas from rock formations by injecting high-pressure water to reduce friction between underground geological faults) in the United States, Canada, and elsewhere has caused significant chemical pollution of the underground aquifers that are increasingly being tapped for domestic, agricultural, and industrial use. In addition, these operations caused a large and unanticipated increase in the number and severity of earthquakes, especially in Oklahoma, which has exceeded California in seismic activity.

Renewables

At the same time, and on the "glass half full" side of the world's energy ledger, there remain several possible routes toward energy sufficiency via renewable sources. The amount of energy reaching the Earth via sunlight is more than enough to meet future demand. Efficient, affordable photovoltaic systems can be designed and employed. And even though US federal energy subsidies for renewable energy are only about one-fifth of those awarded to the fossil fuel industry, the cost of solar energy, for example, has dropped precipitously. In 1977, the average global price of installing solar panels was $76.67 per watt. Less than 45 years later, it is just 52 cents per watt and dropping rapidly, at a rate of 14 percent per year. Similarly, in just 10 years, from 2009 to 2019, the cost of wind power generation fell by 68 percent, at a rate of 7 percent per year. These dramatic declines are more like what consumers have come to expect from digital technology—that is, with computing power increasing and costs decreasing—and they raise the hope for an affordable and renewable energy future. Discounting current federal subsidies for coal, gas, and nuclear power generation, it is now cheaper to build new renewable energy facilities than to continue to operate existing fossil fuel plants.

This means that with a cooperative federal government, a switch to renewables could be accomplished with little or no economic disruption. Prospects are similarly encouraging for eventually harnessing tidal and photosynthetic sources. In the short term, considerable energy savings—equivalent to putting a whole new generation of coal- and oil-fueled power plants on line—could be generated by such simple and low-tech solutions as improving household and industrial insulation, lowering thermostats by 1°F or 2°F, mandating higher automobile fuel-efficiency standards, and so forth. Technological improvements in battery storage and efficient line transmission of electricity are also underway, although government subsidies available for researching and developing such advances are dwarfed by those showered on the fossil fuel and nuclear industries.

Ozone Depletion

When near the ground, ozone (O_3), a molecular form of oxygen, contributes to air pollution, especially photochemical smog. But in the upper atmosphere it is beneficial, absorbing dangerous ultraviolet radiation and preventing it from reaching the ground. (Excessive ultraviolet exposure can cause sunburn, skin cancer, and blindness.) Several decades ago, atmospheric scientists noted that the ozone layer, especially above the Antarctic, was rapidly thinning. Major culprits include chlorofluorocarbons (CFCs), chemicals that are widely used in industry (e.g., as aerosol propellants and refrigerants) and in the manufacture of polystyrene.

The precise causes of ozone depletion have been difficult to establish, and even its effects are diffuse. Unlike wars, epidemics, and famines, atmospheric deterioration generally does not photograph well or lend itself to dramatic 30-second sound bites. But for all its subtlety, atmospheric ozone depletion is no less real. This is once again a kind of tragedy of the commons, in that individuals, or individual industries, have little motivation to behave responsibly toward the atmosphere unless others are persuaded or coerced into behaving similarly. The same applies to countries: Unless all states can be persuaded to act together, there is little motivation for anyone to act separately. There is an immediate economic cost, for example, in forbidding the use of CFCs, or, for that matter, taxing carbon emissions. But the ultimate benefits more than compensate for the costs.

When it comes to ozone depletion, substantial international cooperation has already been achieved. In a great success for the United Nations Environment Programme, most of the world's heavily industrialized countries agreed in 1987 to the Montreal Protocol on Substances that Deplete the Ozone Layer, pledging a dramatic cut in CFC production. Although ozone depletion is only one of the many environmental problems that require attention—and, in the opinion of most experts, overall levels of ozone in the atmosphere will not recover to pre-1980 levels until 2060 to 2075—the Montreal Protocol represents an important victory for environmental consciousness and planetary hygiene, and it serves as a beacon for future pro-environment treaties.

Even in this case, however, the situation remains less than satisfying. Although the Montreal Protocol has greatly reduced the rate at which the ozone layer is deteriorating, hydrofluorocarbons (HFCs), the chemical substances used to replace CFCs, are several thousand times more active than carbon dioxide as a greenhouse gas. And the use of air conditioning, which requires large quantities of HFCs, has skyrocketed in recent years, especially in India and southern China, warm regions that are also undergoing rapid economic growth. Fortunately, environment-friendly alternative chemicals exist, but their introduction has been slowed by patent disputes, government inertia, and political pressures.

Threats to Tropical Rainforests and to Biodiversity

The world's tropical rainforests are the greatest repositories of biological diversity on Earth. Among the most endangered forests, they cover only about 7 percent of the Earth's surface but are home to 50 percent to 80 percent of all plant and animal species (by taxonomic variety, not the total number of individuals). Of the estimated 5 million to 30 million species on Earth, fewer than 2 million have been identified. It is difficult to assess their value to *Homo sapiens,* but seen as entities in themselves, every species is irreplaceable and priceless. Each contributes to the marvel and beauty of the world and many have a beneficial, stabilizing impact on its ecosystem. In addition, rare species often prove to be of direct human benefit—for example, by providing raw materials for the treatment of cancer and other diseases.

More than one-third of all plant and animal species (excluding fish and invertebrates) live exclusively on 1.4 percent of Earth's land surface. These "hot spot" regions are concentrated in the tropics, especially in Madagascar, East Africa, Brazil, the Congo, Borneo, Sumatra, a few other Southeast Asian islands, the tropical Andes, and the Caribbean. This concentration of life forms underscores the risk of extinction but also suggests the possibility that if humanity focuses on the protection of a relatively small total area, substantial amounts of the world's biodiversity can be preserved.

However, the search by agricultural interests for land, combined with governmental support for "development," have resulted in the destruction of vast amounts of tropical rainforests, notably in South America, Africa, and Indonesia. Regions that are most threatened include the island of Madagascar (home to many unique, "endemic" species), where more than 90 percent of the original vegetation is gone; the eastern slope of the Andes; the monsoon-prone rainforests of the low Himalayas; the Atlantic coastal forest of Brazil; and much of Malaysia. Fewer than 5 percent of the world's tropical forests are under any protection whatever, and those that are often are protected on paper only: They remain subject to extensive poaching, lumbering, grazing, and so on, largely because of human poverty and locally dense populations.

Tropical rainforests lie mainly in economically developing countries, which are often very poor and thus eager for economic improvement, even if the "gains" are only short-lived. Moreover, these countries tend to suffer from high national debt and lack funds to make their loan payments. Some Central American countries, for example, clear their remaining rainforests to raise beef so as to earn money from US fast food restaurants, and many Southeast Asian states export teak and mahogany, similarly destroying their own countryside in return for short-term gains (which tend to benefit only a tiny proportion of the local population).

Many economic developers tend to think that because rainforests are so biodiverse, their soils must be highly productive. But these soils—characteristic of hot, wet habitats—are typically high in laterite, consisting of iron and aluminum compounds, with their organic richness contained almost entirely in the organisms inhabiting it, not in the soil itself. (Lateritic soils derive their name from the Latin word for "brick.") Once the above-ground plant material is removed, they revert to a kind of hard, nearly impenetrable, red-brown pavement, unsuitable for agriculture or much else. (The famed temples of Angkor Wat, in Cambodia, which have stood for many centuries, are largely built of lateritic clay.)

About 11 million hectares of tropical forests—roughly the area of the US state of Virginia—are cleared annually. More than 8 million hectares of Brazilian rainforest are burned every year to clear land for cattle ranching. In his book *Earth in the Balance,* former US vice president and Nobel Peace Prize–winner Al Gore asked, "If, as in a science fiction movie, we had a giant invader from space clomping across the rainforests of the world with football field–size feet—going boom, boom, boom every second—would we react?"[2] His point is that the equivalent of this is happening right now in rainforests around the world.

As awareness of the plight of the rainforests has increased, so has international pressure on those countries that are currently devastating their own forests. But this also raises difficulties. For example, having abused their own environment (also making themselves rich in the process), North Americans and western Europeans are on shaky moral ground lecturing Brazilians to refrain from doing to the Amazonian "frontier" what they have done to their own.

A major environmental and social challenge in developing countries is to emulate the prosperity of the industrial states without repeating their mistakes. Conservation efforts must also contend with fierce nationalism, often evoked when the wealthy North lectures the impoverished South about what the latter should do with its land.

Brazil, for example, has its ancient battle cry, *A Amazônia é nossa* ("The Amazon is ours"). Following centuries of destructive ecological, political, and economic imperialism worldwide, Europeans are on questionable grounds in urging the Indonesian government to spare its watersheds. Imagine the response if the British government had sought to prevent the United States from slaughtering its own indigenous bison herds during the 19th century; it would have been good environmental advice but almost certainly deeply resented. Accordingly, it will not be easy to persuade inhabitants and governments in poor countries—or the rest of us, for that matter—that the Amazon, the upper Congo watershed, the New Guinea lowlands, and, indeed, the entire planet, belongs to all of us.

Some global ecological trends are worrisome. Insect populations have plummeted worldwide, with major consequences for the numerous animal species that feed on them, as well as for plant pollination and for ecosystem stability generally. According to the "Living Planet Report" produced by the World Wildlife Fund, the situation for vertebrates "is not for the faint-hearted," with representative populations of mammals, birds, reptiles, amphibians and fish having declined by nearly 60 percent since 1970. Nor has North America been spared: a 2019 study found that roughly three billion birds have disappeared there during that same time frame. Jair Bolsonaro, elected president of Brazil in 2019, has shown no sympathy for preserving the Amazon (the world's richest storehouse of biodiversity) and instead, favors logging, mining, and other forms of "development," while many policies of the Trump Administration were not only unsympathetic but downright antagonistic to the natural world.

But there is also cause for hope. Worldwide awareness of the plight of the rainforests continues to increase. Funds have been established to help preserve these irreplaceable regions. The field of restoration ecology has gathered momentum, investigating ways to restore previously devastated lands. Local governments have started realizing that their own economic, social, cultural, and political health requires that they preserve a healthy environment. Organizations such as the World Wildlife Fund and Conservation International have been experimenting successfully with "debt for nature swaps," in which the external debt of certain developing countries is purchased at a substantial discount (say, 50 cents on the dollar) and then used, in turn, to purchase nature reserves. In this way, such countries as Ecuador and Bolivia have been able to retire some of their debt while also preserving some of their natural environment—to everyone's benefit.

The relatively new field of ecotourism has also been blossoming, giving countries that are wildlife-rich but cash-poor a financial incentive to preserve their living resources. Rwanda, for example, has been able to reap substantial income by providing opportunities for wealthy nature-loving tourists to observe free-living gorillas. (The alternative is to clear the forests and destroy the gorillas for short-lived subsistence farming, which is also less remunerative.) More than 20 percent of Costa Rica's land is now protected, much of it in national parks, and if the worldwide environmental movement continues to be politically influential, other countries can be expected to follow suit. Costa Rica has been able to lead the way in this regard in part because it constitutionally abolished all of its military forces in 1948—retaining only police and a modest coast guard—and has been able to use the money saved to preserve its environment, as well to provide subsidized education and health care for its citizens.

Renewable Resources

A fundamental principle of environmental stewardship is that we must respect the natural cycles on which all life depends. There is no viable alternative to such forms of global balance as those between carbon emissions and carbon fixation; between soil erosion and soil formation; between tree cutting and burning, tree planting and growth; and between births and deaths. In the long run, we cannot take more away from the land than we—or nature—put back. Moreover, we must plan for the long run. A commitment to positive peace recognizes that it is ethically unacceptable, and ultimately impractical as well, to purchase short-term gratification and growth while robbing future generations. Whereas it is relatively easy for most people to see the foolishness of "mining our capital" when it comes to a personal bank account, or such nonrenewable resources as metals and petroleum, it is less obvious, but no less important, to behave responsibly with regard to renewables.

Forests and Food

One of the most important renewable resources involves the production of food. Nontechnological farmers obtain small yields, and are often thought to be inefficient compared with modern high-tech agriculture. In fact, however, much of the productivity of agro-industry is achieved by using vast amounts of energy. On average, every calorie expended by nontechnological farmers (as human and animal labor) yields 5 to 50 calories of food energy. By contrast, the intensive mechanized farming practiced in the United States expends 5 to 10 calories of energy (mostly as petroleum, some as fertilizer and pesticide) to produce just a single calorie of food. The United States grows a lot of food, but it does so by expending even more energy, which not only contributes to global warming but also depletes some of the most important nonrenewable resources, namely fossil fuels, while also adding greatly to the atmosphere's carbon dioxide burden.

Forests and soils are especially worrisome cases of renewable resources that are being disrupted, that is, treated in a nonrenewable manner. Over geological time, for example, soils were formed more rapidly than they eroded, which bequeathed us a life-sustaining layer of topsoil averaging about 6 to 10 inches deep worldwide. But deforestation, erosion, overgrazing, and the like have dangerously degraded this natural legacy. It may be difficult to believe today, but in ancient times, Northern Africa was the granary of Rome. Now, much of North Africa is desert, and desertification is advancing south across Africa at a frightening pace. Unlike drought, desertification—a major threat to soil—is not a natural event but rather the consequence of human mistreatment of the environment, whereby the rich organic material is washed or blown away, leaving relatively coarse rocky materials that cannot retain moisture and sustain plant life, and which in turn contributes to yet more erosion and further degradation. The resulting sand dunes or gullies are nonproductive and very difficult to reclaim, even as a wildlife habitat.

It is possible, fortunately, to turn the tide on forest loss. Tree planting on a massive scale can partially help mitigate anthropogenic climate change, reverse erosion, and improve water and air quality, while also providing fuel and wildlife habitat. South Korea has begun to do just this, China has begun adopting such a strategy, and India has at least developed a forward-looking plan to reclaim its forests. Trees grow back, and reforestation is generally feasible, so long as money is available and developers understand the long-term need for conservation while restraining their short-term search for profits—a tall order.

In the United States today, farmers lose about six tons of topsoil for every ton of produce grown. Atmospheric sensing stations in Hawaii can detect when spring plowing begins in China because of the increased particulate matter in the atmosphere when airborne soil is lost to the land. Worldwide, approximately 25 billion tons of topsoil are lost to erosion every year; this is nearly equivalent to the total topsoil covering the wheat lands of Australia.

As population increases, especially in the poorest countries, marginal land is brought under cultivation, leading to further erosion by wind and water, desertification, and additional loss of long-term productivity. Until the mid-20th century, worldwide crop production increased in part because additional lands were brought under cultivation. Further increases in agricultural yields were achieved during the 1950s and 1960s through the "green revolution," which combined improved genetic varieties and fertilizer use with the cultivation of new land to increase the production of such grains as wheat, especially in India. But the limits of such advances are rapidly being reached: Per capita productivity in much of Africa, for example, has begun to decline, and there are no major new regions—anywhere—that can be brought under cultivation, at least not for long.

Overuse of existing croplands can also exact a heavy price on the land. In addition to desertification and erosion, millions of acres of cropland are being destroyed by salinization: When underground soil drainage is insufficient, irrigation water—loaded with fertilizer and other salts—puddles up and evaporates, leaving a human-made saline desert, which already covers vast areas of previously productive land and is expanding rapidly.

The World Bank has introduced the concept of "food insecure," which refers to those people who lack enough food for normal health and physical activity. Central African states (including Ethiopia, DR Congo, Uganda, Chad, Somalia, Sudan, and Mozambique) are especially food insecure. Moreover, developed states may not be immune to food insecurity. By the end of the 20th century, for example, the US grain harvest fell below consumption for the first time in recent history.

The destruction of productive soil is very difficult, but not impossible, to reverse. Overgrazed and overcultivated land can and should be allowed to lie fallow, sometimes for many years. Land that is especially vulnerable must be taken out of active production. The United States has led the way in this regard; the Food Surplus Act is intended to shift millions of acres of highly erodible land into meadows or forests. (This does not represent a sacrifice. Such land is not highly productive, and, moreover, it cannot produce worthwhile yields for very long before being degraded.)

The principle of sustainability applies to forest and grassland growth and to their regeneration as well. If we destroy more than is created, we are cutting into the productive substance of the planet. And such imbalance cannot continue for long. If we cut and burn more than grows in that same period, the underlying resource is diminished, weakened, and ultimately destroyed.

In most developing countries, forest cover is declining precipitously, through logging, land clearing, and firewood gathering. In only eight years, for example, India lost 16 percent of its forest cover; as a result, fuel wood prices in India's 41 largest cities increased by nearly one-half, exacting a painful toll on that nation's poor. It doesn't take a degree in mathematics or forestry to see that such trends cannot continue for very long without having devastating effects on wildlife, soil formation and maintenance, water quality, atmospheric equilibrium, agricultural productivity, and human well-being.

Acidification

In Central Europe and North America, acid rain generated by industrial air pollution, especially by coal-fired power-generating plants, has already damaged up to 25 percent of the forests and rendered thousands of lakes uninhabitable for fish and other aquatic life. Forest destruction, in turn, leads to soil erosion, degradation of water quality, and increased runoff of water; for example, years of forest destruction in the Himalayan foothills above Bangladesh contribute to frequent and devastating floods, which take an enormous toll in lives and property.

Ocean acidification is another problem. About 25 percent of anthropogenic (human-produced) carbon dioxide dissolves in the oceans, where it produces carbonic acid, which lowers the pH of seawater. It is estimated, for example, that over the past two-and-a-half centuries, the acidity of the oceans has increased by nearly one-third and, at the current rate, is expected to increase to 150 percent by the year 2100. The exact effects of ocean acidification are unclear, but is known to decrease the amount of carbonates dissolved in seawater, which in turn has an effect similar to that of osteoporosis in human beings: It softens and weakens bone and shells produced by animals such as corals, mollusks, and vertebrates, and appears instrumental in the catastrophic decline of coral reefs worldwide. And coral reefs are not just extraordinarily beautiful; they have the highest biodiversity of any ecosystem. Comprising only about 1 percent of the ocean floor, they harbor upwards of 25 percent of its marine life, including spawning grounds for many blue water species.

Some Environmental Principles

These environmental concerns (plus others, too many to be detailed here), exemplify several important general themes:

1. *Political boundaries are virtually irrelevant to the world's ecology.* Forest cutting in northeastern India, Nepal, and Bhutan results in widespread destruction downstream, in Bangladesh. Carbon dioxide emissions in central Beijing contribute to catastrophic rise in sea levels, which threatens to flood the Marshall Islands.

2. *Environmental issues are the legitimate concern of everyone, not only affluent people.* Poor people—and often poor countries—are typically located where the environment has been most severely abused and are

liable to suffer the most from environmental disasters. The concept of "environmental justice" is receiving increasing attention, but warrants considerably more.

3. *Environmental abuse can generate short-term profits but invariably at the cost of long-term declines, both environmental and economic.* Natural systems underpin all national economies; as the former deteriorate, so do the latter. As a result, sensible policies must reflect environmental wisdom no less than economic, social, and political realities.

4. *Natural processes must be respected.* Human beings can intervene in those processes—we can unbalance them and sometimes even restore them—but we cannot transcend them. Francis Bacon (1561–1626) wrote, "Nature, to be commanded, must be obeyed," a useful warning, but with the addition that it is questionable whether in the long run nature can be commanded at all.

Environmental Activism

In the United States

Within the United States, environmental activism is largely expressed through legislation and direct citizen participation. Legislative environmentalism involves the passing of laws designed to protect environmental values, to preserve wild and open space, to restrict pollution by establishing air or water standards to which states and local municipalities are required to comply, to prohibit the sale of materials derived from endangered species, to punish toxic polluters, and so forth. A landmark piece of legislation passed in the early 1970s requires that before the government expends federal funds on any project likely to produce adverse environmental impacts, an Environmental Impact Statement must first be prepared and evaluated; this statement must employ scientific studies to evaluate the extent of the impact and whether harmful effects can be diminished. Such impact statements should also provide impartial assessments whether the project should be permitted to go forward.

Legislative remedies are often incomplete, in part because governments are frequently hesitant to enforce regulations they see as harmful to business interests, which include mining, oil drilling, grazing, and manufacturing. This was especially true of the Trump administration, whose political appointees were often former lobbyists and senior employees of the industries they were supposed to oversee, and who also used executive orders to void or circumvent environmental protections. Moreover, the warnings of scientists—from climate change to the health impact of hazardous chemicals—were deeply undermined by that administration. In such cases, citizens may have access to legal procedures, such as obtaining court injunctions to prevent illegal actions and, in some cases, to force governments to enforce their own laws. Anti-environmental activism also exists and is likely to persist beyond the role of the federal government, manifested, for example, in right-wing militia movements—especially in some Western states—that oppose federal ownership and protection of public land.

Environmental law has nonetheless grown rapidly, and such groups as the Environmental Defense Fund, the Natural Resources Defense Council, and the Center for Biological Diversity regularly bring polluters and habitat despoilers to court; there has also been some progress in identifying environmental values (the right to clean air, clean water, and an environment with wildlife) as having legal standing comparable to personal property rights or the right to privacy.

Finally, there is the question of direct action, analogous in many ways to nonviolent antiwar resistance. Such groups as Greenpeace have blockaded whaling ships and sewage outfalls and, by a variety of dramatic and often courageous acts, including boycotts and sit-ins, called public attention to other environmental abuses, such as the clubbing of baby seals and improper disposal of nuclear waste. These acts of nonviolent resistance often include civil disobedience and can be controversial. For example, the environmental organization Earth First! has resorted to ecological sabotage ("ecotage") by vandalizing land-clearing equipment or "spiking" trees (hammering large nails into the wood, thereby making it dangerous to log them). Governments have occasionally responded with violence and even state terrorism, as when French intelligence agents blew up the Greenpeace vessel *Rainbow Warrior*, which had been protesting French nuclear weapons testing in the South Pacific.

Nonetheless, environmental movements worldwide continue to be strong, although there seems little immediate prospect for US electoral success of a Green Party modeled after its European equivalents, some of which have had considerably electoral and extra-parliamentary successes. There is also a risk that some of the energy and enthusiasm for environmental protection will be co-opted by corporate activities that are environmentally destructive but are misleadingly presented as beneficial: so-called greenwashing.

In Other Countries

Grassroots environmentalism has, if anything, developed more strongly in other countries, especially those less imbued with an ethos of unrestrained and minimally regulated predatory capitalism and the Western-inspired credo that human beings are "created" independent of the natural world. One of the most remarkable examples of grassroots environmentalism is the Chipko, or "Hug-the-Tree," movement of India. Beginning in the 1970s, Chipko developed in remote villages in the southern foothills of the Himalayas. It arose spontaneously, based on a cultural heritage that holds deep respect for the region's lofty mountains, magnificent forests, and clear streams. A series of disastrous floods, resulting from extensive deforestation, induced local activists literally to hug the great trees and, in time-honored Gandhian fashion, to lie down in front of logging operations. The Chipko strategy has since been used to save other natural areas in India and has also spread to other countries, where environmental concern is often most strongly developed among the poor, who rely most deeply on the land.

Similarly, in South America there is a campaign by indigenous Amazonian tribes, rubber tappers (who earn their living extracting the latex secreted by free-growing rubber trees), anthropologists, and environmentalists against land development interests, especially in Brazil. There, ecological exploitation has been intimately connected with violence—notably genocidal extermination of whole villages and indigenous tribes—by private "armies" hired by landowners, often abetted by the military. Since the 2019 election of a right-wing ultra nationalist-populist, Jair Bolsonaro, as president of Brazil, such outrages have become more frequent.

Small-scale grassroots organizing is nonetheless occurring worldwide on behalf of the environment and its people. There are tens of thousands of community development groups in India alone, and their focus, increasingly, is on ecologically sensitive, sustainable development. Similarly, more than 100,000 "Christian base communities" have sprung up in Brazil, while comparable groups in Africa and Asia have been prominent in struggling for local reforestation, soil preservation, and the like. The 2004 Nobel Peace Prize, for example, was awarded to Wangari Maathai, a Kenyan who founded the Green Belt Movement, an environmental organization that combines women's rights with a commitment to sustainable development and countrywide tree planting.

Under United States law, only persons have legal rights. Destruction of a forest, river, or ecosystem cannot be opposed for the sake of the natural feature itself. In American legalese, an entity must have legal standing in order to bring a lawsuit or criminal complaint, and traditionally, only people possess this option. Ironically, therefore, trees do not have standing! Although natural features can be the object of litigation (e.g., injunctions to prevent cutting down a forest or draining a lake), legal action must be brought on behalf of *people* who claim to be harmed thereby, not for the sake of a natural phenomenon itself. And yet, in a controversial 2010 decision (Citizens United v. Federal Election Commission), the US Supreme Court ruled that corporations possess "legal personhood," which overturned previous restrictions when it comes to election spending.

In a number of countries, a movement has developed to expand the concept of personhood to include various natural entities and, as stated by the Earth Law Center, "to recognize and protect nature's inherent rights to exist, thrive and evolve." As a first step, this approach has been applied to rivers, with a proposed Universal Declaration of River Rights, which defines certain basic rights to which all waterways are entitled, as determined by both international legal precedent and ecological principles of river health.

A law passed in Mexico in 2017 recognized that "rivers, channels and streams possess a right to flow, a right to avoid harmful alterations to ecosystems and biodiversity, a right to be free from contamination, and a right to rescue and rehabilitate important water zones." Also in 2017, New Zealand's national legislature bestowed legal personhood on the Whanganui River, passing a law whereby two (human) guardians—one chosen by the government and one by the Maori people—will act as legal representatives of the river system. Ecuador's legislature provided similar legal personhood to that country's Vilcabamba River. These developments represent potentially wide-ranging precedents on behalf of protecting nature more generally from human despoliation.

However, the tide has not yet turned from ecological destruction to environmental protection and sustainability. Every year, the planet seems, on balance, to be losing rather than gaining ground in the struggle for its preservation. There has also been a worldwide tendency for environmental activists—often allied with human rights workers on behalf of indigenous peoples—to be persecuted by governmental authorities, who stand to make large amounts of money by permitting destructive land-use and resource-extraction policies.

Struggling for Sustainability

Some of the world's great ancient civilizations—Sumerian, Mayan, and Roman—appear to have declined in part because they were destabilized internally by depletion of their underlying resource base. Today, very few knowledgeable people question the desirability, or even the necessity, of a sustainable world economy. There is considerable debate, however, over the best route to sustainability as well as about when the limits to growth must be faced.

Some people retain faith that technology will somehow save us, as it was often claimed in the past. Indeed, it is always possible that some technological breakthrough is waiting just around the corner, which, like computers and the Internet, will dramatically change our current way of life, leading to truly clean energy and a sustainable future. Others maintain that the Earth is blessed with abundant resources, natural as well as human, that are sufficient to see us through any crisis that will arise, at least for the foreseeable future, especially because, as resource shortages arise, prices increase, which tends to lead to diminished resource use, along with a more vigorous search for alternatives to the current destruction of the global ecosystem.

Faith in Technology

One line of thinking is that as resources are used up, the ensuing shortages will serve as incentive to (1) find new reserves; (2) reduce the rate of consumption, for example, by increasing efficiency; and (3) substitute abundant resources for those in short supply, such as making telephone lines out of fiberoptic tubes instead of copper. Necessity (or, more precisely, reduced supply and resulting higher prices) may be the mother of invention, as a resource-poor world finds new solutions to old problems. In the recent past, fossil fuels largely replaced wood and animal power in providing energy for heavy industry, and aluminum, to some degree, has supplemented iron as a construction material. New resources, new forms of energy, and new ways of replenishing the Earth may be just over the horizon.

The difficulty with such thinking is that innovations cannot be counted on, whereas the depletion of known resources is certain. Moreover, even when they do prove successful, such "solutions" often carry with them a new array of problems. The advent of automobiles was initially hailed as an environmental triumph in the making, destined to clean up city streets by replacing manure-making horses with "clean" internal combustion engines. Fossil fuels currently pollute the atmosphere, high-technology mining operations are often energy intensive themselves, and so on. A starry-eyed confidence that technology or inventiveness will always save us may well become a tragic disappointment. At the same time, fuel-efficient hybrid cars now exist along with growing numbers of fully electric vehicles (which nonetheless require electricity, however generated), just as hydrogen cell technology may be on the horizon.

Thresholds

Many environmental experts fear that there could be key thresholds in the planetary environment that, once crossed, could permanently impair the Earth's ability to meet our needs in the future. If the atmospheric load of greenhouse gases becomes too high, for example, the ozone layer too sparse, soils too eroded, and air and water pollution too severe (or some combination of these and other factors), or if forest clearing and desertification go too far, at some point the planet may simply become incapable of nurturing life, regardless of subsequent attempts to repair the damage. Thus, the current generation of humans has the responsibility of orchestrating the habitability of our planet, not just for people but also for other living things.

Time is not on our side: Soil, once eroded, can take centuries to be replenished; certain forms of contamination (including plastics, nuclear waste, and long-lived pesticides) will probably be around longer than human history has thus far endured; the atmosphere, once warmed and carrying an excessive carbon dioxide load, may be impossible to cool; and species, once extinct, cannot be reestablished. At the same time, however, there may arise a movement—somewhere between science and wishful thinking—that seeks to engineer the "de-extinction" of certain species, based on DNA technology. Even this seemingly unobjectionable goal may have its drawbacks, if undue confidence in its prospects leads to less concern with preventing species' extinctions in the first place.

Human Perception

Many dramatic human achievements require that a perceptual threshold be crossed. Before this happens, relatively few people have deep dissatisfactions with the status quo; the result is business as usual. Then, charismatic leaders, catastrophic events, and/or successful education campaigns may combine to force a rapid perceptual shift, after which the world appears transformed, and sometimes people then transform it in reality, too. These events often have a distinct ethical/religious component, but self-interest may also be effective: Consider the abolition of slavery and of hereditary monarchies and—increasingly—worldwide revulsion against nuclear weapons. It may be that with the various combined threats to the worldwide environment and the intense publicity they have generated in recent years, ecological wholeness will finally receive the attention—and inspire the action—it warrants.

Interconnections

A world at peace is one in which environmental, human rights, and economic issues all cohere to foster sustainable growth and well-being. Ecological harmony cannot realistically be separated from the defense of human rights and the struggle for economic justice. The right to a safe and diverse environment, clear air, and pure water is no less a human right than the right to freedom of expression or dissent, equal employment opportunity, and participation in the political process.

Ecological well-being and economic justice cannot be achieved piecemeal. The rainforests will continue to be abused so long as there are too many people on too little land; indeed, overpopulation has an impact on most environmental issues. Poverty in developing countries often leads to land degradation as hungry, desperate people are likely to clear and cultivate regions that should be left untouched. The burning of fossil fuels produces air pollution as well as greenhouse gases. Global warming will increase food insecurity by reducing agricultural productivity, perhaps catastrophically; accordingly, solutions to these and other problems must be tied to providing adequate, safe energy. By the same token, poverty in urban, developed regions can also lead to severe environmental injustice.

Environmental degradation is also intimately connected to poverty: Wealthy states are often able to export their most odious environmental abuses (sometimes literally, as in the case of toxic materials), and impoverished states are often forced to accept the situation because they need the payments that they receive in return. The plowing of steep, erosion-prone slopes (which permanently destroys soil) and large-scale intrusions onto wildlife habitats (which contribute to species extinction and loss of biodiversity) are in large part a response to land hunger by the impoverished in rural countries, where a small minority of wealthy people own most of the arable land, thereby pushing the less affluent to engage in environmentally destructive behavior, simply to survive. In addition, wealthy people are able to purchase environmental amenities and thus some insulation from ecological destruction, while the poor find themselves living in polluted, degraded surroundings.

Even within wealthy countries, the poor are often forced to endure environmental abuses that are not only degrading and soul-destroying (due to the absence of attractive natural areas and the presence of persistent trash and other forms of pollution) but also dangerous and possibly life-threatening. Chemical factories and storage sites are usually located in the least affluent neighborhoods, whose inhabitants are accordingly vulnerable to such chronic diseases as asthma, allergies, and cancer.

Environmental racism has likely been involved in some lesser-known scandals in the United States. For example, toxic coal ash from a catastrophic spill in Kingston, Tennessee (majority white), was sent to several landfills in neighboring states, with most of it going to a landfill in Uniontown, Alabama, a rural community with nearly half of the population living below the federal poverty line and which is 80 percent African American. A similar disparity appears to be the major reason African Americans in the part of Louisiana known as "cancer alley" become ill at higher rates than mostly white areas elsewhere in the state, and the most polluted zip code in Michigan is in part of southwest Detroit, which is 84 percent black.

A notorious example of environmental racist destruction occurred in 2014 in Flint, Michigan, which switched its water supply in an effort to save money, and, because appropriate care was not exercised, lead from old pipes then leached into the water and into the bodies of unsuspecting residents, most of whom are poor and African American. This poisoned water will almost certainly have serious, irreversible, long-term medical effects, especially on children. It is unlikely that state officials would have been so cavalier about their actions if the affected population had been largely white and wealthy.

For the most part, however, environmental problems are integrated. Many of the most severe ecological threats, such as global warming, are worldwide in scope. Others, such as the loss of species diversity, although occurring within national boundaries, affect the world economy and/or the global quality of life. Deforestation in Nepal causes flooding in Bangladesh; water overuse by the United States deprives Mexico of the Colorado River; pollution of the Rhine by Swiss and German chemical industries makes its water toxic for the Dutch who live downstream; and whaling by the Japanese and Norwegians destroys these magnificent animals.

Finally, environmental and social issues are interlocking. Population stabilization will likely occur only when poverty is reduced, developing countries will be able to devote themselves to the preservation of their unique wild resources only if their debt burden is relieved, and energy use will be sustainable only if it does not burden the air and water with additional pollutants. World cooperation on issues concerning the environment is as necessary as cooperation on economic and public health matters, or as international solidarity on issues of global security and war prevention.

Tensions Between Economics and the Environment

In the long run, there should be compatibility between economic needs and ecology because what destroys the environment also, in the long run, destroys economies. But economic planners usually look to the near future, and, in the short run, the push for jobs, profits, and development often conflicts with environmental preservation. Air and water pollution controls can be expensive, and installing such preventive measures can make an industry unprofitable (at least in the short run), leading to plant closings and loss of jobs. A sustainable environment may necessitate that wetlands be preserved—to absorb variations in the water table and to control floods, as breeding grounds for fish and other aquatic organisms, etc.—but such preservation may come at the cost of such restrictions on development as fewer new shopping centers, housing sites, and industrial parks.

Ultimately, however, economic development and environmental protection are not incompatible. Millions of people rely directly on the natural surpluses produced by a healthy environment: harvesting fish from wild populations in oceans, rivers, and lakes; hunting game from the land; and obtaining fuel from the forests. A Mauritanian cattle herder does not need advanced training in ecology to know that "the land is tired," nor does a Filipino fisherman require a degree in marine biology to recognize that fish don't thrive where the ocean is polluted. Guatemalan peasants know the consequences of plowing land that is too steep, and it is not only wealthy, amateur bird watchers who mourn the loss of such dazzling animals as the quetzal, a bird that has special significance for many Central Americans.

All of us, not just rural folk in underdeveloped nations, depend on stable hydrological cycles for water, atmospheric processes for air, a stable world climate, and the productivity of organic soils. Nonetheless, battle lines still continue to be drawn between those who see themselves as defending the environment and those who champion jobs and economic development.

For example, China's spectacular economic growth correlated, at least in part, with its enthusiastic embrace of a unique form of state-sponsored, relatively unregulated capitalism, along with considerable indifference toward ecological abuse, especially the world's heaviest reliance on burning coal. Not coincidentally, China has also suffered from some of the world's most horrible environmental problems—notably air and water pollution. For example, in Hebei Province, 75 percent of the premature deaths recorded in 2018 (many of them suffered by infants) were due to the 152 coal-fired power plants in that region. China has been leading the world in the manufacture of solar panels and is also the world's largest consumer of solar energy; simultaneously, air pollution is greatly reducing the efficiency of these devices. On the other hand, one advantage of an authoritarian command economy is that very rapid corrections can be made and hundreds of millions of people quickly mobilized (as during the Covid-19 pandemic, which appears to have first struck central China), and the Chinese government has recently begun moving vigorously to correct its decades of severe environmental abuse.

There is quite often a tension between economic growth and environmental values. In the Pacific Northwest of the United States, for example, a major controversy erupted between conservationists and the timber industry. A rare bird, the northern spotted owl, nests only in relatively large, undisturbed tracts of old-growth forest. But the trees in these forests are also coveted by logging companies. It remains to be seen whether a lasting accommodation can be reached in this and other acute conflicts between economic demands and local ecology. In the long run, like the spotted owl, a successful timber industry requires a continuing supply of trees. Accordingly, it seems not only possible but also necessary that a win-win solution be achieved, because neither the economy nor the environment can survive if the other is decimated.

Political Ideologies

Some Western critics of environmental policies assume that capitalism is largely to blame; after all, an economic and political system that exalts profits above everything seems unlikely to prize environmental values. The industrialization of capitalist states was, and continues to be, intimately connected to a range of environmental abuses. But many "socialist" states have been also been insensitive to environmental issues. For example, rigid adherence to production goals, regardless of environmental consequences, combined with state ownership of the "means of production" made the tragedy of environmental abuse even more widespread in China, North Korea, and the former Soviet bloc than in most market-oriented societies.

A significant difference between traditional economics (whether market-oriented or centrally planned) and sustainable economics is that the former is usually concerned with how to produce as much as possible for as many people as possible at the present time, whereas the latter expands the definition of "for whom" to include future generations.

In the several Asian states that were formerly part of the Soviet Union, the once-majestic Aral Sea has dropped at least 40 feet because of destructive, short-sighted dam and irrigation projects. The Neva River, which runs through the heart of historic St. Petersburg, Russia, has long been befouled with oil. Swimming is regularly curtailed at Black Sea resorts because of typhoid and dysentery contamination. Environmental restrictions on the development of Siberia are almost nonexistent and the few existing ones are often ignored—although environmental conditions are, if anything, even worse on the Chinese side of the border.

The demand, especially by affluent Chinese, for elephant ivory and rhino horns for decoration and use in traditional East Asian medicine have been primary drivers of the decimation of some of our planet's most iconic species. Forest destruction in the former East Germany, the Czech Republic, Slovakia, and Hungary—initiated while those now EU members were under Communist Party–led regimes—is among the most severe on Earth, and many regions of Poland are drastically polluted by chemical and other toxic waste.

It has been said, "The difference between capitalism and communism is that in the former, man exploits man, whereas in the latter, it's the other way around!" In both cases, it is the environment—and, ultimately, everyone—that loses.

Making Environmental Peace and Avoiding Regional Conflicts

A world of increasingly scarce and endangered resources might be one in which people are motivated to cooperate for everyone's benefit. But it could also be one in which conflict and violence are intensified, as wealthy states seek continuing access to raw materials or simply to retain their advantages in the face of growing demands from the "have-nots," while poor nations attempt to exploit fully their scarce existing natural resources for sustenance and survival. There is an increasing risk, especially in large swaths of Asia, South Africa, and Africa, that ecological scarcity will engender regional wars, which, in addition to their human toll, destroy yet more of the environment.

Resource Wars

The prospect of "resource wars"—over water, oil, natural gas, mineral deposits, and so on—looms as a very real threat. In 2012, Sudan and the newly formed South Sudan came to blows over oil fields controlled by the South. Yemen, in addition to experiencing a ruinous civil war, teeters on the brink of becoming the first country to run out of water, and limited water availability (from the Jordan River) has been emerging as a major source of tension between Israel and Jordan. Prior to the outbreak of its devastating civil war, Syria had undergone the severest 4-year drought in its modern history. This, in turn, drove almost a million farmers to the cities, especially to Damascus and Aleppo, where the Assad government was unable or unwilling to provide for them. This, in turn, appears to have fueled the subsequent antigovernment protests and the escalation of hostilities to a full-fledged civil war.

Although governments are only rarely blamed directly for environmental disasters—the Soviet government during the Chernobyl nuclear accident being a notable exception—they threaten to disrupt the implicit social contract whereby citizens expect that their governments will act for their benefit in return for patriotic allegiance. In recent decades, the world has been largely spared the horrors of major interstate wars (civil wars are bad enough, and when it comes to brutal ferocity, often worse). The risk of major resource wars looms as well. Thus, Pakistan has shown substantial internal instability, at least in part because of the social impacts of global climate change on its rural majority. When it comes to the crucial resource of water in an already dry environment, India and Pakistan both depend on the Indus River, whose upstream sources are controlled by India. With increasing global warming, there will almost certainly be reductions in overall flow of the Indus—likely exacerbating lethal tensions between these two already contentious countries—punctuated by occasionally devastating floods. On the other side of the subcontinent, the Brahmaputra River is vital for both southern China and eastern India, and its origin is controlled by China, which has already proposed constructing several dams, threatening to strangle India's water availability.

In Africa, Egypt and Ethiopia have been engaging in an increasingly aggressive dispute produced by Ethiopia's construction of the $4.5 billion Grand Ethiopian Renaissance Dam. When complete, it will be Africa's largest, producing huge amounts of electric power for the Ethiopian economy but also threatening to significantly reduce the water flow downstream in the Nile River, which Egyptian farmers have depended upon for thousands of years, and which most of Egypt's population relies upon for water—an especially precious resource in a desert environment. The resulting political conflict has stoked deep-seated fears, aggressive nationalism in both countries, and even periodic threats of war.

Because of climate change, for the first time in modern human history, the northern ocean will soon be navigable in summer, leading to enhanced overt competition—which has already begun—between claims by the US, Russia, China, and others. Conflicting claims based on international law along with military maneuvering has generated increased activity and positioning of personnel and weapons at US bases in Alaska, northern Norway, and Greenland, matched by Russian countermoves at its large submarine bases in Murmansk and elsewhere. These troublesome actions have been stimulated by expectations that the largely untapped northern polar region has substantial quantities of valuable minerals and vast stores of natural gas.

The future, however, is still salvageable, although this requires the prevention of war and an active dedication to positive peace. This calls for public as well as private commitments to invest heavily in environmental protection and restoration. Such investments require time, effort, and money, none of which can be adequately provided without sufficient awareness of the need. The following goals are minimal but also achievable:

1. Reforesting the Earth and stopping current deforestation

2. Slowing and eventually stabilizing population growth

3. Increasing energy efficiency

4. Further developing and greatly expanding currently available renewable energy sources while reducing reliance on coal, natural gas, and nuclear power

5. Retiring Third World debt (so these countries can invest in environmental protection and restoration)

6. Protecting topsoil from erosion, desertification, and salinization

7. Preserving representative, adequate-sized samples of the planet's pristine ecosystems and its wildlife

8. Protecting the air, water, and land from harmful, persistent pollution

9. Halting, and, if at all possible, beginning to reverse the drastic overheating of the planet

Such accomplishments will not come cheaply. Some estimates suggest that they will require annual expenditures, over the next few decades, in the range of $250 billion per year. (The US Government General Accounting Office estimated in 2019 that it will cost about $377 billion just to clean up the existing mess at US nuclear production facilities.)

A habitable, sustainable planet is clearly worth such an investment in our planet's future. Moreover, even a price tag of $250 billion annually is only about one-fifth of the world's annual military expenditures, more than half of which is spent by the United States alone. If national security is eventually redefined in broader terms than mere military security, to include global human well-being and planetary sustainability, such a transformation would be possible. After all, The Netherlands currently spends about 6 percent of its gross national product defending itself from floods emanating from the Atlantic Ocean, a far greater expenditure for its national security (and a far more relevant one) than its military-related NATO contributions.

Citizens of all countries can begin now to make a major effort toward improving the deteriorating state of the world's environment. A potentially encouraging note is that a total planetary change in awareness and behavior is not immediately necessary. There are key countries that, by acting decisively, could by themselves greatly mitigate our current environmental difficulties. For example, the United States, China, India, and the now autonomous states that constituted the former Soviet Union produce more than 50 percent of the world's carbon dioxide emissions; Brazil, Indonesia, and DR Congo hold 48 percent of all virgin tropical rainforests; China and India together account for 35 percent of the world's annual population increase; and the northern tier of industrial countries is responsible for virtually all the world's acid rain production.

Just as some people claim that "peace begins with me," strides toward environmental peace can begin with the actions of individual countries, not only to showcase what can be done but also to get results. Otherwise, it is possible that before the physical and biological limitations of the Earth take a more direct toll, a period of Hobbesian strife may ensue. Chaos and war—with their profoundly anti-ecological effects along with the better known immediate human catastrophes—would then add to the devastation. It remains to be seen whether environmental threats, even if global, will lead to a viable political mass movement of the inhabitants of our shared and endangered planet.

Environmental Ethics

This chapter—like the others in this book—has been partially motivated by a need to identify real-world problems and to suggest real-world solutions. However, just as there is an underlying ethics to peace studies itself (including the moral desirability of peace, negative as well as positive, and the iniquity of violence), we can also identify deep-seated ethical aspects of enhanced environmental awareness.

In Hindu culture, for example, human activity is, in principle, guided by the three life-affirming values: *artha* (resources), *kama* (the needs and desires of human beings), and *dharma* (right conduct, or what people *ought* to do as opposed to what they *want* to do). *Dharma* also involves the proper utilization of resources, restricting their use to the satisfaction of one's primary needs and not appropriating those of others. To do otherwise is to steal from those others and from the world. In this worldview, *dharma* consists of mediating skillfully and thoughtfully between desires and resources; there is therefore a close link between justice and ecological and social harmony.

As historian Lynn White pointed out in an influential essay,[3] the Judeo-Christian tradition has been quite different from important Asian cultural norms in that it emphasizes separation between human beings on the one hand and the rest of the biological world on the other. According to these mainstream Western religions, human beings were created in the image of God, and people are therefore in sharp contrast with the nonspiritual material world, including organic nature. Christians and Jews were biblically commanded to "go forth and multiply" and to "subdue the Earth." Having articulated distinctions between the human and nonhuman world, certain elements of Judeo-Christian teaching established a context for destruction and exploitation, providing the intellectual and emotional underpinnings to what has since become the planet's ecological crisis. Nonetheless, White concludes his essay by describing an alternative tradition in Western theology: the gentle, nature-centered, and compassionate ministry of Saint Francis of Assisi; he proposes Saint Francis as the patron saint of ecologists.

Other thinkers have also proposed the establishment of ethics on a less human-centered and more species-diverse basis. If human beings saw themselves as *part* of the life process rather than as its most powerful rulers, the result might be a kinder, more tolerant, and gentler way of living. Moreover, a growing trend in liberal Judeo-Christian theology stresses humans' responsibility to act as reliable stewards on behalf of "the creation."

In this regard, Pope Francis has emerged as a spiritual leader of the environmental peace movement, pointing out our collective ethical responsibility to protect the environment as an end in itself and also the extent to which the costs of resource abuse are borne disproportionately by the poor.

512 Part IV ● Building "Positive Peace"

In an address to the United Nations in 2015, he noted that "Any harm done to the environment is harm done to humanity. A selfish and boundless thirst for power and material prosperity leads both to the misuse of available natural resources and to the exclusion of the weak and the disadvantaged." In a Papal encyclical also released in 2015, Pope Francis connected the urgency of fighting global climate change to such issues as combating poverty and worldwide economic inequality. "The Earth, our home," he wrote, "is beginning to look more and more like an immense pile of filth." Chiding those who deny the problem, Francis explicitly blamed a "toxic cocktail" of "overconsumption, consumerism, dependence on fossil fuels and the errant indifference of the powerful and wealthy."

The great environmental struggles on which the future viability of the world's ecology depend will probably be played out during the first half of the 21st century. For the benefit of our planet and those species who depend upon it, humanity will have to see itself as part of planetary processes, not set apart from the Earth. Scholars and scientists should accordingly study the rate of soil erosion as closely as the rate of inflation, expending at least as much concern keeping up with air and water quality standards as with the stock market, as well as reconsidering basic questions about common benefit versus individual rights. Affluent individuals may be able to afford two automobiles, for example, or a large family, but can the planet?

China's current population is 1.4 billion, many of whom used to rely on bicycles as their primary means of transportation. In tandem with China's rapid economic growth has come a skyrocketing increase in automobile ownership, along with a corresponding decline in bicycle use. Given the huge environmental costs of automobiles compared with the comparatively benign impact of bicycles, it is daunting to consider the ecological impact if per capita Chinese automobile ownership begins to approach that of the United States, western Europe, or Japan.

Environmental ethics seeks to respect the natural world as having value in itself, not simply because of its possible utility or threat to human beings. It emphasizes that peace may ultimately require a much broader view of the human community, in which people are responsible not only for their own actions, the actions of other people, and their effects on other people, but also their effects on other life forms.

Judeo-Christianity has long had a code of religious ethics, the Ten Commandments. During the 18th and 19th centuries, it developed contrasting and sometimes conflicting systems of societal ethics: capitalism, democracy, liberalism, conservatism, and socialism. Perhaps what is needed from the 21st century is a code of environmental ethics.

A Final Note on Ecological Well-Being

An important lesson to be derived from the pursuit of ecological well-being is the idea of underlying planetary unity. As poet Francis Thompson wrote, "All things . . . near and far, hiddenly to each other connected are, that thou canst not stir a flower, without the troubling of a star."

Accordingly, any striving for peace must take account of this connectedness: of living things to the soil and the atmosphere, as well as to all other living things; of people to their natural environment, as well as to their human-made social systems and each other; of the past and present to the future of this planet; and of the risks and opportunities for everyone and everything.

Questions for Further Reflection

1. In what ways are environmental concerns also issues of national security as more traditionally defined? In what ways are the two different?

2. Explain how the following serve as examples of the Tragedy of the Commons: deforestation in India, the slaughter of whales, and global climate change. How can these and other situations be made less "tragic"?

3. It has been said that ecological awareness is a luxury to be indulged by the middle and upper classes. Agree, disagree, or take an intermediate position.

4. Demonstrate the connection—or, alternatively, the lack of connection—between ecological wholeness and socioeconomic processes by focusing on a current environmental controversy, either globally or in your local community.

5. It has been suggested that there may be "resource wars" in the future; describe some possible examples. It has also been suggested that there have already been numerous wars over natural resources; describe some possible examples.

Suggestions for Further Reading

Elizabeth Ammons and Modhumita Roy, eds. 2015. *Sharing the Earth: An Environmental Justice Reader*. Athens: University of Georgia Press.

Lester Brown. 2009. *Plan B 4.0: Mobilizing to Save Civilization*, 3rd ed. New York: Norton.

Michael Klare. 2019. *All Hell Breaking Loose: The Pentagon's Perspective on Climate Change*. New York: Metropolitan Books.

Elizabeth Kolbert. 2015. *The Sixth Extinction: An Unnatural History*. New York: Picador.

Aldo Leopold. 2001. *A Sand County Almanac*. New York: Oxford University Press.

Gerry Nagtzaam. 2019. *International Environmental Law*. New York: Routledge.

Peter Raven, David M. Hassenzahl, Mary C. Hager, Nancy Y. Gift, and Linda R. Berg. 2015. *Environment*, 9th ed. New York: Wiley.

David Schmidtz and Dan C. Shahar. 2019. *Environmental Ethics: What Really Matters, What Really Works*. New York: Oxford University Press.

Harriet A. Washington. 2019. *A Terrible Thing to Waste: Environmental Racism and Its Assault on the American Mind*. New York: Little Brown.

Richard T. Wright and Dorothy F. Boorse. 2016. *Environmental Science: Toward A Sustainable Future*, 13th ed. New York: Pearson.

Notes

1. Garrett Hardin. 1961. "The Tragedy of the Commons." *Science* 162: 1243–1248.

2. Al Gore. 1992. *Earth in the Balance: Ecology and the Human Spirit.* Boston: Houghton Mifflin.

3. Lynn White. 1967. "The Historical Roots of Our Ecologic Crisis." *Science* 155: 1203–1207.

picture alliance via Getty Images

The Climate Crisis

Our planet's climate crisis is often called "global warming," a phrase that now seems too mild and reassuring. After all, being warm is mostly desirable, whereas becoming overheated is not. Even "global heating" isn't quite adequate because the climate changes currently underway—not to mention those reliably predicted—are very serious (liable to be catastrophic if not mitigated), multidimensional, and possibly irreversible. Hence: climate crisis.

And it is indeed a crisis, a turning point in humanity's history on Earth, something that demands the attention of individuals, nations, social movements, as well as a planetary response. Although the situation is already dire, it is not yet hopeless. There might not be any quick, easy, and lasting solutions on the horizon, but there remains at least a real possibility of mitigation: in short, trying to keep a situation that is already very bad from getting a whole lot worse.

It is currently settled science that anthropogenic (human-caused) climate change is resulting in unprecedented and deleterious effects, including heating of the atmosphere, land, and oceans; rising sea level; increasingly intense and unpredictably severe climate events; and other harmful consequences. The good news, however (and there is some good news!), is that these effects, once understood and acknowledged, can be mitigated. It is not yet too late.

Causes of Global Climate Change

We start with a brief description of the causes of global climate change, recognizing that although this is not a textbook on climate science, understanding the underlying bases of global heating is in everyone's interest—climate mitigation advocates as well as skeptics and agnostics who aren't sure what to believe. As for the latter, we acknowledge the wisdom of Jonathan Swift when he wrote that people cannot be rationally argued out of a position that they have not been rationally argued into. We nonetheless believe that facts are themselves persuasive, and we hope that once the arguments have been clearly laid out, advocates will find their advocacy strengthened, skeptics will reconsider their views in light of the evidence, and agnostics will also be sufficiently persuaded by the facts that they'll join the great majority of fellow citizens and the scientists who are essentially unanimous in recognizing the existence of the crisis, its sources, and the urgent need for global action to address it. We start with an overview of the carbon cycle because this forms the basis for a scientific understanding of why planet Earth is now heating at an unprecedented level.

The Carbon Cycle

Since the mid-20th century, scientists have warned that human technology and economic "progress" have been disrupting the worldwide carbon cycle, one of many fundamental processes on which life on Earth depends. Under equilibrium conditions, a stable balance is maintained between various biogeochemical carbon "sinks" that store carbon, notably the atmosphere, oceans, living and dead organisms, and inorganic matter. Carbon moves among these natural reservoirs in a variety of ways. For example, atmospheric carbon dioxide (CO_2) is combined with water during photosynthesis to produce such carbohydrates as sugars, which provide energy for plants and, ultimately, all living things.

During metabolism, these carbohydrates are burned: not literally—rather, they are broken down in the presence of oxygen, thereby producing energy-rich molecules that can in turn be used to power the physiology of living things. Carbon is also used to produce the leaves, stems, and roots of plants. It is unusual in its ability to form an immense variety of chemical bonds, and it is the most abundant element found in the key organic compounds of all living things, which is why Earthly creatures are described as carbon-based life forms. When most animals metabolize their carbon-based fuel and then breathe it out, via respiration, carbon is returned to the atmosphere as carbon dioxide.

The carbon cycle also involves other processes. For example, when animals and plants die, their accumulated carbon is returned to the atmosphere via decomposition. Substantial quantities of carbon also accumulate in the soil, from which it eventually returns to the carbon cycle, but often in geological rather than short-term biological time. Carbon is also sequestered in various creatures such as mollusks (e.g., clams), arthropods (notably insects), and marine coral, where it contributes significantly to hard shells and exoskeletons. These, too, eventually rejoin the carbon cycle, but only after much time has passed.

Large quantities of CO_2 are dissolved in water, notably the oceans, to form carbonic acid (H_2CO_3), which contributes to acidification. Most of Earth's carbon is stored inorganically, in rocks (especially as limestone) and minerals; circulation of this form of carbon is the slowest of all. Finally, there is another carbon sink, one that is especially ominous with regard to anthropogenic climate change: fossil fuels.

There are two theories for the origin of hydrocarbon fuels. A minority view is that they were mostly generated by chemical reactions produced deep underground when inorganic ("abiotic") compounds containing carbon and hydrogen were subjected to high temperature and pressure for long periods of time (millions of years). Another, more widely accepted theory, is that hydrocarbons were produced when organic ("biotic") creatures died and were pressed into sedimentary rock, once again under the influence of great pressure and heat.

Coal appears to be largely the result of ancient plants having been squeezed and heated in this manner, while petroleum and natural gas resulted when the bodies of highly abundant small organisms such as diatoms, foraminifera, and planktonic algae underwent similar processes. This is why these commercially and industrially useful hydrocarbons are called "fossil" fuels. Regardless of the historical origin of hydrocarbon fuels, these substances comprise a huge carbon reservoir, one with special significance for global climate change.

Except for occasional meteor or asteroid impacts, the Earth is a closed system with regard to matter (not so for energy, much of which arrives from the Sun as direct solar energy). Therefore, the total amount of carbon on Earth remains constant, although it can be distributed in different ways among the major reservoirs: atmosphere, rocks and minerals, plants, animals, and oceans. In pre-industrial times, the amount of carbon in each of these natural sinks remained pretty much constant, with inputs closely matching outputs. But since the Industrial Revolution, the balance has shifted dramatically; the quantities of carbon compounds have greatly increased, especially atmospheric carbon dioxide, but also, importantly, methane (CH_4), surface-level ozone, nitrous oxides, and fluorinated gases, all of which trap infrared radiation from the sun, resulting in planetary heating.

Mechanism of Global Heating

During the 19th century, Svante Arrhenius, the Swedish scientist who founded the field of physical chemistry, worked out the basic quantitative measurements of how carbon dioxide heats the atmosphere, now widely known as the "greenhouse effect." Thus, the scientific basis for global heating has long been known. What is new is the extent and speed at which it has become a problem and also the ideological and political opposition (especially in the United States) to acknowledging and doing something about it.

Here's how the greenhouse effect works. Energy from the Sun reaches the Earth in several forms, notably as visible and ultraviolet light, along with some infrared (heat) radiation. Reflective surfaces—clouds, ice, and components of the upper atmosphere—bounce about 30 percent of this energy back into space. The remaining 70 percent is absorbed by the Earth's land and water, increasing their total temperature. But although most of the incoming energy from the Sun is not in the infrared spectrum and therefore readily passes through the atmosphere, the heat that is reflected back from the Earth itself is entirely in the form of infrared energy, most of which is then absorbed by certain gases in the atmosphere rather than passing back into outer space. As a result, the atmosphere is heated, and in turn passes much of that energy back to Earth yet again.

The chemicals that do this are called greenhouse gases because they act very much like the glass in a greenhouse: The Sun's rays readily pass through glass, impacting the plants and surfaces inside, but the infrared radiation that emanates from this heated surface is unable to get out. This is why greenhouses are so useful: without needing additional heating, they become significantly warmer than the surrounding air. The same phenomenon happens in a closed car, when energy passes through the windows and then is unable to exit, which is why leaving a person or a pet in a car with the windows up, even on a relatively cool day, is so dangerous.

Under normal, natural conditions, greenhouse heating is not only a good thing, but a necessary one for life on Earth. If it were not for this process whereby atmospheric gases intercept the energy that bounces back from the Earth, so much of the Sun's heat would be lost that our planet would have an average temperature of about -18 degrees Celsius (-0.4 degrees Fahrenheit). The balance between incoming and outgoing radiation maintains the Earth's overall average temperature at about 59 degrees Fahrenheit (15 degrees Celsius).

Neither nitrogen—the most abundant atmospheric gas on Earth—nor oxygen, second in abundance, absorbs thermal infrared radiation, as do the major greenhouse gases: carbon dioxide, water vapor, methane (CH_4), and nitrous oxide (N_2O). In geological time, the amount of carbon dioxide in particular has varied between about 180 parts per million (ppm) during the periodic ice ages to 280 ppm during warm interglacial periods. Since the onset of the Industrial Revolution in the late 18th and early 19th centuries, CO_2 levels have skyrocketed, increasing one hundred times more quickly than they did at the end of the last ice age, when the Earth underwent sustained warming. This immense increase is due almost entirely to the burning of fossil fuels—coal, oil, and natural gas—which had previously served as storage sites for carbon that released carbon dioxide only very gradually, largely as a result of geological forces.

The combustion of fossil fuels in 2019 alone released approximately 37 billion tons of CO_2 (the highest amount on record), which is nearly three times the amount that can be absorbed annually by natural processes (e.g., dissolved in water and incorporated into plants), resulting in an increase in atmospheric CO_2 load during that year alone of roughly 24 billion tons.

Sources of Global Heating

Following is a quick summary of the major greenhouse gases. When it comes to the effect of any particular greenhouse gas on global heating, four factors are especially important:

1. Its chemically based impact on heat retention, per molecule. Neither oxygen nor nitrogen, for example, retains heat and therefore neither is a greenhouse gas, whereas some greenhouse gases are a thousandfold more impactful than others.

2. Its abundance in the atmosphere. A gas that has a small effect, per molecule, but is present in large quantities can have roughly the same impact as one that retains a lot of heat, but is rare.

3. How long it remains in the atmosphere, as well as whether it degrades into another heat-trapping gas or if its byproducts do not retain heat.

4. The rate at which the gas is introduced into the environment.

Gases containing the element fluorine are produced industrially and are more potent, per molecule, than is carbon dioxide. These fluorinated gases include hydrofluorocarbons (HFCs), perfluorocarbons (PFCs), and sulfur hexafluoride. Chlorofluorocarbons (CFCs), which had previously been used as aerosol propellants and as refrigerants, have now been phased out via international agreements. The remaining fluorinated compounds are still being generated, especially in the production of aluminum and semiconductors and by electricity transmission. Fluorinated gases are important because they do not occur naturally, and, per molecule, they can be hundreds of times more effective at trapping heat than is carbon dioxide. They also tend to distribute widely in the upper atmosphere, where they are broken down only very slowly, in some cases lasting for many thousands of years; PFCs, for example, can persist for 50,000 years, retaining heat all the while. Hence, once released, these industrial fluorinated chemicals constitute a very harmful and persistent heat-trapping legacy that will persist for hundreds of human generations.

Methane (CH_4) is another important greenhouse gas. It lingers in the atmosphere for about 12 years and, like the fluorinated gases, is 20 times more effective, per molecule, at trapping heat than is CO_2. Methane is eventually oxidized to form water vapor and carbon dioxide, so it manifests a kind of zombie heat-trapping capability, continuing even after it has been degraded. Methane is naturally emitted from many sources, notably the bacterial decomposition of organic material in wetlands by the action of bacteria in the absence of oxygen, by volcanoes, and because of fires—many of which are anthropogenic (i.e., ignited by humans) and are augmented by global heating itself; this is one of many examples of a positive feedback loop or vicious circle involving global climate change, in which increased heating leads ultimately to yet more heating.

Human activities are responsible for 60 percent of methane emissions, largely through agricultural practices, industry, and waste management activities. Atmospheric methane levels are now roughly two and one-half times pre-industrial levels. A surprisingly large source of methane is the belching of cows—which sounds comical but consists of many millions of tons annually. A particular methane-associated worry is the prospect of catastrophic release from material currently locked in arctic tundra permafrost; such a sudden release would be due to the rapid and unprecedented melting of the permafrost, and it could suddenly push the Earth's climate beyond a tipping point, after which heating could be unstoppable.

Nitrous oxide (N_2O)—familiar to many people as a mild intoxicant and anti-anxiety medication used, for example, in dentistry—occurs naturally in the atmosphere. Per unit weight, it is 300 times more effective in trapping heat than is CO_2. Its atmospheric lifespan is roughly 120 years, and 40 percent of nitrous oxide emissions derive from human activities, especially the use of nitrogen-based fertilizers in agriculture and emissions from various industrial processes, as well as transportation.

Water vapor is the most important greenhouse gas, responsible for about 60 percent of the atmosphere's heat budget. Unlike the other greenhouse gases, water vapor is not significantly impacted by human activities, except as part of a key feedback loop associated with global heating itself. As the atmosphere's temperature increases, more water evaporates from oceans, rivers, lakes, and reservoirs. In addition, the ability of air to absorb water vapor increases with higher temperatures.

Another way of understanding this is to consider the dew point, the temperature below which water vapor cannot remain in gas form, whereupon it condenses out as dew, for example when it contacts a colder surface, such as the ground on a clear, cold night. The key point here with regard to recent changes in global heating is that higher temperatures not only increase evaporation, but also increase the ability of the atmosphere to retain this moisture. Because water vapor is itself a potent greenhouse gas, we have yet another vicious circle: rising temperatures cause evaporation, causing more atmospheric moisture, which in turn causes the atmosphere to hold more moisture, which causes temperatures to rise yet more. This cycle repeats itself indefinitely.

Although the hydrologic (water-water vapor) cycle is well understood, its relationship to global heating is extremely complex and the exact feedback loops are as yet unclear. Thus, on the one hand, increased atmospheric water vapor contributes to cloud formation, which increases ground temperature by absorbing thermal energy radiated from the Earth. But during the daytime, the upper surface of clouds has a cooling effect by reflecting some of the heat energy emanating from the sun. There are abundant data on atmospheric quantities of methane, fluorinated gases, and carbon dioxide; however, quantitative measurements of water vapor—worldwide as well as over time—are considerably less available and more unreliable at present. It does appear, however, that global water vapor levels have been rising.

When it comes to the current climate crisis, carbon dioxide is the most important greenhouse gas because of its abundance compared to the others, as well as its rate of increase in historical times. It also stays in the atmosphere for thousands of years and is responsible for more than 80 percent of the anthropogenic global warming. The bulk of "artificial" CO_2 production (beyond metabolic respiration) is due to the burning of fossil fuels: coal, oil, and natural gas, which combined make up a substantial part of the long-term reservoir associated with the carbon cycle. The second largest source of human-generated CO_2 release is deforestation, especially in the world's rainforests, but occurring elsewhere as well. When trees are cut down for the production of goods for sale (such as housing, paper, furniture, etc.) or simply burned for heat, they quickly release the carbon that is normally stored by photosynthesis and is otherwise released over the course of decades and even centuries. As a result, substantially more than a billion tons of carbon are injected into the atmosphere each year as carbon dioxide.

Beginning in 1958, climate scientist Charles David Keeling began measuring atmospheric CO_2 levels at the Mauna Loa observatory in Hawaii. His findings, now known as the Keeling Curve, provided the first long-term data showing changes in atmospheric carbon dioxide, continuing to the present day. These data have been confirmed by many other measurements worldwide, indicating an ongoing global trend of rapid and unparalleled increase, from 313 ppm (by volume) in early spring, 1958, to 415 by 2020. Climate scientist James Hansen had brought this devastating increase to the public's attention in 1988, when atmospheric carbon dioxide was at 350 ppm. Since

FIGURE 20.1   ●   Carbon dioxide levels from 1958 to 2019, measured from the Mauna Loa Observatory in Hawaii (in black) and the South Pole (in grey). The jagged, saw-tooth pattern in black is explained in the text.

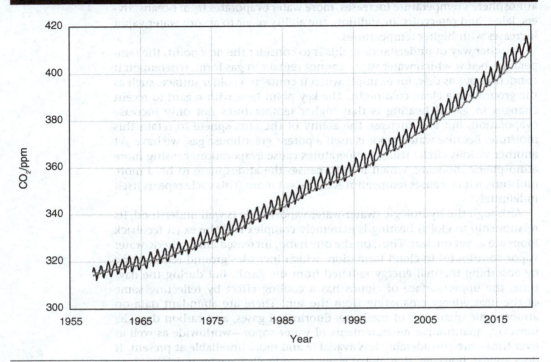

Source: National Academy of Sciences. 2020. *Climate Change: Evidence and Causes: Update 2020.* https://doi.org/10.17226/25733. Reproduced with permission from the National Academy of Sciences, Courtesy of The National Academies Press, Washington, D.C.

then, human activity has added more CO_2 to the global climate burden than had been added in all of human history up to that year. The current rate of increase is roughly 2.5 ppm annually, and, if anything, this *rate of increase* is increasing even further. An almost identical pattern has been obtained from a geographically distant region, the South Pole (see Figure 20.1). The very close correspondence between these measurements, taken at geographically distant locations, shows that they are not a result of local phenomena; rather, they reflect *global* background atmospheric levels.

Underlying the annual increases, there are predictable seasonal changes in atmospheric carbon dioxide in regions distant from the poles, with a cyclic variation of approximately 5 ppm each year. This regular fluctuation is due to seasonal variation: the growth of new plant matter captures CO_2 via photosynthesis in the spring and summer (temporarily reducing atmospheric CO_2 levels), then by September the growing season for most of the world's vegetation ends. At this time, CO_2 levels increase as plants die and decay.

Fires constitute yet another major source of CO_2 emissions, mostly resulting from intentional burning as a means of clearing land (particularly in rainforests in the Brazilian Amazon, the Democratic Republic of the Congo, and Indonesia) as well as unintended wildfires. In recent years, both processes have greatly increased. Land clearing is largely due to economic interests that favor livestock grazing and crop-raising (particularly monocultures such as oil palm, sugar, and soybean plantations). Wildfires are more frequent and intense due to yet another destructive positive feedback loop, in which higher global temperature causes increased desiccation of forests and grasslands, which in turn produces more frequent and intense wildfires, which in turn releases even more carbon dioxide, and which gives rise to yet more fire-stimulating global heating.

Natural tree growth is a potent force for CO_2 removal, and it has been suggested but not yet demonstrated that increased atmospheric CO_2 could contribute to a helpful negative feedback loop: it might increase the rate at which trees accumulate carbon via photosynthesis, which essentially combines carbon dioxide and water in the presence of sunlight to produce energy-rich sugars as well as structural molecules (e.g., wood). However, heightened growth rates (along with increased tree planting), although beneficial with respect to atmospheric carbon dioxide levels, cannot absorb enough carbon to make up for its current overabundance in the atmosphere nor keep up with current fossil fuel emissions.

By analyzing the concentration of carbon dioxide in air bubbles trapped in Arctic and Antarctic ice cores, it has been possible to assess pre-1958 CO_2 levels, which ranged from 275–280 PPM during the Holocene (beginning roughly 9,000 BCE), with a very sharp increase starting early in the 19th century. Figure 20.2 shows global levels of carbon emissions attributable to the burning of fossil fuels between the mid-18th century and early in the 21st century, measured in millions of tons.

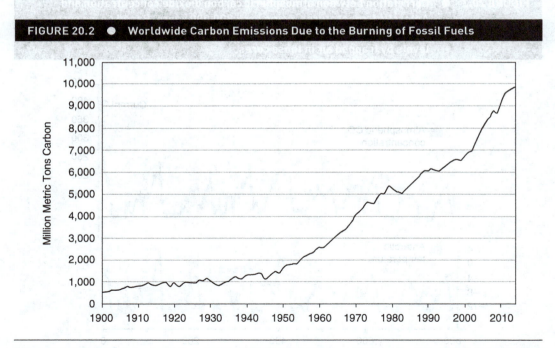

FIGURE 20.2 ● Worldwide Carbon Emissions Due to the Burning of Fossil Fuels

Source: T. A. Boden, G. Marland, and R. J. Andres. 2017. *Global, Regional, and National Fossil-Fuel CO₂ Emissions.* Carbon Dioxide Information Analysis Center, Oak Ridge National Laboratory, US Department of Energy, Oak Ridge, Tenn., U.S.A. doi:10.3334/CDIAC/00001_V2017.

The Effects of Greenhouse Gases on Global Heating

Clearly, global temperatures have been increasing, especially over the last century. It is also clear that atmospheric carbon dioxide levels have also been increasing, and that the former is due almost entirely to the latter. Scientific confidence in this causal connection is extremely high, despite the fact that the actual evidence is correlational. This is because, for one thing, the direct causal relation between CO_2 and temperature is firmly established, both as a result of our understanding of the complex molecular physics of how carbon dioxide molecules interact with infrared radiation and through laboratory experiments. When it comes to effects on a global level, however, we have correlations rather than direct evidence of causation because the worldwide system is simply too large to permit direct experimentation. But the correlations are so abundant, so precise, and based on so many independent sources of evidence, that the causation is incontrovertible.

The paleoclimate record shows a remarkably close correspondence during the glacial cycles of the past few hundred thousand years between temperature and CO_2 concentration: when temperature has risen, so has carbon dioxide level (see Figure 20.3). And when temperature has fallen, the carbon dioxide level has also fallen, in synchrony. Other aspects of paleoclimate also serve as proxies for this connection, notably changes in sea levels and in the advance and retreat of glaciers. In these cases as well as the previous ones, the correlations are extraordinarily precise.

FIGURE 20.3 ● Correlation between atmospheric carbon dioxide concentration and Antarctic temperatures, going back 800,000 years. Based on ice cores: Temperature determined by isotopic content of water and carbon dioxide levels by trapped air in those cores.

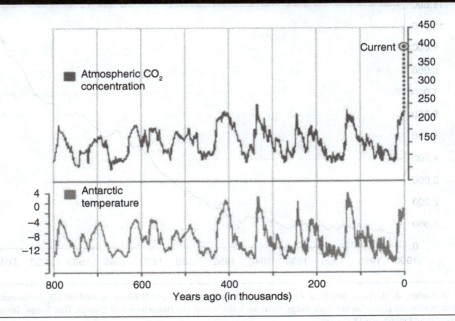

Source: National Academy of Sciences. 2020. *Climate Change: Evidence and Causes: Update 2020.* https://doi.org/10.17226/25733. Reproduced with permission from the National Academy of Sciences, Courtesy of The National Academies Press, Washington, D.C.

Evidence from recent years is no less impressive. Based on the analysis of atmospheric gas trapped in ice cores, we know that CO_2 concentration has increased by more than 40 percent since the start of the Industrial Revolution, with more than half of that increase occurring in the last half-century. Since the beginning of the 20th century, the average global surface temperature has risen by a bit more than one degree Centigrade (1.8 degrees Fahrenheit), which might seem small, but on a worldwide scale is significant and worrying. The 30-year period between 1989 and 2019 appears to have been the hottest three-decade stretch in more than eight centuries, and the most recent decade, 2010–2019, was the hottest 10-year interval ever scientifically recorded since 1850, when record-keeping began (see Figure 20.4). For example, September 2020 was the hottest September ever recorded, beating the record set just a year before. And the years 2019 and 2020 came just short of tying 2016 as the hottest years on record.

Moreover, this pattern of increasing temperature is entirely consistent with detailed predictions of what these increases would be as a result of the observed increases in greenhouse gases.

Not every year shows a temperature increase compared to the one before; in addition, the differences between some years are greater than between others because of fluctuations in such natural weather phenomena as volcanic eruptions, along with El Niños and La Niñas, both of which refer to

> **FIGURE 20.4 ● Global annual temperature (measured average over both land and oceans) from 1880 to 2020. During this time, it has increased by more than 1.5°F (0.8°C). The dark grey bars show temperatures above the 20th-century average, and light grey bars show temperatures below that average. While there is a clear long-term global warming trend, some years do not show a temperature increase relative to the previous year, and some show greater changes than others, due to natural processes.**

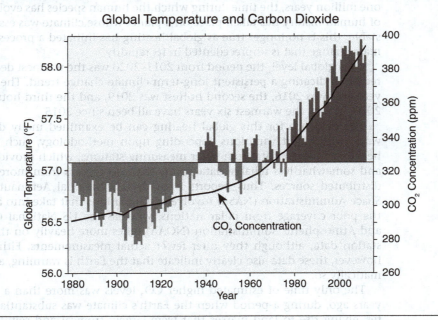

Global Temperature and Carbon Dioxide

Source: Karl, T. R., et al (Eds.). (2009). Global climate change impacts in the United States. Cambridge University Press, used with permission. NOAA National Centers for Environmental Information, US Global Change Research Program.

normal variation in the temperature of the Pacific Ocean (the former involving temporary warming and the latter, temporary cooling). In any event, the long-term global heating trend is as clear as it is undesirable.

These changes in the global climate are demonstrated by such evidence as the following:

- record annual temperatures;

- significant increases in the intensity and frequency of heatwaves and other extreme climate events;

- detailed and unique fingerprint data from tree rings and ice cores;

- poleward and up-mountain shifts in the presence of temperature-sensitive invertebrates, fish, amphibians, mammals, and plants;

- warming of the oceans; and

- a dramatic decline in the Antarctic and Greenland ice sheets, which combined have contributed to the substantial rise in sea levels.

Each of these phenomena is independently and closely linked to changes in greenhouse gas abundance.

Sea ice in the Arctic has declined by 13 percent each decade since 1980, while losses of the Greenland ice sheet, which is more than 110,000 years old and used to cover 660,000 square miles, have nearly doubled in each of the last three decades, from 33 billion tons melted per year in the 1990s to an average from 2010 to 2020 of 254 billion tons annually. One result is that in 2007, for the first time ever, a ship passed through the fabled Northwest Passage without assistance from an icebreaker. The Intergovernmental Panel on Climate Change estimates that by the end of the 21st century, the Arctic in summer will be entirely ice free.

The current level of atmospheric carbon dioxide exceeds that of the past one million years, the time during which the human species has evolved. All of human history has taken place on a planet whose climate was essentially stable; this is no longer true as global heating has initiated a process of climate change that is unprecedented in its rapidity.

On a global level, the period from 2011–2020 was the warmest decade on record, indicating a persistent long-term climate change trend. The hottest year ever was 2016, the second hottest was 2019, and the third hottest was 2020. In fact, the warmest six years have all been since 2015.

The evidence for this global heating can be examined many different ways, with slight variations depending upon methodology, such as how heavily to weight data from polar measuring stations, which provide fewer and somewhat less reliable data points than do reports from more widely distributed sources. Thus, reports from the US National Aeronautics and Space Administration (NASA) involve extrapolations that take into account the poor coverage from polar stations, whereas the US National Oceanic and Atmospheric Administration (NOAA) relies more heavily on the polar station data, although they offer fewer actual measurements. Either way, however, these data also clearly indicate that the Earth is warming, and dramatically so.

The only time of estimated higher CO_2 levels was more than a million years ago, during a period when the Earth's climate was substantially hotter, giving rise to land masses that were largely tropical and semitropical.

Geological and paleontological evidence strongly suggest that the current situation is unprecedented in recorded history; the last epoch in which atmospheric carbon dioxide exceeded current levels of 400 ppm was roughly three to five million years ago, when the Earth's average surface temperature was between 2 and 3.5 degrees Centigrade higher than in pre-industrial times. Going further back in time, CO_2 levels may have reached 1000 ppm, with global temperatures about 10 degrees Centigrade higher than today, when the planet had little or no ice and the sea level was nearly 200 feet above its current levels. As a result, there would have been substantially less dry land, and most of the land on which today's large cities sit would have been under many meters of water. According to climate scientist James Hansen, the Earth's anthropogenic load of greenhouse gases now traps as much energy in a day as would be released by 500,000 Hiroshima-size atomic bombs.

Some Skeptical Questions Regarding Climate Science and Some Replies to Them

At least some climate-change skeptics and agnostics appear to be sincere in their beliefs but are either ignorant of or indifferent to the science behind global heating. Other climate-science deniers are often adherents of ultraconservative, "libertarian" political ideology involving strong commitment to fundamentalist free-market solutions (and therefore are unwilling to accept government actions). Others are reflexive deniers not just of climate science but of virtually all science (especially human evolution) who may also be linked to extreme right-wing personality cults (including supporters of former US President Donald Trump). In addition, there is a very low percentage—according to some estimates, no more than 1 percent—of practicing scientists who deny or are quite skeptical about climate science in general and anthropogenic global heating in particular. This small group is composed of people who are either professional contrarians—who are skeptical about virtually anything—or are funded by fossil fuel companies. Although the arguments provided by such climate-science skeptics are almost always fallacious, and sometimes based on actual lies, there are some legitimate issues raised by well-meaning, concerned citizens that deserve responses:

How do we know that the additional CO_2 is anthropogenic? In addition to a close historical worldwide connection with the Industrial Revolution (which generated local CO_2 spikes predictably associated geographically with industrialization), the carbon dioxide emitted by combustion of fossil fuels has a distinct chemical fingerprint because it contains quantities of the isotope ^{13}C and no ^{14}C. Volcanic eruptions add some atmospheric CO_2, but less than 1 percent of the emission rate provided by fossil fuel combustion; even this amount is roughly balanced by the CO_2 absorbed by the chemical weathering of rocks. In summary, we know that the additional CO_2 is anthropogenic just as it is equally clear that global heating is due to increased amounts of atmospheric greenhouse gases.

Could changes in solar activity, such as sunspots, be responsible for these global heating effects? Satellite measurements since 1970 show no consistent changes in the output of solar energy, while during this period the Earth's surface temperature has risen steadily. During the 11-year solar cycle, the sun's energy output varies by about 0.1 percent before returning to preceding levels.

What about other natural factors, such as volcanos, deviations in the Earth's rotation and orbiting, cosmic rays, and so forth? There have been many detailed climate models simulating the impact on global climate if only natural factors were operating. The results are remarkably consistent: Very little surface warming would take place as a result of any of these "other natural factors," and, if anything, there would have been a slight *decrease* in global temperature during the 20th and early 21st century if such effects had not been overridden by anthropogenic factors. A 2020 report from the National Academy of Sciences concluded that "Only when models include human influences on the composition of the atmosphere are the resulting temperature changes consistent with observed changes."

What about the fact the upper atmosphere (the stratosphere) has actually cooled, while the lower atmosphere (the troposphere) has heated? Climate scientists predicted precisely this stratospheric cooling in 1989, for two reasons. The first reason is that the ozone layer normally absorbs incoming solar energy, but by depleting ozone levels (because of CFCs and other chemicals), human activity has reduced the ability of the stratosphere to retain this energy, which is passed on to lower, troposphere levels, making them hotter and the stratosphere cooler. The second reason is that because the stratosphere is thinner than is the atmosphere at lower elevation, it is less densely packed with gas molecules of all sorts, so the heat absorbed by high-altitude CO_2 is less likely to be intercepted by other, nearby molecules, and is more likely to be radiated into space, thus cooling the stratosphere even as the troposphere is warmed. (Moreover, the fact that the stratosphere has cooled further refutes the notion that global heating is due to increased solar activity because if the sun were radiating more heat, the stratosphere would be made hotter, not colder.)

Given that the climate is always changing, why should we be especially concerned that it is happening now? Change—in everything—is inevitable. It always happens. But the recorded *rate* of current climate change is unprecedented in human history and in the Earth's history as well, excepting such sudden events as asteroid impacts. For example, global temperature changes that occurred since the end of the last ice age (starting 18,000 years ago) took place over thousands of years, not during a stretch of a few decades, as is currently the case. Natural ecosystems as well as human-designed sociocultural, technological, and economic systems are ill-equipped to deal with such rapid changes, which can then become (by definition) catastrophic.

Global heating slowed down somewhat during the first decade of the 21st century; doesn't this mean that climate change is going away? Absolutely not. After the very warm year of 1998, following a powerful 1997–1998 El Niño, the *rate* of heating increase slowed for a time, but the average global temperatures from 2000 to 2009 were nonetheless higher than during the 1990s. Immediately thereafter, temperature increases resumed their record-setting pace.

It is important to distinguish short-term fluctuations from persistent long-term trends, just as it is crucial to distinguish daily changes in weather from changes in overall climate: in a sense, weather is like your most recent meal, whereas climate is your state of nutrition. The fact that the climate is warming does not mean that every day, every week, or even every year will necessarily be warmer than the preceding one. There will still be some unusually cold nights, days, summers, and winters, even as the climate heats up and, as a result, overall there are more hot days, more hot seasons, and fewer cold days and cold seasons. *Complex variations in oceanic and atmospheric circulation, as well as immediate geography, all combine to produce unpredictable short-term effects, but they do not erase the overall climatic patterns.* Taking a longer view over the last half-century, the US as a whole had fewer record high temperatures than lows during the 1960s, whereas during the first two decades of the 21st century, there have been more than twice as many record highs as lows. Similarly, the frequency and intensity of heat waves have increased in most—but not all—of Africa, South America, Europe, Australia, and Asia. As a general pattern, while large areas in Greenland have been melting, much of the Amazon and Australia has been burning.

Changes in sea ice are inconsistent between the Arctic and Antarctic; doesn't this cast doubt on the consistency of global climate change? The Arctic consists of water surrounded by land whereas the Antarctic is land surrounded by water. As a result, their responses differ. And they are also, obviously, at opposite ends of the Earth! Yearly minimal Arctic sea ice has decreased by 40 percent from 1978, when satellite data were first available, to 2020, a decline that has not occurred in at least the past 1,500 years. The expanse of sea ice can be misleading: depth, too, is important, and sea ice is now regularly thinner than has ever previously been measured. There was a slight increase in some but not all regions of Antarctic sea ice from 1979 to 2014, but since then, the quantity of Antarctic sea ice has declined dramatically, reaching the lowest extent ever recorded and remaining low. Moreover, as of 2020, the huge West Antarctic ice shelf is in imminent danger of collapsing due to uniquely rapid melting.

In the summer of 2020, an international group of scientists reported that the huge Antarctic Pine Island and Thwaites glaciers have shown new and enlarged crevasses and fractures along the shear zones that restrain their movement. As a result, these glaciers are sliding more rapidly than ever into the sea, where contact with ocean water will hasten their melting yet more, raising sea levels worldwide. If, as is feared, the entire West Antarctic ice sheet collapses, sea levels will eventually rise by 10 feet—not something liable to happen quickly, but if and when it does, the impact on the world's coastlines (where many of the planet's great cities lie) will be catastrophic. And this doesn't even include the melting of Greenland's vast ice sheet.

The Antarctic ice sheet contains, in total, more than one-half of the Earth's fresh water; if all of it melts (a real, eventual possibility, although not one that is liable to occur sooner than two or more centuries from now), sea levels would rise by 58 meters—an event that would engender an unprecedented worldwide disaster. The best atmospheric modelling, as of 2020, shows that even if the global temperature increase is kept at less than 2°C above pre-industrial levels—which is the goal of the Paris Agreement—the Earth will undergo sea level rises of roughly 2.5 meters, which is guaranteed to be devastating in itself. Moreover, because of feedback loops, the melting of Antarctic and northern polar ice would almost certainly be irreversible.

In addition to its impact on worldwide sea levels, overheated polar regions contribute to yet another vicious climatic circle: snow and ice have a high "albedo" (tendency to reflect incoming energy), whereas dark surfaces such as forests have a low albedo. Decreases in white surfaces reduce the Earth's albedo, resulting in less of the sun's energy being reflected away and therefore increasing global heating even more—which results in more melting and even lower albedo and accordingly higher temperatures.

How can global heating be blamed for more extreme weather events, apart from higher temperatures? No *single* hurricane, tornado, heat wave, flood, and so forth can be attributed entirely to global heating. But like the weather/climate relationship, a *general trend* is clear: there have been more such natural disasters than previously recorded, and they have been more extreme and disruptive. For example, according to a detailed study released in 2020 by the World Weather Attribution Project, based on thousands of data points and the collaboration of scientists in six countries, a half-year of anomalously high temperatures in a vast swath of Siberia—which included a record Arctic temperature of 100.4°F (38°C) in June, 2020—would have been virtually impossible without anthropogenic changes to the global climate. *In short, although no one event can be attributed to global heating, it almost certainly turbocharges most extreme weather events, making them more likely as well as more extreme.*

Increased heat generates more evaporative water loss which, on land surfaces, produces more droughts, while increased desiccation (extreme dryness due to dehydration) results in more and increasingly destructive fires, as well as a longer wildfire season. During each recent summer season, fires have been more frequent and more destructive than the year before. In 2020, for example, the largest fires in the history of the American west burned virtually out of control, not only in California but also throughout the vast regions of the west slope of the Cascade Mountains in the Pacific Northwest, which are normally too wet to have major fires.

At the same time, global heating produces more and increasingly heavy rains, flooding, and local snowfall, which seems counterintuitive but is due to the fact that higher temperature increases the air's ability to hold moisture. Increases in temperature plus the greater energy packed into a given atmospheric volume result in increased intensity and frequency of such climate-related meteorological events as "hundred-year" floods, droughts, tornados, and hurricanes, which would otherwise be expected to occur, on average, only once in a century. Combined with sea level rise, hurricanes ("cyclones" in Asia) are also more likely to generate unusually destructive storm surges.

Why would global heating cause the sea level to rise? First, the increased melting of glaciers, the Greenland and Antarctic ice sheets, and polar icebergs adds to the total volume of ocean water. Also, as water heats it expands, so a given amount of ocean seawater occupies more space, causing the sea level to go up. Since the late 1800s, the global sea level has risen about 16 centimeters (6 inches). As with temperature change, this increase may seem small, but its global geographical impact is immense. The rate of rise in worldwide sea levels has increased in recent decades and is currently increasing about 3.6 millimeters (0.14 inches) per year (see Figure 20.5). These measurements have become more accurate over time, with improved and increased satellite and tidal gauge data.

The oceans absorb carbon dioxide; doesn't this reduce the impact of global heating? The oceans do absorb carbon dioxide. But global heating "is what it is," regardless of the extent to which CO_2 is absorbed by seawater. Accordingly, the extent to which oceanic absorption of CO_2 mitigates global heating is already accounted for in assessing this phenomenon.

The data from scientific studies published in 2019 show that between 1994 and 2007, ocean water absorbed four times more carbon per year than it had from 1800 to 1994 because of the increased amounts of atmospheric CO_2. However, the proportion of emissions absorbed by the oceans has remained stable at 31 percent, while atmospheric CO_2 continued to rise. Hence, the oceans are in no way "gaining" on greenhouse gas emissions. There is also a downside to ocean absorption of CO_2: it increases ocean acidity (lower pH). This is detrimental to most shellfish and corals, which, as a result, are unable to make or maintain their shells. Numerous fish species are also negatively

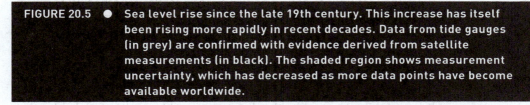

FIGURE 20.5 ● Sea level rise since the late 19th century. This increase has itself been rising more rapidly in recent decades. Data from tide gauges (in grey) are confirmed with evidence derived from satellite measurements (in black). The shaded region shows measurement uncertainty, which has decreased as more data points have become available worldwide.

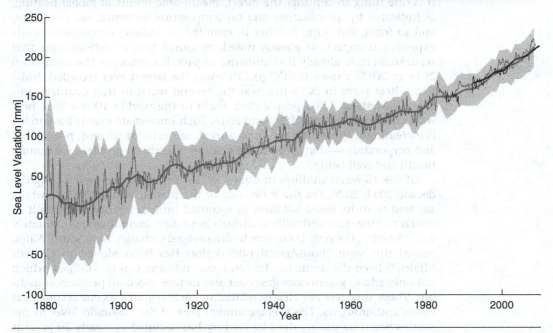

Source: National Academy of Sciences. 2020. *Climate Change: Evidence and Causes: Update 2020.* https://doi.org/10.17226/25733. Reproduced with permission from the National Academy of Sciences, Courtesy of The National Academies Press, Washington, D.C.

affected. It also remains to be seen whether ocean chemistry will permit continued absorption of carbon dioxide as the atmospheric CO_2 load increases. In addition, increased ocean temperatures themselves are having a destructive impact on marine life, partly due to increased metabolic rates and also because warmer water holds less dissolved oxygen, upon which nearly all marine life depends.

Climate change involves just a few degrees. How important can that be? Very important! Just a few degrees may not sound like much, but consider that global temperatures during the last ice age were only 4 to 5 degrees Celsius (7 to 9 degrees Fahrenheit) cooler than at present. Already, wet areas have become wetter and dry areas drier; snowpacks are decreasing (much of south-central Asia, for example, depends on water from Himalayan mountain glaciers, which are rapidly shrinking); sea levels are rising; severe rainstorms are becoming more intense as well as more frequent, and so forth.

In the Atlantic Ocean during 2020 alone, more hurricanes and damaging storms (30) were recorded than during any previous year; naming them used up the English alphabet, and for the first time we had to use Greek letters. Nine of these storms became substantially more intense during a single day, something that used to be exceedingly rare before the current era of global heating. Although the effects of global heating are most apparent over a time scale of years, they continue to occur on a significantly accelerated schedule: For example, in 2020 on Ellesmere Island, in the Arctic, Canada's largest remaining ice shelf—substantially larger than all of Manhattan—collapsed in just two days.

Indirect Consequences of Global Heating

It is one thing to consider the direct, measurable results of global heating, as indicated by quantitative data on temperature increases, sea level rises, and so forth, but quite another to examine its indirect consequences—its experiential impact. As already noted, measured temperature changes that seem small have already had immense impact. For example, the jump from 2014 to 2015, a mere 0.13°C (0.23°F), was the largest ever recorded. India had a heat wave in 2015 that was the second worst in that country's history; upwards of 2,500 people died. Eight of the world's 10 deadliest heat waves occurred between 1997 and 2016. Such immediate events have made it increasingly apparent—except to a small minority of citizens, politicians, and corporations—that greenhouse heating is a critical problem for human health and well-being.

Of the 10 worst wildfires in California history, nine occurred during the decade 2011–2020. On the other side of the planet, during 2019 Australia suffered from its worst wildfires in recorded human history, as a result of which an estimated 480 million animals have died, including approximately 8,000 koalas. (The only bookstore in fire-ravaged Cobargo, New South Wales, posted this sign: "Post-Apocalyptic Fiction Has Been Moved to Current Affairs.") Even the Arctic tundra has been enduring raging wildfires, which not only add to greenhouse gases but also further speed up permafrost melting. These disasters are clearly related to each region's recent record heat waves and droughts. The average annual flow of the Colorado River in the southwestern US during the 21st century has declined by nearly 20 percent compared with 20th-century levels, a result of disappearing mountain snowpack combined with increased evaporative water loss.

What used to be considered worst-case climate change scenarios, especially in the Arctic, have increasingly become regular events. Rapidly melting permafrost has caused roads to buckle, buildings to collapse, and has forced at least two Inuit villages to be abandoned, with others on the verge of doing so. Low-lying shorelines are increasingly imperiled. Nor is this ongoing disaster limited to less-populated regions. Many of the world's great cities are coastal and at sea level, including Los Angeles, San Francisco, New York, Rio de Janeiro, Mumbai, Tokyo, and Manila, as is nearly the entire population of Bangladesh. It is now predicted that as a result of increasing sea level, roughly 150 million people are currently living on land that by 2050 will be underwater during high tides. Scientists tend to be conservative in their estimates of future events; however, when it comes to the degree and impact of global heating, such estimates have nearly always been too low.

If increasing carbon dioxide levels are left unchecked and, as predicted, world temperatures rise by 3°F to 9°F by the year 2050, this would represent a rate of climate change 100 times faster than at any time in recorded history, with predictably catastrophic results: agriculture would be profoundly disrupted on a planet whose human population and domesticated plants and animals are currently adapted to largely temperate environments. Major shifts in world ecosystems, from coral reefs to mountains, have already negatively impacted many living creatures already stressed by pollution, overfishing, and hunting, as well as numerous other threats.

Although many organisms are capable of adapting to environmental change, such evolutionary adaptations typically take thousands of years at a minimum, whereas the current, extraordinary rate of climate change will leave many large, slow-breeding organisms unable to keep up. As a result, many wild species would almost certainly die out: Polar bears, for example, are currently drowning in the Arctic when their ice floes melt, and they are less able to obtain food, which largely involves hunting seals through holes in the ice.

Many of the consequences of global climate change involve impacts on natural ecosystems that are not immediate or intuitively obvious. For example, huge tracts of coniferous forests in the northern hemisphere have died as a result of infestation by bark beetles, whose numbers had previously been held in check by winter die-offs; with less severe winters, more beetles survive to devastate trees. (*This is yet another example of a vicious climate circle*: insofar as trees reduce atmospheric CO_2 by sequestering carbon, fewer trees means more CO_2, which in turn results in yet higher temperatures and yet more tree-killing beetles.)

Although it is likely that heat-adapted organisms will benefit from climate change, it will be unlikely to benefit most other living things, and it will certainly not be beneficial for the great majority of human beings. Contagious diseases, for example, would spread more rapidly than ever because the great majority of pathogens, as well as such important disease transmitters as malaria mosquitoes, find warmer weather conducive to their survival and spread.

Some countries may experience modest economic benefits from moderate global heating; Russian and Canadian agriculture, for example, will be able to grow such crops as corn and soybeans at their more northern latitudes where it is already becoming increasingly feasible. On balance, however, the impact on global food production will be negative. Freshwater supplies will diminish, coastal infrastructures will be threatened and some will disappear altogether, and the enormous human populations currently inhabiting low-lying areas will be threatened and almost certainly forced to relocate. In addition, regions of extreme heat and dryness—such as the Sahara, Atacama, and Gobi Deserts—which now cover roughly 1 percent of the Earth's surface could well expand to cover 20 percent or even more.

Currently marginal farmlands will likely become less productive or even nonproductive, forcing hundreds of millions of people to become climate refugees, resulting in the largest population displacement in human history. Currently, the risk that the world's major grain-growing regions will simultaneously undergo massive crop failures due to severe drought is essentially zero because it is very rare for unusual weather patterns to be experienced on different continents at the same time. But according to the US National Academy of Science, with a 4°C increase, the probability of such simultaneous occurrences rises to 86 percent.

The indirect consequences of climate change are evident not only in their extent but also with respect to their pace. When change is gradual, it is more susceptible to adaptation and adjustment. Although regular seasonal change is very rapid, it occurs within certain well-established limits and is predictable and therefore prepared for—both by natural and human systems—from one season to the next. The rapid baseline changes now underway mean that very little time is available for comparable adaptations and adjustments, even aside from extreme weather events.

There are also geopolitical implications of global climate change. The large increases in the numbers of climate refugees, in addition to being a potential humanitarian catastrophe, also threaten to increase international instability. India and Pakistan are already at odds over the distribution of fresh water that derives from shrinking Himalayan glaciers, and fresh water availability is a growing flash point in the Middle East, especially for Palestinians and Israelis. The anticipated opening of the Northwest Passage, through Arctic polar seas previously closed to ocean shipping, along with competition among such countries as the US, Russia, and Canada over increasingly accessible undersea Arctic minerals, presage further climate-generated instability. The US Defense Department has accordingly identified global climate change as a major national security concern.

India and China illustrate conflicting goals as well as some of the aforementioned problems. On the one hand, these countries, along with other rapidly developing nation-states, are eager to expand their respective citizenry's education, wealth, health, and access to consumer goods, but on the other hand, increasing satisfaction of these human needs and desires may conflict with the need to mitigate climate change. In addition, those countries that currently gain foreign currency by exporting fossil fuels (notably the US, Russia, and Saudi Arabia) stand to lose economically by international agreements to cut fossil fuel use.

The United States, China, and India are also the three largest consumers of oil, and as a result of their economic and military prowess, they dominate international negotiations regarding fossil fuel use and have been active in preventing effective climate control agreements. Meanwhile, the poorer and weaker countries, which are generally least responsible for the current global predicament but have the most to lose as a result of catastrophic climate change and also lack the capital and infrastructure to deal with it, have the least political impact when it comes to worldwide climate decision making.

Financial assistance from developed to developing countries has been largely focused on mitigation rather than adaptation or compensation: Roughly 80 percent of the funding thus far has been directed toward getting these countries to emit less greenhouse gases (which, of course, will benefit the rich countries as well), with only 20 percent concerned with helping the recipients adapt to the consequences of global heating and essentially nothing to compensate them for the costs they have already incurred, mostly through no fault of their own.

The average American is responsible for a global heating footprint of approximately 17.6 tons of carbon dioxide equivalents per year, and the footprint of a European is roughly one-half as large, but that of an average citizen of India is about 1.7 tons. As a result, complaints from developed countries that the lesser developed ones should be held to the same standards ring hollow.

Not only is the problem of global climate change one for which technologically developed countries are responsible, but in the short run, it appears that as usual, the less powerful peoples and nations are at the mercy of the more powerful. Nonetheless, everyone occupies the same planet, so economic, political, cultural, social, and military strength will not serve as ramparts against a shared danger. As the Elizabethan-era English poet John Donne pointed out, "no man [or woman] is an island." And as the inhabitants of the world's low-lying oceanic islands know, to their sorrow, their "tropical paradises" in particular are rapidly disappearing.

What Can We Expect in the Future?

It is now possible to model the Earth's future climate with increasing confidence, under various assumptions of greenhouse gas emissions, while acknowledging the uncertainties inherent in the Earth's very complex climate system and the fact that there is a range of possible outcomes associated with each assumption. Every scientifically reasonable assumption nonetheless projects that the Earth will heat up substantially over the next few decades and probably over the coming centuries. Some consequences of global heating are already (no pun intended) "baked in." Even if greenhouse gas emissions were somehow magically brought to zero, the global climate would not return to its pre-Industrial Revolution levels. Water vapor comes and goes quickly, but it will take thousands of years for current carbon dioxide levels to decline to pre-industrial quantities. As the gas lingers, so will its impact on climate. It would take massive as-yet unanticipated cooling for glaciers, sea ice, and ice sheets to return to their earlier levels and for the sea level to subside. Absent some dramatic and unlikely geo-engineered technological "fix," the current global heating regime appears to be irreversible on human timescales. The amount and pace of future heating will therefore depend almost entirely on the amount and pace of anthropogenic greenhouse gas emissions.

Assuming the current trajectory, average global temperatures will increase in a range from 2.6 to 4.8°C (4.7 to 8.6°F) during this century, changes that will be amplified by the many feedback processes described earlier (see Figure 20.6). Predictions for particular locations are less reliable, although it is nearly certain that inland regions will heat more substantially than will coastal areas because of the meliorating effect of the oceans (bearing in mind that much current coastal geography will be underwater in the future).

Among the recently identified consequences of global heating is a change in the Atlantic Meridional Overturning Circulation (a.k.a. the Atlantic Overturning). This natural cycle has been taking place through geologic time, as warm tropical water moves north and becomes saltier through evaporation, which makes it denser and therefore causes it to sink, whereupon it flows south, is heated and then returns north. Melting of the Greenland ice sheet has been adding unusual amounts of surface fresh water to this system, making the northern Atlantic surface waters less salty and therefore less dense and less prone to sinking. The result is a diminution of the Atlantic Overturning, which is disrupting nutrient flows upon which marine life depends as well as generating unusually high water temperature on the east coast of North America, plus other likely effects, not currently understood or predicted.

It has been calculated that if the atmosphere's total CO_2 burden can be kept below 1,000 gigatons (one billion tons), there would be a two-thirds chance of keeping the average global temperature increase below 2.0°C (3.6°F), and further reducing this increase would, of course, require yet more controls on greenhouse gas production. The current worldwide greenhouse gas burden, however, is 675 gigatons, leaving relatively little room for adjustment; moreover, despite reductions in certain countries—and commitments to achieve yet more declines—greenhouse emissions worldwide have been increasing. In addition, with the melting of glaciers, ice fields, and sea ice, the increased area of darker land and water surfaces (lower albedo) reflect less heat energy and absorb more, which results in higher temperatures, more

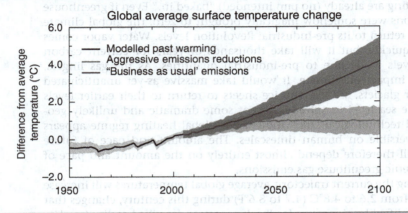

FIGURE 20.6 ● **Worldwide surface temperature change predicted as a result of differing levels of greenhouse gas emissions. All data are shown relative to a reference point (set at 0), indicating the average global temperature between 1986 and 2005. The business-as-usual scenario (dark grey) is compared to one involving aggressive reductions falling nearly to zero by the year 2070. The black line shows past warming, and the shaded areas show standard deviations, a measure of variability.**

Source: National Academy of Sciences. 2020. *Climate Change: Evidence and Causes: Update 2020.* https://doi.org/10.17226/25733. Reproduced with permission from the National Academy of Sciences, Courtesy of The National Academies Press, Washington, D.C.

evaporation, and thus, more atmospheric water vapor—which is a potent greenhouse gas. Clouds can have both negative and positive heating effects, so their impact is currently difficult to model. Also unknown is the long-term capacity of the oceans to absorb CO_2, although it is expected that this will decline over time. All current models therefore predict that feedback processes will amplify global heating.

A major additional possibility is that global climate change will exceed a tipping point leading to sudden, catastrophic events. Uncertainty in this respect is quite high, however, because the atmosphere is changing in ways that appears not to have occurred in millions of years. These include a possible sudden, huge release of methane and carbon dioxide from thawing permafrost and other abrupt changes such as exceptionally rapid melting of Arctic sea ice, or the collapse of the Atlantic Meridional Overturning Circulation by which warmer ocean water travels north in response to the sinking of colder, heavier Arctic water. Such events would throw the world climate system into completely unknown "territory." These and other changes are theoretically possible and consistent with our current knowledge of physics and atmospheric science, although probabilities cannot at present be assessed in any detail—and conceivably not until after they happen!

In this regard, there is also an extreme and utterly terrifying worst-case scenario, worth mentioning but that fortunately need not be taken very seriously: a runaway greenhouse effect in which heightened temperature causes increased evaporation, which leads to increased atmospheric water vapor, which increases the heating, and so on in an unstoppable vicious cycle.

In theory, the result would be a temperature increase in the *hundreds* of degrees, resulting in boiling of the oceans until they are gone along with essentially all life on Earth.

A 2020 report by the US National Academy of Sciences concludes, in characteristically measured tones,

> There are well-understood physical mechanisms by which changes in the amounts of greenhouse gases cause climate changes. The evidence is clear that the concentrations of these gases in the atmosphere have increased and are still increasing rapidly, that climate change is occurring, and that most of the recent change is almost certainly due to emissions of greenhouse gases caused by human activities. Further climate change is inevitable; **if emissions of greenhouse gases continue unabated, future changes will substantially exceed those that have occurred so far**. [emphasis in original] There remains a range of estimates of the magnitude and regional expression of future change, but increases in the extremes of climate that can adversely affect natural ecosystems and human activities and infrastructure are expected.
>
> Citizens and governments can choose among several options (or a mixture of those options) in response to this information: they can change their pattern of energy production and usage in order to limit emissions of greenhouse gases and hence the magnitude of climate changes; they can wait for changes to occur and accept the losses, damage, and suffering that arise; they can adapt to actual and expected changes as much as possible; or they can seek as yet unproven "geo-engineering" solutions to counteract some of the climate changes that would otherwise occur.

Obstacles to Action

The prevention of war, the establishment of greater socioeconomic equity, and the protection of human rights all encounter difficulties that are mostly political. By contrast, responding effectively to the climate crisis (never mind solving it) requires confronting hard scientific realities, not least the degree to which much future climate change is already baked into the Earth's atmospheric system. Nonetheless, confronting the issue also involves questions of political will. High on the list is overcoming some psychological obstacles, notably the peculiar degree to which climate change has become a matter of ideology, with climate denial—especially in the US—closely allied to an anti-science mindset more generally, as well as much right-wing political ideology, which tends to see climate change as "left-wing alarmism," connected to opposition to free-market economics. There is at least some truth here, in that insofar as many of the largest corporations (including not just the fossil fuel industry but also much current manufacturing and transportation) have been built upon the generation of huge quantities of greenhouse gases.

Moreover, just as slave owners have never led the fight to abolish slavery, it is unlikely that those who profit by the unrestricted production of greenhouse gases will take the lead in abolishing their current "business models." Most have, in fact, opposed nearly all efforts to lower their emissions, even by modest amounts, for fear that this would diminish their profits, although the arguments of climate denialists have become so strained that even some of the oil, coal, and gas companies have begun to distance themselves publicly from this perspective, even as they continue to finance the campaigns of politicians who espouse such views. A parallel exists in the vigorous opposition to mandatory seat belts on the part of automobile manufacturers, who claimed for years that such government regulatory imposition would put them out of business. (It did not.)

A more contemporary example is the resistance to wearing masks and to taking other common sense and proven public health measures to protect the health of the citizenry from Covid-19 by those who prize their "freedom of personal choice" over the public good. The Great Recession of 2008 made it clear that private enterprise and market fundamentalism cannot be counted on to always function in the best interests of the citizenry at large. Similarly, it is inconceivable that capitalism by itself—notably the so-called magic of the marketplace—will solve our enormous climate, economic, and public health crises. Substantial government intervention, regulation, and encouragement of alternative technologies are clearly necessary if the public and the planet are to be well served.

Cheap energy is undoubtedly a social good whose benefits rebound not only to the wealthy but to the impoverished as well. At the same time, in view of the planetary costs imposed thus far, not to mention those anticipated for the future, such energy—especially when produced by fossil fuels—is not cheap at all. Furthermore, fossil fuel plants—coal burners in particular—generate huge quantities of toxic byproducts, especially ash laden with heavy metals, which have periodically leaked into fresh water streams and local communities (mostly of color), not to mention the greenhouse gases they generate.

The fossil fuel industry does not represent a triumph of free markets: of the world's 20 largest fossil fuel companies, 12 are state owned. According to the International Monetary Fund, in 2017, government subsidies to the fossil fuel industry worldwide exceeded $5 trillion, an expense that ignores what economists call "externalities." This refers to the costs of an activity or product that are not directly reflected in the market price but rather are passed along to other parties, often the public or the environment. The externalities associated with fossil fuel use are immense, including rising oceans, more severe climate catastrophes, huge numbers of displaced people, and an overheated human and natural environment. It is generally true, however, that externalities are not taken into consideration when most policy decisions are made. (If they were, then they wouldn't be "externalities," but simply the costs of doing the people's business.)

The large number of jobs already created by renewable energy, and the fact that they exceed those produced by fossil fuels, should by itself encourage a rapid transition to the former. However, people currently employed in the traditional energy economy and whose jobs are threatened by conversion to a green economy tend to have especially loud voices and, therefore, outsized political influence. This is similar to the paradox of economic conversion from a military to a civilian economy, in which a large number of potential jobs are often outweighed in the public mind by the smaller number of current jobs that are at risk.

It is also possible that the kind of previously mentioned feedback loops regarding global heating could damage creative responses to climate change. Thus, the negative impacts of increasingly severe climate-based economic and social disruption could lead to major economic losses, which might generate their own feedback loops whereby the ability to prevent further climate-caused damage is in turn undermined, which then causes greater disruption, and so on in a mutually reinforcing vicious circle as economic decline inhibits scientific innovation and technology-based implementation.

Under these conditions, democracy itself could also be at risk, insofar as situations of social and economic stress set the stage for political extremism, especially by the far right (nascent autocracies and national populist fascism). Stressful conditions can lead to greater solidarity, both within a country and internationally, but they can also cause increased intolerance, exclusionary nationalism and, thus, reduced rather than increased cooperation in confronting a problem that does not respect international borders and requires a planet-wide response.

Such a response is especially difficult to generate because cooperation is vulnerable to what economists call the "free-rider problem," which arises when an entity is tempted to benefit from a public good (in this case, reducing global climate change) but without incurring the costs (modifying its economy accordingly). Solutions exist but are difficult to employ: notably public shaming in the court of international opinion and, more strenuously, punishing noncompliance with economic and/or political sanctions.

Religious fundamentalism, usually with a Christian face, also plays a role in climate denial and inaction. A frequent belief, especially among many evangelicals, is that a benevolent God would not permit destruction of that which was divinely created, and if He did, this would represent suitable punishment for human sins. It is sometimes claimed, as well, that it is not the place of humanity to question divine plans—a perspective that is inconsistent with people struggling to improve things, from using medicine to rendering aid to living things in need, or even basic self-help. On the other hand, such attitudes have been, to some extent, countered by movements in favor of environmental stewardship as a religious responsibility.

Some scientists can be stuck in a different kind of fundamentalism, whereby they feel that their public stance should avoid political recommendations and be strictly limited to statements of incontrovertible fact, or circumstances for which they can summon something like a 99 percent confidence level. However, in addition to the difficulty of making accurate predictions, the consequences of the climate crisis are likely to unfold nonlinearly; that is, accumulated effects will probably not vary in a simple straight line with respect to any direct measurement of climate change. These uncertainties, added to those necessarily inherent in a system as complex as global climate, may deter many scientists from proposing solutions, in turn leaving the public stage to those who are less knowledgeable, especially special political and economic interest groups and individuals in a position to profit from inaction. In addition, the natural caution of scientists leads them to couch their findings in probabilistic terms because very little about the natural world can be asserted with absolute certainty; this inclination, in turn, opens public space for climate deniers and self-interested corporate leaders to demand "more research" until the issues are 100 percent guaranteed and universally agreed upon (which is all but impossible), thereby delaying policy decisions indefinitely.

Also, many of those concerned about the climate crisis have been criticized by some mainstream political and business decision makers as "extremists" or as worry-warts, a complaint that derives some credibility from the fact that climate change is not a simple unidirectional process; rather, it proceeds in fits and starts, with occasional short-term reverses. In addition, most contemporary citizens are attuned to rapid, easily identified changes rather than gradual processes, and most people are also rather conservative in their daily lives, preferring to continue living as they have done in the recent past and reluctant to make major changes, especially if those changes require moving in unfamiliar, uncomfortable, and to some extent unpredictable directions.

Personal sacrifice is rarely a popular rallying call, especially when for most people the climate crisis appears to be a wave that may not crash on their shores in the immediate future. The result is additional pressure to under-value the costs of inaction and to overestimate the downsides of responsive and responsible action.

Prospects for Progress

Despite these very real concerns, there is some evidence that millions of citizens—and a considerable number of political leaders—are waking up to the problem. Many ameliorating efforts are therefore under way.

The Paris Agreement of 2015

We don't know the exact dimensions of the climate change threat, but comparable uncertainty has seldom stopped human beings from acting when it came to other threats, such as those posed by nations perceived by one's own political leaders as hostile. The threat posed by climate change may be as great or greater; thus far, however, the collective human response has been much more restrained.

The major culprits—that is, the major carbon emitters—are, in order, China, the United States, India, and Russia. Even though US annual emissions have steadily and slowly declined for the last decade, the US is still responsible for generating far more per capita emissions than other nations: for example, twice as much CO_2 per capita as in China or Europe, and 15–20 times more than someone in Africa. Any state, once it becomes heavily industrialized or highly dependent on coal (especially true of China and the United States), will contribute more than its share to the Earth's carbon load. After much controversy, more than 150 countries (including the United States) signed the Kyoto Protocols in 1997, which established emission reduction targets for 37 industrialized countries. Added up, these targets were relatively modest, accounting for an average 5 percent reduction by 2010, compared to 1990 levels.

The George W. Bush presidential administration refused to comply with these protocols, however, and refused to take responsible action, instead issuing the usual call for more research, while at the same time minimizing and even misrepresenting the established conclusions of technical studies. When it comes to acknowledging climate change and its anthropogenic nature, there is overwhelming scientific consensus. Doing something about it, however, is another story.

A very real political challenge confronted by efforts to mitigate if not reduce global climate change is the opposition by many members of the US Republican Party to meaningful mitigation efforts or, in some cases, to even recognizing the problem. A century or more ago, the Republican Party was quite supportive of environmental protection, beginning notably with President Theodore Roosevelt; after all, "conservation" and "conservative" are etymologically similar, both committed to preserving what is perceived as good (socially, economically, and environmentally). But more recently, the Republican Party, with some exceptions, is the world's most powerful climate-denialist political party, and nearly the only one in a major democracy. As a result, the United States—with its immense international influence as well as its huge greenhouse gas impact—has recently not only failed to lead on this topic, but has become an obstacle to necessary global action.

There is a history of failed attempts to reach international agreement to halt ruinous global heating. For example, a "climate summit" held in Copenhagen in 2009 collapsed in mutual international recriminations. Nonetheless, the possibility exists that an agreement reached in 2015 in Paris (known as the Paris Agreement) represents a turning point in such efforts. At a conference attended by representatives of 195 countries (along with large delegations from nongovernmental organizations and other citizen groups), a number of agreements were reached. These include commitments to hold the increase in the global average temperature to less than 2°C above preindustrial levels and to pursue efforts to limit that increase to 1.5°C. There is near-universal consensus among climate scientists that increases beyond 2°C would be disastrous, and that an increase of at least 1.5°C appears inevitable, with such a rise unavoidable as a result of past emissions, even if greenhouse gas production were somehow to halt globally. Such dire assumptions, however, should not inhibit efforts to do whatever is possible to mitigate the situation.

Despite worldwide criticism, former President Trump announced in 2017 that the United States would withdraw from the Paris Agreement effective November 2020, making the US the only country to do so. However, many countries, as well as individual states within the US, continued to abide by it, and with the election of President Joe Biden, the US rejoined the Agreement in early 2021.

Under the Paris Agreement, countries agreed to "reach global peaking of green-house gas emissions as soon as possible, recognizing that peaking will take longer for developing country parties, and to undertake rapid reductions thereafter." Special consideration is thus allowed for such major greenhouse-emitting developing countries as India, although eventually all countries are expected to participate and to reduce their emissions. The question of liability or compensation on the part of rich, developed countries was not broached, to the disappointment of geographically low-lying and many less economically developed states, which are especially at risk of catastrophic sea-level rise and not responsible for having caused this impending disaster. However, for the first time, the world was put on notice that the special needs of such climate-change victimized peoples will have to be addressed.

All signatories to the Paris Agreement are required to submit plans detailing how they will reduce their greenhouse gas pollution, with a ratcheting-up of limits to be evaluated every 5 years, while acknowledging "common but differentiated responsibilities, and respective capabilities, in the light of different national circumstances." Countries are also required to monitor, verify, and publicly report their emissions and to submit appropriate data to a single global accounting commission. Developing countries, led by India, had urged two separate expectations, a more stringent one for developed countries (whose economies had already benefitted from the industrial development that has brought the world's climate to such a global crisis) and a more lenient one for the others, who, although suffering disproportionately from the actions of the developed countries, have had relatively few of the economic upsides. The developing countries did receive, however, a commitment to establish a fund—starting with a minimum of $100 billion—in climate-related compensatory funding. However, this fund has yet to be even minimally funded.

The Paris Agreement is aspirational and does not constitute a legally binding treaty; this was in large part due to the Obama administration, which realized that Republican opposition in the US Senate made treaty ratification virtually impossible. President Obama described the Agreement as "an enduring agreement that reduces global carbon pollution and sets the world on a course to a low-carbon future." While the Agreement is far from ideal, it may nonetheless represent a triumph of politics, which is sometimes defined as "the art of the possible." It is also historic in many respects; for example, by requiring all states, including the less developed ones, to commit to action to mitigate global warming. Moreover, the Paris Agreement sends a clear message that the international community is mostly united in recognizing the anthropogenic nature of global heating, the danger that it poses, and a determination to fight it. It also sent a clear signal to financial and energy markets about the global imperative to galvanize corporate and research efforts to shift away from a carbon-based economy.

Importantly, most scientists and many world leaders agree that "there is no plan B"; that is, at present, there is no viable alternative to these measures, The Paris Agreement provides a feasible framework for global cooperation on climate change and may prove to be the last, best hope of ameliorating worldwide catastrophe. A hopeful sign is the international agreement reached in Kigali, Rwanda, in late 2016. It greatly restricted the worldwide production and release of HFCs, which—although much less abundant than carbon dioxide—are about a thousand times more potent, per molecule, than CO_2 as a greenhouse gas. When it comes at least to slowing climate change, progress is possible, especially since Donald Trump—who had disparaged it as a "Chinese hoax" while denying the facts of climate science and seeking to discredit individual scientists, and who actually overhauled US government policy to allow *more* atmospheric pollution—was defeated in 2020 by Joe Biden, who includes a robust climate policy in his presidential agenda.

Possible Actions and Solutions

To keep global warming below 2°C will require worldwide success—and thus, international cooperation—in drastically reducing emissions, a process sometimes called "deep decarbonization." A 2019 report from the Intergovernmental Panel on Climate Change stated that emissions would have to be halved by 2030 if heating is to be limited to 1.5°C. As with the prospects for world government, the challenge of climate change isn't so much a lack of specific options as an absence of political consensus and will. Because scientific evidence shows that climate change is mostly anthropogenic, it can be ameliorated, essentially buying time for future generations.

One practical series of solutions is the adoption of the following triad of viable alternatives to the catastrophic status quo: the promotion and global adoption of renewable energy sources (wind, solar, etc.), strict conservation, and reforestation. These suggest many possibilities for action; for example, a tax on carbon emissions would exert economic pressure on corporations for the development and use of noncarbon energy sources. The greater the tax, the greater the pressure. A carbon tax would also be potentially acceptable to dyed-in-the-wool believers in the power of "free markets"—even though it is very unlikely that private enterprise alone will rise adequately to this particular crisis.

Another beneficial change would be to increase automobile fuel economy standards from an average of 27 miles per gallon (in 2010) to 35 miles per gallon as soon as possible, which would save 2.3 million barrels of oil per day in the United States alone, approximately the amount previously imported from the Persian Gulf. Recent relevant developments along these lines include the following:

- The rate of growth of CO_2 emissions in the US slowed significantly in 2019, with the total amount only 0.6 percent higher than in 2018. Growth rates in 2018 were 2.1 percent and in 2017, 1.5 percent. But as promising at it may be for the rate of increase to be declining, current levels of CO_2 emissions need to go *down*, not increase more slowly.

- The rate of fossil fuel emissions in China grew by 2.6 percent, while that of India rose by 1.8 percent in 2019.

- The burning of coal (the dirtiest fossil fuel) has been plummeting in the US and Europe. In the US, it has declined by about 50 percent since 2005. In addition to reducing the rate of CO_2 increase, the resulting cleaner air has saved tens of thousands of American lives by reducing deaths due to such respiratory illnesses as asthma and emphysema. This shift has also created hundreds of thousands of new jobs in renewable energy companies, many more than were lost in the coal industry. Coal nonetheless accounted for 40 percent of global emissions in 2019, with oil contributing 34 percent and natural gas 20 percent.

- In 2018, solar and wind represented 88 percent of the new electricity capacities in the 28 nations of the European Union, 65 percent in India, 53 percent in China, and 49 percent in the United States. In 2019, according to the Bureau of Labor Statistics, the fastest-growing occupation in the United States was solar installer, exceeding the total national average job growth over the previous 5 years by sixfold. The second-fastest-growing job? Wind turbine service technician.

- Repurposing a famous song by Bob Dylan, one answer, my friend, is blowing in the wind: From 2009 to 2020, the price of energy derived from large US wind farms declined by 70 percent and from large-array solar farms by fully 90 percent. These major renewable energy sources (with the addition, to a much lesser extent, of tidal and geothermal energy) constitute 25 percent of global energy production as of 2019, a proportion that is certain to increase, especially because in all probability, it will soon cost less to build renewable energy facilities than to operate existing fossil fuel plants. Wind and solar complement each other: winds are generally stronger at night and during colder, less sunny months; thus, when solar power is less available, there is often more wind available for generating clean energy. There have also been extraordinary reductions in the cost of renewables, such that economic imperatives alone will drive substantial change.

Government policies can make a significant positive impact on reducing the rate of global climate change. For example, steel and concrete production use huge amounts of coal; governments could mandate that a certain percentage of energy used in their manufacture must come from renewables, instead of from coal and oil. Battery efficiency has been improving rapidly, driven in large part by increasing demand for electric cars, and because the cost of batteries represents a large proportion of the cost of such cars, the development of cheaper, more long-lasting batteries will drive yet more demand for electric cars. This is reflected not only in technological innovations, but also in the cost of producing efficient storage batteries, analogous to the price reductions in solar technology. Progress in clean energy can activate a virtuous circle, with innovation driving yet more innovation as well as increased public and political support—which in turn can stimulate more innovation, and so on. But even without major breakthroughs, renewables currently offer highly practical alternatives to carbon-intensive methods of energy generation; accordingly, actionable options currently exist and are not "pie in the sky."

- As of early 2021, and by virtue of its unusual system of "state-controlled capitalism," China is the world's largest investor in renewable energy research and development, and also the world leader when it comes to manufacturing wind turbines, electric vehicles, and the storage batteries on which they depend. China has also become the world's number one producer, exporter, and installer of solar panels. Despite the rapid growth in renewable technology, there is still ample opportunity for immense growth in this industry, whether or not competition with China is a major motivator.

  Speaking to the United Nations General Assembly, Chinese President Xi Jinping pledged that his country would achieve carbon neutrality by 2060 (which means that it would absorb as much carbon from the atmosphere as it spews out). This was an unexpected and unprecedented announcement, although implementing it will not be easy, given that China is the world's biggest emitter of greenhouse gases and burns through more coal than all other countries combined. Mr. Xi stopped short of describing a detailed plan, but he indicated that the Chinese government would shortly be releasing a 5-year roadmap for achieving this goal. For all the downsides of a dictatorial, one-party political system and a "command economy" such as China's, one upside could well be the ability to implement aggressive policies of the sort that appear necessary in order to effectively confront the deep challenges of human-generated global heating.

- The US Democratic Party platform in 2020 (a version of the "Green New Deal") called for requiring that all electricity come from clean sources by 2040 by imposing a national clean electricity mandate that would require utilities to derive a steadily rising percentage of electricity from renewables or from emissions-free nuclear power. The plan also seeks additional spending and regulations to mandate the national adoption of electric vehicles, to promote super-efficient buildings, to plug leaks in the nation's gas infrastructure, and to directly finance the further deployment of renewables. It also invokes such market-based solutions as taxing carbon emissions.

- At a virtual Earth Day Summit in April, 2021, President Joe Biden announced that the US was committing itself to a 50 percent reduction in greenhouse gas emissions compared to its 2005 levels, to be achieved by 2030.

- These last two proposals have, not unexpectedly, been disparaged by many US conservatives as yet another "tax increase." As a result, many American climate activists appear to be moving toward increased emphasis on enhanced direct support for renewable energy, along with establishing standards that mandate limitations on allowable pollution, leaving industry, utilities, and local governments to work out the details of how this is to be achieved. Whether some version of the "Green New Deal" will be implemented during the Biden/Harris term remains to be seen.

- After beginning modestly, a rapidly growing worldwide movement has been promoting divestment from fossil fuel industries, sometimes demanding that large investment and retirement funds sell their holdings in coal, oil, and natural gas, as a result of shareholder insistence. This grassroots pressure from below was a factor in the plunge of the stock prices of many of these companies, which promises (or in the opinion of many of these corporations, threatens) to become a feedback process, whereby fewer people invest in fossil fuels, leading others—regardless of their attitudes toward global climate change— to avoid these companies, if only because they become unprofitable investments as stock prices decline.

A 2020 report from the Shell Oil Company, for example, states that divestment is a material risk to its business, to which climate activists respond that this is poetic and socio-bio-economic justice, given that Shell's business, along with that of other fossil fuel companies, is itself a material risk to the planet. In 2011, ExxonMobil, the gas and oil mega-corporation, was the biggest company on Earth; in 2020, it was dropped from the Dow Jones Industrial Average, after having been a lynchpin of that stock index for 92 years. Also in 2020, BP (formerly British Petroleum), another fossil fuel company, became the first giant international energy corporation to start abandoning its existing business model, having announced that over the coming decade it would cut oil and gas production by 40 percent, while substantially increasing its involvement in low-carbon technology. Borrowing from the movie *Spiderman*, one might say that a growing list of fossil fuel companies have begun to realize that with great emissions comes great responsibilities (if only to their stockholders).

Nonetheless, the challenge to these corporations' immediate "bottom line" is great. Fossil fuel companies currently have access to an estimated 2,795 gigatons (billion tons) of carbon in their underground reserves, all of which they have been planning to burn. By contrast, it has been reliably estimated that a total atmospheric burden of 565 gigatons (about one-fifth the carbon "available" to be released in the future) is the upper limit of what could keep global temperatures from increasing by 2 degrees Celsius—an increase that itself would be not only challenging but ecologically, economically, and socially unsafe. It will be an immense challenge to convince fossil fuel companies to leave their potential profits in the ground.

- Many of the largest universities in the US have already divested from fossil fuel companies or pledged to do so within a few years; however, this process is by no means universal and sometimes involves "greenwashing." (Greenwashing refers to a company or organization spending more time and money on marketing itself as environmentally friendly than on minimizing its environmental impact. It is a deceitful advertising gimmick intended to mislead consumers who prefer to buy goods and services from environmentally conscious brands.) For example, in the spring of 2020, Harvard University pledged to reduce emissions by gradually increasing its investment portfolio with shares in companies developing renewable resources and divesting from environmentally destructive firms, so as to be "greenhouse-gas neutral" by 2050, which pretty much guarantees that such divestment, if it occurs at all, will be too little, too late.

- An indication of the ambiguous nature of "progress" in reducing greenhouse gas emissions is that in the 6 years from 2013 to 2019, the world economy grew by nearly 25 percent, while global greenhouse emissions grew by only 3 percent. So far, so good . . . except that emissions nonetheless grew, whereas they must decrease; otherwise, the planet is still heading toward a climate cliff, just a bit less rapidly than before.

Ironically, one of the most promising reasons for anticipating genuine and sustained efforts to combat global climate change coincides with one of its most worrisome aspects: The fact that the immediate future will bring more devastating floods, droughts, mega-fires, hurricanes, along with yet more destructive sea level rises, heat-caused deaths, and loss of biodiversity, plus other effects not yet experienced or even contemplated. It can be anticipated (and certainly, hoped) that as a result, public pressure in the United States and the world as a whole will pressure political leaders to prioritize the Earth's sustainability over private or corporate profits.

Technology to the Rescue?

Increased political awareness and mobilization are essential for success in confronting the climate crisis. However, there is also room for technological reorientation and advances. Of these, renewables—solar, wind, and tidal—are key, combined with the many inexpensive and immediately practical ways of reducing CO_2 emissions: implementing increases in energy efficiency by improving building insulation, using double-pane windows, otherwise reducing wasteful energy use, increasing the availability of convenient public transportation, and so forth. A seemingly small but exemplary adjustment already under way involves the replacement of incandescent bulbs with high efficiency LED lights, which provide equal or more illumination while using much less electricity. Another example comes from solutions to the "urban heat island effect," a phenomenon whereby building materials characteristic of large cities trap heat, resulting in city temperatures that are consistently five degrees or more above that of the countryside. A simple solution is painting roofs white, which can reduce this potentially lethal effect by as much as one-third.

Other measures have been touted but offer less potential benefit while incurring substantial possible risk. For example, hydraulic fracturing, or "fracking," is a drilling technology that involves injecting water at high pressure into oil shale deposits. It has resulted in substantially increased quantities of natural gas in the United States, Canada, and some other countries. However, it also pollutes underground water supplies and has been responsible for a spike in earthquakes in such locations as Oklahoma, where earthquakes had previously been quite rare. Natural gas is considerably cleaner than coal or oil, and its alternative combustion in power plants reduces greenhouse emissions in the short term, but it nonetheless generates lots of carbon dioxide and cannot be considered a long-term solution.

Unrealistic claims have been made for "clean coal" technologies. However, there is no such thing; the phrase is an oxymoron because even low-sulfur coal is very dirty. Capturing emissions from coal-burning power plants and then somehow storing them underground might offer more potential, but the technology does not currently exist. Electric cars and trucks are already in service and growing in popularity. They operate without producing direct pollution, drawing their power from the electric grid. As of 2020, electric cars comprised 8 percent of new car sales in California (although only about 1.5 percent in the US overall). By contrast, 56 percent of new car sales in

Norway are electric-powered, in large part because the Norwegian government amply subsidizes these purchases—even though that government derives much of its revenue from the sale of North Sea oil.

So long as electricity itself is generated by burning fossil fuels, the benefit is obviously limited, although insofar as electric generation increasingly derives from renewables, the use of electric vehicles is likely to grow. A current stumbling block, however, involves the cost and efficiency of storage batteries, although technological improvements in this regard are rapidly emerging. As a result, some Scandinavian countries are considering banning gasoline-powered vehicles as soon as 2030.

There is no shortage of "options" that currently exist in theory only. For example, one potential solution being examined—but as yet without practical prospects—is somehow to suck carbon dioxide out of the atmosphere and bury it underground indefinitely, possibly in the form of metallic carbonates or some other rocklike mineral. Another series of possibilities, currently more science fiction than science, involves "geo-engineering"— planetary-scale interventions, such as surrounding the Earth with reflecting structures similar to aluminum foil, injecting gaseous material into the atmosphere that would be either impenetrable to or reflect some incoming solar heat, and distributing a kind of inert white material across vast areas of the planet to substitute for the diminishing ice sheets and glaciers as a means of increasing planetary albedo.

Another, marginally more feasible example of geo-engineering calls for spreading rock dust on otherwise bare ground: following rain, silicate and carbonate minerals would dissolve in rainwater, attracting carbon dioxide and forming bicarbonate ions, which would ultimately be washed into the oceans by runoff, storing the carbon for eons. For the foreseeable future, however, such "solutions" are not only pie in the sky (some of them almost literally!), raising unanswerable technological, political, and economic questions, but they also run great risks of unforeseen ecological consequences, were they ever to be attempted.

Another hurdle to dealing with climate change is the political psychology associated with any conceivable time scale. Even in an ideal (and currently unrealistic) scenario in which greenhouse gas emissions are reduced by 5 percent or more each year, many decades would transpire before a helpful impact on global heating would be discernible because of the massive quantities of fossil fuels burned since the Industrial Revolution, combined with the longevity of carbon dioxide in the atmosphere. As a result, any payoff—even from reductions on a heroic scale—would not be quick. The most that can be hoped for is to slow down rather than stave off future climate disruptions.

There is also the fact, of relevance to political psychology, that even under best-case assumptions, people are liable to be impatient when results are not immediately forthcoming, especially if they have made considerable sacrifices in the expectation of positive results. It can therefore be anticipated that climate change deniers and opponents of climate amelioration will take advantage of this built-in lag between action and observed effect to argue against the effectiveness, and therefore the legitimacy, of whatever policies are implemented. This, in turn, makes it all the more important that the public be educated about the problem and prepared both for some inevitable degradation of the planetary system and for the claim that reducing greenhouse gas emissions has not "solved" global heating . . . giving credence to deniers who maintain that these emissions hadn't caused global heating in the first place.

Nuclear Power?

When it comes to technological fixes, at least some—including practical energy conservation, renewables, and electric vehicles—are "shovel ready," available here and now. Yet another "solution" also exists and has been seriously touted as a climate savior. Nuclear power plants have been operating in a number of countries for decades, and many proponents maintain that it is a necessary part of any climate protection program, either as a temporary bridge to a sustainable future based on renewables or even as a solution in itself. Given the growing energy needs of the Global South in particular, a case is readily made that whatever its downsides, the alternative to expanding nuclear energy is expanding the burning of fossil fuels, which is increasingly seen as not merely unsustainable but ultimately catastrophic.

Although the technology of nuclear power generation is quite complex, the basic idea is straightforward: a nuclear reactor, maintained but kept from "going critical" (initiating a potentially dangerous chain reaction), is a constant source of heat, which can then be used to generate electricity by running turbines. As of 2020, there are roughly 450 power-generating reactors operating in 30 different countries, providing about 10 percent of the world's electricity. In some countries, the proportion of national energy generated by nuclear power is much higher, reaching more than 70 percent, for example, in France; in the US it is about 20 percent. Supporters argue that nuclear power is the only way to meet the world's growing energy needs in the short term without continued burning of fossil fuels. They also point to the fact that atmospheric pollution from nuclear power plants is essentially zero.

There are significant downsides, however. For one, there have been at least three catastrophic accidents at nuclear power plants: at Three Mile Island in Pennsylvania (1979), Chernobyl in the former Soviet Union (present-day Ukraine; 1986), and at Fukushima in Japan (2010). Supporters of nuclear energy maintain, on the other hand, that much safer nuclear power reactor designs have already been developed and that such new models would be immune from catastrophic accidents. Nonetheless, no insurance companies have been willing to underwrite new nuclear power plants in the US due to safety concerns, and none have been built there in the last few decades—although about 55 power reactors are currently being constructed in 15 countries, notably in China, India, Russia, and the United Arab Emirates.

In addition, claims that nuclear power is greenhouse gas–free ignore the effects of mining, transporting, and concentrating uranium ore, the last of which is especially energy intensive because it is very difficult to isolate U-235 (uranium used in a reactor) from the much more abundant form of uranium, U-238. In addition, U-235 itself, in sufficient quantities, can produce an atomic bomb. Moreover, plutonium is generated as an inevitable byproduct of power generation, and plutonium is not only highly toxic, it is more easily fissioned than is U-235, which means that it requires less plutonium than U-235 to make a bomb. Nuclear power plants are thus potential bomb-producing factories, possibly contributing to nuclear proliferation, although supporters point out that regular inspections and close monitoring, including tamper-proof cameras, can prevent this. Nuclear power plants also constitute potential high-value targets for terrorists, not so much as a possible source of fissile material for bomb building, but because disrupting their cooling systems or blowing them up with conventional explosives (or by crashing an airplane) would be the equivalent of a highly effective "dirty bomb" that would release huge amounts of long-lived radioactive poisons, even though it is extremely unlikely that such attacks on a nuclear power plant could produce an actual nuclear explosion.

There also remains the as-yet-unsolved problem of disposing safely and reliably of nuclear waste, which will remain lethal for longer than human civilization has thus far existed. According to the International Atomic Energy Agency, there is currently a stockpile of 250,000 metric tons of spent nuclear fuel rods stored in 14 countries, nearly all of them in temporary cooling ponds. On the plus side, unlike solar power, nuclear power is independent of weather and the time of day.

France has announced a substantial decrease in its nuclear plans, while Belgium, Germany, and Switzerland have announced that their nuclear power infrastructure will be completely dismantled, mostly due to public anxiety about long-term safety. Germany has announced a planned *Energiewende* (energy transition) to 100 percent renewables by 2022, and as of 2020, it had approximately doubled its energy production via renewables (notably solar and wind)—and yet, its carbon emissions have remained essentially unchanged, due to growth in demand.

A similar situation exists in Japan. On the one hand, the atomic bombings of Hiroshima and Nagasaki left that country with a kind of collective anti-nuclear trauma, while on the other hand, Japan is both highly industrialized and lacking in domestic energy sources. Tokyo Electric, which operated the Fukushima reactor, had long been criticized for its lax safety procedures, and after the Fukushima disaster, all 50 of Japan's nuclear power stations were shut down and ordered to undergo safety overhauls, during which time coal and gas replaced them and, as a result, greenhouse gas emissions soared. A few nuclear power plants have since been restarted in that country, and it is expected that nuclear energy will account for a minimum of one-fifth of Japan's electricity for at least the next few decades.

Until recently, it appeared that most people failed to appreciate the reality and accumulating threat of global heating while reacting strongly to the threat posed by nuclear energy. The dilemma is real, with most nations stuck between a relatively slow-moving but certain disaster (global heating) and the statistically remote but very visible, high-risk danger inherent in nuclear power. In any event, despite the construction of numerous new nuclear power plants in some countries, it seems unlikely that in the long run there will be many major new investments in nuclear power, at least in part because of economics combined with long construction lead times: new plants are extremely expensive and require a decade or more to construct. Cost overruns in the development of nuclear power plants have also been extreme, whereas investment in energy conservation and in renewables are far more cost-effective, immediately available, and politically palatable. It is nonetheless clear that nuclear power generation will remain part of the global power menu, at least for the next few decades. But given the urgency of instituting greenhouse gas controls combined with the lower costs and much greater public acceptability of renewables, most of today's "smart money" is not currently on nuclear for the long term.

Climate Change Activism

Concern about global climate change has become a worldwide issue, increasingly embraced by perceptive politicians in many countries (albeit opposed by some). It has also emerged as a motivating and organizing issue for activist citizen groups, having become one of those cases in which ordinary people lead and, ideally, most decision makers follow. This is very much a work in process whose actions and impacts are challenging to pinpoint. As of 2020, the most prominent citizens' organizations include the following:

Extinction Rebellion (abbreviated XR) was established in the United Kingdom in 2018, supported by a "call to action" from approximately 100 established scientists. XR has focused on using nonviolent direct action techniques, many involving mass civil disobedience, including the willingness of activists to be jailed to induce national governments, especially the UK and Germany, to take vigorous action on a range of environmental issues. Mitigating global heating is an especially prominent goal of XR—although other issues, notably loss of biodiversity and habitat destruction, are also topics of concern. XR's offshoot, Extinction Rebellion Peace (abbreviated XR Peace), is also concerned with eliminating weapons of mass destruction. This recent development illustrates the close connection between saving the Earth from the existential threats of global heating and nuclear war, hence working for negative peace on the one hand and on the other, developing local peace communities while engaging in nonviolent mass actions that promote positive peace.

Within the United States, as elsewhere, there have been a number of groups concerned with climate change, all of them having been energized by the inaction of the federal government in general and by the overt climate change denial of the Trump administration in particular. For example, 350.org is an organization with international reach founded by the prominent activist and author Bill McKibben. (The "350" comes from 350 ppm of carbon dioxide, which has been identified as the upper limit of atmospheric CO_2 that can keep Earth's climate short of a dangerous tipping point. The existing level in 2019 was already 415 ppm, indicating that the atmosphere's CO_2 burden must be decreased, not simply kept from increasing.) As of late 2020, 350.org had partnered with nearly 190 organizations worldwide. Like similar groups, 350.org is a grassroots movement aiming to end use of fossil fuels and to make progress toward the global adoption of renewable energy. A major focus toward this end has been to demand divestment from fossil fuel companies, thereby making the activities of these corporations unprofitable and necessitating basic changes in their business models.

Also within the US, the Sunrise Movement, which is particularly associated with young activists, emphasizes electing public officials committed to renewable energy and is also attempting to get the Democratic Party to support the Green New Deal. Another organization with global reach is known variously as Youth Strike for Climate, Climate Strike, and Fridays for a Future. Largely led by school-age children, it has organized around boycotting schools on Fridays so that its participants can engage in demonstrations favoring a transition from fossil fuels to renewables, as a way of pressuring adults to act on behalf of climate mitigation. On one day in 2019, this movement attracted more than one million strikers or school boycotters around the world.

A Final Note on the Climate Crisis

The young Swedish climate activist Greta Thunberg (age 16 at the time) addressed the United Nations in 2019, pointing out that because of global heating, entire ecosystems are collapsing and a mass extinction is taking place, so that "business as usual" is no longer acceptable. Ms. Thunberg and other climate activists of all ages represent the hope of humanity as a whole for a more sustainable and prosperous global environment.

Her message to the UN—speaking passionately for a generation destined to feel the full effects of the malfeasance perpetrated by those currently in power—also included a suitable amount of outrage, literally demanding "How dare you?" along with a warning that the world is waking up and change is coming, whether corporate titans and indifferent world leaders want it or not. The question is "What kind of change?" One that damages and erodes, or that fosters and preserves the biosphere and our place in it? Humanity's collective challenge is to steer that change in the right direction.

Questions for Further Reflection

1. Are you persuaded that there's a global climate-change crisis? Why or why not? If so, what would you do to address it? If not, what evidence would persuade you otherwise?

2. Is it a new form of imperialism if developed countries impose climate change regulations upon the less-developed countries (LDCs)? Alternatively, is it unreasonable for LDCs to demand that the more developed ones adopt the strictest climate-control regulations?

3. How would you prioritize these three responses to the climate crisis, and why:

(1) reducing greenhouse emissions, (2) exploring possible geo-engineering to reduce atmospheric carbon dioxide and/or diminish incoming solar heat, and (3) improving adjustment and adaptation to the realities of global heating?

4. Discuss the possible implications of global climate change for human rights, democracy, and economic equity.

5. What are some differences and some similarities between the climate crisis and the Covid-19 pandemic?

Suggestions for Further Reading

Christiana Figueres and Tom Rivett-Carnac. 2020. *The Future We Choose: Surviving the Climate Crisis*. New York: Knopf.

Hope Jahren. 2020. *Climate Change and Where to Go from Here*. New York: Vintage.

Andreas Karelas and Katharine Hayhoe. 2020. *Climate Courage: How Tackling Climate Change Can Build Community, Transform the Economy, and Bridge the Political Divide in America*. New York: Beacon Press.

Naomi Klein. 2019. *On Fire: The (Burning) Case for a Green New Deal*. New York: Simon & Schuster.

William J. Manning. 2020. *Trees and Global Warming: The Role of Forests in Cooling and Warming the Atmosphere*. New York: Cambridge University Press.

Bill McKibben. 2020. *Falter: Has the Human Came Begun to Play Itself Out?* New York: Holt.

Joseph Romm. 2018. *Climate Change: What Everyone Needs to Know*. New York: Oxford University Press.

David Wallace-Wells. 2020. *The Uninhabitable Earth: Life After Warning*. New York: Tim Duggan Books.

Climate Change Websites

The following websites are especially helpful for keeping up with this rapidly changing topic:

Center for Climate & Energy Solutions (C2ES): https://www.c2es.org/

Extinction Rebellion Peace (XR Peace): https://xrpeace.org/

Global Change (US Global Change Research Program): https://www.globalchange.gov/

Intergovernmental Panel on Climate Change: https://www.ipcc.ch/

National Center for Atmospheric Research: https://ncar.ucar.edu/

National Centers for Environmental Information: https://www.ncei.noaa.gov/

Skeptical Science: https://skepticalscience.com/

United Nations Climate Action: https://www.un.org/en/climatechange

21

Economic Well-Being

Peace implies a state of individual and collective tranquility and satisfaction. But it is very difficult to be tranquil or satisfied while lacking such basic needs as food, clothing, shelter, education, and medical care. It is even difficult to establish ethical guidelines—let alone to abide by them—when fundamental necessities are not available. Bertolt Brecht said it clearly (if cynically) in his play *The Threepenny Opera*:

First feed the face, and then tell right from wrong.

Even noblemen may act like sinners,

Unless they've had their customary dinners.

Economic Well-Being

Peace implies a state of individual and collective tranquility and satisfaction. But it is very difficult to be tranquil or satisfied while lacking such basic needs as food, clothing, shelter, education, heat, and medical care. It is even difficult to establish ethical guidelines—let alone to abide by them—when fundamental necessities are not available. Bertolt Brecht said it clearly (if cynically) in his play *The Threepenny Opera*:

> *First feed the face, and then tell right from wrong.*
>
> *Even noblemen may act like sinners,*
>
> *Unless they've had their customary dinners.*

Moreover, even if their bellies are filled, people are rarely peaceful when they perceive that their economic conditions are far inferior to those of others. Not surprisingly, therefore, there is little peace in a world characterized by glaring differences between the haves and the have-nots. Poverty may not lead directly to war, but it certainly is not conducive to peace. Revolutions have been incited and maintained by grinding economic privation. And it seems likely that one of the most important but rarely acknowledged reasons why the rich states maintain large military forces is that they are concerned with preventing any fundamental reorganization in the worldwide distribution of power and wealth. Commenting nine centuries ago on the "plight" of the wealthy, Saint Francis noted that "he who has property also needs weapons and warriors to defend it."

Most of all, inequality in resources and opportunities is a direct burden on the poor themselves (poor people as well as poor countries). When poverty is persistent, degrading, miserable, life-shortening, life-threatening, and life-denying, it is an affront to human dignity. The search for peace must accordingly include a search for human economic and social betterment. At the same time, not all economically "poor" people feel miserable and abused, especially in some Buddhist countries, for example, where material condition is traditionally considered less important than spiritual well-being.

Most of the world's people are so preoccupied with their own immediate problems (of which poverty looms large) that such wider preoccupations as nuclear weapons, peace and war, or the condition of the natural environment seem almost irrelevant. Political imagination is often constrained by a range of immediate issues: for example, in Latin America, debt, democratization, and poverty, and in Africa, famines, displaced persons, debt, epidemics, racial and religious violence. The concrete day-to-day struggles of average people to lead tolerable lives occupy most of the energies of most of humanity. Many Americans, by contrast, know what it is to be *hungry* on occasion but have had blessedly little experience with *hunger*.

Efforts to eliminate poverty or to maximize wealth—which is not necessarily the same thing—have stimulated some of the major socioeconomic ideologies of modern times, notably capitalism and communism. Accordingly, we do not attempt here to reinvent the wheel by drafting blueprints for a preferred world economy. We instead try to sketch out some of the primary issues, identify some of the major controversies, and point toward possible courses of action.

Like war, poverty is not an abstraction, although we often speak of it in general terms. Just as there are specific wars, there are specific, flesh-and-blood people and particular regions of especially bleak poverty, even in so-called wealthy countries. As with war, there are also questions of definition and identification: What is poverty? How do regions and countries differ? Is it getting better or worse? Not surprisingly, as in efforts to understand war, there are many different explanations, some of them conflicting in their interpretations and their recommendations.

The Problem of Poverty

In its simplest terms, poverty exists when people do not have sufficient access to the "good life"; of course, one person's good life is another's luxury. For a middle-class American family, the good life may require two cars, cell phones and laptop computers, at least one satisfying vacation annually, and the ability to send one's children to a college of their choice. For a resident of Manila's Tondo slum, it may be regular meals, a sewer system, one day off per month, and the ability to keep one's children from dying of diarrhea. The official "poverty level"—in terms of annual income—in the United States would be considered luxury in much of the developing world. (At the same time, consider the following figures for the technologically advanced countries of North America and Europe: 80 percent of global suicides, 74 percent of heart attacks, 75 percent of "screen zombies," 56 percent of sexual dysfunctions, 98 percent of illicit drug consumption—out of only 10 percent of the world's population.)

The most dramatic examples of clear-cut poverty on a global scale are the developing nations, mainly in the Southern Hemisphere. Variously labeled "Third World," "underdeveloped," "developing," "have-nots," or "lesser developed countries," these states are significantly poorer than most of their Northern Hemisphere "developed" cousins. It is also clear that they have generally, although not universally, been subject to colonization and exploitation by the wealthier states, at least in the past.

A World Poverty Overview

The following world poverty overview comes from a report issued by the World Bank. Although this organization's mission, "Our Dream Is a World Free of Poverty," is literally carved in stone above its Washington, D.C., headquarters, activists dispute the degree to which its policies contribute to this goal rather than supporting the global economic status quo. Nonetheless, and despite the fact that numbers can be numbing (especially when dealing with information that fails to capture genuine, personal human misery), World Bank data are generally considered accurate and therefore worth presenting here.

There has been marked progress in reducing poverty over the past decades. The world attained the first Millennium Development Goal target—to cut the 1990 poverty rate in half by 2015—five years ahead of schedule, in 2010. Despite this progress, the number of people living in extreme poverty globally remains unacceptably high.

- According to 2020 estimates, 12.7 percent of the world's population lived on $1.90 a day or less. That's a real improvement, down from 37 percent in 1990 and 44 percent in 1981.

- This means that 896 million people lived on less than $1.90 a day, compared with 1.95 billion in 1990, and 1.99 billion in 1981.

- Progress has been slower at higher poverty lines. More than 2.1 billion people in the developing world lived on less than US$3.10 a day, compared with 2.9 billion in 1990—so even though the share of the population living under that threshold nearly halved, from 66 percent in 1990 to 35 percent, far too many people are living with far too little.

Moreover, while poverty rates have declined in all regions, progress has been uneven:

- East Asia saw the most dramatic reduction in extreme poverty, from 80 percent in 1981 to 7.2 percent. In South Asia, the share of the population living in extreme poverty is now the lowest since 1981, dropping from 58 percent in 1981 to 18.7 percent. Poverty in sub-Saharan Africa stood at 42.6 percent.

- China alone accounted for most of the decline in extreme poverty over the past three decades. Between 1981 and 2020, roughly 800 million people moved above the $1.90-a-day threshold. During the same time, the developing world as a whole saw a reduction in poverty for 1.2 billion people.

- In 2020, roughly 75 percent of the extremely poor lived in South Asia (300 million) and sub-Saharan Africa (380 million).

- Fewer than 44 million of the extremely poor lived in Latin America, the Caribbean, Eastern Europe, and Central Asia.

The work is far from over, and a number of challenges remain. It is becoming even more difficult to reach those remaining in extreme poverty, who often live in fragile contexts and remote areas. Access to good schools, health care, electricity, safe water, and other critical services remains elusive for many people, often determined by socioeconomic status, gender, ethnicity, and geography. Moreover, for those who have been able to move out of poverty, progress is often temporary: economic shocks, food insecurity, and climate change threaten to rob them of their hard-won gains and force them back into poverty. It will be critical to find ways to tackle these issues as we make progress toward 2030.

Physical and Psychological Effects of Poverty

One of the most important, if least recognized, aspects of poverty is its psychological effect: the bitter pill of perceived injustice and inequality that must be swallowed by those who observe the affluence of others while mired in poverty. With improved access to communications technologies and transportation, even the most isolated people, living traditional and impoverished lives, are exposed to examples of affluence. The result is often deep mental suffering: envy, shame, and either despair or anger. Moreover, along with "development" in previously impoverished countries, there seems to be an inevitable widening of the gap between rich and poor, something that has been the case in the United States since the early 1980s.

Beyond its psychological consequences, there are the more obvious effects of deep, absolute poverty, of which hunger is the most obvious. Other human deficits usually accompany poverty: Poor housing and inadequate sanitation contribute to disease, as does malnutrition. Health care is often minimal or nonexistent. Educational opportunities are very limited because areas of extreme poverty frequently have few and typically inadequate schools, and also because the very poor often need their children to work, so they are denied whatever limited education might otherwise be available. The result is a deepening cycle of poverty, making it even more difficult for such people or their descendants to escape. Not surprisingly, life spans are significantly shorter among the very poor than for the more affluent.

Infant mortality rates also provide an undeniable measure of poverty's lethal consequence. Data from 2017 show that the countries with the highest infant mortality rates were, in order, Afghanistan, Somalia, Central African Republic, Guinea-Bissau, and Chad (ranging from 111 to 65 deaths per 100,000 births), while the lowest such rates are, in order, Japan, Iceland, Singapore, Norway, and Finland (ranging from 2.0 to 2.5 deaths per

100,000 births). The United States ranks 54th out of 224, the worst among all industrialized countries, at 5.8 infant deaths per 100,000—which is worse, incidentally, than Cuba. An American baby is twice as liable to die during its first year as a Korean or Spanish baby. This gap increases with infant age, being even greater at age 1 than at birth. Moreover—and significantly—the infant offspring of wealthy mothers in the United States suffer much lower mortality than do offspring of financially disadvantaged mothers, and once again this gap increases from birth to a baby's first birthday.

In his book *Ill Fares the Land,* historian Tony Judt notes,

> There has been a collapse in intergenerational mobility: in contrast to their parents and grandparents, children today in the UK as in the US have very little expectation of improving upon the condition into which they were born. The poor stay poor. Economic disadvantage for the overwhelming majority translates into ill health, missed educational opportunity, and—increasingly—the familiar symptoms of depression: alcoholism, obesity, gambling, and minor criminality.

The worldwide economic crisis that began in 2008, often dubbed the "Great Recession," impacted the developed world as well. Even as the US economy began to climb out of this recession—the worst since the Great Depression from 1929 to the late 1930s—it became an increasingly widespread problem in Europe, particularly in the south. Countries most acutely affected by the prolonged economic crisis (notably Greece, Spain, Ireland, and Italy) had a sharp rise in suicide rates. A similar problem has long been reported among impoverished farmers in India, whose debts exceed their incomes.

National and Global Inequalities

Poverty may be measured in absolute terms—sheer deprivation of food, poor health, shortened life expectancy, and so on—or in comparative measures, such as inequality in the distribution of wealth, whereby a small proportion of the population monopolizes more than its share of wealth, leaving the majority with less income and fewer assets per capita. In addition, trends in poverty are also important. The per capita income in most less-developed countries (LDCs) was lower in 2020, for example, than in 1995, even though the total number of severely impoverished people actually declined during the course of those two decades (mostly because of improvement in the situation of tens of millions of Chinese). But relative inequality in *wealth*—that is, in the net financial resources accumulated by a family or an individual—is perhaps even more important, and here, disparities between the very wealthy and those living in absolute poverty are even greater.

As of 2018, slightly more than one-half the world's wealth was in the hands of 1 percent of the population. (Having assets exceeding $3,200 places one in the top 50 percent worldwide.) At the other end of the wealth distribution, the poorest half possess just 1 percent. Yet another way to consider the staggering degree of wealth inequality: The richest 80 individuals on Earth control more wealth than fully one-half the world's total population.

Substantial inequality exists even in the wealthy United States, where the richest 20 percent of the population receives more than 50 percent of the annual gross national product (GNP), while the poorest 40 percent gets less than 15 percent. Interestingly, even Soviet-bloc states during their "communist" phase were not substantially more egalitarian than their Western counterparts. In Bulgaria, for example, the richest 20 percent earned 33 percent of their GNP, and the bottom 40 percent earned 27 percent. (Most countries in the former Soviet bloc were actually more equitable than appears from these statistics, however, because health care, education, housing, and some degree of employment were typically guaranteed.)

Within most fledgling capitalist countries, disparities in wealth have become extraordinarily wide: In Russia, for example, the newly ascendant top 1 percent of the population controls nearly 25 percent of that country's wealth, whereas those at the bottom—notably, elderly people on pensions, rural residents, and children—saw their standard of living plummet as the communist-era socioeconomic safety net was frayed almost to the point of nonexistence. One reason for the generally widespread public support of Vladimir Putin within Russia—in addition to the culturally established valuing of a strong leader—has been that the economic situation of most Russians has improved substantially during his time in office.

In the Developing World

The developing world is one of widespread and appalling contrasts, with gleaming high-tech development alongside unremitting poverty. Moreover, the absolute gap between global rich and poor is widening. In many cases, the degree of deprivation is hidden by government manipulation of statistics. In Chile, for example, instead of assessing malnutrition by considering a child's weight in relation to his or her age, it was long estimated by weight in relation to height; thus, a child whose growth is stunted was declared to be adequately nourished! Examples abound of governmental callousness toward the poor—even in the United States—in part because the poor tend to have very little say in governmental decision making, which generally takes place on behalf of the wealthy and powerful. During the Reagan administration, for example, a notorious effort was made to cut school lunch programs for the poor by declaring ketchup a vegetable.

Although poverty is a worldwide phenomenon, it is not homogeneously distributed. There are poor people living in rich countries (e.g., thousands of homeless persons in the United States) and wealthy people in the poorest countries (e.g., multimillionaire plantation owners in Bangladesh and the Philippines). Poverty, however, is generally easy to identify wherever it is found: high unemployment, poor nutrition, inadequate health care and education, little or no savings, high indebtedness, low investment, inadequate housing, and, often, ecologically depleted environments.

More than half of the world's population—4 billion people—live in cities. Of these, more than 1 billion live in slums, 90 percent of them in developing countries. Although there is no rigid definition for "slum," it is generally taken to mean an urban area characterized by a lack of sanitation, water, social services, and legal rights to housing. Such areas consistently occupy the worst sites for human habitation: steep hillsides, riverbanks that periodically flood, and so on. Cities have huge concentrations of poverty, yet, paradoxically, they also contain some of humanity's best examples of upward mobility.

Although urban slums are devastating in their impact on the impoverished, especially on children, and typically receive the bulk of public attention, in fact the *favelas* of São Paulo, the *barrios* of Mexico City, and the squalid housing of Cairo, Kinshasa, and Karachi are a relatively recent phenomenon. Despite the terrible conditions in which they usually live, the urban poor are generally better off, statistically speaking, than their rural counterparts. This is part of the reason why Third World cities are doubling in size every 10 to 15 years, as impoverished landless peasants flock there, creating slums that become ever more unmanageable.

Even now, however, more than 60 percent of the world's poor still live in rural villages, in India, China, Africa, Indonesia, and elsewhere. Ten percent of the world's population—more than 700 million people—live in rural India alone. And among the rural poor, illiteracy and the most virulent epidemic diseases—malaria, cholera, and tuberculosis—are at an all-time low, but the good things in life (and some of the necessities, such as an adequate diet and opportunities for meaningful work) are today no more available to the global poor than they were before the great migrations from the countryside to the cities.

Historically, rural interests have been overrepresented in Western democratic republics, notably in England and the United States. The state of Wyoming, for example, with a population of just over 500,000, has two US senators, and so does California, with nearly 40 million people; as a result, the average Wyoming resident has 80 times the political voice of a Californian. By contrast, rural people—especially the very poor—are underrepresented in political and economic decision making in most less-developed countries. The rural poor tend to be ignored because their poverty makes them less influential within the "corridors of power" in distant cities and also because they are likely to be seen as irrelevant as well as an embarrassment to those elite decision makers who look to the wealthy North for material goods, for images of their country's future, and, not least, for their own enrichment and advancement.

Although the United States is, by many measures, the wealthiest country in the world, it does not rank very high regarding socioeconomic equity: 5th in literacy, 7th in public school expenditures per capita, 8th in public health expenditures per capita, 14th in life expectancy, 16th in percentage of women enrolled in universities, and 20th in number of teachers per school-age population. From 2000 to 2007, incomes for the bottom 90 percent of earners rose only about 4 percent, once adjusted for inflation. For the top 0.1 percent, incomes climbed about 94 percent. There are more homeless people on the streets of the United States than in China, and an estimated 20 million Americans are functionally illiterate. In the richest country in human history, one child in five lives in poverty.

Causes of Poverty

"The rich are different from you and I," the eminent American writer F. Scott Fitzgerald is said to have commented to his fellow writer Ernest Hemingway, whereupon Hemingway responded, "Yes, they have more money."

It is not terribly useful to conclude that poverty is caused by an absence of money. But what, then, are its underlying causes? There have been many explanations. In certain cases, the natural resources of a country are so inadequate that wealth is virtually impossible to create. The African state of Chad, for example, is so arid as to be agriculturally unproductive; it also lacks significant mineral resources. By contrast, wealthy countries such as the United States tend to be resource rich. But this argument is not altogether satisfying. Japan, for example, has relatively few natural resources; yet, despite recent setbacks, it is an economic giant. The same is true of Hong Kong, South Korea, Singapore, and Taiwan, as well as such wealthy but resource-poor European states as Denmark and the Netherlands.

Some nations can be considered especially resource rich (Venezuela, Norway, Saudi Arabia, and Kuwait), while others are capital rich (Singapore, Luxembourg, Hong Kong, Taiwan, and Japan). Other countries (notably the United States) are rich in both resources and capital, whereas an unfortunate few (e.g., Chad and Bangladesh) appear to be poor in both. Clearly, resources alone do not explain everything. Moreover, it is also possible to be resource rich and yet economically poor, as with Venezuela and the Democratic Republic of the Congo (DRC), due mostly to governmental mismanagement.

Roughly 70 percent of those nations that are deeply impoverished—sometimes called the "bottom billion"—live in sub-Saharan Africa. Explosive economic growth in Asia, although certainly not equally distributed throughout the populations of, for example, India, South Korea, Thailand, and so forth, has nonetheless largely outstripped Africa in terms of the availability of inexpensive labor. Average life expectancy for the bottom billion people is less than 50 years; one in seven children dies before age 5. What to do?

Some progressive Western economists, such as Joseph Stigler and Jeffrey Sachs, argue that impoverished nations could benefit from improved agricultural policies based on widely available, appropriate technology, such as person-operated well pumps and devices for producing fresh water; inexpensive photoelectric systems (especially for rural regions where electric power is not otherwise available); antimalarial mosquito nets; and antiretroviral drugs for those afflicted with AIDS. Others continue to blame the legacy of Western colonialism as well as endemic political corruption by which the wealth of LDCs is often skimmed off and deposited in the personal bank accounts of a small number of political and military leaders.

Yet another likely reason for extreme poverty is war, especially civil war. The World Bank has described war as "development in reverse," and in fact nearly one-half of the bottom billion people either are in the midst of civil war or have only recently emerged from one. War breeds poverty, and poverty in turn may make people more likely to engage in civil war. Moreover, once such a war has occurred, it is more likely to be repeated. The risks of civil war are also increased by a high proportion of young, uneducated, and unemployed men, by an imbalance of power among ethnic groups, and, ironically, by a supply of readily extractable natural resources, which governments are sometimes induced to exploit directly rather than investing in their people. This has been the perverse consequence of, for example, oil in the Middle East and Nigeria and diamonds in Sierra Leone.

Government Policies

Government policies can also have an impact on poverty, ameliorating or enhancing it. Many analysts have attempted to explain the "economic miracle" of Japan. (Even though the Japanese economy has been comparatively stagnant since the 1990s, it nonetheless boasts the third largest GNP, behind only the US and China.) There seems little doubt that social organization—in Japan's case, a powerful work ethic as well as comparatively low defense spending—helped boost economic productivity, as it did in postwar Germany.

Alternatively, where poverty is widespread and has existed for thousands of years with little sign of improvement, a kind of fatalistic lethargy often sets in. Government policies can have substantial impact in such cases, either encouraging grassroots self-help or deepening the plight of a country's majority. The Democratic Republic of the Congo (DRC), for example, is "rich" in natural resources. Yet 80 percent of Congolese are desperately poor, and real wages are less than one-quarter what they were at the time of the DRC's independence from Belgium in 1960. At least some of the responsibility must be borne by longtime dictator Mobutu Sese Seku, who stole more than $5 billion from the national treasury. National wealth was similarly plundered by the likes of Ferdinand Marcos in the Philippines and Suharto in Indonesia. Widespread corruption, and not just at the top of government, has throttled economic development in many countries that have recently emerged from colonial control.

Fiscal mismanagement and irresponsibility—often bolstered by a rigid adherence to discredited ideology—have also resulted in economic degradation. An example is Romania, a country abundantly endowed with natural resources (notably oil) but reduced to poverty by the destructive Stalinist-style policies of the former strongman Nicolae Ceauşescu. Zimbabwe (formerly Rhodesia) suffers from extraordinarily high annual inflation and an agricultural economy—once vibrant—that can no longer feed its people; the predatory policies of erstwhile freedom fighter turned autocrat Robert Mugabe were largely to blame. Zimbabwe is an example of economic collapse due to corruption and social and/or economic insensitivity rather than a shortage of natural resources or its leaders' adherence to a clear-cut political ideology. Similarly, following the devastating Haitian earthquake in 2010, the international community provided billions in aid, but because of corruption and government mismanagement, only a small fraction actually went to alleviate the suffering of the Haitian people.

As already noted, an abundance of natural resources can lead to widespread national impoverishment and wealth for only a tiny minority. For example, "easy money" in the form of oil wealth is often monopolized by a small number of entrepreneurs and predatory government officials (often in collaboration with international corporations), while at the national level, such countries only rarely invest their profits in their own population. In addition, with the dramatic fall in oil prices from 2014 to late 2015 (apparently bottoming out at about $30 per barrel before rebounding), oil-producing countries that had set their budgets based on $80- to $100-a-barrel oil—including Iran, Saudi Arabia, Nigeria, Indonesia, and Venezuela—found themselves vastly underfunded just when their populations surged. By contrast, Norway has frugally managed its large annual income from oil and gas exports; as a result, medical care is essentially free, and that country is the world's wealthiest, per capita.

Political leaders frequently take power by promising to improve the lot of the oppressed and underprivileged who support them. Once in office, however, rulers often find it advantageous to cater to the powerful (i.e., in most cases, the wealthy). There are many reasons for such shifts, including personal payoffs, keeping the military happy—thereby allowing the government to remain in power—and satisfying the demands of foreign bankers, notably the World Bank and the International Monetary Fund, which traditionally insist on domestic fiscal "austerity" in return for loans or debt relief. Short of revolution or the overt threat of it, the very poor generally have a disproportionately small voice in government decision making.

Political Ideology

Social and political factors can also contribute to income disparities. According to Marxists, capitalism is largely to blame. Capitalist societies are stratified by economic class, with the owners of corporations exploiting the workers, thereby keeping them underprivileged, undereducated, divided, and poor. According to mainstream capitalist economic theory, wealth is most likely to be generated by an unfettered free market and poverty results from lack of effort, will, or ability; bad luck; poor individual choices (e.g., drugs, crime, unplanned pregnancies, dropping out of school); or from the allegedly negative influence of government "interference" in the market.

According to the classical economist Adam Smith, private enterprise, if left to its own devices, will act as though guided by an "unseen hand," producing the maximum economic good for the greatest number of people. Implicit in capitalist economic theory is the idea that some people will inevitably do less well than others, a difference that is presumably due, at least in part, to unavoidable differences between them. From this perspective, it is therefore not the job of society to establish socioeconomic equality. Moreover, if government intervenes in market operations to redistribute wealth, this will not only diminish the efficiency with which new wealth is produced, but it will also constitute a major blow to individual liberty.

Even most capitalist societies, however, do not subscribe to classic laissez-faire theories, in which governments are expected to take a completely hands-off attitude. Various "safety net programs" have been established in the United States—for example, Head Start, Temporary Assistance to Needy Families (TANF, the successor to Aid to Families with Dependent Children), Medicare, Medicaid, and the Affordable Care Act ("Obamacare"). Most other Western democracies have governments that are significantly more involved in their economies and in providing social support, especially at the federal level, seeking to maintain and improve the lot of their poorest citizens. In the past, conservative ideologies attributed poverty to alleged natural individual inferiority; more recently, the scapegoating of the less well-off tends to be more subtle, pointing to cultural circumstances such as single-parent families and thereby relieving government of its social responsibility.

Many well-intended people have thought that democracy and capitalism inevitably go together, as appeared to be the case with the United States. But in fact, recent experience suggests that neither democracy nor capitalism is a prerequisite for the other. China, for example, has many gigantic state-owned companies (a kind of state capitalism) and high economic growth but little if any democracy, at least at the national level. The same is true for Singapore. On the other hand, other nations, such as Peru, have taken substantial steps toward democracy but have had relatively disappointing economic growth, while South Korea has both democracy and economic growth. Whatever its connection to economic growth, capitalism in the 21st century has frequently led to greater economic inequality, which in turn is not conducive to democracy. Similarly, political democracy—as in many of the nations spawned from the collapse of the former Soviet empire—doesn't necessarily produce capitalist success, widespread prosperity, or economic equity.

Poverty and War

The relationship between poverty and war is complex. Preparing for war occasionally yields economic benefits. Many advances in the aircraft and electronics industries, for example, were stimulated by military research and development, as were the inventions of Teflon, satellite-based global positioning systems, and even, to some extent, the Internet. But on balance, domestic innovations, if they were the priority, would be generated far more effectively by targeting investment explicitly at domestic needs. Moreover, considering the immense destructiveness of war, there is little doubt that on balance it is impoverishing, essentially a parasite, feeding off the economic and social strength of societies. Like most parasites, war and the preparation for war weaken their host country.

There is also little evidence that poverty leads to war (with the exception, on occasion, of civil war). In fact, the cause and effect relationship may well be in the opposite direction, with impoverished countries being less likely to engage in foreign wars, if only because in an age of elaborate military technology, the equipping of strong military forces requires substantial resources—unless, as in the case of North Korea, a government is willing to allow its people to suffer, and even to starve, while fattening its army.

Socioeconomic Development

"Development" has long been seen by most mainstream economists as the key to an impoverished country's economic future. As President John F. Kennedy put it, "A rising tide lifts all boats." The idea is to improve the economic situation in the world generally, as a result of which some economic benefits would be enjoyed by everyone, including the poorest states and the most deprived segments of society. In a bit of US political jargon from 1980s "Reaganomics," a dynamic world economy would generate benefits that "trickle down" to all inhabitants. On the other hand, when one is chained to the bottom, a rising tide can be less than helpful! Moreover, famed US labor leader George Meany once noted that during his decades as a licensed plumber, he had seen lots of things trickle down, but money wasn't one of them.

Growth and Modernization

During its heyday in the 1960s and 1970s, neoliberal development theory claimed that economic progress would spread from the industrialized states to the LDCs and that foreign aid, as well as enhanced trade and credit provided by the North to the South, would help speed the process. Instead of dividing up the global pie differently, wealthy states would simply help bake a larger pie.

Development theory is closely allied to classical free enterprise economic models, which espouse the basic theme of "grow now, redistribute later (if possible, not at all)." Developing countries, according to this view, should strive to attract foreign capital and should emphasize efficiency and economic growth—not equity—as their policy goals. There have been some success stories in these development models, notably the so-called Asian Tigers (Hong Kong, Singapore, South Korea, and Taiwan), as well as the Asian giants of India and China. Moreover, those economies least integrated into the world free-market system, such as North Korea and, until recently, Myanmar (Burma), have been among the least dynamic.

Disappointments

Development theory persists in various forms, although the great majority of poor countries have not, on balance, benefited recently from global growth and economic development. This in turn has led to dissatisfaction and increasingly militant demands by many poor people and even by some socialist-led governments, particularly in Latin America, for economic equity and social justice.

One of the major disappointing consequences of uneven economic growth and development has been marginalization, whereby modest increases in the size of the middle and upper classes are accompanied by more poverty on the part of those already impoverished. It is likely that there will always be relative poverty—with some people at the poorer end of the income spectrum—just as there will always be those who are comparatively wealthy. The tragedy of marginalization is that it involves an increase in absolute poverty. In short, the benefits of economic growth in the poorest countries typically do not reach the lowest levels of society, with the poorest of the poor pushed more and more to the margins of subsistence. Whatever its causes and correlates, the distressing fact remains that in many cases development policies have been an abject failure, as the already low-income poor face declining incomes.

Globalization

Dramatic advances in communication and transportation, plus the remarkable growth of computer technology, have provided impetus for the denationalization of economies and the advent of globalization. In a globalized economy, a product may be designed in Italy, fabricated in Malaysia using raw materials from Brazil and Kenya, and then sold in Australia—to the economic benefit of a corporation based in Chicago or London (but whose location, in order to avoid taxes, is officially listed as the Cayman Islands or Panama City).

Not surprisingly, globalization is a two-edged sword. On the positive side, it offers the prospect of some employment for impoverished people in nonindustrial countries and, thus, a possible—but often slight and temporary—improvement in their lives. It may connect such people to the world economy and/or to international communication via the Internet, and it may involve them and their government leaders in a web of interconnections that might break down parochialism and reduce the likelihood of armed conflicts. But there are also negative aspects to globalization.

In the absence of carefully enforced international standards, multinational corporations scour the globe for the lowest paid workforce, for the most marginal worker safety and health benefits, and for minimal and sometimes nonexistent environmental protections. The ensuing "race to the bottom" benefits such corporations and, in the short run, many consumers, because products can therefore be produced cheaply. At the same time, more highly paid workers (as in the United States and, increasingly, Europe) suffer in return, as their jobs disappear while workers in poor countries "benefit" from near-starvation wages and minimal, if any, worker safety standards. In many cases—notably China—huge numbers of very poor rural residents have nonetheless greatly improved their economic condition by taking such jobs in newly constructed urban factories, where they accept wages and working conditions that would be rejected by most inhabitants of Western countries; this, in turn, has contributed to the growing de-industrialization of the West, while raising hundreds of millions of people from dire poverty to . . . poverty.

One source of the world's economic dislocation following the 2008 Great Recession has been the integration of billions of these low-wage workers (notably in China and India) into the global economy, as well as increases in productivity stemming from applications of information technology and robotics to the manufacturing sector. These developments, in turn, have pushed global production capacity higher than demand, taking a heavy toll on economies in the industrialized West, where formerly high-paying jobs in manufacturing have been replaced by lower-paying service sector jobs.

In addition, the nature of "production" has often had a depressing effect on job creation. As of early 2015, for example, Facebook's estimated market value was nearly $250 billion; at the same time, this company had roughly 12,000 employees. By contrast, General Motors, valued at about $35 billion, has nearly 80,000 employees in the United States and more than 200,000 worldwide. Similar disparities apply to other high-tech companies such as Google and Apple and indicate how, compared to an earlier generation of industrial production, much of the increased wealth of US cutting-edge companies has not been reflected in comparable levels of job creation.

From the end of World War II until the early 1990s, a primary vehicle for globalization was the General Agreement on Tariffs and Trade (GATT). Currently, trade-related issues are taken up by the World Trade Organization, which concerns itself almost exclusively with lowering trade barriers between countries. Globalization has the potential to help alleviate some world poverty while protecting worker rights and the environment; thus far, however, it has not, on balance, lived up to these hopes and instead has tended to enhance corporate profits over human and environmental values.

Some countries have accordingly begun to move away from a simple pro–growth and development model. Sri Lanka, for example, succeeded in significantly reducing abject poverty by devoting half of its national budget to free rice, education, and health services and to subsidized food and transportation. As a result, life expectancy there has risen dramatically, approaching that of more "developed" countries. (Tragically, ethnic conflict between Tamil and Sinhalese interfered with and, to some degree, overshadowed these remarkable social accomplishments. With the defeat of the Tamil Tiger rebels in 2010—at the cost of tens of thousands of civilian casualties and massive human rights abuses—Sri Lanka is able to focus once again on socioeconomic development for all its citizens, although the Buddhist-majority country tends to discriminate against its Tamil Hindu minority.)

Dependencia Theory

This alternative perspective on international poverty originally came from Latin America, a region that has long tended to be economically, politically, and militarily subservient to the United States. As used by such progressive economic theorists as the German-American social scientist Andre Gunder Frank, the term *dependencia,* based on the Spanish word for dependency, has also been applied to regions in which indigenous peoples and resources are believed by many social critics to be exploited by the wealthier, industrialized states of the North.

The basic idea of *dependencia* is that poverty in the less industrialized South—what peace researcher Johan Galtung and sociologist Immanuel Wallerstein have called the "periphery"—occurs in large part because of the affluence at the "center" or "core": the industrialized North. Poor countries are thus not so much underdeveloped as *overexploited,* such that their poverty is not a result of neglect by the wealthy North but of too much attention. Countries including the DRC, Indonesia, Brazil, India, and Malaysia are rich; only their people are poor!

According to *dependencia* theory, not only did the North exploit the South overtly during the days of colonialism, but such exploitation has continued, covertly, even after direct imperial control was terminated. The wealthy, powerful North is thus seen to take advantage of the South by manipulating markets, credit, and trade balances, all the while depressing local incomes so as to provide cheap labor for northern multinational corporations.

In the past, repressive control of workers in the global South was exerted directly, by armed forces of occupation. Such control is currently indirect, through surrogate local rulers (the so-called *comprador* class) who are clients of the wealthy states and who profit personally by impoverishing their own people while being in league with the Northern powers. In Galtung's terminology, there is an informal but very real alliance between the "center in the periphery" (the *comprador* class in the exploited, ostensibly developing country) and the "center in the center" (the leadership of the wealthy, mostly Western exploiters). As a result, people in most LDCs are victimized directly by their own governments, as well as indirectly by the industrialized states. Unlike the relationship between, say, the United States and France, in which benefits often flow in both directions, exchanges between wealthy Northern powers and Mauritania, for example, are likely to be exploitative and distinctly one-sided.

A way out, according to *dependencia* theorists, would involve collaboration between the "periphery in the periphery" and the "periphery in the center." To some extent, this occurred when Mohandas Gandhi, representing India's poor and exploited workers, visited the United Kingdom and was enthusiastically received by British garment workers, who recognized their common interests despite the fact that Gandhi had been organizing a boycott of British cloth to encourage the growth of an indigenous weaving industry in economically exploited India. But with the rapid growth of right-wing national populism beginning around 2016, such cross-national worker class solidarity has been notably diminished to the point that by the early 2020s, it is barely apparent.

The Debt Problem

In addition to poverty, most of the world's nonindustrialized countries have another problem, one that saps revenues, limits domestic spending options, and sits like a troll inhibiting progress along the path of economic betterment: debt. Forced to pay billions of dollars annually from national economies that barely keep their heads above water, these countries have little hope of achieving prosperity for most of their citizens because they are literally unable to invest in their own economies.

The debt crisis was precipitated several decades ago, in large part by a severe economic recession in the wealthy states. The stage was set during the 1970s, as costs skyrocketed for petroleum, weapons, and food, which were purchased by developing countries, in part using funds that northern banks eagerly made available. By the 1980s, interest rates rose dramatically while commodity prices plummeted, whereupon debtor states found themselves increasingly hard pressed to meet the interest payments on their loans. Ever since then, poor countries have fallen ever further behind in their capacity to pay; their plight has been like that of the coal workers in the folk song "Sixteen Tons": "You load sixteen tons and what do you get? Another day older and deeper in debt." In the 21st century, something similar has occurred even to comparatively developed European countries such as Greece.

Under certain circumstances, the chief international lending agency, the International Monetary Fund, has allowed this crushing debt burden to be rescheduled, but only if the debtor country agrees to "austerity," which typically requires drastic cutbacks in government subsidies of food, transportation, health care, and education, as well as anti-inflation policies that substantially increase unemployment and underemployment. A related strategy has been to provide new loans to enable debtors to pay the interest on old ones—a "solution" that is unlikely to inspire much long-term confidence.

The human cost of international debt has been staggering. A United Nations International Children's Emergency Fund (UNICEF) report estimated that approximately 500,000 children die annually because of economic decline or stagnation in the world's poorest states, conditions that generate government cutbacks in basic health services, primary education, and food and fuel subsidies. These reductions have taken place while family incomes for a billion people have been declining, especially in Africa and southern Asia. Under these circumstances, some of the most impoverished and indebted states have begun to threaten default on their loans. One alternative—debt forgiveness—has been proposed by several religious institutions (notably the Roman Catholic Church), but it has little prospect of widespread enactment.

As a result of the Great Recession that began in 2008, developed countries also began to suffer under a burden of debt, which in turn has led to further frictions. For example, a growing source of friction between the United States and China has been the perceived Chinese reluctance to raise the value of their currency, the renminbi (also known as the yuan), or at least the perceived Chinese hesitancy to allow it to fluctuate on the open market. If they did, and if the renminbi went up, Chinese products would in turn be more expensive, which would mean fewer purchases by the United States and other countries, which in turn would diminish the purchasers' trade imbalances and foreign debt.

In 2014, China began to allow its currency to float; one result, however, has been a slowdown in Chinese economic growth, with its own disruptive effect on the world economy. Disputes have also emerged within developed countries over economic policies, with Western conservatives arguing for austerity (less government spending on social programs, reduced pension allowances, etc.) and progressives arguing for an emphasis on growth, to be achieved by government stimulation of demand (fiscal policy) along with maintaining low interest rates (monetary policy). To this must be added the effect of trade wars initiated by the Trump administration midway in its term. Ostensibly intended to correct trade imbalances, the short-term effect has been to inhibit economic growth in both the US and China—as well as in Europe and Mexico, which have also been impacted.

Ethics, Equity, and a Bit of History

Amid these conflicting ideologies and attempts to reduce global poverty, a fundamental question remains: Why should the wealthy states agree to forgive the debt burden of poor countries or, indeed, agree to any policies designed to reduce worldwide economic inequality? Do wealthy countries have any obligation toward poor ones? An extension of laissez-faire capitalism and the ideology of "rugged individualism" is that poverty is the unavoidable consequence of differences among countries, no less than among individuals, and that inequality should be not only tolerated but even celebrated because it indicates that merit is being rewarded. From this point of view, it is unethical to redistribute wealth because such redistribution necessarily involves taking away resources that rightfully belong to someone who has earned them, while donating resources to others who have not.

But there are many reasons for opposing inequalities in global wealth. One is the notion of distributive justice, that is, the ethical conviction that gross inequity is unfair, even when it might not be the result of unjust practices. Certainly, there is something ethically repugnant about the spectacle of dire, life-threatening poverty coexisting, often side by side, with extreme luxury. For some, redistribution is a moral imperative based essentially on charity: When suffering exists, people have a duty to alleviate it.

Egalitarianism (whether economic or social) has not been a consistent motivating force in United States political history, which has been traditionally committed more to personal freedom and the fruits of successful entrepreneurial striving, along with the inheritance of family wealth. But there have been some notable strains toward economic and social equity, including the Progressive movement of the 1890s and, to a lesser extent, FDR's New Deal of the 1930s, Harry S. Truman's Fair Deal, Lyndon Johnson's Great Society aspirations of the 1960s, and possibly the beginning of the Biden presidency. Even prior to US independence, Tom Paine, one of the inspirational founders of that soon-to-be new country, wrote as follows in *The Rights of Man*:

When it shall be said in any country in the world my poor are happy; neither ignorance nor distress is to be found among them; my jails are empty of prisoners, my streets of beggars; the aged are not in want; the taxes are not oppressive; the rational world is my friend, because I am the friend of its happiness: When these things can be said, then may that country boast of its Constitution and its Government.

Two centuries later, ethicist and political philosopher John Rawls developed an influential theory of rights, according to which "social and economic inequalities are to be arranged so that they are . . . to the greatest benefit of the least advantaged." In his oft-cited book, *A Theory of Justice*, Rawls proposed that we evaluate any social institution from "behind the veil of ignorance," that is, that we consider every system as though we have no foreknowledge of our own specific place within that system. Not knowing whether we would be privileged or not, how would we feel about being part of a given social or economic organization? One's view of the Hindu caste system would probably be biased, for example, if one had a high probability of being an "untouchable" as opposed to an upper-class Brahmin.

Moreover, it is not unreasonable to suggest that the poverty of the many is connected to the extreme wealth of the privileged few. Wealth amid poverty is often the result of extortion, theft, unmerited good luck, graft, collusion, and other factors. The reality is that few countries, if any, offer a truly "level playing field." Although there are inspiring stories of specific individuals who have achieved great success despite having been born financially disadvantaged, the reality is that inherited wealth contributes hugely to the inequality that characterizes the world today. More than a third of the 1,645 billionaires listed by Forbes inherited some or all of their riches.

A much-noted book by French economist Thomas Piketty, *Capital in the Twenty-First Century*, reviewed centuries of Western economic history. Piketty points out that the distribution of wealth in western Europe was highly unequal from the beginning of the Industrial Revolution in the late 18th century, with a comparative handful of wealthy families controlling most of the financial resources. This pattern was only briefly disrupted between World Wars I and II, including during the Great Depression, when wealth inequality declined as a result of higher taxes, inflation, and the growth of welfare states. Piketty shows that by the second half of the 20th century, and even more so in the 21st, the earlier pattern of deep inequality has returned, with levels last seen prior to World War I.

Piketty's theory of capital and inequality proceeds as follows: Wealth generally grows more rapidly than does economic output. This increases inequality. On the other hand, faster economic growth generally reduces the importance of previously accumulated wealth. But because there are no natural forces that act against wealth accumulation, the only way to keep inequality from increasing yet more is rapid economic growth, either via technological progress or vigorous government intervention, "priming the pump" in a manner recommended by the British economist John Maynard Keynes. Piketty recommends a significant global tax on wealth (in addition to the more widespread taxes on income), not only as a matter of basic fairness but to head off increased social disruption in the future if current trends in inequity are not addressed. In the US, the average wage for white workers is about one-third more than that of black workers, while the average financial wealth of white families ($170,000) is roughly ten times that of black families ($17,000).

Beyond the issue of fairness and merit, there looms the question of distributive justice. Should governments take actions to promote a more equitable distribution of wealth? Alternatively, should certain minimum levels of economic welfare be established? If so, how? And what should they include—housing, education, medical care, guaranteed employment? How, under such systems, could societies make room for individual initiative and ensure that people will contribute their "fair share"?

The World Economic Forum, held annually in Davos, Switzerland, hosts the world's wealthiest and economically most influential people, along with representatives from the developed countries. The highly regarded British antipoverty group Oxfam attended and proposed the following seven-point plan:

1. Clamp down on tax dodging by corporations and rich individuals.

2. Invest in universal, free public services such as health and education.

3. Share the tax burden fairly, shifting taxation from labor and consumption toward capital and wealth.

4. Introduce minimum wages and move toward a living wage for all workers.

5. Introduce equal pay legislation and promote economic policies to give women a fair deal.

6. Ensure adequate safety nets for the poorest, including a minimum-income guarantee.

7. Agree on a global goal to tackle inequality.

A classic Marxist maxim is "from each according to their ability, to each according to their need." But in practice, it has proven difficult to assess and reward need and even more difficult to induce people to contribute according to their ability, unless they perceive that a direct personal benefit will flow from their labors. This is one reason for the relatively low productivity of most officially communist economies. A frequent joke heard in the old

Soviet Union was "They pretend to pay me, so I pretend to work," while China, although ostensibly communist and enjoying extraordinarily high rates of economic growth, has in fact become capitalist in most areas of its economy.

Furthermore, is it necessarily true that everyone should be treated equally? With respect to legal entitlements or political rights, most people would agree that the answer is Yes. But in other respects, it is often No. Criminals, for instance, are treated differently from law-abiding citizens. What about rewards for special efforts or skills? Is inequality of compensation in itself unjust? And what about unequal wages and wealth between farmers and factory workers, computer entrepreneurs and ditch diggers, villagers and city dwellers, indigenous hunter-gatherers and high-tech entrepreneurs? And what about differences in the starting conditions (family wealth), in addition to actual income? Is economic inequality any more acceptable between different countries than within a single country? Much more hard thinking about ethics and relevant social-scientific research, not to mention political leadership and public involvement, are needed to answer and address these pressing global concerns.

Hunger

The Extent of the Problem

Approximately 15 percent to 20 percent of the human population suffers from malnutrition, primarily insufficient protein and/or calories. About 70 percent of the world's hunger is found in nine countries: India, Bangladesh, Pakistan, Indonesia, the Philippines, DRC, Cambodia, Brazil, and Ethiopia.

The average person living in a southern Asian nation consumes fewer than 2,000 calories per day, as compared with more than 3,000 for the average American. The average Asian consumes about 400 pounds of grain per year, almost all of it directly as grain. The average American, by contrast, consumes an extraordinary 2,000 pounds of grain per year, but of this only about 150 pounds are eaten directly as grain (the most energy-efficient way); almost 100 pounds are consumed as alcohol, and most of the remainder is eaten much less efficiently, as meat. When calories are transferred from grain to livestock and the meat eaten by human beings, between three-fourths and nine-tenths of those calories are lost. Approximately 1 billion people are chronically undernourished, while worldwide food imports have increased, reinforcing dependence as well as vulnerability to droughts, hurricanes, floods, earthquakes, and other natural catastrophes, in addition to economic disparities.

Unfortunately, per capita food production in many impoverished states, notably in central Africa, went *down* in recent decades, at least in part because, being poor, such states cannot afford modern agricultural technology. Rice yields per acre in India and Nigeria, for example, are only one-third of those in Japan. Approximately one-tenth of the world's land surface is now under cultivation, but little increase can be anticipated because most of the remaining land is desert, mountain, arctic, or otherwise uncultivable. Nonetheless, despite the problems of desertification, erosion, and pollution, worldwide agriculture generates two-and-a-half times the grain needed for human consumption adequate to maintain good health. The problem is, accordingly, inadequate distribution rather than underproduction of foodstuffs. Inequities in such consumption, however, are dramatic.

A Matter of Distribution

To a large extent, the problem of world hunger is not really so much a production problem as it is a distribution problem. In Mexico, for example, about 80 percent of the country's rural children are undernourished and nearly all of the livestock (which consumes more grain than the entire rural population) becomes meat, much of which is then exported to the United States. Throughout much of Africa, land that once grew sorghum and corn for local consumption is now owned by multinational agribusiness conglomerates and used for growing cotton and coffee for export. Local people are thereby denied native grains even as they are left unable to pay for imported wheat and rice. People may have desperate needs, but, in classical economic terms, this doesn't constitute "demand" unless they can pay for what they want. When poor countries are capable of production, there is a tendency to make luxury goods (for export) to be consumed by the rich—whose purchasing power creates economic demand—instead of necessities for domestic consumption because poverty does not generate an attractive, competitive market.

Less than 3 percent of the world's landowners, many of them absentee and/or large agribusiness firms, own nearly 75 percent of all the Earth's cultivatable land. In some areas, this inequity is even greater: 1 percent of the population of northeast Brazil, for example, owns 45 percent of the land, much of it used to grow sugar, which generates money for the owners but provides virtually no food for the population. Peasant farmers, desperate to raise their own food, find themselves forced to cultivate erosion-prone hillsides and infertile terrain, which in turn are quickly depleted, leading to ecological ruin and yet more poverty and famine.

Subsistence farmers typically rely on their own seed, derived from this season's crops, to provide for the next season's planting. Agribusiness companies have developed sterile plant strains, requiring that new seeds be purchased every year. Although public outrage resulted in recall of these "innovations," the pervasive and continuing conflict between corporate profit and human need persists. The politics of scarcity, which dominates the lives of most "Third World" people, has rarely been examined in the overfed "First World." At the same time, even as the wealthy nations have a burgeoning obesity epidemic—particularly among their poorest citizens because of growing consumption of low-quality, high-fat "junk foods," combined with insufficient exercise—a similar public health problem has ironically begun to emerge among many of the world's poorest countries, which, in the 21st century, have endured epidemics of adult-onset diabetes, an illness heretofore unknown.

Measuring Wealth, Poverty, and Income Inequality

It is generally agreed among mainstream social scientists that per capita GNP is a useful index of wealth by which different countries or regions can be compared. Other indexes have also been created, such as the Human Development Index, which is a composite statistic based on life expectancy, education, and income per capita. Nonetheless the GNP and its close relative the gross domestic product (GDP) receive the bulk of attention. (GDP is the GNP with the value of imports and exports omitted.)

If we take GDP as a percentage of total world product, we get a measure of the extent to which a country or a region enjoys more, or suffers from less, than "its share" of the world total. To be meaningful, this figure should then be adjusted for population in each country or region. When this is done, we obtain the "coefficient of advantage"—the percentage of total world product obtained, per capita, by a given country or region. For example, North America contains about 5.5 percent of the world's population; it obtains, however, 30.5 percent of the world's GDP, for a coefficient of advantage of 30.5/5.5 = 5.5. By contrast, Africa has 8.7 percent of the world's population but only 2.0 percent of the world's GDP, for a coefficient of (dis)advantage of 2.0/8.8 = 0.23. A coefficient of advantage of 1.0 would indicate an equitable per capita division of the world's resources. (However, even in this case, divisions of wealth within countries or regions could still be extreme.)

Another important index, the Gini coefficient, is widely used to measure degree of inequality within a larger unit, most commonly a country. Although the calculation of Gini coefficients is mathematically complex, the basics can readily be understood. It is essentially a measure of dispersion (thus conceptually similar to standard deviation and variance, as used in basic statistics). The lower the Gini coefficient, the more equal the distribution, with 0 corresponding to absolute equality in which everyone has exactly the same income. Higher Gini coefficients indicate more unequal distribution, with 1 corresponding to complete inequality, in which a single person gets all of the total income and everyone else gets nothing.

The world's Gini coefficient is estimated to be about 0.6 and the Gini coefficient of the United States is around 0.46. That is, for all the concern about income inequality in the United States, it is actually less than the world average. European countries generally have lower Gini coefficients, whereas those of Latin America and Africa are considerably higher than that of the United States. Gini coefficients can also be calculated for land ownership and accumulated family wealth. When this is done, interesting patterns emerge. For example, the Gini coefficient for European land ownership is substantially higher than for annual income, which reflects historical patterns. The concentration of land ownership in Europe is a holdover from the preindustrial, feudal era, when a landed aristocracy held sway. By contrast, income in many European countries has become more equalized as a result of industrialization and the success of labor unions.

In much of Southeast Asia, agriculture is relatively intensive, with large numbers of small private holdings, but also fabulously wealthy princes, merchants, manufacturers, and miserable impoverished landless peasants. In much of Latin America and Africa, land ownership and wealth tend to coincide, largely through ranching, plantations, and/or mines, leaving the vast majority with no land, income, or other measurable kinds of wealth. One consequence of this inequality, in addition to its manifest unfairness, is the likelihood that many of these countries—especially those that are comparative newcomers to democracy—find themselves politically fragile.

Population

Positive peace involves a web of interconnected relationships. This is especially true of the population problem. Population—the sheer press of human numbers—makes itself felt in every aspect of the human condition, including economics as well as environmental and human rights.

The negative impact that human beings exert on their environment is largely a function of technology. Compare the relatively slight damage done to a tropical rain forest, for example, by 10,000 indigenous hunters, gatherers, and horticulturists, who have lived in relative balance with the forest for thousands of years, with the massive damage wrought by 10,000 people armed with bulldozers, dynamite, asphalt, heavy mining equipment, and guns, who threaten to destroy whole ecosystems in a matter of years.

Even among nonindustrialized countries using minimal technology, the expanding human population threatens wildlife populations because of habitat destruction (e.g., the fencing and plowing of land otherwise needed for jaguar habitat in Belize) and hunting (e.g., poaching of elephants and rhinos in Tanzania). Too many people in too small a space result in too much local consumption, which in turn pollutes the air and water, creates unmanageable quantities of solid waste, and threatens to exceed the ability of any given region—and, ultimately, the entire planet—to provide nourishment, decent living conditions, and an acceptable environment. The Earth's resources are limited. Even with extraordinary future technological innovations (which might not materialize), it is impossible to meet the demands of an indefinitely expanding human population. Many environmental problems can be ameliorated in the short term by social, political, and technological developments, but even with the best of policies, there must ultimately be a stabilization of the human population, or else no solutions will hold for the long term.

This is especially true of attempts at economic self-betterment. All too often, countries seem poised to make real gains in their living standards only to have the progress nullified by an exploding population. No country can "pull itself up by its bootstraps" if the weight of the human population is so great as to tear those straps. The following discussion of population could have been included in the previous chapter on human rights, or on environmental sustainability, but it seems most appropriate here because, as we'll see, excessive population growth adds not only to the burden of poverty but also to economic inequality.

Some Trends in Population Growth

The human species is estimated to be about 200,000 years old. World population, however, did not reach the 1 billion mark until about the year 1600. This increase was due largely to the agricultural revolution, begun around 8000 BCE with the domestication of plants and animals. This in turn resulted in better diets and more reliable food supplies. Although it took almost 10,000 years for humanity to reach its first billion people, it took only 300 years to add the next billion, which happened around 1900, stimulated in large part by the Industrial Revolution (which made energy available via mechanization and the use of fossil fuels), as well as advances in public hygiene and vaccination. The third billion arrived in just one-sixth that time, in 1950, and the fourth by 1975. Human population reached 5 billion in the 1980s, 6 billion at the beginning of the 21st century, 7.3 billion in 2015, and almost 8 billion people in 2021. It is still climbing.

The United Nations has estimated that world population will stabilize at 10 billion in 2100, assuming that birthrates will decline and eventually yield a global average of 2.1 children per woman. At an average global birthrate of 2.6, the number of people will reach 16 billion by 2100. In short, not only has the world population been growing, but the number added each year has itself increased because, as the English economist Malthus pointed out, human population increases geometrically.

In the past 20 years, average fertility in developing countries has declined while use of contraceptives has increased; as a result, the rate of world population increase has slowed from 2.1 percent per year to 1.7 percent. But, importantly, this is a reduction in the *rate of increase,* not in world population itself. Analogously, consider a bus hurtling toward a cliff and accelerating as it goes. Even if the *rate* of acceleration may eventually decline, this is likely to convey little comfort to the occupants! Furthermore, population growth is not evenly spread: States that are already pressing hard on their economic, social, and ecological resource base typically have the most rapid population growth.

In some cases—notably, the developed economies of the West—population levels are stabilizing and even declining, a trend that generates hope in the minds of some while alarming others. It is anticipated, for example, that the US population may decline slightly by the mid-21st century, based on birthrates but not counting possible immigration. Similarly, the population of most northern European states is expected to decline by as much as 10 percent by the year 2025 (even with the arrival of a "flood" of refugees). Some effects of declining birthrate in these countries are already apparent, including the accommodation of increasing numbers of "guest workers" from Turkey, Iran, northern Africa, and Asia, along with attendant ethnic and racial tension and a rise in resentful, right-wing, neofascist ideology on the part of some indigenous Europeans.

On balance, total world population is destined to increase dramatically. About 30 percent of the world's people live in developed countries, although the percentage of world population increase attributable to these countries is less than 10 percent. The world adds the equivalent of Mexico—an additional 100 million people—every year, with more than 90 percent of this growth occurring among the poorest states. "The rich get richer," goes the adage, "while the poor get children." To maintain a constant population size, women must bear, on average, two surviving children in their lifetime. The US average is 1.8, but in countries with rapidly expanding populations, such as Nigeria and Kenya, the numbers reach a whopping 6.6 and 8.0, respectively. The cause of this increase is simply an excess of births over deaths, which leads to a deepening of the planetary ecological crisis plus increasing poverty for rapidly growing populations.

Dramatic population growth has had results that are little short of cataclysmic, making a mockery of efforts at economic and environmental self-improvement. For example, in Nigeria, the most populous country in Africa, the population has grown from 43 million in 1950 to 201 million in 2019, and by 2025 that number is expected to swell to more than 300 million. At that time, Nigeria's population will be about equal to the present-day United States, but will occupy an area the size of Arizona and New Mexico. Nigeria's current unemployment rate for people aged 15 to 24 is nearly 50 percent in its urban areas, which in turn has generated increased crime and discontent. Furthermore, the skyrocketing number of unemployed youth may have contributed to the rapid growth of the terrorist group Boko Haram.

Sub-Saharan Africa has been particularly hard hit by an exploding population. There are currently about 20 countries in which the lifetime birthrate per woman exceeds 5.0; nearly all are in sub-Saharan Africa. And whereas per capita GDP increased between threefold and sixfold in North Africa, Latin America, and Asia, as population numbers have begun to level off, it has increased only marginally if at all in many sub-Saharan African countries, even where economic growth has been rapid overall. The problem is that population growth has been more rapid than the ability of many such nations to provide for them.

Egypt is a troublesome example; its population reached 100 million in 2020, making it the most populous Arab country. Egypt's economic situation is painful, with the government doing a grossly inadequate job of providing housing for the poor, while that country's poverty rate rose from 27.8 percent in 2015 to 32.5 percent in 2020, according to the government's own data. The crisis of poverty and population is made especially severe by Egypt's unforgiving geography, with 95 percent of Egyptians concentrated on roughly 4 percent of its land, along the Nile River, including roughly 20 million people squeezed into Cairo alone.

In Lewis Carroll's *Through the Looking Glass,* Alice is urged by the Red Queen to run, but she doesn't get anywhere. The Red Queen explains that when things are moving so quickly, you must run in order to stay where you are; to get anywhere, it is necessary to run even faster! (In response to this dilemma, the Nigerian government made contraceptives free in 2011, but social pressures, as well as religious condemnation from evangelical groups and the Catholic Church, have restricted their use.) There is also this danger: that in such countries as Nigeria, the existing rich-poor inequality will be widened as richer families have fewer children, who in turn are granted more per capita advantages, while the poor have many children who grow up to be even more impoverished adults in turn.

Some people contend that concern about overpopulation—especially when the worried parties are Caucasian—is actually a concealed form of racism. This accusation is at least plausible, given that rapid population increases are largely occurring in Africa, Latin America, and parts of Asia. But the costs of overpopulation are borne overwhelmingly by those poor and marginalized people whose overpopulation, relative to their country's available economic, social, and environmental resources, is responsible for much of their distress. Countries in which resources are already stretched to the limit are required, by virtue of their expanding human numbers, to increase demands on water, soil, wildlife habitat, education, and health and other human service budgets, which are already severely depleted. Struggling, debt-ridden governments in many cases have already reached or surpassed their abilities to provide even basic services to their people. In 1969, for example, Mexico City had a population of 9 million people; in 2016, there were estimated to be more than 21 million residents. Other "megacities" include Mumbai, Cairo, Lagos, São Paulo, Karachi, Jakarta, and Dhaka, all in developing countries.

Continued high population growth in the poorer countries will not only prevent a closing of the economic gap between rich and poor; it also will actually widen that gap. The rates of income growth in rich and poor countries are roughly comparable; accordingly, it is the different rate of population growth that is largely responsible for the latter's inability to catch up to the former. This problem is particularly acute in the Indian subcontinent, Africa, and parts of Latin America.

A rational population policy commends itself on financial grounds alone. Studies of Mexico, for example, indicate that for every 1 peso spent on family planning, 9 pesos are saved (from maternal and infant health care, not even counting education). Although birth control programs are no substitute for investment in education, health care, and economic and environmental betterment, fertility reduction is essential if the population control measures are to have a significant chance of succeeding.

The Demographic-Economic-Environmental Trap

There is a real danger that some states may never emerge from what might be termed the *demographic-economic-environmental trap*. In these cases, rapid population growth contributes to increased demands on natural and socio-economic systems, which are then overtaxed and begin to collapse. People commonly respond by having more children (hoping for more wage earners, helping hands, potential caregivers, etc.), in turn leading to increased eco-logical and socioeconomic pressures, which ultimately further impoverishes the land and the people. This also stresses the already overtaxed economy (more demands for schools, health care, and so forth), leading to increased mortality, notably from starvation and epidemics, and sometimes to direct violence as well.

Population levels, ecological factors, and economic conditions are all inti-mately related. Thus, every environment can be said to have what ecolo-gists call a carrying capacity: the number of people who can be supported by the soil, forests, grassland, croplands, water, and other resource supplies of that region. If demand exceeds carrying capacity, the effect is of "min-ing capital" rather than sustainably "living off the interest." This cannot be contained for long. For example, in many areas of the world, wood is used for fuel. More people result in more demand for wood, which leads to cut-ting, often in excess of annual growth. As forests dwindle, wood becomes scarce and expensive, adding to the misery of the poor, who cannot afford it. Simultaneously, deforestation diminishes wildlife values, contributes to global warming, and generates erosion and downstream flooding. (Devastat-ing floods in Bangladesh, caused by the destruction of forests in the foothills of the Himalaya Mountains above that country, have become commonplace, periodically killing tens of thousands and making hundreds of thousands homeless.)

Another significant consequence of the demographic-economic-environ-mental trap is the production of large numbers of eco-refugees, people who are forced to leave their ancestral homes because of environmental degrada-tion. Land-hungry farmers are increasingly driven onto wildlife preserves and marginal land that is highly erodible and easily destroyed. The result is desertification, a process that is distinct from drought. In this case, overgraz-ing, over plowing, and deforestation destroy the productivity of the soil, on which whole ecosystems depend. The process is accentuated by natural drought, to which weakened and overcrowded people are especially suscepti-ble. The increasing numbers of eco-refugees congregate in cities and refugee centers, where they rely on government assistance and are highly suscep-tible to disease, and, as has occurred in drought-stricken sub-Saharan Africa, massive starvation when and if relief efforts run into political, economic, or logistic difficulties—not to mention warfare, which itself is often promoted by precisely these complex, interrelated and hurtful conditions.

Uncontrolled population growth in subsistence economies threatens not only a country's environment but also its social and economic system. Universal public education becomes virtually impossible when school sys-tems are overwhelmed with youngsters. When population is constant or declining slightly (as in Germany, Sweden, and Switzerland), a 2 percent increase in economic growth results in increased overall per capita prosper-ity; when the population increases by 3 percent or 4 percent, that same 2 percent economic growth results in painfully *declining* living standards for most people.

It is difficult to make a cogent case that more people are needed, in any part of the world. Those regions that we generally consider to be "underpopulated" usually possess few people because their territories and climates can support only comparatively small populations. Deserts, high mountain slopes, or low-lying marsh or swampland that is regularly inundated by floods cannot—and should not—be heavily populated. There are no Shangri-las on this Earth, regions that are currently unpopulated but that could provide idyllic, well-balanced lives for substantial numbers of people.

On the other hand, overpopulation can be exaggerated as a cause of human misery. Some of the most impoverished regions of the Earth—such as Sudan, northeastern Brazil, and much of Mongolia—are among the most sparsely populated. Ecologists note that such regions, because of their environmental limitations, should not be heavily populated in the first place. Given the extreme susceptibility of tropical soils to destruction and the aridity of northern Africa, the natural carrying capacity of such regions for human population is necessarily low. The extreme poverty of large areas in India, Pakistan, and Indonesia is often blamed on high birthrates and population density, yet these states have fewer people per square mile than do England, Japan, the Benelux countries (Belgium, the Netherlands, Luxembourg), and Singapore. Clearly, then, although population can be a problem and can add to existing problems, it is not the entire story.

The Demographic Transition

Many European states—as well as Japan, those formerly comprising the Soviet Union, and the United States—have virtually attained zero or even negative population growth, whereas in Latin America, Africa, and Asia the population is growing. However, the demographic-economic-environmental trap may be avoidable, and high rates of population increase may decline in the future, as women see improvements in their social and economic status, and if developing countries experience social and economic improvements more generally. This expectation is based on one of the most important trends in human population, known as the demographic transition: Birthrates consistently decline as a result of industrialization, urbanization, and a general improvement in economic conditions.

For nonindustrial, rural societies, both birthrates and death rates tend to be high, and the population is therefore relatively stable. Then, with improved public health measures, immunizations, widespread food distribution, and so on, death rates decline while birthrates remain high. In this second demographic stage, the population surges. But in the final stage of the demographic transition, as social and economic conditions continue to improve and infant mortality declines, there typically arises a demand for smaller families, as growing numbers of parents realize that they do not need lots of children to serve as field hands, to compensate for high mortality, or to serve as a kind of social security in their old age. Moreover, many parents recognize that to provide their children with such benefits as higher education, they must have fewer of them. As a result, in the final stage of the demographic transition, populations eventually level off. In Latin America, for example, requiring girls to finish high school has correlated positively with a sharp drop in birthrates.

Hence, there is a double payoff to improving the socioeconomic conditions of developing countries. On the one hand, there is the direct benefit of human lives being more fulfilling. In addition, there is the beneficial effect of reducing otherwise catastrophic population growth. The demographic transition therefore offers an optimistic aspect to an otherwise dispiriting population picture.

Efforts at Birth Control

Successful birth control requires more than just appropriate technology. As a matter of public policy, it also requires understanding the social causes and effects of population growth. There are five basic theories correlating population growth with socioeconomic status:

1. *Reproduction leads to poverty.* People have too many children, forcing them to try to feed too many mouths and to divide their land and resources across too many individuals.

2. *Poverty leads to reproduction.* People have children because they are needed to work and support their families; moreover, among the very poor, infant mortality is high, which generates pressure for high birthrates.

3. *Oppression of women leads to reproduction.* Women would have fewer children if they had greater control over their lives, especially an increase in status and access to inexpensive, reliable family planning techniques.

4. *Male machismo leads to reproduction* (a variant of theory no. 3). Population growth is due to the influence of men, who equate large families with sexual virility and other "macho" characteristics.

5. *Fundamentalist religious traditions oppose birth control.* For religious fundamentalists, pretty much regardless of their particular belief system, birth control is almost universally condemned. Although this rejection of "planned parenthood" is alleged to derive from a respect for human life, critics contend that it is more associated with short-sighted efforts to maximize the number of their members.

To some extent, all of these theories seem to be true; they are not mutually exclusive. Not only are large families often a result of poverty and low status of women—in which circumstances women often find themselves unable to obtain social respect and a sense of identity—but they also generally lead to a vicious circle of yet more poverty and sexism. Moreover, religious fundamentalism is usually most prevalent among people with low socioeconomic status.

At present, about two-thirds of all birth control users live in the industrialized world. In some cases, people's hesitation regarding birth control can be attributed to such cultural factors as the "macho" tradition in Latin America, which equates manhood with the number of children; opposition by the Catholic Church in such countries as Mexico, the Philippines, and Kenya; as well as to resistance by Islamic fundamentalists in Egypt, Iran, Pakistan, and India. However, there is reason to believe that birth control technology, if more widely available, would be used. UN surveys, for example, consistently find that one-half of all married women do not want any more children. Yet funding for contraceptive research and population assistance has declined in recent decades, in part because conservative politicians in the United States—long antagonistic to family planning, contraceptives, and abortions—are very influential, both domestically and globally. The World Bank estimates that it would cost $8 billion (less than 4 days' worth of US military spending) to make birth control easily available worldwide.

Breastfeeding is a moderately effective means of birth control or, at least, of birth spacing, because lactation tends to inhibit ovulation. This is one reason why Western corporate campaigns to convince mothers in poorer nations to substitute artificial infant formula for breastfeeding have been especially pernicious. (The other reason is that breast milk is healthier for infants than are commercial substitutes, all the more so because the latter is often diluted with water before being administered—plus the fact that such water is liable to be unclean whereas breast milk is essentially free of pathogens.)

Approximately 28 million abortions are performed annually in developing countries and about 26 million in industrialized countries; of these, roughly one-half are illegal and, thus, especially in poor countries, likely to be performed by unskilled people and under unsafe conditions. Abortion is a highly charged issue for many, with even its supporters conceding that it is less desirable than contraception. Nonetheless, when other means of birth control have failed, access to safe abortions seem clearly preferable to enforced childbearing, or to dangerous "back alley" procedures.

Reproductive Rights for Women

Comparatively low social and economic status for women contributes to high birthrates, so perhaps the most effective way to reduce population growth is to improve women's conditions. Thus, married women—who in many developing nations are subordinated to their husbands—are often denied social permission to say "no" to their husband's demands for more children. In much of Africa, for example, social pressures are especially strong, because, at marriage, the husband often purchases his wife's labor as well as her future offspring; each additional child solidifies the mother's place in the household. By contrast, when the government of Bangladesh initiated a program of small-business loans to rural women, thereby helping them achieve a sense of selfhood beyond childbearing, contraceptive use among the recipients increased from an average of 35 percent to 75 percent.

When large numbers of women are denied access to education and other forms of advancement, childbearing may become the only accepted rite of passage to adulthood. As a result, increased education for young women is likely to help reduce fertility rates, thereby diminishing poverty and also helping to prevent further environmental degradation.

Birth control and family planning are advisable as matters of public health alone. For example, complications arising from pregnancy and childbirth are the leading killers of Third World women in their 20s and 30s. More than 3,000 maternal deaths occur per 100,000 live births in regions of Ethiopia and Bangladesh, as compared with 10 in the United States and only 2 in Norway.

Government Policies

China began its "one family, one child" program in 1979. The goal—no more than 1.2 billion people by the year 2000—was achieved. Violators were punished by fines and dismissal from government jobs, while better housing and stipends were available to one-child households. The overall results have been mixed. Such coercive policies are often unpalatable to many people's conceptions of individual liberty. In addition, Chinese population policy was concentrated among urban, ethnic (Han) Chinese, whereas ethnic minorities and rural people were to some extent exempted. Population growth in China, however, decreased, from nearly 3 percent to 1.4 percent, largely because of a contemporaneous Chinese tendency to marry and bear children at a later age and because of the active efforts of the Chinese government.

China's draconian one-child policy caused other serious problems, however, including overall aging of the population in addition to female-selective infanticide. When a family is limited to just one child, in a culture that values boys over girls, infant daughters are liable to be killed, which, in addition to being a humanitarian outrage, results in an unbalanced sex ratio, with disruptive social consequences. As a result, China cancelled its one-child mandate. A similar example of governmental heavy-handedness occurred in India under the leadership of Indira Gandhi; perhaps the worst manifestation was forced sterilization, which eventually generated such outrage that much of the Indian government's population policy was abandoned.

An alternative, more acceptable, yet also effective way of slowing population growth is for women to delay reproduction until later in life—for example, age 32 instead of 17—a cultural tradition that has reduced the population growth of Ireland, for example, which is strongly Roman Catholic, where contraception was long frowned upon and where until 2018 abortion was legal only to save the mother's life.

Although population policies are necessary, for them to be persistent as well as effective, they will likely have to be based on voluntary compliance rather than compulsion; that is, they should educate, provide incentives and technology, and minister to existing demand, without being heavy-handed.

Unmet Need for Contraception

There is, in fact, a large unmet need with respect to family size limitation. For example, women of reproductive age were surveyed in four developing countries: India, Egypt, Peru, and Ghana. The percentages of women who indicated that they did not want any more children were, respectively, 50, 56, 70, and 90, whereas the percentages using contraception were, respectively, 28, 30, 25, and 10. Subtracting the latter from the former, the percentages of women who wish to limit their family size but are not employing any form of birth control are 22 percent, 26 percent, 45 percent, and a staggering 80 percent in Ghana.

Clearly, the unmet need for contraception is enormous, and whereas it can be seen as a personal, family, national, and world tragedy, it also provides population planners with a great opportunity: a chance to reduce the catastrophic increase in human population while at the same time satisfying the desires of those involved.

The Developed Countries

Poor countries tend to reduce their rate of population growth as they become wealthier—the demographic transition—and wealthy countries like those in North America and western Europe have relatively low rates of population increase. However, this is no reason to be complacent or self-righteous, because the wealthy countries use far more resources per capita than do the poor ones, and they also produce proportionately more pollution as well.

The United States is about twice as wasteful as the other developed states; with about 5 percent of the world's population, the United States consumes more than 30 percent of the world's resources, six times its "rightful" share. Or look at it this way: The average US citizen consumes about 20 times the resources as does the average resident of a Third World country.

Clearly, population growth in the world's poorest countries is a serious social, environmental, and economic problem, especially for the residents of these countries. But considering its planetary costs, population growth in such economically developed states as the United States is far more serious. The poor, in short, cannot legitimately be blamed for the world's population plight, because the rich are a disproportionately large part of the problem.

Future Directions

If we don't change direction, states an ancient Chinese proverb, we shall end up where we are headed. An overcrowded, overarmed world, increasingly divided between haves and have-nots, is not a desirable prospect, either in ethical terms or for its tangible consequences: misery, disruption, and, perhaps, increased violence. Granted, poor people are unlikely to march aggressively into the rich countries, especially so long as the latter possess abundant lethal weaponry. Unlike a ghetto riot, in which people's poverty and frustration may erupt, for example, into looting a local department store, poverty is more apt to continue generating its own kind of structural violence, eroding the quality of life. It may also continue to generate political instability.

As with so many other issues in peace and conflict studies, the problem of poverty is easier to diagnose than to cure. It is a major accomplishment just to appreciate the problem, because, like human rights, environmental degradation, and the prevention of war, it is vast and multidimensional. The plight of the poor is unlikely to be temporary, but it also need not be eternal.

In this respect, one of the greatest impediments to effective action is the inclination of powerful governments—representing people who are essentially satisfied with the status quo—to ignore the problem, minimize it, blame its victims, and, if pressed, give only lip service to its urgency. Among the more general and widespread suggestions for reducing global poverty, the following may have particular merit:

- Recognizing that whereas economic growth is to some degree desirable, growth in itself does not necessarily lead to a greater sharing of prosperity, either between states or within them

- Establishing an internationally accepted floor below which poverty shall not be permitted, analogous to the "safety net" currently in place in most Western democracies

- Making birth control universally available, either free or at minimal cost

- Developing and implementing a worldwide literacy program, plus upgrading educational facilities and opportunities, especially in the developing world and particularly focused on women

- Enhancing the role and effectiveness of local, grassroots activities that promote economic growth and environmental protection

- Providing massive debt relief for the poorest states, coupled with reorientation of their economies from being export-oriented to satisfying domestic needs

- Making serious efforts toward achieving self-reliant "eco-development," which is neither stagnation nor ecological exploitation but rather respects the cultural heterogeneity of the local inhabitants as well as their need to work *with* nature rather than against it

- Recognizing that resource-guzzling technologies will likely be harmful for many if not most developing countries as well as for the industrialized world, and, similarly, that high-technology procedures don't necessarily create more jobs than they destroy, and that unemployment contributes significantly to poverty

- Redirecting a large proportion of planetary resources, currently eaten up by military spending, to upgrading the living conditions of the world's people

The Case of Costa Rica

Toward the end of the 20th century, it was widely hoped that with the apparent cessation of East-West military competition, resources previously consumed by the military could be released for desperately needed civilian purposes. Although this optimistic hope was not fulfilled at the global level, the experience of Costa Rica may be instructive.

This small Central American state abolished its army, navy, and air force in 1948. Whereas nearby Guatemala and Honduras, by contrast, spend 15 percent of their GNP on their military, Costa Rica spends less than 2 percent of its GNP on a lightly armed national police. These savings permit Costa Rica to devote 11 percent of its GNP to health and education, more than twice the proportional expenditure of Honduras and three times that of Guatemala. As a result, polio and diphtheria have been eradicated in Costa Rica, and whooping cough, tetanus, and measles are nearly gone as well. Infant mortality has plummeted, as has the birthrate, which declined by nearly 50 percent from 1960 to 2015. Moreover, with the funds saved, Costa Rica now has roughly 23 percent of its land area preserved as either national parks or biological reserves. According to global surveys of "subjective well-being" (sometimes summarized as "happiness"), Costa Rica—despite its moderate per capita economic situation—ranks at or near the top, along with the wealthy, democratic socialist Scandinavian countries. This coincidence of national well-being with demilitarization is probably not a coincidence.

During the 1980s, the US government regularly and unsuccessfully pressured Costa Rica to reverse its priorities and invest in a national army, ostensibly as defense against communism (but, in fact, as part of the Reagan administration's desire to put military pressure on nearby Sandinista-led Nicaragua). However, the demilitarized, prosocial policy of Costa Rica is a surer path to stability and security than is the traditional neoliberal and militarist model of socioeconomic development. Accordingly, it may be hoped that Costa Rica represents a model for the future development of other poor to middle income nations.

A Final Note on Economic Well-Being

Despite the unparalleled wealth enjoyed by some (less than 1 percent), the great majority of the world's people are poor, so much so that many lives are shortened or made miserable. Even more people are prevented from developing their potential. Indirect, or structural economic violence is thus widespread and, in a discouraging number of already-impoverished countries, increasing. Overpopulation exacerbates this problem as well as the disparity between the haves and the have-nots (who, not surprisingly, are also "want-mores").

Solutions, however, do exist, including various redistribution strategies, programs of genuine grassroots development designed to benefit those in need rather than those already well off, and family planning. The problem of poverty—like the problems of human rights, the environment, and war—is ancient but not necessarily intractable. Sufficient resources exist to provide a decent material life for everyone, especially if human population is eventually controlled. The greatest obstacle to economic well-being appears to be the possessive social and political inclinations of some human beings, corporations, and states, usually those with the financial resources to help people in need but who decline to do so. The question is whether these people, corporations, and the governments who represent their interests will acknowledge the aspirations and needs of the "wretched of the Earth" and make the changes needed to improve the lot of their fellow human beings.

Questions for Further Reflection

1. What is meant by "uneven development" or "increased marginalization despite development?" What are some of its causes?

2. Discuss poverty and inequity in ethical terms. Also discuss them in terms of state security, as well as their psychological and social dimensions.

3. Describe several different explanations for why there is so much poverty in the developing world compared with the developed world. Do the same for inequity within the developed world.

4. Why should relatively wealthy people in, for example, Sweden or Norway, Canada or the United States care about starvation in, for example, Sudan?

5. It can be argued that poverty and population lead to mutually reinforcing downward spirals. Show how these disturbing trends could be reversed, leading to mutually reinforcing patterns of amelioration. What are some of the practical obstacles to improving poor people's lives?

Suggestions for Further Reading

Tom Butler, ed. 2015. *Overdevelopment, Overpopulation, Overshoot*. San Francisco: Goff Books.

Cynthia Duncan. 2015. *Worlds Apart: Politics and Poverty in Rural America*. New Haven, CT: Yale University Press.

Mei Fong. 2015. *One Child: The Story of China's Most Radical Experiment*. New York: Houghton Mifflin.

Jeffrey Sachs. 2006. *The End of Poverty: Economic Possibilities for Our Time*. New York: Penguin.

Joseph E. Stiglitz. 2015. *The Great Divide: Unequal Societies and What We Can Do About Them*. New York: Norton.

Joseph E. Stiglitz. 2015. *The Price of Inequality: How Today's Divided Society Endangers Our Future*. New York: Norton.

John Weeks. 2007. *Population: An Introduction to Concepts and Issues*. Belmont, CA: Wadsworth.

Muhammad Yunus and Alan Jolis. 2007. *Banker to the Poor: Micro-Lending and the Battle Against World Poverty*. New York: Public Affairs.

22

Democracy

Winston Churchill once described democracy as "the worst form of government—except for all the others." Citizens of democratic countries have long appreciated Churchill's quip, in part because even as it recognizes democracy's imperfection, it nonetheless notes its overriding merit. Churchill may or may not have been correct, although we, too, admit to being unable to identify a more appropriate candidate for the best form of government. Perhaps there is no "best form," or maybe it varies with local circumstances, or perhaps democracy really is the best—especially if it is a truly comprehensive system of participatory self-governance.

In any event, it seems clear that when given the opportunity—and even when such opportunities are severely restricted by state dictatorship—many

Democracy

Winston Churchill once described democracy as "the worst form of government—except for all the others." Citizens of democratic countries have long appreciated Churchill's quip, in part because even as it recognizes democracy's imperfection, it nonetheless notes its overriding merit. Churchill may or may not have been correct, although we, too, admit to being unable to identify a more appropriate candidate for the best form of government. Perhaps there is no "best form," or maybe it varies with local circumstances, or perhaps democracy really *is* the best—especially if it is a truly comprehensive system of participatory self-governance.

In any event, it seems clear that when given the opportunity—and even when such opportunities are severely restricted by state dictatorship—many people yearn for democracy and are often willing to run great risks and to suffer horribly in the hope of establishing one in their homelands. Because the aspiration for democracy appears to be deep as well as widespread, such that it has become a conspicuous hallmark of international affairs in the early 21st century (albeit with some notable backsliding), and because movements toward democracy have definite implications for both negative and positive peace, we devote this chapter to a brief review of the phenomenon.

What Is Democracy?

A simple definition states that a democratic government is one in which supreme political decision making is ultimately vested in the people (*demos*, in Greek, means "people" and *kratia*, means "rule," as in "technocratic," "meritocratic," etc.), who exercise this power either directly or via decisions made by their chosen representatives. In its classic form, democracy was characteristic of ancient Greek city-states, especially Athens, and during certain periods of the Roman Republic. It still occurs in a small scale among New England town meetings in the United States, and the *jirga* system of many central Asian societies. With increasing local populations, such direct democracy has become more and more unwieldy, so that decision making has typically been the responsibility and privilege of a limited number of individuals expected to represent their constituents—hence, representative or parliamentary democracy.

Despite widespread use of the term, in reality there are many different forms of democracy and variations on what constitutes the "democratic ideal." Thus, truly competitive elections are often seen as a cornerstone of democracy, and yet, there is substantial diversity when it comes to electoral practices. In most countries, for example, only citizens are permitted to vote, thus disenfranchising large numbers of people who may actually constitute an arithmetic majority. In other cases—notably certain Arab states—women are not permitted to vote. In some countries only landowners are "enfranchised," and in others, including, historically, the United States, voters have been required to pay a poll tax that effectively disenfranchises the poor.

Freedom of association, freedom of the press, freedom of political speech and of writing are often considered prerequisites for political democracy, although many countries that proclaim themselves democracies actually restrict such activities. Similarly, even though it is widely assumed that democracy (a political system) implies free-market capitalism (an economic system), this isn't always the case. China provides a dramatic example because the Chinese political system—nominally communist—is rigidly authoritarian, whereas its vibrant, rapidly growing economic system is basically capitalist (so-called state capitalism) with a small number of fabulously wealthy entrepreneurs, a growing middle class, and little or no protection for workers or peasants.

In some countries (e.g., France and the United States) national leaders ("presidents") are chosen via presidential elections, whereas in others (e.g., the United Kingdom, Germany, Israel, and in the world's most populous democracy, India) voting takes place for members of parliament, with the party receiving a parliamentary majority being empowered to "form a government," typically led by an identified prime minister. This not uncommonly involves complex coalitions among two or more parties in the event that no single one achieves an electoral majority of representatives. It isn't clear whether such parliamentary democracies are more or less democratic on balance than those in which national leaders are chosen directly, especially because in the United States, presidents are not chosen by simple majority vote but rather via an electoral college system, which has produced several minority presidents in the past, including George W. Bush in 2000 and Donald Trump in 2016.

Democracy in the United States

Compared to others, the US is not a very old country. It is, however, among the oldest continuous democracies, whose inhabitants by and large take great pride in its political freedoms and democratic governance. Other countries, even those not especially friendly to the United States, paid homage of a sort to the US model by pretending to hold democratic elections and to operate under formal constitutions that were in reality ignored. Nonetheless, the US has had its own difficulties with democracy, beyond the fact that it engaged in chattel slavery until after the Civil War, and that women weren't allowed to vote until 1920.

Within the United States, only two states (Maine and Vermont) permit incarcerated persons to vote, and in 11 states, ex-convicts may lose their right to vote forever. Eight states (Alabama, Arizona, Delaware, Florida, Kentucky, Mississippi, Tennessee, and Wyoming) allow some, but not all, persons with felony convictions to vote after having completed their sentences. Some civil rights advocates maintain that this is a form of politically inspired racism because African Americans are disproportionately represented in this group and their numbers could be sufficient to affect elections if they were permitted to become part of the electoral democratic process. In addition, right-wing pressure has regularly sought to suppress voter turnout among minority communities.

It is also widely assumed that "one person, one vote" is characteristic of democracies, although "vote buying" through various means is not uncommon. In the United States—ostensibly a paragon of democratic political process—political campaigning requires large financial expenditures, leading to well-founded accusations that wealthy people and large corporations, by virtue of their ability to make campaign contributions and/or purchase media advertising, have a disproportionate influence on political elections as well as when it comes to decision making and the crafting of legislation. It has therefore been claimed that when it comes to adherence to democracy, the US often fails to live up to its own standards.

During the presidency of Donald Trump (2017–2021), a variety of democratic norms were persistently violated, leading many—within and outside the US—to worry that American democracy itself was under assault. This difficult situation was italicized following the American presidential election in November, 2020, when Trump lost decisively but then refused to accept this result, claiming falsely that he had actually won. This lie was supported by most leaders of the Republican Party. More worrisome yet, while still president, Mr. Trump incited a violent mob to storm the US Capitol, intending to overturn this election. Two days after this brief but murderous insurrection, *The New York Times* opined that

> To friends and foes, and through triumphs and crises, the United States has stood as the standard of democracy and freedom since the last two world wars. When it was criticized and even reviled—whether over the Vietnam War, the arms race of the Cold War or the Watergate

scandal—it was over its failure to live up to its own standards, and Americans were always quick to reassure its allies that "we're better than that," a cry heard often among Mr. Trump's detractors today. The Soviet Union and tyrants of all stripes paid a perverse homage to the American model by feigning democratic elections and concocting high-sounding constitutions that they never intended to follow.[1]

Although Joseph R. Biden was duly inaugurated president two weeks later, one effect of the January 6, 2021 events was that a country whose democratic institutions had widely been seen as exceptionally strong was revealed to be vulnerable to demagogy. It remains to be seen what effect this will have on the future of democracy in the US and elsewhere around the world.

Is Democracy Desirable?

The desirability of democracy is rarely questioned by Western nations, despite its diversity in practice. Thus, even notoriously undemocratic governments—notably those of North Korea and the former Soviet satellite states of Eastern Europe—incorporated the word "democratic" in their formal state name, as in the Democratic People's Republic of ___. In contrast to such verbal commitment to democracy, typically characteristic of state socialist countries, Fascist and Nazi ideology has a long history of being dismissive of democracy as "degenerate," just as many on the political left criticize the ostensible democracy of right-wing despots as being a sham, whose elections cannot realistically be considered free.

One of the most famous philosophical critiques of democracy occurs in Plato's *Republic*, in which democracy is equated to mob rule, as opposed to a supposedly more just and therefore desirable form of governance by an unelected aristocracy of philosopher-kings. For example, at one point in *The Republic*, Socrates refers scathingly to "democracy, which is a charming form of government, full of variety and disorder, and dispensing a sort of equality to equals and unequals alike." Even the most enthusiastic supporters of democracy—who claim that all people are created equal (for the purpose of electoral influence and ideally, their legal rights)—do not maintain that such equality means that everyone is literally identical.

Participatory Democracy and "Astroturf"

In this chapter, we focus on large-scale, countrywide democracy, which typically involves representative democracy because as group size increases, it becomes less feasible to make political decisions by the direct participation of each citizen. However, a case can be made for the value of direct or participatory democracy, in which every individual has a say in nearly every important decision. The appeal of participatory democracy has been especially strong within the political left; it was a major principle underlying the Port Huron Statement, a manifesto written in 1962 by the young founders of the Students for a Democratic Society. This statement—a now-classic announcement of progressive goals—called for extending participatory democracy from community organizing to the larger realms of economic and foreign policy.

In the 21st century, echoes of participatory democracy can be heard in a range of "shack-dwellers movements," especially in South Africa, Brazil, and India, as well as "landless peasants movements" in South and Central America. In contrast, right-wing activism has also been energized by a vision of participatory involvement, ranging from the extremes of Fascist and Nazi movements of the 1930s to more moderate manifestations of conservative populism such as the Tea Party movement in the United States, replaced a few years later by "Trumpism." It is all too easy for participatory democracy—or at least, the appeal of such participation—to produce demagoguery that appeals to the lowest common denominator of its audience, which in turn threatens to be intolerant or even violent.

Within participatory democracy, the presumption is that decision making still occurs via some form of democratic voting process, in which one person—regardless of gender, wealth, and so forth—casts one vote. In practice, even in so called democratic countries, those in positions of power exercise disproportionate influence, via their wealth (which enables them to purchase political advertising as well as influence via lobbyists and campaign contributions) or the capacity to intimidate their opponents, by controlling media outlets or, not uncommonly, the use of hired thugs. In this regard, a distinction needs to be made between genuine participatory, or grassroots democracy, and its artificial counterpart, sometimes called "astroturf,"[2] whereby wealthy individuals, reigning governments, and corporations use their power to give the appearance of widespread public support when in fact the "movement" is essentially financed and operated by a small minority.

Social Democracy

Another democratic variant is known as social democracy. It is widespread, with many millions of supporters, especially outside the United States. Social Democrats (or "Democratic Socialists" in the US) support a political, social, and economic system that favors active government involvement within the framework of pluralistic democracy and a mixed economy. American social democrats have supported progressive electoral and political reforms as well as such policy proposals as universal single-payer healthcare and the Green New Deal.

The policies and norms social democrats promote involve a commitment to representative and participatory democracy, measures for income redistribution, regulation of the economy in the general interest, and strong social welfare provisions leading to what is often called the "welfare state." Social democracy is especially prominent in Europe, Australia, New Zealand, and even in Canada, with most adherents rejecting authoritarian rule as well as violent, revolutionary tactics. The emphasis is on grassroots (bottom up) participation, in sharp contrast with the repressive top-down, statist (or "democratic centralist") approach characteristic of the Soviet Union under Lenin and Stalin.

There are many Social Democratic and/or Socialist or Labor Parties that subscribe to social-democratic principles and that have also enjoyed electoral success, mostly in advanced industrial Western parliamentary systems. The German Social Democratic Party, for example, although recently declining in popular support (primarily due to large segments of the German electorate voting for parties to its left—The Greens and The Left—or for the far-right Alternative for Germany) has been part of governing coalitions in that country for decades and has produced such acclaimed prime ministers as Willy Brandt and Gerhard Schröder. The British Labour Party has been in and out of power in the United Kingdom for generations. And the New Democratic Party (NDP) in Canada adopts a mixture of social democratic, socialist, and ecological principles and focuses on such issues as LGBTQ+ rights, international peace and social justice, and environmental stewardship. While never in power at the federal level, the NDP held the balance of power in Canada's Parliament following the 2019 election. It governs the Canadian province of British Columbia and has previously formed the government in the provinces of Alberta, Manitoba, Ontario, Saskatchewan, Nova Scotia, and the Yukon Territory.

In sum, social-democratic principles and parties have had considerable influence in many Western democracies and may be gaining adherents, especially among younger Americans, who, for various reasons, are turned off by mainstream politicians.

A Brief Modern History of Democratization

A Series of "Waves"

As the Cold War between the United States and the Soviet Union concluded with the collapse of Soviet-style communism, political theorist Francis Fukuyama proposed that "liberal democracy"—essentially, democracy plus capitalism—had triumphed worldwide. Although not "The End of History," as the title of his book announced, Fukuyama's point was that the competition between democracy and other governmental forms had been resolved in the former's favor. "What we may be witnessing," Fukuyama wrote with hope in 1989, "is the end point of mankind's ideological evolution and the universalization of Western liberal democracy as the final form of human government."

Reality has been more complex, as China's 1.4 billion people have been gradually subjected by the Communist Party elite not to more but to less political democracy, and Russia has moved in a similar direction, while radical Islam has refused to embrace anything approaching liberal democracy. The view that history proceeds toward a fixed point and that the past can therefore be seen (only in retrospect, of course) as aiming at a superior or, in some sense, a more valid outcome has been called "Whig history," and it is generally out of favor among historians.

On the other hand, this approach is meaningful in such nonpolitical domains as science: The Copernican, sun-centered solar system is a better model than the Ptolemaic, Earth-centered version, just as evolution by natural selection is superior to special creation. But political systems are different. Despite the importance of democracy and its widespread appeal (at least in the West), it is important to be wary of the seductiveness of such "Whiggery," and to appreciate that changes in socio-politics do not necessarily exemplify movement from primitive to advanced forms of governance, or from malevolent to benevolent, and so forth.

Political scientist Samuel Huntington argued that democracy advances and recedes in a series of waves. The first such wave began in the early 19th century, with voting rights extended to most white males in the United States and England, reaching its peak in the early 1920s, at which time there were fewer than 30 democracies worldwide. With the Great Depression in the late 1920s and 1930s, came the rise of Fascist, Nazi, and communist dictatorships, along with "strong-man" rule in much of the Balkans, the Baltic States, China, and many countries in Latin America. As a result, according to Huntington, the number of democracies declined to just 12 by the middle of World War II.

Continuing this perspective, a second wave of democratization began with the Allied victory in World War II, associated with decolonization (the breakup of the British, French, Dutch, and Belgian empires in particular) and the transition of postwar Germany, Italy, and Japan to democracy. By the early 1960s, there were 36 identified democracies worldwide, although this number then declined slightly until the mid-1970s. Many countries at that time were only nominally democratic, having sham elections and limited actual political freedom.

A third wave of democratization can be considered to have started in 1974, with the Carnation Revolution that ended Fascist rule in Portugal, followed by democratization in Spain with the death of the Fascist dictator Francisco Franco. This third wave picked up steam in Latin America during the 1980s, when military or one-party regimes collapsed in Argentina, Bolivia, Brazil, Ecuador, Honduras, Paraguay, Peru, and Uruguay, to be replaced by constitutional governments. To some degree, this third wave continued and perhaps even picked up steam after 1989, with the collapse of the Soviet Union and the emergence of numerous former Soviet republics that became independent states. The countries of Eastern Europe—Czechoslovakia (which subsequently split into the Czech Republic and Slovakia), East Germany (which subsequently joined with West Germany to form a united Germany), Poland, Hungary, Romania, Bulgaria, and even rigidly isolated and Maoist Albania—all of which previously had been undemocratic Soviet "satellites," moved rapidly and dramatically toward democracy.

However, with the exception of the Baltic countries (Latvia, Lithuania, and Estonia), the successor states to the Soviet Union, including Russia, did not become notably democratic. They typically established official structures for holding free and fair elections, but in reality, one-party rule persisted, often combined with economic instability, a strong military footprint upon ostensibly civilian affairs, government control of the media, and so forth. This is especially true of the Asiatic "stans" that emerged from the former Soviet Union (Uzbekistan, Tajikistan, Kazakhstan, Turkmenistan, and Kyrgyzstan.), as well as Russia, Moldova, Belarus, and, more recently, Ukraine, where democratic gains are at best fragile, if only because of Russian-backed military pressure on the Russophile eastern parts of that country.

The various waves of democratization don't necessarily exist as clear-cut entities because every country is a unique case. For example, Switzerland is generally considered an early model of democracy and thus part of the first wave, yet Swiss women were not enfranchised (permitted to vote) until 1971. In addition, the exact beginning and ending of each wave is subject to dispute. Whereas some scholars consider, for instance, that the third wave of democratization has continued up to the present, others make a distinction between the events concluding with the breakup of the Soviet Union and those associated with the various "color revolutions," which might therefore warrant being labeled the fourth wave, with yet a fifth wave, the so-called Arab Spring, being the most recent, followed more recently by a palpable antidemocratic retrenchment. In any event, by most estimates there are currently more than 100 functioning democracies in the world, although not all are equally stable or fully democratic. It is always necessary to go beneath the surface to ascertain what governments actually do, as distinct from what they claim.

The "Color Revolutions": A Fourth Wave

Although there was some expansion of democratic governance (notably in the Republic of South Africa) during the 1990s, the most dramatic cases of democratization—especially in the 21st century—included events in a number of different countries, which, despite having followed various paths toward democracy, were similar in several respects:

1. They involved massive, nonviolent street demonstrations and other examples of political (and often economic) protest.

2. They were essentially leaderless, "crowd-sourced" movements, largely involving bottom-up or grassroots protest.

3. Participants tended to be middle class, often students as well as professionals (doctors, lawyers, etc.), but also often included unemployed and otherwise disaffected citizens, with no evidence that their ranks were significantly swelled by extremist ideologues.

4. Mobilization techniques included the widespread use of modern communications technology, including cell phones, Facebook, and Twitter, to coordinate activities as well as to disseminate information—often about recent governmental abuses—that helped mobilize yet more protesters.

5. Popular unrest frequently emerged in the aftermath of a disputed election in which there was strong evidence of major fraud and vote rigging by the ruler in power.

6. In most cases, these prodemocracy protest movements developed characteristic and powerful symbols, often simply involving use of a distinctive color.

These events were foreshadowed, and to some extent inspired by, the nonviolent protests that toppled the autocratic Marcos regime in the Philippines in 1986, sometimes called a Yellow Revolution for the color adopted by Corazon Aquino, widow of assassinated Filipino opposition leader Benigno Aquino. This success, in turn, may have helped inspire the overthrow of the second generation of brutal Duvalier dictators in Haiti, also in 1986, and presaged the various Velvet Revolutions of 1989 that ended Soviet control of Eastern Europe and shortly thereafter led to the dissolution of the Soviet Union itself.

A major event in the history of recent democracy movements was the Bulldozer Revolution in 2000, which led to the deposition of Serb dictator Slobodan Milošević. Opposition groups rallied around the slogan *Gotov je* ("He's finished"), a campaign that galvanized Serbian discontent with Milošević and resulted in his defeat and eventual trial for war crimes by the International Criminal Court.

Next was the Rose Revolution in Georgia, in the aftermath of a disputed election in 2003 and which resulted in a new election in 2004. The Orange Revolution in Ukraine took place after a disputed Ukrainian presidential election in 2004 and led to the annulment of the result and a second election, after which the opposition's leader was declared president, defeating the Russian-backed incumbent (who subsequently was returned to power, only to be deposed after popular protests that were mostly but not exclusively nonviolent, at least on the part of the protesters). In 2014, Russia invaded parts of Ukraine, annexing Crimea and supporting pro-Russian militias in eastern Ukraine, at least in part because pro-European elements in western Ukraine and Kiev seemed ready to embrace Europe rather than Russia.

Many of the former Soviet Republics have had their own, mostly nonviolent, revolutions against Russian-backed autocrats, and in some cases popular movements have installed at least nominally democratic governments. Other massive, mostly nonviolent calls for increased democracy and popular sovereignty have taken place in in Armenia (2008 and 2018), Azerbaijan (2005), Macedonia (2016), Moldova (2009 and 2015), Turkey ("Gezi Park,"

2013), Belarus ("the Jeans Revolution" of 2006), France (the "Yellow Vest" Movement, 2018–2020), Hong Kong (the "Umbrella Movement" of 2014–2015 and 2019–2020), and even sporadically in the urban heart of Russia (2011–2013 and 2017–2019). Some movements have been more successful than others because democratic norms and institutions are quite fragile and could be undermined, if not undone, by Russian aggression and other illiberal forces spreading throughout much of Europe, especially in the Balkans, Poland, Turkey, Hungary, and even in the German-speaking world.

The immediate prospects for democracy in much of post-Soviet Eurasia (Uzbekistan, Kazakhstan, Azerbaijan, Belarus, and Russia) remain bleak. What initially began as a transition from communism to democracy quickly transitioned back to autocracy, often based on family and clan associations of the leaders of each state. There may be a general trend toward democracy worldwide, but its failure to take root in such cases (including the world's most populous country, China) shows that movement of this sort is necessarily erratic, with more than a few reversals. Despite widespread concern about the future of democracy, as well as frequent disagreement over whether specific countries are truly democratic, the number of electoral democracies has generally increased over recent decades, such that somewhat more than one-half of all countries qualify as in some realistic sense democratic, with particular advances in South America and Africa.

In the Middle East, the Cedar Revolution in Lebanon (2005) didn't follow a disputed election; rather, it came after the assassination of a highly regarded opposition leader, in which the Syrian government was widely thought to have been involved. One outcome was the departure of Syrian troops from Lebanon after nearly three decades of semi-occupation. The Lawyers Revolution, consisting almost entirely of upper middle class professionals in Pakistan, initially sought in 2007 to reinstate a judge who had been deposed by military strongman Pervez Musharraf; the nonviolent protests eventually resulted in Musharraf's resignation.

Even though dictatorships were generally decreasing worldwide by the close of the first decade of the 21st century, not all popular movements for democracy were successful. In Iran, popular protests known as the Green Revolution broke out in 2009 following an election widely considered to have been rigged. Unlike many of the other color revolutions, the Green Revolution was militarily suppressed and, as a result, can be considered a failure, although Iran (despite its government being ultimately under conservative theocratic control) has subsequently seen a genuine electoral process when it comes to its secular leadership. On the other hand, another initially unsuccessful color revolution eventually helped induce the military dictatorship of Burma (a.k.a. Myanmar), to ease its repression of that country. This prodemocracy movement became known as the Saffron Revolution because Buddhist monks, who helped lead it, traditionally wear robes of that color. It has resulted in a widespread opening of the country, not only to electoral democracy but also to economic liberalization (at the same time that its Rohingya minority was being brutally suppressed).

The Arab Spring: A "Fifth Wave" That Largely Failed

On December 17, 2010, a young Tunisian man, Mohamed Bouazizi, was in despair because the economic stagnation and unemployment in his country were such that he had been reduced to selling vegetables from a street cart, with no prospect of economic or social advancement. The final straw for

Mr. Bouazizi occurred when his wares were confiscated by a policewoman, whereupon he set himself on fire in protest, an action that almost literally set much of the Arab world ablaze. Two weeks later, Mr. Bouazizi died, after which street demonstrations erupted in Tunisia against a decades-old tyranny (which had been supported by the West), and the protests quickly spread through much of the Arab world, including Libya, Bahrain, Algeria, Yemen, and most notably—because it is the most populous Arab country and in many ways the center of Arab culture—Egypt.

The result became known as the Arab Spring, named in part for its superficial similarity to the Prague Spring, a short-lived, largely nonviolent democratic 1968 uprising in Czechoslovakia. But whereas the Prague Spring was quickly suppressed by Soviet tanks, the Arab Spring (a.k.a. the "Arab Awakening") was far more successful, at least initially. Not since the widespread European revolutions of 1848 have there been so many spontaneous uprisings, although the overthrow of Eastern European communist dictatorships in 1989 offers a similar pattern. In the case of the Arab Spring, the protesters' focus was not Islamic radicalism or antagonism to Israel or to the United States; rather, their demands were limited and clear cut, directed toward their own oppressive governments, many of which had persisted for decades. In Arabic, these demands were summarized by *Kifaya* ("Enough") and *Irhal* ("Leave").

Oil-rich Saudi Arabia has thus far been able to "buy off " protests by providing enhanced financial benefits to Arabian citizens, an option that was not available to the autocratic leaders of either Tunisia or Egypt because both lack oil wealth. And in Bahrain, Saudi troops quelled popular resistance to the monarchy, which, like the Saudi government and most of its populace, is Sunni; in Bahrain, by contrast, the oppressed majority is Shiite.

Although a yearning for democracy played a consistent role in each of the anti-dictator movements within the Arab world, as well as in the color revolutions that preceded the Arab Spring, other factors were also involved. The Arab Spring was not primarily motivated by anti-Western anger but rather was focused on domestic concerns. Protesters typically objected to deep-seated political corruption and cronyism, the concentration of wealth in the hands of hereditary autocrats who had remained in power for decades, sexual frustration deriving in part from few or no prospects for economic growth (which doomed many young men to bachelorhood in societies in which prospective husbands must have a certain level of wealth in order to marry), and more than anything, perhaps, refusal by young people, the downtrodden, disaffected middle class and elites, democracy lovers, and the generally disappointed to accept the status quo. Rapidly rising food prices may also been significant, in addition to the fact that a large proportion of the Internet-savvy youth of these Arab countries had become increasingly inclined to view absolute monarchs and other despots as anachronisms. Most of the deposed despots had been supported by the West, which nonetheless claimed to stand for democracy.

Many decision makers in the West were initially surprised that the Arab world, which had long been considered rigidly hierarchical, indifferent to change, and almost medieval in its outlook and technology, was instead inhabited by serious minded, democracy-loving patriots with access to the Internet, strong antiauthoritarian impulses, and a courageous willingness to take risks and participate in politically sophisticated, mostly nonviolent protest. But an even greater surprise, perhaps, was that several long-standing, highly repressive Arab regimes quickly collapsed. Eventually, the dictators of Tunisia, Yemen, and Egypt relinquished power once it became apparent that they had lost the support of their military in the face of massive and persistent "people power" (an expression that dated from the Yellow Revolution, which ousted the Marcos dictatorship in the Philippines). Popular uprisings against Libyan dictator Moammar Gaddafi evoked a violent response by loyalists within the Libyan military, with Gaddafi eventually defeated (and killed) after a brief but bloody civil war in which NATO forces assisted the rebels.[3] On the other hand, antigovernment protests in Bahrain were brutally suppressed by military force (largely provided by Saudi Arabia).

Events in Tahrir Square—a prominent meeting place in Cairo, which became the epicenter of ongoing protests against longtime Egyptian dictator Hosni Mubarak—were especially dramatic. The government initially responded with violent repression, during which as many as 300 people may have been killed. But an important pattern emerged: When it was clear that large numbers of Egyptian people were willing to risk injury and death for their beliefs, the legitimacy of the regime was lethally undermined. Writing of the events in Tahrir Square, one observer noted,

In Egypt, there were moments of violence when people pushed back against the government's goons, and for a week it seemed like the news was filled with little but pictures of bloody heads. Still, no armies marched, no superior weaponry decided the fate of the country, nobody was pushed from power by armed might. People gathered in public and discovered themselves as the public, as civil society. They found that the repression and exploitation they had long tolerated was intolerable and that they could do something about it, even if that something was only gathering, standing together, insisting on their rights as the public, as the true nation that the government can never be.

It is remarkable how, in other countries, people will one day simply stop believing in the regime that had, until then, ruled them, as African-Americans [and their white supporters] did in the [American] South here 50 years ago. Stopping believing means no longer regarding those who rule you as legitimate, and so no longer fearing them. Or respecting them. And then, surprisingly, they begin to crumble.[4]

A key factor leading to the dissolution of the Mubarak government was the refusal of the Egyptian Army to attack the Egyptian people. By contrast, as of 2012, similar protests against the autocratic government of Bashar al-Assad of Syria temporarily weakened his control, but instead of toppling the government, they precipitated a civil war. Subsequently, despite prominent defections, large segments of the Syrian Army remained loyal to the existing government and turned brutally on protesters, who quickly morphed into armed rebels. The resulting situation in Syria eventually devolved into an intense civil war, during which, as of mid-2020, nearly 500,000 people may have died (exact figures are unavailable) and more than 11 million were displaced. In the process, Iran, Hezbollah (a Lebanon-based, Iran-funded Shiite militia), and Russia entered on the government's side, with Turkey and Saudi Arabia backing the rebels.

These rebels, in turn, include ostensibly moderate, prodemocracy forces supported by the United States and, to a lesser extent, by some other NATO governments, but also radical, violent fighters from ISIS (the self-proclaimed Islamic State). This permitted the Russians and the Assad government to claim that they were fighting Islamic terrorists. Kurdish nationalists—seeking to carve out an independent Kurdistan—are also in the mix, both in Syria and Iraq, as well as to a lesser extent in Iran and Turkey, while the borders between these various states and Kurdish autonomous political entities have become increasingly porous.

Winston Churchill once quipped that the Balkans (Greece, Bulgaria, Serbia, Bosnia, and other small nations) "produce more history than they can consume." Something similar appears to apply—even more so—to the Middle East.

A Complex Legacy

Throughout the Arab Spring, it took some time for the United States and other Western powers to distinguish between the people and their oppressors, or rather, to act on a distinction of which they were surely aware. This may well have been due to the West's concern that these revolutions would produce outcomes equivalent to the Iranian Revolution of 1979, which overthrew the US-backed Shah, and then turned toward anti-American and anti-Western Shiite fundamentalism. The Arab dictatorships that had been toppled, like their Iranian predecessor, were also allied to and supported by the West, which initially reacted to grassroots calls for democracy by condemning the "violence on both sides," whereas nearly always, violence was perpetrated overwhelmingly by the governments in power, not by the protesters.

Following a brief period of enthusiasm and success, much of the Arab Spring turned to "Winter," and not just with the resulting humanitarian disaster in Syria. Thus, Mubarak's overthrow in Egypt was essentially a military coup, after which a new government was democratically elected for the first time in that country's history. That government was essentially fundamentalist and strongly influenced by the previously banned Islamist group the Muslim Brotherhood. The leader of the Muslim Brotherhood, Mohamed Morsi, became president of Egypt in 2012 and instituted a series of unpopular laws, which met widespread resistance. The next year, Morsi was deposed by the military and he died in confinement in 2019. The chief of the Egyptian Army, Abdel Fattah al-Sisi, was installed by the military as president, has been ruling Egypt since mid-2014, and has also staged the most brutal crackdown on his country's Islamist forces in modern history. Al-Sisi, like Mubarak, has been backed by the United States.

Western governments did not hesitate to recognize the restored military dictatorship, which promptly instituted censorship and imposed harsh prison terms for dissenters as well as independent journalists. This represents only the most recent in a long-standing dilemma for alleged Western supporters of democracy. In 1990, a new and popular political party, the Islamic Salvation Front, had received an absolute majority of votes cast by Algerians in local elections. When, 2 years later, it was in the process of winning a general election, a military coup (with the blessing of the United States and France) intervened to prevent a democratic vote and the all-but-certain transition of power to Islamists. Saudi Arabia has long been one of the most despotic and undemocratic regimes in the world; it also has been, along with raucously democratic Israel, one of the linchpins of US policy in the Middle East. Despite their lip service for democracy, the Western powers—including the United States—have long based their foreign policy on perceived *Realpolitik* rather than following a genuine commitment to democratic governance.

In 2012, in the immediate aftermath of the Arab Spring, the former leader of Yemen, who had ruled undemocratically for decades, was ousted as part of the prodemocracy enthusiasm unleashed by the Arab Spring, only to precipitate a governmental crisis that quickly spun into yet another civil war, with Iran supporting the Houthi rebels and Saudi Arabia intervening on behalf of the prior government. After Gaddafi's overthrow, Libya subsequently descended into its own form of violent chaos, with at least two factions claiming to comprise the legitimate government, while the country became a failed state.

One of the few apparently lasting democratic triumphs has been in Tunisia, birthplace of the Arab Spring. It may be significant that the Tunisian military has long been quite small, kept so by the deposed dictator Zine El Abidine Ben Ali, who came to power in a coup and subsequently minimized the size of the army so as to ensure that he would not be similarly overthrown. In contrast, the Egyptian military is huge (450,000 men), consistent with its involvement in overthrowing both the dictator Hosni Mubarak (a former air force general) and his successor. The relative insignificance of the Tunisian military and the fact that it has not been a major factor in repressing popular prodemocracy demonstrations seems to have contributed directly to that country's prodemocracy momentum.

Although the long-term consequences of the Arab Spring are yet to be seen, it is important to acknowledge the courage, tenacity, and overall nonviolence that generally characterized the initial protests and to take heart from their successes thus far. In the words of Russian poet Nadezhda Mandelstam, speaking of Josef Stalin's long and bloody rule in the USSR, "There was a special form of sickness—lethargy, plague, hypnotic trance, or whatever one calls it—that affected all those who committed terrible deeds. All the murderers, provocateurs, and informers had one feature in common: it never occurred to them that their victims might one day rise up again and speak."[5]

More than half a century ago, the philosopher Hannah Arendt described the tipping point in nationwide political revolutions of the sort that characterized the Arab Spring:

The situation changes abruptly. Not only is the rebellion not put down but the arms themselves change hands—sometimes, as in the Hungarian revolution, within a few hours . . . . The sudden dramatic breakdown of power that ushers in revolution reveals in a flash how civil obedience—to laws, to rulers, to institutions—is but the outward manifestation of support and consent.[6]

Possible Lessons From the Arab Spring

The Arab uprisings that began in Tunisia and spread so rapidly through much of the Arab world focused on corruption, poverty, and lack of freedom rather than on Western domination or the Israeli occupation of Palestine. But the fact that they were directed against Western-backed dictatorships meant they posed an immediate threat to the strategic order—at least, as perceived by the West. It is not only the example of the 1979 Iranian Revolution, which kicked out the pro-Western Shah and ushered in an Islamic Republic headed by anti-American Ayatollah Khomeini, that has generated anxiety among some Western elites. Popular discontent in the Middle East has a long history, much of it associated with anti-Western sentiment. The overthrow of the Egyptian monarchy (which had been supported by the previous colonial powers) in 1952 ushered in nearly 60 years of rule by military "strong men," who stifled the growth of promising political institutions and flagrantly disregarded civil rights, culminating in more than 30 years of undemocratic rule by Hosni Mubarak, who was closely associated with US and European interests.

It is always problematic to extract lessons from currently unfolding events because in such cases, only time can provide the necessary perspective, not to mention clarifying outcomes that are presently unresolved. Even so, a few generalities can be hazarded:

1. Just because something is familiar and long-standing, (e.g., the governments of Libya, Yemen, and especially Egypt prior to the Arab Spring) does not mean that it is stable. Saudi Arabia, for example, is now seen as an island of stability and a reliable source of petroleum, despite the fact that this same government often supports violent, fundamentalist Islamist movements in other countries. A more likely assumption is that dictatorships and absolute monarchies may appear stable but are liable to be inherently fragile in the face of democratic yearnings and deep-seated internal discontent. Political and social stagnation can readily be misperceived as stability, and "outside" governments would be well advised to expect change—insofar as they allow themselves to be involved at all in the internal structural affairs of another country.

2. If they are to represent the genuine desires of a significant proportion of a country's population, democracy movements cannot be orchestrated by outside countries, just as their initial outbreak is typically determined by local internal events. For example, even though NATO's participation was crucial to the overthrow of Libya's Gaddafi, the nature and direction of a new Libyan state will ultimately be determined by Libyans. By the same token, the United States could have learned from its experiences in Iraq and Afghanistan that in today's world, outside powers have only limited ability to influence the ultimate governance of another country. Such a limitation may well be healthy because the legitimacy—and thus, the longevity and stability—of those social and political systems that eventually emerge from the Arab Spring will depend on whether they emerge from authentic domestic processes, rather than having been imposed from the outside or by a narrow and privileged internal elite. Trying to keep a dictator in power who has worn out his welcome is nearly always a big mistake.

3. Although the Arab Spring vividly demonstrated what appears to be a widespread human desire for dignity, self-expression, and freedom, the exact nature of each country's preferred system is likely to vary depending on its history, population makeup, economic practices, religious and ideological preferences, and so forth. One size is unlikely to fit all, which further italicizes the unwisdom of "nation building" as something to be done "to" another country. One of the thoroughly bogus rationales for the ultimately disastrous US-led invasion of Iraq in 2003 was that overthrowing Saddam Hussein would lead to the eventual democratization of the Middle East; instead, it led to immense bloodshed, political hatreds, and instability.

4. It seems likely that replacing pro-Western despots with governments that more accurately reflect the political preferences of the "Arab street"

will result in greater distance from the West in general and the United States in particular. This happened, for example, in Egypt with the political ascendancy of the Muslim Brotherhood after Mubarak's removal (before it was later reversed). In any event, this does not necessarily mean that popularly backed governments will be violently anti-Western, anti-Israel, and/or pro-terrorist. Islamist rule is not a victory of jihadism; on the contrary, moderate Islamists tend to undercut the popular appeal of jihadists. It is entirely possible—maybe even likely—that insofar as democracy arrives in the Arab world, it will serve as a deterrent to violent extremism, which flourishes more readily under dictatorship than in a democracy.

5. Although past examples of revolutionary successes and tragedies are instructive, there are no blueprints or reliable forecasts for the outcomes of new revolutionary movements. What happens in Tunisia and Egypt, for example, may or may not prefigure the outcomes of events in, for example, Syria, or even in Bahrain and Saudi Arabia. Historical and political analysis is not an exact science, and forecasting future social and even economic events is far from reliable.

The Occupy Movement

Americans have grown accustomed to being the initiators and exporters of sociocultural trends, from blue jeans, information technology, and rock and roll to corporate and financial capitalism, and even to largely unsuccessful efforts—particularly in the Middle East—to export American-style democracy itself. An interesting exception has been the Occupy Movement, a series of homegrown prodemocracy events that were inspired to some extent by the earlier color revolutions and especially by the Arab Spring, which had been roiling the Middle East for nearly a year before.

This movement, originally known as "Occupy Wall Street" and which subsequently spread to many cities and college campuses, entered public consciousness in 2011. Unlike the Arab Spring, the Occupy Movement did not seek to overthrow the existing (US) government; hence, its actions—and the reactions it generated—were substantially less contested. In fact, many public opinion polls indicated that a majority of Americans supported what they believed to be the goals of the Occupy Movement, a remarkable indicator of widespread discontent with the status quo.

This movement was especially motivated by a widespread perception and dislike of economic inequality in the United States and was notably leaderless and nonhierarchical, functioning via a decentralized array of activists, and localized in various cities and communities. It made conspicuous use of consensus decision making and participatory democracy, with some anarchist overtones. The "Occupiers" attracted attention to their cause by establishing a variety of real and symbolic encampments, drawing public attention to income inequality and their claim that the political system in the United States is biased in favor of "the 1 percent" who are wealthy and politically connected, to the detriment of "the 99 percent." Their popular catchphrase became "We are the 99 percent."

The Occupy Movement was denigrated by some observers and media as made up of "hippie malcontents" who, according to some critics, "need to get a job and pay greater attention to their personal hygiene." As with the Arab Spring—notably in Tahrir Square—the Occupy Movement coalesced around the literal occupation of public spaces, an effective way of gaining attention while highlighting its participatory-democratic credentials. Within a few weeks, it began to resonate with much of the public because of widespread anger that some of the wealthiest Americans, who were largely responsible for the Great Recession that began in 2008, were not punished for their financial misdeeds and, moreover, profited greatly while "the 99 percent" suffered.

In retrospect, a widespread view is that the Occupy Movement failed, having fizzled out without demonstrable accomplishments. A preliminary evaluation, however, suggests that if nothing else, Occupy shifted attention from the previous political focus on government deficits (a concern voiced especially by conservatives) to a newfound concern with economic inequality and how it has increased in recent decades. It also spotlighted how the economic condition of the lower and middle classes has stagnated and often gotten worse while that of the upper classes has dramatically increased over the last generation.

In summary, the Occupy Movement was especially successful in dramatizing economic inequalities rather than pushing a specific policy agenda. Its political goals have been diffuse and free form, its "demands" ranging from reduced college tuition to higher tax rates on the wealthy, to special fees imposed on financial transactions and legislation making it more difficult for banks to foreclose on unpaid mortgages. The Occupy Movement's greatest impact may well be in changing the political discourse, publicizing what is on the American public's mind and thus making it more acceptable as an issue for the political agenda.

In a democracy—even an imperfect one, as every democracy is—such a change in discourse (sometimes known as "consciousness raising") is probably necessary although not sufficient for significant political and social changes to take place. The Occupy Movement no longer exists as an identifiable phenomenon and can therefore be said to have failed. Nonetheless, it remains to be seen whether it will have a lasting impact with respect to public attitudes toward economic inequality as well as whether it will foster specific political efforts to reduce the corporate domination of US politics.

The Democracy "Recession"

Just as prodemocracy movements were making gains in much of the world, democracy itself began to retreat in countries where, ironically, it had seemed well established. A process of de-democratization began in the middle of the "20-teens" in, for example, Brazil, Hungary, the Philippines, and Turkey, where—in the opinion of many worried observers—the rise of authoritarian leaders made these governments into a caricature of themselves, with the show or appearance of democracy but little of their previous substance. Russia and Venezuela, for example, are nominal democracies, and yet neither enjoys free and fair elections, given that media is essentially state-controlled (or monopolized by allies of the government), and potentially effective political dissent is not tolerated. The United States, during the presidency of Donald Trump, also began to experience worrisome challenges to earlier governmental norms, including a free press, an independent judiciary, and the reliable rule of law.

There had been a kind of golden age of democracy following the end of World War II. Whereas only 12 democracies existed worldwide in 1945, there were 87 by the year 2000, largely due to the end of much overt

European colonialism. But by the second decade of the 21st century, democracy not only stopped advancing but suffered substantial reverses. According to a Freedom House report, 2020 marked the fourteenth straight year in which democratic freedoms deteriorated worldwide: they had improved in 37 countries and declined in 64, notably India, which is widely proclaimed as "the world's largest democracy." Ten years earlier, the US had ranked very near the top in measures of democracy, although behind Estonia, Germany, and Switzerland. A decade later, it had slipped substantially, scoring below Greece, Mauritius and Slovakia. Freedom House analysts summarized that during the Trump administration, the US experienced "pressure on electoral integrity, judicial independence, and safeguards against corruption, fierce rhetorical attacks on the press, on the rule of law, and against other pillars of democracy coming from American leaders, including the president himself."

During the 1990s, with the fall of the Soviet Union, the end of Soviet domination of eastern Europe, the overcoming of apartheid in South Africa, and other stunning transitions in international political organization, it became popular to believe that the world was approaching *The End of History*, as the title of an influential book proclaimed, with likely movement toward a universal embrace of liberal democracy. But the reality has been otherwise, with some worried observers suggesting that it is democracy that may be approaching an end.

In their book, *How Democracies Die*, Steven Levitsky and Daniel Ziblatt pointed out how, among those democracies that reverted to authoritarianism, "the referees of the democratic game were brought over to the government's side, providing the incumbent with both a shield against constitutional challenges and a powerful—and 'legal'—weapon with which to assault its opponents." The precise causes of this "democratic recession" are complex and are to a large extent specific to each country involved. For example,

- The election of a right-wing national populist in Brazil was powered in large measure by revulsion at widespread government corruption among previous left-wing administrations.

- The rise of a thuggish president in the Philippines (who has orchestrated thousands of "extrajudicial" killings) was facilitated by popular resentment at widespread drug use and street crime.

- German Chancellor Angela Merkel's humanitarian decision to permit roughly one million refugees to enter that country led to dramatically increased support for the xenophobic, far-right "Alternative for Germany" party, known by its German initials AfD.

- In France, the National Rally political party (previously named the National Front) is a neo-Nazi movement whose power would have been inconceivable just a decade preciously; it emerged as a major political player as a result of concern that immigrants were taking jobs from "real" French citizens.

- Continued public support for the increasingly authoritarian regime of Vladimir Putin in Russia reflected desire for a "strong man" leader as well as resentment over loss of that country's superpower status.

- China (which has never had anything approaching democratic leadership) continued its authoritarian direction under the governance of the Communist Party led by its General Secretary, Xi Jinping, in part because of strong underlying Confucian-related desire for smooth and "harmonious" national leadership, along with rapid economic expansion of the previously tiny middle class, plus brutally effective crackdowns on political dissidents.

● Additional examples of the growth of anti-democratic public sentiment occurred in Turkey, associated particularly with increased Islamist sentiment, and in Italy, Poland, Spain, and the UK, resulting in large measure from anxiety over Muslim and African immigrants.

Right-wing nativist leaders have gained power as well, in Hungary, where Viktor Orbán, a right-wing authoritarian national populist, has spoken openly about building an "illiberal democracy." In the United States, the presidency of Donald Trump showed many authoritarian and anti-democratic tendencies. Although many factors contributed to Trump's election in 2016 (not least the undemocratic nature of the US Electoral College), economic and racial resentment appear to have been especially influential, leading to heightened appeal of nativist and nationalist demagoguery.

Yet another factor, especially prominent in the United States although with components in other countries as well, has been the growth of "conspiracy theories." (Technically, a theory bespeaks substantial credibility, as in number theory, the theory of relativity, or the theory of evolution. Hence, conspiracy "rumors," "falsehoods," or outright "lies" would be far more accurate, but because the phrase has gained currency, it will be used here.)

Lies and false rumors have existed throughout human history, sometimes based on genuine misunderstandings of actual facts and at other times involving intentional lies on the part of those seeking political gain. Often it is difficult to separate these two, notably to ascertain whether the perpetrators of misinformation are aware of the lies they are promoting. In any event, many conspiracy theories were widely circulated in the US during the Trump years, ranging from ludicrous—inflating the size of Trump's inaugural crowd or even the weather at that event—to dangerous, notably repeated claims that Trump had actually won the 2020 presidential election. In any event, truth is important, perhaps especially in democracies, which makes the rise of conspiracy theories especially worrisome.

In addition to factors especially influential in each country, some worldwide generalizations for the widespread retreat of democracy can be identified. These include widespread distrust and even contempt for expertise in general and science in particular by less-educated people who feel marginalized and ignored, along with economic dissatisfaction in the wake of the Great Recession of 2008, after which wealthy individuals and corporations continued to prosper while the "99 percent" benefitted much more slowly or in some cases, actually slipped further back.

Another frequent source of dissatisfaction in Europe, feeding in part on economic unhappiness, has been unusually high levels of immigration, notably Muslims and dark-skinned asylum seekers. In the United Kingdom, white working class resentment toward economic refugees from eastern Europe contributed substantially to the Brexit vote whereby the UK, after much political turmoil, withdrew from the European Union in 2020. Although not anti-democratic in itself (after all, it was the result of a national referendum held in 2016), Brexit was consistent with a growing rejection of pan-European integration.

A case can be made—a troublesome one, for people committed to democracy—that in the past, successful democracies have all been more or less ethnically homogeneous, or when heterogeneous, as in ancient Greece, the minorities did not have one person, one vote political power. Now, Western democracies in particular have been trying to incorporate substantial minority populations, in many cases complete with full rights, including the right to vote and to compete for jobs. This novel situation may in itself be generating social instability and adding to the appeal of authoritarian, nativist populists because of increased dissatisfaction on the part of erstwhile majorities who feel themselves losing the power they used to take for granted.

And of course, perhaps democracy shouldn't be prescribed as the best system in all cases, particularly for societies whose histories and current ideological preferences may favor different patterns of government. Moreover, a cynical perspective suggests that its value has been overrated, even in the West. Here is a caricature from *The Third Man*, a 1949 film noir: "in Italy, for thirty years under the Borgias, they had warfare, terror, murder and bloodshed, but they produced Michelangelo, Leonardo da Vinci and the Renaissance. In Switzerland, they had brotherly love, they had five hundred years of democracy and peace—and what did that produce? The cuckoo clock."

Democracy's horizons are not entirely discouraging, however. The more than 40 million people of Sudan had suffered for decades under the murderous dictatorship of Omar Hassan al-Bashir. After months of courageous and often dangerous protesting, the Sudanese overthrew that government and achieved a commitment for transition to free elections, with Mr. Bashir sentenced to a prison term for corruption. And even in Russia, there has been on-again, off-again agitation for democracy, despite periodic government crackdowns.

The Chinese government, after brutally putting down the Tiananmen prodemocracy protests of 1989, co-opted much of the public dissatisfaction beginning in the early 1990s under Deng Xiaoping by allowing increased economic freedoms but with the implicit understanding that there wouldn't be any significant political activism . . . which has nonetheless occurred, albeit mostly underground. Hong Kong reverted in 1997 from being a British colony to official control by the government of mainland China, but under a "one country, two systems" arrangement, which officially granted Hong Kongers an independent judiciary and a degree of political autonomy. When, in 2019, a bill was passed in Hong Kong that permitted prisoners to be extradited to the mainland, this precipitated prodemocracy protests in which millions took to the streets. The offending bill was withdrawn, and Hong Kongers voted overwhelmingly for prodemocracy candidates in a subsequent local election. Another defining moment was a standoff between police and students who had barricaded themselves on the campus of Hong Kong's Polytechnic University. Here, as elsewhere, the outcome remains uncertain, but it is clear that in many cases, barometers of public opinion—often in the face of severe repression—not uncommonly swing away from authoritarianism, just as under some conditions they embrace it.

In a notable book-length poem, Carl Sandburg reflected on the paradoxes of democracy, on the struggles to maintain honesty and integrity among those representatives tasked to carry out democratic government, and on the hopes and disappointments of the people being represented. He concluded, despite all the difficulties and frustrations, "The People, Yes."

Democracies and Wars

It is unclear whether there is, on balance, a global preference for democracy of one sort or another, reflected in various "democracy movements" worldwide. Despite the aforementioned democracy recession, there is a positive case to be made, recognizing that change in this direction has been and likely will continue to be uneven, with movement both toward democracy and away from it. It is therefore worth examining the implications, if any, that a prodemocracy tendency might have for war and peace. If many people genuinely seek democracy, then success might well constitute progress toward positive peace, especially as a component of human rights—in this case, the right to democratic self-governance. We leave aside the question of whether there are parallel contradictory rights, such as the "right to monarchical rule," the "right to oligarchy," or the "right to theocratic rule," if only because it seems counterintuitive to posit that such "rights" would ultimately contribute to positive peace.

Another and less clear-cut question also arises: What, if anything, is the connection between democracy and negative peace (i.e., the prevention of war)? At least partly because the Western states generally pride themselves in being democracies, and because it is widely believed that democratic governments are more peaceful than nondemocratic ones, it is worth examining the comparative war-proneness of democratic versus more authoritarian nations.

The results are a bit disconcerting, at least for people reflexively believing that political democracies are necessarily peace-loving. Statistically, at least until the second half of the 20th century, no significant difference was demonstrated between the war-proneness of democracies and despotisms.

Some historical examples are illuminating. Authoritarian Sparta was no more aggressive or expansionist than democratic Athens; similarly, Franco's Spain, Somoza's Nicaragua, and Marcos's Philippines, although dictatorships, were not expansionist. By contrast, during the 19th century in particular, Britain and the United States engaged in numerous wars of conquest. For the United States, these included successful campaigns against Native Americans, Mexico, and Spain, as well as the failed War of 1812 against Great Britain (which was undertaken in large part in hopes of annexing what at the time was the British colony of Canada). For its part, Britain completed its acquisition of an immense global empire, it has been said, "in a fit of absent-mindedness," but British imperial expansion nevertheless involved substantial military adventurism on the part of a formal monarchy but one whose actual governance was avowedly democratic.

That said, it remains a valid generalization that democracies very rarely go to war *against other democracies*. Let's look first, however, at why democratic countries are in themselves no less war-prone than others.

Popular Commitment

A direct connection between democracy and war, although perhaps unexpected, should not be all that surprising. In feudal Europe and Japan, the aristocracy had a monopoly on war. This changed substantially with the spread of firearms, which made a commoner capable of stopping a charging horse and penetrating a nobleman's armor. Moreover, the supposed right to keep and bear arms (the Second Amendment to the US Constitution), recently interpreted as inhering in individual citizens, has been seen by many Americans as fundamental to democracy.

One's perception of the peacefulness of democracies may be strongly colored by the 20th century, in which most democracies became "status quo" powers, unlikely to engage in wars of aggression, at least not against other democracies. However, by the end of that century, the United States in particular took on the role of world policeman, thereby becoming embroiled, directly or indirectly, in armed conflicts on every continent but Australia and Antarctica. In addition, democracies have proven to be no less likely than more authoritarian states to fight when provoked, and their prosecution of these wars may be even more brutal than the nondemocratic states against whom they fight. "A democracy is peace-loving," claimed noted diplomat-historian George Kennan (often deemed the intellectual father of "containment" of the former Soviet Union):

> It does not like to go to war. It is slow to rise to provocation. When it has once been provoked to the point where it must grasp the sword, it does not easily forgive its adversary for having produced this situation . . . . Democracy fights in anger—it fights for the very reason that it was forced to go to war. It fights to punish the power that was rash enough and hostile enough to provoke it—to teach that power a lesson it will not forget, to prevent the thing from happening again. Such a war must be carried to the bitter end.[7]

Conservative politicians in particular have long distrusted democracy because of what they saw as its inclination *toward* war. Thus, during the 19th century, when the United Kingdom was debating whether to expand voting rights, British prime minister Benjamin Disraeli maintained that if the electorate were enlarged, "you will in due season have wars entered into from passion and not from reason." And young Winston Churchill pointed out (correctly) in 1901 that "democracy is more vindictive than Cabinets. The wars of peoples will be more terrible than the wars of kings."

In the late 1930s, Britain and France made concessions to and claimed a kind of anti-Soviet partnership with Hitler's Germany. Once war was finally declared, however, and even while Neville Chamberlain was still prime minister, nothing less than the elimination of the Nazi regime was deemed acceptable. The fearsome energy of popular total war, once unleashed, makes it very difficult for accommodations to be made. This is at least partly because as losses accumulate, it becomes all the more important to demonstrate that lives and property have not been expended in vain. During the numerous 17th- and 18th-century European "monarchs' wars" (including such historical curiosities as the Wars of the Austrian and Spanish Succession), rulers were free to end, at their choosing, wars they had often initiated in response to their personal whims or goals. By contrast, once popular passions are ignited—as is necessarily the case when democracies go to war—it is far more difficult to douse the flames.

For democracies, political necessity therefore often demands a commitment to total victory. During World War I, France sacrificed hundreds of thousands of young men without ever seriously considering a compromise that might have allowed for Germany to retain Alsace (mostly German speaking) with France to take back Lorraine, whose inhabitants largely identified themselves as French. And the victors of World War II demanded nothing less than unconditional surrender from the main defeated Axis powers, Germany and Japan.

A major factor prolonging the Vietnam, Iraq, and Afghanistan wars was the view that, having suffered so many casualties and expended so much national treasure, the United States "must not pull out now." National honor was at stake, as well as the very human reluctance for a presidential administration to admit a mistake. Having invested and lost much, American administrations considered it as necessary to invest yet more blood and treasure in military quagmires. Sometimes called the "gambler's fallacy," the principle seems to be a general one, even though it is based on faulty logic: Having suffered losses and incurred costs, whether in a war, a financial investment, or even a gambling episode, it is very difficult to back away. Stuck in a hole of their own making, democratic governments are liable to dig themselves deeper rather than climb out and admit error or defeat. (Critics refer to the First Law of Holes: If you find yourself stuck in a hole, stop digging!)

Why Are Democracy-Democracy Wars So Rare?

Despite the previously mentioned considerations, there is also a potentially important, optimistic, pro-peace aspect of democracy. Simply stated, it is this: Although democracies are not particularly averse to war, it is exceedingly rare for them to go to war against each other. The only clear historical case was the War of 1812, between the United States and the United Kingdom, a war that was relatively insignificant and has largely been forgotten, except in Canada, where it receives more recognition as having successfully rebuffed the Colossus of the South. (Contemporary Russia and Ukraine have been in a violent conflict, possibly a war, for years over the Crimea and Eastern Ukraine, but Russia, at least, may be considered a "democracy" in name only.) It isn't clear why there have been so few democracy-democracy wars, but several possibilities exist:

1. Dictatorships are readily personified by the dictator in charge, a situation that quickly lends itself to a commitment to fighting "evil," as personified by the other side's nefarious leadership. By contrast, democracies by definition are supposed to reflect the will of the people, so that members of a democratic country seeking to go to war against another democratic country are forced to confront the fact that they are endeavoring to kill people like themselves.

2. Wars often involve the comforting mythology that the enemy isn't the other side's population but rather, their malicious leaders. This is more difficult to maintain when the people, rather than a leader per se, are seen as the responsible actors.

3. Even though democracies, once aroused, are prone to pursue their wrath more vigorously than dictatorships, it may be that most people—as the ones most likely to suffer in the event of war—are more reluctant than their leaders to go to war in the first place. If so, then it would seem even less likely that prowar motivation would be generated simultaneously and independently within two different democratic constituencies.

4. Democratic nations and constitutional republics usually have extensive trading, banking, and commercial ties with one another (e.g., among the European Union, Canada, Japan, South Korea, and the United States). It would be very bad for business if governments of one or more of these states or alliances were to initiate military hostilities, other than trade "wars," in order to gain some kind of economic or political advantage.

Whatever the reason(s), it remains possible and perhaps even likely that a world moving toward democracy would as a result also be moving toward greater peace, as some peace theorists have claimed. Beyond whatever domestic benefits democracy may convey, the reluctance of democracies to make war on each other may in itself be a powerful reason to encourage and rejoice in the spread of democratic government.

Democracies in Peace Versus War

Peace is not a prerequisite for democracy, but it seems clear that democracies do better (i.e., they are more democratic) in times of peace than during war. In fact, whereas democracies do not necessarily lead to peace, the tendency may work in reverse: Peace may predispose governments toward democracy. The converse holds as well: Wars often involve abridgment of rights of dissent and due process, even within democracies. War requires increased discipline, secrecy, often unswerving and unquestioning devotion to the state, and obedience to its authority. All of these are easier to achieve with military governments. In fact, the nurturing of democracy in the United Kingdom and the United States may have been facilitated by the fact that in their early history, neither of these nation-states faced constant military threats; most of their wars were "of choice" rather than of necessity.

During World War II, by contrast, Winston Churchill and his cabinet held almost dictatorial power in otherwise democratic Great Britain; that war produced a remarkable convergence in the political systems of all participants, Allies and Axis alike. There was also widespread suppression of dissent within the United States during the Civil War and World War I, along with the forced dislocation and involuntary internment of 120,000 Japanese Americans in "relocation centers" (milder versions of concentration camps) during World War II. Attempts by some American political and police officials to suppress protest movements against the Vietnam War increased as that war's popularity sagged. Since 9/11, comparably repressive measures—especially involving surveillance and the diminution of rights of personal privacy—were adopted by the US government and some of its allies in their global war on terrorism.

Some democracies nonetheless retain an abiding sense that the military is subordinate to the civilian sector. In the middle of the Korean War, for example, President Truman was able to fire General Douglas MacArthur, the most popular and successful military figure in the country, then at the peak of his powers. (After Chinese forces entered North Korea, MacArthur had advocated bombing the Chinese mainland, possibly with nuclear weapons, in defiance of Truman's expressed policy.) Similarly, in 2010, President Barack Obama fired the top US military commander in Afghanistan when the latter made disparaging comments about the US civilian political leadership.

Military leaders are specialists in "legitimate" violence; moreover, career advancement within the military typically is enhanced by successful service during real "shooting wars." It follows that they are often more willing, even eager, to enter wars, and moreover, they are inclined to do so without the public, prolonged, and divisive procedures found in most democracies. In the nuclear age, during which strategic theorists and many decision makers have claimed that they need to respond quickly—almost instantly—to real or perceived threats in order to maintain deterrence, the legal requirement of a formal declaration of war has pretty much been abridged. The War Powers Act, passed in the aftermath of the Vietnam War, requires that the US Congress approve any executive decision to commit combat forces for longer than 60 days. Nonetheless, US military forces have been mobilized by unilateral presidential decisions and without any formal authorization from

Congress or declaration of war, in Serbia, Kosovo, Somalia, Iraq, Afghanistan, and Libya, along with the use of remote controlled killer drones in Pakistan, Yemen, and elsewhere.

More generally, when it comes to the decision to go to war, democracies are not really democratic at all. The following passage, written in the early days of World War I, conveys a strong sense of despair and disillusionment with governmental activities, even in a democracy:

The Government, with no mandate from the people, without consultation of the people . . . . irresistibly slides the country into war. For the benefit of proud and haughty citizens, it is fortified with a list of the intolerable insults which have been hurled toward us by the other nations; for the benefit of the liberal and beneficent, it has a convincing set of moral purposes which our going to war will achieve; for the ambitious and aggressive classes, it can gently whisper of a bigger role in the destiny of the world. The result is that, even in those countries where the business of declaring war is theoretically in the hands of representatives of the people, no legislature has ever been known to decline the request of an Executive, . . . that it order the nation into battle . . . .

The moment war is declared, however, the mass of the people, through some spiritual alchemy, become convinced that they have willed and executed the deed themselves . . . . and the State once more walks through the imaginations of men.[8]

On the other hand, Walter Lippmann, an influential commentator on foreign affairs during much of the 20th century, maintained that democracies are peaceful because of a certain public inertia: "At the critical junctures, when the stakes are high, the prevailing mass opinion will impose what amounts to a veto upon changing the course on which the government is at the time proceeding."[9] This perspective suggests that when democracies are at peace, they tend to remain at peace, just as they may succumb to a kind of popular momentum once committed to war.

There is a paradoxical relationship between democracy and war. Once provoked, democratically elected governments fight fiercely, perhaps even more willingly and with greater enthusiasm than their less democratic counterparts, although as noted, most democracies tend to remain peaceful, at least when it comes to fighting other democracies. American military actions during the latter part of the 20th century, however, suggest a troubling variation on this theme, namely, a penchant by the United States for brief wars of intervention in the affairs of less powerful, undemocratic nations. The 1983 invasion of Grenada, the 1989 invasion of Panama, the 2001 invasion of Afghanistan, and the 2003 invasion of Iraq by the United States were illegal by most standards of international law, as was the American government's support for the *contras* in Nicaragua during the 1980s.

By contrast, NATO's military engagement in Bosnia, Kosovo, and Libya were more in accord with international legal obligations, in that they were undertaken as part of a multilateral international commitment. The Vietnam War is also legally ambiguous, in that, similar to the Soviet "invasion" of Afghanistan in 1979, it occurred in response to a request from the recognized government—although admittedly, both these governments were widely considered illegitimate, even by their own citizens.

Most of these military adventures were quite successful domestically, temporarily boosting the popularity of President Reagan and both Presidents

Bush—at least initially. These belligerent activities were motivated, at least in part, by the perception (accurate, as it turned out) that the presidents in question would benefit politically in the short term, especially as a response to a perception that the United States had been attacked or was otherwise threatened. This raises the "wag the dog"[10] specter: Presidents and other decision makers may seek to offset their domestic political difficulties by engaging in a quick war or "surgical strike" that is relatively painless (at least, for the aggressor) and domestically popular, as President Clinton did in Afghanistan and Sudan in the 1990s, after al-Qaeda supporters attacked the US embassy in Kenya. So long as public opinion responds favorably to such wars, especially around election time, democratically elected governments will be tempted to engage in them.

Nor are democracies unique in this respect: Within-country popularity increased, for example, when the Argentine military junta invaded the Falkland Islands, temporarily displacing British control; this changed dramatically when the UK defeated Argentina in the ensuing Falklands War, which in turn greatly enhanced the popularity of Britain's prime minister Margaret Thatcher, which had previously been seriously waning. The popularity of Russia's Vladimir Putin skyrocketed when that country forcibly annexed Crimea, just as that of President George W. Bush in the immediate aftermath of his administration's invasion of Afghanistan following the 9/11 attacks.

Can Democracy Be Exported? Should It Be?

It is tempting to assume that a yearning for democracy is universal. Even if this is the case (and there is no clear evidence in this regard), there is no "one size fits all" formula for democracy. For example, some long-standing, highly successful democracies—including the United Kingdom, Holland, Denmark, and Norway—are also formal monarchies, whose systems are justified by the claim that hereditary rulers, even when they exercise only symbolic authority, also provide a sense of national unity and continuity. Therefore, it is not necessarily isolationist to oppose "nation building," especially given that it is often difficult, perhaps impossible, for politicians and military leaders in one country to prescribe the optimum and most socially acceptable government system for another, especially when the recipients of such "assistance" (e.g., Iraq, Afghanistan, Libya) have very different histories along with social and religious expectations. What citizens want for themselves seems destined to trump what any country, however well-meaning or imperially strong, wants for them.

It is also widely assumed that democracy and "rule of law" are closely allied, if not synonymous. And yet, many Muslim countries, for example, expect that their laws must be derived from religious texts in order to be valid (*sharia*, or law according to a strict interpretation of the Quran). In Egypt, for example, the briefly incorporated legal system under the Muslim Brotherhood was designed to be *sharia*-based, whereas most Western countries have a far greater degree of separation between church (or synagogue, or mosque) and state. Westerners are tempted to perceive *sharia* law as exemplifying an intolerant refusal to recognize the wisdom of separating church and state. However, there is also a potent tradition in conservative Christianity (especially in the United States) and Orthodox Judaism (in Israel) that also insists on the legitimacy, even the moral necessity, of ending this separation.

In addition to the problem of international heterogeneity (i.e., the reality that different societies have different traditions and expectations), the export of democracy as an avowed policy goal also runs into the problem that it may serve as a smokescreen for less benevolent intentions, such that it could become a *causus bellum* (a reason for war), or at least, what might be called an *excusatum bellum* (an excuse for war)! For example, it was claimed, after the fact, that the Iraq War initiated by the US in 2003 was actually part of a long-term "Freedom Agenda" designed to "bring democracy to the Middle East."

This claim turns out to have been highly questionable, not only because it clearly failed, but also because as it was being made, the United States maintained close relationships with absolute hereditary monarchies (Saudi Arabia, Bahrain), as well as dictatorships that gave lip service to democracy, but whose actual systems were repressive and highly authoritarian (including Egypt, Tunisia before the Arab Spring, Yemen before its civil war, Morocco, and Algeria). Behind the near-universal diplomatic facade of support for democracy, great powers almost always support governments they perceive as being useful to them, regardless of their human rights records. For example, Western governments raised no serious objections to the military coup that removed the democratically elected, Muslim Brotherhood–supported government in Egypt and replaced it with an undemocratic, politically repressive, but pro-Western military regime.

The enthusiasm that surrounds democratic movements worldwide, and that is manifested in the immediate aftermath of "success" (namely, the overthrow or forced abdication of a tyrant), often obscures this sobering fact: In many cases, the hardest part of moving toward democracy isn't the liberation of a country via removal of a despot, but the subsequent establishment of a stable democratic government, however that is defined. It is especially difficult to accomplish this in states that have a low per capita GDP and that lack a tradition of democratic governance, or even of a "civil society."[11] Shortly after the Arab Spring overthrow of the Mubarak dictatorship in Egypt, citizens of that country were glued to their televisions watching with rapt attention the first genuine presidential debate among independent candidates, a first for Egypt and, according to some observers, for the entire Arab world. But this democratic triumph was short-lived.

Historians and political theorists sometimes speak of a "Thermidorian Reaction," referring to a time when power is lost by once-successful revolutionaries, whose regime is then replaced by moderates and sometimes even conservatives, in a kind of pendulum swing back toward pre-revolutionary times. The phrase derives from a time in the French Revolutionary calendar— during the newly designated month of Thermidor—when Robespierre, who had orchestrated much of the "Reign of Terror," was himself overthrown (and beheaded), and which led to a period of relative moderation in response to the violent excesses of the French Revolution. In his book *The Revolution Betrayed*, Leon Trotsky, who had by then broken irrevocably with Stalin, argued that the Soviet dictator had become a "communist tsar" and that his ascension to power was a "Soviet Thermidor" in which that country returned to pre-revolutionary tyranny after a brief experiment with liberalization: the New Economic Policy (1921–1928) under Lenin.

It isn't uncommon for modern democratic revolutions to have their own Thermidorian Reactions after their revolutionary movements have deposed an autocratic government and achieved a degree of democratic governance, during which countries slip back into systems not very different from those they previously had. Examples include Nicaragua under Daniel Ortega and Russia under Vladimir Putin.

A Final Note on Movements Toward Democracy

In the concluding paragraphs of Albert Camus's novel *The Plague*, the residents of Oran (in Algeria) spill into the streets, enthusiastically celebrating the end of a devastating bubonic plague. And yet, the novel's hero, Dr. Rieux, who valiantly fought the plague, observes that such triumphs, although hard won, may only be temporary:

> He knew that the tale he had to tell could not be one of a final victory. It could be only the record of what had had to be done, and what assuredly would have to be done again in the never ending fight against terror and its relentless onslaughts, despite their personal afflictions, by all who, while unable to be saints but refusing to bow down to pestilences, strive their utmost to be healers.
>
> And indeed, as he listened to the cries of joy rising from the town, Rieux remembered that such joy is always imperiled. He knew what those jubilant crowds did not know but could have learned from books: that the plague bacillus never dies or disappears for good; that it can lie dormant for years and years . . . and that perhaps the day would come when, for the bane and the enlightening of men, it would rouse up its rats again and send them forth to die in a happy city.

Following the real-life overthrow of Egypt's long-running autocrat, Hosni Mubarak, in 2011, Egyptians similarly flooded into Tahrir Square to celebrate *their* deliverance. A dispassionate observer, however, could not help noting that in many ways the hard work lay ahead, and indeed, subsequent events have shown how difficult it is to persuade the military (and, alas, military forces generally) to relinquish control and to negotiate genuine democracy.

At the same time, and despite the difficulties, uncertainties, and upheavals of the world's erratic movement toward democracy, it is appropriate to conclude this chapter by citing an observation of Camus's fictional Dr. Rieux, "to state quite simply what we learn in a time of pestilence: that there are more things to admire in men than to despise."

Questions for Further Reflection

1. Do you believe that democracy is the best possible political system? Why or why not?

2. What are some arguments supporting the idea that democracy should be exported to other countries? And what are some opposing arguments?

3. It is widely acknowledged that when given the opportunity to choose their own government, by election, the populations of some countries choose leaders who do not support democracy as it is understood in the West. What implications, if any, should this have for foreign policy?

4. Explore the idea of democracy as something other than a formal electoral system at the national level; that is, what are some implications of "economic" or "social" democracy?

5. Here is a challenging notion, taken from *The Third Man,* a classic film noir: "In Italy, for thirty years under the Borgias, they had warfare, terror, murder and bloodshed, but they produced Michelangelo, Leonardo da Vinci and the Renaissance. In Switzerland, they had brotherly love, they had five hundred years of democracy and peace—and what did that produce? The cuckoo clock." Comment.

Suggestions for Further Reading

Eirikur Bergmann. 2020. *Neo-Nationalism: The Rise of Nationalist Populism.* New York: Palgrave Macmillan.

Juan Cole. 2014. *The New Arabs: How the Millennial Generation Is Changing the Middle East and the World.* New York: Simon & Schuster.

William A. Galston. 2018. *Anti-Pluralism: The Populist Threat to Liberal Democracy.* New Haven, CN: Yale University Press.

Samuel P. Huntington. 1993. *The Third Wave: Democratization in the Late 20th Century.* Norman: University of Oklahoma Press.

Steven Levitsky and Daniel Ziblatt. 2019. *How Democracies Die.* New York: Broadway Books.

Lincoln A. Mitchell. 2012. *The Color Revolutions.* University Park: Pennsylvania State University Press.

Timothy Snyder. 2017. *On Tyranny: Twenty Lessons from the Twentieth Century.* New York: Penguin.

Ece Temelkuran. 2020. *How to Lose a Country: The 7 Steps from Democracy to Dictatorship.* New York: Fourth Estate.

Notes

1. "The Capitol Attack Shocks the World." *New York Times,* January 8, 2021. Retrieved from https://www.nytimes.com/2021/01/08/opinion/world-capitol-attack-trump.html

2. Named for the artificial grass first employed in the Houston Astrodome, a sports stadium in the United States.

3. Consistent with the maxim that states act more out of their own perceived self-interest than from generalized altruism, it has been claimed that among the reasons the prime ministers of France, the United Kingdom, and Italy strongly supported NATO intervention in Libya was that they feared that if Gaddafi succeeded in massacring large numbers of his own citizens, this would generate a mass exodus to Europe at a time when their delicate economies would have had an especially difficult time accommodating large numbers of indigent North African refugees.

4. Rebecca Solnit. 2011, March 20. "Tomgram: Rebecca Solnit, Hope and Turmoil in 2011." *TomDispatch.com.* Retrieved from https://tomdispatch.com/rebecca-solnit-hope-and-turmoil-in-2011/

5. Quoted in Jonathan Schell. 2004. *The Unconquerable World: Power, Nonviolence and the Will of the People.* New York: Henry Holt.

6. Hannah Arendt. 1963. *On Revolution.* London: Faber & Faber.

7. George Kennan. 2012 (1951). *American Diplomacy.* Chicago: University of Chicago Press.

8. Randolph Bourne. 1964. *War and the Intellectuals: Collected Essays 1915–1919.* New York: Harper Torchbooks.

9. Walter Lippmann. 1989. *The Public Philosophy.* New Brunswick, NJ: Transaction.

10. *Wag the Dog* was a 1997 movie in which a US president initiates a fake war in an

effort to distract public attention from his involvement in a sex scandal just weeks before his election.

11. The term *civil society,* which stems from the political theories of Aristotle and the 19th-century French diplomat and writer Alexis de Tocqueville, currently refers to the range of unofficial, cross-cutting nongovernmental systems and structures that function within most advanced societies, providing coherence as well as civic participation. These systems and structures include professional organizations, trade unions, political parties, even book clubs and sports associations, and are considered a significant measure of functioning democracy.

23

PHILIPPE LOPEZ/AFP via Getty Images

National Reconciliation

Just as every human being has a history, so does every society, nation, and country. And just as each person's past will have an impact on his or her present and future, the same applies to societies, nations and countries. This [has] implications for positive peace. We cannot simply direct complex societal systems toward a given goal (assuming of course, that such a goal can even be agreed upon) and assume that those systems will proceed as designed, independent of their histories. Although social history often includes major benefits, all too often it is also marred by massive pain and suffering, which must be ameliorated if a society's future is to incorporate positive peace.

In the opening sentence of his great novel Anna Karenina, Tolstoy wrote, "All happy families resemble one another; each unhappy family is unhappy

National Reconciliation

Just as every human being has a history, so does every society, nation, and country. And just as each person's past will have an impact on his or her present and future, the same applies to societies, nations, and countries. This has implications for positive peace: We cannot simply direct complex social systems toward a given goal (assuming, of course, that such a goal can even be agreed upon!) and assume that those systems will proceed as desired, independent of their histories. Although social history often includes major benefits, all too often it is also marred by massive pain and suffering, which must be ameliorated if a society's future is to incorporate positive peace.

In the opening sentence of his great novel *Anna Karenina*, Tolstoy wrote, "All happy families resemble one another; each unhappy family is unhappy in its own way." Although judgment may be reserved regarding the first part of this famous pronouncement, there have been many distinct sources of societal unhappiness. Moreover, most mental health experts (and growing numbers of political scientists as well) recognize that such discontent—sometimes including anger and even rage—can to some extent be alleviated, but only if they are first acknowledged and confronted. In short, there is a strong argument that for societal structures to effectively embody positive peace, they must take account of any significant past injustices and severe violence, whether direct and physical, or indirect and structural.

Once a people or a country has been traumatized by serious abuses, it is difficult, perhaps even impossible, for the victims to return readily—if at all—to a pattern of peaceful life, especially if their former oppressors are living among them. (It may be difficult for the perpetrators, too, although concern in this regard has focused overwhelmingly on the victims rather than the victimizers.) Could a particularly destructive national history serve as a kind of poison, polluting the future no less than the past?

Regrettably, there is some evidence supporting this gloomy proposition. For example, one reason post–Saddam Hussein Iraq had such difficulty forming a coherent and nonviolent society is the legacy of anger and resentment (among Sunnis, Shiites, and Kurds) bequeathed by a violent past—one for which the West, including not just the United States but also a repressive British colonial regime, has substantial responsibility. In 2016, Colombian voters narrowly rejected a proposed peace treaty with leftist insurrectionists (known as the FARC) because of a feeling that FARC personnel were being given a "free pass" and not held accountable for their earlier violence.

At the same time, however, there have been hopeful examples of national reconciliation, in which people have carved out a largely nonviolent social prospect despite horrific past abuses. In this chapter, we examine some of these successes, the difficulties encountered, and the techniques employed.

Altruism, Aggression, and Reconciliation in Nonhuman Primates

In sharp contrast to the paradigm that human behavior is primarily individualistic and egoistic, altruism denotes activities that are costly to individuals themselves but may benefit others. According to the "empathy-altruism hypothesis," empathic concern (an emotional reaction brought about by the act of perspective-taking and characterized by such feelings as compassion, tenderness, soft-heartedness, and sympathy for another) leads to truly selfless motivation to help another person. In his 1759 book, *The Theory of the Moral Sentiments*, Adam Smith—better known as an early theorist of capitalism—wrote of the universality of such perceptions:

> How selfish soever man may be supposed, there are evidently some principles in his nature, which interest him in the fortunes of others, and render their happiness necessary to him, though he derives nothing from it, except the pleasure of seeing it. Of this kind is pity or compassion, the emotion we feel for the misery of others, when we either see it, or are made to conceive it in a very lively manner. That we often derive sorrow from the sorrows of others, is a matter of fact too obvious to require any instances to prove it; for this sentiment, like all the other original passions of human nature, is by no means confined

to the virtuous or the humane, though they perhaps may feel it with the most exquisite sensibility. The greatest ruffian, the most hardened violator of the laws of society, is not altogether without it.

The distinguished Dutch ethologist Frans de Waal argues against the allegedly antisocial character of aggression and instead proposes a "reconciliation hypothesis," according to which aggression is a well-integrated part of social life. An examination of the dynamics of social interactions among nonhuman primates, according to de Waal, reveals that confrontation should not be viewed as a barrier to sociality but rather as an unavoidable element upon which social relationships can be built and strengthened through reconciliation. Social animals, including human beings, seek contact with former opponents and will, on occasion, engage in such post-conflict reunion practices as kissing, embracing, sexual intercourse, grooming, and so on. Reconciliation serves to decrease aggression and socially destabilizing anxiety. It occurs especially after a conflict between parties whose possible partnership may have a potentially high social value.

De Waal's demonstration of reconciliation in monkeys and apes supports the idea that forgiveness and peacemaking are widespread among nonhuman primates. The evolutionary advantages of reconciliation are obvious for animals that survive through mutual aid, that is, the continuation of cooperation among parties with partially conflicting interests. De Waal's findings regarding nonhuman primates (especially among juveniles) may also have significant potential applications for understanding human conflict resolution, with reconciliation seen as a shared heritage of the primate order.

Truth and Reconciliation Commissions

The most widely used human technique for post-conflict resolution at the political level involves the establishment of so-called truth and reconciliation commissions (TRCs). These commissions generally share certain characteristics. Sometimes they are formed by citizen committees, often locally constituted. More often, however, TRCs are established by a recently empowered national government and are given the job of uncovering past wrongdoing, usually the atrocities perpetrated by an earlier government. Often, the goal is not so much to resolve grievances or right past wrongs as to establish an environment in which the nation's future will not be contaminated by the bitterness and resentment generated by the actions of an earlier regime. The hope is simple, sometimes appearing to verge on cliché, but it is nonetheless profound: to facilitate national healing.

With this in mind, such commissions (under various names) have been planned or established in Argentina, Chile, El Salvador, Fiji, Ghana, Guatemala, Liberia, Morocco, Panama, Peru, Sierra Leone, South Africa, South Korea, East Timor, and the United States. Others may be anticipated. Typically, these efforts take place after a country emerges from difficult periods of civil war, unrest, or dictatorship. It is doubtless significant—and not surprising—that processes of this sort have not, as yet, been seriously attempted in countries who most need them—those that are currently undergoing violent confrontations and within which wounds are literally still raw and being actively inflicted: notably Afghanistan, Iraq, Syria, and Yemen.

Truth and reconciliation commissions are especially intended to provide for the victims of atrocities the partial satisfaction of learning the truth about the past, including clear documentation of abuses, when possible: numbers killed, tortured, forcibly exiled, property confiscated, and so forth. "Failure to remember, collectively, triumphs and accomplishments diminishes us," writes an expert on the process. "But failure to remember, collectively, injustice and cruelty is an ethical breach. It implies no responsibility and no commitment to prevent inhumanity in the future. Even worse, failures of collective memory stoke fires of resentment and revenge."[1] In short, the truth often hurts, but failure to acknowledge the truth can, in the long run, hurt even more.

A further benefit of the truth and reconciliation process is that it may prevent later historical revisionism, namely the erasure or whitewashing of the past. In the absence of an honest investigation of past abuses, wrongdoers can claim that such events never occurred (e.g., Holocaust deniers) or that they were simply the actions of "a few bad apples" (e.g., the official US government explanation of torture at the Abu Ghraib prison camp in post–Saddam Hussein Iraq). Yet another hoped-for payoff of the truth and reconciliation process is that it may help victims and their families achieve a kind of emotional closure. Often, however, success requires expressed apology by the perpetrators, which is often difficult to obtain, especially when this is akin to acknowledging guilt, which might expose the confessors to possible prosecution. In hope of circumventing this problem, the various TRCs—most notably in the pioneering case of South Africa—have been empowered to grant clemency to perpetrators who "come clean" as to their past misdeeds.

In his book *The Magic Lantern*, Timothy Garton Ash summarized the effect of a successful TRC by pointing out that it "symbolically draws a line under the past, without calling for forgetting or even, necessarily, forgiving. It is probably the closest a non-revolutionary revolution can come to revolutionary catharsis."

The Case of South Africa

The standard TRC model is widely acknowledged to be South Africa's Truth and Reconciliation Commission, established by President Nelson Mandela after the fall of that country's apartheid regime. In the South African version of the TRC process, the perpetrators are expected to acknowledge their misdeeds and express contrition, after which, ideally, the victims are expected to offer forgiveness. The intent is consistent with a sentiment often expressed by Holocaust victims: forgive, but do not forget.

To some extent, South Africa's TRC is credited with having contributed to that country's relatively nonviolent transition from white minority to black majority rule, all the more remarkable given the viciousness of the white regime under apartheid. (The word "apartheid" comes from the Dutch word for "separation," later incorporated into Afrikaans, the language of the Boer settlers in that country. It referred to the brutal system of strict racial segregation—with whites on top of that social hierarchy—that characterized South Africa for most of the 20th century, under which the black majority population was kept under conditions of extreme repression.) South Africa's TRC was created by the National Unity and Reconciliation Act in 1995. Here is part of the preamble to that legislation, which provides a good description of the goals of TRCs more generally:

SINCE the Constitution of the Republic of South Africa . . . provides a historic bridge between the past of a deeply divided society characterized by strife, conflict, untold suffering and injustice, and a future founded on the recognition of human rights, democracy and peaceful co-existence for all South Africans, irrespective of color, race, class, belief or sex; AND SINCE it is deemed necessary to establish the truth in relation to past events as well as the motives for and circumstances in which gross violations of human rights have occurred, and to make the findings known in order to prevent a repetition of such acts in future; AND SINCE the Constitution states that the pursuit of national unity, the well-being of all South African citizens and peace require reconciliation between the people of South Africa and the reconstruction of society; AND SINCE the Constitution states that there is a need for understanding but not for vengeance, a need for reparation but not for retaliation.

The commission's motto was "Without truth, no healing; without forgiveness, no future." Headed by Bishop Desmond Tutu—a Nobel Peace Prize winner for his earlier efforts on behalf of ending apartheid—the commission not only took testimony from victims but also was empowered to grant pardons to perpetrators who acknowledged their actions and sought forgiveness. Three years later, in 1998, the commission's final report was delivered to President Mandela. Former president F. W. de Klerk, as well as the African National Congress (ANC, South Africa's post-apartheid governing party), attempted to block publication because de Klerk personally and the ANC, organizationally, were implicated in gross human rights violations. To many observers, the fact that the previous rulers of apartheid South Africa and its post-apartheid black government found the TRC's work objectionable may constitute evidence that the process was fair and impartial!

When it comes to institutionalizing justice and promoting reconciliation in the aftermath of human rights abuses, some people advocate stern prosecution, while others favor amnesty and immunity for perpetrators. South Africa's TRC is widely seen as representing a third way, steering between these two extremes. It is representative of the dilemma facing many new democracies just emerging from past violations of human rights and whose stability requires a response to this past, but whose societies and governments may be so fragile as to be threatened by draconian measures that could be perceived as revenge, even if presented as justice.

The South African TRC had the authority to grant amnesty. As Bishop Tutu put it, "Freedom was exchanged for truth," emphasizing that this referred not only to freedom from apartheid but also to freedom from the social and psychological tyranny of past abuses. This was controversial because, in the minds of many people, it resulted in freedom for violent malefactors to avoid punishment. Tutu emphasized, however, that restorative justice (attempting to make amends to victims) is preferable to retributive justice (punishing the perpetrators) and that the former is consistent with the African cultural tradition of *Ubuntu,* which values healing and the encouragement of social relationships over the satisfaction of punishment. Proceedings of the South African TRC were nationally televised, widely watched, and generally credited with helping establish a shared national conscience.

The German Postwar Experience

One consequence of South Africa's experience with apartheid is that with the end of the white supremacist regime and establishment of a democratically elected government, initially headed by Nelson Mandela, large numbers of victims—mostly, but not entirely, black Africans—found themselves living in close proximity to their victimizers: largely, but not entirely, white members of the South African security service. Each country's experience, however, is different.

The abuses perpetrated by Nazi Germany during World War II, for example, were uniquely horrific and genocidal. Among the innumerable victims of the Holocaust were approximately six million murdered Jews. Other victims included Roma ("gypsies"), gays, the mentally ill, political dissidents, and millions of Slavs. Many others were forcibly deported or emigrated, leaving a population consisting largely of perpetrators or those who were (or claimed to be) unknowing bystanders. Post–World War II Germany was therefore less in need of reconciliation between victims and perpetrators than of society-wide reconciliation with its own past.

Vergangenheitsbewältigung is a characteristically lengthy, composite German word that speaks to the process of dealing with the past (*Vergangenheit* = past; *Bewältigung* = coming to terms with or mastery of), with the added implication that doing so is a struggle. (Note to potentially nervous students: We do not expect you to memorize this word, only to understand the concept!) The philosopher George Santayana famously observed that "those who forget the past are condemned to repeat it."

Vergangenheitsbewältigung describes the effort to respond to Santayana's warning, especially with respect to the Holocaust and other atrocities committed by the Third Reich, as well as the complicity of many German civilians. The postwar Federal Republic of Germany ("West Germany" until its post-communist reunification with its eastern counterpart) assumed the legal obligations of Adolf Hitler's government, and yet the German public's acceptance of its moral responsibilities lagged behind.

Vergangenheitsbewältigung became a goal of many liberal Germans, beginning around the late 1950s, after the most urgent needs of postwar reconstruction were met. German churches—Lutheran as well as Catholic—have played a significant role in the effort to induce Germans to acknowledge their past guilt and to encourage a theology of repentance. German schools constitute another major focus of *Vergangenheitsbewältigung*. Curriculum guides typically provide materials and experiences that expose students to the abuses of the Nazi era, including field trips to concentration camps and lectures from Holocaust survivors.

Much of postwar German literature—including the work of Nobel Prize–winning novelist Günter Grass—has been similarly concerned with coming to terms with that country's past misdeeds. Similarly in the cultural sphere, many sites of atrocities are now commemorated with plaques, and public monuments to Holocaust victims have been widely erected, just as such extermination camps as Dachau, Buchenwald, and Bergen-Belsen are open for visitors on pilgrimages of remembrance. Several years after German reunification in 1999, a Holocaust Memorial was inaugurated in Berlin, to which the German capital had been moved from Bonn. It is informally known as the "Holocaust-Mahnmal," which is noteworthy because *Mahnmal* carries with it an implication that goes beyond "memorial" or "remembrance" to include "warning" or "admonition." In addition, the German state has engaged in a policy of financial reparations, especially to Holocaust survivors living in Israel.

On the other hand, such efforts do not usually include acknowledgments of personal blame on the part of perpetrators. Indeed, denial, convenient amnesia, and lying are more common than confessions of guilt for many Germans and Austrians who collaborated, directly or indirectly, with the

Nazi regime. Notable examples include Kurt Waldheim, once secretary-general of the United Nations and president of Austria, who hid his earlier involvement in a Nazi extermination unit in Greece, and even novelist Günter Grass, who—after frequently excoriating Germans for their widespread complicity in World War II atrocities—only belatedly acknowledged his own enrollment (albeit as a 17-year-old) in the Waffen-SS, a Gestapo-connected military unit.

The German postwar experience of coming to terms—albeit sometimes haltingly—with a regrettable past was revived to some extent after the fall of the Iron Curtain and the reunification of East and West Germany. Thus, the often-brutal actions of employees (notably members of the East German *Stasi*, or secret police) of the former Communist Party–ruled state in eastern Germany have been widely subjected to efforts at *Vergangenheitsbewältigung*.

Japan's Postwar Response to Its World War II Atrocities

Although this process in Germany has not been an unmitigated success, it has constituted an admirable effort. By contrast, the people and government of postwar Japan have by and large been resistant to accepting blame and responsibility for their World War II outrages, including the "rape of Nanking" (from December 1937 to January 1938), mistreatment of Allied prisoners of war, and the forced enrollment of many women (especially Koreans) as sex slaves. The issue remains a sore point in contemporary Japan, with widespread claims that (1) no unethical or illegal acts actually occurred, (2) whatever actually happened was in the context of legitimate military actions of self-defense, and/or (3) far from encouraging national reconciliation, acknowledgment of wrongdoing would set right-wing nationalists against left-wing antimilitarists and thus "tear the country apart."

At the same time, Japan's refusal to engage in a process equivalent to Germany's *Vergangenheitsbewältigung* has emerged as a major stumbling block to political harmony among modern Japan and its neighbors, many of whom—notably Chinese, Koreans, and Filipinos—were wartime victims. Considerable controversy has also been associated with the frequent ceremonial appearance of Japanese prime ministers at the Yasukuni Shrine, a Shinto cemetery and museum that commemorates Japanese war dead. In addition, the Asian victims of imperial Japan during World War II have regularly been incensed by Japanese history textbooks that minimize and whitewash that country's aggression and war crimes; one of these, for example, includes a statement that the Japanese Army "advanced into" rather than invaded China.

One reason why national reconciliation has not been a primary driving force in Japan is that Japanese society is mostly homogeneous and does not include large numbers of victims living in immediate proximity to their previous tormentors. It has also been suggested that traditional Japanese devotion to ancestral generations has prevented thorough acknowledgment of that country's past abuses. As a result, international reconciliation has also been inhibited.

Similar Cases

Japan is not unique in this regard. Russia refuses to apologize for the "Katyn Forest" massacre of thousands of Polish officers early in World War II, after the Soviet Union invaded Poland from the east while Germany invaded from the west. Turkey actively denies that it perpetrated genocide against Armenians early in the 20th century; indeed, it is literally illegal within Turkey to refer to the Armenian genocide, an atrocity that is considered incontrovertible by all neutral historians. Chinese government officials remain largely unrepentant for the many millions killed under Mao Zedong or for the unknown number of pro-democracy protesters slaughtered in Tiananmen Square in 1989. For its part, the US government has not formally acknowledged guilt for its pre–Civil War history of slavery, its massacres of Native Americans, or the atomic bombing of Hiroshima and Nagasaki. Sadly, this list does not come close to exhausting the roster of abuses—by numerous countries—that call for reconciliation.

Latin America and Elsewhere

In Argentina, the report of the National Commission on the Disappeared helped draw attention to governmental abuses during that country's "dirty war" (1976–1983), in which an estimated 30,000 political dissidents were "disappeared" and presumed murdered. Argentina's post-war commission met for nine months, from 1983 to 1984, and its report—*Nunca Mas* (Never Again)—was a crucial component in Argentina's successful transition from tyranny to democracy. Its honesty and sense of moral urgency made it an international bestseller and, to some degree, set the stage for the South African process that followed a decade later.

Democracy now appears to be well established in that country, and most observers agree that even if Argentina were to slip back into dictatorship, a return to comparable abuses is, as a result of the earlier truth telling, unlikely. Similarly, the Guatemalan "Commission of Historical Clarification" not only examined discrimination and marginalization of its indigenous population but has also indicted military authorities for genocide against contemporary Mayans, who constitute a majority of the population. Although not yet accepted by the Guatemalan elite, the commission's report has expanded the national dialogue to include what had previously been unmentionable.

Not surprisingly, it is often easier to come to terms with misdeeds when the perpetrators—not to mention the victims—are elderly, exiled, or deceased. However, there has been a recent trend toward responding more contemporaneously, especially after a transition from dictatorship to democratic rule. During the 1970s and 1980s, for example, many repressive Latin American regimes and other US allies sought to avoid obvious forms of violent repression in order to retain financial and diplomatic support. The result was widespread reliance on clandestine paramilitary death squads and unacknowledged "disappearances" of political opponents. After the fall of these governments, identification of state-sponsored abuses became widespread, although in certain countries—such as Zimbabwe and the Philippines—TRCs have been authorized, but their reports have been either suppressed or never completed.

In some countries, autocrats have successfully insisted that as part of their willingness to relinquish power, they and their henchmen must be guaranteed immunity from prosecution and even from having their misdeeds made public. For example, in Argentina, the National Commission for Forced Disappearances investigated human rights violations, including an estimated 30,000 "disappearances" committed during the so-called dirty war against opponents of the military junta. In nearly every case, however, the commission was empowered only to report on the status of those disappeared and was expressly prohibited from identifying the perpetrators. Next door, in Brazil, a "National Committee on Truth" was established and charged with examining abuses—torture and assassinations—committed by the military dictators who ruled that country from 1965 to 1985. Brazil's committee acknowledged that the earlier murders were committed under a smokescreen of false claims that the country needed to be protected from alleged communist subversion. An interesting outcome of that committee's work was that when its results were made public, it included a formal public apology to Brazilian president Dilma Rousseff for the torture she had suffered following her imprisonment during the 1980s for antigovernment activities.

The Case of the United States

The United States is not exempt from abuses or from occasional attempts to respond to them. In 1979, five African Americans were shot to death and 10 wounded in Greensboro, North Carolina, after which the white defendants were acquitted, even though the shootings had been videotaped. More than two decades later, the Greensboro Truth and Reconciliation Commission—the first such official body ever established in the United States—was formed. Its report, presented in 2005, concluded that

> the passage of time alone cannot bring closure, nor resolve feelings of guilt and lingering trauma, for those impacted by the events of November 3, 1979. Nor can there be any genuine healing for the city of Greensboro unless the truth surrounding these events is honestly confronted, the suffering fully acknowledged, accountability established, and forgiveness and reconciliation facilitated.

Another commission, this one federally appointed, investigated the internment of Japanese Americans during World War II, eventually resulting in the payment of reparations. Also, President Clinton formally apologized for the infamous Tuskegee syphilis experiments, in which African Americans were intentionally left untreated to observe the course of the disease; once again, financial reparations were paid. It remains unclear to what extent such actions constitute mere window dressing or genuine contrition, just as it remains to be seen whether they lead to ultimate reconciliation.

Genocide on the part of the US government against Native American populations is also a regrettable part of early American colonial history, especially during the United States' territorial expansion. It is estimated that approximately 15 million persons were killed in the course of European expansion in North America, a history that tends to get short shrift even in an era of supposed cultural sensitivity. While some groups were wiped out entirely, others were forcibly relocated, often across hundreds and even thousands of miles, and then isolated onto land of marginal value that were politely labeled "reservations." Acknowledgment of such past abuses may make their repetition less likely in the future.

The Australian government organized a commission to report on that country's mid-20th-century policy of taking aboriginal children from their homes and indoctrinating them into Anglo culture. One result has been a "National Sorry Day" and recognition that such acts were grievous misdeeds. Similarly, in 2011, an "Indian Residential Schools Truth and Reconciliation Commission" was established in Canada to explore human rights abuses committed by the Canadian Indian residential school system, which had committed a kind of ethnic genocide against that country's First Nations. Nonetheless, the governments of Australia, Canada, and the United States have yet to make financial reparations to the many victims of their policies.

Within the US in particular, the argument has been raised that because there are essentially no surviving direct victims of slavery or of the genocide of Native Americans, direct reparations—or even current apologies—are difficult to justify.

The Opposite of Reconciliation

Regrettably, instead of truth and reconciliation, some brutal governments are inclined to foster "exaggeration and aggravation," seeking to enhance their public support by playing upon the fears and resentments of their own population. Public celebrations, for example, are often used as opportunities to emphasize past victories over traditional enemies or, alternatively, to remind a populace of their shared outrage vis-à-vis other groups.

Since the 19th century, for example, Northern Irish Protestants ("Orangemen") have paraded to Drumcree each year on the Sunday preceding the 12th of July. Until the recent Good Friday Accords and the subsequent official reconciliation between Northern Irish Catholics and Protestants, this parade, along with others during the "marching season," generated violence and widespread anxiety among Catholics, based upon unreconciled injuries long ago. William of Orange defeated the Irish resistance movement at the Battle of the Boyne in 1690. It is this victory, *more than three centuries ago*, that loyalists persisted in celebrating by their annual marches. Moreover, for decades they went out of their way—literally—to route the victory parades through Catholic communities.

Following France's ignominious defeat in the Franco-Prussian War (1870–1871), the newly unified German state annexed the previously French province of Alsace and most of Lorraine. For decades thereafter, the return of these two regions became a French national obsession, with schoolchildren beginning their day by regularly reciting pledges to achieve this goal. Eventually they did, with the "help" of World War I. It was the French yearning for getting even with the Germans that contributed to the pre–World War I Franco-Russian alliance in support of Serbia against Germany, which dragged much of Europe to war after the assassination of the Austrian archduke in 1914.

The most troublesome national struggles are those that have been going on for a long time, typically fueled by widespread resentment and unreconciled national anger over past abuses, often reciprocal, even though they may also be asymmetric. Israelis mourn the Holocaust, vowing "never again," while Palestinians regularly and painfully remind themselves about *Al-Nakba* ("The Catastrophe") of Israel's founding and the subsequent expulsion of 750,000 Palestinians from their homes in 1948. In the absence of national reconciliation, historical reminiscences loom large, not simply as facts from the past but also because such recollections, especially when painful, generate passions and animosity as well as a felt need for revenge and restitution in the present. As a pair of observers, one Israeli and one Palestinian, put it:

> For Israel's Jewish population, this includes displacement, persecution, the life of the ghetto, and the horrors of the Holocaust; and the long, frustrated quest for a normal, recognized and accepted homeland. There is a craving for a future that will not echo the past and for the kind of ordinary security—the unquestioned acceptance of a Jewish presence in the region—that even over whelming military superiority

cannot guarantee . . . . For Palestinians, the most primal demands relate to addressing and redressing a historical experience of dispossession, expulsion, dispersal, massacres, occupation, discrimination, denial of dignity, persistent killing off of their leaders, and the relentless fracturing of their national polity.[2]

Groups and nations readily tend to ruminate over past wrongs, reminding themselves of their need to right them someday, and not surprisingly, leaders are often eager to manipulate this inclination for their own ends. For example, consider the history of Serbian grievances against Turkish Muslims. In 1989, Slobodan Milošević, then leader of Yugoslavia, announced to an increasingly agitated gathering of Serbs, "No one will ever dare beat you again!" It wasn't lost on Milošević's audience that he was speaking on the precise anniversary of the "Battle of the Blackbirds," near Pristina, the present-day capital of Kosovo. The year of that battle was 1389, when invading armies of Ottoman Turks defeated Serb forces, ultimately pressing far enough north to besiege Vienna. Six hundred years later, Milošević, standing on the same battlefield, orchestrated the violent repression of Kosovars (mostly Muslim) by Serbs (mostly Christian Orthodox). This was not simply an unscrupulous and power-seeking leader reminding his listeners of an unreconciled memory of past pain, but a skillful demagogue literally reviving that pain and anger within them, whereupon it fueled fresh outbreaks of murderous violence.

TRC Downsides and Caveats

At one point in Dante's *The Inferno* (canto XXXIII), Count Ugolino is asked about the abuse he has suffered: "You ask me to renew a grief so desperate," he responds, "that the very thought of speaking it tears my heart in two." He goes on: "But if my words may be a seed that bears the fruit of infamy for him I gnaw, I shall weep, but tell my story through my tears." (In Dante's vision, Ugolino is condemned to spend eternity gnawing on the head of his—equally guilty—opponent; thus both men are punished.) Two disadvantages of TRCs are here revealed: first, the process itself can be painful. And second, to some extent at least, there is powerful motivation to "gnaw" the victimizers and encourage "the fruit of infamy"—that is, revenge—rather than healing. And yet, healing may require precisely such a process.

Another possibly unintended consequence of officially sponsored reconciliation is that insofar as it can help victimizers avoid punishment, it may reduce the deterrent effect that might result from meting out legitimate justice. In many cases, TRCs encourage or require some forms of reparations rather than criminal punishment, a policy that seems more likely to lead to healing. The German government, for example, has paid significant sums to Israel, as partial reparation for the murder of Jews during the Holocaust, and the US government has paid reparations to Japanese American victims of forced resettlement into internment camps (a step up from "concentration camps") during World War II. Financial compensation seems better than its absence, but it also risks trivializing horrendous abuses by suggesting that money can make up for atrocity. The idea of reparations for slavery in the United States has been floated but rejected, although some apologies have been offered. Reconciliation seems unlikely outside a context of social justice. As Desmond Tutu notably put it, "How can I reconcile with you when your foot is on my neck?"

Local cultural traditions in some cases may demand that bad things be ignored rather than confronted in order to be overcome. After the death of the dictator Francisco Franco, for example, Spanish authorities—strongly supported by public opinion—consciously decided not to review the many murders and crimes associated with the Spanish Civil War and the years of Fascist tyranny that followed. "Why pick at old scabs?" goes the refrain, along with "What's been done cannot be undone."

Similarly, a cultural tradition in Mozambique discourages talking about traumatic experiences. Even though more than one million civilians were maimed, tortured, or murdered during the Portuguese occupation of that country and the anticolonial revolution that followed, no public discussion or denunciation of these events has yet occurred; for the most part, nonetheless, the conflicting parties appear at least superficially reconciled. Similar post-genocide silence has characterized Cambodia, in this case partly because some prominent officials involved in that country's notorious "killing fields" under the Khmer Rouge are still in power, and also because the Cambodian style of Buddhism emphasizes that reconciliation can only be hindered by a focus on "justice" or "retribution." One lesson thus appears to be that although much can be learned from the experiences of other cultures, there is no "one size fits all" prescription for national reconciliation.

For example, most of the successful work of TRCs has been in countries that self-identify with a Christian tradition, and reconciliation and forgiveness are explicitly proclaimed to be Christian values, although such values are not universally practiced: witness the readily evoked Serbian anger at Muslims, described above, literally centuries after a painful military defeat. It remains unclear whether similar procedures can succeed in cultures with other expressed values, as well as between different religious and cultural traditions.

Moreover, it is reasonable to ask whether a TRC-type process is even necessary for a country to transition from a violent past to a future society operating under the rule of law. Would TRC-sponsored confrontations inhibit such a transition, for example, by generating a culture of lawless impunity or because the perpetrators (as in the case of post-Pinochet Chile) remain so influential that moving against them may endanger a fragile successor democracy?

On the other hand, are punishments necessary in order to obtain "closure"? Another problem is the selective use of TRCs to further a political agenda. Thus a "Philippine Truth Commission," formed in 2010, was severely criticized by the Philippine Supreme Court as a political witch hunt undertaken by the current government as a way of discrediting its predecessors. And in Sri Lanka, a "Lessons Learnt and Reconciliation Commission" was established to investigate various claims of human rights abuse during the Tamil-Sinhalese civil war. Although this commission's report was quite extensive, it was also roundly criticized by such major human rights organizations as Human Rights Watch, Amnesty International, and the United Nations as representing an effort by the victorious Sinhalese government to co-opt any subsequent inquiry and prevent independent organizations from investigating abuses it had perpetrated.

Some Conceptual Debates About Truth, Reconciliation, and Justice

One position regarding truth and reconciliation is that the only acceptable response to gross violations of human rights (torture, genocide, ethnic cleansing, etc.) is criminal prosecution and punishment; that is, retributive justice. In addition to satisfying a widespread human desire, retributive justice, it is claimed, helps deter comparable abuses in the future. By their nature, however, TRCs don't do this. Instead, they focus on restorative justice, including the payment of reparations as well as acceptance of blame by the perpetrators and forgiveness by the victims. Two relevant poles of human inclination—vengeance on the one hand and forgiveness on the other—may be deep-seated in the human psyche and then culturally elaborated in social institutions.

"The past is never dead," according to Nobel Prize–winning novelist William Faulkner. "It's not even past." If so, it can only be ignored, not avoided, and not only is there a persistent "duty to remember," but a society's encounter with its past is an unavoidable part of its present. But how much farther does this duty go? Is there a duty to achieve justice? And, if so, does this involve only punishment? What about reconciliation? And forgiveness?

Even "truth" can be problematic. When it comes to "dirty wars," every side has its preferred version of what really happened, somewhat like the famous Japanese story and subsequent movie, *Rashômon*, which depicts a murder from numerous perspectives, each with its own version of what actually took place. Martha Minnow has argued that there may actually be different kinds of truth, especially when dealing with complex social phenomena. For example, "empirical truth" refers to whether something happened, and, if so, what were, for example, the actual numbers of rapes, mutilations, murders, and so forth. This is different from "personal truth," the experiences of victims themselves. (Josef Stalin is alleged to have commented that a single death is a tragedy, whereas a million deaths is a statistic.)

Then there is "legal" truth, which refers to the forensic requirements that are required to lead to conviction and punishment of perpetrators and which necessarily varies depending on the evidentiary rules of each country. Is it, for example, a matter of "beyond reasonable doubt," "the preponderance of the evidence," or "realistic certainty"? Finally, there is "meaningful truth," which speaks—in often contradictory ways—to what the events in question actually signify: the South African security forces, for example, have long maintained that their actions were conducted in defense of the country, just as Latin American military dictators argue that they were protecting their homelands from "communist subversion," either indigenous (as in Argentina, Chile, or El Salvador) or "imported" from such venues as Nicaragua or Cuba. Not surprisingly, the victims of these security forces and dictators usually have diametrically opposed interpretations of the "same" events.

Alternatives to Reconciliation

For some, the prospect of genuine reconciliation seems unrealistically optimistic; for others, the downside to such a process is so great that it simply isn't worth it. But what are the alternatives?

One possibility is to ignore the past and attempt to move on. Another is to acknowledge the past, but lightly, and attempt to move on. Yet another—and one that is all too common—is to engage the past but to do so aggressively as a cause of present, future, and escalating cycles of violence, which usually generates a continuing culture of revenge, feuding, and retaliation.

Early in the 20th century, the social scientist R. F. Barton studied a Filipino tribe, the Ifugao; he focused on their social rules and how they settled disputes. His findings have become a classic of legal anthropology. "The

Ifugao," wrote Barton, "has one general law, which with a few notable exceptions he applies to killings, be they killings in war, murders, or executions . . . That law is: A life must be paid with a life."

And here is the testimony of Milovan Djilas, who was born into a perpetually feuding Montenegrin clan and eventually rose to become vice president of the former Yugoslavia. Djilas spanned the interval between ethnic feuding and modernity in his nation, and his insights into vengeance—written nearly 40 years ago—foretell the stubborn enmity that devoured his unhappy land:

> Vengeance—this is a breath of life one shares from the cradle with one's fellow clansmen, in both good fortune and bad, vengeance from eternity. Vengeance was the debt we paid for the love and sacrifice our forebears and fellow clansmen bore for us. It was the defense of our honor and good name, and the guarantee of our maidens. It was our pride before others; our blood was not water that anyone could spill. It was, moreover, our pastures and springs—more beautiful than anyone else's—our family feasts and births. It was the glow in our eyes, the flame in our cheeks, the pounding in our temples, the word that turned to stone in our throats on our hearing that our blood had been shed. It was the sacred task transmitted in the hour of death to those who had just been conceived in our blood. It was centuries of manly pride and heroism, survival, a mother's milk and a sister's vow, bereaved parents and children in black, joy and songs turned into silence and wailing.[3]

Because of the power of such feuding and the vivid historical memory of its participants, in the absence of reconciliation individuals have often been forced to bear the weight of grudges accumulated by earlier generations. Russian anthropologist Sergei Arutiunov described the situation of many distinct ethnic groups in and near the Caucasus mountains, especially Georgians, Abkhasians, Armenians, and Azeris:

> Among the Caucasus highlanders, a man must know the names and some details of the lives and the locations of the tombstones of seven ancestors of his main line. People fight not only for arable land; they fight for the land where the tombstones of their ancestors are located. Revenge is not only for events today, but also for the atrocities from wars eight generations ago.[4]

It is precisely to interrupt such cycles of violence and in the hope of generating a more peaceful future that scholars as well as pragmatic politicians and both secular and religious visionaries have devoted increasing attention to the process of reconciliation.

A Final Note on National Reconciliation

It is remarkably easy to destroy a complex structure, compared with building it or reconstructing it after it has been knocked down. By the same token, it is unfortunately much easier to disrupt society than to repair it after serious damage has been done. Conflict—and, particularly, violence—often does considerable damage to the social fabric, leaving societies in substantial need of repair, even after the perpetrators are no longer in power. There is no simple, universally applicable solution to the problem of achieving reconciliation after national trauma. However, it is increasingly clear that reconciliation is not only necessary but also possible, and that an honest recounting of the past can contribute greatly toward achieving a more peaceful future. In this regard, the newly emerging phenomenon of national reconciliation commissions recommends itself.

Questions for Further Reflection

1. Discuss ways to approach matters of national reconciliation other than through the use of truth and reconciliation commissions.

2. Is it possible to achieve reconciliation without focusing on potentially painful truths?

3. Thus far, the truth-and-reconciliation process has been employed almost exclusively to within-country issues. Describe some issues that might arise if this were applied to tensions *between* states.

4. Most students of peace and conflict studies tend to support some form of restorative justice. Make an alternative case in favor of revenge and retaliation, namely for *retributive justice*.

5. Similarly, make a case for truth and reconciliation with respect to socioeconomic and/or environmental injuries and disputes. Point out some potential disadvantages.

Suggestions for Further Reading

Margaret Soenser Breen. 2005. *Minding Evil: Explorations of Human Iniquity.* Amsterdam: Editions Rodopi BV.

Ronald Niezen. 2015. *Truth and Indignation: Canada's Truth and Reconciliation Commission on Indian Residential Schools.* Toronto: University of Toronto Press.

Samantha Power. 2007. *A Problem From Hell: America and the Age of Genocide.* New York: HarperPerennial.

Imani Michelle Scott, ed. 2014. *Crimes Against Humanity in the Land of the Free: Can a Truth and Reconciliation Process Heal Racial Conflict in America?* New York: Praeger.

Marie Breen Smyth. 2007. *Truth Recovery and Justice After Conflict: Managing Violent Pasts.* London: Routledge (Taylor & Francis).

Desmond Tutu. 2009. *No Future Without Forgiveness.* New York: Doubleday.

Annelies Verdoolaege. 2008. *Reconciliation Discourse.* Philadelphia: John Benjamins.

Notes

1. Martha Minnow. 2003. "Memory and Hate." In *Breaking the Cycles of Hatred: Memory, Law, and Repair.* Princeton, NJ: Princeton University Press.

2. H. Agha and R. Malley. 2009. "Obama and the Middle East." *The New York Review of Books,* LVI (10): 67–69.

3. Milovan Djilas. 1972. *Land Without Justice.* New York: Harcourt Brace Jovanovich.

4. Sergei Arutiunov. 2008. In *Russian and Soviet History: From the Time of Troubles to the Collapse of the Soviet Union,* eds. Steven A. Usitalo and William Benton Wisenhunt. Lanham, MD: Rowman and Littlefield.

Nonviolence

Once the object of skepticism, even scorn, by security specialists and political revolutionaries alike, nonviolence has enjoyed increasing professional and political acclaim since Mohandas Gandhi's successful experiments with nonviolent civil resistance in the first half of the 20th century. As a principled and strategic global "force more powerful" than violence, nonviolence is gradually winning over many former doubters, in large part due to the accomplishments of mass nonviolent movements. In this chapter, we focus on the theoretical and practical dimensions of nonviolence, as well as on some towering figures in its modern history.

What Is Nonviolence?

Nonviolence is a word found in many contexts. In English, it consists of two words most people regard as negative: no(n) and violence. The first known use of "nonviolence" in English was in 1920, probably by Gandhi. Nonviolence has two related and sometimes reinforcing meanings:

1. It can refer, first, to a *general philosophy* of abstention from violence because of ethical or religious principles (e.g., "She believes in nonviolence"). This is called *principled nonviolence*.

2. It can also refer to the *behavior* of people using nonviolent action (e.g., "The demonstrators maintained their nonviolence"). This is called *strategic nonviolence*.

Virtually all the relevant literature on violence and nonviolence assumes that the two are mutually exclusive: either violence or nonviolence. But in real life, the distinction is often less clear-cut. This is relevant for investigations of specific historical and contemporary conflicts where a range of violent and nonviolent strategies and tactics have been adopted. It is also an issue for everyday life situations where both physical force and negotiation may be employed to deal with conflicts at the interpersonal and group levels. Accordingly, violence and nonviolence are not absolutes; they lie on a continuum.

The history of nonviolence has two pacifistic traditions, absolute and pragmatic, with some aspects in common. For absolute pacifists, no goal justifies killing other human beings. They are against all forms of harming humans and often other living beings as well. In the pragmatic tradition, nonviolent actions are evaluated mainly according to their importance and efficacy as political tools, as a collection of techniques, a means of communication, a vehicle for revolutions and social movements, or as a system of defense. Many within the pacifist tradition actively use pragmatic methods, but people using these nonviolent techniques do not necessarily hold absolute pacifist views.

Violence

Violence may be the worst injury that human beings inflict on each other. If a peaceful alien species were to observe human behavior, perhaps they would likely be deeply perplexed by the deliberate infliction of pain, suffering, and death by members of the same species against others of their species, especially when survival is not at stake. (Conversely, of course, belligerent aliens might feel right at home on a warlike Earth!) Identifying violence appears simple: We know it when we see or feel it. But defining it is tricky.

One widely understood definition of violence portrays it in purely physical terms: "The exercise of physical force so as to inflict injury on or damage to persons or property; action or conduct characterized by this."[1] On the other hand, the eminent peace researcher Johan Galtung suggests a wider definition that includes "direct," "structural," and "cultural" violence, as well as a psychological component. To this, the World Health Organization (WHO) adds the phenomenon of self-directed violence.

The WHO has also adopted an expansive definition of violence as "The intentional use of physical force, threatened or actual, against oneself, another person, or against a group or community, that either results in or has a high likelihood of resulting in injury, death, psychological harm, mal-development or deprivation." According to the WHO, four different aspects of violence can be identified: (1) physical, (2) sexual, (3) psychological, and (4) deprivation. The WHO further subdivides each of these into self-directed violence, interpersonal violence, and collective violence.[2]

The Geneva Declaration on Armed Violence and Development (GD) addresses the interrelations between armed violence and development. Although the incidence of armed conflict has declined in recent years, the number of people killed by armed violence has not. Almost 750,000 men, women, and children die each year as a result of armed violence. Almost two-thirds of these deaths occur in countries that are not affected by armed conflicts: The GD was first adopted in 2006 by 42 nations during a Ministerial Summit in Geneva. It is now endorsed by more than 100 nations and is the strongest political statement to date that addresses the impact of armed violence within a development context.

Its report, *The Global Burden of Armed Violence*, examined the tremendous burden imposed on individuals, families, and communities by either armed conflicts or criminality. Wars reduce economic growth by more than 2 percent annually, while the economic cost of armed criminality alone approaches $163 billion annually, and the global cost of all armed violence is approximately $400 billion per year. Most violent deaths occur in non-war situations, due to small- or large-scale violence, either as a result of criminality or political actions. And weapons matter: Approximately 60 percent of all homicides are committed with firearms. Importantly, these numbers should not be allowed to obscure the pain and suffering of individuals that underlie such otherwise bloodless data.

The consequences of armed violence are felt most intensely by the poor and most vulnerable, particularly in Latin America, Asia, Africa, and the Middle East. But armed violence is preventable, and early intervention can reduce suffering and save lives. Thus, it is acknowledged that the following violence-prevention strategies are effective at the interpersonal level:

- developing safe, stable, and nurturing relationships between children and their parents and caregivers;
- reducing access to guns, knives and pesticides;
- changing cultural and social norms that support violence; and
- creating victim identification, care, and support programs.

Arendt on Violence

Hannah Arendt, one of the 20th century's most eminent political thinkers, offered her own reflections on violence, titled—appropriately—*On Violence*. She was writing against the background of "a century of wars and revolutions . . . in which violence is believed to be the common denominator." Arendt claims that "warfare has lost much of its effectiveness and nearly all its glamour" because of the "technical development of the instruments of violence," especially nuclear and biological weapons. She also argues that "the chief reason warfare is with us . . . [is] the simple fact that no substitute for this final arbiter in international affairs has yet appeared on the political scene."[3] Although in her opinion some forms of violence, such as rage, may have "beastly" and/or "irrational" sources, Arendt maintains that political violence in general and revolutionary violence in particular may sometimes be "deliberate" and even "rational," because it "is the only way to set the scales of justice right again."

Arendt was a refugee from Nazi Germany, and her position with regard to the legitimacy of violence against oppression is, not surprisingly, influenced by her own painful experiences as German Jew who survived and analyzed the Holocaust and its perpetrators, especially Adolf Eichmann, about whom she wrote a famous book, *Eichmann in Jerusalem*, in which she notably identified and decried "the banality of evil." This phrase has often been misunderstood. Arendt was *not* suggesting that the immense evil of the Holocaust was banal, but rather, that Eichmann himself was neither "perverted nor sadistic" and was, instead, "terrifyingly normal," lacking in imagination, and unable or unwilling to think for himself. Her point was that monstrous deeds can and have been done by people who are not necessarily demonic or monstrous in themselves, but who, because of their thoughtlessness and "normality," are willing to "go along."

Nonviolent Peace Theorists and Theories

We now examine some leading theorists and practitioners of nonviolence, before considering the varieties of nonviolent movements and their tactics and strategies.

Leo Tolstoy

Lev Nikolayevich Tolstoy, known in the West as Leo Tolstoy (1828–1910), was a Russian writer, primarily of such world-acclaimed novels as *War and Peace*, *The Brothers Karamazov*, and *Anna Karenina*. Later in life, he also wrote political, social, and religious essays. Tolstoy also became noted as a moral thinker and social reformer.

Tolstoy's literal interpretation of the ethical teachings of Jesus, centering on the Sermon on the Mount, caused him in later life to become a fervent Christian anarcho-pacifist. Tolstoy believed that being a Christian required one to be a pacifist; this, combined with the persistent waging of war by government, made him a philosophical anarchist as well. His ideas on non-violent resistance, expressed in such works as *The Kingdom of God Is Within You* and his Address to the Swedish Peace Congress (1909), later had a profound impact on such pivotal 20th-century figures as Mohandas Gandhi and Martin Luther King, Jr.

The Dalai Lama

Tenzin Gyatso (born 1935) is the 14th and current Dalai Lama and thus the leader of Tibetan Buddhism. During the 1959 Tibetan uprising against China's takeover of that country, he fled to India, from which he has since traveled the world, advocating nonviolent resistance to Chinese rule over Tibet, teaching Tibetan Buddhism, and talking about the importance of compassion as the source of a fulfilling life and for what he has called "A human approach to world peace," based on Buddhist principles but accessible to everyone regardless of religious orientation. In his numerous public appearances, the Dalai Lama stresses that during the 20th century, tens of millions of people and animals lost their lives due to violence, while the economies of many countries were unnecessarily ruined. He has proclaimed: "Let the 21st century be a century of tolerance and dialogue"—a fervent hope that has not as yet been fulfilled.

Mohandas K. Gandhi

M. K. Gandhi is revered by most Indians as the founder of their nation and is also venerated by millions of others as the leading exponent and practitioner of nonviolence, and nearly a modern-day saint. He pioneered the modern use of nonviolent resistance as both a spiritual and philosophical approach to life as well as an intensely practical technique of achieving political and social change. Gandhi was widely known among Indians as "Mahatma" (Great Soul), for his courage, simplicity, penetrating insight, and the extraordinary impact of his teachings and his life.

Central to Gandhi's worldview was the search for truth, and, indeed, he titled his autobiography *My Experiments With Truth*. Gandhi thought that nonviolent love (*ahimsa,* literally meaning "not to harm" in Sanskrit) was achievable only through compassion and tolerance for others; moreover, it required continual testing, experimentation, and constant, unstinting effort, undergirded by a degree of courage that many Westerners—unfamiliar with the actual practice of Gandhian nonviolence—frequently fail to credit. His teachings emphasized not just courageous and principled nonviolence but also directness, civility, and honesty. Although Gandhi was himself a devout Hindu, he (like the Dalai Lama) emphasized that nonviolence transcends sectarian beliefs, and that in crucial respects, "all religions are true."

Gandhi's Early Years

Gandhi was born in India, in 1869, to merchant-caste Hindu parents. He remained a committed Hindu throughout his life, although other religious and ethical traditions—especially Jainism, with its doctrinal insistence on non-killing—had a major impact on his thinking. Gandhi was also strongly influenced by pacifist Christian traditions, as well as by the writings of Thoreau and Tolstoy on the rights and duties of individuals to practice civil disobedience when governments violate human rights.

He married very young (he and his wife were both 13) and studied law in London. After a brief time in India, the young barrister went to South Africa, where he was outraged by that country's system of racial discrimination (there was, and still is, a large Asian—especially Indian—population in South Africa). Gandhi remained in South Africa for 21 years, leading numerous campaigns for Indian rights, editing a newspaper, and developing his philosophy of *satyagraha,* or nonviolent action, as well as specific techniques for implementing it. He was physically abused and arrested many times by British authorities but also served courageously on the British side when he agreed with their positions; for example, Gandhi organized an Indian Ambulance Corps during the Boer War (1899–1902) and the Zulu Rebellion (1906), for which he was decorated by the government.

Gandhi's Return to India

After achieving some reforms in South Africa, Gandhi returned to India in 1915 and quickly became leader of the Indian nationalist movement, seeking independence from colonial Britain. When the British government made it illegal to organize political opposition, Gandhi led a successful *satyagraha* campaign against these laws.

In 1919, British troops fired with machine guns into a crowd of unarmed Indian men, women, and children, who had been demonstrating peacefully; nearly 400 were killed in what became known as the Amritsar Massacre. This served to highlight the difference between the steadfast nonviolence of Gandhi's followers and the relative brutality of the British colonial government. It also moved Gandhi to refine his techniques of *satyagraha*. In particular, he took the great Sanskrit epic, the *Bhagavad Gita*, to be an allegory not about war—its literal subject—but about the need for people to devote themselves, unselfishly, to the attainment of the highest goals. He urged his followers to "reduce yourself to zero"—that is, remove the self-will and striving for personal aggrandizement that so often leads so often to arrogance or even tyranny, as well as to cowardice.

Gandhi was a small, slight man with indomitable moral conviction and remarkable physical stamina. He frequently underwent fasts to emphasize the importance of personal self-denial and also against the British colonial authorities, knowing that his renown among the Indian people would generate mass popular unrest if he were allowed to die. This is but one example of the political practicality underlying Gandhi's hard-headed tactics: Risking his life to put the British overlords in a position such that they were pressured to accede to his demands. He also used fasting—potentially to death—to protest the violence that periodically broke out as less disciplined Indian nationalists rioted against British rule, and also, on occasion between Hindus and Muslims. Gandhi was so upset at the latter events that he temporarily called off his struggle for Indian independence.

During the 1920s, Gandhi continued to fight for the rights of the lowest Hindu caste, the *Dalits* ("untouchables"), whom he called the *Harijan* ("children of God"), as well as for miners, factory workers, and poor peasants. He urged Indians to develop cottage industries, especially spinning and weaving, so as to deprive Britain of its major economic advantage in occupying India: markets for English textile products. In addition, hand weaving contributed to the potential of *swaraj* ("self- sufficiency"), while spotlighting the dignity of labor.

In 1930, when the British introduced the Salt Acts, requiring that all salt in India be purchased from the government, Gandhi led a massive march, 320 kilometers to the sea, where he and his followers made salt from seawater, in defiance of the law. In all, Gandhi spent about 7 years in various jails for his numerous acts of nonviolent resistance, making it respectable—indeed, honorable—for protesters to be imprisoned for their beliefs. (It is said that a century earlier, when Henry David Thoreau was imprisoned for refusal to pay federal taxes in protest against the Mexican-American War, his friend Ralph Waldo Emerson visited him in jail and asked "Henry, what are you doing in here?" Thoreau replied "Ralph, what are you doing *out there*?")

Gandhi was ascetic and intensely frugal, possessing a biting sense of humor: Once, when he visited the British king in London, in order to press his campaign for Indian independence, the half-naked Gandhi was asked whether he felt a bit underdressed for the occasion, to which he replied, "His Majesty wore enough for the two of us." Another time, when asked what he thought of Western civilization, he replied, "I think it would be a good idea."

Gandhi was deeply grieved by the intense periodic violence between Hindus and Muslims, and he opposed the partition of British colonial India into an independent Muslim Pakistan and Hindu India. In 1948, a year after India won its independence from Britain, Gandhi was assassinated by a fanatical Hindu, who resented his insistence on religious tolerance. However, Gandhi had accomplished what many thought impossible: gaining independence for a country of 400 million people, without firing a shot. He also showed that a highly spiritual concept—nonviolence—can be an effective practical tool in the quest for peace, even in the 20th-century world of *Realpolitik*, power, and violence.

Satyagraha

Perhaps the most important Gandhian concept is *satyagraha*, literally translated as "soul-force," or "holding firm to the truth." Unfortunately, Gandhian *satyagraha* has often been mistranslated into English as "passive resistance," which is like translating *light* as "nondarkness" or defining *good* as "absence of evil." It omits the essence of its subject, its positive, creative component. *Satyagraha* is passive only insofar as it espouses self-restraint rather than the active injuring of others. In all other respects, it is active and assertive, requiring great energy and fortitude.

Satyagraha requires strong adherence to love and mutual respect, and demands a willingness to suffer, if need be, to achieve these goals. For Gandhi, *satyagraha* necessitated fortitude and persistence in adhering to its precepts. In his words:

> Truth (*satya*) implies love, and firmness (*agraha*) engenders and therefore serves as a synonym for force. I thus began to call the Indian movement *satyagraha*, that is to say, the Force which is born of Truth and Love or nonviolence, and give up the use of the phrase "passive resistance."

According to Gandhi,

> In the application of satyagraha, I discovered in the earliest stages that pursuit of truth did not admit of violence being inflicted on one's opponent but that he must be weaned from error by patience and compassion. For what appears to be truth to the one may appear to be error to the other. And patience means self-suffering. So the doctrine came to mean vindication of truth, not by infliction of suffering on the opponent, but on oneself.[4]

Satyagraha is clearly more complicated than any direct word or phrase can express. For Gandhi, among the major principles of *satyagraha* are

- nonviolence (*ahimsa*);
- truth, which includes situational honesty, but goes beyond it to mean living fully in accord with and in devotion to that which is true;
- not stealing;
- chastity—this includes sexual chastity but also the subordination of other sensual desires to a primary devotion to truth;
- non-possession, notably a lack of attachment to things and thus not the same as poverty;

- a commitment to the legitimacy of one's own physical labor;

- refraining from personal gluttony;

- courage, verging on utter fearlessness;

- absolute respect for all religions;

- persistent economic tactics such as boycotts (*swadeshi*); and

- freedom from untouchability (i.e., elimination of the caste system).

- belief in truth and nonviolence and faith in the inherent goodness of human nature, which may be evoked by suffering;

- a willingness to endure pain, imprisonment, loss of all one's possessions, and even to die;

- abstention from alcohol and other intoxicants;

- willingness to carry out all the rules of discipline that are issued by the *satyagraha* leadership;

- when imprisoned, a commitment to obey all jail rules unless they are specially devised to hurt one's self respect, a determination to respect the humanity of one's jailers;

- harboring no anger and agreeing to absorb the anger of one's opponents, without retaliating or even expressing anger in return;

- refusing to submit, out of fear of punishment or assault, to an order given in anger;

- voluntarily submitting to arrest or confiscation of one's personal property;

- refraining from cursing, swearing, or insulting one's opponent;

- neither saluting nor insulting the flag of one's opponent;

- if anyone attempts to insult or assault one's opponent, defending that opponent (nonviolently) with one's life if need be;

- not asking for special, favorable treatment in prison, and, although fasting is permissible, not to do so in an attempt to gain conveniences;

- not picking and choosing among the orders one obeys, although if one finds the action as a whole improper or immoral, leaving the action;

- not making one's participation conditional on comrades caring for one's dependents while engaging in the campaign or imprisoned;

- not taking sides in communal or sectarian quarrels, but willing to give one's life to protect anyone in danger on either side; and

- not taking part in processions or other actions that would wound the religious sensibilities of any community.

While Gandhi realized the difficulties encountered by most people who attempted to follow the demanding principles and rules of *satyagraha*, he himself tried and seems mostly to have succeeded in doing so. More important, he inspired legions of followers, whose actions—not least, his own—not only discomfited the British authorities but also won their admiration.

Gandhian Nonviolence in Theory and Practice

For some, nonviolence is a principled way of life. When Gandhi established his first communities, called *ashrams*, in South Africa and later in India, it was part of his effort to construct a model for the country as a whole. His hope was to multiply these islands of peaceful, self-sufficient, and disciplined societies, and to create an archipelago of similar ones. For Gandhi, life in the community was integral to his active struggle for a better world, which involved combining the theory and practice of nonviolence into a coherent whole, a strategy that he called the "constructive program." Toward that end, far from isolating himself and his colleagues in their *ashram*, Gandhi argued that it was important to make *ashram* life an enduring action against the malicious aspects of society at large.[5]

Nonviolent Love and Suffering: *Ahimsa* and *Tapasya*

A key to understanding Gandhian nonviolence is the concept of nonviolent love, or *ahimsa*. As Gandhi expressed it, "*ahimsa* is the means; truth is the end." As with the term *passive resistance*, however, defining *ahimsa* as nonviolence or even love does a disservice to the concept, which instead implies a kind of active and embracing love. It is closer to Albert Schweitzer's principle of "reverence for life," which is not only negative (determination not to destroy living things unnecessarily) but, even more so, positive (a commitment in favor of life, especially the life of other human beings, but including all living beings).

Ahimsa requires deep respect for the other's humanity, an insistence upon sympathy and kindness, but also absolute, unwavering firmness. *Ahimsa* is not meek, mild, or retiring. It implies nothing less than the willingness of each individual to take unto themselves responsibility for reforming the planet and, unavoidably, to suffer in the process. Gandhi emphasized that *ahimsa* in its dynamic condition means conscious suffering. It does not mean meek submission to the will of the evil-doer, but it means pitting of one's

> whole soul against the will of the tyrant. Working under this law of our being, it is possible for a single individual to defy the whole might of an unjust empire to save his honor, his religion, his soul, and lay the foundation for that empire's fall or its regeneration.[6]

And,

> Suffering is the law of human beings; war is the law of the jungle. But suffering is infinitely more powerful than the law of the jungle for converting the opponent and opening his ears, which are otherwise shut, to the voice of reason . . . . Suffering, not the sword, is the badge of the human race.[7]

The basis for this suffering, which Gandhi termed *tapasya* (or "being arduous and austere," and based on Hindu spiritual practices), is several-fold. For one thing, unless one is prepared to suffer, the depth of one's commitment can be questioned. Moreover, because any violent conflict must lead to suffering, the nonviolent resister's devotion to justice in the face of violence will almost certainly precipitate suffering. *Tapasya* therefore indicates willingness to undergo this suffering oneself and not to shift its burden onto anyone else, including, notably, the opponent.

Gandhi's emphasis on suffering is especially difficult for many people to understand or accept. It tends, probably more than any other aspect of his thought and practice, to make Gandhian nonviolence relatively inaccessible to many Westerners. Yet *tapasya* should not be altogether alien, especially to Christian tradition, given the central importance attributed to Christ's redeeming agony on the cross. In addition, it is not stretching Gandhi's concept too greatly to substitute "courage" for "willingness to suffer." This has the added benefit of helping dispel the frequent misunderstanding that practitioners of nonviolence are cowards, seeking an easy way out of conflict. The reality is precisely opposite.

Nonviolence as an Active Force

Gandhi strongly emphasized that *satyagraha* must be distinguished from passive acquiescence or the desire to avoid conflict at any price. The middle class in particular has often been scorned as having an excessive fear of conflict and a corresponding desire to be comfortable at all costs. According to a biographer of one of Gandhi's most prominent disciples, Martin Luther King, Jr.,

> The inability of the bourgeois to dream great dreams and ambition noble deeds, is revealed in their timidity in the face of violence and conflict . . . . This cowardice also shows itself in what may be called the mercenary impulse, the impulse to hire others to fight one's own battles. This impulse has such concrete manifestations as hiring additional police to suppress domestic unrest or in spending money for a so-called all volunteer army, rather than personally accepting the obligations of citizenship . . . . [T]hey represent what Gandhi called the nonviolence of the weak. Such nonviolence he took to be counterfeit, a cloak for passivity and cowardice.[8]

Gandhian nonviolence, by contrast, is the nonviolence of the strong, the courageous, and the outraged, not merely passive acquiescence by the weak, the cowardly, or the comfortable. "My creed of nonviolence is an extremely active force," wrote Gandhi. "It has no room for cowardice or even weakness. There is hope for a violent man to be some day nonviolent, but there is none for a coward."[9]

Accordingly, the *satyagrahi* must be prepared to accept beatings and imprisonment in pursuit of what he considered absolute truthfulness. Followers of active nonviolence must take the opponent seriously and seek to engage them in dialogue and self-examination. *Satyagrahis* must respect the opponents and permit them to change direction without loss of face.

Traditionally, when conflicts are resolved by violence, they involve the triumph of one protagonist over the other. Such apparent resolutions may occur via threat or naked force, but the presumption is that one side wins and the other loses: This is what mathematicians call a zero-sum game, as in most competitive sports or board games, where for every winner there is a loser, so the sum total of wins and losses equals zero. Even when overtly seeking a compromise, hence, a win-win or positive-sum solution, each side usually attempts to profit at the other's expense and to compromise only when it has no alternative. By contrast, *satyagraha* aims to identify and address the source(s) of the conflict rather than to defeat or destroy the opponent. The goal is to persuade the seeming adversary that all parties have more to gain by acting in harmony and love than by persevering in discord and violence.

Rather than viewing the other as an enemy to be overcome, the *satyagrahi* considers them a participant in a shared search for a just (i.e., "truthful") solution to the problem at hand.

Ends Versus Means

Not surprisingly, because he attributed so much importance to the *process* of attaining truth and justice, Gandhi was unalterably opposed to any doctrine in which the ends justify the means. He maintained that there was "the same inviolable connection between the means and the end as there is between the seed and the tree." The French philosopher of religion Jacques Maritain wrote that the means of achieving a goal is "in a sense the end in the process of becoming." When the means are pure, the end will be desirable; if the route to political protest is sullied with violence or hatred, the end also will be spoiled. Despite her grudging acceptance of violence in certain very restricted circumstances such as resistance to brutal, warmongering dictatorships, Hannah Arendt concurred, adding that "the practice of violence, like all action, changes the world, but the most probable change is to a more violent world."[10]

For pacifists in the Gandhian tradition, violence is reactionary: The more violence, the less revolution. By using violent methods, revolutions and even antiwar movements can build up reservoirs of resentment and hatred, as well as possibly laying the foundations for additional injustice and yet more violence. This stands not only as a warning against violence but also as a caution against letting frustration drive peaceful protest into violent and often self-destructive avenues.

By contrast, violent political activists of the extreme left and right are often prone to make moral compromises, convinced that their vision of the world-as-it-should-be justifies almost any means of attaining it. Lenin, for instance, announced that "to achieve our ends, we will unite even with the Devil." In "To Posterity," the Marxist playwright and poet Bertolt Brecht lamented how violence corrupted and perverted what were ostensibly the noblest intentions on the part of the Communist government of his native East Germany. He concluded that anger against injustice, even when well-justified, resulted in violence, unkindness, and injustice, and that "we who wished to lay the foundations of kindness could not ourselves be kind."

Neither the violent extreme left nor the far right has shared Gandhi's acute sensitivity to the relationship between means and ends. And whereas most people would agree that it is desirable to avoid aggression and intimidation in pursuit of positive peace, a Gandhian would also question the legitimacy of deploying instruments of violence as means toward that end.

Nonviolence in Practice

Cicero, in *The Letters to His Friends*, asks, "What can be done against force, without force?" Students of nonviolence would answer, "Plenty." Moreover, they would question whether anything effective, lasting, or worthwhile can be done against force *with* force.

The Reverend Martin Luther King, Jr., nonviolent leader of the civil rights movement in the United States during the late 1950s and 1960s, and a visionary who, like Gandhi, was also intensely practical and result oriented, insisted that "returning violence for violence multiplies violence, adding deeper darkness to a night already devoid of stars. Darkness cannot drive out darkness; only light can do that. Hate cannot drive out hate; only love can do that."[11]

This does not mean that the *satyagrahi* is forbidden anger, even hatred; however, these feelings are carefully directed toward the various systems of evil, rather than toward individuals. As Gandhi put it,

> As evil can only be sustained by violence, withdrawal of support requires complete abstention from evil . . . . I can and do hate evil wherever it exists . . . . I hate the ruthless exploitation of India even as I hate from the bottom of my heart the hideous system of untouchability for which millions of Hindus have made themselves responsible. But I do not hate the domineering Englishman as I refuse to hate the domineering Hindus. I seek to reform them in all the loving ways that are open to me. My noncooperation has its roots not in hatred, but in love.[12]

For Gandhi and his followers, it was impossible to elevate oneself by debasing others, just as it debases others by permitting them to dominate one's self. Similarly, as Martin Luther King, Jr., urged, never let anyone push you so low as to make you hate them.

Nonviolent Actions and Government Reactions

In practice, Gandhi's *satyagraha* took many forms: marches, boycotts, picketing, leafleting, strikes, civil disobedience, the nonviolent occupation of various government facilities, vigils and fasts, mass imprisonments, refusal to pay taxes, and a willingness at all times to be abused by the authorities and yet to respond nonviolently with politeness, courage, and determination. This, as Gandhi was fond of pointing out, demanded far more strength than is required to pull a trigger, far more courage than is needed to fight or to fight back. Gandhian techniques thus do not offer an alternative to fighting; rather, they provide other, nonviolent ways of doing so. As a result, the nonviolent struggle is, if anything, more intense than its violent counterpart.

The extraordinary courage and humaneness of the Indian *satyagrahis* contrasted dramatically with the ugly violence of the occupying power, thereby helping sway world opinion as well as the British electorate, which became increasingly sympathetic to Gandhi's cause. This is not unusual: Violent governmental overreaction to nonviolent protest has historically transformed victims into martyrs, who then become symbols of their regime's callous wrongheadedness. For example, in 1819, English soldiers attacked a nonviolent crowd in Manchester, England, who were peacefully listening to speeches calling for the repeal of the Corn Laws, which benefited the nobility and rich landowners while disadvantaging the poor. This so-called Peterloo Massacre became a rallying cry for radicals who eventually succeeded in their demands for repealing the most odious of those laws.

The slaughter of participants in the Paris Commune of 1871 led to greater solidarity among the French working class. Similarly, violence and brutality directed toward US civil rights workers in the 1960s led to widespread revulsion and moral indignation against the system of racial segregation in the South, just as the Kent State and Jackson State University killings of nonviolent antiwar student protesters in 1970 galvanized sentiment opposed to the Vietnam War. The extent to which violence typically delegitimizes those who employ it is demonstrated by the widespread governmental use of *agents provocateurs*: undercover infiltrators in the service of repressive governments who seek to incite nonviolent protestors to engage in self-defeating violence.[13]

Living With and Transforming Violence

For nonviolent campaigns to be successful, the campaigners must have steadfast determination, self-respect, and also (Gandhi would add) respect for the opponent. A favorite expression of 1960s radicals was "power to the people." Followers of nonviolence believe that people are most powerful when they have sufficient moral courage as well as the willpower and training to follow through on their convictions.

Courageous nonviolent "warriors" may gradually become immune not only to the threat of violence directed toward them but also to the inclination to employ violence themselves. The latter comes from having sufficient clarity of purpose (Gandhi would call it "selflessness"). As Gandhi saw it, this does not involve a purging of anger but rather a transforming of it: "I have learnt through bitter experience the one supreme lesson to conserve my anger and as heat conserved is transmuted into energy, even so our anger controlled can be transmuted into a power which can move the world."[14]

When a victim responds to violence with yet more violence, he or she is behaving in a manner that is often predictable, perhaps even instinctive, which tends to reinforce the aggression of the original attacker and even, in a way, to vindicate the original violence, at least in the attacker's mind: Because the "victim" is so violent, presumably he or she deserved it. Moreover, there is a widespread expectation of countervailing power analogous in the social sphere to Newton's Third Law, which states that for every action there is an equal and opposite reaction. Thus, if *A* hits *B* and then *B* hits back, this nearly always encourages *A* to strike yet again.

Gandhi was not fond of the Biblical injunction "an eye for an eye, a tooth for a tooth," pointing out that if we all behaved that way, soon the whole world would be blind and toothless! Instead, if *B* responds with nonviolence, this not only breaks the chain of anger and hatred (analogous to the Hindu chain of birth and rebirth, called *karma*), it also puts *A* in an unexpected position. "I seek entirely to blunt the edge of the tyrant's sword," wrote Gandhi, "not by putting up against it a sharper edged weapon but by disappointing his expectation that I would be offering physical resistance."[15]

Accustomed to counterviolence—and even, perhaps, hoping for it—the violent person who encounters a nonviolent opponent who is courageous and respectful, even loving, toward the aggressor becomes a "victim" of a kind of moral judo in which the attacker's own energy is redirected, placing him or her off balance. "It would at first dazzle him and at last compel recognition from him," wrote Gandhi, "which recognition would not humiliate but would uplift him." And, in fact, many of Gandhi's most bitter opponents were almost inevitably won over.

Continuing this approach, consider this account of a meeting between the young Gandhi and General Jan Smuts, prime minister of South Africa. Gandhi spoke first:

"I have come to tell you that I am going to fight against your government."

Smuts must have thought he was hearing things. "You mean you have come here to tell me that?" he laughs. "Is there anything more you want to say?"

"Yes," says Gandhi. "I am going to win."

Smuts is astonished. "Well," he says at last, "and how are you going to do that?"

Gandhi smiles. "With your help."[16]

Years later, Smuts recounted this meeting, noting—with humor—that Gandhi was correct.

Nonviolence as a Proactive Force

Nonviolence is often described as nonviolent *resistance,* implying that it is a reaction, a response to some initial force. But, in fact, as practiced by Gandhi and his followers (including Martin Luther King, Jr. in the United States), nonviolence is *pro*active much more than *re*active. These practitioners of politically active nonviolence were masters at taking the initiative and keeping their opponents off balance. Their tactics were often unpredictable, spontaneous, radical, and experimental—and, not surprisingly, government authorities found them baffling and exasperating.

It is said—of some people and some nations—that "they only understand force," and therefore they cannot be moved by anything other than force or the threat of force. The truth, however, may be precisely the opposite: Those who understand and expect violent force can generally deal effectively with it; after all, it is typically their stock in trade. *Satyagraha*—soul force rather than physical force—is another matter.

Part of the goal of *satyagraha* is to make the oppressor reflect on his or her possible similarity with the resister and to change, internally. Consider the analogy of an iceberg, which melts below the water line, invisibly, until suddenly, as the weight shifts, it may flip over. Similarly, the consciousness of the oppressor may be changed suddenly and dramatically. "If my soldiers began to think," wrote Frederick the Great, "not one would remain in the ranks." Nonviolence, adroitly and persistently practiced, has the power of inducing soldiers—and government leaders—to think, and, ideally both to learn to love one's opponents and thereby to transform them into one's allies.

Martin Luther King Jr. and the US Civil Rights Movement

In the United States, the most influential modern exponent and practitioner of nonviolence was the Reverend Martin Luther King, Jr., who consciously adapted *satyagraha* for use in the American South. King studied Gandhi's philosophy and methods, traveled to India, and emerged as the chief spokesperson, architect, and spiritual leader of the nonviolent civil rights campaign in the United States.

Like Gandhi, King spent time in prison for his nonviolent defiance of unjust laws supporting racial discrimination. His "Letter From Birmingham Jail" is one of the classic statements of the philosophy of nonviolent civil disobedience and the evils of racial intolerance. In it, King also expressed a sense of courage and urgency:

We know from painful experience that freedom is never voluntarily
given by the oppressor; it must be demanded by the oppressed . . . .

> I guess it is easy for those who have never felt the stinging darts of
> segregation to say "wait." But when you have seen vicious mobs lynch
> your mothers and fathers at will . . . then you will understand why we
> find it difficult to wait.[17]

From the 19th century through the 1950s and 1960s, transportation, restaurants, sports events, restrooms, libraries, and schools were often racially
segregated in the American South, with superior facilities reserved for "whites
only." Voting rights were often denied or severely restricted by poll taxes, literacy tests, and outright intimidation. Lynching of African Americans was
not uncommon and racial violence widespread, often led by the Ku Klux
Klan, a semisecret band of brutal and often murderous white supremacists,
whose legacy lives on in contemporary far-right-wing racist movements.

Perhaps the seminal event in King's leadership of the civil rights movement was the Montgomery, Alabama bus boycott, which started in December 1955, when Rosa Parks refused to take a seat in the back of a public bus.
After thousands of African Americans walked miles to work rather than use
segregated buses, public facilities were eventually integrated. In 1961, "Freedom Riders," seeking to desegregate interstate bus transportation (in accord
with 1946 and 1960 Supreme Court decisions), endured frequent beatings
and mob violence, while state police often failed to provide protection, more
often arresting the Riders instead.

Sit-ins began at segregated lunch counters in 1960, in Greensboro, North
Carolina, at the soda fountain of a five-and-ten-cent store. With King's
encouragement and the guidance and training of local religious and civic
leaders, these nonviolent sit-ins, boycotts, and marches quickly spread to
more than 100 cities and eventually succeeded in integrating restaurants
throughout the South.

In 1963, Alabama's governor George Wallace stood in the doorway of
the University of Alabama to deny admission to black students, and electric
cattle prods, police dogs, and high-pressure water hoses were used against
peaceful demonstrators in Birmingham. Also during the early 1960s, nonviolent civil rights marchers were herded to jail in Jackson, Mississippi, with
the police harassing the marchers and offering them no protection against
abusive crowds. Four young black girls were killed by a bomb blast while
at Sunday school in Birmingham Baptist Church. Throughout, King maintained a steadfast devotion to nonviolence, based on his perception of Christian principles. "Let no man pull you so low," he was fond of saying, "as to
make you hate him."

It is no small task, though, to separate hatred of offenses—or of offending institutions—from hatred of the offenders: to hate murder but love the
murderer, to hate oppression but not the oppressor, to hate torture but not
the torturer. In this, King once again revealed himself a disciple of Gandhi,
showing uncompromising respect, even love, for his opponents, while being
equally uncompromising in pursuit of the truth as he saw it. And like Gandhi before him, Martin Luther King, Jr. was assassinated (in 1968, the year
Robert F. Kennedy was also gunned down).

But also like Gandhi, King mobilized a nonviolent army of followers, captured the conscience of millions, and achieved monumental legal reforms.
He was a founder of the Southern Christian Leadership Conference, which
emphasized grassroots, community action in addition to nonviolence, and,
in 1963, he organized the March on Washington for Jobs and Freedom, also
known as the Poor People's March, which drew about 500,000 demonstrators

to the US capital. This effort represented a new dimension of King's nonviolent campaign: extending it from civil rights to a broader concern with social justice for all. His campaign in favor of the Voting Rights Act also helped lead to its passage in 1965. The year before, King was awarded the Nobel Peace Prize.

Shortly before his death, King also started speaking out in opposition to both the Vietnam War and the nuclear arms race. "If we assume that humankind has a right to survive," he once wrote, "then we must find an alternative to war and destruction . . . . The choice today is no longer between violence or nonviolence. It is between nonviolence or nonexistence."[18]

Some Nonviolent Successes

Clearly, there have been many examples of "successful" violence, if "success" means conquest of territory, booty, and people, the imposition of a particular social system, or the forcible defeat of would-be aggressors. But it can also be argued that violence, by its nature, inhibits lasting success and sows the seeds of its own instability. When a kind of peace is imposed by violence or the threat of violence, it is not really peace but, rather, violence maintained in a temporary disequilibrium, which is to say, structural violence. The situation in apartheid South Africa was a good example: A kind of social stasis was maintained for decades but only through massive violence, structural as well as direct. It is not surprising that the resulting system was not only destructive of humane values but also unstable. (The only surprise, perhaps, is that the demise of South African apartheid was, in the end, relatively nonviolent!) Generally, the record of much human history can be seen as a monument to the *failure* of violence, not to its success.

There have been many cases of successful nonviolent actions, in addition to the well-known examples of Indian independence and the American civil rights movement. Gandhi himself pointed out that nonviolence is far more pervasive in ordinary human life than most of us realize and far more frequent (and successful) than violence:

> The fact that there are so many men still alive in the world shows that it is based not on the force of arms but on the force of truth or love . . . . Thousands, indeed tens of thousands, depend for their existence on a very active working of this force. Little quarrels of millions of families in their daily lives disappear before the exercise of this force.[19]

The Developing World

One notable example of the recent force of nonviolence was the toppling of Philippine dictator Ferdinand Marcos by the "people power" of Corazón Aquino's followers in 1986. This virtually bloodless coup occurred after Marcos loyalists attempted to rig an election in the dictator's favor. The ensuing protest revolved around persistent nonviolence by Filipino civilians, who at one point interposed themselves between armed forces loyal to Marcos and a small band of dissidents who had declared themselves in support of Aquino and her followers. Newspapers worldwide printed photographs showing Catholic nuns inserting flowers in the barrels of automatic rifles carried by Philippine Army soldiers. Marcos relinquished power and went into exile in the United States when it became evident that his own military would not fire on the unarmed populace (also, after the Reagan administration, which had propped up the Marcos regime, indicated that it was withdrawing support).

A few months later, a similar popular expression of discontent drove Jean-Claude Duvalier, son of longtime Haitian dictator "Papa Doc" Duvalier, from power. Regrettably, the departure of Duvalier did not immediately restore democracy to impoverished Haiti, which still has the highest illiteracy rate and lowest per capita income in the Western Hemisphere, as well as a long tradition of autocratic government. In any event, in Haiti and the Philippines, spontaneous nonviolent movements succeeded in deposing military dictatorships that appeared deeply entrenched, such that traditional violent revolution would probably have led to a large number of casualties.

In 1987, popular discontent in South Korea led to a series of largely nonviolent demonstrations, which in turn caused the military dictatorship to relinquish power and permit the first democratic elections ever held in that country. In Haiti, the Philippines, and South Korea, violent repression of popular resistance—often several or more years earlier—on the part of these dictatorships contributed heavily to the nonviolent popular discontent that ultimately toppled their governments.

Eastern Europe

In the spring of 1968, under the Slovak reformist leader Alexander Dubček, the Czechoslovakian government, under the watchful eye of the Soviet Union, began granting a range of political and economic freedoms, seeking to establish "socialism with a human face." In response, the Soviet Union invaded Czechoslovakia in August, crushing the brief "Prague Spring." Although many Americans think of that Soviet-led invasion as an overwhelming victory for the forces of Soviet repression, in fact the people of Czechoslovakia mounted a remarkable campaign of nonviolent opposition.

Although essentially no military resistance was offered to the invading force of nearly 500,000 troops, Czechs and Slovaks for eight months prevented the installation of a collaborationist government, using general strikes, work slowdowns, clandestine radio broadcasts, and noncooperation by government employees. A compromise (the so-called Moscow Protocols) was reached, which allowed most of the reform leaders to remain in authority; only when riots occurred at Aeroflot airline offices in Prague—that is, when nonviolent discipline broke down—did Soviet occupying forces remove the reformists and subdue the country.

Twenty-one years later, in the autumn of 1989, after a decade of nonviolent strikes and civil protest in Poland and elsewhere in the former Eastern European bloc of nations within the Soviet-dominated Warsaw Pact, massive peaceful demonstrations, culminating in "The Velvet Revolution," finally drove the Communist Party from its preeminent place in Czechoslovakia and, ultimately, elsewhere in Central and Eastern Europe. This occurred days after Czech security forces brutally suppressed some prodemocracy demonstrations; outrage at this "police violence" fueled Czech and Slovak determination to replace the discredited government.

The Polish trade union movement "Solidarity" followed a strenuously nonviolent path, one that was ultimately successful in changing the Polish government and that served in many ways as a model for the electrifying events throughout Eastern Europe in 1989. In the words of Polish Solidarity leader Lech Wałęsa, these formidable events, some of the most remarkable in modern times, were accomplished without "so much as breaking a single windowpane."

In contrast to the Czech, Hungarian, Polish, Bulgarian, and East German transformations from Soviet-style communism to fledgling democracies—via political transitions that were almost completely nonviolent—the overthrow of Romanian dictator Nicolae Ceauşescu involved violence, mostly directed toward the government leadership. Significantly, moreover, it was public outrage at the brutal military response to an earlier nonviolent citizens' protest in the Romanian city of Timisoara that ignited the countrywide revolt.

Apparent Failures of Nonviolent Resistance

Also in 1989, the world witnessed the spectacle of the People's Republic of China—the world's most populous country and one that has been in the grip of an authoritarian Communist Party–led government since 1949—convulsed by demands for reform and democratization. For several weeks, nonviolent protesters, led by university students but including a wide cross-section of the population, occupied Tiananmen Square in the heart of Beijing, with popular demonstrations of more than one million people. Prodemocracy protesters also made themselves heard in Shanghai, Nanking, Hunan, and Hong Kong.

Then the Chinese government cracked down with a brutal military assault; the precise number of casualties is not known, but possibly thousands were killed. The government survived these incidents, although it seems likely that the final word on this process has not yet been spoken. Moreover, the bitterness sown by the government's violent repression—which on a larger scale resembles the British Army's Amritsar Massacre in colonial India—may have consequences for the future of China and other governments that practice brutality against nonviolent protesters. More than three decades later, the autocratic Chinese government, dominated by the Communist Party, remains in power, due perhaps to its heavy-handed oppressive power as well as its success in providing substantial economic improvement in the lives of hundreds of millions of everyday citizens.

In contrast, the brutal military dictatorship that oppressed the people of Burma/Myanmar since 1989 has long been challenged by nonviolent protests, spearheaded by thousands of Buddhist monks, in solidarity with longtime nonviolent advocate—and Nobel Peace Prize laureate—Daw Aung San Suu Kyi (revered in Burma as "The Lady"). The results of the 2020 election gave the National League for Democracy (NLD), led by Daw Aung San Suu Kyi, an absolute majority of seats in both chambers of the national parliament, enough to ensure that its candidate would become president. However, as of the writing of this book, the Burmese military has refused to recognize the results of that free and fair election and is engaged in a brutal and violent campaign of repression against the millions of Burmese who, once again, are publicly demonstrating against the coup, and are putting their lives and livelihoods at risk in so doing.

Although Daw Aung San Suu Kyi, the NLD leader, is constitutionally barred from the presidency, a new parliament convened in February 2016, and in March 2016 a close associate of hers was elected as the first nonmilitary president of the country since the military coup of 1962. They, along with thousands of their supporters, have been detained by the military and been charged with various trumped-up violations of public security and other ordinances. It is also important to note that Daw Aung San Suu Kyi, in addition to her pro-democracy activities, spent years colluding with the Burmese military to deny the human rights of the Rohingya Muslim minority in Burma—which many in the West deem genocide—possibly as an accommodation to facilitate a semblance of democracy, which, as of early 2021, has now been aborted. Although the long-term political situation in Burma is unpredictable, it is clear that the greater the violence perpetrated, in this case by the Burmese military, the less secure the legitimacy of the regime. The same may eventually apply to the Chinese occupation and oppression of Tibet, as well as to the many autocratic Arab states.

There is, as Gandhi noted, a special outrage associated with one-sided uses of lethal force. The Tiananmen Massacre, occurring on a Sunday in June 1989, was not the first "Bloody Sunday" in history: In 1905, a mass of non-violent Russian peasants in St. Petersburg, led by Father Gapon, a Russian Orthodox priest and popular political leader who was later assassinated for his alleged links to the czar's secret police, attempted to submit a petition to Czar Nicholas. The czar's troops responded by slaughtering hundreds of unarmed people. This led to a general strike, which ushered in some limited democratic reforms on the part of the government, while also signaling the beginning of the end of czarist rule, culminating ultimately in the Russian Revolution.

A related case is the Kent State Massacre in the United States, although the numbers involved were far smaller, and the public response was far short of revolution. In this incident, Ohio National Guardsmen killed four students who were part of a crowd peacefully demonstrating in opposition to the US bombing of Cambodia in 1970. Eleven days later, two students were killed by police at the largely black Jackson State University in Mississippi. These events generated widespread outrage in the United States and marked one of many turning points in citizen respect for the federal government and its prosecution of the Vietnam War.

Nonviolence, especially when contrasted with a brutal government response, has extraordinary moral and political power, often a force more powerful than violence. Hence, it may well have a profound role to play in practical politics, even—and perhaps especially—against violent, heavily armed, repressive regimes. In 1989 in China, as in Russia 84 years earlier, the general populace, as well as many military leaders, were shocked and infuriated at the heavy-handed use of violence against peaceful demonstrators: "The People's Army," exhorted one communiqué from the Chinese military itself, "absolutely must not attack the people!" When a state does attack its own people, behaving like state terrorists, such a regime is at risk of losing its legitimacy, its popular support, and, ultimately, its power.

Interstate Examples

The above examples of nonviolent successes and near-successes refer to conflicts taking place within a given state, rather than between states. Examples of the successful use of nonviolent tactics between states are harder to come by, although there are some historical examples.

During the mid-19th century, imperial Austria was seeking to dominate its union partner, Hungary. The Hungarians were militarily weaker than the Austrians, and they recognized that physical resistance would be useless and probably counterproductive. Instead, Hungarians responded by boycotting Austrian goods, refusing to recognize or cooperate with Austrian authorities, and establishing independent Hungarian industrial, agricultural, and educational systems. Noncompliance proved a powerful tool. For example, Hungarians refused to pay taxes to Austrian collectors. When the resisters' property was seized, no Hungarian auctioneers would sell them, so Austrian auctioneers were imported. But then, no Hungarian would buy the property, so Austrian buyers were imported as well. In the end, the process proved to be a significant financial cost to the Austrian authorities. Austria also sought to enforce compulsory military service and the billeting of Austrian soldiers in Hungarian homes, but noncompliance was such that in 1867 the Austrian emperor consented to a constitution giving Hungary full rights within the Austro-Hungarian Empire.

Many people associate successful independence movements with war and armed rebellion, such as the American Revolution and the independence struggle of Algeria from France. But there have been numerous examples of independence achieved by nonviolent means, including the peaceful separations of Canada from Great Britain in the 19th century, of many colonies from Western powers in the decades following World War II, and so on. In 1905, Norway was granted independence from Sweden, with no violence whatever. Shortly before, Norwegian nationalists had declared their country to be a free and independent state, almost precipitating a war; in a subsequent plebiscite, all but 184 Norwegians voted for independence, and the Swedish government, acknowledging its defeat, relented. Somewhat analogously, Czechs and Slovaks peacefully separated in January, 1993, forming the independent sovereign nations of the Czech Republic and the Slovak Republic.

During World War II, Norway again became an important site of nonviolent resistance to the Nazis. Germany invaded Norway in April 1940, quickly overcoming Norwegian military resistance. Overcoming the people, however, was much more difficult. A pro-Nazi Norwegian, Vidkun Quisling, was made the nominal head of Norway's German-controlled government (since then, *quisling* has entered the lexicon as a local collaborator who helps form a puppet government). Norwegian society spontaneously and persistently undermined the Quisling-led government, with solidarity on the part of students and the clergy and, especially, by public school teachers, who refused to participate in mandated pro-Nazi indoctrination programs for their students. The Nazis responded by imprisoning and killing many resisters to the regime, but the refusals continued and the country gradually became increasingly ungovernable. As President Franklin Roosevelt put it, Norway became "at once conquered and unconquerable."

Similarly, during autumn 1943, when Denmark was occupied by German armed forces, large numbers of Danes prevented Nazi authorities from seizing 94 percent of the 8,000 Danish Jews and deporting them to concentration camps. Using improvised methods of communication and transportation, the outnumbered and vastly outgunned Danish citizens succeeded in smuggling most of these would-be victims to safety in Sweden. Another successful resistance tactic was for large numbers of Danes to defy the German authorities by wearing the Star of David, intended to identify Jews. Virtually the entire country—the king, government, religious leadership, trade unions, and professionals—opposed the Nazi efforts at liquidating the Jewish population, and they were largely successful. (The Bulgarian resistance movement to Nazi occupation was also somewhat successful, but it combined violent with nonviolent tactics and was mostly pro-Soviet in political orientation.)

Historical evidence suggests that military force has its political and social limits, even when (as in the modern world) such force is technologically almost unlimited. The United States, for example, dropped 8 million tons of bombs on Indochina—the equivalent of about 300 Hiroshima bombs, and 80 times the number of bombs that Germany dropped on Britain during

World War II—but nonetheless lost the Vietnam War. It remains to be seen if a military mailed fist can successfully oppress a resistant population over the long haul. But it remains questionable whether governments will move in the near future to de-emphasize the use of violence or the threat of violence in their internal and international affairs.

Civilian-Based Defense

Advocates of nonviolence are not limited to peace activists and idealistic ethicists. More hardheaded realists are questioning fundamental assumptions about peace, defense, and security, as the limitations and dangers of traditional military "solutions" become increasingly clear. A classic case, epitomizing what for many is the paradox of reliance on military means of defense, was the Vietnamese village of Ben Tre, which, according to a US major, had to be destroyed "in order for us to save it." In particular, the notion of being "defended" with nuclear, biological, or chemical weapons leaves many people skeptical.

If nonviolence is to have a major impact on international affairs, however, it needs to be seen as something more than the idiosyncrasy of uniquely empowered saints and martyrs or as an impractical tactic proposed by politically marginal figures. Rather, practitioners of nonviolence must adopt a realistic approach, feasible for a large number of people.

Among the practical suggestions for applying nonviolence to national defense, one of the most organized and realistic involves so-called civilian-based defense, or CBD. (This must be distinguished from "civil defense," or government plans for protecting citizenry in the aftermath of a nuclear war or equivalent catastrophe, an approach that antinuclear activists describe as neither civil nor defense.) CBD includes a variety of hard-headed nonviolent techniques intended to make it very difficult, if not impossible, for a conquering state to govern another and to gain any benefit from its "victory."

The major theorist of CBD, Gene Sharp, has identified about 200 specific techniques of nonviolent action, ranging from general strikes, boycotts, and nonpayment of taxes to removal of street signs and sabotage of electrical services.[20] Civilian defenders will not violently resist the occupation of their country; accordingly, substantial hardship, suffering, and even death may result. But military defenders must also anticipate considerable hardship, suffering, and possibly death, even in a "successful" defensive war. Advocates of CBD emphasize that substantial training would be required, as well as a populace willing to commit itself to the success of its enterprise.

Again, this is not entirely new: Military training also requires time, effort, and sacrifice, as well as committed participants. (One important distinction is that CBD demands that the public, not just the military, be the participants.) Moreover, most efforts at nonviolent resistance—for example, Hungary in the mid-19th century, Norway in the early 1940s, Czechoslovakia in 1968, segments of the "Arab Spring" and "Occupy" Movements of 2011, and the "Black Lives Matter" Movement of 2020—were spontaneous, unprepared, and largely leaderless. Gene Sharp's writings on civilian-based defense were cited by the Lithuanian, Latvian, and Estonian governments during their separation from the Soviet Union in 1991. Lithuanian defense minister Audrius Butkevicius declared at the time, "I would rather have this book [referring to Sharp's] than the nuclear bomb." But widespread CBD, well-rehearsed and planned in advance, has yet to be seriously attempted.

Given its impressive track record when it was essentially improvised on the spot, the future of CBD might well be bright indeed if it were ever carried out by a populace that is well trained and prepared. Furthermore, the prospects of having one's soldiers face such a populace, who are committed to denying the invader virtually all fruits of conquest, just might serve to deter invasion no less effectively than the amassing of military forces—and at substantially less cost and risk.

Sharp argues persuasively that under traditional military doctrines, "the capacity to defend in order to deter has been replaced by the capability to destroy massively without the ability to defend." By contrast, CBD would aim to

> deny the attackers their objectives and to make society politically indigestible and ungovernable by the attackers . . . . Potential attackers are deterred when they see that their objectives will be denied them, political consolidation prevented, and that as a consequence of these struggles unacceptable costs will be imposed on them politically, economically, and internationally.[21]

Rather than focusing on moral considerations, Sharp has emphasized the merits of CBD relying on serious, well-documented tactical, strategic and cost-effectiveness grounds. He also points out that if nuclear deterrence fails, the results will be utterly catastrophic. By contrast, if deterrence based on CBD fails, the result will be the first opportunity to attempt to implement a truly nonviolent defense.

A national policy of nonviolent CBD would require a state to renounce its interventionist goals in other countries or, at least, to forgo the prospect of any direct military engagement. Such states as the United States, Britain, and France have long deployed military units capable of "projecting power" far from their shores. These forces—including aircraft carriers, long-range fighter-bombers, mobile artillery, and amphibious assault units—are not normally used for defending a state's domestic borders; rather, their purpose is to intervene, or threaten to intervene, in other nations, generally far from home and most often in the developing world and Middle East. A populace trained and organized for CBD might or might not be able to deter an aggressor. But it could not invade or intimidate a distant country, rendering it similar to—but more assertively nonviolent than—nonprovocative defense. For some people, this is an added advantage of CBD; for others, it is a liability.

Although there is presently little chance that CBD will be adopted any time soon as the defense strategy of any major state, there is no reason why CBD training could not be integrated into existing military doctrine, after which it would be available to assume a more significant role as part of a transition from offensively oriented forces to those concerned—at first primarily and then exclusively—with defense. Highly respected military and political planners in a number of European states (mostly Scandinavian) have been studying the prospects for such a transition. CBD represents a revolution in alternative security thinking, one that is currently bubbling just below the level of official policy but that might well emerge in the 21st century.

Counterintuitively, there is some danger that in de-emphasizing the role of traditional military forces and placing the primary burden of defense on the shoulders of the civilian population, CBD could contribute to a kind of militarizing of national cultures, as civilians find themselves forced to confront the essence of national security. The greatest problem, however, is probably a deeply ingrained distrust on the part of the public as well as the military of nonviolence (or even, of less violence) as a workable strategy, combined with a widespread fascination with brute force and a tendency to rely on it whenever, in a revealing phrase, "push comes to shove."

Does Nonviolence "Work"? If So, Why?

When they concern themselves with nonviolence at all, the international media mainly cover such spectacular events as masses of protesters occupying central squares in main cities. Nonetheless, contrary to many popular and media-generated perceptions, it is more the rule than the exception that current revolutionary and social justice movements use nonviolent techniques. The question of whether and how nonviolence works must be placed in an ethical and historical context. What does it mean for something like nonviolence to "work"?

It does not always succeed in achieving short-term political and/or social goals, although the historical record suggests that it does so at least as often as violent methods and with far fewer victims. Neither does it always transform society, but it does so as least as often as do violent methods, and such transformation is far more likely to lead to a desirable, that is, a peaceful outcome, and with far fewer casualties than violent campaigns.

Studying the period from 1900 to 2006, Maria J. Stephan and Erica Chenoweth found that nonviolent struggles against despotism and for self-determination were about twice as effective as violent ones in achieving their goals, even in the Middle East. Moreover, these trends persisted even where most people expected that nonviolent resistance would not be successful, for example, against dictatorships and highly repressive regimes.[22]

Having examined 323 different social change campaigns, Chenoweth and Stephan also concluded that far more people and from more diverse parts of society joined nonviolent campaigns than violent ones. This greater level of participation translates into more people who can demonstrate for change and withdraw their cooperation from an unjust regime. In short, numbers matter; and when nonviolent movements overthrow an unjust regime, the victorious resistance groups are far more likely to establish democracies and to protect human rights and far less likely to lapse into civil war than their violent counterparts have been.

Prospects for Nonviolence

Despite the appeals of nonviolence in its various forms, it is unlikely that most states, especially the great powers, will soon convert their defense to such strategies in the foreseeable future: whether Gandhian *satyagraha*, CBD, or nonprovocative "defensive defense." In the long run, however, it can be argued that nonviolence offers hope for the survival of humankind, whereas violence does not.

Nonviolence is not limited to tactics of defending a given people; rather, it is also directed toward overthrowing a broader and deeper system of relationships based on violence, oppression, and the unjust exploitation of the great majority of humans by privileged elites. Thus, nonviolence is relevant not only to the prevention of war but also to the establishment of social justice, environmental protection, and the defense of human rights. It does not aim merely at achieving a more effective national defense but also at a defense of humanity and of the planet, by seeking to change the terms by which individuals and groups interact.

The destruction of rainforests, the clear-cutting of temperate zone woodlands, the gouging of the earth in the course of strip-mining, the pollution of water and air, the extinction of plant and animal species, and even (among some people) the eating of meat and the use of internal combustion engines may all be considered forms of violence, resulting, in a sense, from a lack of *ahimsa,* in Gandhian terms. As former black power leader H. Rap Brown once pointed out, "violence is as American as cherry pie."

This sentiment can occasionally be presented as seemingly reassuring; that is, violence is nothing new and therefore nothing to get alarmed about. More appropriately, however, it is a warning: Violence is widely considered inimical to humane values. Accordingly, it has become commonplace to decry the prevalence of violence applied not only to international affairs but also to underlying social conditions. Such structural violence includes homicide and abuse of children and spouses, as well as homelessness, drug abuse, environmental destruction, unemployment, poverty, unequal career options, inadequate medical care, poor health outcomes (especially for people of color, as glaringly demonstrated during the Covid-19 pandemic), and low-quality education.

For some persons deeply committed to nonviolence, legitimate outrage against violence is sometimes carried to excess; some would claim, for example, that education is violence, child rearing is violence, marriage is violence, and so on. By this point, however, an important distinction has been trivialized, leaving no alternatives but passivity or else indifference and business as usual. But this is a minority and extreme view; nonviolence is, if nothing else, hardheaded and realistic, demanding that we become immersed, albeit with high ideals, in the actual world.

The leading advocates of nonviolence in the 20th century, Mohandas K. Gandhi and Martin Luther King, Jr., derived the core of their philosophy and the wellsprings of their activism from deeply felt religious faith: Gandhi was a devout Hindu; King was an ordained Southern Baptist minister. Others, by contrast, have emphasized the practical aspects of nonviolence as a tactic for achieving results in the social sphere. For example, Gene Sharp based his commitment to nonviolent CBD and revolutionary change largely on the utilitarian need for alternatives to violence in meeting social injustice, as well as to confront domestic tyranny and international aggression. (Sharp's work, not surprisingly, served as a resource for nonviolent strategies and tactics during the early days of the Arab Spring movement, especially in Tunisia.)

Advocates of nonviolence have been accused by some conservatives as lacking patriotism, not only because in the past they recommended a less bellicose attitude toward the Soviet Union (among other perceived threats to American national security) but also because their efforts appear to some as "subversive" of some mainstream American values. Thus, in an invited memorandum to the Kerner Commission, which was convened by President Lyndon Johnson to investigate the causes of violence in American life following the inner-city riots of the mid-1960s, Catholic monk and nonviolence theorist Thomas Merton warned that the sources of violence can be found "not in esoteric groups but in the very culture itself, its mass media, its extreme individualism and competitiveness, its inflated myths of virility and toughness, and its overwhelming preoccupation with various means of destruction."

Nonviolence, Merton emphasized, is likely to be resisted because it will be seen as weakening the hegemony of the world's great powers. There will also be other challenges. Some government leaders find it easier, for example, to preside over the pillage of national resources, gaining short-term advantage (including election and reelection) rather than facing the daunting task of working toward a self-sustaining natural ecology. A society purged of structural societal violence would also require a sweeping rearrangement of current attitudes toward wealth, property, and social privilege. And imagine a state whose military forces are dismantled and that is prepared to defend itself only nonviolently. Wouldn't it be vulnerable to coercion and attack, leading to loss of freedom and very high casualties if invaded? On the other hand, Costa Rica abolished its army in 1948 (after the military supported an unpopular dictator who was subsequently overthrown). It has persisted as a model democracy and has never been invaded, even though many of Costa Rica's neighbors have been dictatorships and much of the rest of Central America remains quite violent.

Pacifism is currently tolerated in the United States and many other countries only as long as it is practiced by small and relatively marginal groups. As Merton pointed out,

> There is also an implication that any minority stand against war on ground of conscience is ipso facto a kind of deviant and morally eccentric position, to be tolerated only because there are always a few religious half-wits around in any case, and one has to humor them in order to preserve the nation's reputation for respecting individual liberty.[23]

Would it ever be practical to base a state's defense primarily on nonviolent civilian-based tactics and strategies? Some claim that Gandhi succeeded in India and King in the United States only because both Britain and the United States had a long tradition of relatively humane, civilized treatment of others. In fact, the opposite can also be argued: British responses to colonial insurrections (such as the ultimately unsuccessful 1857–1858 Sepoy Mutiny led by indigenous infantrymen in India against the British East India Company and the Crown) were often extraordinarily brutal. The US government and its armed forces did not treat its Native Americans with tolerance and restraint during America's westward expansion, for example at Wounded Knee, South Dakota, in 1890, when the US Army slaughtered hundreds of Lakota civilians. There were also many other well documented, massacres.

It is also questioned whether even a Gandhi-led nonviolent resistance movement could have prevailed against a Stalin or a Hitler, but the Danes nonviolently and successfully resisted German occupation, and the Polish and "Velvet" Revolutions in Eastern Europe during the late 1980s were nonviolent waves of secession from the former Soviet Union. In contrast, CBD would likely be helpless against most bombardment attacks, especially those using weapons of mass destruction—but, of course, military defense would be equally futile. Opponents of nonviolence as a national strategy often point to the slaughter that might take place if a nonviolent country were invaded by a violent opponent. Supporters of nonviolence can point out, however, that in this case the casualties would likely be far lower than if such an invasion were met with countervailing military force.

But the question reappears: Beyond nonviolence as a theoretical ideal or as a profound personal witness, will national security policies ever rest on a collective refusal to engage in violence? It is not appealing to contemplate a strategy that allows an aggressor to take over one's country. But neither is it pleasant to contemplate military defense. It may be that military force is merely something with which we are more familiar, not that it is necessarily more effective, especially if the trillions of dollars now expended globally on military and on such paramilitary forces as contractors and mercenaries were ever redirected toward nonviolent means of individual and collective self-defense. It may also be that governments would vigorously oppose instituting widespread nonviolent training, not only because this would compete with traditional military efforts but also because such training could empower the population to resist the government, thereby posing a threat to the existing state authorities—even in democracies, which, like most governments, are more comfortable responding in kind to violent provocations and armed resistance than to unarmed, nonviolent protest.

A Final Note on Nonviolence

Efficacious nonviolence, not merely as an ideal but as a practical policy—personal as well as national—seems foreign to most Westerners, including even most professed Christians, who claim to follow a fully articulated nonviolent ideal. "Christianity has not been tried and found wanting," noted the English writer G. K. Chesterton, "rather, it has been found difficult and left untried." The same can be said, to some extent, about persistent and courageous nonviolence.

What, we may ask, is the future of nonviolence? That is for all of us collectively to determine. Or, alternatively, we might ask: Does the world have a future *without* nonviolence? In his masterpiece, *Leaves of Grass,* 19th-century American poet Walt Whitman gives this simple answer:

Were you looking to be held together by lawyers?

Or by an agreement on a paper? Or by arms?

Nay, nor the world, nor any living thing, will so cohere.

Only those who love each other shall become indivisible.

Questions for Further Reflection

1. Which aspects of Gandhian nonviolence are most difficult for Westerners to understand? Which aspects are most accessible?

2. Compare several violent and nonviolent resistance movements. Who are the principal actors, and what are their goals, strategies, and tactics? What are the outcomes for these actors, and what do you conclude about the relative success or failure of violence and nonviolence in these movements?

3. Identify common patterns, and differences, between the Indian campaign for independence from Great Britain and the end of Soviet domination in Eastern Europe. Do the same for the overthrow of apartheid in South Africa, the "Orange Revolution" in Ukraine, and democracy movements elsewhere.

4. Suggest nonreligious bases for nonviolence, in the private as well as the public sphere.

5. Evaluate the realistic prospects for civilian-based defense, using actual examples of potential or current international conflict.

Suggestions for Further Reading

Peter Ackerman and Jack DuVall. 2001. *A Force More Powerful: A Century of Non-Violent Conflict*. New York: Palgrave Macmillan.

Judith Butler. 2020. *The Force of Nonviolence: The Ethical in the Political*. New York: Verso.

Erica Chenoweth and Maria J. Stephan. 2011. *Why Civil Resistance Works: The Strategic Logic of Nonviolent Conflict*. New York: Columbia University Press.

James Hanigan. 1984. *Martin Luther King, Jr., and the Foundations of Nonviolence*. New York: University Press of America.

Joseph Lelyveld. 2011. *Great Soul: Mahatma Gandhi and His Struggle With India*. New York: Knopf.

Gene Sharp. 2010. *From Dictatorship to Democracy*, 4th US ed. East Boston: The Albert Einstein Institution.

Gene Sharp and Joshua Paulson. 2005. *Waging Nonviolent Struggle: 20th Century Practice and 21st Century Potential*. Manchester, NH: Extending Horizons Books (Porter Sargent).

Howard Zinn. 2002. *The Power of Nonviolence: Writings by Advocates of Peace*. Boston: Beacon Press.

Notes

1. C. A. J. Coady. 1999. "The Idea of Violence." In *Violence and Its Alternatives*, eds. Manfred B. Steger and Nancy S. Lind. New York: St. Martin's Press.

2. WHO. 2012. "An Internationally Accepted Definition of Violence," from "Preventing Violence and Reducing Its Impact: How Development Agencies Can Help." In *Peace and Conflict Studies: A Reader*, eds. C. Webel and J. Johansen. London and New York: Routledge.

3. Hannah Arendt. 1969. *On Violence*. New York: Houghton Mifflin Harcourt.

4. Quoted in R. K. Prabhu & U. R. Rao, eds. 1960. *The Mind of Mahatma Gandhi*. Ahmadabad, India: Navajivan Trust.

5. M. K. Gandhi. 1955. *Ashram Observances in Action*. Ahmedabad, India: Navajivan Press; and M. Gandhi.

6. Quoted in E. Easwaran. 1978. *Gandhi the Man*. Petaluma, CA: Nilgiri Press.

7. Quoted in N. K. Bose, ed. 1957. *Selections From Gandhi*. Ahmedabad, India: Navajivan.

8. James P. Hanigan. 1984. *Martin Luther King, Jr., and the Foundations of Nonviolence*. New York: University Press of America.

9. Mohandas K. Gandhi. 1940. *An Autobiography: The Story of My Experiments With Truth*. Ahmedabad, India: Navajivan.

10. Arendt. *On Violence*.

11. Martin Luther King, Jr. 1983. "My Pilgrimage to Nonviolence." Reprinted in *The Catholic Worker*, January/February.

12. Mohandas K. Gandhi. 1968 *Selected Works*, ed. S. Narayan. Ahmedabad, India: Navajivan; and Gandhi, *An Autobiography*.

13. David Barash had a personal experience with *agents provocateurs* during

nonviolent anti-nuclear protests in the 1980s. A few individuals continually (and unsuccessfully) pressed for violent demonstrations—and were subsequently revealed to be FBI agents. Charles Webel had a similar experience in Berkeley when a police officer infiltrated the nonviolent training workshops he attended that were being conducted by Nigel Young.

14. Quoted in Erik Erikson. 1969. *Gandhi's Truth*. New York: Norton.

15. Quoted in Joan Bondurant. 1971. *Conflict: Violence and Nonviolence*. Chicago: Aldine Atherton.

16. Quoted in Bose, *Selections*.

17. Martin Luther King, Jr. 1964. *Why We Can't Wait*. New York: New American Library.

18. Martin Luther King, Jr. "My Pilgrimage to Nonviolence."

19. Mohandas K. Gandhi. 1951. *Non-Violent Resistance*. New York: Schocken.

20. Gene Sharp. 2010. *From Dictatorship to Democracy*. 4th US ed. East Boston: The Albert Einstein Institution. Available at http://www.aeinstein.org/organizations/org/FDTD.pdf; also see http://www.aeinstein.org/nonviolentaction/198-methods-of-nonviolent-action.

21. Gene Sharp. 1985. *Making Europe Unconquerable: The Potential of Civilian-Based Deterrence and Defense*. Cambridge, MA: Ballinger; and Gene Sharp (with the assistance of Bruce Jenkins). 1990. *Civilian-Based Defense: A Post-Military Weapons System*. Princeton, NJ: Princeton University Press.

22. Erica Chenoweth and Maria J. Stephan. 2011. *Why Civil Resistance Works: The Strategic Logic of Nonviolent Conflict*. New York: Columbia University Press.

23. Thomas Merton. 1980. *The Non-Violent Alternative*. New York: Farrar, Straus & Giroux.

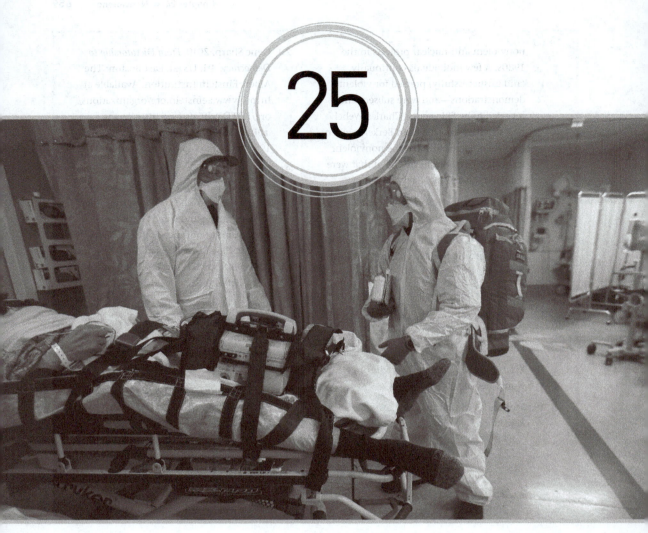

The Coronavirus Pandemic
Catastrophe, Wake-Up Call, or Both?

Baseball great Yogi Berra once observed that "It's difficult to make predictions, especially about the future." Given the complexity of peace (negative as well as positive), reliable analyses are difficult enough to come by, even if limited to the past and the present. And, following Mr. Berra, the future is even harder to predict. This is especially true when it comes to issues surrounding the novel coronavirus pandemic, which began in late 2019 in the region of Wuhan, China, and then quickly spread throughout the world in 2020. The rate of increase in the number of new cases in the

US was slowing somewhat, probably due in large part to vaccinations, as this was being written. The pandemic has affected nearly all aspects of human life around the globe, with no clear end in sight. Attempting to analyze this global event is therefore daunting in the extreme.

Moreover, government responses to the virus varied from far-sighted, to restrictive, to almost nothing—even, in some cases, discouraging any public response. Geographical proximity did not predict which countries were especially impaired. Social engineering, instead, has been crucial: Governments with firm lockdown procedures, mostly in East Asia, had much better outcomes than those with laissez-faire policies, mostly in Europe and the Western Hemisphere.

Creating a clear framework for understanding this global phenomenon is roughly like trying to build an airplane while flying in it. Hence, this chapter will be somewhat different from the others: Rather than laying out facts, consequences, and interpretations, it will outline, briefly, some of the important issues raised by the pandemic, while suggesting possible lessons to be learned, as well as directions that the future may hold. There will be far more questions than answers because literally anything could happen, from stratospheric hospitalization and mortality rates in numerous countries along with substantial social and/or governmental collapse, to a slow and halting rebound induced by appropriate public policy and the development and distribution of one or more safe and effective vaccines. There could be a return to pre-pandemic realities, gradual establishment of a range of "new normals," or dramatic upheavals that disrupt social, environmental, economic, and political norms indefinitely into the future. Only time will tell, but no one even knows how much time will be required—or available.

A Bit of History

An epidemic is a widespread, serious illness, usually within a single region. A pandemic differs in that it is significantly more distributed, often global. There have been many related events in the past, such as the Great Plague of Athens in 430 BCE, an epidemic whose cause is unknown, with likely culprits including influenza, typhus, typhoid, bubonic plague, measles, or smallpox. In the 5th century CE, during the reign of the eastern Roman emperor Justinian, a pandemic occurred, recently revealed to be bubonic plague, a.k.a. the Black Death. This plague returned and devastated much of civilization during the 14th century, killing as much as one-third to one-half of the population of Europe, with unknown mortality rates in Asia, and a global toll of between 75 million and 200 million. It returned repeatedly in succeeding centuries. European explorers brought multiple pandemics to the people of the Western Hemisphere from the 15th to the 19th centuries, notably smallpox, measles, and influenza, diseases for which the indigenous inhabitants lacked immunity and that may well have killed more than 90 percent of the population (approximately 50–90 million people), likely more than were directly killed by European firearms, slavery, and famines combined.

Prior to the Covid-19 pandemic, the most destructive modern worldwide plague was the 1918 influenza pandemic, mistakenly known as the "Spanish flu." It did not originate in Spain; rather, because Spain wasn't a combatant in the First World War, that country did not engage in press censorship and its candid newspaper reports used the incorrect label. This pandemic was responsible for between 50 million and 100 million deaths, while the HIV/AIDS pandemic, which peaked from 2005–2012, killed roughly 20 to 40 million persons.

There are few, if any, useful generalizations that emerge from humanity's experiences with pandemics, except that the human species has continued thus far, with the survivors picking up the pieces. The impact of these events is not only a function of each disease, notably its morbidity and mortality, but also a result of the resilience of the societies where they occur.

For example, the Antonine Plague, 165 to 180 CE—believed to be either smallpox or measles—severely impacted the Roman Empire during the time of the philosopher-Emperor Marcus Aurelius (whose family name was Antoninus, after whom this plague was named). But Rome recovered rather quickly, largely because the Roman Empire at the time was socially and economically robust. When another plague, the Justinianic (apparently a variant of bubonic plague), struck four centuries later during the reign of Justinian in Constantinople, it was not substantially more serious in itself than the Antonine had been, but the Roman Empire was already rickety, and the disease's impact was far more devastating.

Medical science has progressed dramatically when it comes to understanding the pathogens that cause pandemics. Much has been accomplished because of the improvements in public hygiene and disease treatment, largely due to the widespread adoption of appropriate public health measures during the late 19th and early 20th centuries in the Western world, as well as the development and administration of vaccines in the mid- and late-20th centuries. It is nonetheless unclear whether any social or political lessons have been learned from past pandemics, or whether any will be learned from the current one. A lot will depend on how quickly vaccines can be developed and distributed, how effective they will be, and whether a sufficient proportion of the population will consent to be vaccinated, leading to "herd" (population) immunity. In addition, a worrisome development that began in late 2020 and continued into at least 2021 has been the evolution of new, mutant forms of the virus that were capable of spreading more rapidly. It is uncertain whether such new strains will be less susceptible to neutralization by recently developed vaccines. In any event, the outcome is likely to be a continuing "arms race" between vaccine development and the evolution of the virus.

Another crucial and unpredictable factor will be whether societies respond to the pandemic (regardless of the degree to which it is contained and/or suppressed) by making fundamental adjustments or seeking to continue "business as usual." For the rest of this chapter, "pandemic" will be a shorthand referring specifically to the one caused by the novel coronavirus first identified in late 2019.

Although coronaviruses have long been known—certain ones cause the common cold, for example—the first potentially lethal coronavirus was discovered in China in 2002 and identified as the pathogen responsible for Severe Adult Respiratory Syndrome (SARS-CoVid, with "CoVid" shorthand for Coronavirus Disease). It is a relatively simple RNA virus covered with attachment points, called spikes. There are a total of eight known RNA viruses that affect human beings, including the common influenza virus. Another similar one was found in the Middle East in 2012, causing MERS-CoV (Middle East Respiratory Syndrome). The novel coronavirus that recently began to sweep the world is called the Severe Acute Respiratory Syndrome Coronavirus-2 (SARS-CoV-2). The disease itself is properly called coronavirus infectious disease-2019, or Covid-19.

The German social philosopher Theodor W. Adorno wrote that "the splinter in your eye is the best magnifying glass," an oracular observation that, at first glance, seems contradictory. One interpretation of Adorno's quip is that painful experiences can, paradoxically, enhance one's vision and understanding, if people change their previous shortsighted perspective and adjust their behavior. This could apply to the pandemic, if it serves as a wake-up call in a variety of dimensions, subjecting social, political, and economic institutions to an intense stress test. Initially, many of them failed, most noticeably in the US, the UK, Brazil, and India, but also in Hungary and the Czech Republic, European Union members with, as of late spring 2021, the world's highest per capita rates of reported Covid-19-related deaths and infections among nations with more than 1 million citizens. It is not a coincidence that all of these nations were led by right-wing populists mistrustful of science and pandering to their respective business elites. Those countries that dealt best with the pandemic, at least in its initial phases—including New Zealand, Taiwan, Finland, Slovakia, Germany, and Iceland—were led by relatively progressive women supportive of scientific and public health mitigation measures.

Covid-19 and its impacts have, in a sense, unmasked the shaky foundations underpinning much in the modern world, perhaps especially its developed, Western component. This includes much that inhabitants of affluent societies take for granted, from access to health care, safe social gatherings, and in-person education, to reliably safe food at supermarkets, as well as the opportunity to shop in person and to travel with confidence.

Alternatively, it is possible that, assuming some global version of herd immunity eventually comes into effect, the world may gradually return to something closely resembling the *status quo ante*, the prevailing earlier situation. People will disagree whether such a return is desirable, with many maintaining that the st*atus quo ante* was itself greatly flawed and that there might be a silver lining of potential change in the dark pandemic cloud.

Based on the existing evidence as of late spring 2021, here are some discernible and potential consequences of the pandemic, along with a number of possible lessons to be gleaned and provisional predictions that can be made. (We reserve the right to amend or even retract these prognostications should the pandemic develop in ways that are more dire, or, less likely, more optimistic, than seem to be the case as of the writing of this book!)

Socioeconomic Inequality

In his book *The Great Leveller*, historian Walter Scheidel suggested that such severe and enduring events as wars, deep economic depressions, and pandemics tend to have a levelling effect on human inequality, at least partly because existing systems generally funnel wealth unequally, so that any severe disruption, by virtue of shaking things up, is likely to reduce that inequality. By contrast, the Covid-19 pandemic has emphasized the degree to which socioeconomic inequality in the 21st century is deep and widespread. In addition, instead of levelling this inequality, the negative impacts of the pandemic upon people in lower socioeconomic circumstances were considerably more severe than its effects (at least thus far) on affluent populations.

This, in turn, has both highlighted and increased the already lopsided distribution of wealth and power: The negative impact of the pandemic has been much greater on the underprivileged than upon the fortunate and the wealthy, with massive job losses experienced disproportionately by the lowest-paid workers, especially by minorities and women, while the US stock market, for example, has risen along with the wealth of the merely afflu-ent and, especially, the super-rich. Some past pandemics, notably the Black Death in Europe, resulted in higher wages for those who survived (because of labor shortages). It seems unlikely that this will be the case following the current crisis, at least in part because the pandemic's death rate—horrible as it has been and is likely to be, at least in the short run—is substantially lower thus far than that of the world's worst pandemics.

Death rates were substantially greater among minorities and the poor, compared with those able to afford good health care and whose job and liv-ing circumstances made them less vulnerable to contracting Covid-19. Oth-ers who experienced unusually high infection and mortality rates include the elderly and people confined in jails, prisons, elder-care facilities, and migrant detention camps. In addition, many persons whose work involves manual labor are necessarily unable to work at home, compared with white collar workers, who can telecommute. Working conditions for farm and fac-tory workers, for example, or for people who labor in meat packing plants or perform customer service from stocking shelves to checkout lines, unavoid-ably subject them to greater exposure and thus, risk of infection.

This pandemic made it clear that we are not all in the same boat: The rich and powerful continue, for the most part, to sail through these heavy seas on their yachts (sometimes literally) while the rest of humanity had to paddle their own rowboats through a superstorm.

Compared to the various disasters previously experienced in human his-tory, 21st-century Western cultures possess a variety of stabilizers that may well maintain inequality by, ironically, providing just enough of a social safety net to bail out the plutocracy and keep things from threatening the already privileged. This may alleviate pressure for more enduring structural adjustments, making it at least possible that there won't be nearly as sig-nificant a social transformation as some experts predict (and many hope for), resulting in something more like the impact of the Great Recession that began in 2007–2008. Also, the degree to which modern medical science came up with effective vaccines will, perhaps counterintuitively, also likely dampen social pressure for major changes and thus further buttress the sta-tus quo. It may be, therefore, that we shall eventually have relief from the pandemic or from current extremes of inequality, but not both.

There is, on the other hand, some evidence that major social disruptions can open the door to ideas and social policies that were previously outside the mainstream and therefore not taken seriously. In the United States, for example, the Great Depression provided a suitable background for the pas-sage of the Social Security Act of 1935 during the first term of President Franklin Roosevelt (the "New Deal"), along with a number of other reforms that otherwise would have lacked sufficient public support, such as a 40-hour workweek, a minimum wage, worker's compensation, unemployment com-pensation, and a federal law banning child labor.

Social scientists understand that at any given time, only a limited range of sociopolitical approaches are sufficiently acceptable to the public that they are implemented by politicians. This portion of the policy spectrum is known as the Overton Window (named for a libertarian activist who first identified it). Will the pandemic widen the Overton Window in the United States, resulting in greater support for an expanded social safety net includ-ing, among other things, a higher national minimum wage, universal and affordable health care, free childcare and tuition-free college education, even a universal basic income, and the like? Only time (and the degree of exigency and public demands upon hesitant legislators) will tell.

Local and Domestic Consequences

Even if the pandemic is mostly or entirely controlled and mitigated, so that Covid-19 becomes more like the annual flu and less like the bubonic plague, there could well be a number of societal adjustments, such as more telecommuting from home, as many businesses and employees discover that it is often not necessary to be physically present at work. This, in turn, might result in less demand for commercial office space. Would this expense, previously borne by employers, then be shifted from businesses to their employees in their private roles as homeowners or renters? At the same time, direct on-the-job work will necessarily continue for many, beyond the "lap-top elites." This will be especially true for lower-income, lower-status, and "essential" workers who would lose their jobs and homes if they did not work onsite.

Commuting diminished, due largely to the pandemic, and long-distance travel even more so. This resulted in enormous financial losses for the travel and hospitality industry, which might well persist at least to some degree. Post-pandemic, will there also be widespread avoidance of public transportation? Will there be less focus on the traditional 9-to-5 workday, with a reduction in rush-hour congestion? Will vacations be increasingly replaced by "staycations," or, when and if the pandemic relents, will people eagerly embrace their prior lifestyles and spend like there's no tomorrow (which might literally be the case if the pandemic cannot be controlled)?

Many families, especially in the Western and Northern Hemispheres, generally found the loss of in-person schooling, particularly at the K–12 levels, to be very stressful, for children as well as their families. As schools reopen, the revived socialization could be beneficial for all generations, assuming that students do not get infected en masse and bring Covid-19 home to infect the older members of their families, who are considerably more susceptible to this illness than are young people. Before 2020, online education was largely the domain of some adults and college students. However, having discovered some benefits to distance learning for children, many educational institutions are likely to maintain and even increase the use of virtual and hybrid forms of instruction. This, in turn, would make it especially important to expand Internet accessibility to regions and populations currently excluded.

Within most countries, political activity could increasingly shift to online. Will such a transition result in greater efficiency, along with reduced in-person lobbying because many politicians will be less conveniently concentrated in government buildings? Voting by mail and/or by computer may be extended as well, despite pushback by interest groups and political parties—especially Republicans in the US, who have supported policies of voter restriction, rather than expansion, seeking to diminish the impact of marginalized people, who tend to support the other party.

Many of the practices acquired during the spring and summer of 2020 will probably be retained, including, for example, telemedicine for consultations and increased use of home deliveries. Nimble governments and workers—especially those adapting to functioning remotely—will likely continue to flourish; others are liable to fall further behind. In addition, many pre-pandemic social practices are likely to be modified, if not abandoned altogether: for example, the previously widespread tradition of shaking hands, along with the popularity of raucous and crowded social, athletic, and political events at stadiums and convention centers where there is typically little or no social distancing or mask wearing and poor ventilation.

At the same time, another pandemic adjustment—more troublesome—involved gender differences in work. Despite advances in women's equality, men, on average, are paid higher wages than are women, and mothers, on average, are somewhat more inclined than fathers to care for their children. In addition, in the first year of the Covid-19 pandemic, women were more likely to lose their jobs than were men. As a result, it is at least possible that even in a post-pandemic world, women will on balance have lost some of the gains in workplace equality and participation that they had achieved in pre-pandemic society.

Possible Origins of the Pandemic and Human/Animal Interdependency

According to the World Health Organization as well as most—but not all—epidemiologists, virologists, and ecologists, the pandemic is a zoonotic infection; that is, it was caused by the spillover of a pathogen from animals to human beings, likely originating in this case within one or more bat populations in China. Zoonoses—spillovers from animals to humans—know no national boundaries.

On the other hand, because full investigations are still incomplete, in part due to the complexity of the task as well as the apparent reluctance by Chinese authorities to release all relevant data, a minority view at the present time among scientists and intelligence experts is that the pandemic actually originated in a Wuhan, China, virology lab, resulting from genetic manipulation of an existing viral strain. These manipulations, known as "gain of function" experiments, are carried out in a number of laboratories worldwide (including in China, Russia, and the United States) and are directed at engineering natural viruses to make them capable of infecting human beings. Officially justified as defensive research to protect against dangerous variants, however produced, it is an ongoing practice that seems, at best, ethically abhorrent. In this scenario, lab-created virus was then carried an infected worker who, most likely unknowingly, spread it to others, perhaps in a "wet market" (one with live animals for sale) or to family members and friends, in or near Wuhan.

At present, an estimated 70 percent of human diseases are zoonotic, including bubonic plague; bird flu; rabies; African sleeping sickness; malaria; brucellosis; anthrax; HIV/AIDS; Ebola, Dengue, Lassa, and Marburg hemorrhagic fevers; influenza; Lyme disease; MERS; and Zika, West Nile, and yellow fevers. This is just a partial list. In many of these cases, including Covid-19 (assuming that it, too, was zoonotic), the spillover occurred as a result of human-induced disruption of natural ecosystems, along with trade in wildlife, including the now-notorious "wet markets" of China, where a range of species—domestic as well as wild animals such as bats, civets, pangolins, and even nonhuman primates—have long been kept in tortuous and unsanitary conditions and often slaughtered on the spot for human consumption.

Awareness of the key connections between humans and animals could (and should) lead to ending the wildlife trade, which is the third largest illegal international business market, behind drugs and munitions. It should also encourage greater awareness of the wide and deep connections between human beings and the natural environment, resulting in sensitivity to the need of treating all living things and all ecosystems with greater care. It can be hoped—and demanded as a matter of public health—that international policies and regulations will go further in protecting free-living species and their native environments, not only for the sake of the animals and plants, but in the interests of planetary health generally.

Also on the environmental front, the pandemic led, at least temporarily, to some improvements in the urban ecosystem: Less polluted air, safer roads because of reduced car use, and an increase in the visibility of wildlife emboldened by the relative absence of people—all in all, a hint of what a greener future might be like. Because the global economy slowed considerably during the pandemic, 2020 saw a decrease in worldwide carbon dioxide emissions on the order of 10 percent. (It is sobering to learn that such a reduction would be needed every year, and even if the pandemic is entirely ended, if greenhouse heating is to be kept below 1.5°C.)

More Cooperation or Less?

The 1918 flu killed significantly more people than did World War I. The current pandemic disrupted many more lives than have recent wars and, by late spring 2021, had killed more Americans than in all wars combined, except the Civil War. It is possible that such sobering data will induce people worldwide to reconsider what contributes to genuine human security, what constitutes an enemy, to understand that some threats (including global climate change) are more menacing than the traditionally recognized military threats, and that these require the urgent attention of governments. This might optimally result in some redistribution of federal funding from military to civilian needs, or at least the utilization of the military-industrial complex to defend security in human terms, by the increased deployment of military personnel and resources to such civilian purposes as public health and infrastructure repairs.

Similarly, there might be greater recognition of the need for worldwide coordination to fight against worldwide perils. At one (admittedly unlikely) extreme, this could energize a more positive view of world government, or at least of the need for greater international integration and coordination, including a revitalized and empowered World Health Organization (WHO), along with the creation of an entity resembling a global NATO that would be structured to fight the next pandemic. After all, it should be painfully clear that many dangers—including such potential existential threats as pandemic, climate change, and weapons of mass destruction—constitute planetary menaces that are beyond the ability of individual countries to solve. The impact of such threats is worldwide and seamless, transcending state boundaries, which are artificial political creations imposed on an interconnected planet.

On the other hand, some countries responded to the pandemic by pulling back from international cooperation, as the United States did during the Trump administration (e.g., by withdrawing from the World Health Organization). The Biden administration promptly rejoined the WHO as well as a number of other international organizations.

It is quite likely, however, that xenophobia and scapegoating of immigrants, refugees, and foreigners (especially Asians) will nonetheless increase, as xenophobic groups and movements seek recruits by creating scapegoats.

Thus, the Trump administration blamed China for the pandemic ("the China virus" and "kung flu," in Trump's terms), almost certainly in an attempt to divert attention from its own failures to control it. During the Black Death in 14th-century Europe, many local communities responded by a kind of lethal and local xenophobia, scapegoating and murdering large numbers of Jews.

There is a similar risk that global cooperation and solidarity will break down precisely when it is most needed. Some countries responded to the pandemic, at least in its early stages, by closing their borders and banning the export of protective equipment and such life-saving medical devices as ventilators. If effective and safe vaccines continue to be developed, it remains to be seen whether countries will make them widely available or if "vaccine nationalism" will induce them to hoard supplies for their own citizens.

This speaks to the more general question of whether the pandemic will inspire greater collaboration and communication, or increased isolationism and an enhanced "go-it-alone" mentality, both among countries and within them. An ethos of self-reliance can readily morph into selfishness and will almost certainly compete with one of enhanced international solidarity, collective responsibility, and the common good. For a brief period at the beginning of the pandemic, social and political polarization appeared to decrease, but it quickly returned and—at least in the United States—actually increased, as conservative ideology inclined people to ignore medical realities that necessitated mask wearing and social distancing. Also in the US, gun sales spiked, as did hate crimes, mostly perpetrated by extreme right-wing nationalists and xenophobes.

Social distancing is an important technique to reduce the contagious spread of airborne pathogens. But on the international level, most experts agree that the problem has not been too much closeness but not enough: insufficient cooperation among countries and also among individuals. Thus, countries that are more comfortable with collective action, including South Korea, Taiwan, Singapore, Vietnam, and Japan, generally did much better in fighting the pandemic than those committed to "rugged individualism" and an ethos that believes in individual "freedom." The problem arises when freedom is seen to include a right to refuse wearing a protective mask and to engage in potential "super-spreader" activities at the cost of social well-being.

On the other hand, most people don't protest being forced to drive on one side of the road (e.g., right in the US, left in the UK). And although many persons objected when automobile seat belts were mandated in the 1960s, there is essentially 100 percent compliance today. Ditto for the use of bicycle and motorcycle helmets. No one opposes laws against rape, assault, robbery, or murder. In short, even extreme laissez-faire libertarians accept the need for some coordinated restrictions on permissible personal actions in order to establish and maintain a civilized society.

Altered Political Realities, for Better and Worse

There are notable similarities between effective responses to the viral pandemic and to the climate crisis, which is another kind of "pandemic." Both require collective efforts that are national and transnational, and in which individuals also do their part. All of these call for the kind of societal unity typically seen during a war, when industrial capacity along with much of a country's population is mobilized to defeat an outside enemy. In such cases, the citizenry is called upon to make sacrifices, just as governments are called upon to take decisive action. There are also, however, some important differences. Whereas wars and pandemics are immediately and painfully apparent, making concerted responses more feasible in the face of clear and present dangers, climate change is comparatively subtle and slow-moving—except, of course, for superstorms and raging fires—and is therefore less psychologically and politically demanding. In this respect, the fact that even the coronavirus pandemic encountered substantial resistance in some quarters, despite its undeniable impact in real time, does not augur well for universal public responsiveness to the climate crisis.

More than such other crises as global warming and the danger of nuclear war—the former comparatively slow-moving and the latter, currently hidden and mostly undiscussed, although an even greater existential peril—the pandemic had immediate personal impacts upon nearly everyone. It generated widespread distress that led to personal responses associated (if nothing else) with actions intended to minimize risk to self and others, such as mask wearing and social distancing . . . or to refuse such actions. Something comparable occurred on occasion during wars of national survival and, also in 2020, in the antiracism and social justice movements that were energized by police killings of black citizens. Such events can catalyze large-scale movements, such as Black Lives Matter, although their staying power is not guaranteed. The poet Theodore Roethke wrote that "In a dark time, the eye begins to see." Will seeing result in action? This itself remains to be seen.

In light of Covid-19, it might be difficult to argue (as did former US President Ronald Reagan) that "Government isn't the solution; it's the problem." Countries that were generally most successful in fighting the pandemic were those with governments that instituted vigorous measures to protect public health. For example, although the novel coronavirus that causes Covid-19 almost certainly originated in China, following the very beginning of the outbreak that country experienced remarkably low levels of reported morbidity and mortality, despite being the world's most populous nation. This was achieved by instituting strong countrywide restrictions on movement; by requiring masks; by orchestrating an intense public health response of testing, tracing, and isolating; and by strict enforcement, where needed, of those measures—the latter being something anathema to more individualistic Western cultures.

Consistent with the "rally-round-the-flag" effect, many governments experienced an increase in public support, at least in the pandemic's first few months. But as time went on, and following the lead of right-wing populist demagogues, people who also had little respect for science began to assert that such effective public health measures as mask wearing, social distancing, and contact tracing were "totalitarian" intrusions into private life. Laissez-faire, hands-off policies by governments refusing to exert themselves on behalf of the public good—notably Brazil under President Bolsonaro and the US during the Trump administration—became popular among libertarians and others who have focused on "inalienable" personal rights at the expense of the public good.

By early 2021, countries and states without public health mandates began to experience spikes in the numbers of infected persons and deaths from Covid-19. President Trump's failure to deal effectively and realistically with the pandemic during the last year of his term doubtless contributed to his electoral defeat. Far more important, the Trump administration's malfeasances were in all likelihood responsible for tens of thousands and perhaps hundreds of thousands of deaths that could and should have been prevented and that may well have constituted crimes against humanity. In any event, as of mid-2021, the US experienced by far the most Covid-19 deaths worldwide.

The jury is still out on the medium- and long-term socioeconomic effects of the pandemic, especially if efforts to distribute and administer vaccines falter. Other unknowns at the present time include the duration of the extant vaccines' effectiveness, and also if and when even more virulent and lethal variants on SARS-CoV-2 go global and whether they are controllable by current vaccines. Other pandemics may also arise without lessons having been learned about how nations and communities need to prepare for that near certainty. These measures should optimally include the stockpiling of adequate supplies of personal protective equipment as well as emergency medical materials and rethinking the current emphasis upon "just in time" supply chain techniques. In addition, expansion of the social safety net should include more generous provisions for medical leave with pay, thereby reducing the current tendency (especially in the United States) for people to go to work while sick.

As occurs in nearly all global crises, the pandemic catalyzed a general expansion of government power, at least in the short run. Much of this involved responses that are justifiable, even necessary, such as banning large and careless social gatherings, closing many schools, mandating masks, exercising controls over essential industries in a manner more typical of command economies, and so forth. In other cases, however, the responses were what some perceive, particularly in the West, to be overly heavy-handed: Postponing elections, banning mass political rallies (especially protests), restricting press freedom, and possibly employing contact tracing as a surveillance mechanism in some Asian societies, notably China. It has been said that a crisis is too valuable to waste, and autocratically inclined governments were quick to take advantage of the pandemic as precisely such a crisis.

At the same time, many actions, although reducing some personal liberties, also "flattened the curve" of infections and deaths and thereby restricted the growth of the pandemic. Will governments give up such measures if and when the current pandemic ends—or, more likely, is as "normalized" as the annual flu? And what if it doesn't clearly end, as have smallpox and polio, but, on the contrary, mutates into even more infectious and lethal forms? Are governments and policymakers preparing for that possibility? At the present time, that seems unlikely.

Science and Public Health

The importance of science and public health was brought into sharp focus among the majority of informed citizens of advanced industrial countries, while also, paradoxically, catalyzing a backlash against expertise by a significant minority. This is particularly true in the United Sates, where right-wing know-nothing populism, notably manifested and catalyzed by the Trump administration, consistently denied and even mocked medical science—demonstrating lethal irresponsibility by refusing to acknowledge the value of masks and of social distancing, while touting unproven and downright dangerous treatments and also prioritizing short-term political considerations over scientific evidence and objective facts. As a result, certain countries, notably the US, UK, Brazil, and India endured especially high rates of infection and of mortality. It is no coincidence that these countries were led by right-wing populists with little regard for science, who also refused to acknowledge the basic biology of viral infections and even denied statistical data on the prevalence and severity of the pandemic itself.

Reality, as the writer Philip K. Dick once noted, is "that which, when you stop believing in it, doesn't go away." It can therefore be hoped that respect for and adherence to science and science-based public health measures will eventually come back. Science denialism resulted in many thousands of deaths and disabilities that could have been prevented with such inexpensive commonsense, low-tech public health actions as careful hand washing, mask wearing, social distancing, and so on. Highly educated and dedicated scientists create safe and reliable vaccines, and sophisticated public health professionals determine how best to provide them to population groups most at risk. Insofar as successful vaccine development enhances the credibility of science generally, this could conceivably extend to other politically relevant domains as well, notably anthropogenic climate change.

Although safe and effective vaccines were developed in record time, it will likely take at least until 2022–2023 before they are distributed widely enough to achieve sufficient population immunity that a "new normal" might arrive. Even then, it will take longer yet for stability to be achieved. And there is also the daunting, looming prospect that, despite the best efforts of scientists and public health professionals to mitigate and contain the pandemic, Covid-19 will still be a menace. Thus, for example, as of late spring 2021 it remained uncontrolled in many places, notably India and Brazil. Because coronaviruses are based on RNA, which is less stable than DNA, they are more prone to mutate; as a result, insofar as human populations anywhere in the world are left unvaccinated, the prospect exists of new variants arising. In itself, this italicizes the need for a global response, and not merely one based on a narrow and competitive view of national interest.

An interesting possibility is that at some point in a future recovery, pent-up demand will be released, leading perhaps to an explosion of exuberant activity analogous to the "roaring twenties." It is also quite possible that the novel coronavirus, no longer novel, will persist in the human population, perhaps indefinitely, analogous to the coronavirus variants that produce the common cold. Also possible: Public health, previously seen as relatively boring and therefore enjoying comparatively low priority, might well recede in the public mind, perceived as boring and of low priority once again, thus setting the stage for other pathogens to infect and kill millions, in large part because we weren't sufficiently prepared and hadn't learned the lessons of the past.

Experts predict that in the future, other pandemics will occur that could be much more infectious and lethal than Covid-19. There is already a recent precedent for this. In 2012, a new epidemic, MERS—short for Middle East Respiratory Syndrome—emerged in Saudi Arabia, believed to have been a zoonotic spillover from bats, although its immediate animal-human connection was via camels. Like Covid-19, MERS is caused by a coronavirus. However, whereas the mortality rate from Covid-19 is 0.5 to 0.8 percent, that of MERS is roughly 35 percent, and no cure or vaccine exists. Another deadly viral disease, Ebola, has had a fatality rate of about 50 percent; for it, however, both treatments and a vaccine are now available. Fortunately, neither MERS nor Ebola has (yet?) become a global pandemic despite their high lethality, largely because they are substantially less transmissible among human beings than is the Covid-19 virus. If suitably mutated, however, this could happen.

There is no reason, however, why the next pandemic might not also be a coronavirus or some other pathogen as infectious as measles and as lethal as Ebola, which could lead to a global health disaster comparable to the 14th century's Black Plague. It would therefore behoove governments to be better prepared for such eventualities than they were in the case of the Covid-19 pandemic.

Disease transmission is symbolized by R0 (pronounced "R-naught"). It refers to the number of people infected, on average, by an already-infected person. When R0 equals 1, meaning each infected person infects one other person on average, the frequency of a disease remains roughly constant. If it exceeds 1, the disease will increase in transmission exponentially, with the rate determined by the size of R0. If R0 is less than 1, the disease will, all things being equal, eventually peter out or remain mostly dormant. Measles is the most infectious disease known; it has an R0 of 12 to 18, but it is rarely lethal. Because R0 depends on the proportion of a population that is immune, along with the social practices that are followed (frequency of mask wearing, social distancing, etc.), it is extremely difficult to accurately assess R0, especially early in a pandemic. As of mid-2021, the R0 for Covid-19 appears to be in the range of 1.0–1.3.

Because Covid-19 currently does not kill a very high percentage of those infected, many people who harbor the virus are asymptomatic carriers. As a result, the illness can spread widely without raising a red flag. This is unlike Ebola, which is readily identified by the fact that almost everyone who gets the virus shows obvious symptoms, not to mention a very high mortality rate. Paradoxically, a dangerous disease such as Covid-19 that includes many asymptomatic carriers can be more difficult to mitigate, never mind eradicate, than one that generates readily identifiable symptoms.

In addition to R0, another important consideration when it comes to disease epidemiology is "herd immunity." This refers to the fact that once enough people are immune to a given pathogen, the opportunity for it to spread diminishes greatly. If someone carrying the disease is only in contact with others who are immune, the pathogen cannot infect others, and so its R0 tends gradually toward zero. Although herd immunity is certainly a desirable outcome, there has never yet been a case in which it was achieved naturally for a novel human virus. The exact proportion of immune individuals needed for herd immunity is itself unclear, varying with the disease in question. Among the relevant factors, for example, is the R0 for any given illness: herd immunity for a disease with a high natural R0 requires a larger proportion of immunized individuals than does one with a lower R0. Moreover, effective herd immunity depends, among other things, on the extent to which a population engages in such practices as isolating those with disease, social spacing, hand washing, covering one's mouth when sneezing or coughing, and so forth.

In addition, relying on "nature taking its course" to achieve herd immunity could not occur without many people being infected, and therefore suffering and dying, disproportionately the elderly as well as marginalized populations plus those with preexisting conditions such as diabetes, lung disease, and obesity. Such a strategy appears especially difficult to justify given the existence of effective vaccines. As a result, the most ethical approach to controlling such a pandemic is by appropriate social practices combined with mass immunization via vaccines, which could, in theory and probably even in reality, generate the desired herd immunity.

A Final Note on the Coronavirus Pandemic

The more things change, goes the saying, the more they stay the same. The pandemic certainly brought about change, at least in the short term. The long-term consequences remain to be seen . . . and managed.

Questions for Further Reflection

1. In what ways is the coronavirus pandemic different from past global pandemics and local epidemics? In what ways is it similar?

2. Compare the Covid-19 pandemic's possible and likely social, political, and economic impacts with other "game-changing" events.

3. Make your own predictions about what will be different in, say, the year 2025 as a result of the pandemic.

4. Make your own predictions about what will have remained the same in, say, the year 2025 despite the pandemic.

5. How has the pandemic affected your life directly? How has it affected your views of your future, your country, and the world?

Suggestions for Further Reading

Nicholas A. Christakis. 2020. *Apollo's Arrow: The Profound and Enduring Impact of Coronavirus on the Way We Live*. New York: Little Brown Spark.

Peter Hotez. 2021. *Preventing the Next Pandemic: Vaccine Diplomacy in a Time of Anti-Science*. Baltimore: Johns Hopkins University Press.

The Independent Panel for Pandemic Preparedness & Response. 2021. *Covid-19: Make It the Last Pandemic*. Retrieved from https://theindependentpanel.org/mainreport/

Adam Kucharski. 2020. *The Rules of Contagion: Why Things Spread—and Why They Stop*. New York: Basic Books.

Debora MacKenzie. 2020. *Covid-19: The Pandemic That Never Should Have Happened and How to Stop the Next One*. New York: Hatchette.

John Micklethwait and Adrian Wooldridge. 2020. *The Wake-Up Call: Why the Pandemic Has Exposed the Weakness of the West, and How to Fix It*. New York: HarperVia.

David Quammen. 2012. *Spillover: Animal Infections and the Next Human Pandemic*. New York: W. W. Norton.

Walter Scheidel. 2017. *The Great Leveler: Violence and the History of Inequality From the Stone Age to the Twenty-First Century*. Princeton, NJ: Princeton University Press.

David Seedhouse. 2020. *The Case for Democracy in the Covid-19 Pandemic*. Thousand Oaks, CA: SAGE.

Trond Undheim. 2020. *Pandemic Aftermath: How Coronavirus Changes Global Society*. Austin, TX: Atmosphere Press.

Nicholas Wade. 2021. "The Origin of Covid: Did People or Nature Open Pandora's Box at Wuhan?" *Bulletin of the Atomic Scientists*. May 5, 2021. Retrieved from https://thebulletin.org/2021/05/the-origin-of-covid-did-people-or-nature-open-pandoras-box-at-wuhan

David Waltner-Toews. 2020. *On Pandemics: Deadly Diseases From Bubonic Plague to Coronavirus*. Vancouver, BC: Greystone Books.

Fareed Zakaria. 2020. *Ten Lessons for a Post-Pandemic World*. New York: W. W. Norton & Co.

Coronavirus Websites

The following websites are especially helpful for keeping up with this rapidly changing topic:

Centers for Disease Control (CDC) Covid-19 website: https://www.cdc.gov/coronavirus/2019-nCoV/index.html

CDC's Covid Data Tracker: https://covid.cdc.gov/covid-data-tracker

Harvard Medical School coronavirus information: https://hms.harvard.edu/coronavirus

Harvard T.H. Chan School of Public Health Forum: The Coronavirus Pandemic: https://theforum.sph.harvard.edu/?s=Coronavirus

Johns Hopkins University School of Medicine coronavirus resource center: https://coronavirus.jhu.edu/

The Lancet medical journal: https://www.thelancet.com/journals/lancet/home

Nature international science journal: https://www.nature.com/search?q=Coronavirus

The New York Times coronavirus updates: https://www.nytimes.com/news-event/coronavirus

Science journal coronavirus research, commentary, and news: https://www.sciencemag.org/collections/coronavirus

World Health Organization (WHO) coronavirus resources: https://www.who.int/emergencies/diseases/novel-coronavirus-2019

26

The Personal and the Political

This will be a brief chapter, for I realize there isn't much to say but because personal transformations, well, personal. Peace may work differently for each of its. Exposure to peace and conflict studies may, in some cases, not significantly affect the readers' lives. In contrast, it may expand other peoples' consciousness in significant ways, influencing their subsequent behavior and perceptions. We hope that one day you might belong to the latter group.

The Personal and the Political

This will be a brief chapter, not because there isn't much to say but because personal transformation is, well, personal. Peace may work differently for each of us. Exposure to peace and conflict studies may, in some cases, not significantly affect the readers' lives. In contrast, it may expand other people's consciousness in significant ways, influencing their subsequent behavior and perceptions. We hope that one day you might belong to the latter group!

Transformations of Self and Society

When exposed to issues that are particularly relevant or arguments that are especially cogent, or simply when emotions and other unconscious factors "click" in a mysterious and little-known manner, people may suddenly see the world in a different way. Individuals who have undergone a religious conversion experience, for example, often speak of having been "born again," after which everything seems new and different.

Peace and conflict studies does not necessarily aim for a comparable effect, although it sometimes happens. There are many varieties of personal transformation, from the intense and mystical to a practical determination to vote differently, donate money to a particular cause, read another book, take another course, get involved with a social or political movement, or develop a lifelong vocation.

There are many people now working in various ways to help establish a world at peace. The noted legal scholar and peace activist Richard Falk calls them "citizen/pilgrims." They may focus on such specific goals as economic conversion; the abolition of nuclear weapons; an end to military interventionism; the abolition of poverty, malnutrition, political oppression, or environmental destruction (especially anthropogenic climate change); the defense of human rights; opposition to a specific war; or a generally more life-affirming relationship between people and their planet, as well as with each other. The route of such citizen/pilgrims, like that of the earlier pilgrims hundreds of years ago, is likely to be long and difficult but not impossible, and often quite rewarding.

It has frequently been claimed that peace must start within each individual and then spread outward: "Peace begins with me." This implies not only examining one's own life and making changes that seem consistent with one's beliefs but also identifying those personal patterns that reinforce society-wide systems of oppression. Such self-examination may in turn lead to some painful recognitions and decisions: Recognizing how one's life may have at times involved the oppression of others and/or questioning what balance is desirable (and feasible) between relative personal privilege and selfless devotion to a cause. For some people, fighting oppression requires breaking out of their own, sometimes self-induced oppression. Improving one's personal relationships may sometimes contribute to helping alleviate the oppression of others, and it may work the other way around as well.

The world may gradually become a better and less violent place if each individual makes peace in his or her own life. In this way, "outer" and "inner" peace are often interconnected.

Important as this is, however, the personal transformation involved in making inner peace is only part of the necessary equation; peace must be made not only internally but also externally, out there in the real and sometimes nasty world. No amount of "centeredness," "organic living," "alternative lifestyles," or personal peace will solve the problems of surrogate war in the developing world, of poverty, the denial of human rights, or environmental abuse, to say nothing of the danger of nuclear war. One can think pure thoughts, eat only organic foods, and never think ill of another, but this won't prevent destruction of the rainforests, provide a decent education for a little girl in Mozambique, or prevent the next episode of genocide, terrorism, climate change, or "ethnic cleansing." Peace may begin with each of us, but war, at least, is likely to begin elsewhere, and genuine peace must entail significant changes in the world at large. It may be satisfying and even necessary to liberate oneself, but it is not sufficient.

In the course of becoming involved in the struggle for peace, an awkward collision may be unavoidable between a personal ethical commitment to nonviolence and some of the harsh realities of a world in which freedom, equality, justice, and liberation may require conflict—preferably nonviolent—with existing authorities if any significant changes are to occur.

Stumbling Blocks to Personal Transformation and Empowerment

Sometimes a commitment to peace derives from a kind of transformative experience, perhaps a sudden burst of insight, what has been called a moment of epiphany, when things are seen with a unique and breathtaking clarity. At other times, it comes slowly and gradually, with the progressive realization that something long suspected is indeed true, as facts, ideas, and personal experiences fit into a coherent whole. Sometimes the appeal is primarily logical; at other times it is emotional and apparently beyond reason. Optimally, both reason and passion are involved. Religious commitment may or may not be involved.

For others, of course, it never comes at all. Nor need everyone be transformed; for most successful social movements, it is only necessary that a critical number—perhaps 10 percent to 20 percent of the population—become sincerely committed to the cause. Perhaps more are needed for major long-lasting social transformations. In any event, a significant barrier to peace is less the intractability of world problems than the fact that those problems are psychologically and thus politically invisible. Moreover, many concerned people in the affluent West tend to respond to major social and political problems with feelings of either hopelessness or resignation. Others may engage in self-defeating violence, or have a firm conviction that their personal lives are more important and somehow disconnected from these larger issues.

Violence generally evokes its own reaction, comparably violent. As to hopelessness, there are several responses. One is to point out some hopeful and realistic possibilities, as we have tried to do in this book. Another is to adopt an existential view that hopelessness is itself fundamental to the human condition, requiring us to struggle—without hope but with commitment nonetheless—because that is what it means to be human. And yet another is to embrace despair as an indication of our fundamental love for the planet and its living creatures. After all, if we did not care, we would not grieve. Paradoxically, out of that recognition can come renewed strength.

Hopelessness, in turn, can result from two different sources. On the one hand, there is the literal lack of hope, a denial that solutions even exist or could ever be implemented. On the other hand, there is a frustration that derives from facing life as an isolated, seemingly powerless individual in a very large and complicated world. The issue in this case is not so much an absence of hope as a lack of power or, rather, a perception of one's powerlessness. One purpose of *Peace and Conflict Studies*—the book as well as the discipline—is to provide some empowerment at both the personal and the political level.

There are also those who refuse to see the world's plight, possibly worrying that the problem of peace is so vast that if they open themselves to its immensity, they would be sucked in, irresistibly, as into a black hole. To these people, we point out that insofar as they see the problem this way, they have already been engulfed, whether they recognize it or not. Admitting their concerns and anxieties and allowing themselves to act on them may be refreshing in the extreme, even exhilarating, for many skeptics and onlookers. And, of course, one needn't devote oneself 100 percent to global betterment. You can support peace with your votes, volunteer time, make occasional financial contributions, and so forth, without disrupting your entire life. You can also make a deeper commitment, but there is no objective right or wrong about your choices.

Most of us live in a society that in some ways rarely confronts the world's difficulties and, especially, its own complicity in creating them. In such a society, it is relatively easy to avoid thinking about nuclear weapons, environmental deterioration, and world poverty, not to mention genocide against what are (for affluent Westerners) obscure populations in, say, South Sudan, Syria, Myanmar, or Yemen.

It is also easy to perceive the world's ills as inevitable—as part of the natural landscape or human condition—as many people once imagined slavery to be. Similarly, it is easy to practice denial, refusing to recognize what is disconcerting or upsetting because of an understandable inclination to spare oneself emotional pain. Our current planetary plight—including global warming, pandemics, and weapons of mass destruction—constitutes, paraphrasing former US Vice President Al Gore, a huge "inconvenient truth." But a truth is a truth, no matter how inconvenient.

We are rapidly approaching a situation when only a mythological ostrich, head determinedly buried in the sand, will be able to avoid the fundamental issues of preventing war, confronting violence in all its manifestations, stopping global climate change, and establishing a substantive and enduring peace. The Brazilian social activist Paulo Freire coined the term *conscientization* to denote the achievement of first personal and then group awareness. Freire was primarily concerned with the establishment of social justice, and he called, accordingly, for "humanization," which, he lamented in his classic book, *Pedagogy of the Oppressed*, is "thwarted by injustice, exploitation, oppression, and the violence of the oppressors; it is affirmed by the yearning of the oppressed for freedom and justice, and by their struggle to recover their lost humanity."

As Freire emphasized, one of the most important components of personal transformation is empowerment. In some cases, individuals commit themselves to a cause despite a virtual certainty that they will ultimately fail. The most notable example is that of the French existentialist writer Albert Camus, who argued that death and the perceived meaninglessness of the cosmos can make an individual human's life seem absurd. Camus also emphasized that, as a result, it is fundamental to the human condition that we each define ourselves by our struggle against this indifferent universe and that there is happiness, even joy, in our determination never to give up—even though, like the mythological Sisyphus who was condemned forever to roll a boulder up a hill only to have it always roll back down, we are necessarily doomed to unending struggle and repeated failure.

But in the absence of a sense of efficacy and hope, most people are unwilling or unable to summon a personal commitment to action. The image of ultimate failure is not usually considered a reassuring one, likely to recruit many enthusiastic followers! "In order for the oppressed to wage the struggle for their liberation," wrote Freire, "they must perceive the reality of oppression not as a closed world from which there is no exit, but as a limiting situation which they can transform."[1]

Motivating Factors in Personal Transformation

Although oppression is most blatant in the blood-drenched streets of urban conflict zones, in the grinding rural poverty of much of the unindustrialized world, and in the treatment of political prisoners in many countries, it should be clear even to relatively privileged Westerners that we, too, are both contributors to and victims of what has been called "invisible oppression." This form of oppression refers to environmental abuse, the economic maldistribution of goods and services, and the state-sponsored terrorism of nuclear weapons, among the numerous usually unseen but ever-present destructive forces.

Helen Caldicott, an Australian physician and influential peace worker, used to recruit antinuclear activists by urging each individual in her audience to "take the world upon your shoulders, like Atlas." It may be a heavy load, but it is lighter when shared. And, furthermore, if each of us doesn't do it, who will? Law professor and conflict-management specialist Roger Fisher once made an especially effective plea for personal involvement in antiwar activism. He began by recounting a friend's reaction to the title of his presentation, "Preventing Nuclear War." His friend's response was "Boy, have *you* got a problem!"

In response, Fisher recounted a situation he experienced when, as navigation officer, he was test-flying a B-17 during World War II. The pilot had playfully turned off all four engines, demonstrating how the bomber handled with no propulsion. Here are Fisher's own words:

> With all four propellers stationary, we glided, somewhat like a stone, toward the rocks and forests of Newfoundland. After a minute or so the pilot pushed the button to unfeather. Only then did he remember: In order to unfeather the propeller you had to have electric power, and in order to have electric power you had to have at least one engine going. As we were buckling on our parachutes, the copilot burst out laughing. Turning to the pilot he said, "Boy, have *you* got a problem!"

Fisher went on to discuss some of the difficulties as well as the prospects of preventing global war. At the end of his talk, he returned to the hapless B-17, with himself inside, without power and about to crash:

> Well, we didn't crash; we weren't all killed. On that plane we had a buck sergeant who remembered that back behind the bomb bay we had a putt-putt generator for use in case we had to land at some emergency air field that did not have any electric power to start the engines. The sergeant found it. He fiddled with the carburetor; wrapped a rope around the flywheel a few times; pulled it and pulled it; got the generator going and before we were down to 3,000 feet we had electricity. The pilot restarted the engines, and we were all safe. Now saving that plane was not the sergeant's job in the sense that he created the risk. The danger we were in was not his fault or his responsibility. But it was his job in the sense that he had an opportunity to do something about it.[2]

It can be argued that each of us has a duty to contribute to world peace, if only because—like the crew in that stricken B-17—we are all in this world together, and the fate of the Earth is definitely at risk. There aren't even any parachutes. So we all have a problem, but each of us can make a contribution to addressing and working to resolve our common challenges.

Social psychologists have shown that of the various factors likely to motivate people to change their behavior, one of the most powerful is the simple message "You can do it"—that is, evidence that individual behavior will be effective in generating some desirable effect.

For example, in one experiment, participants were given three different kinds of information about cigarette smoking, automobile injuries, and sexually transmitted diseases. The purpose was to determine which information was most effective in changing the behavior of the participants: (1) details about the negative consequences of the events (interviews with lung cancer patients and gruesome photos of automobile accidents and sexually transmitted disease victims); (2) statistical data about the probability of experiencing these outcomes if behavior remains unchanged; and (3) information specifying what preventive measures can be taken and emphasizing their likely effectiveness. The results showed clearly that the third factor, the "efficacy of coping responses," was the most influential in inducing people to change their behavior. Moreover, the first consideration—appeals to fear by emphasizing the noxiousness of the threat—actually served to *reduce* the likelihood that people would engage in adaptive behavior, apparently because such appeals evoked powerful psychological resistance in the participants.[3]

The implications for students, educators, conflict transformers, and practitioners of peace may be important. If significant numbers of people are to change their defeatist mind-sets, to break through their layers of denial and indifference, it may be most effective to appeal to their sense of efficacy rather than simply to their rational evaluation of danger or to their raw fear. An additional motivating factor deserves mention: fun. The surprising (and not at all inconvenient) truth is that it can be great fun trying to bring peace to the world. There are few activities that offer more gratification, self-importance, satisfaction of shared struggle on behalf of a greater good, and, often, gut-level joy.

The Social Efficacy of Individual Action

No one can accurately assess the prospects of establishing enduring global peace. Of course, the problems can be identified, and some of the proposed solutions can be discussed. This we have attempted to do. Some of these proposals may be feasible, especially if initiated in combination rather than alone, including switching to nonprovocative and civilian-based defense; reduced, de-alerted, and gradually eliminated arsenals of all weapons of mass destruction; redistribution of global expenditures from the military to social needs; protection of the environment and of human rights; strengthening various world peacekeeping systems in the context of establishing global human rather than national security; a widespread shift from violent means of addressing conflicts toward nonviolence; and conscientious collective efforts to address and rectify inequities in wealth, income distribution, and power.

As to the efficacy of individual action, individuals *can* make a difference—and not only such apparently larger-than-life figures as Mother Teresa, Martin Luther King, Jr., and the Dalai Lama. Moreover, although powerlessness is often a self-fulfilling prophecy, so is empowerment.

When people are convinced that they are helpless and their behavior is insignificant, they will often behave helplessly and ineffectually. But the opposite can also be true. "It is within our power," wrote Thomas Paine more than 200 years ago, "to begin the world anew." To some degree, that is what happened when a new country was formed based on the principles of democracy and self-government. And the prospect of major transformative change, not only within individuals but in their society as well, is no less true in our time than it was in his. Interestingly, the conservative political theorist Edmund Burke, writing at about the same time as Paine but espousing a very different view of what the world should be like after the American and French Revolutions, noted that "the only thing necessary for the triumph of evil is for good men to do nothing."

In addition, there is some reason for optimism. There have been numerous setbacks, but at the same time, movements for democracy and social justice are spreading in many places around the world, and nuclear weapons are becoming increasingly delegitimized in the minds of some leaders and many citizens alike. War itself may be headed in a similar direction, along with the reduction and possible elimination of major violent conflicts between nation-states, the waning terrorism and terrorists, and, eventually, progress toward positive peace. For this process to continue (to some degree it has already begun), at least four things are needed: (1) belief in the possibility of peace, (2) belief in one's personal power and efficacy, (3) motivation to proceed, whether individually or collectively, and (4) the collective determination of millions of concerned and determined citizens to save the planet and, accordingly, the possibility of a better future for themselves and for their descendants.

A primary obstacle to the establishment of peace is not so much the actual difficulty of achieving it but rather the feeling that it is impossible, resulting in the inability or refusal of many people to imagine peace as a realistic prospect. Before anything can be done, it must first be imagined.

Athletics coaches, business leaders, and many actors on the world stage have come to recognize the value of visualization: imagining one's body perfectly coordinated during a gymnastics exercise, envisioning oneself performing one of Hamlet's soliloquies, or rehearsing a piano piece to be performed publicly may often engender positive results. Subtly, unconsciously, the mind can be essentially "reprogrammed," releasing new potentials and facilitating the accomplishment of things previously thought out of reach. Personal transformation does occur, but usually only after people believe in the possibility of themselves changing, have a positive image of the kind of change they desire, and are positively reinforced by others seeking to accomplish similar goals.

Such a vision need not be fine-tuned in every detail. But it must be realistic and feasible. It must not project so far into the future that it seems irrelevant to the present, and it must not make excessive demands on human capacities as we know them. At the same time, it must be idealistic enough to be inspirational, to be worth striving for.

There are many people who believe that the world today stands at the brink of a major transformation. In less than a quarter century, the Internet, social media, and information technologies have changed many personal habits, not to mention world commerce for billions, with effects that are just being glimpsed. National barriers have fallen, not only with the demise of the Soviet Union but also with the growth of continent-wide collective identity (political, economic, social), especially in Europe with the rise of the European Union (although this is being imperiled by recent refugee and terrorism challenges, as well as by Brexit). South African apartheid is now a bad memory. And the political and social landscape of the Middle East is being transformed, but, regrettably, not only for the better. The very idea that society may change profoundly may itself be one of the most profound of all social ideas, capable of midwifing remarkable improvements in how we and what Buddhists call "all sentient beings" live.

Toward the Future

It has been said that the only constant throughout history is change. The future is not optional. This is to say that there will be *some sort* of future, and, accordingly, the question is, what sort of future?

But since 1945, we are faced with the possibility that there may be no future—at least not for humans nor possibly for much of life on Earth—because of malign human activity (in the case of weapons of mass destruction) or inaction (in the face of global climate change). In a representative democracy, people who do not vote aren't in the strongest position to complain if they don't get the outcome they want. This is also true for people who don't work for a preferred future.

There is nothing immutable about the world as it exists today. A system based on nation-states could give way to one based on local, semiautonomous communities or a global confederation of free peoples, just as reliance on nuclear weapons may be replaced by widespread revulsion toward them, and a confrontational and destructive human relationship with the natural world can give way to one that is healing and sustainable. Nonviolence could swell and violence could shrink in human affairs. Many aspects of a world at peace could be instituted without disruptive alterations in the basic organization of human society as it now exists. As progress is made and new systems are institutionalized, social change could then be evolutionary rather than revolutionary. It may also be long-lasting.

Among recent exciting developments has been the emergence of connections among social activists who used to work in relative isolation. This is evident in such social and political movements as the "Extinction Rebellion" and the "Occupy Movement," despite their shortcomings. In addition, the worldwide women's and lesbian, gay, bisexual, transgender and queer (LGBTQ) movements have gradually emerged from being primarily a concern of middle- and upper-class white people to embrace "sisters" and "brothers" of many different races and economic classes, straight, gay, and otherwise.

Similarly, environmental concerns are increasingly seen as issues that transcend the interests of people who are economically and socially privileged. There is growing recognition that, if anything, "environmental racism" tends to be particularly a burden for the poor and dispossessed. This recognition of shared interests may augur an exciting future of unforeseen empowerment. Most cogent of all, perhaps, is a shared interest in the future, as reflected in Audre Lourd's poem, "A Litany for Survival," in which she urged that we "seek a now" in which our children's dreams "will not reflect the death of ours."

We want to conclude with optimism about life. After all, this is a heady time to be alive. Soviet communism and South African apartheid—both seemingly immutable in their time—have collapsed, essentially without a shot being fired. And millions of people have been in the streets protesting against the economic tyranny of the super-rich and the political tyrannies of autocrats, both near and afar. In a world of unprecedented interconnections, who is to say that monumental accomplishments are impossible?

A Final Note on Transformation and the Future

Achieving sustainable peace is only secondarily a matter of "hardware" involving the manipulation of structures, whether personal, neural, or social. Primarily, the barriers to peace constitute a problem in human "software," in the ways we think and behave and in our often stubborn refusal to do so more compassionately. And herein lies the hope because there is enormous potential within the human species not only to remove the bugs from our own program but also to recreate our lives as we rebuild our world.

In early 2021, the former National Youth Poet Laureate Amanda Gorman recited her poem, "The Hill We Climb," at the inauguration of President Joe Biden. It ends as follows:

The new dawn blooms as we free it

For there is always light,

if only we're brave enough to see it

If only we're brave enough to be it.

There are many ways to "be it." Social organizer Saul Alinsky invoked a valuable phrase for would-be activists: "Think globally, act locally." There are many avenues for personal involvement, additional training to acquire, and numerous organizations to join, a large number of which are active at the local as well as at the national and global levels. Most people find it difficult to persevere alone, and education is empowering; this is a major reason why peace and conflict studies is taught and why various social action groups are also so important.

If a little knowledge is a dangerous thing, try getting a lot of knowledge! Remember, as well, that groups have a larger voice than a solitary individual. If you are a "joiner," join. If not, consider acting alone.

Either way, when was the last time you stood up for something you believed in and that had such enormous implications for your own future, not to mention the future of the world? And do you *really* have anything more important to do?

Questions for Further Reflection

1. If you found yourself personally influenced by the material you have encountered in peace and conflict studies, is this influence likely to change you and/or your behavior? If not, why not?

2. What are some major obstacles to personal involvement in peace and social justice movements?

3. Consider the strengths and weaknesses of some contemporary movements for social and political transformation.

4. Discuss the merits of maintaining a high level of hope and even expectation with regard to future successful movements for peace and justice, as opposed to working without explicit hope but with a sense of responsibility and commitment.

5. Discuss the problem of "compassion fatigue" and how it might be overcome.

Suggestions for Further Reading

Ronald W. Edsforth, ed. 2020. *A Cultural History of Peace*, 6 vols. London: Bloomsbury.

Paulo Freire. 1970. *Pedagogy of the Oppressed*. New York: Continuum.

Sarah J. Jackson, Moya Bailey, and Brooke Foucault Welles. 2020. *#HashtagActivism: Networks of Race and Gender Justice*. Cambridge, MA: MIT Press.

Greg Jobin-Leeds and AgitArte. 2016. *When We Fight, We Win: Twenty-First-Century Social Movements and the Activists That Are Transforming Our World*. New York: The New Press.

Jonathan Schell. 2004. *The Unconquerable World: Power, Nonviolence, and the Will of the People*. New York: Henry Holt.

Randy Shaw. 2001. *The Activist's Handbook: A Primer Updated*. Berkeley: University of California Press.

Alice Walker, Jodie Evans, and Medea Benjamin, eds. 2005. *How to Stop the Next War Now: Effective Responses to Violence and Terrorism*. Novato, CA: New World Library.

Betty Zisk. 1992. *The Politics of Transformation: Local Activism in the Peace and Environmental Movements*. New York: Praeger.

Notes

1. Paulo Freire. 1970. *Pedagogy of the Oppressed*. New York: Continuum.

2. Roger Fisher. 1981. "Preventing Nuclear War." In *The Final Epidemic*, eds. R. Adams and S. Cullen. Chicago: Educational Foundation for Nuclear Science.

3. R. W. Rodgers and C. R. Mewborn. 1976. "Fear Appeals and Attitude Change: Effects of a Threat's Noxiousness, Probability of Occurrence, and the Efficacy of Coping Responses." *Journal of Personality and Social Psychology* 34: 54–67.

• Index •

NASA (National Aeronautics and Space
Administration), 526
Nashville, 449
nasty, 140, 150, 406, 490
nasty world, 677
National Academies Press, 522, 524, 531, 536
National Academy of Sciences, 522, 524, 528,
531, 536
National Aeronautics and Space Administration
(NASA), 526
national agendas, 265, 345
national budget, 260, 326, 566
National Centers, 552
national character, 191–92
National Commission for Forced
Disappearances, 623
national debt, 189, 392, 399
national defense, 84, 258, 652
effective, 654
national defense forces, 46
national faction, 182
national governments, 93, 376, 469–70, 550
current, 377
empowered, 618
national groups, 173, 187
based, 188
isolated, 176
national habit, 63
national habit and militarism, 63
national impoverishment, widespread, 562
national independence, 175, 177–78, 466, 471
national interests, 36, 210, 306, 363, 671
perceived, 353
primary, 209
supreme, 419
vital, 306
nationalism, 163, 171–74, 181–82, 184, 186–88, 190,
192–93, 197, 245, 355–56, 384
aggressive, 131, 509
revived Russian, 258
nationalism and ethnic solidarity, 192–93
nationalism and ethnocentrism, 188, 192
Nationalism and ethnocentrism, 192
nationalism in Eastern Europe, 174
nationalist, 57, 111, 185–86, 190, 338, 366
disciplined Indian, 637
nationalist aspirations, 53, 177
nationalist China, 355
nationalist fervor, stokes violent, 85
nationalist governments, 51, 181
nationalist groups, white, 73
nationalistic world, 445
nationalist movements, 177, 197
nationalist passions, 185–86

nationalist-populist, right-wing ultra, 502
nationalist sentiments, 172–73, 175, 182–83, 187–88,
191, 251
Nationalist Threats, 182
Nationalist Threats to States, 182
Nationalist Wars, 173, 177, 186
nationalities, 171, 183, 190–91, 466
nationalize, 254, 422
national leaders, 61, 106, 130, 186, 209, 280, 299,
304, 306, 323, 587–88
international-minded, 369
National League for Democracy (NLD), 649
national legislature, 415, 503
national liberation, 49–50, 69, 71, 174, 176, 186,
190, 254, 274, 362
national liberation movements, 458
National Missile Defense (NMD), 105
National Oceanic and Atmospheric Administration
(NOAA), 526
national parks, 498, 583
National Peace Council, 22, 281
national policy, 166, 292, 326, 328, 348, 372, 653
national population, 35
national prestige, 178–79
national pride, 179, 182, 472, 482
national reconciliation, 93, 616–31
nationals, 254, 322, 416, 558
foreign, 149, 456
national security, 52, 55, 59, 61, 209, 348–49, 394,
396, 398–99, 409, 484, 488, 510, 513
defining, 409
major, 534
perceived, 126
real, 306
weak on, 287
National Security Adviser, 233
national security adviser Henry Kissinger, 397
national security advisors, 148
National Security Capabilities, 322
National Security Considerations, 398
national security experts, 400
national security interest, 336
national security managers, 397
national security policies, 656
national security rationale, 275
national security state, 198
national security strategy, 334
national security threat, 233
national security to global security, 383
national self-determination, 53, 173, 182, 188–90,
458, 477
national self-interest, 209, 431
national self-interest and power, 431
national statesmen, 61

home-grown, 74
sanctioned, 463
violent acts, 149
violent anti-Semitism, 150
violent appeals, 376
violent attacks, 41, 365
violent backlash, 293
violent behavior, 26, 85, 137, 143, 151, 301
infrequent, 435
violent brain, 137
violent campaigns, 63, 649, 654
violent chaos, 598
violent combat, 433
violent competition, 126, 204
violent conflicts, 9, 19, 27, 32, 52, 63, 65, 168, 170,
435, 441
major, 682
one-sided, 32
overt, 31
smaller-scale, 448
violent conflicts result, 152
violent confrontations, 289, 618
violent consequences, 464
violent constituents, 180
violent crime, 12–13, 412
violent deaths, 54, 634
violent demonstrations, 12, 659
violent dictatorship, 247
violent divisions, 192
violent efforts, 18
violent episodes, 177
violent events, 74, 87
violent eviction, 434
violent excesses, 611
violent extremes, 55
violent extremism, 600
violent fellow citizens, 142
violent fighters, 596
violent fights, 146
violent force, 645
violent groups, 75
violent Hindu nationalism, 437
violent insurgents, 86
violent insurrectionist group, 93
violent interactions, 262
violent Islamist groups, 87
violent Islamists, 37, 92, 107, 225, 263
violent jihad, 82
violent jihadis, 436
violent jihadists, 76
violent malefactors, 620
violent methods, 131, 642, 654
violent mob, 588
violent opponent, 656

violent organizations, 151
violent outcomes, 298
violent person, 644
violent provocations, 657
violent removal, 8
violent repression, 596, 623, 626, 648
government's, 649
justified, 474
violent responses, 88, 292, 596
violent retribution, 88
violent revolts, 85
violent revolution, 249
traditional, 648
violent secessionism, 183
violent state counterterrorism efforts, 91
violent terrorists, 92
violent terrorists to justice, 92
violent test, 199
violent test of strength, 199
violent threats, 74, 87
violent transgressors, 167
violent transition, 245
violent wars, 175
violent withdrawal, 175
violent world, 24, 642
violet, 99
virus, 661–62, 672
vision
alternative, 460
nonconfrontational, 409
visionofhumanity.org/maps/us-peace, 15
visions of disarmament, 321
volunteer time, 679
vote, 370, 375, 459, 462, 468, 473, 587–88, 590, 592,
604, 677, 679, 683
vulnerabilities, 43, 108, 265, 461, 571

Waal, 153–54, 618
wage scales, lowest, 372
waging, 424
Waging Nonviolent Struggle, 658
Waging Peace, 294, 449
Wahhabis, 78
Walker & Company, 65–66
wall, 164, 252, 287–88
Wall Street, 371
Waltz, Kenneth N., 219
war, 2–220, 223–34, 236–81, 283–87, 289–95, 297–
306, 359–61, 364–67, 372–78, 387–90, 394–96,
407–10, 415–17, 423–25, 427–45, 448–49,
464–66, 555, 563–64, 605–11
20th-century Cold, 60
20th-century intra-African, 184
absence of, 4–5, 7, 9, 129, 273, 452

• About the Authors •

David P. Barash (PhD, University of Wisconsin) is a professor of psychology emeritus at the University of Washington. His studies span animal behavior, evolution, and social psychology, with concentrations in sociobiology, psychological aspects of the arms race and nuclear war, and peace studies. A prolific author and researcher, he has written more than 270 technical articles and 40 books ranging from monographs to college textbooks to popular trade titles. His book *Introduction to Peace Studies* (1991) was the first comprehensive undergraduate textbook in the field of Peace Studies. His book *Threats: Intimidation and Its Discontents* (2020, Oxford University Press), is especially concerned with debunking nuclear deterrence.

Charles P. Webel (PhD, University of California, Berkeley) is a professor of international relations and philosophy at the University of New York in Prague. He previously held the Delp-Wilkinson Chair in Peace Studies at Chapman University. A five-time Fulbright Scholar and graduate of the Psychoanalytic Institute of Northern California, he has conducted postdoctoral research at Harvard University, the Max Planck Institute, and the Universities of Paris, Frankfurt, and Heidelberg. He has also taught in the Peace and Conflict Studies Program at Berkeley, the Honors College of University of South Florida, and at Harvard College. He is the author or editor of many articles and nine books, including the forthcoming *The World as Idea: A Conceptual History,* part one of *The Fate of this World and the Future of Humanity* (Routledge).